PEWTER IN AMERICA

Its Makers and Their Marks

PEWTER
IN AMERICA

Its Makers and Their Marks

BY

LEDLIE IRWIN LAUGHLIN

Three Volumes in One

AMERICAN LEGACY PRESS
NEW YORK

Manufactured in the United States of America.

Publisher's Note:
   Pewter in America Volumes I and II were first published in 1940
by The Houghton Mifflin Company of Boston, Massachusetts.
   The marginal annotations in Volumes I and II are
those of the author, inserted to correct errors.
   Volume III, presenting an accumulation since 1940,
of newly-found material about pewterers, their touches or
products and including many new illustrations, was published
by the Barre Publishers in the Spring of 1970.

   Library of Congress Cataloging in Publication Data

Laughlin, Ledlie Irwin.
   Pewter in America.

   Originally published: Barre, Mass. : Barre Publishers,
1969-1971.
   Includes bibliographies and indexes.
   1. Pewter—United States—History.   2. Pewter—Marks.
I. Title.
NK8412.L3 1981   739'.533'0973   81-14894
ISBN 0-517-35063-7 (Crown)   AACR2

CONTENTS
Volume One

Volume Two

Volume Three

PEWTER IN AMERICA

Its Makers and Their Marks

VOLUME ONE

HAMMERED DISH
(*Diameter 15 inches*)
Simon Edgell, Philadelphia, 1713–1742
Collection of Joseph France, Esq.

TO
MY WIFE
ROBERTA HOWE LAUGHLIN

ACKNOWLEDGMENTS

ANY book involving extensive research must, of necessity, be the work of many minds. In this particular undertaking I am under a lasting debt of gratitude to many whose names are unknown to me, members of the staffs of libraries, museums, and historical societies as well as city, town, and state officials in charge of public documents. To all who have helped me I offer my appreciation.

To secure the many photographs and rubbings required, it was necessary to handle hundreds of pieces of pewter. No single collection would have been sufficiently comprehensive. Collectors all over the country have graciously placed their treasures at my disposal for examination, measurement, and photographing, and in many cases have supplied me with the photographs desired. Grateful though inadequate acknowledgment for such courtesies is made to:

The late Mrs. Stanley H. Addicks, Mr. Worth Bailey, Mrs. Harry H. Benkard, Doctor and Mrs. Irving H. Berg, Miss Louise Birch, Mrs. J. Insley Blair, Mr. Dwight Blaney, the late Mr. Albert C. Bowman, Mr. J. G. Braecklein, Mrs. Arthur Brewer, Mr. and Mrs. Carl C. Brigham, the late Mr. Edward Bringhurst, Doctor Madelaine R. Brown, Mrs. Charles A. Calder, Mrs. Edward R. Candor, Mrs. Guy G. Clark, Mrs. F. Cogan, Mr. Morris Cooper, Jr., the late Mr. Howard H. Cotterell, F.R.S., Mr. Charles K. Davis, Mr. H. F. du Pont, Mr. John J. Evans, Jr., Mr. S. Prescott Fay, Mrs. Frederick S. Fish, Mrs. Stephen S. FitzGerald, Mr. Edward C. Ford, Mr. Joseph France, Mr. and Mrs. Paul J. Franklin, Doctor Henry W. Frink, the late Mr. Francis P. Garvan, the late Mr. Frederick K. Gaston, Mr. Burton N. Gates, Mr. George C. Gebelein, Mr. Albert H. Good, Doctor Charles W. Green, Mr. Otis G. Hammond, Director of the New Hampshire Historical Society; Mrs. Ralph P. Hanes, Mrs. H. H. Howe, Doctor Walter Hughson, Mrs. Philip Huntington, Mr. Charles F. Hutchins, the late Mrs. Annie H. Kerfoot, Mr. J. Ritchie Kimball, Mr. Charles H. King, Mr. and Mrs. Earl J. Knittle, Mrs. James H. Krom, Mrs. H. L. Lonsdale, Mr. and Mrs. Frank MacCarthy, Mr. George S. McKearin, the late Mr. Francis Mason, Doctor and Mrs. Warren C. Mercer, Miss V. Isabelle Miller, Curator of the Museum of the City of New York; Mr. Edward E. Minor, Mr. Charles F. Montgomery, Mr. Wilmer Moore, Miss Louise Murray, Mrs. Arthur J. Oldham, Mr. Vincent O'Reilly, Mr. Potter Palmer, 3d, Mr. John M. Phillips, Curator of the Mabel Brady Garvan Collection, Gallery of Fine Arts, Yale University; Mr. Philip G. Platt, Mr. John W. Poole, 3d, Mrs. Chester M. Pratt, the Honorable and Mrs. Richard S. Quigley, Doctor Percy E. Raymond, Mr. John P. Remensnyder, Miss Anna L. Rights, the Reverend Douglas L.

Acknowledgments

Rights, Curator of the Wachovia Historical Society, Winston-Salem, North Carolina; Mr. J. H. Rose, Mr. Herbert M. Rublee, Mr. W. J. Sanborn, the late Mrs. George Sheldon, Curator of the Pocumtuck Valley Memorial Association, Deerfield, Massachusetts; Mr. R. T. Sheldon, the Honorable and Mrs. George V. Smith, Miss Julia D. S. Snow, Mr. W. C. Staples, Mr. Henry H. Stoddard, the late Mr. John F. Street, Capt. A. V. Sutherland-Graeme, Mr. F. L. Thoms, Mrs. Thomas E. Troland, Mr. Stephen Van Rensselaer, Mr. William Mitchell Van Winkle, Mr. Leo E. Wagner, Mrs. Clark Walling, Mr. Lewis A. Walter, Miss Olive Wheeler, Mr. Merton H. Wheelock, Mr. Henry Hall White, and Mr. Ernest W. Young.

To Mrs. Calder and the late Mrs. Kerfoot I am also indebted for the privilege of using again illustrations which appeared in *Rhode Island Pewterers and their Work* and in *American Pewter*.

Aid of various kinds, some of it of great importance to me, was supplied not only by many of the friends listed above but also by Mrs. Helen D. Alexander, Miss Mary C. Alexander, Mr. William Ball, Mr. and Mrs. Peter Beilenson, Mrs. Henri L. Berger, Curator of the Wadsworth Athenaeum, Hartford, Connecticut; Mr. Richard LeB. Bowen, Mr. Francis D. Brinton, Mr. Henry V. Button, Mr. Rudolph E. Condon, Mr. Eugene V. Connett III, Mrs. J. L. Davidson, Mr. William Germain Dooley, Mr. Joseph Downs, Curator of the American Wing, The Metropolitan Museum of Art, New York City; Mr. Laurits C. Eichner, Miss Susan B. Franklin, Mr. Hollis French, Mr. Nelson M. Graves, Mr. William Macpherson Hornor, Jr., Miss Annie Jones, the late Mr. Homer E. Keyes, Mr. Joe Kindig, Jr., Miss Alice D. Laughlin, Mrs. James B. Laughlin, Mr. Herbert Lawton, Mr. S. Harrison Lovewell, Mr. John M. Lupton, Mr. J. H. Martin, Mr. F. P. L. Mills, Mr. Hugh R. Monro, Mr. Lawrence J. Morris, Mrs. John S. Mosher, Mrs. Louis G. Myers, Mr. Frank M. North, Miss Neville C. North, Mr. R. Brognard Okie, Mrs. Eaton H. Perkins, Miss Rebecca A. Richardson, Miss Virginia Robie, Mr. John F. Ruckman, Mr. Harold R. Shurtleff, Director, Department of Research and Record, Colonial Williamsburg, Inc., Williamsburg, Virginia; Mr. Gordon H. Smith, Assistant Regional Director, American Index of Design, Boston; Doctor Henry G. Smith, Mr. Frank F. Starr, Mr. and Mrs. Charles Messer Stow, Mr. J. A. Sweeney, Mr. R. W. Symonds, Mr. L. L. Thwing, Miss Edith M. Tilley, Mr. E. W. Turner, the Honorable Lewis H. Van Dusen, Mr. L. H. Vaughan, Mrs. Charles H. Watkins, Mr. John Whiting Webber, Doctor Thomas J. Wertenbaker, Mr. E. Weyhe, Miss Paige Williams, Mr. Luther B. Williams, Miss Carrie P. Wilson, Miss Alice Winchester, Mr. William F. Worner, Librarian of the Lancaster County Historical Society, Lancaster, Pennsylvania; and Mr. and Mrs. John S. Wright.

Miss Beatrice Shinn with her accurate sketches of the later touch-marks has added to the usefulness of this work.

Mr. Laurits C. Eichner, Mr. Frank D. Halsey, Mrs. J. Bennett Hill, Mr. Philip G. Platt, Mr. John P. Remensnyder, and Doctor Thomas J. Wertenbaker made valuable suggestions and emendations after reading portions of the manuscript.

To my brother, Mr. Henry A. Laughlin, President of Houghton Mifflin Company, to

Acknowledgments

Mr. E. Harold Hugo, of The Meriden Gravure Company, and to all who have been associated with them in the preparation of this publication I offer my congratulations and heartfelt thanks. The dignity, simplicity of design, artistic perfection of typography and illustrations, sturdiness of construction, and careful workmanship which they have put into the making of these volumes would have called forth the admiration of the ablest craftsmen whose stories are told herein. I can offer no greater praise.

I am under a peculiar obligation to two men whom I never knew and to whom I can never express my thanks in this world. The first was a pioneer student of American pewter whose very name is unknown to pewter collectors today. Several years ago Mr. Francis Brinton, knowing about my projected book, wrote that he was sending to me, to use as I saw fit, a large parcel of pewter notes brought in to him by a 'runner.' The package contained correspondence, memoranda, rubbings, and unfinished notes representing a systematic and enthusiastic search among old records for information about Pennsylvania pewterers. This study had apparently been made in 1909 with the evident intention to publish the findings. Fifteen years before *American Pewter* appeared the records of more Pennsylvania pewterers had been unearthed than all other investigators have discovered from that day to this. Although I felt certain that the writer, Mr. Benjamin R. Boggs, would surely have compiled his information and published the results had he still been living, I addressed a note to him at his old address in Harrisburg. As I feared, the letter was returned unclaimed. If Mr. Boggs be still alive I hope that he will see this book, realize my sense of guilt in plucking the fruits of his patient labors, and accept my sincere gratitude for his unwitting help. If he has gone to his great reward I trust that another star will be added to his crown for his otherwise unrewarded contributions to our knowledge of American pewterers.

In much the same manner I came into possession of another sheaf of notes bearing upon American pewterers. The late Mr. Francis Hill Bigelow, noted authority on American silver, had for years been delving into colonial records accumulating information for a comprehensive volume on Massachusetts silversmiths. In the course of his research he discovered in the Suffolk County Court House in Boston an extensive file of court records which had not been indexed and was not normally open to public inspection. It was my good fortune that he jotted down every mention of pewterers as well as silversmiths in the period covering the late seventeenth century and extending up to about 1750. Through the kindness of Mr. John M. Phillips, who is completing Mr. Bigelow's unfinished work, the pewter notes came to me and thus eight Boston pewterers, of whom I had no previous knowledge, were added to the list. It is a matter of sincere regret to me that Mr. Bigelow will never know my appreciation for his assistance.

Words can scarcely convey my feeling of obligation and gratitude to the late Mr. Louis Guerineau Myers. Connoisseur of American craftsmanship in all its forms, enthusiastic student, kindly critic and generous friend, his aid has been all-embracing. He furnished valuable information gathered too late for inclusion in his own book; turned over to me the copper plates used for illustrations in *Some Notes on American*

Acknowledgments

Pewterers; placed his extensive collection at my disposal for study; supplied photographs of the outstanding pieces; read the manuscript in its early form, and with his suggestions saved me from numerous pitfalls. In a thousand and one ways he enhanced what little value this work would otherwise have had.

Many have conspired to make of this book a real contribution to the study of American pewter. Where it has fallen short of that attainment the blame must rest upon its author.

CONTENTS

LIST OF PLATES

[xvii]

List of Plates

INTRODUCTION

I T IS but little more than a hundred years ago that pewter was in daily use in almost every American home. As late as 1850 it was still being manufactured in a few scattered shops. But as the demand died, the surviving makers transferred their energies to more profitable occupations; the household pewter was relegated to the attic or sold to the junkman; and, by the turn of the century, few save the oldest inhabitants knew what pewter was or how universal its use had once been. In such circumstances the histories of the early pewterers were of scant interest to anyone, and even their names, with one or two exceptions, had been long forgotten.

But as America came of age and her people became more conscious of their heritage, even the humblest forms of the handicraft of our ancestors were brought out again with pride and given places of prominence in the home. Pewter became a collectible, and it was but natural that its owners should have wished to know more about the craftsmen who made it. The first real effort to gather information about these forgotten men bore fruit in the publication, by the Wadsworth Athenaeum of Hartford, Connecticut, of a supplement to its *Bulletin* dated March 15, 1923, entitled *American Makers of Pewter and White Metal* compiled by Mme. Henri Berger, Curator of the Museum. As is necessarily the case with all pioneering work, this list was far from complete, but it represented a long step forward and served as a point of departure for one of the most interesting, scholarly, and delightfully written books on collecting that has ever appeared — J. B. Kerfoot's *American Pewter*. Before that volume went to press, however, Charles A. Calder, grandson of an able pewterer, had prepared a brief study entitled *Rhode Island Pewterers and Their Work*, a treatise which still ranks as the authority on the pewterers of that colony. In 1926, Louis G. Myers published *Some Notes on American Pewterers* containing photographs of a number of hitherto unlisted makers' marks (or touches), several rare forms not previously illustrated, together with information, newly discovered, about little-known or unknown pewterers, all so delightfully presented as to inspire even the casual reader. Not only are these three volumes valuable source-books for the student of pewter, but their material has been presented in a manner so entertaining that many a reader, such as myself, who had previously looked upon pewter with the mildest of interest, has become a collector in spite of himself.

In the past fourteen years many new touches have been found, lost forms have been rediscovered, and enough hitherto unpublished material about American pewter-makers and their handicraft has been collected to warrant the publication of *Pewter in America*. The book has been written for the beginner as well as for the advanced student of pewter. In it will be found a pictorial presentation of all the principal surviving forms known to have been made by American pewterers, arranged so as to illustrate the development of every important type of vessel. The shapes made by our early pewterers were, almost without exception, patterned after similar shapes which originated in Europe. For that reason I have attempted to trace in photographs the evolution of the principal forms of American pewter, going back in some cases to English or Continental examples for a starting-point and carrying each series down to its final stage of development in this country.

For the names and histories of the makers of pewter, town records, diaries, early directories, old newspapers, and source-books of every description have been searched. A complete list of our pewterers will never be available, for too many essential records are lost forever, nor is the list in this volume even a close approximation to that which may be available at a later day; but it includes many names that have not appeared in any previous work on the subject and perhaps those of a majority of the pewterers who had shops of their own in this country. Probably very few makers of any importance who were working after 1780 have been omitted.

No arrangement which has suggested itself for the presentation of the makers' histories has seemed ideal. If the names follow one another alphabetically, as must needs be the case with any such unwieldy list as confronted Howard H. Cotterell when preparing his authoritative work on British pewter, *Old Pewter, Its Makers and Its Marks*, the reader's task in finding quickly the history of any particular pewterer is made extremely simple, but at the expense to some extent of the continuity of the story. On the other hand, if the arrangement be chronological or geographical, the narrative advances in a more logical manner and touch-marks similar in character tend to group themselves together, but the reader experiences greater difficulty in turning quickly to the history of any given maker. With a small list covering a wide range in time the latter plan seems the more desirable, but when the names are legion — Cotterell recorded over six thousand British pewterers — such a plan is not feasible.

In this volume a combination of the two methods has been followed. The early men have been grouped geographically, and, within each unit, the stories follow in what approximates a chronological order. The difficulties of intercourse between distant towns were so great before the coming of the railroad that the product of the shops in any one locality tended toward a similarity of design both of forms made and touches used. But after 1830 all was different. Improved means of communication made each new pattern common property throughout the nation within a few weeks of its first appearance. No longer was there a Rhode Island type of porringer handle or a typically Connecticut eagle touch. Everything from shapes of pitchers to forms of marks became standardized the country over. The britannia period, which covered but twenty-five years, has therefore been set apart as a separate study and the brief histories of the many makers of that time have been arranged alphabetically. As an additional aid to

Introduction

the reader, a complete alphabetical list of all known American pewterers and britannia manufacturers, early and late, has been added in an appendix.

To recognize the forms of American pewter and to assimilate a little information about the makers may be all that the casual collector desires, but the student is very much interested in determining from just which shops his specimens have come. That information is to be gleaned primarily from the makers' marks with which the pewter was normally impressed. Consequently the story of every early maker is supplemented by at least one photograph of each touch which that man is known to have used. Although the illustrations show the touches at approximately their actual size, I have carefully avoided any attempt at exactness in measurement as a precaution against the misuse of the photographs by a counterfeiter. The marks of the men of the britannia period (*c.* 1825 and later) are, relatively speaking, so uninteresting, and the likelihood of their being faked is so remote, that sketches alone will suffice for illustrations.

Many a shape made in the colonies has disappeared forever, and many a touch used by an American pewterer has gone beyond recall, but there must still exist, in collections unknown or unavailable to me, numerous shapes and marks which are not illustrated in this volume. I should deem it a great courtesy if the owners or discoverers of any such rarities would bring them to my attention and thus help to plot in the many still uncharted areas of American pewter.

1940

THE EUROPEAN BACKGROUND

IN WHAT land and age the discovery was made that an alloy of tin and lead (or copper) could be worked into durable vessels may never be determined. The Egyptians and Chaldeans are said to have used the metal, and the Chinese were proficient in the art of pewter-making over a thousand years ago. Although Grecian excavations have never yielded any pewter ware, plates, dishes, and ewers, some of which are believed to date from the second century A.D., have been unearthed upon the sites of Roman towns in Great Britain and France. A number of such examples are on display in the British Museum. With the coming of the Goths and the disintegration of the Roman Empire all evidence of pewter-making in Europe vanished for a long period, and it was only after a lapse of many hundreds of years that we come upon the next recorded instance of its existence, when in 1076 the Council of Westminster granted permission for the consecration of pewter chalices for church service. At that time pewter must have been very much of a luxury — in limited use only by the clergy and nobility. As late as the sixteenth century the treen (or wooden) plate was the normal form to be found in the homes of peasants and shopkeepers. Even into the eighteenth century pewter was considered of sufficient value to be bequeathed specifically by will.

The earliest pewterers in England and on the Continent must have plied their trade without supervision, but as standards of quality and workmanship evolved, there arose a need for some central governing body which would, for the benefit of the pewterers as a group as well as for the protection of the buying public, compel the less able or less conscientious makers to live up to the generally accepted standards. Just how early such organizations took form is not known, but in 1348, in London, ordinances regulating the 'Craft of Pewterers' were submitted to and approved by the Mayor and Aldermen.

These original ordinances not only established standards of quality, but also working conditions and selling restrictions. They set up, as overseers, members of the craft, known as wardens, who were given the power of search and seizure, of enforcing the ordinances and of meting out punishments for their infringement. Later ordinances strengthened the hands of the wardens, and in 1473 King Edward IV granted a royal charter to the 'Mistery of Pewterers' (or Pewterers' Company as it came to be known). Under the charter the craft acquired the right to form itself into a corporate body empowered to hold land and was authorized to appoint officers to supervise and control the trade and to 'search' all manner of merchandise exposed for sale, not only in London but throughout the realm. City and town officials were ordered to assist the masters and wardens of the Company in the exercise of their duties. With the wealth that it accumulated, the Company purchased moulds which its members were privileged to borrow or rent, an added incentive for joining the guild and a not inconsiderable factor in enabling the Company to enforce its regulations. By later charters and statutes succeeding sovereigns redefined or enlarged the powers of the Company over the trade until, at the time the colonization of America commenced, this guild had become one of the most powerful trade organizations in the world. Its requirements were so exacting and its ordinances so well enforced, at least in London proper, that London pewter became the standard of excellence for the western world.

As Europe emerged from the Dark Ages the manufacture of pewter began again in many centers on the Continent as well as in England. Just as in London the pewterers in all of the larger towns formed themselves into guilds, and by 1600 every pewter-making center of importance had its organization, which supervised the trade within its jurisdiction. We can assume, therefore, that the pewterers who sailed to our shores were, for the most part, carefully trained, that they brought with them their moulds and tools and as well the customs of the craft in their respective homelands.

Not only did the requirements for pewter-making differ from town to town, but in each district prescriptions for the different alloys were changed by statute from time to time. As J. B. Kerfoot well says, 'there used, in the old days, to be as many formulae for making pewter as there were recipes for mixing rum punch.' But despite minor differences the grades used for any particular form of vessel at any given period in London and, let us say, Limoges or Bruges did not vary greatly. Let us examine a few of the alloys prescribed by the London Company.

From early times it had been recognized that there could not be one set formula for the making of all pewter. The shapes of the vessels and the purposes to which they were to be put dictated in large part the composition to be employed, although occasionally, even in neighboring shops, widely different alloys may have been used for similar articles.

We shall consider some of the alloys used in England, but for a better understanding of such a study we must know what metals were combined to form pewter and what purpose each served. The principal constituent of pewter was always tin, but unalloyed tin is too soft to be worked into serviceable vessels. Very small admixtures, however, of copper, lead, antimony, or bismuth (the 'tin glass' of the inventories) formed satisfactory alloys that could be cast into durable forms. Sometimes two or more of these metals were combined with the tin.

On account of the low cost of lead and the ease in working a tin-lead mixture, such an alloy was preferable if cost was an important factor and stiffness not essential. However, if the lead content was high, the forms made from it were soft, heavy, and easily damaged. The color was dull, the texture coarse, the resonance slight, and some little danger of lead poisoning existed. For this reason, even in the colonies, the use of lead in pewter still-worms was absolutely prohibited.

Copper served to give the alloy tensile strength. A tin-copper alloy gave a smoother surface, closer texture, better color, greater strength, and was the most resonant of all pewter alloys.

Bismuth, which was used by the early pewterers to harden the alloy, also lowered the melting-point and caused brittleness. An improvement was the substitution of brass which introduced zinc with the copper. Both bismuth and zinc were replaced by antimony, a metal unused by the early workers, which served the same purposes as bismuth, guaranteed a metal that was susceptible to a high polish, and did not lower the melting-point.

With this brief explanation of what pewter is, we may turn now to a consideration of the grades that were in general use in London.

The ordinances of 1348 decreed that only the finest quality of pewter could be used in plates, dishes, porringers, salts, and all vessels with flat sides; and specified that fine pewter should consist of tin with the admixture of as much copper 'as of its own nature it will take' (approximately twenty-three per cent). Neither then nor later was the inclusion of lead permitted in fine pewter.

All other vessels, and particularly pots, tankards, and other hollow-ware, each made up of several castings which had to be soldered together, were ordered made from an alloy of tin and a reasonable amount of lead. 'Reasonable amount' was defined as twenty-two pounds of lead to one hundred and twelve of tin, but was presumably varied according to the articles into which it was to be cast. This alloy was known as 'ley metal' or common pewter.

Not mentioned in the first ordinances but early established as a stock grade was 'trifle' — eighty-three parts of tin to seventeen of antimony. This alloy was used in the manufacture of spoons, shakers, buttons, and in general all small articles which could not be finished on the lathe. Men who worked at this branch of the trade were known as 'triflers.'

The successful use of antimony for small items led to its combination with tin and copper in plate manufacture. And so the specifications for fine pewter changed gradually in England until, by the end of the seventeenth century, antimony had all but superseded copper in the making of flatware. A normal specification for fine pewter at that time was one hundred parts of tin to seventeen of antimony. The best hard-metal pewter contained over ninety per cent tin, less than eight per cent antimony, and two per cent copper.

There was one other grade, sometimes known as 'black pewter' because of its color, which was used in the making of organ pipes, candle moulds, and other forms in the manufacture of which the chief consideration was low cost. In this alloy the lead content was high, at times as great as forty per cent.

Such were the principal grades, beginning with fine pewter which contained no lead, and running down to the poorest grade containing forty per cent of that metal.

Throughout its history the Company was involved in prosecuting pewterers who made use of lead in greater proportions than were permitted by law. Until the eighteenth century, when its powers had begun to wane, it had little difficulty in enforcing discipline among its own members, but the records are full of complaints against itinerant journeymen who traveled about the countryside with a few moulds, visiting the country fairs, buying old pewter, melting it up and adding as much lead as they dared 'in deceit of the people and to the disgrace of the whole trade.' This practice, which was even more common in France and elsewhere on the Continent, brought the trade into great disrepute and hastened its downfall. Moreover, it increased the problems of the legitimate pewterers who were compelled to assay every piece of old pewter of unknown origin before returning it to the melting-pot. Because pewter was often sold by weight there was an added temptation to the unscrupulous maker to adulterate his product with lead.

But despite trials such as this the lot of the pewterer of Britain or of the Continent was singularly fortunate. Not only was he strongly protected in his trade by a powerful guild, but also he had ready access to his supplies of raw materials. The English makers in particular enjoyed an enviable location in close proximity to the mines of Cornwall which were producing the purest tin in the world. Just how important these factors were the pewterers who migrated to the colonies were soon to learn.

PROBLEMS OF THE COLONIAL PEWTERER

A PEWTERER in London or Bristol, embarking with his family for the New World, could have had but slight foreknowledge of the manufacturing problems which would confront him once he had set up in business on the other side. Lured by the promise of religious freedom and discouraged perhaps by the severity of the competition with his fellow pewterers at home, many a maker must have set out in high hopes for America, his land of opportunity.

The opportunities did seem limitless. New and fast-growing settlements, in which craftsmen were relatively scarce, gave promise of a demand for pewter which a few local makers could never hope to fill. The need for pewterers was great, but the difficulties in making pewter, far from a source of raw materials and in competition with the product of the English shops, were realities of commensurate magnitude.

As the early colonists sailed from the old country, each took with him as many of his possessions as he felt could be conveniently transported, and particularly those items which to him gave promise of being indispensable in his new home. We can be very certain that pewter spoons, plates, dishes, and pint pots were absolute necessities, part of the required equipment of every immigrant. Almost before the first ship's load had been landed, spoons had undoubtedly been broken or lost, plates had been damaged, and the need for a pewterer already existed. With each new group of arrivals that need increased. And as the settlements grew in numbers and size, and the ravages of time and of normal wear and tear set in, the demand for pewter grew.

For pewter is a soft metal. It cannot long withstand hard usage. John W. Poole has estimated that the average span of life of a pewter plate in daily use was but five years. Even if we were to assume that he may have underrated somewhat the thrifty care of our forebears and if we were to double his estimate, it must still be apparent that the need for replacement of old pewter early became a factor of importance in the lives of the colonists, and a steady flow of old metal to the melting-pot was soon under way.

Unlike china, which was to replace it, pewter, when damaged, commanded a ready market and lost but a relatively small portion of its value. The testimony of the inventories of American pewterers in this connection is convincing. Finished common flatware was never valued at more than twice the value of old pewter, and in some cases the ratio was as low as 100 to 65. In other words, a buyer was able to obtain fifteen to twenty pounds of fine new plates for thirty pounds of old and damaged articles, some of which may have seen service in his family for ten years and upwards. To those who are accustomed at the end of one, two, or three years to turn in automobiles for new models

Problems of the Colonial Pewterer

at the current trade-in rates of exchange, it will be apparent that our ancestors had little incentive to practice their accustomed thrift in preserving carefully their pewter vessels.

Why was old pewter so valuable to the colonial pewterer? Why was he so ready to pay well for it? The difficulties which he faced in securing raw materials for the making of pewter furnish the answers to these questions.

For the word Wales substitute Cornwall.

In the seventeenth and eighteenth centuries the tin deposits in Wales provided the principal tin supply for the western world. The English pewterer had his raw material stock right at his back door; the American maker was thousands of miles from its source. Had the colonial pewterer been dependent upon making his wares from new metal, competition with the pewterers abroad would have forced him out of business. Consider the difficulties confronting him. He had to send to England for bars of tin, pay heavy transportation costs, place his orders far in advance, and depend upon exceedingly uncertain deliveries. He never could predict with even reasonable exactness when his consignments might arrive.

These handicaps were deliberately increased by the British Government. It was part of England's colonial policy to discourage in every possible way all forms of manufacture in the colonies. If the New World were not permitted to make what it needed, England could build up a vast export trade in manufactured goods and thus keep her sons overseas dependent upon and subservient to her. The Government at home watched with suspicion every new undertaking in America, and periodically called for reports from the royal governors on the manufacturing in their respective colonies. By imposts on raw materials and with taxes of various kinds they contrived to make difficult the life of the colonial artisan.

None suffered more from this policy than the pewterer. As early as the reign of William and Mary wrought tin (pewter) was on the duty-free list whereas tin bars carried a five per cent ad valorem duty. The complete absence of tin in every colonial pewterer's inventory that I have examined, and I have seen a good many, is proof of the effectiveness of Great Britain's attempts to shut off the export of raw tin to America. As planned, finished pewter, made in England, could be brought in far more cheaply than like wares made from new metal could be produced by the American pewterer. His only chance for a livelihood was to take old pewter and convert it into new. His problem of supply was to gather up from every household that he could reach every ounce of old metal that could be acquired, and the magnitude of his business was limited by the amount of old pewter that he could buy or take in exchange for new. Consequently, in the country districts where the supply was small the output was low and the pewterer was not justified in purchasing many moulds. Edward Willett of Upper Marlboro, Maryland, is a good example of this limitation in output. He was apparently only a part-time pewterer and had moulds only for spoons, plates, and 'supe' plates.

Thwarted by these limitations of their normal activities and in competition with cheap pewter from abroad, few of our makers, and those mainly in large centers, were able to make a satisfactory living from the manufacture of pewter alone. Most of them found it necessary to branch out into additional lines of work. Few, of course, had moulds enough to furnish all the shapes for which there was a call. Consequently, most makers must have supplemented their stock with purchases from England of shapes which they did not make. In fact several American pewterers so advertised. In many instances the selling of imported pewter led to the stocking of hardware and merchandise of various kinds, and we find records of men such as Simon Edgell of Philadelphia, who, while carrying on the making of pewter to the close of their days, became general merchants on a large scale.

Others of our makers added brass-working, tin-smithing, copper-smithing, or plumbing to the manufacture of pewter, and in some rare cases such disparate occupations as tobacco-growing and pewtering were combined in one individual.

An enlightening article in the magazine, *Antiques*, for October, 1935, furnishes statistical evidence of the success which attended England's efforts to build up her export trade in pewter with the colonies. R. W. Symonds gives a compilation therein, taken from the Public Records Office in London, of the values of English exports to the colonies (exclusive of Georgia) from 1697 to 1767. Before 1700 recorded shipments of pewter from England alone had reached an annual value of over four thousand pounds sterling, and by 1760 this figure had grown to more than thirty-eight thousand pounds per year. When we realize that these were wholesale prices, and that a pound sterling in 1760 had perhaps five or six times the purchasing value of today, we have some idea of the magnitude of Britain's colonial trade in pewter. In value it ran in excess of a million dollars a year in American currency of today, and in weight it was probably in excess of three hundred tons annually. Of further interest is the fact that between the years 1720 and 1767 pewter shipments from England far exceeded in value the exports to America of furniture, silver plate, and tinware combined.

If the supposition advanced first by John W. Poole and enlarged upon herein be correct, that the colonial pewterer rarely had pure tin on hand, he must have found it most difficult to make pewter to any exact formula. And yet the one test made as a check on the composition of American pewter indicates just how accurately analyses could be duplicated.

I owned a badly battered plate bearing the marks of Joseph Danforth of Middletown, which was offered as a sacrifice on the altar of science, in order that we might obtain some idea of the practice of American pewterers, and Frank MacCarthy kindly supplied for a similar purpose a fragment of an Edward Danforth plate. Although these makers were brothers, trained in the same shop, and although there was every reason to expect that the chemical analyses would not vary greatly, the findings of the laboratory disclosed a similarity that is amazing:

	Tin	Copper	Lead	Antimony
Joseph Danforth plate........................	88.52	0.67	8.33	2.47
Edward Danforth plate.....................	88.43	0.97	8.39	2.15

It will be seen that the tin content varied by less than one tenth of one per cent, the lead content by but six hundredths of one per cent. It is difficult to believe that this could have been just a coincidence. To one who has seen a melter in an openhearth steel plant take a sample from a heat, break it in half and determine by a glance at the grain structure the percentage of carbon, phosphorus, and sulphur contained therein, it is easy to realize how accurately the trained eye can assay metal. The colonial pewterer may have developed just such keenness, and may have been able by judicious selection from his stocks of old pewter to bring each melt to approximately the analysis desired. Whatever his method for controlling his quality, he was able to furnish metal very close to specification.

It is of especial interest that the Danforths used over eight per cent of lead in pewter for plates. Other pewterers, notably those of New York, made a finer quality of pewter, but the Danforths measured up well with the majority of small-town makers, and it is probably fair to say that the inclusion of small quantities of lead, even in the manufacture of flatware, was normal in the colonies.

Pewter-making in America, in one other respect, took place under conditions differing from those in Britain. In England the Pewterers' Company not only established the standards for the trade and supervised every phase of the business, but even dictated to the pewterer in many matters of his personal life. In America, as far as we now know, there was no pewterers' guild (with the possible exception of a small organization in New York, on which comment will be made later), and, barring the limited supervision of the local assay masters, each pewterer was left free to produce metal of any composition desired and to conduct his business as he saw fit. Is there any cause for wonder that American pewter, made under such circumstances, varies far more widely in quality than does the pewter of England?

It would be very satisfactory, very comforting, to be able to write truthfully that colonial pewter was fully the equal of the London product. Occasionally we find examples of which any London maker would have been proud, but an unbiased observer would be compelled to report that the cruder American specimens fell far below English standards, both in quality and workmanship. No other result could have been expected of pewter made under no external supervision, in the face of trials with which English pewterers were never confronted. The miracle is that so much really fine pewter was produced in America; that our men were able to compete at all with the pewterers in the homeland.

Despite all his handicaps, the local pewterer still found for himself a place in the scheme of life in colonial America. What percentage of the going business in pewter he was able to handle we cannot guess with any degree of accuracy, but certain it is that in the two hundred years of pewter-making on these shores several hundred men worked at the trade and some few of them became wealthy in so doing. Kerfoot estimated that for every marked American plate that he found in this country he had to examine one hundred to one hundred and twenty-five English specimens. Though appearing upon the scene at a later date, after stocks in antique shops had been picked over for American pewter, I should judge that American plates turn up with slightly greater frequency than one in a hundred; that a considerably greater percentage of mugs, tankards, and flagons found in this country are American; and that nineteen out of every twenty marked porringers that come to light are of local manufacture. That is simply my own experience; others, whose searches have carried them into different fields, may have cause to dispute my estimates. We may say with assurance, however, that the great bulk of pewter used in colonial America was imported from abroad, particularly in the case of flatware, which lent itself readily to compact shipment in casks. Not until after the Revolution, when the demand for pewter was everywhere dwindling, were our makers in a position to dominate the trade in this country.

THE BUSINESS OF A PEWTERER

TWO hundred years ago, when every large town and many a smaller community had its pewter shop and the small boys watched the pewterers at work just as small boys of every generation (except the present) have stood in curious wonder around the door of a smithy, pewter-making was such a normal trade that none realized that there would ever come a day when the written records would be painstakingly combed for any scrap of information as to what took place in a pewterer's shop. Otherwise at least one American pewterer might have preserved for us the story of a routine day in his life. The background of the picture here drawn was built up, with Howard H. Cotterell's aid, from inventories, advertisements, and old books, particularly a treatise published in 1788 by M. Salmon, a pewterer of Chartres, entitled *L'Art du Potier d'Étain*. The manuscript was then submitted to Laurits C. Eichner, a gifted craftsman in metals. His practical knowledge of modern pewtering, coupled with extensive research into the methods of early metal-workers, enabled him to amend and clarify the descriptions of the actual operations and to give to this chapter whatever authority it may now have.

Prior to the Revolution and, with few exceptions, prior to 1810, each maker was bound, in youth, as an apprentice to the trade and spent seven or more years learning the business under the supervision of a master pewterer. His father or guardian had to put up a sum of money (in London in 1743 the figure was twenty pounds) for the training, and the master was required to find for the boy board, lodging, and clothes. If, when his apprenticeship terminated, he had insufficient capital to set up in business for himself, he worked as a journeyman pewterer until he was in position to open a shop. If, on the other hand, he had several hundred pounds of his own he prepared at once to establish himself in business.

Few trades in that day required such a large initial outlay. The tools and 'furniture' were many, and the moulds, in particular, were expensive. The moulds for stock shapes were usually made of brass both on account of the resistance of that alloy to wear and because of the ease of finishing brass with hand tools; but, owing to the high cost of that metal, moulds of iron, soapstone, and other less expensive materials were sometimes used, especially for articles that were made infrequently or in small quantities. No doubt many an American pewterer commenced business with a minimum of tools and with only a couple of spoon moulds and three or four moulds for plates and dishes. But the typical shop of a small-town maker (of which Thomas Danforth, Second, of Middletown, Gershom Jones of Providence, and David Melville of Newport can be cited as examples) had from three hundred to eight hundred pounds of moulds, and in such prosperous establishments as that of Thomas Byles of Philadelphia the moulds weighed over half a ton. In addition to the moulds every shop had its wheel, lathe, large pots, ladles, benches, anvils, planishers, burnishers, soldering irons, floats, and numerous other tools as well as its stock of raw materials. Then there was the rent of the shop, the outlay for a certain minimum stock of finished wares, and the board and lodging for the apprentice or apprentices as well as for the master and his family. So, to commence in business even in a small way, a pewterer required a capital of at least two hundred to three hundred pounds, and five hundred pounds would have been required to set him up handsomely. But five hundred pounds in the eighteenth century was a great sum of money, and few tradesmen of that time could spare such an amount to establish a son in business.

Let us assume, however, that the fledgling pewterer had the necessary capital; had rented a shop; had acquired by inheritance or by purchase, possibly from a retired pewterer, a set of moulds and the necessary tools; had laid in a stock of raw materials; had secured under indenture the service of 'a likely lad' as his apprentice; and had advertised the opening of his shop.

Presumably he had already finished enough examples of his craftsmanship to make a brave showing of his work in the shop window before his sign went up, and, within the front door, at least one side of the room was lined with shelves on which the finished stock was to be stored. (See Plate IV, 11, 12.) The room was divided by a counter as any country store of today, and on the counter were scales, for pewter was frequently sold by weight. A partition perhaps divided the store from the shop proper.

The shop itself, except in large establishments, probably consisted of but one large room. In one corner or along one wall were bins or piles of raw materials — principally old pewter, but also small supplies of lead, copper, and antimony or bismuth (frequently both). No evidence of tin bars is found in the early inventories and apparently the pewterers were entirely dependent upon old pewter for their tin supply. Each shop also had its stock of fuel — wood, charcoal, and, occasionally in Pennsylvania, coal.

At one side of the room was the hearth with furnace and wide projecting hood and about it the pots or crucibles in which the metals were melted, a bellows, and the ladles in which the molten metal was carried to the moulds. (Plate I, 2; Plate III, 7; and Plate IV, 9.)

The pewterer's first operation was, of necessity, the preparation of his metal. If his old pewter had not been sorted and graded, that step was required before he could prepare his bath. Plate I, 1, shows a pewterer assaying the returned old metal. Seated beside a small furnace he has several iron tools with diamond-shaped heads heating over the fire. These he changes off as fast as the tool which he is using cools. A hollow wooden handle is slipped over the tool to be used and is transferred to the next one as the first is returned to the grill above the coals. On his leather-aproned lap the pewterer takes the piece of metal to be tested. Holding it with one hand he takes with the other a red-hot tool and presses it into the pewter. From the rapidity of melting and congeal-

PLATE I — *Pewter-Making*

The illustrations are from an eighteenth-century French treatise, *L'Art du Potier d'Etain*,
by a pewterer of Chartres, M. Salmon. Courtesy of J. Ritchie Kimball, Esq.

1. Assaying and sorting old metal. The workman is assaying each piece and depositing it, according to quality, in the proper stock pile.

2. Casting pewter plates.

   7 with a brush is coating a mould.

   23 is tightening a mould with a jack screw preparatory to pouring.

   10 is pouring.

   15 is tapping a casting from a mould.

   Note the hearth where the metal is prepared; also the shelves of moulds not in use.

3. Turning pewter dishes.

   4 is heating a casting over a brazier and filling in pits in the casting with small particles of solder, which are being prepared for that purpose by 1.

   7 is a 'turn-wheel' — the power for the lathe.

   8 is turning a pewter dish. Note the use of an arm-rest fixed perpendicular to the casting. In front of the workman are four more turning hooks with varied faces, while others are on a rack on the wall.

PLATE I

1

2

3

4. 8 is soldering together separate castings of hot-water plates.
   2 is removing a 'tadge' or 'sprue' from a casting.
   5 with a float is smoothing rough surface of dish casting.
   6 and 7 are burnishing by hand, the latter using a two-handled burnisher.

5. Hammermen at work. Note the shape of the hammers.
   D shows an ingenious contrivance in which a porringer is clamped for hammering.

6. Engravers decorating flatware using burins of varied types.

PLATE II

4

5

6

ment of the drop of pewter which is scooped up on the iron, and the form and color of the same while congealing, the workman can, from long training, determine the quality of the metal with sufficient accuracy to classify it as fine, good, ley, or black pewter.

The assay completed, the pewterer selects from his stocks of old metal a sufficient amount for the task involved, the quality depending upon the specification to which he proposes to work. This metal he dumps into a large iron cauldron over the fire, adding to the bath such other ingredients as may be required, and, while the metal is melting, takes down from the shelves, on which the moulds were normally stored when not in use (see Plate I, 2), the particular moulds into which the metal is to be run.

Let us assume that our man is about to cast plates as in the illustration in Plate I. The mould was first carried to one of the benches and the inside of both cover and base was coated. Various preparations were used for this purpose. One of the oldest and most efficient methods was to form a paste out of Venetian red or yellow ochre, white of egg and vinegar, and to apply this mixture evenly over the surface with a paintbrush. Then the mould was taken to the hearth, thoroughly heated, and the coating baked on. The albumen in the egg underwent changes in baking which gave it a lasting quality and made recoating necessary only at long intervals.

This form of coating was used only for moulds from which the castings were to be finished on a lathe or by hand. When only a minimum of finish was required, as for common spoons, the mould was coated with soot from a smoking flame. Pine knots were excellent for this purpose. The soot wore off easily, however, and had to be renewed frequently.

Coating was essential to prevent direct contact between the mould and the molten metal. Wherever such contact occurred, shallow characteristic blisters formed, blisters very different in appearance from those caused by enclosed air. The latter were occasioned by imperfect ventilation of the mould or improper position of the mould during pouring. Ventilation was usually provided after an examination of the first sample casting. Notches, wide at the outside and tapering down to deep scratches where they entered the cavity, were filed in the mould. Sometimes additional vents had to be added until a casting came out free from blisters.

Before casting could begin, great care had to be exercised to make sure that mould and metal were at just the right temperature. If either was too cold, the metal would not flow sufficiently freely to cover the entire inner surface; if too hot, time was lost waiting for castings to solidify. Proper temperature of the metal was determined by thrusting into it a dry pine stick. The degree of the charring of the wood gave a sufficiently close indication of temperature. Before use the mould was heated to a point where vapor would not condense on its surfaces.

Having satisfied himself that all was in readiness, the pewterer carried the mould to the casting bench (Plate I, 2, Fig. 12) and clamped the sides together, the pour uppermost. From the pot on the hearth he dipped out just enough metal in a ladle to complete one casting and carried it to the bench. With tongs held in the other hand he steadied the mould while he poured in the molten metal until it filled the pour.

The Business of a Pewterer

As soon as the pewter hardened, the clamps were released. Top and bottom of the mould were tapped with a mallet to loosen the casting; the cover was then raised and the mould turned over permitting the casting to drop onto a piece of felt. The first pouring usually served no other purpose than to heat the mould, and ordinarily the casting was too defective for use.

The mould was then set again and casting continued until the temperature of the mould reached a point where the castings were too slow in cooling, usually evidenced by their breaking as they were being removed from the mould. The mould was then set aside to cool in a drafty place while another mould was started.

Every piece, as it came from the mould, was rough indeed, and, before it could be taken to the wheel for the finishing operations, fins, sprue, and other imperfections had to be removed. First of all the 'tadge' or sprue, the excess metal which had protruded above the casting hole, was melted off with a heated tool (Plate II, 4, Fig. 4), or, if it was small, was removed with a pair of nippers. Secondly, any bubble holes or other indentations were carefully filled (Plate II, 3, Fig. 4) and finally the entire surface of each casting was smoothed down with large two-handled floats, i.e., single coarse-cut files (Plate II, 4, Fig. 6). Unlike a rasp or file in which the cutting is done by a series of points, the float has a series of scrapers which remove the excess metal in diagonal cuts, leaving a smooth surface with no deep scratches. This procedure was necessary to prevent the tools from jumping in the lathe operations which followed. After all the castings had been thus treated, they were stamped with the touches of the shop and carried to the lathe.

The lathe was usually operated by man power (Plate I, 3, Fig. 7), sometimes by an apprentice, but frequently by a 'turn-wheel,' a cripple or feebleminded man, who was capable of no higher form of labor. In some few shops the wheel was turned by a horse (usually blind) on a treadmill, and a few favorably located establishments used water power.

The casting was slipped over a wooden chuck which had been hollowed out to take the shape of the piece to be turned and was carefully centered. The chuck was provided with a metal ring onto which the casting was tacked with solder, the tacking being cut away as the final operation. This was the method used for both hollow-ware and flatware. Onto the chuck was screwed a metal disc and onto this disc the first plate was tacked with solder.

The pewterer then selected from a row of long-handled 'hooks' (or cutting tools) the particular cutting face which he required. (Plate VI shows some of the hooks of Samuel Pierce.) With the handle of the tool under his arm and the arm supported on a crossbar, the workman, with his other hand, held the tool blade against the revolving casting. This crossbar was peculiar to the pewterer's lathe, which in all other respects resembled closely the lathe of the woodturner. The bar was permanently fastened to the head and tail stock of the lathe with no up-and-down adjustment as of the T-rest on the woodturner's lathe. The pewterer's technique in turning was different from that of other trades in that it involved scraping and a consequent pull on the tools, while in wood-

Plate II 3, fig. 4, should read
Plate I 3, fig. 4

Plate II 4, fig. 6, should read
Plate II 4, fig. 5

turning and that of all other metals turned by hand the tools were held against the direction of the turning and sustained a push. Working from the outside toward the center the pewterer scraped the entire surface of the casting. Next he took a blunter cutting tool and repeated the skimming process (see Plate I, 3).

*See Plate I 3,
should read
See Plate I 3, fig. 8*

The ensuing operation, in which the wheel also played a part, was burnishing. The tools employed in this operation resembled the cutting tools, but had smooth, rounded, highly polished faces instead of sharp edges (see Pierce's burnishers, Plate VI). The marks of these tools can frequently be seen today in the spiral ridges on the bottoms of porringers, mugs, and even plates which have had little use. After lubricating the particular burnisher which he desired to use by dipping it in soapy water or stale beer, the workman pressed it against the revolving casting (which had also been moistened) until the piece had acquired a bright appearance over its entire surface. If he desired to adorn the plate with incised lines, he did so at this stage of manufacture, but any elaborate engraving was performed after the plate was otherwise finished (see Plate II, 6). The plate then received a polish with rotten stone or other abrasive and the face was in its finished form.

Instead of being removed now from the lathe, the plate was made to serve as a chuck for the next casting which was lightly soldered to it at three points, equidistant on the rim. The face of the second casting was then turned, burnished, and polished, when it, in turn, became a chuck for the third casting. This procedure continued until the pewterer had finished the faces of as many plates as the lathe could conveniently carry. Then the bottom plate was cut loose from the chuck, the pile reversed, and the bottom plate (just previously the outside one) was soldered to another hollow chuck which it fitted snugly. The operator then skimmed, burnished, and polished the bottom just as he had done the face of the plate, trimmed the edges, and, as he finished each plate, cut it loose at the soldering points from its fellow. The method of fastening plates in a lathe as described above was used extensively in France and probably in England. I have no doubt that it was also the normal method employed in the colonies. It was, however, applicable only to flatware. Other forms were fitted singly over wooden chucks and could not be made to serve as chucks for identical castings.

One further process was required for such flatware as was to be hammered either on the booge alone or over the entire surface. Hammering closed the pores of the metal, made a closer grain structure, and consequently added strength to the portion hammered. The tools required were stake anvils and hammers, the faces of which had to be kept smooth and highly polished. I do not know of the existence of any pewterer's hammers in this country today, but hammermen can be seen at work in Plate II, 5. As the illustration shows, each hammer had two faces and every pewterer had hammers of different sizes and with varied curvature of face. Choice of which face to use depended upon the contour and size of the surface to be hammered and also upon whether hammering or planishing was desired.

Plates that were to be hammered were turned first on the lathe, but on the back of each casting only. The hammerman (or sadware man as he was known in England) took a casting in one hand and held it with the booge resting on the anvil stake. With the other hand he selected the proper hammer and struck a blow on the booge. As he slowly turned the plate, each succeeding blow fell above the same spot on the anvil but farther around the circle of the booge. When each ring of indentations had been completed, another, just above or below it, was commenced until the entire booge had been hammered. When struck by a master of the craft, the circular impression made by each blow overlapped the next circle in each direction so accurately as to give an appearance of almost square indentations. If you have the same difficulty as the author in striking a nail twice in the same spot with the same force of impact, you can perhaps realize the precision required to cover a pewter plate with marks of equal depth and size which overlapped in every direction to exactly the same extent. If you desire to see how accurately this was done, examine either of the surviving hammered dishes of Simon Edgell, early Philadelphia pewterer (see Frontispiece, volume I). In England hammermen comprised one branch of the trade, the highest caste in the pewter hierarchy; in the colonies hammering was but one detail of the art in which every pewterer was supposed to be proficient.

When the planishing was completed, each plate was returned to the lathe and finished inside, thus obliterating all marks left by the stake.

There were, of course, occasions for making flatware in odd sizes, sizes for which there were no moulds. Such plates were hammered out from a flat sheet. The pewterer would cast a flat circle in a mould made for that purpose. From that he would cut a blank of the size wanted and raise it with a raising hammer on the stake. As more force and less precision was required during the raising process, the elbow served as the pivot for the hammer, but in planishing, where precision was essential, the wrist served as the pivot, with the elbow close to the body. So much for the manufacture of flatware.

The making of hollow-ware involved the same general methods, but was more complicated, because no item of hollow-ware could be cast in a single two-part mould. Either a number of separate castings had to be soldered together to make the finished whole or moulds of more than two parts with cores had to be employed. For many forms a combination of the two methods was necessary. It must be apparent, for instance, that any such form as the belly of a Queen Anne teapot must needs have been made up of two castings. These were soldered together at their widest diameters after each section had been cast in a mould of several parts, usually a cover and bottom and a two-part core. The latter formed the solid center around which flowed the metal inside the mould to make the finished casting. The casting operation differed but little from plate casting, but involved the additional precaution of seeing that moulds and cores fitted together perfectly. As with plates the tadge had to be removed after casting, all depressions filled, and the surface smoothed with floats.

Suppose that we follow the operations involved in finishing a teapot of early design. After the castings had been smoothed off, they were taken to the lathe. Let us assume that the workman decided to skim first the upper portion of the pot proper. Over the chuck, which in this case was a sort of face plate with a center recess just able to receive

PLATE III — *Pewter Shop Interior Views*
From *L'Art du Potier d'Etain*.

7. Making hollow-ware.
   2 is pouring.
   4 and 5 are soldering.
   6 is casting a solid handle directly onto a vessel.
   7 is burnishing by hand.

8. Finishing hollow-ware.
   F is the turn-wheel.
   1 is 'slush-moulding' (casting a hollow spout or handle).
   2 is skimming or burnishing a pot on the lathe.
   3 is tacking a spout to a teapot with solder.
   4 is soldering the spout in place with a blowpipe.

PLATE III

7

8

PLATE IV — *Pewter Shop Interior Views*

9 and 10 are from *L'Art du Potier d'Etain*; 11 and 12 were furnished through the courtesy of the late Howard H. Cotterell.

9. Spoon-making.
   1 is crunching old metal for the bath.
   2 is casting an ingot.
   3 and 4 are casting spoons.

10. Finishing spoons.
   1 and 2 are scraping by hand.
   3 is burnishing by hand.
   4 and 5 are polishing.
   6 is packing.

11. Trade card of Robert Peircy showing store front with scales on counter.
   (Reproduced from *Old Pewter, Its Makers and Its Marks*.)

12. Store front, from an old Dutch engraving.

PLATE IV

10

12

9

11

the opening that eventually was to be covered with the lid, he slipped the pot and tacked it in position. With a hook or other scraping tool he smoothed off the seams where the cores had met and then skimmed and burnished as much of the inside as could be reached conveniently. The casting was then reversed and tacked, perhaps, to the same face plate, which would have been designed with an additional recess to take the belly of the teapot. The inside of the neck was then scraped and burnished. In like manner the lower half of the pot and the casting for the base were finished and all pieces were carried to the furnace to be soldered.

Soldering required a steady hand, an accurate eye, a well-heated iron, and pewter with scrupulously clean edges. Some makers did their welding with a soldering iron and a solder which fused at a lower temperature than the pewter to be welded. Others used as the welding agent the edges of the pewter shapes on which they were working. In the latter method the pewterer, before the soldering operation began, turned up the edges to be joined, forming a very narrow flange perpendicular to the surface of the casting. The two parts (in this instance the lower and upper halves of the belly) were butted against one another after every care had been taken to see that their surfaces were wiped clean. On the inside where the two castings were to be joined was placed a piece of felt about an inch wide, cut to a length so that it fitted exactly the inside circumference. Its purpose was to prevent any molten metal from dripping through to the inside. Then the pewterer spread a flux of fresh pine resin or rancid tallow along the juncture, and, as he turned the castings with one hand, he ran the soldering iron with the other around the circumference, melting down the flanged lips and completing the entire welding operation without once lifting his tool from the castings. Undoubtedly a blowpipe and candle flame were used at times instead of a soldering iron as may be seen in Plate III, 8, Fig. 4. In like manner the base was welded to the belly; the rest of the castings on hand went through the same routine; and then once more the embryo teapots were carried to the lathe.

At the lathe the workman clamped a pot in position over forms, like cores, which exactly fitted the interior contours of the vessel. His first operation was to trim the soldered circle, then the remainder of the exterior surface, a planer with slightly rounded edge serving to skim the joints, fillets, etc. Then the pot was burnished, polished, and set aside to await the attachment of handle, hinge, and spout.

The lids, usually made up of two or more castings each, were also finished on the lathe. The remaining parts, handle, spout, hinge, and hinge pin, on account of size and shape, could not be lathe-finished and were of necessity scraped, burnished, and polished with small hand tools.

Handles varied in form and in method of manufacture. On many of the early teapots the handles were of wood held in place by pins run through two small pewter sleeves, which had been soldered to the pot. Less frequently a solid pewter handle was applied. In some shops it was cast separately and then soldered on. The more usual practice — and this applies with equal or greater force to porringer, mug, and tankard handles — was to cast the handle directly onto the pot (or bowl). The mould for such a handle was open at both top and bottom and was held in position on the pot while a 'stop rag' or 'tinker's dam,' a piece of burlap or other coarse cloth filled with wet sand, was held firmly against the area inside the pot directly under the points where the hot metal would impinge upon and be sweated to the pot. Then the casting was poured. The mark of the tinker's dam may be seen on many a piece today, particularly on the inside of porringer bowls. In Plate III, 7, Fig. 6, a workman is shown casting a handle upon a ewer in the manner described above.

The casting of hollow handles, which came into great favor in the eighteenth century, required a special technique — a method known as slush-moulding, that was also used for the manufacture of spouts. In developing this method the pewterer made use of the well-known fact that all molten metal cools more quickly on the exterior, leaving the central core liquid after the outer edges have solidified. The casting began in the normal manner, but, soon after the start of solidification, the workman, with a deft flick of the wrist, turned the mould upside down, ejecting all metal still in a molten state and leaving in the mould a hollow pewter shell in the shape of a handle. A slush-moulder at work will be noted in Plate III, 8, Fig 1.

The process required not only a special method but also a special alloy. To attempt to make hollow handles in this manner with a normal alloy would be foredoomed to failure because, as ordinary pewter solidifies, the crystals tend to cling to one another, and if a casting that had just begun to cool were up-ended the semi-molten fluid could not be quickly ejected. With the particular alloy employed in slush-moulding the exterior hardened quickly while the inner mass remained in a molten state. For a homely analogy recall to yourself the differences in action of fresh-water ice and salt-water ice as they melt. The former changes abruptly from ice to water; the latter melts first into a spongy state where it seems to be neither water nor ice.

Just what the exact formula for this alloy was I do not know, for I have had no hollow handles assayed, but I am told that the tin content was lower than in the standard grades.

After casting in this manner, handles and spouts were finished by hand; hinges were cast separately in two parts or directly onto pot and cover; and hinge pins were cast and finished. All parts were then assembled; the various members soldered in place, and the teapot made its last trip to the lathe to have the regions about the soldering points scraped, burnished, and polished once more. The lid was then attached with hinge pin and the teapot was finally ready to be carried to a shelf in the front store.

In much the same manner all forms of hollow-ware were manufactured and prepared for market. One other branch of pewter-making, the work of the triflers, or spoon-makers, requires but brief comment. The story is told pictorially in Plate IV, 9 and 10.

The illustrations are those of a large French establishment. The operations are almost precisely such as would have taken place in a colonial pewterer's shop except that few of our makers, prior to the nineteenth century, had more than two or three employees at one time or shops of more than two rooms.

In this country prior to 1825 there were just two methods of disposing of the finished product. One was to sell it over the counter direct from the shop; the other was to carry

PLATE V — *Pewter Moulds and Tools*

13. Moulds of John Philip Reich, Salem, North Carolina, 1797–1867. Courtesy of the Wachovia Historical Society, Winston-Salem, North Carolina, the Reverend Douglas L. Rights, Director. Shown in the illustration are a dish mould, basin mould, spoon mould, and also a mould for a small object that was probably made on order.

14. One of Reich's Plate Moulds. Courtesy of the Wachovia Historical Society. The illustration shows the mould in closed position with the 'pour' at the top.

15. Some small moulds and tools of Samuel Pierce, Greenfield, Massachusetts, 1767–1840. Collection of the author.

   Top row (left to right): wooden mould for casting small pewter ornament, a casting made in same, small eagle die, soapstone mould for teapot finial, brass porringer handle mould, three-part mould for sleeve for teapot handle.

   Bottom row: porringer handle mould (brass), soapstone mould for beaker base, and base of beaker cast therein.

PLATE V

15

13

14

PLATE VI — *Tools of Samuel Pierce*

Greenfield, Massachusetts, 1767–1840. Collection of the author.

16. *Above:* porringer tongs for holding porringer while attaching handle, etc. The cloth-padded arms fit snugly inside porringer bowls.

Left to right: 1, long-handled burnisher; 2, hawk-bill burnisher; 3, two-handled burnisher; 4, wood file; 5 and 6, soldering irons; 7 and 8, turning hooks; 9, knurl; 10, chasing tool for making threads. (Note the corncob handle on 6.)

17. *Left to right:* 1, float for smoothing castings; 2 and 3, two-handled hooks for skimming; 4 to 10, turning hooks.

Most of the heads have been ground down by Pierce from discarded files and other hard steel tools. Note how ingeniously they have been fastened to the wooden handles (4 to 10). At the top of the handle two or three circular grooves were cut, intersecting other channels at right angles to the circular openings. The head was then inserted and the tool plunged into molten pewter. A cross-banding of pewter, which filled the channels and remained after the tool was withdrawn from the pot, holds each head firmly in place.

PLATE VI

16

17

the goods to the public in a peddler's cart. In the larger cities the peddler's cart was probably rarely employed, but the country maker had no recourse but to hawk his wares far and wide, for his local trade would never have furnished sufficient business. Some men like Thomas Danforth, Second, of Middletown, had their own carts; others hired peddlers to merchandise their goods. As evidence of the way in which peddlers operated, the following copy of a contract made September 3, 1816, between William and Samuel Yale of Meriden, Connecticut, and one of their peddlers, Amos Francis, is illuminating:

> Articles of Agreement made and entered into by and between William and Samuel Yale of Meriden in New Haven Co. on the one part and Amos Francis of Wallingford in said County on the other part witnesseth viz: I, the said Amos Francis agree on my part to hawk, peddle and vend such articles as the said Yales shall deliver me for that purpose in any part of the United States they shall see fit to send me for the term of ten months from the first day of October next and to furnish a good horse, waggon and harness and be faithful in their said employ during said term of time to be fully completed and ended.
>
> And we, the said William and Samuel Yale agree to pay the said Amos Francis for his said services thirty dollars per month certain wages, forty dollars per month if said Francis clears it over and above the first cost of his load and expenses and one half of all profits over and above said forty dollars, that he, said Francis, shall actually clear.
>
> Dated at Meriden this 3rd day of September, 1816
>
> William Yale
> Samuel Yale
> Amos Francis

Trudging at his horse's head, day in and day out, over hill and dale, in all kinds of weather, the peddler reached every little hamlet east of the Alleghenies. He played no small part in the sales program of the country pewterer.

THE MARKS ON PEWTER

COLLECTORS there are who love pewter for the forms in which it was cast, for its texture, its color, and its associations, who care not a whit for the marks which the individual pieces bear. This chapter is not for them. But the majority of us are not satisfied with merely admiring our possessions. We want to know when and where they were made and what manner of men were the pewterers who fashioned them. Only by a study of the touches can we find the answers to such questions.

To trace the origin of the custom of marking pewter, it is necessary to revert to the history of the *Worshipful Company of Pewterers*. When, in the fifteenth century, the Company had obtained a royal charter and had been granted wide powers over the manufacture and sale of pewter throughout England, efforts were made to enforce their regulations. But at times the vigilance of the Company's searchers to seek out the source of inferior metal must have been brought to naught by their inability to fix the blame definitely upon the guilty pewterers. It is therefore not surprising to find a statute (dated 1503) in which it is ordained:

> ... (9) that the Makers of such wares shall mark the same Wares with several Marks of their own, to the Intent that the Makers of such Wares, shall avow the same Wares by them (as above said) to be wrought; (10) and that all and every such Wares not sufficiently made and wrought, and not marked in Form aforesaid found in the Possession of the same Maker or Seller to be forfeited;

Thereafter English pewterers were required to impress upon their metal (barring, of course, such small objects as salts, etc.) the touches of their respective shops.

When active settlement began in America in the first quarter of the seventeenth century, the Pewterers' Company was all-powerful within the trade in England. It specified the percentage of the different metals that should go into the making of each form of vessel; it dictated the methods and conditions of sale; prescribed just what form of marking should be employed; and haled before the courts the offenders who broke its regulations.

Trained in such a rigid school were our first pewterers. I am satisfied that in theory, at least, every reputable pewterer in the colonies with a trade of any magnitude normally stamped upon his wares his own identification touches. Yet had there existed in the colonies a central governing body of the craft, comparable to the London Company, the quality of American pewter would have been uniformly higher, we should now find far fewer unmarked pieces, and our knowledge of the American makers would be immeasurably greater. It is a matter of congratulation, however, that, in the absence of a guild with even local power in the colonies, American pewterers should have turned out such creditable work and should have been sufficiently proud of their wares to stamp upon them their names.

It is not surprising that much pewter that we find is unmarked. Some country makers probably never had individual touches, and we can be certain that those who had did not always bother to mark their work. For evidence I have seen a pair of chalices, alike as two peas, which had apparently always been together. One bore the touch of Peter Young of Albany and the other was unmarked. Again, I secured a communion set that contained three beakers, identical to all outward appearance, and, though two had the touches of T. D. Boardman, the third showed no evidence of ever having been stamped. Many such cases might be cited, and we can say without reservation that it was normal for the larger shops, at least, to mark their wares, but that through carelessness and the absence of a Pewterers' Company in America a great quantity of metal from these same shops was allowed to reach the public without any identification marks.

Marks themselves are of various kinds, applied for various purposes. There are those which the pewterer used to identify and advertise his wares; there are the marks which indicate a superior grade of hard metal; and there are the initials of the purchasers, usually stamped or engraved by the seller at the time of sale, but occasionally added afterward by the owners themselves.

Of primary importance are the makers' touches which were struck cold with a die after the casting came from the mould. The dies were so cut as to leave the designs in relief on the pewter. Some of the touches are very handsome and nearly all are interesting. The best of them represent exceedingly fine work by the die-cutters, and it is a pity that we know practically nothing about the men who cut and, in some cases, designed the marks of our pewterers.

Every shop of any importance had at least two touches, one used on plates, dishes, and other large surfaces; the other, somewhat smaller, reserved for porringer handles, beakers, etc. The larger touches usually included the maker's name and frequently the place where he worked, though the town's name was sometimes added in a separate touch. In the small marks the man's name is usually omitted, his initials being substituted therefor. When not even the initials are shown, identification is extremely difficult unless the mark has been found in conjunction with previously identified touches.

In addition to the regular touches many makers, prior to 1800, stamped their pewter with sets of from two to four very small rectangular or shield-shaped marks, which we have been accustomed to call hall-marks, deriving our terminology from marks of a similar nature found on silver and ordered to be impressed thereon in Goldsmiths' Hall, London. The silver marks, however, indicated not only the maker's initials, the town in which he worked, and the sovereign whom he served, but even the year in which that particular piece of silver was made. Pewter hall-marks (so called) give us no such exact information. They represent nothing more than an additional identification mark (or group of marks) of one particular shop. Even in London hall-marks were never prescribed on pewter. In fact, in the records of the Goldsmiths' Company during the seventeenth century we find that the workers in the fine metals objected strenuously to this aping of their customs and petitioned the Lords of the Council to correct the evil. The pewterers were ordered to abstain from the practice and professed obedience to the order, but apparently winked at those who failed to observe it, and before 1700 the use of pewter hall-marks had become general. In this country they were continued until about the year 1800.

Early in the nineteenth century, when the shapes of pewter vessels began to undergo marked changes, marks also ceased to retain their early character. The tendency at first was toward smaller touches; then to mere rectangles enclosing the maker's name, though still with raised letters; and the last stage was reached when the latter were replaced by the names intaglio. Practically all pewter, so marked, belongs to the britannia period.

The pewterer's marks, then, included at least two touches, often an additional touch indicating the town in which he worked, and from about 1750 to 1800 a set of so-called hall-marks. In addition it often happened that the original dies became marred or were lost or the maker tired of the touches which he had been using, or finally that a change in political conditions made it desirable that touches of new design be substituted for the old. As a good example of a wholesale change, note how the rose and crown and the rampant lion and unicorn, symbols of the sovereignty of England, were discarded in favor of eagles by almost every American pewterer soon after the Revolution. Consequently, it happened that most makers used a variety of touches, and in some cases we can follow a man's career in the changes in his marks, dating almost exactly many of the pieces which he made.

Since the types of touches varied in different sections, and marks of one locality often showed distinct differences in design from those of a neighboring community, and since, further, the marks of any section changed with the changing times, it is often possible to make a fairly accurate surmise of the age and place of manufacture of any given example of pewter if only the specimen bears a maker's mark. This can frequently be done even when the touch is one that has not been recorded previously.

A second and less important group of marks comprises those used by a few of our pewterers to indicate a superior quality of metal. In England various makers used a mark in addition to their normal touches in which the words 'Hard Metal' appear where we should normally find the maker's name. Such a touch was used by Samuel Hamlin of Providence (Plate XLIX, 333) on what he considered his best quality plates and dishes. It was also a practice in England to stamp a crowned X (occasionally an X alone) on the finer wares. This custom was followed in America, although there was no Pewterers' Company here to see that the quality symbol was legitimately used. We find such marks (always intaglio) on pewter of the Danforths, the Boardmans, Henry Will, Peter Young, D. Curtiss, Nathaniel Austin, and others.

Finally there were the initial marks of the owners, usually in the form of a triad. The upper letter of the triangle represented the initial letter of the surname of the owners, while the lower letters were the initials of the Christian names of the husband and wife. Although sometimes these were engraved by the pewterer at the time of sale or by the owner after he had returned to his home with his purchases, the normal procedure was for the pewterer to stamp the initials (intaglio) on the metal when the sale was made. In examining the inventories of pewterers it will be found that each usually included a set of twenty-four letter punches which were used for just this purpose.

To the collector who really desires to know his possessions the study of the touches is invaluable. There still are and always will be bargains in American pewter. Any dealer knows enough to put a good price on an eagle-marked piece, assuming it to be American, but how many have the requisite knowledge to differentiate among the rose and crown of America, of England, and of the Continent? The early pieces are the real rarities, and, fortunately for the student of pewter, they are the very ones which can be obtained the most reasonably if only the purchaser knows the touches.

PEWTER-MAKING IN AMERICA

THE colonization of America may be said to have begun in earnest with the landing of the Pilgrims at Plymouth in 1620. We find no record of a pewterer in the ship's company of the *Mayflower*, but Richard Graves had a shop at Salem as early as 1635, and by 1640 at least four pewterers were at work in the Massachusetts Bay Colony. During the rest of the seventeenth century probably very little pewter was made in this country except in and around Boston. In fact we have record of but five pewterers in other colonies prior to 1700 — two each in Pennsylvania and Virginia and one in Maryland.

Until recently nothing made by these early artisans was known to be in existence today. The discovery on the site of Jamestown, Virginia, of a fragment of a spoon bearing the touch of a Virginia pewterer who was at work as early as 1675 furnished the first specimen of American pewter of the seventeenth century. That spoon conforms in a general way to the contemporary design of English spoons, and since every American pewterer of that period, whose record has been authenticated, was an Englishman by birth or descent, their product surely followed closely in design the forms then current in England.

By the first quarter of the eighteenth century, Boston, grown to a populous town, could boast at least ten pewter-making establishments and might well have supported a local pewterers' guild, though no record of such an organization exists. In the same period New York and Philadelphia had at least half a dozen shops apiece and individual pewterers are known to have operated in Taunton (Massachusetts), Newport (Rhode Island), Upper Marlboro (Maryland), and Charleston (South Carolina). The combined output of these shops must have been great, but the period is represented in collections today by only a few examples.

In the hundred years that followed, the century in which most of our surviving examples of pewter were made, Boston, New York, and Philadelphia retained their preeminent position in the industry, shared after 1760 by Middletown (Connecticut) and to a lesser degree by Newport, Providence, and Albany. Also in Norwich (Connecticut), Lancaster (Pennsylvania), Annapolis (Maryland), and Norfolk (Virginia) there were individual pewter-making shops prior to the Revolution.

During the early days of the Republic the pewter trade in the larger cities declined precipitately, hastened to its end by the importation from England of china and other substitutes. In Boston, Newport, and New York the recession seems to have been especially rapid. In the country districts, on the other hand, the demand for pewter ap-

PLATE VII — *Four Pewterers*

18. John Dolbeare, Boston, *c.* 1664–1740. From *A Few Facts Relating to the Origin and History of John Dolbeare of Boston*.

19. Colonel John Carnes, Boston, 1698–1760. From *History of the Military Company of the Massachusetts*.

20. Spencer Stafford, Albany, 1772–1844. From *Collections on the History of Albany*.

21. Squire William Yale, Meriden, 1784–1833. From *A History of Wallingford and Meriden, Connecticut*.

PLATE VII

18

19

Ames. 1805

Spencer Stafford

20

21

PLATE VIII — *Plates, Dishes, and Basins*

22. An English plate with narrow rim and multiple reeding; marks in well. Diameter $9\frac{3}{16}$ inches, rim width $\frac{5}{8}$ inch. Robert Clothyer, Chard, Somerset, *c.* 1670–1710. Collection of the author.

23. Early English dish with wide rim and narrow reed on reverse. Diameter $18\frac{1}{4}$ inches, rim width 6 inches. Maker unknown; late seventeenth century. Collection of Mr. and Mrs. Carl C. Brigham.

24. English plate of normal rim width with multiple reeding; marks on upper face of rim. Diameter $9\frac{1}{4}$ inches, rim width $1\frac{3}{16}$ inches. Edward Leapidge, London, 1699–1724. Collection of the author.

25 and 26. Standard American plates with single reed on upper face of rim. Collection of the author.

    25. Diameter $7\frac{15}{16}$ inches, rim width $1\frac{3}{16}$ inches. Parks Boyd, Philadelphia, 1795–1818, mark 544.

    26. Diameter $7\frac{7}{8}$ inches, rim width $1\frac{5}{16}$ inch. Thomas Badger, Boston, 1786–1810, mark 308. The comparative shallowness of well and narrowness of rim of the Badger plate are typical of Boston flatware.

27, 28, and 29. American dish, deep dish and basin. Collection of the author.

fig. 27.
Mark should read
422a instead of 542a

    27. Diameter 11 inches, rim width 1 inch, depth $1\frac{3}{16}$ inch. James Porter, Connecticut(?), *c.* 1800, mark 542a.

    28. Diameter $11\frac{1}{8}$ inches, rim width $1\frac{1}{4}$ inches, depth $1\frac{3}{8}$ inches. Daniel Curtiss, Albany, 1821–1840, mark 522.

    29. Diameter $11\frac{1}{2}$ inches, depth 3 inches. Robert Palethorp, Jr., Philadelphia, 1817–1822, mark 561.

PLATE VIII

22

23

24

25   26

27   28   29

parently kept up, perhaps even increased; and, because the importation of pewter had dwindled, many country makers did a tremendous business. Connecticut, with large shops in Middletown, Hartford, Meriden, and Wallingford, did not reach the peak of its production until well into the nineteenth century, and during these same years the shops of Philadelphia and Baltimore found a ready market for their product in the Central and Southern States. Providence, Albany, Fayetteville (North Carolina), and Augusta (Georgia) were other pewter-making centers of that period.

About 1825 the character of the industry changed completely. In the old days no man was qualified to set up a shop of his own until he had served seven years to a master-pewterer and was sufficiently wealthy to purchase a set of moulds and tools, for which a considerable outlay was required. It was not a business which any irresponsible work-man could enter. Those who did become pewterers usually followed the trade for the rest of their lives. But with the introduction of 'spinning' on a large scale, all this was changed. Before 1800 our makers had ceased to hammer their wares, and after 1825 the operations of casting and turning became obsolete also. Cheap blocks replaced the expensive moulds and the laws of apprenticeship were no longer enforced. Even the name of the industry was changed. Pewterers had become high-sounding 'britannia manufacturers.'

All over the country fly-by-night opportunists with little capital and, frequently, with a meager knowledge of their craft opened small factories. Some of these makers limited their output to candlesticks and whale-oil lamps, and many of them worked at the trade for but a few years. Certain establishments, operated by pewterers of the old school, notably the Boardmans in Hartford, Calder in Providence, and Gleason in Dorchester (Massachusetts), were very successful. But for every shop that prospered half a dozen failed. In this last period of the industry the center of manufacture shifted back to its starting-point in New England. There were a few successful shops in New York, Philadelphia, Albany, Cincinnati, and one or two other towns of the Middle States and the new West, but the trade in the South, never large, had dwindled to almost nothing. Portland (Maine), Providence, Boston and its environs, Taunton (Massachusetts), and particularly the towns of the Connecticut Valley were the last outposts of the industry. Today Reed and Barton of Taunton, who can trace a direct industrial descent from the little shop of Babbitt and Crossman (established in 1824), is the one survivor of an age and an industry that have passed.

HOUSEHOLD PEWTER

FROM the settlement of Plymouth in 1620 until the founding of the Republic (or later), pewter was probably the commonest metal that entered into the lives of our colonial forebears. It was cast into every conceivable form and was ready at hand in one shape or another all day long every day.

In many homes practically every vessel or utensil that came on the table (except knives and forks) was made of pewter. There were pewter plates, dishes, basins, porringers, spoons, ladles, mugs, tankards, beakers, pitchers, teapots, creamers, sugar bowls, salts and peppers, syrup jugs, and gravy boats. For illumination there were pewter lamps and candlesticks, sconces and tinder-boxes. Sundials and clock dials, clock hands and spandrels also were often made of pewter. There were barbers' bowls and shaving-mugs, inkwells, inkstands, and sanders. Commodes, bedpans, and spittoons were of the same metal. Liquor was distilled in stills equipped with pewter worms. Pewter infusion pots were advertised for those afflicted with colds, and when doctors bled their patients they gauged the letting of blood in pewter bleeding-bowls. Clothes were held in place with pewter buttons, and pewter buckles adorned the shoes and hats of that day. For the men there were pewter dram bottles and snuffboxes; for the women, patch-boxes, spool-holders, and linen-markers. The children had toy tea-sets made of pewter and the babies received their nourishment from pewter nursing-bottles. Today it is difficult for us to realize how universal the use of pewter once was.

It will be needless here to attempt a description of all the shapes that are known to have been made in the metal, but it may prove profitable to consider the principal stock forms, to show the changing styles in each, and to point out merits and faults of representative examples that have survived.

PLATES, DISHES, AND BASINS

The great majority of surviving specimens of American pewter, made prior to 1825, are flatware, and unquestionably this division of the business made up the bulk of the average colonial pewterer's trade. Flatware is the comprehensive term which includes every article of pewter, cast in a single piece, which could serve as a food-container. In this category are all those items variously known to us as plates, platters, dishes, saucers, trenchers, chargers, bowls, and basins. These terms have undergone changes

PLATE IX — *Plates, Dishes, and Basins*

30 to 39. Series of plates and dishes to show the range of size in American flatware. Collection of the author.

Top row:

30. 11-inch dish, 1-inch rim. James Porter, Connecticut(?), *c.* 1810, mark 422a.

31. 9-inch plate, 1-inch rim. Parks Boyd, Philadelphia, 1795–1818, mark 544.

32. 8⅞-inch plate, 1⅛-inch rim. Peter Young, Albany, *c.* 1780–1813, marks 512, 513.

33. 8-inch plate, 1⅛-inch rim. James Porter, Connecticut(?), *c.* 1800, mark 423.

34. 6¼-inch plate, 1¹³⁄₁₆-inch rim. Parks Boyd, Philadelphia, mark 545.

35. 4⅞-inch plate, ¹⁹⁄₁₆-inch rim. Samuel Green, Boston, 1779–1820, mark 303.

Bottom row, left to right:

36. 16⅜-inch dish, 1¹⁵⁄₁₆-inch rim. Frederick Bassett, New York, 1764–1800, marks 464, 466, and 467.

37. 15-inch dish, 2-inch rim. Henry Will, New York, 1760–1793, marks 488, 491.

38. 13⅜-inch dish, 1⁷⁄₁₆-inch rim. Thomas Badger, Boston, 1786–1810, marks 309 and 287b.

39. 12⅛-inch dish, 1½-inch rim. Thomas Danforth Second, Middletown, Connecticut, 1755–1782, marks 362, 363.

40 to 47. Series of basins to show range of size in American basins. Collection of the author.

Top row, left to right:

40. Diameter 7¾ inches, depth 2¹⁄₁₆ inches. Richard Lee, Springfield, Vermont, 1788–1805, mark 410.

41. Diameter 6⅝ inches, depth 1¹¹⁄₁₆ inches. William and Samuel Yale, Meriden, Connecticut, 1813–1820, mark 440.

42. Diameter 6 inches, depth 1⅝ inches. Samuel E. Hamlin, Providence, Rhode Island, 1801–1825, mark 337.

43. Diameter 3⅝ inches, depth 1⅛ inches. Same maker, mark 337.

44. Diameter 2¹³⁄₁₆ inches, depth ¾ inch. Same maker, mark 337.

Bottom row, left to right:

45. Diameter 11⁹⁄₁₆ inches, depth 3 inches. Thomas S. Derby, Middletown, Connecticut, 1815–1825, mark 441.

46. Diameter 10⅜ inches, depth 2⅝ inches. John Bassett, New York, 1720–1761, mark 458.

47. Diameter 9 inches, depth 2⅛ inches. Joseph Danforth, Middletown, Connecticut, 1780–1788, mark 378.

PLATE IX

30   31   32   33   34   35
   36   37   38   39

40   41   42   43   44
   45   46   47

PLATE X — *Smooth-Rim Plates*

48 to 50. Three Smooth-Rim Plates, 1760–1790. Collection of the author.

> *Left to right:*

> 48. Diameter 9⅝ inches, rim 1$\frac{3}{16}$ inches. Nathaniel Austin, Charlestown, Massachusetts, 1763–1810, marks 297, 298, and 299.

> 49. Diameter 9¼ inches, rim 1⅜ inches. Samuel Hamlin, Providence, Rhode Island, 1772–1801, marks 330, 333.

> 50. Diameter 8⅞ inches, rim 1⅛ inches. John Skinner, Boston, 1759–1790, marks 293 and 294.

48a to 50a. Reverse of same. The comparatively wide reed on the rim of 48a is unusual.

51. Smooth-rim small plate, diameter 5⅝ inches, rim $\frac{15}{16}$ inch. Colonel William Will, Philadelphia, 1765–1798, mark 539. Unusual in its small size, smooth rim, and marking on rim. Collection of Mr. and Mrs. Richard S. Quigley.

52. Oval dish, 15¼ inches × 11⅝ inches. Henry Will, New York and Albany, 1760–1793, marks 491 and 492. The only example of record of an oval dish of American manufacture. Collection of John W. Poole, Esq.

PLATE X

50a 49a 48a

52

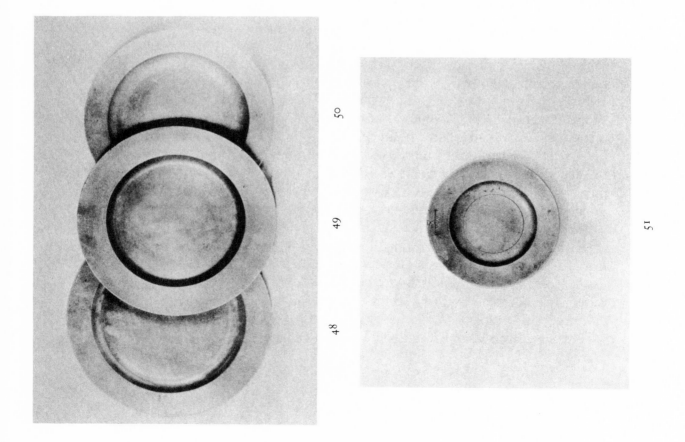

50 49 48

51

in meaning with the passing of the centuries, and our forefathers of pre-Revolutionary days would be surprised and perplexed by the use, or rather misuse, of some of these words as we employ them today. This current looseness of expression may possibly be corrected to some extent by an explanation of how, according to newspaper notices and town records, these specific terms were used in colonial America.

One of the commonest errors, of which almost every one of us is guilty, is to denote as a plate any piece of flatware, regardless of size, except a basin. Consider how often you have been asked to buy 'a 13-inch plate'; properly no such thing exists. Howard H. Cotterell, foremost English authority, who made the study of pewter his life-work, wrote me that a plate is a piece of flatware from which food was consumed directly by the individual, as differentiated from the larger pieces on which the food was carried to the table and from which it was distributed — the collective food-containers for the family. The significance of the term lies in the use to which the piece in question may have been put rather than its actual size, but it may be set down as an established fact, proved by the weight of plate moulds in numerous inventories, that plates never measured over 10 inches in diameter. Although we do find some plates (measuring approximately 9 inches in diameter) which are semi-deep, the normal plate was shallow and was never intended for food of a liquid or semi-liquid nature. Plates 6½ inches or smaller were butterplates, and occasionally served as patens.

Anything in flatware over 10 inches (except of course the large basin) is rightly termed a 'dish.' This division holds true irrespective of depth, for the inventories mention both the 'dish' and the 'deep dish.' We find some that are as shallow as the normal plate, while the rims of others may be over 1½ inches above the table. American dishes vary in size from 10 inches to 16½ inches. Just as the plate was the unit for individual service, the dish was the container of the food for a family.

Supplementing the plate and the dish, and used primarily for puddings, stews, and other forms of semi-liquid foods, was the 'basin,' a bowl-shaped container with narrow, moulded rim. In its smaller diameters it substituted for a deep plate; in the larger forms for a deep dish. The standard sizes were the pint (about 6¼ inches in diameter), quart (8 inches), three-pint (9 inches), two-quart (10½ inches), and three-quart (11½ to 12 inches). We do find basins measuring just 3¾ inches in diameter, and large specimens bearing American touches run up to 14 inches in diameter, but those under 5½ or over 11 ½ inches across are decidedly rare. It should be understood that a basin was essentially a food-container and not, as we are now accustomed to consider it, a bowl in which to wash. It is true, however, that in some of the poorer parishes basins served as baptismal bowls.

These three terms — plate, dish, and basin — are adequate to describe almost any form of American flatware which we are ever likely to find, and in this book we shall use any other but sparingly. As a matter of record, however, and in the hope of furthering a more correct usage of various terms, I shall attempt to throw some clearer light on the meaning of such words as 'charger,' 'trencher,' 'platter,' 'saucer,' and 'bowl.'

A 'charger' was a large dish upon which a whole turkey, a roast pig, or other form of

Plates, Dishes, and Basins

game or meat was carried in bulk to the banquet table. In England the term 'charger' is not used for pewter flatware under 18 inches in diameter, and as we have yet to find an American dish of that magnitude the word will have no place in this volume.

'Trencher' is a word frequently misused both by collectors and dealers. The term is derived from the French *trencher*, meaning 'to cut'; it was applied to the wooden blocks upon which the individuals cut their food, and, later, to the wooden plates which supplanted the hollowed blocks; in the sixteenth century it was used in England of any plate, whether wood or pewter, during the period when wood was giving way to the metal. No colonial records which I have examined apply the word 'trencher' to pewter except in the term 'trencher salts,' and I believe that we should do well to reserve its use for woodenware.

We are on debatable ground when we attempt to define a platter. In seventeenth-century England, and possibly also in America, 'platter' may have been synonymous with 'plate,' as Howard H. Cotterell believed. Such a view is supported by the inventory of Henry Shrimpton, Boston pewterer, which was taken in 1666. The shop contents included platters, dishes, and basins — but plates were not mentioned. From that time until about 1770 the term 'platter' is rarely found in colonial inventories or newspaper notices. Thereafter, however, it was back in common usage, apparently in place of the term 'dish,' for most of the later makers advertised plates and platters, but not dishes. It is also worth noting that in David Melville's inventory, taken in 1800, the platter mould weighed 62 pounds, whereas the plate moulds weighed from 9 to 26 pounds. It must be apparent, therefore, that, although a platter may have been merely a plate in the seventeenth century, the term implied a dish, usually a large dish of 14 or 15 inches in diameter, at the close of the eighteenth century.

Exactly what was meant by a 'sawcer' is even less certain now. The word was unquestionably applied to a diminutive plate, but there appears to be no proof now as to the point on the descending scale of sizes where the plate ceased to be a plate and became a saucer. It would be the part of wisdom to avoid the use of words such as this, the meaning of which remains ambiguous.

Last in our flatware glossary comes the 'bowl.' Here again is a term for which the collector of American pewter will have scant need. The term was very rarely used in early records except when preceded by some limiting term, as 'christening bowl,' 'sugar bowl,' etc. It should be emphasized that the basin, which was made by almost every pewterer from Henry Shrimpton's day to the close of the pewter period, was not a bowl. The basin was one of the commonest stock forms, the bowl a specialty, the exact shape of which is now a question. The inventory of the shop of Thomas Byles of Philadelphia (1771) included 'Hd Bowles,' but this was a very small item as compared with his 'Basons.' Incidentally Byles's inventory is the only one in which I have found the term 'bowl' used alone. It may therefore be dismissed as irrelevant to any study of existing shapes in American pewter.

During the period from 1650 to 1825, plates and dishes in many shapes and of varied proportions and details were produced in Great Britain and on the Continent of Europe,

[27]

PLATE XI — *Porringer Basin and Two-Handled Porringer*

53 and 54. Basin and porringer basin.

    Left: Pint basin, diameter $5\frac{7}{8}$ inches, mark 410.

    Right: Similar basin with handle, marks 411, 412. Richard Lee, Springfield, Vermont, *c.* 1788 to *c.* 1805. As far as now known this design of handle is found only on Lee porringer basins. Formerly in the collection of the late Albert C. Bowman, Esq.

55. Two-handled porringer with cover. Diameter 6 inches. Unmarked. Probably made in Rhode Island about 1800. Collection of the author.

55a. Same, with cover used as a stand.

PLATE XI

53   54

55

55 a

PLATE XII — *Porringers*

56. $5\frac{1}{4}$-inch porringer. Mark 587. Maker unknown. Eighteenth century. Type of handle rare. Collection of Mrs. James H. Krom.

57. $4\frac{5}{8}$-inch porringer. Mark 356. Attributed to John Danforth, Norwich, Connecticut, 1773 to 1793. Type of handle rare. Collection of the author.

58. $4\frac{13}{16}$-inch porringer. Richard Lee or Richard Lee, Jr., Springfield, Vermont, 1795–1813, mark 413. Type of handle rare. Collection of Charles F. Hutchins, Esq.

59, 60, and 61. Porringers in the collection of the author.

    59. $5\frac{7}{16}$-inch porringer. Gershom Jones, Providence, Rhode Island, 1774–1809, mark 341. This form of handle was used in Middletown and later by Newport and Providence pewterers.

    60. $4\frac{5}{8}$-inch porringer. Mark 575. Maker unknown. New England late eighteenth and early nineteenth centuries. A form of handle in common use in New England and New York.

    61. $4\frac{3}{8}$-inch porringer. Thomas Danforth Third, Stepney, Connecticut, 1777–1800, mark 368. Least rare of all forms of American porringer handles.

62. 4-inch porringer. Joseph Belcher or Joseph Belcher, Jr., Newport or New London, 1769–1784, mark 314. A form of handle peculiar to the Belchers. Collection of Mrs. J. Insley Blair.

63. $5\frac{5}{8}$-inch porringer basin with dolphin handle. Mark 357a. Attributed to John Danforth, Norwich, Connecticut. Rare. Collection of the author.

64. Rare, perhaps unique, four-handled miniature porringer. Diameter $2\frac{1}{2}$ inches, Richard Lee, Grafton, New Hampshire, or Ashfield, Massachusetts, 1788–1793, mark 408. Formerly in the collection of W. C. Staples, Esq.

PLATE XII

56

57

58

59

60

61

62

63

64

Household Pewter

but only three distinct variations of American plates are known to exist. The great majority are of the circular type with single-reeded, medium-width rim (Plate IX), a form that made its first appearance in England about 1700 and was discontinued there some fifty years later. The earliest of identified American plates are of this type, as are also the very latest. There was a period from about 1740 to 1790 or shortly thereafter when the smooth-rimmed plate, particularly in the 9-inch size (Plate X, 48 to 50), was made by many American pewterers, but not to the exclusion of the older form, and American dishes with smooth rim are so rarely found that they could never have had any great vogue.

Unfortunately we know of no American flatware of the seventeenth century. If it exists we can be very sure that it differs in design from the plates and dishes that we have thus far found. For the single-reeded rim and the smooth rim with wide, flat reed underneath were unknown in England prior to 1700. Since our earliest plates must have been cast in moulds that were brought from the 'old country,' it seems desirable to illustrate the types of flatware which were most prevalent in England from 1650 to 1700, for the hope persists that we may eventually find and be able to distinguish one or two examples made by the seventeenth-century pewterers of Massachusetts Bay. The first type shown (Plate VIII, 23), which became obsolete soon after 1675, had a very wide smooth rim, on the under face of which was an extremely narrow reed, quite unlike the wide, flat reed of the later smooth-rim plates. This design was followed by a plate with very narrow rim (c. 1650 to c. 1705) (Plate VIII, 22), which in turn gave way to a medium-rim plate with multiple reeding on the upper face (c. 1660 to c. 1705). Several different varieties of the multiple reeding exist, but the plate illustrated (Plate VIII, 24) will serve our purpose.

These, then, were the seventeenth-century forerunners in England, and probably also in America, of the single-reed plate — the standard plate of the colonies in the eighteenth century. In some one of these designs was cast the flatware of Graves, Shrimpton, Grame, Bumstead, Clarke, Paschall, the Comers, and the Dolbeares.

The third surviving form of American plates or dishes is the oval dish (Plate X, 52), the last new form discovered before this book went to press. Since we know of but the one example we can be certain that the number made in the colonies was relatively small. Octagonal, scalloped, or wavy-edged plates, and all those other plate forms which had a vogue in Europe but required elaborate turning equipment, seem never to have been experimented with in America.

Basins changed but little if any in shape either in England or America from 1650 until 1825. Typical examples are illustrated in Plate VIII, 29, and Plate IX, 40 to 47, and require no further comment here.

In London it was ordained early by the Pewterers' Company that on flatware the booge should be hammered. In country districts, however, the London edicts were not always obeyed and enforcement was extremely difficult, so it is problematical whether the earliest American pewterers hammered their flatware. It is worthy of note, however, that two surviving dishes of Simon Edgell (Frontispiece, Vol. I), made before 1742,

[28]

are hammered not only on the booge but over their entire surface. After 1750 and until the Revolution, hammering of the booge was normal on American plates. (See Plate X, 50.) Then, with the war, men began to look for short cuts; the same careful craftsmanship was no longer demanded; and all the younger makers laid aside their hammers, only a few old-timers, notably John Skinner and Peter Young, continuing the practice that had been all but universal before the Revolution. I have never seen evidence of hammer-marks on an American pewter plate or dish that had been made by a man who began work after the war.

Although many English basins were hammered, just as were the plates, the practice was not normal in this country. I have never seen a hammered American basin, though such a piece bearing Joseph Danforth's touch has been reported to me.

Prior to 1725 it was not unusual for the maker in England to stamp his touch or hallmarks in the well of the plate (Plate VIII, 22), and even more frequently the marks appeared on the rim (Plate VIII, 24). But thereafter the normal place for the touch was on the bottom of the plate or dish, and existing American plates, if marked at all, were 'touched' in that manner. The only exceptions known to me are the 8-inch plates of Samuel Hamlin stamped in the well, one 6-inch plate by William Will similarly marked, and one 5⅝-inch plate by the same maker with the touch on the rim. (See Plate X, 51.) This plate is unique also in that it is the only American plate under eight inches in diameter, thus far reported, which has a rim with smooth face. With basins, however, just the reverse holds true. Ordinarily the touch was placed in the center of the well, but on a few early specimens it is found on the outside bottom.

Roughly, this covers the story of American flatware. We shall find that the proportions of rim width to plate diameter vary slightly from one section of the country to another and that plates were made shallower in Boston, for instance, than in any of the Connecticut shops; but a true variety in style is all but non-existent, and the plates, dishes, and basins of one American pewterer are much like those of any other. It is for that reason that our chief interest in American flatware will probably always lie in the touches which the items bear, rather than in the pieces themselves.

PORRINGERS

So alluring has the collector of American pewter found the search for rare marks that, in many cases, he has failed to make due note of the forms on which these touches are impressed. Some shapes are so definitely American, in fact so definitely the work of specific pewterers, that they may be identified without need for examining the touches upon them. It is merely a matter of comparing their characteristics with those of examples already classified on the basis of their marks. Of all forms made by American pewterers, the porringer, with its exceptional diversity of handle designs, lends itself most readily to such a study.

Plate XIII — *Porringers*

65 to 69 inclusive. Group of small porringers. Collection of the author.

66. Diameter 3⅞ inches. Thomas D. Boardman, Hartford, 1806–1820, mark 426.

66. Diameter 3⅜ inches. Richard Lee or Richard Lee, Jr., Springfield, Vermont, 1788–1820, mark 413.

67. Diameter 2⅞ inches. Same maker, mark 413.

68. Diameter 2⅜ inches. Same maker, mark 414.

69. Diameter 2¼ inches. Isaac C. Lewis and Company, Meriden, Connecticut, *c.* 1840.

Each shape of handle in this illustration seems to have been an exclusive design of the shop to which it is here attributed.

70. Solid-handle porringer, diameter 5½ inches. Mark 292. Maker unknown. Rare form of handle. *C.* 1750–1780. Mabel Brady Garvan Collection, Museum of Fine Arts, Yale University.

71. Solid-handle porringer, diameter 5½ inches. David Melville, Newport, 1775–1794, mark 316. A form of handle found rarely on any but Newport porringers. Collection of Dwight Blaney, Esq.

72. Solid-handle porringer, diameter 5⅜ inches. Thomas Danforth Third, Philadelphia, 1807–1813, mark 373. Marked abnormally in well. Only recorded exception to rule that handles of this design are of Newport origin. Formerly in the collection of Philip G. Platt, Esq.

73. Solid-handle porringer basin, diameter 5⁷⁄₁₆ inches. Elisha Kirk, York, Pennsylvania, *c.* 1780–1790, mark 547. Type of handle made only in Pennsylvania. Collection of the author.

74. Solid-handle porringer basin, diameter 5⁵⁄₁₆ inches. Attributed to John Andrew Brunstrom, Philadelphia, 1783–1793, mark 548. Collection of the author.

75. Solid-handle porringer basin, diameter 5½ inches. Maker unknown, Pennsylvania, *c.* 1780–1800, mark 598. Collection of Mrs. J. Insley Blair.

fig. 74.
This solid-handle porringer basin is a modern fake and should be so classified

PLATE XIII

65   66   67   68   69

70   71   72

73   74   75

Plate XIV — *Flat-Top Tankards*

76. Fine English Stuart tankard with low flat lid, crenate lip, flaring base, graceful solid handle ending in a boot-heel terminal of early form. Height 5 inches, top diameter 3¾ inches, bottom diameter 5 inches. Maker unknown. Second half of seventeenth century. The earliest American tankards were probably of this general type. Collection of J. Ritchie Kimball, Esq.

77. An unusually fine, early, quart tankard, probably American, first half of eighteenth century. The handle with Stuart terminal is earlier in design than any other tankard handle here illustrated except 76. Height 5$\frac{9}{16}$ inches, top diameter 4⅜ inches, bottom diameter 5 inches. Mark not illustrated. Maker unknown, initials W. B. (?), possibly William Bradford, Jr., New York, 1719–1758. Collection of Edward E. Minor, Esq.

78. Fine flat-top tankard of type made by several New York pewterers. Height 6⅛ inches, top diameter 4½ inches, bottom diameter 5 inches. Frederick Bassett, New York and Hartford, 1761–1800, mark 465. Collection of Mrs. J. Insley Blair.

fig. 79.
Mark should read
502 instead of 510.

79. Similar tankard in the same collection made by another New York pewterer, William Kirby, 1760–1793, mark 510.

80. Front view of another Frederick Bassett tankard, identical with 78, illustrated to show details of thumb-piece and crenate lip. Collection of the author.

81. A tankard of the same period differing only in details. An open thumb-piece replaces the ram's-horn pattern and a bud terminal is substituted for the dolphin tail in 78–80. Height 6$\frac{1}{16}$ inches, top diameter 4⅜ inches, bottom diameter 5 inches. Henry Will, New York and Albany, 1761–1793, mark 491. Collection of Edward E. Minor, Esq.

82. Tankard of later design without crenate lip and with late form of thumb-piece. Height 5$\frac{13}{16}$ inches, top diameter 4 inches, bottom diameter 4¾ inches. Frederick Bassett, New York and Hartford, 1761–1800, mark 468. Collection of Edward E. Minor, Esq.

83. Last in point of design of the flat-top tankards. The top is not as flat as in its predecessors and the beginning of a dome has appeared. Height 6⅛ inches, top diameter 4$\frac{5}{16}$ inches, bottom diameter 5 inches. Peter Young, New York and Albany, 1775–1795, mark 514. Collection of the author.

PLATE XIV

79

83

78

82

77

81

76

80

Household Pewter

Porringers were used by the earliest settlers in America, and were, with little doubt, made by our first pewterers. The form became virtually obsolete in England soon after the middle of the eighteenth century. We do find in this country a few English porringers of Bristol manufacture which date from the final quarter of the eighteenth century, but these were presumably made for export after the demand had ceased in Great Britain. On the other hand, most of the surviving American specimens were made after 1800. In Philadelphia and the South there was, apparently, little demand for these vessels after the Revolution; and existing New York specimens, all of them made prior to 1800, are rare. But in New England, porringers were turned out generously until about 1825. For a few years longer their manufacture continued in Connecticut and Rhode Island, though on a declining scale; and then, about 1830, abruptly ceased, not to be resumed.

In an article in *Antiques* I made the statement that the porringer was ordinarily cast in two parts, the bowl and the handle. No less an authority than Howard H. Cotterell (who has saved me from many pitfalls) insisted that the bowl alone comprised at least two sections, the handle a third. It is probable that a close study of the earlier porringers would substantiate his belief, but a careful examination of many American specimens furnishes internal evidence to prove that the bowl was cast in one piece. The question is controversial and is of interest only to the close student of pewter.

We shall not tarry long over the bowl. Its function was purely utilitarian — to hold food; and after a vessel had been evolved satisfactorily to serve that purpose, succeeding makers deviated but little from the standard form. We find, in general, but two shapes of porringer bowl: first, the typical container with bulging sides, contracted at top and bottom, surmounted by a narrow perpendicular lip, the bottom consisting of a flat circular gutter with domed center; second, the basin with handle, which is in reality not a porringer at all, but a porringer-basin. The latter type of bowl is usually found only in the larger porringers, with a diameter of $5\frac{1}{2}$ to 6 inches, and in diminutive tasters or doll-size porringers.

But whereas the shape of the bowl invited little experimentation, the handle was a feature well adapted to individual decorative treatment. It afforded such endless opportunity for diversification of pattern under favorable circumstances that each pewterer might easily have devised a design peculiar to his own product. Unfortunately, however, moulds were very costly in early days. A fledgling pewterer, on completing his apprenticeship, usually started out with an old set of moulds, either inherited or purchased, and these in turn he passed on to his successor, so that the same moulds were forced to serve one generation after another. And even when the young pewterer had to buy an entire new equipment, custom and the conservatism of his trade led him to select shapes to which the public was accustomed. Consequently, instead of hundreds of different designs in porringer handles, we have thus far found less than two dozen varieties impressed with the touches of American pewterers.

Even at that we may congratulate ourselves, for no such multiplicity is known in England; and it is probably greater than can be matched among surviving porringers of any Continental country. The reason is perhaps discoverable in the fact that our pewterers were men of divers nationalities, catering to buyers who naturally preferred the styles to which they had been accustomed in their respective homelands. Hence the American output embodied English forms, Continental forms, and variations upon, or combinations of, the two.

We may roughly divide all porringer handles into two distinct classes: first, the solid type; and second, the 'flowered,' or openwork, type. The former was an inheritance from the Continent of Europe. Howard H. Cotterell wrote me that he had never seen an English porringer with solid handle. It is the openwork handle which is characteristic of British porringers. To be sure, this latter form is found also on some Continental pieces; but, generally speaking, the British handle is perforated, the Continental solid. In this country we find both forms, with the perforated decidedly in the majority and evidently the favorite.

Though it is counter to the usual opinion, I am satisfied that the earliest form of American handle was pierced rather than solid; for the majority of our early settlers, and the earliest American pewterers of record, were Englishmen, who would naturally have followed English custom. But in the districts where Continental influence was strong we might reasonably expect to encounter solid handles, and it is in those very sections that they come to light.

In the country districts of Pennsylvania, largely settled by Germans and Swiss, solid-handle porringers were the normal form. Likewise the only Philadelphia porringer thus far identified has a solid handle. It is probable, however, that Philadelphia pewterers of English birth or extraction made porringers with openwork handles. But that matter can be determined only if, and when, other Philadelphia porringers are identified.

Substitute the word Swedes for Swiss.

In one other section of the colonies the solid handle was apparently in general use; and there it did not supplant the pierced form, but was manufactured in competition with it. Newport, in 1770, was the most cosmopolitan town in New England, with a foreign trade greater than that of New York. It is therefore not surprising that the solid handle should have obtained recognition among the pewterers of the Rhode Island city.

In time we may possibly learn that early pewterers of Dutch lineage in New York or Albany employed the solid handle. But it would be, to say the least, surprising were we to find such a form stamped with the touch of a pewterer of Massachusetts, Maryland, or any of the Southern colonies, where the great majority of settlers were of English extraction.

An examination of the accompanying illustrations (Plates XI, XII, and XIII) will give an idea of the forms most frequently found in America. It will also enable the reader to distinguish between the solid handles of Newport and those of Pennsylvania; the pierced handles of Rhode Island and the shapes made in other colonies; and in some instances to determine by pattern alone the handiwork of individual pewterers.

Cast as part of the handle was the support or bracket, that member which strengthened the handle at the point where it was attached to the bowl. Here, too, we find considerable variety which can be studied in the photographs of the Rhode Island, Connecticut, and New York touches, Plates XLVII, LVI, LIX, LXII, and LXIX.

PLATE XV — *Domed-Top Tankards*

84. Unusually fine domed-top quart tankard. Height $6\frac{7}{8}$ inches, top diameter $4\frac{5}{16}$ inches, bottom diameter $5\frac{1}{8}$ inches. Mark undecipherable, maker unknown. (A similar tankard in the collection of H. F. du Pont, Esq., is marked 'I. L.,' possibly Joseph Leddell of New York, 1712–1753.) Noteworthy are the fine early thumb-piece and graceful handle with Stuart terminal. Collection of Edward E. Minor, Esq.

85. Splendid three-and-one-half-pint domed-top tankard — largest of American tankards. Height $7\frac{5}{8}$ inches over all, top diameter $4\frac{7}{8}$ inches, bottom diameter $5\frac{5}{8}$ inches. John Bassett, New York, 1720–1761, mark 458. Collection of Potter Palmer III, Esq.

86. Another three-and-one-half-pint domed-top tankard differing only in the addition of a crenate lip. Measurements the same. Frederick Bassett, New York and Hartford, 1761–1800, mark 465. Collection of John P. Remensnyder, Esq.

87. Fine quart tankard with domed cover and crenate lip. Height $6\frac{5}{8}$ inches, top diameter $4\frac{3}{8}$ inches, bottom diameter 5 inches. Mark 582. Maker unknown, not improbably William Bradford, Jr., New York, 1719–1758. Collection of Edward E. Minor, Esq.

88 and 89. Pair of quart tankards with domed cover, crenate lip and bud handle terminal, made from the same moulds. 89 is particularly interesting on account of the engraved decoration. Height $6\frac{5}{8}$ inches, top diameter $4\frac{7}{16}$ inches, bottom diameter 5 inches. John Will, New York, 1753–1766, marks 480 and 483. Collection of Mrs. J. Insley Blair.

90. Quart tankard similar in design to 87. Height $6\frac{9}{16}$ inches, top diameter $4\frac{7}{16}$ inches, bottom diameter $4\frac{15}{16}$ inches. William Kirby, New York, 1760–1793, mark 503. Collection of Edward E. Minor, Esq.

PLATE XV

90

86

89

85

88

84

87

PLATE XVI — *Domed-Top Tankards*

91. Quart tankard with domed cover and finial. Height without finial $6\frac{3}{4}$ inches, top diameter $4\frac{5}{16}$ inches, bottom diameter $4\frac{7}{8}$ inches. Mark 312. Attributed to Benjamin Day of Newport, 1747–1757. Apparently hammered all over, this is one of the finest of American tankards. Collection of Edward E. Minor, Esq.

92. Quart tankard with domed cover and finial. Height over all 8 inches, top diameter $3\frac{15}{16}$ inches, bottom diameter $4\frac{3}{4}$ inches. Maker unknown, probably New England, *c.* 1740–1760. Unusual in its proportions, with fine thumb-piece and handle with boot-heel terminal. Collection of Edward E. Minor, Esq.

93. Quart tankard with domed cover and finial. Height over all $6\frac{7}{8}$ inches, top diameter $4\frac{3}{16}$ inches, bottom diameter $4\frac{5}{8}$ inches. Maker unknown, initials 'IC' cast in handle. Probably New England, *c.* 1750–1780. Collection of the author.

   Finials are found on the covers of silver tankards made in New England in the same period, 1740–1780. There is very little doubt that 91, 92, and 93 are of New England provenance.

94. Quart tankard with domed cover. Height 6 inches, top diameter $4\frac{3}{8}$ inches, bottom diameter $4\frac{3}{4}$ inches. Mark 526a. Attributed to Simon Edgell, Philadelphia, 1713–1742. Perhaps earliest of all surviving American tankards. Both thumb-piece and handle terminal are early variants of standard forms. Courtesy of Warren C. Mercer.

95. Quart tankard with domed cover. Height $6\frac{7}{8}$ inches, top diameter $4\frac{5}{16}$ inches, bottom diameter $5\frac{1}{8}$ inches. Mark 526. Attributed to Simon Edgell, Philadelphia, 1713–1742. Except for a very heavy base this tankard is later in design than many American tankards made after 1770. It was undoubtedly the 'newest thing' in tankards in Edgell's day. Collection of Edward E. Minor, Esq.

96. Quart tankard with domed cover. Height $6\frac{1}{2}$ inches, top diameter $4\frac{1}{2}$ inches, bottom diameter 5 inches. Henry Will, New York and Albany, 1761–1793, mark 491. Collection of Edward E. Minor, Esq.

97. Quart tankard with domed cover. Height $6\frac{5}{8}$ inches, top diameter $4\frac{7}{16}$ inches, bottom diameter $4\frac{15}{16}$ inches. Cornelius Bradford, Philadelphia and New York, 1753–1784, mark 496. Collection of the author.

PLATE XVI

97

96

95

94

93

92

91

Household Pewter

Although the great majority of surviving pewter plates in this country were made in Europe, quite the reverse holds true of porringers. Barring Continental examples, for the most part brought to America in recent years, almost all porringers which we find today are of native workmanship, and the collector is reasonably safe in classifying as American any unmarked piece with a handle design similar to any handle illustrated as American in this volume.

TANKARDS, POTS, AND MEASURES

When the colonization of America began, the principal forms of pewter hollow-ware in use in the homes and inns of England were the tankard, the pot, and the measure. The same shapes were transplanted to our shores, and were made in the colonies from moulds that had been brought from England. So, although all colonial hollow-ware of the Pilgrim century seems to have vanished, we can be certain that the shapes departed little if any from English designs.

Aristocrat among drinking-vessels in seventeenth-century England and America, the covered tankard is today the form in pewter most generally sought after by American collectors. As long as pewter had its place upon the tables of the well-to-do, tankards were made in great numbers, but as the eighteenth century progressed and pewter was driven from the board of the élite, being tolerated by the poor only on account of its economy, the cheaper and less imposing open-topped mug (or pot, as it is usually termed in the old inventories) almost completely supplanted, at least in the colonies, the splendid covered tankard with which it had long been in competition, and by the close of the eighteenth century the latter was practically obsolete. Consequently we have very few marked American examples today.

Sets of liquid measures were also turned out by many of the early pewterers, but these went the way of the tankards, and before 1790 mugs were serving the dual purpose of drinking-vessel and measure. In fact, I do not know of one marked American measure that was made prior to 1820. Occasionally we hear of a measure bearing one of the later Boardman touches, but even these are extremely rare, and no other nineteenth-century maker appears to have continued the manufacture of such forms.

Pots, though not plentiful, are obtainable. All the larger shops, at least after 1700, must have had moulds for the quart and pint sizes and some few men made three-pint or 'pottle' pots, and half-pint pots.

The body of the seventeenth-century English tankard or pot was a masterpiece of simplicity (Plate XIV, 76). The desirability of many later American drinking-vessels lies in the fact that their makers, probably from the dictates of their pocketbooks — we should like to attribute it to considered choice — were slow to discard the early designs and never adopted some of the least meritorious shapes developed in England and on the Continent. Although in the sixteenth and early seventeenth centuries tall slender tank-

Tankards, Pots, and Measures

ards were made occasionally in England, the form in common use when the American story begins had a plain drum with the bottom diameter little if any larger than the top. It may be stated as a general, though not infallible, rule that in England the earlier the vessel the more squat its body, the more nearly perpendicular its lines, and the more marked its simplicity.

Toward the close of the seventeenth century, British pewterers began to depart from the standards of simple design. There came a growing tendency toward more prominent base mouldings, and the drum was elaborated with an encircling fillet. These changes became general in England soon thereafter and the simpler design ceased to be made. Although the rib is often found on American mugs and tankards, some of our pewterers, even as late as 1820, clung to the earlier form.

About 1735 in England, and probably a decade or two later in America, tankards and pots of a very different design made their appearance. The 'tulip' form (see Plate XVII, 100 and 101), as Howard H. Cotterell has designated this shape, had great vogue in England from about 1755 to 1780, although it never completely supplanted the straight-sided body. Late in reaching America, the 'tulip' mug proved but a passing fancy. Few of our pewterers discarded their old moulds for those of new design, and even they, after the Revolution, returned to the earlier shape. In fact, I can recall having seen tulip-shaped drinking-vessels made by but four American shops, all of which date from the period 1760 to 1785.

The dates should read 1735 to 1780 instead of 1755 to 1780.

Substitute four for six shops.

Dates should read 1745 to 1785 instead of 1760 to 1785.

The bell-shaped body and the exaggerated tulip form which had their day in England seem, fortunately, never to have been adopted on these shores. The only additional variations in body design found impressed with American touches are illustrated in Plate XX, 128 and 129, and in each case the shape appears to have been made in Philadelphia only. The first, a 'barrel' mug, was the work of Parks Boyd, Philadelphia, about 1800. On a trade card of John Alderson of London, printed in 1792, a mug with body of the same design can be seen, but the shape apparently enjoyed no greater popularity in England than in America. The second, from the shop of Robert Palethorp, Junior, Philadelphia (1818-1822), has no counterpart, so far as I know, in England, but was made also by Brunstrom and perhaps other Pennsylvania pewterers. For the most part our makers were ultraconservative, and the shape of the body of the pots of 1825 was in most cases little different from the design in general use one hundred years earlier.

Substitute the name Boyd for Brunstrom.

Just as we have no American flatware of the seventeenth century (which must needs have been different in rim design from our existing plates), so also we regret the absence from our collections of a pot or tankard dating from the period when the graceful solid handle was in general use on such vessels in England. And because there is still a possibility that a seventeenth-century American tankard may come to light, it is well to study surviving English vessels of that period.

The handles of the Stuart tankards were solid castings with a bold, graceful sweep from lip to base, curling into terminals of varied and interesting forms. Such a handle, the shape of which has been aptly likened by Howard H. Cotterell to the curve of a

[33]

PLATE XVII — *Late Tankards*

98. Quart tankard of late design with double-domed cover, open thumb-piece and tall, slender body. Height 7⅛ inches, top diameter 3⅞ inches, bottom diameter 4¹¹⁄₁₆ inches. William Will, Philadelphia, 1764–1798, mark 541. Collection of the author.

99. Quart tankard with double-domed cover and a finial that is badly proportioned to the design of cover. Height 6¾ inches, top diameter 4⅜ inches, bottom diameter 5 inches. Samuel Danforth, Hartford, 1795–1816, marks 401 and 404. Collection of the author.

100. Quart tankard with double-domed cover, tulip-shaped body. An excellent example of its type. Height 7½ inches, top diameter 4 inches, bottom diameter 4½ inches. William Will, Philadelphia, 1764–1798, mark 539. Collection of Edward E. Minor, Esq.

101. Quart tankard with double-domed cover, tulip-shaped body. Height 7½ inches, top diameter 4¼ inches, bottom diameter 4⅝ inches. Mark 595. Maker unknown, probably New England or New York. Late eighteenth century. Collection of the author.

102. Pint tankard with domed cover and unusual thumb-piece of late design. Height 5⅝ inches over all, top diameter 3⅜ inches, bottom diameter 4⅛ inches. Peter Young, New York and Albany, 1775–1795, mark 514. Courtesy of the Mabel Brady Garvan Collection, Gallery of Fine Arts, Yale University.

103. Quart tankard with flattened dome cover. Height 6¾ inches, top diameter 3⅞ inches, bottom diameter 4⅝ inches. Parks Boyd, Philadelphia, 1793–1819, mark 546. Collection of Edward E. Minor, Esq.

104. Quart tankard with flattened dome cover. All dimensions the same as for 103, except that the bottom diameter measures 4⅞ inches. Same mark, maker, and owner.

105. Quart tankard with flattened dome cover. Dimensions, mark, and maker the same as for 104. Collection of the author. A comparison of 104 or 105 with 103 illustrates well the unfortunate results of over-elaboration which began to manifest itself about 1800.

PLATE XVII

101

105

100

104

99

103

98

102

PLATE XVIII — *Pots and Tankards*

106, 107, 108. An exceptionally fine group of hollow-ware made by Henry Will, New York and Albany, 1761–1793, from the collection of Mrs. J. Insley Blair. The bottom diameter of the quart pots is $4\frac{7}{8}$ inches, of the tankard $4\frac{15}{16}$ inches. 106 is unusual among New York pots of the Revolutionary period in the absence of any banding around the drum. 108, with typical New York banding, has a handle terminal of a form rarely seen on American pewter.

109. Splendid massive lidless tankard, or pot, holding slightly more than a quart. Bottom diameter $5\frac{1}{16}$ inches, height $5\frac{5}{16}$ inches exclusive of handle, $5\frac{3}{4}$ inches over all. Mark 312. Attributed to Benjamin Day, Newport, 1744–1757. Collection of John W. Poole, Esq.

110. Quart pot with solid handle of rare type, provenance unknown. Height $5\frac{7}{8}$ inches, top diameter $3\frac{7}{8}$ inches, bottom diameter $4\frac{3}{4}$ inches. Mark 578 (believed to be American). Collection of Edward E. Minor, Esq.

111. Half-pint pot. Height $3\frac{1}{8}$ inches, top diameter $2\frac{11}{16}$ inches, bottom diameter $3\frac{1}{16}$ inches. Boardman and Hart, New York, 1827–1850, mark 437. Collection of the author.

112. Pint pot with early form of boot-heel handle terminal. Height $4\frac{5}{8}$ inches, top diameter $3\frac{1}{4}$ inches, bottom diameter $3\frac{3}{4}$ inches. Mark erased. Maker unknown. Collection of the author.

113. Quart pot with plain drum. Height $5\frac{5}{8}$ inches, top diameter 4 inches, bottom diameter $4\frac{1}{2}$ inches. Thomas Danforth Third, Stepney, Connecticut, and Philadelphia, 1780–1818, marks 367 and 373. Collection of the author.

PLATE XVIII

106   107   108

109   110

111   112   113

Plate XIX — *Pots*

114. Quart pot. Height $6\frac{1}{8}$ inches, top diameter $3\frac{7}{8}$ inches, bottom diameter $4\frac{3}{4}$ inches. Francis or Frederick Bassett, 1754–1800, mark 457. The heavy fillet on this pot is typical of New York manufacture. Collection of Mrs. J. Insley Blair.

115. Pint pot of similar lines to 114. Height $4\frac{1}{2}$ inches, top diameter $3\frac{5}{16}$ inches, bottom diameter $3\frac{7}{8}$ inches. John Will, New York, 1752–1766, mark 481. Collection of the author.

116. Pint pot with late double C form of handle. Height $4\frac{1}{4}$ inches, top diameter $3\frac{1}{4}$ inches, bottom diameter $3\frac{7}{8}$ inches. Samuel Hamlin or Samuel E. Hamlin, Providence, 1771–1820, mark 331. Collection of Edward E. Minor, Esq.

117. Quart pot with fillet at line of handle juncture; a sturdier vessel than most of the New England pots that have survived. Height 6 inches, top diameter $4\frac{1}{8}$ inches, bottom diameter $4\frac{7}{8}$ inches. Samuel Hamlin, Providence, 1771–1801, marks 330 and 331. Collection of Edward E. Minor, Esq.

118. Quart pot. Height $5\frac{5}{8}$ inches, top diameter $3\frac{7}{8}$ inches, bottom diameter $4\frac{3}{4}$ inches. Mark 590. Maker unknown, Philadelphia, about 1775. Engraved 'Liberty or Death.' 'Huzza for Capt. Ickes.' Of unusual interest because of its patriotic decoration. Collection of Albert H. Good, Esq.

119 and 120. Identical quart pots made from the same moulds. Height $5\frac{7}{8}$ inches, top diameter 4 inches, bottom diameter $4\frac{3}{4}$ inches. Marks, 374 on left-hand pot, 382 on right-hand pot. Joseph Danforth, 1780–1788, and Jacob Whitmore, 1758–1790, Middletown, Connecticut. Their moulds were owned jointly. Collection of the author.

121. Quart pot with solid handle of late design. Height $5\frac{7}{8}$ inches, top diameter $4\frac{3}{16}$ inches, bottom diameter $4\frac{13}{16}$ inches. Gershom Jones, Providence, Rhode Island, 1780–1809, mark 342. Collection of Edward E. Minor, Esq.

PLATE XIX

117

121

116

120

119

115

114

118

PLATE XX — *Pots*

fig. 122. Quart pot. Mark should read 296 instead of 306.

122. Quart pot with solid strap handle. Height $5\frac{3}{4}$ inches, top diameter $3\frac{7}{8}$ inches, bottom diameter $4\frac{3}{4}$ inches. Nathaniel Austin, Charlestown, Massachusetts, 1763–1805, mark 306. Collection of Edward E. Minor, Esq.

123. Quart pot with strap handle, decorated at top of grip with anthemion design. Height $5\frac{7}{8}$ inches, top diameter $3\frac{7}{8}$ inches, bottom diameter $4\frac{1}{2}$ inches. Major Gershom Jones, Providence, Rhode Island, 1774–1800, mark 341. Collection of Morris Cooper, Jr., Esq.

124. Quart pot with strap handle. Height 6 inches, top diameter $3\frac{7}{8}$ inches, bottom diameter $4\frac{13}{16}$ inches. Richard Lee or Richard Lee, Jr., Springfield, Vermont, 1788–1810, mark 413. Collection of the author.

125. Pint pot with strap handle. Height $4\frac{5}{8}$ inches, top diameter $3\frac{5}{16}$ inches, bottom diameter $3\frac{15}{16}$ inches. Mark 292. Maker unknown. Probably New England, second half of eighteenth century. Collection of the author.

126. Pint pot with tulip-shaped body. Height $4\frac{9}{16}$ inches, top diameter $3\frac{7}{16}$ inches, bottom diameter $3\frac{1}{2}$ inches. Cornelius Bradford, Philadelphia and New York, 1752–1784, mark 496. American pint pots with tulip-shaped body are extremely rare. Collection of the author.

127. Quart pot with tulip-shaped body and 'double C' handle with acanthus leaf decoration. Height $6\frac{1}{4}$ inches, top diameter 4 inches, bottom diameter $4\frac{3}{8}$ inches. Colonel William Will, Philadelphia, 1764–1798, mark 541. One of the handsomest of the later pot designs. Collection of the author.

128. Quart pot with barrel-shaped body. Dimensions not recorded. Parks Boyd, Philadelphia, 1793–1819. Perhaps unique in American pewter. Formerly in the collection of Philip G. Platt, Esq.

129. Pint pot with pinched barrel-shaped body. Height $4\frac{1}{4}$ inches, top diameter $3\frac{3}{8}$ inches, bottom diameter $3\frac{5}{16}$ inches. Robert Palethorp, Jr., Philadelphia, 1818–1822, mark 560. Collection of the author.

PLATE XX

125

129

124

128

123

127

122

126

swan's neck, can be seen on the English tankard pictured in Plate XIV, 76. This, un-doubtedly, was the type used on the vanished hollow-ware of our early pewterers.

The form which made its bow in England late in the seventeenth century, supplant-ing the solid handle and continuing in favor there until about 1760, is the handle used on the great majority of surviving American vessels. It was introduced in this country early in the eighteenth century and remained the favorite for over a hundred years. In outline it differs from its predecessor chiefly in its greater massiveness and more care-fully modulated curves. In method of manufacture, however, it represented a very radical departure. The new handle was cast hollow in one piece as described on page 17. This handle had one marked advantage over the solid handle — a greater gripping surface, permitting a more secure grasp.

Contemporaneous in England with the tulip body was the 'double C' handle, a form better adapted for use with that type of body than with the cylindrical drum. It was employed, however, in England on tankards and mugs of all kinds for upward of a hundred years, beginning about 1730. There is no evidence as yet that it was used at all in this country prior to the Revolution, and even after that period few shops adopted it, and none to the exclusion of the earlier design. It may be studied in an elaborate form in the fine quart mug of William Will of Philadelphia (*c.* 1770–1796, Plate XX, 127). At its worst, especially where two struts intervene between body and handle, it represents a long step downward from the grace, simplicity, and architectural integrity of the earlier forms.

The complete debasement of the pewter handle occurred in its final form, which ap-peared at the beginning of the britannia period in this country. In this last phase the hollow handle has lost all charm of line and terminates in a characterless blunt stub, soldered flush against the body. In Great Britain this handle is found occasionally on tankards, frequently on late mugs. In America it was not adopted until after tankards had ceased to be made and just at the close of the days of mug manufacture. Its occur-rence, therefore, is fortunately rare except on water pitchers (see Plate LXXIII) and very late flagons.

During the second half of the eighteenth century several American shops, notably those of Nathaniel Austin, Gershom Jones, and Richard Lee, manufactured a mug handle of a design which never seems to have been employed in England. This handle was solid as in the very early forms, but its curves follow the lines of the contempora-neous hollow handle. In the upper ends of the moulds used for these handles a beaded design was usually cut out so as to leave a pleasing raised decoration on the upper face of the grip of the casting. An otherwise interesting design was marred, however, by the interpolation of a strut between the lower end of the handle and the body of the vessel (see Plate XX, 122 to 125). This design of handle is exceedingly rare.

Tankard covers furnish another field for study. Most of the early covers in England, like the early tankard bodies, were exceedingly squatty. The rim was flat, with or without a slight projection at the lip. In the center, extending only about a quarter of an inch above the rim, was a shallow cylinder absolutely flat on top (Plate

Tankards, Pots, and Measures

XIV, 76). This was the tankard cover in use in England in the second quarter of the seventeenth century. It was succeeded by the later Stuart cover. In the latter form the projecting lip becomes more elaborate, the central portion is raised higher, and, with the appearance of a pronounced curve between rim and top surface, we have the beginnings of a dome (see Plate XIV, 83). By about 1690 the double-domed cover (Plate XV, 84 to 90) had appeared in England. This shape is the same as its predecessor except for the addition of a second dome. Soon thereafter many shops eliminated the crenate lip, and by approximately 1710 that elaboration was obsolete. The final development, which dates from about 1715, was a change from a flat to a curved rim. To quote from Howard H. Cotterell, 'whereas all the former [covers] had a flat brim of some $\frac{3}{8}$ of an inch in width, before the dome mouldings commenced, in the latter such mouldings start flush, at the outer edge, with a cavetto.' This change was not adopted by the colonial pewterers and I have no record of any covers of this type which antedate the Federal period. Even then the curve of the outer rim was so slight that it can scarcely be perceived in the illustrations of the William Will and Samuel Danforth tankards in Plate XVII, 98 and 99. It can be studied to better advantage on the T. D. Boardman flagon in Plate XXXIV, 229.

These were the types of tankard covers used in England and, generally speaking, it is possible to date an English tankard fairly accurately by its design of cover alone. Unfortunately there is no such rule of thumb for determining the age of an American tankard.

For although most of the English designs appeared later in American pewter, they did not displace one another in this country, but were used contemporaneously. While I have never seen one of our tankards with an early cover similar to that illustrated on the English tankard in Plate XIV, 76, every succeeding British type has been found on at least one American tankard; in fact, each type appears on the vessel of at least one American pewterer who was in business as late as 1790. The explanation lies in the fact that our makers could not afford to scrap outmoded moulds. Although occasionally our craftsmen bought moulds of new design, most of our pewterers inherited or purchased second-hand equipment. Consequently, many moulds in use in 1800 had probably been doing duty in this country for fifty to a hundred years. We can only say, therefore, of each design of cover that it probably did not appear in America until a few years after its inception in England. On the other hand, it may have continued in use until close to the end of the eighteenth century.

There are two types of cover design, found occasionally on American tankards, which are variations of the double-dome cover previously described. The first group comprises the covers surmounted with finials of which at least four distinct forms are known. The splendid quart tankard attributed to Benjamin Day, Newport (c. 1744–1757, see Plate XVI, 91), is set off by a well-designed finial; a second form that is also well-proportioned may be seen in Plate XVI, 92. The third of these finial-capped tankards is also undoubtedly of New England origin; the maker is an unidentified pewterer, 'I. C.,' who was probably working at about the time of the Revolution. The

PLATE XXI — *Small Mugs, Beakers with Handles, Measures*

130. Pint mug with handle of late form. Height 4 inches, top diameter $3\frac{7}{16}$ inches, bottom diameter $3\frac{7}{8}$ inches. Roswell Gleason, Dorchester, Massachusetts, 1822–1840. Collection of Charles K. Davis, Esq.

131. Half-gill mug. Height $2\frac{1}{16}$ inches, top diameter $1\frac{9}{16}$ inches, bottom diameter 2 inches. Samuel Danforth, Hartford, Connecticut, 1795–1816, mark 401. Smallest of American marked mugs. Collection of Mrs. Stephen S. FitzGerald.

132. Beaker with handle. Height $2\frac{13}{16}$ inches, top diameter 3 inches, bottom diameter $2\frac{1}{4}$ inches. William Calder, Providence, Rhode Island, 1817–1856, mark 361. Collection of Charles K. Davis, Esq.

133. Beaker with handle (one of a set of six). Height 4 inches, top diameter $3\frac{7}{8}$ inches, bottom diameter $2\frac{13}{16}$ inches. Eben Smith, Beverly, Massachusetts, 1841–1856. Collection of John P. Remensnyder, Esq.

134. Beaker with handle. Height $3\frac{3}{16}$ inches, top diameter 3 inches, bottom diameter $2\frac{1}{2}$ inches. Boardman and Hart, New York, 1827–1850, marks 445, 446. Collection of Charles K. Davis, Esq.

135 to 141. Set of lidded measures from half-gill to one gallon. Heights (exclusive of thumb-piece and handle, $2\frac{7}{8}$, $3\frac{3}{8}$, $4\frac{3}{8}$, 5, $7\frac{1}{4}$, $9\frac{1}{4}$, and $11\frac{1}{2}$ inches respectively). Maker unknown. Possibly American and typical of the form we should expect for American measures of that period, dated 1732. Formerly owned by the Colony of New Hampshire. Collection of the New Hampshire Historical Society; courtesy of Otis G. Hammond, Director.

142 to 146. Set of open-top measures from half-gallon to gill. Heights $8\frac{7}{8}$, $6\frac{7}{8}$, $4\frac{7}{8}$, $3\frac{3}{4}$, and 3 inches respectively. The pint measure was made by Timothy Boardman and Company, New York, 1822 to 1825, and is dated 1824. The others are unmarked, except that all are stamped with the same owner's initials and bear dates from 1824 to 1826. Collection of Albert H. Good, Esq.

PLATE XXI

130

131

132

133

134

135   136   137   138   139   140   141

142   143   144   145   146

PLATE XXII — *Beakers*

A group of beakers in the collection of the author

Back row, left to right:

147. Height $4\frac{3}{8}$ inches, top diameter $3\frac{3}{4}$ inches, bottom diameter $3\frac{7}{16}$ inches. Ebenezer Southmayd, Castleton, Vermont, 1802–1820, mark 416.

148. Height $6\frac{3}{4}$ inches, top diameter 4 inches, bottom diameter $3\frac{3}{8}$ inches. John Bassett, New York, *c.* 1720–1761, mark 458.

149. Height $5\frac{3}{16}$ inches, top diameter $3\frac{9}{16}$ inches, bottom diameter 3 inches. Samuel Danforth, Hartford, 1795–1816, mark 401.

Middle row, left to right:

150. Height $3\frac{3}{8}$ inches, top diameter 3 inches, bottom diameter $2\frac{3}{8}$ inches. Samuel Kilbourn, Baltimore, 1814–1839, mark 568.

151. Height $3\frac{5}{16}$ inches, top diameter $2\frac{7}{8}$ inches, bottom diameter $2\frac{1}{4}$ inches. Babbitt and Crossman, Taunton, Massachusetts, 1824–1826.

152. Height $3\frac{1}{8}$ inches, top diameter $2\frac{7}{8}$ inches, bottom diameter $2\frac{7}{8}$ inches. Samuel Danforth, Hartford, 1795–1816, mark 399.

153. Height $3\frac{1}{16}$ inches, top diameter 3 inches, bottom diameter 2 inches. Cornelius B. de Riemer and Company, Auburn, New York, *c.* 1833.

Bottom row, left to right:

154. Height $3\frac{1}{8}$ inches, top diameter 3 inches, bottom diameter $2\frac{1}{2}$ inches. Boardman and Hart, New York, 1827–1850, marks 437, 438.

155. Height $1\frac{9}{16}$ inches, top diameter $1\frac{9}{16}$ inches, bottom diameter $1\frac{1}{2}$ inches. Unmarked. Maker unknown.

156. Height 2 inches, top diameter $1\frac{7}{8}$ inches, bottom diameter $1\frac{9}{16}$ inches. Unmarked. Maker unknown.

PLATE XXII

153

156

149

152

148 155

151

147

154

150

PLATE XXIII — *Beakers*

fig. 157.
Beaker Mark should
read 407 instead of
415.

157. Beaker. Height $4\frac{7}{16}$ inches, top diameter $3\frac{11}{16}$ inches, bottom diameter $3\frac{1}{4}$ inches. Samuel Pierce, Greenfield, Massachusetts, 1792–1831, mark 415. Collection of Edward E. Minor, Esq.

158. Sturdy beaker with heavy base. Height $4\frac{5}{8}$ inches, top diameter $3\frac{3}{4}$ inches, bottom diameter $3\frac{13}{16}$ inches. Frederick Bassett, New York and Hartford, 1761–1800, mark 465. A fine, rare piece. Collection of Mr. and Mrs. Richard S. Quigley.

159. Tall beaker. Height $6\frac{3}{4}$ inches, top diameter 4 inches, bottom diameter $3\frac{3}{8}$ inches. John Bassett, New York, 1720–1761, mark 458. One of the finest of surviving beakers. Collection of the author.

160. Japanned beaker or small vase. Height just $3\frac{1}{2}$ inches. George Coldwell, New York, 1787–1811, mark 508. Perhaps unique in shape and one of two known pieces of marked American pewter that had been japanned. According to tradition the piece belonged to General Washington and later to his bodyservant, 'Billy.' Collection of Lewis A. Walter, Esq.

161. Excellent example of the tall flare-mouthed beaker, the standard beaker design of Connecticut and perhaps other colonies. Height $5\frac{3}{16}$ inches, top diameter $3\frac{9}{16}$ inches, bottom diameter 3 inches. Samuel Danforth, Hartford, 1795–1816, mark 401. Courtesy of the Mabel Brady Garvan Collection, Gallery of Fine Arts, Yale University.

PLATE XXIII

160

161

159

157

158

PLATE XXIV — *Spoons*

162 to 168. A group of seventeenth-century English spoons from the Port Collection, reproduced with the permission of the late Howard H. Cotterell, Esq., from *Old Pewter, Its Makers and Its Marks*. These spoons are contemporary with the Chuckatuck spoon pictured below.

169 and 170. Bowl and handle of identical spoons unearthed on the site of Jamestown, Virginia, by the National Park Service, and illustrated through the courtesy of the Service and of Worth Bailey, Esq. Diameter of bowl 2⅛ inches, length of handle 5½ inches. On the handle is the still identifiable touch (563) of Joseph Copeland, Chuckatuck, Virginia, 1675–1691. This is the earliest piece of existing marked American pewter now of record.

171 and 171a. Obverse and reverse of slip top spoon, measuring 6½ inches in length, long diameter of bowl 2⅜ inches, short diameter 2 inches. John Bassett, New York, 1720–1761, mark 458. Except for the Chuckatuck spoon, this is the only marked American spoon antedating 1760, the maker of which has been identified. Courtesy of the New Hampshire Historical Society, Concord, through its Director, Otis G. Hammond, Esq.

PLATE XXIV

162   163   164   165   166   167   168

169   170   171   171a

fourth and last of the finials (see Plate XVII, 99) is a grotesque, topheavy cone which does little credit to the sense of proportion of its maker, Samuel Danforth of Hartford (1795–1816).

The second group is composed of the covers with flattened dome, examples of which can be observed in Plate XVII, 103, 104, and 105. This form, made by Parks Boyd, Philadelphia (*c*. 1795–1816), has little to commend it beyond its oddity and rarity. Some Swedish tankard covers have a coin inserted on a flattened dome, and inasmuch as there was a large Swedish settlement in eastern Pennsylvania one of their tankards doubtless furnished the inspiration for Boyd's design.

The illustrations in Plates XIV to XVII will serve as the most satisfactory mediums for acquainting the reader with the various designs of body, cover, handle, thumb-piece, and handle terminal found upon American hollow-ware.

It may seem tedious to examine so minutely the varied details of tankard and mug design, but an accurate knowledge of the different forms, with the dates when they were current in England as well as America, may prove most valuable to the seeker after the extreme rarities in pewter.

BEAKERS

A beaker was a drinking-vessel without handle or cover which ordinarily, though not invariably, was wider at the top than at the bottom. American beakers range in height from $1\frac{1}{2}$ to $6\frac{7}{8}$ inches, but those under $2\frac{1}{2}$ inches were rarely if ever impressed with the maker's mark. In fact very few beakers under 4 inches have touches to identify them. Throughout the two centuries of pewter-making on this side of the Atlantic, beakers were a stock shape, for we find such items listed in Henry Shrimpton's inventory in 1666, and the Boardmans and others were still turning them out after 1830. The small beakers (under 4 inches) may be entirely the product of the nineteenth century, for most of them are of thin metal and none that I have ever seen bore early touches. Samuel Danforth of Hartford (after 1794) made tall beakers, and he has also left us shorter ones which were very patently large beakers cut down, cups which would have been much improved by the addition of a moulded rim to give them a finished appearance. It is not at all improbable that this cut-down beaker was the forerunner of the small beaker for which there seems to have been so great a demand during the first thirty years of the last century.

In Plate XXII is shown a group of representative beakers in my own collection. In the central background is one of a pair of tall tumblers made not later than 1760 by John Bassett of New York. They are probably the earliest and in some respects the finest of surviving American beakers. No later examples were so capacious and none so stoutly made. (See also Plate XXIII, 159.)

Of slightly later date and more graceful lines are the flare-mouthed vessels of two unidentified makers, 'R. B.' and 'I. W.' The shape is patterned closely after the design of contemporary silver beakers and was continued well down into the nineteenth century by Samuel Danforth and later the Boardmans. One of Samuel Danforth's beakers is shown in the right background in Plate XXII and another in Plate XXIII, 161. In the latter this maker added a band of reinforcement around the lip to give needed strength and a more finished appearance. Of much the same type, though shorter and with a fine heavy flaring base, is the beaker in Plate XXIII, 158, made by Frederick Bassett of New York (1756–1800).

Another design of tall beaker which was in use late in the eighteenth and early in the nineteenth century was made by Samuel Pierce in Greenfield, Massachusetts, and by Ebenezer Southmayd at Castleton, Vermont. These beakers are wider, have a less pronounced taper, and lines that are, in general, less satisfying, but they are nevertheless sturdy honest vessels of great rarity. A Pierce beaker can be seen in Plate XXIII, 157. The beaker in the left background in Plate XXII was made by Southmayd.

About 1815 the demand for large beakers all but ceased, and, except for those made for communion sets by the Boardmans at Hartford, few were turned out after that date in this country. The drinker of ale was superseded by the whiskey drinker and the pewterers were compelled to meet the changing habits of the times. Accordingly, we find that the nineteenth-century vessels are small affairs; many are of thin metal and poorly made, the great majority lacking any mark of identification. Notable exceptions are the graceful little beakers of Samuel Kilbourn of Baltimore, one of which is pictured in Plate XXII, 150. A small beaker (if we may term it that, for it hardly seems adapted for use as a drinking-vessel, either in shape or decorative treatment) is illustrated in Plate XXIII, 160. This item is perhaps unique both in design and surface decoration. Comment upon it will be found in the story of its maker, George Coldwell, volume II, page 25. Other makers whose product was well above the average were the Boardmans, T. Melville, Babbitt and Crossman, Calder, Hamlin, H. Yale, and J. Weekes.

All of the early beakers were marked on the inside bottom, while the touches on the later pieces are usually found by turning the beakers upside down.

SPOONS, LADLES, AND DIPPERS

Although spoons were made in the colonies by the hundred thousand, marked specimens which antedate the britannia period are among the real rarities of American pewter. They were so easily broken or lost and their value was so slight in the eyes of their owners that very few eighteenth-century examples have been preserved and, with rare exceptions, these are post-Revolutionary. Moreover, in the country districts it was common practice for several families to club together, buy a spoon mould, and turn out crude spoons for everyday use, purchasing perhaps a few well-made spoons which were brought out only on festal occasions. Many such moulds are still to be found, and

Plate XXV — *Spoons*

172. Spoon made by John Yates, an English pewterer, for the American trade. Length $7\frac{7}{8}$ inches. Collection of the author.

173 and 174. Spoons with patriotic decoration made by George Coldwell, New York, 1787–1811. The bowl of each measures $1\frac{9}{16}$ inches in width; the lengths are $7\frac{5}{8}$ and $7\frac{7}{8}$ inches respectively; the marks 509 and 510. Collection of Albert H. Good, Esq.

175. Another spoon with eagle decoration. E. Whitehouse, location of shop not known. Nineteenth century. Courtesy of Philip G. Platt, Esq.

176. Small spoon. Length $4\frac{1}{2}$ inches. Richard Lee or Richard Lee, Jr., Springfield, Vermont, 1788–1820, mark 411. Collection of Mrs. J. Insley Blair.

177 and 178. Two small spoons with eagle decoration, probably made in England for the American trade. Courtesy of Philip G. Platt, Esq.

179. A well-made little spoon. Length $4\frac{1}{4}$ inches. Unmarked. Late eighteenth or early nineteenth century. Collection of Mrs. J. Insley Blair.

PLATE XXV

172

173

174

175

176

177

178

179

PLATE XXVI — *Ladles*

180. Ladle with maple handle. Length over all about $15\frac{1}{2}$ inches, diameter of bowl $3\frac{1}{2}$ inches. Unmarked. Maker unknown, *c.* 1770–1800. Fine early ladle. Collection of Mr. and Mrs. Carl C. Brigham.

181. Ladle with wooden handle. Length over all about 14 inches, diameter of bowl $3\frac{9}{16}$ inches. Unmarked. Maker unknown. Probably New England, *c.* 1770–1800. Fine early ladle. Collection of the Honorable and Mrs. George V. Smith.

182. Pewter ladle. Length over all about 15 inches, diameter of bowl $3\frac{1}{2}$ inches. Colonel William Will, Philadelphia, 1764–1798, mark 542. Fine ladle with beaded rim. Collection of Mrs. Henry H. Benkard.

183. Ladle with wooden handle. Length over all about $13\frac{1}{2}$ inches, diameter of bowl $3\frac{5}{8}$ inches. Richard Lee or Richard Lee, Jr., Springfield, Vermont, mark 411. Collection of W. C. Staples, Esq.

184. Pewter ladle. Length over all 14 inches, diameter of bowl $3\frac{11}{16}$ inches. Thomas D. Boardman, Hartford, 1805–1825, mark 425. Fine example of the period. Collection of Charles K. Davis, Esq.

185. Dipper with wooden handle. Length over all about 13 inches, top diameter of bowl $3\frac{1}{8}$ inches. J. Weekes, New York and Poughkeepsie, 1820–1835. Collection of the author.

186. Gravy ladle. Length over all about 7 inches, diameter of bowl $2\frac{1}{2}$ inches. J. Weekes, New York and Poughkeepsie, 1820–1835. Collection of Mrs. J. Insley Blair.

PLATE XXVI

184

183

186

182

181

185

180

quantities of spoons now on the market have been made within the past fifteen years from these old moulds.

Our ancestors turned to England for the models for most of their pewter forms, but this does not seem to have been true of spoons. A comparison of the fragments of the now famous Chuckatuck spoon, made in Virginia about 1675 (Plate XXIV, 169 and 170), with English spoons of the same period (Plate XXIV, 162 to 168), shows a family resemblance, but, if Worth Bailey's reconstruction of the Chuckatuck spoon is a replica of the original, the handle end does not correspond exactly to that of any English spoon that I have been privileged to see and the bowl is nearer a true round than in contemporary English spoons. The latter feature may be traceable to the Dutch influence as exemplified in the round-bowled spoons of Holland.

It is our misfortune that we know of no American spoon that was made in the first half of the eighteenth century. Our second example (Plate XXIV, 171 and 171a), made about 1750 to 1760, again shows the Dutch influence, which is perhaps natural because its maker, John Bassett, was catering to a trade in New York that was as largely Dutch as English. The bowl does not approach a true round as in the spoons of Holland, but is slightly pear-shaped and very shallow while the handle is extremely narrow and thick, a type of handle known in England as 'slip-top.' This spoon was marked, as many early specimens were, in the face of the bowl. Touches on later spoons are almost invariably found on the handles.

About the time of the Revolution or earlier, these interesting but rather unwieldy spoons were replaced by a shape, then current in silver, which has remained to this day as the normal spoon shape. Two dessert spoons of this type, made by George Coldwell (*c.* 1785–1810), are illustrated in Plate XXV. The handles, impressed with patriotic devices, are unusually elaborate. An interesting small spoon, made by one of the Lees, probably for a toy, early in the nineteenth century, may be seen in Plate XXV, 176.

Coldwell was not the only pewterer who turned out spoons with eagle-bedecked handles. Several varieties exist, examples of which are illustrated in Plate XXV. With the exception of Coldwell's and those marked 'Whitehouse,' an unidentified maker believed to be American, all such spoons that I have seen were of English make, but designed expressly for the American trade. Even though English these spoons appeal to the collector of American pewter for the same reasons that impel the collector of Lowestoft or Liverpool wares to pay a premium for a pitcher or jug upon which an American merchantman or eagle is represented.

Pewter spoons can be had today almost for the asking. Every antique shop has its quota, but with rare exceptions these are crude country specimens, late britannia, or new spoons cast in old moulds.

Occasionally I have come across long-handled serving spoons, well designed and handsomely finished, but all were unmarked or else bore the touches of English pewterers of the eighteenth century. Any American prototypes which may have existed have apparently disappeared.

Early ladles and dippers have met much the same fate, although examples made in the britannia period are not scarce. The first two pictured (Plate XXVI, 180 and 181), with graceful maple handle and turned finials, are unfortunately not marked, but probably date from the last half of the eighteenth century; the next (Plate XXVI, 182), a ladle made by William Will in the last quarter of the eighteenth century, was the type with solid handle that the britannia makers of the nineteenth century used as a model; this example has been tastefully finished with a beaded rim around the top of the bowl; the fourth (Plate XXVI, 183) was made by one of the Richard Lees, probably Richard, Junior, about 1800. The next specimen (Plate XXVI, 184) is a later ladle similar in type to 183 but of simpler design, made by Thomas D. Boardman about 1815. Similar ladles, but usually of poorer design, were made by Josiah Danforth, L. Kruiger, J. H. Palethorp, and other late workers. Plate XXVI, 185, illustrates a dipper of about 1830 with a very deep bowl spun from thin metal and marked 'J. Weekes, N.Y.,' and in 186 is shown a dainty, well-designed little gravy or sauce ladle by the same maker, which is worthy of one of the earlier pewterers. Most welcome would be the discovery of a few more spoons and ladles bearing the impress of the dies of colonial pewterers.

COFFEE-POTS, TEAPOTS, CREAMERS, AND SUGAR BOWLS

Though it is difficult to believe now, Englishmen were not always tea-drinkers. Both tea and coffee were introduced in London about the middle of the seventeenth century, and prior to 1700, perhaps until 1725, were luxuries indulged in only by the wealthy. Silver tea caddies and sugar bowls of that period were made with locks, an indication of the value placed on their contents.

None of our earliest pewterers can be presumed to have made any of the forms discussed under this head. Such shapes probably did not take their place as stock articles in colonial shops until the second quarter of the eighteenth century. By 1750, however, all of the larger shops made teapots and some of them creamers and sugar bowls. Robert Boyle of New York in 1755 and Cornelius Bradford of Philadelphia in the following year advertised 'teapots of all sorts.' Bradford also listed 'sugar pots'; but at that date coffee-pots and creamers were still apparently specialties for which there was little demand.

The earliest marked survivals among American teapots date approximately from the Revolutionary period and are of the so-called Queen Anne type with pear-shaped body and wooden handle; they probably vary but little in design from the earliest teapots made in colonial America. Three fine examples are illustrated in Plate XXVIII, 188, 189, and 190. The first is attributed to William Kirby of New York; the other two are the handiwork of William Will of Philadelphia. The handle of the Kirby pot is of pewter instead of wood, but in all other respects the design is early. The third pot is unusual, not only in the addition of feet, but because the claw-and-ball feet are patterned after the designs of Philadelphia furniture rather than contemporary forms in pewter or silver.

PLATE XXVII — *Coffee-Pot*

187. Coffee-Pot. Height over all 15$\frac{3}{4}$ inches, top diameter 3$\frac{3}{8}$ inches, bottom diameter 4$\frac{1}{2}$ inches, greatest width of bowl 6 inches. Colonel William Will, Philadelphia, 1764–1798, mark 541. Splendid tall coffee-pot, the only form of American coffee-pot of the eighteenth century that is known to have survived. Collection of the author.

PLATE XXVII

187

PLATE XXVIII — *Teapots*

188. Fine pear-shaped teapot with pewter handle. Height over all 6⅝ inches, length over all about 8 inches. William Kirby, New York, 1760–1793, mark 503. Collection of Mrs. James H. Krom.

189. Fine Queen Anne teapot with wooden handle. Height over all 6½ inches, length over all 8½ inches. Colonel William Will, Philadelphia, 1764–1798. Collection of John W. Poole, Esq.

190. Rare teapot of early form. Similar to 189, but with the addition of three lion's feet. Height over all 7 inches, length over all about 8 inches. Colonel William Will, Philadelphia, 1764–1798. Collection of Dr. and Mrs. Irving H. Berg.

191. Teapot of later form with pewter handle. Height over all 7½ inches, length over all about 8½ inches. William Calder, Providence, Rhode Island, 1817–1830, mark 350. Collection of Mrs. Charles A. Calder.

192. Another step in the evolution from the Queen Anne type. This pot has the beginning of a footed base. Height over all 7¼ inches, length over all about 8 inches. G. Richardson, Boston, 1818–1828, mark 310. Formerly in the collection of Philip G. Platt, Esq.

193. First of the tall teapots of the britannia period. Height over all 9¼ inches, length over all 9¼ inches. Thomas D. Boardman, Hartford, 1805–1830, mark 427. This form was also made by Boardman's uncle, Samuel Danforth. Collection of the author.

PLATE XXVIII

188

189

190

191

192

193

PLATE XXIX — *Circular Teapots and Sugar Bowls*

194. Handsome round teapot of the Federal period. Height over all $6\frac{7}{8}$ inches, bottom diameter 5 inches. Mark erased. Maker unknown, probably New York, 1750–1790. Collection of the author.

195. Smaller teapot of similar design to 194. Height over all $6\frac{1}{2}$ inches, bottom diameter $4\frac{11}{16}$ inches. Colonel William Will, Philadelphia, 1764–1798, mark 542. Collection of Mr. and Mrs. Richard S. Quigley.

196. Round teapot in transition stage of design from the Federal to the britannia period. Height over all $6\frac{1}{4}$ inches, bottom diameter $4\frac{1}{4}$ inches. Thomas D. Boardman, Hartford, 1804–1820. Collection of Dr. and Mrs. Irving H. Berg.

197. Rare early sugar bowl. Height over all $5\frac{3}{4}$ inches, top diameter without lid $4\frac{1}{4}$ inches. Johann Christopher Heyne, Lancaster, Pennsylvania, 1754–1780, mark in lid 533. Collection of the author.

198. Fine sugar bowl of same period. Height over all $4\frac{5}{8}$ inches, top diameter without lid $4\frac{3}{8}$ inches. Unmarked, probably Pennsylvania. Collection of Albert H. Good, Esq.

199. Fine sugar bowl. Height over all $4\frac{7}{8}$ inches, top diameter without lid $4\frac{1}{2}$ inches. Unmarked, but undoubtedly made in Philadelphia, 1770–1810. Collection of John W. Poole, Esq.

200. Choice little sugar bowl of early form. Height over all 4 inches, top diameter $3\frac{1}{4}$ inches. Thomas Danforth Third, Stepney, Connecticut, 1777–1800, mark 369. Collection of the author.

Numbers 198 and 199 follow closely the designs of contemporary Philadelphia silver sugar bowls.

PLATE XXIX

196

195

194

200

199

198

197

Plate XXX — *Creamers, Salts, etc.*

201. Fine early creamer. Height over all 4 inches. Mark 484. Attributed to John Will, New York, 1752–1766. Collection of Mr. and Mrs. Richard S. Quigley.

202 to 206. Five creamers in the collection of the author.

202. Height over all $4\frac{7}{8}$ inches. Peter Young, New York and Albany, 1775–1796, mark 524.

203 and 205. Similar in body and spout, vary principally in their supports. Both are the work of an unidentified pewterer, about 1760–1800, mark 594. The over all heights are $3\frac{7}{8}$ and 4 inches respectively.

206. $4\frac{1}{16}$ inches high over all, touch obliterated, maker unknown, late eighteenth century.

204. The central pitcher, unmarked and probably later than the others, early nineteenth century. Height over all $4\frac{3}{4}$ inches.

207 and 208. Pair of very fine shakers. Height about $5\frac{1}{2}$ inches. Maker unidentified, probably American, late eighteenth century. Collection of Edward E. Minor, Esq.

209. Large shaker. Height $5\frac{5}{8}$ inches. Thomas Danforth Third, Stepney, Connecticut, and Philadelphia, 1777–1818, mark 373. Collection of Joseph France, Esq.

210. Salt. Height $2\frac{3}{8}$ inches. Unmarked, but probably of Philadelphia origin, 1775–1820.

211. Late salt. Height $2\frac{1}{16}$ inches. J. Weekes, New York or Poughkeepsie, 1815–1835.

212. Shaker. Height $4\frac{1}{4}$ inches. Boardman and Company, New York, 1825–1827, mark 431.

213. Shaker. Height $5\frac{5}{8}$ inches. Unmarked. Maker unknown, possibly American, probably nineteenth century.

214. Small shaker. Height 4 inches. Mark 594. Maker unknown, late eighteenth century.

210 to 214 are from the author's collection.

PLATE XXX

Household Pewter

John W. Poole, at a recent meeting of the Pewter Collectors' Club, made the pertinent observation that in the mad scramble to acquire a colonial tankard the average collector forgets that there are other forms which are fully as desirable from an aesthetic point of view, far more difficult to find, and yet when discovered can usually be purchased more reasonably than a tankard of the same period. Such a piece is the early teapot, one of the rarest and — to my mind — most desirable shapes in American pewter.

Shortly before the Revolution a handsome teapot of new design, patterned after a silver model, came upon the market. An invoice of Frederick Bassett, dated May 13, 1773, includes 'Tea potts' and 'Round dᵒ' (Plate LX). Two examples of what I believe to have been the 'round' teapot are illustrated in Plate XXIX, 194 and 195, one the work of an unknown maker, the other from the shop of William Will. There is no existing evidence that the round teapot was made in any of the colonies except New York and Pennsylvania.

To the same period, 1770 to 1795, belongs the magnificent coffee-pot, also made by William Will, illustrated in Plate XXVII, bearing additional testimony to the skill and taste of its designer. Unfortunately no other American pewterer of the eighteenth century is known to have manufactured either coffee-pots or coffee-urns.

Successive steps are shown in Plate XXVIII, 191, 192, and 193, in the transition from the early Queen Anne teapot to the tall teapots of the period of britannia. Though both desirable and rare, the later examples lack the crispness in outline and the grace of form of the earlier pear-shaped vessels. They foreshadow the decline in craftsmanship that was already under way at the close of the eighteenth century. Pewter handles replace handles of wood and the carefully modulated curves of cover and pot begin to lose their well-rounded appearance.

The pot shown in Plate XXVIII, 193, deserves special comment. Although this particular example bears the touch of Thomas D. Boardman of Hartford, the design probably originated in the shop of his uncle, Samuel Danforth, who has also left us marked examples of this type. Here is an excellent illustration of the care used by our early craftsmen to make the most of the limited equipment available to them. There was apparently a demand for larger teapots than had been supplied previously. Without the purchase of any new moulds, Danforth met the need, and in doing so developed a new design. He simply took two castings made from his old teapot mould, inverted one, and soldered the bottoms together, adding the handle, spout, cover, and base which would have been used on the teapot of earlier shape.

The pot designated as 196, Plate XXIX, also affords an exceedingly interesting study in the evolution of teapot design, for here are commingled a spout of the Queen Anne style, a handle to match but of pewter instead of wood, a round pot of the Federal years, tapered inward slightly at top and bottom, but still beaded as in the earlier form, all capped with a cover the sharp contours of which are characteristic of many lids of the britannia period. We are most fortunate in having these links in the chain which bridged the gap from the choice little pear-shaped pot of colonial days and the chaste round teapot of the early Republic to the countless varieties (many of them graceless) of elongated teapots and coffee-pots with which the country was flooded by the makers of the nineteenth century. Examples of some of the more desirable designs of this later period may be studied in Plates LXXI and LXXII.

Even rarer than early teapots are sugar bowls and cream pitchers which can be identified positively as American. Only two distinct designs of sugar bowl have been reported to date and my limited knowledge of English and Continental forms will not permit me to say whether either design had its origin across the sea or can be claimed for native pewterers.

The bowls numbered 197, 198, and 199 in Plate XXIX, are three varieties of a type that was made in Pennsylvania and possibly in New York. In these bowls there is some similarity to the glass bowls of Baron Stiegel and a very close resemblance to the contemporary Philadelphia sugar pots in silver of such makers as John Letelier and Joseph Richardson. Number 197, an unusually fine early specimen, is the work of Christopher Heyne of Lancaster (1754–1780). Neither 198 nor 199 is marked, but the latter particularly shows such marked characteristics of Philadelphia design that we can have little hesitation in attributing it to William Will, Parks Boyd, or one of their contemporaries.

Number 200 in Plate XXIX was termed by Louis G. Myers in his *Notes* an herb box, but I believe it to have been made for use as a small sugar bowl. The maker was Thomas Danforth, Third, of Stepney, Connecticut (1777–1807). Even if it were unmarked this appealing little sugar pot could be ascribed to New England just as certainly as the three larger bowls can be set down as of middle colonies origin. Later forms may be studied in Plate LXXII.

Early pewter creamers also followed silver designs. They were usually of inverted pear-shaped body with narrowed neck and wide-flaring mouth, standing on three legs. Plate XXX shows four such creamers, varying slightly from one another; number 201 is attributed to John Will of New York (1752–1766), and number 202 was made by Peter Young of New York and Albany (1775–1790); numbers 203 and 206, as well as the little footed creamer (number 205), are the work of unknown makers. All five are rare desirable little pieces. The sixth creamer shown (number 204), which bears no maker's mark, is undoubtedly later but superior in design and decoration to most of the nineteenth-century cream pitchers.

After the advent of the spinning process, permitting the use of thinner metal, simple curves gave way to sharp edges and broken lines. Although many of the later teapots, coffee-pots, sugar bowls, and creamers show considerable originality and in some cases decided charm and grace, others are lacking in merit of any kind. Examples of the better types are discussed in the study of the britannia period.

PLATE XXXI — *Flagons*

215. Fine early English flagon. Height over all 14 inches, top diameter $4\frac{9}{16}$ inches, bottom diameter 6 inches. Mark Cotterell 5614 A. Maker unknown. Probably London *c.* 1635. Found at Whitman, Massachusetts, and probably used in one of the earliest churches in the colony. Collection of the author.

216. English flagon of early eighteenth century design. Height over all $13\frac{7}{8}$ inches, top diameter $4\frac{3}{8}$ inches, bottom diameter $6\frac{15}{16}$ inches. Maker unknown, possibly William Newham, London, *c.* 1725. If flagons were made in the colonies from 1720 to 1750, they were probably of this general form. Collection of the author.

217. American flagon of Germanic design. Height over all $11\frac{1}{2}$ inches, top diameter $3\frac{1}{2}$ inches, bottom diameter $6\frac{1}{8}$ inches. Johann Christopher Heyne, Lancaster, Pennsylvania, 1757–1781, marks 531, 532. The flaring base, narrow top, spout, and mascarons used as feet are all Teutonic. The handle, however, is distinctly English, a normal tankard handle, that is too short for the body of a flagon. Collection of John W. Poole, Esq.

218. Another flagon giving evidence of the Germanic origin of its maker. Height over all $9\frac{1}{2}$ inches, top diameter $3\frac{7}{8}$ inches, bottom diameter $5\frac{1}{16}$ inches. Colonel William Will, Philadelphia, 1764–1798, marks 538, 535. Except for the spout and spout cover, this flagon is English (or American) in design. Marred unfortunately by the loss of its finial and part of the thumb-piece. Collection of Mrs. James H. Krom.

PLATE XXXI

215

216

217

218

PLATE XXXII — *Henry Will Flagon*

219. A flagon of dignified simplicity. Height over all $11\frac{1}{4}$ inches, top diameter $4\frac{1}{4}$ inches, bottom diameter $5\frac{5}{8}$ inches. Henry Will, New York and Albany, 1761–1793. The one flaw in design is the use of a handle, designed for a tankard, that is too short for the flagon body. Courtesy of the Mabel Brady Garvan Collection, Gallery of Fine Arts, Yale University.

PLATE XXXII

PLATE XXXIII — *Flagons*

220, 221, and 222. The flagons of Trinity Church, Lancaster, Pennsylvania. Height over all about 12½ inches, top diameter 3½ inches, bottom diameter 6⅛ inches. The mark on the central vessel is that of Heinrich Mueller, Rothenburg, Germany, *c.* 1720; the marks on the other two (530, 531, 532) those of Johann Christopher Heyne, Lancaster, Pennsylvania, 1757–1781. Made presumably to match the earlier German flagon, this pair of Heyne flagons have ball thumb-pieces which were replaced by English types on all other surviving Heyne flagons. Courtesy of Trinity Church and John J. Evans, Jr., Esq.

220a, 221a, and 222a. The bases of the same flagons contrasting two methods of construction. Heyne used his normal 6⅛-inch plate as a flagon base.

223. A late flagon. Height over all 13½ inches, top diameter 4⅛ inches, bottom diameter 6¼ inches. Thomas D. Boardman, Hartford, 1806–1820, mark 425. An excellent design marred by a spout and a too-heavy finial. The same design was made by Samuel Danforth of Hartford, 1795–1816. Collection of the author.

224. Albany flagon, a design found bearing the touches of three Albany pewterers. Height over all 10¾ inches, top diameter 4⁵⁄₁₆ inches, bottom diameter 6³⁄₁₆ inches. Timothy Brigden and Spencer Stafford, Albany, *c.* 1816, marks 517, 519. Collection of Charles K. Davis, Esq.

PLATE XXXIII

220   221   222

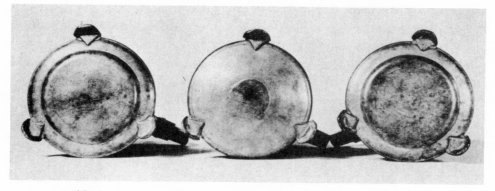

220 a   221 a   222 a

223

224

Plate XXXIV — *Communion Vessels*

225. Beaker. Height $4\frac{3}{4}$ inches, top diameter $3\frac{3}{4}$ inches, bottom diameter $3\frac{5}{8}$ inches. Peter Young, New York and Albany, *c.* 1775–1795, mark 514.

226. Quart tankard. Height $6\frac{1}{8}$ inches, top diameter $4\frac{5}{16}$ inches, bottom diameter 5 inches. Same maker, mark 514.

fig. 227. The Baptist Church was in Cheshire, Mass. and not Cheshire, Conn.

227. Beaker. Mate to 233. This fine communion set, formerly used in the Baptist Church of Cheshire, Connecticut, is now in the collection of Dr. and Mrs. Irving H. Berg.

228. Two-handled beaker or church cup. Height 5 inches, top diameter $3\frac{3}{4}$ inches, bottom diameter 4 inches. Thomas D. Boardman, Hartford, 1805–1830.

229. Tall flagon. Height $12\frac{1}{2}$ inches, top diameter 4 inches, bottom diameter $6\frac{1}{4}$ inches. Same maker. Fine nineteenth-century flagon.

230. Two-handled beaker. Mate to 236. Collection of Dr. and Mrs. Irving H. Berg.

PLATE XXXIV

225 226 227

228 229 230

ECCLESIASTICAL PEWTER

ADIVISION between household and church pewter is indeed an arbitrary one, for vessels that were made for use in the home were frequently bought by or presented to the churches as parts of communion services. There were, however, certain forms which were made primarily for use in the churches.

In the wealthier parishes the communion services were made of silver, but in country districts pewter vessels were used. The number of pieces to the set varied with the size and wealth of the congregation, but ordinarily consisted of at least one flagon for wine (for which a tankard was often substituted), two or more (sometimes as many as twelve) church cups, chalices, or beakers, one to four dishes (usually eleven inches to thirteen inches in diameter), and a basin or bowl for baptismal use. In addition some congregations owned a number of six-inch plates that served as patens.

Only occasionally do we hear of a set of which all the pieces were the work of the same shop. This is because of the fact that most services were acquired piecemeal as gifts from individuals, and rounded out by purchases as required. Even when an entire set was bought at one time there was little likelihood of any uniformity in the pieces, for the purchase would be made at the nearest country store, the stock of which was intermittently added to as different peddlers came that way. No examples of marked American church pewter antedating 1750 are known to be in existence, and comparatively few pieces that were made prior to 1800.

Two handsome communion sets in the collection of Doctor and Mrs. Irving H. Berg are illustrated in Plate XXXIV. The fine pair of beakers in the upper group were made by Peter Young in Albany about 1785 to 1795 and were used for many years in a church in Cheshire, Massachusetts. They differ in shape from any beakers illustrated and commented upon earlier. Thomas D. Boardman of Hartford was the maker of the vessels in the lower group, probably between the years 1805 and 1815. To my mind the design both of flagon and cups was superior to that of any of similar forms made by Boardman's contemporaries and successors.

But let us return and examine the types of communion vessels used in America prior to the nineteenth century. In Plate XXXI, 215, is shown a very fine English flagon, found near Plymouth, Massachusetts, and until recently in the possession of the Alden family. A pair of identical flagons bearing the mark of the same unidentified maker and inscribed with the date 1635 are illustrated in Cotterell's *Old Pewter*. Vessels of much this same type must have been in use in many an early colonial church. Another flagon found in this country and probably also English (*c.* 1725) is illustrated in Plate XXXI,

216, as the type of flagon that was in general use in the colonies early in the eighteenth century.

Of the eighteenth-century American flagons just four types have come to my notice. First are the Lancaster flagons, closely resembling the flagons of Alsace, made in the third quarter of the eighteenth century by Christopher Heyne, a Pennsylvania German. Such a flagon is illustrated in Plate XXXI, 217, and commented upon in greater detail in volume II, pages 44–46. The second type is the splendid tall flagon of Henry Will, really an elongated tankard, which was made in about the same period in New York (Plate XXXII). Its simple dignity gives it great charm. This flagon is early in form, the absence of a spout emphasizing its early lines. Plate XXXI, 218, shows a flagon made by William Will of Philadelphia. Despite the loss of its finial and part of the thumb-piece, it is still a handsome vessel. The spout bears evidence of the Germanic heritage of its maker.

In the 'eagle period' (1790 to 1825) we find flagons by but four makers, Spencer Stafford and Timothy Brigden of Albany and Samuel Danforth and T. D. Boardman of Hartford. Since Stafford's and Brigden's flagons are apparently identical in design, and since Boardman probably used Danforth's moulds after the latter's death, we have just two types to describe. The Albany flagon (made about 1818 by Timothy Brigden, Plate XXXIII, 224) is a very plain serviceable vessel, and would probably have more appeal had it not served as a model for the modern aluminum and enameled coffee-pots in daily use in our kitchens today. Two Boardman flagons (*c*. 1816–1820), differing only in details, are shown in Plate XXXIII, 223, and Plate XXXIV, 229. The base of each is too heavy, and the finial of 223 shows too great a striving for originality, but the other proportions are very fine and their maker might have been deservedly proud of them. Except for some of the later vessels made in the same shop, American communion flagons never again attained the same dignity and grace. In some of the later Boardman flagons (*c*. 1820–1830) the lines were improved by narrowing the bulging base, but in other respects these vessels are less successful in design than the earlier Boardman product and the thinner walls foreshadowed the decline that was already on the way. As an example of one of the better designs of late flagons I have illustrated in Plate LXXIII, a vessel made by Israel Trask (Beverly, *c*. 1830).

The drinking-vessels into which the wine was poured from the flagons were of three generic types — church cups, chalices, and tall beakers. Exceedingly rare are the marked examples of any of these forms.

In the collection of the Pocumtuck Valley Memorial Association at Deerfield, Massachusetts, is a set of four superb church cups impressed with an unidentified touch formerly attributed to Robert Boyle, New York pewterer. The cups (Plate XXXV, 232) are of early design, decorated most effectively with rope bandings and gadrooned ornamentation, a pattern copied from the silver caudle cups that were being fashioned in England and the colonies at the close of the seventeenth century. Note also the raised, beaded motif on top and bottom of each handle. No finer examples of the craftsmanship of the American pewterer have survived.

Plate XXXV — *Ecclesiastical Pewter*

231. Unusually fine church cup of early design. Height $4\frac{1}{4}$ inches, top diameter $4\frac{1}{16}$ inches, bottom diameter $2\frac{13}{16}$ inches. Maker unknown, probably New England, *c.* 1750–1780, mark 292. The same design was current in England about 1700. Formerly in the collection of Herbert M. Rublee, Esq.

232. A similar cup to 231, with handles. Extreme width $7\frac{1}{8}$ inches. Same maker. One of a set of four unusually handsome cups. Courtesy of the late Mrs. George Sheldon, formerly Curator of the Pocumtuck Valley Historical Society, Deerfield, Massachusetts.

233. Large two-handled cup. Height $6\frac{1}{4}$ inches, top diameter $6\frac{1}{2}$ inches. A rare form. Mark indistinct. Maker unknown, but probably American. Courtesy of the late Mrs. George Sheldon, formerly Curator of the Pocumtuck Valley Historical Society, Deerfield, Massachusetts.

234 and 235. Individual communion set. Height of cup $2\frac{1}{8}$ inches, top diameter $2\frac{1}{16}$ inches; height of tray $1\frac{1}{8}$ inches, top diameter $3\frac{3}{4}$ inches. Both items unmarked. Maker unknown, probably Connecticut, early nineteenth century. Said to have been carried by a minister or priest for administering communion to parishioners who were ill. Collection of the Honorable and Mrs. George V. Smith.

236 and 237. Obverse and reverse of two communion tokens which measure 1 inch by $\frac{7}{8}$ inch and $\frac{7}{8}$ by $\frac{7}{8}$ inch. Dated 1807 and 1824, and presumed to have been used in a church in Hebron, Connecticut. Collection of the author.

PLATE XXXV

231

232

233

234   235

236   237

236 a   237 a

PLATE XXXVI — *Chalices*

238. Early chalice of Germanic design. Height $8\frac{3}{4}$ inches, top diameter 4 inches, bottom diameter $4\frac{1}{2}$ inches. Johann Christopher Heyne, Lancaster, Pennsylvania, 1754–1780, marks 531 and 532. Collection of John W. Poole, Esq.

239. Similar but slightly later chalice by same maker, perhaps unique among American chalices in having a lid. Height $8\frac{7}{8}$ inches, with lid $10\frac{7}{8}$ inches, mark in lid 533. Collection of the author.

240. A chalice of dignified simplicity. Height 8 inches. Unmarked. Maker unknown, but with its mate this chalice was found with the William Will (1764–1798) flagon shown in Plate XXXI, 218. Contemporaneous even if not made by Will. Collection of Mrs. James H. Krom.

241. Chalice with slender stem. Height 9 inches, top diameter $4\frac{1}{4}$ inches, bottom diameter $3\frac{7}{8}$ inches. Unmarked. Maker unknown, probably Pennsylvania, 1760 to 1800. Collection of the author.

242. An Albany chalice. Height $8\frac{9}{16}$ inches, top diameter $4\frac{1}{16}$ inches, bottom diameter $4\frac{1}{4}$ inches. Peter Young, Albany, *c.* 1780–1790, mark 514. A very similar form was made also by Timothy Brigden of Albany. Collection of the author.

243. New England chalice. Height $8\frac{11}{16}$ inches, top diameter $3\frac{3}{4}$ inches, bottom diameter $3\frac{11}{16}$ inches. Unmarked. Maker unknown, New England, *c.* 1800–1820. Of heavy pewter. Many britannia chalices in much the same design have survived. Collection of the author.

PLATE XXXVI

238

239

240

241

242

243

PLATE XXXVII — *Baptismal Bowls*

244. Fine English baptismal bowl. Diameter 14 inches, width of rim $2\frac{3}{8}$ inches, depth $2\frac{1}{4}$ inches. Engraved 'The Gift of the Revd Thomas Cary of Newburyport to the Church of Christ in Waterford, 1805.' Made fully one hundred years earlier by Erasmus Dole of Bristol, England (Cotterell, 1679–1697). Collection of the author.

245. Baptismal bowl formed from two normal 8-inch basins. Samuel Danforth, Hartford, 1795–1816, mark 403. Collection of Charles F. Hutchins, Esq.

246. Footed baptismal bowl. Height $4\frac{9}{16}$ inches, top diameter $7\frac{1}{4}$ inches, bottom diameter $5\frac{1}{4}$ inches. Thomas D. and Sherman Boardman, Hartford, 1810–1825, mark 428. The forerunner of many footed bowls of the britannia period, many of them of more elaborate but less pleasing designs. Collection of Albert H. Good, Esq.

PLATE XXXVII

The Gift of the Revd. Thomas Cary of Newburyport, to the Church of Christ in Newburyport 1802

244

245

246

PLATE XXXVIII — *Early Baptismal Bowl*

247. Two views of the finest and earliest of American baptismal bowls. Diameter 13 inches, width of rim 1 inch, depth 2¾ inches. Joseph Leddell, New York, 1712–1753, or Joseph Leddell, Jr., New York, 1740–1754, mark 455. The sides slope more than in the ordinary basin and a narrow plate rim supplants the normal basin rim. Collection of Mrs. J. Insley Blair.

PLATE XXXVIII

247

247a

Ecclesiastical Pewter

The maker of these cups supplied them with or without handles. A specimen of the latter type, at one time a part of a service of an early Connecticut church and recently owned by H. M. Rublee, is pictured in Plate XXXV, 231. A pair of identical vessels, said to have been used in a church in Tiverton, Rhode Island, is in the collection of Carl C. Brigham. A larger cup, simpler in design but of pleasing lines, is illustrated as number 233. Although the maker is unknown, the cup gives evidence of American workmanship. I have no record of the survival of American church cups in any other design.

Church cups and chalices are among the loveliest forms in pewter, and the pity of it is that so few have come down to our time. Chalices are only less rare than cups, and probably none thus far reported antedates 1760. The first of those illustrated (Plate XXXVI, 238 and 239) were made by Christopher Heyne of Lancaster, Pennsylvania (*c.* 1760–1770). The cover is a most unusual feature. Noteworthy also is the knopped stem, a definite indication of the Teutonic origin of their maker.

The unmarked chalice in Plate XXXVI, 240, is one of a pair that were found with a flagon made by William Will of Philadelphia and may also have been from his hand, though such attribution is little more than guesswork. The slenderness of their stems denies the possibility of English origin. All the evidence points to a colonial maker of Continental birth or extraction.

Also unmarked, but almost certainly American and of the same period (last quarter of the eighteenth century), is the chalice in Plate XXXVI, 241; number 242 is the form that was made in Albany by Peter Young and Timothy Brigden. Last of the chalices is number 243, from a church in New Hampshire, and possibly typical of the chalices of New England. Though perhaps of nineteenth-century manufacture it is of thicker metal than any of its kind that I have seen. Unfortunately it is not marked. These drinking-cups of the eighteenth century are lovely things; those of a later time are graceless by comparison.

Beakers have already been described under 'Household Pewter' (see page 36), and require no further comment here. And what is true of beakers applies with equal force to dishes. Identical forms were used in church and home. Many of our best-preserved dishes in the 11-inch, 12-inch, and 13-inch sizes owe their unmarred surfaces to the fact that they never saw harder service than as trays for communion bread or as plush-lined collection plates.

This statement was in error when written, because a Leddell baptismal basin is illustrated in Plate XXXVIII and at least one other similar basin was then known.

In many of the earlier church sets the baptismal bowl must have been an ordinary basin or deep dish. If the pre-Revolutionary pewterers made a form just for this purpose, no example is known to have survived, nor have I ever seen such an item advertised. I am illustrating, however (Plate XXXVII, 244), an English baptismal bowl made by Erasmus Dole of Bristol (*c.* 1700). On its rim is engraved 'The Gift of the Revd Thomas Cary of Newburyport to the Church of Christ in Waterford, 1805.' This bowl must have been made a full century before its presentation to the Maine congregation. Any early American baptismal bowls which may still exist are probably of the same general pattern as the Waterford bowl.

Ecclesiastical Pewter

The one early eighteenth-century piece that we have that may have been used for baptismal purposes is the well-preserved and unusual bowl illustrated in Plate XXXVIII. Its maker was Joseph Leddell of New York (1712–1753) or his son, Joseph, Junior, who died in 1754.

During the 'eagle period,' however, at least two men, Samuel Pierce and Samuel Danforth, did make baptismal basins which were in reality basins to which a base or foot was added. An example by Danforth is illustrated in Plate XXXVII, 245.

Just at the dawn of the britannia period the bowl was raised on a footed standard to form a very pleasing design. An excellent example of this type, made by T. D. and S. Boardman, may be seen in Plate XXXVII, 246. At the sale of the collection of the late A. C. Bowman in New York in February, 1938, another bowl on standard, from the shop of Oliver Trask of Beverly, Massachusetts (c. 1830), deservedly brought a handsome price. Its lines and proportions were so well conceived that any of the older school of pewterers might well have been proud of the composition. This general form was made also by Israel Trask, Gleason, Boardman and Company, and others. Had their examples been executed in heavier metal after the manner of the earlier makers, they too would be much sought for today.

In Plate XXXV, 234 and 235, a small cup and tray have been illustrated. These are said to have been used by a member of the cloth as a little individual communion set with which he administered last rites to dying parishioners.

We cannot close a chapter on ecclesiastical pewter without a brief discussion of church tokens, two of which are also illustrated in Plate XXXV. These particular tokens, dated 1807 and 1824 respectively, are presumed to have been used in a church in Hebron, Connecticut. The tokens themselves have no great merit, but are interesting reminders of a custom unknown to the present generation, and perhaps the following brief digression on the purpose they served will be not altogether out of place.

In older times it frequently happened that, through the death of a pastor or a scarcity of ministers, congregations would find themselves without any ordained clergyman to preside over their services. It was also true that not all ministers were permitted to administer communion. The result was that several congregations would meet at one central place of worship for communion service. The presiding churchman could not have been expected to distinguish the 'sheep' from the 'goats,' and accordingly a deacon of each congregation distributed tokens, similar to those illustrated, to such members of his own parish as were qualified to take communion, and each communicant, as he came to the table, returned his evidence of fitness.

THE PEWTERERS OF MASSACHUSETTS BAY

THE beginnings of pewter-making in this country date back with certainty almost to the days of the arrival of the first of the Pilgrim Fathers at Plymouth. We have nothing to show that pewter was made during the first decade of the settlements along Massachusetts Bay, but by 1640 there were at least four pewterers dwelling, and presumably working at their trade, in those earliest New England towns.

Richard Graves came to this country in 1635 and settled in Salem; Henry Shrimpton landed at Boston in 1639; Samuel Grame (or Greames) was in the same town at least that early; and Thomas Bumstead arrived at Roxbury from the old country in 1640. Thus, over fifty years before the witchcraft excitement was to reach its climax in Salem, the making of pewter appears to have become an established industry on these shores. Boston thus became the first important pewter-making center in the colonies and for over one hundred years appears to have maintained that pre-eminence.

The fullness of early Massachusetts records, their careful preservation and ready accessibility have made possible a much more nearly complete list of the early pewterers there than can be compiled for any other colony. More than fifty men can now be thus classified who worked in or near Boston prior to 1825. Some of them, of course, were factors of little consequence in the trade, perhaps journeymen only, of whom we have but the most meager information, but the majority were substantial citizens, holders of office in the town government, property owners, and, in a few instances, proprietors of large pewter-making and braziery establishments.

Although it may be true, as J. B. Kerfoot believed, that the early workers were dealers in and menders of imported ware rather than makers of pewter, I am inclined to think otherwise. That may have been the situation for a few years, but as worn and damaged pewter accumulated, this cheap form of raw material and the growing demand for replacements would have guaranteed a profitable business to a pewter-maker at a very early date. The very fact that our earliest pewterer of record, Richard Graves, owned brass moulds, is well-nigh convincing proof that the first of our makers was a fashioner of pewter. I believe further that our earliest pewterers, trained in England, would have brought with them to their new land not only their moulds and tools, but also the customs of their trade. And since they marked their metal in England with individual touches, I can see no reason for doubting that they would have continued the same practice after their arrival here. The recent discovery at Jamestown, Virginia, of a seventeenth-century American-made spoon stamped with its maker's mark is strong evidence in favor of such an assumption.

The Pewterers of Massachusetts Bay

Very different were many of the shapes in pewter of the seventeenth century from those that we now know. The inventory of Henry Shrimpton's shop taken in 1666 furnishes a very fair list of the forms that were in common use in Boston at that date. Among the items there listed were 'beere Bowles, Wine Cupps, Bed Panns, Sawcers, New Fashion Potts, Flaggons, Alcamy Spoons, Pewter Spoones, Candelsticks, Salts, Trencher Salts, Pint Potts, Goadards, Beakers, Potts without Lids, Dram Cupps, Porringers, Basons, Platters, Flat brimd Chamber Potts, Qt. Bottles, Suckling Bottles, Thorondell Potts and Dishes.' The comparative preponderance of drinking-vessels enumerated testifies to the extensive use of liquor by our forebears.

It is difficult now to picture the appearance of many of these forms, for some of them were soon to become obsolete. Even such familiar items as 'candelsticks' and salts were very different in shape from the candlesticks and salts which we find today. As for such forms as 'goadards' and 'thorondell potts' I question whether there are a half-dozen people in this country who could tell offhand what such names stood for. My own slight knowledge about them has been gleaned from Halliwell's *Dictionary of Archaic and Provincial Words* and from H. J. L. J. Massé's *Chats on Old Pewter*. The former gives:

> *Goddard* . . . A kind of cup or goblet.
> *Thirdendales* . . . (1) A third part. (2) A measure containing three pints.

Massé says:

> In the middle of the fifteenth century thurndells or thurendales of a new fashion, and in two sizes, some being hooped, were in use in England. . . . Goddards were tankards, some upright, others round, the largest of which had Dolphin ears. . . .

At the date of Shrimpton's death, pewter was the universal ware, found in all homes except those of the very poor, who still were using wooden plates and vessels. Even the wealthy, who could afford silver, probably saved the latter for special occasions, using pewter for everyday service. China, porcelain, tin, and all the other substitutes were to come later, but in the seventeenth century pewter was in its heyday. Shrimpton, you will note, made no teapots, coffee-pots, sugar bowls, or creamers. They all belonged to a period that was only just dawning. In 1652 the first coffee-house was opened in London, and in 1661 Samuel Pepys in his *Diary* speaks of having a cup of tea, 'a new Chiny drink that I have never tasted before.'

Before the death in 1677 of Thomas Bumstead, last of the earliest group of Boston pewterers, Thomas Clarke, John Comer, and perhaps others whose records are now lost had become established in the trade in Boston, and from 1700 until after the Revolution there were never less than a half-dozen shops in operation and at times a dozen or more.

Boston records indicate that in that town the trades of pewter-making and brass-working were usually combined. Many of the workers are indiscriminately termed 'pewterer' or 'brazier' in public documents. Some few of our pewterers — Thomas Bumstead, John Comer, and John Skinner, for example — are invariably described as pewterers, but they are exceptions rather than the rule. Similarly, there were some braziers who were never termed pewterers. I have refrained from including any such men in our lists except when their inventories included pewter-making equipment or when there was other incontrovertible evidence that they carried on both trades. Nevertheless there is no doubt in my mind that some of the men believed now to have been braziers only were pewter-makers also. For example, Thomas Simpkins is invariably termed a brazier in public documents in which his name appears, but we have two pewter plates impressed with touches that include his name. Incidentally those plates are two of but four or, at the most, five which can be classified with reasonable certitude as of Boston manufacture prior to 1760.

It is not surprising, perhaps, that no Boston pewter of the seventeenth century has come down to us, but it is amazing that so little flatware and not one piece of hollow-ware has been spared from the tremendous output of the first six decades of the eighteenth century. For this condition I can offer no logical explanation. The suggestion has been advanced that the early pewterers in Massachusetts made very little beyond flatware and that the other forms which they advertised and sold in such large quantities were imported from England. That argument can be refuted, at least in part, by the testimony of inventories which, in several cases, included moulds for hollow-ware.

Coming down to Revolutionary times and later, Boston is well represented with flatware in collections today. John Skinner, Nathaniel and Richard Austin, Samuel Green, Thomas Badger, and George Richardson have left us a great many plates, dishes, and basins; but even for this late period there is no hollow-ware except a few quart mugs by Nathaniel Austin and some very late forms bearing Richardson's mark; and that despite the fact that we have many splendid examples of hollow-ware made by contemporary pewterers in other colonies. Even such a small pewter-making center as Albany, New York, for instance, or Lancaster, Pennsylvania, can make a braver showing as far as variety goes than Boston with its large group of pewterers. Perhaps we have a right to expect that before long some fortunate collector will report the discovery of a measure or two, an early tankard or some other of the rarer shapes stamped with a touch of a Boston maker of the eighteenth century. Such a hope may soon be fulfilled, for there now is evidence that the fine examples marked with the initials 'R. B.,' a rose and crown (Plate XLIV, 292), a touch which has long been attributed to Robert Boyle of New York, may in reality be the work of an unidentified Boston pewterer. If such a claim can be established, the pewter of Massachusetts will warrant the recognition which the written records indicate that it deserves, and the Bassetts, the Wills, and the Danforths may have to look to their laurels.

Boston flatware, by which alone we can judge the Boston pewterers, was of very good quality and carefully finished, superior in general to the flatware of most of the other colonies. As a rule the Boston plate has a narrower rim than was in general use on the contemporary plates of Providence, Middletown, New York, or Philadelphia, and almost all Boston flatware is unusually shallow. The normal range in size was from about 8 to 15 inches in diameter. The latter size was not an unusual form there as elsewhere in colonial America. In fact every Boston maker of the second half of the eighteenth century who has left us any pewter at all is represented by at least one 15-inch dish.

Richard Graves of Salem

One other feature of Boston pewter deserves at least passing recognition. The man (or men) who designed the handsome touches used by John Skinner, Nathaniel Austin, Richard Austin, and Thomas Badger (Plates XLV and XLVI) was a die-cutter of unusual ability. No other colony has left us as fine a group of bold, tasteful, well-proportioned touch designs.

Ten or fifteen years earlier than in Rhode Island or Connecticut, the Boston pewterers gave up their unequal struggle with the potteries of Staffordshire, and after 1815 we find the successful Massachusetts shops (with one late exception) located in the smaller towns of Beverly, Dorchester, Malden, and Taunton. Their product was principally britannia metal, and their work will be considered later. In the remainder of the present chapter we shall confine our attention to the individual histories of the early pewtermakers of Massachusetts.

RICHARD GRAVES OF SALEM

One summer day some fifteen years ago I picked up by chance J. B. Kerfoot's *American Pewter* and opened it at the history of Richard Graves. This ne'er-do-well of Salem was such a delightfully irresponsible character and his brief story was so enchantingly told that I went on to read the book from cover to cover. Ever since, in my travels about the country, I have been turning pewter plates upside down in a search for American marks. It does not necessarily follow that a reading of this sketch of Graves's life will have the same impelling effect on someone else that it had on me, but the temptation to reprint it here is too strong to be resisted.

Graves came to Massachusetts in the *Abigail*, arriving in July, 1635. He settled at Salem and was a proprietor there in 1637. . . . He got into trouble with the authorities very soon and in December, 1638, was sentenced to sit in the stocks for beating Peter Busgutt in his own house. . . . In 1641 Graves was brought into court again, and William Allen testified that 'he had herd Rich Graves kissed Goody Gent twice.' Richard confessed that it was true, and for this unseemly conduct was sentenced to be fined and whipped. . . . He was presented at a quarterly court on February 28, 1652–3, for 'oppression in his trade of pewtering, and acquitted of the charge. Then he was accused of neglecting to attend the ferry carefully, so that it would seem that pewtering occupied only part of his time. This he acknowledged, but said that he had not been put to it by the Court and also that it was necessary to leave the ferry when he went to the mill, a quite apparent fact. He seems to have been a somewhat reckless fellow in his dealings with his neighbors, for he was accused of taking fence rails from Christopher Young's lot and admonished by the Court. At the same time he was fined for stealing wood from Thomas Edwards and for evil speeches to him, calling him 'a base fellow, & yt one might Ruun a half pike in his bellie & never touch his hart.' . . . In 1645 he was in Boston in connection with some brazen molds that were in dispute. . . . On another occasion, a few years later, when Graves went to Boston, he got drunk at Charlestown, and in consequence, was mulct by the Quarterly Court. Only a month later he was complained of for playing shuffle-board, a wicked game of chance, at the tavern kept by Mr. Gedney in Salem, but this time he escaped the vengeance of the law, for the case against him was not proved. He was still pursuing his trade of pewterer in 1665 when he so styled himself in a deed to John Putnam, and some time between that date and 1669 he passed out of reach of the courts to that bourne from which no pewterers ever return.

Graves was twenty-three years old when he sailed from England, and was therefore born about 1612. His pewter has disappeared long since. There is little likelihood that a single piece exists today. But who, upon reading his story, and in particular the item about a dispute over some 'brazen molds,' can doubt that he was more than a mere mender of imported metal?

SAMUEL GRAME (OR GREAMES)

'The 29th day of 2nd month, called Aprill, 1639 . . . Samuel Grame is Allowed for an Inhabitant.' Such is the wording in Boston records of this early pewterer's admission to citizenship in the town. A prior Boston document records the birth of 'Mary, daughter of Samuel and Francis Greames' two days before his acceptance as an inhabitant. In January, 1640, 'Samuel Grame hath a great Lott granted unto him for 4 heads at the Mount,' and just two years later Samuel and Frances Grame joined the church and their daughter, Mary, was baptized.

The pewterer's name is found just once thereafter on a surviving town record. In the 'Book of Possessions,' which was commenced in 1645, 'Samuel Greames' great Lott' is described. He therefore was living at least until that year, but perhaps not much later.

Although Grame's occupation is recorded in the church records, we do not know — and probably never shall know — the extent of his business or the forms in pewter which he made.

HENRY SHRIMPTON

The next man on our list, Henry Shrimpton, born about the year 1615, came to Boston in 1639 from Bednall Green, Middlesex, England. At a selectmen's meeting on the 25th of March of that year it was voted that 'one Henry Shrimpton, a Brayser, is allowed to be an Inhabitant in this Towne.' Nine children were born to Henry and Ellinor Shrimpton between 1641 and 1660, and about the latter date Mrs. Shrimpton must have died, for in 1661 Henry married a widow, Mrs. Mary Fenn.

At the time of his death in 1666, Shrimpton was one of Boston's wealthiest and most influential citizens. His funeral expenses amounted to over £134, a tidy sum as money went in those days, and a sufficient answer to those who imagine that none of the early settlers were accustomed to luxuries. The inventory was valued at just under £12,000. I can recall only one other pewterer who attained such affluence.

Thomas Bumsteed (or Bumstead)

Thomas Bumstead, another pewterer, was a witness to the will and helped take the inventory. Among the shop contents at the time of Shrimpton's death were 2782 pounds of pewter worth at that time over £235.

Although in deeds and other public documents Shrimpton called himself a brazier, almost all of our early pewterers combined brass-making with pewtering. The existence of such an amazing stock of pewter in the man's shop at the time of his death would assuredly indicate that he too worked at both trades. But far more significant evidence is the provision in his will leaving to his son Samuel 'all my tools for pewter and Brasse.'

Colonel Samuel Shrimpton, Henry's son, may also have been a brazier and pewterer in his early years, but he is styled 'merchant' or 'gentleman' in public documents. He amassed a very large fortune, and his fleet of merchantmen unloaded cargoes from all corners of the world.

Jonathan Shrimpton, Henry's nephew, was also a well-to-do brazier. As in the case of his uncle, this man, at the time of his death in 1674, had an inventory that included a large quantity of finished pewter, and it is quite possible that his name properly belongs on our lists.

THOMAS BUMSTEED (OR BUMSTEAD)

The name of Thomas Bumsteed has appeared on many lists of American pewterers, but his dates have been vaguely given and his story has so far been untold.

Thomas Bumsteed came to this land with his wife Susan and two small children, Thomas and Jeremiah, in July, 1640, and settled in Roxbury. In the next three years three more children were born to the couple. Then Thomas moved with his growing family to what was to be their permanent home, now the corner of State and Washington Streets in Boston, and there the family was swelled by the arrivals of three more little Bumsteeds.

Somewhat irrelevant, but possibly entertaining, is the following extract from Governor John Winthrop's *Journal* written in 1644:

> It may be of use to mention a private matter or two which fell out about this time because the power and mercy of the Lord did appear in them in an extraordinary manner. . . . A child of one [Thomas] Bumstead, a member of the Church, fell from a gallery in the meeting house about eighteen feet high and brake the arm and shoulder, and was also committed to the Lord in the prayers of the Church, with earnest desires, that the place where his people assembled to his worship might not be defiled with blood and it pleased the Lord also that this child was soon perfectly recovered.

Thomas became a member of the Ancient and Honorable Artillery Company in 1648 and must have been making pewter in Boston for many years — that is, when he was not busy taking inventories of his late neighbors' estates; for on inventory after inventory in the old Boston records we find that 'Thomas Bumsteed, pewterer,' was one of the appraisers. He is styled a pewterer on many deeds also.

Bumsteed died in Boston in 1677, and the inscription on his gravestone in the Old Granary Burial Ground indicates that he was born in England in 1610. He must have given up pewtering and sold his tools before his death, for his shop contents were valued at only seven pounds. For those collectors who may imagine that prices of antiques have been thoroughly deflated in these recent years of depression, the value of the furniture in one room of Bumsteed's home as determined by the appraisers of his estate is submitted herewith. That room contained a press cupboard, two small tables, nine 'old chayres and stools,' one glass case (an unusual item for those days, we should think), and a settle — all lumped together with a total valuation of £2 10s.

THOMAS CLARK (E)

On several previous lists, Thomas Clark's name has appeared as that of an early Boston pewterer. Men of that name, and with no middle initial to help identify them, were commoner in Boston in the last quarter of the seventeenth century than John Smiths would be in any town of the same size in this country today. Consequently it has been impossible to determine in many cases whether specific documents had reference to Thomas Clark the pewterer or to the merchant, the mariner, or the tailor of that name.

However, a few papers give the occupation also and the following facts in the life of the pewterer have been established: 'Thomas Clarke, ye Pewterer,' appears on Boston's tax list for 1674, our earliest record of the man in Boston; at a public meeting in March, 1679, 'Thomas Clark, pewter^r,' was elected constable for the ensuing year; and in 1685 'Thomas Clark, pewterer,' joined the Ancient and Honorable Artillery Company. It was apparently the same Thomas Clark who contributed one pound to the erection of the first King's Chapel in 1689 and was one of the twenty founders of the Brattle Square Church eleven years later.

Thomas Clark and his first wife, Jane (maiden name unknown), had at least four children — Thomas, Jane, a second Thomas, and Anne, the first Thomas and Anne dying in infancy. The first Mrs. Clark lived only until July 21, 1691, and on April 30 of the following year Clark married the widow Smith (née Rebecca Glover), who bore him one daughter, another Anne. In 1711 the second Mrs. Clark passed on, and on August 13, 1713, the widower embarked upon his third matrimonial venture, taking in marriage Mrs. Abigail Keech.

In deeds until 1720 Clark described himself as a pewterer, after that date as a merchant, whereas in the inventory appraisal he was termed a brazier. His shop was at the Town Dock. The only items of interest to the student of pewter in Clark's inventory were

211 *lb* Pewter a 2/9
19 *lb* Course do at 20d

The Two John Comers

Thomas Clark died December 16, 1732, aged about eighty-seven. He had outlived three wives and all but one of his children. The records indicate that he was a man of very considerable prominence in Boston. He was, for instance, one of three permitted to select pews in the Brattle Square Church in advance of the other members. His real estate holdings in Boston were large. In his will he mentions 'My Mansion House, Brick Ware-house, Shops, Coach-House and Land thereto belonging,' 'my certain Farm in Charlestown,' 'all my land at the Eastward' (shown in his inventory to have been at Wells, Maine), 'and all the Residue or Remainder of my Estate both Real and Personal.' With the possible exceptions of Henry Shrimpton, John Dolbeare, and Jonathan Jackson, Thomas Clark seems to have been the most prosperous of the American pewterers. It is regrettable that no example of his handicraft is known to have survived.

THE TWO JOHN COMERS

Earlier lists have included the name of John Comer. The *Wadsworth Athenaeum Bulletin* correctly placed him in Boston in the year 1678, but no further light on his history can be gleaned therefrom nor from any of the other lists of American pewterers.

The first of the family to emigrate to these shores was John Comer of Oake in the diocese of Bath and Wells, County of Somerset, England. This man was evidently a farmer. He was in or near Boston as early at least as 1652, when his name is found in the list of debtors to the estate of Robert Button.

His son John, the pewterer, must have been born about 1650, but whether in England or in Massachusetts we do not know. The date of his marriage is also unknown, but between the years 1674 and 1685 five children of whom we have record were born to John and 'Ellener' Comer in Boston. His first appearance in the Town Records was on the tax list of 1674, where he is described as a 'puterer.' He became a freeman of the town in 1678. From 1686 to 1691 Comer was 'Overseer of Chimneys,' and in 1690 he was also 'Clarke of the Market.' In 1709 and 1710 he was 'Tithing Man' and in 1712 'Constable.' His death occurred August 7, 1721, when he must have been about seventy years of age. His name appears on many Suffolk deeds, and always as a pewterer.

His eldest son and namesake, born August 12, 1674, followed the same trade. This we know from his inventory, taken in 1706, which included a wheel, tower, spindle, pewterer's tools, old pewter, etc. The younger John married Mary Pittom in 1698 and had one son, born in 1704, who was brought up by the grandfather and later became a famous Baptist divine in Rhode Island.

In the Suffolk County Court Files is the following letter, which was admitted to probate in lieu of a will:

South Carolina, July the 3ᵈ 1706.

Ever Honʳᵈ Father & Mother

My humble duty to you & love to Brother and Sisters. This is to give you to understand that we are safe arrived and had 3 weeks passage. I have not been ashore yet, for it is very sickly here

PLATE XXXIX — *Bottles*

248. Dram bottle. Height over all 4⅝ inches. Maker unknown, possibly John Bassett, New York, 1720–1761, mark 580. Collection of the author.

249. Infusion pot. Height 4⅝ inches, top diameter 3 5/16 inches, bottom diameter 3⅞ inches. Robert Pale-thorp, Jr., Philadelphia, 1817–1821, mark 560. The patient, with a severe cold, croup, 'the rheum,' etc., inhaled the vapors from the pot. Courtesy of the Mabel Brady Garvan Collection, Gallery of Fine Arts, Yale University.

250. Dram bottle. Height 4½ inches. Johann Christopher Heyne, Lancaster, Pennsylvania, 1754–1780, mark 533. Collection of John J. Evans, Jr., Esq.

251. Early nursing bottle. Height over all 5⅜ inches, bottom diameter 2¼ inches. Maker unknown, probably American, eighteenth century. Collection of Mr. and Mrs. Carl C. Brigham.

252. Nursing bottle. Height 6 inches. Frederick Bassett, New York and Hartford, 1761–1800, mark 465. Courtesy of the Mabel Brady Garvan Collection, Gallery of Fine Arts, Yale University.

253. Nursing bottle. Height not recorded. Timothy Boardman and Company, New York, 1822–1825, mark 432. Collection of the late John F. Street, Esq.

254. Nursing bottle with flat sides and long nipple. Height 6⅞ inches. Maker unknown, probably American, 1775–1825. Collection of the author.

PLATE XXXIX

250

254

249

253

252

248

251

PLATE XL — *Boxes*

255. Circular box, probably a soap container. Height 1¾ inches, diameter 4 5/16 inches. Maker unknown, possibly William Bradford, New York, 1719–1758, mark 583. A fine early example. Collection of Mrs. Guy G. Clark.

256. Tinder box with compartments for flints and tinder. Height 1 inch, 4 inches long by 3 inches wide. Unmarked, probably New England, early nineteenth century. Collection of the author.

257. An unusual circular box; purpose unknown. The three lugs must have carried a tray or separator at one time. Measurements not recorded, but the diameter was probably 6 or 7 inches. Parks Boyd, Philadelphia, 1795–1819, mark 544. This box is not in scale with other items illustrated on this plate. Formerly in the collection of Wilmer Moore, Esq.

258. Soap box. Height 1¾ inches, top diameter 4½ inches, bottom diameter 3⅝ inches. Ashbil Griswold, Meriden, 1807–1835, mark 420. Fitted inside in the depression in the lid there was originally a circular mirror. Collection of the author.

259. Small box, possibly used as a patch box. Height 1¼ inches, length 3 inches, width 1½ inches. Thomas Danforth Second, Middletown, Connecticut, 1755–1782, mark 363. Collection of the author.

260. Fine nutmeg box with dainty engraving. Height 4⅝ inches, long diameter of base 1¾ inches, short diameter 1¼ inches. George Coldwell, New York, 1787–1811, mark 508. Collection of John P. Remensnyder, Esq.

PLATE XL

255

256

257

258

259

260

PLATE XLI — *Hot-Water Plate, Inkstands, Sundials*

261. Hot-water plate. Diameter $9\frac{7}{16}$ inches, depth $1\frac{1}{4}$ inches. Henry Will, New York and Albany, 1761–1793. Collection of John W. Poole, Esq.

262 and 262a. Two views of an inkstand on feet. Height over all $2\frac{1}{4}$ inches. Top when closed measures $7\frac{7}{8} \times 4\frac{11}{16}$ inches. Henry Will, New York and Albany, 1761–1793, mark 491. The only known example of a marked American ink tray of this type. Collection of John W. Poole, Esq.

263. Standish. Inkwell with trays below for sand and wafers. Height $3\frac{3}{4}$ inches, base $3\frac{1}{4} \times 3\frac{1}{4}$ inches. A. G. Whitcomb, Boston, nineteenth century. Probably very late, though early in form. Collection of the author.

264. Inkwell. Height $3\frac{1}{2}$ inches, both diameters $4\frac{3}{4}$ inches. Boardman and Hall, Philadelphia, 1844–1845. Collection of Mrs. J. Insley Blair.

265. Sander. Diameter $2\frac{3}{8}$ inches, height $2\frac{1}{4}$ inches. W. Potter, location and dates unknown; after 1825. Collection of the author.

266. Early sundial. Dated 1762. Diameter $4\frac{1}{2}$ inches. Maker unknown. Collection of Edward E. Minor, Esq.

267, 268, and 269. Three later sundials measuring in diameter $4\frac{1}{2}$, $4\frac{7}{8}$, and $3\frac{1}{8}$ inches respectively. 268 is dated 1820. The others are probably of the same period. Hagger, whose name is stamped on 267, was a merchant of 'astronomical, nautical, mathematical, and philosophical instruments' in Baltimore. Collection of the author.

PLATE XLI

261

262

262a

263

264

265

266

267   268   269

PLATE XLII — *Household Articles*

270. Shaving mug with soap dish fitted in top. Height of mug 4½ inches, top diameter 3¼ inches, bottom diameter 3⅞ inches, depth of soap dish 1½ inches. G. Richardson, Cranston, Rhode Island. Collection of Joseph France, Esq. Formerly in the Bowman Collection.

271. Funnel. Height 7¼ inches, diameter 6 inches. Frederick Bassett, New York, 1765–1800, mark 465. Courtesy of the Mabel Brady Garvan Collection, Gallery of Fine Arts, Yale University.

272. Foot-warmer. Length 11¾ inches, height 6⅝ inches without handle, width at bottom 5⅞ inches. Henry Will, New York and Albany, 1761–1793, marks 487a and 492. The only recorded example of a marked American foot-warmer. Courtesy of the Mabel Brady Garvan Collection, Gallery of Fine Arts, Yale University.

273. Gravy or sauce boat. Height over all 4⅝ inches, length 7⅝ inches including handle. Mark 594. Maker unknown. Probably American, late eighteenth century. Collection of the author.

274. Covered water pitcher. Height over all 8½ inches, bottom diameter 4½ inches. Parks Boyd, Philadelphia, 1795–1819. Earliest of recorded marked American water pitchers. Collection of J. W. Poole, Esq.

272 is not in scale with the other items.

PLATE XLII

273

274

272

270

271

acct to the plague for they dont lye past three or four days and many of the Inhabitants are dead. Abundance of Indians, but tell Brother I hope to get one for him. I understand that we cant get Freight for London nor is Freight quick for Boston. I am much afraid whether we shall lye a great while here and that doth much startle me, for there is but few of the Vessels but what hath lost men by the Distemper.... If it should please God to take me out of this World before I should see you again My Will and desire is that my son John Comer should have two hundred pounds & Improved for him and I hope there will not be much less for my Wife for if I should dye she will be poorly of it. She will get another husband but he will be little the better. So not in large but Desiring your Prayers to God for me. So I rest and remain your ever Dutifull Son till death.

John Comer Junr

Superscribed for Mr. John Comer, Senr, Pewt^r in Boston p. Capt. Lalline.

Just nine days after the writing of that letter John Comer, Junior, was dead, and within two years his widow fulfilled his prediction by marrying a husband who proved 'little the better.' But let his son tell the story. The Rhode Island Historical Society owns the Reverend John Comer's *Diary*, from which the following is quoted:

My dear & honoured father, Mr. John Comer, engaged in a voyage to England but touching first at South Carolina was soon taken sick with ye prevailing sickness of y^t country and in a few days exchanged as I trust Earth for Heaven on ye 12th of July 1706, in ye 32nd year of his age.

· · · · · · · · · ·

This summer [1714] my mother with my father-in-law [stepfather] went over to South Carolina to live. One principal reason was because he had got two hundred pounds in money from my mother y^t my own father left for my education, and upon my grandfather's hearing of it he pursued him to get it; but he went away thither privately. So I was abused. But God has promised to avenge ye wrongs of ye fatherless. He lived there about two years and at ye expiration of y^m, he having been out on his horse came home in a dark evening and going into the house came out to look after his horse with a long pipe in his mouth, it being very dark fell over a log, ye pipe stem ran down his throat and broke and all means y^t could be used could not get it out. It being Saturday, he continued until Monday without speaking and died. Thus ye Lord found out a way in his Providence (tho awful) to meet with him. I always thought it a judgment ...

· · · · · · · · · ·

After ye going down of ye sun I visited my Grandfather, who was then sick and laboured under ye infirmities of old age; whom it pleased God to call hence as I trust into ye joy of his Lord, on Monday, Augt ye 7th 1721....

THE DOLBEARE FAMILY

John Dolbeare was one of those pewterers who appeared in the Kerfoot list with a question-mark and without dates. The doubts concerning his actuality were removed, however, by the examination of a number of interesting papers, once the property of the Dolbeare family, now in the custody of the Massachusetts Historical Society. Out of these documents John Dolbeare not only emerged as a maker of pewter, but was also disclosed as but one of a family of workers in that metal.

Edmund Dolbeare, a native of Ashburton, Devon, England, came to this country with his wife and two small sons, Joseph and John, probably about the year 1670. The first appearance of the name in Boston records is in 1671. In that year Edmund Dolbeare, aged twenty-nine, made a deposition concerning the collision of two vessels in Boston Harbor. That record furnishes us with Edmund's approximate year of birth — 1642. Apparently he did not prosper, for in 1682 'John Baker, brasier,' became surety to the town for 'Edmund Dolbeare, pewterer, and his family.' About that time the first wife died and Sarah (last name unknown) took her place. Edmund's name is on the list of heads of families in Boston in 1695 and on the tax list for 1700. The Record Commissioners' Reports for Boston contain the following notation by the tax assessor for the latter year, giving further evidence that Edmund Dolbeare was having hard sledding in his adopted country:

> Edm^d Dolbear, Aged and poor, his Rates amo^t: to 24. Propably upon reassuming ye Consideration of his Circumstances, reason may be seen for abatement

The tax, which amounted to £1 4s., was abated, as was that of the son Joseph. Edmund, however, was not so infirm as the tax assessor was led to believe, for in 1702 his wife, Sarah, gave birth to twin daughters. Sometime between 1705 and 1711 Edmund Dolbeare died.

We do not know what became of Joseph Dolbeare after he learned his trade except that he married Hannah Hewes (or Hughes) prior to 1690, and had at least four children — Joseph, Edmund, Elizabeth, and Hannah. The last-named was born in 1704, and there the record of Joseph Dolbeare ceases. That he did work for a while as a pewterer is evidenced by the following excerpt from the Suffolk County Court Files for the year 1694:

> Sampson Pentz, aet. 30 or thoroabout testyfyeth & saith that he the said Pentz did on the twenty-second day of Novemb^r last past being on Thursday did see Caleb Ley prison keeper off the Gaoal off Boston deliver to Joseph Dolbeir, putirer in Boston the son of Edward Dolbeir, an Indian Man named James Wampatuck with a great Iron chain with good ho---lock upon his Legg and giving him a strict charge that he should look after him and bring him again at night and farther saith not.

Both Edmund and Joseph Dolbeare were poor men. John, on the other hand, became a property owner in 1716, added to his holdings from time to time, and before his death had piled up a sizeable fortune. He had been born in England about the year 1664. In 1698 he married Sarah, daughter of John Comer, pewterer, and raised a large family. A son John, who died in 1728 at the age of twenty-six, probably followed the pewterer's trade also.

Although in deeds John Dolbeare the elder is termed a brazier, his son Benjamin has stated in a letter dated 1772 that 'My father and Uncle Joseph served their times with my Grandfather to the Pewterers Trade, in which Business my Father set up & added to it the Ironmongery Trade, both which he carried on to the year 1740.' However, we are not compelled to rely on his word alone. Among the Dolbeare papers is an old bill of lading book in John's handwriting in which are set down shipments made by water from 1718 to 1740. These cover consignments of pewter, copper, brass, iron, beeswax, and gunpowder to various settlements in America, as well as shipments of copper, brass, gold, silver, 'train-oyl,' and beeswax to England. After 1729 no shipments of pewter are recorded, and from that date braziery seems to have represented the bulk of the business.

Dolbeare's principal out-of-town pewter customers were located in Southold (Long Island), New London (Connecticut), Piscataqua (Maine), and Charleston 'in South Caralinah.' It is interesting to note that, although shipments of other goods were made to Newport, New York, and Philadelphia, pewter was not included. For this, of course, there was a very good reason. Resident pewterers in all three towns were able to supply the local trade.

Further proof that John Dolbeare was well-to-do and, in addition, something of a philanthropist is furnished by the record of his contribution of twenty-five pounds for the new Town Work House in Boston in 1727. He owned Lot 51 in the South Burying Ground, and no doubt it was there that his remains were laid to rest. His portrait is shown in Plate VII.

The statement was made above that John Dolbeare was born about 1664. This date may be out of the way by ten years, for the Dolbeare papers demonstrate a need for extreme caution before accepting family records at their face value. Benjamin, John Dolbeare's son, writing in 1772 gave his father's age at date of death (1740) as seventy-five, which would make the year of his birth 1664 or 1665. In the same letter he stated that his father was nine years of age when he came to this country 'about the year 1664,' which would, of course, place the year of his birth some nine or ten years earlier than the first statement indicated. To complicate matters further, Benjamin's son, John, listed the dates of birth of members of the family and recorded '1669 Feb. 9th' as the day on which his grandfather was born.

Although Benjamin Dolbeare carried on his father's business and may have made pewter in his early years, all of the deeds in which he figured recorded him as a merchant. In any event the evidence is too meager to warrant the inclusion of his name in a list of pewterers.

Just as this manuscript was scheduled to go to press, Mr. John Marshall Phillips, Curator of the Garvan Collection, Yale University, wrote me that he had found among the Browne Manuscripts, 1678–1836, a bill of July 12, 1729, for quart pots and basins made out and signed by John and James Dolbeare. So probably John's son, James, should also be classified as a pewterer, though termed a brazier in deeds. He was born in 1705 and died sometime prior to 1775.

JOHN BAKER

At the time when Thomas Clark and John Comer, pewterers, first appeared on Boston tax lists (1674), John Baker was listed as exempt from tax, and he and 'Nathaniell Ellkin' were coupled as 'Mr. Shrimpton's men.'

William Man(n)

Baker, born in Boston October 1, 1654, a son of Thomas and Leah Baker, was just twenty years old at the time of the above tax-taking. Without doubt he was then an apprentice of Shrimpton and must have completed his time about 1676. In 1681 he, with Shrimpton, went surety to the town for Edward Briscoe, founder, and in the following year performed a like service for Edmund Dolbeare, pewterer. In 1684 he was chosen one of Boston's eight constables and in 1685 a 'tythingman.'

John Baker died, apparently unmarried, in 1696, and the inventory of his shop was taken on January 4, 1696/7, by John Comer and Edmund Dolbeare. Though Baker was termed a brazier in deeds and probate records, his inventory proves that pewter-making was his principal occupation. His equipment included the usual wheel, tools, furnace, anvils, and 1280 pounds of moulds; also old copper, lead, spelter, old pewter, and 'damnified tankards.' Interest-provoking forms listed in the inventory were alchemy spoons, 'pewter bottels,' sucking bottles, 'pewter ure,' 'half quartern pots,' and 'pease basons.'

There were also 'three-pint,' 'small quart,' and 'four inch' tankards both plain and 'graved,' the latter valued at a premium of ten pence each over the plain vessels.

Serene as John Baker's life would appear from this brief account, his death precipitated a scandal in the Baker family. Thomas Baker, ironmonger, an older brother of John, discovered soon after the appraisal that property from the shop which had been on hand at the time of his brother's death was missing. He appealed to the court and accused John Dolbeare, a pewterer and son of one of the appraisers. Dolbeare had no difficulty in clearing his name, and when the true identity of the culprits was discovered Thomas Baker found himself in the ignominious rôle of prosecutor against his own son, Thomas, Junior, and his nephew, John Waldron, late apprentices of the deceased, both of whom made signed confessions and promised full restitution to the estate.

WILLIAM MAN(N)

When tracking down the history of Thomas Byles, Philadelphia pewterer (of whom more later), I found that he had been apprenticed in the sixteen-nineties to a 'Mr. Man' and I knew that his youth had been spent in Boston. A perusal of Boston records for that period turned up several men named Man who were braziers, but none whom I could also prove to have been a pewterer. It was only after a more exhaustive search some five years later that I was rewarded by the finding of a deed of 1704 given by William Man, pewterer.

William, son of Nathaniel and Deborah Man, was born in Boston, February 19, 1671. The Boston Registry Department has record of the births to William and Rebecca Man of three children, Thomas, John, and Rebecca, in the years 1694, 1696, and 1697 respectively, and we know from other sources that another son, William, Junior, had preceded his brothers and sister into the world.

In 1696 William Man, brazier, bought property from Samuel Shrimpton near the Town Dock on what was later known as Shrimpton's Lane. There he had his home and shop for over forty years. Like most of the Boston makers, Man took his fair share of civic responsibilities and between the years 1698 and 1714 served as tithingman, constable, and clerk of the market. Our last record of him is in 1738 when he mortgaged his home. His probate records are not on file in Boston.

The son William was also a brazier and not improbably a pewterer. He bought property near Oliver's Dock in 1716 and disposed of it ten years later. At that time he and his wife Hannah were residents of Marblehead. Their later history has not been traced.

JONATHAN JACKSON

In Jonathan Jackson we have a prominent, wealthy merchant and brazier whose inventory indicates that he also made pewter or hired journeymen to manufacture it for him in his shop.

Jonathan was a grandson of Edward Jackson, a nailmaker of White Chapel, London, who came to America about 1642. The subject of this history was born in Boston December 28, 1672, third child of Jonathan and Elizabeth Jackson, and on March 26, 1700, he married Mary Salter, who bore him eight children.

In the town government of Boston Jackson served four years as tithingman and annually from 1726 to 1733 he was elected one of the overseers of the poor.

On January 9, 1699, Jonathan Jackson and John Dolbeare bought jointly from John Wiswall wharves and real estate near the Town Dock, and there, whether in one or in separate shops, conducted their braziery and pewter-making businesses. Jackson's name is on many later deeds, but in all he is termed a brazier. He died May 4, 1736, perhaps the wealthiest of all American pewterers, leaving an estate of over £30,000.

The inventory is divided into three categories: (1) 'Goods of the English Manufacture'; (2) 'Goods of the New England Manufacture'; and (3) 'Household Furniture and Real Estate.' Of very particular interest to us is the inclusion, under the 'Goods of the New England Manufacture,' of a great quantity of finished pewter, more than half a ton of old pewter, a small quantity of old lead, pig lead, 'Sett Pewterers Tools' valued at £33. 11s., and over 1500 pounds of 'Pewt' Moulds.' Consequently there can be no doubt that Jackson's name belongs on our lists. The stock of pewter included ordinary plates, dishes, and basins; 'New England hard mettle plates'; three-pint, wine quart, quart, pint, half-pint, gill, and half-gill 'potts'; porringers in five sizes; 'bekers'; tobacco 'potts'; and 'Chamber Potts.' Pewter teapots were not on the list and presumably had not yet become stock articles of the American pewterer.

By his will Jackson left twenty pounds to the poor of Boston and fifty pounds each to the two pastors of the First Church. The bulk of the estate went to his wife, his son Edward, and two married daughters.

Thomas Smith

Jonathan Jackson's wife was the Mary who has been carried for years on our list of American pewterers. Perhaps she is entitled to such listing, for she advertised as a brazier after her husband's death; but until there is more definite proof that pewter was made in her shop — she offered for sale 'London pewter' — I feel that her name should not be included as that of a manufacturer of pewter.

THOMAS SMITH

When in 1692 Thomas Clarke, pewterer, was married to his neighbor in Dock Square, the widow Rebecca Smith, the union of the two families provided not only a mistress for his household but probably also a new apprentice for his shop. Rebecca's first husband, Captain Thomas Smith, a mariner, had died four years earlier leaving five small children. The oldest boy, Thomas, born in Boston May 13, 1678, was not fourteen years old when his mother remarried. Soon thereafter his pewter-making career commenced. As soon as young Thomas was qualified to start in business for himself (*c.* 1700), the executors of his father's estate apparently consented to the use for that purpose of his childhood home in Dock Square, which had been held in trust for the Smith children. In 1707 four fifths of the property was set off to the children then of age and eventually Thomas bought the interests of his brother and three sisters.

On May 9, 1701, Smith married Mary Corwin and in the following year joined the Ancient and Honorable Artillery Company. During the next two decades he was plying his trade as pewterer and brazier and establishing himself as a responsible member of his community. Eight children were born of his first marriage, and, after Mary Smith died in 1716, he married, April 30, 1717, Sarah Oliver, who bore four more.

Thomas Smith rose through the various grades in the Artillery Company to become captain in 1722 and usually thereafter was termed in documents Captain Thomas Smith. He served terms in 1711 and 1712 as town scavenger, and for six years, commencing in 1713, was one of the overseers of the poor. In 1717 he joined the Old South Church and was a benefactor of Harvard College.

From the Selectmen's Minutes for 1739 we learn that Captain Smith had as serious plumbing problems as does any of us today:

> Liberty is granted to Thomas Smith, Esq' to Dig up the Pavement and open the Ground before his House in Dock Square in order to repair the Boxing and Stop the Tides from flowing into his Cellar.

The Captain died at the age of sixty-three without leaving a will. Papers of administration were granted in March, 1742. Unfortunately the inventory contained nothing of interest to the student of pewter and Smith's handiwork, like that of all the early Boston pewterers, awaits identification if still in existence.

[59]

The Pewterers of Massachusetts Bay

JOHN HOLYOKE

Nothing is now known about the pewter of John Holyoke and in history he basks only in the reflected glory of a younger brother, Edward, who became the eighth President of Harvard College.

His descent is traced from Edward Holyoke of Tamworth, Warwickshire, who settled at Lynn in 1638. The pewterer's father was Elizur, a shopkeeper and brazier and one of the founders of the Old South Church in Boston. John, the fourth child, was born in Boston February 10, 1683, and probably began his long pewter-making career about 1706. In 1714 he joined the Ancient and Honorable Artillery Company, but never rose beyond the rank of fourth sergeant. The Company's historian states that Holyoke married a Mrs. Green of Cambridge, a statement which I have been unable to verify. If this was a fact, he was married twice, for in 1727 his marriage to Joanna Walker was recorded. He seems to have had no children.

In deeds from 1716 to 1760, Holyoke described himself usually as a pewterer, occasionally as a brazier. His shop, like that of most of his competitors, was in Dock Square. On three different occasions he was chosen a constable, but begged off and paid a fine. He served as clerk of the market in 1729 and thrice later was elected to the office of scavenger.

President Edward Holyoke kept a diary in which on two occasions John's name appears; under date of December 1, 1758, 'My bro^r John's wife died'; and on March 30, 1768, 'My Bro. J. Holyoke went to live at Newtown.' John was then eighty-one years old and must have retired from pewtering long before. He died March 2, 1775, one of the longest-lived of American pewterers. All of his working years were devoted to the manufacture of pewter and brass and some evidence of his craftsmanship must still be in existence.

SAMUEL CARTER

On June 3, 1712, the ship *Marlborough* from Bristol arrived in Boston Harbor, carrying as one of her passengers, 'Saml Carter, puterer.'

It is not at all likely that Carter was a figure of any importance in the history of American pewter, for as far as I can learn he never owned property in Boston, never filled any town office, and may never have had a shop of his own. However, he must have followed the same trade in his adopted country, for the will of 'Samuel Carter, pewterer,' was probated in Boston thirty-five years after his arrival (October 7, 1747). His sole heirs were his nieces, Hester and Philadelphia Carter, of South Hampton in Hampshire, England, and his executor was Benjamin Dolbeare, merchant. The inventory contained merely personal belongings and cash.

JONAS CLARK(E)

Jonas Clark was another brazier and pewterer who apparently preferred to be called a brazier; for again it is only the evidence of his inventory that places him in the list of pewterers.

Born in Boston September 8, 1690, son of Captain Timothy and Sarah Clark, he married Grace Tilley November 24, 1715. By her he had two children, Sarah and Timothy. No record is found of the first wife's death, but on October 2, 1749, 'Jonas Clarke, Esq.,' married Elizabeth Lillie. In deeds until 1737 he was termed a brazier, thereafter simply 'Jonas Clark(e), Esq.'

Clark held many positions of trust in Boston and served at various times as assessor, tithingman, constable, and selectman. In 1746 he received the thanks of the town for his long and useful service in the last-named office.

Papers of administration of Clark's estate were granted on January 4, 1760. Although he had retired before that time and although there was no new pewter in the inventory, his possessions included 'One Pewterer's Wheel and Appurtenances' and shop tools.

GEORGE RAISIN

To the late Francis H. Bigelow we are indebted for the discovery that George Raisin belongs in the list of Boston pewterers. Termed both a pewterer and a brazier, Raisin figured in six minor cases that were brought before the Suffolk County Courts between the years 1718 and 1727. One of these suits was over the ownership of two casks of pewter.

He is believed to have been a son of George Raisin, gunsmith, and Eliza Dyer, who were married in Boston May 21, 1689. The elder Raisin died in 1695 and consequently the son must needs have been born between the years 1690 and 1696. Beyond the brief court and probate records we have no knowledge of Raisin's history. His will, which was dated March 9, 1727, was admitted to probate February 10, 1728. He apparently was unmarried, for the only relative mentioned by name in the will was a cousin, Hannah Dyer. The inventory, which furnished definite proof of Raisin's occupation included a wheel and tower, 'vises, shears, hammers, hood and bellows, 43 hooks, 355 pounds of brass moulds, stakes, old pewter,' etc.

RICHARD ESTABROOK

In the appendix to volume II will be found a very full inventory of the shop contents of a brazier named Richard Estabrook, a 'find' made by chance while searching for another man's records. Estabrook, as the inventory proves, was a pewterer as well as a brazier. The stock was evaluated on October 11, 1721, by Jonathan Jackson, John Holyoke, and William Tyler. Papers for administration of the estate were granted to the mother of the deceased, Abigail Treat, widow.

No record of Estabrook's birth was found and nothing is known about his life. The complete absence of information about him and the evidence that he was unmarried point to the probability that he was a young man who had but recently embarked on a business career when death overtook him.

One interesting deduction can be made from an examination of the inventory. Included therein are 'Quart Potts' and 'Quart Potts, hollow handle.' The hollow handle had been introduced in Great Britain only a few years earlier. Finding both types of handle in this inventory helps us to date very accurately the passing of the solid handle on pots and tankards.

Another interesting item is the '8 doz 9 Blood Porringers.' One would think that supply of bleeding-bowls would have taken care of the need of every physician in all the colonies for a long time to come.

JONES, FRANCIS, DURNINGER, EDGELL, AND PAVEY

Hidden away in the files of the Suffolk County Court of Common Pleas is a wealth of information about early citizens of Boston. Below is given the meager information that we have on five pewterers mentioned in those records who, but for 'their day in court,' would not appear in our lists.

In 1714 John Dolbeare and Jonathan Jackson, braziers, filed a writ of attachment for £69 against Daniel Jones, pewterer. A Daniel Jones, possibly the same man, married Ann Pickring in Boston, February 23, 1705.

Joseph Watson, mariner, brought suit in 1718 against Thomas Francis, pewterer, to recover '6 fine pictures (being Landskips) of the value of 8 pounds' which said Watson lost and Francis found.

In the one case in which the next man was involved his name was spelled in so many different ways that it is impossible to determine now which was the accepted version. Daniel Durninger (alias Darminger, Derringer, and Durringer), pewterer, was defendant in July, 1723, in a suit over the ownership of sixty-nine pounds of pewter. Boston church records reveal that on July 7 of the previous year the marriage intentions of Daniel Durninger and Sarah Button were published.

Fourth of these little-known pewterers was William Edgell (or Edgehill), who was a defendant in a suit in 1724.

Fifth and last of the group was George Pavey, mentioned as a 'pewterer or gentleman,' in a suit in 1733.

Please note that none of these men served in the town government or owned real estate in Boston and that no probate record could be located for any one of the five. There is little reason to believe that they were factors of any moment in the pewter trade of Boston.

JOHN CARNES

George Francis Dow's interesting and illuminating work, *Arts and Crafts of New England*, with its careful culling of pertinent items from early Boston newspapers, has supplied us with the names of several forgotten pewterers, the earliest of whom was John Carnes.

Fortunately we can furnish Carnes with an excellent ancestry. His great-grandfather, John, had been a native of Orchardtown, Scotland, where he owned large estates. Entering the Royal Navy, he rose to the rank of post-captain and spent much time in American waters. He had joined the Ancient and Honorable Artillery Company in Boston in 1649, and when, in 1652, he lost his heart to a Boston girl, he decided to sell his property in Scotland and move permanently to America. Having now risen to the rank of commodore, he married and sailed away for England on what was to have been his last eastward voyage. Such the voyage proved to be, for Commodore Carnes died at sea, his posthumous son, Thomas, becoming the ancestor of the Carnes family of New England.

Strangely enough, history repeated itself in the story of the father of the pewterer. He too was a John Carnes; he too was a captain in the Royal Navy; and, just as in the case of his grandfather, he died at sea, his only son arriving after his death.

So John, the pewterer, born April 3, 1698, was left to carry on the race; and a very thorough job he made of it, for he took unto himself three wives: (1) Eliza Greenough, October 5, 1720; (2) Sarah Baker, July 26, 1722, who bore him fourteen children; and (3) Mrs. Dorothy Farnum, September 15, 1741.

In 1723 the loss of some paper money was advertised by John Carnes, pewterer, and we know from Suffolk deeds that, like most of the early Boston pewterers, he was also a brazier.

As his great-grandfather had done before him, he joined the Artillery Company. In time he rose through the successive grades to lieutenant-colonel, and was in command of the organization at the time of his death, March 4, 1760. This Artillery Company, upon which many later military organizations have been patterned, was social in its nature as well as military, and its commanding officer without any question would have been one of the most distinguished members of the community.

Carnes also filled at various times the positions of 'Clarke of the Market,' 'Scavenger,' and 'Fire Ward' in the town government. It is recorded in the Selectmen's Minutes for 1740 that 'Mr. William Salter, the keeper of the Powder-house, Informs that sometime ago the Fire Wards seized Three half-barrels of Gun Powder in the House of Mr.

John Carnes.' Perhaps it was to make Carnes a little more conscientious that he himself was chosen a fire ward for the following year.

For several years he was a member of a committee of prominent citizens to make periodically 'a Walk or Visitation of the Town,' starting at 'Nine o'Clock in the morning if the weather be fair,' and 'to meet at Faneuil at Five o'Clock in the Evening to report the State of the Town.'

At the time of his death Colonel Carnes owned a stone house with garden on Ann Street, two brick tenements, a large shop, and several stores. He was evidently no longer active in business, but his inventory included a pewterer's wheel, tower, blocks, etc., as well as 695 pounds of pewterer's moulds — almost twice as many moulds by weight as were left by Richard Austin and Samuel Green combined, or by Thomas Green or William Danforth — pretty fair evidence of the large trade enjoyed by some of these early pewterers. Moreover, their inventories prove that their business was frequently a most lucrative one.

Shortly before this volume went to press John W. Poole found in a junk shop an unquestionably early Boston plate. Unusual in its size, $7\frac{1}{2}$ inches, it is also deeper than the average Boston plate and does not have a hammered booge. The interesting design of its mark (Plate XLIV, 285) bears no close resemblance to the known touch of any pewterer, American or English. Enough of the maker's name is still visible to warrant its attribution to John Carnes.

A reproduction of a portrait of Colonel Carnes, as photographed from a plate in the *History of the Ancient and Honourable Artillery Company* may be seen in Plate VII.

JOHN TYLER

On March 2, 1723, the heirs of John Coney, Boston silversmith, sold for one thousand pounds to John Tyler, 'Pewterer and Brazier,' a messuage, tenement, land, and privileges on Ann Street near the Town Dock. But for the record of the deed for that property we should not have Tyler's name in our list of pewterers. All other public records which I could find gave his occupation simply as 'Brazier.'

Thomas Tyler, a mariner and native of Budleigh, Devonshire, England, came to Boston in the last quarter of the seventeenth century. He married Miriam, daughter of Pilgrim Simpkins, and had at least six sons, three of whom became workers in metals — William, a brazier; Andrew, a goldsmith; and John, the subject of this sketch.

John Tyler was born in Boston, June 11, 1695, and on August 1, 1720, he married Sarah Brame. Their family of ten children included seven boys, none of whom appears to have followed his father's occupation. Tyler and his wife joined the New Brick Church in 1722 and all of their children were baptized therein. The Ann street property, which he purchased in 1723, was sold to a group of Boston merchants in 1734. John Tyler's will, written in 1753, was admitted to probate in April, 1757.

David Cutler

THOMAS SIMPKINS

Several years ago I saw in a shop in New Bedford an eight-inch plate impressed with the mark illustrated in Plate XLIV, 289. Because the plate looked American and because its shallow well and narrow rim pointed to the possibility of a Boston origin, it was hastily purchased. Examination of the English records disclosed no pewterer named Simpkins and the search was transferred hopefully to Boston. From a brief examination of Suffolk County documents pertaining to the Simpkins family the following facts were gleaned:

Nicholas Simpkins, a tailor living in Boston as early as 1634, was appointed the first commander of the fort on Castle Island. He had one son, Pilgrim, who carried on the male line of the Simpkins family. Thomas, the man in whom we are interested, was born in Boston, January 27, 1702, a grandson of Pilgrim and son of Thomas (a mariner) and Margery (Barton) Simpkins.

Thomas learned the brazier's trade, married, and opened a shop on Ann Street. In all documents he is styled a brazier. In the town government he held office as clerk of the market in 1728, constable in 1734, and scavenger in 1742. When he died intestate in 1766, his brother William, a goldsmith, who acted as administrator of the estate, reported that the liabilities exceeded the assets by some ninety-one pounds.

Only recently J. P. Remensnyder has found another Boston plate measuring $8\frac{1}{2}$ inches, impressed with a different Simpkins touch (Plate XLIV, 288), which is believed to be another mark of the same maker. Neither of the Simpkins plates is hammered; in fact they are not unusual in any respect; but they provide us with the name of another American pewterer, two new touches that bear no close resemblance to any known American marks, and a warning to be very careful about rejecting as a pewterer any New Englander simply because he styled himself a brazier. In all probability most of the early braziers were trained and equipped to work in pewter as well as brass.

DAVID CUTLER

Another new name among the Boston pewterers is that of David Cutler, who worked at his trade for many years. David was born in Boston, September 28, 1703, the son of David and Abigail Cutler, and grandson of John Cutler who came to this country from Sprowston, County of Norfolk, England, in 1637.

Cutler was twice married; first in 1732 to Lydia Belknap, who bore him twelve children; secondly, after Lydia's death, to her cousin, Polly Belknap. Boyle's *Journal of Occurrences in Boston* contains the following entry: '(1770) Dec. 27th. Married, Mr. David Cutler, Pewterer, to Miss Polly Belknap, a Maiden of 45.'

David held at various times the positions of scavenger, constable, and assay master

PLATE XLIII — *Miscellaneous Objects*

275. Continental dollar. Diameter $2\frac{1}{2}$ inches. Collection of Dr. Percy E. Raymond.

276. School medal. Diameter $1\frac{7}{16}$ inches. Collection of the author.

277. Drawer pull — two views. Measurements not recorded. Courtesy of Mrs. Earl J. Knittle.

278 and 279. Henry Clay and William Henry Harrison campaign medals. Diameters $\frac{3}{4}$ and $1\frac{7}{16}$ inches respectively. Collection of the author.

280. Medal celebrating the opening of the Erie Canal, 1825. Diameter $3\frac{3}{16}$ inches. Collection of the author.

281 and 282. Pair of shoe buckles. Initials 'J. T.' cast in corner of each. Length $2\frac{1}{4}$ inches, height $1\frac{5}{8}$ inches. Collection of the Honorable and Mrs. George V. Smith.

283. Fife. Length $16\frac{3}{8}$ inches. Collection of the author.

284. Hunting Horn. Length over all $14\frac{3}{4}$ inches. Collection of Albert H. Good, Esq.

The makers of all items shown above are unknown. Figures 283 and 284 are in scale with each other, but not with the other objects illustrated.

PLATE XLIII

277 a

282

281

284

277

280 a

278 a
279 a

276 a

276

280

283

275

278
279

PLATE XLIV

285

286   287

288

289

290
287 a

290 a
291

290 b
292

in the town government, occupying the latter office for almost twenty years. Upon his retirement in 1764, the vacancy was filled by another pewterer, Thomas Green. It is a rather interesting fact that from 1747 to 1793 at least one of the assay masters was always a pewterer, and in some years both incumbents of that office followed that trade.

Cutler's active career may have ended in 1764 when he retired from public office. In any event his retirement occurred sometime before his death, February 27, 1772, for no evidence of pewter-making or of a shop was found in the inventory. Thomas Green, pewterer, was one of the bondsmen for the administrators, and both he and Nathaniel Austin owed small sums to the estate.

The widow Cutler died in 1794, aged eighty. Consequently the age recorded by Boyle in his *Journal* was in error. The error, however, is readily understandable, for what maiden of fifty-five in any era would not forget for publication a half-score companionless years?

I am indebted to George Francis Dow's *Arts and Crafts in New England* for the following advertisement, which first appeared in the *Boston Gazette* of March 14, 1757:

> To be sold by David Cutler, Pewterer, at the Sign of the Great Dish (with his name on said Dish) in Union Street, near the Town Dock; all sorts of Pewter, Viz. Dishes, Plates, Basons, Porringers, Quart Pots, Pint Pots, Cans, Tankards, Closestools, Pans, &c. by Wholesale or Retail, at the cheapest Rates for Money or old Pewter, and the Ware made thick and substantial.

Recently I acquired an 8¾-inch plate, very carefully finished, with hammered booge and of excellent metal, which is here attributed to Cutler.

An exceedingly interesting feature of the touches (Plate XLIV, 286 and 287) is the appearance of the Boston scroll which was later employed by 'Semper Eadem,' Richard Austin, and Thomas Badger. Apparently this same die, passed on from one pewterer to another, was in almost continuous use for over seventy years — possibly much longer.

ROBERT BONNING (OR BONYNGE)

In the Boston Selectmen's Records for the year 1739 the following notation is found:

> Mr. John Davis appearing. Desires he may have the leave to admit Mr. Robert Bonning, Pewterer, an under tenant in the Shop he hath lately leased from the Selectmen, vizt. Number 6 in Dock Square — who desires to hire of him the chamber over the same and
>
> Mr. Bonning appearing at the same time Desires the Selectmen would please to give him the leave at his own Cost and Charges to raise the front part of the roof of said Shop, the better to accommodate him in setting up his Wheel for carrying on his said Business.

But one other item could be found in Boston records which seemed to have reference to this man. On December 10, 1731, a Robert Benning (spelled Bonynge in the marriage intentions) was married to Sarah Henderson.

Had Bonning worked for any great length of time in Boston and had his business prospered, we should surely have found record of real estate which he purchased; and if he had been a man of any importance or responsibility he would have held at least one minor office in the town government. Absence of probate records for anyone of this name may indicate that his later years were passed in some other town.

JOSEPH RANDLE (OR RANDALL)

Joseph Randle was presumably one of the lesser lights of American pewter, a man about whom little could be learned, who must have worked in Boston for a brief period only.

Boston vital statistics furnish dates of birth for two men of this name. Joseph, son of William, a japanner, and Elizabeth (Hall) Randoll, was born December 10, 1691. Another Joseph, son of Robert and Elizabeth Randall, was born May 4, 1712.

The pewterer married Mary, only child of Samuel Plumer, cooper, on August 8, 1738. Less than a month later, Joseph Randle of Boston, brazier, and Mary, his wife, sold property in Shrimpton's Lane, and in the following year 'Joseph Randle, Puterer,' and Mary disposed of the property in Royal Exchange Lane which she had inherited from her father. And right there our knowledge of Joseph Randle's history ends.

THOMAS GREEN

When Boston's first printed directory appeared in 1789, it listed two pewterers by the name of Green — Thomas at 17 Dock Square and Andrew in Temple Street. By 1798 Samuel Green was enrolled as a pewterer in Milk Street. Recent research has proved that the three men were closely related and that at least seven members of the family made pewter in Boston — a father, five sons, and a grandson.

Thomas Green, so we learn from the *Independent Chronicle* in its issue of September 15, 1794, died in Boston during that week at the age of seventy-nine and was buried in the Old Granary Burial Ground. Most of his pewter must therefore have been made before the Revolution. His birth would have occurred about 1715. Unfortunately, the Boston birth records are sadly wanting in Thomas Greens at just the period in which we should like to find one, and so it is not unlikely that Thomas made his first appearance in the world at some other port of entry.

Though still lacking positive proof, I am convinced that the pewterer was born in New London, Connecticut. About 1712, or perhaps earlier, Samuel Green, a printer of Cambridge, Massachusetts, with his wife Sarah, son Timothy, also a printer, and the latter's family, moved to New London. There on January 31, 1715, a son, Thomas, was born to Timothy and Mary Green. At that time there were at least two older children, Samuel and Nathaniel, and in 1719 and 1721 respectively John and Mary were born. These names are here presented for a purpose. Among the children of the Boston pewterer were two Timothys, a Samuel, Sarah, Nathaniel, Mary, and John. If the New London Thomas, who was born in 1715, was not the Boston pewterer, the striking identity of surnames in the two families and the amazing fact that both Thomas Greens were born in the same twelvemonth represent coincidences that are to say the least startling. One other straw blowing in the same direction is the note in a Boston paper in 1763 of the arrival from Connecticut of Joana, 'daughter of Mr. Green, Brasier.'

If we are warranted in our surmise that these facts represent something more than remarkable coincidences — if indeed the Thomas Green of New London became the Boston pewterer — it is a natural assumption that the printer sent his son, while still a youth, back to relatives in Cambridge or Boston to be apprenticed to a pewterer. At any rate, Thomas Green on October 11, 1739, married Mary Brown in Boston. Mrs. Green joined the Brattle Square Church in 1741; her husband five years later. Mary Green died in 1760 after having borne eleven children. On April 8, 1762, the widower married Mrs. Esther Trevett, by whom he had four more sons, fifteen children in all.

As early as 1756 Thomas Green purchased property near the Town Dock in Dock Square, where he and his sons were making pewter for over forty years. During the Revolution Green had charge of the town's lead supply, and from 1775 to 1791 he served jointly with another pewterer, John Skinner, as town assay master; in 1778 he was also elected a scavenger, and in 1779 and 1780 was one of the city's constables.

Prior to the Revolution, Green owned several pieces of property and probably enjoyed a trade of sufficient size to take care of the needs of his large family, but after the war he fell upon evil days and by 1788 was listed in the tax records as 'poor,' his tax abated. At the time of his death he owned 368½ pounds of 'brass pewterers Moulds,' a wheel, tower, spindle, and blocks, all of which were purchased from the estate by his son Samuel. As no pewter was listed in the inventory, it seems likely that Samuel merely took title to equipment which he had been using.

It is almost inconceivable that no example of Thomas Green's pewter has survived, but thus far no mark has been positively identified as the touch of this man.

'SEMPER EADEM'

One of the most puzzling problems of American pewter is the question of the identity of the Boston pewterer who substituted for his own name on his rose-and-crown touch the words 'Semper Eadem.' Although this touch rightfully belongs among the unidentified marks, the story of its use is so closely interwoven with that of several of the known Boston makers that I shall follow J. B. Kerfoot's procedure and comment upon it here in the stories of the Boston pewterers.

This touch normally accompanies a Boston-in-scroll design (Plate XLIV, 290 and 287), the same scroll which, as we have just learned, is found on pewter attributed to David Cutler. As this identical Boston mark was employed also by Thomas Badger and Richard Austin, it was long believed that one of these men must have hidden behind the Latin pseudonym. In this, however, we have been in error, as the Boston records clearly prove.

We can speedily dismiss Austin from further consideration. He was not born until 1769 or 1770. That a man entering upon his career in the seventeen-nineties would have adopted any device so reminiscent of the recently overthrown English dominion is unthinkable.

Badger's claims require more careful examination. Thomas Badger the elder, born in 1735 and reported by Louis G. Myers as having died in 1809, would have commenced his business activities at a date when such a touch might well have been used. There is plenty of existing Badger flatware impressed with eagle touches and a few plates with a somewhat earlier Badger scroll, but there are no Badger marks definitely pre-Revolutionary in appearance. It would therefore be quite logical to think that this rose-and-crown touch might be the elder Badger's early mark, for all that is needed is to prove that the first Thomas was a pewterer.

The information gleaned about Badger from the Boston records is interesting but disappointing. After his marriage to Mary Beighton in 1762 his name is not found again on public documents until 1781. On a deed dated May 1 of that year 'Thomas Badger, blockmaker,' sold property in Boston to David Speare, cooper. On April 18 of the following year 'Thomas Badger, blockmaker,' and Mary, his wife, transferred property in Dorchester to Samuel Clap, housewright. But one more mention of the man was found. In the Selectmen's Minutes for 1782, the following entry appears:

> At a meeting of the Selectmen, Nov. 6 . . . Capt. Hunt of Engine No. 2 proposes John Cade & Jacob Clough in the room of Henry Swift and Thomas Badger, deceased, as suitable persons for their Engine Comp^y.

There can be but one deduction. Thomas Badger the elder was a blockmaker, not a pewterer, and his death, instead of occurring in 1809, took place sometime between April 18 and November 6, 1782. All the Badger pewter was therefore made by Thomas, Junior, who came upon the scene too late for a rose-and-crown touch. Thus do we eliminate all the former pretenders to 'Eadem's' crown.

Not until the summer of 1937 did a new clue come to light. I learned then of a plate in the collection of Mrs. Stephen S. Fitz Gerald which bears the 'Semper Eadem' mark coupled with an 'R. B.' rose-and-crown touch (Plate XLIV, 290b and 292); and the problem seemed very near solution. That 'R. B.' touch had long been attributed to Robert Boyle, New York pewterer, and with apparent justification. To the best of my knowledge Boyle is the only American pewterer who advertised 'church cups' and the 'R. B.' touch has been found on vessels which answer that description, but those church cups as well as practically all the 'R. B.' pewter had been turning up in New England rather than New York. Because Boyle's history could be traced in the New York records only up to 1758, I rushed up to Boston convinced that I should learn there that Boyle, alias Semper Eadem, had deserted New York for Boston about 1760. The exhaustive search of Boston records which followed shattered those short-lived hopes. Not only did I fail to find trace of Boyle in Boston, but not one of the many eighteenth-century Bostonians with initials 'R. B.,' whose histories I explored, gave any indication of having worked in pewter or brass in Boston after 1740. It is, of course, possible that a Boyle plate was later sent to 'Eadem's' shop to be straightened or mended and that the touches were applied at different times in different shops. Whatever the answer this new combination of touches has merely confounded worse an already perplexing problem.

'Semper Eadem' remains unidentified. We do know that he probably worked in Boston; we believe on the basis of the large number of surviving Eadem plates that he enjoyed a good trade; and we can approximate with reasonable exactness the period of his activity. The Boston scroll touch which frequently is found in conjunction with the 'Eadem' mark was apparently used by David Cutler, who retired not later than 1770. After 'Mr. Eadem' had ceased to have need of it, we find the scroll cropping out anew on the plates of a man whose career commenced about 1790. 'Eadem,' then, must have been at work in Boston during most of the two decades prior to the latter date and he may have started his pewter-making long before 1770.

If the R. B. touch on the Fitz Gerald plate was not applied by 'Semper Eadem,' the latter was probably some Boston pewterer whose records are well known to us, possibly Thomas Green, John Skinner, or Edward Kneeland. It may be significant that Thomas Green, for whom we have no touches, was making pewter in Boston at least as early as 1764 and that he succeeded as assay master David Cutler, the earliest known user of the Boston scroll. Furthermore, he was a bondsman for Cutler's executors and might well have acquired the Boston scroll die from Cutler's estate. Then, too, we know that Green lived until 1794, just about the time when the scroll first appeared on Richard Austin's pewter. These observations may prove to be absolutely irrelevant to the question of the 'Semper Eadem' identity; on the other hand, they may be clues of value to some later investigator.

One more phase of the 'Semper Eadem' riddle requires consideration. During the past few years several plates have come to light bearing what seems to be the identical 'Semper Eadem' impression with which we are familiar, but accompanied by a London mark instead of the normal Boston-in-scroll. For the purposes of comparison photographs of both combinations of touches are shown in Plate XLIV. The same imperfections that are found in one appear in the other, and there can be little question that the same rose-and-crown die was used in each case.

Since the London plates turned up, more than one person has remarked that the new touch proved conclusively that 'S. E.' was a London maker who turned out some pewter with a Boston mark purely for New England consumption. I do not hold with that opinion. Louis G. Myers proved most conclusively that Austin, Badger, and 'Semper

Eadem' all used an identical Boston touch. This would not have been possible if one of the three had been working in London. Moreover, there is, I believe, a reasonable explanation for the use by an American pewterer of a London mark.

Prior to the Revolution there was throughout the colonies a strong prejudice in favor of London-made pewter, and rightly so. In London, standards of manufacture were set and enforced by the Pewterers' Company. No similar organization ever existed on this side of the water. There were some colonial pewterers who maintained just as high a standard, but generally speaking the London pewterers as a group excelled the provincials. Consequently, the demand for London metal created a problem that our struggling craftsmen had to face, as is evident in an advertisement of Samuel Hamlin of Providence wherein he offers his metal as 'superior to any Imported except from London.' John Skinner and Nathaniel Austin went even further. In their newspaper notices they list the various forms which they make and then tell us that they also carry 'London Pewter.' We are all of us prone to buy a trade-mark, not a product; and so it may have been with our forefathers. It would not have been much of a trick to stamp and sell, as imported, pewter that had been made in this country. As a precedent for such action we know that Stephen Maxwell of Glasgow stamped some of his export pewter with a London die, and the practice was so prevalent among the country pewterers of England that the Pewterers' Company in London considered taking measures to prevent them from using a London touch.

The conclusion forced upon us is that 'Semper Eadem,' identity still unknown, was a colonial pewterer who impressed most of his metal with a Boston touch. Upon occasion, however, he was not above substituting a London mark for his Boston scroll. Thus did he provide for those customers who demanded the London-made article.

The recorded 'Eadem' items are 7$\frac{7}{8}$-inch and 8$\frac{1}{2}$-inch plates, 12$\frac{1}{4}$-inch and 15-inch dishes and quart basins.

DAVID AND WILLIAM NORTHEY

Up to this point our story of eighteenth-century pewter-making in Massachusetts has been confined to workers in Boston and Charlestown and perhaps there were no large pewter shops north of Boston; but we have very definite information about two goldsmiths, working respectively in Salem and Lynn, who mended pewter and quite possibly fashioned the baser metal while carrying on the goldsmith's trade.

David Northey of Salem was married in Lynn in 1732 to Miriam Bassett of that town. The eldest of their sons, William, was born about 1734 and, like his father, learned the goldsmith's trade. Soon after completing his apprenticeship, William must have returned to his mother's home town, where he was married in 1764 to Rebecca Collins.

In all public documents both David and William Northey are termed goldsmiths, but, when David died in 1778, his inventory included a number of items of finished pewter, eleven hundred pounds of old pewter, a lathe, wheel, and 'Pewter tools,' as well as normal equipment for a goldsmith.

The son William died at Lynn in 1804 and, although his inventory was not found, he bequeathed by will to his son Ezra 'all my tools for the Goldsmiths, Pewterers and Tin-mans Business.' The Northeys undoubtedly had a large repair trade in pewter and some-day we may learn that they actually fashioned pewter vessels as well.

PETER BLIN AND DAVID FLAGG

In the files of the Suffolk County Court House there is record, under date of February 12, 1757, of the transfer of a piece of property in Prince Street, Boston, by two pewterers, Peter Blin and David Flagg, and the latter's wife Margaret, to Samuel Brown, house-wright.

Peter Blin, as further research indicated, was born in Boston, October 30, 1733. He was a son of a shopkeeper, William, and grandson of James Blin, a mariner, who had been successful enough to acquire several valuable pieces of Boston real estate. Young Blin must have just started in business, probably as a partner or employee of Flagg, at the time of the aforementioned transaction. On but two later documents, deeds of 1758 and 1759, was his name found and in each he called himself a pewterer. Blin's probate records are not on file in Boston and his later history could not be traced.

Of David Flagg a little more is known, although the date of his birth has not been established. He was probably descended from Thomas Flagg, who settled in Watertown in 1643, and in all likelihood was born in one of the settlements near to but outside the town of Boston. When David's father, Thomas, a Boston merchant, died in 1747, David Cutler, pewterer, apparently a close friend of the family, was appointed executor of the estate. This may be a leading clue to the source of Flagg's training.

At some time prior to 1750 David Flagg had married Margaret, only sister of Peter Blin, by whom he had at least four children, David, Junior, Peggy, Sarah, and Rachel. In 1759 he was chosen and sworn in as hogreeve, apparently the only position which he ever held in the town government.

Flagg's shop, like that of Cutler, was in Union Street near the Mill Pond and hard by the Green Dragon Tavern on property inherited by his wife from James Blin. In deeds of 1748 and 1749 he was termed a brazier; thereafter until 1772 a pewterer. Just as in the case of Blin, Flagg's probate records are missing, but since his daughters sold in 1782 and 1783 property formerly owned by Margaret Blin Flagg, there can be little doubt that David Flagg died prior to that time.

We have no knowledge of the existence of any pewter made by either Blin or Flagg.

John Skinner

JOHN SKINNER

Although John Skinner's career continued after the Revolution, the major portion of his working years fell in the earlier period. The early Boston pewterers made a great variety of shapes. Of this we have plenty of evidence in the inventories and advertisements, even though their handiwork has all but disappeared. But about the time of the Revolution the demand in Boston for everything but flatware seems to have fallen off badly. As a result, the men whose careers commenced after the Revolution got along with comparatively few moulds. There is very little hope that we shall come across unusual forms bearing the touches of Badger or Richard Austin, for instance, but Skinner was of the older school. We know that he had many moulds. We dare hope that some of his unusual pieces will yet be found.

John, son of Richard and Martha Burrill Skinner, was baptized at Marblehead May 6, 1733. He was descended from James Skinner, a fisherman, who settled in that town prior to 1665, and the pewterer's grandfather, Richard, was the wealthiest merchant of his generation in Marblehead. Skinner may have been making pewter in Boston as early as 1756, for he was apparently well established there by 1761, when he advertised the removal of his shop to Union Street. The exact date of his marriage to Sarah Holyoke of Boston is not known, but the intentions were published March 20, 1762. They joined the West Church in Boston in 1768, and in that church are recorded the baptisms of six of their seven children. In 1759 Skinner joined the Artillery Company, became 4th sergeant in 1763 and ensign in 1773.

In 1765 he was chosen one of Boston's assay masters, and for twenty-nine years was annually re-elected to that office. He also served several terms as hogreeve and as hayward, holding three town offices at one time from 1786 to 1788. Although listed as a pewterer in the directory of 1789, he probably made little if any pewter after 1785.

John Skinner died in Boston, January 25, 1813, but must have retired from pewter-making many years before. No tools were found in his inventory. Even so he probably worked at his trade for over thirty years and was one of the few eighteenth-century workers who did not combine either brass-, copper-, or tin-working with his manufacture of pewter. As his estate amounted to almost seventeen thousand dollars, we are probably safe in believing that he turned out a great quantity of the metal in his day.

In those days the death of an ordinary mortal was passed unheralded by the daily papers, or received at most a line or two of comment. It may help us, therefore, to understand the position of this man in his community to quote in part from his obituary notice:

Deaths: — Mr. John Skinner, aged 80. In him his children mourn the loss of a discreet and most affectionate parent; his numerous acquaintance a friend greatly endeared by a benevolence of heart that knew no interruption or abatement; and society a citizen of an integrity of character against which even suspicion never whispered a censure....

The Pewterers of Massachusetts Bay

In George Francis Dow's *The Arts and Crafts of New England* are two advertisements by this maker which should prove of interest to the pewter collector. Both notices are quoted in full below:

> John Skinner, Pewterer, adjoining on the North-side of the Mill-Bridge, next to Deacon Barrett's in Boston, Makes and Sells by Wholesale or Retail, very cheap for Cash or Old Pewter,
>
> Plates of different sizes, hammer'd the same as London, very neat Canns, Quart and Pint Potts, Quart and Pint Basons, Porringers of five different sizes — pewter Beakers, &c. all warranted the best of fine Pewter; also Rum Measures, from Quart to Jill Pots; — also sells Tea-Kettles, the best London Pewter; etc.,
>
> Gentlemen Traders may be supplied at the above Place at the very lowest Rate. — *Boston News-Letter*, July 7, 1763.

The second notice appeared in the *Boston Gazette* of July 1, 1765:

> John Skinner, Pewterer, Hereby informs his Customers and others,
>
> That he has removed from the front of the House adjoining the Mill-Bridge, to his work-shop at the back end of said House, in the Lane leading to the Mills; where he continues to make hammer'd Plates the same as London, of different Sizes; also Wine Measures from Quarts to Jills, with all other sorts of Pewter Ware usually made in New England, where Gentlemen and Ladies that trade in Pewter may be supplied with large or small Quantities, at the very lowest Rate for Cash or Old Pewter.
>
> N.B. The highest Price is given by said Skinner for Old Pewter.

These advertisements bring out several points that might bear elaboration. We are interested, for instance, in the implied 'sales-resistance' to the purchase of American-made pewter and the steps which Skinner took to offset it. The public preferred the London-made article, so John not only hammered his plates but advertised the fact also. However, he was not going to lose any sales just because some fastidious individuals demanded the imported ware. For them he carried pewter made in London.

Compared with the long array of stock shapes, the number of Skinner pieces now known to exist is pitifully small. At the time when *American Pewter* was written, J. B. Kerfoot knew of but one Skinner plate, and even that he had not seen. Since then a number of $8\frac{7}{8}$- and $9\frac{1}{4}$-inch smooth-rim plates have turned up, two or three plates measuring $7\frac{3}{4}$ and 8 inches, and several dishes or platters measuring 12, $13\frac{1}{4}$, and $15\frac{1}{16}$ inches. All of these are 'hammer'd same as London.' One $9\frac{1}{4}$-inch basin and several in the quart size have also appeared, one of which bears the very clear impression of Skinner's rarer touch, which has been illustrated in Plate XLV, 295. But what has become of all of Skinner's hollow-ware? Who knows but that some dusty attic may still conceal one of those 'very neat Canns' or perhaps a rum measure or two!

NATHANIEL AUSTIN

The superior craftsmanship observed in the flatware of Nathaniel Austin and the refined taste in design of the touches thereon have been erroneously attributed to the fact that the maker was a goldsmith as well as a pewterer. The error, however, can be readily explained as a case of mistaken identity.

In the early years of the eighteenth century there lived in Charlestown, Massachusetts, a large family of Austins, and a frequently recurring name in the family history is Nathaniel. By chance it happened that a child of that name was born in 1739. Just two years later, in another branch of the family, another boy was baptized Nathaniel Austin. The elder of these cousins chose as his life-work goldsmithing, as his father had done before him; the younger became a pewterer. Both men opened shops in their native town, and there each lived and worked until the arrival of the British in 1776. In the bombardment of the town each lost his house and shop. The goldsmith then moved to Boston and opened a shop in Back Street. His cousin fled to Lunenburg, returning to Charlestown after the departure of the British. Presumably he rebuilt the establishment which had been destroyed and spent the rest of his days at the trade to which he had been trained. Since there are no early directories of Charlestown, it was a very natural mistake to assume that the goldsmith of Boston was the Nathaniel Austin whose name is impressed on existing pewter.

The man in whom we are particularly interested, baptized July 19, 1741, was the youngest child of Ebenezer and Mary (Smith) Austin. He set up as a pewterer in 1763 and three years later married Margaret Rand. Of their six children at least two were to attain some measure of prominence. William Austin was a state senator and well-known author in his day, and Nathaniel, Junior, became a brigadier general of militia, a state senator and representative, and high sheriff of Charlestown.

The handsome touch-marks hitherto found on 'N. A.' flatware are post-Revolutionary in character, but J. B. Kerfoot pointed out in *American Pewter* that Austin was thirty-five when the war began and might well have made pewter prior to that date, a fact that would have to be determined by the 'discovery of earlier records bearing on the case, or of manifestly pre-Revolutionary pieces.'

Fortunately I am in position to supply the documentary evidence and at the same time illustrate two groups of pre-Revolutionary marks (Plate XLV, 297, 298, and 299) as found respectively on a smooth-rim 9¾-inch hammered plate and an 8¾-inch plate with normal rim.

The announcement of the opening of Austin's first shop appeared in the *Boston Gazette* for October 3, 1763, and is quoted in full:

> Nathaniel Austin, Pewterer; next door to Mr. Boylston's in Charlestown, makes and sells (as Cheap for Cash or Old Pewter, as any Person in Boston) the following Articles, viz, Quart and Pint Pots, Quart and Pint Basons, Plates and Porringers of all Sizes &c.
> He has also to dispose of at a Reasonable Rate, a small Assortment of Brazier's Ware, viz: —

The Pewterers of Massachusetts Bay

Brass Kettles, Warming Pans, Skillets, Frying Pans, Tea Kettles, Iron Pots and Kettles, Shovel and Tongs, Candlesticks, best London Glue, Bellows, Hand-saws, Files, Rasps, Aul Blades, Tax, Brads, best shoe Knives, Pen-Knives, Knives & Forks, London Pewter, &c.

Please note that Austin followed John Skinner's example and carried 'London Pewter' for those who insisted upon the imported article.

As stated above, Austin lost heavily when the British shelled Charlestown; buildings, trees, and fences were destroyed. Soon after that date each Massachusetts town was apparently called upon to give the names of all strangers within its limits capable of bearing arms. We find in the list of the village of Lunenburg, dated December, 1776, 'Nath¹ Austin & his apprentice' of Charlestown. We lost a bit of interesting information when that Lunenburg town official neglected to record the name of Mr. Austin's apprentice. It was in Lunenburg also in 1780 that Nathaniel's son, William, was born. Soon thereafter the pewterer must have returned to Charlestown with his family to rebuild his house and shop, and in Charlestown he died, March 5, 1816. His inventory is not on file, so we do not know whether he was still making pewter just prior to his death, but as he was then seventy-five years old, it is probable that he had retired from active business.

In Louis G. Myers's *Notes* is illustrated a quart mug made by Austin with a circular name-touch (Plate XLV, 296) impressed on the handle. Half a dozen similar mugs are now in various collections. The handles on these vessels are solid, and early in form except for the strut at the base of each (Plate XX, 122).

Quart mugs and basins, plates and dishes represent the existing output of Austin's shop so far recorded. The flatware range, however, is most complete. Sizes known to me are 7½-inch, 8-inch, 8⅝-inch, 8¾-inch, 9½-inch (smooth rim), 9¾-inch (smooth rim), 12-inch, 12-inch (smooth rim), 13½-inch (flat), 13½-inch (deep), and 15-inch (flat). All of Austin's plates and dishes, except the 13½-inch deep dish, are extremely shallow and have a rim that is narrower in proportion than the plate rims normal to the other colonies. This same statement holds true for the flatware of almost all the Boston pewterers.

On the 9¾-inch smooth-rim plate illustrated in Plate X, 48, the bead on the under side of the rim is exceptionally wide, measuring a full half-inch across, a deviation from standard for which I have no explanation.

Austin touches and so-called hall-marks (which latter were apparently used throughout his career) are shown in Plate XLV, 296 to 301. Examine any one of the marks, from the early lion, so full of action, to his classic eagle, perhaps the handsomest of all eagle touch-marks, and one must be impressed with the fact that this man was endowed with taste and imagination not given to the average artisan. Austin's pewter was of fine quality, his workmanship superior, and his touches are always found accurately centered, one form of evidence of a master workman.

The Younger Greens

EDWARD KNEELAND

Here again we have a Boston pewterer whose name has not appeared in earlier lists. Edward Kneeland was descended from John Neland, who settled near Boston about 1630.

Edward was the tenth of the thirteen children of John Kneeland, shopkeeper, and the eldest by John's fourth wife, his birth occurring October 20, 1747. As early as 1768 he had a shop in Union Street, where, so ran his advertisement, 'he makes and sells the best New England Pewter.' He joined the Ancient and Honorable Artillery Company in 1772 and it is recorded that he had charge of the arms for Ward 6 at the time that the British troops landed in Boston in 1775. In February of the same year he was published to marry Sarah Baxter. In 1779 he was captain of a company of Boston Guards under General Gates.

The Boston tax files of 1784 and 1787 list him in Ward 6 as a 'pewterer, very poor.' Consequently he may have been only a journeyman after the Revolution. According to the census of 1790 Kneeland's household consisted of one 'female,' presumably his wife, and two 'males under sixteen years of age.' A deed of September, 1791, in which he is termed a pewterer, is the last record of him that could be found in Boston. No will or letters of administration are on file.

Though Kneeland worked in Boston for many years, his poverty in later life would indicate lack of success in business, and perhaps explains in part the disappearance of all examples of his workmanship.

THE YOUNGER GREENS

Thomas Green the elder, whose story has already been told (page 67), was probably never at a loss for an apprentice. With a family which included ten boys he had only to draft another son into the business when an 'opening' in his shop occurred.

Thomas, Junior, the oldest of the second generation, was baptized November 2, 1746. His history is obscure, but in the 'Assessors Taxing Books for the year 1780' he is set down as a pewterer. Whether he merely worked as a journeyman or had an establishment of his own we may never know. His name is not found in the Directory of 1789 and appears on the tax lists for 1786 for the last time. Inasmuch as Thomas Green, Senior, was appointed guardian in 1790 for Thomas and Rebecca, minor children of Thomas Green, Junior, one of whom was residing 'outside the state,' it is probable that Thomas, Junior, left Boston about 1786 to earn a living elsewhere and died not later than 1790. He was evidently a poor man, of little importance to the student of American pewter.

Andrew Green, whose twin brother Timothy died in infancy, was baptized August 5,

PLATE XLV — *Massachusetts Touches — John Skinner and Nathaniel Austin*

293 and 294. Touches of John Skinner, Boston, 1760–1790. From a dish in the collection of the author.

293a and 293b. Other impressions of Skinner's normal touch. From a dish in the collection of the author.

295. Unusually fine impression of Skinner's rarer mark. From a basin in the Mabel Brady Garvan Collection, Gallery of Fine Arts, Yale University.

296. Touch used by Nathaniel Austin, Charlestown, 1763–1807, on quart mugs. Collection of John W. Poole, Esq.

297, 298, and 299. The early touches of Nathaniel Austin. From a plate in the collection of the author.

297a and 298a. Another impression of Austin's rare Charlestown touch. Collection of the author.

297b. An unusually fine impression of Austin's lion touch. From a plate in the collection of John W. Poole, Esq.

300 and 299a. Austin's cartouche (300) replaced the lion touch probably during the Revolution. From a plate in the collection of Mrs. Charles A. Calder.

301. Austin's last touch, the least rare of all of his marks. From a plate in the collection of the author.

PLATE XLV

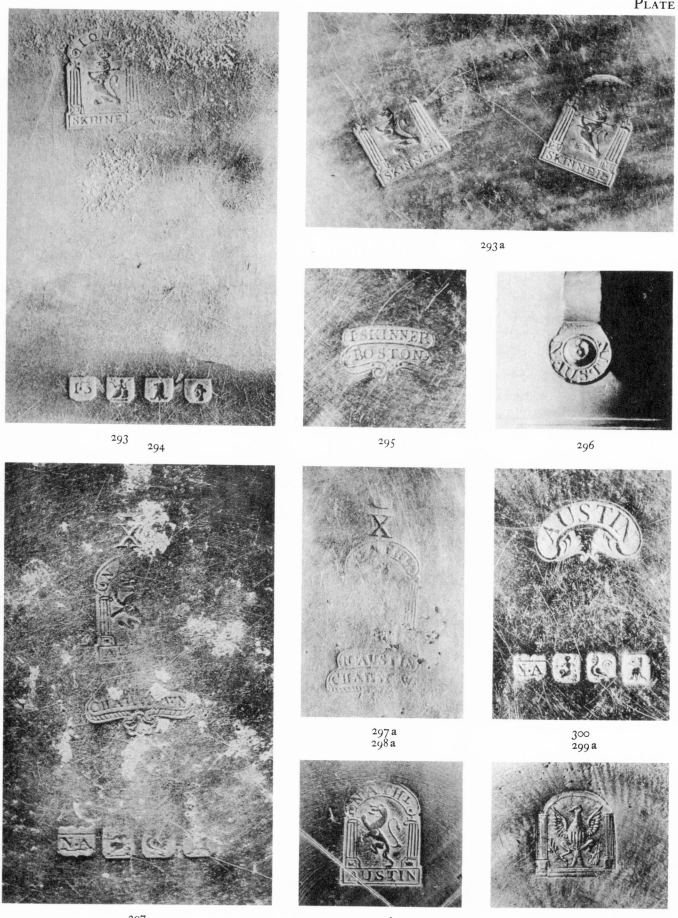

293

294

293 a

295

296

297
298
299

297 a
298 a

300
299 a

297 b

301

PLATE XLVI — *Massachusetts Touches — Samuel Green, Richard Austin, Thomas Badger, and George Richardson*

302. Touch attributed to Samuel Green, Boston, 1779–1828. From a dish in the collection of Vincent O'Reilly, Esq.

303. Another touch attributed to Samuel Green. From a basin owned by John W. Poole, Esq.

304. Early touch of Richard Austin, Boston, 1793–1817. From a plate in the Mabel Brady Garvan Collection, Gallery of Fine Arts, Yale University.

304a. Another impression of same touch. From a plate in the collection of Charles F. Hutchins, Esq.

305. An impression of Austin's name-touch. Collection of the author.

305a and 306. Richard Austin's lamb and dove mark and a second impression of his name-touch. From a plate formerly in the collection of the late Albert C. Bowman.

307. Rarest and probably latest of Richard Austin's touches. From a dish owned by John W. Poole, Esq.

308 and 287b. Earlier touches of Thomas Badger, Boston, 1787–1815. The Boston scroll was used also by David Cutler, 'Semper Eadem,' and Richard Austin. Collection of the author.

309 and 287c. Combination of touches used by Badger in his later years. From a dish in the collection of the author.

310. Touch of G. Richardson of Boston, 1818–1828. From a teapot formerly in the collection of Philip G. Platt, Esq.

Massachusetts touches — 308 and 287b should read 308 and 287a in order to correspond with the numbering under the illustrations on the opposite page.

PLATE XLVI

302

303

304

304 a

305

305 a   306

307

310

308   287 a

309   287 b

1750. He served as a 'matross' in Colonel Richard Gridley's Artillery Regiment at Boston in 1775 and 1776, was at Valley Forge in 1777, and in the Rhode Island campaign in 1779 and 1780. He was discharged with the rank of first lieutenant December 1, 1781, near West Point, New York.

He had married Meletiah Bradley in Boston March 7, 1773, and upon his return to Boston after the Revolution they lived in and presumably owned a house at the corner of Temple and Derne Streets. Though listed as a pewterer in the Directories of 1789, 1796, and 1798, it is doubtful whether he was ever anything more than a journeyman. In 1784 he was working with (or for) Joshua Weatherly, a pewterer, coppersmith, and founder. He paid a tax on personal property assessed at only twenty-five dollars in 1787. In the tax lists of 1792 he was shown to be a journeyman pewterer with five children and 'poor.' In 1795 he was marked 'very poor' and not taxed at all. He seems to have left Boston, as did his brother Thomas, to gain a livelihood, for we find him there no more after 1798. Though his estate was not settled until 1808, his wife was described as a widow in the Directory of 1805. The property distributed by the administrators of his estate was valued at only $416.89.

The third of Thomas Green's sons to take up pewtering was Timothy, the second child in the family so named. This Timothy was baptized in the Brattle Square Church April 20, 1755. With his brother Andrew he enlisted as a 'matross' in Colonel Gridley's Artillery Regiment in 1775 and served throughout the war. He was discharged in the grade of second lieutenant.

He married Mary Allen in Boston on October 12, 1779, and apparently learned the pewterer's trade, for such was his given occupation in 1780. Earlier than his brothers, however, he read the trend of the times, and on July 30, 1782, in a petition describing himself as a shopkeeper who was then furnishing his store in Dock Square with 'India Goods,' he applied in writing for a license to dispense liquors because the traders chose to sip rum or wine while making purchases. The India goods soon became a minor issue, and after 1784 Timothy's occupation was given as wine merchant. He proved that then as now a very nice competence can be made from the sale of liquor. Timothy Green died in 1818. He may never have made pewter on his own account, and if he did so it was for but a year or two at most.

The next son, Samuel, baptized April 24, 1757, married Susannah Raymond on July 16, 1778. He apparently went to work for his father and succeeded to the business when the latter retired. In a deposition made in the year 1799, having reference to a boundary dispute in connection with the Dock Square property, Samuel testified:

> ... in the year 1779 I was in possession under my father, the late Thomas Green, of a certain shop and the land under the same and the yard behind it. ... I continued in possession of said shop until the present time excepting that my said brother John has occupied the lower part of it for several years past. ...

In 1792 Samuel succeeded his father as one of Boston's assay masters, but held the position for just two years. His only other public office was that of town constable in 1812. In 1794 he purchased from his father's estate the latter's tools and moulds. Until about 1798 his shop was at Dock Square. Thereafter we find him at various addresses. About 1814 he became a partner of Richard Austin, and when the latter died in 1817 the shop's moulds, jointly owned, weighed within ten pounds of the amount purchased by Samuel Green from his father's estate. Their description and the list of stock in the shop indicate that their owners made plates and dishes, basins (two sizes), porringers, teapots, and tumblers. In 1818 Green joined forces with George Richardson in a shop on Hawley Street, but the partnership lasted for only one year, after which Samuel Green worked alone. In 1828 he was taxed as a journeyman pewterer in rear of Fifth Street, and in 1834 was described as 'gentleman,' Fifth Street, 'old & poor.' No will or letters testamentary are on file in Boston, but he probably died about the latter date.

Pewter marked 'S. G. Boston,' which has been attributed to this maker, is rare, and judging from the few examples that I have seen the metal is not as good as that of his contemporaries, Skinner, the Austins, and Badger. A few plates are semi-deep, an exception to the general rule that all Boston flatware is markedly shallow. The 'S. G.' items reported thus far are a quart basin, a pint basin, 15-inch flat dish, two dishes measuring $13\frac{1}{2}$ inches in diameter, a $12\frac{3}{16}$-inch dish, several $7\frac{1}{2}$-inch, 8-inch and $8\frac{1}{8}$-inch plates, some of which are semi-deep, a 6-inch plate, and a rare little saucer measuring just $4\frac{7}{8}$ inches in diameter, to the best of my knowledge the smallest marked American plate. It is my belief that Samuel Green, during his father's lifetime, worked for the latter and used his dies, and that neither of the 'S. G.' touches (Plate XLVI, 302 and 303) was used prior to 1794.

One other son of Thomas Green worked in pewter for a very brief season. Jonas, baptized August 12, 1764, was listed as a pewterer, working for his father, in 1786 and 1787. He soon thereafter became a mariner and in later life was a successful sea-captain and trader. He died in 1818.

The history of the pewter-making Greens will be brought to a close with the story of Samuel Green, Junior, son of Samuel and grandson of the first Thomas. Though no record of his birth or baptism could be found, he must have been born about 1779. He apparently married and was a merchant in Roxbury in the second decade of the nineteenth century. His name appears in the Boston directory of 1821, but no occupation is listed. From 1826 to 1829 he is described as a pewterer and from 1833 to 1835 as a block tin manufacturer in the rear of Fifth Street, South Boston. Since the tax lists of 1828 show him to have been a 'journeyman pewterer,' it is probable that he never had a pewtering establishment of his own. After 1835 he was the proprietor of a small hat store in South Boston. He died, a poor man, April 18, 1862, and was buried in a five-dollar grave in Mount Auburn Cemetery.

Members of the Green family were making pewter in Boston for almost one hundred years. That they have left us almost no examples of their work need cause little wonderment, for none, save possibly the senior Thomas, appears from the records to have prospered at the trade.

JOSHUA WITHERLE (OR WEATHERLY)

Various deeds from 1784 to 1793 record transactions made by Joshua Witherle, pewterer. Witherle was not a common Boston name and this man probably was born elsewhere. He appears for the first time in town documents in the record of his marriage on May 10, 1776, to Mrs. Rebecca How. From tax lists of the seventeen-eighties we know that another pewterer, Andrew Green, was working with or for Witherle.

In the 1789 Directory the listing is as follows:

Witherle, Joshua & Co., coppersmiths, house Washington St., shop in Kilby St.

In the Directories for 1796 and 1798 Witherle is called a wire manufacturer, and apparently this trade represented a promotion in the social scale, for in deeds made in those years he styled himself 'Joshua Witherle, Gentleman.' In 1800 his name appears for the last time in Boston Directories. No probate records were discovered. Had his pewter business been large, we should have found before this some examples of metal bearing his touch.

AUSTIN, BOWLES, AND BRADFORD

Boston records of the seventeen-eighties supply the names of three more pewterers who probably never figured prominently in the pewter trade of the city.

In a deed of 1785 'John Austin, pewterer, of Boston,' sold property on Belknap Street to Prince Watts of the same city. Since both John and his wife 'Silvia' made their marks on the deed in lieu of signatures, I assume that the man was uneducated, a journeyman only, and probably related in no way to Nathaniel or Richard Austin.

Samuel Bowles, whose history has also defied search, was termed a pewterer in the tax lists of 1787 and 1788. At that time he had two rooms in a boarding-house in Ward 1. There is no record of his having owned any real estate in Boston and little likelihood that he had a shop of his own.

John Bradford, who married Sarah, daughter of Paul Revere, on March 20, 1783, was listed as a pewterer in Ward 6 in 1784; in 1788 he was living in Mr. Kimble's house in Ward 3, 'a pewterer, poor.' Later he had a small hardware store. I suspect that he was a journeyman only, and if pewter ever was made in Paul Revere's shop Bradford was probably the man who turned it out.

THOMAS BADGER, JUNIOR

It seems apparent now, as explained in the note on 'Semper Eadem,' that there was but one pewterer in the Badger family and that man Thomas the younger. Born in 1764, he presumably commenced his pewter-making about 1786. Louis G. Myers illustrated in his *Notes* an early Badger touch (see also Plate XLVI, 308). Its form is such that we might well have guessed it to be pre-Revolutionary, and it may yet develop that the first Thomas Badger was not only a block-maker, but also a pewterer and the user of this mark. In the light of present knowledge, however, I should say that it was a touch used by the younger Thomas when he opened his first shop, and was discarded soon thereafter in favor of the patriotic eagle.

Descended from Giles Badger, who settled in Newbury, Massachusetts, in 1635, Thomas Badger, Junior, was born in Boston in 1764 and married in 1786. His shop from 1789 until 1815 was on Prince Street; after that date he is listed in the directories as a grocer.

The records show that Badger was a public-spirited man, and when not busy making pewter he seems to have been taking part, and a leading part, in town activities. As did many of our pewterers, Thomas joined the militia, rose to the rank of captain in 1806, and by 1813 was a colonel. In 1812 he was defeated for the office of county treasurer, and he also ran unsuccessfully several times for state senator. It is apparent that his contemporaries thought well of his judgment and common sense, for between 1815 and 1819 he served on almost every special committee appointed by the selectmen. The duties of these committees covered such varied matters as the adoption of regulations for carts and trucks, the selection and purchase of sites for a new burial ground and for an armory, regulations for town health, for market inspection, etc. In 1819 Badger was chairman of a committee that applied to the selectmen for permission to use Faneuil Hall on Independence Day 'for the purpose of a collation and patriotic meeting,' and in 1822 he was elected an overseer of the poor. Taken by and large, Colonel Thomas Badger must have been a credit to the community. He died in Boston in 1826.

His pewter trade would seem to have been large, but we have no evidence yet that he made anything but flatware. Basins are found in the quart size (8-inch), and plates and dishes come in the following diameters: $7\frac{3}{4}$, $7\frac{7}{8}$, $8\frac{5}{16}$, $8\frac{1}{2}$, $12\frac{1}{4}$, $13\frac{1}{4}$, $13\frac{1}{2}$, $14\frac{3}{4}$, and 15 inches.

RICHARD AUSTIN

In spite of recent careful investigation we are unable to say definitely when or where Richard Austin was born. The historian of Boston's Ancient and Honorable Artillery Company tells us that Richard, born in 1764, was a son of Thomas Austin of Charlestown (and hence a distant relation of Nathaniel Austin), but the notice of his death in the Boston newspapers of 1817 gave his age as forty-seven, which would place his birth in 1769 or 1770.

Whether Boston-born or not, he took an active interest in state and civic affairs. In 1792 he joined the Artillery Company and was a member of the organization for many years, holding the rank of captain when he died. In 1800 Austin was appointed to the city government position of sealer of weights and measures and continued in that office for seventeen years. During the last eight years of his life he was also one of Boston's two assay masters. In 1801 he married Deborah Lee of Salem.

Richard Austin's life was darkened by many sorrows. Although we know nothing of his youth, we are fortunate in having a contemporary account of him written in 1820 by a fellow member in the Artillery Company, which gives in some detail the trials he passed through in later years.

He must have opened his first shop on Marlborough Street, about 1792, soon became well and favorably known, and seemed headed toward a successful career. About 1800, however, the pewtering trade began to feel with steadily increasing pressure the competition of china, tinware, and other cheaper substitutes. Austin saw the handwriting on the wall, and decided to give at least part of his time to some more lucrative calling.

In the year 1810 he entered into partnership with George Blanchard, a fellow member of the Artillery Company, who was, we are told, a rough-spoken, haughty individual who had accumulated a good deal of property through successful real estate deals. Austin and Blanchard opened a brokerage office at 6 State Street. Through their wide acquaintanceship they soon built up a high-class clientèle. Many friends placed large sums in their hands with no more security than their faith in the partners, and in a very short period the house had gained general confidence. Suddenly they failed. Although all of their private property was attached, very little of the money was ever found and no satisfactory explanation of its disappearance was ever vouchsafed. Suspicion never pointed to Austin, but Blanchard was thrown into prison. Despite questionings and investigations, sufficient evidence could not be found to convict the man and he was finally permitted to take the poor debtor's oath. Austin's associates believed him to have been the dupe of an unscrupulous partner.

And so, at middle age, his fortune gone, his good name tarnished, he was compelled to start again at the one trade he knew — pewtering. It is probable that he had to sell all his tools to satisfy his creditors, but he made some sort of arrangement with Samuel Green, and at the time of his death in 1817 he and Green were sharing a shop, part of the inventory of which I give below:

27 teapots	@ .75	20.25
79 pint and 96 half pint porringers	Weighing	
27 quart " 24 pint basins	120 lbs @ .25 per lb	30.00
38 tumblers	@ 1/1	6.33
101 lbs pewter (probably flatware)	@ .17	17.17
3 dish moulds, 2 plates do, 1 bason do and 2 porringer do weighing 359 lbs @ .25		89.75
Balance of shop contents (listed by name in inventory)		78.37
		241.87
Deduct one half the property of Mr. Green		120.94

After all debts had been paid, the widow, Deborah Austin, received but $34.09.

The inventory indicates that these men in their later years were not equipped to manufacture any great range of shapes. But what have become of all the Austin and Green porringers, teapots, tumblers, and pint basins? Austin's plates and dishes have been found in the following sizes: $7\frac{13}{16}$, $8\frac{3}{8}$, $8\frac{1}{2}$, $12\frac{1}{4}$, $12\frac{1}{2}$, $13\frac{1}{4}$, $13\frac{3}{8}$, and 15 inches, all of the shallow variety; his basins in the quart size (8 inches) only. His metal is good, and, though rarer than that of Thomas Badger or Nathaniel Austin, is not infrequently met with.

Two of the Richard Austin touches are great rarities. There is record of only about a half-dozen examples of the interesting 'Massachusetts Coat-of-Arms' mark (Plate XLVI, 304), which I take to be the earliest of this pewterer's touches, and but one plate is known with the initials in saw-tooth border (number 307). On account of its similarity in design to a touch (number 303) of Austin's latter-day partner, Samuel Green, I assume that the die dates from the partnership period (1814–1817). No record of any business connection between Austin and Badger was found, and we still are in the dark as to the explanation of their having used the same Boston scroll touch.

Z. G. Whitman's brief account of Richard Austin is not only interesting to us as coming from a friend and contemporary — and incidentally Whitman lost all he had when Austin failed — but it dates fairly accurately for us the end of pewter-making as a competitive industry in Boston. I quote in part from his narrative written in 1820:

> The trade in pewter had been a lucrative branch of manufacture but about this time began to go out of fashion. The better sort of people used pewter platters, spoons, plates, porringers, etc., and it was a mark of poverty not to see a dresser abundantly furnished with pewterware. . . . Captain Austin was a man of strict honesty and honor as well as liberality. When his trade declined he entered into copartnership with George Blanchard and followed the business of a broker. Disaster followed and Mr. Austin, deeply in debt, suffered much depression during the latter part of his life. . . . Although the lack of offspring, the misfortunes of business, the treachery of his partner, and the severity of bodily pain cast a secret gloom over his warm heart, yet he always wore the same cheerful countenance and died with great fortitude and resignation.

NATHANIEL BOWMAN

Nathaniel Bowman, a pewterer of Charlestown, was a descendant of a man of the same name who is said to have come over in the fleet with Governor Winthrop and is known to have become a freeman of Watertown in 1630.

The subject of this brief sketch was a son of Samuel and Elizabeth (Robbins) Bowman and was born prior to 1785. In Charlestown deeds from 1806 to 1814 he was termed a pewterer. One of these, dated 1807, records the transfer to Bowman by Nathaniel Austin, pewterer, of property on a new street which was being laid out through land which Austin owned.

Bowman died, unmarried and intestate, shortly before January 8, 1816, when an administrator of his estate was appointed. In the probate records he is called 'a gunsmith alias pewterer.' Since the shop contents included principally a turner's tools and rifle parts I believe that the man gave up pewter-making prior to 1815.

No pewter that could be attributed to this maker is known to be in existence.

GEORGE RICHARDSON

George Richardson, Boston pewterer and block-tin manufacturer, appears in Boston records for the first time in 1818. In that year Samuel Green, whose partner, Richard Austin, had just died, took Richardson in with him in a shop on Hawley Street. A few months later Green and Richardson advertised pewter at a new location, 5 and 9 Marlboro Place. Soon thereafter they parted company, and in a newspaper notice of 1821 Richardson announced the manufacture of block tin at 27 Newbury Street. By 1825 he had moved to Oliver Street at which address he was listed until 1828. We could hardly be criticized for assuming, as most students of pewter had assumed, that Richardson was a comparatively young man in 1828. It was a distinct surprise to learn from an article by Mrs. Lura Woodside Watkins in the *Antiques* magazine for April, 1937, that Richardson died in Boston April 10, 1830, at the age of eighty-three and was buried in Copp's Hill Burial Ground. The date of death and age at the time are confirmed by an obituary notice in the *Columbian Centinel* for April 17 of that year. If we can believe — I find it difficult to do so — that the George Richardson who died in 1830 was the pewterer, we must also believe that he was over seventy years old when he joined forces with Samuel Green and was over eighty when still actively engaged at his trade.

Existing pewter marked 'G. Richardson Boston' (Plate XLVI, 310), includes teapots of at least three different designs, pint pots, 9⅝-inch deep dishes and a shaving-mug and dish. Richardson's advertisements inform us that he also made pitchers, washbowls and ewers, tumblers and lamps — the earliest newspaper notice (1821) of pewter lamps that I have seen. The wares were well made, but the designs were in no way distinguished.

There are in existence also a good many pieces of pewter marked 'G. Richardson' which bear the additional touches of 'Glennore Co.' and 'Cranston, R.I.' Items so marked include the famed sugar bowls (Plate LXXII, 616) upon which J. B. Kerfoot lavished well-merited praise, pitchers of two varieties and teapots in several different designs. Generally speaking, the Cranston pewter is more pleasing in outline, though definitely of later design, than the pieces bearing the Boston touch.

Several searches through Rhode Island have thus far thrown very little light on the Cranston pewter-maker and no evidence whatever has been found of the Glennore Company whose name is stamped on Richardson pewter. Doctor Madelaine Brown, Mr. and Mrs. Paul J. Franklin, and Professor Percy E. Raymond made a trip to Cranston and examined what were said to be the ruins of Richardson's factory at the corner of

George Richardson

Natick and Phenix Avenues. A George W. H. Richardson was found on the Cranston tax lists for 1860, but there is no positive proof that this was the pewterer. The deed for the factory site mentioned above was not found, and we still do not know just when the Cranston pewter was made.

It does seem possible now, however, to deny upon reasonable grounds some previously held opinions on the subject of Richardson and his wares. First of all the Cranston maker could not have been the man who worked in Boston from 1818 to 1828, if the latter died in 1830, for the Rhode Island pewter belongs very definitely to the period after 1825.

Secondly, I have not seen, and no one has reported to me teapots, mugs, or other forms identical in design, one example bearing the Boston touch, another the Cranston marks. There is strong support, therefore, for the supposition that George Richardson, pewterer, of Boston, and G. Richardson, Cranston pewterer, were not one and the same man as was long believed.

While the above story of George Richardson was in galley proof an informing article about this pewterer by Edward H. West appeared in the October issue of *Antiques*. With the deductions reached therein, I am in full accord. The gist of Mr. West's findings is that the Richardson who died in Boston in 1830 was not the pewterer; that the George Richardson, pewterer of Boston, and the Cranston maker of that name were one and the same man; that he was born in England about 1782; worked continuously at pewtering from 1818 until his death; was in Cranston in 1840 and perhaps much earlier; had a britannia-ware shop with his sons, George B. and Francis B. Richardson, at 207 High Street, Providence, in 1847 and 1848; and died in that city on July 15, 1848.

THE RHODE ISLAND PEWTERERS

WHEN a British expedition landed at Newport in 1777, a town official, in his anxiety to safeguard the public documents of the colony, attempted to carry them to a point safe from marauders. Unfortunately the vessel on which they were temporarily placed was lost in the Hell Gate channel and we are now deprived of much valuable information bearing upon the early history of Rhode Island.

There seems little doubt that Newport was one of the earliest pewter-making centers in the colonies, but the evidence to support that belief has disappeared. Thomas Byles, who was a prominent pewterer in Philadelphia after 1740, is known to have been living in Newport as early as 1710. But nothing could be gleaned about Byles's early years from the existing records of Newport nor could any trace be found of a pewterer or pewterers who may have preceded him there.

The earliest Newport pewter-maker of verified record was Lawrence Langworthy, who became a freeman in 1735; a few years later Benjamin Day and John Fryers appear in documents as pewterers. No pewter of Langworthy's has been found, and although several collections contain items which can be attributed with reservations to Day or Fryers, positive ascription is not at present possible. Any real appreciation, therefore, of Rhode Island pewter must be confined to the years of the Revolution and later, the period for which we have authenticated examples.

Relatively speaking, a great quantity of marked Rhode Island pewter of the early days of the Republic still survives; sufficient examples, certainly, upon which to base a fair estimate of the ability of the makers.

Before we pass judgment it will be well to note several unusual features of the Rhode Island output. In that state there seems to have been a tremendous demand for porringers. It is no overstatement to say that there are more Hamlin porringers in existence today than the combined surviving total of marked porringers by all American pewterers (the Boardmans of Hartford excepted) who dwelt outside the confines of Rhode Island. Furthermore, there are twenty or thirty Hamlin porringers to every existing small Hamlin-marked plate. The case of the Hamlins is an extreme example, but the product of every maker in the state shows an unusually high proportion of porringers to small plates. Particularly is this true of the Providence men.

It is therefore perhaps only natural that their porringers are the most interesting forms that they have left to us. As explained elsewhere, these Rhode Island vessels can be distinguished almost as far as they can be seen. They had their own individual form of handle; this was fastened to the bowl by a bracket, which also differs in shape from that employed by the pewterers throughout the other states of the Union. But among themselves — and this also is particularly true of the Providence group — there is little if any variation from the fixed Rhode Island standards.

Porringers excluded, the Rhode Island pewterers appear to have made nothing that differed to any great extent from the forms produced in the neighboring states of Massachusetts and Connecticut. Variations between the pewter of Newport and that of Providence should, however, be pointed out. In Newport, as in Boston, the dishes and plates were almost always of the flat variety. Providence pewter, on the other hand, shows the influence of the Connecticut training of Samuel Hamlin and Gershom Jones. Dishes, 11-inch and larger, are of the semi-deep variety — a compromise between the flat specimens of Newport and the deep dishes of Connecticut. The scale of sizes differs also. In Newport we find 8-inch, 9-inch, 12-inch, and 14-inch flatware, whereas in Providence the scale runs 8-inch, 9-inch, 11-inch, 13-inch, and 15-inch. In one other respect the two groups differ. Although porringers under 5 inches in diameter, whether made in Newport or Providence, are practically identical in design, the Newport men frequently employed on their larger sizes a distinctive trefoil-shaped solid handle, whereas in Providence all porringers, large and small, were made with what we might term the standard Rhode Island handle.

Excluding the pewter made after 1825, i.e., William Calder's later forms and the work of George Richardson, we have nothing left but flatware, porringers, a few mugs, and two or three beakers — a great quantity of pewter but remarkably little variety. This is indeed surprising, for Rhode Island was wealthy. Her furniture of those early days has in some respects more distinction than that of any other colony. Hence we wonder at the paucity of forms made by her pewterers. The failure upon the part of the native makers to have supplied a demand that must have existed for pewter in its finest forms implies a lack of ability, a lack of imagination, or, more probably, as the records of the settlements of their estates would indicate, a lack of funds sufficient to purchase the moulds required for a varied product. We may state, then, that the Rhode Island pewterers made final metal and showed high ability, but only within the limited scope which they set for themselves.

LAWRENCE LANGWORTHY

On what is said to be the only colonial gravestone in Rhode Island that is engraved with a coat of arms the following inscription appears:

> In memory of Lawrence Langworthy of Ashburton in ye County of Devonshire. Died Oct. ye 19, 1739 in ye 47 year of his age. Also of Mary, his wife, of Dartmoor in ye County of Devonshire died Jany ye 16, 1732–3 in ye 37 yr of her age.

Langworthy was a pewterer, brazier, and iron founder in Newport. A court record in that city dated September, 1731, proves that he was in residence there at least as early as May of that year. On July 3, 1734, he was married to Mary Lawton in Trinity Church and on May 6, 1735, was admitted as a freeman of Newport. The General Assembly on July 10, 1739, voted that his account of £183 18s. 6d. for powder supplied to Fort George be allowed. His only son, Southcote, was a brazier and may have made pewter also. These few facts constitute the sum of our knowledge of Langworthy's sojourn in Newport.

None of the pewter which Langworthy made in this country has been found as yet, but several iron pots made in his shop are known to be in existence. Howard H. Cotterell illustrated in *Old Pewter* a sketch of the touch of a Lawrence Langworthy of Exeter in which the date 1719 appears. In all likelihood this was the man who later made pewter in Newport and through the courtesy of Captain A. Sutherland-Graeme I am illustrating this touch (Plate XLVII, 311) as it appears on an English plate.

JOHN FRYERS

In the *Newport Mercury* for May 6, 1776, the following obituary notice appeared.

> Died — Last se'nnight at Voluntown John Fryers, late of this place, upwards of ninety years of age.

No information has been gleaned about John Fryers's antecedents or early history, but the obituary notice would place his birth about 1685. It is unlikely that he was a native of Newport, for the name first appears in the local records when in 1735 he married Susanna Macneal in Trinity Church. In the same year John Fryers, tinman, settled out of court a suit brought against him by Elizabeth Lee, widow. At that time he would have been fifty years of age. Three years later, according to the Rhode Island Colonial Records, Fryers became a freeman of Newport. It is not until 1749 that records show his occupation as that of pewterer. In all earlier documents he is termed a tinman.

His house in Newport was advertised as 'to let' in 1769, and the natural supposition is that he moved soon afterward across the Connecticut border to Voluntown, where his death occurred.

A mug, formerly in the Myers Collection and now in the Garvan Foundation Collection at Yale University, bears the initials 'I. F.' (Plate LXIX, 585.) This may well be the work of Fryers and the touch is here attributed to that maker, with reservations.

BENJAMIN DAY

The known facts about Benjamin Day, Newport pewterer, are not many, and his story must needs be brief.

His tombstone at Newport gives his age as fifty at the time of his death in 1757, thus placing his birth about 1706. The earliest mention of the name in the annals of Newport is found in the court records for 1744, where he is described as a pewterer.

Benjamin's first wife, Ann, died in 1745, and two years later in Trinity Church he married Rebecca Shuttleworth.

When Day died intestate in 1757, Joseph Belcher, another pewterer, was one of those who took the inventory of his estate. Only a torn and faded fragment of that document now remains, carefully sewn between transparent sheets and filed away among the records of the Newport Historical Society, but we can still read that his moulds were valued at over one hundred pounds and the rest of his pewterer's equipment at approximately one hundred and fifty pounds; so there is every reason to believe that he made a great variety of shapes and that he had a business of some magnitude.

An impressive fact in the study of these inventories is that the pre-Revolutionary pewterers made a far larger range of shapes than most of the later men, and if we may judge from the few existing examples of their handicraft they were, as a group, more finished and capable workmen.

Three unusual items, all marked with the initials 'BD' in an octagon (Plate XLVII, 312 and 312a), have been attributed tentatively, and with seeming justification, to Benjamin Day. John W. Poole owns a splendid mug, or lidless tankard, with capacity of slightly more than a quart (Plate XVIII, 109); Edward E. Minor has a quart tankard with double-dome cover which is unusual in having a finial (Plate XVI, 91); moreover, the drum appears to have been hammered; and finally I have a porringer with solid handle, similar to that illustrated in Plate XIII, 70.

Arguments in favor of attributing the 'B. D.' touch to Benjamin Day are three. All three pieces were found within fifty miles of Newport; the initials would fit no other American pewterer now listed, with the possible exception of Benjamin Dolbeare of Boston, who may or may not have worked in pewter; porringers with solid handles were made, as far as now known, nowhere in New England except in Newport.

JOSEPH BELCHER, FATHER AND SON

Back in the third quarter of the eighteenth century, when Newport was one of the wealthiest and most thriving of colonial ports, one of her prosperous and prominent citizens was Joseph Belcher, brazier and pewterer.

Descended from Jeremy Belcher, who settled in Ipswich, Massachusetts, in 1635, Joseph was born in Boston, April 13, 1729, the eldest son of Joseph and Elizabeth (English) Belcher. We know nothing about his early life, but as a young man he moved to Newport, where he married Hannah Gladding on February 14, 1751. In 1756 he was admitted as a freeman of Newport, and in the same year he commanded a company in an expedition against Crown Point and served as a member of the Rhode Island Assembly.

Plate XLVII — *Newport Touches — Lawrence Langworthy, Benjamin Day, the Belchers, and David Melville*

311. Touch used by Lawrence Langworthy, Newport, 1731–1739, before he left England. From a plate in the Royal Albert Memorial Museum, Exeter, England. Courtesy of Mrs. Paul J. Franklin and Captain A. Sutherland-Graeme.

312. Touch attributed to Benjamin Day, Newport, 1744–1757. From a tankard in the collection of Edward E. Minor, Esq.

312a. Another impression of touch attributed to Day. Collection of the author.

313. Initial touch attributed to Joseph Belcher, Newport, 1769–1776, and to Joseph Belcher, Jr., Newport and New London, 1776–1785. Collection of the author.

314 and 315. Touches of Joseph Belcher, Jr., Newport and New London, 1776–1785. 314 may have been used also by his father. Collection of Edward E. Minor, Esq.

316. An early touch of David Melville, Newport, 1776–1794, the only recorded example of this touch. Collection of Dwight Blaney, Esq.

317 and 318. Another David Melville porcupine touch (almost equally rare) and his hall-marks. From a dish in the collection of the author.

PLATE XLVII

311

312

312a

313

314   315

316

317
318

PLATE XLVIII — *Newport Touches — The Melvilles*

319. Rare initial touch attributed to David Melville, Newport, 1776–1794. From a basin in the collection of the author.

320. Another rare mark used by David Melville. From the collection of S. Prescott Fay, Esq.

321. Initials cast in the support of a Melville porringer handle. No other example recorded. Formerly in the collection of the late J. B. Kerfoot, Esq.

322 and 318a. Least rare of the David Melville touches. Collection of the author.

323. Melville initial touch. Collection of the author.

324 and 318b. Probably the last touch used by David Melville. Later employed by his brothers and son. Courtesy of Mrs. Charles A. Calder.

325. Initials cast in the handle support of a porringer. Employed by David's brother, Thomas, 1793–1796, or by David's son, Thomas, 1796–1824. Collection of Dwight Blaney, Esq.

326 and 327. Touch and hall-marks of Samuel Melville, 1793–1800, and his brother, Thomas (or nephew, Thomas). From a plate in the collection of the author.

328 and 329. Touch and hall-marks of the younger Thomas Melville, 1796–1824. From a plate in the collection of the author.

PLATE XLVIII

319

320

321

322   318a

323

324   318b

325

326   327

328   329

The Rhode Island Pewterers

In all early documents Joseph Belcher is termed a brazier, but he may have combined pewter-making with his work in brass, as did many Boston braziers. On the other hand, his advertisement in the *Newport Mercury* in 1763, quoted by Charles A. Calder in *Rhode Island Pewterers*, makes no mention of pewter-making in his shop on Thames Street, and the wording of a notice that appeared in 1769 is such as to indicate that the manufacture of pewter may have been a new departure for him at that time. It is at least probable that it then took on an added importance, for John Fryers, an old man of over eighty and, as far as we know, Newport's only other pewterer in the seventeen-sixties, is supposed to have retired in that year to Voluntown, Connecticut.

In 1775 Belcher was a colonel of militia, but was superseded or retired in the following year and apparently played no part in the Revolution. In 1776 and again in 1777 he was elected a colonial deputy. When the British occupied Newport he removed with his family to Brookline, Massachusetts, where his death took place September 27, 1778. Upon the evacuation of Newport by the British the family moved back to the old home, but in July, 1781, the homestead was disposed of at sheriff's sale, to satisfy Belcher's creditors, and to make proper division of the estate between his wife and the nine surviving children in a family of fourteen.

But our story does not end here. The eldest of the children of 'Joseph Belcher, pewterer,' was his namesake, who followed the same trade. The date of Joseph Junior's birth is not found in Newport church records, but must have occurred in 1751 or 1752, for in 1772 he married Lydia Cahoone. He learned his trade in his father's shop, probably worked a few years longer with the elder Belcher, and took over the business when the latter moved to Brookline.

In Newport young Joseph did not prosper, for he was too busy skylarking to spend much time at the shop, and unfortunately for him a hard-working competitor, if we may judge from the number of existing examples, began the making of pewter at about this time; for David Melville came of age in 1776. The scarcity of Belcher pewter alone might indicate that its maker's industry was not all that might have been hoped for, but we have additional evidence in documentary form.

I quote from Book F, page 236, of the Superior Court Records for Newport. On March 6, 1784:

> Cometh Lydia Belcher of Newport in the County of Newport and preferreth her certain petition and therein sheweth forth that in June A.D. 1772 she intermarried with Joseph Belcher of said Newport, Pewterer, that since that time the said Joseph regardless of his marriage Covenant entered into with the said Lydia hath treated her with great cruelty and abuse and hath not afforded her that maintenance & Support to which she hath been entitled, and hath otherwise Wickedly & Willfully broken & violated his said Marriage Covenant — Wherefore the said Lydia prayeth the interposition of this Court and that sentence of Divorce may be pronounced dissolving the bonds of Marriage....

The sheriff was ordered by the court to serve a summons on Joseph, but reported back that the latter could not be found and that his whereabouts were unknown. The divorce was accordingly granted. And thus we know why Joseph Belcher left Newport. We had previously been unable to explain the use of a New London touch on a few of the Belcher plates.

The only further record of the man I found among Barbour's *Vital Statistics* in the State Library at Hartford. There I discovered that in August, 1788, Joseph Belcher, late of Newport, married Hannah Wood of Lyme, Connecticut. I hope that someone reading this sketch will be sufficiently curious to dig out the facts of Joseph's later career, tell us how he fared with wife No. 2, and during what years he made his New London pewter. It would be somewhat of a surprise to learn that his pewter-making career extended into the nineteenth century.

Of the elder Belcher's moulds, which weighed two hundred and fifty pounds at the time of his death, one half were left to Joseph, Junior; undoubtedly the tools and touches descended to the son also, and we shall probably never be able to distinguish the work of the two men except in the case of those items to which Joseph, Junior, added the 'N. London' mark (Plate XLVII, 315).

Belcher pewter is of good quality and remains exceedingly rare. No new shapes have been found since J. B. Kerfoot's *American Pewter* was published, and only a few additional pieces have come to light. The existing forms of record are 8-inch plates, 13- and 13¼-inch deep dishes, 4- and 5-inch porringers with open handle, 5- and 5¼-inch porringers with solid handle, and one quart basin. A 4-inch porringer with unusual handle of effective design is illustrated in Plate XII, 62.

DAVID MELVILLE

In the year 1691 the history of the Melville family in America commences with the arrival of David Melville at Barnstable, Massachusetts. He soon moved to Eastham and finally to Boston, where he married a daughter of Doctor Willard, President of Harvard College. Early in the eighteenth century his two sons left for Newport. The members of the family in whom we are interested were descended from Thomas, who was admitted as a freeman of Newport in 1719 and styled a housewright.

The first Melville to work in pewter was David, born in 1755. Just as his apprenticeship must have been drawing to a close, the British occupied Newport, partially destroying the town. Melville secured a commission as an ensign in Captain Lemuel Bailey's company of Colonel Lippitt's Rhode Island regiment, but the extent or nature of his service I have not been able to learn. His release from the army on account of illness, countersigned by General Charles Lee, was kept in the family for nearly one hundred and fifty years and is now preserved in the Newport Historical Society files. In 1779 the British withdrew from Newport, and presumably Melville then returned, opened his shop on Thames Street, and married. In 1783 he advertised the removal of his shop to 'Long-Wharf.' His brief business career was devoted to pewter-making, and he died at the early age of thirty-seven, November 22, 1793.

The inventory of David Melville's shop is given in great detail. Though too lengthy to include here, it does give such a clear picture of a pewterer's equipment at the close of the eighteenth century that I am showing it in an appendix at the end of the book. A study of that paper proves that Melville was equipped to make five sizes of flatware (exclusive of basins), ranging from a platter — undoubtedly his 14-inch size — to a butter plate, basins in three sizes (with handles if so desired), five porringer sizes from the beer-pint to the gill, quart, and pint mugs, tablespoons, and teaspoons. A point worth mentioning, already confirmed by existing pewter, is that he could offer for the larger porringers either 'plain' or 'flowered' handles. Melville pint basins, basins with handles, gill and half-pint porringers, pint mugs, and spoons are still among the missing forms made by this pewterer. The 14-inch platter seems to have been a size peculiar to the Melvilles. I have never found one bearing any other American touch. Flatware in the following sizes has been found bearing David Melville's touches, $6\frac{1}{8}$, $8\frac{1}{4}$, $8\frac{1}{2}$, $8\frac{7}{8}$, $12\frac{3}{16}$, and 14 inches; also basins of $3\frac{3}{4}$, 8, and $8\frac{7}{8}$ inches. The quality and finish of this man's product are well above the average, and that he had a large trade and was prospering when death overtook him is evidenced not only by the number of surviving examples, but also by the fact that he owned three slaves when the first census was taken in 1790.

David Melville had a great variety of touches. Plate XLVIII, 318, 322, and 324, are not uncommon, but the others are extreme rarities. Plate XLVII, 316 and 317, and Plate XLVIII, 319, 320, and 323, have never before been shown: number 323, taken from a $5\frac{1}{2}$-inch porringer, is so typical of Rhode Island marks that we can be almost certain of its correct attribution to Melville; number 319 is from an $8\frac{7}{8}$-inch basin which, like many Rhode Island basins, is abnormally deep for its diameter. This particular basin is unusual also in the design of the rim. An identical basin, formerly owned by Louis G. Myers, is impressed with one of David Melville's known large touches. There can be no doubt, therefore, of the correct attribution of the newly discovered mark, which resembles Belcher's initial touch (Plate XLVII, 313), particularly in the use of the dots.

Unfortunately no piece of pewter bearing any of the above marks can be positively set down as the work of David, for, as we shall see in a later sketch, his brothers used his moulds and even his touches.

SAMUEL AND THOMAS MELVILLE

Samuel and Thomas Melville Hereby informe the Public that they carry on the Pewterers' Business in the Shop belonging to Mrs. Carr, at the Corner of the Ferry Wharf; where they make Pewter-Ware, Brass and Leaden Weights. Mend Pewter, Brass and Copper Kettles. They also work in the Plumbers Business such as, Hawser, Scupper and Deep-Sea Leads &.&.

They also give cash for old Pewter, Brass, Copper and Lead.

Those who favor them with their Custom will meet with the strictest attention to their Commands and the smallest Favours gratefully acknowledged.

The above notice appeared in the *Newport Mercury* for December 31, 1793, just five weeks after David Melville's death. Who were Samuel and Thomas Melville? Assuredly not David's sons as has been suggested, for he was but thirty-seven years old when he died. There can be little doubt now that they were younger brothers who had been working in David's shop.

Although Newport vital records furnish no information whatever about the births or baptisms of these brothers, it was my good fortune recently to have word from Miss Susan B. Franklin, a descendant through another line of the Melville family, who kindly sent me a copy of an unpublished Melville family history, compiled about 1840 by another David Melville, a distant relation of the pewterers. According to his records, David, Samuel, and Thomas, children of Thomas and Elizabeth (Yeats) Melville, were born in 1755, 1760, and 1764 respectively.

In the year 1785 Samuel married Rhoda Spooner in the First Baptist Church and, when the first census was taken in 1790, both Samuel and Thomas were living on 'the Hill' near David, the former with a wife and three small children, and Thomas apparently single.

My supposition is that immediately after David's death his younger brothers took over his business, even to the extent of using the dies which bore his name or initials. This belief is based on the existence of a number of porringers impressed on the upper surface of the handle with David's touches, but bearing the initials 'S. M.' or 'T. M.' cast in the handle or handle support.

In the *Newport Mercury* for October 14, 1800, another Melville advertisement appeared:

> Samuel and Thomas Melville — Pewterers — Inform their Friends and the Public at Large that they have removed from their shop on the Hill, to one on the Long Wharf, directly opposite the Brick Market, where may be had Pewter of all kinds, of a good quality, and as low as can be purchased in the State.
>
> Likewise Hawse-Leads and Scuppers of any dimentions at the shortest notice; Deep-Sea Leads and Lead Weights.

It would seem apparent from a reading of this notice in conjunction with the advertisement of 1793 that Samuel and Thomas worked at three different locations, first in Mrs. Carr's shop on the Wharf, then up on 'the Hill' where they lived, and finally on the Wharf opposite the Brick Yard. But the explanation is not so simple as that, for if we may believe the Melville historian, the Thomas Melville of this sketch died in 1796, four years before the second advertisement appeared. If the family history compiled in 1840 was correct — I have been unable to verify Thomas's date of death in other existing records — there were two Samuel-and-Thomas partnerships. The first, 1793–1796, was a combination of David's brothers; the second, *c.* 1799–1800, was a merger of Samuel's interest in the earlier shop with that of his nephew Thomas, David's son (of whom more later).

From the Newport court records we learn the occasion for Samuel's first departure from the Wharf. In 1799 the Widow Carr had recourse to the courts to collect from him fifteen months' back rent which he admitted owing. Presumably she had her unsatisfactory tenant evicted and he, no doubt, then threw in his lot with his nephew Thomas.

After 1800 the curtain drops on Samuel's activities. There is no headstone for either Samuel or his brother Thomas in the family plot in the cemetery and no probate records for either man are on file in Newport.

In addition to the Melville touches previously described, there is an anchor touch and a set of so-called hall-marks used by S. and T. Melville. These touches (Plate XLVIII, 326 and 327), are found on $8\frac{7}{8}$-inch basins and on flatware measuring $7\frac{11}{16}$, 8, $8\frac{5}{8}$, and 12 inches. The plate dimensions vary somewhat from those bearing David Melville's marks. I believe, therefore, that the brothers made use of David's moulds for a short time only and that, in anticipation of the acquisition by David's son of his father's equipment, they found it necessary to purchase moulds of their own.

DAVID MELVILLE'S SONS

The Melville history now returns to David's house on 'the Hill.' The pewterer's will contained the following pertinent clause:

> I give and bequeath to my three sons, Thomas, Andrew and William and to the child or children with which my wife is now pregnant should it be a male all my Pewter-making tools, implements and apurtenances equally to be divided between them as they shall severally arrive to lawful age, that is to say if each of my sons and that which may be born a son should learn the Pewterer's trade. . . .

A few months after David's death his widow followed him to the grave, and the post-humous son David, Junior, lived but a short time longer. Of the six remaining children, the three boys all grew to manhood and all three followed, for a period at least, the trade of their father.

The eldest, Thomas, was born in 1779, and on January 12, 1796, his first advertisement appeared before he was seventeen years of age:

> Thomas Melville Informs the Public at large that he now carries on the Pewterers Business, in all its Various Branches; where may be had Pewter of all Kinds, Lead Weights & Also The Plumbing Business such as making Hawse-Leads, Scuppers, Deep-Sea Leads & &.
>
> He would be happy to serve his Customers and gratefully acknowledges their Favours. Cash, or any of the above, Wares, given for old Pewter, Lead, Brass & c.
>
> N.B. — He now carries on The Business at the House and Shop just above the Church on the Hill, formally occupied by his Father, David Melville, deceased.

Here we have evidence that the old laws of apprenticeship were no longer enforced — a youth of seventeen advertising himself as a full-fledged pewterer. With a family of five younger brothers and sisters depending upon him for support, it is much to his credit that he should have shouldered the responsibility at such an early date.

As pointed out in the story of Samuel and Thomas Melville, David's son Thomas may have worked with his uncle Samuel for a few months in 1799 and 1800, probably not longer. In 1800 Thomas Melville married Clarissa Dean of Taunton. Records of real estate transactions and minor civil suits (in which he invariably played the rôle of defendant) describe him as a pewterer right up to the time of his death, November 24, 1824. He apparently never prospered and was frequently running afoul of the courts.

Only just recently have we been able to identify what is believed to be this man's work. An 8⅞-inch plate has turned up with a touch once thought to have been David's, but here accompanied by a partly obliterated set of hall-marks, showing the initials 'T. M.' (Plate XLVIII, 328, 329). The same touch is found also on 8¼-inch plates and on footed cup-shaped beakers.

Two more pewter-making Melvilles remain, neither of them mentioned in any previous list of American pewterers. Both Andrew and William, David's second and third sons, elected to follow their father's trade.

Andrew Melville had much the same sort of record, in court and out, as his brother Thomas. He was born in 1782, and up to 1810 is termed a pewterer in existing records. After that time he tried his hand at various businesses with indifferent success. He died February 3, 1851.

William L. Melville, the last pewterer of the family, was born in Newport in 1786. For a few years he worked at pewter-making, but, as in the case of Andrew, his identity must have been merged in that of the older brother, Thomas. I should be grateful for any evidence that Andrew or William ever had pewter shops or touches of their own. My belief is that when the house and shop, which had been built by David, were sold in 1810 by his children, Thomas purchased outright his brothers' interests in the tools and moulds which they had jointly owned. In any event, William, described up to that date as a pewterer, is afterward called a tinplate worker. One Newport historian states that William Melville had in his day the largest tin-working shop in the town. His death occurred March 2, 1857.

SAMUEL HAMLIN AND SAMUEL E. HAMLIN

Descended from Giles Hamlin, one of the earliest settlers of Middletown, Connecticut, Samuel Hamlin, son of Charles and Ann (Hosmer), was born in that town September 9, 1746. He is supposed to have been trained in the shop of Thomas Danforth, Second. In 1771 he married Thankful Ely, moved soon afterward to Providence, and set up in business at the head of Long Wharf as a pewterer, brazier, and coppersmith. In 1774 he took in as a partner his brother-in-law, Gershom Jones, a business arrangement which continued until 1781. Jones was also a brazier as well as a pewterer, and it is rather interesting to note that chests of drawers have been found in Rhode Island with brasses the bails of which are impressed with the letters 'H. J.,' attributed to the partnership of Hamlin and Jones. Perhaps some day we shall find pewter that bears a touch combining both names. At least it is something for which we should be on the lookout.

When Thomas Danforth, Second, died in 1782, his son Joseph, administrator of the estate, made a trip to Providence to secure some of his father's moulds which Hamlin had been using — a fact which supports the belief that Hamlin had worked for Danforth.

During at least two years of the Revolution, 1778 and 1779, Hamlin served his country as a lieutenant in Captain Peck's company of the First Rhode Island Regiment.

Samuel Hamlin died insolvent April 1, 1801. One son, William, was an engraver of at least local prominence, while another, Samuel Ely Hamlin, carried on his father's business.

Samuel Ely Hamlin was born at Providence in 1774. He apparently worked in his father's shop until the latter's death, continuing the business thereafter even to the extent of using his father's touches. It is therefore impossible now to distinguish, in some instances, between the work of the father and that of the son.

In 1807 Hamlin, the younger, 'informed the Public' through the *Providence Gazette* that he carried 'a good assortment of Pewter Ware, Superior to any imported, except from London.' He advertised 'Platters, Plates, Basins and Porringers of different sizes, Quart and Pint Pots, Soup Ladles, Tumblers and sundry other articles. Also at retail Bed Pans and Teapots of different sizes and kinds, Hard Metal, Iron and pewter spoons and various Articles in the Brass Line' in his shop 'nearly opposite the Episcopalian Church, next door North, Mr. Henry Russell.' On July 27, 1811, although still offering pewter in various forms, he announced also the manufacture of 'Brittania Metal' teapots and tumblers. Strangely, it seems, none of these teapots is known to have survived, and that in spite of the fact that Hamlin is supposed to have worked almost to the close of the britannia period. For over fifty years he had a shop on Main Street and after 1841 is listed only as a maker of britannia. Nothing that I have seen touched with his mark is of thin metal or of a design that could not have been made prior to 1820.

Of the nine Hamlin touches here illustrated, three (Plate XLIX, 332, 335, and 338) are shown for the first time. Although some of the marks of Hamlin, Senior, may have been used after his death by his son, there can be little doubt that number 332 was discarded soon after the Revolution. Number 334 shows thirteen stars above the eagle, which dates the touch about 1790. If, as believed, the number of stars in the touch is significant, that mark was superseded about 1795 by number 336. Probably both of the other eagles, and certainly the small name-touch, were marks of the younger man exclusively. There is ground for believing that all other Hamlin touches were employed first by the father and later by the son.

Hamlin porringers are more frequently found than those of any other identified American maker. In fact, the rarity of Hamlin plates as compared with porringers is amazing. Dishes are not uncommon, but until comparatively recently the existence of plates of this maker had not been verified. The range of flatware as now established seems almost complete with the probable exception of butter plates. The ascending scale of sizes runs as follows: 8-inch flat, 9¼-inch smooth rim flat, and deep dishes of 11½, 13, 13¼, 13½, 14, 14¾, and 15 inches. It is a curious fact that most of the Hamlin 8-inch plates are marked in the well rather than on the bottom, as we should have expected. Why this custom, discarded in England several generations earlier, should have been revived by Hamlin and then applied to but one size of flatware is difficult to fathom. Pint and quart basins, pint and quart mugs, porringers from 4 to 5½ inches in diameter, small beakers, and doll-size basins make up the remainder of the known Hamlin output. I have not seen any of the eagle touches on plates, dishes, or mugs.

Hamlin pewter is of fine quality, and we honor the younger man for maintaining the standard of his father right through the britannia period. His death did not occur until April 14, 1864, when he had almost reached his eighty-ninth milestone.

GERSHOM JONES

Gershom Jones was born in Somers, Connecticut, in 1751, the son of Ephraim and Elizabeth Jones. He is said to have 'served his time with a coppersmith in Norwich,' and the striking similarity of his early touch to that of John Danforth of Norwich leaves little doubt as to the source of his training. He moved to Providence at the age of twenty-one, was married September 25, 1774, to Desire Ely of Middletown, Connecticut, and was taken into partnership in that year by his brother-in-law, Samuel Hamlin, who had a shop on Long Wharf, Providence.

During the early years of the Revolution, Hamlin was in the Continental Army, and upon his return in 1780 Jones obtained a commission as lieutenant in the Providence United Train of Artillery. He was promoted to a captaincy in 1781, and in 1790 we find him a major, a position that he held until 1794.

Jones's absence in the army was probably largely responsible for his falling out with his partner, Samuel Hamlin, in 1781, and for the suit for two thousand pounds which he instituted against Hamlin. In December of that year, through his attorneys, 'Gershom Jones of Providence, Rhode Island, Pewterer and Brazier Complains against Samuel Hamlin of said Providence, Yeoman, alias Pewterer and Brazier, in the Custody of the Sheriff in an Action of the Case for the Recovery of the Sum of £799 2s. 2d. 3 farthings' and other sums. The use of the words 'alias' is a nice touch, indicative of the state of mind of the man who has reached the 'I'll sue him' stage.

Jones, it seems, had advanced monies to Hamlin which the latter refused repeatedly to repay, stating that they were lent not to him personally but as capital needed in the business. The truth of the matter probably is that during Jones's absence in the army Hamlin was unsuccessful in conducting the business, and that Jones blamed him entirely for circumstances some of which, on account of the war, were beyond Hamlin's control. The decision was placed in the hands of three referees, who adjudged that Hamlin should pay the Captain £100 15s. and costs of 'sute.'

The Rhode Island Pewterers

In 1784 Jones advertised 'at the sign of the Pewter Platter near Mr. Jacob Whitman's Hay Scales.' Later he moved his shop to the corner of Westminster and Pleasant Streets, and in 1806 took into partnership with him his sons, James and Samuel. A few months later the copartnership of Gershom Jones and Sons was dissolved, and thereafter the older man carried on alone the making of pewter, while the boys set up as coppersmiths, founders, and plumbers.

Major Jones was one of the charter members of the Providence Association of Mechanics and Manufacturers and for two years was its vice-president. Writing in 1860, E. M. Stone said of him:

> Major Jones was a large, portly man, of active habits, and interested himself in the passing events of the day. He was fond of music, and persons still living who attended Rev. Dr. Hitchcock's Meeting in the recently demolished old Town House, remember the resonance of his deep voice. . . . His funeral was attended by his Masonic brethren of various lodges, the Mechanics Association, and many other of his fellow citizens.

Providence in 1800 must have still been too small to support two pewtering establishments, much less three. The result was that Hamlin, Jones, and Job Danforth all died insolvent. Jones's inventory, and probably his trade, was greater than that of Hamlin, Senior, but not sufficient to offset his debts. It included 47 plates and basins, 30 wine-pint porringers, 6 quart pots, and 2 pint pots. I have seen but two quart mugs ('pots' as they are termed in the inventory) bearing a Jones touch, no pint mugs, and no basins. His plates have been found in 8-inch, $8\frac{3}{16}$-inch, $8\frac{5}{16}$-inch, and $9\frac{1}{8}$-inch diameters, platters or deep dishes of diameters of $13\frac{1}{2}$, $14\frac{1}{4}$, and 15 inches. The known porringer sizes are $4\frac{1}{4}$, 5, $5\frac{3}{8}$, and $5\frac{1}{2}$ inches in diameter.

Worthy of comment is the crudity of the touches (Plate L, 339 to 345), which nevertheless seem to exemplify the vigor and individuality of this soldier of the Revolution.

Gershom Jones died May 6, 1809. His obituary notice in the *Providence Gazette* was as follows:

> The character of the deceased, in the varied lights of the friend, the husband and the parent, was peculiarly endearing. His friends will long regret the loss of one whose kindness and hospitality they had so often enjoyed.

Soon after the Major's death his sons moved away from Providence. James Green Jones, who was born in Providence October 23, 1782, is listed as a coppersmith at various addresses in New York from 1812 until his death May 9, 1820. Samuel Ely Jones, a year younger, was recorded as a coppersmith in Utica's earliest directory, that of 1817. He died there April 4 of that year. I have found no proof that either of the younger Joneses made pewter in a shop of his own.

WILLIAM BILLINGS AND JOB DANFORTH, JUNIOR

William Billings was born, probably in Newport, in 1768, a date determined by his age at time of death.

[98]

Josiah Keene

Our first and most vivid impression of him is furnished by the naïvely delightful newspaper announcement of the opening of his first shop in 1791:

> William Billings, Pewterer, Coppersmith and Brazier. In the Main Street, Providence, near Messieurs Joseph and William Russell Store, and directly opposite Col. Knight Dexter.
> Makes and sells all kinds of Pewter Ware warranted as good as any made in town or country.
> Young in life and having a desire to be employed as well as to please, he flatters himself that those gentlemen who wish to promote industry and the young, will honor him with their commands, which will be gratefully acknowledged and attended with despatch and fidelity.

On November 29, 1799, Billings married Amy Burr in the First Congregational Society Church, Providence. A year earlier he had announced the formation of a partnership with Job Danforth, Junior, in a shop 'a few doors North of the Baptist Meeting House'; but the association was of short duration, for death called Danforth on September 5, 1801. For a few years longer Billings worked alone, and on April 12, 1806, his shop was offered for sale. He died in Pawtucket, Rhode Island, June 19, 1813.

Billings's pewter, still comparatively rare and confined to plates, platters, and porringers, is of good quality. His flatware ranges in diameter from $7\frac{7}{8}$ to 15 inches, and the porringers have been found in the beer-pint, wine-pint, and half-pint sizes. His marks are illustrated on Plate L.

Job Danforth, Junior, was a member of that largest of all pewtering clans, the Danforths of Connecticut, whose ancestors had settled at Taunton, Massachusetts, in the seventeenth century. This man's father, Job, born at Taunton, was a nephew of the first pewter-making Danforth, Thomas of Taunton and Norwich. Job, Junior, was born in Providence in 1774 and, immediately after setting up in business with Billings, he married Miss Sally Barse of Boston. He died at the early age of twenty-seven, intestate and insolvent. We know of no pewter made by Job Danforth, and it is possible that the touches of the senior partner were used on all pewter that was turned out by the firm.

JOSIAH KEENE

Josiah Keene, son of Charles and Anna (Hunt) Keene, was born in 1778 or 1779. The date is based on his age at the time of death as shown in Rhode Island Vital Records.

Keene was essentially a coppersmith and brass-founder, but for a few years early in life he made pewter also. Charles A. Calder reproduced in *Rhode Island Pewterers* an advertisement that was taken from an October, 1802, issue of the *Providence Gazette* in which Keene announces that he continues to carry on the pewterer's business, at his shop 'directly opposite Isaac Everleth and Sons Tobacco Manufactory.' But in all public documents he is termed a coppersmith or founder, and after his early business years pewtering, if continued at all, must have been essentially a sideline.

Louis G. Myers's *Notes* contain a photograph of a $5\frac{3}{8}$-inch porringer marked 'I. K.,' here illustrated again (Plate L, 349), that is identical in construction and design with other Rhode Island porringers and can, without hesitation, be attributed to this maker. One of the most recent discoveries of hitherto unlisted touches is the partially obliterated mark shown in Plate L, 348, as photographed from an 8¼-inch plate in the possession of Doctor Madelaine R. Brown. There can be little question that an unmarred impression would have shown the maker's name to have been Josiah Keene.

One of Calder's illustrations is of a receipt from Josiah Keene for moulds that he sold in 1817 to William Calder, pewterer. As a brazier and founder Keene would naturally have made pewterers' moulds, but it is my belief that the receipt in question was for moulds in which he had cast his own pewter; that he had had little if any use for them for several years preceding; and that he had finally decided to sell his pewter-making equipment. This opinion is strengthened by the wording of the bill. One mould and one mould only, and that the last on the list, is specifically called 'new.' Had they all been made on order for Calder, the word would hardly have been used where it was. It is worth noting that our one Keene plate is identical in all its proportions with the 8¼-inch plates of William Calder.

Inventory lists or receipts such as this are most valuable to us when they name the various moulds. In that way we can determine what shapes were regularly made and stocked. This particular receipt lists a 'Butter-plate Mould.' Who can report the existence of a butter plate made by either Josiah Keene or William Calder?

Almost all of the Rhode Island pewterers not only served in the state militia, but held commissions therein, and Josiah Keene was no exception. As early as 1809, when only thirty-one, he held the rank of major in the Second Regiment.

Keene was twice married, first to Miss Abby Hall at Providence February 9, 1808, and secondly to Miss Ann W. Wilkinson, also at Providence, May 25, 1830. Two daughters, Anna and Harriet, died before coming of age, and at least two sons, Charles L. and Stephen S., grew to manhood. Keene seems to have retired from the founder's business about 1838, but lived on until June 5, 1868, when he died at the age of eighty-nine.

WILLIAM CALDER OF PROVIDENCE

William Calder, last of the early Rhode Island pewterers, was descended from a William Calder who was born at Aberdeen, Scotland, in 1690 and settled in Boston prior to 1732.

The pewterer was born in Providence July 18, 1792, and, as a boy, went to work for Samuel E. Hamlin. When his apprenticeship was completed, he journeyed to Philadelphia, where, for about a year, he presumably plied his trade in one of the local pewter-making establishments. By 1817 or earlier he had returned to Providence and in that year he purchased a set of moulds from Josiah Keene and opened a shop of his own.

William Calder of Providence

There on Main Street, opposite Smith Street, near-by the shop of his old master, Hamlin, William Calder was turning out his wares for almost forty years.

He married, first, Eliza Treadwell Spencer September 23, 1818, and second, Mary Whitmarsh on August 23, 1829.

He was a founder of the First Universalist Church of Providence and a captain of a local fire company. His death occurred December 5, 1856.

Charles A. Calder tells us that his grandfather was 'a very quiet, stately old gentleman,' and from another source we learn that he was a great reader, unusually well-informed and a convincing arguer. He also seems to have been conservatism itself, for he never advertised and in his long career is known to have used but three touches.

When Calder set up in business he had moulds for the manufacture of eight- and nine-inch plates, butter plates, quart pots, and pint, wine-pint, and half-pint porringers. As time passed he equipped himself to manufacture many other forms. From his day book (now owned by Mrs. Charles A. Calder), in which record was kept of business transactions from 1826 until 1838, we learn not alone the shapes which the pewterer made, but we gain a glimpse therefrom of the changing trends in pewter fashions. Doctor Percy E. Raymond made a careful study of the entries and presented his observations thereon at a meeting of the Pewter Collectors' Club. To him I am indebted for the substance of the comments which follow.

The variety of Calder forms is great, and it is, of course, probable that prior to 1826 and after 1838 he made other shapes not recorded in the day book. In addition to the articles for which moulds were purchased in 1817, the following forms appear among the entries: 10-, 11-, and 12-inch 'plates,' platters (probably 15-inch); pint, quart, three-pint, and two-quart basins; gill and three-gill porringers; pint, and two-quart pots; pewter, britannia, 'best' and 'no. 2' tumblers; teaspoons and tablespoons of both pewter and britannia; ladles of pewter and block tin; teapots and coffee-pots of several designs and sizes, tea 'earnes,' coffee biggins, and percolators; sugar bowls and creamers; flagons, christening bowls, communion basins, and fonts; handled, britannia, church, and molasses cups; bottles and nursing-bottles; plain, nurse, and britannia lamps; candlesticks, tinder-boxes, shaving-boxes, quart pitchers, gravy dishes, funnels, molasses gates, skimmers, syringes in two sizes, urinals, spindle caps, and trumpets (probably ear trumpets).

The gross sales of the shop in 1826 amounted to $1174.68. Although we have no evidence that Calder made teapots in 1817, over sixty per cent of his output in 1826 was accounted for by such articles. The falling off in demand for what had been his 'best sellers' a few years earlier — a change which was taking place at that time throughout the country — is exemplified by the records of plate and porringer sales. Only seven per cent of his business in 1826 was in plates and but thirteen per cent in porringers.

The day book disclosed that britannia lamps were made as early as 1826; that no water pitchers (definitely a late form) were manufactured before 1834; and that tumblers in 1838 outstripped even teapots in numbers sold. 'Tumblers,' I take it, are what we are accustomed to term small beakers.

PLATE XLIX — *Providence Touches — The Hamlins*

330 and 331. Name-touch and hall-marks of Samuel Hamlin, Providence, 1771–1801. Probably used later by his son, Samuel E. Hamlin, 1801–1856. Collection of Edward E. Minor, Esq.

332. The initial touch of the elder Hamlin. Collection of Charles F. Hutchins, Esq.

330a and 333. The combination of touches used on hard metal plates by both Samuel Hamlins. Collection of the author.

334. Hamlin eagle. Probably the earliest of the Hamlin eagle touches. Collection of Albert H. Good, Esq.

335. Late name-touch. Probably used only by the younger Hamlin after 1820. Collection of Mrs. J. Insley Blair.

336. Probably second of the Hamlin eagle touches. First used in 1794 or 1795. Collection of the author.

337. Another eagle used probably only by Samuel E. Hamlin after 1800. Collection of Edward E. Minor, Esq.

338. Probably last and certainly rarest of the Hamlin eagles. Collection of Mr. and Mrs. Richard S. Quigley.

PLATE XLIX

330
331

332

330 a
333

334

335

336

337

338

PLATE L — *Providence Touches — Gershom Jones, William Billings, Josiah Keene, and William Calder*

339. Early touch of Major Gershom Jones, Providence, Rhode Island, 1774–1809. Collection of Charles K. Davis, Esq.

339a. Another impression of 339. Collection of Mrs. Stephen S. FitzGerald.

340. Jones's early hall-marks, 1774–*c.* 1785. Reproduced from *American Pewter* through the courtesy of the late Mrs. J. B. Kerfoot.

341. Jones's early initial touch. Collection of the author.

342, 343, and 344. Post-Revolutionary touches and hall-marks used by Jones. Collection of Charles F. Hutchins, Esq.

342a and 343a. Other impressions of 342 and 343. Collection of Charles F. Hutchins, Esq.

345. Another late touch, usually found only on large dishes in conjunction with 342, 343, and 344. Collection of the author.

346. The initial touch of William Billings, Providence, 1791–1806. Collection of the author.

347. Billings's normal touch, usually impressed three times on each piece. Collection of John W. Poole, Esq.

348. Touch attributed to Josiah Keene, Providence, 1801–1817. The only known example of this touch. From a plate in the collection of Dr. Madelaine R. Brown.

349. Touch attributed to Josiah Keene, Providence, 1801–1817. The only known example of this mark. Courtesy of the Mabel Brady Garvan Collection, Gallery of Fine Arts, Yale University.

350. The normal touch of William Calder, Providence, 1817–1856. Collection of the author.

351. Calder's later name-touch. Collection of Albert H. Good, Esq.

PLATE L

339

339a

340

341

342a

343a

342

344

343

345

346

347

348

349

351

350

The word 'britannia' was used but sparingly in Calder's early entries, frequently in 1828 and 1829, and distinctions between pewter and britannia were seldom made after 1830. Professor Raymond undoubtedly inferred correctly that after the latter date the entire product of the shop was britannia. For those who are accustomed to 'raise the eyebrow' at britannia, it is worth noting that vessels made of that alloy commanded a premium over common pewter articles of like form.

During the day-book years Calder did not record the names of any apprentices, but we do find that he employed Elkins Leslie as a journeyman for a few months in 1827 and 1828, and during the summer of 1829 he paid Charles Plumly fifteen dollars a month for making pewter. Both Leslie and Plumly, as we shall learn later, had previously worked in Philadelphia.

Surviving Calder forms of which I have record are 8-inch plates, 11-inch deep dishes, pint and quart pots; quart and two-quart basins; pint, three-gill, and half-pint porringers; flagons and chalices; teapots and lamps of various designs; small beakers, one coffee percolator, and one pair of candlesticks.

In addition to the eagle touch (Plate L, 350), Calder had a small name-in-rectangle mark (number 351) which probably supplanted the eagle mark about 1825 or soon thereafter. The diminutive Providence intaglio mark is found only on very late forms (see volume II, page 99).

THE PEWTERERS OF
THE CONNECTICUT VALLEY

THE story of pewter-making in Connecticut is virtually the story of the Danforths, their partners, and their apprentices. It may be and probably is true that pewter was made in the colony before the first Thomas Danforth moved from Taunton, Massachusetts, to Norwich, Connecticut, in 1733, but if there were pewterers who antedated him, their records are still to be found.

We shall start, then, with Thomas Danforth of Norwich, the sire of the largest and, in some respects, the most interesting group of pewterers that America ever produced. At least twelve and possibly fourteen men of that name followed the trade, and when we add the three Boardmans and Otis Williams, who were sons of Danforth women, we have a race of pewterers, extending through five generations, that no other family on this side of the Atlantic ever approached in number. But they themselves were only the nucleus — though a large one — of the Connecticut pewter industry. The Danforths trained a legion of men who opened shops as far west as Buffalo and as far south as Augusta, Georgia. In fact, they turned out pewterers faster than Connecticut could absorb them, and before the day of the eight-inch plate had passed, offshoots of the Middletown nursery had blossomed in at least nine of the original thirteen states. Hamlin and Jones had set up in Providence, where they trained a whole school of Rhode Island makers; Samuel Pierce moved to Greenfield, Massachusetts; Ebenezer Southmayd worked in Castleton, Vermont; the third Thomas Danforth and B. Barns demonstrated to staid old Philadelphia the meaning of quantity production; Samuel Kilbourn and S. Griswold opened shops in Baltimore; Otis Williams in Buffalo, New York; Joseph Danforth, Junior, in Richmond, Virginia; Jacob Eggleston, Jehiel Johnson, and William Nott in Fayetteville, North Carolina; and Giles Griswold, John North, and Adna Rowe in Augusta, Georgia.

It is not solely in their numerical strength, though, that the Danforths stand out. They made pewter at an even more amazing rate than they did pewterers; it would be no exaggeration to say that over seventy-five per cent of all our marked American pewter is the work of natives of Connecticut. Chance alone could never explain the unduly large proportion of existing Connecticut pewter. The answer lies in the makeup of the men themselves.

The Connecticut Yankees seem to have been traders by instinct; what may be said here about the pewterers or tinsmiths applies with equal force to the clock-makers, button manufacturers, braziers, etc. About 1740 two brothers named Pattison came from Ireland to this country and settled in Berlin, Connecticut. After they had 'saturated' the near-by towns with their wares, they hired carts and horses and peddled their surplus stock far beyond the borders of the colony. Perhaps the Pattisons did not introduce into this country the peddler method of extending sales; it is even possible that the Danforths themselves were the first to use it; but, regardless of what individual or industry originated this method of selling on our side of the Atlantic, we must give credit to Thomas Danforth of Middletown and his sons for their early use of the peddler's cart. They were wide-awake merchandisers as well as pewterers, worthy forerunners of the twentieth-century business 'go-getter.' By the time of the Revolution, Connecticut peddlers were carrying tin and pewter to every little hamlet east of the Alleghenies, and the Middletown Danforths were building up a business probably far beyond anything ever dreamed of by old Thomas of Norwich.

Later this sales service was to be carried one step further by the Boardmans, who opened up branch offices in New York and Philadelphia — early exponents, as J. B. Kerfoot points out, of the chain-store system.

And so if one is hunting for Connecticut pewter, he is likely to meet with almost as much success by combing Pennsylvania or Maryland, for instance, as by searching in the state where it was made.

What of the metal itself that the pewterers of Connecticut fashioned? Of the early work we know little or nothing It is questionable whether a single existing example can be proved to be pre-Revolutionary. Since Thomas Danforth, Second, died just as peace was dawning, it seems reasonable to believe that most of his plates antedate the war, but that is mere surmise. All the other makers whose pewter survives worked for a few years at least after the Revolution. There is no basis, therefore, for a consideration of any earlier forms that may have been made.

We can say, however, that an amazingly large number of Connecticut pieces manufactured between 1775 and 1790 are still in existence, perhaps more than the combined total of Massachusetts, New York, and Pennsylvania for the same period. Beginning, then, with the War of the Revolution, and ending only with the passing of pewter-making as an industry, we have a great many examples by which to judge the makers.

Probably no other group of American pewterers has left us a greater variety of forms. We have marked Connecticut inkwells, tankards, beakers, mugs, porringers, porringer-basins, two-handled porringers, sugar bowls, teapots, christening bowls, and flagons, as well as plates, dishes, and basins in many sizes. As might be expected, the bulk of the product was flatware. The plates are almost never as shallow as those of Boston or Newport, and the shallow dish or platter in the 15-inch size was apparently never made in the colony. The largest size of flatware, a form made by almost every Connecticut pewterer, was the 13-inch or 13¼-inch deep dish.

Generally speaking, the metal was good, though not always of the best, and the quality of the workmanship and finish varied with the individual maker. Men such as Thomas Danforth, Third, maintained a uniformly high standard in spite of large production, and if at times some of his apprentices or relatives seem to have sacrificed quality to quantity, let us remember that we of the twentieth century are hardly in a position to criticize those hard-working Yankee craftsmen, early exponents of the theory of mass production.

THOMAS DANFORTH, FIRST

The earliest of the known Connecticut pewterers, the first Thomas Danforth, opened a shop at Norwich in 1733. Himself a pewterer, he was to become father, grandfather, great-grandfather, and great-great-grandfather of men who followed the same trade.

His descent is traced from Nicholas Danforth, who settled at Cambridge, Massachusetts, in 1634. Thomas, ninth of the Reverend Samuel Danforth's fourteen children, was born in Taunton, Massachusetts, May 22, 1703. We do not know where his apprenticeship was served, but he opened a brazier's and pewterer's shop in Taunton, and in that town he married Sarah Leonard, November 6, 1730. In the following year the first of his fourteen children was born. This child, Thomas, and a younger brother, John, were the Danforth pewterers of the second generation. In 1733 Thomas Danforth moved across the Connecticut border to Norwich. After the death of his first wife he married Hannah Hall in 1742 and joined the First Congregationalist Church of Norwich. When he finally retired from business, presumably in 1773, his son John carried on the work of the shop.

Thomas Danforth died at Norwich in 1786. His inventory amounted to three hundred pounds, but his debts more than offset these small assets. The inventory included a few items of a pewterer's stock in trade, among them a 'dial mould.' This was probably, as Louis G. Myers suggests, a mould for sundials. Such forms are still found occasionally, but I have record of only one that was impressed with the maker's mark. This was not a standard shape made by all pewterers, and its presence in the inventory may indicate that Danforth in his day could have supplied his customers with a large variety of forms. Long before his death he had undoubtedly sold, or otherwise conveyed, to his son John the major portion of his shop equipment.

It may surprise some readers to be told at this late date that there is considerable doubt as to whether any pewter bearing the touch of the first Thomas Danforth has been correctly identified. For reasons which will be discussed on a later page, there are strong grounds for the belief that we have yet to find this maker's mark. There are in existence, however, a number of unmarked items of pewter which probably were the work of this man. Several painted chests have come to light which are marked 'R. C. — Taunton' with dates ranging from 1729 to 1742. The earliest of these have pewter escutcheons and, as Thomas Danforth left Taunton about 1733, it seems more than possible that the escutcheons came from his shop, for there would scarcely have been two pewterers in such a small town as was Taunton in 1730.

PLATE LI — *Norwich Touches — John and Samuel Danforth*

352 and 353. Touch and large hall-marks. John Danforth, Norwich, 1773–1793. From a plate in the author's collection.

352a and 354. Another impression of 352 with Danforth's lion touch. Collection of John W. Poole, Esq.

355. The same maker's small hall-marks. From a plate formerly in the collection of the late Francis Mason, Esq.

356. Initial touch attributed to John Danforth, but possibly a touch of his nephew, Joseph. Collection of the author.

357. Similar touch from a different die. Collection of Albert H. Good, Esq.

357a. Another impression of 357. Collection of the author.

352b and 358. Touches of Samuel Danforth, Norwich, 1793–1802. Impressed on a plate in the collection of Mr. and Mrs. Richard S. Quigley.

352c and 359. The name-place touch is here accompanied by what was presumably a crude eagle mark, attributed to Samuel Danforth. Collection of John W. Poole, Esq.

PLATE LI

352a   354

352   353

355

356   357

357a

359   352c

352b   358

Middletown June 9th 1773

Mr. Vestelde, Sir   I went from Boston to Providence and have given Mr. Samuel Hamlin orders to Sell that old Brass that was their and Send the money to you as Soon as Possible But the man Lives ten miles from Providence and its unsortin when he will git the Brass; so that I have put on Board Capt. Tyle one Borriall with 118 lbs. old Copper and 221 lbs. old Pewter and have Paid the Frait Martin Gay will give you 7/old tenner for the Copper and Thomas Green will Take the old Pewter I beleave and aLow near 10 per lb for it and I Hope you will do well as you can with it and give me Credit for the same I Have also sent you seaven Pounds in Cash by Capt. Tyle. He has a letter for you with the Recat in it which you may give up I have Ben to Mr. Hanshaw & he Hath Put some Rum & Suger on Board said vessel for you which I hope will over dew his Part so much as to settle the note if Hamlin money should be sent to you I should Be glad you will Deliver it to Mr. John Timmins and Take his Recait after your note is setted. I got Hom Last Fryday and Had my Copper & Pewter Rady the next day But The vessel was not Rady untill this Day So that I have dun Everything possible I could Help you I recived your Letter Last Night By Mr. Burr dated 28th May 1773 so I Remain yours & c.

Thomas Danforth

PLATE LII

JOHN DANFORTH

Although Thomas Danforth, Second, was the senior member of the second generation of this family of pewterers, it was John, a younger son, who remained in Norwich and who, with his descendants, there carried on the father's trade. It will therefore be just as well, perhaps, to conclude the history of the Norwich Danforths before proceeding to the account of the second Thomas and his sons.

These Norwich makers may have been just as capable pewterers as were their brothers and cousins who settled farther west, but they all seem to have lacked the enterprise and business ability which characterized the elder branch of the family.

John, born in Norwich, March 12, 1741, was the fifth and youngest child by the senior Thomas Danforth's first marriage. His own marriage to Elizabeth Hartshorn took place September 10, 1767. John worked in his father's shop and carried on the business after the old gentleman retired in 1773, giving up pewtering himself some twenty years later in favor of his son, Samuel. His death is said to have occurred January 31, 1799, at Ellsworth, Ohio, though probate records are on file in Connecticut. As his father before him had done, John died insolvent.

In addition to two sets of hall-marks (Plate LI, 353 and 355), he employed a lion-in-gateway touch (number 354) and a Norwich mark (number 352). These latter touches, sometimes alone but frequently together, have been found on flatware measuring $7\frac{5}{8}$, $8\frac{5}{16}$, and $12\frac{3}{16}$ inches, and on $13\frac{1}{4}$-inch deep dishes.

Two other touches, unquestionably Danforth marks, are attributed with a good deal of confidence to this maker. The first, illustrated by Louis G. Myers in *Some Notes on American Pewterers*, was found upon a wine-pint porringer then in his collection. I own a dolphin-handle porringer-basin that bears the same impression (see Plate LI, 357). The second of these touches (number 356) has not been illustrated before. It was photographed from a wine-pint porringer formerly owned by W. C. Staples. The touches are alike except for details in the lower half of the impression.

Although it is more than probable that these marks have been correctly attributed to John Danforth, there are reasons for hesitating to accept the attribution as definitely settled. In the first place, the same initials and the same form of rampant lion could have been employed by John Danforth's nephew, Joseph. Furthermore, a porringer-basin was not a stock shape. It was made by Richard Lee and a few others, but not by the general run of pewterers. The only inventories in which I have seen listed a mould for such a vessel are those of Gershom Jones and Joseph Danforth. While John also may have owned such a mould, that fact remains to be proved. The makership could be definitely established if some collector were to find an example combining one of these circular 'I. D.' lion touches with a set of John Danforth's known hall-marks.

Thomas Danforth, Second

SAMUEL DANFORTH OF NORWICH

We shall spend little time over Samuel Danforth, Norwich pewter-maker, who worked independently but a few years. The scarcity of his pewter is probably traceable to a meager business, which in turn can be partly explained by Danforth's unfortunate habit of looking upon the wine when it was red: his cousin, Thomas Danforth, Fourth, wrote of him in 1818, in a letter still preserved, that he was drinking heavily.

Second son of John and Elizabeth (Hartshorn) Danforth, Samuel was born in Norwich in 1772. He was trained in his father's shop and took over the management of the business in a new shop in 1793. On Christmas Day, 1797, he married Lucy Hartshorn at Mansfield. He continued his pewter-making at Norwich until 1803, when he sold out. Thereafter he seems to have been a journeyman only. He died August 5, 1827, at Ellsworth, Ohio. Samuel's son John was probably a pewterer also, but we have no reason for believing that he ever had a shop or touch of his own.

Samuel Danforth's pewter is extremely rare. I have record of plates — six in number — which measure $7\frac{5}{8}$ inches or $8\frac{5}{16}$ inches in diameter and one $13\frac{1}{8}$-inch deep dish. His Norwich touch seems to have been made with the die used by his father. The new eagle mark, shown in Plate LI, 359, accompanied by the Norwich touch which both John and Samuel Danforth used, has been tentatively attributed to the younger man, but may have been used by the father in his later years. In its crudity it bears close resemblance to the other Norwich touches as well as to those of Gershom Jones, who learned his trade from John Danforth.

THOMAS DANFORTH, SECOND

Thomas Danforth, Second, was not only the son and brother of a pewterer, but holds also the distinction of having furnished five sons to the trade, a record equaled by but one other American maker.

He was born in Taunton, Massachusetts, June 2, 1731, the eldest son of the first Thomas and Sarah (Leonard) Danforth. He served his apprenticeship in his father's shop at Norwich and very soon thereafter moved to Middletown, where he set up in business for himself. In 1756 he married Martha Jacobs.

During the Revolution Danforth manufactured 'musquet balls' for the Continental Army, and for over twenty years he served his town as sealer of weights and measures, which office he still was holding at the time of his death, August 8, 1782. In his latter years his son Joseph was taken into partnership with him and some of the shop's moulds were jointly owned with Jacob Whitmore. Thomas's moulds were left at his death to his two oldest sons, Thomas and Joseph.

If, as suggested below, the second Thomas made all the pewter which we formerly accredited to his father, there can be little doubt that his business was large. Moreover, his pewter is scattered far beyond the confines of Connecticut — my best example came from a farmhouse in South Jersey — indicating that he made extensive use of the peddler's cart.

Until comparatively recently nothing by this maker beyond flatware was known to exist — $7\frac{7}{8}$-inch and 9-inch plates, 9-inch and $9\frac{3}{16}$-inch plates with smooth rim, 12-inch flat dishes, and 11-inch and $13\frac{1}{4}$-inch deep dishes. The Garvan Foundation Collection, Yale University, owns an inkwell, and I have acquired a small box with lid (Plate XL, 267) that might have served any one of a number of uses. The two latter pieces are marked only with the hall-marks. Although Danforth's metal and workmanship are above the average, he has left us nothing that would enable us to classify him with the Wills or the Bassetts or even to place him upon the same plane of ability with his son Thomas.

THE THOMAS DANFORTH LION MARKS

One of the great charms in collecting American marked pewter lies in the study of the various marks and the attempts to attribute these touches correctly to specific individuals. The more difficult the problem the more engrossing it becomes. One may build up a cleverly conceived theory based on a few meager facts only to have someone unearth a specimen with a hitherto unknown mark that completely upsets the most elaborate deductions. Exactly that is what seems to have happened in connection with the Thomas Danforth marks.

The proper allotment of the various 'T. D.' lion marks to the different Thomas Danforths has perplexed every student of American pewter. After much study and with but few misgivings I now feel ready to say that the preponderance of evidence is against the previously accepted theories. My own belief is that the lion-in-circle touch was the early mark of the third Thomas; that all the pewter formerly attributed to Thomas the first was made by the second of that name; and that we must look for another touch for the father of the Danforth clan.

Louis G. Myers in his *Notes* has told us much about the Danforths, and without drawing heavily on that source of information and repeating a large part of what he has already said, it would be difficult indeed to present properly these theories of mine. In this, as in many other connections, I am heavily in his debt.

Three Thomas Danforths had shops of their own, should have had individual touchmarks, and hence are contenders for the various 'T. D.' lion-marked touches. The first Thomas is supposed by the Danforth family genealogist to have retired in 1773 after perhaps forty-eight years of activity. His son, the second Thomas, died in 1782 after approximately twenty-eight years of pewter-making; and the third Thomas, whose story will be told later, commenced work during the Revolution and retired in 1818 with some forty-five working years to his credit.

The Thomas Danforth Lion Marks

To be divided in some manner among these men are three general groups of lion touches: (1) lion-in-gateway (Plate LIII, 362), (2) lion-in-oval (number 364), and (3) lion-in-circle (number 368). That arrangement represents the order in which they probably first appeared, if we may judge by the wear of the metal on which each is found and the general form and characteristics of the designs and lettering. In addition, two sets of hall-marks were employed; the earlier in appearance (number 363) is found in conjunction with both the gateway and oval touches, the other set (number 369) with the lion-in-circle touch or the small eagle-in-circle (number 370).

One point that proves helpful in solving our problem of ascribing correctly the lion touches is the knowledge that, as soon as the second and third Thomas Danforths had learned their trade, each deserted his father's shop and moved to another town. Of necessity these three shops, miles apart, would have required individual touch-marks. We can therefore discard at once any attribution that assumes the use by any of these men, one generation later, of an older Danforth's dies.

The simplest method of procedure will be to deal first with the third Thomas, the man who moved in 1777 from Middletown to Rocky Hill. He was unquestionably the user of all the Thomas Danforth eagle marks. But touches of that form did not come into use prior to 1790, certainly not before 1785. We must have a touch for him to represent the first ten or fifteen years of his pewter-making. We therefore award to this man the small lion-in-circle (the latest in appearance of the lion marks, and a counterpart of the touch used by his younger brother, Joseph; cf. numbers 368 and 375). As evidence that this deduction is correct, plates have been found stamped with the small eagle of the third Thomas accompanied by the hall-marks that are normally found with the circular lion. In the Garvan collection and that of the author are plates thus marked. The proof seems conclusive that the small lion was used by the third Thomas Danforth prior to his adoption of the eagle touches.

We are left now with the lion-in-gateway and lion-in-oval touches, and the question is whether to attribute both marks to Thomas of Norwich or to award them to his Middletown namesake. As explained above, the coupling of the same set of so-called hall-marks with both the lion-in-gateway and lion-in-oval prevents us from dividing the touches between the two men.

I had felt for some time that the accepted attribution of both touches to Thomas of Norwich was incorrect, but I had no data to support my views. Although the elder Thomas worked for a longer period than his son, it seemed of greater importance that Thomas of Norwich retired before the Revolution while his son worked until 1782. During the war the country was combed for everything containing lead to supply munitions for the Continental troops. Little beyond the absolutely essential, and probably new, pewter would have escaped the melting-pot. How many pre-Revolutionary pieces of marked American flatware — positively identified as pre-Revolutionary — are known to exist today? Certainly a smaller group than the total of Thomas Danforth lion-in-gateway plates, to say nothing of the oval-marked pieces. Would it not seem more surprising that we should have say fifty or more examples by a pre-Revolutionary

PLATE LIII — *Danforth Touches — Thomas Danforth, Second, Thomas Danforth, Third, and Joseph Danforth*

361 and 362. Touches of Thomas Danforth, Second, of Middletown, 1755–1782, as found on a plate which had been converted into a crude handle for a bedpan. Formerly owned by the late Louis G. Myers, Esq.

362a, 363. The same lion touch with Danforth's hall-marks. Collection of Albert H. Good, Esq.

364 and 363a. Another touch, probably later (*c.* 1770–1780), of the same maker. Collection of Philip G. Platt, Esq.

365. Similar touch with initials 'T. I.,' attributed to the partnership of Thomas Danforth and his son, Joseph, 1780–1782. From the collection of Albert H. Good, Esq.

366. Eagle touch of Thomas Danforth, Third, Stepney, Connecticut, and Philadelphia, Pennsylvania. 1777–1818. Collection of Philip G. Platt, Esq.

367. Initial touch of the same maker. From a pot in the author's collection.

368 and 369. Early small touch and hall-marks of Thomas Danforth, Third. Courtesy of the Mabel Brady Garvan Collection, Gallery of Fine Arts, Yale University.

370. The Third Thomas Danforth's small touch which superseded 368 about 1790. Collection of John W. Poole, Esq.

371 and 372. Large eagle and Philadelphia touches of the same maker. 371 was probably not used before 1800; 372 from 1807 to 1813 only. Collection of John W. Poole, Esq.

373. Another touch by the same maker and of the same period. Collection of John W. Poole, Esq.

374. Initial touch of Joseph Danforth, Middletown, 1780–1788. From a quart pot in the collection of Edward E. Minor, Esq.

375 and 376. Small initial touch and small hall-marks of the same maker. Collection of John W. Poole, Esq.

377 and 378. Normal touch and hall-marks of Joseph Danforth. From the collection of John W. Poole, Esq.

PLATE LIII

361   362   362 a   363   364   363 a

365   366

368   369

367   375   376

370

371   372   373   377   378

                    374

PLATE LIV — *Middletown Touches* — *Joseph Danforth, Junior, Edward Danforth, Jacob Whitmore, Amos Treadway, and Jacob Eggleston*

379 and 380. Touches attributed to Joseph Danforth, Jr., Richmond, Virginia, 1807–1812. From a plate in the collection of Mr. and Mrs. Richard S. Quigley.

381. Another touch attributed to the same maker. Collection of Albert H. Good, Esq.

382. Initial touch of Jacob Whitmore, Middletown, Connecticut, 1758–1790. From a quart pot in the author's collection.

383. Jacob Whitmore's normal touch. Collection of John W. Poole, Esq.

384 and 361a. Touches of Amos Treadway, Middletown, Connecticut, dates uncertain, but between 1760 and 1790. Note that the die for 361a was used also by Thomas Danforth, Second. Collection of Joseph France, Esq.

384a. Another impression of 384. From the collection of John W. Poole, Esq.

385. Touch attributed to Jacob Eggleston, Middletown, Connecticut, 1795–1807, and Fayetteville, North Carolina, 1807–1813. Collection of the author.

386. Touch of Jacob Eggleston. Collection of Miss Anna L. Rights.

386. Another impression of the same touch. Collection of Mr. and Mrs. Richard S. Quigley.

387 and 388. Normal touch and hall-marks of Edward Danforth, Middletown and Hartford, Connecticut, 1788–1794. Collection of the author.

389. Edward Danforth's small touch. From a basin in the author's collection.

389a. Another impression of the same touch. From a mug in the collection of Edward E. Minor, Esq.

390 and 391. Edward Danforth's small hall-marks as illustrated in *Some Notes on American Pewterers* by the late Louis G. Myers, Esq. The incised marks below were used by Danforth's nephews, Thomas and Sherman Boardman, of Hartford, 1815–1830.

PLATE LIV

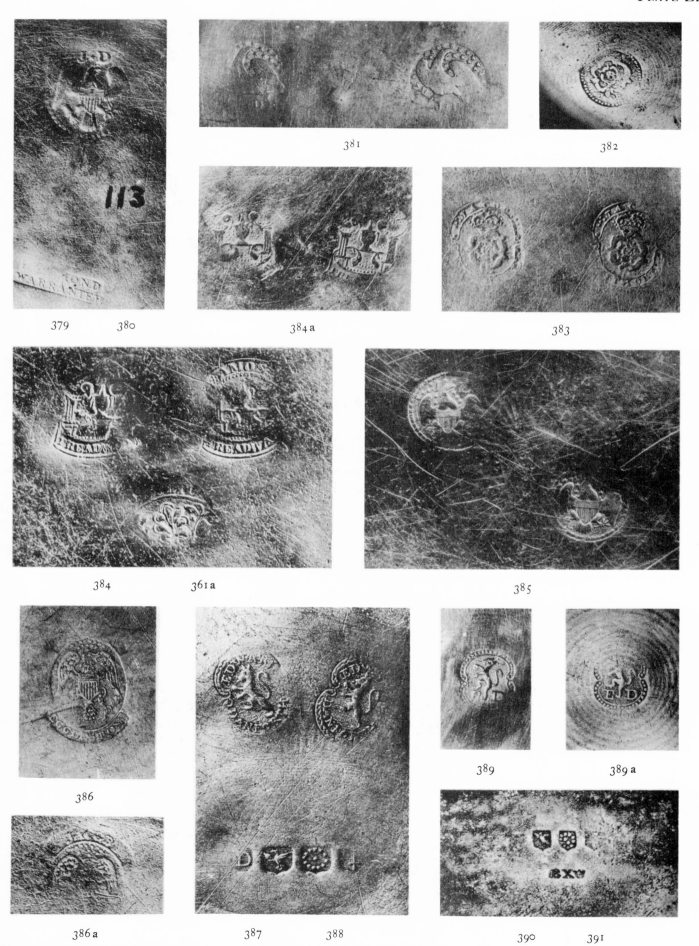

379   380

381

382

384 a

383

384   361 a

385

386

389   389 a

386 a

387   388

390   391

pewterer, no matter how prolific, than that we should be unable to find any of his pewter whatever?

By measuring carefully a group of Thomas Danforth lion-marked plates and comparing these measurements with similar determinations made from a study of the plates of John Danforth of Norwich (who inherited the first Thomas's moulds), I was convinced by the differences that the existing Thomas Danforth plates could never have been made in the moulds from which John's specimens were cast. Conversely, I satisfied myself that they could very easily have come from the moulds which turned out Jacob Whitmore's plates; and Whitmore, as we learned from Louis G. Myers's *Notes*, owned his moulds jointly with Thomas Danforth, second. Try this experiment yourself when you have an opportunity to do so. The result was conclusive enough for me, but I wanted proof that would be still more evident.

Thanks to Mr. Myers, that proof was not long in presenting itself. He secured the remnant of a plate which goes far toward settling the problem. This plate, by the way, gives a striking demonstration of how fortuitous are the opportunities for solving some of our pewter dilemmas. A dealer sent to Mr. Myers on approval a bedpan made by Jacob Eggleston of Middletown. At some time, many years ago, the handle had been lost, and for it had been substituted an old plate crudely rolled up into a handle. Had the handle never been lost, or had the plate been so rolled as to bring the marks inside, we might still be blindly groping for the Danforth lion-touch solution. But chance was kind to us.

On the plate in question are the familiar lion-in-gateway and a hitherto unlisted Middletown touch (Plate LIII, 361) strikingly similar to John Danforth's Norwich mark. And so it would seem that we have no touches at all for the first Thomas Danforth. To quote from a letter of Mr. Myers on the subject: 'There is a pleasant thrill awaiting the collector who discovers a specimen marked "Thomas Danforth" and "Norwich" or "T. D." and "Norwich."'

The only remaining feature of the problem that requires comment concerns the oval-shaped touches in which we find the initials 'T. I.' instead of 'T. D.' (Plate LIII, 365). Until recently they were presumed to have represented the marks of the first Thomas and his son John, working as partners in Norwich. But the mark could just as well represent the combination of the second Thomas and his son Joseph. When the latter completed his apprenticeship in his father's shop at Middletown, his position became exactly analogous to that of his uncle John in Norwich one generation earlier — the second son helping the father to carry on the business.

It is therefore my contention, fully endorsed by Mr. Myers, that the lion-in-circle was an early touch of Thomas Danforth of Rocky Hill, that the lion-in-gateway and lion-in-oval were the marks of the Middletown Thomas, and that the missing clue which will settle the matter for all time will be the eagerly awaited discovery of a Thomas Danforth-Norwich touch.

THOMAS DANFORTH, THIRD

Of the many Danforths who followed the trade of pewter-making, probably none excelled the third Thomas in quality of work, none ever had a larger trade, and certainly no one of them has left us so many examples of his handiwork.

He was born in Middletown June 2, 1756, the eldest son of the second Thomas. At the age of nineteen he married Elizabeth Tellman of New London, and in 1777, his apprenticeship completed, he opened a shop in Rocky Hill (at that time named Stepney), a hamlet outside the ancient town of Wethersfield. In May of the following year he moved his little family to the new home. Apparently he prospered from the start, for in 1783 he built a fine house there. This new home, lying between Hartford and Middletown, became a frequent stopping-place for all members of the Danforth connection.

Danforth made not only pewter, but also tinware, copper, and brass goods. The lathe was turned by a horse on a treadmill. In 1794 he took into business with him his son-in-law, Richard Williams, and among his apprentices at different times were Ashbil Griswold and Charles and Hiram Yale. If we but knew all the facts we should probably be justified in adding to this list Samuel Danforth, William Nott, Samuel Kilbourn, and many other Connecticut pewterers.

In 1807 Thomas Danforth opened a second shop at Thirteenth and High Streets in Philadelphia. We still have so many pieces of his pewter bearing the Philadelphia stamp that there can be little doubt that the venture was eminently successful; and yet, strange to say, he returned to Rocky Hill in 1813. In 1818 he is supposed to have retired.

In 1833, Thomas, then a man of seventy-seven, took a journey by land and water to visit his nephew, Joseph Danforth, Junior, at Richmond, Virginia. His diary of that trip, handed down in the family, is now in the possession of Luther B. Williams of New Britain, Connecticut, who very kindly permitted me to examine it. This journal in the old gentleman's neat handwriting gives an insight into his character. Each letter is as carefully formed as were his pewter vessels. The diary not only tells in detail what he did and saw, but also gives us his opinions on many subjects and includes quotations from the Bible, from well-known authors, and from the daily newspapers. We see Danforth as a methodical, conservative, highly religious man, fond of his home and family, interested in all that he saw and heard, and probably quite out of sympathy with opinions that differed from his own. He felt, as most elderly men do, that the country had fallen on evil times. In politics he was a staunch supporter of Henry Clay, and recorded of one acquaintance that he was 'a very worthy man, esteemed much more for not being a Jackson man.' The diary closes on June 15, 1834, with the following characteristic statement: 'Took New England Steam Boat for Rocky Hill, Conn., the land of steady habbits.'

Thomas Danforth died in 1840, the last pewterer of the Revolutionary times. His probate records could not be found, but there is little doubt that he left a large estate.

On preceding pages the attribution of Danforth's touches has been discussed. To his early years from 1777 until about 1790 belong the lion touch, his hall-marks, and the initials in a rectangle. The hall-marks are found on a few pieces that bear also the smallest of the eagle touches. Their use was probably discontinued prior to 1800, and the small eagle itself must have been discarded soon after the Philadelphia shop was opened. The largest eagle would hardly have been used much prior to 1800, whereas the other two touches probably date from the years in Philadelphia. I have a quart mug which is impressed on the inside bottom with the eagle shown in Plate LIII, 373, and on the outside upper rim next the handle is the T. D.-in-rectangle (number 367), evidence that the small initial touch may have been used throughout Danforth's career.

Danforth's pewter still exists in a variety of forms. There are flat plates with normal rim measuring $6\frac{1}{8}$, $7\frac{1}{2}$, $7\frac{3}{4}$, $7\frac{7}{8}$, $8\frac{5}{8}$, and 9 inches; $9\frac{1}{4}$-inch smooth-rim plates; deep dishes measuring 11, $11\frac{9}{16}$, and 13 inches; basins of diameters of 8, 9, 10, and 12 inches; pint and quart mugs, quart tankards, three sizes of porringers, beakers, teapots, and sugar bowls. Although Thomas must have made a great many porringers and should have had moulds for five or six different sizes, I know of only four examples, two of which are here illustrated (Plate XII, 61, and Plate XIII, 72). The first belongs to his early period and is stamped on the under side of the handle with the lion touch. The second, formerly owned by P. G. Platt, and shown here with his kind permission, illustrates Danforth's ability to adapt himself to the requirements or whims of his customers. There you see a form of handle peculiar to the Newport pewterers, an adaptation of a Continental form. This porringer was unquestionably made in the Philadelphia shop and is one of the few surviving Philadelphia porringers.

For the use of this type of handle I believe that there is a sound explanation. In eastern Pennsylvania there was a large population of Germans and Moravians. Accustomed in the old country to porringers with solid handles, they desired nothing different here. Thomas Danforth was too clever a salesman to try to force upon them the handsomer English types which he had been accustomed to make in Connecticut. So he ordered a mould of the Newport type (such as he must have seen often in New England), and made for the Pennsylvania Dutch trade a porringer that was less crude than the Chester and York types (of which more later) and at the same time a form that more closely resembled the porringers made on the Continent. It may be noted here that even without the touch no one would long mistake this particular porringer for a Rhode Island example, for it lacks the Rhode Island type of handle support.

The third Thomas's only son, Thomas Danforth, Fourth, born at Rocky Hill, July 6, 1792, was also a pewterer. He worked in Philadelphia for his father and later for B. Barns. In 1818 he was turning out pewter plates for North and Rowe in Augusta, Georgia. There seems, however, to be no evidence that he ever made pewter on his own account. His death took place at Rocky Hill, March 23, 1836.

JACOB WHITMORE

Jacob Whitmore, one of the men whom Louis G. Myers in his *Notes* placed in 'Pewterers' Hall' and furnished with ancestry and touch-marks, was born in Middletown, May 6, 1736, the son of Captain Jacob and Rebecca (Hurlbut) Whitmore. He would have been nineteen years old when the second Thomas Danforth arrived from Norwich. So, unless he started rather late to learn his trade, there must have been early pewterers in Middletown whose names and records still await discovery.

Whitmore married Elizabeth King, June 15, 1758. He served as an officer during the Revolution, commanding a company in Colonel Beebe's regiment in 1775, and was a captain under Colonel Comfort Sage in 1779. On June 19, 1781, he advertised as follows in *The Connecticut Courant:* 'To be Sold (for hard money only). At the shop of the subscriber in Middletown. A good assortment of New Pewter among which are one article of Tea-Potts of the best sort.'

He was elected a deacon of the First Congregational Church in 1782 and in later Middletown documents is referred to as 'Deacon Jacob Whitmore.' In 1788, for one year only, he served as sealer of weights and measures in the town government, succeeding Joseph Danforth in that office. He owned his moulds jointly with Thomas Danforth, Second, and the form of his touch would indicate that he retired from pewter-making about 1790 or earlier.

In 1804 Jacob and his wife Elizabeth bought property in Middletown from William Danforth, but the outlay apparently took all his available cash, for two years later Webster and Catlins, merchants, having failed to collect on notes of Whitmore, secured a judgment against him. To save himself from prison, the deacon had to sell his last piece of property. His name continued on the tax lists only until 1807, but he lived until September 25, 1825, just short of ninety years.

During the past few years a number of this man's plates, hitherto overlooked on the presumption that they were English, have passed into collections. The examples thus far found are $7\frac{7}{8}$-inch plates, 11- and 12-inch flat dishes, and $13\frac{1}{4}$-inch deep dishes. Three 8-inch basins, one 9-inch basin, and one butter plate have also been reported. Whitmore should, of course, have had a small initial touch. In Plate LIV, 382, is portrayed a new rose touch with initials 'J. W.' and with characteristics so similar to the large Whitmore mark that there can be little if any hesitation in ascribing it to this maker. The touch was photographed from a quart mug that appears to be identical with similar items made by Joseph Danforth (who shared moulds with Whitmore). Other quart mugs and one in the pint size are known. A porringer similarly marked is owned by Mrs. Thomas Troland. It is an interesting fact that the handle of this vessel is of that particular design which in this volume is designated as the Rhode Island type. It therefore seems probable that the design was carried from Middletown to Providence by the senior Hamlin and afterward adopted not only by all later Providence pewterers, but also by the Melvilles in the near-by town of Newport.

The Pewterers of the Connecticut Valley

AMOS TREADWAY

Seven or eight years ago I found a dish marked with an unidentified touch on which only the name Treadway was decipherable. The mark was unlike any known American or English touch, but the piece itself gave evidence that pointed to American workmanship. The discovery of another plate with the same touch (Plate LIV, 384) in the collection of Mrs. H. L. Lonsdale whetted my desire to learn who Treadway was. Unfortunately the upper half of the touch, which would have shown the maker's surname, was erased as completely on Mrs. Lonsdale's specimen as on mine. One example had been found in Andover, Massachusetts, the other in Colchester, Connecticut.

A genealogical search indicated that the New England Treadways were, with few exceptions, descended from Nathaniel, an original settler of Sudbury, Massachusetts, in 1639. Exhaustive examination of Treadway wills and inventories in Massachusetts turned up no pewterers. However, James, a grandson of Nathaniel, was found to have removed about 1700 from Watertown, Massachusetts, to Colchester, Connecticut, and by 1750 his many descendants had spread into the neighboring towns of Salem and Middletown. Middletown, a known pewter center, seemed a promising field of search, but its records furnished no helpful clues.

It became necessary to wait for the discovery of another Treadway piece with a sufficiently clear impression of the upper portion of the touch to determine the surname of the pewterer. Recently two such plates have come to light, and we now know that Amos was the first name of the elusive maker; but we still are left the problem of determining which of two Amos Treadways used the touch, and no discoverable papers aid us in the solution.

On February 19, 1738, Amos, second child in a family of twelve and grandson of the Watertown maltster, James, was born to Josiah and Eunice (Foote) Treadway in Colchester. He married Elizabeth Blake in the same town on June 16, 1760, and the second of their nine children, born on August 6, 1762, was also christened Amos. Soon thereafter the family moved to Middletown. There both father and son were living with their families when the first census was taken in 1790. Amos, Junior, died in 1808, his father six years later, and nothing in either inventory gives evidence of pewter-making.

And so, for the time being, positive identification of the pewterer is held up awaiting proof that must still exist in some well-hidden record. But in the meantime I am inclined to believe that the elder Amos, a contemporary of the second Thomas Danforth, was our pewterer; for in the group of touches on Mr. France's Treadway plate (Plate LIV, 384a, 361a) is an impression of the 'Middletown' mark that is also found on early examples of Danforth's pewter.

Treadway's touches have been found on 8-inch plates and on 11- and $12\frac{3}{16}$-inch flat dishes.

[114]

Joseph Danforth, Father and Son

JOSEPH DANFORTH, FATHER AND SON

Joseph, second son of Thomas and Martha Danforth, was born in Middletown, August 17, 1758. After serving his apprenticeship he worked with his father until the latter's death in 1782 and succeeded him as sealer of measures in Middletown. The lion-in-oval touch of Thomas Danforth with the initials 'T. I.' is now thought to have been used by this father-and-son combination for a brief period prior to the elder man's death.

By the terms of Thomas's will, Joseph, his executor, inherited a one-half share in his father's moulds. One of the documents filed with the will verifies in an amusing way the trait of carelessness that is evident in the finish of a few of Joseph's plates, and also in the occasional haphazard stamping of his metal. It seems that Joseph in settling the estate was called upon to make a trip to Providence to secure from Samuel Hamlin moulds that had belonged to the father, Thomas. On his way home he may have spent a convivial evening with a few choice spirits. Whatever did occur, we at least know that when he reached Middletown and unloaded his wagon a thirty-pound quart basin mould was missing, all as set down in Joseph's accounting of his stewardship.

However much we may criticize him for occasional carelessness, he stands out as one of the most prodigiously energetic and productive of all American pewterers. When we stop to think that he had a shop of his own for but six years — seven at the most — and that he died before the coming of the eagle period, it seems incredible that so much of his work should have survived.

We are now prepared to furnish Joseph with three touches (Plate LIII, 374, 375, and 377), as well as two sets of hall-marks (numbers 376 and 378). The large hall-marks and lion-in-gateway are found on $7\frac{7}{8}$-inch, 8-, $8\frac{1}{2}$-, and 9-inch plates, $9\frac{3}{16}$- and $9\frac{1}{2}$-inch smooth-rim plates, $11\frac{1}{4}$- and $12\frac{1}{4}$-inch flat dishes, 13-inch deep dishes, and 9- and $10\frac{1}{4}$-inch basins; both sets of hall-marks on 9-inch basins.

The Mabel Brady Garvan Collection contains a $6\frac{1}{8}$-inch butter plate impressed with the lion-in-circle, and the same touch is found on quart and pint mugs. On the outer rim of these mugs, near the handle, is an impression of Joseph's rectangular mark, and other quart mugs are known which have the rectangular touch alone.

On April 12, 1781, Joseph Danforth married Sarah King of Middletown, and on December 17, 1788, when his death occurred at the early age of thirty, Joseph, with six children, had made a splendid start toward building up a family of typically Danforthian proportions.

Among Joseph's children was a son, Joseph, Junior, one of twin brothers born March 14, 1783, the other twin dying in infancy. According to the *Danforth Genealogy*, Joseph, Junior, learned his trade from his uncle William; and 'Uncle William,' as we know, was a pewterer, and not, as the writer of that volume believed, a carpenter. The Danforth historian further states that Joseph moved to Virginia about 1805. This date is probably a little too early, for Joseph's name is on the Middletown tax lists from 1803 to 1807.

In the latter year he married, at Petersburg, Virginia, Frances Heath of Prince George

County. He served during the War of 1812 in Captain Andrew Sherman's battery and from 1812 until his death, November 11, 1844, he was superintendent of the capitol at Richmond.

There can be little doubt that Joseph Danforth, Second, was a pewterer. In Massachusetts, Rhode Island, and elsewhere the early deeds, wills, records of lawsuits, etc., when mentioning the names of the principals, usually give the occupation beside the name. Unfortunately Connecticut records, so complete in other respects, invariably omit this valuable information. It was so in all papers pertaining to Joseph. Although we cannot be certain that we have discovered in this man another pewterer in the Danforth family, the evidence all points that way.

Not only do we know that Joseph learned his trade (whatever it was) from a man who has left us marked pewter, but it is also recorded in the administration papers of the senior Joseph's estate that Edward Danforth, the executor, with the approval of the court, set off in trust for Joseph, Junior, all of his father's braziery and pewter-making tools — surely an incentive to the boy to take up that trade.

If young Joseph did for a few years try his hand at pewter-making, we need not look far for touches to attribute to him. Louis G. Myers formerly owned an $8\frac{3}{4}$-inch plate, illustrated in his *Notes*, which is impressed with two marks, one a large eagle and the letters 'J. D.' in a circle, the other a rectangle enclosing the words 'Richmond Warranted.' A duplicate of that plate passed into the collection of Mr. and Mrs. Richard S. Quigley, and the touches of the latter piece are here shown through the courtesy of the owners (Plate LIV, 379 and 380). Those marks fit, in every particular, the history of Joseph Danforth, Second. To illustrate my reasons for attributing the Richmond eagle to this man, I refer the reader to a comparison of the 'J. D.' eagle with a well-known touch of Thomas Danforth, Third (Plate LIII, 371) and a mark attributed to Jacob Eggleston of Middletown (Plate LIV, 385).

Examine these eagles carefully. There can be little doubt that all three birds came from the same nest. Thomas Danforth of Rocky Hill used in Philadelphia from 1807 until 1812 the mark illustrated in number 371. It may have been adopted in Connecticut a year or so earlier — let us say 1805; Jacob Eggleston died in 1813, so his eagle dates from the same period; and young Joseph, if he made pewter in Virginia at all, would have done so from 1807 to 1812. The evidence of the touches parallels exactly the historical evidence. So much for the eagles.

Now we know of no pewterers who were at work in Virginia when Joseph Danforth moved to that state. The use of the 'Richmond Warranted' touch would have been a logical scheme for inducing Richmond housewives to patronize local industry. In this new light the touch for the first time assumes real significance. In my mind there is no question but that 'J. D. — Richmond Warranted' and Joseph Danforth, Junior, were one and the same man, an opinion that was shared by the late Mr. Myers.

The last new touch to come to light before the publication of this book was another 'J. D.' eagle (number 381) which I am also attributing to the younger Joseph Danforth. Again all available evidence points to the correctness of this assumption. Mr. Good found the plate at Hagerstown, Maryland, within the probable distribution area of Danforth's wares; the plate measures 8¾ inches as did Mr. Myers's plate; and lastly this eagle and the general design of the touch are typical of other Danforth marks.

EDWARD DANFORTH

Edward was the third son of Thomas and Martha Danforth. His birth occurred in Middletown March 20, 1765. Undoubtedly his apprenticeship began in his father's shop and was completed under his older brother, Joseph. The latter died in 1788, Edward acting as administrator of the estate. In the following year Edward's name is on the Middletown tax lists for the last time, and, according to the census of 1790, he had then settled in Hartford. His marriage to Jerusha Mossly of Glastonbury, Connecticut, took place in 1791.

Edward Danforth made fine pewter, and his flatware with its amusing lion touch (Plate LIV, 387) is comparatively rare. I know of but five sizes that he made, 8-inch, 8⅞, 11, 12⅛, and 13¼-inch — the last being of the deep variety. His small touch (Plate LIV, 389) has been found on pint and quart mugs, on tall beakers, on a 7¼-inch basin, and on half-pint porringers.

On account of the design of Edward's touch and the rarity of his metal I believe that he never made pewter after leaving Middletown. In any event he could have given but a year or two at Hartford to his early trade, for otherwise we should find eagle-marked pieces bearing his touch. This supposition is greatly strengthened by the discovery in the *Connecticut Courant* for February 1, 1796, of the following advertisement:

> Edward Danforth
>
> Has for sale coarse Salt of an excellent quality by the hundred or single bushel cheap for cash or short and approved credit.

Furthermore, he was listed simply as a 'trader' in the Hartford directory of 1799. Edward Danforth died insolvent in 1830.

WILLIAM AND JOSIAH DANFORTH

Our next Danforth is William, fifth son of Thomas of Middletown, who entered this world in 1769. The Danforth genealogist tells us that William is supposed to have been a carpenter. This, however, I very much doubt, for we have pewter marked with his name, and from 1792 until his death, December 9, 1820, practically his entire working life, he held the office of sealer of weights and liquid measures in Middletown, a position invariably filled by a worker in metals. Moreover, his inventory includes a normal pewterer's equipment with no evidence of carpenter's tools.

[117]

Although I have never seen pewter bearing either of William's touches (Plate LV, 392 and 393) in any forms except $7\frac{7}{8}$- and $8\frac{3}{4}$-inch plates, $11\frac{1}{4}$- and $13\frac{3}{16}$-inch deep dishes, and quart basins, his inventory shows him to have been also a maker of teapots, porringers, quart and pint pots, and spoons. It is difficult to understand why his metal is so much scarcer than that of his brothers, Joseph and Samuel, both of whom lived shorter lives.

In 1793 William married Huldah Scovil at Middletown. Of their six children, Josiah, born July 18, 1803, was to be the last of the long line of Danforths to make pewter.

Upon the settlement of William Danforth's estate each child in the distribution received a little more than one hundred dollars. Josiah, then a boy of seventeen and presumably an apprentice in his father's shop, received his share in pewterer's moulds. In 1825 his name was first placed on the town electoral list and his pewter-making, with a touch of his own, must date from about that time.

He it undoubtedly was who marked his well-made ware with a small circular touch showing an eagle encircled by 'J. Danforth Midd. Ct.' (Plate LV, 394). His early forms include 8-inch plates, pint and quart basins, 4-, 5-, and $5\frac{1}{8}$-inch porringers, and pint and quart mugs, all of them comparatively rare. As did most of the men who worked into the britannia period, he made teapots, cuspidors, and other forms that are of lesser interest to the average collector. His porringers display an excellent feature that I have seen in the work of no other maker. Down the center line of the handle, on the under face, there is a tapered rib of reinforcement that gives added strength to the weakest part of a comparatively frail vessel.

The touch which I am attributing to this newcomer in the Danforth lists has long been known. Louis G. Myers in his *Notes* suggested that it might have been used by John, son of Samuel Danforth of Norwich. However, there is no record of a John Danforth in the Middletown documents between 1810 and 1830, whereas Josiah's name is frequently found. The new evidence seems to me to justify the change in ascription of the mark.

Josiah Danforth married Almira Camp in November, 1831, and had seven children. He continued in the manufacture of pewter until February, 1837, when he sold to Jasper Graham of Wethersfield and William H. Savage of Middletown his lot and shop at the corner of Main and Mill Streets, together with the 'steam engine and fixtures thereon.' In later life he was a successful manufacturer of trusses and a prominent citizen. His death occurred in Middletown, May 11, 1872.

SAMUEL DANFORTH OF HARTFORD

The youngest son of Thomas and Martha Danforth was born in Middletown in 1774. We cannot say now which of his brothers taught him his trade, but in December, 1795, when he had but just attained his majority, he advertised at Hartford that 'Samuel Danforth & Co. have for sale a good assortment of New Pewter by wholesale and retail at the New York prices.' It would be interesting to know now who were represented by the '& Co.' Soon thereafter Danforth married Melinda Seymour, and until his death in Hartford, April 11, 1816, he was busy turning out his eagle-marked wares. As fast as he tired of one eagle, he discarded it for another in a vain search for a satisfactory touch.

There has been some question as to whether or not some of the marks attributed to this maker may not be the later touches of his cousin, Samuel Danforth of Norwich. However, the Hartford touch has been found with the 'S. D.' hall-marks, and with one exception every one of the Samuel Danforth eagles has at one time or another been noted in conjunction with either the Hartford impression or the hall-marks. The exception mentioned is the eagle touch illustrated on Plate LV, 398. I believe this touch should go to the same maker, and I should welcome information from any collector who is in a position to confirm my opinion.

From a financial standpoint Samuel was a most successful pewterer. He had a large stock of finished metal on hand when he died, and his estate was valued at over eleven thousand dollars net. We have record of existing plates in the following sizes: $6\frac{1}{8}$, $7\frac{3}{4}$, $7\frac{15}{16}$, and $8\frac{3}{4}$ inches, 9-inch with smooth rim; 12-inch flat dishes; and $11\frac{1}{4}$- and $13\frac{3}{16}$-inch deep dishes; $6\frac{1}{4}$-, $6\frac{5}{8}$-, 8-, and $10\frac{1}{2}$-inch basins; quart, pint, and half-pint pots; $3\frac{5}{8}$ to 5-inch porringers; quart tankards, christening bowls, and cups (the latter tall beakers), communion flagons, tall teapots, doll-size mugs, and small beakers. Among the articles mentioned in his inventory and not yet accounted for in existing metal are sugar bowls, half-gill and beer-gill porringers, and spoons.

At the time of the division of the estate, the executors, one of whom was Thomas D. Boardman, held a note from Boardman for $220.18 and another from T. D. & S. Boardman for $552.18, indicating perhaps that the Boardmans, as may also be surmised from other evidence, purchased many of Danforth's moulds.

Samuel's work, as J. B. Kerfoot states in *American Pewter*, is uneven in quality. I have seen, for instance, one of his beakers of fine metal in almost mint condition, which had a large sliver on the side due to faulty casting. A more particular maker would have thrown this piece back into the melting-pot when it became evident that the defect was too deep for removal on the lathe. There is no question of Samuel's ability to make good pewter, but that he was frequently satisfied with less than his best is apparent.

RICHARD WILLIAMS

So far as I know, the touch of Richard Williams has not yet come to light. Perhaps he never had a shop of his own, but we are informed in the Danforth genealogy that he was at one time a partner of the third Thomas Danforth.

He was born in Wethersfield, December 3, 1771, the son of Captain Othniel Williams. He married Thomas Danforth's third daughter, Hannah, and became associated with his father-in-law in business. A son, Otis (of whom more later), followed the same trade.

We do not know how long Williams lived at Rocky Hill, but it was probably sometime late in the seventeen-nineties that he moved with his family to Hartford. For one year only, 1809, he served as sealer of weights and measures in Hartford. There his death occurred on November 1, 1812.

JACOB EGGLESTON

A few years after the settlement of Middletown, Connecticut, there arrived in the village Samuel Eggleston, shoemaker. The following extract is taken from the Town Records:

> At a town meeting in Febbieary 9, 1658, theer was granted to the shoomecker eagellston a peas of meddow that was intendid for a shoomecker formerely, leying from creack to creack butting on the bogey medow as allso a howse lot beyond goodman meller in cace not by and if by then to give him upland answerabell to a howse lot and he ingaging to inhabit it seven yeer upon it as also doth ingag to indeevour to sut the town in his tread for making and mending shooese.

Among the descendants of the 'shoomecker' was the subject of this sketch, Jacob Eggleston, recently identified as the user of the touch once known as 'Unidentified Eagle No. 4.'

When J. B. Kerfoot's *American Pewter* was published but one example of this touch was known. The illustration of it showed the final letters 'STON' beneath an eagle, the upper name being entirely erased. As any of us would, Kerfoot assumed that the incomplete word was 'Boston.' Then, shortly before his death, he acquired another specimen with the same touch (Plate LIV, 386). In this case the full word showed beneath the eagle and we learned that its user was named Eggleston. But who was Eggleston and where did he work? The form of his touch suggested Connecticut, and Lucius Barbour's valuable statistics in the State Library at Hartford furnished the desired information.

Jacob Eggleston was born in Middletown, February 10, 1773, the son of Bennett and Phoebe Eggleston. In 1792, when only nineteen years of age, he married Sarah Whitmore. Hence it seems not unlikely that he served his apprenticeship in Jacob Whitmore's shop. Middletown land records show that he purchased property there in 1796. He probably opened a shop of his own at that time. From then until 1810 we find him buying and selling land, but in the latter year his record in Middletown ceases.

It was, therefore, most fortunate that his will and inventory were also found on file in Hartford. From these records it is apparent that Eggleston moved to Fayetteville, Cumberland County, North Carolina. An examination of Fayetteville land records uncovered a deed of May 4, 1807, confirming the sale to 'Jacob Eggleston of Fayetteville' of property on the south side of Cross Creek. He presumably continued to make pewter there and very probably also conducted a general store.

His will, dated March 13, 1813 (six days before his death), was made at Fayetteville.

By its terms he left to his parents the property in Middletown on which they were living and released them from all debts to him. The rest of the estate was willed to his wife and children. The Southern business venture must have been quite successful, for over eleven thousand dollars in real and personal property went to his family after the payment of all debts. Pertinent items included in the inventory were: 'Two horses — $95.00, One waggon and harness — $25.00, One peddlar's box — $6.00, 334 lbs. pewter moulds @ $0.40, $133.60. 333 lbs. new pewter @ .36 — $119.88.' There were also the usual pewterer's tools, old pewter, etc., as well as a long list of tinware, drygoods, etc. — just such a stock as any country store might carry.

An examination of Eggleston's probate records was like turning the pages of a memory book. What a gathering of old friends it proved to be! Here was a note of William Danforth for $23.13, and there (classified, alas, as worthless) one for $35, signed by Jacob Whitmore. Another sheet listed the debts which Eggleston owed, disclosing among his creditors Samuel Danforth, William Nott, and Blakslee Barns, the latter known to us heretofore as B. Barns of Philadelphia. Another paper showed that Nott accepted his payment in pewterer's moulds. And last of all was an accounting by the executors for the remainder of the moulds which they sold to William and Samuel Yale. We should know much more about Connecticut pewter and its makers could we but have been administrators of that estate.

Jacob Eggleston's body was brought back to his native town for burial and his grave may still be seen, close to the Danforth plot, in the cemetery on Liberty Street, Middletown.

The author owns a 13-inch deep dish marked with a large eagle and the initials 'J. E.' In design and general appearance the mark is so similar to one used by Thomas Danforth, Third, as well as to Louis G. Myers's 'Richmond Warranted' eagle (which is now attributed to Joseph Danforth, Junior), that I am convinced all three were the work of the same die-maker, probably a Middletown man. Plate LIV, 385, illustrates this new touch which we are attributing to Jacob Eggleston. Thus far, recognized examples of this man's pewter are limited to 8-inch and $8\frac{13}{16}$-inch plates, 12-inch flat dishes, 11-inch and 13-inch deep dishes, and bedpans.

THE RICHARD LEES

At the time that *American Pewter* appeared, two Richard Lee touches had been identified, but the Lee history was little known and most of the information that we had was erroneous.

I did not have the pleasure of ferreting out the truth about this maker, for a more energetic investigator was before me. Harold G. Rugg discovered an autobiography of the pewterer, entitled *A Short Narrative of the Life of Mr. Richard Lee; containing a brief account of his Nativity, Conviction and Conversion . . . printed for the Author 1821.* It will

PLATE LV

392

392 a

393

394

394 a

395

398

399

400

396   397

401

402

403

404   397 a

405

406 a

407

406

PLATE LVI — *Touches of the Connecticut Valley — The Lees, Ebenezer Southmayd, Stephen Barns, Ashbil Griswold, and James Porter*

408. An early mark of the elder Richard Lee, probably used at Grafton, New Hampshire, or Ashfield, Massachusetts, 1788–1793. From a four-handled diminutive porringer formerly in the collection of W. C. Staples, Esq.

409. An early touch of the elder Lee, 1788–1795. From a 2½-inch porringer formerly owned by the late Albert C. Bowman, Esq.

410. A touch probably used by the elder Lee at Springfield, Vermont, and earlier, 1790–1816. From a basin in the author's collection.

411 and 412. Small name-touch and handsome fleur-de-lis mark used by Richard Lee or his son Richard, Jr., Springfield, Vermont, 1795–1816. Formerly in the collection of the late Albert C. Bowman, Esq.

413. Name-touch used by Richard Lee or his son. From a small plate in the author's collection.

411a. Another impression of 411. From a brass skimmer owned by John P. Remensnyder, Esq.

414. Another Lee touch used by father. or son. Collection of the author.

415 and 416. Large and small touch of Ebenezer Southmayd, Castleton, Vermont, 1802–1820. From the author's collection.

417. Touch of Stephen Barns, residence not known, but probably the Middletown-Wallingford district, Connecticut, about 1792–1800. Collection of Charles F. Hutchins, Esq.

418. Large touch of Ashbil Griswold, Meriden, Connecticut, 1807–1815. Collection of Joseph France, Esq.

419. Another Griswold touch that was probably discarded prior to 1820. Collection of the author.

420 and 421. Later touches, about 1820 to 1830, used by Ashbil Griswold. Collection of the author.

422. Touch of James Porter, who was in Baltimore in 1803 and probably worked in or near Hartford for a few years prior to that date. From a plate formerly owned by Wilmer Moore, Esq.

422a. Another impression of the same touch. The author's collection.

423 and 423a. Two impressions of another touch of the same pewterer. From dishes in the author's collection.

PLATE LVI

408

409

410

411   412

413

411a

415

414

416

417

418

419

420

421

422

422a

423

423a

not be out of place to review briefly that history, adding a few details of minor importance which have since come to light.

It must first be stated that there were two Richard Lees, father and son, both of whom worked in pewter. Of the younger man's life we know very little. Richard, Senior, on the other hand, has given us a lengthy account of his wanderings, but the story unfortunately is given up in very large part to his spiritual tribulations, and furnishes us with but little more historical fact than could be gleaned from a reading of *The Pilgrim's Progress*.

Richard Lee the elder was born in Scituate, Rhode Island, January 27, 1747, the oldest boy in a family of sixteen children. He tells us that at five years of age 'I was put at work as steady as a man.' During his youth and early married years he lived at various times in Swansea, Rehoboth, Dighton, Taunton, and Dartmouth. When the war came he enlisted at Rehoboth in 1775 and served several enlistments, and, although his narrative tells us nothing of the type of service he performed, he complains bitterly of his broken health, which never recovered from the hardships in the army. How Lee earned his living prior to the war is not related in his autobiography.

The second period of his life was again one of wandering. He lived in many towns and plied many trades. We find him tanning hides in Gloucester, Rhode Island, in 1782, speculating in real estate in Springfield, Vermont, in 1785, keeping store, trading in wild land, and making hardware buttons in Grafton, New Hampshire, about 1788. Here in the narrative he first mentions the trade which has kept alive his memory. He writes: 'My next object was pewtering with my son,' and he says it in such a way as to lead us to believe that he had never had any previous training for this type of work. How did Lee secure the knowledge and experience to enable him to become a pewterer? And back in the woods, far from any pewter-making center, where did he acquire his moulds and how did he pay for them?

After a short sojourn in Grafton, Lee again set off on his travels, spending a year at Ashfield, Massachusetts, and two years at Lanesborough. Misfortune still followed him. His tools were seized to pay what he claimed were unjust debts, a thirty-pound quart basin mould bringing only $2.25 at forced sale.

Finally in 1802 he returned to Springfield, Vermont, married for the third time, and earned a meager living in his later years by peddling pewter and brass for his son, Richard, Junior. He died in Springfield in 1823 and is buried in the North Springfield Cemetery.

Pursued by misfortune which seemed to keep right at his heels no matter how fast he traveled, Richard Lee was one of those individuals who cannot settle down. The end of the rainbow was always just on the other side of the hill. In spite of ill health he had no lack of energy, for, in addition to his many vocations listed above, he was at times an itinerant preacher, an herb doctor, and a maker of children's books.

Richard, Junior, eldest son of Richard and Mehitabel Lee, was born in Rehoboth, Massachusetts, May 6, 1775. He accompanied his father on many trips, settling in Springfield, Vermont, sometime prior to 1795. There he married Olive Brown, January

10, 1796. For over twenty years he lived in Springfield making pewter and brass ware. However, I could not find his name on the tax lists after 1816, and his grave is not in the lot with the other members of the family.

The metal of the Lees is of fine quality, but the workmanship is not always of the best. Some pieces, as we might expect, betray the work of country pewterers. Lee pewter is nevertheless eagerly sought for; and rightly so, for individuality is always evident in the forms that were made.

Most marked is the Lee flair for the diminutive. The Lee saucers (or butter plates), unusual on account of the absence of reeding on the rim, measure but $5\frac{3}{8}$ inches in diameter. Only one smaller marked American plate is known. The same fondness for the smaller forms is evidenced in the spoons, ladles, and porringers. Other makers rarely made (or, if they did, they rarely marked) porringers under $3\frac{3}{4}$ inches in diameter. I have seen but one Lee porringer that was over $3\frac{3}{4}$ inches, and the size most frequently found is the tiny $2\frac{1}{4}$-inch model (Plate XIII, 68). Described as tasters or, even more erroneously, bleeding-cups, these attractive little vessels were, I feel sure, intended to serve some purpose now unknown; possibly they were toy porringers. Certainly Mr. Staples's little four-handled example would have made a most unsanitary and awkward wine-taster.

Homer E. Keyes, in 'Richard Lee, Pewterer,' in *Antiques* magazine, called attention to the variety of Lee porringer handles. I would point out further that each form of handle made by the Lees is absolutely distinctive. The initiate can distinguish a Lee porringer the full length of an ordinary room. Another point well taken by Mr. Keyes is that Lee porringers are in reality little basins with handles. With the exception of the $3\frac{3}{8}$- and $4\frac{13}{16}$-inch sizes, they never have the raised bosses and bulging sides of the typical New England porringer.

Even in the larger forms the Lee individuality persists. The porringer-basin, itself an uncommon vessel, has on the Lee pieces a very handsome and distinctive handle (Plate XII, 54). On his quart mug (Plate XX, 124), too, Lee used a strap handle such as is rarely found, a handle reminiscent of an earlier period. The discovery of this large mug came as a surprise. We should have expected from Lee's proclivities that the half-pint or pint size would have fitted more satisfactorily into his program.

The Lee output is just as unusual for the forms that it omitted as for the varied range made. We have found no plates larger than the $8\frac{3}{16}$-inch size, no basins of greater dimension than the quart, and, as pointed out above, only one porringer within the normal range, 4-inch to $5\frac{1}{2}$-inch. Large moulds were very expensive and the Lees were rarely out of debt. So perhaps they had few opportunities for purchasing the equipment required to turn out large vessels.

With the possible exception of 8-inch plates and $2\frac{1}{4}$-inch porringers, Richard Lee pewter is exceedingly scarce.

It will probably never be possible to determine whether both Lees used the same dies, or whether certain marks were employed only by the father and certain other touches by the son. There can be little question, though, that numbers 408, 409, and 410, of

Plate LVI, are much cruder and earlier-looking than the marks which follow. Number 408 shows the name cast in the bracket, which supports a frail porringer handle of early design. It is taken from Mr. Staples's four-handled specimen and has also been seen on a vessel with only one handle. The diameter of the bowl in both pieces, 2½-inch, is most unusual. Number 409 is from a 2¼-inch porringer formerly owned by the late A. C. Bowman. Although the second letter appears to be an 'I,' it is apparent that the uneven surface of the handle prevented a clear impression of what was assuredly a letter 'L.' The fleur-de-lis (number 412) is found on porringers and porringer-basins, the deer's head (number 414) on 2¼-inch porringers, and the full name (numbers 410 and 413) on porringers over 2½ inches in diameter, plates, basins, and mugs. The last touch (number 411) appears on porringer-basins, small porringers, ladles, and spoons, as well as on the brass skimmers and ladles which are presumed to have been made by Richard Lee, Junior. Here it should be reported that Louis G. Myers informed me that he once saw a brass ladle marked 'R. Lee' and the date 1830, indicating that the younger man must have still been at work after our record of him ceases. The Lee touches are almost always clearly impressed upon the metal, and the fleur-de-lis is, in my opinion, one of the most appropriate and well-designed of American touch-marks.

Because so much of the Lee pewter is found in the vicinity of Providence, Rhode Island, I think it likely that Richard, Junior, closed his days in the section of the country in which he was born.

SAMUEL PIERCE

'Samuel Pierce, Pewterer, and His Tools,' in the February, 1927, issue of *Antiques* is the title of the most absorbing article on American pewter that it has ever been my good fortune to read. To anyone desirous of an interesting and exciting half-hour, I recommend that he experience with Miss Julia D. S. Snow the thrill of her discovery of Pierce's eagle die in a barn in Greenfield, Massachusetts. Miss Snow has also resurrected for us from the records of the past a most complete account of Pierce's life, which I shall but tersely summarize here.

Samuel Pierce was born in Middletown, Connecticut, July 8, 1767, the son of Stephen and Hannah Pierce. It seems more than probable that Samuel learned his trade in the shop of Joseph Danforth. In 1790 he married Anne Joyce and soon thereafter was lured to Greenfield, Massachusetts, by the promises of prosperity which the budding town held forth. There we find him engaging in various enterprises. He was in turn a riverman carrying freight up and down the Connecticut, an oil and salt merchant, a cooper, a farmer, a miller, and a groceryman, and always, in his spare time, a coppersmith, tinsmith, and pewterer. He retired about 1831 and died in Greenfield March 25, 1840, at the age of seventy-two.

Pierce's touches are shown in Plate LV, 405 to 407. Although the initial touch and large eagle are great rarities and his metal is far from common, plates and basins impressed with the smaller bird may be found in a good many collections. The forms thus far reported include 8-inch plates, 11¼-inch and 12 3/16-inch flat dishes, 13-inch deep dishes, quart basins, pint and quart mugs, beakers, and christening basins. I have yet to hear of a Pierce porringer, although moulds for such are with his tools. The man's metal and workmanship are both of a high standard of excellence.

In Plates V and VI are illustrations of Pierce's tools and moulds. These were pictured first in Miss Snow's article in *Antiques*. With Pierce's tools was but one die, his small eagle touch. The absence of dies for his other two touches, which are, incidentally, rarer than the small eagle, strengthens the belief that the latter superseded the large eagle and the initials-in-circle.

STEPHEN BARNS

The identification of the users of certain touch-marks has been exceedingly difficult, in some cases impossible, when the touches included no clues beyond the initials. But when a man's name is spelled out in full upon the touch, the problem of tracking him down to the particular town where he worked and to the family to which he belonged has in most cases been merely a matter of research. Success has usually crowned our efforts; but Stephen Barns is an exception. Here is a maker whose touch, though not common, is by no means rare. At one time he probably had a fairly large trade, and yet all efforts to determine where that business was conducted have thus far been unavailing.

Barns's eagle touch (Plate LVI, 417), however, gives some important secondary evidence as to his provenance. There are fourteen stars over the eagle's head. Since Vermont entered the Union as the fourteenth state in 1791 and Kentucky was admitted the following year, we can date exactly when Barns's die was prepared for him. Moreover, the eagle seems to be closely related in type to Ashbil Griswold's straggly bird, and shows more than a nodding acquaintance with the eagle of William Danforth. The resemblances are so marked that I feel certain that the man worked in the Middletown-Meriden district. There was a Stephen Barns in Middletown in the first decade of the nineteenth century, but no records thus far found mention the man's occupation. It is possible that the pewterer was a kinsman of Blakslee Barns (son of Moses of Wallingford), but unfortunately I have not been able to locate baptismal records of Moses Barns's family.

The Barns pewter is typical of the Connecticut makers in form and is, if anything, somewhat below that general average in quality. I have seen his mark on 8-inch and 10-inch basins, on 7⅞-inch and 8¾-inch plates, and on 11⅛-inch and 13¼-inch deep dishes, as well as on a pewter separator in a lead tobacco jar — never, however, on hollow-ware.

EBENEZER SOUTHMAYD

An entirely new name in our lists of pewterers is that of Ebenezer Southmayd. An 11-inch deep dish came to light which was impressed with the name of E. Southmayd below a full-rigged ship (Plate LVI, 415) — a touch that was somewhat reminiscent of (though cruder than) the ship mark of John Will of New York. The plate had all the evidences of Connecticut workmanship, and there was reason for belief that it might lead to the discovery of a maker who was a contemporary, or even a forerunner, in Connecticut of the first Thomas Danforth.

Sure enough, a large Southmayd family was discovered in Middletown, that great pewter center of the colonial and Federal periods, but the maker proved to be a far later worker than might have been anticipated from the early form of his touch.

Ebenezer, son of Jonathan and Martha (Sage) Southmayd, was born in Middletown, January 23, 1775. His great-great-grandfather, William Southmayd, a sea-captain, had moved from New London to Middletown about 1670, and in 1683 was master of the sloop *John and Mary*. Ebenezer, so we are told, was a seaman himself in early life. It was therefore most appropriate that a ship should be the Southmayd device on pewter even when most makers of that day were stamping their handiwork with eagle touches.

In 1797 Southmayd married Elizabeth Starr in Middletown, and it is recorded that they had fourteen children. About 1802 — the exact date is uncertain — Ebenezer Southmayd and his family moved to Castleton, Vermont. According to Middletown land records, he still owned property there in October, 1803, but a Castleton historian states that he made pewter in the latter town from 1802 until his death. In Vermont he not only was a pewterer, but also a block-tin factor, a brass-founder, and a farmer. His lathe was turned by horsepower, and as late as 1887 his shop on the south side of the village green was still standing. Southmayd died September 30, 1831.

Since the discovery of the first Southmayd dish four more examples of his work have been found, all of which are impressed with a smaller touch showing the initials only (Plate LVI, 416). This mark appears on two $7\frac{7}{8}$-inch plates and two $4\frac{3}{8}$-inch beakers. The beakers are well finished and of good quality, but the flatware is very patently the work of a country pewterer.

JAMES PORTER

After the publication of *American Pewter* several more unidentified eagle touches were added to the group which Kerfoot illustrated. In the past three years clearer impressions of some of these eagles have come to light, and two designs are now known to be the work of a James Porter.

A pewterer of that name was listed in the Baltimore directory for 1803, but the man was apparently not a native of that city, for the name was found in but the one directory and in no other Baltimore records of that time.

Of the eight or ten Porter plates and dishes which have thus far been reported, over half turned up in the Connecticut Valley, and the character of the touches tends to confirm my belief that their user hailed from that district. Plate LVI, 422, shows an eagle that is very similar to one of Samuel Danforth's (Plate LV, 396). The second Porter touch (number 423) if unmarred would show sixteen stars above the eagle, evidence that the touch was first used between the years 1795 and 1803. James Porters were plentiful in Connecticut records of the eighteenth century, but I have thus far failed to prove that any of them made pewter.

The Porter marks have been found on 8-inch plates, on 11-inch flat dishes with comparatively narrow rim, and on 13⅛-inch deep dishes. That Porter hailed from Connecticut is all but confirmed by the fact that he made narrow-rim 11-inch dishes; for that form was apparently a specialty of the Connecticut Valley.

ASHBIL GRISWOLD

Ashbil Griswold was born in Rocky Hill, Connecticut, April 4, 1784, the second son of Constant and Rebecca (Boardman) Griswold. As a boy he was apprenticed to Thomas Danforth, Third, and in 1807 moved to what was then Clarksville on the outskirts of Meriden and commenced the manufacture of pewter-ware. He ate his first meal there in the residence of James Frary, whose daughter, Lucy, he later married.

Griswold was an energetic business man, built up a large trade, and became a prominent citizen of the town. He was the first president of the Meriden Bank, a warden of the Episcopal Church, justice of the peace, and representative in the State Legislature in 1831 and again in 1847.

About the year 1830 Griswold took in as partner a man named Couch under the firm name of Griswold and Couch. At that time he employed ten or twelve men and his gross sales were close to twenty-five hundred dollars per month. The power in the shop was supplied by a blind horse traveling around a beam which operated the lathes on the floor above. Griswold's goods were sold mainly by peddlers who traveled as far south as Georgia. In 1842 he retired from active business. Ashbil Griswold's death occurred May 30, 1853.

Few American pewterers have left us so many marked pieces. Why he should have enjoyed such a large trade we are at a loss to understand. Certainly his workmanship was not always of the best and the quality of his metal varies. Perhaps the answer lies in superior salesmanship.

Griswold used the eagle touches which are illustrated in Plate LVI, 418 to 420. The small 'A. G.' initial touch (number 421) was also his. He made the usual Connecticut range of plates and dishes, 8-inch to 13-inch; basins, 8-inch to 12-inch. Only the three-gill porringer has been reported thus far, although he must have made other sizes. His touches are found on many teapots and small beakers and upon occasional sugar bowls, inkwells, and soap boxes.

THE BOARDMANS

In the history of American pewter by all odds the largest single enterprise was that of the Boardmans of Hartford. Two brothers, great-grandsons of that patriarch of Connecticut pewter, Thomas Danforth of Norwich, worked for almost fifty years on Main Street, Hartford, and not only lived to see the passing of pewter, but were even present at the burial of that ill-begotten stepchild of the pewter industry, britannia metal.

Oliver Boardman, soldier of the Revolution, and his bride, Sarah Danforth, settled in Litchfield, Connecticut, about 1784. Then as now Litchfield was a town of lovely setting and unusual culture, and there Boardman built a fine home. There, too, the first law school in the country was founded at just about the time of the arrival of the Boardmans. The first son, Thomas Danforth Boardman, was born in Litchfield, January 21, 1784; his brother, Sherman, July 10, 1787. Oliver Boardman was a God-fearing man of very strict principles, and he watched with dismay the increase in consumption of wine and toddy by the students and townspeople. To him it seemed an unwholesome atmosphere in which to raise a family, and in 1795 he left his comfortable home and moved to Hartford. There the sons are presumed to have been apprenticed to their uncle, Samuel Danforth, pewterer.

In 1804 Thomas D. Boardman completed his apprenticeship and soon thereafter commenced his long business career in Hartford; a few years later Sherman became associated with him. On May 28, 1812, the older brother married Elizabeth B. Lewis; Sherman's marriage to Henrietta Richards took place on May 29, 1817.

Specimens of pewter bearing Thomas's touches alone (Plate LVII, 424 to 427) are so numerous, comparatively speaking, that there can be little doubt that he prospered early, and by 1822 the Boardmans had such a large local trade that they decided to open a branch store in New York. A younger brother, Timothy, acting presumably under the Hartford management, was put in charge of the New York branch, and the comparatively rare 'T. B. & Co.' touch (number 432) dates from that year. Upon Timothy's death, two years later, the New York firm name was changed to Boardman and Company. The active manager was Lucius Hart of Rocky Hill, whose stepmother was a Boardman, and in 1827 Hart was admitted to partnership in the concern, the business continuing under the name of Boardman and Hart until its dissolution in 1850.

All of the evidence that we have indicates that Boardman pewter was never made in New York, but was stamped at the Hartford factory with the touches reserved for the New York shop and then shipped to the latter city for sale. Meanwhile the Boardmans in Hartford not only were selling pewter direct from the shop as well as through peddlers and the New York branch, but also seem to have had agents in other cities, in some cases even stamping their metal with the names of their dealers. Witness particularly John H. Whitlock of Troy, New York, who is listed as a merchant in that city from 1836 to 1844.

Finally, in 1844, these enterprising brothers opened a second branch store. This agency was located at Philadelphia under the name of Boardman and Hall, the local representatives being Sherman's son, Henry S. Boardman, and F. D. Hall. The name was later changed to Hall, Boardman and Company, and finally to Hall and Boardman, and under the latter title was still listed in the Philadelphia Directory when the elder Boardmans closed out their business in Hartford in 1854. Sherman died March 20, 1861, but Thomas survived until September 10, 1873.

The touches employed by the shop are numbered in the order in which they are believed to have been first used, except that numbers 431 and 434, Plate LVII, should be transposed, an arrangement which the photographs will not permit. Numbers 428 to 434 inclusive must have made their first appearance between the years 1810 and 1830. Since very often two different eagle touches are found impressed upon the same article, these marks may all have been used contemporaneously. Differing from J. B. Kerfoot's opinion, I believe the lion touch (number 435) to be later than any of the eagle marks and contemporary with the Boardman and Hart name touch. This reasoning is based on the fact that those Boardman communion flagons which are late in form and light in weight usually bear the lion touch. Moreover, Boardman water pitchers, unquestionably late forms, are found, as far as I know, with only one of two touches, the late Boardman and Hart name touch (number 437) or the seated lion. It is worth recalling also that large eagle touches had been discarded by all other makers by 1832 at least, and perhaps earlier.

Boardman pewter far outnumbers, in quantity of existing pieces and variety of design, the existent output of any other shop in this country. For almost every known American form manufactured during the nineteenth century the Boardmans appear to have had models.

The pewter from this shop deserved the wide distribution which it received. All of the early pieces are well fashioned and of excellent quality. That Thomas Boardman purchased his uncle Samuel Danforth's moulds from the latter's estate in 1816 seems almost certain, for the early Boardman flagons and tall teapots are identical with those of Danforth, and beakers, otherwise alike, may bear the touch of Samuel Danforth, 'T. D. B.,' 'T. D. & S. B.,' 'T. B. & Co.,' or 'Boardman & Hart.'

Although some of the later Boardman ware is thin, I have seen but one piece, a teapot, which could be condemned as poorly made and of bad design. For the most part the Boardmans remained pewterers, not britannia-makers, to the close of their days. They are so listed, to their credit, in the mercantile directories of the eighteen-forties when all their competitors were described as makers of britannia ware, and as late as 1847 Hall, Boardman and Company were advertising 'pewter' plates. Much of this later Boardman pewter is as fine as the metal made by the shop in its early days, and some forms, such as communion flagons, were never equaled in line nor bettered in quality by any other makers of the britannia period.

Through the kindness of Mrs. Arthur Brewer, great-granddaughter of Thomas Danforth Boardman, I am privileged to reproduce (see Frontispiece, volume II) a portrait of this last pewterer of the old school. Not only was he one of the ablest of American pewterers, but he was also a respected and eminent citizen, a gentleman who looked every inch the part.

THE YALE FAMILY

It is a difficult matter to know just where the line should be drawn in preparing a list of pewterers. In this volume, however, it has been decided to eliminate from serious consideration those men who cannot be expected to have had touches of their own. There must have been plenty of men, such as Henry and Silas Grilley of Waterbury or Samuel Yale, Senior, of Meriden, who apparently made nothing in pewter but buttons. They would have needed no touch-mark for work of that nature, so out they go. But although we eliminate Samuel Yale, Senior, his five sons apparently qualify as *bona-fide* pewterers.

William and Samuel, Junior, born respectively on March 13, 1784, and April 4, 1787, at Meriden, worked in their youth as button-makers in their father's shop, and then branched out as partners in an establishment of their own. They had a shop together at least as early as 1813, when they purchased moulds from the estate of Jacob Eggleston. We also have record of a contract made in 1816 with one of their peddlers. They were probably still making pewter in 1820 or later.

Both men married; had families; and were prominent in civic and religious affairs of the town. Squire William Yale was a mountain of strength in the church (First Baptist), and is said to have possessed the only 'sale-carpeted' house in Meriden. He was looked upon with a great deal of respect by his neighbors, for he entertained the visiting ministers and in a room in his house the Meriden National Bank had its beginnings. He represented his town in the State Legislature for many years, and upon his death, January 23, 1833, he left to his family a handsome estate accumulated in the manufacture of pewter and tinware.

Samuel Yale, although apparently less prominent, also took part in public affairs, serving a number of terms as sheriff's deputy for New Haven County. In later life he was a manufacturer of japanned tinware and lamp trimmings. He retired in 1858 and died on March 12, 1864.

The eagle touch of these brothers (Plate LVII, 440) first illustrated by Louis G. Myers in his *Notes*, has been found on 7⅞-inch and 8⅜-inch plates, also on pint and quart basins. It was probably used for only a few years (*c.* 1814–1820).

The Yale Family

The three younger brothers — Charles, born April 20, 1790; Selden, February 29, 1795; and Hiram, March 27, 1799 — moved from Meriden to Wallingford after completing their apprenticeships. Charles and Hiram certainly, and Selden probably, learned the trade of pewter-making in the shop of Thomas Danforth, Third, at Rocky Hill. Charles may have had a business of his own in Wallingford prior to 1815, but no early touch-mark of his has been found. About that time he took his brother Selden into business with him and they opened what may have been a branch store in Richmond, Virginia. They manufactured tinware and perhaps some pewter, though no touch-mark of this pair is known. Selden, who had married Sarah Kirtland of Wallingford in 1822, died November 1, 1823, leaving his wife and one small child. His half share in the firm of C. & S. Yale was worth slightly more than seven thousand dollars, and the value of the pewter-making tools in the shop was placed at one hundred and fifty dollars.

Hiram Yale, who had married Rosetta Robinson on April 6, 1821, must have commenced the manufacture of pewter prior to Selden's death. Soon thereafter Charles joined his younger brother in the firm of H. Yale and Company.

There can be little doubt that Hiram was the moving spirit of the organization which bore his name, and an enterprising young man he must have been, for he imported workmen from England to instruct his apprentices in the manufacture of the finest britannia ware. According to one historian, it was in the shop of H. Yale and Company that the spinning of britannia was first successfully performed in this country. Unfortunately Hiram died in 1831, when only thirty-two years of age. Among the creditors of the estate were Thomas S. Derby and his son, Thomas, Junior, of Middletown, and Hiram's older brothers, William and Samuel Yale. The shop inventory included 'suspending lamps,' a coffee-urn, 'old fashion coffee pots,' 'old fashion and new fashion teapots,' tankards, christening basins, goblets, pitchers, plates, 'baskets,' 'new fashion coffee pots,' and quantities of tools and raw materials. Included among the latter were:

| 1 Lot Block Tin | | $2127\frac{1}{2}$ lbs @ $15\frac{3}{4}$ | 335.08 |
| 1 " Castings. | Rolled Mettle | $710\frac{3}{4}$ lbs @ 17 c | 120.82 |

furnishing proof that Yale's product was made by the spinning process. If, as may be assumed, the 'suspending lamps' were whale-oil swinging lamps and the pitchers were large water pitchers, this inventory supplies the earliest evidence of the manufacture of such forms. On the other hand, it is most surprising to find that tankards were being made at such a late date.

After Hiram's death, Charles Yale moved the plant outside the town in order to take advantage of the waterpower which the new site offered. The hamlet which grew up around the factory was named Yalesville in his honor. Charles, however, seems to have been unable or unwilling to carry on the business, and was in the midst of negotiations for the sale of the company to his foreman, Lorenzo Williams (an Englishman, who later opened a shop of his own in Philadelphia), and to Samuel Simpson, a former apprentice, when his death occurred November 2, 1835. Williams and Simpson then acquired the shop, operating it in partnership for a year, after which Simpson ran it successfully alone until 1845, when he in turn sold out to John Munson.

Although Charles Yale was listed as a britannia-maker at 80 Pine Street in the New York City directory for 1832, he undoubtedly was supervising at the same period the business of H. Yale and Company. It is my supposition that the New York establishment was merely a shop for the sale of britannia made at Yalesville, just as the Boardmans of Hartford were operating a New York warehouse and salesroom at that same date. The one known mark of Charles Yale contains the word 'Wallingford,' and is found principally upon teapots of just this period.

An early touch of Hiram Yale, mentioned by Charles A. Calder in *Rhode Island Pewterers*, but never before illustrated, is shown in Plate LVIII, 444, and with it H. Yale's later uninteresting incised marks (number 445). The new touch has been found on 8⅜-inch and 11-inch deep dishes of good quality. The later marks appear on 11-inch dishes, small beakers, communion sets, teapots, and an unusual two-handled mug which Louis G. Myers illustrated in his *Notes*.

Elsewhere comment was made upon the energy of the Danforths and other Connecticut pewterers in peddling their wares far and wide, and a copy was exhibited of a contract between William and Samuel Yale and one of their peddlers. Here we are fortunate in being able to present also a 'business conditions' letter, or salesman's report, which would no doubt startle — though perhaps not unpleasantly — the average sales manager of the twentieth century.

Newburgh, West Branch of
the Susquehanna River
May 11, 1814

Worthy Patron:

Where to begin or end my uncouth epistle I know not, but upon reflection will try to compose my mind while I inform you that I shall sink one hundred dollars at least unless fortune turns the scale in my favor.

R. Baldwin and I have traversed the country from Dan to Beersheba, besides going to Albany, and I have not sold either buttons or spoons to any amount. The reason which people give for not purchasing these articles is that the embargo is repealed, an armistice on foot and peace at the very door, when all these things are to be showered down upon them as manna was to the Israelites.

Moses [Baldwin] has gone to Pittsburg to see what may be done there while I am cruising about here and there wherever the spirit moves as I thought it would hardly quit cost for me to go any farther. Tin goes extremely well.

Your well wisher til Death

Warren P. Stone

Mr. Samuel Yale.

We should like to know more about Warren Stone. One who could write such a letter to a pillar of the church in Meriden was surely wasting his talents serving as a mere peddler.

One statement in the letter will bear enlargement. Stone mentions only buttons and spoons and later speaks of tinware. From this we should naturally assume that he was not peddling pewter flatware. William and Samuel Yale, as we know, made buttons for their father and probably had no early training in the manufacture of other forms in pewter. It seems more than likely that the purchase of Eggleston's moulds in 1813 was the occasion of their branching out, and that the actual production of pewter plates in their shop commenced at about the date of Warren Stone's letter.

THE NOTTS AND JOHNSONS

Among the pewterers rescued from oblivion by Louis G. Myers was William Nott of Stepney, Connecticut, who, according to an extant letter of Thomas Danforth, Fourth, was working for B. Barns in Philadelphia in 1812. Myers acquired several plates stamped with an eagle above a masonic emblem and the name William Nott (Plate LVIII, 450); and very naturally he attributed this touch to the Stepney pewterer whom he proved to have been a founder of Columbia Lodge No. 25, F. & A. M., at Stepney in 1793.

In my efforts to throw more light upon this man's history I have become very much involved in a genealogical problem, for it now appears that there were two William Notts, both of them masons, working in pewter in different towns at approximately the same period, and it is difficult to differentiate between the two. I shall set down the facts as I have found them and explain my deductions therefrom, but shall leave to another the problem of determining definitely whether there were one or two William Notts who made pewter, and if two, which was the user of the known Nott touch.

One of the earliest settlers in Wethersfield, Connecticut, was a John Nott. For several generations the name William recurs in the Nott family, and in the census of 1790 we find a William Nott of Wethersfield (which included Stepney) and another William near-by in Middletown. Each man had a son of the same name. The Stepney Nott married Elizabeth Goodrich at Wethersfield in 1784, but further than that I can add nothing to Louis Myers's information about the man.

The elder of the William Notts of Middletown does not enter into our story, but we are interested in his son, William, who was born in Middletown, February 10, 1789, and married Betsey Gaylord of the same town April 11, 1809.

After the death of Jacob Eggleston, Middletown pewterer, in Fayetteville, North Carolina, in 1813, a William Nott purchased the pewter-making tools from the executors of the estate.

On October 15, 1817, William Nott of Middletown gave a lease to Samuel Babcock of one half of a building 'lately erected by said Nott, Babcock and Jehiel Johnson for carrying on the business of plating and pewtering.'

On April 11, 1818, 'Jehiel Johnson and William Nott, both of Fayetteville, North Carolina,' purchased property on Hay Street in that town and on August 5 of the same year a William Nott became a member of St. John's Lodge No. 2, F. & A. M., in Middletown.

PLATE LVII — *Touches of the Connecticut Valley — The Boardmans and Yales*

424. Touch of Thomas D. Boardman, Hartford, 1805–1820. Collection of John W. Poole, Esq.

425 and 404a. Boardman's name-touch and the Hartford mark, used earlier by his uncle, Samuel Danforth. From a flagon in the author's collection.

426. The same maker's small initial touch as found on a beaker in the author's collection.

427 and 427a. Two impressions of Boardman's small eagle touch as taken respectively from examples in the collection of Albert H. Good, Esq., and Mrs. Arthur Brewer.

428 and 429. Touches of the partnership of Thomas D. and Sherman Boardman, Hartford, 1810–1830. From the author's collection.

430 and 431. 430 was used by the Boardmans after about 1820 both on pewter sold direct from Hartford and that made for their New York agency. 431 was used exclusively by the New York house, Boardman and Company, 1825–1827. Collection of the author.

432. Touch presumed to have been used on pewter sold by Timothy Boardman and Company, New York, 1822–1825. Collection of the author.

433. Boardman touch used about 1820 to 1830. Collection of John P. Remensnyder, Esq.

434. Another Boardman eagle that was probably first used when Sherman was taken in as a partner about 1810. From a dish in the author's collection.

435. Last of the Boardman Hartford touches, probably not used prior to 1830. Collection of the author.

436. Earliest touch of Boardman and Hart, New York, used first about 1827. Has been found on same plates with the touches of its predecessor, Boardman and Company. Collection of Albert H. Good, Esq.

437 and 438. Least rare of the Boardman and Hart touches. Used from about 1830 to 1850. The New York mark was replaced, perhaps before 1840, by the smaller New York touch in the adjoining illustration 439. Courtesy of the Mabel Brady Garvan Collection, Gallery of Fine Arts, Yale University.

437a and 439. See comments directly above. The marks are from a beaker in the author's collection.

440 and 440a. Two impressions of the touch of William and Samuel Yale, Meriden, Connecticut, 1813–1820. From plates in the Mabel Brady Garvan Collection, Gallery of Fine Arts, Yale University.

PLATE LVII

424

427

425   404 a   426   427 a   428

430   431   429

432   433   434   435

436   437   438   437 a   439   440   440 a

PLATE LVIII — *The Later Touches of the Connecticut Valley*

441. Early touch of Thomas S. Derby, Middletown, Connecticut, 1816–1820. From a basin in the collection of the author.

442. Derby's second Jackson touch, adopted about 1820. From a plate in the collection of Miss Anna L. Rights.

442a and 443. Photograph of another plate in the collection of Miss Rights, showing the same touch and the name-touch which is found on Derby's later work.

444 and 444a. Two impressions of the early touch of Hiram Yale, Wallingford, Connecticut, 1822–1825. The former was in the collection of the late Frederick N. Gaston, Esq.; the latter is the author's.

445. Hiram Yale's later uninteresting mark, 1825–1831. Collection of the author.

446. Touch of J. and D. Hinsdale, Middletown, Connecticut, about 1815. From a plate in the author's collection.

447 and 447a. Touch attributed to Jehiel Johnson, Middletown, Connecticut, and Fayetteville, North Carolina, 1815–1825. Collection of the author.

448. A second touch attributed to Jehiel Johnson. From a plate in the collection of Charles F. Hutchins, Esq.

449. Another touch attributed to Johnson. From a plate in the collection of Mrs. Ralph P. Hanes.

450. Touch of William Nott, Middletown, Connecticut, and Fayetteville, North Carolina, 1813–1825. From a plate in the collection of John P. Remensnyder, Esq.

451. Touch of Otis Williams, Buffalo, New York, 1826–1831. From a plate in the author's collection.

430a and 452. Touches of I. Curtiss. Residence of maker not known, probably Connecticut, about 1818–1825. Courtesy of the Mabel Brady Garvan Collection, Gallery of Fine Arts, Yale University.

453. Touch of Samuel Campmell (or Campbell). Residence of maker unknown, probably Connecticut, about 1825. From a plate in the author's collection. In *American Pewter* this touch was designated as unidentified eagle number 3.

453a. Two faint impressions of the same touch. From a small plate (or saucer) owned by Joseph France, Esq.

PLATE LVIII

441

442

442 a   443

444

444 a

445

446

447

447 a

448

449

450

451

430 a   452

453

453 a

The Pewterers of the Connecticut Valley

In the *Middlesex Gazette* of July 7, 1819, published in Middletown, the following notice appeared:

> The copartnership heretofore existing under the firm name of Johnson & Nott is this day dissolved by mutual consent.
>
> Jehiel Johnson
William Nott

On October 26, 1822, as a resident of Middletown, Nott mortgaged the property in Middletown mentioned above to Jehiel Johnson, and on September 10, 1825, Johnson released the mortgage to 'William Nott, late of Middletown, now of Fayetteville, North Carolina.'

In August, 1824, when Blakslee Barns died at Berlin, Connecticut, the estate held a note of a William Nott amounting to over one thousand dollars, advanced for the purchase of stationery, books, shoes, etc., indicating that at least one man of this name had given up pewtering prior to that date.

In October, 1826, William Nott and John D. Starr, of the firm of Nott and Starr of Fayetteville, took title to land in Middletown and on August 12, 1836, William Nott of Fayetteville disposed of the last of his Connecticut real estate. He died at some time between the latter date and January 5, 1841, when his widow received her division of the estate in Fayetteville.

I do not know in what section Mr. Myers found his William Nott plates, but all others that have been seen by or reported to me — perhaps fifteen plates — came to light in North Carolina, in several cases with 'J. J.' eagle-marked plates, which I attribute to Jehiel Johnson. The William Nott plates are of good quality and are found in diameters of $7\frac{7}{8}$ and $8\frac{13}{16}$ inches; deep dishes measuring $11\frac{1}{4}$ and $13\frac{1}{8}$ inches.

My feeling, therefore, is that two William Notts made pewter; that the Wethersfield man was never more than a journeyman; and that all known William Nott pewter was made by the one-time partner of Jehiel Johnson in Middletown and Fayetteville.

Let us now turn to Johnson's history. Jehiel, son of Constant and Thankful (Whitmore) Johnson, was born in Middletown in 1784 or 1785. He married Betsey Bidwell in 1809 and had seven children. Of his early years we know nothing, but from March 3, 1814, until September 9, 1815, he was in the grocery business with his brother, Constant Johnson, Junior. On September 19, 1815, the *Middlesex Gazette* announced the formation of the firm of Johnson, Hall and Company with Jehiel and Constant Johnson and John H. Hall as partners. The notice failed to state the nature of their business, but on April 3, 1817, they advertised as follows:

> To the Patrons of Domestic Manufactures. — The Subscribers offer for sale a large assortment of Plain and Japan'd Tin Ware, Blocktin Tea Pots & Ladles. Together with a general assortment of Pewter Ware warranted to be of a good quality. The above Wares will be sold as cheap as can be bought elsewhere, for cash or country produce or approved Notes.
>
> Johnson Hall & Co.
>
> N.B. Old Pewter, Copper & Brass taken in exchange.

Jehiel Johnson must have left the firm early in 1817 to join forces with Nott and Babcock as related above, and not improbably the new firm took over Johnson, Hall and Company's pewter-making business. Babcock's association with the enterprise was brief, and the partnership of Johnson and Nott, with shops in both Middletown and Fayetteville, lasted only until July, 1819. After the latter date Johnson's name is not found in Fayetteville records. He presumably returned to Middletown and continued his pewter-making for a few years longer. His death took place in Middletown, July 1, 1833, at the age of forty-eight.

Louis G. Myers in his *Notes* illustrated a touch showing an eagle and the initials 'J. J.' (Plate LVIII, 447). This he ascribed to James Jones, a Newport coppersmith, who in his youth worked in his father's pewter shop. We now know, however, that soon after Gershom Jones's death in 1807 James left Newport and opened a coppersmithy in New York City, following that trade until his death in 1820. There is no evidence that he made pewter in a shop of his own. Furthermore the 'J. J.' plates are found usually in North Carolina or the Connecticut Valley, and frequently with pewter of William Nott. Had Johnson's history been known to Myers, I believe that he, too, would have attributed to this maker, as I am doing, the rare 'J. J.' touch.

Two other 'J. J.' eagle touches (Plate LVIII, 448 and 449), which have been seen in North Carolina collections, are here attributed to Jehiel Johnson. The various 'J. J.' marks have been found on 7$\frac{7}{8}$-inch basins, 7$\frac{7}{8}$-inch and 8$\frac{13}{16}$-inch plates, 11$\frac{3}{16}$-inch flat dishes, and 13$\frac{1}{8}$-inch deep dishes.

THOMAS S. DERBY

Thomas S. Derby's questionable fame has hitherto been based upon his teapots, cuspidors, and other late forms, stamped with the name-touch 'T. S. Derby.' J. B. Kerfoot in *American Pewter* wrote of him: 'I should say that he is of greater importance to the completeness of our records than to the beauty of our shelves.' But then Kerfoot had not seen any of Derby's early work, the pewter that he had made before succumbing to the doubtful charms of the siren, britannia.

In Plate LVIII, 441, is a photograph from an 11$\frac{1}{2}$-inch basin of excellent pewter and careful finish of one of the most interesting and certainly the most historical of all American touches — a bust of General Jackson in uniform in a circle of eighteen stars, with the old hero's name and the initials 'N. O.' above the head. Jackson's famous victory at New Orleans occurred in 1815. Indiana was admitted to the Union as the nineteenth state in 1816. The date of the first use of the touch is therefore very accurately determined. At that time Jackson was the idol of the nation, and the use of his bust in the touch-mark was a clever move by the pewterer to capitalize the General's popularity. The basin, however, gave no clue to its maker. Where might we turn in our search for this unknown Jackson admirer?

Through the kindness of Mrs. J. B. Kerfoot, I learned of the existence of a set of six 8-inch plates bearing not only a head of Jackson, but also the normal T. S. Derby mark. Their owner, Miss Anna L. Rights of Winston-Salem, North Carolina, has courteously permitted me to illustrate this combination of touches (numbers 442 and 443). The Jackson touch found on her plates differs in details from that on my basin. It shows twenty-two stars instead of eighteen, and consequently indicates that it was impressed with a later die which was first used in 1818. Both touches are here illustrated.

We now had the pewterer's name and his approximate working dates, but still no knowledge as to the location of his shop. His pewter had been found in New England, New York, New Jersey, and North Carolina. When any maker's wares have been scattered so widely it is a gamble worth backing that they were distributed by Connecticut peddlers. Lucius Barbour's statistics in the State Library at Hartford confirmed this supposition. There it is recorded that on November 3, 1847, 'Thomas S. Derby, britannia manufacturer, aged 61, married Ruth S. Russell, aged 47, both of Middletown.'

Thomas Scovel, son of Patrick and Elizabeth (Ward) Derby, was born about 1786 and baptized in the First Congregational Church of Middletown, January 28, 1787. On November 2, 1808, he married Mary Porter and in 1818 was admitted as a freeman of the town. During the same twelvemonth he voted in Middletown for the first time and is first listed as a taxpayer. He was then thirty-two years of age. It would seem, therefore, that some of his early years were spent elsewhere. It is not at all unlikely that he operated a shop for a few years in one of the Southern states, just as did Jacob Eggleston, William Nott, and other Connecticut pewterers.

In addition to the 8-inch plates and large basins previously mentioned, I have seen a 13¼-inch deep dish and have knowledge of a pint basin both of which bear a Jackson impression. The late Derby pieces that have come to my attention have little to commend them.

Thomas Derby died in Middletown April 17, 1852, aged sixty-five. At least one son, Thomas S., Junior, followed the same trade.

I. CURTISS

I. Curtiss's marks (Plate LVIII, 430a and 452) were known to J. B. Kerfoot and, as he pointed out, the same eagle touch, either before or after its use by Curtiss, was stamped on pewter of the Boardmans of Hartford about 1825.

Although this man may be identical with the Joseph Curtiss, Junior, who sold pewter in Troy, New York, in 1828, and later worked in Albany, it is difficult to believe that at that date he would have used the old-fashioned 'I' instead of a 'J' for his initial. It is my belief that the man's first name actually did commence with the letter 'I,' that he worked in or near Hartford about the year 1820, and that the Boardmans later acquired his eagle touch.

His mark has been found only on 6-inch and 8-inch plates of a very good quality and finish.

Samuel Campmell

J. AND D. HINSDALE

Another touch, new to collectors, is that of J. and D. Hinsdale (Plate LVIII, 446). Unlike any other Connecticut eagle, the touch is elliptical in outline and bears some resemblance to the marks of Robert Palethorp, Junior, of Philadelphia. The photograph is from an 8¾-inch plate in my own collection.

John and Daniel Hinsdale, sons of the Reverend Theodore and Anne (Bissel) Hinsdale, were born in Windsor, Connecticut, in 1778 and 1785 respectively. No records that I could find indicated that they were pewterers. Though they may have made pewter in their early years at Middletown, they were essentially merchants who had a large trade with the West Indies. From 1813 to 1815 we find them advertising in the *Middlesex Gazette* a great variety of articles including hardware, groceries, lead, glass, block-tin, iron, leather, Antigua rum, cook-stoves, etc. Later on they offered a new eighty-one-ton sloop for sale, and at another time advertised for 'twenty shipping horses.' The Hinsdale brothers were apparently merchants on a large scale, but they overreached themselves; in 1826 they failed, carrying with them to disaster the Eagle Bank of New Haven. Soon thereafter John Hinsdale moved with his family to Brooklyn, where he died in 1851. Daniel's death occurred in 1837 at Rising Sun, Indiana.

Though the Hinsdale pewter may have been made for them by some other man, the fact that they had a touch of their own entitles the brothers to be listed here. The character of the mark indicates a date between 1810 and 1820. The three surviving plates of record bearing this touch measure 8¾ inches in diameter.

SAMUEL CAMPMELL

J. B. Kerfoot in his *American Pewter* showed among his unidentified touches a mark which he termed 'unidentified eagle, number 3.' In the original touch, reproduced here again (Plate LVIII, 453) from an 8-inch plate, it is apparent that the maker's first name was Samuel. More than twelve years were to pass before another plate of the same maker came to light. Joseph France now owns a 5¼-inch butter plate with a badly worn impression of the same touch (number 453a) on which the last name seems to be decipherable as 'Campmell' or possibly 'Campbell.'

As this book goes to press Samuel Campmell, pewterer, has not been located, but the evidence of both the plates and the mark point to the Connecticut Valley as the probable place of origin during the period from 1810 to 1825.

The Pewterers of the Connecticut Valley

OTIS WILLIAMS

When *American Pewter* was published, we learned that the Danforth family could boast three generations of pewterers. Somewhat later Louis G. Myers unearthed four more pewter-making Danforths and extended their period of activity through four generations. Data now at hand prove that a grandson of the third Thomas Danforth worked early enough to make eagle-marked 8-inch plates.

A chance examination several years ago of the earliest Directory of Buffalo, New York, that of 1828, disclosed that the growing frontier village boasted among its industries of that day a block-tin and pewter manufactory. In the Directory proper the proprietor of the shop in question was listed as 'Otis Williams, blocktin manufacturer, Main St.' Buffalo's next Directory is dated 1832 and makes mention neither of a pewter manufactory nor of Williams. The aforesaid facts were jotted down but with very little expectation that a marked example of Williams's handicraft would ever be found, for he had apparently worked but a brief period in a small town. Furthermore, it was my belief at that time that just such country makers as this man were responsible for much of the unmarked pewter which we find.

It was therefore with no little delight that I learned from P. G. Platt that he had seen an 8-inch plate marked with an eagle and 'O. Williams, Buffalo.' That plate is now in my possession, and in Plate LVIII, 451, is illustrated a cut of the touch that it bears. The striking similarity of the mark to the small eagle used by Boardman and Company led to the belief that Williams might have worked in the Boardman shop and might possibly have been a relative of the R. Williams of Rocky Hill, Connecticut, who was listed by J. B. Kerfoot.

The facts gleaned from Connecticut records proved these surmises to be justified. Otis Williams was born in Rocky Hill, Connecticut, March 13, 1799, the only son of Richard and Hannah Danforth Williams. His mother was a daughter of the third Thomas Danforth, and his father is said to have been Danforth's partner for several years. The family moved to Hartford soon after Otis's birth, and there the father died while the boy was still in his 'teens.

We cannot be absolutely certain when the younger Williams started West to seek his fortune, but we have two leading clues. Once a month the *Buffalo Emporium* printed the names of the addressees of unclaimed mail at the post-office. Otis Williams's name is on the list of December 1, 1826. Just one month later, in the same newspaper, the following advertisement appeared:

Block Tin and Pewter Manufactory.

Otis Williams, second door north of the National Hotel near the Canal Basin, has on hand and is constantly manufacturing Britannia Coffee Urns, Tea Pots, Ladles, and Tumblers, Quart and Pint Cups, Basons, Platters, Plates, Porringers, etc.

Merchants of the Western Country are invited to supply themselves at his establishment. All orders thankfully received and punctually attended to.

Otis Williams

Williams lived but four years longer, and after his death, May 12, 1831, following a lingering illness, his debts were found to be in excess of the value of his possessions.

Among the Erie County records are papers for the administration of the estate, one of which is an inventory. Williams owned little apart from his shop equipment. Included in the latter were moulds valued at one hundred and fifty dollars, approximately one hundred and fifty pounds of finished pewter, and eight hundred twenty-eight pounds of old pewter, as well as the necessary tools and the shop appurtenances.

The Williams plate measures exactly eight inches, and would be in almost mint condition had not some Victorian housewife had it buffed to save the labor of frequent cleaning. It is of excellent metal made by a pewterer of the old school.

To include a Buffalo maker's history among those of the pewterers of the Connecticut Valley may be stretching a point, but Williams, by birth and training, was rightfully of the Connecticut tradition, and it would be certainly more absurd to give to Buffalo a heading all by itself on the basis of only one surviving pewter plate.

END OF VOLUME I

PEWTER IN AMERICA

Its Makers and Their Marks

VOLUME TWO

THOMAS DANFORTH BOARDMAN

1784–1873

From a portrait painted in 1843 by Hinsdale, and now owned
by THOMAS DANFORTH BOARDMAN, Esq., of San Francisco

Courtesy of Mrs. Arthur Brewer

CONTENTS

LIST OF PLATES

THE PEWTERERS OF NEW YORK CITY

THE date when pewter was first made in New York City is a matter of conjecture. Perhaps there were Dutch pewterers working there when the town was still called New Amsterdam. The earliest resident pewterers of whom we have knowledge were William Diggs and William Horsewell, two Englishmen, whose occupation as pewterers was shown in New York records dating from the opening years of the eighteenth century, over sixty years after Richard Graves began to mix pewter-making with philandering in Salem, Massachusetts. The products of these shops must have followed closely the designs of vessels made in England at the close of the seventeenth century. Horsewell's apprentice, who opened his own establishment a few years later, was Francis Bassett, the first of a famous family of pewterers, and by 1740 there were almost as many men earning their livelihood by pewtering in New York as in the older and larger town of Boston.

Boston and New York present interesting contrasts both in the histories of the workers and in the forms of their work that have survived. In Boston, as has been pointed out, most of the pewter-makers were men who learned two trades, brass-founding and pewtering. In New York not a single record has been found of a pewterer who 'doubled in brass.' Some few of the late makers (the McEuens and the Youles, for instance) combined plumbing with pewtering, but in general the New York pewterers were pewterers only.

That difference in training may account, in part at least, for the contrast in survival between early Boston and New York hollow-ware. The Boston makers have left us almost nothing; the New York pewterers, a small but impressive group of splendid pieces in a variety of shapes. For the quarter-century prior to 1765 not a single example of Boston hollow-ware is known to be in existence, whereas at least fifteen to twenty pieces bearing witness to the skill and versatility of the New York men of that period are scattered through collections that I have examined. The metal of these early men is of fine quality and workmanship; the walls are thick, and the pieces sturdy and well designed. Had we but a score more of varied examples of their craftsmanship I feel quite certain that no one would doubt that the 'golden age' of American pewter came — and passed — before the Revolution.

New York had one more outstanding group of pewterers, the men whose working years spanned the struggle for independence, the immediate successors to the Leddells, to John Will, and to the early Bassetts. It is a matter for congratulation that, although existing examples by this group are nearly as scarce as those of their predecessors, the range in form is again surprisingly wide. The Boston contemporaries of these men have left us only flatware and a few quart pots, whereas New York touches are found also on flagons, tankards, chalices, beakers, teapots, creamers, porringers, hot-water plates, ink-stands, and other interesting shapes. As in the case of the earlier New York pieces the workmanship is of a high order.

Louis G. Myers, in his *Notes*, illustrated a banner, now in the New York Historical Society's custody, which was carried by the pewterers in the parade that celebrated the ratification of the Federal Constitution in 1788. Whether the 'Pewterers' Society' which owned the banner was a social organization, hurriedly formed to represent the trade in the parade, or an active trade guild which had been in existence for many years, we do not know. The discovery of its records and particularly its membership lists would be an outstanding event in the pewter world.

About the time of the Revolution, pewter-making in New York started downhill. It would seem that the competition of china and other substitutes was first seriously felt in that city. Just prior to the war at least nine workers in the metal were plying their trade in New York. Twenty-two years later but one man remained of what seems to have been the most versatile group of pewterers that this country produced. Cornelius Bradford, the first to desert the ranks, turned innkeeper in 1776; his partner, Malcolm McEuen, became a plumber; Peter Kirby died; William Kirby, bent on holding his customers, sold them china and glass instead of pewter; Henry Will became a dry-goods merchant; Peter Young moved to Albany; and William Elsworth and Francis Bassett retired, leaving Frederick Bassett as the sole survivor. With the death of the latter in 1800, New York pewter-making virtually died also. The giants had gone, and the pygmies who remained had not the business ability to maintain the unequal battle against the growing popularity of china.

To be sure, the making of pewter had not altogether ceased in Manhattan by 1800. On the contrary, we know of at least eight men who were listed in the Directories as pewterers between the years 1800 and 1822, but, except for a few spoons, a beaker, a snuffbox, and a nutmeg box of George Coldwell (all of which may have been made before 1800) and one mug bearing the mark of Moses Lafetra, none of the work of these men is known to have survived. This dearth of New York pewter is particularly astonishing in contrast with the hundreds of contemporary pieces made in Massachusetts, Rhode Island, Connecticut, Pennsylvania, and Maryland. That this absence of New York pewter for the first quarter of the nineteenth century must be laid to the lack of ability of the New York men themselves, rather than to competitive conditions, is proved even more conclusively by the record of the amazing business built up there after 1820 by those enterprising pewter-makers and super-salesmen of Connecticut, the Boardman brothers.

New York did have a few resident pewterers of the 'coffee-pot era' (after 1825), principally makers of lights, of whom by all odds the most noteworthy were J. Weekes, Endicott and Sumner, and Henry Hopper. Endicott and Sumner made just about the most pleasing of all whale-oil lamps, and Henry Hopper's candlesticks have a great deal of merit. Broadly speaking, though, the trade of pewter-making ceased in New York when the last of the Bassetts died, and we shall be concerned here principally with eighteenth-century pewterers.

No survey of New York pewter would be complete without some word concerning the tankards her makers produced. Basing our conclusions solely upon examples identified to date, we can say that many more tankards were made in New York in the second half of the eighteenth century than in all the other colonies combined. These display wide variation in design of cover, handle, thumb-piece, and handle terminal. Lids with crenate lip were manufactured by at least six different shops, but strangely enough, although in England many forms of crenate outline can be found, all six New York pewterers used but one design (Plates XIV and XV), a design which is found, though rarely, on English tankards. Consequently, the collector fortunate enough to pick up a tankard with lid of this type may be sure that the laws of chance are strongly in favor of his having acquired a New York piece.

The versatility and capability of the New York pewterers were by no means confined to tankard manufacture. They have left us examples of almost every stock form that was made anywhere else in the colonies, and many of their unusual shapes have no prototypes in the surviving pewter of other sections of the country.

WILLIAM DIGG(E)S AND WILLIAM HORSEWELL

According to Louis G. Myers's *Notes*, William Diggs in 1702 and William Horsewell in 1705, both described as pewterers, were admitted as freemen of the city of New York.

Our information about both Diggs and Horsewell is extremely meager, however, for very few early New York records remain. There seems little doubt that the New York Diggs is the same man whom Howard H. Cotterell lists as William Digges, a London pewterer, who joined the yeomanry of the Pewterers' Company in 1699. The earliest record of him in New York dates from December, 1701, when, as one of a group of citizens of the city, he signed a petition to the King. In another record, dated 1702, his name appears among 'ye chiefest Inhabitants and Freeholders of the City.' This man's touch is still preserved on Plate II of the London touch-plates in Pewterers' Hall and, as he probably carried the die with him to these shores, the mark is reproduced, with the late Mr. Cotterell's permission, in Plate LIX, 454. We know nothing whatever of Diggs's history after 1702 nor of the pewter that he made.

Horsewell's story is just as brief. Louis G. Myers states in his *Notes* that the earliest pewterer in the Bassett family, Francis, Senior, was bound as an apprentice to William Horsewell, pewterer, in 1707, but, before young Bassett's training could have been completed, his master died. The latter's will, dated March 20, 1708, and proved February 4, 1710, is still on file in New York City. By its terms fifty pounds were left to a daugh-

454. Touch of William Digges, London, struck in 1699 on London Touch-Plate II. This is believed to be the same William Digges who was in New York, 1701–1702. Courtesy of the late Howard H. Cotterell, Esq.

455. Touch of Joseph Leddell, New York, 1712–1753, or Joseph Leddell, Jr., 1740–1754. From Mrs. J. Insley Blair's christening bowl (Plate XXXVIII).

456. A Bassett touch attributed to Francis Bassett, New York, 1718–1758, or to the younger Francis, 1754–1799. Three examples are known. Courtesy of the Mabel Brady Garvan Collection, Gallery of Fine Arts, Yale University.

457. Another Bassett mark, used by one of the Francises or by Frederick, 1761–1780. Not quite so rare as 456. Courtesy of Mrs. J. Insley Blair.

457a. Another impression of 457. From a tankard in the collection of Edward E. Minor, Esq.

458. Touch of John Bassett, New York, 1720–1761. From the tall beaker illustrated in Plate XXIII. Collection of the author.

459 and 460. Touches of Francis Bassett the elder or his younger namesake, as they appear on a 16-inch dish in the author's collection. Only this one example of 459 is recorded.

461 and 460a. Another combination of touches of the same maker from a 9-inch plate formerly in the collection of Wilmer Moore, Esq.

462 and 462a. Two sets of impressions of a rare F. Bassett touch attributable to either Francis Bassett. 462 is from a plate in the collection of Albert H. Good; 462a from a plate belonging to Mrs. Roger Fish, photographed through her courtesy and that of Ernest W. Young, Esq.

463 and 464. Touches of Frederick Bassett. From a plate in the collection of Edward E. Minor, Esq.

463a. Another impression of 463. From the author's collection.

465. A touch of Frederick Bassett. From a tankard in the collection of Edward E. Minor, Esq. Compare 458.

466. Frederick Bassett's hall-marks. From the author's collection.

467 and 464a. Frederick Bassett's normal touches. Courtesy of the Mabel Brady Garvan Foundation, Gallery of Fine Arts, Yale University.

468. An excellent impression of the Frederick Bassett initial touch which is presumed to have superseded his fleur-de-lis mark (465). Courtesy of John W. Poole, Esq.

PLATE LIX

454

455

456

457

457 a

458

459 460

461 460 a

463 464

462

462 a

463 a

465

466

467 464 a

468

PLATE LX — *Invoices of Pewterers*

469 and 470. Invoices of Frederick Bassett to Hinman and Osbourn, merchants of Woodbury, Connecticut. Of particular interest is the item of 'Round Teapotts.' No teapot of Frederick Bassett in any shape is known to be in existence today.

471. Invoice of George W. Will for sand boxes and inkstands. Today no collection boasts a marked American sand box and only two early inkstands are known.

472 and 473. Invoices of Samuel Danforth. Mention is made of block tin platters at fifty per cent higher price than pewter platters. It would be enlightening if we could differentiate between and compare samples of each today.

PLATE LX

471

472

473

469

470

ter in England. It is reasonable to assume, therefore, that Horsewell had not been in America many years, and was probably no longer young when he first arrived in New York. The discovery of any of his metal would be little short of a miracle.

JOSEPH ISLY

Letters of administration were granted on October 19, 1715, to Garrett de Baere on the estate of Joseph Isly of New York, pewterer, who died intestate at de Baere's house and was indebted to him for board and lodging.

Isly's name does not appear on the New York tax lists for 1699 nor have I found it on any other early New York document.

THE LEDDELLS

Joseph Leddell, Senior, was born, probably in Hampshire, England, prior to 1690. He married Maria Vincent in New York in 1711 and became a freeman of the city in 1716. In 1720 he was a petitioner for the incorporation of the earliest Presbyterian Church in the colony, and from 1736 to 1738 held the elective office of assessor for Dock Ward. Until 1744 his shop was at 'The Sign of the Platter' in Dock Street. In that year he moved to the lower end of Wall Street near the Meal Market. From various documents in which the name and occupation of this man are given, we can be certain that he was a maker of pewter throughout his working years. Upon his death in 1754 he left to his son Joseph 'all my brass moulds for pewter work and all my working tools,' and he left to his former apprentice, Robert Boyle, the joint use with Joseph, Junior, of the moulds and tools which he had bought in England. As he speaks in his will of land in Gosport, Hampshire, given to him by his father, there is reason for believing that he was not a native of New York. Leddell's will was dated November 16, 1753; proved January 22, 1754.

Joseph, Junior, also a pewterer, was born in New York in 1718. In 1752 he married Mary Patterson and in the same year was advertising the sale of pewter from his house in Smith Street. The advertisement in question closes in the following manner:

> ... and makes ... any uncommon Thing in Pewter, in any Shape or Form as shall be order'd ...
> He also engraves on Steel, Iron, Gold, Silver, Copper, Brass, Pewter, Ivory or Turtle-shell, in a neat manner and reasonably.

The younger Leddell died intestate May 10, 1754.

Just one example of Leddell pewter has been definitely identified, and by a rare stroke of good fortune this piece appears to have been one of those 'uncommon Things in Pewter' which the younger Joseph was offering to make in 1752. The vessel, owned by

Mrs. J. Insley Blair, and illustrated in Plate XXXVIII with her kind permission, was probably used as a baptismal bowl. An unusual feature, for American pewter, is the impression of the touch upon the upper face of the rim, and a very handsome and well-preserved touch it is (Plate LIX, 455). The mark has been ascribed here to the younger Leddell, though it may just as well have been the touch of the father.

Were we never to find another example of pewter by the maker, we still could not withhold from him a seat among the elect at the head of the board in Pewterers' Hall.

Listed among the unidentified touches is a circular mark with initials 'I. L.' (Plate LXIX, 579) similar in design to other New York touches. It was found on the bottom of a handle on a 4⅞-inch porringer in the collection of Mrs. Ralph P. Hanes. Positive attribution to either of the Leddells is not warranted, but if other examples, similarly marked, should come to light, the chances seem good that evidence will appear which will enable us to place the touch in the Leddell column.

THE BASSETTS

Over a span of ninety-four years — from 1707 until 1800 — members of the Bassett family were making pewter in New York City, and the metal of Frederick, the last of the line, has epitomized for many collectors the pewter of America.

This story of the family has been taken principally from Louis G. Myers's *Notes* and begins with the arrival of John Bassett, aged nineteen, at Barbados in 1635. Later in life he moved to New York and secured title to sixty acres of land on the East River. The first John Bassett had at least two sons, Francis and Michael, both of whom followed the sea for their livelihood and both of whom had sons who worked in pewter.

Francis, son of Francis and Marie Magdalen (Vincent) Bassett, was born in New York in 1690, according to the records of the French Church, and in 1707, with the consent of his widowed mother, was apprenticed to William Horsewell, pewterer. In 1718 he became a freeman of the city. Nothing else is known of his history except that he served as constable for the East Ward in 1732 and died in New York in 1758, leaving his estate to his wife, Elizabeth Mary Bassett.

His first cousin, John Bassett, son of Michael, was baptized in 1696 and married Elizabeth Fisher in 1724. He did not become a freeman until 1732 and his name is not found among the lists of town officials. His occupation, however, is given as 'pewterer' in numerous documents. Of his seven children, the oldest and youngest, Francis and Frederick, were to carry on the family trade. John died in 1761, leaving to his son Frederick his pewter-making tools and a slave, 'Tom.'

The second Francis, born in 1729, married Mary Hestear, April 26, 1757. Since Francis, Senior, died without issue in the following year, it is not unlikely that his kinsman and namesake acquired his tools and touches. On December 12, 1749, Brandt Schuyler, Esquire, and Margaret his wife sold to Francis Bassett, pewterer, a house and lot on Queen Street in the East Ward, apparently the same property, 218 Queen Street, on which he was living at the time of his death, some fifty years later. Bassett became fireman for the East Ward in 1762 and served in that capacity until 1776. At the outbreak of the Revolution he was appointed one of the General Committee (of Safety) for the City and County of New York. He was one of the founders of the New York Hospital in 1771 and at a later date became a member of the board of governors of that institution. Though his occupation is invariably given as pewterer in all public documents, the metal of Francis Bassett is so scarce that it is difficult to believe, as the Directories seem to indicate, that he worked at his trade until his death in 1800.

Frederick, youngest child of John Bassett, was baptized in New York in 1740. His father's death provided him with tools and a shop just as he came of age. On March 15, 1764, he married Janetje Vredenburg and, after her death, was married, on March 26, 1772, to Susannah Bubelot. In 1769 he became a freeman of New York.

At some time during the Revolution, Bassett moved to Hartford, Connecticut, for in a deed of April 12, 1781, 'Frederick Bassett, late of the City and County of New York now of Hartford,' purchased a house and lot in Cooper Lane. As late as January 18, 1785, Bassett was advertising in the *Connecticut Courant*, but stating therein that his house in Hartford was for sale. By February, 1786, when the Hartford property was sold, Frederick was again back in New York, and when the first Directory of that city appeared in 1787 his shop was at 7 Burling Slip. Later he moved to 218 Pearl Street. Frederick Bassett died in New York in 1800, leaving no son to carry on the business.

Though his pewter is not common, it is more plentiful than that of any other New York maker. His workmanship was of the highest order and he was unquestionably one of our ablest pewterers. However, it may be doubted whether his craftsmanship merits the position on a pinnacle by itself which some collectors are disposed to accord to it. The discovery within the past few years that equally meritorious work has been left behind by other New York and Pennsylvania makers has challenged Bassett's supremacy, though it cannot detract from his reputation.

The problems encountered in our attempts to attribute properly the Danforth touches to the different members of that family who bore the same initials and, in some instances, the same surnames, are repeated when we try to allot the Bassett marks to the individual pewterers of that name. At the risk of doing slight violence to the correct chronological order we take up first a touch (Plate LIX, 458) attributed to John Bassett. This mark is his beyond question, for the same design, except for the substitution of the letter 'F' for an 'I,' was used by his son Frederick. In fact the crowded appearance of the letter 'F' in the younger man's touch lends credence to the opinion of H. V. Button that John's die may have been altered by Frederick for his own use. Among the unidentified touches on Plate LXI is one (number 580) which was photographed from the bottom of a dram bottle (Plate XXXIX) which exhibits details characteristic of New York workmanship. Despite the similarity in design to other New York touches, this can be attributed only with decided reservations to John Bassett and, for the present, I prefer to classify it among the unidentified. At least ten surviving examples of this pewterer's

Plate LXI
should read LXIX.

[6]

handicraft bear witness to his ability and versatility; two $3\frac{1}{2}$-pint tankards (Plate XV); two quart tankards; a slipped-top spoon (Plate XXIV) — except for a seventeenth-century Virginia example, the earliest of our marked spoons; a funnel (Plate XLII), a rare shape in pewter today, marked or unmarked; two splendid tall beakers (Plate XXIII), most massive of American drinking-cups; and a pair of 3-pint basins, marked, as the early basins were, upon the bottom instead of in the well. These ten items, together with the dram bottle, which may have been his, form an extremely interesting group. The existence of that many examples of such varied shapes by a maker who died more than one hundred and seventy-five years ago is sufficient evidence that John Bassett's trade was large. Moreover, his metal is of the finest. It is worth noting that few, if any, American pewterers, even of the nineteenth century, have left us pewter so free from corrosion although that may be merely a coincidence. There may have been in the colonies pewterers whose ability matched that of John Bassett, but it is doubtful whether any excelled him.

Touches 456, 457, 459, 460, 461, and 462 (Plate LIX) are those which are attributed to the two Francises. At this writing there is no means of determining which, if any, were used by the elder and which by the namesake. As pointed out before, the younger man may have used the dies of the first Francis after the latter's death. There is also the possibility that numbers 456, 457, and 462 were early marks of Frederick Bassett, though I am inclined to believe otherwise. The mark 462, which has been found on five plates, is unlike any other American touch. Its design bears a close resemblance to a touch of Spackman and Grant struck in London about 1709, just a few years before the first Francis became a freeman of New York. Such evidence, however, is insufficient for allotting the mark definitely to the earliest of the Bassetts. The initial touch, number 464, appears upon a splendid flat-topped tankard, a porringer, and a basin which came *464 should read 456.* from one household and apparently had always been together. I have seen the rampant lion on one pint mug, one quart mug, one three-pint tankard, several quart tankards, and two porringer handles. The 'Frans Bassett' mark (number 460) is from an 8-inch plate. Two other plates of the same size show only the lion-and-fleur-de-lis. The most recent group of Francis Bassett touches to come to light, found on a $16\frac{3}{8}$-inch platter, is illustrated as numbers 459, 460.

Last in the Bassett group are the marks which were used by Frederick (numbers 463 to 468). One or two of the initial touches may have seen service first in the shop of his brother or cousin, but all have been found accompanying Frederick Bassett's hall-marks or the touch in which his name is spelled out in full.

Just as the Richard Lees had a predilection for the diminutive in pewter forms, so the Bassetts seem to have had an equally strong leaning toward the massive. Frederick's $16\frac{3}{8}$-inch platters, at least four of which are in existence, represent the limit in size, now known, of American flatware. Noteworthy too are his flat-topped tankards, which have the characteristics of English pieces made a full century earlier. My list of Frederick Bassett flatware includes the following sizes: $6\frac{1}{2}$, 8, $8\frac{1}{4}$, $8\frac{7}{16}$, 9, $9\frac{1}{4}$ (smooth rim), $12\frac{1}{4}$, $13\frac{3}{8}$, $14\frac{3}{4}$, 15, and $16\frac{3}{8}$ inches, all of the shallow type. Some, but not all, of his flatware was hammered. I have record also of 9-inch deep plates by this maker. Other surviving forms are pint and quart basins, pint and quart mugs, 3½-pint tankards, quart tankards of several varieties, 4¼-inch, 4½-inch, and 5-inch porringers, 4⅝-inch beakers, funnels, a nursing bottle, and a commode 8 inches in height.

From a group of four surviving invoices (see Plate LX), made out in the handwriting of Frederick Bassett to Hinman and Osbourn of Woodbury, Connecticut, for pewter which he sold to them in the years just prior to the Revolution, we have evidence that, in addition to the forms in pewter which have already come to light bearing this man's touches, we may also hope to find teapots (in two varieties).

Frederick Bassett was the last of a succession of master-pewterers. Just as any one of his splendid tankards today dwarfs into insignificance the work of his later competitors and successors, so completely did he dominate the pewter trade of his native city during the closing years of his life. When Bassett died there was none to carry on his work. The craft of pewter-making in New York had been dealt its deathblow.

WILLIAM AND CORNELIUS BRADFORD

Louis G. Myers, in a delightful paragraph in his *Notes* about Malcolm McEuen, wrote:

> There were three Malcolms in all. The first was a book binder; then came Malcolm, the pewterer, and finally Malcolm, the plumber. Thus in father, son and grandson, we see a typical case of American evolution, with the grandson landing at the top.

In a companion frame could be hung the portrait of the Bradfords — father, son, and grandson. First, William, printer and newspaper publisher; his son, William, Junior, a printer who turned pewterer; and in the third generation, Cornelius, who, beginning as a pewterer, realized no doubt that he was not fulfilling his destiny and added plumbing to his pewter business. And perhaps it was just to give me the pleasure of linking my story more closely with that of Mr. Myers that Cornelius obligingly chose Malcolm McEuen as his partner.

In 1682 William Bradford, a printer of Leicestershire, England, emigrated with William Penn to Philadelphia, where in 1685 he set up the first printing press in the middle colonies. Not long afterward he moved to New York, was appointed the royal printer for that colony, and in 1725 published New York's first newspaper. A son, Andrew, returned to Philadelphia and established the first newspaper in that town.

Another son, William Bradford, Junior, born in Philadelphia in 1688, is said to have learned the printing trade in New York, but his health was too poor for such confining work and he turned to the sea for his livelihood. Just when he abandoned the sailor's life we do not know; but on November 25, 1716, he married Sytie Santvoort in New York, and in 1719 he became a freeman of the city. His occupation as shown on the records was that of a pewterer, and a pewterer he remains in all subsequent documents in which his name appears. In the closing years of his life his home was in Hanover Square at the corner of Stone Street. William Bradford's will was probated in 1759.

No pewter has yet been found with touches which include this maker's full name, but included among our unidentified marks are four with the initials 'W. B.' (Plate LXIX, 581 to 584), any or all of which may have been struck in Bradford's shop. The three small circular initial touches are so similar to one another, so much like other New York touches, and are found on articles so characteristic of New York workmanship, that I am attributing them, though with some reservations, to William Bradford. Number 584 is from a quart tankard owned by Wilmer Moore. I have seen a similar tankard which bears the touch shown in number 581, as do also two porringers which I have handled. The mark 582 is from a domed-top quart tankard which is owned by Edward E. Minor. Another impression of this same touch, found by Louis G. Myers on a domed-top quart tankard, was illustrated in his *Notes* and attributed to Bradford. The fourth touch (number 583), which I would also like to award to Bradford, but which for the present will be listed among the *incogniti*, is a most unusual touch and was impressed on a very interesting and rare form — a circular box, perhaps a soap box, owned by Mrs. Guy G. Clark and illustrated in Plate XL. The eight-pointed star is a detail found in several New York touches and the tooling on this unusual piece is also typical of the New York makers.

William Bradford, Third, a son of the pewterer, returned to the family trade of printing, became a newspaper publisher in Philadelphia, and eclipsed even the reputation of his famous grandfather. During the trying days which preceded the Revolution his newspaper admonished the colonies to 'Unite or Die'; and his tavern, the London Coffee House, became a hotbed of patriotism. When the war came, he received a commission, served under General Washington at Trenton, Princeton, and elsewhere, and rose to the rank of colonel.

It is little wonder, therefore, that Cornelius Bradford has remained in the background, his story overshadowed by the careers of his more distinguished relatives. But he, too, played a man's part in the events of his time, and deserves at least brief recognition.

Cornelius, fifth and youngest child of the pewterer, William Bradford, Junior, was born in New York, October 18, 1729. Unquestionably he served his apprenticeship in his father's shop. On April 23, 1752, he married Esther Creighton, and later in the same year advertised the manufacture and sale of pewter at his father's shop in Hanover Square. Soon thereafter he must have left for Philadelphia, his father's birthplace. Reasons for deserting New York in favor of Philadelphia were plentiful. In the former town in 1753 there was already a plethora of pewterers at work — William Bradford, Francis Bassett the elder, John Bassett, the two Leddells, and John Will, to name but a few. In the Quaker City, on the other hand, Simon Edgell had passed on, and we know definitely of but one man, Thomas Byles, who was at that date making pewter in Philadelphia. Another incentive for the move would have been the presence in Philadelphia of relatives and friends of the family upon whom young Bradford could count for patronage and help. But the crowning motive for the change was unquestionably the fact that an uncle, Andrew Bradford, with whom Cornelius had always been a favorite, died in 1742 and by the terms of his will provided that if he left no direct heirs Cornelius should inherit his Philadelphia property. So here was a home and shop ready and waiting for the boy to finish his apprenticeship and take possession.

In the spring of 1753, possibly a little earlier, Bradford opened his shop on Second Street, Philadelphia, and his first newspaper notice in that town is found in the *Pennsylvania Gazette* for May 3 of that year.

In the same journal on October 14, 1756, the following notice appeared:

To be sold by

Cornelius Bradford, Pewterer,

At the sign of the Dish in Second St. opposite the sign of the George wholesale or retail at the most reasonable rates all sorts of pewter ware, viz: Dishes and plates of all sizes, basons, tankards, quart and pint mugs, porringers, tea pots, sugar pots, cullanders, bed pans, stool-pans, half pint and gill tumblers, wine measures, salt sellers, spoons, milk pots, pint and half-pint dram bottles, slop bowls and all sorts of other pewter.

Said Bradford makes the best of pewter or block-tin worms, of all sizes for distilling, as shall be ordered, as also cranes for hogsheads or bottles, candle molds of different sizes. All persons may have pewter mended at a reasonable price, and ready money given for old pewter or exchanged for new.

Another advertisement, in 1758, is almost identical, but with the addition of 'ink pots' to the announced stock in trade. From later notices we get the impression that Bradford became a general merchant; and in 1769, when he is taxed for property in High Street Ward, his name occurs for the last time as a resident of Philadelphia.

The records of Christ Church show that between 1754 and 1759 four children were born to Cornelius and Esther Bradford. In 1765 the wife died. About five years later the widower, with his children, returned to New York, where in 1771 he was married again, this time to Catherine, widow of Captain Dennis Candy. That he was living in New York in 1773 and working there at his trade we have certain knowledge, for in that year he disposed of most of his Philadelphia property, the rest being sold in 1783. The deeds covering both transactions, on file at City Hall, Philadelphia, mention the grantor as 'pewterer, formerly of the City of Philadelphia, but now of the State of New York.'

Whatever his position had been in Philadelphia, Cornelius became one of the most prominent New York figures of his day. If the city had required a Paul Revere, no doubt Bradford would have filled that rôle. In the years just before the Revolution he was the trusted dispatch-bearer between the Committees of Correspondence in New York and Boston, and in New York and Philadelphia.

We have already told how the brother William, in his inn, the London Coffee House, in Philadelphia, became a central figure in the city's patriotic councils. Cornelius Bradford was to play a similar part in New York. The Merchants' Coffee House, at the corner of Wall and Water Streets, had long been the business rendezvous of the city. Early in 1776 Bradford purchased the inn and the property on which it stood. Upon its reopening in May, it became the headquarters for those ardent spirits who desired no temporizing with the British Government; and we are told that Bradford proved himself an energetic and enterprising host.

But his tenure was short at this time. War had come in earnest. The British fleet arrived and troops were landed in New York, necessitating the withdrawal of the Continental forces. Bradford might have remained to enjoy a thriving business catering to His Majesty's soldiers and to Tory citizens. Instead, when Washington's troops marched out, Bradford deserted his inn and went with them. For seven years thereafter he and his family lived at Rhinebeck, some distance up the Hudson. In 1783, the war over, Cornelius returned to New York and took charge again of the famous hostelry.

To W. Harrison Bayles's interesting *Old Taverns of New York* I am indebted for much of the preceding information. He tells us further that Bradford

> prepared a book in which he proposed to enter the names of vessels on their arrival, the ports from which they came, and any particular occurrences of their voyages, so that merchants and travellers might obtain the earliest intelligence. Bradford's marine list appears in the newspapers of that period. He also opened a register of merchants and others on which they were requested to enter their names and residences, the nearest approach to a city directory that had yet been made. Bradford, by his energy and intelligence, revived the good name of the house. . . .

We now return to the starting-point of our story. In New York's earliest Directory, that of 1786, Bradford and McEuen are listed as plumbers at 147 Water Street. This McEuen was the second Malcolm, who spent most of his days as a pewterer. The two men were working together at least as early as 1773, as evidenced by the recorded approval of a bill presented by the firm in that year for sales made to the New York Almshouse. I doubt, however, if Bradford gave much time to either pewter-making or plumbing after 1775. The shop was closed during the war, and his duties as host of the Coffee House would have required most of his energies after the return of peace. It is therefore my belief that any examples of Bradford's pewter that come to light may be identified, with reasonable assurance, as pre-Revolutionary.

Although, until very recent years, the existence of any such examples was unknown, there is now record of at least seven pieces of the man's handicraft — three quart tankards, a pint mug of bellied form, a 10-inch smooth-rim plate, and two plates with normal rim, measuring $8\frac{9}{16}$ and $8\frac{7}{8}$ inches respectively. All three plates have hammer-marks on the booge.

The late Francis Mason made the first Bradford discovery, and to him we are indebted, not only for a new touch, but also for a brand-new mystery. Examine the marks reproduced from the Mason plate (Plate LXII, 496, 497). Why should the initials in the hall-marks (so called) be 'D. S.' instead of 'C. B.'? Possibly English precedent affords the answer. In England, when a pewterer succeeded to another man's business, he frequently applied for and received permission from the Pewterers' Company to adopt the touches used by his predecessor — to capitalize, as it were, the good-will of a going establishment. It seems not improbable, therefore, that 'D. S.' was an earlier Philadelphia maker whose business Bradford acquired; but thus far I have been unable to find trace of such a man.

The other Bradford touch (number 495), found as yet on but one $8\frac{9}{16}$-inch plate, could have been used only in Philadelphia, and hence unquestionably antedates the Revolution. The other mark, while dating from the same period, may have done duty in New York as well as in Philadelphia.

Bradford's pewter is of good quality and workmanship. One of his tankards and a pint mug are illustrated in Plates XVI and XX respectively. The latter is of a shape that must have been common in the colonies about the time of the Revolution, but very few examples have survived.

On the ninth of November, 1786, Cornelius Bradford died. In his will, witnessed by Malcolm McEuen, he styled himself 'Keeper of the Coffee House.' Under its terms a large estate, including several parcels of property and five negro slaves, was divided among his widow, his sons, William and James, and his daughters, Tace and Catherine.

In an obituary notice the *New York Packet* wrote of Bradford that not only

> ... was he distinguished as a steady patriot during the arduous contest for American Liberty, but that he always discovered a charitable disposition toward those who differed from him in sentiments....
>
> The Coffee House under his management was kept with great dignity and he revived its credit from the contempt into which it had fallen during the war.

THE WILLS OF NEW YORK

The records of the Reformed Dutch Church in the city of New York have preserved for us the information that on the nineteenth of February, 1750, 'Johannes Will, Junior, van Nieuwied in Hoog Duitschland' joined the church, and that on the twenty-second of September, 1752, 'Johannes Will & Anna Judith Bomper, Egte Lieden met hare 3 kinderen, Hendrik Bernhard, Margaretha Elizabeth & Philip Daniel Will van Niewit in Duitsland,' also became members of the congregation.

Tracing the family back to Germany, J. P. Remensnyder found, in the Register of the Reform Church Congregation in Nieuwied on the Rhine, record of the following baptisms of children of Johannes Will, 'Zinngeister' (pewterer) and Johanna Judith his wife:

Philipp Daniel, born Nov. 2, baptized Nov. 9, 1738
Johann Wilhelm, born Jan 27, baptized Feb 4, 1742
Johann Christian, born Nov. 14, baptized Nov. 21, 1744

Christian's godfather was his grandparent, Johann Christian Will, 'Citizen of Herborn.' In all likelihood the Wills moved to Nieuwied from Herborn shortly before Philip Will's birth, and anyone desirous of determining the dates of birth of John Will, pewterer, and his older children Gertrude, John, Junior, Elizabeth, and Henry, should seek for them in the Herborn records. The Will family appears in the Nieuwied Register for the last time in this significant entry:

> Johanetta Maria, daughter of Johannes Diers, citizen of Nieuwied, and his wife, Anna Elisabeth, was born on March 19, 1752, and baptized on March 25, 1752. The baptismal witnesses were Anna Maria, wife of the merchant, Mathias Ernst in Neujorck, and Johanna Judith, wife of the pewterer and citizen Johannes Will. The baptismal witnesses, as well as the pewterer Johannes Will, were to depart for America immediately following the christening.

John Will's daughter Gertrude had been married in 1746, so the pewterer was at least forty-five years of age when he emigrated with his family and set up his business in the New World. He became a freeman of New York in 1759. Although his chief occupation was the manufacture of pewter, an advertisement in the *New York Gazette* of September 27, 1756, quoted in full below, proves that he was also a seller of spirits and an active agent for Amelung's ill-starred glass enterprise:

> To be sold by Johannes Will, Pewterer, living in Smith's Fly opposite Mr. Robert Livingston, a Parcel of the best New-York distill'd Rum, by the Hogshead, Barrel, or smaller Quantity, not less than Five Gallons; as also a Variety of Glass Ware, manufactured at the Glass House in New Windsor. N.B. Said Johannes Will gives ready Money for good Wood Ashes, and broken Window and Bottle-Glass, as also old Pewter. Any Person wanting any Particulars of Glass Ware made may apply to the said Will, and they shall be served with all possible Expedition.

Instead of "Amelung's ill-starred glass enterprise" substitute "the factory in Ulster County of The Glass House of New York".

John Will's name continued to appear in various New York records up to the year 1763, soon after which his death must have occurred.

Of John Will, Junior, nothing is known after he joined the Dutch Church. He may have been the 'John Michael Will, Cordwainer,' who became a freeman of New York May 6, 1760.

Henry Will, however, was to take his place with John the elder as one of the most gifted of American pewterers. We can assume that he was born about 1735, probably in Herborn, Germany. He married Magdalena Haan in the Reformed Dutch Church on November 25, 1761, and four years later became a freeman of the city. His civic duties included four years' service, 1768 to 1772, as a fireman for Dock Ward. At that time his shop in the Old Slip was advertised as 'The Sign of the Block-tin Teapot.' Will sold a great deal of merchandise to customers in Albany, received a commission as lieutenant in the Tenth Albany Militia in 1775, and moved to that city late in the same year or early in 1776. A son, Johannes, was baptized in New York November 7, 1762, and at least two daughters were baptized in Albany in 1776 and 1780. In August, 1783, John Townsend, New York merchant, and Margaret his wife sold to 'Henry Will of Albany, pewterer,' property at 3 Water Street, New York, at which address Will was advertising the manufacture of pewter wine measures in 1786. It is probable, therefore, that eight of his working years were spent in Albany.

In 1785 Henry Will served as assistant alderman in the East Ward, New York, was elected to the Assembly in 1789, and was re-elected thereafter until 1797, with a break of one year in 1795. In 1793 he moved his shop to 41 Chatham Street; after that date pewter-making, if continued at all, was a side issue, for in the later Directories Will is variously listed as a shopkeeper, proprietor of a drygoods store, and merchant. His name appears for the last time in New York records in 1802.

Just one mention of Philip Will is found in New York archives after he joined the Reformed Dutch Church in 1752. On June 26, 1766, 'Philip Will of the City of New York, Pewterer,' and Nicholas Steagg of the same city, butcher, were bound for fifty pounds to the estate of Nicholas Duyckman. In 1763 a Philip Will advertised the manufacture of pewter in Philadelphia and a pewterer of that name died there in 1787. It is my opinion that but one Philip Will made pewter in this country; that he served his apprenticeship in New York, moved to Philadelphia in 1763, returned to New York for a brief period about 1766, and spent the remainder of his days in Philadelphia (see page 51).

William Will, whose history will be found on pages 51–55, moved to Philadelphia also, where he achieved pre-eminence in the pewter-making trade in that city.

The youngest brother, Christian, was also a pewterer, but, by comparison, an insignificant craftsman, who probably worked as a journeyman only. With his wife, 'Rebekka Bokee,' he was a witness at a baptism in 1770, and in the New York Directory of 1789 he is listed as 'Christian Will, pewterer and collector of Montgomery Ward, Franklin's Wharf.' During the following year Christian must have died, for thereafter in the Directories the name of his widow, Rebecca, appears alone.

John and Henry Will are represented in collections today by a number of splendid examples. Their pewter is extremely rare, but fortunately enough pieces have survived to prove that each was a pewterer of exceptional ability.

Selected for illustration as examples of outstanding merit from the shop of John Will are the superb quart tankards in Mrs. J. Insley Blair's collection (Plate XV, 88 and 89). Cast in the same moulds they differ only in details. Particularly interesting is the engraving on the right-hand tankard. The decoration around the top and bottom of the drum was made to represent the cut-card design found on silver tankards of such early New York goldsmiths as Peter Van Dyke and Jacob Boelen. If the decoration was not done by Will himself, it was at least contemporaneous. A competitor, Joseph Leddell, Junior, advertised 'engraving on pewter' and may have done such work for the other New York makers.

The crenate lip on the cover of each tankard is worthy of comment. In American pewter it has been found thus far only on New York tankards. This feature, current on drinking-vessels of the Stuart period, disappeared from use in England about 1710, an excellent illustration of the persistence in the colonies of forms long outmoded on the other side of the Atlantic.

Another rare form with a touch attributed to this maker is the graceful little creamer (Plate XXX, 201) owned by Mr. and Mrs. Richard S. Quigley. It is stamped inside with a tiny initial touch illustrated as number 484 on Plate LXI. Other items made by, or at least attributed with some confidence to, this maker are an 8-inch plate, an $8\frac{5}{18}$-inch plate, two $9\frac{1}{8}$-inch plates, a $13\frac{1}{8}$-inch semi-deep dish, a $3\frac{1}{2}$-pint tankard, several quart tankards, a $3\frac{1}{2}$-pint mug, several quart mugs, and a pint mug.

The Wills of New York

Louis G. Myers, having learned that Henry Will's father was also a pewterer, was the first to resurrect an example of John's work. His fine 9⅛-inch plate with hammered booge furnished a remarkable keyplate to John Will touches, which are shown again in Plate LXI, 478, 479, 480. At almost the same time Charles A. Calder found an 8 5/16-inch plate with an entirely different set of John Will touches which appear to be even earlier in design (numbers 482, 483). The angel touch with initials 'I. W.' is typically Continental and may well have been used by Will in Germany as well as in this country. And now, almost simultaneously, two more sets of what are also apparently John Will touches have just come to light. One group is on an 8-inch plate with hammered booge owned by Dr. Madelaine Brown, the other on a dish in Mrs. Stephen S. FitzGerald's collection. An identical New York touch (number 475) is found in each group.

Mrs. J. Insley Blair owns a pair of John Will tankards, commented upon above. One bears the circular initial touch as found on the Myers plate, its mate the Will name-in-rectangle touch as in the Calder group of marks. A variation of the circular initial touch (number 481), as photographed in a fine pint pot in my own collection, is so similar to a touch of John's son, Henry, and the mug in which it appears is so typical of New York workmanship, that I am attributing the mark to John without more ado.

We now have identified so many touches that we are attributing to this man that the question may well be asked whether it is not possible that both John Will and his eldest son of the same name were New York pewterers and that some of these touches were used by John the elder and some by the younger John. I admit that a case could be made for such an hypothesis, but it is worthy of note that Henry and William Will each had a penchant for getting out new dies and the trait may have been inherited. This is one of the problems that is left for settlement to some future student of American pewter.

The high standard of excellence seen in the work of John Will was ably maintained by Henry. The latter's pewter is only less rare than that of the elder man, and fortunate is the collector who owns an example. Judging solely from authenticated survivals I should assume that Henry Will was equipped to supply a wider diversification of forms than any other American pewterer of the eighteenth century.

Louis G. Myers illustrated two of this maker's rare shapes, both considered unique in American pewter when the *Notes* were published. The superb flagon (Plate XXXII) now in the Mabel Brady Garvan Collection is still the finest American vessel of its kind. Its design indicates that Will had no flagon moulds, but he overcame that difficulty by superimposing one tankard body upon another, forming what might well be termed a tall tankard. The tankard handle which he used seems too short for such an attenuated drum, but the general impression left by the composition as a whole is one of dignity and simplicity.

Mrs. Mary Sampson's hot-water plate was the other Henry Will rarity illustrated in Myers's little volume. Since that date two similar items by the same maker have

Plate LXI — *New York Touches — John and Henry Will*

474 and 475. Touches of one of the Wills, presumably John Will, New York, 1752–1766. Collection of Mrs. Stephen S. FitzGerald.

476, 475a, and 477. The same New York die with a lion touch and hall-marks attributed to the same maker. Collection of Dr. Madelaine R. Brown.

478, 479, and 480. Another group of John Will touches. Courtesy of the Mabel Brady Garvan Collection, Gallery of Fine Arts, Yale University.

481. Touch attributed to John Will. From a mug in the author's collection.

482 and 483. Probably the earliest of the John Will touches. 482 is typically German. Collection of Mrs. Charles A. Calder.

484. Small initial touch attributed to John Will. From Mr. and Mrs. R. S. Quigley's creamer, illustrated in Plate XXX.

485, 486, and 487. Group of early touches of Henry Will, New York and Albany, 1761–1793. From a plate in the collection of John W. Poole, Esq.

488 and 489. Touches of Henry Will. The die for 488 was apparently discarded by Will in Albany during the Revolution. It was used thereafter on Spencer Stafford's pewter. Courtesy of the Mabel Brady Garvan Collection, Gallery of Fine Arts, Yale University.

487a. Beautifully preserved Henry Will touch on a foot-warmer in the Mabel Brady Garvan Collection, Gallery of Fine Arts, Yale University.

490. Initial touch of Henry Will. From a tankard formerly owned by Wilmer Moore, Esq.

491. Hall-marks of Henry Will. From a tankard in the collection of Edward E. Minor, Esq.

492. Another Henry Will touch. From the Garvan foot-warmer (487a).

PLATE LXI

481

484

490

492

480

479

478

483

482

487a

491

477

475a

476

489

488

475

474

487

486

485

PLATE LXII — *New York Touches — Robert Boyle, Cornelius Bradford, and the Kirbys*

493 and 494. The touches of Robert Boyle, New York, 1752–1758. From a plate in the collection of John P. Remensnyder, Esq.

495. A touch used by Cornelius Bradford in Philadelphia, 1753–1770. Collection of the author.

496 and 497. Touch and hall-marks used by Cornelius Bradford, probably both in New York and Philadelphia, 1751–1785. To date, the former user of these hall-marks, 'D. S.,' has not been identified. From a plate formerly owned by the late Francis Mason, Esq.

498. Touch attributed to Peter Kirby, New York, 1736–1788. Note that the porringer handle on which it appears is almost identical with the William Kirby handle in 502. Collection of Mrs. J. Insley Blair.

499. Initial touch attributed to William Kirby, New York, 1760–1793. From a tankard in the author's collection.

500 and 501. Normal touch and hall-marks of William Kirby. Courtesy of the Mabel Brady Garvan Collection, Gallery of Fine Arts, Yale University.

502. Another Kirby initial touch. (Compare 582, Plate LXIX.) Collection of Mrs. J. Insley Blair.

503. Least rare and probably latest of the Kirby initial touches. Collection of the author.

PLATE LXII

493 494

495

496 497

498

499

500
501

502

503

come to light. In Plate XLI is such a plate as photographed in the collection of John W. Poole.

Another form, perhaps unique, is the foot-warmer in the Mabel Brady Garvan Collection, illustrated in Plate XLII. Despite its homely use this piece was beautifully made of an excellent quality of metal and is still in unusually well-preserved condition. Just as rare in American pewter is a marked double-lidded inkstand. Undoubtedly many were made in this country, but few were marked. Mr. Poole, who has come very close to cornering the market on Henry Will rarities, is the owner of this item impressed on the lid with Will's touches (Plate XLI, 262). He, too, turned up what I would have wagered an impossible find in American pewter — an oval platter. Such a form required, I have been led to believe, elaborate expensive turning equipment and it hardly seemed likely that the demand for such a form would have warranted the initial outlay. I am grateful to Mr. Poole for making his discovery before I stated in print, as I surely should have done, that we should never find an American oval platter. This fine piece (Plate X, 52) measures $15\frac{1}{4} \times 11\frac{1}{4}$ inches and has a hammered booge. Of less importance but nevertheless unusual also is a $16\frac{3}{8}$-inch deep dish, the largest known American deep dish. Although most of Henry Will's flatware was hammered around the booge, this dish is an exception to the rule.

A rare group of Will hollow-ware, owned by Mrs. J. Insley Blair, is pictured in Plate XVIII. The tankard is from moulds used by John Will, and would be accepted as the elder man's work were it not for the Henry Will hall-marks found on the base inside the tankard. The quart mugs vary considerably in details. That on the left has the form of handle characteristic of American pots of that time, but the right-hand example is supplied with a handle terminating in an unusual scroll. Just such differences in detail and variations in design add interest to the work of John and Henry Will, a distinction that will be found also in the pewter of William Will of Philadelphia.

Another Henry Will tankard of different design, owned by Edward E. Minor, is illustrated in Plate XIV, 81. Please note the pierced thumb-piece — a feature found also on some of William Will's tankards.

In addition to the forms listed above, Henry Will's touches have been found on $8\frac{3}{4}$-inch, $8\frac{7}{8}$-inch, $9\frac{1}{4}$-inch, and $9\frac{7}{16}$-inch plates, 9-inch smooth-rim plates, $12\frac{1}{8}$-inch deep dishes, $13\frac{3}{16}$-inch and 15-inch flat dishes, pint basins and pint mugs. It seems almost certain that we shall discover his touches on still unlisted shapes.

This maker had almost as wide a variety of touches as of forms. Among those shown on Plate LXI, 485–492, are four which were unknown when the last book on American pewter appeared. Three of the four (numbers 485, 486, and 487) were found together on a smooth-rim 9-inch plate. The rarity and early character of these marks point to the probability that they were used in Will's early working years. A second illustration of the rectangular name-touch, beautifully preserved on the back of the Garvan foot-warmer is shown in number 487a. The fourth new touch (number 490) was found on a pint mug in my collection and on a quart tankard owned by Wilmer Moore. Mr. Moore's tankard is a mate in all details to a tankard in Edward E. Minor's collection which is impressed with Henry Will's hall-marks. I have no hesitation, therefore, in listing this touch with the authenticated Henry Will marks.

Of this pewterer's better-known touches, the rose-and-crown (number 488) is found also on pewter of Spencer Stafford of Albany, and, as suggested by Louis G. Myers in his *Notes*, was apparently discarded there by Will prior to his return to New York in 1784.

A great deal of space has been allotted here to the account of John and Henry Will, but certainly no more than is owed to two of our most gifted and versatile pewterers.

PETER AND WILLIAM KIRBY

To the earlier lists of New York pewterers may be added the name of Peter Kirby. When and where he was born we are unable to state. He first appears in New York records on December 24, 1736, when his marriage to Margaret, widow of Joseph Ellison, took place. Although he had at least one son, William, no record of the birth or baptism of any member of the family is now to be found. Kirby's shop in 1746 was near the North River. In 1759 and again in 1760 Peter Kirby was elected an assessor for the West Ward, and from 1765 to 1776 he was a tax-collector for the same ward. In all existing documents in which his occupation was given he is listed as a pewterer. Letters for the administration of his estate were granted to his son, William, on October 13, 1788.

Mrs. J. Insley Blair acquired a 4¼-inch porringer marked as in Plate LXII, 498. The handle is identical with one found with William Kirby's touch and the design of the mark has characteristics of other New York initial touches. I believe this to be a mark of Peter Kirby.

As in the history of his father, nothing is known about William Kirby prior to his marriage on February 6, 1760, to Catharine, daughter of Nicholas Roosevelt. In all probability he was a successful pewterer with a good-sized trade, for he owned at various times properties on Dock Street, First Street next to Trinity Church Burying Ground, Crown Street, and Pearl Street. An interesting attestation to Kirby's business reputation was recently discovered by Henry V. Button and kindly relayed to me for inclusion here. The entry which is quoted in part below was taken from a letter in the order book of John Thurman, Junior, one-time New York merchant. Under date of December 9, 1772, he wrote to his London agent, John Stark:

> The Inclosed Order from Wᵐ Kirby for sundry Goods in your way. Shall be Glad you would Execute on the Best Terms as I can recommend him for a safe customer & do not doubt but he may become a considerable one his Business is a Pewterer he has a most Excellent stand & a Toyshopman rents one small front room in his House, & if Mʳ Holmes will please to execute the order for Pewter on the Lowest Terms at 12 Mos. Credit I dont in the Leaste doubt but he will find him very punctual & if they can settle terms agreeable I dont doubt but he [has?] it in his power to Vend more Pewter than any Merchᵗ in this City.

In 1786 Kirby's shop was on Great Dock Street, and the census of 1790 shows that at that time he was living in Dock Ward with a family of three females and one male over sixteen years of age. The latter was apparently Nicholas Roosevelt Kirby, whose name is found as a witness to a deed for property which William Kirby sold in 1795. In or about 1794 he gave up pewtering and opened a china and glass store, and thereafter is described in all documents as a merchant. His name is listed in the city Directories only until 1804, at which date his shop was in Pearl Street. In that year he was sued by Thomas Hewett, a merchant, who was awarded $935 and costs. To meet this judgment the sheriff sold Kirby's property at 105 Pearl Street. One other deed testified to the fact that he was still alive in 1811. His probate records are not on file in New York City.

William Kirby's large touch (number 500) and pseudo-hall-marks (number 501) have been found on a few $8\frac{3}{16}$-inch and 9-inch hammered plates of very fine metal. In addition, three 'W. K.' initial touches have been tentatively attributed to this maker. The first of these, of which I have seen but one impression (number 499), is from a domed quart tankard with crenated lip. The next touch (number 502), only slightly less rare, is found on pint and half-pint porringers. Number 503, photographed from a porringer also, has been observed upon a very fine tankard of early design with flat top and crenated lip, in several domed tankards (Plate XV, 90), in a quart mug, in a pint basin, and on the bottom of a very fine early little teapot (Plate XXVIII). Kirby's work was of a high order and is doubly desirable on account of its rarity.

ROBERT BOYLE

> It is my will and pleasure that, for the help and encouragement of my Late apprentice Robert Boyle that he shall have the free use of my molds during the time that my Son Joseph and the said Robert shall continue to Live in New York.

The above extract from the will of Joseph Leddell, written on November 16, 1753, indicates that Robert Boyle's business career in New York began shortly before the date of the will. Nothing is known about his birth or parentage, but since Joseph Leddell also mentioned in his will 'my friend, Solomon Boyle,' a skinner by trade, who became a freeman of New York November 11, 1729, the natural assumption is that Robert was a son of Solomon. On October 21, 1755, Robert Boyle became a freeman of the city and on March 9, 1758, he married Affie Waldron. There is no record of his ever having owned property in New York. In fact I have no evidence whatever of his existence in that city after the date of his marriage, although earlier lists of pewterers place him in New York as late as 1784.

In 1755 he offered for sale, at 'The Sign of the Gilt Dish' in Dock Street between the Old-Slip and Coenties's Market:

> Dishes, and Plates of all Sorts, Basons, Tankards, and Porringers of all Sizes, Quart and Pint Mugs, Tea-Pots of all sorts, Cullenders, Bed Pans, Infusion Pots so much approved of in Colds and Con-

sumptions, Cups and Flaggons for Churches, Half-pint and Jill Tumblers, Wine Measures from a Quart to a Half-jill, salts and Ink Stands, Spoons of all sorts, Limbecks and Cold Stills, Candle Molds of different Sizes, Hogshead, Barrel and Bottle Cranes, Pewter or Block-Tin Worms of all sizes . . .

We have long attributed to this maker the fine examples of pewter which are touched with an 'R. B.' rose-and-crown mark. The recent discovery of this touch on the plate of a Boston pewterer has cast grave doubt upon the validity of our attribution (see volume I, pp. 69 and 70).

If we deny to Boyle the small 'R. B.' mark, he is left with but one recorded example of his work, a 9-inch plate with hammered booge, now in the collection of J. P. Remensnyder. Compare his ship touch (Plate LXII, 493) with a similar design (Plate LXI, 478) used by his New York contemporary, John Will.

BLAUN, BLAND, HENRY, AND MERRYFIELD

The muster rolls of the provincial troops for the colony of New York, 1755 to 1764, have supplied the names of four men who gave their occupation as pewterer at the time of enlistment. No other evidence of pewter-making or even of their existence has been found in New York records. In spite of the fact that I cannot be certain that they worked at their trade on these shores, the data from the muster rolls are given herewith.

James Blaun from Ireland, age twenty-five, enlisted March 16, 1759, in Captain Bloomer's Company of Westchester County Militia.

Robert Merryfield, born in England, age forty-four, height five feet eight inches, complexion fair, enlisted April 30, 1760, in Captain Hubbell's Company of New York County Troops.

James Bland, from 'Old England,' age twenty-nine, height five feet eight inches, enrolled April 4, 1761, in Captain Williams's Company of Westchester County Militia.

Andrew Henry from Ireland, age twenty-five, height five feet six inches, enlisted May 1, 1761, in Captain Lent's Company of Orange County Provincial Troops.

If, as seems probable, James Bland was the same man who, as James Blaun, served a 'hitch' in Westchester County in 1759, it would appear that the ordeal of military service aged him very rapidly.

GEORGE HARNER

George Harner, pewterer, became a freeman of the city of New York in 1761. So much Louis G. Myers records in his *Notes*. The paucity of New York records has made further search unproductive, and not one additional scrap of information about this pewterer has been found.

The Pewterers of New York City

WILLIAM J. ELSWORTH

William J. Elsworth was a direct descendant of Theophilus Elswaert, a free-holder in New Amsterdam at least as early as 1655. The pewterer was born in 1746, son of John and Hester Roome Elsworth. In 1767 he became a freeman of the city and two years later was married to Ann Van Dalsam, by whom he had eight children.

As Louis G. Myers states in his *Notes*, Elsworth represented the pewterers on the General Committee of Mechanics in 1786, was the treasurer of that organization from 1790 to 1792, and became one of the incorporators of its successor, the General Society of Mechanics and Tradesmen of the City of New York, in 1792. He also served in the city government as an assistant ward alderman, fireman, superintendent of fire engines, and coroner.

From 1786 until 1798, the last year in which Elsworth's name is found in the Directories, his shop was in Cortlandt Street. On June 20, 1793, 'William J. Elsworth, Pewterer, and Ann his wife' sold property in New York, and soon thereafter the first Mrs. Elsworth must have died. The widower did not remain single long. In September, 1798, he married Jane Smith and at a subsequent date moved across the river to New Jersey, for in his will, dated March 9, 1814, and proved November 13, 1816, he gave his address as 'Township of Harrington, County of Bergen, New Jersey.' The wife received all possessions that she had brought to her consort and five hundred pounds in lieu of a dower. The principal devisees were the children, John, William, Richard, and Ann. John received among other bequests the tinman's tools then in his possession. Pewter moulds and tools were not mentioned, and it is reasonable to suppose that disposition had been made of them many years earlier.

The banner of the Society of Pewterers, mentioned elsewhere, came down through the family of William Elsworth and is supposed to have been carried by him in the Federal parade in 1788.

Although Elsworth's hall-marks and lamb-and-flag touch have been known to collectors for a number of years, they had not been illustrated in any publication until Albert H. Good's article on 'William Elsworth; His Rose and Crown' appeared in the March, 1939, issue of *Antiques*. There was shown also the even rarer rose-and-crown mark (Plate LXIII, 504) which has been found only on one 15-inch dish in Washington's Headquarters at Morristown, New Jersey. The same illustrations have been reproduced here through the courtesy of Mr. Good and the National Park Service. The scroll design enclosing the lamb device (number 506) is very similar to that in Kirby's mark (Plate LXII, 500) and was probably designed by the same die-cutter. This touch has been observed on flatware in the following sizes: $7\frac{7}{8}$-inch, $8\frac{1}{4}$-inch, 9-inch, $13\frac{1}{8}$-inch, and 15-inch. The hall-marks appear alone in the base of a quart tankard with domed cover and crenate lip that resembles closely tankards made by John and Henry Will. There may be some significance also in the observation that, as far as I know,

Henry Will was the only other American pewterer to impress hall-marks on the bottom of hollow-ware.

Among the unidentified touches are two (Plate LXX, 592 and 593) which the dictates of conscience have placed in that category. In all probability they were marks of William Elsworth and some day they may be awarded to him outright. Number 592 was photographed in the bottom of Mrs. Blair's quart tankard with flat top similar to a tankard cover used by Peter Young. The stars in this touch are characteristic of New York initial touches. The second, illustrated previously in Louis G. Myers's *Notes*, is from a quart basin now in the Mabel Brady Garvan Collection.

MALCOLM McEUEN AND SON

The year of birth of Malcolm McEuen (or McEwan) has not yet been established, but must have been about 1740, a date estimated by Louis G. Myers from other and known facts of the man's life. In 1762 he married Mary McKenzie in the First Presbyterian Church of New York and became a freeman of the city in 1770. In 1772 he formed a partnership with Cornelius Bradford, who had just removed from Philadelphia to the city of his birth.

McEuen appears to have been an uncompromising patriot of the same stamp as Bradford, for it is on record that 'Malcolm McEuen, a pewterer,' was recognized by Samuel Loudon as one of those who in April, 1776, took away forcibly and burnt some of his (Loudon's) pamphlets simply because they portrayed dispassionately both sides of the question of the desirability of independence.

Bradford and McEuen were pewterers and plumbers with a shop on Water Street, and were still listed at that address when Bradford died in 1786. From then until 1792 McEuen's name appears alone.

On October 30, 1793, McEuen announced the formation of a partnership with his son, Duncan, under the name of Malcolm McEuen and Son. They advertised proficiency in various types of plumbing and in the manufacture of block tin and pewter worms for distillers and pewter ware of all sorts in their shop at 160 Water Street, corner of Beekman Slip. Their stock at that time included twelve pewter worms of different sizes, a gross of quart teapots, and an equal number of quart and pint mugs and quart and pint basins. After 1798 the McEuens appear in the Directories as plumbers only. In the *New York Herald* for May 7, 1803, the following obituary notice was found:

> Died. On Wednesday last by a fall from the scaffold of a ship Mr. Malcom McEuen, an old respectable inhabitant of this city.

Duncan McEuen, who was born in New York May 28, 1769, remained in business on Water Street many years longer, but his pewter-making career apparently ended before the turn of the century.

The Pewterers of New York City

I acquired a pewter plate touched with the marks shown in Plate LXIII, 507 and 497a. The maker's name has unfortunately been erased by wear, but the tops of what appear to be the letters 'D' and 'M' are still visible. I believe this plate to have been made by the firm of Malcolm and Duncan McEuen. It will be noted that the hall-marks are those once used by Malcolm's former partner, Cornelius Bradford. Unusual in this plate is the combination of an eagle touch and a hammered booge.

PETER YOUNG

Peter Young, last of the New York pewterers who began work before the Revolution, has hitherto been listed as an Albany maker. It was only with the publication of the New York Historical Society's *Early Craftsmen of New York* that we learned that Young worked in New York before moving to Albany. I quote in full the evidence as it appeared in *The Constitutional Gazette* for December 13, 1775:

> For the Benefit of the Public in General, I Peter Young, of the City of New York, Pewterer, living at Mr. Fisher's, Barber, in Spring Garden, commonly called Chatham-Street, was afflicted with an imposthume or sore in my breast with such a violent cough, that I could not rest day or night, spitting and vomitting matter constantly for three months, that I thought I was in a consumption. I applied to several, and tried various kinds of Physick until I applied to the French Doctor Blouin who advised me to make use of his Anti-Venereal Pills, so well known by the name of Keyser's Pills. I followed his advice, and by the use of those pills alone, in a short time I recovered my former health. Witness my hand, Peter Young

Inscrutable are thy ways, O Lord, whether of curing an 'imposthume' or preserving the minor facts of history!

Peter Young was born on the nineteenth of October, 1749. That much we know from the inscription on his tombstone in Albany, but where he was born and where he learned his trade are matters of conjecture only. The known date of birth nullifies the previously accepted belief that he was the Peter Young who was born in Albany in 1746. No record of births or baptism could be found in New York church files and it seems not improbable that Young, like Henry Will, came to this country as a child. Nor do we know when he moved to Albany. He was married in 1785 to Eva Moore and their first child was baptized in the Reformed Dutch Church of Albany in August, 1786. Henry Will, it will be remembered, returned to New York from Albany about 1783. Perhaps Young moved up the Hudson at that time to a market which Will had developed.

In 1792 Peter Young bought property on Columbia Street. It is a matter of small moment to us but was no doubt of primary importance to the pewterer that in the great fire of Albany, August 4, 1797, he lost his house and barn. Since all of Young's flatware is hammered after the early manner, and since but two examples of his eagle-marked pewter are known to have survived, it seems probable that he never re-established his pewtering business after that disaster. The fact that he deeded to his daughters in 1799 the Columbia Street property, vesting a life interest therein in his wife, may indicate that he was in failing health, a possible explanation for the scarcity of his later metal. He died September 26, 1813, and was buried in the Reformed Protestant Dutch Burial Ground.

Peter Young was not just another pewterer. He was a maker of taste, ability, and considerable originality. His chalices, one of which is illustrated in Plate XXXVI, 242, are lovely vessels. Their exquisite design was, as far as we now know, Young's own composition — one of the few designs made in America that is not known to have a counterpart in European pewter. His creamers (Plate XXX, 202) are also distinctive, and I have seen no quart tankards by any other maker with the form of cover (Plate XIV, 83) used by Young except a single example which is attributed to William Elsworth, and one made by Henry Will. Other surviving products of this man's craftsmanship are $8\frac{3}{4}$-inch plates, $13\frac{1}{2}$-inch deep dishes, quart basins, flagons, beakers, pint tankards, and pint mugs; probably many other shapes made in his shop have been lost.

All of Young's plates and dishes have hammered booges. His so-called hall-marks are as bold and as interesting as those of any maker, American or European, and all of his work is of the best quality and finish.

In addition to the touches illustrated in earlier works (Plate LXIV, 512, 513, and 514), a new initial-touch with saw-tooth edge is shown in number 515. It has been found on chalices and on one basin, and is probably later than the touch with initials in beaded rim. The tiny rectangular initial-touch (number 518) was photographed from a creamer and has also been found on chalices. It is cause for regret that the only known impressions of Young's rare eagle touch (number 516) are so very faint.

As time passes and other examples of his work come to light, Peter Young's fame should grow. We are just beginning to realize that he was one of the real masters of American pewter.

GEORGE COLDWELL AND MOSES LAFETRA

Two American pewterers, and two only, are known to have used the Liberty cap as a symbol impressed on their metal. Perhaps that bond between George Coldwell and Moses Lafetra should have pointed us to a relationship between the men, a relationship which might still be unknown to us but for the finding of Coldwell's will.

Nothing is known about George Coldwell's antecedents or early history. He may have been the pewterer of that name who was listed by Howard H. Cotterell in *Old Pewter* as of Cork, Ireland in 1773, but I am inclined to think not. The first trace of him found in New York is in the Directory of 1789 in which he was listed as a pewterer at 218 Queen Street, which incidentally was the address of Francis Bassett. At that time he was probably a journeyman in Bassett's employ or had leased from the latter his shop. At the time of the census-taking in 1790, Coldwell was living in Montgomery Ward with a household of 'three females' and three small boys. In the following year his shop was on Gold Street, where he remained until 1795, termed sometimes a pewterer, but more frequently a 'pewter, spoon, and candle mold mnfr.' In 1800 and from 1807 to 1811 his address was 7 Beekman Street. Why he is not listed at all from 1796 to 1799 and again from 1801 to 1806 is an omission which must probably be charged up to the carelessness of the directory-takers.

On November 22, 1794, Coldwell advertised in the *New York Daily Advertiser*, from which I quote in part:

Block Tin

Candlemould Manufactory &c.
George Coldwell, Pewterer, No 86 Gold Street in the Swamp manufactures and sells by wholesale and retail the following articles, viz. block tin and common pewter candlemoulds, 20 different sizes, beer and wine measures, block tin quart and pint pots, British metal, table, desert and tea spoons, elegantly ornamented and plain, common pewter table and tea spoons, various sizes, plain and figured, pewter buttons, suitable for sailors on slops and working clothing, handsome patterns. . . .

. . . .

Beginners in the Tallow business, will find it essential to their interest to apply to him, as his is the only manufactory on the continent, where they can be supplied with moulds as to smoothness, number of sizes, exact weights, proportion and gloss. His being principally used by the Tallow Chandlers throughout the United States. . . .

His will, in which he calls himself a pewterer, was dated October 31, 1808, and proved April 29, 1811. Most wills make dry-as-dust reading; not so this one. Only rarely do we stumble upon any public document that gives such insight into a man's history and character.

Coldwell's story as it unrolls in the will takes us back to the days when he once had a lawful wife, Anne Cotterill, and five small boys, the youngest of whom he never knew by name. 'Through many vicissitudes in life,' he tells us, he had long been separated from them and they from him, eight years having passed since his wife had darkened his door. Because of the estrangement, and because his family had in no way contributed to his estate or welfare, he ordered that 'one dollar each be paid to them when called for.'

He appointed as executrix of his estate his 'dearly beloved female friend Rebekah Lafetra.' Coldwell was apparently a bit modern in thought, or at least in action, for without going through the formality of divorce he was enjoying a companionate marriage with his 'dearly beloved female friend.' The bulk of the estate was left in trust to a son, Joseph Lafetra Coldwell, who came to grace this alliance. According to the terms of the will the interest was to be paid to the boy's mother for her own use and that of her son. But Coldwell had had one unfortunate experience with women, and so he provided a guardian for the boy, to whom the money was to be paid in case Rebekah should marry. At this point the pewterer seems to have taken thought of the hereafter and stipulated that should Rebekah marry and Joseph die in his minority, Trinity Church, New York, should become the principal beneficiary under his will.

George Coldwell and Moses Lafetra

One other beneficiary is mentioned by name in the document: 'To Moses Lafetra, brother of my beloved female friend,' he bequeathed the sum of fifty dollars 'together with such of my Books and Pamphlets of every kind as his sister shall think fit to give him.' As this clause was later expressly revoked by codicil, it would seem that Coldwell found it as difficult to get along with young Lafetra as with his own family. The will affords that one brief glimpse into the man's life and character. What little more we know is furnished by examination of the surviving examples of his workshop.

These few specimens tend to confirm our suspicion that Coldwell was an unusual fellow, a man who did not run with the crowd. We know from his advertisement that he was a specialist, a maker, primarily, of spoons and candle moulds. In a day when the bulk of almost every American pewterer's output consisted of flatware, Coldwell advertised neither plates nor basins and neither of these forms has been found impressed with his mark. In fact just seven examples of his craftsmanship are known, all unusual in their decoration, three of the group perhaps unique in form among marked American pieces.

The little beaker, if we may so term it, illustrated in Plate XXIII, was a center of interest in the pewter display at the Harvard University Tercentenary Exhibition in the fall of 1936. On many counts it deserves special comment. It is perhaps the earliest surviving small beaker, a form little used in the eighteenth century, and in addition to that distinction the shape has no counterpart in American pewter. Even more striking is the vessel's decoration. Few American makers employed any adornment that was applied after casting other than the occasional use of incised lines, but Coldwell had to be different. The outer surface of this beaker was japanned. Occasionally we find Continental pewter which has been thus treated, but I know of no other example made by an American pewterer save a Coldwell snuffbox which will be commented upon later.

Japanning is an imitation of lacquering in which the desired result is obtained by the application of several coats of varnish, usually black, but in this case dark green. After each coating the vessel is placed in an oven and the varnish baked on and then polished. The japanning of this beaker served primarily as a background for the display and accentuation of Coldwell's skill with an engraver's tool. Below the rim is a band of conventional foliate design and, centered beneath the banding, a wriggle-work circle enclosing an engraved wreath. The design is simple but effective.

Undoubtedly this item was made on special order, perhaps a presentation piece. In fact, according to its present owner, Lewis A. Walter, it was a gift from Coldwell to George Washington, passed thence to the General's body-servant, Billy, and has had but three other owners in the past century and a quarter. Whatever the occasion of its manufacture, this little vessel is an important addition to our knowledge of the craft of the American pewterer.

Another japanned Coldwell piece, a snuffbox, the only marked American snuffbox of which I have record which antedates the britannia period, was among the items in the recent sale of the collection of the late Albert C. Bowman.

The third Coldwell rarity (Plate XL, 260), equally unusual in form, engraved like the beaker with a formal design, is a well-nigh flawless little piece, a box of elliptical cross-section probably used as a container for nutmeg from which its former owner spiced his drinks. The engraved decoration is tastefully designed and well proportioned to the surface which it adorns. This piece, incidentally, is the earliest item of American pewter on which I have seen a catalogue number and must therefore have been a stock shape made by Coldwell.

The four remaining articles are dessert spoons, 'elegantly ornamented,' as Coldwell's newspaper notice boasted. Even ordinary marked pewter spoons, once so plentiful, are now exceedingly rare. The Coldwell spoons not only were elaborately decorated, but the decoration in both patterns here illustrated (Plate XXV, 173 and 174) was designed to appeal to the newly aroused consciousness of nationalism in the prospective customers. The first spoon is of particular historical significance, a souvenir of the ratification of the Constitution. On the second (a mate to a spoon illustrated in *American Pewter*) is impressed another patriotic design.

In taking leave of Coldwell and his work, let us consider the decoration of this second spoon. How fitting as a symbol of his own life was the cap of Liberty, but what ironic sense of humor prompted him to combine with it a scroll bearing the words 'Peace and Amity?' The known Coldwell touches are illustrated in Plate LXIII.

In the year following Coldwell's death, Moses Lafetra blossomed out as a full-fledged pewterer in Coldwell's old shop at 7 Beekman Street. His career, however, was brief. For four years he maintained an establishment of his own, and in 1816 he is listed jointly with Anthony Allaire under the firm name of Lafetra and Allaire at 277 Water Street. After that he disappears from the records. It is probable that his death occurred about that time, for a widow Lafetra is found in the Directories for a few years longer. On the other hand, no will nor letters of administration are on file either in New York or in Monmouth County, New Jersey.

Search of the records was made in Freehold, Monmouth County, because Edmund Lafetra, a Huguenot, had been one of the original purchasers of land from the Indians of Monmouth in 1667. One branch of the family took root at Shrewsbury, where Rebekah was living in 1808. Although no trace of Moses Lafetra was found, I feel positive that he was a native of New Jersey.

Except for the pint mug illustrated by Louis G. Myers in his *Notes*, no example of Lafetra's work is known. His touch is reproduced as Plate LXIII, 511.

ROBERT PIERCY

Between the years 1792 and 1797 the New York Directories list a pewterer whose name is variously spelled or misspelled Piercy, Pierse, Peirse, Pierce, and Pearse at the apparent whim of the Directory-takers. He worked at three different addresses on Chatham Street and for one year, 1793, was at 11 Warren Street. His given occupation varied between pewterer, pewter toy-maker, and toy-maker. I found no Directory for 1798, but in 1799 Mary Pierce is listed as a toy-maker at 17 Bowery Lane. The name is not found in Directories before 1792 nor after 1799. I suspect Piercy (or Pierce) was in this country for a few years only.

Howard H. Cotterell, in *Old Pewter*, listed a Robert Peircy of London, pewter toy-maker, 1722 to 1760, whose trade card I have reproduced in Plate IV. I believe that the New York pewterer was either the toy-maker of London or his son, but I cannot substantiate that belief with proof.

THE YOULES

Of the Youles, George and Thomas, we have little information. Father and son presumably, of the eagle period, each had a shop on Water Street, New York — George for over thirty years, 1793 to 1828; Thomas from 1813 to 1819.

New York probate records show that both Youles died intestate; and the last year of Directory listing was, in each case, the year of death.

On June 3, 1793, George Youle advertised himself as a plumber and pewterer at 54 Water Street. Neither in that newspaper notice nor in another that appeared on May 17, 1794, does he mention any forms in pewter other than distilling worms, spoons, and candle moulds, and it seems quite probable that neither Youle ever made plates, mugs, and the other stock shapes on which we have been hoping to find touch-marks bearing their names.

Louis G. Myers in his *Notes* states that in 1803 George Youle was a member of the Society of Mechanics and Tradesmen of New York.

The only other bit of information about either man was gleaned from the Military Minutes of the Council of Appointment of the State of New York, where it is recorded that George Youle in 1793 held a commission as ensign in the First Regiment of the City and County of New York.

EIGHT LATE WORKERS

Eight men, listed in the New York Directories as pewterers, have left no other evidence that they are entitled to such designation.

The first of this colorless group was Thomas Grindell, listed in the 1789 Directory as a pewterer at '67 Broad way.' His name appears for two years longer, spelled 'Grennell,' at other addresses and with no occupation given.

The next man is André Michel (or Michal), who was working as a tinsmith and pewterer at 255 Broadway from 1795 to 1797.

[27]

PLATE LXIII — *New York Touches — William J. Elsworth, the McEuens, George Coldwell, and Moses Lafetra*

504 and 505. Rare and probably early touch of William J. Elsworth, New York, 1767–1798, and his hall-marks. From a 15-inch dish at General Washington's Headquarters, Morristown, New Jersey. Courtesy of the National Park Service and Albert H. Good, Esq.

506 and 506a. Two impressions of Elsworth's normal touch.

505a. Fine impression of Elsworth's hall-marks. All the above are here shown through the courtesy of the National Park Service.

507 and 497a. 507 is a touch attributed to the partnership of Malcolm and Duncan McEuen, New York, 1793–1803. The hall-marks were used earlier by Malcolm McEuen's partner, Cornelius Bradford. From a plate in the author's collection.

508. Small touch of George Coldwell, New York, 1787–1811. From the bottom of the nutmeg box illustrated on Plate XL. Collection of John P. Remensnyder, Esq.

509 and 510. Two Coldwell touches. From spoons in the collection of Albert H. Good, Esq.

511. Touch of Moses Lafetra, New York, 1812–1816. From a pint mug in the Mabel Brady Garvan Collection, Gallery of Fine Arts, Yale University.

PLATE LXIII

506

506a

504   505

505a

507   497a

508

509

510

511

PLATE LXIV — *The Albany Touches — Peter Young, Timothy Brigden, Spencer Stafford, and Daniel Curtiss*

512 and 513. Touches of Peter Young, New York and Albany, 1775–1795. From a plate in the author's collection.

514 and 515. Initial touches of Peter Young. From chalices owned by the author.

516 and 513a. Rare eagle touch of Peter Young. From a plate owned by John W. Poole, Esq.

518. Young's small initial touch. From a creamer in the author's collection.

488a and 517. Touches of Spencer Stafford, Albany, used prior to 1800 (1794–1800). 488 was previously used by Henry Will. Collection of the author.

512a and 517a. Another combination of Stafford touches, possibly used on Young's pewter sold by Stafford. Courtesy of the Mabel Brady Garvan Collection, Gallery of Fine Arts, Yale University.

519. Touch of Timothy Brigden, Albany, 1816–1819. From a chalice owned by the author.

519a and 517b. Marks in a flagon owned by Charles K. Davis, Esq., indicating that Brigden also probably made pewter for Stafford.

517c and 520. A later combination of Stafford marks. The Albany touch was probably not used before 1820. Collection of Charles K. Davis, Esq.

521. Last of the Stafford touches, 1817–1824. From a basin owned by the author.

522. Handsome touch of Daniel Curtiss, Albany, 1822–1840. This touch was probably not used after 1830. Collection of Charles K. Davis, Esq.

522a. Another impression of the same touch. Collection of the author.

523. Curtiss's later mark. Collection of the author.

PLATE LXIV

512   513

514

515

513a   516

488a   517

518

519

512a   517a

519a   517b

517c   520

521

522

523

522a

The Pewterers of New York City

In 1796 Abraham Young was a plumber and pewterer at 57 Chapel Street. His name is found in the city Directories from 1789 to 1801, but, except for the 1796 listing, his occupation, where recorded at all, was given as that of plumber or laborer.

In the 1797 Directory, for one year only, the name of Elijah Knapp appears as a pewterer in Mulberry Street, and in the 1799 issue a pewterer named Philip Fields was at 16 Bowery Lane.

The sixth of these little-known pewterers, Luke Kiersted, is recorded as a pewterer and plumber at 14 Upper Chambers Street in the Directory for 1805.

There is a little more evidence of Anthony J. Allaire's having been a real pewterer, though his early days in New York indicate no serious preparation for the work. His name first appears in the 1814 Directory as a milkman, disappears in 1815, and comes back as a pewterer and partner of Moses Lafetra at 277 Water Street in 1816. In 1817 James Jones, Providence coppersmith, son of Gershom Jones, pewterer, replaced Lafetra, and the firm name of Jones and Allaire is listed, with a plumber's shop on Water Street. For the next four years we find Allaire, now partnerless, plying the trade of pewterer at various addresses on Water Street, after which he is listed only as a plumber. He died in New York in 1859.

The last of the group is James Bird. Recorded from 1816 to 1819 as a plumber at 77 Harman Street, he graduated into pewtering in 1820, continued that trade in 1821, but at 76 Eldridge Street, and thereafter is listed as a plumber only. His death occurred in 1862.

ALBANY PEWTERERS

IN ALBANY, as in New York, there were probably Dutch pewterers at work long before the earliest established date of pewter-making in that city.

Our history of the craft there goes back only to the eve of the Revolution when Henry Will moved up the Hudson River from New York. Shortly thereafter he was followed by another able New York pewter-maker, Peter Young. The pewter of both men is distinguished and alone would be sufficient to place Albany among the important pewter-making centers in this country.

Prior to the britannia period at least three other shops which have left us pewter of better than average quality and workmanship were established in Albany. The proprietors of these later shops were Spencer Stafford, merchant and only incidentally a pewterer; Timothy Brigden, a silversmith who worked also in the baser metal; and Daniel Curtiss, pewterer and bell-founder.

The distinctive Albany form in pewter, and that for which the city is most noted, is Peter Young's chalice design, which, in but slightly modified form, was turned out also by Timothy Brigden. Without question it was one of the most pleasing shapes made in this country and, barring the Lancaster chalice, was the only type of such a vessel that has been found with the marks of an early American pewterer. Young may have made chalices in New York prior to moving to Albany, but thus far all examples known have been found in upstate New York and western New England.

The work of all five Albany makers is worthy of inclusion in any collection of American pewter.

HENRY WILL AND PETER YOUNG

The histories of these men were related in the chapter on New York City pewterers (pages 12–17 and 22–23). Will was in Albany from 1775 to 1784. Young moved there at an undetermined date after 1770, probably during the Revolution. Undoubtedly there was some close association between these men. A striking similarity is evidenced in their handle designs and in other forms that they made. Young may have been one of Will's apprentices and perhaps went with the older man to Albany as a journeyman, or he may simply have moved up there in 1784 to take over Will's trade when the latter returned to New York. At that time Will's rose-and-crown touch was left behind and was used later, as was Peter Young's, on the pewter of Spencer Stafford, an indication perhaps that Young made for Stafford much of the pewter bearing the latter's name.

SPENCER STAFFORD

Spencer Stafford, whose likeness is shown in Plate VII, was born May 10, 1772, at Cheshire, Massachusetts, the son of Joab Stafford and Susannah Spencer. The family moved to Albany in 1783. Young Stafford in 1788 was apprenticed to his brother-in-law, Thomas Spencer, a merchant, and under the latter's supervision learned the manufacture of tin plate and copper. On September 7, 1790, Stafford, then only eighteen years of age, married Dorothea Hallenbake, a reigning belle of Albany.

When his apprenticeship expired in 1792, he removed with his wife to Deerfield, near the present site of Utica, where he manufactured potash. His home was a log house, oiled paper serving as window glass, and by the light of pine torches he read the books received from Albany. These were sent to him with the necessities of life in exchange for the goods that he had to sell — potash, tinware, and molasses. The frontier life soon proved intolerable to his bride, and in 1793 the Staffords returned to Albany.

In 1794 he informed the public of a resumption of business in his old line, namely, 'Tinplate, sheet iron, copper and brass manufacture,' at his shop 'east side of Market,' a few doors north of the Dutch Church. Stafford prospered greatly, became a bank director in 1811, and put up a five-story building in 1814–1815. In 1820 he was making, at a foundry on the corner of Washington and Central Avenues, stoves that represented an improvement upon the fashionable nine-plate stove.

During these years Stafford was busy forming and dissolving partnerships. In 1795 he was associated with James Minze. Their shop was at 45 Court Street with a branch store in Schenectady. That partnership was dissolved in the following year, and Spencer's brother, John, joined him. Together they built up a very successful business. In 1815 the firm name was Staffords, Rogers and Company. In a naïvely worded advertisement on May 7 of that year John and Spencer Stafford and George and Thomas Spencer announced the dissolution of their company, 'owing to a misunderstanding between one of the persons composing the firm of Staffords, Rogers & Co. and the other persons of said firm.' Spencer Stafford was the senior partner of this organization and of its various successors, Stafford, Spencer and Company, Spencer Stafford and Company, and Stafford, Benedict, and Company. In 1824 the last-named partnership was dissolved, and Stafford continued the business alone until his retirement in 1827.

The first Mrs. Stafford had died in 1806, and in the following year the widower married Harriet Romeyn. Spencer Stafford's sons, Hallenbake and Joab, and his son-in-law, Lewis Benedict, were associated with him in business after 1817.

There is no question as to the social and business prominence of Stafford in Albany.

Timothy Brigden

I quote in part from a leading article that appeared in the *Albany Argus* of February 12, 1844, two days after his death:

> For more than forty years he was engaged in extensive mercantile pursuits; and although he retired several years since from the active cares of business, took a deep interest in the prosperity and advancement of the city. He was an enterprising merchant, and a citizen of intelligence and high respectability. He leaves a numerous body of relatives and friends to mourn his death, with whom our citizens generally will unite their regrets....

At no point in the documentary record of Stafford's life do we find any mention of pewter-making, and I agree heartily with Louis G. Myers's statement in his *Notes* that Spencer Stafford 'was evidently a captain of industry and let his high privates make his pewter.'

I believe that in his early days he sold pewter that was made for him and stamped with his name by Peter Young (see Plate LXIV, 488a, 517, and 512a, 517a); that for a few years Timothy Brigden made pewter for him (numbers 519a, 517b); and that he later employed in his own shop journeymen pewterers to turn out his wares. Under this latter arrangement Stafford's touches were used alone (numbers 517c, 520). To the period between 1815 and 1824 belongs the touch shown in number 521, a very early use of the uninteresting incised form of marking.

Stafford's marks have been found on $7\frac{7}{8}$-inch and $8\frac{7}{8}$-inch plates, $13\frac{1}{2}$-inch deep dishes, $6\frac{5}{8}$-inch and $10\frac{1}{2}$-inch basins, quart tankards, and communion flagons (Plate XXXIII, 224). The plates bearing Henry Will or Peter Young touches have a hammered booge; the others have not.

TIMOTHY BRIGDEN

In J. B. Kerfoot's *American Pewter* occurs the following comment upon the product of Thomas Badger's shop: 'I once heard much talk of a communion set by him, but I was unable to run it down.'

There is a strong suspicion in my mind that the Thomas Badger communion set yarn was put in circulation by someone who had seen a pair of communion chalices marked 'T. B.' in a saw-tooth circle, four or five pairs of which are now known to be in existence. These handsome vessels are almost identical with the chalices of Peter Young of Albany, but vary slightly in dimensions from the work of that man. In fact they are so similar in design that it was almost a foregone conclusion that the maker eventually would be found in or near Albany, particularly inasmuch as the chalices themselves have been found in that region. I communicated this belief to H. V. Button, and to him goes the credit for locating an Albany pewterer with initials 'T. B.'

Timothy, fourth child of Thomas and Elizabeth (Banks) Brigden, was born August 14, 1774, in Middletown, Connecticut. We know nothing about his youth or early working years, but he must have been apprenticed to a silversmith. He never owned property in Middletown, and the family may have moved to Albany soon after the Revolution as did so many natives of Connecticut. In Albany's earliest Directory, that of 1813, Brigden is listed as a silversmith at 106 Beaver Street and was following the same trade in 1815, though he may have begun many years earlier to supplement his income by the manufacture and sale of pewter. In the Directory issues from 1816 to 1818 his address remains the same, but his occupation is changed to that of 'pewterer,' and in 1819 the widow Brigden is listed at 106 Beaver Street. The sudden death of 'Mr. Timothy Brigden, formerly of Middletown, Connecticut,' was reported in the *Albany Gazette* of May 13, 1819. Of his history I can add nothing more except that his name appears with that of Spencer Stafford among the members of the Albany Mechanics' Society, founded in 1796.

In Plate LXIV, 519, is the touch which I attribute without hesitation to Brigden. Its resemblance to one of Peter Young's marks is as striking as the similarity in the work of the two men. Unfortunately the touch has been found thus far on only a small group of pieces: one transition-type teapot, two or three flagons similar to those which bear Stafford touches (see Plate XXXIII), and a number of chalices, but chalices of exquisite early design made of fine metal and finished with the care that might be expected of a man trained in the silversmith's art.

The last of the 'T. B.' flagons to be reported to me is marked with the Brigden touch and also with Stafford's name touch indicating that Brigden as well as Young made pewter for Stafford.

THE CURTISSES

In the search for the history of the maker of the superfine pewter which is stamped with a graceful urn and the name D. Curtiss, there was little from which to start beyond a shrewd guess by Louis G. Myers that the man would be located in the neighborhood of Albany. But Myers's guesses, with amazing regularity, have turned out to be realities, and this case was no exception.

Prior to 1820 no Albany record of Curtiss could be found, and no directories were issued for the years 1820 and 1821. In the 1822 Directory and succeeding issues up to 1832, Daniel Curtiss is listed as a pewterer at 566 South Market Street. In the latter year his business address changes to 23 Church Street, and there he worked until his death in 1872.

Among the advertisements in the front of the Directory for 1822 the following notice appears:

Daniel Curtiss

Fancy Pewterer

No. 566 South Market St.

Respectfully informs the Public that he keeps constantly on hand a general assortment of Pewter Ware of various descriptions, which he will furnish his customers at the New York prices.

The Curtisses

And if any of the later pewterers is entitled to call himself a 'fancy pewterer' surely Daniel Curtiss is the man. He was not only a maker of pewter of the finest grade and finish; he had also a sense of line and proportion that most of the other later makers lacked. Compare, for instance, the handsome covered pitcher (Plate LXXIII), now in the Mabel Brady Garvan Collection, with the finest that such able craftsmen as Roswell Gleason or the Boardmans have left us.

As the day of pewter was passing, Daniel Curtiss was preparing to go into a new line of work, and in 1843 he advertised that 'The subscriber is prepared to furnish Church Bells, with improved cast iron yokes, warranted in tone and durability equal to any made. Steamboat and factory bells constantly on hand. Also brass and composition castings. . . .' Thereafter he is listed as a bell-founder and pewterer until 1850, and in later years as a bell-founder only.

Following up Daniel Curtiss's history led to the finding of his brother Joseph, possibly the man whose 'I. Curtis' touch was illustrated by J. B. Kerfoot in *American Pewter*. Louis G. Myers once showed me a plate marked I. Curtiss on which the second *s* is plainly visible, and it is now apparent that on the example photographed by Kerfoot and shown again here (Plate LVIII, 452), the last *s* had been obliterated by wear.

Joseph Curtiss did not appear upon the scene in Albany until 1832, when he was listed in the Directory as a pewterer at the address of his brother. This seemed so unduly late that I had to find him an earlier place of business.

In the *Troy Sentinel* for July 3, 1827, appeared a notice from which the following is quoted:

New Hardware Store

Joseph Curtiss having taken a store 10 rods south of E. & P. Dorlon's Fourth Ward House, River St., Troy, offers for sale . . . britannia tea-pots, plated and britannia spoons . . . coffee and teapots, pewter platters, plates, basins, porringers, tumblers, ladles, spoons, inkstands, cups, measures, syringes, bed and chair pans, together with many articles usually found in a Hardware Store.

Whether or not Curtiss made the pewter which he offered for sale cannot be determined from the notice. The store could not have been a success, for in 1832 Joseph joined his brother in Albany. In 1838 he separated from Daniel, opening a shop of his own at 77 Ferry Street. Until 1859 he is listed as a pewterer at three or four different addresses, and from then until 1879, the probable date of his death, his occupation was given as that of a clerk.

To return to Daniel Curtiss, two helpful facts appear in his obituary notice in the *Albany Evening Journal* of September 14, 1872. It tells us that Daniel was in his seventy-third year, making his year of birth 1799 or 1800, and it mentions, among the family that survives him, his brother Joseph. Except for that notice we could not be certain how the two men were related.

In the deeds covering the purchase and sale of his Troy real estate, Joseph appears as Joseph, Junior, from which we infer that his father bore the same name. However, we have no information as to where the elder Joseph lived or in what town or even state his sons were born.

[33]

Albany Pewterers

I am by no means satisfied that Joseph Curtiss of Albany is the 'I. Curtiss' whose pewter we have found. First of all it would be most surprising to learn that a maker of the eighteen-thirties should use the old form letter 'I' for a 'J.' Secondly, no I. Curtiss pewter yet found belongs to the britannia period. Such as I have seen is flatware (6-inch and 8-inch plates), made, one would judge, prior to 1825. I think it not improbable that this Albany pewterer has left no marked examples and that the maker of the I. Curtiss pewter was a Connecticut man who died or retired about 1825.

The metal of Daniel Curtiss remains exceedingly rare. His work is represented by at least two $6\frac{1}{2}$-inch butter plates, a number of $7\frac{7}{8}$-inch plates, $11\frac{1}{16}$-inch deep dishes, pint and quart basins, together with such later forms as teapots, coffee-pots, and water pitchers. His touches are illustrated on Plate LXIV.

THE PEWTERERS OF PENNSYLVANIA

ONE hundred and fifty years ago Pennsylvania was the most cosmopolitan of the American colonies. Unlike Massachusetts, for instance, which was settled so largely by men of one stock, one language, and even one religious belief, Pennsylvania was an asylum for the persecuted of many faiths, refugees from almost every country and principality in Europe.

The first permanent European settlement had been made by the Swedes at Upland (now Chester), but the entire territory passed under the control of the Dutch a few years later, only to be wrested in turn from them by the English.

In 1680 William Penn besought and received from the Crown, in payment of debts long owed to his father, a grant of land on the Delaware River. He immediately prepared plans for a city, and agents in London and Bristol sold lots in the wilderness which was to become the city of Philadelphia.

In the following year the first of Penn's company sailed for the new land, and among the number was Thomas Paschall of Bristol, Pennsylvania's earliest pewterer of record. He settled on the Schuylkill in March, 1682, and soon thereafter opened a shop for the manufacture of pewter in Philadelphia. By 1690 the new town boasted two pewter-making establishments. Some twenty years then elapsed before the arrival of the earliest pewterer whose metal has survived.

Simon Edgell, a native of London, was at work in Philadelphia as early at least as 1713, and for thirty years he was a prominent craftsman and merchant of the city. We now know that at least five other makers worked in Pennsylvania during the first half of the eighteenth century, but four of the group are little more than names to us, for their histories are obscure and their metal has vanished.

Those early pewterers were all of Anglo-Saxon stock, but by 1750 conditions were changing. Immigration from the Continent of Europe had been increasing by leaps and bounds. The influx of Swiss, Bohemians, Moravians, Alsatians, and men of the Palatinate had become so great that in some districts English was rarely spoken. It was therefore but natural that this Teutonic tide should have carried in with it a number of pewterers, of which at least five are known to us by name, and one of the number, William Will, was to become an outstanding figure in the history of American pewter. To the same period belong also two or three makers of Anglo-Saxon stock, of whom the most prominent was Cornelius Bradford.

In such an environment and under such conditions it would have been most surprising had the pewterers slavishly followed English models, as did their fellow-craftsmen of Massachusetts. We find, to be sure, Pennsylvania pewter which differs but little from that of New England, but our collections are also enriched and varied by forms that were never made in America outside of Pennsylvania; such, for instance, as the church flagons of Christopher Heyne of Lancaster, Alsatian in their outline, but displaying certain details that are more English than German (see Plate XXXI, 217). In other Pennsylvania forms we see the same mingling in different degrees of English and Continental influences. The result is a variety in shape and detail which is always interesting and frequently most pleasing.

This third quarter of the century was the high-water mark of Pennsylvania pewter. The peak in production may not have been reached until 1810, but no post-Revolutionary maker has left us such interesting shapes as did Heyne, the Moravian of Lancaster, nor did the successors of William Will ever approach the grace, the dignity, and the finished workmanship of that pewterer's better pieces. After the Revolutionary War Colonel Will lived but a few years. In that time he had the field almost to himself in Pennsylvania. In fact his principal competition probably came from England and from peddlers of Connecticut pewter.

By the turn of the century, however, a new crop of makers was springing up. With a few exceptions these men were pewterers of limited ability who undertook the manufacture of only the simplest forms.

In that period three figures stand out, by no means the equals of Will, to be sure, but makers of some originality, the better examples of whose work are extremely desirable. These three were Parks Boyd, Thomas Danforth, Third (whose story has already been told in the chapter on Connecticut pewterers), and Robert Palethorp, Junior. Palethorp died in 1822, a date which corresponds closely to the beginning of the decadent period of pewter-making, not only in Philadelphia, but throughout the country. His successors, lesser lights all of them, will be considered in the history of the britannia period.

Pennsylvania pewter displays no marked characteristics common to all its makers as does, for instance, the flatware of Massachusetts. Nor should we have expected any such regularity, for its makers came from different countries and were trained in different schools, and each probably catered specifically to communities settled by his own countrymen, who would naturally have had predilections for shapes in pewter that resembled those which they had brought from the old country.

Not only is the variety in form more pronounced than in the output of any other colony, but we find also an extremely wide range in quality and workmanship. The worst Pennsylvania pewter is not worthy of a place in any collection, but to capture an Edgell dish or a Will coffee-pot is the goal of every collector. It is to be doubted that the craftsmanship of pewter-making ever attained a higher degree of perfection elsewhere in America than in the work of Pennsylvania's ablest pewterers.

THOMAS PASCHALL

In the outskirts of Bristol, England, there lived during the seventeenth century a family named Paschall, most of whose bread-winners were pewterers by trade. In December, 1681, one of this group, Thomas Paschall, with his wife Joanna (Sloper), his sister, Elizabeth, his apprenticed sons, William and Thomas, Junior, and a daughter, Mary, set sail for America and took up five hundred acres on the west side of the Schuylkill River, some five miles from the newly laid-out town of Philadelphia.

Thomas Paschall was born near Bristol May 13 (third month, thirteenth day, 'old style'), 1635, and was baptized in the following December in Saint Mary Redcliffe Church. He was a son of William Paschall, also a pewterer, to whom he was apprenticed on November 16, 1652. He was therefore working at his trade as a master-pewterer for over twenty years prior to his departure for America.

During his first year in Pennsylvania, Paschall must have been too busy establishing himself, clearing and cultivating his land, to do much in the trade in which he was schooled. An existing letter which he wrote to a friend in England in 1683 comments at length upon crops, the bounty of nature in the new land, and kindred subjects. It also records the safe arrival of William Penn.

Paschall's property, as shown on a map of 1681, prepared by Thomas Holme, Penn's surveyor-general, was situated near the present site of Mount Moriah Cemetery. On it he built a log cabin that first spring, and he was fortunate in being able to rent a house for his family not far distant on the Schuylkill. Philadelphia was then just a city on paper, and preparatory to the construction of permanent homes some of her earliest citizens were digging temporary shelters for themselves in caves along the waterfront. Very soon thereafter Paschall must have bought or rented property in the town, for his name appears as that of the only 'putorer' on an old 'List of Coopers, House Carpenters, etc., in Philadelphia, 1682.' It seems highly improbable, therefore, that we shall ever find evidence of an earlier pewter-maker in Philadelphia.

Farming must have been his principal occupation in the early years, for in deeds up to 1686 he is termed a yeoman, thereafter a pewterer. In 1690 he bought property on the riverbank at Front Street, and toward the close of his career his shop was near the corner of Second and Walnut Streets.

Thomas Paschall was a citizen of prominence in the early government of the province. From 1685 until 1689 he was a member of the Assembly, and under the first charter of the city of Philadelphia, dated '3rd month, 20, 1691,' he was named one of the twelve common councilmen. In 1705 he served on a committee that divided the city into wards.

In the Bible of Thomas Say, an early Philadelphian, the following entry appears:

Thomas Paschall S[r]. departed this life the 13th of 7[ber] 1718 about 4 o'clock in the morning in the 83rd year of his age and was buried upon his wife.

His will was dated September 12, 1716, and in it he described himself as of the 'City of Philadelphia and Province of Pennsylvania, Pewterer.'

Both sons, William and Thomas, Junior, had been apprenticed to their father in England, but no evidence could be found that either followed the pewterer's trade. William, in Philadelphia, was a silversmith, while Thomas is described in deeds as a yeoman (occasionally as a maltster) of Blockley Township.

The Paschall Bible, dated 1599, is today in the possession of one of the pewterer's descendants, Lawrence J. Morris of Philadelphia.

THOMAS BADCO(C)KE

The value of printed propaganda to the real estate salesman is no new discovery. William Penn realized and made use of it two hundred and fifty years ago, and his campaign to advertise Pennsylvania might be studied to advantage by promoters of today. One of the devices he employed was to turn to his own use the personal letters written by colonists to friends in England describing the blessings of the new country. He seized upon these eagerly, had them printed, sometimes in several languages, and scattered them throughout England and the Continent of Europe. Two letters, thus preserved, are of especial interest to the pewter collector. One, mentioned previously, was written by the pewterer, Thomas Paschall. It dealt primarily with the beauty of the country and the natural advantages of Pennsylvania. The second letter, written in 1690 by a man named Goodson, dwelt at some length upon the growth of Philadelphia and enumerated enthusiastically the many crafts which had already been established in the town. It recorded among other facts the existence at that date of two pewterers' shops. One, of course, was Paschall's; to find the second a search was made of the earliest Philadelphia will books, a search which was not entirely without results.

In a will dated January 2, 1707/8, and proved on March 9 of the same year, 'Thomas Badcoke of the City of Philadelphia, Pewterer,' left the bulk of his small estate to his cousin, 'Henry Badcoke, Brewer,' and among the specific legacies was a gift of ten pounds to his friend, Thomas Paschall. Badcoke apparently was a bachelor and had no close relatives. His may have been the second pewter-making establishment in Philadelphia mention of which was made by Goodson in 1690. On the other hand, it must be admitted that his name is found in no Philadelphia records except the will books and is missing from the existing tax lists of 1693.

Reference to Howard H. Cotterell's *Old Pewter* establishes the fact that a Thomas Badcocke, pewterer, joined the yeomanry of the Pewterers' Company in London on October 4, 1688, after which all record of him in the books of the Pewterers' Company ceases. It is conjectural therefore that this man may be the Thomas Badcoke who died in Philadelphia in 1709.

Simon Edgell and James Everett

SIMON EDGELL AND JAMES EVERETT

The next earliest Philadelphia pewterers whose records have been found are Simon Edgell and James Everett. Both were born in England, where they learned their trade, and both were admitted as yeomen to the Pewterers' Company in London — Edgell in 1709, Everett in 1711.

Edgell came first to this country; he was in Philadelphia at least as early as 1713. Everett, however, was not given leave to strike his touch in Pewterers' Hall, London, until October, 1714. Soon thereafter he must have sailed from England, for we learn from the records of Christ Church, Philadelphia, that 'John, son of James Everitt,' was buried November 7, 1716.

In May of the following year Simon Edgell and James 'Everet,' both described as pewterers, were admitted as freemen of the city. With this all record of Everett in Philadelphia ceases. It is a fair surmise that he soon moved to some other town in the colonies or else returned to England.

With the kind permission of the late Howard H. Cotterell, I am showing a cut (Plate LXV, 524), taken from his book, *Old Pewter*, of Everett's touch as photographed from Plate 3 in Pewterers' Hall, London. No doubt this same mark would have been impressed upon the pewter which he made in this country.

Edgell's history is somewhat less obscure. In the Minutes of the Common Council of Philadelphia, under date of January 29, 1717, the following entry appears:

> Upon the Peticon of Simon Edgill, Setting fforth that there is a vacancy of the Office for Sealing Weights & Measures within this City, Craved that this Board Would please to appoint him to Execute ye s'd Office, w'ch s'd peticon is referred to ye next Council.

Politicians seem to have changed but little in two hundred years, for there is no record that Edgell's 'peticon' ever again saw daylight.

Edgell unquestionably prospered. In 1718 he purchased property on High Street, and upon several occasions in the succeeding twenty years he added to his holdings. His name appears a number of times in newspaper notices. In 1730 he was one of a number of Philadelphia merchants who agreed to accept in trade the paper currency of the lower counties of the Delaware, and he advertised in the following manner in the *Pennsylvania Gazette* of September 11, 1735:

> All Persons indebted to Simon Edgell, of this City, are desired to come and settle, and pay the Balance of their Accounts, with said Edgell, or they must expect to be sued.

> N.B. There is to be sold at his Store, opposite to William Fishbourn's Wharff for ready Money, Ozenbrigs, Nails, Shot, Window Glass, Looking-Glasses, Irish Linnens, Woollens and sundry other Merchandize at very reasonable Rates, he intending to depart this Province the latter end of November.

PLATE LXV — *Early Pennsylvania Touches — James Everett, William Cox,*
Simon Edgell, Johann Christopher Heyne, and William Will

524. The touch of James Everett, Philadelphia, 1716–1717, which was struck on Touch-Plate II in Pewterer's Hall, London, October 29, 1714. The same mark may have been used in Philadelphia. From *Old Pewter, Its Makers and Its Marks.* Courtesy of the late Howard H. Cotterell, Esq.

525. The touch of William Cox, London, struck in Pewterer's Hall about 1710. This was probably the William Cox(e) who was making pewter in Philadelphia from 1715 to 1721 and the same mark may well have been used on his Philadelphia pewter. From *Old Pewter, Its Makers and Its Marks.* Courtesy of the late Howard H. Cotterell, Esq.

526. Initial touch, attributed with confidence to Simon Edgell, Philadelphia, 1713–1742. From an early domed-top tankard that has come down in the family of Dr. Warren C. Mercer and illustrated in Plate XVI, through Dr. Mercer's courtesy.

526a. Another impression of the same touch. From a tankard in the collection of Edward E. Minor, Esq.

527, 528, and 529. The large touches of Simon Edgell. From a plate in the author's collection.

530, 531, and 532. The large touches of Johann Christopher Heyne, Lancaster, 1754–1780, as found on a flagon in the Mabel Brady Garvan Collection, Gallery of Fine Arts, Yale University.

533. Heyne's small touch as photographed on the top of a dram bottle (250, Plate XXXIX), owned by John J. Evans, Jr., Esq.

533a. Another impression of the same touch. From the lid of the author's sugar pot, illustrated as 197, Plate XXIX.

534, 535, and 536. A group of early touches of Colonel William Will, Philadelphia, 1764–1798. From a large dish formerly owned by the late M. Brix, Esq., and illustrated through the courtesy of Philip G. Platt, Esq. Of particular interest are the unexplainable hall-marks with initials 'I. C.' or 'T. C.'

PLATE LXV

524

525

530   532

526   526 a

527   528   529

533

533 a

534   535   536

PLATE LXVI — *Philadelphia Touches — William Will, the Heras, and Parks Boyd*

534a. A second impression of this early touch of Colonel William Will, which was illustrated in Plate LXV. The same illustration appeared in *American Pewter*, and is reproduced through the courtesy of the late Mrs. J. B. Kerfoot.

535a. A second impression of Will's early lamb and dove touch. From the bottom of a quart pot owned by Mrs. James H. Krom.

537. Another Colonel Will touch. From the Mabel Brady Garvan Collection, Gallery of Fine Arts, Yale University.

538 and 539. Will touches. Photographed in the bottom of Mrs. James H. Krom's flagon which has been illustrated through her courtesy as 218, Plate XXXI.

540 and 537a. Will touches. From a plate in the collection of Mrs. Stephen S. FitzGerald. 540 is probably one of the earliest of all eagle touches.

541. An initial touch of William Will, which is found usually on hollow-ware. Collection of Charles F. Hutchins, Esq.

541a. Another impression of the same touch. Collection of the author.

542. Last of the Will touches, which is also found on hollow-ware and spoons. This impression is from Mrs. H. H. Benkard's ladle which is pictured as 182, Plate XXVI.

542a. Another impression of the same mark. From a round teapot owned by Mr. and Mrs. Richard S. Quigley.

543. Touch of Christian and John Hera, Philadelphia, 1800–1812. From a smooth-rim plate, also in the collection of Mr. and Mrs. Quigley.

544 and 544a. Two impressions of the normal touch of Parks Boyd, Philadelphia, 1795–1819. From plates owned by the author.

545. Boyd's small eagle touch. From a 6-inch plate owned by the author.

546. The Boyd touch usually found on his hollow-ware. From a quart pot in the collection of Edward E. Minor, Esq.

PLATE LXVI

534 a

537

535 a

538   539

540   537 a

541

541 a

542

542 a

543

544

544 a

545

546

The Pewterers of Pennsylvania

N.B. A parcel of likely servants just arrived from Milford on board the Brigt. Britannia, John Bond, Master; whose Times are to be disposed of by said Simon Edgel or said Master at Market-street Wharff.

Again, in 1737 and 1738, Edgell advertised his departure for London, promising trouble to those who did not pay their accounts. In those years he also offered to book space for passengers or freight in the brig *Constantine*. It is therefore evident that Edgell had become a merchant on a large scale, and it is likely that he made periodic visits to London to purchase merchandise. In spite of his increased activities, however, he remained a pewterer to the end of his days, or at least he so styled himself as late as 1741. His death occurred in 1742. Edgell's will throws an interesting sidelight upon the social circles in which he moved, for witnessing the document is the signature of Benjamin Franklin.

Exclusive of real estate Edgell owned at the time of his death possessions valued at almost forty-five hundred pounds. The inventory is most interesting to a student of pewter but too lengthy for insertion here. It will be found in Appendix II, page 155.

It is a matter for congratulation that at least six examples of this early pewterer's handicraft have already come to light. Two splendid dishes, probably the finest, and perhaps the earliest, survivals of American flatware, bear testimony to the high quality of Edgell's work. One, measuring 16⅜ inches in diameter, now in the Mabel Brady Garvan Collection at Yale University, was illustrated by Louis G. Myers in his *Notes*. The other, a 15-inch dish, owned by Joseph France, is the frontispiece of volume I. Both are hammered all over — not simply on the booge, the normal procedure — and undoubtedly commanded a premium over unhammered wares. To evaluate properly Edgell's skill as a hammerman, place alongside one of these dishes a dish or plate of such an able workman as Frederick Bassett or William Elsworth. The perfection of the Quaker's work will at once be apparent.

The third Edgell item, a 9¼-inch smooth-rim plate, has a hammered booge and bears not only the normal Edgell touches, but also a Philadelphia mark (Plate LXV, 529). A second plate, similarly marked, has just been reported to me, and with it was found a domed-top tankard, with the previously unlisted touch illustrated as number 526. The owners of plate and tankard believe that they have always been together and the touch undoubtedly is one used by Simon Edgell. This tankard has an unusually heavy base and also an unusually heavy hinge for the cover. A long step toward the confirmation of this attribution was made with the discovery of another very fine early tankard (Plate XVI, 94), bearing the same touch (Plate LXV, 526a) in the home of Doctor Warren C. Mercer, Philadelphia. The tankard had come down through generations of his family from Ann Michener, whose initials it bears, member of an early Philadelphia family.

WILLIAM COX

In Jane Logan's account book, now in the archives of the Pennsylvania Historical Society, the following entries appear:

> 1715, 5 mo. (July) 1st — Paid Wm Cox Pewterer Peter's Note on me £7.12.6
> 1715, 10 mo. 17th   — Wm Coxe Pewterer Dr. to Cash £5.3.5 his Note to R^d. Clymer in full £5.3.5.

We find also the following entry in the accounts of Mary Coates, widow, of Philadelphia:

> 1721 1 m° 28th   Sundry pewter ware, bought of William Cox £2.4.4 a Large Dish W^t 7^lb at 20^d. £0.11.2

The public records of Philadelphia give us but little additional information about Cox. On July 3, 1720, Richard Anthony of Philadelphia, merchant, and Sarah his wife, of the one part, sold to John Leech, of Philadelphia, merchant, and William Cox of said city, pewterer, of the second part, for four hundred pounds property 50 feet by 250 feet on King Street extending to the riverbank, with buildings, messuages, and wharves thereon. On December 12, 1727, a William Cox married Anne Richard in the First Presbyterian Church, and on August 26, 1745, letters of administration were granted on the estate of William Cox, 'late Merchant of Philadelphia,' to George Roth of Maryland, 'Gentleman,' and Mary his wife, daughter of William Cox.

It may also be of interest to note that a William Cox, pewterer of London, joined the yeomanry of the Pewterers' Company on the sixteenth of December, 1708, and that his touch was struck about 1710. The touch (Plate LXV, 525) is illustrated here on the possibility that its user may have been the pewterer of Philadelphia.

THOMAS BYLES

The next name, like that of William Cox, has appeared in no previous history of American pewterers. Thomas Byles owes his escape from oblivion to an advertisement which appeared in the *Pennsylvania Gazette* of November 19, 1741. In that issue 'Thomas Byles, Pewterer,' in Market Street offered for sale 'a good Still and Worm containing near 70 gallons.'

The examination of Pennsylvania records which followed this discovery disclosed nothing about Byles's early life; but an excerpt from a letter of one of his relatives, Doctor Jeremy Belknap, written October 12, 1783, furnished a leading clue which carried the search to Boston.

In or about the year 1693 Josias Byles, a saddler, of Winchester, England, sailed for Boston with his wife Sarah (Auber) and sons, Josias and Thomas. The date of Thomas's birth in England is not definitely known, but it was within the period from 1683 to 1690, for when Josias died in 1707 he left a will, dated 1704, mentioning his son, Thomas, under age, 'who is apprenticed with Mr. Man, Brazier.'

Josias had been thrice married, and Mather Byles, half-brother of Thomas, became one of the most conspicuous figures in Boston's provincial history. Educated at Harvard, this young man entered the ministry. In addition to being a gifted preacher, he was a poet of note, an exceptionally able prose writer, and one of the greatest humorists in the colonies. His Tory sympathies ended in his trial and sentence to deportation, but the sentence was later rescinded. He died in Boston in 1788.

Thomas himself can be positively identified as the Philadelphia pewterer by the previously mentioned Belknap letter, from which the following is quoted:

> My grandfather Byles had a brother Thomas, who lived and died in Philadelphia. He was a pewterer and lived in Market Street; he had a son Daniel, who is dead, and left a son who, I am told, has been a Major in the army in this war.

Among the Massachusetts Historical Society records is a letter from Thomas Byles written at Newport, Rhode Island, January 16, 1711/12, to his 'loving brother and sister.' Unfortunately it makes no mention of pewter.

It would seem that Byles moved to Newport very soon after his apprenticeship to William Mann of Boston was ended, and there he married Elizabeth White. Why and when he deserted Newport for Philadelphia are questions that remain unanswered, but in 1738 he purchased property in High Street in the latter city.

When the First Baptist Church of Philadelphia was organized May 15, 1746, Thomas and Elizabeth Byles were among the charter members. They are known to have had but two children, Daniel and Elizabeth. There is no evidence as yet that the son ever followed the pewterer's trade. In a deed of 1755 registering his purchase of property in Merion, he is described as a merchant of Hopewell, New Jersey. He married Margaret Lambert and inherited from her father, Thomas Lambert, property in New Jersey. Daniel died in Merion in 1757, leaving one son, Thomas Lambert Byles.

According to Thomas Byles's will, dated June 13, 1770, and probated June 11, 1771, he was survived by his wife, a daughter, Elizabeth, and a minor grandson, Thomas Lambert Byles. In the document he termed himself 'a pewterer, aged and infirm.'

A lengthy inventory of the contents of his shop is given in Appendix II, pages 156–158. He carried a tremendous stock in a great variety of shapes and his moulds alone weighed over half a ton. Although we can only surmise as to the extent of his business, available records indicate that Byles was one of the most important of the colonial pewterers.

It is hard to believe that not one example of this man's craftsmanship has survived and I am tempted to attribute to him a 'T. B.' touch which has been found on a half-dozen or more plates with hammered booge which have been picked up in Pennsylvania and New Jersey. The large crown in this design (Plate LXIX, 586, 586a) is unlike anything on British pewter, and can be set down as the work of a colonial or a Continental die-cutter. But until we have more convincing proof as to its user it will be listed among the unidentified touches.

SIMON WYER

In Watson's *Annals of Philadelphia* mention is made of the shop sign of 'Simon Myer, pewterer.' An unsuccessful search was made through Philadelphia records for traces of a man of that name, but the mystery was not cleared up until the publication of *Arts and Crafts in Philadelphia*. That valuable volume contains a notice which was inserted in the *Pennsylvania Gazette* on May 15, 1746, by Simon Wyer (not Myer). The advertisement in question reads as follows:

> Simon Wyer, Pewterer, at the Sign of the Globe in Market-street, Philadelphia, all sorts of old pewter plates and dishes &c that by long use or neglect of servants are batter'd, bruised, melted or damaged, shall be mended (if possible) neat and cheap; care shall be taken to give general satisfaction. N.B. Ready Money is given for old pewter.

Of Wyer's antecedents and early history nothing has been learned, but on January 1, 1740, he married Hannah Pearson in Christ Church, Philadelphia. He appears to have figured in just one transfer of property in Philadelphia. On July 6, 1749, a tripartite deed was executed by 'Simon Wyer of the County and City of Philadelphia in the Province of Pennsilvania, Pewterer of the one Part, Hannah Pearson, Spinster, who intermarried with the said Simon Wyer, of the Second Part and Thomas Day of the City afors^d Merchant of the third Part.' The property on High Street covered by the deed had been inherited in 1739 by 'Hannah Pierson alias Wyer' and improved by buildings erected by Wyer. Upon this occasion its ownership was transferred to Thomas Day. Wyer lived but a few years longer. On November 30, 1752, Marcus Kuhl, principal creditor, was granted letters of administration upon the estate of the late pewterer. It is difficult to determine why Hannah Pearson was termed a spinster in the deed of 1749, nine years after the recorded date of her marriage to Wyer, and also why the deed was not drawn up as a two-party agreement between Simon Wyer and wife Hannah of the one part and Thomas Day of the second part. Nor is the problem in any way clarified by the fact that a Dorothy Wyer renounced her dower rights in favor of Marcus Kuhl at the time of the pewterer's death.

Nothing at all is known about Wyer's metal.

MUNGO CAMPBELL

On the fourteenth of May, 1752, the following notice appeared in the *Pennsylvania Gazette:*

> Mungo Campbell, from Dublin, makes and mends all sorts of pewter, at reasonable rates; or exchanges new for old: Likewise tinns all sorts of brass and copper work. N.B. The said Campbell

has almost 4 years of a servant lad's time to dispose of, who is fit for country business. Enquire at Thomas Overend's at the corner of Second-street in Chestnut-street.

It was apparently the same Mungo Campbell who three years earlier advertised in the *Maryland Gazette* that he had for sale 'at the House of John Campbell, Pewterer, in Annapolis' various choice groceries.

I have been unable to find any other record of the man in either Annapolis or Philadelphia, and although I imagine that Mungo was a blood-relation of John Campbell, I cannot establish the connection.

CORNELIUS BRADFORD

This maker's story will be found with those of the New York pewterers. He made pewter at his shop in Second Street, Philadelphia, from 1753 to about 1773, and in one of his two known touches (see Plate LXII) the word Philadelphia appears.

JOHANN CHRISTOPHER HEYNE

The frontispiece in the issue of *Antiques* for February, 1928, pictured a very unusual example of American pewter, a church flagon showing decidedly Continental influence, engraved with the date 1771, and impressed with touches at that time new to most collectors — the initials 'I. C. H.,' a crown, and the word 'Lancaster.' The flagon, then owned by the late Howard Reifsnyder, is now in the Mabel Brady Garvan Collection at Yale University.

Until then Lancaster had not been on our pewter map, and the search which followed threw no light on the identity of the flagon's maker. But as other examples of the man's work were found and studied, it became possible to piece together from the testimony of the pewter a fragmentary pattern of the craftsman's life, a pattern which has since been verified and amplified in detail as the result of the careful and exhaustive search of Lancaster records by J. J. Evans, Junior.

The maker of the flagon, Johann Christoph Heyne, was born December 3, 1715, in the village of Funtschen, Bohra, in Saxony. On March 15, 1742, he sailed from London in the snow *Catherine*, as a member of what Moravian writers term 'The First Sea Congregation' and arrived at Philadelphia on June 7 of that year. In 1746 he was married to 'Maria Margr. Schiefeun.'

We do not know now whether Heyne remained in Philadelphia several years or whether he settled almost immediately in Lancaster. Our earliest record of him in the latter town was found in the 'Adition'l Tax of ye Borough of Lancaster for ye King's use, Lodwick Lowman, Collector, 1757,' wherein 'Chris'r Heiny' was listed for fourteen shillings. At a 'Supream Court' held in Philadelphia, April 10, 1761, 'Jno Christ'r Hayne of Lancaster, a foreigner,' was naturalized as a subject of King George, having complied with the regulations stipulated by Parliament for Quakers and others with conscientious scruples against taking an oath, one of which required a seven-year residence in the colonies.

On January 7, 1764, Mrs. Heyne died, and six months later her widower and the widowed wife of Christian Frederick Steinman were married. In 1765 Heyne, as a member of the Sun Fire Company, signed a petition to Lieutenant-Governor John Penn asking him to refuse to repeal the law providing for a night watch in the borough of Lancaster.

'Christopher Heyne of Lancaster, tinman and pewterer,' became a property-owner on June 22, 1767, when he purchased for six hundred pounds a lot and 'Brick Messuage or Tenement' thereon on West King Street, Lancaster.

On October 27, 1775, John Hubley, commissioner of purchases in Lancaster County, 'paid Christopher Hayne, Caspar Fordney and Nicholas Miller for making canteens, etc. for riflemen, £9, 13s, 10d.'

On January 11, 1781, Heyne was stricken with apoplexy and died suddenly at the age of sixty-six. He was buried in the Moravian graveyard, Lancaster.

Heyne apparently never had children of his own. A stepson, John Frederick Steinman, probably worked in his stepfather's shop and carried on the business for a few years after the latter's death. Steinman was one of the administrators of Heyne's estate, and was termed a pewterer in a deed of 1783 conveying to himself the home and shop on King Street in which Heyne's wares had been made.

The inventory of Heyne's possessions, exhibited at the office of the register of wills, January 30, 1781, accounted for personal property valued at approximately £182 and included also bills against the state of Pennsylvania, running from 1777 to the time of his death, for $6500 in Pennsylvania currency.

Let us turn our attention now to the Reifsnyder flagon mentioned above. Commenting upon it, Homer E. Keyes wrote:

> It is not alone the pre-Revolutionary date upon its surface which gives this venerable specimen of pewter its outstanding importance. As a document in the history of style development in the American colonies the flagon is of quite inestimable value, for it exemplifies ... that mingling of Teutonic and English motives which, though one might well expect to find it in many eighteenth century products of Pennsylvania craftsmanship, usually eludes assured discovery.

And that flagon is now but one of a group of such 'documents' in which can be traced with certitude the gradual cumulative effect of environment upon the craftsmanship of an alien pewterer. Step by step the growing influence of the English designs about him can be followed in the product of this German-American's shop. At first his vessels were almost pure Teutonic in line and detail. Then, as he himself became naturalized and absorbed English ideas, changes crept into his designs until the work of his closing years was differentiated only by touch-mark from the pewter of contemporary makers of English birth or extraction. Almost unparalleled in the annals of American antiques is the unusual opportunity presented by Heyne's work to study in detail the gradual evolution from the Teutonic to the Anglo-Saxon styles.

For the first decade of this man's working years in America we have no metal positively identifiable as such. Such pieces, if they do exist, probably conform very closely to contemporary German designs, but following rapidly upon the heels of his own naturalization came the first changes in the Americanization of the designs of his shop.

In Plate XXXIII are the communion flagons of the Evangelical Lutheran Church of the Holy Trinity, Lancaster. The vessel in the center was presented to the congregation in 1733 and is described in the church records as follows:

> September 30: John Martin Weybrecht presented a pewter flagon, having a lid and a wreath on it. It rests on three feet of angel-heads, and holds about two quarts. There is a lamb, with a banner and a cross engraved upon it: also the letters I.C.S.

That flagon, as can be seen in the illustration, is German in all its details. Its touch, unlike any known American mark, has proved to be that of Heinrich Mueller of Rothenburg ob der Tauber, Bavaria, who began the making of pewter in 1719.

Now let us examine the other two flagons, twin pieces, which are impressed with 'I. C. H.'s' touches. The church has no record of their presentation, but the authorities have assumed that they date from about 1766 or possibly a few years earlier, a surmise in which I concur. In the year 1761 the congregation, which had outgrown its building, purchased additional property and commenced the construction of a magnificent new edifice. It seems highly probable that at about that time additional flagons would have been required, and it was only fitting that they should have been provided in time for the dedication of the new church. The building was consecrated May 4, 1766, and the procession was headed by the schoolmaster and children, followed by the deacons solemnly bearing the sacred vessels.

The deacons quite naturally commissioned the manufacture of the new flagons to their fellow-townsman, Heyne, and a comparison of these pieces with the original vessel, which unquestionably served as their model, will show that the influence of his surroundings was already at work upon the designs of his shop. To quote from Mr. Evans in an article, 'I. C. H., Lancaster Pewterer,' in *Antiques*, volume 20:

> In executing this commission, our craftsman departed slightly, yet significantly, from the design of the original, a procedure which may be attributed, in part, to changes in style that had occurred during the preceding third of a century; in part, to his limited equipment; and, in part, perhaps, to his own conscious or unconscious absorption of English ideas.

An examination of the Trinity Church flagons gives an insight into the problems with which Heyne was beset when he agreed to manufacture communion vessels. There can be little doubt that prior to that undertaking he had no flagon moulds. German churches in Pennsylvania were still few and far between, and the decision to embark upon a venture which would have entailed the purchase of expensive moulds for a type of vessel for which only an extremely limited market existed must have been made only after careful deliberation. The result of those deliberations, as exemplified in the Trinity Church flagons, is a tribute to the resourcefulness of the Lancaster pewterer.

Johann Christopher Heyne

For the drum of his new design new moulds were essential. The model was followed closely except for the addition of banding midway down the side, a detail frequently found on Alsatian flagons, one of which may have served as his inspiration. The cover also differs but little from the design of the original, but in the base of the newer vessels a very marked structural change can be observed. Instead of a normal flagon base the Lancaster man ingeniously made use of a butter plate which exactly fitted the opening at the bottom of his vessel.

But the most radical departure in the new composition was in the design of handle and hinge. Yielding to the trend of the times and to the influence of English styles, Heyne replaced the earlier strap handle with the hollow-cast type of England and the colonies and at the same time substituted a flatter type of hinge. Unquestionably these changes tied together flagon and handle more successfully than in the earlier design, giving a feeling of sturdiness that is lacking in Mueller's model. English though it be, such a handle would never have been found on a London flagon. Rather is it the handle of a tankard (for which moulds were probably already on hand), and its use on the taller vessels was a makeshift to keep down expenses. Not improbably the banding on the drums of Heyne's flagons was added primarily as a seeming structural device, to which the bottom of a too-short handle could be anchored, and only secondarily as a form of decoration.

One other feature requires comment — the ball thumb-piece and its method of attachment. Acting under the influence of his early training or perhaps instructed to cap his vessels in true German fashion, the Lancaster pewterer applied a ball thumb-piece as on the original vessel. That he had no mould for such an item is evident from the fact that the balls on the two later vessels differ not only from that on the original, but also from one another, which led to Homer E. Keyes's suggestion that they may have been appropriated for the purpose from existing tankards. Real difficulty was encountered in attaching these adornments to the high-projecting English handles, a problem which the earlier flat handle never presented. To permit the ball to clear the handle when the lid was fully raised, it became necessary to set it back farther and to build for it a little platform on stilts. That the awkwardness of this arrangement was apparent to its designer is evidenced by the fact that all other existing flagons of this maker omit the ball. The Reifsnyder vessel and its counterpart (Plate XXXI, 217), in the collection of John W. Poole, illustrate this second step in the Americanization of a German flagon design. Note also that the cover in this second type is of the double-domed pattern.

In Plate XXXVI are pictured two of the fine Lancaster chalices, at least seven of which are still in existence. They have no counterpart, as far as I know, in the pewter of England or America. The cup proper and the base might well have been copied from English models, but distinctly Teutonic is the stem with its unusually large knop, resembling a flattened ball thumb-piece of some German tankard. Nor is there record of chalices with cover to match made by any other American pewterer.

Another form made by this pewterer which exhibits both German and English influence, is the sugar bowl pictured on Plate XXIX, 197. Though not unlike designs in glass of that other famous German-American artisan, Baron Stiegel, the shape is even more reminiscent of certain sugar bowls made by contemporary colonial silversmiths in Philadelphia. Sugar bowl and chalice afford additional testimony to their designer's ability to make the most of a limited equipment, for their covers were cast in the same mould.

A porringer with a handle of typical English design (of which no photograph could be secured) represents the final phase in the work of our Lancaster pewterer. Though he worked amid people of Continental extraction, and though all known porringers made by his Pennsylvania competitors are fashioned after Continental patterns, this particular example is as English in design as the porringers of the Danforths of Connecticut. As eloquently as through the medium of the spoken word the German pewterer of Lancaster has testified, in the pewter which he fashioned, to his gradual conversion to and complete acceptance of the customs and ideas of his adopted country.

Among the missing forms listed in the shop inventory are spoons, quart and pint pots, chamber pots, and basins. In addition to items mentioned previously, Heyne's metal known to me includes five flagons, a dram bottle (perhaps one of the 'canteens for riflemen' for which he was paid in 1775), three 6-inch plates, and two $7\frac{7}{8}$-inch plates.

Heyne's known touches are shown in Plate LXV. Number 589, Plate LXX, shows another 'ICH' mark from a $9\frac{5}{16}$-inch plate in the collection of J. P. Remensnyder. This touch may have been used by Heyne, but there is just as much reason for its attribution to Johann Christian Höran of Philadelphia, and it is therefore classified as unidentified.

Many another American pewterer enjoyed a more lucrative business and many a competitor may have attained greater prominence in his own community, but none has enriched us with such a significant group of unusual pewter forms. Christopher Heyne's vessels are the acme of laboratory material for the student of colonial pewter.

JOHANN CHRISTIAN HÖRAN (HERA)

J. B. Kerfoot in his *American Pewter* introduced to us what he rightly termed a 'hide-and-seeky sort of family' of Philadelphia pewterers whose last name he found to be variously spelled Hero, Herroe, Heavo, or Hera in different Directories, while sandwiched in among Christians and Johns, who jumped in and out of the lists, were Christophers, Charlottes, and Christianas, all presumably pewterers. Mr. Kerfoot tantalized us with just enough information about this tribe to lead, as he no doubt intended, to a further research — an investigation that is hardly warranted by the few identified examples of Hera pewter, all of them 9-inch smooth-rimmed plates, made by Christian's sons, whose story will come later.

Let me put down, therefore, the few facts gleaned from Philadelphia records, which seem to have a bearing on the family history.

On September 24, 1751, one 'Johannes Höring' took the oath of allegiance in Philadel-

Johann Christian Höran (Hera)

phia, having just arrived from Rotterdam in the ship *Neptune*. Whether this be the first of our family of pewterers it is difficult to say, but the date seems about right and the name is close enough to warrant consideration.

In December, 1758, according to the records of Saint Michael's and Zion Church, 'Johann Christian Herrang' was a witness to a marriage. In the following year 'Christian and Charlotte Hera' acted as god-parents at a baptism, and again from the same church records we learn that 'Dorothea Hera' was baptized April 13, 1762, 'Christian and Charlotte Hera' being sponsors. Although we now know that a son, Christian, Junior, was born about 1763, the date of his baptism was apparently never entered on the church records. On February 12, 1767, 'Joh: Andreas Höran' was baptized, his birth having occurred on January 2 of that year. He is recorded as the son of 'Christian and Charlotta Louisa Höran.'

Of greater interest is the following newspaper notice which was printed in the *Staatsbote*, March 5, 1764:

> Christian Höran, pewterer, who began the pewterer's business in partnership with Mr. Philip Alberti for a few years, and has worked at it until the present time, herewith gives notice that he will take the next ship to London, and will travel by way of Hamburg or Frankfort to Leipzig (his native city); he expects (D.V.) to return by the latest fall ship: If he can serve his friends, fellow citizens and acquaintances on his journey, without self-interest, it will be a pleasure to him.

In the tax records for 1769 (the earliest complete returns for Philadelphia that I have been able to locate), 'Christian Hero, pewterer,' is listed in the division for Mulberry Ward. He apparently owned no taxable property, for no tax was assessed. He so appears again in the lists for 1774 and 1779, paying a small tax in the latter year. In 1782 the name is spelled Heron and a tax is imposed on property valued at one hundred pounds in the Northern District of Philadelphia.

In 1777 'Christian Herro' was enrolled as a private in Captain Jacob Bright's Company of Colonel Nicola's City Guards.

There remains one document with a real bearing on the case — the will of 'Johann Christian Höran, Pewterer,' dated September 20, 1784, proved February 10, 1786. By the terms of that paper the estate is left to his wife 'Charlotte Louisa,' daughter 'Dorothy Elizabeth,' and sons 'Johann Christian' and 'Johann Andrew.' The witnesses to the will signed themselves 'Elizabeth Heron,' 'Christian Heron junior,' and 'John Heron.'

It may seem far-fetched to the reader that Johannes Höring, who landed in 1751, should be accepted as the Christian Höran of the will just mentioned, but spelling was free and easy in the eighteenth century. Even at the time of his death this man signed his name in German script and probably spoke little if any English. It should cause little wonder that recorders failed to follow any uniform method of spelling his name. Unquestionably the children anglicized the name first to Heron, as it appears in their signatures to the will, and finally to Hera, as we shall find it on their touch-mark and in all the later Directories.

As Höran seems never to have had many of this world's goods it is natural to assume that his trade was not large. This may account for the fact that, to the best of my knowledge, none of his pewter, definitely recognizable as such, has yet turned up. On the other hand, Plate LXX, 589, shows an 'I. C. H.' touch-mark which is listed as unidentified because it could be attributed with equally good reasons to either Höran or Johann Christopher Heyne of Lancaster (see pages 44–48). It was photographed from a 9$\frac{5}{16}$-inch plate in the collection of J. P. Remensnyder.

JOHANN PHILIP ALBERTI

Philip Alberti is another man who was unknown to Mr. Kerfoot when he wrote *American Pewter*. He took the oath of allegiance to his new country in Philadelphia on December 13, 1754, having just arrived from Hamburg in the ship *Neptune*. Soon thereafter he opened a pewterer's shop, taking into partnership Christian Höran. It was apparently in 1764 that this firm was dissolved, for on June 11 of that year the following notice appeared in the *Pennsylvania Staatsbote*:

> John Philip Alberti, pewterer, has moved from Front St. to 3d St. between Arch and Market Sts., in the 2d house from the inn, the City of Rotterdam. He asks his former customers, and those who will honour him with their favour, to encourage him; he will furnish each one with good work. He also tests all kinds of metals, and for the cheapest price gives the most accurate analysis.

Soon after his arrival in America, Alberti married, for we learn that in 1761 and 1765 Carl Friedrich and George Friedrich were born to Philip and Anna Barbara Alberti. Alberti's name appears as that of a pewterer on the tax lists of Mulberry Ward from 1768 to 1779. If the amounts of the taxes which he paid are any indication of the magnitude of his business, Alberti never had a large trade, one equal, perhaps, to that of Christian Höran, but far less than that of his younger competitor, William Will. Further evidence that Alberti did not prosper is found in the records of Philadelphia mortgages, for on April 8, 1768, he found it necessary to mortgage the property on Arch Street to which he must have moved subsequent to the date of his newspaper notice, quoted above.

Philip Alberti died in 1780, and in his will, dated July 14 of that year and proved August 9, he styled himself a pewterer. None of his pewter has as yet been identified. The appraisal of his shop inventory was made by two pewterers, Christian Höran and Adam Koehler, and included various tools, 274 pounds of pewter, and but 42$\frac{3}{4}$ pounds of brass moulds. The supposition is, therefore, that Alberti was not a large factor in the pewter trade of Philadelphia. We know of no pewter that can be attributed to him.

William Will

PHILIP WILL

Although proof is still lacking that Philip Will, pewterer of Philadelphia, was a member of the family of Wills who worked at the same trade in New York, I am convinced that he was the Philip Daniel, son of John Will, who was born in Nieuwied, Germany November 2, 1738, and, with his family, joined the Reformed Dutch Church in New York in 1752. Nothing has been learned about his early life, but on September 19, 1763, the following notice appeared in the *Pennsylvania Staatsbote*, German newspaper of Philadelphia:

> Philip Will, pewterer, at the Dish and Worm, in 3d St. opposite the Inn, the City of Rotterdam, makes all kinds of new and repairs old hollow and flat pewterware; likewise the various parts of distilleries and brandy distilleries, such as worms &c. Any who choose to favour him with his custom may be assured that he will give the best work at the cheapest price. He gives the highest price for old pewter or tin.

On August 3, 1764, Will covenanted with Thomas and Ann Willing to pay an annual rent of seven and one-half Spanish pistoles of fine coined gold for property on the west side of Third Street — no doubt the site mentioned in his newspaper notice — with an agreement that he would erect thereon within three years a two-story brick house and with the privilege of buying the property within ten years at a price of one hundred and fifty Spanish pistoles.

Philip Will and his wife Charlotta were members of the First Reformed Church of Philadelphia. The pewterer died in 1787, and on July 5 of that year letters of administration were granted to his brother, William Will.

Thus far no pewter made by Philip Will has been identified.

WILLIAM WILL

William Will is one of the outstanding figures in the history of American pewter. No other has left a more impressive evidence of ability, and few approached the craftsmanship which his pewter displays. Gifted beyond most of his fellows, he unselfishly subordinated his business to a life of service to his community and demonstrated that he was not only a superior craftsman, but also a splendid soldier, a capable statesman, and an executive of unusual ability.

He was born in the town of Nieuwied on the Rhine January 27, 1742, fourth son of John Will, pewterer, who migrated with his family to New York in 1752. William's apprenticeship was probably served in the shop of his brother Henry in New York, and it is perhaps worthy of comment that on several surviving examples of his pewter he used the double line of tooling as a decorative feature exactly as we find it on most of the New York pewter. He must have moved to Philadelphia with his brother Philip, for within a few months of the announcement in the *Staatsbote* of the latter's business venture, William Will's marriage to Barbara Culp was solemnized in the First Reformed Lutheran Church of Philadelphia. We have record of his second marriage, this time to Anna Clampher in 1769. There is no evidence that he owned property or had a shop of his own prior to that date, nor does his name appear in the city tax lists for 1769, but by 1772 he was well established, for in the issue of the *Staatsbote* for April 28 of that year he announced the removal of his shop to the west side of Second Street next door to Vine.

At a surprisingly early age this young German had gained the respect and confidence of his neighbors, and when the differences with the Crown reached a climax in 1776 he organized a company of infantry known as 'Captain Will's Company of Associators.' In 1777 he was Lieutenant-Colonel of the First Battalion, and later of Colonel Jacob's Third Battalion, which he himself afterward commanded, and in 1780 he commanded the Third Regiment of Foot. In 1777 he was appointed, with Charles Wilson Peale and four others, 'Commissioner for the Seizure of the Personal Effects of Traitors' for the city of Philadelphia, and in the following year this same committee was put in charge of forfeited estates as well as personal property — the Alien Property Custodians of an earlier day. In the same year the Pennsylvania Council delegated William Will as storekeeper at Lancaster for the Continental Army, and in 1779 'Commissioner for Collecting Salt.' For his able handling of the latter office he was thanked by President Reed in a letter still preserved among the Pennsylvania Archives. In spite of these many positions of trust which had fallen to the young colonel, Will found time in 1780 to run for high sheriff of Philadelphia, to which office he was duly elected. In 1781 and again in 1782 he was re-elected.

By this time he had accepted more duties than he could possibly handle, and in November, 1781, the State Council took cognizance of the situation in the following record:

> The Council taking into consideration the circumstances of William Will, Esq., one of the Agents for Forfeited Estates, he being sheriff of the city and county of Philadelphia, and his time consequently taken up by the duties of the said office,
>
> Ordered that William Will be discharged from said office and the thanks of this Board given him for the faithful discharge of the duty therein.

In addition Will was chief councillor in a political organization known as 'The Society of the Sons of Saint Tammany.'

That William Will, like many another prominent man of his day, had not completely mastered the art of letter-writing is attested by the following note to President Reed written in 1780:

> Sir:
>
> From some Conversation i have just heard there is a Certain Bertlis Shinn, who is a suspitious Carracter, and has a vessel now Lying at Warden's Wharf, Cleared for Boston, But her Cargo would suit New York. Information may be had from Coll. Rice at Kensington and John Thompson, Cooper, near Peter Knight. I am Sr. your
>
> Very Humble Servt.
Wm. Will

William Will

In 1785 the people of Philadelphia elected as councillor their world-citizen, Benjamin Franklin, and at the same election sent as representatives to the General Assembly Robert Morris, 'the financier of the Revolution,' and William Will, the pewterer.

Once again, in 1788, Will ran for sheriff, but was defeated by a narrow margin. So close was the result that the Colonel demanded a recount, insisting that his opponent, James Ash, had been elected by the votes of non-taxpayers including even those of sailors from ships in the bay — an early warning of what that city's politics would become. Will's witnesses were heard, the voting lists rechecked, and the ballots recounted; but Ash was declared elected.

After this defeat Colonel Will retired to private life. For a brief period he appears to have been a tavernkeeper as well as a pewterer, but his closing days were devoted to the making of pewter in his shop on North Second Street.

During the early years of the Revolution, Will was absent from Philadelphia with his regiment, and upon his return he found that his shop had been ransacked. The notice which follows was taken from *Dunlap's Packet* of December 31, 1778:

Pewterer

Taken from the shop of the subscriber at the corner of Arch and Second Streets, while the enemy was in possession of the city. Three Pewterer's Wheels with all the furniture thereto belonging, one pair of bellows, a number of hammers, steel and iron tools, an iron ingot and many other things for carrying on the pewterer's business. Those who are base enough to withold any of said property from the right owner after this publication, may depend on having little favor shown them by William Will in Second Street.

Despite Will's many public activities during the years immediately following, he apparently managed in some way to keep his shop in operation, for we have records from an old account book, dated April and May, 1780, evidencing sales of pewter by Will's agent, receipts for payment being in the Colonel's handwriting.

William Will's death occurred in 1798. The following extract is from the notice that appeared in the *American Daily Advertiser* for February 14, 1798:

On Saturday morning departed this life after a lingering indisposition which he bore with Christian fortitude, Col. William Will, in the 56th year of his age.... On Monday his remains were interred in the burial ground of the German Reformed Congregation attended by the members of the German Incorporated Society and a very large number of respectable citizens.

The estate amounted to but one thousand pounds, mute testimony to the honesty of this man through whose hands had passed thousands of dollars of the taxpayers' property.

Other American pewterers turned out metal of just as fine quality, but very few were capable of such a high order of workmanship and, to the best of my knowledge, none attempted such ambitious designs. Will was an artisan, not a mere pewterer who followed accepted standards. Like the work of most American pewterers, his forms followed in the main the English tradition, but unlike his contemporaries he lost no time in securing up-to-date moulds as fast as new models were imported from England.

Nor did he hesitate to borrow ideas from the pewterers of the Continent or the silver-smiths of England and America. As a result his work illustrates a distinction and an originality not found thus far in the pewter of any other American maker.

Let us examine the photographs of a few of his finest examples. The coffee-pot illustrated in Plate XXVII represents a pewterer's adaptation of a contemporaneous design in silver. Although its lines are not as satisfactory as those of many silver coffee-pots of the same period, it nevertheless is one of the most imposing and magnificent examples of the art of the American pewterer. Plate XXXI, 218, shows a flagon (now unfortunately marred by the loss of its finial) owned by Mrs. James H. Krom. Found with the flagon were a pair of fine unmarked chalices (Plate XXVI, 240) which may have come from Will's shop. Here again we see pieces that are unlike any other American examples. The body and handle of the flagon are English in form, but no British pewterer ever embodied in his work a spout of such unmistakably German origin. And yet Will merged that detail so successfully into his composition that the result is a handsome as well as an unusual piece. The graceful cups of the chalices are supported upon baluster stems far slenderer than are ever found on English chalices.

(Plate XXVI, 240)
should read
(Plate XXXVI, 240)

On Plate XXVIII, 189 and 190, are shown two of the finest surviving American tea-pots. Of slightly later design, a piece which must have had its inspiration in some model in silver, is the cylindrical pot, Plate XXIX, 195, four examples of which are now known.

The mug pictured in Plate XX, 127, though also late in form, represents probably the most ambitious of all American mug designs. The acanthus leaf embellishment on the handle, though found occasionally on the handles of English pewter hollow-ware, was essentially a silversmith motif.

Other surviving forms bearing this maker's touches include a unique $5\frac{5}{8}$-inch smooth-rim butter plate (Plate X, 51), two $6\frac{1}{8}$-inch butter plates with single-reed rim (one of which is marked abnormally in the well), 8-inch and $8\frac{3}{8}$-inch plates of normal rim, a $9\frac{3}{8}$-inch smooth-rim plate, a 12-inch dish, $12\frac{1}{4}$-inch deep dish, $16\frac{3}{8}$-inch flat dish, tea-spoons, a ladle (Plate XXVI), a bed-warmer illustrated in *American Pewter*, pint basins, pint and quart mugs, and pint and quart tankards. Quart mugs and tankards come in the tulip-shaped as well as cylindrical body. For an American pewterer this represented a great variety of moulds, especially when we consider the variety of thumb-pieces, handles, etc., that varied with the types on which they were used. In spite of the number of pieces enumerated above, William Will's pewter is exceedingly rare. Perhaps three dozen examples would cover his known surviving output and, rather strangely, it seems, we have found but half a dozen plates in the normal 8-inch to 9-inch range. Forms listed in the inventory but still unreported are: sugar bowls, cream jugs, salts, chamber pots, bottle-cranes, measures from a gill to a half-gallon (five sizes), pocket bottles, funnels, inkstands, soup spoons, syringe pipes, quart basins, goblets, pewter cranes, crane cocks, candle-moulds, britannia metal candlesticks, and, most surprising of all, 'Ice Cream Moulds.'

Will's touches are almost as varied as his designs in pewter. The last of the Will touches to come to light, though probably the earliest in point of usage, is the lamb-and-dove mark (Plate LXV, 535), similar to that used by John Townsend of London, reproduced here from the 16⅜-inch dish owned by the late M. Brix. The accompanying hall-marks are apparently those of an earlier pewterer whose dies Will had acquired; but who 'T. C.' (or 'I. C.') was still remains a matter of conjecture.

In Plate LXVI, 540, is shown a mark from a plate in the collection of Mrs. Stephen S. FitzGerald. The same touch was illustrated in J. B. Kerfoot's *American Pewter*, but all lettering had been obliterated from the impression there shown. It is apparent from this photograph that the word above the eagle is FEDERAL and a perfect touch may disclose the word CONVENTION below. If such a find should be made we shall be able to date Will's eagle very definitely as 1787 or soon thereafter, unquestionably one of the earliest of the eagle marks. Another rare touch of Colonel Will is the tiny hall-mark from the Krom flagon (Plate LXVI, 538). The remaining touches of this maker, illustrated earlier by Mr. Kerfoot, may be seen on Plate LXVI.

William Will typifies all that is best in the history of American pewter. The surviving examples of his work are of a standard of quality as high as our pewterers ever attained, and he as a man exemplified in his life the spirit we admire, the spirit which carried an immigrant boy to the chief legislative council of his adopted state.

THE HASSELBERG GROUP

In the burial record of Old Swedes' Church, Philadelphia, the following entry appears under date of July 23, 1790:

> Elizabeth Kehler, widow of Hasselberg, a Swede who was her first husband; a pewterer by trade.

But for this record we might never have known that Abraham Hasselberg was a Philadelphia pewterer. On May 5, 1762, he was married in that city to Elizabeth Mets, and in Old Swedes' Church are recorded the burials of two of their children (in 1774 and 1777). Except for the administration of his estate in 1779 no other record of Hasselberg's activities has been found.

On January 27, 1780, the widow Hasselberg married Adam Kehler (or Koehler) in the Moravian Church in Philadelphia. Later in that year Kehler was one of the appraisers of the estate of Philip Alberti, pewterer. On February 20, 1782, 'Adam Kehler, pewterer,' leased a building in Pewter Platter Alley from 'John Redman, Practitioner of Physick,' but in 1783 the property passed into the hands of another pewterer, John Andrew Brunstrom. Whether or not Kehler continued the making of pewter after that date is problematical. Subsequent records bearing the name either omit the occupation or list Kehler as a baker. My own opinion is that he gave up pewter-making in 1783.

The last of this group was another native of Sweden, John Andrew Brunstrom. On

January 16, 1783, in Old Swedes' Church he married Elizabeth, daughter of Abraham Hasselberg, deceased, and stepdaughter of Adam Kehler. Four months later he purchased from Doctor Redman the property in Pewter Platter Alley which Kehler had been occupying. In the deed he was described as a pewterer; also in a deed of 1786 when he bought property on the north side of High Street. The records show that in the same year he was a private in the Philadelphia militia. In the census of 1790 'John Bromstone, Pewterer,' was living in Elfreth's Alley. The city Directory of 1791 shows his residence at the same address, his shop at 133 North Second Street. The yellow fever plague of 1793, which carried off one-tenth of the city's population within a few months, cut short the life of this obscure maker on September 13 of that year. His age at time of death was given as 'about 40.'

Second paragraph beginning "Recently a pair. . . ." Disregard completely this paragraph. The IAB initial mark, 548, is a modern fake. Beware this spurious touch.

Recently a pair of crude porringers with solid handle of a type made by the country pewterers of Pennsylvania has been found impressed with an equally crude touch — an irregular rectangle enclosing the initials 'IAB' (Plate LXVII, 548), a mark which is here attributed to Brunstrom. If that attribution be correct and if the porringers (one of which is illustrated in Plate XIII) are representative of the man's workmanship, he was probably a factor of little importance in the pewter trade of his adopted city. The same mark has also been found in a basin and in a mug, similar in design to the Palethorp mug in Plate XX, 129.

WILLIAM BALL

William Ball's name has long been on the list of Philadelphia artisans, but as a goldsmith rather than a pewterer. Recent research proves that he was both, and a wealthy merchant into the bargain.

He was born in Philadelphia on October 6, 1729, the eldest child of William and Mary (White) Ball. His father, probably a native of Devonshire, England, settled at 'Hope Farm' (now Balltown) prior to William, Junior's, birth. His mother was a daughter of Daniel White of Newport, Rhode Island, and a sister of Mrs. Thomas Byles. The details of Ball's early life are unknown, but by 1754 he was carrying on the goldsmith's trade in Philadelphia. His shop was at that time on Front Street between Market and Chestnut. By 1766, when he notified the public that he had moved next door to the London Coffee House, he had made at least one trip to London and had branched out as a general merchant selling hay, clover, drygoods, etc., as well as the products of his goldsmithy.

In 1771 he married his cousin, Elizabeth Byles, daughter of Thomas Byles, pewterer (recently deceased), and moved into the more commodious quarters offered by Byles's old shop on Market Street. Because of the discovery of a notice in the *Pennsylvania Packet* for May 29, 1775, portions of which follow, we have listed William Ball as a pewterer:

Just opened and to be sold by William Ball at his New Ware house of Gold, Silver, Pewter, Copper and Brass Wares, the north side of Market-street, three doors below Hall and Seller's Printing-Office, being the place late of Mr. Thomas Boyle, Pewterer and Brasier, deceased. All the Stock in Trade of the late Thomas Boyles, consisting of pewter and hard metal dishes, plates, basons, porringers, tankards, mugs &c. of all sizes; sacrament cups, cullenders, barbers pots and basons, sealed measures from a gallon to jill, bottle cranes, pint pocket bottles, half pint ditto, sucking bottles for children. Table and tea spoons, ink stands, tea and coffee pots, mustard and pepper casters, salts, sugar and chocolate bowls, wash basons, bed pans, close stool pans, chamber pots, urinals &c.

N.B. He wants to employ a journeyman silversmith that is a neat hammerman; also a Pewterer if a good workman.

Again in 1777 Ball advertised a general assortment of pewter, concluding his notice with the following statement:

Said Ball will give employ to a pewterer to work up a quantity of pewter.

His final newspaper notice, signifying, no doubt, his retirement, was published in the *Packet* on May 2, 1782:

Silversmiths, Brasiors & Pewterers Tools. To be sold at Public Vendue at the house of William Ball, the north side of Market-street, between Front and Second-streets, Thursday the 9th Day of May inst. The Sale to begin at 9 o'clock in the Forenoon — a general assortment of Silver smiths Brasiors and Pewterers Tools — Among which are the following Articles, viz. — Two turning lathes, A variety of Turning Tools and Burnishers, a very large assortment of brass Moulds for Pewter dishes, plates, basons, tankards, mugs, porringers &c.

In the celebration of the ratification of the Federal Constitution, at Philadelphia in 1788, William Ball took a prominent part as the senior member of thirty-five gold-smiths.

Ball must have been a rich man, for as early as 1774 he had five servants and in 1779 paid a tax of £375 — a very considerable figure for that day.

He died May 30, 1810, in his eighty-first year, and after a magnificent funeral was interred in the burial ground of the Baptist Congregation. The cortége was headed by the Society of Free Masons, of which Ball had been a member for upwards of fifty-nine years. In fact, he was appointed on July 15, 1761, by the Earl of Kellie, Grand Master of England, to be the first Provincial Grand Master of the Ancient Order of Free Masons of Pennsylvania.

We have not yet found any pewter bearing this man's name, and, although he probably had touches of his own, I doubt whether he ever soiled his own hands with pewter-making. For Ball was not trained in the business of pewtering; he married into it.

JOHN THORNTON

On the passenger list of the ship *Catharine*, which docked in Philadelphia in November, 1774, was John Thornton, pewterer of London, aged thirty. Unfortunately no evidence of his existence has been found in any Pennsylvania record.

THE YOUNGER HERAS

Christian Hera, the second of that name, was born in Philadelphia in 1762 or 1763. Record of the date of his birth has not been found, but his age at time of death was given as fifty-four. No doubt he and his brother John (born January 2, 1767) were apprentices in their father's shop, and the older boy would have just about completed his training when the parent died.

On August 13, 1788, Christian married Catharina Powell in Saint Michael's and Zion Church, Philadelphia. In the census of 1790 we find him recorded as living in the Northern District of Philadelphia and accredited with a household of one male under sixteen years of age and two females — presumably a wife and small daughter. In the same return Charlotte Hera, his mother, is listed with family of one female, undoubtedly her daughter Elizabeth. Where John was at this time we are at a loss to know.

On September 1, 1792, Charlotte Hera, widow, bought from Isaac Warner of the Northern Liberties property on Second Street for which she paid five hundred pounds. To the new home Christian and his family moved also. In 1793 and 1794 Christian Hera was on duty as a private in the Seventh Company of Philadelphia Militia Artillery. The mother, Charlotte, must have died in 1798, the last year her name appears in a directory. We may never know where John Hera was or how he was employed from the time of his father's death in 1786 until his name first appears in 1800 in the Philadelphia tax list and Directory. There is, however, in the Pennsylvania Archives record of a warrant for four hundred acres in Luzerne County dated March 15, 1794, in the name of John Hero. Thus it may be that John tried his luck at farming and found it no more profitable than many farmers are finding it today. It may be, too, that at least part of the time was spent in his brother's shop and no recognition was given to him in the Directories because he was not the head of a family.

In spite of the fact that from 1802 until 1804 only the younger brother's name is listed in the Directories, the partnership seems to have extended from about 1800 until John's death in 1812. This was the period of the 'C. & I. Hera' touch-mark, illustrated in Plate LXVI, 543. John's estate, of which Christian was administrator, amounted to only a little over three hundred dollars, and Christian himself, who passed on July 3, 1817, leaving no will, had only about thirty-five hundred dollars to bequeath to his family. On August 6 of that year at the house of the late Christian Hera his household goods and furniture, together with 'a large number of Pewterer's Brass and Block Tin Moulds, and a variety of Tools and implements, necessary to conduct the Business,' were sold at auction by order of the administrators of the estate.

We now come to the third generation of pewterers in the Hera family. They must have been the children of the second Christian, for when the latter found it necessary in 1813 to mortgage his one-half interest in the home on Second Street inherited from his mother, mention was made of the share formerly owned by his late brother John, who died 'unmarried and without issue.' Little is known about these later Heras, for records of birth, baptism, and with one exception death have not been found, but from other records we learn that there were at least six. The marriages of Eliza, Charlotte, Charles, and Thomas took place between the years 1815 and 1819, and Joseph, in 1821, was the administrator of the estate of John (presumably his brother).

John is the member of this generation in whom we are most interested. He unquestionably was the eldest of the family. During the War of 1812 he served as a corporal in Captain John Martin's company of the 132d Regiment of Pennsylvania Militia. He later served at least one enlistment in the Navy, for in the *American Daily Advertiser* of March 23, 1821, the following obituary notice appears:

> Died on the 20th inst., in the 34th year of his age, John Hera, late second gunner of the U.S. Ship Adams.

John Hera, Second, left no will, but in the letters of administration granted to Joseph Hera, John is termed a pewterer, and Thomas Hera, pewterer, is one of the sureties. It would therefore seem that John worked for his father and uncle during his early years, but had the *wanderlust* and deserted the shop to see the world. Upon Christian's death John came home to run the shop. True sailor that he was, he left an estate inventoried at a value of less than fifty dollars. Thomas, barely out of his teens and with no capital, was evidently unable to carry on the business, and after John's death the name of Hera disappears from all Philadelphia records.

To correct previous lists of pewterers I believe we are now justified in spelling Christian the elder's name as he himself did in his will — Höran — and in determining upon the anglicized form, Hera, for the younger members of the family. Of the 'christian' names that have appeared on earlier lists, there seems to be justification for dropping Christopher, Christiana, and Charlotte. I am convinced that the first two were typographical errors or corruptions of the name Christian. Charlotte, of course, did exist, but that she herself ever made pewter seems highly improbable. On tax lists and deeds her title is 'widow.' Nor is the young Thomas Hera entitled to listing. That he ever had a shop or touch of his own is unlikely.

A correct record of the pewterers of the Hera family should, I believe, read something like this:

Christian Höran, Senior	(*c.* 1728–1786) working		1754–1785
Christian Hera, Junior	(*c.* 1763–1817)	"	1785–1817
John Hera	(*c.* 1767–1812)	"	1800–1812
John Hera, Second	(*c.* 1787–1821)	"	1817–1821

The elder Christian should have had a touch-mark or marks of his own. Christian, Junior, may have continued to use the same touch or to have adopted a new one. That used by the brothers when working together is well known. After John's death we should expect to find another change in touch, but not after Christian, Junior's, for we know that the younger John's capital would never have warranted any such unnecessary expenditure as a new die if the old could be made to serve.

This leaves us, then, four pewterers whose activities in Philadelphia covered an unbroken range of approximately sixty-five years. That we should now have but five or six examples (all of them 9¼-inch smooth-rim plates) as evidence of those sixty-five years of work is indeed surprising. It confirms what the meagerness of their estates indicated: that no Hera ever enjoyed a big trade, that no member of the family ever attained eminence in business.

GEORGE WASHINGTON WILL

Despite the one-time prominence of Colonel William Will, it is extremely difficult now to glean information about his family. According to church records he had one daughter, Elisabetha, by his first marriage, and four children, baptized respectively 'Wilhelm, Maria, Heinrich, and Waschington,' were born of his union with Anna Maria Clampher. In further proof of the relationship of the Philadelphia Wills to the pewter-making family of the same name in New York, it is perhaps significant that, at a period when no Henry Will appears on Philadelphia tax lists or public records, the Colonel should have given that name to a son and that one of the god-parents should have been a Heinrich Will.

George Washington Will, the Colonel's youngest child and the only one of his sons who grew to manhood, was born in Philadelphia, May 22, 1779, and named for his father's commander-in-chief. He was probably an apprentice in the Colonel's shop when the latter died in 1798. George Will, undeterred by his tender years — for he was not yet twenty — opened a shop of his own immediately at 95 North Second Street. From the beginning he must have found his business venture unprofitable, for in 1803 he placed a mortgage on this property, which he and his sisters had inherited jointly.

In 1795 Anna Maria Clampher, widow, had deeded to her daughter and son-in-law, Anna and William Will, for occupancy and use during their lives and thereafter outright to their children, a house and lot at 22 Elfreth's Alley. At that address George Will was listed as a pewterer in 1801, and in 1804 he obtained clear title to the property. However, soon thereafter he sold this house and lot and in the Directories subsequent to 1807 he is listed as a comb-maker.

Although I own a receipted bill of George Will's (dated 1799) for four inkstands and four sand boxes, we have yet to find a piece of pewter marked with a touch which can be definitely assigned to this maker. However, in Plate LXVII is a group of interesting touches as photographed from a 13¼-inch deep dish owned by the late Edward Bringhurst. Two of the touches are well-known marks of Blakslee Barns, whose story will be told later (see page 64), but the central design (number 552) has not been illustrated before. The natural supposition on first glance at the marks is that all three touches were applied at the same time in Barns's shop. But if that is the case what possible reason can be advanced for the use by Barns, who did not move to Philadelphia until 1809, of a touch showing the initials of the first President with the meaningless

Last paragraph — 8th line from bottom beginning "However in Plate LXVII . . . etc. . . . and succeeding sentences through the second paragraph on page 61. Kindly disregard those sentences. The touch, 552, there attributed to George W. Will is really a button mould impression. If young Will had a touch of his own it is still unknown.

inscription 'Long live the President'? For George Washington died in 1799. On the other hand, what more appropriate design could Will have employed than a touch which identified him with the great man for whom he had been named, and whose days were already numbered when Will was setting up in business.

It is my belief that this was George Will's touch; that the dish in question, for reasons unknown to us, passed through Barns's hands some ten years later, and was then stamped with his marks. It is perhaps worth noting that the Barns touches were not accurately centered as was the central mark. If the above surmise be correct, it is a vagary of fate that the one known example of Will's touch should be found in conjunction with the marks of another maker.

An invoice for inkstands and sand boxes, sold and presumably made by G. W. Will, is illustrated in Plate LX.

PARKS BOYD AND THE PALETHORPS

Very little new information has been unearthed about either Parks Boyd or Robert Palethorp, Junior. We can, however, furnish their dates and repeat what J. B. Kerfoot has written in *American Pewter*: that their metal is excellent and existing examples are by no means easy to find. What little we have learned of their lives is furnished principally by the obituary notices which appeared in the daily newspapers.

Boyd was born in 1771 or 1772, but which of the many Philadelphia Boyds was his father has not been determined. On June 6, 1793, he married Sarah Loudon in Saint Paul's Episcopal Church. In 1797 he first appeared in the Philadelphia Directories at 35 Elfreth's Alley, moving later to various locations on High, Mulberry, and Second Streets. He worked at his trade of pewtering and brass-founding until his death, which occurred June 6, 1819. His estate went to his unmarried daughters, Sarah Maria and Eliza, previous provision having been made for a married daughter.

The following notice of his death is taken from the *American Daily Advertiser* of June 7, 1819:

> Died, last evening, the 6th inst., Mr. Parkes Boyd, after a long and severe illness.
>
> His friends and acquaintances are invited to attend his funeral from his late dwelling No. 50 North Second Street this afternoon at four o'clock.
>
> His Masonic brethren are particularly invited to attend.

Boyd's known forms include $6\frac{1}{4}$-inch, $7\frac{15}{16}$-inch, $8\frac{5}{8}$-inch and $9\frac{1}{2}$-inch plates — the latter size having a smooth-rim — $13\frac{1}{4}$-inch and $13\frac{9}{16}$-inch flat dishes, and 9-inch and 11-inch deep dishes. He made pint and quart mugs in standard forms as well as a rare barrel-shaped mug shown in Plate XX. Two other unusual shapes made by this pewterer are the circular covered box illustrated in Plate XL and the tall covered pitcher in Plate XLII. Quart tankards of three designs (Plate XVII) complete the list of this man's work thus far established. These tankards, though well made, are interesting chiefly for their variation from type. The two bands of triple reeding around the drum of number 104 are found, so far as I know, on no English mugs or tankards and upon no examples of any other American maker. They may represent an outgrowth of the banding found on Alsatian flagons (cf. the 'ICH' flagon, Plate XXXI, 217), though Boyd's use of the motif is less satisfactory. The other unusual feature is the flattened boss on the cover.

In the record of the administration of Boyd's estate there is evidence that Robert Palethorp, Junior, bought out the contents of the shop, for the executor listed receipts for over two hundred dollars paid by Palethorp, together with a note for five hundred dollars additional.

Robert Palethorp's excellent pewter was the work of a mere boy, for he died at an age when college graduates of today are just commencing their careers. He was born in 1797, the son of Robert Palethorp and Sarah Harrison. As his father and Parks Boyd were neighbors, it seems probable that Palethorp learned to make pewter in Boyd's shop. In 1817, when just twenty years old, he opened a shop of his own in the same district (444 North Second Street), and on June 24, 1819, he married Abigail Kessler. In 1820 a daughter Mary was born and in the following year her sister Martha arrived. Then, just on the threshold of life, Robert Palethorp, Junior, died.

The following notice is from the *Philadelphia Union* of March 2, 1822:

> Died, on Wednesday the 27th of February Robert Palethorp, Jr., in the 26th year of his age, of a very severe illness of ten months which he bore with patient resignation. His friends are invited to attend his funeral, from his late residence, No. 50 N. Second St., this afternoon at two o'clock.

It is a strange coincidence that Parks Boyd and Robert Palethorp, Junior, were buried from the same house.

The list of Palethorp's shapes includes 7¾-inch, 8½-inch and 9-inch plates, 13½-inch flat dishes, 13-inch deep dishes, 10-inch and 11⅜-inch basins, 4-inch beakers, pint and quart mugs, and an infusion pot (Plate XXXIX). A mug of unusual shape made by this pewterer is illustrated in Plate XX, 129. Palethorp's touches are found at the foot of Plate LXVII.

Although we cannot place either Boyd or Palethorp on the same plane of ability with William Will, both men turned out metal of a quality as fine as any produced in this country. Boyd's workmanship was excellent, but his taste was not always of the best. Palethorp's hollow-ware is very heavy and most carefully finished. For that reason it is rather surprising that some of his flatware was not turned with the same precision. However, both men deserve to be rated high among nineteenth-century pewterers.

In 1820 Robert Palethorp, Junior, had taken his younger brother John Harrison Palethorp, into partnership with him. When the former died in 1822, Robert Palethorp, Senior, who had been an ink-powder manufacturer, took over the interests of his deceased son, and the firm continued as Robert and J. H. Palethorp, 'Ink Powder and Pewter Manufacturers,' until the elder Palethorp died in 1825. Probably pewter-making was the more profitable portion of the business, for Robert, Senior, termed himself a pewterer in his will. John continued the business many years longer, but most of his working days fall in the britannia period and his record will therefore be taken up later.

THE HARBESONS

There were four Harbesons: Benjamin and his three sons, Benjamin, Junior, Joseph, and Robert, all of them Philadelphia coppersmiths. Benjamin, Senior, was a prosperous craftsman at the time of the Revolution and earlier. The two older sons opened a shop of their own in 1793, while Robert remained with his father. Just which Harbeson or Harbesons made the pewter marked with the name (Plate LXVII, 549), has not been definitely established, but it seems likely, as J. B. Kerfoot suggested in his *American Pewter*, that it was made in the shop of Benjamin, Junior, and Joseph between the years 1793 and 1803.

Benjamin Harbeson, Junior, was born about 1763 and died in 1824. After 1819 he is listed in the Directories as 'agent for the inland transportation of merchandise.'

Joseph was born in 1770 and baptized in the Second Presbyterian Church. He died in 1822. After 1803 he is listed as an ironmonger. Known examples by the Harbesons are limited to flatware — 6⅝-inch and 10¼-inch basins, 5⅞-inch, 7⅞-inch and 8¾-inch plates, and 11-inch and 13⅛-inch deep dishes. I fully agree with Kerfoot that Harbeson pewter has little to commend it beyond its well-deserved rarity. The metal contains much lead, the workmanship is poor, and the marking is slipshod.

THOMAS DANFORTH, THIRD

For this maker's history, see volume I, page 111. He had a shop at the corner of Thirteenth and Filbert Streets, Philadelphia, from 1807 to 1813, and, judging from the surviving examples bearing his touches, had a large local trade.

THREE COUNTRY PEWTERERS OF PENNSYLVANIA

In several communities west of Philadelphia pewterers were at work in the last quarter of the eighteenth century. With the exception of Heyne of Lancaster, whose history has been related, all these men probably had other occupations, and made no attempt to produce pewter beyond the requirements of the local settlements in which each lived. Nor is it at all likely that any one of them owned more than a few moulds. In any event, we have not yet found more than one shape for each man here mentioned.

Elisha Kirk of 'Yorktown,' a watchmaker by trade, has left behind at least five or six 5½-inch porringer-basins impressed with his touch to bear witness to his versatility. Nothing is known of the man's early life. His name appears on the York tax lists for the first time in 1781, and in 1783 he owned a house, half an acre of land, five servants, and two negroes. A man of parts, Elisha Kirk served from 1783 until 1788 as a private and 'Minister of the Gospel' in Captain Ephraim Pennington's company (the 7th) of York County Militia. He died in 1790 when probably still in his early thirties.

One of Kirk's porringers is reproduced in Plate XIII. Compared with New England examples this piece in appearance is crude indeed, but it has been finished much more carefully than many of those with elaborate handles. Bowl and handle seem to have been cast in one instead of two pieces as was usually done, and there is no supporting bracket beneath the handle. Kirk's touch is illustrated on Plate LXVII, 547.

Not far from York, probably in Chester or Westtown, there lived at about the same period another maker of porringers whose design differs but slightly from that of Kirk. Several examples of this variant have come to light, all in the same neighborhood; the touch (Plate LXX, 598), shows the initials 'S. P.,' and the maker is said to have been Samuel Pennock of Westtown. I regret to say that I have not been able to confirm that supposition and I am consequently listing the mark among the touches of unidentified makers.

The last of these country makers of whom we have any knowledge is 'I. Shoff,' whose touch, shown in Plate LXVII, 550, was found on an 11-inch dish in the Mabel Brady Garvan Collection. Louis G. Myers found record in Lancaster County of the marriage of a John Shoff in 1793. In the Pennsylvania Archives and Pennsylvania Colonial Records I came across the following data about men of the same name:

A John Shoff owned 150 acres in Bedford County in 1774. In 1779, 1781, and 1784 a John Shoff, 'blacksmith,' was taxed for property in West District Township, Berks County. In 1781 a John Shoff was a private in the 6th Company, Captain Snyder commanding, Chester County Militia; and in 1782 a man of the same name was a private in Captain Jacob Metzger's company, Lancaster County Militia. It has been impossible for me to determine which John Shoff made the Garvan dish, but there can be little doubt that it was the work of a Pennsylvania 'Dutchman' during the period from 1775 to 1800.

BLAKSLEE BARNS

In Philadelphia, between the years 1812 and 1817, there worked on Thirteenth Street, a few doors from Thomas Danforth's shop, a man who was listed in the Directories simply as B. Barns, tinsmith and pewterer. Though he has left us a good many surviving plates and basins, their touches give no further clue to the maker's identity. Who this man was and whence he came to build up such a trade have been among the unsolved problems of American pewter.

Blakslee Barns

One day, with time to spare in Philadelphia, I went to the City Hall to try to unravel the Hero-Hera tangle. At the same time I made a note of all the deeds recorded between 1800 and 1830 in which any Barns with a first initial 'B' figured. One after another — Barnaby a merchant, Benjamin a farmer, and Blair a wigmaker — were discarded as their occupations appeared on the deeds. But the next document rewarded the search. This deed covered the purchase by Blakslee Barns, 'manufacturer,' of a piece of property on Thirteenth Street improved with brick dwelling and large frame building with kitchen in the rear. The date of the deed was December 28, 1809. As 'B. Barns' first appeared in the Philadelphia Directories in the issue of 1810 as a tinplate worker and japanner on Thirteenth Street, there seemed little doubt that Blakslee was the mysterious B. Barns.

Two more deeds threw a little additional light on the problem. On May 31, 1813, Blakslee Barns, 'tinplate worker,' was the high bidder at sheriff's sale for property 20 × 128 feet on Cherry Street. The price paid was thirty-one hundred dollars. Thirteen months later Blakslee and Almira his wife sold the same property for six thousand dollars. Here was a stroke of business worthy of B. Barns the pewterer, who in five years built up one of the largest pewter trades this country has known and yet had foresight enough to sell out before the day of pewter had quite passed.

With something definite from which to start, a fresh search of Philadelphia records followed, but without a single bit of new evidence resulting. The smoke screen had settled down as completely as before. So there for the time being the matter rested.

Some time later the quest for pewter information took me to Hartford, Connecticut. In the State Library are filed and catalogued, so as to be readily accessible, all vital statistics, wills, administration papers, etc., for the entire state. Just on a chance I looked for Blakslee Barns. The rest was simple.

Blakslee Barns was born in Wallingford, Connecticut, in 1781. His parents, Moses, and Phoebe (Blaksley) Barns, were poor and the boy was sent to Berlin, Connecticut, at an early age to learn the tinplate business. At that time Berlin was the center of Connecticut's tinware industry, and there, when his apprenticeship was ended, Barns opened a small shop. In 1807 he married Almira Porter. Barns must have known Thomas Danforth, Third, who had a large pewter business in the near-by hamlet of Stepney. From Philadelphia and the South peddlers were, no doubt, bringing back stories of the business opportunities in that section. England and France were at war. Imports were falling off and pewterers south of New York were few. We may be sure Barns watched with interest Danforth's Philadelphia venture, and doubtless its success influenced him in 1809 to close his shop in Berlin and leave for Philadelphia, where, as we have seen, he bought property in the same block with his old-time neighbor.

We know from the correspondence of the fourth Thomas Danforth that he and a 'Mr. Nott of Stepney' were working for Barns early in 1812. It seems highly probable that the latter, successful in his Philadelphia venture in tin-manufacturing, had just decided to add pewter-making as a side line. It was only natural for him to have sent to his home in Connecticut, a section already overcrowded with struggling pewterers, for trained

The Pewterers of Pennsylvania

men to make his pewter. Starting the pewter business, in 1812, perhaps in a small way, Barns made the fortunate real estate deal before mentioned which added three thousand dollars of new capital. And at just about the time of this windfall Thomas Danforth suddenly closed his shop and returned to Stepney. Does it seem unreasonable to believe that Barns bought Danforth out, taking over both his trade and his apprentices, journeymen, pewterers, and peddler contracts? This would go far toward accounting for the tremendous number, relatively speaking, of existing B. Barns plates. If the shop ever turned out anything but flatware, it is surprising that our collections have nothing to show for it when far less prolific makers are represented. That Barns ever cast or turned a pewter plate himself seems questionable. He was a tinman by trade, and he had in Nott a master-pewterer to take care of that end of the business.

In 1817 we find Barns back in Berlin, a member of the Harmony Lodge of Masons, paying the third largest tax in that town, and buying property in Berlin and Meriden. No doubt he planned to settle on the land and enjoy the rest of his days as a gentleman farmer — the Utopia of which many a business man dreams. This surmise gains strength from an examination of his inventory. It listed nothing required for the making of pewter and a very meager tinsmith's equipment; whereas it did include a nine-acre farm, a 'new barn,' livestock, and a 'patent plow.'

B. Barns did not long enjoy his rural life. His death occurred August 1, 1823, and his gravestone can be seen in the North Cemetery at Berlin. The will was probated at Middletown in 1825, when $34,701.66 was distributed to his heirs — his wife Almira and four children (all minors), Laura, Almira, Jane, and Blakslee.

At his death Barns held among other notes one of William Nott for $1,282.92 advanced for books, maps, shoes, etc. From this it would seem that Nott also gave up pewtering and that Barns helped set him up in a general store. One of the accounts of the administrator of the estate reads as follows:

> To 5 days in Phila. collecting and settling account of books, stationery, etc.............. $7.50

Before the estate was settled, over five hundred dollars of Nott's debt had to be written off as a total loss. The estate, large for those days, included stock in two Hartford banks and real estate in Indiana and Illinois, as well as Connecticut.

The inventory is indeed that of a man of wealth. It included, for instance, over sixty chairs, tables of all kinds, sofas, mirrors, sideboard, pianoforte, maps (including one of Philadelphia), and many books listed by name, together with innumerable items of lesser value including one that piques our interest — a 'washing machine.'

But we cannot leave the inventory quite yet. What better evidence could we ask of a fortune rapidly acquired in the manufacture of pewter than three brief items which together tell a story in themselves?

> Silver plate.................$210.00
> 1 Set Cut Glass.............. 90.00
> Old Pewter.................. 2.00

Barns's metal is good and his work carefully finished, but he seems to have made nothing but flatware. His plates measure $6\frac{1}{8}$, $7\frac{3}{4}$, 8, $8\frac{7}{8}$, and $9\frac{1}{4}$ inches, deep dishes

11-inch and 13-inch, and basins 6⅝-inch, 8-inch, 9-inch, 10-inch, and 13-inch. The latter, owned by P. G. Platt, is the largest of American basins if we except the remarkable 14-inch Boardman covered basin illustrated by J. B. Kerfoot in *American Pewter*. The various touches which Barns used are shown in Plate LXVII. The rarest is the circular touch, similar to the Harbeson mark, which appears as number 555.

PLUMLY AND BIDGOOD

Several years ago a pint mug with touch as shown in Plate LXVII, 562, was offered for sale at an auction in Bucks County, Pennsylvania, and since then I have seen a 7½-inch plate similarly marked. Both pieces were made some time prior to 1830.

The new mark furnished the names of two hitherto unlisted Philadelphia pewterers, 'Plumly & Bidgood.' Both Plumly and Bidgood were Bucks County names, but an investigation of the records of both families at the county seat, Doylestown, failed to furnish any clue as to which individuals might have worked in pewter. So the search returned to Philadelphia.

Apparently the earlier examination of the city Directories had not been sufficiently thorough, for in the issues from 1825 to 1833, inclusive, Charles Plumley, pewterer, was found recorded as living at 9 Kunckle Street, Northern Liberties.

The next discovery was the record of an assignment by Charles Plumly in 1822 of all his real and personal property to Michael Baker, coppersmith, principal creditor of the bankrupt pewter-maker. The inventory included '2 Plate molds, 1 quart ditto, one pint ditto [probably the mould in which my mug was cast], 3 spoon molds, 2 inkstand molds 1 lamp mold, 2 still worm molds, 1 shaving box mold, etc.' This list is of particular interest because of the inclusion at such an early date of a 'lamp mold.' J. B. Kerfoot, in *American Pewter*, noted:

> . . . the invention [of the whale-oil lamp] must have been little known and seldom applied until the second quarter of the nineteenth century . . . and it is strongly indicative of the late entry of the craft of pewterers into the lamp game in America to find that no single one of the twenty-eight pewterers by whom marked lamps have so far turned up, and whose dates we know, began to work before 1828.

The writer owns a pewter 'betty' lamp, found in the Pennsylvania Dutch district, which was probably made in this country during the eighteenth century or very early in the nineteenth (Plate LXXVI). Plumly's mould may have been for a lamp of that type. If, however, his lamp was of the whale-oil variety, and unless he was a pioneer in such manufacture, the earliest appearance of that form can be moved back into the second decade of the last century.

Charles Plumly may have been descended from the man of the same name who settled on Neshaminny Creek, Bucks County, in 1682; on the other hand, I think it quite probable that he was one of the New England family of Plumlys and joined the pewter in-

PLATE LXVII — *Late Pennsylvania Touches*

547. Touch of Elisha Kirk, York, about 1785, as impressed on a porringer in the collection of Mrs. J. Insley Blair.

548. Touch attributed to John Andrew Brunstrom, Philadelphia, 1783–1793. From the author's collection.

fig. 548.
Shun this touch.
It is a spurious mark.

549. Touch attributed to Benjamin (Junior) and Joseph Harbeson, Philadelphia, about 1800. From a plate in the collection of Philip G. Platt, Esq.

550. Touch on a plate formerly in the collection of the late Louis G. Myers, Esq. The maker is believed to be a John Shoff working west of Philadelphia, late in the eighteenth century.

551, 552, and 553. This remarkable combination of touches is from a dish in the collection of the late Edward Bringhurst, Esq. 551 and 553 are touches of Blakslee Barns, Philadelphia, 1812–1817. 552 is believed to be a mark of George Washington Will, Philadelphia, 1799–1807.

fig. 552.
This is a button mould
impression which was
erroneously attributed
to G. W. Will as a
touch.

554, 555, and 551a. An unusual combination of Barns touches. 554, the only Barns mark in which the name is spelled with an *e*, and 555, the small circular mark, are the rarest of the Barns touches. Both, as shown here from a plate in Mr. Charles K. Davis's collection, are in mint condition.

551b. A fine impression of Barns's large eagle. From the collection of Mr. and Mrs. Richard S. Quigley.

556. Another eagle touch used by Blakslee Barns. From a plate in the collection of John J. Evans, Jr., Esq.

557 and 553a. Two more unusually fine impressions of touches of B. Barns. From a plate owned by George C. Gebelein, Esq.

557a and 558. 558 is the last and least interesting of the Barns touches, one of the earliest of the intaglio marks which are found on metal of the britannia period. Collection of Philip G. Platt, Esq.

559. Large touch of Robert Palethorp, Jr., Philadelphia, 1817–1821. Collection of Albert H. Good, Esq.

559a and 560. Another impression of the same mark, with Palethorp's small touch. From a plate owned by Charles K. Davis, Esq.

561. A Palethorp touch, probably of later date, which may have been used also by R. & J. H. Palethorp, 1820–1825, after the death of Robert, Junior. From a plate in the collection of Albert H. Good, Esq.

562. Touch of Charles Plumly and —— Bidgood, Philadelphia, about 1825, as photographed in a pint mug belonging to the author.

PLATE LXVII

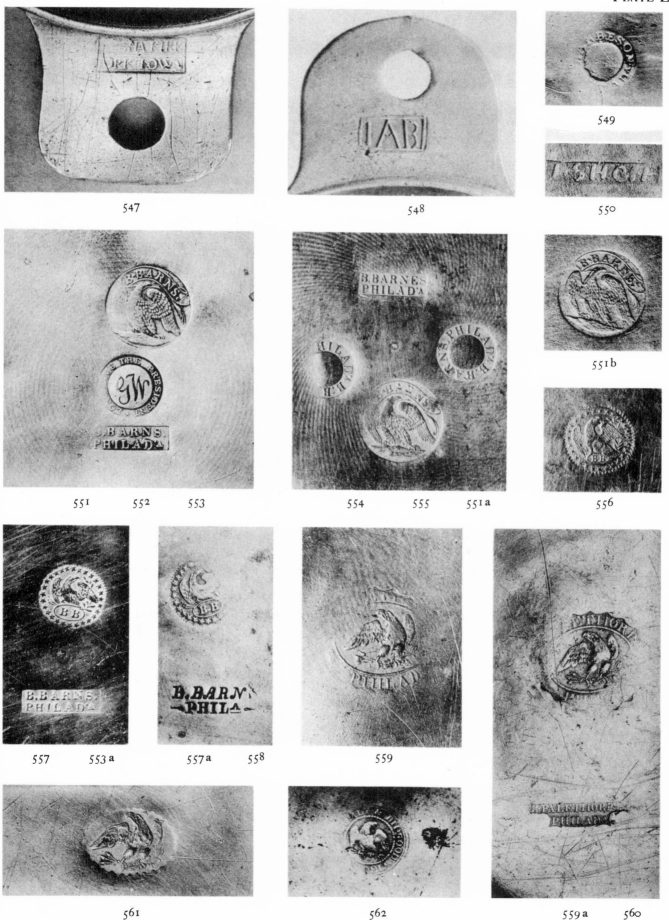

547

548

549

550

551 552 553

554 555 551a

551b

556

557 553a

557a 558

559

561

562

559a 560

PLATE LXVIII — *Southern Touches and the Initialed Porringer Marks*

563. Reconstruction of the mark of Joseph Copeland, Chuckatuck, Virginia, 1675–1691, as found on the handle of a spoon (169, Plate XXIV), unearthed at Jamestown, Virginia. Courtesy of Worth Bailey, Esq., and the National Park Service.

564. Touch struck in Pewterer's Hall, London, by Edward Willet, 1684 or 1685. This was undoubtedly the Edward Willett who was making pewter in Upper Marlboro, Maryland, 1692–1743, and the touch may have been used in this country. Reproduced from *Old Pewter, Its Makers and Its Marks*, through the courtesy of the late Howard H. Cotterell, Esq.

565. A touch of a maker whose history has not been traced. The name appears to be J. W. Olcott of Baltimore, early nineteenth century. Present location of the plate upon which this mark appears is not known. Illustrated through the courtesy of George S. McKearin, Esq.

566. Large eagle touch of George Lightner, Baltimore, 1806–1815. From a plate or dish owned by Philip G. Platt, Esq.

566a. Another impression of the same mark. Collection of Albert H. Good, Esq.

567. Lightner's smaller eagle touch. From a plate in the collection of Joseph France, Esq.

568. A touch of very similar design used by Samuel Kilbourn, Baltimore, 1814–1830. Collection of Dr. Walter Hughson.

569. Better known touch of Samuel Kilbourn. From a deep dish owned by the author.

570. A mint condition impression of the rare touch of Sylvester Griswold, Baltimore, about 1820. From a quart basin in the collection of Mrs. J. Insley Blair. Compare the design with 551 (Barns) and 569 (Kilbourn).

571. The only known example of the touch of John Philip Reich, Salem, North Carolina, 1820–1830. From a plate in the collection of the Wachovia Historical Society. Courtesy of the Reverend Douglas L. Rights and Miss Anna L. Rights.

572 to 577 are marks found cast in the handles of porringers of New England origin. With the exception of 574, which is from the collection of Edward E. Minor, Esq., all are reproduced with the permission of the late Mrs. Annie H. Kerfoot from her husband's volume, *American Pewter*. The users of these marks are unknown. Most of the porringers so marked are of late eighteenth- or early nineteenth-century manufacture.

PLATE LXVIII

563

564

565

566

566a

567

568

569

570

571

572

573

574

575

576

577

vasion of Philadelphia and the Southern states along with Thomas Danforth, Blakslee Barns, and others in the early years of the nineteenth century. In any event, it may be of interest that a Charles Plumly worked as a journeyman for William Calder in Providence in 1829, and that a man of the same name sold to William R. Smith of Middletown, Connecticut, in 1848, his tools and equipment for the manufacture of britannia.

Bidgood I have not been able to find. No man of that name who could be presumed to have been a pewterer has been located in Philadelphia in the period from 1810 to 1830. This maker may have belonged to the Bucks County family of Bidgoods, but further careful research will be required before his identity can be determined.

EIGHT OBSCURE PHILADELPHIA PEWTERERS

We have told at some length the stories of the early Philadelphia makers who qualify without question as pewterers. There still remains a handful of men of the early period whose only claim to listing is based on their classification as pewterers in the city Directories or tax lists. They were probably of little more prominence in their own time than they are today. Apparently they never owned real estate in Philadelphia; their probate records are not on file in City Hall; and they have left us no marked pewter. Most of them were probably journeymen or tinkers, and indeed one of the number, Wolfe, is termed a tinker in two Directories. Leslie was, without much doubt, the E. Leslie, journeyman, whom William Calder of Providence employed in 1828. But, for the sake of those who collect names as well as pewter, the addresses of these men, as recorded by the Directory compilers, are given herewith:

Bouzigues (first name not given)	454 North Second Street	1810
Leslie, Elkins	Little Boys Court	1821
McIlmoy, John		1793
Moore, Luke	501 South Second Street	1819 to 1822
Peal (or Peel) Henry	119 Swanson Street	1822
	294 South Second Street	1825 to 1833
Seip, Jacob	455 South Second Street	1820 to 1822
Seltzer, Abraham	32 Cresson Alley	1793
Wolfe, John	Coates Street	1801

THE PEWTERERS OF THE SOUTH

I T HAS been said that the dearth of Southern pewter may be chargeable to confiscation by agents of the Confederate Government of all available metal that could be used in the manufacture of munitions during the Civil War. There is probably a great deal of truth in that statement; on the other hand, it is at best but a partial explanation. Conditions were never favorable for a local pewter trade of any proportions in any one of the Southern colonies, and in all probability the amount of pewter manufactured south of Philadelphia was small indeed.

An essential prerequisite for a profitable venture in pewter-making was a readily accessible market. New England and the middle colonies, settled for the most part by men of little wealth — yeomen whose small farms dotted the countrysides and shopkeepers who congregated in densely packed towns — furnished just such a market. Along the seacoast from Portsmouth to Philadelphia a traveler in 1775 was rarely out of sight of habitations for long, and the roads, though poor, were at least passable. Boston, Newport, Middletown, New York, and Philadelphia were centers of population from which, with the aid of a peddler's cart, a pewterer could easily reach a large market.

How different were conditions in the Southern colonies! In a far longer coastline, deeply indented by wide bays, sounds, rivers, and creeks, there was but one large town, Charleston, and even the smaller towns and villages were few and far between. Overland communication was slow and difficult. Such roads as existed were little more than trails; and bridges in the Southern colonies in the middle of the eighteenth century were scarce indeed.

The type of the settlers and the nature of their commercial ties with England also militated against any demand for local pewter. Maryland and Virginia in particular were peopled largely by well-to-do or wealthy landowners and their slaves, and their indentured servants. The plantations were extensive and in some cases all but self-contained villages, housing not only the slaves for ordinary labor but indentured servants, fresh from the old country, whose services were purchased for from three to seven years. Many of these men had been craftsmen in England, and each of the larger estates had its own masons, carpenters, joiners, tailors, cordwainers, coopers, blacksmiths, etc. A few certainly must have employed resident pewterers to mend their English-made wares, and fashion for the use of their retainers the simpler forms such as spoons, plates, and dishes. In fact, we have evidence, in the registers of the ships *Fleetwood* and *Mermaid*, of the arrival in Maryland in 1775 of two pewterers under indenture as servants for periods of four years each.

[69]

The Pewterers of the South

Tobacco, the principal crop, was so universally cultivated in Maryland and Virginia that it served as the normal currency of those colonies. Since London was the great tobacco market of the world, the wealthy planters, located, as most of them were, on tidewater, found it convenient to ship their crops to London, receiving in exchange not only luxuries but many of the necessities of life, which were delivered by water almost at their very doors. Under such conditions a colonial pewterer must have found competition with London metal all but prohibitive. In only three centers does it seem possible that pewtering, on a small scale at least, might have been financially successful prior to the eve of the Revolution: in Charleston (South Carolina), at Annapolis (Maryland), and in the Norfolk-Williamsburg area of Virginia; but even in each of those localities one or two shops could probably have supplied amply all the pewter needs of the community.

It is therefore my belief, partially confirmed by a cursory examination of the records, that comparatively little pewter was made in the South, that shops were few, and that the range of forms manufactured was extremely limited.

We know that there were pewterers in the Southern colonies even in the early days of the settlements. Howard H. Cotterell found record of a John Lathbury, pewterer, who died in Virginia in 1655; Worth Bailey has recently recorded the finding of portions of spoons at Jamestown, Virginia, made by Joseph Copeland about 1675; and the story of Edward Willett, seventeenth-century Maryland pewterer and planter, will be told later. However, we can supply the names of but three other Southern makers who had shops of their own prior to 1770.

The first alarms of the Revolution were to increase vastly the opportunities for colonial pewterers. After the passage by the British Government of the hated tax on tea, one colony after another adopted resolutions against the importation of British manufactures, and among the contraband articles was pewter. Virginia took this step in 1769, and existing records prove that local pewter-making was given a new impetus. As evidence I submit John Norsworth's advertisement of the opening of a shop in Norfolk in 1771 (page 76); the will of John Sclater of York County, dated 1773, specifically devising '6 Virginia made pewter plates'; the newspaper notice of William Smith and Brother of Stafford County, advertising in 1774 'all sorts of moulds for casting pewter'; and the entry in the diary of Colonel Landon Carter of Williamsburg under date of July 19, 1776:

> Pd. This day a pewterer from Middx. recommended here by Mr. Giberne for new casting 22 plates at a bit a plate 13/9. I don't think his work well done; but it seems our parson paid the same and for no better work....

What was transpiring at this period in Virginia probably had its counterpart in Maryland, the Carolinas, and Georgia. In fact, we know that a Francis Hendricks opened a pewter shop in Charleston in 1771. What we do not know, however, and have reason to doubt, is that any one of these men profited from the disruption of commerce with Great Britain sufficiently to build up a successful pewter trade in the South. At any rate, but one example of their handicraft has been identified.

So, up to the nineteenth century, the history of Southern pewter-making is little better than a blank. But with the turn of the century came the period of the Napoleonic Wars and the second interruption of commerce with Europe. Pewter had to be secured. At first the demand was supplied largely by Yankee peddlers. As the shortage continued, Connecticut pewterers, hard pressed at home by an oversupply of men trained in the craft as well as by the competition of dealers in china, glass, and tin, moved South to better fields. For the first quarter of the nineteenth century we have record of a dozen or more shops in the South, most of which have left at least one marked example of their work; but with four exceptions these shops were operated by Connecticut pewterers, and only two who may have been Southerners by birth, George Lightner of Baltimore and Philip Reich of Salem, North Carolina, are represented by existing pewter.

We must therefore reserve for the present, and possibly for all time, any estimate of the abilities of the Southern pewterers as a group, contenting ourselves with brief recitals of the few established facts in the lives of the men who are known to have worked in this metal.

JOHN LATHBURY

On September 9, 1654, John Lathbury, citizen and pewterer of London, 'intending to take a voyage to sea,' made his last will and testament. According to the Probate Registry Records of London, as transcribed in George Sherwood's *American Colonists*, second series, the will was proved July 26, 1655, the testator having died in Virginia.

Lathbury would scarcely have had time to begin the making of pewter in the new land, and may possibly have been on a visit only, with no intention of settling in America, but his is the earliest name, thus far uncovered, of a pewterer in America south of Massachusetts Bay.

JOSEPH COPELAND

The story of the amazing discovery at Jamestown, Virginia, of a fragment of a pewter spoon, made by an American pewterer prior to 1692 and impressed with his still-legible touch, was related in the April, 1938, issue of *Antiques* by Worth Bailey, technician of the museum erected at Jamestown to house articles of interest which the National Park Service is unearthing on the site of that ancient town.

Fragments of other spoons (Plate XXIV), found in the same area which, though unmarked, appear to be of the same pattern as the marked item, have made it possible for Mr. Bailey to reconstruct one of these spoons. As stated in volume I, page 38 the handle is a variant of the trifid type in general use in contemporary England and the bowl is rounder than on the normal English spoon of that period.

The mark, as redrawn by Mr. Bailey (Plate LXVIII, 563), is the only small touch of the seventeenth century, known to me, which includes the maker's full name, place of work, and date. It is unusual also in that it was stamped on the handle rather than in the bowl as was usually the case on seventeenth-century English spoons. The touch enabled Mr. Bailey, after painstaking research, to piece together Copeland's story. Here I shall but summarize that interesting account.

By 1635 the settlement at Jamestown had become firmly established and new colonists coming out from England were beginning to spread to outlying districts, not only up and down the James River, but along many another stream of Tidewater Virginia. The region 'over the water' (the south bank of the James) became at an early date a haven for Quakers and other dissenters, one of whom was John Copeland, now believed to have been an uncle of the pewterer.

The senior Copeland embarked from London for New England in 1635, but, because of his religious beliefs and practices, was jailed in Boston and was sentenced to have one ear cut off by the local hangman. Thence he fled to Virginia and settled in the little parish of Chuckatuck, on a small stream of the same name in Nansemond Shire, about eighteen miles due south of Jamestown. His disfigurement and the stories of his persecution immediately established him as a martyred hero in his new home.

To Chuckatuck also came Joseph Copeland, maker of pewter spoons. From the records of the Worshipful Company of Pewterers in London, Mr. Bailey learned that Joseph, son of Thomas, a spectacle-maker, was apprenticed on May 17, 1666, for a term of seven years to John Mann, London pewterer. Instead of practicing his trade in London young Copeland must have decided to join his uncle in Virginia almost as soon as his apprenticeship was completed; for the date on his spoon, 1675, unquestionably represents the year in which he set up in business in his new home.

Joseph Copeland's first wife, Mary, died at Chuckatuck in 1678 and soon thereafter he married Elizabeth, daughter of Major Thomas Taberer. About 1688 the family moved to Jamestown, and the Journals of the Virginia House of Burgesses show Copeland's appointment as overseer of the State House and custodian of the key of the Assembly Room. Apparently pay for such service was slow in forthcoming, for in 1691 the pewterer prayed 'to be allowed for looking after & keeping cleane the Assembly roome and utensils.' That represents the last recorded evidence of Copeland's existence in Virginia. He died presumably in that year. His son Joseph, who was also short-lived, died in 1725, and in his inventory was an item of '2 old Spoon-molds,' in all likelihood the moulds in which the father's spoons were cast. There is nothing in any surviving record that would indicate whether Copeland was equipped to make forms other than spoons.

Many another American pewterer, who worked in a much later period and turned out far greater quantities of finished pewter, passed on without leaving us a shred of evidence of his existence. And so I cannot close this account without commenting further on the miracle of the Copeland discovery. It is probably not surprising that fragments of pewter spoons were found at Jamestown, but in order that we might identify their maker and trace his history an amazing combination of circumstances had to be present.

First of all, a spoon handle must needs have borne the touch of its maker. Many spoons of that period were not marked at all and the majority of those that were had the touch in the bowl.

Secondly, the mark must have been struck in such manner as to leave a clear impression and must also have been sufficiently well preserved as to be easily decipherable. Thousands of pieces left the shops with the touch impressed so carelessly as to be illegible and the marks on other thousands, once clear, cannot be read today because of ordinary wear and tear. But this particular spoon handle, after what we may assume was a normal spoon life, was thrown away and had been buried for perhaps two hundred and fifty years. During all that time it had been subject, not to the ordinary corrosion caused by changes in atmospheric conditions, but to the more insidious action of the acids in the soil. The odds against finding on it a mark that could be deciphered at all were almost too great for the imagination.

Thirdly, it was necessary that the maker's mark should include his name. On the oldest touch plate still preserved in London are three hundred and fifty-one different marks struck by London pewterers who were at work between the years 1640 and 1680 (or thereabouts) — in general, the period of the Chuckatuck spoons. Fewer than one hundred of those touches show a maker's name that can now be read, and, almost without exception, those ninety-odd touches are too large to be impressed on a spoon handle.

Fourthly, in order to know when Copeland began his work the touch had to show a date. Less than one in four of the contemporary London marks include a date in the touch.

Fifthly, a place name had to be included in the touch if we were to know where to look for Copeland's history. Just seventeen of the three hundred and fifty-one London touches mentioned above give the place of work. The odds were therefore greater than twenty to one against finding the name of Copeland's town in his touch. In fact, on only one of the three hundred and fifty-one can we read the maker's name, place of work, and date, and in that one the touch is far too large for a spoon handle.

Finally, it seems almost too good to be true that Mr. Bailey, after discovering from the touch three cardinal facts about the maker, was able to verify from existing records in Virginia and London the story which the spoon handle told.

Surely we are still living in an age of miracles.

THE WILLETTS

Maryland's earliest pewterer of record was Edward Willett. Nothing has as yet been learned about his ancestry or whence he came. His name first appears in existing Maryland records in the year 1692, when he is mentioned as 'Clerk of the Vestry, St. Paul's

Parish, Charles Town,' apparently a man of some education and standing in his community at that time. In a letter to the Crown bearing the signatures of all the military and civil officers of the colony, written in 1696, Edward Willett's is found among the 'Civill Officers & Magistrates of Prince George's County.'

In that same year he bought from Colonel Ninian Beall property just outside the town of Upper Marlboro, paying for his purchase in tobacco. At that time Colonel Beall was probably the most prominent man in Prince George County. Influential in both Church and State, he was also commander-in-chief of the Rangers. When the Revolution of 1688 in England overturned the Stuarts, a committee of seven Protestant Freemen, among them Colonel Beall and John Campbell (father of a Maryland pewterer), temporarily seized control of the colonial government. That Willett was not only a neighbor but probably a close friend and possibly a relative of the Colonel is proved by the fact that he witnessed the old gentleman's will and named one of his sons in his honor.

Edward Willett's name appears on a number of the early Prince George County records. In some he is termed a pewterer, in others a planter. The district in which he lived was sparsely settled, and the demands of the small pewter trade open to him could probably have been provided for in the seasons when tobacco took up but little of the planter's time.

Although nothing is known of Willett's early life, it seems probable that he was the same Edward Willett who was given leave to strike his touch in Pewterers' Hall, London, in 1684/5. That touch is reproduced in Plate LXVIII, 564. Howard H. Cotterell, in *Old Pewter*, stated that Willett's name is not in the existing yeomanry or livery lists, an omission which could be readily explained by his departure for America soon after he learned his trade.

Willett's will, dated June 16, 1743, and proved February 7, 1744/5, mentions his wife Tabitha, his sons, Ninian, Edward, Thomas, William, and James, and a daughter, Ann (Swan). Of particular interest is the following clause:

> I further give and bequeath to my said son William Willett all my Pewterers Moulds and other Tools thereunto Belonging provided he doth make what necessary Pewter the rest of my Children shall want for their own proper use in their houses they finding Mettle.

In addition to small quantities of both old and new pewter and a 'parcele of Pewterers Tools,' the inventory included 'Dish Molds' weighing one hundred and ten pounds and one hundred and thirty pounds respectively, a plate mould of forty-seven pounds, two spoon moulds, and one 'Soop Mould.' There is no evidence that Willett was prepared to make any hollow-ware.

The son, William, like his father before him, was both tobacco-grower and pewterer. Most of the surviving Willett records indicate that tobacco-raising was his principal occupation, but the following notice from the *Maryland Gazette* for January 8, 1756, proves that he did carry on at least a small business in pewter:

> William Willett, Pewterer, Living about two miles from Upper-Marlborough on the Bladensburg Road, new Moulds, old Pewter at 9d. per pound, or will return one half good new Pewter for

any quantity of old, and to be cast in whatever Form, The Employer pleases, either flat or soup Dishes, or flat or soup Plates. N.B. He will wait on any employer within 20 or 30 miles to receive their old, or return their new Pewter. And they may depend on being faithfully and honestly dealt with.

William Willett's will, dated July 10, 1772, was proved on August 27 of the same year. The entire estate was held in trust for the widow, Mary, for the term of her natural life, unless she should remarry. Seven sons were mentioned by name as the ultimate inheritors of Willett's possessions, and to the third, Edward, was left 'my whole set of Pewterer's Tools and Moulds' upon conditions similar to those imposed upon William by his father one generation earlier.

In the *Maryland Gazette* of February 25, 1773, Mary Willett advertised:

The Pewterer's Business is still carried on at the Subscriber's House in the same manner, and at the same Rates as were in my deceased Husband's Life.

I have no knowledge as to how long Mary Willett continued at the pewterer's trade or whether the son, Edward, ever made use of his legacy. Existing deeds give his occupation as 'planter' right up to the time of his death in 1816.

ANTHONY CORNE

The earliest pewterer in Charleston, South Carolina, whose record has been found was Anthony Corne.

On November 28, 1735, he advertised as follows in the *South Carolina Gazette*:

Anthony Corne, brazier lately come from London and living in Elliott Street in Charleston maketh and selleth all sorts of Brass, Pewter &c and Tinneth and mendeth any of the aforementioned ware at the lowest prices.

Corne's name was not found in the English lists, and I can report nothing further about his life in Charleston.

JOHN CAMPBELL

The one known Annapolis pewterer, John Campbell, appears to have been a native of Maryland, and a son of an early prominent Scotch settler of the same name. Records of his birth and early life were not found, but he was well established in Annapolis and may even have reached middle age when mentioned as a pewterer in a notice in the *Maryland Gazette* for January 4, 1749. He was a member of the Church of England and is recorded as a vestryman of Saint Ann's Parish in 1767 and 1769.

Upon the outbreak of the Revolution he was appointed by the Associators of the City of Annapolis as one of a committee of seven to arrange with the Council of Safety for the defense of the city. He lived but a short time longer, for his will, dated October 14,

1774, was proved November 1, 1777. In it he makes mention of his wife Frances, three sons, Robert Eagle, Daniel, and John, and three daughters. The inventory included nothing indicative of pewter-making, and he may have given up that trade several years before his death. No example of his pewter has been identified.

JOHN NORSWORTH

The Subscriber begs leave to inform the Publick that he has just opened Shop opposite Maximilian Calvert's Door in Norfolk, where he makes and sells different sizes of Dishes, Basons, and Plates, either hammered or turned. He likewise makes and mends Still Worms, Candle Moulds, Soup Spoons, Table and Tea do, etc. Any persons may be supplied by wholesale much cheaper than they can import from England. He also works up old Pewter at a reasonable Rate, makes House Lead and Lead Work for Ships.

All persons who please to favour him with their Demands, may depend upon being served in the neatest manner, and with great Expedition.

The above notice, for a copy of which I am indebted to Miss Paige Williams of Richmond, Virginia, appeared in the *Virginia Gazette* issue of March 28, 1771, published at Williamsburg. It represents all that we know of John Norsworth.

FRANCIS HENDRICKS

On April 30, 1771, the following notice appeared in the *South Carolina Gazette & Country Journal*, published in Charleston:

Francis Hendricks, Pewterer, Who can be well recommended in his trade, Informs the Public in general, and those Merchants who may please to employ him in the Pewtery Business, that he will allow 2s. 6d. a Pound for old Pewter. As he is just come into this Country, he will be much obliged to all those who chuse to encourage so useful an undertaking. Apply at Michael Keller's Shop in King-Street near the corner of Queen-Street.

Francis Garlieb Hendricks (also spelled Henricks) was presumably a native of the Continent of Europe and most probably of one of the German states. At some time after his arrival in this country or shortly prior thereto he married Anna Catherine, widow of William Sauer, but apparently was not blessed with any children. In 1772 he paid two thousand pounds for the property of Richard Beresford, deceased, on Archdale Street, and in December, 1784, he witnessed the will of his former landlord, John Michael Keller. That is the last definite date that we can assign to him. Sometime prior to July 9, 1795, his death took place, for at that time his property on Archdale Street was sold by his widow.

Perhaps an intensive search of Charleston attics would discover pewter of marked Continental appearance impressed with the touch of this long-forgotten maker.

An interesting statement in the advertisement quoted above is the price offered for old pewter. The inventory of Thomas Byles taken in Philadelphia in the same year allowed but tenpence per pound.

THEODORE JENNINGS AND JAMES EDWARD SMITH

Elsewhere we recorded the fact that ships' passenger-lists have furnished the names of two pewterers who were shipped to Maryland as indentured servants in 1775.

In April Theodore Jennings, a pewterer of Middlesex, aged forty, came to Maryland in the ship *Fleetwood*, and in the following month the *Mermaid* landed James Edward Smith, aged thirty-one, a pewterer of London. Both men were under indenture for four years. I have found no record to prove what became of them after reaching this country, but both probably had had a thorough training in the manufacture of pewter. According to Howard H. Cotterell's *Old Pewter*, a Theodore Jennings joined the yeomanry in London March 24, 1757, and James Edward Smith did likewise on December 13, 1764. The latter was gazetted in London as insolvent on June 25, 1774. The English dates and records match so well with the facts given in the ship registers that there can be little doubt that they apply to the same men.

LEWIS GEANTY

Although I feel certain that careful research will disclose pewterers at work in Baltimore before 1800, no such record has as yet been found. A David Evans is said to have made pewter buttons for the Continental Army, but substantiating proof has not been forthcoming.

The first pewterer mentioned in the city Directory — that of 1800 — is Lewis Geanty (sometimes spelled Ganty). Since Baltimore at that time had a large French population, I take it that Geanty, a man of some education, emigrated from France a few years before we first find record of him. In 1796 he purchased property in Baltimore and in the deed is styled 'gentleman.' Although listed as a butcher in the Directory of 1799, all other papers prior to 1800 omit the occupation. In the 1800 Directory we find him at 72 French Street, a 'Pewterer and Philosophical Instrument Maker,' and in 1802 he is termed a pewterer only. How, in the brief space of one year, the metamorphosis from butcher to pewterer and philosophical-instrument maker was accomplished, we are compelled to leave to the imagination.

Geanty was apparently no business man. The sale of pewter and philosophical instruments was not bringing in sufficient returns, and in December, 1802, he advertised in the *Federal Gazette* a course of 'Philosophical Lectures and Experiments at Mr. Priestly's

College in St. Paul's Lane — tickets to be had at Mr. Conrad's book store or at the subscriber's manufactory, Old Town, near Mr. Williams', dyer, foot bridge.'

Alas, even the lectures could not stave off the impending disaster, and in the following May Geanty was declared insolvent, all of his property, real and personal, except necessary wearing apparel, being turned over to William Woods, trustee for the creditors.

Geanty's later history is unknown, and none of his pewter has as yet been identified.

J. W. OLCOTT (OR J. WOLCOTT)

The correct name was J. W. Olcott, not J. Wolcott.

The touch illustrated in Plate LXVIII, 565, is our sole record of this obscure Baltimore pewterer. The impression is not sufficiently complete to determine whether the name was J. Wolcott or J. W. Olcott.

Whoever the man was, his sojourn in Baltimore must have been brief. He is listed in none of the Directories, and neither Olcott nor Wolcott was a Baltimore name. My guess — and it is nothing more than that — is that the family name was Olcott and that the pewterer was a native of Connecticut who for a very brief period (about 1800) worked in Baltimore.

Two plates measuring approximately eight inches in diameter are the only known survivals of this man's work.

GEORGE LIGHTNER

The first mention of George Lightner, found in Baltimore records, was in a deed dated 1791 in which he was termed a tavern-keeper; and although his occupation was omitted in practically all later documents, he appears once, in 1804, as a carpenter and the town records show payments to him for keeping the bridges in repair. Carpentry, therefore, seems to have been his early trade.

Lightner must have been one of that group of men, who, profiting from the disruption of foreign trade caused by the Napoleonic Wars, saw an opportunity advantageously to set aside his other work and turn to pewter-making; for on November 21, 1806, he advertised a 'Tin and Pewter Manufactory' on 'North Street, Old Town, near the Hay Scales, Baltimore.' In all likelihood this notice heralded his entry into the business which he carried on for the few remaining years of his life.

According to the *Baltimore American* he died after a brief illness on January 26, 1815, in the sixty-sixth year of his age. His birth would therefore have been in 1749, but whether at Baltimore or elsewhere we cannot say.

Lightner was evidently doing a big business in pewter when he died. His inventory included over fifteen hundred pounds of finished pewter, five hundred and nineteen pounds of metal cast but not finished, and three hundred and twenty-three pounds of old pewter. Since he owned 'Pewter Casting Moulds' that weighed four hundred and nineteen pounds, we can be certain that he made other forms than the plates and basins that have thus far been found. His plates measure 6, $7\frac{7}{8}$, $8\frac{3}{4}$, and $9\frac{3}{8}$ inches in diameter, deep dishes 11 and 13 inches, and basins 8, 10, and $11\frac{3}{4}$ inches. His plates are heavy and seem to have a fairly high lead content, but all that I have seen were well made. His touches are illustrated in Plate LXVIII.

Lightner apparently was childless. He left his estate, valued at over fourteen thousand dollars, to his wife with the provision that upon her death one half should go to his brother John, the balance to be divided among his married sisters and their children.

Now as to this brother. For one year only, 1816 — and that the year of George Lightner's death — John's name is found in the Directory as a pewterer and tinman. Prior to that year he is listed as a laborer and afterward as a tinman. It is quite possible that he advertised himself as a pewterer just long enough to dispose of his late brother's unsold wares. It would be surprising if pewter bearing his name should come to light, and there seems ample justification for removing his name from our lists.

SAMUEL KILBOURN

Hitherto we have thought of Samuel Kilbourn only in connection with Baltimore pewter, for his known touches bear the name of that city. When, however, no early Kilbourns could be found among the Maryland records, a search was made in that land of lost pewterers, Connecticut, and with the same success that rewarded the hunt for Jacob Eggleston and others of the 'Yankee-Dixie' group.

Samuel Kilbourn was a descendant of Thomas Kilborne, who settled in Wethersfield in 1635. The father of the pewterer was Stephen, who owned a farm in East Hartford. Although no record of Samuel's birth has been found, he apparently had come of age by 1794, as evidenced by a Hartford deed of that date bearing his name.

In 1799 Samuel Kilbourn was living on Ferry Street, Hartford, and his name is on many records of that city from 1794 to 1813, but town officials in Connecticut had an unfortunate habit of omitting a man's occupation when preparing public records, so we are left in the dark as to how his early years were employed. It would not be at all surprising if it should be discovered that a new Kilbourn eagle had been found unaccompanied by the word Baltimore, for when Samuel moved to Maryland with his family in 1813 or 1814 he must have been at least forty years of age.

Among the unclaimed mail at the Baltimore post-office on March 1, 1814, as advertised in the *Baltimore American* on the fourth of that month, was a letter for Kilbourn and Porter. Apparently the partnership of these two men was formed immediately upon Kilbourn's arrival. Jephtha Porter was a tinman who was associated with Kilbourn until 1816 only. From that time on the latter worked alone, moving to different locations on Howard, Saratoga, and Baltimore Streets.

The following advertisement, which encourages us to keep our eyes open for a number of lost Kilbourn forms, first appeared in the *Baltimore American and Commercial Advertiser* of December 29, 1819:

Samuel Kilbourn

Pewterer & Tin Manufacturer
No. 93 North Howard St.

Manufactures and has constantly on hand for sale
Pewter Dishes, Plates and Basins of all sizes
" Quart and Pint Mugs.
" Inkstands of a great variety of sizes and patterns
" Spoons, Teapots, Ladles and Syringes
" Bed Pans
" Candle Moulds
and a large assortment of
Tinware.

All of which are offered for sale at such prices and on such terms as cannot fail to give satisfaction. Families in the city can have any particular article of tinware made to order at short notice. Country merchants are respectfully requested to call.

After 1831 Samuel is listed in the Directories as a tinplate worker only, and he appears to have retired in 1836. The genealogist of the family gives the date of his death as July 8, 1839. No will or letters of administration have been found.

Until recently we have had no evidence that the pewterers who worked south of the Mason and Dixon line ever made anything but flatware. The graceful little flare-mouthed beaker bearing on the inside bottom Kilbourn's rarer touch, and illustrated in *Plate XXII, 155* should read *Plate XXII, 150.* Plate XXII, 155, convincingly demonstrates that at least one Southerner, even if a Southerner by adoption, was fully the equal in ability of many of his Northern competitors. I have also seen quart and pint mugs made by this man.

Kilbourn's plates measure $7\frac{3}{4}$, $8\frac{5}{8}$, and $9\frac{1}{8}$ inches in diameter, deep dishes 11 and 13 inches, and basins 8, 10, and 12 inches. All of this pewterer's ware is of a good quality, carefully and accurately finished. His touches appear as numbers 568 and 569, Plate LXVIII.

SYLVESTER GRISWOLD

In S. Griswold of Baltimore we have another new man of the 'eagle' period. His touch (Plate LXVIII, 570), which bears such a striking resemblance to that of his contemporary, Samuel Kilbourn, first came to light shortly after the appearance of Louis G. Myers's *Notes*, and has since been observed on $7\frac{3}{4}$-inch flat plates, 13-inch deep dishes, and 8-inch basins.

No trace of the man — not even of the family name — has been found in Baltimore records for the first quarter of the nineteenth century, but as Mr. Myers had previously located another Griswold — Ashbil — in Connecticut, it seemed logical to search there for S. Griswold also.

In the Connecticut State Library at Hartford the papers for the administration of the estate of a Sylvester Griswold, 'late of Meriden,' were found. The first document examined was the appointment by the court on August 25, 1822, of our old friend Ashbil as administrator. This looked promising. But, alas, the inventory was of no assistance! It amounted to but $326.87 and consisted merely of clothes and personal belongings; no evidence at all of pewter-making. One paper, however, did indicate that we had the right man. This was a claim for $4553.47 against the estate from Clark and Haskell of Baltimore — Griswold's only creditors. After Ashbil's expenses had been deducted — and these included a small charge for a trip to Brooklyn to attend Sylvester in his last illness — the balance was turned over to the Baltimore firm.

A second bit of information was gleaned from the records of the Stepney Society Congregational Church of Wethersfield, Connecticut. There we learn that Sylvester, younger brother of Ashbil and fourth son of Constant and Rebecca (Boardman) Griswold, was baptized December 11, 1791.

Returning to Baltimore Directories, we find Clark and Haskell listed for the first time in the issue of 1817. They appear as tinsmiths with a shop on Union Street. The same listing is found in 1819. The next Directory is dated 1822–1823, and in it John Haskell is given as working alone at the same address. Sometime, therefore, during those directory-less years from 1819 to 1822 Sylvester Griswold must have made his Baltimore pewter.

How, in such a short period, Griswold became so deeply involved in debt must remain a mystery. The cost of his tools and two years' rent would never have amounted to anything like forty-five hundred dollars. That he did fail is certain, and whatever the cause we cannot attribute it to his metal, which seems to be of good quality and workmanship.

NORTH AND ROWE

In Louis G. Myers's account of the Danforth family he quotes the following excerpt from a letter written by Thomas Danforth, Fourth, from Augusta, Georgia, under date of November 27, 1818, to his father in Rocky Hill, Connecticut:

> I am working for North and Rowe in a new shop, built since I left home last spring, especially for tin and pewter business. Peddlers are doing extremely well. North & Rowe had one come in that was gone three weeks and brought them $1200 in cash.

That letter gave us the first information that there were pewterers at work in Augusta; but who were 'North and Rowe'? To three descendants of John North, Mrs. T. W. Alexander, Miss Neville North, and Frank M. North, I am particularly indebted for the information in this sketch.

John North, second son of John and Rhoda Merrill North, was born in Farmington,

Connecticut, in 1779. An ancestor, John North, had come to this country from England in 1635 and had been an original settler of Farmington.

Our John had worked as a young man in his father's blacksmith shop, but was threatened with consumption, and upon the advice of his doctor decided to take a long ocean voyage and then live in the South. To quote from a letter of Frank North:

> He [John North] therefore embarked for Cuba, and incidentally, while enroute the vessel was boarded by pirates, who however took nothing except a live pig, which was the property of my grandfather, he having been advised by the Captain to invest in that property, and to sell it to the sailors at a profit when they became tired of eating salt pork. On the return voyage my grandfather disembarked at either Charleston or Savannah, the latter most likely, and came to Augusta. Augusta was then the farthest inland point to which there was practical transportation for Georgia, the Carolinas and Tennessee.... Cattle and even Turkeys and geese in great quantities were driven through the country on foot.

In Augusta, North found an old neighbor, Isaiah Rowe. The latter was born in Farmington in 1755 and had probably been a friend of the family. To him the senior John North must have sent his son. At this time (1812), Rowe had a general merchandise and trading business and gave young North employment in his store. As part of his training, North, we are told, traveled around the country in a high-wheeled gig trading with the Indians and the frontier settlements.

In 1817 John North married Laurana Rowe, daughter of his employer, and was taken in as a partner in the business. Mr. and Mrs. North are said to have been passengers on the first steamboat trip up the Savannah River.

Apparently the senior Rowe died or retired about 1817, for thereafter the firm name appears as 'North and Rowe' or 'North, Rowe and Company.' So far as we can determine, the partners were John North and Adna Rowe, the latter a son of Isaiah. To the period of this later partnership belongs the shop built 'especially for tin and pewter business.'

The tax digests for Richmond County furnish us with the following information: North, Rowe and Company were taxed in 1818 and 1820 on stock valued at four thousand dollars; in 1823, at eight thousand dollars. The next list discovered shows Adna Rowe taxed on fifteen thousand dollars, while the name of his erstwhile partner had disappeared from the records.

North, it appears, moved to New York. As a son was born to him there in 1823, we can state very accurately that the pewter-making activities of this firm were confined to the period from 1818 to 1823. That they had a big business, for a short while at least, is indicated from Danforth's letter. Like Spencer Stafford in Albany, these men were really successful merchants, not pewterers, and as a side line to their general business they called in journeymen pewterers to manufacture in their own shop one of their principal lines of stock. Though neither North nor Rowe may have had any great knowledge of pewter-making, it seems likely that wares made in their shop would have been stamped with their own touch, and we may yet find North and Rowe eagle-marked pewter.

In New York, North's prosperity continued. As the senior partner in a drygoods house he built up a good-sized fortune for those days. In later life he retired to an estate at New Haven, where he died April 4, 1865.

Whether Adna Rowe's pewter activities continued after North's departure we cannot say, but he remained at Augusta, and the records of the settlement of his estate indicate that he died there about the year 1835.

GILES GRISWOLD

Giles Griswold is another man whose sole record as a pewterer has been preserved in the correspondence of the fourth Thomas Danforth. Writing from Augusta in November, 1818, to his father in Rocky Hill, Connecticut, Danforth made the following observations: 'Giles Griswold is setting the pewter business agoing by horsepower'; and again: 'Griswold wants to engage Danforth [Samuel] for the winter.'

As might be expected, no traces of native Griswolds could be found in Augusta. Giles's name was found only in the two earliest tax digests — those of 1818 and 1820; it is missing from the list of 1823, the third earliest on file in Augusta.

Everything pointed to a Connecticut origin. Two other Griswolds of Connecticut had been pewterers; the South was dotted at that time with opportunist craftsmen from the Nutmeg State; and lastly, Danforth, in his letter, would hardly have written to his father without some explanation about a pewterer who would have been unknown to the older man.

So to Connecticut the search took us, and although I could not definitely connect any Giles Griswold with pewter-making, I found in Meriden one whose dates and provenance exactly met our requirements. I shall introduce, then, a man who may have been and probably was the pewterer of Augusta.

Giles O. Griswold, son of Giles and Eunice, was born in Meriden, October 8, 1775. On Christmas Day, 1797, he married Lucy Brocket, who bore him three children. For 1809 and 1810 Meriden Land Records exhibit deeds for property purchased by Griswold, and in the years 1816 and 1822 he disposed of the same parcels of land. Sometime between the last two dates I suspect that this man was in Augusta making pewter. He died in Meriden, November 13, 1840.

EGGLESTON, NOTT, JOHNSON, AND DERBY

Although Jacob Eggleston, William Nott, and Jehiel Johnson certainly, and Thomas S. Derby probably, were working in North Carolina for brief periods in the first quarter of the eighteenth century, all four were Middletown men whose careers began in Connecticut. Their stories will therefore be found with those of the Connecticut pewterers.

The Pewterers of the South

JOHN PHILIP REICH

The study of the lives of the early craftsmen of this country frequently necessitates excursions into the history of their times and environments. The story of John Philip Reich is a case in point.

Almost two centuries ago the Moravian Church, which had already planted little settlements of refugees in Bethlehem, Nazareth, and other Pennsylvania towns, determined upon a more ambitious program of colonization. Under the guidance of its leader, Count Zinzendorf, the Church purchased from Lord Granville, proprietor under the British Crown, a tract of approximately one hundred thousand acres in what is now the northwestern corner of North Carolina. To this new colony, named Wachovia, in honor of Count Zinzendorf's ancestral home in Austria, twelve colonists were sent out from Pennsylvania in 1753. Despite great hardship they overcame all obstacles, and their numbers were soon swelled by other settlers both from Pennsylvania and the old country. The first houses were built at Bethabara, but the earliest town was soon overshadowed by the growing settlement at Salem (founded in 1766), now part of the city of Winston-Salem.

In Wachovia the land was all owned by the Church, and it was thus possible to limit the population to citizens who were considered desirable. Even as late as 1849 the Church had complete control over trade and industry within the tract, a remarkable experiment of church control over lay matters which lasted for over one hundred years.

Into this Moravian community at Salem on September 3, 1797, John Philip, son of Christopher and Catherine Transon Reich, was born. Of his life little has been learned. On June 17, 1824, he entered into matrimony with 'the single sister, Sybilla Cecilia Dull,' and he had been at work for perhaps a decade when the following notice appeared in the *Weekly Gleaner* of September 22, 1829:

J. & P. Reich
Copper-Smith and Tin-Plate Workers

Respectfully inform their friends and the public generally, that they still carry on the above business in Salem, in all its various branches and will supply their customers on the shortest notice with Stills & Worms, Hatters', Dyers' Wash & Tea Kettles & &. Which will be executed in a durable and workmanlike style, and on accomodating terms. All kinds of repairing in any of the above articles done with punctuality and despatch.

Also a variety of Tin Ware is constantly kept on hand, at wholesale or retail. Old pewter will be taken and run into plates, dishes and spoons for those who desire it.

Old copper and Beeswax received in exchange for any of the above work.

Soon thereafter Reich must have given up this limited manufacture of pewter, for in later years he appears to have been a tinsmith only. He died in Salem February 7, 1867.

The control of industry by the Church has proved most happy for the student of early life in Wachovia, for the Church had the foresight to preserve for future generations

John Philip Reich

many tools used by its early artisans. In the interesting collection of the Wachovia Historical Society at Winston-Salem are on view today the moulds in which Reich 'ran' his spoons, plates, and dishes, and with them is an $8\frac{3}{4}$-inch plate bearing his touch, the only known example of his handiwork.

Through the courtesy of the Society's president, the Reverend Douglas L. Rights, I am enabled to show a photograph of that touch (Plate LXVIII, 571). Some of Reich's moulds are illustrated in Plate V.

Thus it has been our good fortune to discover in John Philip Reich not alone the story of a forgotten maker, but also an unlisted touch and the moulds which the man employed.

THE INITIALED PORRINGERS

ANY times the question has been asked whether anything definite has been discovered as yet concerning the makers of the New England porringers which are marked only by initials cast in the bracket or in the underface of the handle. With regret I have been compelled to reply in the negative. I am not, however, without opinions as to the origin of these pieces.

Through the kindness of the late Mrs. Annie H. Kerfoot five examples of such marks have been reproduced in Plate LXVIII from J. B. Kerfoot's *American Pewter*, and a new photograph of the 'S. G.' touch secured from Edward E. Minor. It will be noted that three sets of initials are applicable to three very early Massachusetts pewterers, Richard Graves, Samuel Grame, and John Comer. It is, of course, unthinkable that these three makers of the seventeenth century are responsible for the surviving 'R. G.,' 'S. G.,' or 'I. C.' pieces. Had even one example of such a frail vessel endured from their day it would be little short of a miracle. However, it is not at all improbable that seventeenth-century moulds should have continued in use into the nineteenth century, and I am inclined to believe that the initials may be those of six early Massachusetts pewterers whose porringer moulds were handed down from one generation to another and were still in use after the Revolution.

Does it not seem surprising that we have not found a single porringer bearing an identifiable touch of a Boston maker when numerous examples from Newport, Providence, Hartford, and New York shops still exist? Furthermore, we know that John Skinner and Nathaniel Austin advertised the manufacture of porringers and that such forms were listed in the inventory of the shop jointly owned by Samuel Green and Richard Austin. There can be but one conclusion, namely, Boston pewterers did make porringers, probably in large quantities, and some of those porringers must have survived to the present day. It is also worthy of notice that we have plates made by six Boston pewterers of the last quarter of the eighteenth century (Nathaniel and Richard Austin, Thomas Badger, 'Semper Eadem,' Samuel Green, and John Skinner), and we have an equal number of unidentified marks on porringers purported to have been made in or near Boston.

I therefore suggest as a possible explanation of the initialed porringer mystery that the moulds from which these vessels were made date from the seventeenth or early eighteenth century, that the initials are those of the first users of the moulds, and that each of the latter passed by sale or inheritance to a line of successive pewterers, none of whom felt it necessary to have his second-hand mould recast simply because it bore inappropriate initials. If such a surmise be correct, it stands to reason that the initials on the porringers are not those of the men who made them, but of the first owners of the moulds from which they came. For instance, Nathaniel Austin may have owned the 'I. C.' mould, whereas the porringers marked 'S. G.' (the least rare of the six touches) may have been made by Badger rather than by Samuel Green, as some suppose. These opinions are merely conjectural, but they represent the only tenable explanation thus far advanced for a problem that seems to defy solution.

The problem, by the way, is no longer limited to porringers, for I own a tankard illustrated in Plate XVI, 93, which has the initials 'I. C.' cast one on either side of the handle.

PLATE LXIX — *Unidentified Touches*

578. Touch of what appears to be a horse with foreleg raised, as found in an early pint pot in the collection of John W. Poole, Esq. The same touch is in a quart pot with unusual handle owned by Mr. Minor (see Plate XVIII, 110); possibly American, probably early or mid-eighteenth century.

579. Assuredly an American touch and quite possibly a mark of Joseph Leddell or Joseph Leddell, Jr., New York, 1712–1754. From the collection of Mrs. Ralph P. Hanes.

580. A touch from the bottom of a dram bottle owned by the author (Plate XXXIX, 248). Maker unknown, but probably American, mid-eighteenth century. This may be another touch of John Bassett, New York, 1720–1761.

581. Touch of an unknown maker, unquestionably American, found on porringers and in tankards. This impression is from a porringer in the collection of Joseph France, Esq. Probably early or mid-eighteenth century. This and the three succeeding touches may all have been used by the same man, possibly by William Bradford, New York, 1719–1758.

582. 'W. B.' mark from a fine domed-top tankard that exhibits characteristics of New York craftsmanship (Plate XV, 87). Collection of Edward E. Minor, Esq.

583. An interesting touch as photographed from the interior of Mrs. Guy G. Clark's soap box illustrated in Plate XL. Probably American.

584. Another 'W. B.' touch that seems definitely American and probably is that of a New York maker It was taken from the inside bottom of a domed-top tankard with crenate lid and fish-tail handle terminal, formerly in the collection of Wilmer Moore, Esq.

585. A touch attributed by the late Louis G. Myers, Esq., to John Fryers, Newport, 1749–1768, and reproduced by permission of Mr. Myers from *Some Notes on American Pewterers*. There is no reason to doubt the correctness of this attribution, but I should like to find further supporting evidence before placing it definitely in Fryers's column.

586 and 586a. Two impressions of a crude touch, with initials 'T. B.,' found on a number of plates and dishes that invariably have come to light in New Jersey and eastern Pennsylvania. It may well be a touch of Thomas Byles, Philadelphia, 1738–1771, who should have left some examples of his work. The illustrations are from plates owned by Philip G. Platt, Esq., and the author.

587. Touch from the under side of the handle of Mrs. J. H. Krom's unusual porringer illustrated in Plate XII, 56. The porringer is early in appearance. The mark bears no resemblance to other New York initial touches, which makes it doubtful that John Will was the user. I should be equally hesitant in attributing it to Jacob Whitmore of Middletown.

588. A very similar touch struck with a different die and probably used by the same maker. From a tall beaker owned by John W. Poole, Esq.

292a. An almost mint impression of this touch which was formerly attributed to Robert Boyle, New York City. From a porringer in the Mabel Brady Garvan Collection as illustrated in Plate XIII, 70. Probably the work of a now unknown pewterer of Boston or Newport, about 1760.

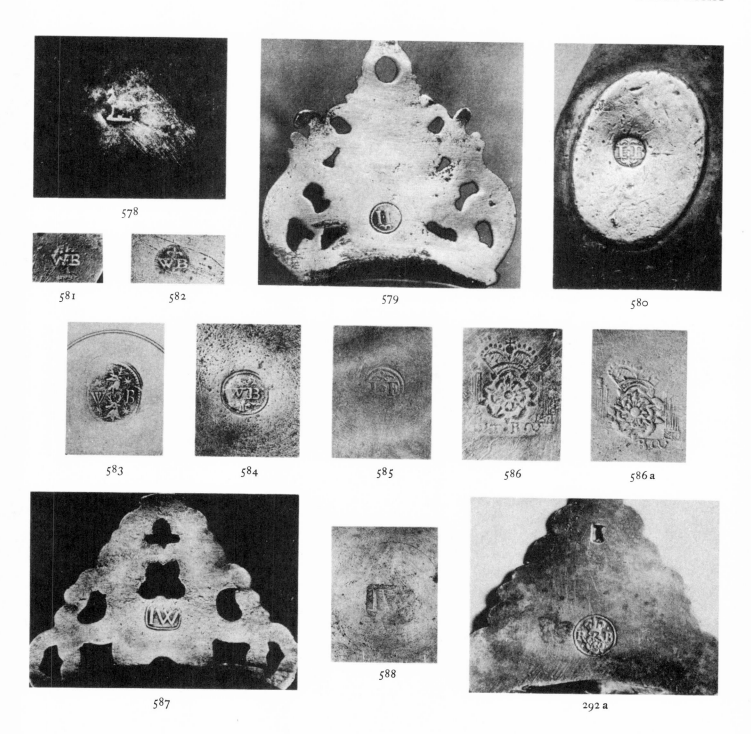

PLATE LXIX

578

581   582

579

580

583   584   585   586   586 a

587   588   292 a

PLATE LXX — *Unidentified Touches*

589. Touch probably used either by Johann Christian Höran, Philadelphia, 1758–1786, or his contemporary, Johann Christopher Heyne, Lancaster, Pennsylvania, 1754–1780. From a plate owned by John P. Remensnyder, Esq. Please note that Höran's sons, Christian and John Hera, used a shield for their touch (Plate LXV, 543).

"Plate LXV" should read "LXVI".

590. A Philadelphia touch of an unidentified maker as found in the Captain Ickes mug illustrated in Plate XIX, 118, and owned by Albert H. Good, Esq. Date about 1775.

591. The so-called Paul Revere touch. From a spoon owned by George C. Gebelein, Esq. The illustration is included with misgivings, for I am more than skeptical of its proper attribution to Paul Revere and am far from convinced that it can even be classified as an early American touch.

592. Touch from a tankard in the collection of Mrs. J. Insley Blair. The tankard is almost identical with the Peter Young tankard (Plate XIV, 83), and the touch is in character with other New York marks. There is considerable justification for awarding it to William Elsworth, New York, 1767–1798.

593. Another touch, attributed by Mr. Myers to Elsworth. From a basin owned by him and now in the Mabel Brady Garvan Collection at Yale University. The touch is less characteristic of New York marks than 592, and it seems best to list it among the unidentified until further proof of the ascription is found.

594. Probably the commonest of these unidentified marks, found on flagons, gravy boats, creamers, shakers, etc. The mark of an able maker who may or may not have been American, 1750–1780. From a gravy boat in the author's collection.

595. Mark found in inverted pear-shaped tankards and mugs that come to light usually in upper New York State or western Connecticut; 1760–1780. From a quart tankard in the author's collection.

596. The touch of an unknown maker, 'T. L.' From a quart pot owned by John W. Poole, Esq. Probably late eighteenth or early nineteenth century.

597. A late Philadelphia touch (nineteenth century), probably used by some maker already well known to us. From a pint mug in the collection of John J. Evans, Jr., Esq.

598. Touch of an unknown maker of porringers who worked in or near Westtown, Pennsylvania, late in the eighteenth century. From the collection of Mrs. J. Insley Blair.

599. Crude touch, probably of a German-American pewterer, found on an English plate, made by Townsend and Giffin of London, 1773–1800, which must have passed through his hands. Collection of the author.

600. The late Mr. Kerfoot's unidentified eagle, number 1. The maker is still unidentified. The touch, not uncommon, is found only on basins. The character of the mark and the total absence of basins made by Gershom Jones, Providence, 1774–1809, lend credence to the supposition that he may have been its user. Collection of Edward E. Minor, Esq.

601. A rare Griswold touch. From a plate formerly in the collection of the late Albert C. Bowman. It may have been used by any one of the three Griswolds.

602. A touch from a plate found by the late Mr. Kerfoot in Hagerstown, Maryland, and now in the author's collection. If we could prove that Aaron Burdett, who was listed as a pewterer in Baltimore in 1838, was working there fifteen years earlier, the touch would be attributed to him. Date 1815–1825.

PLATE LXX

589

590

591

592

593

594

595

596

597

598

599

600

601

602

UNIDENTIFIED AMERICAN TOUCHES

PERFECT impressions of pewterers' touches are extremely rare. Even if the die had been perfectly struck, as must have happened only occasionally, the wear to which the metal was subjected has usually been sufficient to obliterate entirely or in part the mark which once stood out so boldly. Consequently, when only one or two examples of any particular touch have survived, it is not surprising that in some few instances portions of the mark, essential for identification of the maker, are no longer visible. In such cases all that we can do is to wait for the discovery of a more perfect impression.

There are also the touches which we cannot positively assign to any particular man no matter how perfect the touch may be — those on which no lettering appears; touches with initials which fit no known American pewterer; and finally the initialed touches which would be applicable perhaps to specific makers, but which can be attributed only with decided reservations.

These are the unknown touches, some of which will eventually be definitely and accurately identified.

The earliest in appearance of these marks (Plate LXIX, 578), showing what appears to be a horse with one foreleg raised, was photographed from the inside bottom of a pint pot with solid handle, a vessel that is early in all its details. This piece is now in the collection of John W. Poole. We should like, of course, to attribute this touch to William Horsewell, early New York pewterer, but there is little likelihood that any work of this man, who was in New York but a few years and died more than two and a quarter centuries ago, has survived. These misgivings are increased by a later discovery by Edward E. Minor of another mug (Plate XVIII, 110), similarly marked, which seems too late in design for Horsewell's period.

The next touch (number 579) shows the initials 'I. L.' This may have been used by one of the Leddells as suggested on page 5.

Plate XXXIX, 250 should read Plate XXXIX, 248.

Touch number 580, upon which observations were also made earlier (page 6), is from the dram bottle illustrated in Plate XXXIX, 250, and may possibly have been a mark of John Bassett.

The interesting deer's head design with initials 'W. B.' (number 583) is from the circular box illustrated in Plate XL. William Bradford may have been its user.

Touches numbered 581, 582, and 584 may all have been used by the same man, possibly William Bradford and have been commented upon on page 9.

Touch number 586, possibly a mark of Thomas Byles, Philadelphia pewterer (c. 1740–1770), was commented upon on page 42.

[88]

Unidentified American Touches

The next two unattributed marks (numbers 587 and 588), similar in design, but apparently struck with different dies, were probably used by the same man, possibly John Will of New York or Jacob Whitmore of Middletown, Connecticut. Number 587 was found on a porringer handle of early and unusual design in the collection of Mrs. James H. Krom; number 588 was photographed from one of a pair of beakers owned by John W. Poole. The same beaker design was employed at a later date by various members of the Danforth and Boardman families. (See Plate XXIII, 161.)

Number 585 is a mark which Louis G. Myers in his *Notes* attributed to John Fryers of Newport, Rhode Island (1749–1768). It is to be hoped that confirmation of this attribution can soon be found.

Number 292a is the touch formerly attributed to Robert Boyle of New York. For two reasons it has been taken from that maker and placed among the unknown. In the first place, a plate bearing this 'R. B.' mark, coupled with the touch of 'Semper Eadem,' unknown Boston maker (Plate XLIV), was recently acquired by Mrs. Stephen S. FitzGerald. Secondly, 'R. B.' pewter almost invariably comes to light in New England rather than in New York. There is no doubt at all in my mind that the user of this touch was an American. Howard H. Cotterell wrote me that he had never seen the mark in England and that the form of the coronet was such that he felt sure that the design was either provincial or colonial. If we could only prove that Robert Boyle, whose later history has not been traced, moved from New York to some New England city or town, and particularly if we could place him in Boston, we should have no hesitation in awarding this touch to Boyle once more.

Whoever 'R. B.' was he deserves recognition as one of our ablest pewterers. He made fine church cups of early design both with and without handles (Plate XXXV, 231 and 232). Incidentally it is a matter worth consideration that Boyle is the only American pewterer who is known to have advertised the sale of church cups. This same touch has also been found on pint basins, pint tankards, pint mugs with strap handles, beakers similar to the 'I. W.' beakers described above, and on at least one solid-handle porringer. The last three forms are so definitely American that we can place 'R. B.' positively in the American lists.

Touch number 589, Plate LXX, is with little question a mark of either Johann Christian Höran of Philadelphia (1751–1786) or Johann Christopher Heyne of Lancaster (1754–1781). The claims of both men are equally good. So for the time being, the touch must be classified as that of an unidentified maker. The photograph is from a $9\frac{5}{16}$-inch plate owned by J. P. Remensnyder.

Number 590 is the mark of an unknown Philadelphia pewterer who was working in 1775 or earlier. It was photographed in the bottom of Mr. Good's historic 'Ickes' mug (Plate XIX, 118).

I realize that I am treading upon extremely dangerous ground in listing as unidentified the 'P. R.' touch, here illustrated as number 591. It has been found on a porringer impressed abnormally in the well of the bowl (formerly in the collection of W. J. Sanborn) and on the handles of at least three spoons of early design. Each of these items,

I believe, is considered by its owner to have come from the shop of Paul Revere, Boston patriot, silversmith, engraver, coppersmith, bell-founder, dentist, and merchant.

Although Revere's name has appeared in practically every previous list of American pewterers, I doubt whether the man ever worked in that metal. We do know that as a merchant he advertised the sale of pewter along with other items of merchandise from tacks to looking glasses, but assuredly that gives us no more warrant for listing him as a pewterer than for stating that he was a looking-glass manufacturer. It may be significant that upon at least one occasion he offered for sale 'Imported Hardware,' specifically listing pewter under that heading. Moreover, his day books, which fortunately have been preserved, disclose no evidence of pewter-making. But, for the sake of argument, let us assume that Paul Revere did make pewter. What sort of designs should we expect from a man, reared in Boston, trained in the goldsmith's art, capable of noteworthy engraving, and generally considered a master of grace and line in silver? Surely not the 'P. R.' spoons which have been attributed to him. Interesting though they be, these spoons are more massive, clumsier, and earlier in design than any surviving spoon with an identifiable mark of an American pewterer. And what is said of the design of the spoon is equally true of the character of the touch. Consequently, I am forced to believe that although the mark may be American it certainly was not struck by Paul Revere.

Unidentified touches numbered 592 and 593 have been discussed in the story of William Elsworth. There are grounds for believing that one probably, and both possibly, were touches of that New York pewterer.

Touch number 594, perhaps the least rare of all the early unidentified marks, was employed by a pewterer of considerably more than average ability whose range of shapes was large. The touch was found on a fine communion flagon, once used by the old First Church of Springfield, Massachusetts, a vessel that was probably made about the time of the Revolution or earlier. I have seen the mark also on creamers, sprinklers, peppers, gravy boats, and other unusual forms. (See Plate XXX, 203, 205, and 214; and Plate XLII, 273.) The fact that such small items as peppers and creamers were rarely, if ever, marked in England lends credence to the belief that this was probably a touch of an unidentified American pewterer, perhaps one of our ablest makers.

Number 595 shows the initials 'T. S.' as found in quart pots and quart tankards with tulip-shaped bodies. The few examples that I have seen were traced to Connecticut or to New York near the Connecticut state line. They probably date from the period of the Revolution or the early Federal years.

Number 596, with initials 'T. L.' in a heart-shaped border or between the flukes of an anchor, is from a quart mug owned by John W. Poole. If the central design is an anchor, as it appears to be, the maker probably worked in Rhode Island. (Late eighteenth century.)

Number 597 is a very late touch, nineteenth century almost assuredly, of a Philadelphia pewterer. It bears close resemblance to a mark of J. H. Palethorp, but does not correspond exactly to that or any other previously listed mark.

Unidentified American Touches

Number 598 is found only on solid-handle porringers made in or near Westtown, Pennsylvania, probably late in the eighteenth century.

Touch number 599, last of the early marks, was photographed from a plate found in the Pennsylvania-Dutch country. The piece was formerly part of a communion set in a small church just west of York. Curiously enough, the plate is English and bears the touches of Townsend and Compton of London. The 'M. L.' mark is patently that of some local maker, through whose hands the English plate had passed. (Date *c.* 1810.)

All the remaining touches are positively American and all belong to the period from 1790 to 1830. Following J. B. Kerfoot's nomenclature, I shall designate them 'unidentified eagles' and number them to distinguish one from another.

Eagle number 1 (600) was illustrated in *American Pewter*. It is probably the mark of a man whose record is well established, whose other touches have long been known to us. It is by no means rare, but has been found only on basins, both the pint and quart sizes. The design of the touch should place it in the first half of the eagle period (1785 to 1805). The fact that this eagle is as crude as are all Gershom Jones's touches may be significant, for I have never seen a basin with a known touch of that maker, whereas Jones's fellow-townsman and contemporary, Samuel Hamlin, has left us many marked basins; and this despite the fact that Hamlin's plates are far rarer than those of Jones.

Unidentified Eagle number 5 (601) is a touch that should not remain among the unknown for long. The pewterer's last name was Griswold. The presumption is that this is another touch used by Ashbil Griswold of Meriden, but it may have been a mark of his brother, Sylvester, or his cousin, Giles. It was photographed from an $8\frac{5}{16}$-inch plate that was formerly in the collection of the late A. C. Bowman.

Eagle number 6 (602), last of the unidentified marks, furnishes the initials of its user 'A. B.' Its striking resemblance to touches of those two Connecticut-Pennsylvania makers, Thomas Danforth, Third, and Blakslee Barns, places it accurately in time (about 1810 to 1815) and provenance. If we could prove that Aaron Burdett, who was making pewter in Baltimore in the eighteen-thirties, was a Connecticut pewterer and started his career before 1820, there would be a justifiable basis for attributing this touch to him. The photograph is from one of three 8-inch plates found in Hagerstown, Maryland, by J. B. Kerfoot shortly before his death.

THE BRITANNIA PERIOD

ABOUT the year 1825 the trade of pewter-making in America was revolutionized by a radical change in methods of manufacture, a new process for shaping the metal. For hundreds of years pewterers had succeeded one another, each learning from his master the secrets of the trade. One generation after another used the same moulds, the same formulae, the same methods of working the metal. As time passed, various articles had undergone gradual changes in design, and during the eighteenth century horse- or water-power had succeeded the foot-treadle in turning the lathes; but, generally speaking, designs, tools, methods, and materials were much the same in 1800 as they had been three centuries earlier. Plates, dishes, spoons, mugs, tankards, and porringers were the backbone of the pewterer's business in the days of the Pilgrim Fathers, and the same forms (tankards excepted) made up the bulk of the pewter-maker's stock when James Monroe became President in 1817. But the period of the steamboat, of invention, and of mass production was at hand, and pewter-making, like everything else, was to be affected by the spirit of the times.

About 1800 in America, and probably several decades earlier in Great Britain, there came on the market a grade of pewter termed britannia metal. This composition, at the time of its introduction, was neither new nor untried. Practically the same formula — of exceptionally fine quality, high in its content of tin — had been used for many years in the manufacture of 'hard metal' plates. Most logical is J. B. Kerfoot's surmise that the British pewterers, in casting about for some means of stemming the onrushing popularity of china and glass, decided to dignify a superior grade of pewter with the patriotic and high-sounding trade-name of 'Britannia' metal.

At first no change in method of manufacture was entailed, but it was soon found that by further increasing the tin content, with but a small admixture of antimony, vessels could be made with thinner walls than in the past. It was but a short step then to the final change which revolutionized the industry — the forming of the metal in the shape desired after, not during, casting. The method was to cast the metal into flat sheets, regardless of the shapes in which it was to be finished, and to form the parts by pressing the sheets with blunt tools over inexpensive revolving blocks, made in the shape in which the parts were to be finished. This process, known as 'spinning,' had probably been in use in a limited way in America before 1800, but it was not until about 1825, when Hiram Yale imported English workmen to instruct his men in the technique of the new method, that the older processes gave way to the new. This innovation meant not only a great saving in the original cost of equipment (for it required no expensive brass moulds), but permitted greater production, and made possible thin, light vessels which could be readily fashioned into intricate shapes and designs with sharp edges and abrupt contours, such as pewter had never known.

That this change in process should have occurred when taste in design was approaching its lowest ebb was little short of a calamity. In the hands of such a master as William Will the new forms might have been converted into graceful compositions, but there were few men with the ability of the Wills making pewter in 1825.

Right here allow me to emphasize the fact that britannia — the metal itself — was a splendid ware. When cast (not spun) in a well-designed shape and in a vessel with thick walls it was the equal of the best contemporary pewter. I will go further and say that there are few if any who can distinguish by sight or touch the best britannia from the best pewter of the same period. It is for the shapes that the metal so frequently took that we should reserve our criticism.

With the coming of the new period we find an entirely new set of shapes. Instead of mugs, dishes, plates, basins, and porringers, the principal forms manufactured were tea-sets, coffee-pots, water pitchers, small beakers, whale-oil lamps, and candlesticks. Thin britannia spoons replaced those of pewter, and the communion sets of dignified design of the earlier day gave way before the more elaborate 'tin-panny' services which were turned out in such large numbers in the second quarter of the nineteenth century. A few pewterers, notably the Boardmans of Hartford, who had been taught in the old school, clung to the old traditions, and continued to make pewter plates, basins, porringers, etc., just as they had always done. Not that the Boardmans refused to accept the new order; but they sold lathe-turned pewter as well as spun britannia. They, however, were outstanding exceptions. In the main the new makers quickly adopted the new methods, discarding all too willingly the moulds, the shapes, and the traditions of an industry whose days were numbered.

J. B. Kerfoot in *American Pewter* termed this new period the 'Coffee-pot Era' because of the thousands of surviving examples of what nearly all of us had believed to be coffee-pots. In *Some Notes on American Pewterers*, Louis G. Myers made the observation that perhaps these coffee-pots were in reality large teapots. It was left to Percy E. Raymond to prove the correctness of that surmise, which he did most convincingly in the magazine *Antiques* (October, 1936, issue) in a study of the day book of William Calder. His analysis of Calder's entries of sales from 1826 to 1838 shows that the 'best sellers' throughout that period were teapots: the quart size in 1826, the three-pint in 1831, and the two-quart teapot in 1838. What we have been terming Calder coffee-pots hold only slightly more than two quarts, and there can be little doubt now that they were sold as teapots. To be sure, Calder did make coffee-pots, but such items represented a very small proportion of his trade. The infrequency of their sales and their considerably higher price prove pretty conclusively that they were of a more intricate design, probably percolators for drip coffee, of which one or two examples have been found. In this volume, therefore, what were formerly described as coffee-pots will be illustrated as tall teapots. Many are the designs of britannia teapots, but too few, unfortunately, are of real merit. In Plates LXXI and LXXII representative examples are illustrated.

Second only in importance to the teapot during this period and perhaps more truly American than any form in pewter made in this country was the whale-oil (or camphene) lamp. Lamps were made in Europe, but they bear little resemblance to most of the shapes developed in this country. So amazingly varied are the American designs that a collector might confine his activities to lamps alone with little hope of corralling an example of each variation — and an interesting collection he could make. Only a few of the many types can be illustrated here (Plates LXXV to LXXVII).

Of the other late forms, perhaps the pitcher was the most successful. Examples with and without cover are shown in Plate LXXIII. Small beakers were made by the thousand after 1830, but very few bear makers' marks.

One other large division of the britannia-maker's trade was composed of communion sets. Most of these sets are tragic illustrations of the decadence of the pewterer's art and craftsmanship, but the Trasks, the Boardmans, and a few other makers have left us well-designed and well-fashioned examples of their skill.

Although we note in general the evidence of a striving for originality, at the expense of the simplicity and well-rounded lines of the vessels formed by the earlier makers, it must not be assumed that the products of these years were devoid of taste. The water pitcher, usually made of thick metal, is a most satisfactory shape in spite of a graceless handle; many of the lamps (for instance, those of Endicott and Sumner or the Taunton Britannia Manufacturing Company) were not only of appropriate but graceful design; and the oft-praised Richardson sugar bowls were worthy of a master-pewterer of the eighteenth century. This list might be much further extended, but the truth remains that the nineteenth-century designs that were in good taste were outnumbered by the inartistic forms of that period, a statement which holds equally true for silver, furniture, or any other work of the craftsman.

MAKERS OF THE BRITANNIA PERIOD

WHEN communication was difficult and travel infrequent, when expensive moulds were never 'scrapped' simply because the forms for which they had been made were out of style, it is natural that the pewter of any particular locality should show at times marked characteristics which differentiated it from that of other districts. But, with the coming of the railroad and the steamboat and the utilization of inland waterways, all geographical barriers disappeared. Workmen moved freely and frequently from one section to another, and a new design that had originated, let us say, in Boston was soon common property in Baltimore or Cincinnati. The water pitchers of William McQuilkin of Philadelphia (to use an illustration) are almost identical with those of Rufus Dunham of Portland, Maine, and the touch of one is as uninteresting as that of the other; for that matter practically all late marks are merely makers' name-plates and catalogue numbers, devoid of character and lacking in individuality.

We shall, therefore, list the late workers alphabetically rather than geographically, and since our interest lies chiefly in the forms that were made and but incidentally in the makers, the comment upon each shop will be briefer than that allotted to the early men. Where the touches are known to the author, a sketch of each will accompany the text. After 1850 the major portion of the britannia manufactured was plated. I am therefore including in my list only a few shops which commenced business subsequent to that date, and then only because they have left us marked examples which were not plated. The list follows:

Andrew Allison. Listed as a pewterer at 65 George Street in Philadelphia Directories, 1837 to 1841.

John Allison. A pewterer on Hope Street, Philadelphia, 1835 to 1836.

Benjamin Archer. Listed as a britannia-ware manufacturer in St. Louis, Missouri, 1847.

Ellis S. Archer. A lamp has been found marked 'Archer's Patent, Philada., June 18th 1842.' Ellis S. Archer sold camphene oil and lamps at 32 North Second Street from 1843 to 1847. In the 1850 Directory he was at 119 Chestnut Street. For several years thereafter Archer and Warner sold gas fixtures and lamps at the same address.

Makers of the Britannia Period

Archer and Janney. Lamps have been found so marked. N. E. Janney and Company were listed as importers of and wholesale dealers in britannia and German silver ware in St. Louis in 1845. Benjamin Archer presumably manufactured britannia that was sold by N. E. Janney and Company.

Armitages and Standish. Location unknown. Probably working about 1840 or later. Their mark is from a late teapot owned by Charles F. Hutchins.   ARMITAGES & STANDISH

Babbitt and Crossman. Isaac, son of Ziba Babbitt, was born in Taunton, Massachusetts, July 26, 1799. He learned the watchmaker's trade, but in 1814 en-   BABBITT & CROSSMAN
tered into copartnership with William W. Crossman, a mechanic of
Taunton, for the manufacture of britannia ware. They made inkstands, shaving-boxes, looking-glass frames, beakers, teapots, and many other shapes. Their work was of excellent quality. The shop continued under virtually the same management until 1828, although the name was changed prior to that date to Babbitt, Crossman and Company. They were succeeded by Crossman, West and Leonard. Babbitt and Crossman were the founders of what grew to be the present firm of Reed and Barton, the only survivor of the pewter industry from early days.

The date 1814 should read 1824.

Babbitt, Crossman and Company. See Babbitt and Crossman.   BABBITT CROSSMAN & Cº

Timothy Bailey. Timothy Bailey was born in Westmoreland, New Hampshire, September 20, 1785. In early life he was a farmer and schoolmaster. From about 1807 to 1815 he peddled tinware and pewter for Burrage Yale of South Reading, Massachusetts. From 1815 to 1819 he made tinware in his own shop in Roxbury and then moved to Malden, Massachusetts, where he continued the business and became a prominent citizen of the town. About 1830 he took into business with him his nephew, James H. Putnam, under the firm name of Bailey and Putnam. They separated soon thereafter and each had a shop of his own. Bailey was town treasurer and a bank president in later life, and probably made little if any britannia ware after 1840, but at one time he employed eight workmen and sixteen peddlers. He died in Malden November 19, 1852. I have never seen any article marked with Bailey's name alone, but examples by Bailey and Putnam exist.

Bailey and Putnam. See above. Their shop was at the corner of Main and Madison Streets, Malden, Massachusetts, about 1830 to 1835.   BAILEY
&
PUTNAM

L. G. Baldwin. A britannia-maker of Meriden, Connecticut, employing five hands in 1849.

William Bartholdt. A maker of candlesticks and perhaps other forms at Williamsburgh, New York, 1850–1854.

Morris Benham. Listed in the *New England Mercantile Directory* of 1849 as a britannia manufacturer at West Meriden, Connecticut.

Benham and Whitney. Advertised in the *New England Mercantile Directory* of 1849 as britannia-makers at 272½ Pearl Street, New York. They were probably New York sales agents for Morris Benham's shop in West Meriden, and possibly for J. B. Graves in Middletown.

Henry S. Boardman. Born in Hartford, Connecticut, in 1820, a son of Sherman Boardman. He is listed as a pewterer at 67 Trumbull Street in the Hartford Directory of 1841, but was probably in his father's employ at that time. He was in Philadelphia in 1844 as a resident member of the firm of Boardman and Hall, supposedly a sales office for T. D. and S. Boardman of Hartford. He is presumed to have been a member of the firms which succeeded Boardman and Hall, namely, Hall, Boardman and Company, and Hall and Boardman. In 1845 he   BOARDMAN PHILADA
apparently worked alone for one year at 106 North Third Street and
later had a shop at 243 Arch Street. He was selling britannia at the latter address as late as 1861. One beaker of a very poor quality of britannia, marked with his individual touch, is illustrated in J. B. Kerfoot's *American Pewter*. Henry Boardman died in 1895.

J. D. Boardman. Listed as a pewterer at 58 Main Street in the Hartford Directory of 1828. He was related to Thomas and Sherman Boardman and was probably only an employee in their shop, which was directly across the street from the address given above.

Luther Boardman. Born at Rocky Hill, Connecticut, December 26, 1812. He was apprenticed to Ashbil Griswold at Meriden, where he learned the britannia trade. In 1833 he was in the employ of Burrage Yale at South Reading, Massachusetts, operated the shop for Yale, and became its proprietor in 1836. He employed four hands in the shop. In 1837 he returned to Meriden and married Lydia Ann Frary of that city. In 1838 he was employed by Russell and Beach at Chester, Connecticut, and later made britannia, principally spoons, in his own shop in that town. In 1842 he moved to East Haddam, Connecticut, continuing the same business, but most of his product thereafter was plated ware. He died March 29, 1887. I have seen a few teapots by this maker which were probably made in South Reading or Chester and a great number of spoons of late appearance bearing a small   L.B
initial touch, 'L.B.,' attributed to Luther Boardman.

Sherman Boardman. See volume I, page 128.

Thomas D. Boardman. See volume I, page 128 and Plate LVII.

T. D. and S. Boardman. See volume I, page 128 and Plate LVII.   B X w

Timothy Boardman and Company. Timothy Boardman, younger brother of Thomas and Sherman, was born in Hartford in 1798 and died in New York City,   TB&Cº
February 24, 1825. He was sent to New York in 1822 as local agent for

his brothers and opened a shop at 178 Water Street. Pewter marked 'T. B. & Co.' was made in Hartford for sale through Timothy Boardman and Company in New York.

Boardman and Company. Listed at 178 Water Street, New York, 1825 to 1827, successors to Timothy Boardman and Company. Controlled and probably owned by the Boardmans of Hartford. Its pewter, manufactured in Hartford, covered the complete Boardman line and included practically everything that was made in pewter at that period. No contemporaries excelled, and few equaled, the Boardman quality. See Plate LVII.

Boardman and Hall. At 436 High Street, Philadelphia, 1844. The Philadelphia branch store of T. D. and S. Boardman of Hartford. The local agents were Henry S. Boardman and Franklin D. Hall. They sold the full Boardman line and probably made no pewter locally.

Boardman and Hart. At 178 Water Street, New York, from 1827 until 1831, and at 6 Burling Slip from 1831 until 1850; successors to Boardman and Company. Lucius Hart, a native of Rocky Hill, Connecticut, was a partner in the firm and local manager for the Boardmans of Hartford. See Plate LVII.

John Bouis. Listed as a 'Lamp Manufacturer and tinplate worker' at 106 Baltimore Street in the Baltimore Directory of 1829. In 1831–1832 the name is John Bouis and Son at the same address. In 1833–1834 John Bouis is listed as a 'double block tin ware and lamp manufacturer' at 16 South Street.

John Bouis and Son. See above.

Joseph Bouis. A lamp-maker on South Street, Baltimore, in 1834. Presumably a son of John Bouis.

Brook Farm. Brook Farm was a co-operative community established at West Roxbury, Massachusetts, in 1841. Nathaniel Hawthorne, Charles A. Dana, and many other prominent men of that day interested themselves in the experiment. At some time during the span of its existence from 1841 to 1847 an attempt, not wholly successful, was made to manufacture britannia teapots and lamps.

David S. Brooks. Listed as a pewterer at 27 Trumbull Street in the Hartford Directory of 1828. Thereafter he was a dealer in tinware and stoves.

Browe and Dougherty. Listed as 'Lamp-makers and Britannia Ware' in the Newark, New Jersey, Directory of 1845.

Townsend M. Buckley. A lamp-maker of Troy, New York, 1854–1857. Burton N. Gates reported a lamp marked with this man's name.

Bull, Lyman and Couch, successors to Lyman and Couch. In a list of britannia factories in Meriden, Connecticut, dated 1845, this concern was recorded as having a shop inventory valued at three thousand dollars and a force of seven men. The partners were Bull, William W. Lyman, and Ira Couch.

Makers of the Britannia Period

A. Burdett. A pewterer at 27 South Liberty Street, Baltimore, 1838 to 1841.

J. W. Cahill and Company. The mark of this firm was found upon a teapot made about 1830 to 1840. Nothing whatever is known about the makers.

William Calder. Main Street, Providence, Rhode Island, 1817 to 1856. (See volume I, page 100.)

PROVIDENCE

John Calverley. A britannia-maker on Parrish Street, Philadelphia, in 1840 and on Orange Street in 1841.

William E. Camp. Listed as a britannia manufacturer at Middletown, Connecticut, in the *New England Mercantile Directory* of 1849.

Ephraim Capen. A partner in Capen and Molineux who, just before or just after the duration of the partnership, must have manufactured britannia ware in a shop of his own. Lamps and teapots of no particular merit have been found marked 'E. Capen.'

E·CAPEN

Capen and Molineux. Lamp-makers at 132 William Street, New York, 1848 to 1854. The partners were Ephraim Capen and George Molineux. Their lamps are plentiful, but none that I have seen was in any way distinguished.

Oren Colton. A partner of J. B. Woodbury in Philadelphia in 1835 and 1836. Prior to that time (from 1826 to 1835) he was a 'shuttle maker and brass-founder.' I have seen a well-fashioned baptismal bowl stamped with his name alone, and assume that for a short time he made britannia in a shop of his own.

O.COLTON

S. L. Cone. Listed as a britannia-maker employing four hands in Meriden, Connecticut, in 1849.

Thomas Connell. Listed as a pewterer at 48 Duke Street in Philadelphia Directories from 1829 to 1831. In 1837 he was following the same business at 55 North Sixth Street. In 1839 and 1840 he was a partner of J. H. Palethorp in J. H. Palethorp and Company at 144 High Street.

Ira Couch, Meriden, Connecticut. See Bull, Lyman and Couch.

Crossman, West and Leonard, successors to Babbitt, Crossman and Company at Taunton, Massachusetts. In 1828 William W. Crossman was joined by William Allen West and Zephaniah A. Leonard, Isaac Babbitt remaining with the firm as a metallurgist, in which capacity he invented 'Babbitt metal.' The product of the firm consisted chiefly of britannia coffee-pots, tea services, and communion sets. The firm was reorganized in 1830 as the Taunton Britannia Manufacturing Company.

CROSSMAN
WEST&LEONARD

[99]

PLATE LXXI — *Late Teapots*

603, 604, and 605. Three teapots of the 1825–1830 period in the author's collection. 603 and 604, measuring respectively 6¾ inches and 7⅝ inches over all in height, were made by Daniel Curtiss, Albany, New York, 1822–1840. 605, 7½ inches tall, was made by John H. Palethorp, Philadelphia, 1820–1845. This rather ingenious form was made from a pint-mug mould, a simple and dignified design that was marred by a handle of grotesque silhouette.

606. A fine teapot of late design (after 1830) made by Roswell Gleason, Dorchester, Massachusetts, 1822–1860. The pot alone is a well-proportioned piece of pleasing outline. The author feels that the composition would have been even finer had not Gleason, in his design of spout and handle terminals, been catering to the desire of his generation for 'elegance.' Assuredly one of the handsomest of the later teapots. Height 8¾ inches over all. Collection of Mrs. Chester Pratt.

607 and 608. Two of the most desirable shapes of the period. From the collection of Charles F. Hutchins. 607, a form aptly termed by Mr. Kerfoot a pigeon-breasted pot, is 9⅛ inches high over all, and was also made by Gleason in Dorchester. 608, popularly termed a lighthouse pot, measures 12 inches in height. Its design is honest, simple, and dignified. Maker, Israel Trask, Beverly, Massachusetts, 1825–1856.

609, 610, and 611. Three tall teapots in the author's collection, made respectively by Boardman and Company, New York, 1825–1827, Daniel Curtiss, Albany, 1822–1840, and Josiah Danforth, Middletown, Connecticut, 1825–1837. Their heights are 11¾, 10½, and 9⅞ inches respectively. The design of the handle of 611 seems particularly unfortunate.

PLATE LXXI

603   604   605

606   607   608

609   610   611

Plate LXXII — *Tea Sets*

612. Another example of the skill of Roswell Gleason, Dorchester, Massachusetts, 1822–1860, as a designer and a craftsman. An exquisite little teapot of the britannia period. Measurements and present location not known. Formerly in the collection of J. G. Braecklein, Esq.

613 and 614. Sugar bowls of the britannia period measuring approximately 7 and 6 inches respectively in height. 613 was made by the Taunton Britannia Manufacturing Company, Taunton, Massachusetts, 1830–1835, and is owned by Miss Alice D. Laughlin. 614 was made by Boardman and Company, New York, 1825–1827. The lid seems too small and may not have been made for this bowl. Collection of the author.

615. Unusual teapot on ball feet which follows the design of silver teapots of the final quarter of the eighteenth century. Height 6⅛ inches over all. Made by Israel Trask, Beverly, Massachusetts, 1825–1856, and is almost certainly one of his early pieces. Note the chiseled decoration which Trask so often used with taste and restraint. Collection of Mrs. Arthur J. Oldham.

616 and 617. Sugar bowl and pitcher, formerly in the collection of the late Albert C. Bowman, measuring approximately 5 and 7¼ inches respectively in over-all height. Maker, G. Richardson, Cranston, Rhode Island, probably about 1825–1835. It is interesting to note that the lower sections of both pieces are from the same moulds. Richardson's sugar-bowl design is generally considered one of the most desirable forms of the period.

618 to 621. Handsome tea set of late design made by the Taunton Britannia Manufacturing Company, Taunton, Massachusetts, 1830–1835. Heights of pots 8¾ and 10⅞ inches respectively, sugar bowl 7½ inches, creamer 5⅜ inches. Collection of the Honorable and Mrs. George V. Smith.

PLATE LXXII

615

614

613

612

621

620

619

618

617

616

Edwin E. Curtis. Had a small shop in Meriden, Connecticut, from about 1838 to 1845.

Enos H. Curtis. Probably a brother of Edwin. Employed two hands in a small shop at Meriden, Connecticut, in 1845.

Lemuel J. Curtis. From 1836 to 1838 Curtis was a partner of Isaac C. Lewis in Meriden, Connecticut, under the name of Lewis and Curtis. From 1838 until about 1840 he worked with his brother, Edwin. He had a small shop of his own in Meriden from about 1840 to 1845. In 1846 he joined forces with William W. Lyman. On the formation of the Meriden Britannia Company in 1852, Curtis became one of its directors. I have seen several teapots marked 'L. J. Curtiss.'

L.J.CURTISS

Curtis and Lyman. See Lemuel J. Curtis.

Daniel Curtiss. Albany, New York, 1822 to 1850. See page 32. An outstandingly able maker of his period. His quality, design, and workmanship were of the best.

Joseph Curtiss, Junior. Brother of Daniel. Troy, New York, 1827 to 1832; Albany, New York, 1832 to 1858. (See page 33.)

Josiah Danforth. Middletown, Connecticut, 1825 to 1837. (See volume I, page 117.)

Thomas S. Derby. Middletown, Connecticut, 1818 to about 1850. (See volume I, page 135.)

Thomas S. Derby, Junior. Middletown, Connecticut. Son of Thomas S. Derby. He was born in 1820 and became associated with his father. The firm name in 1849 was Thomas S. Derby and Son. I have heard of a teapot marked 'T. S. Derby, II,' so the younger man may have worked alone for a short time. He died in Middletown in 1850.

Thomas S. Derby and Son. See Thomas S. Derby, Junior.

C. B. De Riemer and Company. Cornelius Brouwer De Riemer, born in New York, June 14, 1804, was a silversmith and jeweler with a shop in Ithaca, New York, in 1831. He moved soon thereafter to Auburn, New York, where he died in 1872. Small beakers made in Auburn, testify to his work in pewter, at least for a short period.

C.B.DE RIEMER&C° AUBURN

E. Dunham. A lamp marked with this name was included in the Twentieth Century Club Exhibit of Pewter in Boston in 1924.

Rufus Dunham. Born in Saco, Maine, May 30, 1815. As a boy he ran away to Portland and bound himself for three years as an apprentice to Allan Porter in Stevens Plains, Westbrook, Maine, in 1831 for two suits of clothes per annum, his board, and fifty dollars in cash. In 1833 he broke the contract because he was not paid for overtime work. For the next four years he was working at first for Roswell Gleason at Dorchester and later in a shop in Poughkeepsie, New York. In the latter town he purchased moulds and tools in 1837 and returned to Stevens Plains to open a shop of his own, with his brother John as his helper. At first his lathe was operated by foot-power,

R.DUNHAM   R DUNHAM

then by a horse on a treadmill, and finally by a steam engine — he was the second man in Maine to use steam-power. At one time he employed twenty or thirty men and his wares were peddled in northern New England and Canada. In 1861 his buildings were burned and the business was moved to Portland. His sons, Joseph S. and Frederick, were taken in as partners, under the firm name of *Rufus Dunham and Sons*, sometime subsequent to that date. The business was liquidated in 1882.

Rufus Dunham was twice married, first to Emiline Stevens of Westbrook, second to Emma B. Sargent of Portland. He had eleven children. Long before his death he had become one of the most respected citizens of Portland. I have seen Dunham teapots, water pitchers, lamps, candlesticks, and communion flagons. A great many examples of his work have survived, and in quality they are well above the average for that period.

R. Dunham and Sons. See Rufus Dunham.

Eli Eldredge. Eldredge had a shop at 15 Hawley Street, Boston, for one year only, 1849. In 1860 he was working in Taunton, Massachusetts.

John Ellison. Listed as a pewterer at 246 North Second Street in the Philadelphia Directory for 1837. Possibly the same as John Allison, *q.v.*

Edmund Endicott. See Endicott and Sumner.

Endicott and Sumner. Edmund Endicott and William F. Sumner made lamps and candlesticks first at 106 Elm Street, later at 195 William Street, New York City, from 1846 until 1851, and Endicott worked alone at the latter address for two years longer. Probably no lampmakers turned out such uniformly well-designed pieces. Their swinging lamps in particular are much sought for today. Taste is evident in all of their work, and even their touch-mark is reminiscent of the heyday of pewter.

Gaius and Jason Fenn. 35 Peck Slip, New York, about 1840. Makers of inkwells, molasses gates (see Plate LXXVII) and faucets.

Asa F. Flagg. An Englishman by birth who made britannia ware in Cincinnati, Ohio, from 1842 to 1846. From 1846 to 1854 he was associated with Henry Homan in H. Homan and Company, britannia and plated wares, Cincinnati.

Flagg and Homan. See above.

Thomas Fletcher. A britannia-maker of Philadelphia, Pennsylvania. His address was 83 St. John Street in 1837, 22 Pegg Street in 1841.

Makers of the Britannia Period

Daniel Francis. A partner in Whitmore and Francis, 9 Ellicott Square, Buffalo, New York, in 1833. From 1835 to 1842 he worked alone at 239 Main Street.

James A. Frary. In 1845 in West Meriden, Connecticut, James Frary employed eight hands in a shop, the inventory of which was valued at four thousand dollars. He is listed as a britannia manufacturer in the same town in the *New England Mercantile Directory* of 1849.

Frary and Benham. Britannia-makers of Meriden employing ten men in 1849. This firm probably represents a merger of the shops of James A. Frary and Morris Benham.

Fuller and Smith. This firm is listed in the *Connecticut Business Directory* of 1851 as makers of a complete line of britannia ware including tea-sets, goblets, lamps, candlesticks, etc. Their shop was at 'Pequonoc Bridge, New London County.' They may have commenced business a few years earlier. I have seen nothing but lamps and candlesticks bearing their mark.

–y and Gardner. I have a rubbing of a mark on a teapot for this partnership. The makers and their place of work are now unknown.

Anthony George, Junior. A britannia-maker of Philadelphia. His addresses as given in the city Directories are as follows: 1839, 7 Pennsylvania Avenue; 1844, 25 Plum Street; 1847, 607 South Second Street.

Gerhardt and Company. Makers of snuffboxes, etc. Location unknown. After 1840.

Roswell Gleason. Born in Putney, Vermont, April 6, 1799. Roswell Gleason settled in Dorchester, Massachusetts, in 1818 and worked at the tinware trade under a Mr. Wilcox. He married Rebecca T. Vose of Dorchester in 1822. In the same year Gleason began the manufacture of block tin and pewter in his own shop, and about 1830 britannia-making was commenced. In 1837 the Massachusetts Charitable Mechanic Association awarded a medal and diploma to Gleason for his products. Although he had but six employees working for him that year, the concern grew soon thereafter to be one of Dorchester's leading industries. At one time one hundred and twenty-five men were employed. After 1850

ROSWELL GLEASON

most of the product was plated ware. The business was wound up in 1871. Roswell Gleason died January 27, 1887, a prominent, wealthy, and respected citizen.

With the possible exceptions of the Boardman establishment at Hartford and Reed and Barton at Taunton, Gleason's was the largest britannia manufactory in this country. Most of his work was fine and some of it displays considerable originality. The frequency with which examples of his work have been pictured in Plates LXXI to LXXVII testifies to my high regard for Gleason's skill in design.

Glennore Company. Cranston, Rhode Island, after 1828. (See G. Richardson, page 111.)

Jasper Graham. See Graham and Savage.

John B. Graham. See Graham and Savage.

Graham and Savage. On February 10, 1837, Josiah Danforth of Middletown, Connecticut, sold to Jasper Graham of Wethersfield and William H. Savage of Middletown property at the corner of Main and Mill Streets, Middletown, with his britannia factory and the steam engine and fixtures thereon. Seven months later Jasper Graham disposed of his one-half interest therein to John B. Graham of Middletown, and the firm name was changed from Graham and Savage to Savage and Graham. In 1838 Savage and Graham took a mortgage on the property from William Savage of Berlin, who apparently operated the plant for about a year; but in February, 1839, the latter failed to meet his interest payments and the property was quitclaimed to William H. Savage. Whether or not the business was continued after that date remains undetermined. Teapots resembling in design those of Ashbil Griswold of Meriden are found with the marks of Savage and Savage and Graham.

H. H. Graves. Henry H. Graves of Middletown, Connecticut, is listed as a pewterer in the *New England Mercantile Directory* of 1849. He made teapots, candlesticks, and other forms of average merit. (See J. B. and H. H. Graves.)   `H.H.GRAVES`

J. B. Graves. Joshua B. Graves, of Middletown, assigned ownership to a lot in Westfield, Middletown, with the britannia factory thereon, to a number of creditors, including Benham and Whitney, on February 6, 1849.   `J.B.GRAVES`
(See J. B. and H. H. Graves.)

J. B. and H. H. Graves. It is my supposition that Joshua and Henry Graves worked independently prior to the former's insolvency in 1849, and that the latter event was the occasion for their partnership.   `J.B.&H.H.GRAVES`
At any rate, a Middletown deed of 1852 indicates that they were working together in that year. Comments upon the pewter of Henry Graves are applicable also to that of the partnership.

Samuel Green, Junior. Pewterer and block-tin manufacturer of Boston, Massachusetts. His shop was at 14 Second Street, South Boston, in 1826, and in Fifth Street from 1828 to 1835. (See volume I, pages 78–79.)

Ashbil Griswold. A pewterer and britannia-maker of Meriden, Connecticut, 1807 to about 1835. (See volume I, page 127.) His later work included teapots, ladles, small beakers, soap boxes, sugar bowls, and inkwells. The quality and design of his wares was somewhat above the average of the later makers. Griswold seems to have had a very large trade.

Griswold and Couch. Although Ashbil Griswold is said to have taken Ira Couch into

PLATE LXXIII — *Pitchers, etc.*

622, 623, and 624. Open-top pitchers measuring $7\frac{5}{8}$, $6\frac{7}{8}$, and $5\frac{3}{8}$ inches respectively to top of pitcher, exclusive of spout and handle. The makers (left to right) were J. H. Palethorp (marked 'Palethorp's'), Philadelphia, 1820–1845, Daniel Curtiss, Albany, 1822–1840, and Henry Hopper, New York, 1842–1847. Collection of the author.

625 and 626. Two small covered pitchers. 625, smallest of covered pitchers, measuring just $5\frac{1}{2}$ inches over all, made by T. Sage and Company, St. Louis, Missouri, 1847, was formerly in the collection of William Mitchell Van Winkle, Esq. — a rare little piece. 626, height $7\frac{5}{8}$ inches, Boardman and Company, New York, 1825–1827, belongs to the author.

627. One of the handsomest of covered pitchers. Height 11 inches, Daniel Curtiss, Albany, 1822–1840. Courtesy of the Mabel Brady Garvan Collection, Gallery of Fine Arts, Yale University.

628. A dignified communion flagon in the best taste of the britannia period. Height $11\frac{7}{8}$ inches over all, bottom diameter $5\frac{11}{16}$ inches. Israel Trask, Beverly, Massachusetts, 1825–1856. Collection of Charles K. Davis, Esq.

629. A well-proportioned coffee-urn. Height 14 inches, exclusive of wooden base. Roswell Gleason, Dorchester, Massachusetts, 1822–1860. Collection of the author.

630. A most unusual form of decidedly Continental appearance which bears the mark of James H. Putnam, Malden, Massachusetts, 1830–1855. Nothing even roughly approximating such a shape has been found heretofore with an American touch. Height 10 inches over all. Collection of Mrs. J. Insley Blair.

PLATE LXXIII

622   623   624

625   626   627

628   629   630

PLATE LXXIV — *Candlesticks*

631. An unusually fine eighteenth-century candlestick, one of a pair in the collection of Albert H. Good, Esq. Height 6 inches. We have no means of determining the provenance of these candlesticks, but illustrate one as a form which antedated the shapes in use in this country in the nineteenth century.

632. A saucer candlestick with opening for scissor snuffers and form for conical snuffer. Maker unknown. Late eighteenth or early nineteenth century. Height $3\frac{3}{4}$ inches over all. Collection of the author.

633. Well-designed small candlestick. Height $4\frac{1}{2}$ inches. Fuller and Smith, New London County, Connecticut, 1851. Collection of Charles K. Davis, Esq.

634. Saucer candlestick with candle ejector. Height $4\frac{5}{8}$ inches. Lewis and Cowles, Meriden, Connecticut, 1834–1836. Collection of John P. Remensnyder, Esq.

635. Fine tall candlestick. Height 12 inches. Henry Hopper, New York, 1842–1847. Reproduced from *American Pewter* through the courtesy of the late Mrs. J. B. Kerfoot.

636. Handsomest of all American tall candlesticks. Height $12\frac{1}{4}$ inches. The Taunton Britannia Manufacturing Company, Taunton, Massachusetts, 1830–1835. Reproduced from *American Pewter* with the kind permission of the late Mrs. J. B. Kerfoot.

637. Saucer candlestick. Height $4\frac{1}{8}$ inches. Charles Ostrander, New York, 1848–1854. Courtesy of J. G. Braecklein, Esq.

638. Saucer candlestick. Height 4 inches. Roswell Gleason, Dorchester, Massachusetts, 1822–1860. Collection of the author.

639. Another Henry Hopper candlestick (see 635) in a smaller size. Height 10 inches. Collection of the author.

640. A candlestick of interesting design. Height $9\frac{1}{2}$ inches. Boardman and Hart, New York, 1827–1850. Collection of the author.

641. A candlestick made by Roswell Gleason, Dorchester, Massachusetts, 1822–1860. Height $8\frac{5}{8}$ inches. Collection of the author.

642. Another Gleason shape. Height about 10 inches. Courtesy of J. G. Braecklein, Esq.

PLATE LXXIV

631

632

633

634

635

636

637

638

639

640

641

642

partnership with him at Meriden about 1830, I have heard of no pewter marked Griswold and Couch.

G. & W. The mark in the inset is from a late teapot. The W may stand for Whitlock. See under that name.

Franklin D. Hall. Listed in the Hartford, Connecticut, Directory of 1840 as a pewterer, Hall was probably at that time an employee of the Boardmans, whom he later served as a Philadelphia agent. (See Boardman and Hall.)

Hall, Boardman and Company. Successors to Boardman and Hall, at 104 North Third Street, Philadelphia, from 1846 to 1848. In an advertisement in the front of the Philadelphia Directory of 1847 they offered for sale many forms including five gallon pitchers and 'pewter plates.' They were distributors for T. D. and S. Boardman of Hartford, Connecticut.

Hall and Boardman. Britannia ware. Successors to Hall, Boardman and Company, 104 North Third Street, Philadelphia, 1849 to 1855, and at 95 Arch Street, in 1856 and 1857.

Hall and Cotton. Location unknown. Probably worked about 1840 and later. An inkwell of their manufacture was illustrated in J. B. Kerfoot's *American Pewter*. A handsome syrup jug which they made may be seen in Plate LXXVII, 670.

Samuel E. Hamlin. Pewterer and britannia-maker on Main Street, Providence, Rhode Island, from 1801 to about 1856. (See volume I, pages 95–97.)

Joseph Harrison. Pewterer and britannia-maker of Philadelphia. His shop was in Baker's Court from 1829 to 1833, at 10 Perkenpine's Court from 1834 to 1844, at 3 Baker's Court again in 1847, and thereafter until 1852 at 589 North Front Street.

Lucius D. Hart. Born at Stepney, Connecticut, July 31, 1803; will probated in New York City February 23, 1871. A partner in Boardman and Hart, *q.v.*

S. S. Hers(ey?). The late A. C. Bowman owned a nineteenth-century teapot marked with this name (partially obliterated). The maker has not been identified.

John Hill. John Hill sold and presumably made britannia ware at 61 Elizabeth Street, New York City, in 1846. In 1848 his shop was at 44 Eldridge Street.

Charles Hillsburgh. A plumber and pewterer at 342 Water Street, New York, in 1837.

Robert Holmes and Sons. Makers of britannia ware at 15 East Pratt Street, Baltimore, in 1853 and 1854. Their work has little merit.

Thomas R. Holt. Although I have seen nothing but spoons bearing this man's mark, he had the largest britannia manufactory in Meriden, Connecticut, in 1845. At that time he was employing eight men.

Henry Homan. See Homan and Company.

Homan and Company. Henry Homan and Asa Flagg made britannia ware under this firm name in Cincinnati, Ohio, from 1847 to 1854. Flagg retired in 1854 and thereafter the major portion of the product was plated ware. The company made teapots, communion flagons, water pitchers, etc. The Homan pieces are well made, but in some instances have the mid-Victorian tendency toward overdecoration. Two Homan lamps are to be seen in Plate LXXV.

HOMAN & CO
CINCINNATI

HOMAN & CO
CINCINNATI

Henry Hopper. Hopper was a maker of candlesticks, lamps, water pitchers, and probably other britannia forms. His shop was at 234 Second Street, New York, from 1842 to 1847. His tall candlesticks are among the choice examples of the best work of this period. (See Plate LXXIV.)

H·HOPPER

E. N. Horsford. Nothing is known about this maker. I have record of one lamp marked 'E. N. Horsford's Patent.'

Houghton and Wallace. Thomas Houghton and John F. Wallace of Philadelphia took out a patent on a lamp in 1843. I am told that at least one such lamp has been reported.

Edwin House. Listed as a pewterer on Union Street, Hartford, Connecticut, from 1841 to 1846; probably an employee of the Boardmans.

Willis Humiston. Son of Ephraim A. Humiston of North Haven, Connecticut. He moved first to Wallingford and later to Troy, New York. In the Troy Directory of 1857 he is listed as a candle-mould manufacturer. I have seen one or two teapots, marked 'W. Humiston, Troy, N.Y.,' which must have been made about 1840.

W. HUMISTON
TROY N.Y

S. Hunt. A teapot of little merit and of late design has been found impressed with this man's name.

S HUNT

George Hunter. Listed as a pewterer in the Troy, New York, Directory of 1831.

Martin Hyde. Hyde was a britannia manufacturer at 44 Eldridge Street, New York City, in 1857 and 1858. His work is not distinguished.

M·HYDE

D. M. H. I have record of one teapot made after 1830, marked as per inset. The maker has not been identified.

DMH

Daniel H. Jagger, James H. Jagger, Walter W. Jagger. Listed as pewterers in Hartford Directories from 1839 to 1846. These men were in all probability merely employees of the Boardmans.

Edward Jones. A lamp manufacturer at 80 Elizabeth Street, New York City, from 1837 to 1841. In 1842 and 1843 his shop was at 54 Elizabeth Street. He was still in the lamp business as late as 1850. The mark shown here is presumed to have been his.

JONES

De Witt Kimberly. Kimberly employed three men in a small britannia factory in Meriden, Connecticut, in 1845. The mark shown here, found on a teapot owned by Mrs. Frank M. Colman, is attributed with reservations to this maker.

D.W.K

W. W. Knight and Company. William Knight was a hardware dealer at 229 High Street, Philadelphia, from 1839 to 1850 and later. At some time in that period he sold britannia teapots stamped with his name.

Lewis Kruiger. Listed as a pewterer at 119 Callowhill Street, Philadelphia, in 1833. I have seen nothing that he made except ladles.

Leonard, Reed and Barton, successors to the Taunton Britannia Manufacturing Company of Taunton, Massachusetts, in 1835. The partners were Gustavus Leonard, Henry G. Reed, and Charles E. Barton. They employed about twelve men. The principal products were communion vessels, tea-sets, and lamps. At the exhibition of the American Institute in New York in 1838 they were awarded a gold medal for quality, neatness, and elegance of finish. Upon Leonard's death in 1840 the firm name was changed to Reed and Barton. (See under that title.)

Isaac C. Lewis. Isaac C. Lewis was born October 19, 1812, and at the age of fifteen was apprenticed to Hiram Yale at Wallingford, Connecticut, to learn the britannia trade. In 1834 he opened a shop at East Meriden with George Cowles as partner. In 1836 the firm name became Lewis and Curtis, Lemuel J. Curtis replacing Cowles. With Daniel B. Wells, a former apprentice, Lewis organized in 1839 I. C. Lewis and Company, an establishment which remained in business until absorbed in 1852 by the newly formed Meriden Britannia Company, of which Lewis himself became president. The shop of I. C. Lewis and Company employed five men in 1845, eight men in 1849. I have seen nothing made in the Lewis shops except teapots and two or three diminutive tasters which were rather crudely made — souvenirs, perhaps, for some anniversary celebration.

I. C. Lewis and Company. East Meriden, Connecticut, 1839 to 1852. (See Isaac C. Lewis.)

Lewis and Cowles. East Meriden, Connecticut, 1834 to 1836. (See Isaac C. Lewis.) An unusual candlestick made by this firm is illustrated in Plate LXXIV, 634.

Lewis and Curtis. East Meriden, Connecticut, 1836 to 1839. (See Isaac C. Lewis.)

J. D. Locke. Listed at various addresses in New York City from 1835 to 1860 and later. A maker of teapots of no distinction.

Locke and Carter. From 1837 to 1845 J. D. Locke's partner was a man named Carter. Their shop was on Water Street, New York.

I. Love. Very crude and, it would seem, thoroughly impractical pewter cups and saucers of poor quality were made by this man in Baltimore, Maryland. Probably after 1840.

For the words "large syringe" substitute "sausage stuffer"

I. Lowe. The touch of this maker was found on a large syringe. He probably worked prior to 1840.

William W. Lyman. Born at Woodford, Vermont, in 1821. At the age of fifteen he moved to Meriden, Connecticut, to learn the britannia business in the shop of Griswold and Couch. In 1844, with Ira Couch, he made spoons 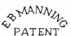 at Meriden, and in the following year the firm became Bull, Lyman and Couch. At about 1846 he was associated with Lemuel J. Curtis, and in 1849 had a shop of his own that employed six hands. He became a director of the Meriden Britannia Company upon its organization in 1852. I have seen one tall teapot marked 'Lyman,' and hope that its quality and lines are not representative of its maker's taste and ability.

Lyman and Couch. Meriden, Connecticut, 1844. (See William W. Lyman.)

William McQuilkin. 91 North Second Street, Philadelphia, from 1845 to 1853; a maker of teapots and water pitchers whose work is representative of the period.

E. B. Manning. A britannia manufacturer of Middletown, Connecticut, about 1850 to 1862 and later.

Thaddeus Manning. A britannia manufacturer of Middletown, Connecticut, in 1849.

Manning, Bowman and Company, of Middletown, Connecticut, listed in the *Connecticut Business Directory* of 1866 as britannia ware manufacturers. Their mark was found on a chalice of late design.

Marston. I have seen a lamp and have heard of a teapot marked 'Marston, Baltimore.' All of the Marstons in the directories of that city from 1825 to 1850 were engaged in the glass, china, and crockery business. At least one member of the family, however, seems to have sold pewter also, for a brief period, probably after 1840.

Marcus Maton. Listed as a pewterer in the Hartford, Connecticut, Directory of 1828.

Meriden Britannia Company. This company represented a merger in 1852 of the principal britannia shops of Meriden, East Meriden, and Yalesville, Connecticut. I. C. Lewis was its first president, and among the directors were L. J. Curtis, W. W. Lyman, John Munson, and Samuel Simpson. The concern is listed in the *New England Business Directory* of 1860. It later became a unit of the International Silver Company. Most of its wares were plated and naturally late in form.

Morey and Ober. Britannia makers at 5 and 7 Haverhill Street, Boston, from 1852 to 1855. Partners: David B. Morey and R. H. Ober. Successors to Smith, Ober and Company and one of the many firms which succeeded Smith and Morey. For further comment refer to that concern.

Morey, Ober and Company, successors to Morey and Ober at 5 Haverhill Street, Boston, in 1855. Partners: D. B. Morey, R. H. Ober, and Thomas Smith. Succeeded by Morey and Smith in 1857.

Makers of the Britannia Period

Morey and Smith, successors to Morey, Ober and Company at 5 and 7 Haverhill Street, Boston, in 1857. Partners: D. B. Morey and Thomas Smith. The shop remained at the same location until 1860 and the firm continued in business until 1885. (See also Smith and Morey.)

Henry Morgan. Listed as a britannia manufacturer at Groton, Connecticut, in the *New England Mercantile Directory* of 1849.

John Munson. John Munson purchased from Samuel Simpson in 1846 the plant at Yalesville, Connecticut, which the latter had bought from Hiram Yale and Company in 1837. Munson operated the shop until 1852, when it became the nucleus of the newly formed Meriden Britannia Company. Munson joined the directorate of the latter organization. I have seen this man's name on teapots only.

I. Neal. I know nothing of this maker except that a very unusual whale-oil lamp (Plate LXXVI, 654) is marked on the bottom 'I. Neal's Pat. 1842.' The same mark has also been found on brass and tin lamps of similar design.

George Norris. See Ostrander and Norris.

Charles Ostrander. A britannia-maker of New York City whose product seems to have consisted principally of lamps and candlesticks. His shop was at 234 Second Street. From 1848 to 1850 his partner was George Norris. Thereafter he worked alone until 1854.

Ostrander and Norris. 234 Second Street, New York, 1848 to 1850. See Charles Ostrander.

J. H. Palethorp. John Harrison Palethorp, son of Robert and younger brother of Robert Palethorp, Junior, was a pewterer and britannia-maker in Philadelphia from 1820 to 1845. He was a partner of his brother at 50 North Second Street under the name of R. and J. H. Palethorp from 1820 until Robert's death in 1822. The firm continued at the same address and under the same name until 1826, Robert Palethorp, Senior, taking the interest of his deceased son, Robert, Junior. The Palethorps were listed as 'Ink Powder and Pewter Manufacturers.' From 1826 to 1836 John H. Palethorp worked alone in the same shop and in 1837 he moved to 55 North Sixth Street. Thereafter until 1845 his place of business was 144 High Street. For three years — from 1839 to 1841 — Thomas Connell was associated with him under the firm name of J. H. Palethorp and Company, and during that period the mark used on their wares was 'Palethorp and Connell.' The touches of Robert Palethorp, Junior, were probably used until 1826. Thereafter J. H. Palethorp used his own name except for the three-year period mentioned above. In 1829 Palethorp was a director of the Bank of Pennsylvania. I have seen, by this maker, mugs of early form, beakers, ladles, spoons, teapots, slop bowls and water pitchers. Palethorp's pewter is generally good, particularly his early work. The touch, 'Palethorp's,' was undoubtedly used after 1830. It appears principally on spoons, ladles, and water pitchers, forms which were not made in quantity before that date. A Palethorp water pitcher is illustrated in Plate LXXIII.

J. H. Palethorp and Company. 144 High Street, Philadelphia, 1839 to 1841. (See J. H. Palethorp.)

R. and J. H. Palethorp. 50 North Second Street, Philadelphia, 1820 to 1826. (See J. H. Palethorp; also Robert Palethorp, Junior, page 62.)

Palethorp and Connell. See J. H. Palethorp.

Charles Parker and Company. Makers of britannia spoons at Meriden, Connecticut, in 1849 and probably for several years before and after that date.

J. G. Parker. Rochester, New York, 1840 or later. His mark was found on a lamp in the collection of Charles F. Hutchins.

W. Parkin. Charles F. Hutchins owns a teapot impressed with this man's name. Other than that nothing is known about the maker.

Parkin was a British maker of Britannia. His name should be omitted from our lists.

W. H. Parmenter. A lamp of late appearance in the Pennsylvania Museum, Philadelphia, bears this maker's name. We have no other information about him.

Charles Plumley. This man, who was working in Middletown, Connecticut, in 1844 and sold to William R. Smith on October 17, 1848, his lathes, turning tools, vices, furnace, pewterers' moulds, and other equipment for the manufacture of britannia and block tin in the factory of Ames and Russell, may have been the Charles Plumly who worked in Philadelphia at an earlier date. (See page 67.)

Allen Porter. Early history unknown. He settled at Stevens Plains, Westbrook, Maine, about 1830 and engaged in the manufacture of pewter.
In March, 1835, his brother, Freeman Porter, became associated with him under the partnership name of A. and F. Porter.
A few years later Allen Porter was in Hartford, Connecticut, but there is no evidence that he continued to make pewter after separating from his brother. He deserved a greater trade than he apparently enjoyed. He made teapots of

good design and quality and his lamps are among the handsomest survivals of the period.

A. and F. Porter. See Allen Porter.

Freeman Porter. Freeman Porter, younger brother of Allen, was born at Colebrook, New Hampshire, July 1, 1808. He joined his brother in the partnership of A. and F. Porter at Westbrook, Maine, in 1835. In the same year he married Mary Ann (Buckley) Partridge, who lived almost into the twentieth century. About 1840, or perhaps a year or two earlier, Allen Porter retired, but persuaded Elizur B. Forbes of Hartford to move to Westbrook and become Freeman Porter's foreman. The shop was still in operation as late as the Civil War as evidenced in the *New England Business Directory* of 1860. Freeman Porter made a great variety of shapes, including lamps, candlesticks, teapots, and water pitchers. In quality and design his work ranks with the best of that period.

W. Potter. I own a small sander bearing this maker's touch (Plate XLI, 265). Nothing is known about the location of the shop. Period, about 1835 or later.

J. H. Putnam. James Hervey Putnam was born in Charlestown, New Hampshire, in 1803. He was apprenticed to his uncle, Timothy Bailey, in Malden, Massachusetts. About 1830 he became the partner of Bailey. (See Bailey and Putnam.) A few years later he established his own shop at the corner of Main and Haskins Streets, Malden, and continued the britannia business there until his death in 1855. At that time he employed eighteen hands and his annual product was valued at eighteen thousand dollars. Putnam made lamps, candlesticks, pitchers, teapots, and many other forms. A most unusual demijohn bearing his touch is illustrated in Plate LXXIII. Putnam was one of the ablest of the later makers. Some of his small nursing lamps — sparking lamps, as they are frequently mistermed today — are of especially pleasing design. (See Plate LXXVII.)

Reed and Barton. This firm was the final flowering, after several changes in management, of the partnership of Isaac Babbitt and William Crossman, in Taunton, Massachusetts, in 1824. The immediate predecessors were Leonard, Reed and Barton. Established in 1840, this concern is in the same business under the same name today. In their early days Reed and Barton were makers of communion sets, tea-sets, coffee-pots, etc. Their wares were beautifully made, but the designs, like those of practically all of their contemporaries, seem to us today a degeneration from the earlier and simpler shapes.

Renton and Company. F. P. L. Mills once owned a small saucer-lamp marked 'Renton & Co. N.Y.'

B. Richardson and Son. This name has been found on a britannia teapot. The Richardsons were listed as cutlers at 77 South Second Street in the Philadelphia Directory of 1839.

Makers of the Britannia Period

G. Richardson. This is probably the George Richardson who was working in Boston from 1818 to 1828. He moved soon thereafter to Cranston, Rhode Island, where he was working in 1840. In 1848 Richardson and his sons, George B. and Francis B. Richardson, had a britannia factory at 207 High Street, Providence. George Richardson died July 15, 1848. Much of his pewter was marked 'Glennore Co.' — either a trade-name or a firm through whom the pewter was merchandised. (See also volume I, page 84.) Richardson made teapots, sugar bowls, mugs, shaving mugs, inkwells and many other forms. (See Plates XLII and LXXII.) Surviving examples testify to the large trade that he must have had.

John Rodgers. Listed as a britannia manufacturer in 1839 to 1840 at 2 Williamson's Court, Philadelphia, Pennsylvania.

Rogers, Smith and Company. Britannia-makers of Hartford, Connecticut, about 1850. Their mark has been found on a chalice of late design.

Russell and Beach. Britannia-makers at Chester, Connecticut, for whom Luther Boardman worked in 1838.

John N. and Samuel Rust. Lamp-makers at 77 William Street (and 38 Gold Street), New York City, 1842 to 1845.

Leonard M. Rust. Lamp-maker at 8 Dominick Street, New York City, in 1849.

Samuel Rust. Lamp-maker at 125 Fulton Street, New York City, 1837 to 1842.

T. Sage and Company. In the St. Louis, Missouri, Directory of 1847, T. Sage and Company are listed as manufacturers of britannia ware at 62 Green Street. In 1848 Timothy Sage appears as a britannia manufacturer at 62 Green Street. Sage was a maker of teapots and water pitchers. A diminutive pitcher of very good quality of metal is illustrated in Plate LXXIII.

Sage and Beebe. Britannia-makers, possibly successors to T. Sage and Company, St. Louis, Missouri, about 1849 to 1850. Neither Sage nor Beebe is listed in the Directory of 1850–1851.

William Savage. Middletown, Connecticut, 1838. A maker of teapots. (See Graham and Savage.)

William H. Savage. Middletown, Connecticut. (See Graham and Savage.)

Savage and Graham. Middletown, Connecticut, 1837. (See Graham and Savage.)

[III]

Sellew and Company. In about the year 1832 Enos and Osman Sellew, who had received their training in Connecticut, opened a shop for the manufacture of britannia ware in Cincinnati, Ohio. Later they were joined by William Sellew. In the thirties they made teapots of eighteenth-century design, eight-inch plates after the early manner, and even had an eagle touch. In 1836 their shop was on Fifth Street between Walnut and Vine; in 1840 at 194 Main Street. In 1841 the firm employed eight men and its annual product was valued at $12,840. The britannia they made was typical of that time. Some of the work was excellent, and all of it exhibits a commendable restraint that was rare in the eighteen-forties. Sellew and Company's range of products was wide and included communion sets, tea-sets, lamps, and candlesticks. They were still in business after 1860.

Sheldon and Feltman. 35 Dean Street, Albany, New York, 1847 and 1848. The partners were Smith Sheldon and J. C. Feltman, Junior. They advertised as makers of 'Argentina and Britannia Wares.' They made tea-sets, communion flagons, and plates, and other pieces of thin metal and inferior design.

Sickel and Shaw. A lamp of late design marked with this firm's name has recently been reported. In 1849 they were listed as lamp-makers at 33 North Fourth Street, Philadelphia. In 1850 the shop was at 32 North Second Street. Thereafter until 1854 H. G. Sickel worked at the same address alone.

Samuel Simpson. An apprentice of H. Yale and Company at Yalesville, Connecticut. In 1837 Francis A. Gale, Lorenzo L. Williams, and Samuel Simpson purchased the H. Yale plant from the executors of the estate of Charles Yale and operated it under the name of Williams and Simpson until 1838, when Williams moved to Philadelphia. Thereafter Simpson owned the shop outright until he sold out to John Munson in 1845. From 1843 until 1845 he was listed at 272½ Pearl Street, New York City, possibly acting as his own New York agent while another ran his shop. From 1845 to 1847 he was at the same address in New York under the firm name of Simpson and Benham. He became one of the directors of the Meriden Britannia Company when that organization was formed in 1852. Occasionally teapots marked S. Simpson or Simpson and Benham come to light. They are, however, in no way distinctive.

Simpson and Benham. 272½ Pearl Street, New York, 1845 to 1847. The partners were Samuel Simpson and Morris Benham. This was presumably a sales agency for Simpson's shop at Yalesville, Connecticut.

Makers of the Britannia Period

Eben Smith. Smith was at one time an employee of Israel Trask in Beverly, Massachusetts. Later, probably in the early forties, he commenced a britannia business of his own and was still operating as late as 1856. He was an able maker of teapots and lamps. (See Plate LXXV.)   `E.SMITH`

William R. Smith. A britannia-maker of Middletown, Connecticut, who in 1848 purchased the tools and equipment of Charles Plumley.

Smith, Ober and Company. Britannia-makers at 3 Haverhill Street, Boston, 1849 to 1852. Successors to Smith and Company. Partners: Thomas Smith, David B. Morey, and R. H. Ober. Ober, the new partner, was a native of Washington, New Hampshire. He was active in the concern only until 1856, when he moved to South Newbury, Ohio, leaving his capital in the business of his former partners. The firm of Smith, Ober and Company was succeeded by Morey and Ober. See Smith and Morey.

Thomas Smith and Company. 4 Market Street, Boston, 1842; Charles Street, corner of Cambridge Street, 1842 to 1847. Successors to Smith and Morey, q.v. Partners: Thomas Smith, David B. Morey, and Henry White. Succeeded by Smith and Company.

Smith and Company (1). 3 Haverhill Street, Boston, 1847 to 1849. Successors to Thomas Smith and Company; succeeded by Smith, Ober and Company. Partners: same as in Thomas Smith and Company. See Smith and Morey.   `SMITH&CO`

Smith and Company (2). Britannia-makers at 542 Broadway, Albany, New York, 1853 to 1856. Successors to Smith and Feltman, q.v.

Smith and Feltman. Britannia-makers at 23 Dean Street, Albany, New York, 1849 to 1852. Successors to Sheldon and Feltman, q.v. Partners: George W. Smith and J. C. Feltman, Junior.   *SMITH &FELTMAN ALBANY*

Smith and Morey. This was the first of a succession of firms, located in Boston, which in the course of twenty-four years operated under seven different names with very little change in personnel. Thomas   `SMITH & MOREY` Smith, an Englishman, and David B. Morey (born in Malden, Massachusetts, 1807, married Almira, daughter of Timothy Bailey, britannia-maker, in 1842, and died in Malden in 1885) founded the business at 4 Market Street, Boston, in 1841. They were joined in 1842 by H. White, and the name was changed to Thomas Smith and Company. After two more reorganizations, R. H. Ober took White's place in the partnership at the new shop in Haverhill Street in 1849. The name was then Smith, Ober and Company. For a brief period, from 1853 until 1856, Smith seems to have left the organization, returning upon Ober's departure for Ohio, and becoming junior partner to the man with whom he had embarked in the business over fifteen years earlier. The partnership was thereafter known as Morey and Smith, and the address at the time of liquidation in 1864 was 49 Haverhill Street.

J. B. Kerfoot, in *American Pewter*, has said of Smith and Company: 'They did uniformly tasteful and craftsmanlike work. Their designs are simple and clean-cut. Their metal is of the best.' What was true of Smith and Company may be said of all the organizations which Thomas Smith or David Morey sponsored. They were makers primarily of lamps and teapots.

J. H. Stalkamp and Company. 69 East Fifth Street, later 247 West Fifth Street, Cincinnati, 1853 (and possibly a few years earlier) to 1856; manufacturers of 'Britannia and Silecia Ware.' John H. Stalkamp's partner in 1853 was John F. Wendeln; in 1856 William C. Pomroy.

Alexander Standish. I can give no information as to this man's place of work. A britannia coffee-urn of about 1840 or later is impressed ALEX^B STANDISH with his name.

William H. Starr. A maker of lamps at 67 (later 77) Beekman Street, New York, 1843 to 1846. I have seen just one example by this man, a small nursing lamp.

S. Stedman. In the collection of R. R. Endicott is a birch-handled ladle marked 'S. Stedman.' I know nothing about its maker.

Frederick Stoddart. Listed as a pewterer at 4 Holmes Alley, Philadelphia, in 1833.

William F. Sumner. See Endicott and Sumner.

——Sykes. A pocket flask of about 1850 bears this name. Nothing is known of the maker.

Taunton Britannia Manufacturing Company. Taunton, Massachusetts, about 1830 to 1835. Successors to Crossman, West and Leonard. This concern was one of the predecessors of the present firm of Reed and Barton. Their communion flagons are graceless affairs, and although their coffee-pots, teapots, sugar bowls, etc., are rather handsome and quite distinctive, they illustrate the tendency of that period to depart from the simple, clear-cut designs of the early makers. On the other hand, the 'T. B. M.' candlesticks and lamps are among the handsomest survivals of the britannia period. (See Plates LXXII, LXXIV, LXXV, and LXXVII.)

John Thomas. A maker of britannia ware at Shippen Lane, Philadelphia, in 1841.

——Tomlinson. Charles K. Davis recently acquired a lamp marked 'Tomlinson's Patent, 1843.' Nothing is known of the maker or where his place of business was.

Israel Trask. Born in Beverly, Massachusetts, October 24, 1786. As a boy he was apprenticed to John W. Ellingwood, a silversmith and bought out Ellingwood's stock in trade in 1807. He commenced the manufacture of pewter and britannia in that town about 1825 and his designs and decorations of pewter testify to his training as a silversmith. His shop was in Cabot Street. As late as 1856 he was listed as a britannia manufacturer in the *New England Mercantile Directory*. His death occurred in 1867. Trask made teapots, communion flagons, christening bowls, castors, lamps, and probably a great many other forms. A dignity and honesty of design is apparent in all his work. (See Plates LXXI and LXXIII.)

Oliver Trask. A younger brother of Israel. He was born in Beverly June 13, 1792, and is said to have received his training in his brother's shop. His actual working dates are not known, but in a deed of 1832 he called himself a teapot manufacturer and in deeds from 1837 to 1839 a britannia-plate worker. A baptismal bowl, by this maker, which was in the sale of Mr. Bowman's collection in 1937, is to my mind one of the finest examples of its type and period. Trask also made communion flagons, teapots, lidded boxes, and other forms which evidenced careful workmanship. He died in 1847.

Vose and Company. Albany, New York, after 1840. Britannia that I have seen, so marked, was of little merit.

Lester Wadsworth. Listed as a pewterer in the Hartford, Connecticut, Directory of 1838.

R. Wallace and Company. This concern made britannia and German silver at Wallingford, Connecticut. Commencing business about 1855, the same firm is operating successfully today. Except for an occasional spoon I have never seen anything bearing their name that was not plated.

H. B. Ward and Company. J. B. Kerfoot, in *American Pewter*, placed this concern at Guilford, Connecticut. They may have been established there at one time, but in 1849 the shop, according to the *New England Mercantile Directory*, was at Wallingford, Connecticut. Ward's mark is found occasionally on teapots.

——Warren. W. H. Chubbuck owns a lamp marked 'Warren's Hard Metal.' Nothing is known about the maker.

C. P. Wayne and Son. Caleb P. Wayne, who died in Philadelphia in 1849, aged seventy-two, was by turns a printer, hardware merchant, and proprietor of a 'Looking Glass and Fancy Store' in Philadelphia. I have seen one teapot bearing his name. I should judge that it was made about 1835.

J. Weekes. There are in existence a great many pieces of pewter and britannia marked 'J. Weekes, N.Y.' or 'J. Weekes & Co.' I have also seen one teapot marked 'J. Weekes, Brooklyn.' Although the New York Directories of the period from 1818 to 1840 list a number of James and Joseph Weekes (or Weeks), none is termed a pewterer or britannia-maker. The man to whom attribution

PLATE LXXV — *Tall Whale-Oil and Camphene Lamps*

643. 8¾-inch lamp, an example of the excellent design of the shop of Endicott and Sumner, New York, 1846–1851. Reproduced from *American Pewter* through the courtesy of the late Mrs. J. B. Kerfoot.

644. One of a pair of lamps with camphene burners. Height not recorded. Homan and Company, Cincinnati, Ohio, 1847–1864. Courtesy of J. G. Braecklein, Esq.

645. The only marked American double bull's-eye lamp in my records. Height 8¼ inches. Roswell Gleason, Dorchester, Massachusetts, 1822–1860. The magnifying glasses were supposed to increase greatly the light, but must have been a trial to the housewife. Courtesy of the Mabel Brady Garvan Collection, Gallery of Fine Arts, Yale University.

646. A fine 'lemon-top' whale-oil lamp on a handsome standard of a type employed by the Beverly and Dorchester makers. Note the decoration of base. Height about 9 inches. Roswell Gleason, Dorchester, Massachusetts. Collection of Vincent O'Reilly, Esq.

647. Whale-oil lamp with cylindrical font. Height 9 inches. William Calder, Providence, 1817–1856. Collection of the author.

648. Lamp with hexagonal font on typical candlestick base and standard. One of the finest designs of the period. Height 13¼ inches. The Taunton Britannia Manufacturing Company, Taunton, Massachusetts, 1830–1835. Reproduced from *American Pewter*. Through the courtesy of the late Mrs. J. B. Kerfoot.

649. 'Lozenge-top' lamp, one of a pair measuring 10 inches in height. Eben Smith, Beverly, 1841–1856. Collection of the author.

650. A most unusual lamp of patently Dutch design, but bearing the mark of Henry Homan and Company, Cincinnati, 1847–1864. Height not recorded. Courtesy of Leo F. Wagner, Esq.

651. Skirt lamp. Maker and height unknown. Reproduced from *American Pewter* through the courtesy of the late Mrs. J. B. Kerfoot.

652. One of a fine pair of 12¼-inch lamps made by Roswell Gleason, Dorchester, Massachusetts, 1822–1860. Now in the collection of Charles F. Hutchins, Esq.

PLATE LXXV

647

652

646

651

645

650

644

649

643

648

PLATE LXXVI — *Lamps*

653. Unmarked pewter 'betty' lamp for burning lard; probably Pennsylvania late eighteenth century. Height 4⅝ inches. Collection of the author.

654. An unusual lamp patented by I. Neal in 1842. Height not recorded. Similar lamps in tin and brass are found with the same mark. Courtesy of Philip G. Platt, Esq.

655. Unmarked patent lamp. Formerly in the collection of the late John F. Street.

656. 'Acorn-top' lamp. Height 6 inches. Roswell Gleason, Dorchester, Massachusetts, 1822–1860. Collection of the author.

657, 658, and 659. Three saucer lamps in the author's collection. The heights, respectively, from left to right, are 6¾, 7¼, and 5 inches. The makers, Smith and Company, Boston, 1847–1849, Thomas Wildes, New York, 1832–1840, and William Calder, Providence, 1817–1850.

660. Fine swinging lamp. Diameter of saucer 5 inches, height when flat 4 inches over all. Endicott and Sumner, New York, 1846–1851. Courtesy of Philip G. Platt.

661. Ship's lamp with double swivel, also made by Endicott and Sumner. Dimensions the same as 660. Courtesy of the Mabel Brady Garvan Collection, Gallery of Fine Arts, Yale University.

662. Another swinging lamp made by the Boardmans of Hartford, mark 430. Height 4⅞ inches. Collection of the author.

PLATE LXXVI

653 654 655 656

657 658 659

660 661 662

for pewter-making is given in this volume is listed as follows in the Directories:

1822–1824 James Weeks, drygoods, 406 Pearl Street
1824–1828 James Weeks & Co., drygoods, 390 Pearl Street
1828–1830 James Weeks, Merchant, 80 Pine Street
1830–1831 James Weeks, Merchant, 93 Pearl Street
1831–1833 James Weeks, Merchant, 2 Cedar Street

His name is missing from succeeding New York Directories, but on June 26, 1833, a James Weeks advertised general fancy goods on Main Street, Poughkeepsie, and on September 4 his advertisement mentions a variety store on Main Street and a block-tin manufactory at the corner of Main and Bayeux Streets. On April 23, 1834, J. Weekes and Company, corner of Main and Perry Streets, Poughkeepsie, advertise that they make, at their manufactory of block tin and britannia ware, coffee-pots and teapots, soup ladles, molasses gates, beer mugs, tumblers, teaspoons and tablespoons, faucets, etc. On March 4, 1835, J. Weeks advertised the sale at auction of his remaining stock of goods. He may then have moved to Brooklyn. It is, of course, possible that the James Weeks, merchant of New York, was not the same man as the britannia manufacturer of Poughkeepsie, but if not it is a striking coincidence that the former appears for the last time in New York Directories in the issue of 1832–1833 and the Poughkeepsie man advertises in the latter town for the first time early in 1833.

It is a matter of passing interest that Rufus Dunham (*q.v.*) was working as a journeyman in Poughkeepsie about 1835 and purchased his tools there. In all likelihood James Weekes was his employer.

Every example of Weekes pewter or britannia that I have seen is well made. His designs display character, originality, and taste. Although in some of his later pieces the metal is thin, the quality seems to have been invariably high. I have seen a basin (indicating that he was making pewter before 1830), the teapot with a Brooklyn touch, spoons, dippers, gravy ladles, salts, small beakers, lamps, and candlesticks. So far as I know Weekes did not make pitchers, communion flagons, or other large hollow-ware forms, but he was an able specialist in small articles and his work is worthy of a place on the shelves of the most discriminating collector. (See Plates XXVI and XXX.)

J. Weekes and Company. See above.

A. G. Whitcomb. Although we know from Whitcomb's mark that he worked in Boston, I have been unable to find out who he was or when he made pewter. The little ink chest illustrated in Plate XLI is a most unusual form in American pewter; although early in form it may have been made after 1835, for I have had report of inkwells bearing his name which are late both in design of well and of marking.

E. Whitehouse. Spoons marked with this man's name, some of which may have been made as early as 1800, are found occasionally. I believe that he was an American pewterer, but cannot substantiate my belief with proof. (See Plate XXV.) WHITEHOUSE WHITEHOUSE WARRANTED

G. and J. Whitfield. Listed as plumbers at 262 or 266 Water Street, New York, from 1836 to 1865. An old trade card fastened to a stand of pewter candle-moulds gives their occupation as 'Plumbers and Pewterers.' George B. Whitfield was listed alone as a plumber at 342 Water Street from 1828 to 1833.

J. H. Whitlock. A merchant with store at 231 River Street, Troy, New York, from about 1836 to 1844. As pointed out by J. B. Kerfoot, in *American Pewter*, Whitlock was probably not a maker of pewter or britannia. The articles stamped with his name were made presumably by the Boardmans of Hartford, for whom he acted as agent or distributor. WHITLOCK TROY. N.Y. WHITLOCK TROY. N.Y.

Lewis Whitmore. A maker of teapots and other britannia and block-tin wares in Rocky Hill, Connecticut, in the early eighteen-forties.

Whitmore and Francis. The partners — Whitmore and Daniel Francis — advertised the opening of a block-tin and britannia factory at 9 Ellicott Square, Buffalo, New York, in 1833. Francis is listed alone in the Directory of 1835.

Thomas Wildes. Thomas Wildes made lamps, candlesticks, spoons, and perhaps other forms at the corner of Hester and Second Streets, New York, from 1833 to 1840. One of his lamps is illustrated in Plate LXXVI. T.WILDES T.WILDES

Thomas Wilds. Probably identical with Thomas Wildes. Listed as a pewterer at 30 Kunckle Street, Philadelphia, from 1829 to 1833.

Lorenzo L. Williams. A foreman in the shop of Hiram Yale at Wallingford, Connecticut, in 1835. He was one of the artisans brought from England by Yale to teach the spinning of britannia. In 1837 with Samuel Simpson he bought the plant of H. Yale and Company at Yalesville. In the following year he sold out to Simpson and opened a shop of his own at Third Street and the Railroad in Philadelphia. He turned out britannia tea-sets until 1842. His work is of average merit. L. L. WILLIAMS. PHILAD^A

Williams and Simpson. L. L. Williams and Samuel Simpson, Yalesville, Connecticut, 1837 and 1838. The 'W & S' touch, here shown and tentatively attributed to this concern, was found on a teapot owned by Miss Olive Wheeler. W&S

Thomas Willis. A pewterer at 3 Northampton Court, Philadelphia, 1829 to 1833.

J. B. Woodbury. We know little of Woodbury's history. The fact that one of his touches is strikingly like a mark of Roswell Gleason; that some of his teapots resemble those of Israel Trask; and that his product is found more frequently in New England than in Pennsylvania leads to the belief that he probably worked near Boston before opening a shop in Philadelphia in 1835. His place of business in the latter city was at 22 Library Street and his partner was Oren Colton. In 1837 and 1838 he worked alone at 361 Cedar Street. Woodbury made lamps, candlesticks, coffee-pots, teapots, and beakers.

The last-named are sometimes found with handles. His designs are simple and tasteful. One of the most desirable of American 'lights' is a Woodbury lamp which J. B. Kerfoot illustrated in *American Pewter*.

Woodbury and Colton. 22 Library Street, Philadelphia, 1835 to 1836. (See J. B. Woodbury.)

Woodman, Cook and Company. Portland, Maine, after 1830. I know nothing of this concern except that J. B. Kerfoot listed them as makers whose work had already turned up.

Burrage Yale. Born in Meriden, Connecticut, March 27, 1781. Married Sarah S. Boardman in 1808 and moved to South Reading, Massachusetts, where he manufactured tinware and later britannia. He died September 5, 1860. Timothy Bailey was one of his peddlers and Luther Boardman was his shop foreman from 1833 to 1835, purchasing the business from him in the latter year.

Charles Yale. Wallingford (Connecticut), Richmond (Virginia), and New York City, about 1818 to 1835. (See volume I, pages 131, 132.)

Charles Yale. Probably a New York sales office for H. Yale and Company, 80 Pine Street, New York, 1832.

H. Yale and Company. Wallingford, Connecticut, 1824 to 1835. (See volume I, pages 131, 132.)

William Yale. A lamp-maker at 115 Beekman Street (later 271 Pearl Street), New York City, 1830 to 1832. This was probably the William Yale of W. and S. Yale of Meriden, Connecticut, who died in that town in 1833. (See vol. I, p. 130.)

Yale and Curtis. Henry Yale and Stephen Curtis, Junior, made lamps of all types, including the swinging variety, at 67 Beekman Street, New York, in 1858. They moved later to 90 Fulton Street and the business was continued under the name of Yale and Curtis until 1867.

DETHRONED PEWTERERS

THE foregoing chapters include all the names of American pewterers and britannia-makers, working prior to 1850, that I have been able to verify to my own satisfaction. Earlier lists, however, included many names which I have omitted, and I have also failed to include a number of men whose names have been given to me as those of pewterers. The omissions have been made for one of the following reasons:

(1) The men were not American pewterers.
(2) Their work is too late both in time and form to interest the average collector.
(3) They were makers of buttons only and probably had no individual touch-marks.
(4) They were presumably journeymen or dealers only.
(5) Records could not be found showing that they worked in pewter. In some cases I have been unable to prove that such men ever existed.

Unquestionably some few of these names belong among the elect, but the surest way to gain for them such recognition is to say that they were not American pewterers, and thus give opportunity to their protagonists to come forward with the information which will substantiate their claims. Let us proceed, then, to an examination of the list of names which are hereafter to be eliminated for cause:

NAMES FROM PREVIOUS LISTS OF PEWTERERS OMITTED FOR CAUSE FROM THE NEW LISTING

Names	Addresses (as reported on earlier lists)	Dates (as reported on earlier lists)	Reasons
Thomas Badger, Sr.	Boston, Mass.	Eighteenth century	Was a block-maker in 1782. No evidence of pewter-making.
O. & A. Bailey 'Lamps'	New York	1845	Probably dealers only.
C. Bancks	Chelmsford, Mass.	?	Probably confused with C. Bancks of Bewdley, England.
S. Bast	New York	Nineteenth century?	No information.
—n Brigh	?	?	Allen Bright of Bristol, England.
Robert Bush	—	—	Of Bristol, England (c. 1765–1790).
Bush & Perkins	—	—	Bristol, England (c. 1775).
William Calder (lion touch)	Charlestown, Mass.	Eighteenth century	Bristol, England. Died in 1752.
Cleveland & Brothers	Providence, R.I.	After 1825	Cabinet-makers and warehousemen in the eighteen-forties. No evidence of pewter-making except for buttons marked with the firm's name.
Robert Crocker	Boston	Late eighteenth century	Dealt in pewter, but was a founder by trade.
James Dixon & Sons	—	Nineteenth century	Britannia-makers of Sheffield, England, who during the eighteen-fifties had a branch store in New York and a large trade in this country.

Dethroned Pewterers

Names	Addresses (as reported on earlier lists)	Dates (as reported on earlier lists)	Reasons
Eastman & Co.	Albany, New York	After 1830	No information.
Edgar, Curtis & Co.	—	—	Bristol, England (*c.* 1793–1801).
Glenmore Co.	Cranston, R.I.	After 1825	Should read Glennore Co. (See p. 111.)
Henry and Silas Grilley	Waterbury, Conn.	1790	Button-makers only.
Hall, Elton & Co. (spoons)	Wallingford, Conn.	1860	Too late for consideration.
William Hamlin	Providence, R.I.	*c.* 1800	An engraver; not a pewterer.
Peter Harby	New York	1746	Probably in error for Peter Kirby.
— Harris	—	—	English (and very late).
Christian Heave	Philadelphia	Early nineteenth century	Corruption of the name Christian Hera.
Charlotte Hera (Hero)	Philadelphia	1796	Widow of Christian Höran. No evidence that she herself made pewter.
Christopher Hero	Philadelphia	1797–1798	In error for Christian Hera.
Christianna Herroe	Philadelphia	1785	In error for Christian Höran.
John Holden (Halden)	New York	1743	A brazier named John Halden was working in New York in the seventeen-fifties and later moved to Boston, where he died in 1780. He may have been a pewterer also, but proof to that effect has not been found.
Mary Jackson	Boston	Early nineteenth century?	The Mary Jackson who lived in Dock Square, Boston, in 1796 seems never to have been in business. A brazier of this name, Cornhill, Boston (*c.* 1730–1760), sold pewterers' moulds and London pewter. No evidence of pewter-making.
Knowles & Ladd	—	—	No information.
James Leddel	New York	1744–1780	Error for Joseph Leddell.
Richard Lee	Providence, R.I.	1832	Probably Richard Lee, Jr., of Springfield, Vermont, who may possibly have worked in or near Providence in 1832. His later history has not been traced. (See volume I, pp. 121–124.)
John Lightner	Baltimore, Md.	1814	A tinsmith, brother of George Lightner. For one year only he was listed as a pewterer while selling off his brother's stock.
D. Locke	New York	—	Error for J. D. Locke.
J. B. Locke	New York	—	Error for J. D. Locke.
Bartholomew Longstreet	Bucks County, Pa.	*c.* 1810?	No records of any Longstreet could be found in Bucks County dating back to 1710 or earlier, but a Bartholomew Longstreth, who was not a pewterer, died in that county in 1749. His cousin, Martin Longstreth, a journeyman-brazier, had a son Bartholomew, who was living one hundred and fifty miles west of Philadelphia (probably in Bedford County) in 1769. He may possibly have made pewter.
Daniel Melvil	Newport, R.I.	1788	In error for David Melville. (See volume I, p. 91.)
Joshua Metzger	Germantown, Pa.	1806? 1820?	No information.
G. I. Mix & Co. (Spoons)	Yalesville, Conn.	After 1860	Too late for consideration.
S. Moore	Kensington, Conn.	*c.* 1820–1830?	No information.
C. Parker (Whitesmith)	New York		Confused with Charles Parker & Co. of Meriden, Connecticut.
Porter Britannia and Plate Co.	Taunton, Mass.	1860	Too late for consideration.
Edmund Porter (1)	Taunton, Mass.	*c.* 1800	Died in Taunton in 1833. Termed a yeoman in deeds. No evidence of pewter-making.

Dethroned Pewterers

Names	Addresses (as reported on earlier lists)	Dates (as reported on earlier lists)	Reasons
Edmund Porter (2)	Taunton, Mass.	c. 1847	Probably a proprietor of Porter Britannia and Plate Co. (See above.)
F. Porter	Westbrook, Conn.	After 1825	In error for Freeman Porter of Westbrook, Maine.
Lincoln Porter	Taunton, Mass.	c. 1800	Brother of Edmund, Sr. Died in 1823. Termed a yeoman in deeds. His inventory that of a farmer.
Samuel Porter	Taunton, Mass.	c. 1800	Father of Lincoln and Edmund. Died in 1800. Termed a yeoman. His inventory that of a farmer.
Quilkin	Philadelphia	—	Error for William McQuilkin. (See p. 107.)
Paul Revere	Boston	1735–1818	(See pp. 89, 90.)
Thomas Rigden	Philadelphia	Early nineteenth century?	Died in Philadelphia in 1805. Is termed a shopkeeper in his probate records. There are two Philadelphia Directories for 1799. In one he is listed as a pewterer, in the other as a fruiterer. I believe that the second was correct and that the mistake in the first was due to euphonic similarity in the terms. In Directories for the other years Rigden is carried either as a shopkeeper or a carpenter.
Sellers & Co.	Cincinnati, Ohio	—	In error for Sellew & Co. (See p. 112.)
Aaron Smith	Philadelphia	1729	A merchant who sold pewter. No evidence of pewter-making.
H. Snyder	Philadelphia	—	No information.
Jireh Strange	Taunton, Mass.	c. 1800	Died in Taunton after 1830. Described as a yeoman or laborer. No indication of pewter-making.
Joseph Strange	Taunton, Mass.	c. 1800	Died after 1830. Termed a blacksmith. No evidence of pewter-making.
John Trask	Boston, Mass.	1822–1826	Described in Directories as a 'composition worker.' No proof of pewter-making.
James Ward	Hartford, Connecticut	1795	A silversmith and jeweler who advertised for old metals, including pewter. No evidence of pewter-making.
George and William Wild	Bucks County, Pennsylvania	Nineteenth century	The names do not appear in Bucks County records but are found on the lists of warrantees of land for Bedford County in 1786. No data as to their occupation was found.
A. Williams	'Bitheford'	?	A pewterer of Bideford, England.
Samuel Yale, Sr.	Meriden, Connecticut.	1790–	A maker of buttons only.
John Yates (or Yeates)	—	—	A pewterer of Birmingham, England.
Widow Youle (of Thomas)	594 Water Street, New York	1821–1822	Listed as a pewterer while settling up her husband's estate.

PLATE LXXVII — *Small Lamps and Miscellaneous Objects*

663. Small nursing lamp of compact design, made by J. H. Putnam, Malden, Massachusetts, 1830–1855. Height 3 inches. Collection of the author.

664 to 668. A remarkable group of miniature lamps. Frequently termed 'sparking' lamps today, they appear as nursing or nurse lamps in contemporary records. 667 bears the mark of William Calder, Providence, 1817–1850; the others are unmarked. Their heights are 3, $2\frac{7}{8}$, $4\frac{1}{4}$, $4\frac{1}{16}$, and $\frac{15}{8}$ inches respectively, exclusive of burners. This unexcelled group is in the collection of the Honorable and Mrs. George V. Smith.

669. Another unusually small nursing lamp, its burner unfortunately missing. Height $1\frac{3}{4}$ inches. The Taunton Britannia Manufacturing Company, Taunton, Massachusetts, 1830–1835. Formerly in the collection of the late Albert C. Bowman, Esq.

670. A syrup jug in the best taste of the period. Height 6 inches over all. Hall and Cotton, place of work unknown, after 1830. Collection of the Honorable and Mrs. George V. Smith.

671. Vessel with handle, used possibly as a flower vase. Height $6\frac{1}{2}$ inches, exclusive of handle. The piece is unmarked, but is believed to have been made by the Boardmans. Mrs. Arthur Brewer, a great-granddaughter of Thomas D. Boardman, recalls a number of pieces in the Boardman home with the same raised decoration as on this handle. According to tradition they were made by the Boardmans. Collection of the author.

instead of 672
read 672 and 673

672. Silhouette frames measuring $3\frac{1}{4}$ and $2\frac{1}{2}$ inches in diameter respectively. Almost invariably these frames come to light in Vermont, New Hampshire, or western Massachusetts.

instead of 673
change to 674

673. Ingenious molasses gate, the flow regulated by a ratchet with handle, which closes the gate when handle is raised. Height when closed $6\frac{1}{4}$ inches, length $4\frac{1}{2}$ inches. G. and J. Fenn, New York, *c.*1840. Collection of Dr. Percy E. Raymond.

instead of 674
change to 675

674. Britannia baptismal bowl. Height $5\frac{1}{4}$ inches, top diameter $8\frac{1}{4}$ inches. Roswell Gleason, Dorchester, Massachusetts, 1822–1860. Collection of the author.

instead of 675
change to 676

675. Spool-holder and pincushion. Height $5\frac{1}{4}$ inches. Unmarked, probably made after 1830. Collection of the author.

instead of 676
change to 677

676. Cruet stand or caster of unusual shape. Unmarked and probably late, but of considerable merit in design. Collection of the Honorable and Mrs. George V. Smith.

PLATE LXXVII

663

664 665 666 667 668

669

672 673

670 671 674

675 676 677

PLATE LXXVIII — *Fakes*

In this plate are shown fake touches of five American pewterers
and alongside each is a photograph of the genuine touch

678. A very crude imitation of Parks Boyd's large eagle touch as found on a porringer that resembles no American porringer. This counterfeit was applied to new pewter in odd shapes by a workman in either England or Germany upon order from an American merchant about fifteen years ago. Note the block letters, heavy lines, and lack of any niceties in design.

679 and 680. Fake Bassett marks executed by the same man. Found on two-handled porringers and other 'rarities' as well as on plates of Continental design.

681. Fake Lightner touch from the bottom of the cup illustrated as 682 — a cup which Lightner could never have been presumed to have made. A Baltimore mechanic is said to have been guilty of this counterfeit. Courtesy of Dr. Walter Hughson.

681a. Through the kindness of Joseph France, Esq., another impression of this touch was secured. An intermediary, who knew both Mr. France and the fakir, obtained this sample for illustration here.

683. Fake William Will touch by same man who was responsible for the Boyd and Bassett marks. Found on the bottom of an oval platter. A similar platter was on display recently (presumably as genuine) in a large eastern museum.

684. Fake mark of Thomas Badger on the bottom of a heavy antique Continental plate. Though crude in comparison with the original, it is a cleverer reproduction than any other here illustrated. The source is not known. Courtesy of Mrs. Philip Huntington.

PLATE LXXVIII

537 b

309 a

680

679

683

684

468 a

464 a

544 b

682

678

567 a

681

681 a

FAKES

IT IS NOT my intention to place any emphasis on the 'faking' of pewter; for the pewter collector, to a far greater extent than his fellow collector of silver, glass, or furniture, has thus far been spared the pitfalls laid by the unscrupulous individuals who make a living by the sale of modern 'antiques.'

With the artisans who carefully and honestly turn out by hand faithful replicas of the craftsmanship of other days and stamp and sell such work as reproductions, we are entirely in sympathy. In the present scheme of things there is a real need for such men, for most of us will never be able to buy original Randolph 'sample chairs' or Gilbert Stuart portraits of George Washington. But unfortunately the lure of money leads many able men to turn out reproductions which they sell or allow to be sold as antiques. Even more insidious is the practice of taking the honest skeleton of an old piece, repairing it, doctoring it up with embellishments such as the poor old thing never knew, and marking it with the name or label of a maker of long ago. Every field of antiques has been invaded by these doctored wares, and the collector now feels that he must become a first-class detective before he is qualified to make a purchase.

At some stage in the making of a collection, every one of us has been, or is likely to be, taken in by one or two of these spurious pieces. It is my hope that my own experience with fakes may forewarn some prospective purchaser. Otherwise there would be no excuse for the inclusion of this chapter.

In England and on the Continent of Europe there still exist many moulds used by the early pewterers. In some few instances these moulds have fallen into the possession of unscrupulous individuals or firms who are turning out modern pewter in the exact shapes of the early pieces — pewter which is being sold today as antique. But although the shapes can be accurately reproduced, it has been found impossible to imitate the evidence of time, the tiny specks of corrosion which will be found on any genuine piece. The new pewter may be scratched and battered, it may be blackened to imitate age, but the roughness of the old metal to the hand and eye will not be there.

In this country few early moulds have survived, and those that have are happily safe from the machinations of the counterfeiter. The only exceptions are spoon moulds. Many of the latter are still at large, and some of the 'antique' pewter spoons on the market today have been made in recent years from the old moulds.

But unmarked pewter brings no high prices in this country. The fakers' big field lies in imitating the touches of the early men and there he encounters well-nigh insurmountable obstacles. J. B. Kerfoot performed a great service for the collectors of

Fakes

American pewter when he photographed all the known makers' marks — a practice which has been followed by every succeeding writer on the subject. These photographs will always serve as foils to the counterfeiter. Examine any one of the marks and you will see minute irregularities due to the inaccuracy of the die-cutter. Such slight deviations from the original sketched design are safeguards against the faker for all time.

Up to the present writing we have had little need for such protection. Most of the fakes that have thus far appeared are the work of ignorant men of little ability. But it is conceivable that the masterpieces of American pewter may, in time, become sufficiently valuable to tempt more skillful men to enter the field, and for them we must be ready.

At present there are on the market two distinct types of 'undesirables' of which the collector should beware. Most insidious, because most likely to pass as genuine, are the spurious imitations of known touches which have been stamped on old pewter. At least two and perhaps three men, ignorant tinkers all of them, have tried their hands at this sort of work. One of these, said to be a resident of Baltimore, experimented a number of years ago with a fake Lightner mark, and is also, I believe, the sponsor of fraudulent touches of the third Thomas Danforth. Shown side by side on Plate LXXVIII, 567a and 681, are the original Lightner touch and the spurious. The new dies are passable imitations of the old, and at first glance even an expert might be deceived, but close examination shows at once many defects and a general lack of refinement as compared with the genuine. The marks are usually found on well-worn pieces from which the original touches had long been obliterated. Now the stamping of pewter is a trick in itself. Many of the early makers were not always able to accomplish it without allowing the die to slip, and this novice has made a double impression upon almost every occasion. This slipping of the tool has helped, however, to hide some of the faults in the touch itself. Furthermore, our man seems unable to make an impression without striking the die so hard that the outline of its face appears on the under surface of the pewter, a fault not found in the work of the old pewterers. What hastened the exposure of these fakes was the finding of the Lightner mark on a mug of the Victorian era (Plate LXXVIII, 682) and the Danforth touches on whale-oil lamps. The mere presence of early marks on late forms laid them open to suspicion. This error on the part of the user is an indication of his level of intelligence. A very small number of such pieces have been reported to me — the mug described above, a few lamps, and six or eight plates and dishes.

At an exhibition given by the Pewter Collectors' Club in the Curry Galleries in New York in February, 1938, a new fraudulent touch (number 684) was shown. The mark gives evidence of the work of a different hand and has been struck squarely without wobbling the die. It closely resembles the original (number 309a), but is larger and shows marked differences when placed alongside its pattern. Nevertheless, it is a good imitation. Its user fell into the same error as the Baltimore faker — he stamped the touch on a piece which Badger could never have been presumed to have made — a patently Continental plate.

Fakes

This group of marks should present no problem now that they have been exposed. By comparison the other recognized counterfeits are ridiculously amateurish.

Group two, which first appeared more than a dozen years ago, includes touches of Badger, B. Barns, Frederick Bassett, Parks Boyd, Thomas Danforth, Third, and William Will. They are found on new pewter only which has been blackened and scarred to simulate age. For the same reason some items have been left rough-cast or but partially skimmed. Another trick used was to buff the piece, after blackening with acid, thus leaving what might seem to be evidences of age embedded in the polished surface. Not only is the pewter new, but the forms are incorrect and the touches so crude as scarcely to resemble the originals from which they were copied. The lettering in the touches is entirely of the block type and all the lines in the designs are heavy, wide, and regular, characteristics never found in pewter made before 1800. The shapes on which the marks were struck are in many cases unlike any on which American touches have ever been found — footed porringers with two solid handles, coasters, and other rarities which would bring fancy prices if genuine. Examples of these touches are shown in Plate LXXVIII, 678 to 680 and 683. The illustrations of the genuine marks beside the fraudulent show very clearly how far short of perfection this man's work falls.

Unfortunately a good many examples of this group are on the market and one of the principal offenders in their early distribution was a large, and presumably reputable, department store in the heart of New York City's shopping district. There I have seen as many as a dozen fake pieces mixed indiscriminately with genuine marked American pewter. The salesgirls could not distinguish the old from the new and the buyer for the department, when summoned for an explanation, brazenly admitted that the pieces which I criticized had been made to order in Germany. No excuse whatever was offered for placing such wares on sale at prices fully as high as might be expected for the genuine.

The third group comprises items which are not really fakes at all. These bear modern marks impressed on modern pewter with no intention to deceive. They became problems to the collector only when they had passed into the hands of unscrupulous or ignorant middlemen who sold them as antiques at antique prices. In this category are two varieties, Paul Revere tablespoons and various forms marked with a small eagle.

The P. Revere-in-rectangle mark (of which there is no illustration here) is found only on the handles of teaspoons, spoons which I am satisfied are comparatively modern. It is my supposition that they were manufactured as souvenirs to commemorate some anniversary of Paul Revere's ride or as presents for guests at a reunion of the Revere family. It is unthinkable, as some of their owners believe, that they were the work of the Patriot himself.

The small eagle touch with initials enclosed in a circle, was used for a short time by a silversmith and pewterer on new metal which he was fashioning. As soon as he realized that dealers were selling his wares to a gullible public which believed the touch a newly discovered mark of an unknown old master he discarded the die.

This concludes the known range of questionable American touches and it is my hope that the illustrations accompanying this text will aid in removing from the market all of the fraudulent wares.

THE CLEANING AND CARE OF PEWTER

ONE of the first questions asked by any collector is, 'How do you clean your pewter?' So much has been written, after careful experimentation and investigation of this subject, that I hesitate to include even a brief chapter thereon. For I have no new and easy cure-all to suggest. Many recipes have been tried with reputed success. Descriptions of the best-known may be found in Cotterell's *Old Pewter*, Massé's *The Pewter Collector*, Kerfoot's *American Pewter* and in an article in *Antiques* for November, 1938, by John W. Poole, entitled *The Care of Pewter*.

My own experience has been limited, but I have found two methods which have been satisfactory for my needs and would, I presume, be adequate for the average collector. The choice of these treatments depends upon the condition of the piece to be cleaned.

If the article is merely dirty or dull but not corroded, gentle treatment will suffice. With a soft cloth and an application of any good metal polish (Noxon, for instance) rub the entire surface vigorously, using a brush if necessary to get into crevices. While the piece is still covered with the resulting black paste, a combination of the polish and grime, lather thoroughly with soap flakes and then immerse and scrub in warm water. It is essential that every vestige of polish and dirt be removed from the pores of the metal in the rinsing operation. Then dry thoroughly and polish with a soft, clean, dry cloth. Once thoroughly cleaned in this manner, the pewter should remain untarnished for a long period and, unless food is to be served from it, need not be polished again for six months or more.

But if the article to be cleaned has corroded, no amount of rubbing with metal polish will do the trick. For corrosion is a disease of the metal, the result of oxidation which is believed to be caused, and certainly is accelerated, by exposing pewter to low temperature in a moist climate. Once begun, the disease spreads until large areas are affected and, as with many ailments of the human body, elimination of the diseased sections is the only cure. The corrosion appears as a crust or as a group of small excrescences of a dark greenish or brownish black color on the surface of the metal.

Until recently very little was known about the cause of 'tin disease,' but Doctor Sven Brennert of Stockholm made a careful study of the subject, which was made available to the English-reading public in a bulletin, dated August, 1935, published by the International Tin Research and Development Council, which in turn was summarized for the layman by Doctor Percy E. Raymond in Bulletin no. 7 of the Pewter Collectors' Club. Doctor Brennert established three facts that are pertinent to a study of pewter. First of all, 'tin disease' is caused by an electrolytic action which occurs in the presence of moisture, dilute acids, or alkalis or salt solutions; secondly, once that action is under way very dilute solutions will continue it; and thirdly, tin in the presence of less noble elements, such as lead, is not as readily subject to attack as in the pure tin state.

The lessons which these findings teach us are: (1) that our collections will be best preserved in a dry climate; (2) that if pewter is used on the table or for flowers, it should be carefully cleaned and dried afterward; and (3) that our finest pewter — that which is freest from lead — is most subject to tin disease, and consequently requires the most care.

The removal of pewter scale requires the use of some penetrating agent (such as paraffin oil, dilute hydrochloric acid, or lye), which will eat into and soften it without affecting the sound metal. Paraffin, though safe, is slow. Hydrochloric acid, quickest in action of the three, requires great care. It should be used only by the expert or by the amateur who has some knowledge of chemistry, and who, by successful experimentation upon valueless pewter, has learned how to use the acid and to know what results to expect from its use under varying conditions. Lye, which is less dangerous, will ordinarily give just as satisfactory results.

To clean pewter with lye, take a wash-boiler, a large galvanized pail, or other container, that is considerably larger than any of the pieces to be cleaned, and fill with very hot water to a point where the pewter, when immersed, will be entirely covered. The hotter the water the quicker will be the action of the solution. Add about half a can of lye to a pail of water — careful measurement is not necessary — and stir with a stick until all particles of the lye are dissolved. Since lye has the same action upon flesh as upon corroded metal, the hands should be protected by rubber gloves, and, as a precaution against splashing when removing pewter from the bath, old clothes should be worn.

The bath is now ready for the pewter. Immerse the pieces in such manner that all surfaces will be exposed to the action of the lye. Do not, for example, drop in a stack of plates and allow them to lie flat on the bottom of the pail. A plate rack, similar in form to a large toast rack, can be improvised out of pieces of wire, and the rack, filled with plates, can be lowered into the solution. If that cannot be contrived, move the pewter frequently with a stick so as to permit the lye free access to all surfaces. Above all else make sure that no part of the pewter protrudes above the bath, for, if a piece is left in that position for any length of time, an ineradicable line of discoloration will appear on the pewter just at the water line.

The length of time recommended for the immersion will vary with the depth of the corrosion and with the temperature and strength of the solution. Half an hour or less will be sufficient in some cases, but no harm will come to the metal if it is permitted to stand overnight. Allowing the pewter to remain in the solution longer than is actually necessary is preferable to removing it too soon and scratching the surface needlessly in an effort to remove the scale before the latter has been thoroughly softened.

Use sticks or tongs to remove the pewter from the bath; rinse in clean water and then scrub with soap and brush. If the pewter has soaked long enough in the lye, the corrosion and dirt will come off in a black stream with the aid of but slight pressure on its surface. If, however, the corrosion seems to resist the brush, the piece should be returned to the bath for longer immersion or, better still, should be dropped into a stronger solution. Until the scale has disintegrated into fine particles and crumbles at the touch, the lye has not completed its work. In some obstinate cases, where corrosion extends deeply into pits or crevices too fine to admit the coarse bristles of a brush, steel wool must be substituted for the brush. Even then only the lightest pressure is necessary and the grade of steel wool used should never be coarser than triple O.

Removal of all extraneous particles in this cleansing operation leaves a uniformly clean but often rough surface of a dull light gray color. If the disease was deep-seated, pockmarks will be evident where disintegration of the pewter took place, and in some instances the metal will have been eaten clear through, leaving a hole. Such a result is, of course, unfortunate, but preferable to dirty pewter in which disease may still be spreading.

Return of the pewter to its original color and luster is obtained by cleaning with metal polish and soap and water exactly as prescribed for metal which did not require a lye bath.

I have said above that cleaning with lye is generally satisfactory. There are three types of articles, however, which should never be dropped into lye solutions. Teapots or other forms of hollow-ware, with handles or lid buttons made of wood, should be painted with acid because lye will not only discolor the wood, but will also open up in it cracks and seams. Similarly pewter that has been japanned or has a japanned or painted metal handle should not be immersed in lye unless the owner desires to have the japanning removed. The third group comprises all forms of hollow-ware which have defective hollow handles. The word defective is used here to denote a handle that has a hole or crack which, when immersed, would admit and bottle up the lye, and from which the lye would later drain drop by drop, subjecting the surface upon which it drained to the danger of discoloration exactly as on the plate which is permitted to extend above the surface of a lye bath. Unless the holes can be stopped up thoroughly before the piece is immersed, removal of the corrosion with acid is much safer.

Every collector should clean his own pewter, first, in order to ensure proper treatment of his possessions, and, secondly, because of the educational value of his labors. He will thus learn, as in no other way, what individual pieces feel like. The comparative ease or difficulty with which pewter takes a polish will teach its owner how to estimate roughly the lead content of any given item, and as he concentrates upon the surfaces which he is polishing his attention will be directed to peculiarities in design or methods of manufacture which might otherwise have escaped his notice. Best of all, if after hours of labor he succeeds in restoring as a thing of beauty an object which was ready for the junk heap, he will have recaptured in so doing some of the feeling of pride of the craftsman who fashioned it.

In closing this chapter I wish to stress, as others before me have done, the fact that the high crime of which any pewter collector can be guilty is to permit his pewter to be buffed. If for any reason you cannot or will not clean your own pewter, do make certain that those to whom you entrust it do not put it on the wheel. That is ruining, not cleaning, pewter, and, as Kerfoot truly warned, 'a buffed piece is a buffed piece forever.'

RANDOM NOTES ON COLLECTING

RARE indeed must be the collector of pewter who, looking over his possessions, can honestly say that he regrets none of his purchases. In almost every collection are certain undesirable items which the owner would gladly exchange for the purchase money. These he possesses today because his acquisitive enthusiasm, particularly in the early stages of his collecting, far outstripped his discriminatory powers. Almost all of us began to collect before we knew what we really wanted. To the beginner the suggestion is therefore offered that he buy with extreme caution until he has acquired, by examining the collections of others, a general knowledge of pewter forms and at least some slight discernment between good and poor metal.

There is no royal road to such knowledge. The written word may teach us somewhat, but the particular value of books on pewter lies in the illustrations, which most assuredly may be studied to advantage. There is, however, no other medium for enlightenment comparable to the actual examination and handling of the metal. To quote J. B. Kerfoot, in *American Pewter*:

> The unquenchable desire and the unending quest . . . of the student and collector of pewter should be opportunity, and more opportunity, and still more opportunity to handle pewter — pewter of all types and grades, of all nationalities and periods. Opportunity to hold it and heft it; to run inquisitive fingers over its differing surfaces; to take in its varying sheens with discriminating eyes; to test its many tensions and listen to its revealing rings. This and the firm resolve to take no man's word for it, but to find out for one's self what pewter does to one's own senses. For only so can come to us the joy of feeling our own sensitivenesses develop and refine.

As soon as the collector has acquired a general knowledge of forms and touch-designs, his progress toward connoisseurship will be rapid, provided he has access to pewter other than his own and uses such opportunity intelligently. As often as he picks up a piece of pewter, let him blind his eye to the touch-mark until eyes and fingers have assayed the object as a whole and the mind has made note of its probable period and provenance. The ensuing examination of the touch-mark will in many cases determine the maker and confirm or correct the collector's guess. Thus, by the method of trial and error, he accumulates knowledge of the forms that were made in the different countries and learns in time to observe those minute variations in quality, design, and detail (apparent to the trained eyes and fingers), some of which are sufficiently individualistic to permit a correct attribution to one particular craftsman.

At the outset every collector should define for himself the scope of his collection. Is it to include the pewter of only one period, one locality, or one general shape? Or are his tastes to be catholic, limited only by the size of his pocketbook and the space for display at his disposal? There are collections — interesting collections, too — which include only the work of one shop; others that are limited to one form. Anyone who sets out to collect porringers, let us say, or whale-oil lamps, will be amazed at the variety of design that is open to him. His choice, whatever it be, should be determined early, before he shall have made purchases which he will at a later date have cause to regret.

With few exceptions the collector of American pewter, when first setting forth upon his quest, harbors the hope that he will some day find an example of seventeenth-century pewter made in this country. Because the possibility of such a discovery does exist, I would rob no one of his hope, but the mathematical probabilities that so early a piece has survived are very slim indeed, and even slimmer are the chances that it could be recognized for what it is. For it must be remembered that there was very little incentive to preserve early pewter. The metal itself was not cheap, but the conversion charge was low. A pewterer's advertisement almost invariably included an offer to accept old pewter in exchange for new. So from time to time each household sent back to the shop accumulations of damaged and worn pieces which were exchanged for new wares of the latest fashion. If any really early piece has survived, its most likely hiding-place is in one of the early churches.

Assuming that such items do exist, how can they be identified? Even if they originally bore touches, the odds by now are very great that such marks have been obliterated by wear. But allowing for miracles, it is possible that an example will be found showing a clear impression of its maker's mark. Let us consider, therefore, the touches on the earliest London touch-plate; for our seventeenth-century makers were English by birth or extraction, and would probably have used touches of the same general design as those employed by the London craftsmen.

We find that of the marks struck in 1670 or earlier on the oldest of the existing London touch-plates not one in seven gives the maker's name. Initials were considered sufficient identification in those early days. So must it have been with our own pewterers also. Consequently, even though seventeenth-century American pewter, stamped with a well-preserved impression of its maker's touch, may have survived, we can hope for little more than that the mark includes the initials of a pewterer whose name is already known; and even then positive identification would be hazardous.[1]

But, although we may never find colonial pewter made before 1700, a sufficiently large group of pre-Revolutionary pieces of varied design has come to light in the past few years to assure us that the future still holds for us many an interesting discovery.

In the pages which immediately follow, a few suggestions will be offered which may, upon occasion, aid the collector in distinguishing American from foreign wares or give him some clue to the probable provenance and approximate dates of certain pieces which he has identified as American.

---

[1] Since this paragraph was written the now-famous seventeenth century Copeland spoon has been found at Jamestown, Virginia. This I hold to be a miracle which does not, to any great extent, invalidate the observations made above.

Random Notes on Collecting

The scarcity of American pewter proves definitely how dependent upon Europe the colonists were for the fulfillment of even their simplest wants. The bulk of the pewter which we find in America today was manufactured abroad. Consequently, one of the most valuable assets to him who limits his collection to American pewter is the ability to recognize the American product when he sees it. The attainment of such discrimination requires first of all a knowledge of American forms and touches and familiarity with the names of American pewterers whose touches are still unknown. Only less essential, however, is an understanding of the shapes made, the details of construction and design employed, and the general types of touches used by the craftsmen of those countries upon which the colonists were in large measure dependent for their pewter — Germany, the Netherlands, France, and particularly Great Britain.

London pewter in the eighteenth century was the standard of quality for the western world. The bulk of what is offered for sale to us today was made in England. The study of British pewter is therefore strongly recommended to the American collector. In *Old Pewter, Its Makers and Its Marks*, the late Howard H. Cotterell has listed thousands of British makers with their touches, but for those to whom that volume may not be accessible, a very brief list is given herewith of pewterers of Great Britain whose work is sufficiently common in this country to lead to the inference that their trade with the colonies was large. The quality of metal and workmanship of these shops was almost invariably high, but their work is of interest to the collector of American pewter chiefly because of what it teaches us. The list follows, headed by four shops (or successions of partnerships) any one of which has probably left behind more pewter in America than any equally early establishment of our own.

1. John Townsend of London, his partners and successors (Townsend and Giffin; Townsend and Reynolds; Townsend and Compton; Thomas Compton; Thomas and Townsend Compton), 1748–1817. I do not believe I should be guilty of overstatement in estimating that over fifty per cent of the marked antique pewter in this country bears a touch of John Townsend or of one of his successors.
2. Samuel Ellis of London and his successor, Thomas Swanson, 1721–1783. Only less plentiful than the pewter of the Townsend firms is that of Samuel Ellis.
3. Richard King of London, 1745–1798.
4. The group of Bristol firms of which Robert Bush, Preston Edgar, and James Curtis were owners or partners (Robert Bush and Company; Bush and Perkins; Curtis and Company; Edgar, Curtis and Company; Edgar and Company; and Edgar and Son, *c.* 1770–1850.)

The secondary list which follows, arranged alphabetically, includes the names of British makers whose pewter, though no longer plentiful in this country, is found not infrequently:

Burford and Green, London, 1748–1780.
Stephen Cox, Bristol, 1735–1754.
Erasmus Dole, Bristol, 1679–1697.
Samuel Dunscomb, Birmingham, *c.* 1740–1780.
John Fasson, London, 1745–1792.
Graham and Wardrop, Glasgow, *c.* 1776–1806.

Random Notes on Collecting

Henry and Richard Joseph, London, 1787.
Stephen Maxwell, Glasgow, c. 1780–1800.
Francis Pigott, London, 1741–1784.
James and Joseph Spackman, London, c. 1780–1785.
John Watts, London, 1725–1760.
A. Williams, Bideford, c. 1730.
James Yates, Birmingham, c. 1800–1840.
John Yates, Birmingham, c. 1835.
Richard Yates, London, 1772–1824.

The collector of American pewter should know something about the British touches, not only in order to differentiate between British and American items, but also in order that he may in a general way determine, in advance of their discovery, the probable character of early (and unlisted) American marks. For the marks of most of our pre-Revolutionary makers and even those of a few later men resemble closely touches of contemporary Englishmen. In some cases the designs were direct steals from makers in England or on the Continent. For instance, the lamb-and-dove touch of John Townsend of London served as the model for marks of William Will of Philadelphia and Richard Austin of Boston, and John Will's angel touch had its counterpart in many Continental marks. These are but random examples of a practice prevalent among American pewterers of the eighteenth century. And since the pieces bearing unlisted touches can usually be purchased cheaply, becoming sought-after rarities when their touches have been identified, the knowledge of the European marks and the selective ability which such knowledge engenders are doubly desirable.

And now it may not be amiss to comment upon several fallacious beliefs which are given credence by many collectors and dealers.

Perhaps the most persistent and at the same time the most erroneous is the belief that, because English and Continental pewterers were required to stamp their touches on their wares, any unmarked pewter must be American. Such an opinion has little foundation in fact. Although most foreign flatware, particularly that of Great Britain, was marked, many a piece bearing every characteristic of European workmanship has been found without a semblance of a touch. Furthermore, we have all had the experience of hearing some dealer say of a badly worn piece, 'I know this is American because it is unmarked.' If such a statement were necessarily true, a bit of coarse steel wool would be all the equipment required to transform European into American pewter. It should be noted also that, although London flatware was almost always marked, the same practice was rarely if ever followed on small articles such as creamers, peppers, sprinklers, etc.; and even the larger forms of hollow-ware, for instance, teapots and mugs, are occasionally found unmarked in England. While on the subject of the marking of hollow-ware I should like to point out that in England the excise officers assayed and measured mugs, tankards, and other hollow-ware destined to be used in public houses or for measuring purposes generally, and, as evidence that the vessels were of satisfactory size and quality, stamped beneath the lip of each, near the handle, the capacity of the piece, together with the official marks of the local bureau. Such a touch is the 'W. R.' (William, Rex) crowned, which is frequently mistaken in this country for a maker's mark. I have never seen marks of that nature upon American mugs or tankards, though early newspapers prove that such a practice was followed, at least in Philadelphia.

There is a current belief, probably only partially justified, that a hammered American plate is necessarily early, and that absence of hammer-marks indicates comparatively late manufacture. It is indeed true that flatware made by American pewterers whose careers began after the Revolution was apparently never hammered, and equally true that most of those makers whose careers spanned the Revolution usually did hammer their plates, but among recent discoveries are several earlier pieces of flatware which show no indentations of the hammer. I own a basin made by John Bassett, who died in 1761, and a plate impressed with the touch of Thomas Simpkins, whose death occurred in 1766. Hammer-marks are not visible on either of these items, yet they are among the earliest examples of American flatware thus far reported.

Let us say, then, that normally flatware was not hammered in this country after about 1785; that most flatware (except basins) made in the period from 1760 to 1785 was hammered; and that further discoveries alone will provide a basis for the determination of how common the use of the hammer was in the earlier days. It is my own belief that prior to 1760 much flatware was never hammered at all; that such treatment was given in the early years only to a piece which sold at a premium; that the competition of London pewterers shortly before the Revolution compelled our markers to hammer their wares; and that finally (about 1785) hammering had to be discarded when the low price of pottery and china forced American pewterers to cut to a minimum the cost of manufacture.

One more fallacy is the belief that hall-marks on American pewter necessarily indicate early workmanship. Just as in the case of hammering, the use of hall-marks on nineteenth-century metal was rarely if ever employed. I know of one exception, a pitcher, made after 1830, which strangely enough is stamped with the touches of Thomas and Sherman Boardman and also with the hall-marks of their uncle, Edward Danforth, who retired before their pewter-making began. This pitcher may have been, as Louis G. Myers suggested, in his *Notes on American Pewterers*, a presentation piece to the older man, stamped with his discarded dies merely as a compliment to him. Barring that one exception, I have never seen or heard of a hammered or hall-marked piece of American pewter impressed with the touch of a man whose career began after 1796.

The use of hall-marks and hammer appears to have gone hand in hand; where we find one we frequently find the other. Most of our pewterers of the Revolutionary years used hall-marks, but their predecessors apparently did not. Although hall-marks are found on many English plates of the seventeenth century, not one among our earliest examples bears touches of that nature. They are lacking on the surviving work of Simon Edgell, John Carnes, David Cutler, Thomas Simpkins, 'Semper Eadem,' John Bassett, Francis Bassett, and Robert Boyle. We are therefore probably on firm ground in saying that hall-marks were rarely used in this country before 1750 or 1760, were almost universally employed thereafter until 1785, were gradually discarded after the Revolution, and had been completely abandoned by 1800.

One more peculiarity of American touch-marks is sufficiently interesting to warrant comment. This point, which escapes the notice of many collectors, is the significance of the number of stars in the touches (principally eagle marks) which made their appearance in the Federal period. Just as we can date any American flag by the number of stars in its field, so we can determine the approximate date of first use of almost every touch which includes in the field or border thirteen or more stars. Each star in any given touch represented a state, and the total number of stars indicated the number of states in the Union when the touch was designed. There are a few exceptions, touches in which the stars form a complete or almost complete circular border. In those cases (one touch each of Samuel Danforth, Thomas Danforth, Third, and Joseph Danforth, Junior, and two of Blakslee Barns) the stars were evidently used as a decorative feature with no other significance, but barring those exceptions the stars were included with the definite intention of dating the designs.

To take an example, George Lightner first advertised as a pewterer in 1806. His large touch shows seventeen stars. Ohio was admitted as the seventeenth state in 1803; Louisiana as the eighteenth in 1812. Hence, without the evidence of directories or newspapers we could be certain that Lightner first used the touch in question between the years 1803 and 1812. By similar deductions we know that Parks Boyd had secured his die, and probably had opened his shop, at least two years before his name was listed for the first time in a Philadelphia Directory.

A careful examination and comparison of details of construction, design, and touch will elicit many other facts of interest, and will develop in the collector a keenness which should make him a master of his subject.

UNSOLVED PROBLEMS OF
AMERICAN PEWTER

ALTHOUGH many names have been added to the first comprehensive list of American pewterers, many new forms and touches have been discovered since 1924, and much additional information about the makers then known has been gathered, most of the problems inherited from Mr. Kerfoot still defy solution. In fact, their number has grown with the intervening years.

We still wish to know what has become of all of the hollow-ware of Boston; we still wonder why no one can find an early American measure; we still seek a reason for the disappearance of all pewter made in New York in the first two decades of the nineteenth century; and we know no better than Mr. Kerfoot did the identity of 'Semper Eadem,' of 'Unidentified Eagle No. 1,' and of the makers of the New England porringers with initials cast in the handles. And to those problems we have added that of twenty or more additional unidentified touches which we wish to attribute to American pewterers. May the next volume on this subject contribute some satisfactory answers to our queries, and lay to rest a few of those intriguing ghosts which the study of this fascinating subject has called forth.

APPENDIXES
Volumes One and Two

APPENDIX I

CHECK LIST OF AMERICAN MAKERS OF PEWTER, BRITANNIA, OR BLOCK TIN

IN THE list which follows are the names of all men in my records who are known to have made pewter, britannia, or block tin prior to 1850 and who had or might conceivably have had shops of their own. Those names that are starred have left marked examples of their work.

NAME OF INDIVIDUAL OR FIRM	LOCATION OF SHOP	APPROXIMATE WORKING DATES
Alberti, Johann Philip	Philadelphia, Pa.	1754–1780
Alberti and Höran (Philip Alberti and Christian Höran)	Philadelphia, Pa.	1758–1764
Allaire, Anthony J.	New York, N.Y.	1816–1821
Allison, Andrew	Philadelphia, Pa.	1837–1841
Allison, John	Philadelphia, Pa.	1835–1836
Archer, Benjamin	St. Louis, Mo.	1847
*Archer, Ellis S.	Philadelphia, Pa.	1842–1850
Archer and Janney (Benj. Archer and N. E. Janney)	St. Louis, Mo.	1847
*Armitages and Standish	Location unknown	1840 or later
Austin, John	Boston, Mass.	1785
*Austin, Nathaniel	Charlestown, Mass.	1763–1807
*Austin, Richard	Boston, Mass.	1793–1817
*Babbitt, Crossman & Co. (Isaac Babbitt and William W. Crossman)	Taunton, Mass.	1826–1828
*Babbitt and Crossman (same partners as above)	Taunton, Mass.	1824–1826
Badco(c)ke, Thomas	Philadelphia, Pa.	1707
*Badger, Thomas	Boston, Mass.	1787–1815
Bailey, Timothy	Malden, Mass.	1830–1840
*Bailey and Putnam (Timothy Bailey and James H. Putnam)	Malden, Mass.	1830–1835
Baker, John	Boston, Mass.	1676–1696
Baldwin, L. G.	Meriden, Conn.	1849
Ball, William	Philadelphia, Pa.	1775–1782
*Barns, Blak(e)slee	Philadelphia, Pa.	1812–1817
*Barns, Stephen	Unknown	1791–1800
*Bartholdt, William	Williamsburgh, N.Y.	1850–1854
Barton, Charles E. (partner in Leonard, Reed, and Barton)	Taunton, Mass.	1835–1850 and later
Bassett, Francis	New York, N.Y.	1718–1758

Appendix I

American Makers of Pewter, Britannia, or Block Tin

Name of Individual or Firm	Location of Shop	Approximate Working Dates
*Boyd, Parks	Philadelphia, Pa.	1795–1819
*Boyle, Robert	New York, N.Y.	1752–1758
*Bradford, Cornelius	New York, N.Y.	1752–1753, 1770–1785
	Philadelphia, Pa.	1753–1770
Bradford, John	Boston, Mass.	1784–1788
Bradford, William, Junior	New York, N.Y.	1719–1758
Bradford and McEuen (Cornelius Bradford and Malcolm McEuen)	New York, N.Y.	1772–1785
*Brigden, Timothy	Albany, N.Y.	1816–1819
*Brook Farm	West Roxbury, Mass.	1841–1847
Brooks, David S.	Hartford, Conn.	1828
Browe and Dougherty	Newark, N.J.	1845
*Brunstrom, John Andrew	Philadelphia, Pa.	1783–1793
*Buckley, Townsend M.	Troy, N.Y.	1854–1857
Bull, Lyman and Couch (—— Bull, William Lyman, Ira Couch)	Meriden, Conn.	1845–1849
Bumste(a)d, Thomas	Roxbury, Mass.	1640–1643
	Boston, Mass.	1643–1677
Burdett, Aaron	Baltimore, Md.	1838–1841
Byles, Thomas	Newport, R.I.	1711–1712
	Philadelphia, Pa.	1738–1771
*Cahill, J. W., & Co.	Location unknown	after 1830
*Calder, William	Providence, R.I.	1817–1856
Calverley, John	Philadelphia, Pa.	1840–1841
Camp, William E.	Middletown, Conn.	1849
Campbell, John	Annapolis, Md.	1749–1770
Campbell, Mungo	Philadelphia, Pa.	1752
*Campmell, Samuel	Connecticut ?	c. 1820
*Capen, Ephraim	New York, N.Y.	c. 1848
*Capen and Molineux (Ephraim Capen and George Molineux)	New York, N.Y.	1848–1854
*Carnes, John	Boston, Mass.	1723–1760
Carter, Samuel	Boston, Mass.	1712–1747
Clark(e), Jonas	Boston, Mass.	1715–1737
Clark(e), Thomas	Boston, Mass.	1674–1720
*Coldwell, George	New York, N.Y.	1787–1811
*Colton, Oren (see Woodbury and Colton)	Philadelphia, Pa.	1835–1838
Comer, John	Boston, Mass.	1674–1721
Comer, John, Junior	Boston, Mass.	1700–1706
Cone, S. L.	Meriden, Conn.	1849
Connell, Thomas (see Palethorp and Connell)	Philadelphia, Pa.	1829–1840
Cook —— (see Woodman, Cook & Co.)	Portland, Maine	after 1830
*Copeland, Joseph	Chuckatuck and Jamestown, Va.	1675–1691
Corne, Anthony	Charleston, S.C.	1735
Cotton (see Hall and Cotton)	Location unknown	after 1830

Appendix I

Name of Individual or Firm	Location of Shop	Approximate Working Dates
Couch, Ira (see Griswold and Couch)	Meriden, Conn.	1830–1845
Cowles, George (see Lewis and Cowles)	East Meriden, Conn.	1834–1835
Cox(e), William	Philadelphia, Pa.	1715–1721
Crossman, William W. (see Babbitt and Crossman)	Taunton, Mass.	1824–1835
*Crossman, West and Leonard (William W. Crossman, William A. West, and Zephaniah A. Leonard)	Taunton, Mass.	1828–1830
Curtis, Edwin E.	Meriden, Conn.	1838–1845
Curtis, Enos H.	Meriden, Conn.	1845–1849
*Curtis(s), Lemuel J.	Meriden, Conn.	1836–1849
Curtis, Stephen (see Yale and Curtis)	New York, N.Y.	1858–1867
Curtis and Curtis (Edwin E. and Lemuel J. Curtis)	Meriden, Conn.	1838–1840
Curtis and Lyman (Lemuel J. Curtis and Wm. W. Lyman)	Meriden, Conn.	1846
*Curtiss, Daniel	Albany, N.Y.	1822–1840
*Curtiss, I.	Location unknown	c. 1820
Curtiss, Joseph, Junior.	Troy, N.Y.	1827–1832
	Albany, N.Y.	1832–1858
*Cutler, David	Boston, Mass.	1730–1765
*Danforth, Edward	Middletown, Conn.	1788–1790
	Hartford, Conn.	1790–1794
Danforth, Job (see Billings and Danforth)	Providence, R.I.	1798–1801
*Danforth, John	Norwich, Conn.	1773–1793
*Danforth, Joseph	Middletown, Conn.	1780–1788
*Danforth, Joseph, Junior	Richmond, Va.	1807–1812
*Danforth, Josiah	Middletown, Conn.	1825–1837
*Danforth, Samuel	Norwich, Conn.	1793–1802
*Danforth, Samuel	Hartford, Conn.	1795–1816
Danforth, Thomas	Taunton, Mass.	1727–1733
	Norwich, Conn.	1733–1773
*Danforth, Thomas, Second	Middletown, Conn.	1755–1782
*Danforth, Thomas, Third	Stepney, Conn.	1777–1818
	Philadelphia, Pa.	1807–1813
Danforth, Thomas, Fourth	Philadelphia, Pa.	1812
	Augusta, Ga.	1818
*Danforth, William	Middletown, Conn.	1792–1820
*Day, Benjamin	Newport, R.I.	1744–1757
*Derby, Thomas S.	Middletown, Conn.	1816–1850
Derby, Thomas S., Junior	Middletown, Conn.	1840–1850
Derby, Thomas S. & Son	Middletown, Conn.	1849
*De Riemer, Cornelius B. & Co.	Auburn, N.Y.	1833
Digg(e)s, William	New York, N.Y.	1701–1702
Dolbeare, Edmund	Boston, Mass.	1671–1702
Dolbeare, James	Boston, Mass.	1727–1740
Dolbeare, John	Boston, Mass.	1690–1740

American Makers of Pewter, Britannia, or Block Tin

Name of Individual or Firm	Location of Shop	Approximate Working Dates
Dolbeare, Joseph	Boston, Mass.	1690–1704
Dougherty (see Browe and Dougherty)	Newark, N.J.	1845
*Dunham, E.	Location unknown	after 1825
*Dunham, Rufus	Westbrook, Me.	1837–1860
*Dunham, R. & Sons (Rufus, Joseph, and Frederick Dunham)	Portland, Me.	1861
Durninger, Daniel	Boston, Mass.	1722–1723
*'Eadem, Semper'	Boston, Mass.	1760–1780
*Edgell, Simon	Philadelphia, Pa.	1713–1742
Edgell, William	Boston, Mass.	1724
*Eggleston, Jacob	Middletown, Conn.	1795–1807
	Fayetteville, N.C.	1807–1813
Eldredge, Eli	Boston, Mass.	1849
	Taunton, Mass.	1860
Ellison, John	Philadelphia, Pa.	1837
*Elsworth, William J.	New York, N.Y.	1767–1798
*Endicott, Edmund	New York, N.Y.	1846–1853
*Endicott and Sumner (Edmund Endicott and William F. Sumner)	New York, N.Y.	1846–1851
E(a)stabrook(e), Richard	Boston, Mass.	1720–1721
Everett, James	Philadelphia, Pa.	1716–1717
Feltman, J. C., Junior (see Sheldon and Feltman)	Albany, N.Y.	1847–1848
*Fenn, G. and J. (Gaius and Jason Fenn)	New York, N.Y.	1831–1843
Fields, Philip	New York, N.Y.	1799
Flagg, Asa F. (see H. Homan & Co.)	Cincinnati, Ohio	1842–1854
Flagg, David	Boston, Mass.	1750–1772
*Flagg and Homan (Asa F. Flagg and Henry Homan)	Cincinnati, Ohio	1842–1854
Fletcher, Thomas	Philadelphia, Pa.	1837–1841
Francis, Daniel (see Whitmore and Francis)	Buffalo, N.Y.	1833–1842
Francis, Thomas	Boston, Mass.	1718
Frary, James A. (see Frary and Benham)	Meriden, Conn.	1845–1849
Frary and Benham (James A. Frary and Morris Benham)	Meriden, Conn.	1849
Fryers, John	Newport, R.I.	1749–1768
*Fuller and Smith	Poquonock Bridge, Conn.	1849–1851
*—— and Gardner	Location unknown	after 1830
Geanty, Lewis	Baltimore, Md.	1800–1803
George, Anthony, Junior	Philadelphia, Pa.	1839–1847
*Gerhardt & Co.	Location unknown	after 1840
*Gleason, Roswell	Dorchester, Mass.	1822–1871
*Glennore Company (see G. Richardson)	Cranston, R.I.	after 1825
Graham, Jasper (see Graham and Savage)	Middletown, Conn.	1837
Graham, John B. (see Savage and Graham)	Middletown, Conn.	1837–1838
*Graham and Savage (Jasper Graham and W. H. Savage)	Middletown, Conn.	1837

Appendix I

NAME OF INDIVIDUAL OR FIRM	LOCATION OF SHOP	APPROXIMATE WORKING DATES
Grame (or Greames) Samuel	Boston, Mass.	1639–1645
*Graves, Henry H.	Middletown, Conn.	1849–1851
*Graves, Joshua B.	Middletown, Conn.	1849
*Graves, J. B. and H. H.	Middletown, Conn.	1852
Graves, Richard	Salem, Mass.	1635–1667
Green, Andrew	Boston, Mass.	1773–1798
Green, Jonas	Boston, Mass.	1786–1787
*Green, Samuel	Boston, Mass.	1779–1828
Green, Samuel, Junior	Boston, Mass.	1826–1835
Green, Thomas	Boston, Mass.	1740–1794
Green, Thomas, Junior	Boston, Mass.	1769–1786
Green, Timothy	Boston, Mass.	1780–1782
Green and Austin (Samuel Green and Richard Austin)	Boston, Mass.	1812–1817
Green and Richardson (Samuel Green and George Richardson)	Boston, Mass.	1818
Grindell (or Grennell), Thomas	New York, N.Y.	1789–1791
*Griswold, Ashbil	Meriden, Conn.	1807–1835
Griswold, Giles	Augusta, Ga.	1818–1820
*Griswold, Sylvester	Baltimore, Md.	1820
Griswold and Couch (Ashbil Griswold and Ira Couch)	Meriden, Conn.	1830
Hall, Franklin D. (see Boardman and Hall)	Hartford, Conn.	1840
	Philadelphia, Pa.	1842–1857
Hall, John H. (see Johnson, Hall & Co.)	Middletown, Conn.	1815–1817
*Hall, Boardman & Co. (Franklin D. Hall and Henry S. Boardman)	Philadelphia, Pa.	1846–1848
*Hall and Boardman (same partners as above)	Philadelphia, Pa.	1849–1857
*Hall and Cotton	Location unknown	after 1830
*Hamlin, Samuel	Providence, R.I.	1771–1801
*Hamlin, Samuel E.	Providence, R.I.	1801–1856
Hamlin and Jones (Samuel Hamlin and Gershom Jones)	Providence, R.I.	1774–1781
*Harbeson, ——	Philadelphia, Pa.	1800
Harner, George	New York, N.Y.	1761
Harrison, Joseph	Philadelphia, Pa.	1829–1852
Hart, Lucius D. (see Boardman & Co. and Boardman and Hart)	New York, N.Y.	1828–1850
Hasselberg, Abraham	Philadelphia, Pa.	1762–1779
Hendricks, Francis G.	Charleston, S.C.	1771–1784
Henry, Andrew	Orange Co., N.Y.	1761
Hera, Christian	Philadelphia, Pa.	1791–1817
*Hera, C. and J. (Christian and John Hera)	Philadelphia, Pa.	1800–1812
Hera, John	Philadelphia, Pa.	1800–1812
Hera, John, Second	Philadelphia, Pa.	1817–1821
*Hers —, S. S.	Location unknown	after 1830
*Heyne, Johann Christopher	Lancaster, Pa.	1754–1780

American Makers of Pewter, Britannia, or Block Tin

Name of Individual or Firm	Location of Shop	Approximate Working Dates
Hill, John	New York, N.Y.	1846–1848
Hillsburgh, Charles	New York, N.Y.	1837
*Hinsdale, J. and D. (John and Daniel Hinsdale)	Middletown, Conn.	1815
*Holmes, Robert, and Sons	Baltimore, Md.	1853–1854
*Holt, Thomas R.	Meriden, Conn.	1845–1849
Holyoke, John	Boston, Mass.	1706–1760
*Homan, Henry	Cincinnati, Ohio	1847–1864
*Homan & Co. (Henry Homan and Asa F. Flagg)	Cincinnati, Ohio	1847–1864
*Hopper, Henry	New York, N.Y.	1842–1847
Höran, Johann Christian (see Alberti and Höran)	Philadelphia, Pa.	1758–1786
Horsewell, William	New York, N.Y.	1705–1709
*Horsford, E. N.	Location unknown	after 1830
*Houghton and Wallace	Philadelphia	1843
House, Edwin	Hartford, Conn.	1841–1846
*Humiston, Willis	Troy, N.Y.	after 1830
*Hunt, S.	Location unknown	after 1830
Hunter, George	Troy, N.Y.	1831
*Hyde, Martin	New York, N.Y.	1857–1858
Isly, Joseph	New York, N.Y.	1715
Jackson, Jonathan	Boston, Mass.	1695–1736
Jagger, Daniel H.	Hartford, Conn.	1844–1846
Jagger, James H.	Hartford, Conn.	1843
Jagger, Walter W.	Hartford, Conn.	1839–1846
Janney, N. E. (see Archer and Janney)	St. Louis, Mo.	1846
Jennings, Theodore	Maryland (?)	1775
*Johnson, Jehiel	Middletown, Conn.	1815–1825
	Fayetteville, N.C.	1818–1819
Johnson, Hall & Co. (Jehiel and Constant Johnson and J. H. Hall)	Middletown, Conn.	1815–1817
Johnson and Nott (Jehiel Johnson and William Nott)	Middletown, Conn.	1817–1818
	Fayetteville, N.C.	1818–1819
Jones, Daniel	Boston, Mass.	1705
*Jones, Edward	New York, N.Y.	1837–1850
*Jones, Gershom (see also Hamlin and Jones)	Providence, R.I.	1774–1809
Jones, Gershom and Sons (Gershom, James, and Samuel Jones)	Providence, R.I.	1806–1807
*Keene, Josiah	Providence, R.I.	1801–1817
Kehler, Adam	Philadelphia, Pa.	1780–1783
Kiersted, Luke	New York, N.Y.	1805
*Kilbourn, Samuel	Baltimore, Md.	1814–1839
Kilbourn and Porter (Samuel Kilbourn and Jephtha Porter)	Baltimore, Md.	1814–1816
*Kimberly, De Witt	Meriden, Conn.	1845–1849

Appendix I

American Makers of Pewter, Britannia, or Block Tin

Name of Individual or Firm	Location of Shop	Approximate Working Dates
*McEuen, Malcolm, and Son (Malcolm and Duncan McEuen)	New York, N.Y.	1793–1803
McIlmoy, John	Philadelphia, Pa.	1793
*McQuilkin, William	Philadelphia, Pa.	1845–1853
Mann, William	Boston, Mass.	1690–1738
*Manning, E. B.	Middletown, Conn.	after 1840
Manning, Thaddeus	Middletown, Conn.	1849
*Manning, Bowman & Co.	Middletown, Conn.	after 1850
*Marston, ——	Baltimore, Md.	after 1830
Maton, Marcus	Hartford, Conn.	1828
Melville, Andrew	Newport, R.I.	1804–1810
*Melville, David	Newport, R.I.	1776–1793
*Melville, Samuel	Newport, R.I.	1793–1800
*Melville, S. and T. (Samuel and Thomas Melville)	Newport, R.I.	1793–1800
*Melville, Thomas	Newport, R.I.	1793–1796
*Melville, Thomas, Second	Newport, R.I.	1796–1824
Melville, William L.	Newport, R.I.	1807–1810
*Meriden Britannia Company	Meriden, Conn.	1852 and later
Merryfield, Robert	New York, N.Y.	1760
Michel, André	New York, N.Y.	1795–1797
Minze, James (see Stafford and Minze)	Albany, N.Y.	1794–1796
Molineux, George (see Capen and Molineux)	New York, N.Y.	1848–1854
Moore, Luke	Philadelphia, Pa.	1819–1822
Morey, David B. (see Smith & Co. etc.)	Boston, Mass.	1841–1860 and later
*Morey and Ober (D. B. Morey and R. H. Ober)	Boston, Mass.	1852–1855
Morey, Ober & Co. (D. B. Morey, R. H. Ober, Thomas Smith)	Boston, Mass.	1855–1857
*Morey and Smith (D. B. Morey and Thomas Smith)	Boston, Mass.	1857–1860 and later
Morgan, Henry	Groton, Conn.	1849
*Munson, John	Yalesville, Conn.	1846–1852
*Neal, I.	Location unknown	1842
Norris, George (see Ostrander and Norris)	New York, N.Y.	1848–1850
Norsworth, John	Norfolk, Va.	1771
North, John	Augusta, Ga.	1818–1823
North and Rowe (John North and Adna S. Rowe)	Augusta, Ga.	1818–1823
Northey, David	Salem, Mass.	1732–1778
Northey, William	Lynn, Mass.	1764–1804
Nott, William	Philadelphia, Pa.	1812
*Nott, William (see Johnson and Nott)	Middletown, Conn.	1813–1817
	Fayetteville, N.C.	1817–1825
Nott, Babcock and Johnson (William Nott, Samuel Babcock, and Jehiel Johnson)	Middletown, Conn.	1817

Appendix I

Name of Individual or Firm	Location of Shop	Approximate Working Dates
Ober, R. H. (see Morey and Ober, etc.)	Boston, Mass.	1849–1857
*Olcott, J. W. (or J. Wolcott)	Baltimore, Md.	1800
*Ostrander, Charles	New York, N.Y.	1848–1854
*Ostrander and Norris (Charles Ostrander and George Norris)	New York, N.Y.	1848–1850
*Palethorp, John H.	Philadelphia, Pa.	1820–1845
*Palethorp, J. H. & Co. (J. H. Palethorp and Thomas Connell)	Philadelphia, Pa.	1839–1841
Palethorp, Robert	Philadelphia, Pa.	1822–1826
*Palethorp, Robert, Junior	Philadelphia, Pa.	1817–1821
Palethorp, R. and J. H. (Robert, Junior, later Robert, Senior, and J. H. Palethorp)	Philadelphia, Pa.	1820–1825
*Palethorp and Connell (see J. H. Palethorp & Co.)	Philadelphia, Pa.	1839–1841
*Parker, Charles & Co.	Meriden, Conn.	1849
*Parker, J. G.	Rochester, N.Y.	1840 or later
*Parkin, W.	Location unknown	after 1835
*Parmenter, W. H.	Location unknown	after 1840
Paschall, Thomas	Philadelphia, Pa.	1686–1718
Pavey, George	Boston, Mass.	1733
Pearse, Robert (see R. Piercy)	New York, N.Y.	1792
Peel, Henry	Philadelphia, Pa.	1822–1833
*Pierce, Samuel	Greenfield, Mass.	1792–1831
Piercy, Robert	New York, N.Y.	1792–1797
Plumley, Charles	Providence, R.I.	1829
	Middletown, Conn.	1844–1848
Plumly, Charles (probably same as above)	Philadelphia, Pa.	1822–1833
*Plumly and Bidgood (Charles Plumly and —— Bidgood)	Philadelphia, Pa.	1825
Pomroy, William C., partner in J. H. Stalkamp & Co.	Cincinnati, Ohio	1856
*Porter, Allen	Westbrook, Me.	1830–1838
Porter, A. and F. (Allen and Freeman Porter)	Westbrook, Me.	1835–1838
*Porter, Freeman	Westbrook, Me.	1835–1860 and later
*Porter, James	Location unknown	1795–1803
Porter, James (probably same as above)	Baltimore, Md.	1803
Porter, Jephtha (see Kilbourn and Porter)	Baltimore, Md.	1814–1816
*Potter, W.	Location unknown	after 1825
*Putnam, James H. (see also Bailey and Putnam)	Malden, Mass.	1830–1855
Raisin, George	Boston, Mass.	1718–1728
Randle (or Randall), John	Boston, Mass.	1738–1739
Reed, Henry G. (see Leonard, Reed, and Barton)	Taunton, Mass.	1835–1860 and later
*Reed and Barton (H. G. Reed and C. E. Barton)	Taunton, Mass.	1840 to present

American Makers of Pewter, Britannia, or Block Tin

NAME OF INDIVIDUAL OR FIRM	LOCATION OF SHOP	APPROXIMATE WORKING DATES
*Reich, John Philip	Salem, N.C.	1820–1830
Reich, J. and P. (John and Philip Reich)	Salem, N.C.	1829
*Renton & Co.	New York, N.Y.	after 1830
*Richardson, B. and Son	Philadelphia, Pa.	1839
Richardson, Francis B.	Providence, R.I.	1847–1848
*Richardson, George	Boston, Mass.	1818–1828
*Richardson, George (probably same as above)	Cranston, R.I.	1830–1845
Richardson, George B.	Providence, R.I.	1847–1848
Rodgers, John	Philadelphia, Pa.	1839–1840
*Rogers, Smith & Co.	Hartford, Conn.	after 1840
Rowe, Adna S. (see North and Rowe)	Augusta, Ga.	1818–1828
Russell and Beach	Chester, Conn.	1838
Rust, John N. and Samuel	New York, N.Y.	1842–1845
Rust, Leonard M.	New York, N.Y.	1849
*Rust, Samuel	New York, N.Y.	1837–1845
*Sage, Timothy	St. Louis, Mo.	1847–1848
Sage, T. & Co.	St. Louis, Mo.	1847
*Sage and Beebe	Location unknown	after 1840
Savage, William	Middletown, Conn.	1838–1839
*Savage, William H. (see Graham and Savage)	Middletown, Conn.	1837–1840
*Savage and Graham (William H. Savage and John B. Graham)	Middletown, Conn.	1837–1838
Seip, Jacob	Philadelphia, Pa.	1820–1822
*Sellew & Co. (Enos, Osman, and William Sellew)	Cincinnati, Ohio	1832–1860
Seltzer, Abraham	Philadelphia, Pa.	1793
Shaw (see Sickel and Shaw)	Philadelphia, Pa.	1849–1850
*Sheldon and Feltman (Smith Sheldon and J. C. Feltman, Junior)	Albany, N.Y.	1847–1848
*Shoff, I.	Eastern Pennsylvania	Late 18th century
Shrimpton, Henry	Boston, Mass.	1639–1666
Sickel, H. G.	Philadelphia, Pa.	1849–1853
*Sickel and Shaw (H. G. Sickel and —— Shaw)	Philadelphia, Pa.	1849–1850
*Simpkins, Thomas	Boston, Mass.	1727–1766
*Simpson, Samuel	Yalesville, Conn.	1835–1852
*Simpson and Benham (Samuel Simpson and Morris Benham)	New York, N.Y.	1845–1847
*Skinner, John	Boston, Mass.	1760–1790
*Smith, Eben	Beverly, Mass.	1841–1856
Smith, George W. (see Smith and Feltman)	Albany, N.Y.	1849–1856
Smith, James E.	Maryland (?)	after 1775
Smith, Ober & Co. (Thomas Smith, R. H. Ober, and D. B. Morey)	Boston, Mass.	1849–1852
Smith, Thomas	Boston, Mass.	1700–1742
Smith, Thomas (see Morey and Smith, etc.)	Boston, Mass.	1841–1862

Appendix I

Name of Individual or Firm	Location of Shop	Approximate Working Dates
Smith, Thomas & Co. (Thomas Smith, D. B. Morey, and Henry White)	Boston, Mass.	1842–1847
Smith, William R.	Middletown, Conn.	1848
*Smith & Co. (Thomas Smith, D. B. Morey, Henry White)	Boston, Mass.	1847–1849
Smith & Co. (another) (George W. Smith and associates)	Albany, N.Y.	1853–1856
*Smith and Feltman (G. W. Smith and J. C. Feltman, Junior)	Albany, N.Y.	1849–1852
*Smith and Morey (Thomas Smith and D. B. Morey)	Boston, Mass.	1841–1842
*Southmayd, Ebenezer	Castleton, Vt.	1802–1820
Spencer, George B. (see Stafford, Spencer & Co.)	Albany, N.Y.	1815–1817
Spencer, Thomas (see Staffords, Rogers & Co.)	Albany, N.Y.	1815
Stafford, Benedict & Co. (Spencer and Joab Stafford and Lewis Benedict)	Albany, N.Y.	1824
Stafford, Hallenbake (see S. Stafford & Co.)	Albany, N.Y.	1815–1824
Stafford, Joab (see Stafford, Benedict & Co.)	Albany, N.Y.	1824
Stafford, John (see Staffords, Rogers & Co.)	Albany, N.Y.	1815
*Stafford, Spencer	Albany, N.Y.	1794–1830
Stafford, Spencer, Junior (see S. Stafford & Co.)	Albany, N.Y.	1817–1824
*Stafford, S. & Co. (Spencer, Spencer, Junior, and Hallenbake Stafford and Lewis Benedict)	Albany, N.Y.	1817–1824
Stafford, Spencer & Co. (Spencer and Hallenbake Stafford, George B. Spencer, Lewis Benedict and Sebastian Tymiesen)	Albany, N.Y.	1815–1817
Stafford and Minze (Spencer Stafford and James Minze)	Albany, N.Y.	1794–1796
Staffords, Rogers & Co. (John and Spencer Stafford, Thomas and George B. Spencer and —— Rogers)	Albany, N.Y.	1814–1815
*Stalkamp, J. H. & Co.	Cincinnati, Ohio	1853–1856
*Standish, Alexander	Location unknown	after 1830
*Starr, William H.	New York, N.Y.	1843–1846
*Stedman, S.	Location unknown	after 1800
Steinman, John Frederick	Lancaster, Pa.	1783–1785
Stoddart, Frederick	Philadelphia, Pa.	1833
Sumner, William F. (see Endicott and Sumner)	New York, N.Y.	1846–1851
*Sykes, ——	Location unknown	after 1840
*Taunton Britannia Manufacturing Company	Taunton, Mass.	1830–1835
Thomas, John	Philadelphia, Pa.	1841
Thornton, John	Pennsylvania (?)	after 1774

American Makers of Pewter, Britannia, or Block Tin

NAME OF INDIVIDUAL OR FIRM	LOCATION OF SHOP	APPROXIMATE WORKING DATES
*Tomlinson, ——	Location unknown	1843
*Trask, Israel	Beverly, Mass.	1825–1856
*Trask, Oliver	Beverly, Mass.	1832–1839
*Treadway, Amos	Middletown, Conn.	1760–1790
Tyler, John	Boston, Mass.	1720–1756
Tymiesen, Sebastian (see Stafford, Spencer & Co.)	Albany, N.Y.	1815–1817
*Vose & Co.	Albany, N.Y.	after 1840
Wadsworth, Lester	Hartford, Conn.	1838
*Wallace, R. & Co.	Wallingford, Conn.	1855
*Ward, H. B. & Co.	Wallingford, Conn.	1849
*Warren, ——	Location unknown	after 1830
*Wayne, C. P. & Son	Philadelphia, Pa.	1835
*Weekes, J.	Brooklyn, N.Y.	after 1830
*Weekes, J. (perhaps the same as above)	New York, N.Y.	after 1820
*Weekes, J. & Co. (perhaps the same as above)	Poughkeepsie, N.Y.	1833–1835
Wendeln, John F., partner in J. H. Stalkamp & Co.	Cincinnati, Ohio	1853
West, William A. (see Crossman, West and Leonard)	Taunton, Mass.	1828–1830
*Whitcomb, A. G.	Boston, Mass.	after 1820
White, H. (see Smith & Co.)	Boston, Mass.	1842–1849
*Whitehouse, E.	Location unknown	after 1800
Whitfield, George B.	New York, N.Y.	1828–1865
*Whitfield, G. and J.	New York, N.Y.	1836–1865
*Whitlock, John H.	Troy, N.Y.	1836–1844
*Whitmore, Jacob	Middletown, Conn.	1758–1790
Whitmore, Lewis	Rocky Hill, Conn.	1841
Whitmore and Francis (—— Whitmore and Daniel Francis)	Buffalo, N.Y.	1833
Whitney (see Benham and Whitney)	New York, N.Y.	1849
*Wildes, Thomas	New York, N.Y.	1832–1840
Wilds, Thomas (possibly same as above)	Philadelphia, Pa.	1829–1833
Will, Christian	New York, N.Y.	1770–1789
*Will, George W.	Philadelphia, Pa.	1799–1807
*Will, Henry	New York, N.Y.	1761–1775
	Albany, N.Y.	1775–1783
	New York, N.Y.	1783–1793
*Will, John	New York, N.Y.	1752–1763
Will, Philip	New York, N.Y.	1766
Will, Philip (probably same as above)	Philadelphia, Pa.	1763–1787
*Will, William	Philadelphia, Pa.	1764–1798
Willett, Edward	Upper Marlboro, Md.	1692–1743
Willett, Mary	Upper Marlboro, Md.	1773
Willett, William	Upper Marlboro, Md	1744–1772
*Williams, Lorenzo L.	Philadelphia, Pa.	1838–1842

Appendix I

Name of Individual or Firm	Location of Shop	Approximate Working Dates
*Williams, Otis	Buffalo, N.Y.	1826–1831
Williams, Richard	Stepney, Conn.	1793–1800
*Williams and Simpson (Lorenzo L. Williams and Samuel Simpson)	Yalesville, Conn.	1837–1838
Willis, Thomas	Philadelphia, Pa.	1829–1833
Witherle (or Weatherly) Joshua	Boston, Mass.	1784–1793
Wolfe, John	Philadelphia, Pa.	1801
*Woodbury, J. B.	Philadelphia, Pa.	1835–1838
*Woodbury and Colton	Philadelphia, Pa.	1835–1836
*Woodman, Cook & Co.	Portland, Me.	after 1830
Wyer, Simon	Philadelphia, Pa.	1740–1752
Yale, Burrage	South Reading, Mass.	1808–1835
*Yale, Charles	Wallingford, Conn.	1817–1835
Yale, Charles (probably same as above)	New York, N.Y.	1832
Yale, C. and S. (Charles and Selden Yale)	Wallingford, Conn. Richmond, Va.	1817–1823
Yale, Henry (see Yale and Curtis)	New York, N.Y.	1858–1867
*Yale, Hiram	Wallingford, Conn.	1822–1831
*Yale, H. & Co. (Hiram and Charles Yale)	Yalesville, Conn.	1824–1835
Yale, Samuel (see W. and S. Yale)	Meriden, Conn.	1813–1820
Yale, Selden (see C. and S. Yale)	Wallingford, Conn. Richmond, Va.	1817–1823
Yale, William	Meriden, Conn.	1813–1830
Yale, William (probably same as above)	New York, N.Y.	1830–1832
*Yale, W. and S. (William and Samuel Yale)	Meriden, Conn.	1813–1820
*Yale and Curtis (Henry Yale and Stephen Curtis)	New York, N.Y.	1858–1867
Youle, George	New York, N.Y.	1793–1828
Youle, Thomas	New York, N.Y.	1813–1819
Young, Abraham	New York, N.Y.	1796
*Young, Peter	New York, N.Y. Albany, N.Y.	1775 1785–1795

APPENDIX II

REPRESENTATIVE INVENTORIES OF AMERICAN PEWTER SHOPS

Pewter and Pewter Equipment in the Inventory of Possessions of Richard Estabrooke

FILED OCTOBER 11, 1721, IN BOSTON, MASSACHUSETTS, BY JONATHAN JACKSON, JOHN HOLYOKE AND WILLIAM TYLER

6 Doz. and 5 large belly Porringers	@ 20/	6–8–4
6 Doz. and 2 middling Ditto	@ 18/	5–11–0
6 Doz. and 3 small Ditto	@ 14/	4–7–6
4 Doz. and 6 smaller Ditto	@ 12/	2–14–0
1 Grindstone, Spindle & Frame	@ 20/	1–0–0
1 Casting bench & screws 5/ 1 lead piece & 2 mallets 5/		0–10–0
3 Iron Kettles & 3 Ladles	20/	1–0–0
1 Wheel and Tower and 33 blocks		5–0–0
A parcell of Hooks and hammers and small Tools & pr. sheers		5–10–0
A pr. of Bellows 40/ andirons 7/		2–7–0
3 Doz. and 4 Chamber Potts	@ 45/	8–16–3
9 Doz. and 3 quart Potts	44/	20–7–0
3 Doz. pint Potts N.F	at 28/	4–4–0
367 (lbs) of Rough Basons & Plates	at 20	30–11–8
45 Quart Potts hollow handles	at 3/8	8–5–0
30 Tankards	at 5	7–10–0
10 Quart Potts	at 3/8	3–6–0
19 Pint Potts hollow handles	at 2/4	2–4–4
17 Round brim Chamberpots	at 3/9	3–3–9
6 Doz. & 8 pint Porringers	at 1/8	6–13–4
5 Doz. & 7 middling Do	at 1/6	5–0–6
4 Doz. & 2 small Ditto	at 1/2	2–18–4
8 Doz. & 5 smaller Ditto	at 12/	5–1–0
8 Doz. & 9 Blood porringers	at 5/6	2–8–1
5 Beaker cups	5/	5
4 Doz. 2 Soope plates	at 32/	6–13–4
14 Ditto flatt		1–2–8
8 doz. 1 smaller	at 22	8–17–10
8 doz. Ditto "	at 17	6–16
2 bottom and side stake and 2 horseheads wt 135 lb	at 15d	8–8–9
16 2 Quart Basons	at 4/6	3–12–0
3 Doz. & 2 3 pint Basons		6–13

15 large Quart Ditto	at 2/6	1–17–6
22 small " "	at 2/	2–4
5 Doz. large pint do.	at 1/4	4–0–0
7 " Ditto Smaller	at 13d	4–11–
30 large Sawcers	at 12d	1–10–
2 Doz. 8 smaller	at 8d	1–1–4
59 lbs Old fine pewter	at 1/4	3–18–8
2 Setts of Letters 20/ Wire 27/ 1 Square bit 3/		2–10–0
Old lay mettle 49^{lb} at	12d	2–9–0
1 Beam 8 Scales	8/	–8–0
1 Pewter Standish	2/	2–
A parcell Moulds		37–0–0

Representative Inventories of American Pewter Shops

Pewter Listed in the Inventory of Simon Edgell

Taken August 27, 1742, in Philadelphia by Evan Morgan and Myles Strickland

			£ S.d.
1635 Dishes	5014 lbs.	at 19d	313. 3.10
407 Basons	583 "	" "	21.17.3
146 doz. & 4 Porringers and Bassons		" 20s doz.	146. 6.8
15 Doz. Small Cupps & Porringers		" 8s doz	6. 0.0
12 Doz. Qt. Tankards		" 5s	36. 0.0
2 Doz. & 9 Pint do		" 3s	4.19.0
8 half Gallon Potts		" 11s	4. 8.0
28 Doz & 10 Qt. do		" 3.9	64.17.6
19 Doz & 11 Pint do			22. 0.0
7 Doz & 11 Half Gill do		" 12d	4.15.0
3 Doz. Gill Glasses		" 5s doz.	0.15.0
164 doz. Spoons		" 4s doz.	34.16.0
9 Gross Tea Spoons		" 2s. 2 gross	9.18.0
4 Soop Spoons		" 1/8 pr.	0. 5.0
7 Doz. Pewter Forks		" 2/ doz.	0.14.0
10 Doz. & 5 Tea potts		" 4s	24. 3.4
4 Doz. Mustard Potts		" 2s	4.16.0
5 Doz & 9 Salt Sellers		" 16s doz.	4.12.0
7 Punch Bowles		" 2/6	0.17.0
5 Doz & 10 Dram bottles		" 2/6	8.16.0
2 Doz. & 9 Sucking do		" 3/	4.19.0
7 Barbers Potts		" 5	2. 0.0
8 do Basons		" 5	2. 0.0
18 Cullenders		at 11	9.11.0
11 Bottems for Cullenders		" 1	0.11.0
6 Funnells		3/6	1. 1.6
4 Fine Wrought Plats & 2 Cans for Sacrament Table			1. 0.0
1 Large Water Plate			0. 2.0
1 Pewter Tea Kittle			0. 4.0
13 Syringes		at 2/6	1.12.6
14 Close Stool Panns		at 10	7. 0.0
9 Doz & 8 Chamber Potts		4.9	27.11.0
3 Bed Panns		14	2. 2.0
14 Bed Pan Handles		1	0.14.0
3 Gross Curtain Rings		at 2s Gross	0. 6.0
800 lbs. Old Pewter		10d	33. 6.8

Appendix II

Pewter and Pewter Equipment Listed in the Inventory of Thomas Byles

Presented September 10, 1771, at Philadelphia by Benjamin Harbeson, Jr. and William Will

Old pewter	10 lbs.	at 10d	0. 8.4
Do	2328 do	" 9d	87. 6.0
Pew^r Ware rough Cast	687 "	" 13d	37. 4.3
Pewter plates	567 "	" 18d	42.10.6
Do basons	610 "	" 18d	45.15.0
Wrought dishes	419 "	" 20d	34.18.4
do basons	318 "	" 20½d	27. 3.3
do plates	792 "	" 19d	62.14.0
H^d plates	68 "	" 2s	6.16.0
19 Watter plates		8d	7.12.0
1 Gall Wine Measure			0.15.0
3 ½ Gal do do		10	1.10.0
19 Qt do do		6	5.14.0
30 Pt. do do		3/6	5. 5.0
39 ½ Pt. do do		2	3.18.0
24 Gill do do		20d	2. 0.0
87 Quart Potts		3.6	15. 4.6
12 Pint Potts		2	1. 4.0
63 Quart H^d Mugs		4	12.12.0
13 Quart H^d do		5	3. 5.0
25 H^d Pint do		3	3.15.0
31 Common Qt Bellied mugs		3.6	5. 8.6
38 Qt H^d Tankards		5.6	10. 9.0
28 Qt Common do		5	7. 0.0
58 Strait Bodied do		5	14.10.0
5 Bellied Pt do		3	0.15.0
3 Pt H^d do		3/6	0.10.6
89 Quart H^d Bowles		2s.	8.18.0
82 Pint do		18d.	6. 3.0
55 Lg. Close stool pans		10	27.10.0
3 Sm. do do do		7	1. 1.0
7 Lg. Bed pans		15	5. 5.0
4 Sm. do do		12	2. 8.0
18 Cham^r potts		5	4.10.0
20 H^d do do		6	6. 0.0
42 doz 6 Porringers			30.10.0
28 doz H^d do		24s per doz.	33.12.0
37 Tea Potts			8.14.0
4 2 Qt Coffee Potts		18	3.12.0
8 3 Pt do do		15	6. 0.0
9 Qt do do		10	4.10.0
3 Pt do do		6	0.18.0
44 Sugar Basons with **Covers**		2s	4. 8.0
24 Qt Black Jacks		2/6	3. 0.0

Item	Weight	Price	Value
24 ½ Pt. Cup with handles		1s	1. 4.0
15 ½ Pt. Cups no handles		10d	0.12.6
14 Sm. Pewʳ Cups		9d	0.10.6
48 Pt. Dram Bottles		2s	4.16.0
7 ½ Pt. do do		20d	0.11.8
15 Sucking do		3/6	2.12.6
6 Challices pewʳ		6	1.16.0
23 Soop spoons		2	2. 6.0
43 Hᵈ Table do			0.17.6
36 doz. Com. do do		3/6	6. 6.0
46 doz Tea spoons			2. 6.0
1 Cullinder			0.12.0
2 Cullinders			1.10.0
86 Pewʳ Salts		10d	3.11.8
1 Plate Cover & funnel			0. 6.6
7 doz 8 Candlesticks		7	2.13.8
8 Bottle cranes		3.6	2. 8.0
39 pr Cotton & wool cards		3	5. 8.0
9 pr. flasks & screws			0.12.0
12 Barbers basons		5	3. 0.0
3 do Potts		5	0.15.0
1 Oval Standish			1. 2.6
9 Lg. Chest Standishes			5. 8.0
2 Lead Inkstands			0. 5.0
Pewter curtain rings	14 lbs		1. 1.0
Brass molds	1183	2/6	147.17.6
Pewter do	188	13d	10. 3.8
Brasier stakes & Beak Irons	lbs. oz. 454.12	9d	17. 0.9
1 Pewterers anvil	29		1. 9.0
9 Brasiers heads	44.8		2. 4.6
2 Vices	56	4d	0.18.8
130 files		6d	3. 6.0
1 Pr. Shears			1. 1.0
1 Sm. Anvil	31	4d	0.10.4
28 Hammers		6d	0.14.0
12 Pewterers do		2/6	1.10.0
1 Upright Drill			0. 5.0
1 Solder Mortar & pestle			0. 2.6
Punches, Chisels &c.		66 at 2d	0.11.0
30 New Hooks		18d	2. 5.0
27 Hooks Usefull			1. 7.0
32 Hook shanks		1½d	0. 4.0
5 Wheel burnishers			0. 7.6
Old Iron	500 lbs.	1½d	3. 2.6
101 Sundry Iron tools		4d	1.13.8
1 Cast Iron Stand			0.10.0
2 pʳ Shears 2 pʳ Pinchers			0. 9.9
24 Molds and Paterns		13d	1. 6.0

50	Blocks with Burnings		2.10.0
8	Spoon Bows &c.	18d	0.12.0
10	Graters & Burnishers	4d	0. 3.4
2	Pr Lg. Bellows		2. 0.0
1	Old Brass Ketle		0. 5.0
	Cast Iron Weights		0. 7.6
1	Pewterers Wheel &c		2.10.0
1	Pewterers Anvill & Spoon test	321 lbs. 15d	2. 0.0
	Sundry files, floats, Ladles &c		0. 9.6
1	Small Anvill	10 lbs. 6d	0. 5.0
2	Screw plates & taps		0. 5.0
	Old Lead Weights	34 lbs. 3d	0. 8.6
	Brass do	14 lbs.	1. 8.0
12	Scale Beams &c.		4. 0.0
46	Nest Crucibles		2. 6.0
15	Black Lead do		2. 4.0
	Rotten stone &c.	22 lbs.	1. 2.0
60	Bushel Coal		1.10.0
	Tin glass & Bismuth	10.4 2/6	1. 5.7

Total Inventory £1517.   18.5

Representative Inventories of American Pewter Shops

INVENTORY OF THE 'FRONT SHOP' OF WILLIAM WILL

FILED JANUARY 7, 1799, IN PHILADELPHIA BY JOHN BAKER AND LEWIS FARMER

Item		Unit	Total
8 Chamber potts & 2 Chairpans		$1.50	$15.00
3 Bedpans		3.50	10.50
2 Ice-Cream Moulds		6.00	12.00
43 Sugar Bowls		.50	21.50
12 Coffee Potts		2.00	24.00
18 pr Salts		.31	3.58
40 Tea Potts		.80	32.00
4 Bottle cranes		.50	2.00
17 Half Gallon Measures		1.67	28.39
8 Quart "		.80	6.40
9 Pint "		.67	6.03
22 Half pints and Jills		.43	9.46
22 Quart Mugs		.67	14.74
26 Pint Mugs		.43	11.18
5 Pocket Bottles		.53	2.65
5 Goblets		.40	2.00
15 Cream Jugs		.53	7.95
1 Funnel			.67
20 Soop Spoons		.50	10.00
2 Ink Stands		.25	.50
4 Syringe Pipes		.25	1.00
7 doz. Butter Plates		1.33	9.31
3¼ doz. Pint bassons		2.67	8.68
5 pr Bretania metal Candlesticks		3.00	15.00
5 Quart Bassons		.40	2.00
12 doz. 12 lb. Plates			
1 do 11 " "			
8 " 9 " "			
3 " 8 " "	251 lbs	.25	62.75
2 10 lb. Dishes		.25	52.50
44½ Gross Tea Spoons		1.33	59.18
20 doz. Table ditto		.50	10.00
2 Pewter Cranes		6.00	12.00
22 Crane Cocks		.33	7.26
5 Church Cups & 2 Stands			2.00
1 Pewter Dish and 2 doz. Ink Stand Glasses			.67
9 doz. Candle Moulds		2.67	24.03
1 Brass Scales and Weights			6.00
205 lbs. lead		.06	12.30
10 lbs old pewter		.16	1.60

Appendix II

PEWTER AND EQUIPMENT IN THE SHOP OF DAVID MELVILLE

AS REPORTED IN NEWPORT DECEMBER 11, 1801, APPRAISED BY WILLIAM BURROUGHS, THOMAS TILLEY AND THOMAS GODDARD

1 Quart Pot Mould, bottom and handle w. 51 lbs 6 oz		
1 Pint do bottom & 2 handles w. 34.6	85	12
1 Three pint Bason Mould 46.8 1 Quart		
Bason do 40.8 1 Pint do 19.4	106	4
1 Platter do 62.12 Plate do 26.1.9		
Plate 19.12.8 Plate 25.6 Plate do. 9.12	142	9
Beer pint Porringer do plain & flowered		
2 handles 30.8 Wine pint & 1 handle 26.4	56	12
3 Jill do & 1 Handle 22.12 half-pint do		
and 1 handle 21.12 Jill Porringer mould 9.	53	8
	444.5	

	@ 50 cts	$221.15
1 Curtain Ring Mould 1 Bullet do: 25 cts		
2 large spoon moulds 1 poor 75		1.00
3 Tea spoon do 50 cts Bason handle do 25 cts		
Lathe, Spindle Wheel & Standard 9 Dolls		9.75
Inch Driver 50 cts Iron rest for turning 1 Doll 50 cts		
Hawks bill Burnisher 1 flat ditto 75 cents		2.75
12 Turning Hooks 2 Dolls 4 Large Stamps 2 Dolls		
3 small do 50 cts 24 Letters, & figures 1 Doll		5.50
2 Rasps & old files 75 cts, 1 Anvil & hammer		
3 dolls Iron vise & 2 hand do 5 dolls.		8.75
1 Pr Large forge Bellows 4 dolls, 1 pr large shears		
2 dolls large cannipers and small do 20 cts		
iron square 25 cts		6.45
Steel frame saw 6 inches long 25 cts 1 pr		
compasses 75 cts. Grindstone & frame 3 dolls		4.00
Old iron kettle broke 25 cts 1 pr. furnace		
tongs 1 doll Mortar Irons 1 doll Brass do 50		2.75
1 large Iron State 56# 4 Dolls 1 large old		
Ladle 12 cts 5 Hammers 75 cts 5 Copper Solders 75 cts		5.62
2 Steed Irons 62 Cents Scales Beam & Chains		
5 Dolls (various weights) 3.50		9.12
1 Pr large Tin Scales 1 doll 1 pr small do 50 cts		
Brass weights 7# — 2 dolls 1 Iron hod 1 doll		
Ivory Rule 40 cts		3.90
1 Set Brass Patterns 2 Dolls 1 Small vise 50 cts		
1 Turkey Oil, Stone 50 cts 20 Turning Blocks 4 dolls		7.00
1 Pr Bullet cutters & piece of Iron 20 cts		
1 Pr Large Steelyards 2 Dolls 1 pr Spring Tongs 25 cts		2.45
Sundry small matters in the Shop 1.50 Sand Box and casting sand 50 cts		2.00
6 Platters 14 Pewter Plates 3 Basons 3 Porringers		
Tankard & Sundrys of Pewter		9.00

BIBLIOGRAPHY
Volumes One and Two

BIBLIOGRAPHY

THE EUROPEAN BACKGROUND

Encyclopaedia Britannica, fourteenth edition, 1929, vol. 17, p. 684.

Major C. F. Markham, F.S.A., *The New Pewter Marks and Old Pewter Ware*, second edition, Charles Scribner's Sons, New York, 1928, pp. 15–36.

J. B. Kerfoot, *American Pewter*, Houghton Mifflin Company, Boston, Mass., 1924, pp. 16–17.

H. J. L. J. Massé, *Chats on Old Pewter*, T. Fisher Unwin, Ltd., London, 1911, pp. 107–110.

THE BUSINESS OF A PEWTERER

M. Salmon, *L'Art du Potier d'Etain*, Moutard, Paris, 1788.

H. J. L. J. Massé, *op. cit.*, pp. 117–127.

PROBLEMS OF THE COLONIAL PEWTERER

John W. Poole, 'Early American Pewterers Used Old Pewter as Supply,' *New York Sun*, February 8, 1936.

John W. Poole, 'Early Pewterer Governed in his Output by Economics,' *New York Sun*, February 15, 1936.

Henry Crouch, *A Complete View of the British Customs*, fourth edition, The Custom House, London, 1745, p. 288.

R. W. Symonds, 'The English Export Trade in Furniture to Colonial America,' *Antiques*, vol. 28, p. 156.

Upper Marlboro, Maryland, *Probate Records*, vol. 1, p. 358.

Charles Welch, F.S.A., *History of the Worshipful Company of Pewterers of the City of London*, Blades, East and Blades, London, 1902, vol. 2, p. 135.

THE MARKS ON PEWTER

Major C. F. Markham, *op. cit.*, pp. 24, 33–34.

Howard H. Cotterell, F.R.S., *Old Pewter, Its Makers and Its Marks*, B. T. Batsford, Ltd., London, 1929, pp. 51–52.

HOUSEHOLD PEWTER

Plates, Dishes and Basins

Charles Welch, *op. cit.*, vol. 2, p. 135.

Porringers

Ledlie I. Laughlin, 'The American Pewter Porringer,' *Antiques*, vol. 17, pp. 437–440.

Tankards, Mugs and Measures

Howard H. Cotterell, 'Dating the Pewter Tankard,' *The Connoisseur*, April, 1932.

Beakers

Louis G. Myers, *Some Notes on American Pewterers*, The Country Life Press, Garden City, New York, 1926, p. 34.

Bibliography

ECCLESIASTICAL PEWTER
  Howard H. Cotterell, *Old Pewter*, p. 104.

THE PEWTERERS OF MASSACHUSETTS
  Suffolk County Probate Records, vol. 5, pp. 15, 30.

  James O. Halliwell, F.R.S., *A Dictionary of Archaic and Provincial Words*, seventh edition, George Rutledge & Sons, Ltd., London, 1924, pp. 407, 864.

  Encyclopaedia Britannica, fourteenth edition, vol. 5, p. 973; vol. 21, p. 857.

  H. J. L. J. Massé, *op. cit.*, pp. 178, 179.

Richard Graves
  J. B. Kerfoot, *op. cit.*, p. 32.

  George F. Dow, 'Notes on the Use of Pewter in Massachusetts During the Seventeenth Century,' *Old Time New England*, July, 1923.

  John C. Hotten, *The Original Lists of Persons of Quality; Emigrants etc. Who went from Great Britain to the American Plantations 1600–1700*, Chatto & Windus, London, 1874, p. 92.

Samuel Grame
  Boston Record Commissioners' Reports, vol. 2, part 1, pp. 40, 46; part 2, p. 17; vol. 9, pp. 7, 14.

  Charles Henry Pope, *The Pioneers of Massachusetts*, Boston, 1900, p. 196.

  James Savage, *A Genealogical Dictionary of the First Settlers of New England*, Little, Brown & Co., Boston, 1862, vol. 2, p. 290.

Henry Shrimpton
  James Savage, *op. cit.*, vol. 4, p. 90.

  Boston Record Commissioners' Reports, vol. 2, p. 40; vol. 9, pp. 12, 16, 20, 38, 45, 55, 60, 64, 74, 77, 82.

  Suffolk County Probate Records, vol. 1, pp. 465, 469; vol. 5, pp. 15 to 30; vol. 7, pp. 337, 346, 347.

  Justin Winsor, *The Memorial History of Boston*, Ticknor & Co., Boston, 1880, vol. 1, pp. 195, 573, 582.

  Oliver Ayer Roberts, *History of the Military Company of the Massachusetts, now called the Ancient and Honorable Artillery Company of Massachusetts, 1637–1688*, Alfred Mudge & Son, Boston, 1895, vol. 1, p. 215.

Thomas Bumstead
  Boston Record Commissioners' Reports, vol. 6, pp. 84, 114; vol. 9, pp. 19, 30, 45.

  Governor Winthrop's Journal, edited by James K. Hosmer, Charles Scribner's Sons, New York, 1908, vol. 2, p. 20.

  Thomas Bridgman, *The Pilgrims of Boston*, D. Appleton & Co., New York, 1856, p. 9.

  Oliver Ayer Roberts, *op. cit.*, vol. 1, p. 165.

  Suffolk County Probate Records, docket 902.

Thomas Clarke
  Boston Record Commissioners' Reports, vol. 1, pp. 33, 42; vol. 7, p. 137; vol. 9, pp. 132, 145, 154, 159, 162, 192, 198, 214; vol. 10, p. 68; vol. 28, p. 44.

  Henry W. Foote, *Annals of King's Chapel, Boston*, Little, Brown & Co., Boston, 1882, vol. 1, pp. 89, 137.

  Oliver Ayer Roberts, *op. cit.*, vol. 1, pp. 274, 276.

Bibliography

Diary of Samuel Sewall, Massachusetts Historical Society Collections, 6th series, vol. 6, pp. 324, 399.

Suffolk County Deeds, vol. 27, p. 197; vol. 34, p. 203.

Suffolk County Probate Records, docket 6352.

The Two John Comers

Mme. Henri Berger, *American Makers of Pewter and White Metal*, supplement to the Bulletin of the Wadsworth Athenaeum, Hartford, March 15, 1923.

J. Henry Lea, 'Genealogical Gleanings Among the English Archives,' *New England Historical and Genealogical Register*, vol. 54, p. 193.

William B. Trask, 'Abstracts from the Earliest Wills on File in the County of Suffolk, Massachusetts,' *New England Historical and Genealogical Register*, vol. 8, p. 59.

The Diary of John Comer, Collections of the Rhode Island Historical Society, vol. 8, pp. 15, 17.

Boston Record Commissioners' Reports, vol. 1, p. 33; vol. 7, pp. 189, 199, 201; vol. 8, pp. 70, 77; vol. 9, pp. 131, 145, 151, 165, 243.

Suffolk County Probate Records, vol. 16, pp. 171, 172, 446; vol. 17, p. 167; vol. 22, p. 266.

Records of the Early Files, Supreme Judicial Court, Suffolk County, file 6900.

Unpublished volume of *Suffolk County Court Records*, in Boston Athenaeum (reference for 'freeman').

The Dolbeare Family

J. B. Kerfoot, *op. cit.*, p. 56.

Arthur D. Osborne, *A Few Facts Relating to the Origin and History of John Dolbeare of Boston*, privately printed, New Haven, 1893.

Edward Doubleday Harris, 'The Dolbeares of Boston,' *New England Historical and Genealogical Register*, vol. 47, pp. 24–27, 495.

Ellen A. R. Stone, 'Dolbear Records,' *New England Historical and Genealogical Register*, vol. 83, p. 511.

Records of the Early Files, Supreme Judicial Court, Suffolk County, files 1071, 1423, 4235.

John Dolbeare's Bill of Lading Book, Massachusetts Historical Society, Boston.

Boston Record Commissioners' Reports, vol. 1, p. 158; vol. 8, pp. 41, 136, 196, 225; vol. 9, pp. 162, 206, 243; vol. 10, pp. 72, 97, 98; vol. 12, p. 183; vol. 13, p. 185.

Suffolk County Deeds, vol. 30, p. 248.

Records of Old South Church, Boston.

John Baker

Boston Record Commissioners' Reports, vol. 1, p. 47; vol. 7, pp. 173, 177; vol. 9, p. 254; vol. 10, pp. 70, 72.

Suffolk County Probate Records, vol. 11, p. 268; vol. 14, p. 76; vol. 4, new series, pp. 200–207.

William Mann

Boston Record Commissioners' Reports, vol. 7, pp. 229, 239; vol. 8, pp. 27, 36, 100; vol. 9, pp. 119, 215, 227, 248; vol. 11, pp. 3, 18, 58; vol. 13, p. 55.

Suffolk County Deeds, vol. 18, p. 197; vol. 33, p. 41; vol. 57, p. 158.

Suffolk County Common Pleas Court, 12730 (1718), 15631 (1721).

Jonathan Jackson

Oliver A. Roberts, *op. cit.*, vol. 1, pp. 187–188.

Boston Record Commissioners' Reports, vol. 8, pp. 130, 136, 162, 170, 201, 215; vol. 9, p. 123; vol. 12, pp. 1, 11, 18, 28, 38, 55; vol. 24, pp. 8, 18, 29, 35, 42, 49, 106; vol. 28, p. 2.

'Researches Among Funeral Sermons,' *New England Historical and Genealogical Register*, vol. 8, p. 368.

Bibliography

Suffolk County Probate Records, docket 6861; vol. 38, pp. 312–317; vol. 32, p. 445.

Suffolk County Deeds, vol. 21, p. 167; vol. 25, p. 56; vol. 32, p. 80; vol. 35, p. 252; vol. 36, p. 24; vol. 42, pp. 86, 313, 314; vol. 46, pp. 119, 206; vol. 49, p. 163; vol. 50, p. 155; vol. 51, p. 248.

Thomas Smith

Boston Record Commissioners' Reports, vol. 8, pp. 75, 88, 97, 218; vol. 9, p. 146; vol. 11, p. 242; vol. 15, p. 188; vol. 23, pp. 5, 72; vol. 24, pp. 11, 24, 37, 58, 64, 78, 93, 108.

Suffolk County Deeds, vol. 15, p. 91; vol. 23, pp. 174, 175, 176, 178; vol. 27, pp. 298, 299, 301; vol. 28, p. 36; vol. 34, p. 177; vol. 37, p. 198.

Oliver A. Roberts, *op. cit.*, vol. 1, p. 347; vol. 2, p. 467.

Suffolk County Probate Records, vol. 35, p. 618; vol. 36, pp. 121, 124.

Arthur H. Nichols, 'Christ Church Bells,' *New England Historical and Genealogical Register*, vol. 58, p. 69.

John Holyoke

Andrew Nichols, *Genealogy of the Holyoke Family*, Essex Institute Historical Collections, vol. 3, pp. 57–59.

Oliver A. Roberts, *op. cit.*, vol. 1, p. 389.

Boston Record Commissioners' Reports, vol. 12, pp. 5, 13, 20, 29, 100, 215; vol. 14, p. 8; vol. 19, p. 29.

Suffolk County Deeds, vol. 35, p. 84; vol. 37, p. 54; vol. 42, p. 13; vol. 48, p. 287; vol. 53, p. 113, vol. 69, p. 63; vol. 80, p. 193; vol. 82, p. 207; vol. 94, p. 119.

George F. Dow, *The Holyoke Diaries*, The Essex Institute, Salem, Massachusetts, 1911, pp. 21, 30.

'Boyle's Journal of Occurrences in Boston 1759–1778,' *New England Historical and Genealogical Register*, vol. 85, p. 7

Samuel Carter

New England Historical and Genealogical Register, vol. 31, p. 310.

Suffolk County Probate Records, vol. 40, pp. 204, 205.

Jonas Clark(e)

Boston Record Commissioners' Reports, vol. 8, pp. 30, 35, 45, 49, 58, 64, 74, 89, 93, 130, 136, 158, 219; vol. 9, p. 189; vol. 12, pp. 12, 19, 28, 38, 58, 96, 127, 152, 184, 209, 243, 262, 285; vol. 14, pp. 2, 27, 63, 78, 95, 108; vol. 24, pp. 135, 154; vol. 28, pp. 57, 242.

Suffolk County Deeds, vol. 34, p. 183; vol. 35, p. 267; vol. 55, p. 233.

Suffolk County Probate Records, docket 12207; vol. 56, p. 35; vol. 58, pp. 39–43.

George Raisin

Boston Record Commissioners' Reports, vol. 9, p. 187.

Records of the Early Files, Supreme Judicial Court, Suffolk County, vol. 115, p. 30; vol. 187, p. 112.

Suffolk County Probate Records, vol. 27, pp. 52, 53, 144.

Richard Estabrooke

Suffolk County Probate Records, vol. 22, pp. 241, 272.

Durninger, Edgell, etc.

Suffolk County Common Pleas Court, 1718, p. 120; 1714–1715, p. 136; 1722, p. 236; 1726, p. 388.

Records of the Early Files, Supreme Judicial Court, Suffolk County, vol. 150, pp. 57, 140; vol. 153, p. 128; vol. 95, p. 19; vol. 177, p. 104.

Boston Record Commissioners' Reports, vol. 28, pp. 11, 159.

Bibliography

John Carnes

George Francis Dow, *The Arts and Crafts in New England, 1704–1775*, The Wayside Press, Topsfield, Massachusetts, 1927, p. 73.

Oliver A. Roberts, *op. cit.*, vol. 2, p. 49.

Boston Record Commissioners' Reports, vol. 8, p. 182; vol. 9, p. 240; vol. 12, p. 56; vol. 15, pp. 230, 276; vol. 19, p. 3; vol. 24, pp. 159, 238; vol. 28, pp. 86, 105, 240.

Boston Gazette, October 28, 1723.

Suffolk County Probate Records, vol. 56, p. 406.

'Diary of Robert Culley,' *New England Historical and Genealogical Register*, vol. 6, p. 36.

John Tyler

New England Historical and Genealogical Register, vol. 8, p. 102.

Boston Record Commissioners' Reports, vol. 9, pp. 176, 182, 223; vol. 24, pp. 153, 157, 167, 173, 184, 195, 205, 219, 231, 241; vol. 28, p. 90; vol. 12, pp. 5, 292, 294.

Thomas B. Wyman, Junior, 'Records of New Brick Church, Boston,' *New England Historical and Genealogical Register*, vol. 19, p. 328.

Suffolk County Deeds, vol. 37, p. 182; vol. 43, p. 179; vol. 46, p. 21; vol. 48, pp. 40, 184.

Suffolk County Probate Records, docket 11521; vol. 52, pp. 276–279, *incl.*

Thomas Simpkins

Heads of Families at the First Census of the United States, 1790, Massachusetts, U.S. Government Printing Office, Washington, D.C., 1908, p. 187.

James Savage, *op. cit.*, vol. 4, p. 101.

Boston Record Commissioners' Reports, vol. 12, pp. 3, 11, 284; vol. 14, p. 8; vol. 24, pp. 17, 205, 219.

Suffolk County Probate Records, vol. 65, p. 304.

Suffolk County Deeds, vol. 27, p. 208; vol. 79, p. 258; vol. 90, p. 68.

David Cutler

Nahum S. Cutler, *A Cutler Memorial*, Press of E. A. Hall & Co., Greenfield, Massachusetts, 1889, p. 338.

Boston Record Commissioners' Reports, vol. 12, pp. 56, 216; vol. 14, pp. 80, 137, 157, 172, etc.; vol. 28, p. 176.

'Boyle's Journal of Occurrences in Boston,' *New England Historical and Genealogical Register*, vol. 84, p. 268.

The Boston Gazette and Country Journal, March 2, 1772.

Suffolk County Probate Records, vol. 71, pp. 232, 453.

George Francis Dow, *op. cit.*, p. 73.

Robert Bonning

Boston Record Commissioners' Reports, vol. 15, p. 209; vol. 28, p. 170.

Joseph Randle

Boston Record Commissioners' Reports, vol. 9, pp. 199, 202; vol. 24, p. 85; vol. 28, p. 208.

Suffolk County Deeds, vol. 56, p. 237; vol. 58, p. 68.

Thomas Green

Boston Directories, 1789, 1798.

Independent Chronicle and Universal Advertiser, September 15, 1794.

Bibliography

Tombstone Inscriptions of Granary Burial Ground, Boston, published by Essex Institute, Salem, Mass., 1918.

Annie Holt Smith, 'Green Family Items from the Records of New London, Connecticut,' *The Genealogical Advertiser*, vol. 4, p. 51.

Boston Gazette, May 14, 1763.

Records of Brattle Street Church, Boston, pp. 101, 112, 163–185, 251, 280, 281.

Boston Record Commissioners' Reports, vol. 28, p. 211; vol. 30, p. 42; vol. 31, pp. 8, 56, 103, 138, 163, 186, 223, 248.

Suffolk County Deeds, vol. 89, p. 167; vol. 97, p. 97; vol. 102, p. 234; vol. 141, pp. 137, 236.

Suffolk County Probate Records, vol. 93, pp. 174, 185, 234, 409, 493, 542, 633; vol. 94, p. 79.

Boston Tax Lists, 1788.

'Semper Eadem'

John Cogswell Badger, *Giles Badger and his Descendants*, John B. Clarke Company, Manchester, N.H., 1909, pp. 5, 18, 39.

Boston Record Commissioners' Reports, vol. 25, p. 198; vol. 30, p. 45.

Suffolk County Deeds, vol. 132, p. 166; vol. 134, p. 181.

Louis G. Myers, *op. cit.*, pp. 1, 4.

Charles A. Calder, *Rhode Island Pewterers and Their Work*, E. A. Johnson & Co., Providence, R.I., 1924, p. 14.

Boston News Letter, July 7, 1763, and October 3, 1763.

Howard H. Cotterell, *op. cit.*, p. 27.

J. B. Kerfoot, *op. cit.*, pp. 92, 93.

David and William Northey

Essex County Probate Records, 1638–1840, dockets 19597, 19606.

Essex County Deeds, vol. 60, p. 269; vol. 134, p. 214; vol. 136, p. 179.

Salem and Lynn vital records.

Blin and Flagg

Boston Record Commissioners' Reports, vol. 16, p. 19; vol. 24, pp. 12, 215, 273.

Henry Bond, *Genealogies of the Families and Descendants of the Early Settlers of Watertown, Massachusetts*, Little, Brown & Co., Boston, 1855, vol. 1, p. 219.

Suffolk County Deeds, vol. 76, pp. 206, 209; vol. 89, p. 221; vol. 92, pp. 102, 200; vol. 121, p. 106; vol. 136, p. 10; vol. 139, p. 103; vol. 189, p. 274.

Suffolk County Probate Records, docket 8942; vol. 41, p. 84.

John Skinner

Harriet S. Topley, *Richard Skinner, an Early Eighteenth Century Merchant of Marblehead*, Essex Institute Historical Collections, vol. 67, p. 329.

Elizabeth Ellery Dana, 'Richard Skinner of Marblehead and His Bible,' *New England Historical and Genealogical Register*, vol. 64, pp. 416–418.

Boston News Letter, October 1, 1761.

Suffolk County Probate Records, vol. 3, pp. 485, 486.

Records of West Church, Boston.

Oliver Ayer Roberts, *op. cit.*, vol. 2, p. 97.

Bibliography

Boston Record Commissioners' Reports, vol. 16, pp. 136, 168, 204, 236, 270; vol. 18, pp. 11, 43, 68, 114, 156, 221, 232, 273; vol. 26, pp. 6, 52, 113, 178, 230, 297; vol. 30, p. 419; vol. 31, pp. 7, 8, 55, 56, 103, 137, 138, 163, 186, 187, 223, 248, 280, 322.

Boston Directories, 1789 to 1813 inclusive.

Boston Gazette, January 28, 1813.

George Francis Dow, *op. cit.*, p. 74.

J. B. Kerfoot, *op. cit.*, p. 95.

Nathaniel Austin

Thomas Bellows Wyman, *The Genealogies and Estates of Charlestown in the County of Middlesex and Commonwealth of Massachusetts, 1629–1818*, David Clapp and Son, Boston, 1879, vol. 1, pp. 30, 32, 38.

Boston Gazette, October 3, 1763.

Francis Everett Blake, 'Gleanings from Massachusetts Archives,' *New England Historical and Genealogical Register*, vol. 55, p. 389.

J. B. Kerfoot, *op. cit.*, p. 85.

George Francis Dow, *op. cit.*, p. 73.

Louis G. Myers, *op. cit.*, p. 42.

James F. Hunnewell, *A Century of Town Life, A History of Charlestown, Massachusetts, 1775–1887*, Little, Brown & Co., Boston, 1888, pp. 155, 164.

Edward Kneeland

Stillman Foster Kneeland, *Seven Centuries in the Kneeland Family*, privately published in New York, 1897, p. 55.

George Francis Dow, *op. cit.*, p. 73.

Boston Record Commissioners' Reports, vol. 22, p. 476; vol. 30, p. 372.

Massachusetts Soldiers and Sailors of the Revolutionary War, compiled from the Archives by the Secretary of the Commonwealth, Boston, 1899, vol. 9, p. 339.

Oliver Ayer Roberts, *op. cit.*, vol. 2, p. 170.

Suffolk County Deeds, vol. 170, p. 129.

Boston Tax Lists, 1784, 1786, 1787.

The Younger Greens

Records of Brattle Square Church, pp. 170, 173, 175, 176.

Assessors' Taking Books of the Town of Boston, 1780, Bostonian Society Publications, vol. 9, pp. 33, 37.

Boston Directories, 1789 to 1840 inclusive.

Suffolk County Deeds, vol. 89, p. 253; vol. 136, p. 106; vol. 179, p. 235; vol. 191, pp. 255, 256; vol. 249, p. 220.

Massachusetts Soldiers and Sailors of the Revolutionary War, pp. 794, 837, 838.

Boston Record Commissioners' Reports, vol. 30, pp. 51, 81; vol. 31, pp. 280, 322; vol. 38, p. 74.

Boston Tax Lists, 1784, 1786, 1787, 1789, 1792, 1795, 1798, 1828, 1834.

Suffolk County Probate Records, vol. 106, pp. 582, 588; vol. 116, p. 483; vol. 93, p. 174; docket 25204.

Records of the Early Files, Supreme Judicial Court, Suffolk County, file 93899, dated July 30, 1782.

New England Historical and Genealogical Register, vol. 55, p. 147.

Tombstone Inscriptions of the Granary Burial Ground, Essex Institute Publications, Salem, Mass., 1918.

Bibliography

Joshua Witherle

  Boston Directories, 1789 to 1800.

  Boston Record Commissioners' Reports, vol. 30, p. 437.

  Suffolk County Deeds, vol. 143, p. 270; vol. 167, pp. 86–88; vol. 171, p. 36; vol. 173, p. 182; vol. 186, pp. 205, 206; vol. 189, p. 185.

Austin, Bowles and Bradford

  Suffolk County Deeds, vol. 156, p. 152.

  Boston Tax Lists, 1784, 1787, 1788.

  Boston Record Commissioners' Reports, vol. 30, p. 145.

Thomas Badger

  Louis G. Myers, *op. cit.*, p. 3.

  John Cogswell Badger, *op. cit.*, pp. 5, 39.

  Boston Directories, 1789 to 1815 inclusive.

  Boston Record Commissioners' Reports, vol. 30, p. 456; vol. 35, pp. 310, 339, 340; vol. 37, pp. 30, 52, 71, 73, 95, 97, 109, 115, 123, 154, 161; vol. 39, pp. 73, 247.

  Suffolk County Probate Records, vol. 124, p. 454.

Richard Austin

  Oliver A. Roberts, *op. cit.*, vol. 2, p. 263.

  Columbian Centinel, March 29, 1817.

  Thomas Bellows Wyman, *op. cit.*, vol. 1, p. 39.

  Boston Record Commissioners' Reports, vol. 30, p. 478; vol. 33, pp. 56, 101, 143, 178, 226, 264, 283, 299, 333, 371, 406; vol. 35, pp. 248, 263, 282, 300, 331; vol. 37, pp. 3, 27, 52, 67; vol. 38, pp. 14, 54, 85, 109, 138, 179.

  Suffolk County Deeds, vol. 247, p. 94.

  Boston Directories, 1794 to 1817 inclusive.

  Boston Probate Records, docket 25204.

Nathaniel Bowman

  Thomas Bellows Wyman, *op. cit.*, vol. 1, p. 104.

  James Savage, *op. cit.*, vol. 1, p. 224.

  Middlesex County Deeds, vol. 172, p. 247; vol. 177, p. 213; vol. 178, p. 226; vol. 206, p. 180.

  Middlesex County Probate Records, docket 2366.

George Richardson

  Boston Directories, 1818 to 1828 inclusive.

  J. B. Kerfoot, *op. cit.*, p. 173.

  Lura Woodside Watkins, 'George Richardson, Pewterer,' *Antiques*, vol. 31, pp. 194–196.

  Columbian Centinel, April 17, 1830.

  Madelaine R. Brown, M.D., 'G. Richardson, Cranston Pewterer,' Rhode Island Historical Society Collections, vol. 32, pp. 1–2.

  Edward H. West, 'George Richardson, Pewterer,' *Antiques*, vol. 38, pp. 176–177.

THE RHODE ISLAND PEWTERERS

  Letter of Thomas Byles, 1711, Massachusetts Historical Society Collections.

Bibliography

Superior Court Records, Newport, R.I., vol. B, p. 489.

Newport Land Evidence, vol. 3, p. 265.

Lawrence Langworthy

Superior Court Records, Newport, R.I., vol. B, pp. 410, 480, 545.

Records of the Colony of Rhode Island and Providence Plantations in New England, edited by John Russell Bartlett, Secretary of State, Providence, Knowles, Anthony & Co., 1860, vol. 4, pp. 505–559.

Boston Evening Transcript, Genealogical Section, February 26, 1936.

James N. Arnold, *Vital Records of Rhode Island, 1636–1850*, Narragansett Historical Publishing Company, vol. 10, p. 457.

Town Council Records of Newport, Collections of Newport Historical Society, vol. 8. (Will of Lawrence Langworthy.)

Newport Historical Magazine, vol. 2, p. 186.

John Fryers

Newport Mercury, May 6, 1776.

James N. Arnold, *op. cit.*, vol. 10, p. 449.

Superior Court Records, Newport, R.I., vol. A, p. 464.

Records of the Colony of Rhode Island, *op. cit.*, vol. 4, p. 450.

Newport Land Evidence, vol. 3, p. 265.

Benjamin Day

H. E. Turner, M.D., Newport Cemetery Records, unpublished manuscripts in Newport Historical Society Collections.

Newport Town Records, Newport Historical Society, vol. 3, p. 155.

Superior Court Records, Newport, R.I., vol. B, p. 489.

James N. Arnold, *op. cit.*, vol. 10, p. 445.

Town Council Records of Newport, Collections of Newport Historical Society, vol. 12, pp. 115, 116.

Joseph Belcher, Father and Son

Joseph Gardner Bartlett, 'The Belcher Families in New England,' *New England Historical and Genealogical Register*, vol. 60, pp. 126, 360.

James N. Arnold, *op. cit.*, vol. 8, p. 458.

Joseph Jenckes Smith, *Civil and Military List of Rhode Island, 1647–1800*, Preston, Rounds & Co., Providence, 1900, vol. 1, pp. 172, 180, 200, 286, 317, 319.

Records of the Colony of Rhode Island, *op. cit.*, vol. 5, p. 487.

Charles A. Calder, *op. cit.*, p. 6.

Suffolk County Probate Records, vol. 79, p. 560.

Newport Land Evidence, vol. 1, pp. 37, 86.

Superior Court Records, Newport, vol. F, p. 236.

Connecticut Vital Records, Lucius B. Barbour, Librarian, Connecticut State Library, Hartford, Conn.

David Melville

'The First Settlers of Eastham, Massachusetts,' *New England Historical and Genealogical Register*, vol. 6, pp. 169–170.

Records of the Colony of Rhode Island, *op. cit.*, vol. 5, p. 19.

Joseph Jenckes Smith, *op. cit.*, vol. 1, pp. 337, 503, 523.

Bibliography

Newport Mercury, November 3, 1783.

H. E. Turner, M.D., *op. cit.*

Newport Probate Records, vol. 3, p. 335.

Heads of Families at the First Census of the United States Taken in the Year 1790, Rhode Island, U.S. Government Printing Office, Washington, D.C., 1908, p. 21.

Unpublished records of the Melville Family in the possession of Miss Susan B. Franklin of Newport.

Samuel and Thomas Melville

Newport Mercury, December 31, 1793, and October 14, 1800.

Marriage Records, First Baptist Church, Newport, Newport Historical Society Collections.

Heads of Families at the First Census, op. cit., p. 22.

Superior Court Records, Newport, R.I., vol. K, p. 475.

Thomas Spooner, *Records of William Spooner and his Descendants*, Press of F. W. Freeman, Cincinnati, O., 1883, vol. 1, p. 384.

David Melville's Sons

Newport Probate Records, vol. 2, p. 337.

H. E. Turner, M.D., *op. cit.*

Newport Mercury, December 31, 1793, January 12, 1796, October 14, 1800, and September 9, 1916.

James N. Arnold, *op. cit.*, vol. 21, p. 398.

Superior Court Records, Newport, R.I., vol. L, p. 241; vol. 14, pp. 614, 615; vol. 16, p. 410.

Newport Land Evidence, vol. 11, pp. 498, 528.

Samuel Hamlin

H. Franklin Andrews, *The Hamlin Family, a Genealogy of Captain Giles Hamlin of Middletown, Connecticut, 1654–1900*, privately printed, Exira, Iowa, 1900, pp. 14, 73, 104, 105.

Charles A. Calder, *op. cit.*, pp. 12, 14.

Connecticut Probate Records, Middletown District, docket 1149, Connecticut State Library, Hartford.

Joseph Jenckes Smith, *op. cit.*, pp. 366, 376.

James N. Arnold, *op. cit.*, vol. 15, p. 510; vol. 20, p. 28.

Providence Probate Records, Inventories, vol. W 8, p. 472.

Providence Gazette, October 24, 1807; July 27, 1811.

Providence Directories, 1824, 1841, 1845.

New England Business Directory, 1856.

Gershom Jones

Connecticut Vital Records, op. cit.

E. M. Stone, *An Account of the Seventy-First Anniversary of the Providence Association of Mechanics and Manufacturers*, 1860, p. 46. (In New York Public Library.)

Charles A. Calder, *op. cit.*, pp. 16, 17.

Quarterly Court Records, Providence, February Term, 1782.

Joseph Jenckes Smith, *op. cit.*, pp. 393, 407, 486, 537.

James N. Arnold, *op. cit.*, vol. 2, pp. 103, 230; vol. 21, pp. 311, 312, 313.

Providence Probate Records, Inventories, vol. W 10, p. 406.

Providence Gazette, May 6, 1809.

Bibliography

New York City Directories, 1812 to 1819 inclusive.

Utica (New York) *Directory*, 1817.

William Billings and Job Danforth, Junior

Providence Gazette, November 5, 1791; November 10, 1798.

James N. Arnold, *op. cit.*, vol. 10, p. 157; vol. 13, p. 1771; vol. 15, pp. 23, 494.

Charles A. Calder, *op. cit.*, pp. 19, 20.

Providence Probate Records, docket A 3581.

John Joseph May, *Danforth Genealogy*, Charles H. Pope, Boston. 1902, pp. 54, 90.

Josiah Keene

Charles A. Calder, *op. cit.*, pp. 20, 21.

Louis G. Myers, *op. cit.*, p. 49.

Joseph Jenckes Smith, *op. cit.*, vol. 2, p. 135.

James N. Arnold, *op. cit.*, vol. 15, p. 176; vol. 20, p. 105; vol. 21, p. 317.

Providence Gazette, June 7, 1868.

William Calder

Charles A. Calder, *op. cit.*, pp. 23, 31.

James N. Arnold, *op. cit.*, vol. 10, p. 186.

William Calder's Day Book, Rhode Island Historical Society Collections.

Percy E. Raymond, 'William Calder, a Transition Pewterer,' *Antiques*, vol. 30, pp. 209–211.

Representative Men and Old Families of Rhode Island, J. H. Beers & Co., Chicago, 1908, vol. 2, pp. 1142, 1143.

THE PEWTERERS OF THE CONNECTICUT VALLEY

Catharine M. North, *History of Berlin, Connecticut*, Tuttle, Morehouse and Taylor Company, New Haven, Conn., 1916, p. 73.

Richardson Wright, *Hawkers and Walkers in Early America*, J. B. Lippincott Company, Philadelphia, Pa., 1927, p. 71.

J. B. Kerfoot, *op. cit.*, p. 129.

Thomas Danforth

John Joseph May, *op. cit.*, p. 42.

Louis G. Myers, *op. cit.*, pp. 19–21.

Connecticut Probate Records, Norwich District, docket 3094, Connecticut State Library, Hartford.

John Danforth

John Joseph May, *op. cit.*, p. 62.

Louis G. Myers, *op. cit.*, pp. 20, 23.

Connecticut Probate Records, Norwich District, docket 3093, Connecticut State Library, Hartford.

Samuel Danforth of Norwich

John Joseph May, *op. cit.*, p. 112.

Louis G. Myers, *op. cit.*, p. 30.

Thomas Danforth, Second

John Joseph May, *op. cit.*, p. 56.

Records of the State of Connecticut, vol. 1, p. 342.

Bibliography

Middletown Town Records, City Hall, Middletown (unpublished).

Connecticut Probate Records, Middletown District, docket 1149, Connecticut State Library, Hartford.

The Thomas Danforth Lion Marks

Louis G. Myers, *op. cit.*, pp. 32–36.

Thomas Danforth, Third

John Joseph May, *op. cit.*, pp. 94–96, 186.

Henry R. Stiles, M.D., *History of Ancient Wethersfield*, The Grafton Press, New York, 1903, pp. 906, 907, 934.

Philadelphia Directories, 1807 to 1813.

Thomas Danforth 3rd, Journal of My Visit to Virginia Containing a Description of the City of Richmond, also Compiled Many Interesting and Instructive Pieces from Various Authors, 1834. (MSS. in possession of Luther B. Williams, New Britain, Conn.)

Louis G. Myers, *op. cit.*, pp. 25, 31, 32.

Jacob Whitmore

Connecticut Vital Records, *op. cit.*

Record of Service of Connecticut Men in the War of the Revolution, compiled by the Adjutant General, Hartford, 1889, pp. 547, 616.

Statistical Account of the County of Middlesex, Clarke and Lyman, 1819. (A pamphlet in the New York Public Library.)

Middletown Town Records, City Hall, Middletown (unpublished).

Middletown Land Records, vol. 38, p. 4; vol. 39, p. 76.

Middletown Tax Lists, City Hall, Middletown.

The Connecticut Courant and Weekly Intelligencer, Hartford, June 19, 1781.

Amos Treadway

William T. Tredway, *History of the Tredway Family*, privately published, Pittsburgh, Pa., pp. 2, 12, 14, 19, 207.

Heads of Families at the First Census, Connecticut, *op. cit.*, p. 86.

Joseph Danforth, Father and Son

John Joseph May, *op. cit.*, pp. 56, 100, 104, 186.

Middletown Town Records, City Hall, Middletown.

Connecticut Probate Records, Middletown District, dockets 1147, 1149, Connecticut State Library, Hartford.

Connecticut Vital Records, *op. cit.*

Louis G. Myers, *op. cit.*, p. 24.

Middletown Tax Lists, 1803 to 1807, City Hall, Middletown.

Edward Danforth

John Joseph May, *op. cit.*, pp. 56, 100.

Connecticut Probate Records, Middletown District, docket 1147, Connecticut State Library, Hartford.

Hartford Probate Records, vol. 37, pp. 137, 139, 210.

Middletown Tax Lists, 1788 to 1790, City Hall, Middletown.

Heads of Families at the First Census, Connecticut, *op. cit.*, p. 45.

Louis G. Myers, *op. cit.*, pp. 24, 27.

Bibliography

Connecticut Courant, February 1, 1796.

Hartford Directory, 1799.

William and Josiah Danforth

John Joseph May, *op. cit.*, pp. 56, 104, 189.

Middletown Town Records, City Hall, Middletown.

Louis G. Myers, *op. cit.*, p. 24.

Connecticut Probate Records, Middletown District, docket 1151, Connecticut State Library.

Connecticut Vital Records, *op. cit.*

Middletown Land Records, vol. 67, p. 154.

Samuel Danforth of Hartford

John Joseph May, *op. cit.*, pp. 56, 104.

Connecticut Courant, December 21, 1795.

Louis G. Myers, *op. cit.*, p. 24.

Hartford Probate Records, vol. 32, p. 160; vol. 33, pp. 24 to 33.

J. B. Kerfoot, *op. cit.*, p. 112.

Hartford Town Votes, City Hall, Hartford, vol. 3, pp. 47, 57, 65, etc.

Richard Williams

John Joseph May, *op. cit.*, p. 96.

Connecticut Vital Records, *op. cit.*

Henry R. Stiles, *op. cit.*, vol. 1, p. 907.

Hartford Town Votes, *op. cit.*, vol. 3, p. 57, etc.

Jacob Eggleston

J. B. Kerfoot, *op. cit.*, p. 126.

Connecticut Vital Records, *op. cit.*

Middletown Land Records, vol. 32, pp. 74, 258; vol. 41, pp. 266, 267, 485.

Fayetteville (N.C.) *Land Records*, vol. 23, p. 122.

Connecticut Probate Records, Middletown District, docket 1288, Connecticut State Library, Hartford.

The Richard Lees

Homer E. Keyes and Harold G. Rugg, 'Richard Lee, Pewterer,' *Antiques*, vol. 13, pp. 493–495.

Massachusetts Soldiers and Sailors of the Revolution, *op. cit.*, vol. 9, p. 640.

Grand List for State Taxes, Vermont, 1810, 1816, 1817, 1818, Springfield, Vermont.

Samuel Pierce

Julia D. S. Snow, 'Samuel Pierce, Pewterer and His Tools,' *Antiques*, vol. 11, pp. 124–127.

Connecticut Vital Records, *op. cit.*

Francis M. Thompson, *History of Greenfield, Massachusetts*, privately printed, Greenfield, Mass., 1904, vol. 2, p. 843.

Ebenezer Southmayd

Unpublished records of Southmayd Family, Middletown.

Commemorative Biographical Record of Middlesex County, Connecticut, J. H. Beers & Co., Chicago, Ill., 1903, p. 522.

Epitaphs in Castleton, Vermont, Churchyard, privately printed, Pamphlet in New York Public Library.

Bibliography

James Porter

 Baltimore Directory, 1803.

Ashbil Griswold

 Henry R. Stiles, *op. cit.*, vol. 2, p. 401.

 Louis G. Myers, *op. cit.*, p. 46.

 Charles H. S. Davis, *The History of Wallingford and Meriden, Connecticut*, privately printed, Meriden, 1870, pp. 593, 594.

 C. Bancroft Gillespie and George Munson Curtis, *A Century of Meriden*, Journal Publishing Company, Meriden, 1906, part 2, p. 107; part 3, pp. 37, 38.

The Boardmans

 Charlotte Goldthwaite, *Boardman Genealogy*, published by W. F. J. Boardman, Press of the Case, Lockwood and Brainerd Company, Hartford, 1895, pp. 354-356, 447, 448.

 J. B. Kerfoot, *op. cit.*, p. 141.

 New England Mercantile Directory, 1849.

 Hartford Directories, 1825, 1828, 1842, 1846, 1849.

 New York Directories, 1822 to 1854.

 Philadelphia Directories, 1844 to 1854.

 Louis G. Myers, *op. cit.*, pp. 15, 16.

 Hartford Daily Courant, September 11, 1873.

The Yale Family

 Rodney H. Yale, *Yale Genealogy and History of Wales*, privately printed, Beatrice, Nebraska, 1909, pp. 162, 163, 222-224.

 C. Bancroft Gillespie, *op. cit.*, vol. 1, pp. 346, 347.

 Charles H. S. Davis, M.D., *op. cit.*, pp. 475, 587.

 Connecticut Probate Records, Wallingford District, dockets 1662, 1676, Connecticut State Library, Hartford.

 Connecticut Probate Records, Middletown District, docket 1288, Connecticut State Library, Hartford.

 Louis G. Myers, *op. cit.*, p. 75.

 Wallingford Land Records, vol. 43, p. 453.

The Notts and Jehiel Johnson

 Louis G. Myers, *op. cit.*, pp. vi, 61.

 Heads of Families at the First Census, *op. cit.*, pp. 53, 86.

 Unpublished records of Middletown Families, compiled by Frank F. Starr, Middletown, Conn.

 Connecticut Vital Records, *op. cit.*

 Middletown Land Records, vol. 44, p. 527; vol. 51, p. 505; vol. 52, p. 169; vol. 64, p. 544.

 Fayetteville (N.C.) *Land Evidence*, vol. 28, pp. 788, 1069; vol. 30, pp. 91, 201; vol. 34, p. 377.

 Connecticut Probate Records, Middletown District, dockets 268, 1288, Connecticut State Library, Hartford.

 Unpublished records of St. John's Lodge #2, F. & A. M., Middletown.

 Middlesex Gazette, March 3, 1814; September 9, 1815; September 19, 1815; April 3, 1817; July 7, 1819.

Bibliography

Thomas S. Derby

J. B. Kerfoot, *op. cit.*, p. 157.

Connecticut Vital Records, op. cit.

Unpublished records of Middletown families, compiled by Frank F. Starr.

Middletown Town Records, City Hall, Middletown.

Middletown Tax Lists, 1815 to 1818.

New England Mercantile Directory, 1849.

I. Curtiss

J. B. Kerfoot, *op. cit.*, p. 139.

J. and D. Hinsdale

Herbert C. Andrews, *Descendants of Robert Hinsdale*, privately printed at Lombard, Illinois, 1906, pp. 94, 124–126.

Middlesex Gazette, Middletown, various issues, 1813 to 1815.

American Sentinel, Middletown, various issues, 1823 to 1826.

Samuel Campmell

J. B. Kerfoot, *op. cit.*, p. 125.

Otis Williams

Buffalo Directories, 1828, 1832.

John Joseph May, *op. cit.*, p. 104.

Buffalo Emporium, December 1, 1826; January 1, 1827.

Buffalo Journal and General Advertiser, May 18, 1831.

Erie County Probate Records, docket 24472.

William Diggs and William Horsewell

Louis G. Myers, *op. cit.*, pp. 10, 42.

The Freemen of New York, Collections of the New York Historical Society, 1885, pp. 82, 86.

Howard H. Cotterell, *op. cit.*, p. 196.

Documents Relating to the Colonial History of the State of New York, procured in Holland, England, and France, vol. 4, pp. 936, 1006.

Indentures of Apprenticeship, 1695–1708, Collections of the New York Historical Society, 1885, p. 619.

New York Wills, Liber 7, p. 567.

Joseph Isly

New York Wills, Liber 8, p. 1715.

The Leddells

E. B. O'Callaghan, M.D., *Documentary History of the State of New York*, arranged under the direction of Christopher Morgan, Secretary of State, Albany, New York, Weed, Parsons & Co., 1850, vol. 3, p. 278.

The Freemen of New York, op. cit., p. 95.

Minutes of the Common Council of the City of New York, Dodd, Mead & Co., New York, 1905, vol. 4, pp. 346, 386, 442.

New York Wills, Liber 18, p. 430.

Bibliography

Names of Persons for Whom Marriage Licenses Were Issued by the Secretary of the Province of New York Previous to 1784, printed by order of Gideon J. Tucker, Secretary of State, Weed, Parsons & Co., Albany, 1860, p. 228.

Louis G. Myers, *op. cit.*, pp. 54–56.

Weekly Post Boy, New York, May 7, 1744, and June 1, 1752.

New York Administrations, Liber 1½ B, p. 501.

The Bassetts

Louis G. Myers, *op. cit.*, pp. 9–12.

The Freemen of New York, op. cit., pp. 98, 120, 218.

Indentures of Apprenticeship, op. cit., p. 619.

New York Wills, Liber 21, p. 37; Liber 22, p. 427; Liber 43, p. 210.

Minutes of the Common Council, op. cit., vol. 4, p. 152; vol. 6, p. 308; vol. 7, p. 384.

Calendar of Historical Manuscripts Relating to the War of the Revolution, Weed, Parsons & Co., Albany, 1868, vol. 1, pp. 4, 315.

Names of Persons for Whom Marriage Licenses Were Issued, op. cit., p. 191.

New York Directories, 1787 to 1798 inclusive.

Hartford Town Records, vol. 15, p. 418; vol. 17, p. 418.

The Connecticut Courant and Weekly Intelligencer, Hartford, January 27, 1784, and December 21, 1784.

Homer E. Keyes, 'Francis Bassett II, Man of Affairs,' *Antiques*, vol. 33, p. 321.

Henry V. Button, 'Concerning the Pewtering Bassetts,' *Antiques*, vol. 17, p. 242.

'Records of Burials in the Dutch Church, New York,' *Year Book of the Holland Society of New York*, 1899, p. 143.

The Bradfords

Louis G. Myers, *op. cit.*, p. 57.

Henry Lewis Bullen, 'Famous American Printers,' *The American Collector*, vol. 1, pp. 164–166.

Henry Darrach, *The Bradford Family*, privately printed, Philadelphia, 1906, pp. 4, 5.

Alice Delano Weekes, 'Bradford Genealogy,' *New York Genealogical and Biographical Record*, vol. 56, pp. 61, 62.

The Freemen of New York, op. cit., p. 99.

New York Wills, Liber 21, p. 190; Liber 39, p. 358.

'Records of the Reformed Dutch Church in the City of New York,' *New York Genealogical and Biographical Record*, vol. 21, p. 70.

Philadelphia Deeds, vol. I 11, p. 312; vol. D 8, p. 42.

Pennsylvania Archives, third series, vol. 14, p. 185.

W. Harrison Bayles, *Old Taverns of New York*, Frank Allaben Genealogical Company, New York, 1915, pp. 266, 278, 279, 318–322.

The Arts and Crafts in New York, 1726–1776, New York Historical Society, New York, 1938, p. 101.

Pennsylvania Gazette, Philadelphia, May 3, 1753; October 14, 1756.

New York Conveyances, Liber 42, p. 279.

Minutes of the Common Council, op. cit., vol. 7, p. 404.

Ledlie I. Laughlin, 'Cornelius Bradford, Pewterer,' *Antiques*, vol. 18, pp. 144–145.

Bibliography

The Kirbys

Names of Persons for Whom Marriage Licenses Were Issued, op. cit., p. 215.

Minutes of the Common Council, op. cit., vol. 6, pp. 183, 222, 431; vol. 8, p. 107.

New York Administrations, Collections of the New York Historical Society, 1905, p. 353.

New York Conveyances, Liber 33, p. 222; Liber 48, p. 511.

New York Mortgage Records, vol. 3, p. 479; vol. 8, p. 517; vol. 80, p. 107; vol. 90, p. 272; vol. 297, p. 98.

New York Directories, 1786 to 1803 inclusive.

Heads of Families at the First Census, op. cit., New York, p. 117.

The Arts and Crafts in New York, 1726–1776, New York Historical Society, 1938, p. 102.

Robert Boyle

New York Wills, Liber 18, p. 430.

The Freemen of New York, op. cit., pp. 113, 183.

Names of Persons for Whom Marriage Licenses Were Issued, op. cit., p. 40.

Louis G. Myers, *op. cit.,* pp. 55, 56.

The Arts and Crafts in New York, op. cit., p. 100.

The Wills

Heads of Families at the First Census, op. cit., New York, p. 117.

'Records of the Reformed Dutch Church in the City of New York,' *New York Genealogical and Biographical Record,* vol. 28, pp. 221, 224; vol. 29, p. 157; vol. 61, pp. 74, 79.

Register of the Reform Church Congregation, Nieuwied-on-the-Rhine.

The Freemen of New York, op. cit., pp. 193, 208.

Names of Persons for Whom Marriage Licenses Were Issued, op. cit., p. 460.

Minutes of the Common Council, op. cit., vol. 6, p. 436; vol. 7, pp. 101, 386.

Calendar of Historical Manuscripts, op. cit., vol. 1, p. 174.

New York Gazette or The Weekly Post-Boy, September 27, 1756.

The Arts and Crafts in New York, op. cit., pp. 104, 105.

A List of Members of the City Government from Its Incorporation to the Present Time: A Manual of the Corporation of the City of New York, published by D. T. Valentine, New York, 1864, p. 555.

New York Directories, 1786 to 1802.

New York Conveyances, Liber 39, p. 185; Liber 41, p. 265; Liber 52, p. 38.

Louis G. Myers, *op. cit.,* p. 80.

'Records of the Reformed Dutch Church of Albany, New York, 1924–1925,' *Year Book of the Holland Society of New York,* p. 13.

Bland, Blaun, Henry and Merryfield

Enlistments in New York Muster Rolls of Provincial Troops, New York Historical Society, 1891, pp. 188, 306, 360, 404.

George Harner

Louis G. Myers, *op. cit.,* p. 42.

The Freemen of New York, op. cit., p. 197.

William J. Elsworth

Howard L. F. Randolph, 'The Elsworth Family of New York City,' *New York Genealogical and Biographical Record,* vol. 64, pp. 155, 265.

Bibliography

Records of the Reformed Dutch Church in the City of New York, *op. cit.*, vol. 25, p. 70.

The Freemen of New York, *op. cit.*, p. 214.

Names of Persons for Whom Marriage Licenses Were Issued, *op. cit.*, p. 218.

Louis G. Myers, *op. cit.*, p. 40.

Minutes of the Common Council, *op. cit.*, vol. 7, p. 101.

New York Directories, 1786–1798.

New York Conveyances, Liber 103, p. 192.

New York Wills, Liber 53, p. 381.

Malcolm McEuen and Son

Louis G. Myers, *op. cit.*, p. 57.

Names of Persons for Whom Marriage Licenses Were Issued, *op. cit.*, p. 247.

The Freemen of New York, *op. cit.*, p. 232.

Minutes of the Common Council, *op. cit.*, vol. 7, p. 404.

Calendar of Historical Manuscripts, *op. cit.*, vol. 1, p. 282.

New York Directories, 1786 to 1800.

New York Herald, May 7, 1803.

New York Daily Advertiser, October 30, 1793.

Peter Young

Louis G. Myers, *op. cit.*, pp. 78, 79.

The Arts and Crafts in New York, *op. cit.*, p. 106.

Albany Deeds, vol. 14, p. 187; vol. 19, p. 57.

'Records of the Reformed Dutch Church of Albany,' *Year Book of the Holland Society of New York*, 1906, p. 113; 1924–1925, p. 58; 1926–1927, pp. 27, 50.

Joel Munsell, *Annals of Albany*, published by Joel Munsell, Albany, 1855, vol. 6, p. 199.

The Herald: A Gazette for the Country, New York, August 12, 1797.

George Coldwell and Moses Lafetra

Heads of Families at the First Census, *op. cit.*, New York, p. 122.

New York Directories, 1789 to 1816.

New York Wills, Liber 49, p. 252.

J. B. Kerfoot, *op. cit.*, p. 104.

Louis G. Myers, *op. cit.*, p. 53.

New York Daily Advertiser, November 22, 1794.

Robert Piercy

New York Directories, 1792 to 1797.

Howard H. Cotterell, *op. cit.*, p. 281.

The Youles

New York Directories, 1793 to 1828.

New York Administrations, Liber 17, p. 39; Liber 24, p. 212.

Louis G. Myers, *op. cit.*, p. 95.

New York Daily Advertiser, June 3, 1793; May 17, 1794.

Bibliography

Eight Late Workers

New York Directories, 1789 to 1822.

New York Administrations, Liber 74, p. 151.

New York Wills, Liber 127, p. 368.

Spencer Stafford

Joel Munsell, *op. cit.*, vol. 3, p. 164; vol. 6, p. 121; vol. 8, pp. 103, 117.

Joel Munsell, *Collections on the History of Albany*, Joel Munsell, Albany, 1870, vol. 3, pp. 444 to 450.

George R. Howell and Jonathan Tenney, *History of the County of Albany, New York*, W. W. Munsell & Co., New York, 1886, pp. 526, 529, 566.

Albany Register, June 21, 1793.

New York Evening Post, May 17, 1815.

Albany Argus, February 12, 1844.

Louis G. Myers, *op. cit.*, p. 77.

Timothy Brigden

J. B. Kerfoot, *op. cit.*, p. 93.

Connecticut Vital Records, *op. cit.*

Stephen G. C. Ensko, *American Silversmiths and Their Marks*, privately printed, New York, 1927, p. 68.

Albany Directories, 1813 to 1819.

Albany Gazette, May 13, 1819.

The Curtisses

Louis G. Myers, *op. cit.*, pp. 17, 18.

J. B. Kerfoot, *op. cit.*, p. 132.

Albany Directories, 1819 to 1860.

Troy Sentinel, July 3, 1827.

Albany Evening Journal, September 14, 1872.

THE PEWTERERS OF PENNSYLVANIA

Robert C. Moon, M.D., *The Morris Family of Philadelphia*, privately printed, 1898, vol. 2, p. 545.

Some Letters and an Abstract of Letters from Pennsylvania Containing the State and Improvement of That Province, printed and sold by Andrew Soule, London, 1693.

Thomas Paschall

Robert C. Moon, M.D., *op. cit.*, vol. 2, p. 545.

Howard H. Cotterell, *op. cit.*, p. 279.

Collection of Various Pieces Covering Pennsylvania, printed in 1684, *Pennsylvania Magazine*, vol. 6, p. 323.

Philadelphia Deeds, vol. E 1–5, pp. 231, 233, 486; vol. E 1–10, pp. 187, 188.

Howard W. Lloyd, *Lloyd Manuscripts*, New Era Printing Company, Lancaster, Pa., 1912, p. 231.

Pennsylvania Archives, first series, vol. 9, pp. 714, 730.

'Records from the Bible of Thomas Say,' *Pennsylvania Magazine*, vol. 29, p. 216.

Philadelphia Wills, vol. D, p. 101.

Bibliography

Thomas Badcock
 Philadelphia Wills, vol. C, p. 76.
 Howard H. Cotterell, *op. cit.*, p. 152.

Simon Edgell and James Everett
 Howard H. Cotterell, *op. cit.*, pp. 202, 205.
 Louis G. Myers, *op. cit.*, pp. 37 to 39.
 Minutes of the Common Council of the City of Philadelphia, 1704–1776, pp. 125, 130, 141.
 Philadelphia Deeds, vol. F 1, p. 162; vol. F 5, p. 6; vol. F 6, p. 287.
 Pennsylvania Gazette, Philadelphia, March 26, 1730; September 4, 1735; August 4, 1737; September 21, 1738; May 3, 1739; July 23, 1741.
 Philadelphia Wills, vol. F, p. 297 (Probate file 1742, docket 269).

William Cox
 Jane Logan's Account Book, Collections of Pennsylvania Historical Society.
 Mary Coates's Account Book, Collections of Pennsylvania Historical Society.
 Philadelphia Deeds, vol. F 3, pp. 157, 163.
 Philadelphia Administrations, vol. F, p. 6.
 H. H. Cotterell, *op. cit.*, p. 190.

Thomas Byles
 Records of the First Baptist Church, Collections of Pennsylvania Historical Society.
 Pennsylvania Gazette, Philadelphia, November 19, 1741.
 Arthur W. H. Eaton, D.D., 'The Byles Family,' *New England Historical and Genealogical Register*, vol. 69, p. 103.
 The Belknap Letters, Massachusetts Historical Society Collections, fifth series, vol. 2, p. 262.
 Magazine of American Genealogy, vol. 16, p. 143.
 Philadelphia Deeds, vol. D 4, p. 244; vol. F 10, p. 183; vol. I 3, p. 242.
 Philadelphia Wills, vol. P, p. 105 (Probate file 1771, docket 75).

Simon Wyer
 John F. Watson, *Annals of Philadelphia and Pennsylvania in the Olden Time*, published by E. S. Stuart, Philadelphia, 1898, vol. 3, p. 368.
 Alfred Coxe Prime, *The Arts and Crafts in Philadelphia, Maryland and South Carolina, 1721–1785*, The Walpole Society, 1929, p. 111.
 Records of Christ Church, Philadelphia, Collections of Pennsylvania Historical Society.
 Philadelphia Deeds, vol. G 12, p. 83.
 Philadelphia Administrations, vol. F, p. 469 (Probate file 1752, docket 86).

Mungo Campbell
 Alfred Coxe Prime, *op. cit.*, vol. 1, pp. 108, 109.

Johann Christopher Heyne
 John J. Evans, 'I. C. H., Lancaster Pewterer,' *Antiques*, vol. 20, pp. 150–153.
 John J. Evans, 'I. C. H., Lancaster Pewterer,' *Lancaster County Historical Society Magazine*, vol. 35, no. 13, pp. 301–313.
 Unpublished records of Trinity Lutheran Church, Lancaster, Pennsylvania.

Bibliography

Pennsylvania Archives, second series, vol. 2, pp. 347, 418; vol. 9, p. 140; third series, vol. 17, pp. 7, 293, 458, 608; vol. 24, p. 690.

Records of the Moravian Churchyard, Lancaster, Collections of the Lancaster Historical Society.

Lancaster Probate Records, File H, 1781.

Lancaster Deeds, vol. P, p. 391; vol. Z, p. 488.

John H. Carter, 'Johann Christoph Heyne, Pewterer,' *Antiques*, vol. 33, no. 1, p. 13.

Johann Christian Höran

J. B. Kerfoot, *op. cit.*, p. 105.

Pennsylvania Archives, second series, vol. 18, p. 342; third series, vol. 14, pp. 202, 296, 660; vol. 16, p. 514; sixth series, vol. 1, p. 584.

Records of Saint Michael's and Zion Church, Philadelphia, Collections of Pennsylvania Historical Society.

Alfred Coxe Prime, *op. cit.*, vol. 1, p. 109.

Philadelphia Wills, vol. T, p. 283 (Probate file 1786, docket 168).

Johann Philip Alberti

Pennsylvania Archives, second series, vol. 17, p. 450; third series, vol. 14, pp. 208, 286, 539, 815; vol. 15, p. 339.

Alfred Coxe Prime, *op. cit.*, pp. 107, 109.

Records of Saint Michael's and Zion Church, op. cit.

Philadelphia Mortgages, vol. X 9, p. 506.

Philadelphia Wills, vol. R, p. 316 (Probate file 1780, docket 316).

Philip Will

Records of the Reformed Dutch Church in the City of New York, op. cit., vol. 61, p. 79.

Alfred Coxe Prime, *op. cit.*, p. 110.

Philadelphia Deeds, vol. H 20, p. 555.

Records of the First Reformed Church, Philadelphia, Collections of the Pennsylvania Historical Society.

Philadelphia Administrations, vol. I, p. 192 (Probate file 1787, docket 54).

William Will

Philadelphia Staatsbote, September 19, 1763; April 28, 1772.

Pennsylvania Archives, first series, vol. 7, p. 729; vol. 8, p. 638; vol. 11, p. 410; second series, vol. 8, p. 729; vol. 13, pp. 569, 670, 763; third series, vol. 14, pp. 282, 784, 818.

Colonial Records of Pennsylvania, Minutes of the Supreme Executive Council, vol. 11, pp. 330, 423; vol. 12, p. 506; vol. 13, pp. 85, 106, 391; vol. 15, pp. 567, 579.

Records of the First Reformed Church of Philadelphia, Collections of the Pennsylvania Historical Society, vol. 1, pp. 214, 257, 392, 443, 498, 598.

Philadelphia Directories, 1785–1797.

Louis G. Myers, *op. cit.*, p. 73.

Francis von A. Cabeen, 'Society of the Sons of Saint Tammany of Philadelphia,' *Pennsylvania Magazine*, vol. 26, p. 346.

J. B. Kerfoot, *op. cit.*, p. 88.

Dunlap's Packet, Philadelphia, December 31, 1778.

American Daily Advertiser, Philadelphia, February 14, 1798.

Philadelphia Administrations, vol. H, p. 308 (Probate file 1798, docket 63, and 1799, docket 20).

Bibliography

The Hasselberg Group

Burial Record, Old Swede's Church, Philadelphia, Collections of the Pennsylvania Historical Society, pp. 52, 63.

Baptismal Record, Old Swede's Church, Philadelphia, Collections of the Pennsylvania Historical Society, pp. 125, 836.

Pennsylvania Archives, second series, vol. 2, p. 132; vol. 8, p. 316; vol. 9, p. 150; sixth series, vol. 3, p. 1022.

Philadelphia Administrations, vol. I, pp. 22, 333.

Philadelphia Probate Records, file 1780, docket 316.

Philadelphia Deeds, vol. D 7, p. 318; vol. D 18, p. 281.

Philadelphia Mortgages, vol. M 2, p. 159.

Heads of Families at First Census, Pennsylvania, op. cit., p. 231.

William Ball

Magazine of American Genealogy, vol. 16, p. 143.

Pennsylvania Gazette, Philadelphia, September 26, 1754.

Pennsylvania Archives, second series, vol. 2, p. 23; third series, vol. 14, p. 522.

Pennsylvania Packet, Philadelphia, May 29, 1775; May 2, 1782.

Pennsylvania Evening Post, Philadelphia, February 4, 1777.

Stephen G. C. Ensko, *op. cit.*, p. 120.

Poulson's American Daily Advertiser, Philadelphia, June 1, 1810.

Richard F. Seybolt, 'Schoolmasters of Colonial Philadelphia,' *Pennsylvania Magazine*, vol. 52, p. 367.

John Thornton

Emigrants from England, transcribed by Gerald Fothergill, *New England Historical and Genealogical Register*, vol. 64, p. 227.

The Younger Heras

Burial Records, Philadelphia Board of Health, Collections of the Pennsylvania Historical Society, vol. 367, p. 599.

Records of Saint Michael's and Zion Church, op. cit., vol. 36, p. 415.

Pennsylvania Archives, second series, vol. 9, p. 398; third series, vol. 24, p. 233; sixth series, vol. 5, pp. 471, 557; vol. 10, p. 556.

Heads of Families at the First Census, Pennsylvania, op. cit., p. 220.

Philadelphia Directories, 1791–1822.

Philadelphia Deeds, vol. D 36, p. 313.

Philadelphia Probate Records, 1812, docket 95; 1817, docket 174; 1821, docket 142.

Poulson's American Daily Advertiser, Philadelphia, August 3, 1817; March 23, 1821.

Philadelphia Mortgages, vol. M 9, p. 44; vol. I C 12, p. 107.

George Washington Will

Records of the First Reformed Church, op. cit., vol. 1, pp. 214, 257, 392, 443, 498, 598.

Philadelphia Directories, 1799–1808.

Philadelphia Mortgages, vol. EF 7, p. 74; vol. EF 20, p. 372.

Parks Boyd and the Palethorps

J. B. Kerfoot, *op. cit.*, pp. 103, 117.

Bibliography

Poulson's American Daily Advertiser, Philadelphia, June 7, 1819.

Pennsylvania Archives, second series, vol. 9, p. 489.

Philadelphia Directories, 1797 to 1825.

Philadelphia Wills, vol. 7, p. 76 (file 1819, docket 124); vol. 7, p. 450 (file 1822, docket 28); vol. 8, p. 610.

Burial Records, Board of Health, op. cit., vol. 367, pp. 750, 1020.

Records of St. John's Protestant Episcopal Church, Northern Liberties, Philadelphia, Collections of the Pennsylvania Historical Society, vol. 377, pp. 23, 398.

Philadelphia Union, March 1, 1822.

The Harbesons

Philadelphia Directories, 1793 to 1815.

Records of Second Presbyterian Church, Philadelphia, Collections of the Pennsylvania Historical Society, vol. 32, pp. 22, 291, 323, 427, 460, 467.

J. B. Kerfoot, *op. cit.*, p. 99.

Three Country Pewterers of Pennsylvania

Louis G. Myers, *op. cit.*, pp. 51, 64.

Pennsylvania Archives, third series, vol. 17, pp. 354, 543, 896; vol. 18, pp. 300, 557, 611; vol. 21, pp. 330; 371, 665; vol. 22, p. 120; vol. 25, pp. 622, 623, 634; fifth series, vol. 5, p. 540; vol. 6, p. 428; vol. 7, p. 437; sixth series, vol. 2, p. 445; vol. 3, pp. 1418, 1421, 1478.

Blakslee Barns

Philadelphia Directories, 1812 to 1817.

Philadelphia Deeds, vol. I C 7, p. 52; vol. I C 31, pp. 287, 290.

Connecticut Vital Records, op. cit.

James Shepard, *History of Saint Mark's Church, Wethersfield and Berlin, Connecticut*, privately printed, New Britain, Conn., 1907, p. 220.

Trescott C. Barnes, *The Barnes Family Year Book*, Winsted Printing and Engraving Company, Winsted, Conn., 1910, vol. 3, p. 33.

Louis G. Myers, *op. cit.*, p. 61.

Catharine M. North, *History of Berlin, Connecticut*, Tuttle, Morehouse and Taylor Company, New Haven, Conn., 1916, p. 208.

Connecticut Courant, Hartford, August 6, 1823.

Connecticut Probate Records, Middletown District, docket 268, Connecticut State Library, Hartford.

Plumly and Bidgood

Philadelphia Directories, 1825 to 1833.

Philadelphia Deeds, vol. I H 5, p. 549

J. B. Kerfoot, *op. cit.*, p. 209.

Middletown (Conn.) *Deeds*, vol. 79, p. 86.

Eight Obscure Philadelphia Pewterers

Philadelphia Directories, 1793 to 1833.

THE PEWTERERS OF THE SOUTH

John Fiske, *Old Virginia and Her Neighbours*, Houghton Mifflin Company, Cambridge, Mass., 1897, vol. 2, p. 210.

Bibliography

Virginia Gazette, Williamsburg, June 1, 1769, and March 28, 1771.

York County (Virginia) *Wills*, vol. 22, 1773.

Collection of Robert Carter of Nomini Hall, Memorandum Book 13, 1773–1776, Duke University, Durham, N.C.

Diary of Colonel Landon Carter, *William and Mary Quarterly Historical Magazine*, first series, vol. 21, p. 174.

John Lathbury

George Sherwood, *American Colonists*, second series, London, England, 1933, p. 151.

Joseph Copeland

Worth Bailey, 'Joseph Copeland, 17th Century Pewterer,' *Antiques*, vol. 33, pp. 188–190.

The Willetts

Howard H. Cotterell, *op. cit.*, p. 337.

Alfred Coxe Prime, *op. cit.*, p. 111.

Upper Marlboro (Md.) *Land Records*, vol. A, pp. 152, 154, 374, 376; vol. C, pp. 25, 26; vol. M, p. 324.

Upper Marlboro (Md.) *Probate Records*, vol. 1, p. 358; vol. T 1, p. 47.

Archives of Maryland, Proceedings of the Council of Maryland, published by authority of the state under the direction of the Maryland Historical Society, vol. 20, p. 546; vol. 22, p. 79.

Bernard C. Steiner, 'The Chief Executive Officers of Maryland During the Provincial Period,' *Maryland Historical Magazine*, vol. 7, p. 325.

Mrs. Joseph Rucker Lamar, 'Bellevue, the Home of the National Society of Colonial Dames,' *Maryland Historical Magazine*, vol. 24, pp. 100–102.

Anthony Corne

South Carolina Gazette, Charleston, South Carolina, November 28, 1735.

John Campbell

Mrs. Rebecca Key, 'A Notice of Some of the First Buildings, with Notes of Some of the Early Residents,' *Maryland Historical Magazine*, vol. 14, p. 259.

Maryland Gazette, Annapolis, January 4, 1749.

'Vestry Proceedings, St. Anne's Parish, Annapolis, Maryland,' *Maryland Historical Magazine*, vol. 10, p. 41.

Elihu S. Riley, *The Ancient City, a History of Annapolis in Maryland*, Record Printing Office, Annapolis, Md., 1887, p. 181.

Anne Arundel County Wills, vol. EV 1, p. 33.

John Norsworth

The Virginia Gazette, Williamsburg, Virginia, March 28, 1771.

Francis Hendricks

South Carolina Gazette and Country Journal, Charleston, South Carolina, April 30, 1771.

Charleston Mesne Office, vol. 53, pp. 309, 310; vol. D 5, p. 94; vol. O, p. 6.

Charleston Wills, vol. A, page ref. missing; vol. C, p. 361.

Theodore Jennings and James Edward Smith

Emigrants from England, transcribed by Gerald Fothergill, *New England Historical and Genealogical Register*, vol. 65, pp. 122, 131.

Howard H. Cotterell, *op. cit.*, pp. 244, 308.

Bibliography

Lewis Geanty

    Baltimore Directories, 1799 to 1802.

    Baltimore Land Records, vol. 20, pp. 698, 701; vol. 76, p. 92.

    The Federal Gazette, Baltimore, December 2, 1802.

George Lightner

    Baltimore Land Records, vol. GG, pp. 179, 181; vol. 82, p. 594.

    W. F. Coyle, City Librarian, *Records of the City of Baltimore*, Press of Meyer and Thalheimer, Baltimore, Maryland, 1909, pp. 23, 50, 55.

    Baltimore American, November 21, 1806, and January 27, 1815.

    Baltimore Directories, 1796 to 1817.

    Baltimore Wills, vol. 9, p. 521.

    Baltimore Inventories, vol. 29, p. 244.

Samuel Kilbourn

    Payne Kenyon Kilbourne, *The History and Antiquities of the Name and Family of Kilbourn*, Durrie and Peck, New Haven, Conn., 1856, p. 225.

    Heads of Families at the First Census, Connecticut, op. cit., p. 46.

    Hartford Deeds, vol. 19, pp. 239–240.

    Hartford Directory, 1799.

    Baltimore Directories, 1814 to 1835.

    Baltimore American, March 4, 1814, and December 29, 1819.

Sylvester Griswold

    Connecticut Probate Records, Wallingford District, docket 615, Connecticut State Library, Hartford.

    Baltimore Directories, 1817, 1819, and 1822.

    Henry R. Stiles, M.D., *op. cit.*, vol. 2, p. 401.

North and Rowe

    Louis G. Myers, *op. cit.*, p. 32.

    Dexter North, *John North of Farmington and his Descendants*, privately printed, Washington, D.C., 1921, pp. 35, 68.

    Connecticut Vital Records, Lucius B. Barbour, Librarian, Connecticut State Library.

    Ruth Blair, State Historian, *Some Early Tax Digests of Georgia*, published by the Georgia Department of Archives and History, 1926, p. 140.

    Richmond County (Georgia) *Deeds*, vol. X, p. 189.

Giles Griswold

    Louis G. Myers, *op. cit.*, p. 32.

    Ruth Blair, *op. cit.*, p. 140.

    Connecticut Vital Records, op. cit.

    Meriden Land Records, Warranty, vol. 1, p. 337; vol. 2, pp. 15, 18, 540; vol. 5, pp. 30, 45.

John Philip Reich

    Home Moravian Church Records, Winston-Salem, North Carolina.

    The Weekly Gleaner, Salem, North Carolina, September 22, 1829.

THE INITIALED PORRINGERS

    J. B. Kerfoot, *op. cit.*, p. 205.

Bibliography

UNIDENTIFIED AMERICAN TOUCHES

Florence T. Howe, 'Some Early New England Church Pewter,' *Antiques*, vol. 22, pp. 92–94.
Paul Revere advertisements.
J. B. Kerfoot, *op. cit.*, pp. 123–125.

THE BRITANNIA PERIOD

C. H. S. Davis, *op. cit.*, p. 475.
J. B. Kerfoot, *op. cit.*, p. 146.
Louis G. Myers, *op. cit.*, p. 91.
Percy E. Raymond, *op. cit.*, pp. 209–211.

THE MAKERS OF THE BRITANNIA PERIOD

Andrew Allison. Philadelphia Directories, 1837 to 1839.

John Allison. Philadelphia Directory, 1836.

Benjamin Archer. St. Louis Directory, 1847.

Ellis S. Archer. Philadelphia Directories, 1842 to 1855.

Archer and Janney. J. G. Braecklein, 'Ohio and Missouri Pewter Data,' *Antiques*, vol. 14, p. 333.

Babbitt and Crossman. Taunton (Mass.) *Vital Records.* Samuel H. Emery, D.D., *History of Taunton, Massachusetts*, D. Mason & Co., Syracuse, N.Y., 1893, pp. 652–654.

Timothy Bailey. Charles L. Woodside, 'Marked American Pewter,' *Antiques*, vol. 9, p. 317.

L. G. Baldwin. C. H. S. Davis, *op. cit.*, p. 494. G. W. Perkins, *Historical Sketches of Meriden*, Franklin E. Hinman, West Meriden, Connecticut, 1849, p. 117.

William C. Bartholdt. 'Riddles and Replies,' *Antiques*, April, 1938.

Morris Benham. New England Mercantile Directory, 1849.

Benham and Whitney. New England Mercantile Directory, 1849.

Henry S. Boardman. Charlotte Goldthwaite, *op. cit.*, p. 449. *Hartford Directory*, 1841. *Philadelphia Directories*, 1844 to 1861. J. B. Kerfoot, *op. cit.*, p. 137.

J. D. Boardman. Hartford Directory, 1825. Charlotte Goldthwaite, *op. cit.*, p. 358.

Luther Boardman. Commemorative Biographical Record of Middlesex County, *op. cit.*, p. 435. Charlotte Goldthwaite, *op. cit.*, pp. 495, 496. *New England Mercantile Directory*, 1849.

Timothy Boardman & Co. New York Directories, 1822–1825. Charlotte Goldthwaite, *op. cit.*, p. 854.

Boardman & Co. New York Directories, 1825 to 1827.

Boardman and Hall. Philadelphia Directory, 1844.

Boardman and Hart. New York Directories, 1827 to 1850.

John Bouis. Baltimore Directories, 1829 to 1834.

David S. Brooks. Hartford Directory, 1828.

Browe & Dougherty. Newark (N.J.) *Directory*, 1845.

Bull, Lyman and Couch. C. Bancroft Gillespie, *op. cit.*, part 1, p. 359.

A. Burdett. Baltimore Directories, 1838 to 1841.

John Calverley. Philadelphia Directories, 1840 and 1841.

William E. Camp. New England Mercantile Directory, 1849.

Capen and Molineux. New York Directories, 1848 to 1854.

Oren Colton. Philadelphia Directories, 1826 to 1836.

S. L. Cone. C. H. S. Davis, *op. cit.*, p. 494. G. W. Perkins, *op. cit.*, p. 117.

Bibliography

Thomas Connell. Philadelphia Directories, 1829 to 1840.

Crossman, West and Leonard. S. H. Emery, *op. cit.*, pp. 653, 654.

Edwin E. Curtis. C. Bancroft Gillespie, *op. cit.*, part 1, p. 359; part 3, p. 40.

Enos H. Curtis. C. Bancroft Gillespie, *op. cit.*, part 1, p. 359.

Lemuel J. Curtis. C. Bancroft Gillespie, *op. cit.*, part 1, p. 359; part 2, p. 299; part 3, p. 40. C. H. S. Davis, *op. cit.*, p. 592.

Thomas S. Derby, Junior. New England Mercantile Directory, 1849.

C. B. de Riemer & Co. Stephen G. C. Ensko, *op. cit.*, p. 115.

Rufus Dunham. C. L. Woodside and Lura Woodside Watkins, 'Three Maine Pewterers,' *Antiques,* vol. 22, p. 9. *New England Mercantile Directory*, 1849. *New England Business Directory*, 1860.

Eli Eldredge. Boston Directory, 1849. *New England Business Directory*, 1860.

John Ellison. Philadelphia Directory, 1837.

Endicott and Sumner. New York Directories, 1846 to 1853.

Asa F. Flagg. J. G. Braecklein, *op. cit.*, p. 331.

Thomas Fletcher. Philadelphia Directories, 1837 to 1841.

Daniel Francis. Buffalo Directories, 1833 to 1842.

James A. Frary. New England Mercantile Directory, 1849. C. H. S. Davis, *op. cit.*, p. 494.

Frary and Benham. C. H. S. Davis, *op. cit.*, p. 494.

Fuller and Smith. Connecticut Business Directory, 1851.

Anthony George, Junior. Philadelphia Directories, 1839–1847.

Roswell Gleason. John Barber White, *Genealogy of the Descendants of Thomas Gleason of Watertown, Massachusetts*, Press of the Nichols Print, Haverhill, Mass., 1909, pp. 256, 257. John Whiting Webber, 'Roswell Gleason,' *Antiques*, vol. 20, p. 87. J. B. Kerfoot, *op. cit.*, Plate 3.

Graham and Savage. Middletown (Conn.) *Land Records*, vol. 65, p. 493; vol. 67, pp. 154, 356; vol. 68, p. 13.

H. H. Graves. New England Mercantile Directory, 1849.

J. B. Graves. Middletown (Conn.) *Land Records*, vol. 79, p. 112.

Samuel Green, Junior. Boston Directories, 1826 to 1835.

Griswold and Couch. Louis G. Myers, *op. cit.*, p. 46.

Franklin D. Hall. Hartford Directory, 1840.

Hall, Boardman & Co. Philadelphia Directories, 1846 to 1848.

Hall and Boardman. Philadelphia Directories, 1849 to 1857.

Hall and Cotton. J. B. Kerfoot, *op. cit.*, p. 162.

Joseph Harrison. Philadelphia Directories, 1829 to 1852.

Lucius D. Hart. New York Wills, Liber 204, p. 33. Henry B. Stiles, *op. cit.*, p. 418.

John Hill. New York Directories, 1846 to 1848.

Charles Hillsburgh. J. Disturnell, *New York as It Is in 1837.*

Robert Holmes and Sons. Baltimore Directories, 1853 and 1854.

Thomas R. Holt. C. Bancroft Gillespie, *op. cit.*, part 1, p. 359.

Homan & Co. J. G. Braecklein, *op. cit.*, p. 333.

Henry Hopper. New York Directories, 1842 to 1847.

Houghton and Wallace. Edward A. Rushford, '15 Lamps Patented in 1843,' *The New York Sun*, December 1, 1934.

Bibliography

Edwin House. Hartford Directories, 1841 and 1846.

Willis Humiston. C. H. S. Davis, *op. cit.*, p. 823. *Troy* (New York) *Directory*, 1857.

George Hunter. Troy (New York) *Directory*, 1831.

Martin Hyde. New York Directories, 1857 and 1858.

D. H., J. H., and W. W. Jagger. Hartford Directories, 1839 to 1846.

Edward Jones. New York Directories, 1837 to 1843.

De Witt Kimberly. C. Bancroft Gillespie, *op. cit.*, part 1, p. 359.

W. W. Knight & Co. Philadelphia Directories, 1839 to 1850.

Lewis Kruiger. Philadelphia Directory, 1833.

Leonard, Reed and Barton. S. H. Emery, *op. cit.*, p. 654.

Isaac C. Lewis. C. Bancroft Gillespie, *op. cit.*, part 1, p. 359; part 3, pp. 40, 41. C. H. S. Davis, *op. cit.*, p. 573. *New England Mercantile Directory*, 1849.

J. D. Locke. New York Directories, 1835 to 1860.

William W. Lyman. C. H. S. Davis, *op. cit.*, p. 575. C. Bancroft Gillespie, *op. cit.*, part 2, pp. 298, 299; part 3, p. 40. *New England Mercantile Directory*, 1849.

William McQuilkin. Philadelphia Directories, 1845 to 1853.

Thaddeus Manning. New England Mercantile Directory, 1849.

Marcus Maton. Hartford Directory, 1828.

Meriden Britannia Company. C. Bancroft Gillespie, *op. cit.*, part 3, pp. 40, 41. *New England Business Directory*, 1860.

Morey and Ober. Boston Directories, 1852 to 1855. Charles L. Woodside, *op. cit.*, p. 316.

Morey, Ober & Co. Boston Directories, 1855 to 1857.

Morey and Smith. Boston Directories, 1857 to 1885.

Henry Morgan. New England Mercantile Directory, 1849.

John Munson. New England Mercantile Directory, 1849. C. H. S. Davis, *op. cit.*, p. 477. C. Bancroft Gillespie, *op. cit.*, part 3, p. 40. *Wallingford* (Conn.) *Deeds*, vol. 46, pp. 35, 233, 234; vol. 47, p. 248; vol. 49, p. 349.

Charles Ostrander. New York Directories, 1848 to 1854.

Ostrander and Norris. New York Directories, 1848 to 1850.

J. H. Palethorp. Philadelphia Directories, 1820 to 1845.

Charles Parker & Co. G. W. Perkins, *op. cit.*, p. 115. C. H. S. Davis, *op. cit.*, p. 494.

Charles Plumley. Middletown Land Records, vol. 79, p. 86.

Allen Porter. Charles L. Woodside and Lura Woodside Watkins, *op. cit.*, p. 8.

Freeman Porter. Charles L. Woodside and Lura Woodside Watkins, *op. cit.*, p. 8. *New England Business Directory*, 1860.

J. H. Putnam. Charles L. Woodside, *op. cit.*, p. 319.

Reed & Barton. S. H. Emery, *op. cit.*, p. 654.

B. Richardson & Son. Philadelphia Directory, 1839.

G. Richardson. Edward H. West, 'George Richardson, Pewterer,' *Antiques*, vol. 38, pp. 176–177.

John Rodgers. Philadelphia Directories, 1839 and 1840.

Russell and Beach. Commemorative Biographical Record of Middlesex County, *op. cit.*, p. 435.

John N. and Samuel Rust. New York Directories, 1842 to 1845.

Leonard M. Rust. New York Directory, 1849.

Bibliography

Samuel Rust. New York Directories, 1837 to 1842.

T. Sage & Co. J. G. Braecklein, *op. cit.*, p. 333.

Sellew & Co. Cincinnati Directories, 1834, 1836, and 1840. J. G. Braecklein, *op. cit.*, pp. 331, 332.

Sheldon and Feltman. Albany Directories, 1847 and 1848.

Sickel and Shaw. Philadelphia Directories, 1849 to 1853.

Samuel Simpson. C. H. S. Davis, *op. cit.*, pp. 475–477. *Wallingford* (Conn.) *Deeds*, vol. 43, pp. 392. 453; vol. 46, pp. 35, 234. *New York Directories*, 1843 to 1845.

Simpson and Benham. New York Directories, 1845 to 1847.

Eben Smith. New England Mercantile Directory, 1849. *Massachusetts Register*, 1852 and 1853. *New England Business Directory*, 1856. J. B. Kerfoot, *op. cit.*, p. 60.

William R. Smith. Middletown (Conn.) *Land Records*, vol. 79, p. 86.

Smith, Ober & Co. Boston Directories, 1850 to 1853. Charles L. Woodside, *op. cit.*, p. 316. Editor's Attic, *Antiques*, vol. 10, p. 272.

Thomas Smith & Co. Boston Directories, 1842 to 1846. Charles L. Woodside, *op. cit.* r 315.

Smith & Co. Boston Directories, 1847 to 1849. *New England Mercantile Directory*, 18.). Charles L. Woodside, *op. cit.*, p. 316.

Smith & Co. Albany Directories, 1853 to 1856.

Smith and Feltman. Albany Directories, 1849 to 1852.

Smith and Morey. Boston Directory, 1841. Charles L. Woodside, *op. cit.*, p. 315. J. B. Kerfoot, *op. cit.*, p. 180.

William H. Starr. New York Directories, 1843 to 1847.

Frederick Stoddart. Philadelphia Directory, 1833.

Taunton Britannia Manufacturing Company. S. H. Emery, *op. cit.*, p. 654.

John Thomas. Philadelphia Directory, 1841.

Israel Trask. J. B. Kerfoot, *op. cit.*, p. 60. John Whiting Webber, 'A Massachusetts Pewterer,' *Antiques*, vol. 5, pp. 26 to 28. *Beverly* (Mass.) *Vital Statistics. New England Business Directory*, 1856. John Whiting Webber, 'The Real and the Legendary I. Trask,' *Antiques*, vol. 35, p. 224.

Oliver Trask. Beverly (Mass.) *Vital Statistics.* J. B. Kerfoot, *op. cit.*, p. 60. *Essex County Deeds*, vol. 264, p. 85; vol. 302, p. 178; vol. 305, p. 154; vol. 313, p. 83.

Lester Wadsworth. Hartford Directory, 1838.

R. Wallace & Co. C. H. S. Davis, *op. cit.*, p. 477.

H. B. Ward & Co. J. B. Kerfoot, *op. cit.*, p. 60. *New England Mercantile Directory*, 1849.

C. P. Wayne & Co. Philadelphia Directories, 1829 to 1849.

J. Weekes & Co. New York Directories, 1822 to 1833. *Intelligencer and Republican*, Poughkeepsie, New York, June 26, 1833; September 4, 1833; April 1, 1834; April 23, 1834; March 4, 1835.

G. and J. Whitfield. New York Directories, 1828 to 1865.

J. H. Whitlock. Troy (New York) *Deeds* (references missing).

Lewis Whitmore. Henry R. Stiles, *op. cit.*, vol. 1, p. 934.

Whitmore and Francis. Buffalo Republican, January 12, 1833. *Buffalo Directory*, 1835.

Thomas Wildes. New York Directories, 1833 to 1840.

Thomas Wilds. Philadelphia Directories, 1829 to 1833.

Lorenzo L. Williams. Wallingford (Conn.) *Deeds*, vol. 43, pp. 133, 213, 392, 405, 453. *Philadelphia Directories*, 1838 to 1842.

Bibliography

Thomas Willis. Philadelphia Directories, 1829 to 1833.

J. B. Woodbury. Philadelphia Directories, 1835 to 1838.

Woodman Cook & Co. J. B. Kerfoot, *op. cit.*, p. 61.

Burrage Yale. Rodney H. Yale, *op. cit.*, pp. 154, 203. Charles L. Woodside, *op. cit.*, p. 319. *Commemorative Biographical Record of Middlesex County*, *op. cit.*, p. 435.

Charles Yale. New York Directory, 1832.

William Yale. New York Directories, 1830 to 1832.

Yale and Curtis. New York Directories, 1858 to 1867.

THE CLEANING AND CARE OF PEWTER

H. H. Cotterell, *op. cit.*, pp. 61–62, 75–76.

H. J. L. J. Massé, *op. cit.*, pp. 135–140.

H. J. L. J. Massé, *The Pewter Collector*, Herbert Jenkins, Ltd., London, 1921, pp. 35–39.

J. B. Kerfoot, *op. cit.*, pp. 214–215.

John W. Poole, 'The Care of Pewter,' *Antiques*, vol. 34, pp. 248, 249.

Sven Brennert, *Black Spots on Tin and Tinned Ware*, Technical Publications of the International Tin Research and Development Council, series D, number 2.

Percy E. Raymond, *Pewter Disease*, Bulletin number 7, The Pewter Collector's Club of America.

RANDOM NOTES ON COLLECTING

J. B. Kerfoot, *op. cit.*, pp. 20, 30.

H. H. Cotterell, *op. cit.*, various references.

Pennsylvania Gazette, Philadelphia, April 27, 1738.

Louis G. Myers, *op. cit.*, p. 16.

INDEX OF SYMBOLS AND INITIALS IN THE EARLY TOUCH-MARKS

Volumes One and Two

INDEX OF SYMBOLS AND INITIALS IN
THE EARLY TOUCH-MARKS

[195]

Index of Symbols and Initials in the Early Touch-Marks

Index of Symbols and Initials in the Early Touch-Marks

Index of Symbols and Initials in the Early Touch-Marks

Index of Symbols and Initials in the Early Touch-Marks

INDEX OF MAKERS OF PEWTER
SHOWN IN PLATES
Volumes One and Two

INDEX OF MAKERS OF PEWTER
SHOWN IN PLATES

Index of Makers of Pewter Shown in Plates

GENERAL INDEX
Volumes One and Two

GENERAL INDEX

Abigail, ship, I, 49

Addicks, Mrs. Stanley H., vii

'A. G.,' touch of Ashbil Griswold, I, 127

Albany Evening Journal, obituary notice of Daniel Curtiss, II, 33

Albany Gazette, II, 32

Albany Mechanics' Society, II, 32

Alberti, Anna Barbara, wife of Johann Philip, II, 50

Alberti, Carl Friedrich, son of Johann Philip, II, 50

Alberti, George Friedrich, son of Johann Philip, II, 50

Alberti, Johann Philip, Philadelphia pewterer, II, 49; in partnership with Johann Christian Höran; dies, 50; 55

Alberti and Höran, partnership mentioned, II, 50

Alden family, its English flagon, I, 42

Alderson, John, London pewterer, his mug design, I, 33

Alexander, Mrs. Helen D., viii

Alexander, Miss Mary C., viii

Alexander, Mrs. T. W., descendant of John North, II, 81

Allaire, Anthony J., in partnership with Moses Lafetra, pewterers, II, 26, 28

Allen, Mary, married wine merchant Timothy Green, I, 78

Allen, William, I, 49

Allison, Andrew, listed as pewterer, II, 95

Allison, John, listed as pewterer, II, 95; probably identical with John Ellison, 101

Alloys, in pewter-making, I, 2–4

Amelung, John Will agent for, II, 13

American Colonists, by George Sherwood, II, 71

American Daily Advertiser, obituary of William Will, II, 53; of John Hera, 59; of Parks Boyd, 61

American Makers of Pewter and White Metal, xv

American Pewter, viii, ix, xv; I, 49, 74, 75, 91, 119–21, 126, 135, 137, 138; II, 26, 31, 33, 50, 54, 55, 61, 63, 67, 86, 91, 93, 130

American Pewterers, Check List of, II, 139–52

Ames and Russell, factory of, II, 109

Ancient and Honourable Artillery Company, I, 51, 52, 59, 60, 63, 73, 77, 81, 82

Ancient Order of Free Masons, of Pennsylvania, II, 57

Annals of Philadelphia, its error of Myer for Wyer, II, 43

Anthony, Richard, merchant, and his wife Sarah, II, 41

Antimony, its use in pewter-making, I, 3

Antiques, quoted on England's export trade in pewter with the colonies, I, 7; statement on porringers, 30; on George Richardson, 84, 85; article on Richard Lee, 123; on Samuel Pierce, 124, 125; 'William Elsworth: His Rose and Crown,' by Albert H. Good, II, 20; church flagon, 44, 46; on the Jamestown spoon, 71; study of the day book of William Calder, 93; on 'The Care of Pewter,' by John W. Poole, 126

Apprentices, in pewter-making, I, 10, 11; laws no longer enforced, 24

Archer, Benjamin, record of, II, 95; manufactured pewter for N. E. Janney, 96

Archer, Ellis S., a lamp-maker, II, 95

Archer and Janney, lamp-makers, II, 96

Archer and Warner, listed as lamp-makers, II, 95

Armitages and Standish, made teapots, II, 96

L'Art du Potier d'Etain, treatise on pewter, I, 10

Arts and Crafts in Philadelphia, clears up mystery of name Myer, II, 43

Arts and Crafts of New England, I, 63, 66; advertisement of John Skinner quoted, 73

Ash, James, defeated William Will for sheriff, II, 53

Assay of metals, I, 8

Auber, Sarah, married to Josias Byles, II, 41

Austin, Deborah, widow of Richard, I, 82, 83

Austin, Ebenezer, father of the pewterer Nathaniel, I, 75

General Index

Austin, John, Boston pewterer, I, 80

Austin, Margaret Rand, wife of Nathaniel Austin, I, 75

Austin, Mary Smith, mother of the pewterer Nathaniel, I, 75

Austin, Nathaniel, Charlestown pewterer, I, 21, 34, 48, 49, 66, 71; identity confused with goldsmith of same name, 75; sketch of his life, 75, 76; 83; II, 86, 87

Austin, Nathaniel, goldsmith, mistakenly identified as a pewterer, I, 75

Austin, Nathaniel, Jr., son of the pewterer, I, 75

Austin, Richard, Boston pewterer, I, 48, 49, 64, 66; his use of the 'Boston scroll' touch, 69, 70; 73; became partner of Samuel Green, 79; sketch of his life, 81; ruined in brokerage business, 82, 83; his death, 84; II, 86, 133

Austin, Silvia, wife of John, I, 80

Austin, Thomas, father of Richard, I, 81

Austin, William, state senator and author, son of the pewterer Nathaniel, I, 75, 76

Babbitt, Isaac, Taunton pewterer, II, 96; invented Babbitt metal, 99; of firm of Babbitt and Crossman, 110

Babbitt, Ziba, father of Isaac Babbitt, II, 96

Babbitt & Crossman, New England pewterers, I, 24; their beaker design, 37; II, 96

Babbitt, Crossman and Company, succeeded Babbitt and Crossman, II, 96, 99

Babcock, Samuel, Connecticut tinman, I, 133-35

Badcoke, Henry, Philadelphia brewer, cousin of Thomas, II, 38

Badcoke, Thomas, Philadelphia pewterer, provisions of his will, II, 38

Badger, Giles, ancestor of the pewterer Thomas, I, 81

Badger, Mary Beighton, wife of Thomas Badger, Sr., I, 69

Badger, Thomas, blockmaker, I, 69

Badger, Thomas, Jr., Boston pewterer, I, 48, 49, 66; his use of the 'Boston scroll' touch, 69, 70; 73, 79; sketch of his life, 80, 81; his supposed communion set, II, 31; 86, 87, 123, 124

Bailey, Almira, married to David B. Morey, II, 113

Bailey, Capt. Lemuel, I, 91

Bailey, O. and A., probably dealers only, II, 119

Bailey, Timothy, sketch of life, II, 96; J. H. Putnam partner of, 110, 113; a peddler for Burrage Yale, 118

Bailey, Worth, vii; his reconstruction of the Chuckatuck spoon, I, 38; II, 70-72

Bailey and Putnam, pewterers of Malden, Mass., II, 96

Baker, John, Boston pewterer, becomes surety for Edmund Dolbeare, I, 55; sketch of his life, 56, 57

Baker, John, of Philadelphia, inventory of William Will's shop filed by, II, 159

Baker, Leah, mother of John, I, 57

Baker, Michael, Philadelphia coppersmith, creditor of Charles Plumly, II, 67

Baker, Sarah, second wife of the pewterer John Carnes, I, 63

Baker, Thomas, father of John, I, 57

Baker, Thomas, Boston ironmonger, brother of John, I, 57

Baker, Thomas, Jr., apprentice pewterer, I, 57

Baldwin, L. G., britannia maker of Meriden, Conn., II, 96

Baldwin, R., I, 132

Ball, Elizabeth, wife of William Ball, II, 56

Ball, William, viii

Ball, William, and Mary White, parents of William, Jr., II, 56

Ball, William, Jr., Philadelphia goldsmith and pewterer, becomes general merchant, II, 56; first Provincial Grand Master of Free Masons in Pennsylvania, 57

Baltimore American and Commercial Advertiser, notice of death of George Lightner, II, 78; advertised letter for Kilbourn & Porter, 79; advertisement of Samuel Kilbourn, 80

Bancks, C., of Bewdley, Eng., II, 119

Banks, Elizabeth, married to Thomas Brigden, II, 31

Baptismal bowl presented to the Church of Christ in Waterford, Plate XXXVII, No. 244

Baptismal bowls, forms made in America, I, 44, 45

Baptist Church of Cheshire, Conn., communion set formerly used in, Plate XXXIV, No. 227

Barbour, Lucius, his *Vital Statistics*, I, 91, 120, 136

Barns, Almira, wife of Blakslee, II, 65, 66

Barns, Barnaby, merchant, II, 65

Barns, Benjamin, farmer, II, 65

Barns, Blair, wigmaker, II, 65

Barns, Blakslee, Philadelphia pewterer, I, 103, 112, 121; possible kinsman of Stephen Barns, 125;

General Index

Billy, body-servant of George Washington, II, 25

Birch, Miss Louise, vii

Bird, James, New York pewterer, II, 28

Bismuth, its use in pewter-making, I, 3

Bissel, Anne, married to Theodore Hinsdale, I, 137

'Black pewter,' I, 3

Blair, Mrs. J. Insley, collector, vii; II, 5, 14, 15, 16, 17, 21

Blake, Elizabeth, married Amos Treadway, I, 114

Blaksley, Phoebe, wife of Moses Barns and mother of Blakslee Barns, II, 65

Blanchard, George, defrauds the pewterer Richard Austin in brokerage business, I, 82, 83

Bland, James, pewterer, without record, II, 19

Blaney, Dwight, vii

Blaun, James, pewterer, without record, II, 19

Blin, James, mariner, grandfather of Peter, I, 72

Blin, Margaret, sister of Peter, married David Flagg, I, 72

Blin, Peter, Boston pewterer, sketch of his life, I, 72

Blin, William, Boston shopkeeper, father of Peter, I, 72

Blisters, in casting pewter, I, 12

Bloomer, Captain of Militia, II, 19

Blouin, French doctor, his patent medicine, II, 22

Boardman, Elizabeth, wife of Thomas D. Boardman, I, 128

Boardman, Henrietta, wife of Sherman Boardman, I, 128

Boardman, Henry S., son of Sherman, I, 129; II, 97, 98

Boardman, J. D., a pewterer of Hartford, II, 97

Boardman, Luther, sketch of his life, II, 97; worked for Russell and Beach, 111; foreman for Burrage Yale, 118

Boardman, Lydia, wife of Luther Boardman, II, 97

Boardman, Oliver, soldier of the Revolution, married Sarah Danforth, I, 128

Boardman, Rebecca, wife of Constant Griswold, I, 127; mother of Sylvester Griswold, II, 81

Boardman, Sarah, wife of Oliver Boardman, I, 128

Boardman, Sarah S., married to Burrage Yale, II, 118

Boardman, Sherman, partnership with his brother Thomas D., I, 128; his death, 129; II, 97, 134

Boardman, Thomas Danforth, Hartford pewterer, I, 20; 32; 35, 39; touch on teapot, 40; his beaker design, 42; flagon designs, 43; an executor of the estate of Samuel Danforth, 119; in business with his brother Sherman, 128, 129; 130; II, 97, 134

Boardman, Timothy, younger brother of the Boardmans, I, 128–30; II, 97, 98

Boardman & Co. I, 45, 128–30, 138; II, 98

Boardman & Hall, a Boardman branch store, I, 129; II, 97, 104

Boardman & Hart, I, 128, 129; II, 98, 104

Boardman, T. D. & S., Hartford pewterers, their baptismal bowl designs, I, 45; in debt to Samuel Danforth, 119; history of, 128–30; II, 97, 98, 104, 134

Boardmans, pewterers, I, 21, 24, 32, 36, 37, 86, 103, 104, 119, 128–30, 136; II, 2, 33, 67, 89, 93, 94, 98, 102, 104, 105

Boelen, Jacob, New York goldsmith, II, 14

Boggs, Benjamin R., ix

Bokee, Rebekka (Rebecca), married Christian Will, II, 14

Bomper, Anna Judith, joined the church, II, 12

Bond, John, master of brigantine, *Britannia*, II, 40

Bonning (Benning or Bonynge), Robert, Boston pewterer, I, 66, 67

Bonning, Sarah Henderson, wife of Robert, I, 66

Bonynge, *see* Bonning

Booge, in pewter-making, I, 14, 15; regulations on hammering, 28, 29

Boston Gazette, quoted on David Cutler, I, 66; notice of John Skinner, 74; announcement of Nathaniel Austin quoted, 75

Boston News-Letter, advertisement of John Skinner quoted, I, 74

Boston Selectmen's Records, I, 66

Bouis, John, block-tin maker of Baltimore, II, 98

Bouis, John, and Son, block-tin makers of Baltimore, II, 98

Bouis, Joseph, of John Bouis and Son, II, 98

Bouzigues, Mr., Philadelphia pewterer, II, 68

Bowen, Richard LeB., viii

Bowl, I, 26; not identical with basin, 27

Bowles, Samuel, Boston pewterer, I, 80

Bowman, Albert C., vii; collection of pewter, I, 45; 124; his Coldwell snuffbox, II, 25; 91, 104, 115

Bowman, Elizabeth Robbins, mother of Nathaniel, I, 83

Bowman, Nathaniel, Charlestown pewterer, I, 83; his death, 84

Bowman, Samuel, father of Nathaniel, I, 83

Bowman, of Manning, Bowman and Company, II, 107

Boyd, Eliza, daughter of Parks Boyd, II, 61

General Index

Bruges, in pewter-making, I, 2

Brunstrom, John Andrew, Philadelphia pewterer, I, 33; II, 55; marriage to Elizabeth, daughter of Abraham Hasselberg, 56

Bubelot, Susannah, second wife of Frederick Bassett, II, 6

Buckley, Townsend M., a lamp-maker of Troy, N.Y., II, 98

Buffalo Emporium, I, 138

Bull, Lyman and Couch, britannia makers of Meriden, Conn., II, 98, 107

Bumstead, Thomas, *see* Bumsteed, Thomas

Bumsteed, Susan, wife of Thomas, I, 51

Bumsteed (or Bumstead), Thomas, early Boston pewterer, I, 28, 46; his death, 47; sketch of his life, 51, 52

Bumsteed, Thomas and Jeremiah, children of Thomas, I, 51

Burdett, Aaron, Baltimore pewterer, II, 91, 99

Burford & Green, London pewterers, II, 132

Burr, Amy, married William Billings, I, 99

Burr, Mr., mentioned in letter of Thomas Danforth, 2d, Plate LII

Burrill, Martha, wife of Richard Skinner, I, 73

Burroughs, William, Melville's shop appraised by, II, 160

Busgutt, Peter, I, 49

Bush, Robert, Bristol pewterer, II, 119, 132

Bush & Perkins, Bristol pewterers, II, 119, 132

Button, Henry V., viii; II, 6, 17, 31

Button, Robert, I, 53

Button, Sarah, intended wife of Daniel Durninger, I, 62

Buttons, of pewter, I, 3

Byles, Daniel, son of Thomas, II, 42

Byles, Elizabeth, daughter of Thomas, II, 42; married William Ball, Jr., 56

Byles, Elizabeth, wife of Thomas Byles, II, 42, 56

Byles, Josias, saddler, and his wife Sarah Auber, II, 41; thrice married, 42

Byles, Josias, Jr., II, 41

Byles, Margaret Lambert, wife of Daniel Byles, II, 42

Byles, Mather, half-brother of Thomas, deported as a Tory but allowed to return, II, 42

Byles, Thomas, Philadelphia pewterer, I, 11, 27, 57, 86; records relating to him, II, 9, 41, 42; daughter Elizabeth married to William Ball, Jr., 56; 77, 88; inventory of, 156–158

Byles, Thomas Lambert, grandson of Thomas, II, 42

Cade, John, I, 69

Cahill, J. W. & Co., makers of teapots, II, 99

Cahoone, Lydia, married the pewterer Joseph Belcher, Jr., petitions for divorce, I, 90

Calder, Charles A., his *Rhode Island Pewterers and Their Work*, xv; quotes *Newport Mercury* on Joseph Belcher, I, 90; 99; describes his grandfather William Calder, 101; 132; II, 15

Calder, Mrs. Charles A., vii, viii; I, 101

Calder, Eliza, wife of William Calder, I, 101

Calder, Mary, wife of William Calder, I, 101

Calder, William, ancestor of the pewterer William Calder, I, 100

Calder, William, of Bristol, Eng., II, 119

Calder, William, Providence pewterer, I, 24; his beaker design, 37; 87; sketch of his career, 100–02; II, 68; study of his day book in *Antiques*, 93; later listing, 99

Calverley, John, a britannia maker of Philadelphia, II, 99

Calvert, Maximilian, shop next door to John Norsworth, II, 76

Camp, Almira, married Josiah Danforth, I, 118

Camp, William E., britannia maker of Middletown, Conn., II, 99

Campbell, Daniel, son of John, II, 76

Campbell, Frances, wife of John, II, 76

Campbell, John, pewterer, II, 44; his will, 75, 76

Campbell, John, Jr., II, 76

Campbell, Mungo, Philadelphia pewterer, II, 43, 44

Campbell, Robert Eagle, son of John, II, 76

Campmell (or Campbell), Samuel, Connecticut pewterer, I, 137

Candor, Mrs. Edward R., vii

Candy, Catherine, widow of Capt. Dennis, second wife of Cornelius Bradford, II, 10

Candy, Capt. Dennis, II, 10

Capen, Ephraim, lamp-maker of New York, II, 99

Capen and Molineux, lamp-makers of New York, II, 99

'Care of Pewter, The,' by John W. Poole, in *Antiques*, II, 126

Carnes, Dorothy, married to John Carnes, I, 63

Carnes, Eliza Greenough, married to John Carnes, I, 63

General Index

Hewett, Thomas, New York merchant, his judgment against William Kirby, II, 18

Heyne, Johann Christopher, Pennsylvania pewterer, his sugar bowl design, I, 41; flagon designs, 43; chalice design, 44; II, 36; sketch of his life and work, 44–48, 50; 63, 89

Heyne, Maria, wife of Johann Christopher Heyne, II, 44; death of, 45

Hill, Mrs. J. Bennett, viii

Hill, John, britannia maker of New York, II, 104

Hillsburgh, Charles, britannia maker of New York, II, 104

Hinman and Osbourn, Connecticut pewter merchants, II, 8; invoice of pewter shipped to, Plate LX, Nos. 469, 470

Hinsdale, painter, portrait of T. D. Boardman painted by, II, frontispiece

Hinsdale, Mrs. Anne Bissel, mother of John and Daniel, I, 137

Hinsdale, John & Daniel, firm of Connecticut pewterers, I, 137

Hinsdale, Rev. Theodore, father of John and Daniel, I, 137

History of the Ancient and Honourable Artillery Company, I, 64

Hitchcock, Rev. Dr., Providence minister, I, 98

Holden, John, *see* John Halden

Hollow-ware of pewter, methods of manufacture, I, 15, 17

Holme, Thomas, William Penn's surveyor-general, II, 37

Holmes, Mr., II, 17

Holmes, Robert and Sons, britannia makers of Baltimore, II, 104

Holt, Thomas R., britannia-maker of Meriden, Conn., II, 104

Holyoke, Edward, ancestor of the Holyokes, I, 60

Holyoke, Edward, 8th President of Harvard College, I, 60

Holyoke, Elizur, Boston brazier, father of the pewterer John, I, 60

Holyoke, Joanna Walker, married to John Holyoke, I, 60

Holyoke, John, Boston pewterer, his career, I, 60, 62; II, 153

Holyoke, Sarah, married John Skinner, I, 73

H. Homan and Company, Cincinnati pewterers, II, 101, 105

Homan, Henry, Cincinnati pewterer, II, 101, 104, 105

Hopper, Henry, New York pewterer, II, 2, 3, 105

Höran, Charlotte Louisa, wife of Johann Christian Höran, II, 49; died in 1798, 58

Höran (spelled also Hero, Herroe, Heavo, Hera), Johann Christian, Philadelphia pewterer, family history, II, 48–50; 89, 120

Höring, Johannes, arrived from Rotterdam in ship *Neptune*, II, 48

Hornor, William Macpherson, Jr., viii

Horsewell, William, New York pewterer, II, 1; his short career and death, 3, 4, 5; 88

Horsford, E. N., made patent lamps, II, 105

Hosmer, Ann, married Charles Hamlin, I, 95

Houghton, Thomas, a partner of John F. Wallace, II, 105

Houghton and Wallace, lamp-makers of Philadelphia, II, 105

House, Edwin, pewterer of Hartford, II, 105

Household utensils of pewter, I, 25 ff.

How, Rebecca, married Joshua Witherle, I, 80

Howe, Mrs. H. H., vii

Hubbell, Capt., II, 19

Hubley, John, II, 45

Hughson, Dr. Walter, vii

Hugo, E. Harold, ix

Humiston, Ephraim A., father of Willis Humiston, II, 105

Humiston, Willis, britannia maker of Wallingford, Conn., and Troy, N.Y., II, 105

Hunt, Anna, wife of Charles Keene, I, 99

Hunt, Capt., of Engine No. 2, I, 69

Hunt, S., britannia maker, II, 105

Hunter, George, a pewterer of Troy, New York, II, 105

Huntington, Mrs. Philip, vii

Hurlbut, Rebecca, wife of Captain Jacob Whitmore, I, 113

Hutchins, Charles F., vii; II, 96, 109

Hyde, Martin, britannia maker of New York, II, 105

Hydrochloric acid, dilute, for removing pewter scale, II, 127

'I. C.,' pewter touch, II, 86, 87

'I. C. H.,' touch of Johann Christopher Heyne, II, 44, 45, 62

[225]

General Index

General Index

Parker, C., a whitesmith of New York, II, 120

Parker, Charles & Co., makers of britannia spoons, II, 109

Parker, J. G., his mark found on a lamp, II, 109

Parkin, W., a maker of teapots, II, 109

Parmenter, W. H., maker of a patent lamp, II, 109

Partridge, Mary Ann Buckley, married to Freeman Porter, II, 110

Paschall, Elizabeth, sister of Thomas, II, 37

Paschall, Joanna Sloper, wife of Thomas, II, 37

Paschall, Mary, daughter of Thomas Paschall, II, 37

Paschall, Thomas, Pennsylvania pewterer, I, 28; II, 35; his death, 37; legacy from Thomas Badcoke, 38

Paschall, Thomas, Jr., II, 37, 38

Paschall, William, English pewterer, father of Thomas, II, 37

Paschall, William, son of Thomas, II, 37, 38

Paschall family, II, 37

Patterson, Mary, married Joseph Leddell, Jr., II, 4

Pattison brothers, their peddling method of sales, I, 104

Pavey, George, Boston pewterer, I, 62

Peal (or Peel), Henry, Philadelphia pewterer, II, 68

Peale, Charles Wilson, II, 52

Pearse, Robert, see Piercy, Robert

Pearson, Hannah, married Simon Wyer, II, 43

Peck, Capt., Revolutionary soldier, I, 96

Peddler's cart, for sale of pewter-ware, I, 18, 104; convenience in reaching large markets, II, 69; supplying the South, 71

Peirse, Robert, see Piercy, Robert

Penn, John, Lieut.-Gov. of Pennsylvania, II, 45

Penn, William, emigrates to Philadelphia, II, 8; receives grant of land on Delaware River, 35; 37; his use of propaganda, 38

Pennington, Capt. Ephraim, Pennsylvania Militia, II, 64

Pennock, Samuel, II, 64

Pennsylvania Gazette, advertisement of Cornelius Bradford, II, 10; advertisement of Simon Edgell, 39; advertisement of Thomas Byles, 41; advertisement of Mungo Campbell, 43

Pennsylvania Historical Society, Jane Logan's account book, II, 41

Pennsylvania Packet, notices of William Ball, Jr., II, 56, 57

Pennsylvania Staatsbote, on Johann Philip Alberti, II, 50–52

Pentz, Sampson, I, 55

Pepys, Samuel, his Diary quoted, I, 47

Perkins, see Bush and Perkins

Perkins, Mrs. Eaton H., viii

Pewter, its use in American homes and as a collectible, xv; its discovery and antiquity undetermined; bequeathed by will, I, 1; metals used in its making, 2, 3; exchange values, 5, 6; quality of American below that of London product, 8; bulk in colonial America imported from abroad, 9; control over manufacture and sale in England, 19; marks and touches of makers, 19 ff. (see also Makers of the Britannia Period, II, 95–118); variety of forms in household use, 25; cleaning and care, II, 126–29; Random Notes on Collecting, 130–35; unsolved problems, 136

Pewter Collector, The, cleaning and care of pewter, II, 126

Pewter Collectors' Club, I, 40; addressed by Dr. Percy E. Raymond, 101; II, 123, 126

Pewter in America, xvi

Pewterers, craft regulated by ordinances in London, I, 1; downfall of their industry through adulteration, 4; migration to New World, 5; handicapped by government restraints, 6; their place in colonial America, 8; from apprentice to master, 10; methods of manufacture, 11 ff.; marks and touches, 19–22 (see also Makers of the Britannia Period, II, 95–118); early 18th century establishments in America, 23, 24; their history in the South, 69–71; list of the dethroned, 119–21

Pewterers' Company, I, 1; power as a trade organization, 2; prosecution of lawbreakers, 3, 4; established standards for the trade, 8, 71; power over manufacture and sale in England, 19; 21; rule on booge, 28; II, 3, 11, 38, 39, 41

Pewterers' Hall, in London, II, 3, 39, 74

'Pewterers' Society,' carried banner in parade celebrating ratification of the Constitution, II, 2, 20

Pewter scale, means of removal, II, 127

Philadelphia Union, death notice of Robert Palethorp, Jr., II, 62

Phillips, John Marshall, vii, ix; I, 56

Pickring, Ann, supposedly the wife of Daniel Jones, I, 62

[232]

Pierce, Anne, wife of Samuel Pierce, I, 124

Pierce, Hannah, mother of Samuel, I, 124

Pierce, Mary, II, 27

Pierce (or Pierse), Robert, *see* Piercy, Robert

Pierce, Samuel, New England pewterer, I, 13, 14; his beaker design, 37; baptismal basin designs, 45; 103; his various occupations, 124; standard of workmanship, 125

Pierce, Stephen, father of Samuel, I, 124

Piercy (Pierse, Peirse, Pierce, Pearse), Robert, New York pewterer, II, 26, 27

Pierson, Hannah, *see* Pearson

Pigott, Francis, London pewterer, II, 133

Pilgrims, at Plymouth, I, 23

Pilgrim's Progress, The, cited, I, 122

Pitcher marked 'Palethorp's,' Plate LXXIII, No. 622

Pitchers, II, 94

Pitton, Mary, married John Comer, Jr., I, 53, 54

Planishing, in pewter-making, I, 14, 15

Plates, of pewter, I, 3; their need in New World, 5; forms made, 25–29; types made in Boston, 48

Platt, Philip G., vii, viii; I, 112, 138; II, 67

Platter, I, 26; ambiguity of meaning, 27

Plumbing, as an addition to pewter-making, I, 7

Plumer, Mary, married Joseph Randle, I, 67

Plumer, Samuel, Boston cooper, I, 67

Plumly, Charles, pewter-maker with William Calder, I, 102; II, 67, 68, 109, 113

Plumly & Bidgood, Philadelphia pewterers, II, 67

Pocumtuck Valley Memorial Association, its collection of church cups, I, 43

Pomroy, William C., a partner in J. H. Stalkamp & Co., II, 114

Poole, John W., 3d, vii; estimate of span of life of pewter in daily use, I, 5; 7; on the acquisition of tankards, 40; discovery of an early Boston plate, 64; 89; his Henry Will rarities, II, 16, 47; 88, 90; on 'The Care of Pewter,' in *Antiques*, 126

Porringers, I, 3; greater proportion are of American manufacture, 9; diversity of handle designs, 29; cast in two parts, 30; types of handles, 31, 32

Porter, Allen, employed Rufus Dunham, II, 100; sketch of his life, 109, 110

Porter, Almira, married Blakslee Barns, II, 65

Porter, A. and F., pewterers of Westbrook, Maine, II, 109

Porter, Edmund, a yeoman of Taunton, II, 120, 121

Porter, Edmund (2), a proprietor of Porter Britannia and Plate Company, II, 121

Porter, F., of Westbrook, Conn., II, 121

Porter, Freeman, associated in pewter business with his brother Allen, II, 109; sketch of his life, 110

Porter, James, Connecticut pewterer, I, 126, 127

Porter, Jephtha, Baltimore tinman, in partnership with Samuel Kilbourn, II, 79

Porter, Lincoln, a yeoman of Taunton, II, 121

Porter, Mary, married Thomas S. Derby, I, 136

Porter, Mary Ann, wife of Freeman Porter, II, 110

Porter, Samuel, a yeoman or farmer of Taunton, II, 121

Porter Britannia and Plate Company, late britannia makers, II, 120

Pots, of pewter, I, 3; their need in New World, 5

Potter, W., maker of a sander, II, 110

Powell, Catharina, married Christian Hera, II, 58

'P. R.,' touch attributed to Paul Revere, II, 90

Pratt, Mrs. Chester M., vii

Priestly's College, in Baltimore, II, 77, 78

Providence Association of Mechanics and Manufacturers, I, 98

Providence Gazette, I, 96; obituary on Gershom Jones, 98; announcement of Josiah Keene, 99

Public Records Office, London, values of exports of pewter to the colonies, I, 7

Putnam, James H., in business with Timothy Bailey, II, 96; sketch of his life, 110

Putnam, John, I, 50

Queen Anne teapot of pewter, belly of two castings, I, 15; type made in colonial America, 39; 40

Quigley, the Hon. and Mrs. Richard S., vii; their Danforth plate, I, 116; their John Will creamer, II, 14

Raisin, Eliza Dyer, mother of George Raisin, I, 61

Raisin, George, Boston gunsmith, father of the pewterer George, I, 61

Raisin, George, Boston pewterer, I, 61

Rand, Margaret, married the pewterer Nathaniel Austin, I, 75

Randle, Elizabeth, wife of Robert, I, 67

Randle (or Randall), Joseph, Boston pewterer and brazier, I, 67

Randle, Mary, wife of Joseph Randle, I, 67

Rublee, Herbert M., viii; church cup, I, 44

Ruckman, John F., viii

Rugg, Harold G., discovers an autobiography of Richard Lee, I, 121

Russell, Henry, I, 96

Russell, Joseph and William, I, 99

Russell, Ruth S., married Thomas S. Derby, I, 136

Russell, Mr., of the firm of Ames and Russell, II, 109

Russell and Beach, employed Luther Boardman, II, 97; britannia makers at Chester, Conn., 111

Rust, John N. and Samuel, lamp-makers in New York, II, 111

Rust, Leonard M., lamp-maker in New York, II, 111

Rust, Samuel, lamp-maker in New York, II, 111

Sadware man, hammerman in pewter-making, I, 14

Sage, Col. Comfort, soldier in the Revolution, I, 113

Sage, Martha, married to Jonathan Southmayd, I, 126

Sage, Timothy, a britannia manufacturer in St. Louis, II, 111

Sage, T. & Co., made britannia in St. Louis, II, 111

Sage and Beebe, britannia makers, location unknown, II, 111

St. John's Lodge No. 2, F. & A. M., I, 133

Salmon, M., French pewterer, his *L'Art du Potier d'Etain*, I, 10

Salter, Mary, married the pewterer Jonathan Jackson, I, 58, 59

Salter, William, keeper of the Boston Powderhouse, I, 63

Salts, of pewter, I, 3

Sampson, Mrs. Mary, her Henry Will hot-water plate, II, 15

Sanborn, W. J., viii; II, 89

Santvoort, Sytie, married William Bradford, Jr., II, 8

Sargent, Emma B., married to Rufus Dunham, II, 101

Saucer, I, 26, 27

Sauer, Anna Catherine, widow of William, married Francis Hendricks, II, 76

Savage, William, a maker of teapots, II, 103, 111

Savage, William H., bought the business of Josiah Danforth, I, 118; II, 103, 111

Savage and Graham, Middletown pewterers, II, 103, 111

Say, Thomas, Bible entry of Thomas Paschall, II, 37

Schiefeun, Maria Margr., married Johann Christopher Heyne, II, 44; 45

Schuyler, Brandt, and wife Margaret, sell real estate to Francis Bassett, pewterer, II, 5, 6

Sclater, John, will disposing of Virginia pewter plates, II, 70

Scovil, Huldah, married William Danforth, I, 118

'S. E.,' I, 70

Seip, Jacob, Philadelphia pewterer, II, 68

Sellers & Co., in error for Sellew and Company, II, 121

Sellew, Enos, a partner in Sellew and Company, II, 112

Sellew, Osman, a partner in Sellew and Company, II, 112

Sellew, William, joined Enos and Osman Sellew, II, 112

Sellew & Co., Cincinnati pewterers, II, 112

Seltzer, Abraham, Philadelphia pewterer, II, 68

'Semper Eadem,' Boston pewterer, identity unknown, I, 66, 68–71; II, 86, 89, 134, 136

Seymour, Melinda, married Samuel Danforth, I, 119

'S. G. Boston,' a pewter touch, I, 79; II, 86, 87

Shakers, of pewter, I, 3

Shaw, Mr., a partner in Sickel and Shaw, II, 112

Sheldon, Mrs. George, viii

Sheldon, R. T., viii

Sheldon, Smith, a partner in Sheldon and Feltman, II, 112

Sheldon and Feltman, britannia makers of Albany, II, 112, 113

Sherman, Capt. Andrew, I, 116

Sherwood, George, his *American Colonists*, II, 71

Shinn, Miss Beatrice, viii

Shinn, Bertlis, II, 52

Shoff, I., or John, Pennsylvania pewterer, II, 64

Short Narrative of the Life of Mr. Richard Lee, A, autobiography of the pewterer, I, 121

Shrimpton, Ellinor, wife of Henry, I, 50

Shrimpton, Henry, Boston pewterer, I, 27, 28; his beaker, 36; 46; his death, 47; sketch of his life, 50, 51; 53, 57

Shrimpton, Jonathan, nephew of the preceding, I, 51

Shrimpton, Mary, wife of Henry Shrimpton, I, 50

General Index

General Index

Sykes, Mr., a pocket-bottle marked 'Sykes,' II, 114

Symonds, R. W., viii; compilation of English exports of pewter to the colonies, in *Antiques*, I, 7

Taberer, Elizabeth, second wife of the pewterer Joseph Copeland, II, 72

Taberer, Major Thomas, II, 72

'Tadge,' in pewter-making, I, 13, 15

Tankards, of pewter, I, 3; principally American, 8; one of the principal forms of hollow-ware in England, 32; American forms in common use, and the Stuart, 33; handle designs, 33–36; cover designs, 34–36; New York tankards, II, 3

Taunton Britannia Manufacturing Co., II, 94, 99, 106, 114

'T. B.,' touch ascribed to Thomas Brigden, II, 31; to Thomas Byles, 42

'T. B. & Co.,' a Boardman touch, I, 128, 129

'T. C.' (or 'I. C.'), identity a problem, II, 55

'T. D.,' as a Danforth mark, I, 110

T. D.-in-rectangle touch, I, 112

'T. D.' lion marks, ascribed to Thomas Danforth, 2d, I, 108

'T. D. B.,' a Boardman touch, I, 129

'T. D. & S. B.,' a Boardman touch, I, 129

Teapots, methods of manufacture of, I, 15, 16; early American, 39, 40, 41; II, 93

Tellman, Elizabeth, married to Thomas Danforth, 3d, I, 111

Thomas, John, a britannia maker of Philadelphia, II, 114

Thomas and Townsend Compton, London pewterers, II, 132

Thompson, John, Philadelphia cooper, II, 52

Thoms, F. L., viii

Thornton, John, London pewterer, II, 57

Thurman, John, Jr., New York merchant, II, 17

Thwing, L. L., viii

'T. I.,' as a Danforth mark, I, 110

Tilley, Miss Edith M., viii

Tilley, Grace, married Jonas Clark, pewterer, I, 61

Tilley, Thomas, appraised inventory of David Melville's Shop, II, 160

Timmins, John, mentioned in letter of Thomas Danforth, 2d, Plate LII

Tin, as a principal constituent of pewter, I, 2

'Tinker's dam,' use on pewter teapot, I, 17

Tin-smithing, as an addition to pewter-making, I, 7

'T. L.,' pewter touch, unidentified, II, 90

'T. M.,' touch of Thomas Melville, I, 95

Tobacco-growing, as an addition to pewter-making, I, 7

'Tom,' a slave bequeathed to Frederick Bassett, II, 5

Tomlinson, Mr., made patent lamps, II, 114

Touches, stamp of pewterer, I, 13; regulations for their use, and variety of designs, 19–22; Boston productions of a die-cutter, 49; perfect impressions rare, II, 88. (*See also* Makers of the Britannia Period, II, 95–118)

Townsend, John, London pewterer, his lamb-and-dove mark, II, 55, 133

Townsend, John and Margaret, II, 13

Townsend & Compton, London pewterers, II, 91, 132

Townsend & Giffin, London pewterers, II, 132; touch used by, Plate LXX, No. 399

Townsend & Reynolds, London pewterers, II, 132

Transon, Catherine, married to Christopher Reich, II, 84

Trask, Israel, New England pewterer, his flagon design, I, 43; baptismal bowl designs, 45; II, 94, 113–115, 118

Trask, John, a composition worker in Boston, II, 121

Trask, Oliver, New England pewterer, his baptismal bowl designs, I, 45; II, 94, 115

Treadway, Amos, Connecticut pewterer, problem of his identity, I, 114

Treadway, Amos, Jr., I, 114

Treadway, Elizabeth, wife of Amos Treadway, I, 114

Treadway, Eunice Foote, mother of Amos, I, 114

Treadway, James, grandson of Nathaniel, I, 114

Treadway, James, maltster, I, 114

Treadway, Josiah, father of Amos, I, 114

Treadway, Nathaniel, settler, I, 114

Treat, Abigail, mother of the pewterer Richard Estabrook, I, 62

Trencher, I, 26; its misuse in application, 27

Trevett, Mrs. Esther, second wife of Thomas Green, I, 68

'Trifle,' as a grade of pewter, I, 3

'Triflers,' in pewter-making, I, 3, 17

Trinity Church Burying Ground, II, 17

Trinity Church, Lancaster, Pa., flagons of, Plate XXXIII

Troland, Mrs. Thomas E., viii; I, 113

'T. S.,' pewter touch, unidentified, II, 90

Turner, E. W., viii

[238]

General Index

108; II, 12, 14, 15, 16, 35, 36, 50, 51; his marriage to Barbara Culp as his first wife, Anna Clampher the second, 52; his political activities, 53; his death, 53; 54, 55, 60, 62, 93, 124, 133, 156, 159

Will family, I, 48, 108; II, 12, 13, 51, 93

Willard, Dr. Samuel, President of Harvard College, I, 91

Willett, Ann, daughter of Edward Willett, II, 74

Willett, Edward, his difficulties as an American pewterer, I, 6; ancestry and early life unknown, his will, II, 70, 73, 74

Willett, Edward, Jr., II, 74, 75

Willett, Edward, 3d, inherited his father's tools and moulds, II, 75

Willett, James, son of Edward, II, 74

Willett, Mary, widow of William, II, 75

Willett, Ninian, son of Edward, II, 74

Willett, Tabitha, wife of Edward, II, 74

Willett, Thomas, son of Edward, II, 74

Willett, William, Maryland pewterer, son of Edward, II, 74; his will, 75

William and Mary, import duties in their reign, I, 6

'William Elsworth: His Rose and Crown,' by Albert H. Good, in *Antiques*, II, 20

Williams, A., Bideford (England) pewterer, II, 121, 133

Williams, Capt., of Militia, II, 19

Williams, Hannah Danforth, wife of Richard Williams, I, 119, 138

Williams, Lorenzo, I, 131, 132; II, 112, 117

Williams, Luther B., viii; I, 111

Williams, Capt. Othniel, father of Richard, I, 119

Williams, Otis, Buffalo pewterer, I, 103; son of Richard, and Hannah Danforth, 119; sketch of his career, 138, 139

Williams, Miss Paige, viii; II, 76

Williams, Richard, partner of Thomas Danforth, 3d, I, 111, 119; married Thomas's daughter Hannah, 119; his death, 120; 138

Williams, Mr., dyer in Baltimore, II, 78

Williams & Simpson, pewterers, I, 131, 132; II, 112

Willing, Thomas and Ann, II, 51

Willis, Thomas, a pewterer in Philadelphia, II, 117

Wilson, Miss Carrie P., viii

Winchester, Miss Alice, viii

Winthrop, Gov. John, his *Journal* quoted, I, 51, 83

Wiswall, John, I, 58

Witherle (or Weatherly), Joshua, pewterer, coppersmith and founder, I, 78; becomes wire manufacturer, 80

Witherle, Rebecca, wife of Joshua Witherle, I, 80

'W. K.,' touch of William Kirby, II, 18

Wolcott, *see* Olcott

Wolfe, John, Philadelphia pewterer, II, 68

Wood, Hannah, married Joseph Belcher, Jr., I, 91

Woodbury, J. B., partner of Oren Colton, II, 99; brief history, 118

Woodbury and Colton, pewterers in Philadelphia, II, 118

Woodman, Cook & Co., pewterers in Portland, Maine, II, 118

Woods, William, II, 78

Worner, William F., viii

Worshipful Company of Pewterers of London, its regulations for marking pewter, I, 19; II, 72

'W. R.' (William, Rex), mistaken for a maker's touch, II, 134

Wright, Mr. and Mrs. John S., viii

Wyer, Dorothy, relict of Simon Wyer, II, 43

Wyer, Hannah, wife of Simon Wyer, II, 43

Wyer, Simon, Philadelphia pewterer, and his wife Hannah Pearson, in transfer of property, II, 43

Yale, Burrage, employed Timothy Bailey, II, 96; employed Luther Boardman, 97, 118

Yale, Charles, as an apprentice of Thomas Danforth, 3d, I, 111, 131; his 'Wallingford' mark, 132; II, 112, 118

Yale, Charles, of New York, II, 152

Yale, Henry, a partner in Yale and Curtis, II, 118

Yale, Hiram, pewterer, his beaker design, I, 37; as an apprentice of Thomas Danforth, 3d, 111, 131; 132; imported English workmen, II, 92; 106, 117

Yale, Rosetta, wife of Hiram Yale, I, 131

Yale, Samuel, pewter button-maker, I, 130; II, 121

Yale, Samuel, Jr., pewterer, served as sheriff's deputy for New Haven County, I, 130–33

Yale, Sarah, wife of Selden Yale, I, 131

Yale, Sarah Boardman, wife of Burrage Yale, II, 118

Yale, Selden, pewterer, I, 131, 132

Yale, William, of New York, prominent in public affairs, I, 130–33; a lamp-maker, II, 118

Yale, William and Samuel, partnership for selling pewter products by peddler's cart, I, 18; buy

General Index

PEWTER IN AMERICA

Its Makers and Their Marks

VOLUME THREE

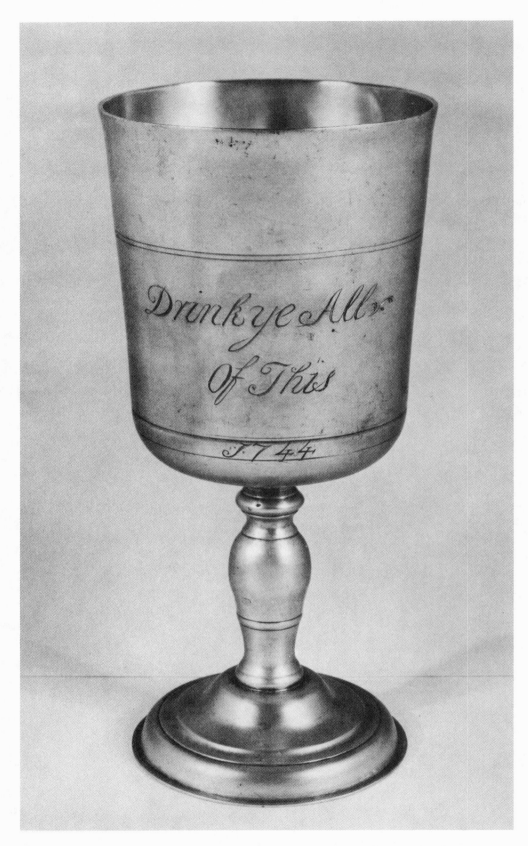

Chalice of Christ Church Parish, West Haven, Connecticut. Height 10¼ inches overall; top diam. 4¾ inches; bottom diam. 4¼ inches. Touch 856. Joseph Leddell, New York, 1711–1753. Engraved "Drink ye All Of This, 1744." Largest and one of the finest of surviving marked American chalices. Courtesy New Haven Colony Historical Society.

PREFACE

WHEN the decision was reached to update *Pewter in America*, a book which had been published thirty years ago, questions arose as to how best to present the new material in the interests, not only of those who owned copies of the original edition, but also of those who had been trying, some of them for ten or fifteen years, to obtain a set of the long-out-of-print books.

The ideal arrangement would have been for me to have told the story of American pewter from start to finish as though it had never been told before, using the original volumes as an outline into which would be woven in logical order all the new makers, touches, and forms, based on information accumulated from many sources by many collectors, dealers, and other students of early American craftsmanship.

The great disadvantages of a comprehensive orderly history were that such a plan would involve the complete overhauling and rewriting of the first edition, a labor that would have kept me occupied for a far longer period than I was willing to be so employed. In addition it would delay for a seemingly needless length of time an opportunity for the newer collectors to obtain copies of the earlier work, which are particularly useful because of the many excellent illustrations.

And so a not-altogether-satisfactory compromise was adopted. Volumes One and Two would be reprinted at the earliest possible date with the addition of only a few errata notes in the margins. Volume Three, which would include all the additions to our knowledge of American pewter that have turned up in the past thirty years, would follow Volumes One and Two as soon as the material, including the illustrations, could be assembled and organized. The arrangement of Volume Three would follow the same chapter and division headings as in the earlier volumes. The great disadvantage of this plan is that the material about any particular maker, form, or touch might be found in any one or all of the three volumes. This naturally necessitated the preparation of a separate index for Volume Three. Any inquirer, seeking information about the history, product or marks of a particular pewterer, would have to turn first to two different indexes for his references and, in many cases, would find it necessary to turn back and forth from one volume to another for complete coverage of our knowledge of the matter under consideration. The plan is far from ideal but for many of us, "it is later than we think"; time seemed the prime interest to be considered, and the plan adopted represented the best workable compromise.

And so this third volume of *Pewter in America* has been prepared and published

Preface

with the intention of correcting and supplementing the original volumes, adding all pertinent available material, unreported in 1940, which has accumulated about pewterers, their products, and their marks during the past thirty years.

In presenting the new material it has seemed best, as I said above, to follow the original arrangement of Volumes One and Two, correcting and adding to each chapter in the order in which it appears in the earlier work. Where no correction or addition seems desirable in any particular chapter, that chapter or heading will be omitted in this volume.

1970

CONTENTS

LIST OF PLATES

List of Plates

ACKNOWLEDGMENTS

THE preparation for publication of this third volume of *Pewter in America* loomed at one time as a tremendous undertaking but, following the eminently successful example of Tom Sawyer, the author handed out bucketfuls of whitewash to friends and acquaintances who have painted in for him much of the needed background.

In fact, one of the rewarding contributions made by the publication of the first two volumes in 1940 was the incentive which it apparently gave to collectors to learn more about their prized possessions by doing their own research, frequently uncovering enough new material to warrant the preparation of articles for publication. The successive editors of the *Bulletin* of the Pewter Collectors' Club of America welcomed such articles and a goodly number appeared in the magazine *Antiques*.

So here were two sources, easily available, from which could be culled a wealth of information, unreported prior to 1940. From these lode veins have been extracted much of the ore which has eventually found its way into the construction of Volume Three. My deep thanks go out to those contributors who have become, in some cases unwittingly, my collaborators and partners in the preparation of this book, as well as to Miss Alice Winchester, editor of *Antiques*, and to the succession of editors of the *Bulletin* for permission to reproduce in print information which originated in their publications.

Very special thanks are offered to a number of diligent delvers into the past whose findings have widened appreciably our heretofore limited knowledge of the histories of specific pewterers, of groupings of pewterers or of the makers of certain geographical areas not adequately studied in the past—able investigators whose discoveries, not yet publicized elsewhere, have been generously turned over to me for my use. In this group are John P. Remensnyder and Donald Noble, whose investigations in Germany as well as in this country have made possible a very full history of John Will, New York pewterer, and of his pewter-making sons, Henry, Philip, and William.

Special thanks go also to Eric de Jonge, curator of the William Penn Memorial Museum in Harrisburg, whose knowledge of German must have been invaluable in his study of the records of the Moravian Church in Bethlehem, Pennsylvania, with the resulting clarification and enlargement of the histories of three Pennsylvania Moravian pewterers—Heyne, Hasselberg and Brunstrom.

In like manner, Joseph K. Ott's study of early Rhode Island manuscripts has provided us with further details about the work of pewterers of Newport and Providence,

Acknowledgments

including the discovery of the man who now becomes Providence's earliest pewterer of record, Joseph Randle.

Harold B. Gill, research associate at Williamsburg, Virginia, made an extensive study of Virginia records in a search for early craftsmen. He graciously turned over for inclusion in this volume all references to pewterers that he had found, in that colony, an area which had been scarcely tapped before.

Last of these men to whom I am so indebted for information not published before is Wendell Hilt, who has gone through the records of Connecticut with a fine-tooth comb and uncovered enough new material about Connecticut pewterers and britannia makers to have published a volume on the subject. In fact, he had contemplated seriously that project but self-effacingly and most generously submitted all this material to me with each item meticulously catalogued as to its source. No thanks are adequate for his invaluable assistance.

Our story of the britannia period is very much fuller and more accurate today than thirty years ago, thanks primarily to George S. Gibb's *The Whitesmiths of Taunton* (the history of Reed & Barton) and Nancy A. Goyne's researches and writings, in particular her monograph *Britannia in America*, which appeared in the *Winterthur Portfolio II* (1965), a definitive exposition of the subject.

To the late Carl Jacobs and his wife, now Mrs. Celia Stevenson, I am indebted not only for the information gleaned from *A Guide to American Pewter*, but also for their generosity in turning over to me photographs of pewter, in furnishing leads as to the location of rare pieces, and a kind offer to help in any way possible in the preparation of this volume.

Although it is not possible to thank everyone who has assisted me in making possible the presentation of this volume, I do wish to offer sincere thanks and appreciation to those listed below.

Dr. Adelbert C. Abbott; The Albany (New York) Institute of History and Art, J. D. Hatch Jr., Director, Norman A. Rice, Curator, and Kenneth H. MacFarland, Librarian; Mrs. Neal Almgren; Norton Asner; Paul M. Auman; John L. Barry Jr.; Herr Becker, Bürgermeister of Herborn, West Germany; Alexander J. Bennett; the Beverly (Massachusetts) Historical Society, Miss Ruth Hill, Historian-Librarian; Clifton Blake; Willard O. Brewer; Mr. and Mrs. Paul Brunner; Birger W. Bruzelli; John W. Charlton; the late Arthur W. Clement; the late H. Douglas Curry; Marshall B. Davidson; the late Walton Deckelman; Mrs. John R. Dyer; F. Farny Eilers Jr.; Dean A. Fales Jr.; the late Hugh S. Ferguson; the late Mrs. Paul J. Franklin; Dr. Reginald F. French; Rockwell Gardiner; Wendell D. Garrett, Managing Editor of *Antiques* magazine; Titus C. Geesey; Mrs. Daniel H. Giffen; Robert G. Goelet; Stanley Goldsmith; John M. Graham IV, Director of Collections, Williamsburg, Virginia; Roger H. Hallowell, President of Reed & Barton; N. Vance Harper; George L. Heigis, Secretary, Lancaster (Pennsylvania) Historical Society; George T. Heussner; John Hill; C. P. Hinshaw; the late Rudolf P. Hommel; Frank L. Horton, Director of Restoration, Old Salem, Inc., North Carolina; Miss Myrtle M. Jillson; Joseph Kindig Jr.;

Acknowledgments

Sam Laidacker; Mrs. Bertram K. Little; Charles W. Lyon; Mrs. Fred McClaskey; Ronald F. Michaelis, Hon. Librarian, The Pewter Society, Great Britain; Edward E. Minor; Dr. William A. Monkhouse; Moravian College, Bethlehem, Pennsylvania, Vernon Nelson, Curator of Archives; Richard Mundey; Rudolph F. Papa; Marius B. Péladeau; Dr. Warren M. Poland; John W. Poole; the late Dr. Percy Raymond; the late Mrs. Edwin M. Rothschild; the late John F. Ruckman; Dr. Jerome Seliger; Donald A. Shelley, Curator, Henry Ford Museum, Dearborn, Michigan; Sleepy Hollow Restorations, Joseph T. Butler, Curator; Miss Helen B. Smith, Miss Julia D. S. Snow; the late William G. Snow, Director of Historical Research, International Silver Company; John Carl Thomas; Mrs. Ralph L. Thresher; Robert S. Trim; Peter N. Vanden Berge, Librarian, New Brunswick Theological Seminary; Lura Woodside Watkins; Jack H. Weil; Wenham (Massachusetts) Historical Association and Museum, Inc., Mrs. Irene Dodge, Executive Secretary; Mrs. Laura N. Bell; and Robert N. Whittemore, Captain, U.S.N. Retired.

However informative any new material in this volume might be about our makers of pewter and britannia, it would have but a very limited appeal to collectors if not accompanied by illustrations of representative and unusual examples of the handiwork of our makers. To the individuals and institutions listed below I am deeply indebted for permission to show treasures from their collections. Many of the same group were my benefactors in various other ways in this undertaking and will, I hope, realize how important their help has been to me.

George Abraham; Mrs. Peter H. Alderwick; The Antiquarian and Landmarks Society of Connecticut, Arthur W. Leibundguth, Director; Mr. and Mrs. Charles W. Baughn; Mrs. Charles Beaven; Mr. and Mrs. William O. Blaney; The Brooklyn Museum, J. Stewart Johnson, Curator of Decorative Arts; the late Dr. Madelaine R. Brown; Henry V. Button; Currier Gallery of Art, Manchester, New Hampshire, Melvin H. Watts, Curator; Charles K. Davis; Eric de Jonge; Mr. and Mrs. Oliver W. Deming; Henry Francis du Pont Winterthur Museum, Winterthur, Delaware, Charles F. Montgomery, Senior Research Associate, John J. Evans Jr., Research Associate; John J. D. Feyko; the late Mrs. Stephen S. Fitzgerald; Lloyd W. Fowles; Joseph France; Mrs. Paul Glazier; William M. Goss Jr.; Mrs. Melvin H. Gulbrandsen; Mr. and Mrs. Ralph P. Hanes; Raymond Hellenek; Mr. and Mrs. Wendell Hilt; Harry Hirsch; Historical Foundation of the Presbyterian and Reformed Churches, Montreat, North Carolina, T. H. Spencer Jr., Historical Director; the late Carl Jacobs; Dr. and Mrs. S. Harris Johnson III; William F. Kayhoe; Mrs. Amos Clark Kingsbury; Dr. Joseph H. Kler; the late Mark LaFountain; Louis Lyons; Dr. and Mrs. Robert Mallory III; Mrs. George A. Marks; John H. McMurray; Metropolitan Museum of Art, New York, American Wing, Miss Mary Glaze and Berry B. Tracy, Assistant Curators; Museum of Early Southern Decorative Arts, Winston-Salem, North Carolina, Frank L. Horton, Director of Restoration, Old Salem, Inc.; New Haven Colony Historical Society; Donald Noble; Joseph K. Ott; Stanley P. Paddock; Pilgrim John Howland Society, Mrs. W. Russell Greenwood, Secretary-Treasurer; Plimoth Plan-

Acknowledgments

tation, Plymouth, Massachusetts, Dr. James Deetz, Assistant Director; Mrs. Ralph B. Post; Dr. Lola S. Reed; William Reed; John P. Remensnyder; Dr. and Mrs. William B. Rice; Mr. and Mrs. Richard A. Rockwell 2nd; Salem Lutheran Church, Aaronsburg, Pennsylvania; John A. Schneider; Mrs. Lawrence R. Schumann; Dr. William P. Shelton; Mr. and Mrs. Edgar Sittig; Amory S. Skerry; Smithsonian Institution, Washington, D.C., C. Malcolm Watkins, Curator, Division of Cultural History, Richard E. Ahlborn, Assistant Curator; Charles V. Swain; General Assembly of the United Presbyterian Church, Philadelphia, Pennsylvania, William B. Miller, Manager of the Department of History; Mr. and Mrs. Richard F. Upton; William S. Wilcox; William Penn Memorial Museum, Harrisburg, Pennsylvania, Eric de Jonge, Curator; Mr. and Mrs. Thomas D. Williams; Lothrop Withington Jr.; Mrs. Peter Woodbury; Yale University Art Gallery, Garvan and Associated Collections, Graham Hood, Associate Director; Mr. and Mrs. Paul M. Young.

Of this group Charles V. Swain and Thomas D. Williams have, over the years, notified me many times of their own recent acquisitions or of those of other collectors about which they had learned and have supplied me with many photographs that have done much to make possible the very comprehensive pictorial display presented in this volume.

Once again, as thirty years ago, I cannot give too great praise to Harold Hugo and his talented associates of The Meriden Gravure Company, particularly to John F. Peckham, for the high quality of the reproduction of the photographs from which they had to work; and this time Meriden also did all of the printing as well as the illustrations.

To Alden Johnson and the staff of Barre Publishers I offer my deep and sincere thanks for their cooperation in preparing the manuscript for publication and for overseeing the many details of publishing and promoting this book.

But the one man to whom I feel most deeply indebted is my long-time friend, Charles F. Montgomery, Senior Research Associate and former Curator of the Winterthur Museum, scholar, teacher, and author, preeminent in his knowledge of American craftsmanship, who has helped me with information and advice over the years. As Warren Stone peddled pewter for the Yale brothers across the countryside years ago, Charles in the days of the depression did his best to dispose of *Pewter in America*, then a drug on the market.

Last of all I would like my loving and devoted helpmate of a happy married life to see in print my thanks and recognition for all her help and encouragement in the writing, proofreading, and advice in the preparation of all three volumes. I regret now that I did not dedicate the earlier volumes as I had seriously considered doing: "To my loving wife, Roberta Howe Laughlin, but for whose encouragement and prodding these volumes would never have been written; but for whose charms they might have been finished long ago."

PROBLEMS OF THE COLONIAL PEWTERER

FIRST of all a correction must be made under this heading in line 6, page 6, Volume One. I inadvertently wrote that Wales was the source of English tin, when in fact the mines are in Cornwall, as I had stated correctly on page 4. This may be as satisfactory a point as any at which to comment upon a few terms that occur occasionally in articles and books on pewter, in old newspaper advertisements, directories, etc.—terms that are not clear to many collectors. Reference is made particularly to the words *block tin, white metal,* and *whitesmiths.*

Just as iron is cast into what are termed pigs, oblong masses of a size and shape that are convenient for handling, so refined tin in its solid state, after smelting, was converted into what were termed blocks or bars, rather than pigs, in a shape and size easily manageable for remelting. These blocks were known as blocktin.

Very little tin was imported into the Colonies as long as they remained under British rule. Our pewterers were compelled to rely for their raw materials upon being able to gather up old and damaged pewter plates and vessels which they remelted, as explained on pages 5 and 6 in Volume One. After the Revolution, however, tin bars were imported more freely and the term blocktin came into much more frequent use in inventories, advertisements, etc. Hitherto it had not been possible to make pewter to any specific formula. Now that was to become possible with the importation of tin. The use of refined tin raised a lot of new problems for our pewterers, most of whom, without any training in England or on the Continent, had had no experience in working to a fixed formula. It was a mystery to them as to how much copper or antimony should be added to the bath of molten tin. Among the papers of Thomas D. Boardman in the Connecticut State Library is one which tells in some detail of his own difficulties in meeting this problem. It will be found verbatim on page 84 in this volume in the section on Boardman.

To return to blocktin—that term had two very different meanings. The first and obvious meaning was that this was the term applied to refined tin in solid blocks.

The second meaning refers to one particular combination of metals in the manufacture of teapots, mugs, beakers, canisters, etc. When the makers, George Coldwell for instance, advertised blocktin teapots and other blocktin vessels, they did not intend to imply that those products were made from unalloyed tin. That would not have been feasible because tin is too soft and lacks the strength and machineability of pewter.

In the second half of the eighteenth century a new and revolutionary method was adopted for the manufacture of hollow-ware that would be thinner, brighter, and stronger than the cast pewter bodies. This was termed blocktin.

The central idea in the manufacture of this new material was to take a sheet of malleable iron and coat it with tin, the forerunner of the tin plate of today. Several different processes were used to obtain this tinned sheet which, when finished, could be formed into the bodies of teapots, beakers, and other vessels.

The quotation which follows was taken from *The Complete Book of Trades*, published in London in 1837:

> Block tin consists of two plates of tin and one of malleable iron, all rolled to a desireable thinness, and brought together with the iron in the middle, by any method which should exclude oxydation by the action of atmospheric air. This was effected in the old way, by first covering the cleaned iron plates with tallow, and immersing these in melted tin, when the tallow would consume as the iron took up the coating of the liquid tin. . . . An improved and more scientific method, however has superseded the old process, whereby a saving of time, tallow and the fusion of the tin, is effected. Thus, the iron plates having been rolled to the required substance, are immersed together in a trough of water impregnated with sulphuric acid; and being there scrubbed with a hard brush to get rid of any loose particles on the surface, they are brought together, two tin to each iron plate, piled and pressed—always under the water. Adhesion and oxydation immediately take place, with absorption of the tin, by the iron at an uncertain period. Of this, however, we may be assured . . . the affinity is strong and inseparable; inasmuch as the plates have no sooner undergone the final operation of one more rolling, than the edge of any cut made by the Tinman's shears, presents no appearance whatever of the iron plate, which we know resides in the centre, and gives, strength, substance and durability to the goods that are made from these plates.

It is my opinion, although no positive proof to substantiate this belief can be given, that many pewterers in this country, when advertising blocktin teapots, etc. did not mean vessels with an iron core clad with tin, but rather finished pewter made from tin bars with small additions of copper, antimony, bismuth, etc. which could be made to an exact formula, in contrast to the ordinary cast pewter which was made from scrap metal and could not be made to any precise analysis. It is of interest in this connection that blocktin articles were usually sold at a slight premium above the price for similar articles described merely as pewter.

In all probability those very same teapots with which Thomas D. Boardman had so much difficulty, when learning how to use the pure tin bars, were sold by him as blocktin teapots. Also it seems probable that the blocktin teapots which George Coldwell advertised were made without any iron core. In other words "blocktin" may have had three different meanings: (1) the blocks of unalloyed tin; (2) vessels made from iron coated with tin; and (3) vessels made from new tin bars to which other elements were added in small quantities, as contrasted with pewter articles made from remelted scrap pewter. So much for an explanation of what blocktin was; now for comment upon white metal and whitesmith.

White metal, in its original meaning was, purely and simply tin. As a consequence a tinsmith or tinplate worker was termed a whitesmith. Later that term was used loosely to refer to a man who burnished or polished metals, rather than one who smelted or cast them. In its earlier restricted meaning the term whitesmith was certainly not synonymous with pewterer or britannia manufacturer.

PLATE LXXIX

Two views of double spoon mould, patented by Luther and Norman S. Boardman,
East Haddam, Connecticut 1870. Collection of William F. Kayhoe.

686. Inner face of top half of a patented double spoon mould. The cheeks may be unscrewed and replaced by others with different designs of handle decoration.

687. Top and bottom halves of same mould with rough casting of a pair of spoons from this mould. The spoons measure $5\frac{3}{4}$ inches.

688. Top and bottom of spoon mould bearing an impression on handle of head of King William III. A newly cast spoon from this mould is illustrated on Plate XC. The spoon measures $7\frac{3}{8}$ inches. Collection of Lothrop Withington. The same collector owns an almost identical mould but with a different head, purporting to be that of Queen Mary. Probably Massachusetts, c. 1690–1705.

689 and 690. Covered water pitcher and sugar bowl made by Parks Boyd, Philadelphia, 1795–1819. Illustrated in Volume One as Plate XXIX, Fig. 198, and Plate XLII, Fig. 274. Shown again here to illustrate one way in which an unmarked item—in this case the sugar bowl—may be identified as to maker. The lids are interchangeable. Courtesy of The Brooklyn Museum.

PLATE LXXIX

686

687

688

689

690

THE BUSINESS OF A PEWTERER

IN THE chapter under this title in Volume One errors were made in correlating the text with the accompanying illustrations of the plates. The following corrections should be made:

Page 13, line 15 (Plate II, 3, Fig. 4) *should read* (Plate I, 3, Fig. 4).
Page 13, line 17 (Plate II, 4, Fig. 6) *should read* (Plate II, 4, Fig. 5).
Page 14, line 4 (See Plate I, 3) *should read* (See Plate I, 3, Fig. 8).

The original chapter on the pewterer's business covered the shop operations as well as the author was able to present that story. There is nothing new to add. However it is a privilege to illustrate here on Plate LXXIX closer views of two unusual spoon moulds, one that dates from the closing years of the seventeenth or early years of the eighteenth century; the other dating from 1870 and representing surely the final refinement in britannia spoon casting.

THE MARKS ON PEWTER

IN RECENT years there has been a growing realization of the importance of pewterers' secondary touches, in identifying the makers of pieces which lack the shop's normal touches. For example, Charles V. Swain owns a small creamer, which is marked only by five small connected dots, just as they appear above a quality X on the inside of a Colonel Will flagon, see Plate LXVI, Fig. 538, Volume Two. This is a very small identification, but sufficiently definite and distinct to enable determination that Will was the maker of the Swain creamer.

Another piece, whose maker has been rescued from anonymity, is the teapot illustrated as Fig. 768 of Plate XCIII. Its principal touch is too badly detrited for identification, but it still bears a worn crowned quality mark, which is distinctive and different in design from most normal quality touches. It can be identified easily as a mark found frequently on the pewter of the Pennsylvania pewterer or pewterers who used the "Lovebird" touch (see Plate CIX, Fig. 869) and by John A. Brunstrom, Philadelphia pewterer.

There must be many other rarities in American pewter, still unidentified as to maker, which bear telltale indications of their origin, an origin which might be determined, if only the secondary marks were studied carefully.

There are, besides, many examples which bear no marks of a pewterer, primary or secondary, which can be identified as to maker, simply by careful comparison with other vessels that bear identifiable touches of known pewterers.

Charles V. Swain and the late John F. Ruckman, in studies published in bulletins of the Pewter Collectors Club of America, demonstrated pictorially how identification may be made of the makers of some of these unmarked examples. One of the most impressive of these demonstrations was made by comparing an unmarked lidded sugar bowl with a covered water pitcher which was impressed with a touch of Parkes Boyd, Philadelphia pewterer, both pieces in the collection of the Brooklyn Museum. The comparison of the lids of the two vessels can be seen again in Plate LXXIX, Figs. 689, 690 through the courtesy of the Museum. Here is demonstrated clearly the identity of the maker of the unmarked sugar bowl. Interestingly enough, an almost identical sugar bowl, also unmarked, was illustrated as Fig. 199 of Plate XXIX in Volume One and the very same lidded pitcher was shown as Fig. 274 of Plate XLII. No one, myself included, had the perspicacity to note then or during the next thirty years, how similar the lids of the two vessels were.

If any collector were to note carefully the likenesses of different forms, whose makers are unidentified, and would have the patience to compare them with marked examples, he might be able to satisfy himself that the same mould or moulds had been used in making his unidentified piece and some other vessel whose maker had been positively identified. It should be noted, for instance, that some of the presently unidentified salts with beaded rim, give every appearance of having come from the same moulds as were used for the upper portion of the lids of William Will's coffee pots. Similarly it may be possible to identify the makers of certain unmarked chalices or candlesticks because their bases appear to have been cast from the same moulds as those which were used for tankard covers. These are but a few of the possibilities which could provide a fascinating experiment in detective work.

HOUSEHOLD PEWTER

PLATES, DISHES, AND BASINS

WHEN the first two volumes of *Pewter in America* were published, all surviving American plates and dishes of record were made in one of two standard designs, either (1) with a brim of normal width ending in a single bead on the face of the brim, or (2) with a smooth brim having a rather wide bead on the under surface of the brim. They varied in diameter from a tiny saucer up to a dish sixteen and one-half inches wide. Only a handful bore the touches of pewterers whose careers could have begun as early as the first decade of the eighteenth century.

However it seemed probable that some few plates or dishes made in the Colonies in the seventeenth century might have survived. Consequently, in order that collectors might be forewarned as to the probable appearance of any such rarities, three examples, typical of English design in the last half of the seventeenth century, were illustrated as Figs. 22, 23, and 24 in Plate VIII.

As a result of what seems a near miracle, not just one or two, but at least twelve to fourteen, separate discoveries of early plates and dishes, that have come to light in the past twenty-five years, have widened significantly our knowledge of the range in form and size made by our early craftsmen, and have extended back into the seventeenth century the date of manufacture of our earliest examples of identifiable American flatware, or as it was termed in England, sadware.

These discoveries added four new forms to our known list of American sadware shapes, namely:

1) The dish or plate with multiple reeding on the outer edge of the brim, Plate LXXXI, Fig. 694;
2) The dish or plate with smooth brim of unusual width, Plate LXXXI, Fig. 693;
3) The rosewater dish with raised boss in well, Plate LXXXII, Fig. 697;
4) The fluted sweetmeat dish, Plate LXXX, Fig. 692.

At least ten of these early dishes (in categories 1 to 3), which in the past may have been seen and passed over by more than one collector of American pewter on the assumption that they were English, have passed into collections in recent years. Not only are the designs of the plates and dishes different from the eighteenth-century American examples that we had known previously, but the size, design, and location of the touches on the brims represented practices that must have been discarded by the eighteenth-century Colonial pewterer before 1725.

It is noteworthy that every one of these ten early examples was marked on the upper face of the brim. Furthermore just one small initial die was used on each dish; in every example the die was struck four times, leaving the impressions in a slightly irregular line; and all three dies, used by three different shops, were similar in size and design to one another. Thus far, such touches have been found on one plate, on a number of dishes with multiple-reeded rims, on several dishes with wide smooth brim, and on one rosewater dish, which latter may possibly have been used as a christening basin.

These initial-touched pieces have been attributed probably correctly, to three early Boston pewterers. Six dishes, the one plate, and the only American rosewater dish are impressed with a small shield-shaped touch enclosing the initials E.D., Plate CIV, Fig. 831. They are presumed to have been made by Edmund Dolbeare, whose working years, 1671–*c.* 1705, were divided between Boston and Salem, Massachusetts. One dish each is attributed to John Baker, Boston, *c.* 1670 to 1690 and Joseph Dolbeare, Boston, *c.* 1690–1704 or his brother John *c.* 1690–1740. The initials I.B. in a shield (Fig. 876 of Plate CX) and I.D. in a heart may be seen in Fig. 832 of Plate CIV. I concur in these attributions even though positive proof may never be forthcoming.

The fourth of these rare early forms, probably comparatively scarce in the period when it was made, was the so-called fluted sweetmeat dish, of which two examples are now known, both illustrated on Plate LXXX. This type of dish was never a stock form; rather it was made on special order and engraved as a gift to commemorate a wedding, wedding anniversary, baptism, or other festive occasion.

A cast disc or circular slab of pewter was placed over wooden blocks and raised with hammers, to shape it into dish form, with arrises running from rim to well and extending evenly around the circle to form a fluted pattern, circling the entire brim. The plates pictured measure $8\frac{1}{2}$ and $8\frac{3}{4}$ inches in diameter and have thirty-four and thirty-six flutings respectively. The rim of each plate and the base of the booge, where the fluting ends, are decorated with a tasteful punched design, and the entire well is engraved with a circlet of flowers and leaves, enclosing the initials of the celebrants, for whom the dish was designed, and the numerals of the year of presentation.

The earlier and larger dish gives evidence of superior workmanship, with more pronounced and even fluting than is evident in the 1732 plate. Unfortunately any touch that it may once have had, has vanished, and there is no positive proof that it is even American, despite its very close resemblance to its slightly smaller counterpart, which bears the worn but clearly identifiable lion touch of Francis Bassett of New York, Plate LIX, Fig. 461.

So similar in design and feeling is the decoration of the 1732 plate to that of the earlier example that one is compelled to assume that the 1728 dish was brought into Bassett's shop with instructions to the pewterer to make one just like it. Certainly the engraver of the later plate could not have dreamed up a design so nearly identical to that on the earlier plate.

It was stated earlier that new discoveries had extended upward the range in size of American dishes by two and one-half inches or more. The Henry F. duPont Winterthur Museum owns a magnificent 19-inch charger, bearing touches of Simon Edgell, early Philadelphia pewterer, Plate CVII, Figs. 528a, 529a, and, as in the cases of the best of Edgell's dishes, this example was hammered all over. Strangely enough the larger of the Edgell touches is flanked by two impressions of a hitherto unknown touch of André Michel, little-known New York pewterer, whose career in this country probably commenced after Edgell's death. The explanation for the presence of the Michel touches on the earlier dish is still to be determined.

Even this tremendous dish is in danger of losing its briefly-held record. In the spring of 1966 an auction was held of the contents of a house owned by a family long established in Fairhaven, Massachusetts, a seaport across the bay from New Bedford. In the sale was a dish measuring twenty inches in diameter, impressed with the touch of Lawrence Langworthy, a pewterer of Ashburton, Devon, England, who emigrated to Newport, Rhode Island, at some point prior to May, 1731. On it were two impressions of the mark illustrated in Cotterell's *Old Pewter* as no. 2839 and reillustrated in Volume One of *Pewter in America* as Fig. 311 of Plate XLVII. The one flaw in any claim that this is the largest of all American dishes, is that it bears a touch which Langworthy used first in England, and we have no certain knowledge he stamped his pewter with the same touch after his arrival on these shores. A strong argument in support of such a claim is that the dish turned up within forty miles of Newport, where Langworthy worked. It is not difficult to believe that it had always been in that area. Were the dish mine, I would be dissuaded with difficulty from believing it to have been made in this country.

Attention is called to a correction that should be made in the description of the pewter illustrated as Fig. 27 of Plate VIII in Volume One. The touch that was reported as appearing on that dish was recorded as 542a. It should have read 422a.

One further minor correction should be made on Plate IX, Fig. 45. The basin there illustrated was marked with touch 441, a head of General Jackson. Prior to 1940 that touch had been found in conjunction with a name touch of Thomas S. Derby. Since then the same touch has been found alongside the eagle mark of Hiram Yale of Wallingford, Connecticut, and Richmond, Virginia. (See Plate CVI, Figs. 442b, 444b.) We have also learned that Derby was at one time a journeyman working for Yale. Inasmuch as this particular basin was found in the same house as five Yale plates in western Maryland, it may be assumed that this particular piece was made by Yale, probably in Richmond, and not by Derby, who apparently acquired at a later date the Jackson dies used by his master.

PLATE LXXX—*Early Fluted Presentation Dishes*

691. 8¾-inch presentation dish, possibly designed as a sweetmeat dish. The plate was hammered out expertly over wooden blocks to form thirty-five flutings. Inscribed "I.Z. C.Z. 1728." No identifiable touch. Maker unknown. It is possibly the work of Joseph Leddell, New York pewterer, who advertised his facility at engraving, or it may have been of English or Dutch origin. Used in or near New York, quite possibly by members of the Zabriskie or Zenger families. It undoubtedly served as the model for the dish illustrated as Fig. 692. Collection of William M. Goss, Jr.

692. 8½-inch presentation dish. Inscribed "$\begin{smallmatrix} & G. & \\ Z & & M \end{smallmatrix}$ 1732." Has thirty-three flutings. Touch 461. Maker Francis Bassett, first, New York. It would seem apparent that the dish, illustrated as Fig. 691 above, was brought in to Bassett with instructions that he copy the original as far as proved feasible. Compare the design and quality of the engraving of each; the beautifully even scalloping of the 1728 dish with the comparatively straight edge of the 1732 specimen; and the more expert hammered-out fluting of the earlier work. Collection of Dr. Joseph H. Kler. Courtesy Smithsonian Institution, United States National Museum.

It is amazing that two such fine and fragile dishes of such rare design and decoration should have survived to this day.

PLATE LXXX

691

692

PLATE LXXXI — *Early Dishes*

Two early dishes which exemplify the two forms of rim design in general use both in England and the colonies during the late seventeenth and early eighteenth centuries.

693. $15\frac{3}{8}$-inch dish with smooth, wide brim and narrow bead on underside of brim, hammered all over. One of the finest of surviving American dishes. Touch 831. Edmund Dolbeare, Boston and Salem, Massachusetts, 1671–c. 1710. Courtesy Henry Francis du Pont Winterthur Museum.

694. Hammered $16\frac{3}{4}$-inch dish with multiple-reed brim which measures $2\frac{7}{16}$ inches. Touch and maker same as for Fig. 693. Unusually fine example of a multiple-reeding dish. Collection of Dr. Joseph H. Kler. Courtesy of the Smithsonian Institution, United States National Museum.

PLATE LXXXI

693

694

PLATE LXXXII — *Dishes and Basins*

695. 15-inch dish with multiple-reeded rim. Engraving on brim. Edmund Dolbeare, Boston and Salem, *c.* 1671–*c.* 1710, touch 831. Collection of Lloyd W. Fowles.

696. 15-inch dish with multiple-reeded rim. Attributed to Joseph Dolbeare, Boston, 1694–1704, or to his brother John Dolbeare, Boston, *c.* 1694–1720. Touch 832. Courtesy of the Henry Francis du Pont Winterthur Museum.

697. Rosewater dish with raised central boss. Diameter $12\frac{11}{16}$ inches, width of brim $1\frac{3}{16}$ inches. Believed to be unique in American pewter. Edmund Dolbeare, Boston and Salem, Massachusetts, *c.* 1671–1710. Touch 831. Collection of Mrs. Peter H. Alderwick.

698. Covered basin, 14 inches diameter, height 8 inches including cover. $4\frac{1}{4}$-inch depth of basin alone. Boardman and Co., Hartford, Connecticut, *c.* 1825 to 1835. Touch 433. First illustrated in J. B. Kerfoot's *American Pewter*. Courtesy of the Henry Francis du Pont Winterthur Museum.

PLATE LXXXII

695

696

697

698

PORRINGERS

Although many fine porringers have been lured out of obscurity and into collections in the past thirty years and although a few additional variations in handle design or form of handle support have been found, no startling discoveries, such as those in the designs of plates and dishes, have been reported.

Before comment is made upon the newly-illustrated porringers, errors, that appeared in the section on porringers in the text of Volume One, should be corrected.

On page 31 mention was made of the fact that the country districts of eastern Pennsylvania were settled largely by Germans and Swiss. This misstatement was apparently caused by an error in typing, because the manuscript read correctly "Germans and Swedes."

Immediately following that sentence on page 31, the statement was made that the only Philadelphia porringer, which thus far could be identified as to maker, has a solid handle. That statement must now be modified. If the pewter marked with the so-called lovebird touch (see Plate CIX, Fig. 869) was made in Philadelphia—and some of it almost certainly was—then the crown-handle porringer was a form made in Pennsylvania as well as in New York and New England. This is proved by the porringer handle illustrated as Fig. 704 of Plate LXXXIII, which bears the lovebird touch. It still remains a mystery why so very few Philadelphia porringers have survived.

The third, and most glaring, error in the discussion of porringers in Volume One, was in illustrating and attributing to John Andrew Brunstrom, Philadelphia pewterer, the solid-handle porringer shown as Fig. 74 of Plate XIII. The experts are now in pretty general agreement that the crude initial touch, Plate LXVII, Fig. 548, as impressed on the handle of this porringer, is a modern fake and that this porringer and, in fact, many of the forms on which this mark appears were newly cast some thirty or forty years ago.

Two other minor revisions may now be made to the captions for illustrations on Plate XIII. In Fig. 70, the R.B. touch on the porringer there illustrated is definitely of New England origin and is now attributed with reservations, to Robert Bonynge, Boston, 1731–*c.* 1764.

Similarly it is generally agreed that touch 598, as impressed on the solid-handle porringer shown in Fig. 75, was almost certainly the mark of Samuel Pennock of East Marlborough Township, Chester County, Pennsylvania, or of his son Simon, *c.* 1780–*c.* 1815.

With those corrections noted, the road is clear for comments upon the porringers illustrated in this volume.

Attention is called first to a porringer which, if American, has no counterpart in handle design among recorded American examples. It is illustrated as Fig. 699 of Plate LXXXIII. The touch with initials I.L. is shown in Fig. 882 of Plate CX. Just three Colonial pewterers with those initials, working in the period to which this porringer can be assigned, could be considered as possible makers, Joseph Leddell and Joseph, Jr. of New York, and Ivory Lucas of New London, Connecticut. We already have one initial touch which the elder Leddell definitely used and a second that is attributed to him with considerable assurance. They bear no resemblance whatever to this touch. It would seem that if this porringer is American, the maker is Lucas or some man whose records are unknown to us. Of course it may have been of English origin, but as explained below, porringers of a different handle design have been found with this same I.L. touch.

Let us consider next a group of four porringers, varying slightly from one another in the details of the fenestration of the handles, but essentially of one general handle pattern, a design that was in very common use in England late in the seventeenth century and in the first quarter of the eighteenth. It may have been a standard pattern in New England also during that period, but, by the time of the American Revolution, it had all but disappeared. When *Pewter in America* was published in 1940, I knew of but one porringer, believed to be American, which had a handle of this roughly-triangular form. It was illustrated as Fig. 56 of Plate XII, Volume One. The maker, with initials I.W., was then, and still remains, unidentified.

First of the four new examples to be shown and discussed here is Plate LXXXIV, Fig. 708. This is a 5-inch porringer, with eight openings in the handle, marked on its underside with a very clear impression of Fig. 292, definitely a Boston touch, and now attributed with some slight reservations to Robert Bonynge, 1731–c. 1764.

Fig. 709 shows a handle which is even more triangular in general outline which also has eight openings. The bowl measures $5\frac{7}{16}$ inches in diameter. The initials T.B. are cast in the bracket, the shape of which seems to have been peculiar to Newport (see Plate XLVIII, Fig. 325). Consequently this specimen is attributed here, with only slight reservations, to Thomas Byles, Newport and Philadelphia, 1710–1771.

The third porringer in this group, Fig. 700 of Plate LXXXIII, also measures $5\frac{7}{16}$ inches in diameter. Though very similar in handle outline to the last, it has twelve holes, instead of eight within the frame. It bears no touch or cast-in initials that might help to identify its maker, but, as with Fig. 709, it has a support that is typical of Newport. This support however has a feature that is not found on any marked American porringer that I have seen. Projecting above the surface of a bracket of typical Newport shape are three ribs, rising to sharp ridges which fan out from the base or apex of the support to their juncture with the handle proper. Undoubtedly their purpose was to provide added strength where the handle most needed support.

Last of this group, and almost certainly the latest in date of manufacture, is another $5\frac{7}{16}$-inch porringer illustrated as Fig. 710. The handle is almost identical with that of Fig. 700 except for its addition of one more small opening just below the center. This handle bears a touch of David Melville, Newport, 1775–1794.

On the basis of the limited evidence that we have, it would seem that porringers,

PLATE LXXXIII — *Porringers and a Basin*

699. 5-inch porringer with rare design of early handle. Touch 882. Maker unidentified but possibly Ivory Lucas, New London, Connecticut, *c.* 1732–1747. Collection of Mrs. Peter Woodbury.

700. 5¼-inch porringer with what might be termed a triangular form of handle. Variants of this general design may be seen in Plate XII, Fig. 56, Volume One, and in Figs. 708, 709 and 710 of Plate LXXXIV in this volume. This form of handle seems to have been used on these shores only in Massachusetts and Rhode Island, mid-eighteenth century. Maker unidentified. The support for the handle with unusual rayed ribs is illustrated as Fig. 703 on this plate. Collection of Amory S. Skerry.

701. 4⅝-inch porringer with coronet-shaped handle of most delicate tracery. A rare and fine porringer. Maker unknown, his initials T.B. cast in the bracket supporting the handle (see Fig. 880); probably first half eighteenth century. Collection of William S. Wilcox.

702. 5½-inch basin with an almost perpendicular side wall. Height 1⅝ inches. No basin of similar design has been reported. Maker William Bradford Jr., New York, 1719–1758. Gift of Mrs. Stephen S. Fitzgerald to the Metropolitan Museum of Art, New York.

703. Handle of 5¼-inch porringer, unidentified as to maker, illustrated as Fig. 700 above.

704. Handle of coronet type; dimensions not recorded. Marked with the lovebird touch, illustrated as Plate CIX, Fig. 869. The maker remains unidentified but is assuredly a Pennsylvania pewterer, possibly Abraham Hasselberg. Second half of the eighteenth century. One of the very few surviving porringers of Pennsylvania origin. Formerly in the collection of Joseph France, since presented by him to William Penn Memorial Museum, Harrisburg, Pennsylvania.

705, 706, and 707. Three 5-inch porringers with so-called old English type of handle. Despite the fact that the three appear to be identical and may even have come from the same mould, they bear the touches of three different makers. Reading from left to right they are William Bradford Jr. (touch 582), New York, 1719–1758, Francis or Frederick Bassett (touch 861), New York, 1754–1799, or Hartford, 1780–1785, and Samuel Danforth, Hartford, 1795–1816 (touch 398). Collection of Amory S. Skerry.

PLATE LXXXIII

699

700

701

702

703

704

705

706

707

PLATE LXXXIV — *Porringers*

708. 5-inch porringer with early type of handle that was current in England in the second quarter of the eighteenth century. American variants, all rare, are illustrated as Fig. 56, Plate XII, Volume One, Fig. 700, Plate LXXXIII, in this volume, and Figs. 709 and 710 on this plate. This general design has been found thus far only on porringers of Boston or Newport origin. Touch 292, attributed to Robert Bonynge, Boston, 1731–1763. Collection of the author.

709. $5\frac{7}{16}$-inch porringer. Marked T.B. on underside of handle (Fig. 881) and attributed to Thomas Byles of Newport and Philadelphia, 1710–1771. One fact supporting the attribution to Byles is the shape of the supporting rib, a shape found elsewhere only on porringers made later by the Melvilles of Newport. Collection of John H. McMurray.

710. $5\frac{7}{16}$-inch porringer. Maker David Melville, Newport, 1775–1793. Similar to the porringers just discussed but slightly more elaborate in handle design. Collection of the Henry Francis du Pont Winterthur Museum.

711. 5-inch porringer. Made by Richard Lee or Richard Lee, Jr. Various locations in New Hampshire, Vermont, and western Massachusetts, 1788–1820. Touch 410. This is another of the handle designs employed by Lee, that were, seemingly, peculiar to his shop. Collection of John H. McMurray.

PLATE LXXXIV

708

709

710

711

with the general design of handle which we have just considered, were standard forms in Newport prior to 1780 and, quite possibly, in Boston also in the early decades of the eighteenth century.

One other early porringer, illustrated as Fig. 701, deserves special comment here. If this porringer is, as I believe, of American manufacture it is one of our finest. The diameter of the bowl is 4⅝ inches and the handle is of the coronet design with perhaps the most open, airy, and graceful of all American porringer handles. A very similar porringer, but with a handle of less airy fenestration is owned in London by the Worshipful Company of Pewterers and is illustrated at the bottom of page 68, catalogue no. 388, in Ronald Michaelis' recently published *Short History of the Worshipful Company of Pewterers of London.* It bears no maker's mark, but is given the approximate date of 1695–1700.

The American porringer, Fig. 701, has the initials T.B. cast in the handle bracket (see Plate CX, Fig. 880). Here again, as in the case of Fig. 709 discussed above, attribution might be made with reservations to Thomas Byles. Attention is called however to a comparison of the handle supports as illustrated in Figs. 881 and 880. They differ markedly in shape. The first is typical of Newport; the second, triangular with somewhat rounded edges, varies slightly from the shape of bracket that was normal to most porringers made in Boston, New York, and in central Connecticut.

This porringer is so very different in design from the other T.B. example (Fig. 709) and the finish so superior, that it is difficult to believe that the same pewterer could have been responsible for both. Two men, who were trained in England and whose dates would qualify them as possible makers of this specimen, are Thomas Burroughs of Boston and New York, *c.* 1684–1703, and Thomas Badcock, early Philadelphia pewterer (died in 1703).

An interesting study could be made of the relative merits, as craftsmen, of different pewterers by comparing the finish of handles of marked porringers. Reference is made to the way in which the openings in the coronet design and "flowered" handles were left. The less exacting makers were careless about how they removed excess metal in the openings. The conscientious, well-trained pewterer reamed out each hole carefully leaving a sharply-cut finished design. Compare, for instance, the handle of the T.B. porringer just commented upon, with the handle illustrated as Fig. 341 of Plate L, Volume One, made by Gershom Jones of Providence, who not infrequently was guilty of just such slipshod work. This absence of careful finish, although not often so pronounced, can be seen in the porringer handles of many New England pewterers, including Belcher, David and Thomas Melville, John and Joseph Danforth, Samuel Danforth of Hartford, and the Boardmans, to name but a few. It is of interest to note that Jones's partner, Samuel Hamlin and the latter's one-time apprentices, Samuel E. Hamlin and William Calder, almost invariably cleared the excess metal from the handles. As far as my observation goes the same comment can be made of the pewterers of New York as a group.

Household Pewter

TANKARDS, POTS, AND MEASURES

Although we still await the finding of a seventeenth-century drinking vessel that can be identified positively as the work of a Colonial pewterer, our knowledge of the forms in general use after 1730 has been broadened, as more and more marked identifiable examples have emerged from their long hiding.

Until recent years the tankard seemed to be one of the rarest of surviving shapes in American pewter. When J. B. Kerfoot's *American Pewter* was published in 1924, he was able to illustrate but one covered tankard. Of it he wrote: "[L]ike its aristocratic silver relative [it] belongs among the greater rarities; and the flat-topped variety of the breed, marked by one of the early men, is only to be mentioned with reverence." In spite of the fact that there must be over two hundred marked American tankards in collections today, they are still "mentioned with reverence," that is, if reverence can be measured by the prices which collectors are willing to pay for them.

But before offering any comments about tankards that have turned up since 1940, correction should be made of the errors that cropped up in Volume One in the section devoted to these drinking vessels.

In the description of the tankards illustrated in Plate XIV, an error was made in reporting the mark found on the tankard illustrated in Fig. 79. The mark should have read Fig. 502 instead of 510.

A number of revisions must be made in the text on page 33, Volume One. On line 15 the dates should be shown as 1735 to 1780 instead of 1755 to 1780. In line 19 please substitute six for four, as the number of shops making tulip-shaped vessels, and in line 20 the dates should be changed to read 1745 to 1785 instead of 1760 to 1785. One further correction needs to be made on that page; for Brunstrom substitute Boyd in line 30. Finally a revision is required in the comments on the page facing Plate XX. Fig. 122 is an illustration of a quart pot made by Nathaniel Austin. The mark should have been recorded as Fig. 296 instead of 306.

At long last we know what mid-eighteenth-century Boston tankards looked like, providing that the John Carnes quart tankard with double-dome cover, now in the Winterthur Museum, is representative of the tankards of that time and place. This example, Plate LXXXV, Fig. 714, has an unusually heavy boot-heel handle terminal. Otherwise the tankard displays no unusual features.

One tankard cover peculiarity, found thus far only on New York tankards, is a crenate projection of the lid, which was frequently found on both flat-top and domed covers. Although such a feature must have disappeared in England about 1720 or earlier, it persisted in New York until about the time of the Revolution. No less than nine different shops are known to have made tankard lids in this long-outmoded design and yet not one such tankard has been reported bearing a touch of a New England or Pennsylvania pewterer. No logical explanation can be offered for this anomaly.

Plate LXXXV — *Tankards*

712. Quart tankard with double-dome cover. Height $6\frac{1}{2}$ inches, top diameter $4\frac{5}{16}$ inches, bottom diameter $4\frac{15}{16}$ inches. Touch 878. Attributed to Thomas Byles, Newport, Rhode Island, Philadelphia, 1710–*c.* 1770. Courtesy of the Metropolitan Museum of Art, gift of Mrs. J. Insley Blair, 1940, in memory of J. Insley Blair.

713. Splendid two-quart tankard with double-dome cover. Height $7\frac{1}{2}$ inches, top diameter $4\frac{7}{8}$ inches, bottom diameter $5\frac{5}{8}$ inches. Frederick Bassett, New York, 1761–1800, touch 468. Collection of William M. Goss Jr.

714. Quart tankard with double-dome cover and heavy boot-heel handle terminal. Height $6\frac{1}{2}$ inches, top diameter $4\frac{1}{8}$ inches, bottom diameter $4\frac{1}{2}$ inches, touch 285. Col. John Carnes, Boston, *c.* 1720–1760. Courtesy of Henry Francis du Pont Winterthur Museum.

715. Bellied quart tankard with double-dome cover, chair back open thumb rest and broken double C handle, abnormally marked near handle at rim. Touch 483. Height overall $7\frac{1}{8}$ inches, diameter of base $4\frac{7}{16}$ inches. Maker John Will, New York 1752–*c.* 1774. This is the only New York quart tankard with bellied body and reversed C handle thus far reported.

716. Quart pot or mug by the same maker, and bearing the same touch. Height $6\frac{1}{4}$ inches, top diameter $3\frac{7}{8}$ inches, bottom diameter $4\frac{7}{8}$ inches. Unusual among New York mugs in that no rib or fillet encircles the drum. Both pieces are in the collection of William M. Goss Jr.

717. Quart tankard with flat cover and crenate lip; height $6\frac{3}{16}$ inches, bottom diameter $4\frac{15}{16}$ inches. Probably unique among American pewter tankards, in that a medallion, illustrating a biblical scene, has been let into an opening in center of lid. John Will, New York, 1752–1774. Touch 483. Collection of Donald Noble.

718. Medallion on lid of John Will tankard above showing detail of the biblical scene of the prophet Elijah being fed by an angel of the Lord and by a raven. The medallion is, of course, out of proportion to the tankards illustrated on this plate. It is shown at approximately actual size.

PLATE LXXXV

714

718

713

717

712

716

715

PLATE LXXXVI — *Tankards*

719. Quart tankard with flat top and crenate lip; ram's-horn thumbpiece. The drum has been tastefully engraved with the cypher of the owners within a floral design. Height $7\frac{1}{16}$ inches, top diameter $4\frac{3}{8}$ inches, bottom diameter 5 inches. Touch 582. William Bradford Jr., New York, 1719–1758. Courtesy Henry Francis du Pont Winterthur Museum.

720 and 721. Pair of quart tankards, unmarked, maker unidentified. Similarity of lids and thumb rests point to the likelihood that both are from the same shop. Provenance probably Massachusetts or Rhode Island, mid-eighteenth century. Compare Fig. 93, Plate XVI, Volume One. Measurements of left-hand tankard, height $7\frac{1}{4}$ inches, top diameter $4\frac{1}{8}$ inches, bottom diameter $4\frac{5}{8}$ inches; right-hand tankard, height $8\frac{1}{4}$ inches, top diameter 4 inches, bottom diameter $4\frac{7}{8}$ inches. Collection of William M. Goss Jr.

722. Pint tankard, double-domed cover, height $4\frac{5}{8}$ inches, top diameter $3\frac{3}{8}$ inches, bottom diameter $3\frac{7}{8}$ inches. Touch 495. Cornelius Bradford, Philadelphia and New York, 1752–1785. One of the very few marked American pint tankards that has survived. Collection of William M. Goss Jr., photograph courtesy of Carl Jacobs.

723. Quart tankard with flat top. Height $6\frac{5}{16}$ inches, top diameter $4\frac{1}{4}$ inches, bottom diameter 5 inches. Touch 539. Colonel William Will, Philadelphia, 1764–1798. Closely resembles tankards of Henry Will and Peter Young. Collection of John J. Evans Jr.

724. Quart tankard with flattened double-dome cover. Height $6\frac{3}{4}$ inches, bottom diameter $4\frac{3}{4}$ inches. Compare Figs. 103, 104, and 105, Plate XVII, Volume One. Touch 870. Maker John A. Brunstrom, Philadelphia, 1781–1793. Formerly in the collection of Mr. and Mrs. Ralph P. Hanes, since presented by them to the Museum of Early Southern Decorative Arts, Winston-Salem, North Carolina. Photograph courtesy of Thomas D. Williams.

725. Bellied quart tankard with double-domed lid. Height $7\frac{3}{8}$ inches, bottom diameter $4\frac{1}{16}$ inches. Touch inside 869. Touches outside near handle 871. Positive identification of maker not possible but attributed probably to Abraham Hasselberg, Philadelphia, 1763–1779, or John Brunstrom, Philadelphia, 1781–1793. Collection of Dr. and Mrs. Robert Mallory III.

PLATE LXXXVI

722

725

721

720

724

719

723

Tankards, Pots, and Measures

Of outstanding importance among the newly-found tankards is the John Will flat-topped example illustrated as Fig. 717 of Plate LXXXV. As far as presently known it is unique in American pewter in that its lid is decorated with a medallion cast into a depression in the center of the lid. Depicted there in bas-relief is the story of an Angel of the Lord appearing with food and drink for the sleeping prophet, Elijah, and even a raven is shown flying in with food in its mouth. Elijah, upon waking, would surely have been no more surprised at seeing an angel before him than at the sight in the background of a four-square modern house with chimney. An enlargement of the medallion is shown in Plate LXXXV, Fig. 718. It would be interesting to find the original engraving which must have furnished Will with the design for his composition.

Two more examples of Will's hollow ware are shown as Figs. 715 and 716 of Plate LXXXV. The tankard is unusual on three counts. It is the only New York tankard of record with a tulip-shaped body, the only one with a double-C acanthus leaf handle (such as John's son, William, was to use on quart pots and loving cups at a later date), and the only New York tankard that is marked abnormally on the body near the handle. The quart pot, which is shown with it, is one of the comparatively few surviving New York mugs that was made without a heavy encircling rib.

Earlier assumptions that the straight-sided cylindrical drum of tankard and pot was the normal form in the Colonies, and the bellied body something of a specialty, have been confirmed by a study of the larger collections of today. Extant examples of the bellied form are limited to just six shops, and five of those six also made the commoner drum-shaped form. It is of interest, though, that the tulip shape was not just a passing fad. I own a pewter mug with the R.B. touch attributed to Robert Bonynge, which, according to its engraved inscription, was presented to the Church in Southborough, Massachusetts, in 1747; yet William Will was making tankards, as well as pots of similar contour in Philadelphia at least as late as 1790.

Three fine early tankards are illustrated in Figs. 712, 713 and 714 of Plate LXXXV. Fig. 712 has an early form of handle terminal and low dome cover. Its touch, illustrated as Fig. 878, Plate CX, shows the initials T.B. and the date 1710 within a diamond. The touch is attributed here, with some reservation, to Thomas Byles of Newport and Philadelphia, 1710–1771. Of course it might possibly be the touch of an English pewterer, even though not illustrated in Cotterell.

Fig. 713 has a two-quart capacity and is impressed with a touch of Frederick Bassett, New York, 1769–1800. The handle is of an early type, which would not have been expected from the shop of such a late worker. It is just possible that this touch, Fig. 465, may have been used earlier by Frederick's uncle, the first Francis Bassett, 1718–1758. The third of these early tankards, Fig. 714, was commented upon above.

Fig. 719, Plate LXXXVI, bears a touch that has been attributed to William Bradford of New York, 1719–1759. The engraved decoration on its drum is particularly fine. Figs. 720 and 721 of Plate LXXXVI, present two unmarked tankards, made by an unidentified New England pewterer. The similarity in designs of the lids, with identical finials, points to a common origin. Compare them with Plate XVI, Figs. 92 and 93, Volume One. Noteworthy is the long flat area at the top of the handle, a feature of Fig. 93 as well as of the pair just illustrated. The late Dr. Percy Raymond owned a tankard with domed cover, but with no finial and with a handle of this same flat-top design. Engraved on the drum was the inscription "This Belongs to Voluntown Church, 1730." Perhaps that date provides a clue as to the approximate period of manufacture of tankards of this general type.

The bellied quart tankard, illustrated as Fig. 725 of Plate LXXXVI, has been of real value in linking the unidentified Pennsylvania pewterer or pewterers, who used the lovebird touch, Plate CIX, Fig. 869, with John A. Brunstrom, Swedish-born Philadelphia pewterer. Here you may see, to the left of the handle, very clear impressions of a distinctive crowned X which is frequently found on pewter bearing the lovebird mark, together with a rampant lion in diamond lozenge, struck four times.

A tankard with flattened dome top, similar to Fig. 104 of Plate XVII is in the Museum of Early Southern Decorative Arts in Old Salem, North Carolina. It bears the very same marks as shown on the bellied tankard to its left, Fig. 725, and also a hitherto unknown touch with the name I. Brunstrom in a serrated arc, Plate CIX, Fig. 870.

As we take leave of the covered tankards, your attention is called to a magnificent lidless flagon with an unusually graceful, beautifully-proportioned, early handle, illustrated as Fig. 726 of Plate LXXXVII. This particular vessel, impressed with small marks of an unidentified pewterer, is probably English, but we would like to hope that the same type of flagon may have been made on these shores and is now simply awaiting identification of its maker.

A few early pewter pots (or mugs) deserve comment but a few revisions should be made to captions for Plates XVIII and XX in Volume One, before we take up the new illustrations.

For Fig. 110 of Plate XVIII, the caption reads "provenance unknown." In the light of present knowledge that statement should be changed to read "Definitely of New England origin, probably Boston or Newport."

For Fig. 122 of Plate XX the touch mark should have read 296 instead of 306.

Fig. 125, same plate, touch 292 is now attributed, though with reservations, to Robert Bonynge, Boston, 1731–*c.* 1764.

One of the earliest of American drinking vessels is illustrated as Fig. 743 of Plate LXXXIX. It is unfortunately in damaged condition and the handle has been clumsily repaired. There is evidence that it may once have had two handles and perhaps been designed as a loving cup, rather than a pint pot. It is distressing that we cannot see this early form as it looked when new. It has the distinction of bearing a hitherto unknown initial touch of Lawrence Langworthy, Exeter, England, 1719 and Newport, Rhode Island *c.* 1730–1739. The newly discovered touch is illustrated as Fig. 841 of Plate CV.

PLATE LXXXVII — *Covered and Open-Top Drinking Vessels*

726. Extremely fine lidless flagon with gracefully sweeping handle ending in a boot-heel terminal. Height $8\frac{3}{4}$ inches, top diameter $4\frac{7}{16}$ inches, bottom diameter $4\frac{13}{16}$ inches. Maker unknown, probably English, late seventeenth century or early eighteenth. A shield-shaped coat of arms hall mark was struck three times; the fourth mark encloses the initials I.K. Engraved within a cartouche is "Ipswich Second Ch^{h} 17^{34}." Courtesy Henry Francis du Pont Winterthur Museum.

727, 728, and 729. A group including a pair of presumably identical quart pots or cans with solid handles of broken-C design ending in double volutes; in center a pint pot or can with hollow handle ending in "fish-tail" terminal. Measurements of the quart pots: height $5\frac{3}{4}$ inches, top diameter $3\frac{7}{8}$ inches, bottom diameter $4\frac{3}{4}$ inches; of pint pot, height $4\frac{5}{8}$ inches, top diameter $3\frac{1}{8}$ inches, bottom diameter $3\frac{5}{8}$ inches. The quart pots seem to have been made in the same moulds, although not necessarily in the same shop. The vessel on the left bears touch 838, the mark of a still unidentified Boston pewterer with initials I.S. and is from the collection of John J. Evans Jr. Its counterpart on the right is from the collection of Mrs. George A. Marks and bears a very clear impression of the stag mark, illustrated as Fig. 578a. The touch is that of an unidentified Massachusetts or Rhode Island pewterer working about the middle of the eighteenth century. The same touch appears on the pint can, which was formerly in the John W. Poole collection, now owned by the Brooklyn Museum. Photograph courtesy of Thomas D. Williams.

730. Quart double-domed tankard. Height $6\frac{1}{2}$ inches, top diameter $4\frac{1}{4}$ inches, bottom diameter $4\frac{7}{8}$ inches. Touch 356 together with quality mark. Thomas Danforth 3rd, Rocky Hill, Connecticut and Philadelphia, 1777 to 1818. Similar tankards, probably from the same moulds, have been found bearing the touches of Samuel Hamlin, Edward Danforth and Samuel Danforth of Hartford. Present location of tankard is not known. Photograph courtesy of Carl Jacobs.

731. Quart pot with plain solid handle. Height $5\frac{13}{16}$ inches, top diameter $3\frac{7}{8}$ inches, bottom diameter $4\frac{13}{16}$ inches. This is the same pot as Fig. 727 above except for the plainer handle. Touch 838, unidentified Boston pewterer of *c*. 1750–1760. Collection of John H. McMurray.

732. Late quart tankard. Height $7\frac{1}{4}$ inches, top diameter $4\frac{1}{8}$ inches, bottom diameter $5\frac{1}{16}$ inches. Marked "T. Wildes, N. York" within a circular frame. 1833–1840. Despite the fact that this tankard was made of spun britannia and with thin walls, it retains the simplicity of form of the earlier tankards. Collection of Charles V. Swain.

733. One of the latest of pint mugs. Height $4\frac{7}{8}$ inches, top diameter 4 inches, bottom diameter $4\frac{7}{8}$ inches. Apparently cast, not spun. Marked R. Gleason, *c*. 1820–1830, Dorchester, Massachusetts. Note elaborate handle with two struts. Collection of Charles V. Swain.

PLATE LXXXVII

726

727　　　　　728　　　　　729

730

731

732

733

PLATE LXXXVIII—*Pots and Measures*

734. Quart pot; solid handle ends in a boot-heel terminal, has cast-in rayed decoration at base of thumb rest. Height $6\frac{1}{16}$ inches, top diameter 4 inches, bottom diameter $4\frac{5}{8}$ inches. Unmarked. Maker unknown, probably Boston or Newport, mid-eighteenth century. Collection of John H. McMurray.

735. Pint pot with strap handle, terminating in a grotesque mask. Height $4\frac{5}{8}$ inches, unmarked, maker unknown. Collection of the Metropolitan Museum of Art, the gift of Mrs. Stephen S. Fitzgerald.

736. Pint pot, illustrated to show decoration of handle terminal. Height $4\frac{11}{16}$ inches, top diameter $3\frac{1}{4}$ inches, bottom diameter $3\frac{13}{16}$ inches. Touch 292, attributed to Robert Bonynge, Boston, 1731–1763. Courtesy of Yale University Art Gallery, the Mabel Brady Garvan Collection.

737. Pint pot with hollow handle ending in boot-heel terminal; height $4\frac{3}{8}$ inches, top diameter $3\frac{3}{8}$ inches, bottom diameter $3\frac{7}{8}$ inches; touch 502, William Kirby, New York, 1760–1793. Collection of John A. Schneider.

738, 739 and 740. Group of three lidded baluster measures attributed to Rhode Island pewterers. The quart measure on the left is marked with initial touch 842, attributed with confidence to Lawrence Longworthy, Newport, 1731–1739. The central measure with a half gallon capacity, touch 883, attributed to John Fryers, Newport, 1749–1768 and the half-pint measure on the left, touch 847, is believed to have been used by Thomas Melville of Newport 1793–1796 or by his nephew and namesake, Thomas 2nd, 1796–1824. This measure is 5 inches to top of thumbpiece, $4\frac{3}{16}$ inches to top of lid; bottom diameter $2\frac{9}{16}$ inches. The larger measures were formerly in the collection of the late Dr. Madelaine Brown; the T.M. measure is owned by J. K. Ott. All three were shown in an exhibition of Rhode Island Pewter at the John Brown House, arranged by the Rhode Island Historical Society in the summer of 1959. This illustration is reproduced with the Society's permission from the bulletin of that exhibition and with the concurrence of Mr. Ott.

741. Quart lidded baluster measure. Height without thumbpiece $7\frac{1}{8}$ inches, top diameter $3\frac{3}{4}$ inches, bottom diameter $3\frac{7}{8}$ inches. Marked on lid with touch 869, unidentified but attributed with reservations to Abraham Hasselberg, Philadelphia 1762–1779 and/or J. A. Brunstrom, Philadelphia, 1781–1793. The top is also stamped with the initials C.P. as placed there by the Sealer of Weights and Measures of the city of Philadelphia. Collection of the author.

PLATE LXXXVIII

737

741

736

735

740

739

738

734

Tankards, Pots, and Measures

Another early form, if we may judge from its slender solid handle, is the mug illustrated as Fig. 731 of Plate LXXXVII. It bears the I.S. Semper Eadem touch, Fig. 838 of Plate CIV of a still unidentified Boston pewterer and probably dates from 1760 or slightly earlier.

The third of these early pots is illustrated in Fig. 737 of Plate LXXXVIII. Its touch, Plate LXIX, Fig. 292a, has been attributed, with reservations, to Robert Bonynge, who was working in Boston as early as 1731 and for at least three decades thereafter. The handle terminal is a definite indication of its early manufacture.

A group of three drinking vessels, two quart pots and one in the pint size, definitely of New England (and probably Boston) origin, made about 1730 to 1760, are illustrated as Figs. 727, 728 and 729 of Plate LXXXVII. They are shown here, primarily, to help identify eventually the users of their touches, which to date, cannot be assigned positively to any particular shop or shops.

Compare first Figs. 727 and 729. They appear to be as alike as two peas with every indication of having come from the same moulds. But the touches are different and the pots may have been made years apart and in two different shops. Fig. 727 is marked with the I.S. Semper Eadem touch, found also on Fig. 731 commented upon above; Fig. 729 has a touch showing what seems to be a stag with one foreleg raised (Plate CX, Fig. 578a). So very different are these two touches—in subject, feeling and quality of workmanship—that it seems highly improbable that one pewterer was the user of both.

The same stag touch is found on the pint pot illustrated as Fig. 728. This complex "Semper Eadem" problem is discussed at some length on pages 39–41.

Three more pots, all of New England provenance, are presented in Figs. 734, 735 and 736 in order to illustrate unusual decoration of handle, thumb rests, or terminals.

When the first two volumes of *Pewter in America* were published, no American measure made prior to 1824 had been reported. Now there is record of at least six marked American measures, five attributed to Newport makers, the sixth made in or near Philadelphia. All are of the baluster type with hammerhead thumbpiece.

In the larger illustration, Plate LXXXVIII are three Rhode Island measures, attributed to three different makers, all of Newport—Lawrence Langworthy, John Fryers, and Thomas Melville. In each case the touch was impressed on the upright rim just below the lid.

Fig. 741 presents the one Philadelphia measure. In this case the touch, Plate CIX, Fig. 869, showing a pair of love-birds, was impressed on the top of the lid. Also stamped on the lid are the large initials C.P., the mark of the Sealer of Measures of the City of Philadelphia, testifying that the vessel met the Sealer's standards.

The known marked measures range in capacity from a gill made by Lawrence Langworthy of Newport up to a half-gallon that bears a touch which has been attributed to John Fryers, also of Newport.

[16]

Household Pewter

BEAKERS

There have been no startling discoveries in the past thirty years that affect in any way what was written about beakers in Volume One.

However half a dozen beakers are being illustrated on Plate LXXXIX largely to show slight variations in design in different shops.

Before leaving this subject one error should be corrected in the captions for Plate XXIII in Volume One. In Fig. 157 the touch on the Samuel Pierce beaker should have been recorded as 407, instead of 415.

SPOONS, LADLES, AND DIPPERS

When one considers that hundreds of thousands of pewter spoons must have been made in the Colonies, it is scarcely believable that so very, very few were preserved and are in collections today.

The more significant of the spoon discoveries in recent years are examples that have been excavated and are consequently badly worn by erosion. A second Chuckatuck spoon (the first was described on pages 71–73, Volume Two) has been identified and, like the earlier discovery, had been broken in two pieces. Because of its long exposure to the acids of the soil, erosion has obliterated practically all of the lettering of the touch on the handle but, because of the unusual design of the handle end, there can be no doubt that this is another Copeland spoon. Actually, except for the erosion at the handle tip, this spoon is in a much better state of preservation than the earlier discovery. The bowl is rounder than the illustration in Volume One, Plate XXIV, indicated and there is a decided curve in the handle, that is not apparent in the spoon at Jamestown.

Probably not quite so early, but made perhaps before 1700, is a spoon on display at the Plimoth Plantation Museum, Plymouth, Massachusetts, on loan there from the Pilgrim John Howland Society. This so-called Howland spoon was dug up at the site of the Joseph Howland House at Kingston, Massachusetts. Artifacts such as broken clay pipes, etc., found with the spoon, enabled experts to date it as probably made between the years 1690 and 1710.

Although not as miraculous as the story of the Chuckatuck spoon at Jamestown, with the name of the pewterer, his date, and place of work still preserved on the handle, this tale of the Howland spoon belongs, itself, in the realm of fairy tales.

One day, not so long ago, Lothrop Withington, Jr., a collector of spoon moulds, chanced to enter the Plimoth Plantation Museum at Plymouth, Massachusetts. In a

PLATE LXXXIX — *Pot, Cup and Beakers*

742. Pint mug, height $4\frac{5}{8}$ inches, touch 867 attributed to John A. Brunstrom, Philadelphia, 1782–1793. One of a pair of mugs, formerly in use in the Allamance Church, North Carolina. Courtesy of the Historical Foundation of the Presbyterian and Reformed Churches, Montreat, North Carolina.

743. Pint mug, or possibly a small two-handled loving cup of which one handle is now missing. The second handle was damaged and repaired badly. Height of cup $4\frac{5}{8}$ inches, top diameter 3 inches, bottom diameter 4 inches. It is regrettable that the cup is not in better condition because it is one of the earliest surviving examples of Rhode Island pewter. The rather badly eroded touch with initials L.L. (Fig. 841, Plate CV) shows the same general design that was used by Lawrence Langworthy in his large touch used in England, prior to his coming to this country, and at Newport, Rhode Island, 1731–1739. Collection of Mrs. Lawrence R. Schumann.

744. One of a pair of very fine tall unmarked beakers. Height 6 inches, top diameter $4\frac{7}{8}$ inches, bottom diameter $4\frac{1}{4}$ inches. Probably American, eighteenth century. Collection of Dr. and Mrs. Robert Mallory III.

745. Beaker with handle. Mark erased. Probably American, late eighteenth or early nineteenth century. The handle may have been a later addition but the resulting combination provided a very satisfactory design and a vessel that should have been more useful than the handleless beaker. One wonders why it was not adopted as a stock form. Bottom diameter $3\frac{1}{16}$ inches. Formerly in the collection of Edward E. Minor.

746. Tall beaker, height $6\frac{1}{2}$ inches, top diameter $3\frac{3}{4}$ inches, bottom diameter $3\frac{1}{8}$ inches, touch 482, John Will, New York, 1752–1774. One of the largest of marked American beakers. Courtesy of Henry Francis du Pont Winterthur Museum.

747. Sturdy small beaker. Height $4\frac{1}{4}$ inches, top diameter $3\frac{7}{16}$ inches, bottom diameter $2\frac{5}{8}$ inches. Touch 533, Johan Christopher Heyne, Lancaster, Pennsylvania, 1754–1780. Courtesy of the Henry Francis du Pont Winterthur Museum.

748. Beaker with slightly flaring lip. Height $4\frac{3}{4}$ inches, top diameter 4 inches, bottom diameter $3\frac{3}{4}$ inches. Maker Henry Will, New York and Albany, 1761–1793. Collection of Dr. Joseph H. Kler, courtesy of the Smithsonian Institution, United States National Museum.

749. Small beaker or cup. Height $3\frac{1}{16}$ inches, top diameter $2\frac{11}{16}$ inches, bottom diameter $2\frac{1}{4}$ inches. Touch 328, Thomas Melville II, Newport, 1796–1824. Courtesy of Yale University Art Gallery, Mabel Brady Garvan Collection.

PLATE LXXXIX

742

743

744

745

746

747

748

749

PLATE XC—*Spoons and a Ladle*

750 and 751. Two rat-tail spoons from the same mould, one new-cast recently by Ellis Withington, the other made probably in Massachusetts about 1690–1705. The head on the handle is said to portray King William III of England. The spoon, which came to light in New Bedford, Massachusetts is owned by Lothrop Withington Jr. The same owner also acquired a companion mould, almost identical except that it bore a different head, purporting to be that of William's consort, Queen Mary. This latter mould was found at Newburyport, Massachusetts.

The ancient spoon was excavated in 1959 on the site of the Joseph Howland house at Rocky Nook, Kingston, Massachusetts and is now on loan by the Pilgrim John Howland Society, Inc., to the Plimoth Plantation Museum in Plymouth, Massachusetts. Thanks are due to the Pilgrim John Howland Society for permission to illustrate their spoon and for the photographs used to the Plimoth Plantation and to Lothrop Withington, Jr. See Plate LXXXIX for illustration of the mould.

752 and 753. Reverse side of the bowls of the same spoons, showing the rat-tails and elaborate decoration around their juncture with the bowls. The latter are $1\frac{7}{8}$ inches in width.

754. Another rat-tail spoon of approximately the same period, unearthed on the site of an early house at Haddam, Connecticut. Length $7\frac{1}{4}$ inches. Collection of Raymond Hellenek.

755 and 756. Pair of rather crudely decorated tablespoons, $7\frac{3}{8}$ inches in length. Maker unidentified. One spoon was found in Vermont, the other in western Massachusetts. The mould in which they were cast, now in the Henry Francis du Pont Winterthur Museum, was acquired in New Britain, Connecticut. The origin was probably central or eastern Connecticut, *c.* 1800–1810. Collection of Mr. and Mrs. Oliver W. Deming.

757. Small spoon, measuring $4\frac{3}{16}$ inches in length, with the name "R. Lee" in script cast on the handle. Note raised decoration at juncture of bowl and handle. Made by Richard Lee or his son Richard Jr., who worked at various locations in New Hampshire, Vermont, Rhode Island, and Massachusetts, *c.* 1788–1820. Courtesy Henry Francis du Pont Winterthur Museum.

758. $7\frac{7}{8}$ inch tablespoon, excavated at the Buttolph-Williams House, Wethersfield, Connecticut. Touches 369 and 849. Attributed to Thomas Danforth 3rd, Rocky Hill, Connecticut and Philadelphia, 1777–1818 or possibly to his father, Thomas Danforth 2nd of Middletown, Connecticut. Courtesy of the Antiquarian and Landmarks Society, Inc., of Connecticut.

759. Ladle 16 inches long with 4 inch diameter bowl. Touches 512, 513, and 514; Peter Young, New York and Albany, 1775–1795. Courtesy Henry Francis du Pont Winterthur Museum.

PLATE XC

750   751   754   755   756

752   753

757

758

759

display case there he noticed a pewter spoon which, although now badly worn, must once have been a rather elaborately-decorated utensil, Figs. 751, 753, Plate XC. It recalled at once to him a spoon mould, which he owned and which had seemingly similar decoration. He hurried home excitedly, gathered up his mould, returned to the Museum and arranged to have the display case opened. The spoon dropped right into the opening which it had left almost three hundred years earlier. Who made it? Where? When? Some mystery must be saved for solution in our next installment.

The last of these long-buried spoons, illustrated as Fig. 758 of Plate XC was found when the Buttolph-Williams House was restored at Wethersfield, Connecticut. It was made perhaps one hundred years later than the Howland spoon. Its principal significance is that, despite erosion, it has preserved, and identified as to user, a touch, known previously to collectors, which could not previously be pinned on any particular shop. The new touch, see Plate CV, Fig. 849, is a rosette design which bore no accompanying initials which would have helped to identify the maker. But, with the rosette on this spoon, are the small hallmarks that were used by the third Thomas Danforth of Rocky Hill, Connecticut, and possibly by his father before him, the second Thomas of Middletown.

COFFEEPOTS, TEAPOTS, CREAMERS, AND SUGAR BOWLS

When *Some Notes on American Pewterers* by Louis G. Myers appeared in 1928, illustrated therein was an unmarked teapot of early design, believed to be of the type turned out by our early teapot makers. That illustration should have been reproduced again in Volume One of *Pewter in America* for the edification of those collectors who were not fortunate enough to own a copy of Mr. Myers' valuable little book. That very same teapot, now in the collection of Charles F. Swain, is illustrated here as Fig. 767 of Plate XCIII.

Also from the Swain collection, which has come very close to cornering the market on early American pewter teapots, are two other pots of the same general pattern. Fig. 764 is almost identical with the Myers-Swain specimen, except for the handle; Fig. 764 has a wooden handle, the Myers-Swain teapot a flat solid pewter handle. It is of interest that even the buttons or finials of the lids appear to be exactly alike. Fig. 764 was found in a New Jersey farmhouse along with a John Bassett porringer. It does not necessarily follow that John Bassett made the teapot, but it is assuredly of a form that might have been expected from his shop.

This brings us to the earliest form of teapot of which marked examples exist, a pot with a slightly taller, more elongated belly than those just described. At least two such marked teapots have been reported in recent years. We are privileged to illustrate both examples, Plate XCII, Figs. 761 and 762. Both teapots are impressed with Bassett touches. Of the two, Fig. 761 which would seem to be the earlier in design, bears the F.B. rampant lion touch, Fig. 457 of Volume Two, which has been attributed to Francis Bassett the elder of New York, 1718–1758 or to his nephew of the same name, 1754–1799. The teapot illustrated as Fig. 762 is similar in general design and differs mainly in its finial, a more prominent cone-shaped ornament encircled from top to bottom by shallow horizontal grooves. This teapot is impressed with the F.B. and fleur-de-lis touch, Fig. 465 of Volume Two, of Frederick Bassett of New York and Hartford, 1760–1800.

The statements in the above paragraph obviously alter and supersede the observations in the last paragraph of page 39, Volume One, where it was stated that the earliest marked American teapots date approximately from the Revolutionary period.

An exceedingly interesting little teapot of a design that was being made in silver in the Colonies around the middle of the eighteenth century, and perhaps slightly earlier, is illustrated as Fig. 765 of Plate XCIII. This particular pot may not be of American origin. It bears no maker's touch, but on its bottom is a quality mark, struck three times in the form of a triad, a practice that is common on Continental pewter. We should expect that just such a teapot would have been made in the Colonies and it is not too much to hope that a marked American example may yet come to light.

Other teapots illustrated in Plates XCIII and XCIV are variations of forms illustrated in the earlier volumes and require no special comment here. In the earlier edition the handsome Federal-style teapot, made by Israel Trask of Beverly, Massachusetts, shown as Fig. 615 of Plate LXXII in Volume Two should more properly have been grouped in Volume One with the earlier examples. Teapots illustrated as Figs. 770, 771 and 772 are variations of the Trask pattern.

Here I must make an embarrassing confession of an error, that was not even corrected in the second edition of Volumes One and Two. The teapot, illustrated as Fig. 194 of Plate XXIX, is recorded as being in "the collection of the author." This is assuredly an error, because I own no such teapot today and have no record of ever owning it. What is distressing is that the real owner never reported to me the faulty attribution and will not even now be acknowledged as the owner, because of my inability to trace the ownership in my old records. To the unknown owner my humble apologies.

A few more William Will coffeepots have been reported, including two with square plinths, one of which is shown as Fig. 760 of Plate XCI. It is worth pointing out here that William Will was not the only maker of large coffeepots. Two of his contemporaries in Philadelphia also made such a form, though we do not know now to what extent their patterns resembled his design. Thomas Byles' inventory, taken in 1771, shows that he had in stock, at the time of his death, four two-quart coffeepots (the same capacity as those made by William Will), eight of the three-pint size, nine of quart capacity, and three holding just a pint.

The other maker of tall coffeepots was John Brunstrom. In his inventory, taken in 1793 by William Will and John Hera, was "1 coffee pot mould complete" which

PLATE XCI

760. Splendid tall coffee pot on square plinth. Height 15¾ inches. Length of a side on base 4¼ inches. Diameter of the rounded base 3¼ inches. Compare with similar coffee pot on round base, Plate XXVII, Volume One. Maker in each case William Will, Philadelphia, 1764–1798. Collection of Dr. and Mrs. Robert Mallory III.

PLATE XCI

760

PLATE XCII — *Two Early Teapots*

761. Earliest surviving marked American teapot as reported to date. Height 6¼ inches, width overall 8¼ inches. Touch 457. Francis Bassett 1st, 1718–1758 or Francis Bassett 2nd, 1754–1799, New York. Collection of Charles V. Swain.

762. Another early teapot of slightly later design. Height 7 inches, diameter of base 3 inches. Touch 465, Frederick Bassett, New York, 1761–1800. Courtesy of New Haven Colony Historical Society.

PLATE XCII

761

762

PLATE XCIII — *Teapots*

763. Early teapot, illustrated first in Louis G. Myers', *Some Notes on American Pewterers.* Height overall 6⅛ inches, width overall 8 inches, bottom diameter 3 inches. Unmarked, maker unknown, collection of Charles V. Swain.

764. Another teapot of approximately the same period, i.e. 1740–1760. Overall height 6¼ inches, overall width 9 inches. When found in a New Jersey farmhouse, this teapot was with a John Bassett, New York, 1720–1761, basin. It is unmarked but of the period when Bassett was working. Courtesy of Henry Francis du Pont Winterthur Museum.

765. Small so-called "skittle ball" teapot. Height 5½ inches, bottom diameter 2¾ inches, top diameter 2¼ inches, overall width 7⁹⁄₁₆ inches. No maker's mark. This teapot may be of Continental origin but similar teapots were made in the colonies in silver in the middle of the eighteenth century and it should not come as too great a surprise, if such a pot with touch of a well-known American pewterer should come to light. Collection of Mrs. Ralph B. Post.

766. Squatty pear-shaped teapot on three feet. Height overall 7¼ inches, width overall 8½ inches. Touch 496, Cornelius Bradford, New York and Philadelphia 1752–1785. Courtesy Henry Francis du Pont Winterthur Museum.

767. Teapot of slightly later form. Height overall 7 inches, width overall 9 inches. Touch 869, maker unidentified but quite possibly Abraham Hasselberg, Philadelphia, 1764–1779, or John Brunstrom, Philadelphia 1784–1793. Collection of Charles V. Swain.

768. Another teapot by same maker. Height overall 7¼ inches, bottom diameter 5 inches. Collection of Mr. and Mrs. Robert M. Laughlin.

PLATE XCIII

763

764

765

766

767

768

PLATE XCIV — *Teapots of the Federal Era*

769. Teapot of transitional design. Height overall 7 inches, width overall 10 inches. Touch 519, Timothy Brigden, Albany, 1816–1819. Courtesy of the Brooklyn Museum.

770. Boat-shaped teapot. Measurements not available. Touch 837, Lee and Creesy, Beverly, Massachusetts, *c.* 1810. Formerly in the collection of Mark La Fountain.

771. Boat-shaped teapot. Height overall $5\frac{1}{2}$ inches, length of base $4\frac{7}{8}$ inches, width of base $3\frac{5}{8}$ inches. Touch 508, George Coldwell, New York, 1787–1811. Collection of Mrs. Ralph B. Post.

772. Boat-shaped teapot of a different pattern by the same maker. Height overall $6\frac{1}{8}$ inches, height to cover 5 inches, long diameter of base $4\frac{1}{8}$ inches. Courtesy of the New York Historical Society and Thomas D. Williams.

PLATE XCIV

770

772

769

771

PLATE XCV—*Sugar Bowls and Creamers*

773. Pair of covered sugar bowls of late eighteenth century. The bowl on left measures $4\frac{1}{2}$ inches in height overall, top diameter $4\frac{1}{4}$ inches, bottom diameter $2\frac{3}{4}$ inches, unmarked except for a small quality mark identified as one used by Peter Young, New York and Albany, 1775–1795. Collection of Charles V. Swain.

774. A covered sugar bowl, also $4\frac{1}{2}$ inches high, top diameter $4\frac{1}{2}$ inches, bottom diameter $2\frac{7}{8}$ inches, touch 888. The maker with initials D.S. was almost certainly a Pennsylvanian of German origin, working in eastern Pennsylvania in the last quarter of the eighteenth century. Collection of Charles V. Swain.

775. Covered sugar bowl. Height $5\frac{5}{8}$ inches overall, top diameter $4\frac{3}{8}$ inches, bottom diameter $3\frac{3}{8}$ inches. Attributed to William Will, Philadelphia, 1764–1798, because the lid appears to have been made from the same mould as for the base of his chalices. Collection of Charles V. Swain.

776 and 777. Two Philadelphia creamers that are also in the Swain collection. No. 776, the creamer on left, is pear-shaped with crenate rim, standing on three feet. The height is $3\frac{7}{8}$ inches overall, the width $4\frac{1}{2}$ inches. Touch, the quality mark shown with Fig. 538, William Will, 1764–1798.

No. 777 on the right is a taller creamer on round base. Height $5\frac{3}{8}$ inches, width also $5\frac{3}{8}$ inches. Unmarked but attributed to the same maker, because the lower section of the body and the base appear to have been made from the same moulds as those used for William Will salts.

778. Small creamer on circular foot. Height $3\frac{7}{8}$ inches, diameter of body $2\frac{3}{8}$ inches. Unmarked but attributed to John Will, New York, 1752–1774 because of shape. Courtesy of Yale University Art Museum.

Group of three items, shown at the exhibition of pewter at the Currier Gallery of Art, Manchester, New Hampshire in the fall of 1968, all believed to have been made at Beverly, Massachusetts.

779. Small oval-shaped creamer with fluted body on four ball feet. Length $5\frac{3}{8}$ inches overall marked with name touch of Israel Trask, Beverly, *c.* 1813–1856. Collection of Mr. and Mrs. Paul M. Young, courtesy of Currier Gallery of Art.

780. Covered tapered bowl, perhaps a sugar bowl. Height 7 inches to top of finial. Believed to have been made in Beverly. Courtesy of Currier Gallery of Art, Manchester, New Hampshire.

781. Boat-shaped creamer on four ball feet, overall length $5\frac{1}{2}$ inches. Marked with a small T and attributed to Israel Trask, Beverly, 1813–1856. Collection of Mr. and Mrs. Richard F. Upton.

PLATE XCV

773   774   775

776   777   778

779   780   781

weighed forty-six pounds, largest of all the moulds in the inventory. This surely turned out castings for a large coffeepot. It may indeed have been the same set of moulds from which Byles's largest coffeepots were made, for it has been surmised that Brunstrom acquired, eventually, moulds and dies which Byles had once owned.

To return to Byles's inventory, one wonders what has become of all of those medium-sized coffeepots; what did they look like and how did they vary in design from what he sold as teapots?

In Figs. 773, 774 and 775 of Plate XCV are shown three more sugar bowls, differing from one another only slightly and all made presumably in the last two decades of the eighteenth century.

Similarly three more eighteenth-century creamers can be seen in Figs. 776, 777 and 778 of Plate XCV. Note the similarity of the William Will creamer, Fig. 776 to another little creamer by William Will's father which was illustrated as Fig. 201 of Plate XXX in Volume One.

The following revisions should be made in the captions recorded for the pewter objects illustrated in Plates XXIX and XXX.

Fig. 198 — identification of the maker of this sugar bowl has been made as a result of comparison with a marked ewer, the base of which was from the same mould that was used to produce the base of this bowl. The maker was Colonel William Will, Philadelphia, 1764–1798.

Fig. 199 — this sugar bowl has been identified recently as the work of Parks Boyd, Philadelphia, 1795–1819, see pp. 145, Volume Three.

Fig. 203, 205, and 214 of Plate XXX — all of these items, bearing the same H.I. touch, Fig. 594, once believed to have been American, are now attributed to Henry Joseph, London pewterer, *c.* 1740–1780, all as presented by J. Carl Thomas in an article in the Pewter Club Collectors' *Bulletin* for June 1967. The evidence is pretty conclusive and the supposition is that the H.I. touch was reserved for pewter made for export to this country.

Fig. 210 of Plate XXX — this small salt is now attributed with considerable assurance to William Will. Compare its outlines with the cover of the William Will coffeepot Plate XXVII, Volume One. A slightly larger salt of similar shape, not illustrated, compares even more closely with the lid of the Will coffeepot.

ECCLESIASTICAL PEWTER

SOME of the most exciting discoveries in American pewter in the past thirty years have been rare forms, long hidden in small country churches, with congregations that were never large enough or sufficiently wealthy to replace their original pewter services with silver. And even today the most likely hiding places in which to seek for rare unrecorded pewter items are in just such little churches in rural areas within two hundred miles of the Atlantic coast line.

Not only have the churches preserved rare forms for us, but the condition of the pieces is usually very fine, with touches as clear as when first impressed, all because of the limited use and special care which the vessels had been accorded. The individual items, for instance, in the service of the Hill Evangelical Lutheran Church, Cleona, Pennsylvania, now in the William Penn Memorial Museum at Harrisburg, Pennsylvania, and illustrated here in Plate XCVI were found still in their original cloth wrappers, just as they must have been delivered at time of purchase, and, except for one flagon, looking as though they had never been used.

Another favorable feature, found occasionally on church pewter, and a boon to students of American pewter, has been the engraving, at time of gift, of the date and name of the donor.

Earliest of these later discoveries is the splendid tall chalice of Christ Church Parish, West Haven, Connecticut, now in the custody of the New Haven Colony Historical Society and here illustrated as the frontispiece to this volume. This magnificent drinking vessel stands $10\frac{1}{4}$ inches high. It is not only the largest of all recorded Colonial chalices, but, engraved with the date 1744, is the earliest chalice that can be definitely assigned to an American pewterer. The maker was Joseph Leddell, Sr., New York, 1711–1753. The touches found on the chalice and accompanying paten are shown as Figs. 855a, 854b and 856 of Plate CVII.

Even more amazing were the discoveries of two pairs of tall church candlesticks, $22\frac{1}{4}$ inches high, of definitely Germanic design, which are now in the Henry F. du Pont Winterthur Museum, candlesticks which, without much doubt, once stood together on the same altar in some Pennsylvania country church. Both pairs turned up in the neighborhood of Reading, Pennsylvania. They bear an initial touch and place touch used by Johan Christopher Heyne, German-American pewterer of Lancaster. One pair may be seen in Plate C. The hollow bases, which stand on flattened ball feet, were made from thin, cast, sheet-like sections which were then soldered together.

The composition of this form is so foreign to anything that might be expected of an English or Colonial pewterer, that it is difficult to convince some dealers and collectors, that the candlesticks could have been made on these shores, in spite of the Lancaster touches which they bear. There have been suggestions by competent students of American pewter that either the sticks had been brought from Germany by immigrants, had then been damaged and taken to Heyne for repairs when his touches were applied, or else that Heyne, to fill a church's order, sent to Germany for the decorated cast sections and, upon their arrival, made the simpler sections and then assembled the parts, soldered them together, and stamped them with his Lancaster touches.

For my part I see no reason for doubting that Heyne was the maker. It should be remembered that this man served his apprenticeship in Saxony, presumably to a competent master pewterer, then travelled later to northern German states and Sweden, working as a journeyman pewterer and, perforce, broadening his knowledge of how to design and make the forms then current throughout all those areas. It seems reasonable to assume that he had made similar candlesticks before migrating to Pennsylvania and consequently was well qualified and able to make them in this country.

Indicative of the possibility of finding other rare and beautiful forms in pewter in the still unexamined closets of country churches are four very fine communion services, each from a rural Pennsylvania church, illustrated here as Figs. 782–800 inclusive, Plates XCVI and XCVII. Three of the sets show forms that were still unreported when Volumes One and Two of *Pewter in America* were published.

The first of these eighteenth-century services, entirely the product of Colonel William Will's shop, Plate XCVI, Figs. 782–785, was illustrated and commented upon in some detail in an article by Paul M. Auman entitled "The Aaronsburg Communion Service" in the April 1950 issue of *Antiques.* The service had been presented by Aaron Levy to the Salem Lutheran Church of Aaronsburg, Pennsylvania, during the years 1789–1794. When that article appeared, all forms in the set, except the basin, were unrecorded William Will designs, and, to this day, no replica of the beautifully proportioned pitcher has been reported. A side view of this lovely vessel is shown as Fig. 801 of Plate XCVIII. Illustrated as Fig. 819 of Plate CII is a chalice very similar to that in the Aaronsburg service. From the Hill Church, Cleona, Pennsylvania, this chalice also was found accompanying a Will flagon of the Aaronsburg type. Such a flagon, as viewed from the side, may be seen in Fig. 802 of Plate XCVIII, a flagon that differs from the Aaronsburg example mainly in the addition of a square plinth.

The second set shown, Plate XCVI, Figs. 786–790, and commented upon above, was used in the Hill Evangelical Lutheran Church, Cleona, Pennsylvania, and is in almost mint condition. All items were made by Christian Heyne of Lancaster, *c.* 1755–1781. The paten is a 6¼-inch saucer. It is noteworthy that one of Heyne's sugar bowls was supplied as the pyx or ciborium.

The third service, Plate XCVII, Figs. 791–795, was used by the Oxford Presbyterian Church. It consists of two patens or collection plates made by John Belson, mid-eighteenth-century London pewterer, a flagon bearing the marks of William Will of Philadelphia, 1764–1798, and two chalices, which, though unmarked, are of a design found on other occasions with Will pewter and are here attributed to him with considerable confidence. It should be noted that the flagon is an unmarred replica of Plate XXXI, Fig. 218 in Volume One; also it should be noted that the chalices are from the same moulds as that shown as Fig. 240 of Plate XXXVI.

The next and last service (and a fine one it is), Plate XCVII, Figs. 796–800, was used in the little Lost Creek Presbyterian Church; it, like the Oxford service described above, is now in the custody of the Presbyterian Historical Society of the United Presbyterian Church, through whose kindness both sets are illustrated here.

All five pieces in this service were made by William Will. The two-handled church cups and the unusual little dish-top patens are forms made by Will, which have not been illustrated previously, except in one of the Presbyterian Church's bulletins. Only the patens are marked, but the tankard is a standard William Will form and the handles of the cups are proof positive that Will was their maker.

Last of the communion sets to be shown here, and latest in time to be manufactured, is that shown as Figs. 803, 804 and 805 of Plate XCVIII, made by Israel Trask of Beverly, Massachusetts, *c.* 1820. Although of thin metal and late design, Trask's vessels retain the simple lines of earlier forms, a comment that is equally true of his two-handled loving cup, illustrated as Fig. 815 of Plate CI.

The last important discovery, made shortly before this volume went to press, consisted of a communion set comprising a tall flagon with two tall beakers recently acquired by Mr. and Mrs. Oliver Deming. According to tradition these vessels had been used in a small church in western Connecticut. Even after the statement had been prepared about the newly found Philip Will flagon, still another flagon turned up, bearing a touch of Samuel Danforth of Hartford. This rare, important vessel, illustrated as Plate XCIXA, is discussed on page 61.

The imposing flagon illustrated on Plate XCIX and commented upon on page 104 bears the hallmarks of Philip Will, New York and Philadelphia pewterer. The accompanying beakers are unmarked but are of the same design and dimensions as a similar pair, made by John Will and now in the Brooklyn Museum.

A number of chalices are presented in Figs. 813–822 to illustrate the wide variations in design to be found in these lovely drinking cups.

And finally this pictorial story of the pewter vessels used in the churches of early America will be rounded out with illustrations of four baptismal basins, Figs. 809, 810, 811, and 812.

Before taking leave of this subject, two corrections should be made of errors that appeared in Volume One.

In the last paragraph on page 44, Volume One, the statement was made erroneously that no pre-Revolutionary pewterers made a form specifically for baptismal purposes, and yet just a few pages later the caption for Plate XXXVIII reads correctly "Early Baptismal Bowl."

782 to 785. Chalice, pitcher, flagon and baptismal basin. All made by Colonel William Will, Philadelphia, within the period from 1789–1794. In some respects this is the finest of surviving American services. Each piece is engraved as follows:

Das Geschenke
Zudenen
Deutschen Gemeinden
in Arensburg
von Aron Levy

Measurements: flagon, height 13$\frac{11}{16}$ inches, bottom diameter 5$\frac{9}{16}$ inches; pitcher, height 10$\frac{3}{4}$ inches, bottom diameter 5 inches; chalice, height 7$\frac{5}{16}$ inches, diameter 3$\frac{9}{16}$ inches; diameter of basin 10$\frac{5}{16}$ inches. The chalice is not marked, but this and other chalices of the same design have been found with other Will pewter and are almost certainly from his shop. The flagon is extremely rare and the beautifully proportioned pitcher is the only recorded example of this form. Courtesy of the Salem Lutheran Church, Aaronsburg, Pennsylvania, and Paul Auman.

786, 787, 788, 789, and 790. Service of the Hill Evangelical Lutheran Church, Cleona, Pennsylvania, consisting of two flagons, measuring 11$\frac{1}{2}$ inches in height overall, 3$\frac{1}{2}$ inches top diameter, 6$\frac{1}{8}$ inches bottom diameter; a covered chalice measuring 11$\frac{5}{8}$ inches with cover, a sugar bowl serving as pyx or ciborium, height about 5$\frac{1}{2}$ inches with cover, and a paten 6$\frac{3}{8}$ inches in diameter. All five pieces were made by Johann Christopher Heyne, Lancaster, Pennsylvania, *c.* 1754–1780. Except for the flagon on the right all pieces are in mint condition and still in their original wrappings. Courtesy of William Penn Memorial Museum, Harrisburg, Pennsylvania.

PLATE XCVI

782   783   784   785

786   787   788   789   790

PLATE XCVII — *Church Communion Services*

792 to 795. Communion service of the Presbyterian Church of Oxford, Pennsylvania. The flagon with covered spout, rococo finial and open thumbpiece, bears the touches of Colonel William Will, Philadelphia, 1763–1798. It is 10½ inches high overall, with bottom diameter of 5⅛ inches (cf. the similar though damaged Will flagon, Fig. 218, Plate XXXI, in Volume One; also the chalice which accompanied it, Fig. 240, Plate XXXVI). The Chalices are 8⅛ inches high, top diameter of 5⅛ inches and bottom diameter of 4⅛ inches. Although unmarked, such chalices are, when they turn up, almost invariably with other William Will forms and are attributed to him with confidence. The plates, used as patens, are English and have the touches of John Belson, London, 1734–1782. Illustrated through the courtesy of the Department of History, General Assembly of the United Presbyterian Church in the United States of America, Philadelphia.

796 to 800. Communion Service of Lost Creek Presbyterian Church, Presbytery of Huntingdon, Pennsylvania. One of the finest of surviving American church services. As so rarely occurred in the small country parishes, this church apparently purchased the set complete at one time and from just one shop, that of Colonel William Will, Philadelphia, 1763–1798. Only the patens are marked, but the tankard, used as a flagon, was a standard Will form and any student of his work would recognize his individualistic acanthus leaf handles on the cups, just as he used them on quart mugs and other vessels. Surviving American loving cups with two handles are exceedingly rare and none made by William Will has been reported heretofore.

796, 797, and 798. The measurements of the quart tankard are height overall 7½ inches, top diameter 4 inches, bottom diameter 4½ inches. The cups measure 5⅜ inches high, 5 inches top diameter, 3⁹⁄₁₆ bottom diameter.

799 and 800. The patens are an even more surprising discovery. As can be seen, they are not true plates. A strip of thin metal, ¾ inch wide, has been formed into a circle to make a miniature dish ring and to the top of the ring has been welded a dished circular sheet of 6-inch diameter. The design is perhaps unique in American pewter. The fact that all five units are decorated with beaded edges at the joints gives a unity of composition to the set that can be equalled by few if any other church services. Courtesy of the Department of History, General Assembly of the United Presbyterian Church in the United States of America, Philadelphia.

PLATE XCVII

791   794   792   795   793

796   799   797   800   798

Plate XCVIII — *Church Pewter*

801. Side view of tall pitcher illustrated in the Aaronsburg communion service, Plate XCVI. Perhaps the finest of all known American pitchers or ewers, a design of great dignity, simplicity and charm. Height 10¾ inches, diameter of base 5 inches. Courtesy of the Salem Lutheran Church, Aaronsburg, Pennsylvania, and Paul Auman.

802. Fine communion flagon on square plinth. Height 14 inches, base 4⅛ inches square. Engraved:
Evangel. Lutherische Zion Church,
Penns Township, Northumberland
Co. 1795.
Maker William Will, Philadelphia. Compare with similar flagon in Fig. 785, Plate XCVI, and with the Will coffee pot, Plate XCI in this volume. Collection of Charles V. Swain.

803, 804, and 805. Handsome late communion service. Height of flagon 12½ inches, bottom diameter 6¼ inches. Chalices, height 6¾ inches, diameter of top and bottom 4 inches. Israel Trask, Beverly, Massachusetts, *c.* 1813–1856. Collection of Charles V. Swain.

PLATE XCVIII

801

802

803 804 805

PLATE **XCIX**—*Communion Flagon*

806. Unusually fine flagon. Height overall 12¾ inches, height without lid 10 inches, top diameter 4¼ inches, bottom diameter 5½ inches. Touch 477a, the hallmarks of Philip Will, probably made in New York during his early years, *c.* 1760–1768. Said to have been used in a small church in western Connecticut. For comment, see page 104. Collection of Mr. and Mrs. Oliver W. Deming.

PLATE XCIX

806

Plate XCIX a

806a and 806b. Two views of probably the finest known Connecticut flagon. Height overall 12⅛ inches, height to cover 9½ inches, top diameter 4¼ inches, bottom diameter 6 inches. Touch Fig. 400. Maker, Samuel Danforth of Hartford, 1795–1816. The handle and thumbpiece are of surprisingly early design for a nineteenth-century flagon. Almost as unexpected on a Connecticut piece is the elaborate, sophisticated engraving of the cypher with initials P.R. For additional comment see page 61. Collection of Abraham Brooks.

806a

806b

PLATE C — *Tall Altar Candlesticks*

807 and 808. One of two pairs of tall candlesticks formerly used in a church in eastern Pennsylvania, probably near Reading. Now in the Henry Francis du Pont Winterthur Museum. The height of each candlestick is 22¼ inches overall. So definitely Continental is the style of these sticks that any collector, interested only in American pewter, would probably have failed to examine them; but on each stick is impressed on one of the panels of the base with touches 532 and 533, used by the Lancaster pewterer Johann Christopher Heyne, 1756–1780. Courtesy of the Henry Francis du Pont Winterthur Museum.

PLATE C

807   808

PLATE CI — *Baptismal Basins and Chalices*

809. Baptismal basin with wide bead on upper face of the brim. Diameter 11$\frac{3}{8}$ inches, height 3$\frac{1}{16}$ inches. Touch 490, Henry Will, New York and Albany, 1761–1793. Courtesy of the Henry Francis du Pont Winterthur Museum.

810. Shallow baptismal basin with beaded brim. Diameter 10$\frac{5}{8}$ inches, height 1$\frac{5}{8}$ inches. Touches 537, 540, Colonel William Will, Philadelphia, 1763–1797. Courtesy of the Henry Francis du Pont Winterthur Museum.

811. Baptismal bowl with beaded brim on footed circular base. One of the handsomest of baptismal bowls, diameter, 10$\frac{7}{8}$ inches, height 5$\frac{1}{4}$ inches. Oliver Trask, Beverly, Massachusetts, 1832–1839. Collection of Mrs. Amos Kingsbury; courtesy of the Currier Gallery of Art, Manchester, New Hampshire.

812. Covered baptismal bowl. Height overall 6$\frac{1}{4}$ inches, diameter of bowl 7 inches. Hiram Yale, Wallingford, Connecticut, 1822–1831. Collection of Dr. and Mrs. Robert Mallory III.

813. A chalice of simple, chaste design. Height 7$\frac{1}{2}$ inches, top diameter 3$\frac{7}{8}$ inches, bottom diameter 4 inches. Unmarked but attributed to Henry Will, New York and Albany, 1761–1793. On two different occasions a chalice of this design has been found accompanying a marked Henry Will flagon. Collection of John H. McMurray.

814. An unmarked chalice of pleasing lines. Height 7$\frac{3}{4}$ inches, both top and bottom diameters measure 4 inches. Unmarked, but found near Lancaster, Pennsylvania, and believed to be of Pennsylvania origin, mid-eighteenth century. Collection of Eric de Jonge. Illustrated courtesy of him and the William Penn Memorial Museum, Harrisburg, Pennsylvania.

815. Two-handled loving cup or communion cup of late but dignified design. Height 6$\frac{3}{4}$ inches, top diameter 3$\frac{1}{2}$ inches, bottom diameter 4$\frac{3}{8}$ inches. Israel Trask, Beverly, Massachusetts, *c.* 1813–1830. Collection of Charles V. Swain.

PLATE CI

809

813

810

814

811

812

815

PLATE CII — *Chalices*

816. Covered chalice. Height $8\frac{3}{4}$ inches without lid, $11\frac{1}{2}$ inches when covered. Top diameter $4\frac{3}{4}$ inches, bottom diameter $3\frac{7}{8}$ inches. Formerly used in the Hill Lutheran Evangelical Church, Cleona, Pennsylvania. Unmarked, but probably of Pennsylvania or German origin, *c.* 1750–1770. The cup proper resembles, in size and shape, those found on the chalices of Heyne, the Lancaster pewterer, but in this design the stem is too short, the base too small, and both stem and base are marred by the use of too many horizontal lines. Courtesy of William Penn Memorial Museum, Harrisburg, Pennsylvania, and of Eric de Jonge.

817 and 818. Two handsome chalices that are unmarked but believed to be of Pennsylvania origin. The chalice on left is $7\frac{1}{8}$ inches high, top diameter $3\frac{1}{8}$ inches, bottom diameter 4 inches. That on the right measures $8\frac{7}{8}$ inches, $11\frac{1}{2}$ inches overall with lid, top diameter, $3\frac{7}{8}$ inches, bottom diameter $4\frac{3}{16}$ inches. A similar chalice, but lacking a cover, was illustrated as Fig. 241, Plate XXXVI, Volume One, *c.* 1750–1770. Both chalices shown here are in the collection of Charles V. Swain.

819. An unmarked chalice that has been attributed to Colonel William Will, Philadelphia, 1763–1798. Height $8\frac{1}{4}$ inches, top diameter $3\frac{1}{2}$ inches, bottom diameter $4\frac{1}{4}$ inches. The beading around lip of cup, base and central knop on stem is a customary decoration on Will's pewter. This chalice, as well as one in the Aaronsburg service (cf. Plate XCVI) are attributed to Will with confidence. Formerly used in the Hill Evangelical Lutheran Church, Cleona, Pennsylvania. Courtesy of William Penn Memorial Museum, Harrisburg, Pennsylvania, and Eric de Jonge.

820, 821, and 822. Group of three late chalices, collection of Charles V. Swain. Although all three are of nineteenth century manufacture, the designs are simple and tasteful. The chalice on the left, Fig. 820, once was attributed, probably erroneously, to Samuel Pierce, Greenfield, Massachusetts. It consists of a flare-mouthed beaker similar to, but not identical with, the small beakers of Samuel Pierce, which has been raised up on a short stem with circular base. The height overall is $6\frac{1}{2}$ inches, top diameter $3\frac{1}{2}$ inches. Probably of New England provenance, early nineteenth century. The central chalice, Fig. 821, is $7\frac{1}{8}$ inches high, top diameter $3\frac{11}{16}$ inches, bottom diameter $3\frac{1}{2}$ inches, Reed and Barton, Taunton, Massachusetts, 1840 or later (still in business today). The lines are simple and graceful in a period of over-elaborate decoration. The right-hand chalice, Fig. 822 measures $7\frac{1}{2}$ inches high, top diameter 4 inches, bottom diameter $3\frac{11}{16}$ inches. The chalice is marked "Palethorp's" — J. H. Palethorp and Company, Philadelphia, 1820–1841.

PLATE CII

816

817   818

819   820   821   822

Another example of inadvertence and faulty editing is to be found in the caption for Fig. 227 of Plate XXXIV. A beaker is there illustrated as part of a service "formerly used in the Baptist Church of Cheshire, Connecticut," whereas that same service is correctly stated on page 242 to have been in use in Cheshire, Massachusetts.

Although there are no errors to correct in the captions supplied for Plates XXXV and XXXVI, some additional information, now available, might be given about certain of those cups and chalices.

Touch 292, which was impressed on the church cups illustrated in Figs. 231 and 232 is now attributed, with reservations, to Robert Bonynge, Boston, *c.* 1731–*c.* 1764.

Figs. 238 and 239 show but two of the many variations, that might be illustrated, in the stems and bases of Heyne chalices. He probably had brass moulds for the cup of his chalice but used moulds of short-lived materials for making the knops and other sections between cup and base. As a result his chalices vary considerably in height and the knops differ both in shape and size.

Fig. 240, thought to have been made by William Will, can now be attributed to him with greater confidence, because of further discoveries of similar chalices found with marked Will flagons.

Fig. 243 has been identified as a form made by the Boardmans of Hartford.

Before taking up consideration of individual pewterers and their work, we should make one correction to a caption that accompanied an illustration on Plate XLII. Fig. 273 pictured a gravy boat, marked with touch 594 which, according to the caption, was "probably American." It now seems well established that this was a touch of Henry Joseph, London pewterer.

THE PEWTERERS OF MASSACHUSETTS BAY

ONE of the most interesting developments in recent years, in the history of American pewter, has been a succession of discoveries of dishes of early form, now believed with confidence to have been made in Massachusetts, all of them certainly before 1710 and some, with little doubt, during the final quarter of the seventeenth century.

The first published announcement of such discoveries was made by Dr. Reginald F. French in an article entitled "The Dolbeares," which appeared in the May 1954 issue of the *Bulletin* of the Pewter Collectors' Club of America. Therein were illustrated two dishes of patently early form, one with extremely wide smooth brim, the other with multiple-reeded brim (see Plate LXXXI, Figs. 693 and 694), designs that had been in vogue in England throughout the second half of the seventeenth century, though destined to be supplanted about 1705 by a medium-width rim with single reed on its upper face. In other words the form of these dishes was exactly what should have been looked for in Colonial plates at the close of the seventeenth century.

Both dishes illustrated, as well as two others with multiple reeding and one with a smooth brim, were owned or had been examined carefully by French and all were commented upon in the text.

All five examples had turned up separately at different locations in Massachusetts or Connecticut and, strikingly, all were marked abnormally, as far as our experience with Colonial marking was concerned, by the stamping on the upper face of the brim, of a very small initial touch or pseudo-hallmark, struck four times on each dish in what was intended to be an even line, but the spacing of the touches was in all cases slightly uneven, clear evidence of the work of men who had not been subjected to the rigid apprenticeship training of a London pewterer. In each case, only one die was used to strike the four individual impressions. On four of the dishes the design of the little pseudo-hallmark was a shield enclosing the initials E.D. above five stars; the fifth was in the shape of a heart with the initials I.D. and three stars below. Attribution of the E.D. touch was made to Edmund Dolbeare, native of Ashburton, England, who made pewter in Boston and Salem from about 1670 until 1706 and possibly as late as 1710. The I.D. mark was ascribed to one of Edmund's sons, either John or Joseph Dolbeare. (See Figs. 831 and 832, Plate CIV.)

Reference to Cotterell's *Old Pewter* with its illustrations of hundreds of British marks, disclosed only four examples in which a single die was struck four times and in which the outline of that die was shield- or heart-shaped enclosing initials alone or initials with stars. In not one of those four cases was the place of work of the pewterer known. All presumably were country pewterers.

Another point made by French to support the attribution of these touches to the Dolbeares was that a number of the leading goldsmiths of Boston—John Coney, Jeremiah Dummer, and John Hull for examples—were marking their silver in the second half of the seventeenth century with their initials enclosed in a heart. What more natural than that a pewterer, seeking a design for his touch, should adopt a similar identification mark?

As French reported, these Boston dishes were hammered all over, though a little unevenly, and the final skimming was done haphazardly so that incisions were made under the reed. Here again is evidence that the makers were not London-trained pewterers.

Since 1954 five more examples, and possibly others unknown to me, all stamped with the E.D. shield have been reported. One of the five is an $8\frac{3}{8}$ inch smooth-rim plate, which, unlike the dishes, seems to have been hammered only around the booge. In addition to the E.D. touch, another early shield mark, impressed four times on the brim of a 17-inch dish with multiple reeding, shows the initials I.B. within the shield. This might well be the mark of John Baker, early Boston pewterer, who went surety to the town for Edmund Dolbeare and his family in 1682, when Dolbeare apparently was unable to meet his commitments. If this I.B. touch has been correctly attributed to Baker, the dish on which it appears must of necessity be of seventeenth-century manufacture, because Baker died early in 1697.

All of the available evidence and clues tend to confirm French's assumption that these early dishes are of Massachusetts origin and, particularly in the case of the Dolbeares, the attribution of the initial touches seems especially convincing. The special combination of the initials E.D. for pewterers of record, not only in the Colonies but throughout Great Britain, is found so rarely that no known pewterer except Dolbeare could be presumed to have used such a touch. Furthermore when French made inquiry of Ronald F. Michaelis, Honorable Librarian of the Society of Pewter Collectors, London, the latter wrote: "I am intrigued with your news of the multiple reed plates with marks of ED and ID and I will say right away that I have no trace of these ever having turned up in England. . . ."

From whatever viewpoint these dishes are studied, they fit so well the pattern of what might have been expected, that it seems all but certain that French's identification of them as of Massachusetts origin is thoroughly sound.

Far less successful has been the search for early Massachusetts hollow-ware. At least one tankard with double-dome lid, made by John Carnes in Boston at sometime prior to 1760, has been found (Plate LXXXV, Fig. 714) but, surprisingly, that is the only surviving tankard that can be positively identified as of Boston manufacture prior to the Revolution. Even more difficult to explain away is the scarcity of pewter pint and quart pots with touches of Massachusetts makers, and yet such vessels must have been turned out by the thousands in Boston during the eighteenth century. Today there are in collections perhaps half a dozen quart pots bearing a mark of Nathaniel Austin of Charlestown, as many more in quart or pint size attributed to Robert Bonynge of Boston, and a small number attributed on even less certain evidence to John Skinner. But why have we none by Cutler, Carnes, Simpkins, and their contemporaries? And must we believe that the later makers, Badger, Richard Austin, and Samuel Green, made no pots at all?

The story about Boston porringers is equally unclear. There have been no discoveries in the past quarter of a century that have shed any new light on this enigma. We have literally hundreds of porringers, believed to be of Massachusetts origin, that are marked only by initials cast in the handle or handle support, porringers which, in most cases, must have been made in the last half of the eighteenth century or the early years of the nineteenth, and yet the initials on the porringers do not correspond, except in one instance (S.G., which could be Samuel Green) to the initials of the more prominent Massachusetts pewterers who were active in that period. For instance, the two men who, on the basis of surviving plates and dishes, probably had the largest pewter-making businesses in the Boston area in the last quarter of the eighteenth century were Nathaniel Austin of Charlestown and John Skinner of Boston. In the H. F. du Pont Winterthur Museum is an account book of Benjamin Clarke, Boston brazier. In the years from 1769 to 1772 many transactions are recorded with both Austin and Skinner, Clarke purchasing pewter — mostly basins, pots and porringers — in exchange for old pewter. On one occasion Clarke purchased from Austin as many as eight dozen porringers in various sizes and from Skinner he bought six dozen porringers. Presumably Clarke was but one of the many customers of Skinner and Austin. And yet no porringer has been found with a known touch of either of these men, nor have the initial combinations of N.A. or I.S. been reported on any of the so-called Boston initial porringers. In fact there are but two porringers, known to the author, which bear a known touch of any Boston pewterer, two porringers differing greatly in design of handle from one another and from any of the initial porringers. Both have the R.B. touch (Plate XLIV, Fig. 292) which is attributed to Robert Bonynge.

We are therefore forced to return reluctantly to the not very happy explanation offered over twenty-five years ago, that the hundreds of surviving initial porringers must have been made — most of them — in Boston and Charlestown shops, late in the eighteenth and early in the nineteenth centuries, by pewterers whose initials do not correspond to those cast in the porringer handles, from moulds descended, in some cases, from much earlier makers, whose initials really did coincide with those on the mould.

For example, three of the commoner combinations of initials on those handles are R.G., which might have stood for Richard Graves of Salem and Boston; S.G., Samuel Graeme of Boston; and I.C., John Comer, Jonas Clarke, or John Carnes of Boston. This is only conjecture and perhaps very farfetched, but what more reasonable explanation can be offered for an enigma which seems to defy solution.

PLATE CIII — *Tea Caddies, Inkwells, etc.*

823. Lidded oval tea caddie with engraved decoration. Height with cover $5\frac{1}{2}$ inches, height without cover $3\frac{5}{8}$ inches, overall length 5 inches, overall width $3\frac{1}{2}$ inches. A handsome piece embellished at top and bottom with bandings of classic design. Marked "G. Coldwell, N.York," 1787–1811. Courtesy of Thomas D. Williams.

824. An almost identical caddie, even to the design of engraving. Measurements same as in Fig. 823. Faintly marked "Thompson." This is presumably, but not necessarily, the Andrew Thompson who was making pewter in Albany, New York, 1811–1817. Thompson first appeared in Albany in the same year in which George Coldwell died in New York. So strikingly similar in form, size, and decoration are the two caddies that one must wonder whether Thompson did not secure his training in Coldwell's shop. A search of New York directories for the years in which Coldwell was working in that city failed to disclose any Andrew Thompson working in any metal trade. Courtesy of Thomas D. Williams.

825. Engraved oval teapot stand on four feet. Greatest length $6\frac{3}{4}$ inches. An I. Trask teapot has long rested on this stand. Its owner has assumed that, although unmarked, the stand was made by Trask. However, note how similar the decoration is to that seen on the Coldwell and Thompson caddies, Figs. 823 and 824. It may well be that either Coldwell or Thompson was the maker. Collection of Mrs. Melvin H. Gulbrandsen, photograph courtesy of the Currier Gallery of Art, Manchester, New Hampshire.

826. Dishring, height $3\frac{7}{16}$ inches, top diameter $6\frac{9}{16}$ inches, bottom diameter $6\frac{3}{4}$ inches. Provenance unknown, possibly American. Probably late eighteenth or early nineteenth century. Collection of J. H. McMurray.

827. Inkstand or standish, $4\frac{1}{4}$ inches high with square base measuring $3\frac{3}{16}$ inches on a side. The drawers were used for sand and wafers. Touch 593, which had been attributed to William J. Elsworth, New York, 1767–1798, is found on one of the drawers. It is believed now however that the touch may be English. Collection of Louis Lyons, photograph courtesy of Thomas D. Williams.

828. Circular inkwell with central hole for filling and three holes near rim for quills. Height $2\frac{1}{4}$ inch base, $4\frac{1}{4}$ inch diameter. Touch 363, attributed to Thomas Danforth 2nd, Middletown, Connecticut, 1755–1782. Courtesy of Yale University Art Museum.

829. Priest's can with screw top and removable wafer compartment. Height with cover $4\frac{5}{8}$ inches. Maker Roswell Gleason, Dorchester, Massachusetts, 1822–1871. Collection of Dr. and Mrs. William B. Rice.

830. Funnel with rounded bowl and ring for hanging, diameter 5 inches, height $7\frac{1}{4}$ inches. Touch Plate CX, Fig. 882. Maker I.L. unidentified but possibly Ivory Lucas, New London, Connecticut, 1732–1747. Courtesy of Mr. and Mrs. Edgar J. Sittig.

PLATE CIII

823

824

825

826

827

828

829

830

The Dolbeare Family

Boston public records were so full, so carefully preserved, and so readily accessible for study, that the lists of pewterers, made over thirty years ago still stand practically unchanged. The few additional names of Massachusetts makers which will be added here now are, for the most part, men who worked outside of Boston and in most cases, part-time pewterers at best.

RICHARD GRAVES OF SALEM

Just to make slightly more complete our story of Richard Graves, his wife, whom he probably married shortly before coming to these shores, was named Dorothy, maiden name unknown. According to the vital records of Salem the following baptisms of children of Richard and Dorothy occurred: Joseph, 16th day, 8th mo. 1642; Benjamin and Elizabeth, 6th day, 6th mo. 1645; Mary, 16th day, 2nd mo. 1648; Richard, 6th day, 8th mo. 1650; Hanna, bp. 15th day, 6th mo. 1652; and Deliverance, 16th day, 5th mo., 1654. An older daughter Ruth, for whom no record of baptism was found, was married in Boston in June 1656.

Since the daughter Elizabeth died in Boston on January 2, 1661, it would seem that Richard moved to Boston from Salem with his family between 1654 and 1661, even though he still owned property in Salem as late as 1665.

THE DOLBEARE FAMILY

In a very carefully documented article entitled "Early Dolbeares," which appeared in the *New England Historical and Genealogical Register* — Volume CXII, pp. 170–178 (July 1958) — Winifred Lovering Holman has supplied so much additional detail about Edmund Dolbeare, his children and grandchildren, that it is possible now to revise and enlarge the family history that had been recorded in Volume One of *Pewter in America.*

Presumably Edmund was born about 1644, for, according to the Parish Register of St. Andrew's Church, Ashburton, Devon, England, Edmund Dolbeare, son of John, was baptized there June 26 of that year. His name first appears in Boston records September 16, 1671, when, in a deposition, he gave his age as twenty-nine, which, if correct, would push his date of birth back to 1642. In Ashburton also there is record of the birth of a son, John, on the ninth (or eleventh) of February 1669/70 and of a second son, Joseph, about 1672. Because the father was in Boston in 1671 it must be assumed that Mrs. Dolbeare (maiden name unknown) did not follow her husband to Boston until after Joseph's birth.

As reported in Volume One, Edmund apparently did not prosper in Boston and on August 15, 1682, John Baker, brazier and pewterer, went surety to the town for

Edmund Dolbeare and his family. It is conjectural that Edmund, in financial straits, was then merely working as a journeyman in Baker's shop.

A new chapter in Edmund's life, unknown to me in 1940, opened soon after 1682. The first Mrs. Dolbeare must have died and Edmund married Sarah (maiden name unknown). About 1684 the Dolbeares moved to Salem. There is record in Boston of the birth there of Elizabeth, daughter of Edmund and Sarah Dolbeare, October 28, 1684, but Salem Vital Records list the birth there of Elizabeth, daughter of Edmund and Sarah, on October 3, 1684. They also record the births in Salem to Edmund and Sarah of four other children in the years 1686, 1687, 1689, and finally on September 19, 1691. The discrepancy in dates and place of birth for Elizabeth cannot be explained, but it seems probable that she was born in Boston and incorrectly registered a second time in Salem. Because of this error we cannot be sure when the Dolbeares moved to Salem, but probably that took place about October 1684. From Land Court evidence we know that in a deed of August 13, 1688, "John Dolbeare, now of Salem, in ye county of Essex in New England, Shipwright, do acknowledge myself indebted unto Edmund Dolbear of ye Same towne and county aforesaid, pewterer, the full and just Sume of eight pounds seven shillings. . . ." In other existing Essex County records Edmund Dolbeare is shown to have been a resident during the years 1690, 1691, and 1692, in which latter year his tax was abated.

Soon thereafter the Dolbeares must have returned to Boston, for the birth of the sixth child of Edmund and Sarah was recorded in Boston, February 23, 1693. There is also record in Boston of deeds which Edmund witnessed in May and August 1694. Prior to that year there is no indication that the Dolbeares had been members of any church in either Salem or Boston, but, on July 5, 1697, in Boston, Thomas, Bernard, Elizabeth, Sara, and Martha of Edmund and Sara Dolbier [sic] were baptized in the Old South (Third) Church and younger children were baptized there in later years.

The last record of Edmund in Boston was a deed dated June 17, 1706, which he witnessed. He must have died at some time between that date and July 24, 1711, the date of birth of his grandson, Benjamin Dolbeare, who wrote in 1772 that "my grandfather died before I was born."

It can be stated, then, with reasonable accuracy, that Edmund Dolbeare made pewter in Boston from 1671 to *c.* 1684, in Salem from *c.* 1684 to *c.* 1693 and thereafter in Boston until his death which must have occurred between the years 1706 and 1711.

Earlier in this volume, pages 25–26, comment was made about the significant discoveries of at least eight flat dishes, a plate and a rosewater bowl with raised central boss, all of early form and all similarly impressed on the upper face by a single die, struck four times in a slightly uneven line. The mark, similar in design to marks of contemporary Boston silversmiths, shows a shield-shaped frame enclosing the initials E.D. above five small stars (Plate CIV, Fig. 831). All of the dishes were hammered all over, the plate only on the booge. The plate measures $8\frac{3}{8}$ inches in diameter; the dishes vary from $13\frac{1}{8}$ inches to $16\frac{13}{16}$ inches in diameter; the rosewater dish $12\frac{11}{16}$ inches.

The Dolbeare Family

The E.D. touch is found on two different types of plates or dishes, both designs normal in England in the second half of the seventeenth century and consequently just what we should expect of American pewterers, working at the close of that century.

At least three of the newly found dishes have an unusually wide smooth brim with only a very narrow bead on the undersurface. The plate and all of the other dishes, with brim widths comparable to what we would expect to find in eighteenth-century dishes, have multiple reeding instead of a single reed on the upper face of the rim. The two types of brim design can be studied in Figs. 693 and 694 of Plate LXXXI.

There seems no cause for questioning the attribution of this E.D. pewter to Edmund Dolbeare, but what we will never know is whether any given piece was made in Boston or in Salem. So much for Edmund Dolbeare and his pewter.

As we know, Edmund's two oldest sons, John and Joseph, were both pewterers. John had been born in Ashburton, England, in February 1669/70, Joseph c. 1672. Both sons would have been in their early twenties when the family moved from Salem and, up to that time, would presumably have been working for their father. As recorded on page 55, Volume One, Benjamin Dolbeare, son of John, wrote in 1772: "[M]y father and Uncle Joseph served their times with my Grandfather to the Pewterers Trade, in which Business my Father set up & added to it the Ironmongery Trade, both which he carried on to the year, 1740."

Benjamin did not state that his Uncle Joseph set up in business for himself and, because we know that he was a poor man and his record could not be traced beyond 1704, it seems altogether probable that he never had a shop of his own.

John, on the other hand, became a wealthy and prominent citizen of Boston and must have made a great deal of pewter, though pewter-making had probably become a sideline long before his death in 1740. There is nothing new to add to John's history, but a few excerpts from his will may throw some light on the man's character. Bequests were made to his wife Sarah, to seven children, and to one grandchild. In the following manner three of the legacies were recorded: "to my son Thomas Dolbeare, five shillings and no more because he misimproved £2000 which I advanced him from my estate . . . to son David Dolbeare five shillings, and the reason why I give him no more is because he has behaved himself very Disobedient to my self & my wife & still persists therein and because he married contrary to my mind & will and he would not in any wise take my advice therein . . . to grandchild John Dolbeare, son of Samuel Dolbeare, dec'd, 5 shillings and no more because said son Samuel, his father married contrary to my mind and consent." John was apparently a very demanding and trying parent.

Soon after the first of the Edmund Dolbeare dishes was reported, a very similar 15-inch multiple-rim hammered dish came to light, marked just as the E.D. dishes had been by a die struck four times in line on the upper surface of the brim, but in this case the initials were I.D. above three stars within a heart-shaped frame (Plate CIV, Fig. 832). So closely does this dish follow the E.D. pattern in design, workmanship, character of touch, and manner of marking that it may be attributed out of hand to a Dolbeare, probably to John, although there is an outside chance that it was made by his brother Joseph.

Two, and quite possibly three, of John's sons learned the pewterer's trade. James Dolbeare, born October 18, 1705, was working for or with his father in 1729 when he signed with his father a receipt for pewter pots and basins. In 1732 he married Mary Valentine from whom he was divorced in 1738.

On December 22, 1739, "James Dolbeare of Boston, Brazier" sold to Richard Smith of Roxbury, a dwelling house, shop, and land in Roxbury. His will, drawn November 7, 1740, was proved November 8, 1743. Whether he ever made pewter or was actually a brazier only, after leaving his father's shop, we may never know.

Benjamin Dolbeare, John's tenth child, was born January 24, 1711. At the time of his father's death he had not married and had had no occasion to bring down upon himself his father's irascible temper. He therefore inherited a large portion of his father's estate and, upon his mother's death in 1745, his father's braziery shop and business were left to him. In all of the surviving Benjamin Dolbeare records, that I have examined, he was termed a merchant. It is to be doubted that he ever made pewter in a shop of his own even in his early years. He became not only a wealthy merchant but also a prominent citizen of Boston. He was twice married and had eleven children, only four of whom were living at the time of his death in Boston in 1787.

Last of the Dolbeare pewterers was David, twelfth of John's children, who was born January 5, 1714, and had the misfortune to marry against the wishes of his parents, for which he was cut off with five shillings in his father's will.

We know very little about this man except that his wife's first name was Charity and that the couple had at least two daughters, born in 1738 and 1742. David is listed here as a pewterer on the authority of a Suffolk County deed of August 20, 1760, in which Thomas Dolbeare of Dorchester, Felmonger, Benjamin Dolbeare, merchant, David Dolbeare, pewterer, both of Boston, and John Dolbeare of same, shipjoiner, son of Samuel Dolbeare, late of same, deceased, convey property in Boston to John Scollay, Esquire, which property had been in the John Dolbeare estate. In another deed, dated 1758, David was termed a brazier. He died June 17, 1778. Because he was cut off in the wills of both his father and mother there is little reason to believe that he was ever able to set up in business for himself. He never owned any property in his own name and took no part in the town government.

Any pewter made by a Dolbeare, which may have come down to our day, was probably from the shop of Edmund or of his son, John.

JOHN BAKER

There is nothing new to report about the history of John Baker, early Boston pewterer, but a few years ago Dr. Joseph H. Kler acquired a 17-inch dish, now on loan to the Smithsonian Institution, Washington, which may be the work of this man.

[31]

PLATE CIV — *Massachusetts Bay Touches*

831. Touch attributed with confidence to Edmund Dolbeare, Boston and Salem, Massachusetts, *c.* 1671–*c.* 1710. Photographed from upper face of wide-brim $15\frac{5}{16}$-inch dish. Henry Francis du Pont Winterthur Museum, photograph courtesy of Professor Reginald F. French.

832. Touch attributed with reservations to Joseph or John Dolbeare, Boston, *c.* 1690–*c.* 1710. Photographed from upper face of 15-inch dish with multiple-reeded brim. Henry Francis du Pont Winterthur Museum, photograph courtesy of Professor Reginald F. French.

833 and 834. Coat-of-arms of Holyoke family as engraved on smooth brim of plate, marked with touches 290 and 291, "Semper Eadem." Collection of the author. Cypher S. Holyoke engraved on same plate.

835 and 292b. Touches found on similar plate. Attributed with reservation to Robert Bonynge, Boston 1731–*c.* 1763. Collection of John H. McMurray.

836 and 291a. Touches from dish of unidentified Boston pewterer *c.* 1750, possibly Thomas Simpkins. Collection of Mr. and Mrs. Paul R. Glazier.

837. Touch of Philip Lee and — Creesy, Beverly, Massachusetts, *c.* 1807–1812, from bottom of Federal period teapot, illustrated as Fig. 770, Plate XCIV. Collection of the late Mark La Fountain. Present location unknown.

287c and 292c. Another combination of touches believed to have been used by Robert Bonynge, Boston, 1731–*c.* 1763. Collection of John P. Remensnyder.

291b and 838. Touches used by an unidentified Boston pewterer, *c.* 1750–*c.* 1770, doubtfully attributed to John Skinner. Note that this London touch has been found in conjunction with "Semper Eadem" (290), R. Bonynge (292), T.S. Semper Eadem (836) as well as in this combination. Collection of John H. McMurray.

839. A touch of Samuel Green, Boston, 1779–1828. A slightly different die from that used for Figs. 302 and 303, shown in Plate XLVI, Volume One, from a 15-inch dish in the collection of Mr. and Mrs. William O. Blaney.

PLATE CIV

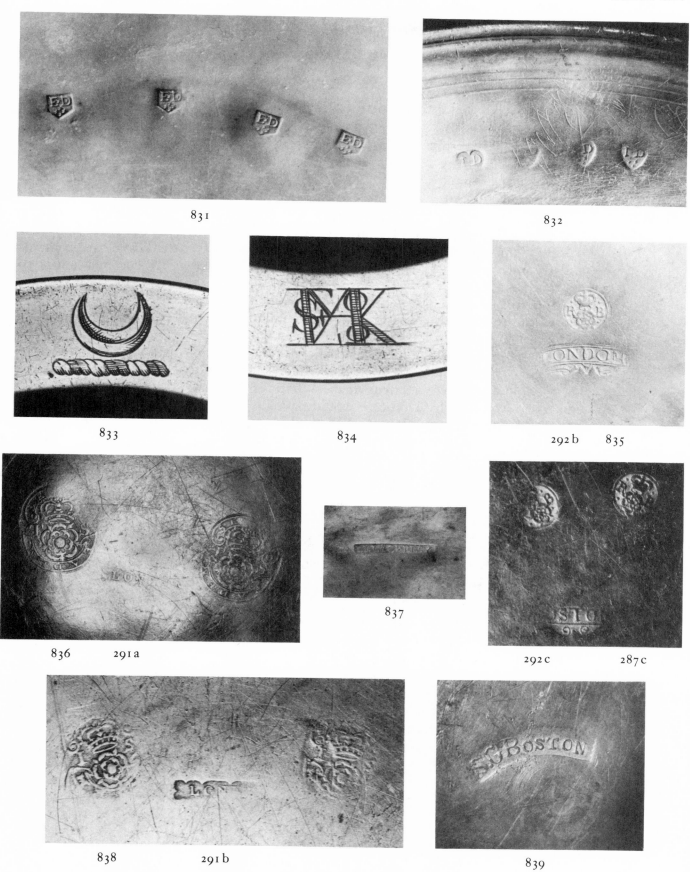

831

832

833

834

292 b   835

836   291 a

837

292 c   287 c

838   291 b

839

Somewhat worn and considerably corroded, this dish is marked in the same manner as the dishes, which have been attributed to the Dolbeares, see page 25, with a small initial touch, struck four times in series on the upper face of the brim. The die, very similar to that attributed to Edmund Dolbeare, is a shield-shaped frame that encloses the initials I.B. over five stars. The brim of the dish is not a true multiple-reeded rim, as was the case in the Dolbeare examples, but is an even earlier form, showing scarcely any reed on the upper surface and illustrated as "Type 1" on the late Howard Cotterell's composite plate, shown on Plate LIII, page 121, of *Old Pewter* —a type current in England early in the seventeenth century.

There must be greater reservation in attributing this dish and its marks to Baker, than was the case with the Edmund Dolbeare dishes, both because of the very early design of the plate rim and, more particularly, the fact that there were many British and Colonial pewterers with the initials I.B., whereas the E.D. combination is exceedingly rare.

On the other hand it seems more than a coincidence that the E.D. touch is so very similar to the I.B. mark, differing only in the initials. We know that Baker went surety to the town for Edmund Dolbeare and his family in 1682. There may have been a very close business relationship between these two men. If, as seems indicated, Dolbeare was in straitened financial circumstances at that time, Baker may have been employing him as a journeyman. Whatever the relationship, it was surely close enough to explain why Dolbeare would have been inclined to use a touch similar to Baker's. So, with reservation, the I.B. touch (Plate CX, Fig. 876) is attributed here to John Baker. The dish may be the earliest example of surviving Colonial-made sadware.

TWO NEW PEWTERERS—AND A SCANDAL

In the search for names of early pewterers in the court records of Suffolk County, I missed two men who appeared in cases before the Inferior Court of Pleas for Suffolk, late in the seventeenth century. To C. H. Paige we are indebted for rescuing them from oblivion and building a fascinating story around their activities, as he did in an article in The Pewter Collectors Club *Bulletin* for November 1950.

On the docket of the Court at a session held in December 1683 at Boston were two cases involving pewter.

The first was against Jonathan Fairbanks of Sherborn, now part of Millis, who was accused of putting false impressions on pewter. He was found guilty, sentenced to stand an hour in the pillory, pay a fine of ten pounds to the County, pay the fees of the Court, and make restitution to those whom he had defrauded.

The second was against Margaret Fairbanks, also of Sherborn. She was found guilty of putting marks on pewter with intent to lead the customer to believe that it was silver. For punishment she was fined five pounds and costs, but escaped the pillory.

The Pewterers of Massachusetts Bay

Mr. Paige found a more complete abstract of the judgment against Jonathan which read as follows:

> Jonathan Fairbanks of Sherborn, convicted of notorious cousinage by cheating in casting off pewter pieces with a stamp or impression upon them for good silver. Sentanse, to stand one hour in the pillory immediately after the next lecture in Boston, with a paper of his crime fastened to the pillory. To pay 10 pounds in money, five to the county, and to make satisfaction to the several persons whom he hath cheated, and likewise that he do give bond of 40 pounds to pay good money, for all the pewter pieces of any of his stamps that shall be brought into the Clerk's office within one month next coming and also that he shall bring in and deliver his moulds, and pay charges of prosecution and fees of court and prison standing committed until his sentanse be performed.

What was this heinous crime for which Jonathan and his sister, Margaret, were punished so severely? As Mr. Paige writes: "It is particularly interesting to see the long arm of the Worshipful Company of Pewterers stretching across the sea to catch these inconspicuous Colonials in an obscure hamlet. We do not know the exact nature of their offence, but intent to deceive must have been proven.... It is interesting to note that John Blackwell was fined 20 shillings at a Court of the Worshipful Company in London in 1683 for selling plates with no other than the silver mark...." However, very soon thereafter, the pseudo-silver marks were in almost general use by pewterers in London and we here are attributing to the Dolbeares and other early Boston makers plates and dishes which show no other identifying marks except small pseudo-hallmarks with initials.

And where did the Fairbanks duo secure the moulds in which their metal was cast? Well that brings us to the second new pewterer. In July 1691, Joseph Damon of Dedham, husbandman, brought suit against Michael Metcalf of Dedham, pewterer, but later withdrew his complaint.

I quote again from Mr. Paige's article:

> But let us have recourse to *The Fairbanks Family in America* by Lorenzo Sayles Fairbanks, Boston, 1897 . . . it would appear that the Jonathan and Margaret involved in this unfortunate incident were the children of George Fairbanks and grandchildren of the Jonathan who brought his family from Yorkshire to Boston in 1633 and established himself at Dedham in 1636. George . . . was drowned on January 10, 1682/3. His son Jonathan, born May 1, 1662, was the first physician in Sherborn, a most highly respected man, Selectman for several years, and Town Clerk for a time. He was drowned December 18, 1719.... Margaret was a younger sister born June 27, 1664. She married in 1684 William Holbrook of Mendon.
>
> From these data it becomes obvious that Jonathan was a little over 21 at the time of the trial . . . that Margaret was only 19, and their father had been dead for 11 months. Probably the whole episode was an ill-advised mercantile adventure of immature unguided youths. They certainly repented their crime, and led exemplary lives thereafter. . . .
>
> But we still have not explained where they got their moulds. It is of course only surmise, but Michael Metcalf was a first cousin. His mother, Mary, was a sister of George Fairbanks, and the first of her two husbands was Michael Metcalf, born in England, August 29, 1620. Their son Michael, born in January 1645, was the pewterer. Metcalf, rather than the Fairbanks children,

may have been the real culprit, standing in the wings and sending out his young cousins to sell wares stamped by him in a manner forbidden by law. If the pun may be forgiven, it is easy to understand now why Jonathan was charged with 'notorious cousinage.'

A further search among Suffolk County records failed to locate any information of a Michael Metcalf described as a pewterer. His listing must be based on that one court case of 1691. In my own mind it is highly doubtful whether Jonathan Fairbanks qualifies as a pewterer. Assuredly his sister Margaret does not.

JOHN HOLYOKE

Although John Holyoke was both a pewterer and brazier, pewter-making was assuredly his primary business, as evidenced by the many Suffolk County papers in which he is termed "John Holyoke, Pewterer." His business career must have begun in the first decade of the eighteenth century and there is reason to believe that he was still active as late as 1760. In his day he is thought to have had a large business and yet, strangely, no surviving piece of pewter can be positively identified as his.

Recently, however, Rockwell Gardiner acquired a pair of $9\frac{1}{2}$ inch smooth-brim plates, which may furnish a clue that eventually could solve one of our most baffling problems of touch identity and at the same time prove that examples of Holyoke's work have survived. The plates in question—and there are said to be four others that were once part of the same set—have a hammered booge and are each stamped with two impressions of the Semper Eadem touch, used by some unidentified Boston pewterer or pewterers, and in this instance accompanied also by a London touch and a crowned X quality mark (Plate XLIV, Figs. 290a, 291). On the face of the brim are engraved on each plate a Holyoke coat-of-arms and a cypher which seems to spell out S. Holyoke. (See Plate CIV, Fig. 834.)

What members of the Holyoke clan, living in Boston in the eighteenth century, might logically have used a cypher, spelling out S. Holyoke? Reference was made to a Holyoke genealogy in which were found four names anyone of whom might conceivably have been the first owner of the plates. The most likely candidate is Samuel, younger brother of the pewterer, who was born in 1693, died in 1768. Another possibility is a nephew Samuel, born in 1726 who died in the Carolinas in 1751, when only twenty-five years of age. It seems doubtful that he would have taken a half dozen plates with him to Carolina or that they would ever have found their way back to New England if he had done so. The other possibilities were Sarah, a sister of the pewterer, who married a bookseller in Boston, named Elliott and a niece, Sarah, who married the pewterer, John Skinner, in 1762. Although either Sarah might have used the cypher up to the time of marriage, it would not have been appropriate thereafter.

It is of no importance to us as to who first owned the plates. What is of interest is that the only residents of Boston who might conceivably have used that cypher prior to the Revolution were very closely related to the pewterer, John Holyoke. It does not necessarily follow that all members of the Holyoke family, when purchasing pewter, would have patronized John, but that would be a very natural assumption. If therefore these Semper Eadem plates were made during John Holyoke's working years, and if the engraving is contemporaneous, as it seems to be, it is a reasonable deduction that Holyoke was the maker of the plates and the user, probably the first user, of the "Semper Eadem" touch, which has long provided one of the most puzzling problems for the American collector.

One more thought on the subject. John Holyoke was reared in a family of considerable culture for the Boston of that day. His father, a brazier, became both wealthy and prominent and was one of the founders of the Old South Church. An uncle of the pewterer, in preparation for the ministry, had graduated from Harvard and John's younger brother, Edward, became Harvard's eighth President. The pewterer must have had a better education than most artisans of that day and the use of a Latin motto, as his trademark, would have come more naturally to a man of Holyoke's background, than to the average Boston pewterer.

There is no intention here to attribute to Holyoke the Semper Eadem touch on such tenuous evidence and reasoning, except with considerable reservation, but a better case can now be made in his behalf than for any other early Boston pewterer, except possibly Robert Bonynge, whose claims are presented on pages 36–38.

JOHN CARNES

In 1940 Colonel Carnes was represented in collections by but one example of his work in pewter, a $7\frac{1}{2}$ inch plate. Since that time at least three more plates of the same size have come to light and the Henry F. du Pont Winterthur Museum has acquired a quart tankard with dome cover and boot-heel handle terminal. This vessel, illustrated as Fig. 714 of Plate LXXXV is the only pre-Revolutionary tankard that can be attributed positively to any specific Boston pewterer.

THOMAS SIMPKINS

The latest discovery, among early Boston touches, is a hitherto unreported rose-and-crown mark that includes in its design the words "Semper Eadem" and the initials T. and S., Plate CIV, Fig. 836, all as impressed on a $13\frac{1}{2}$-inch deep dish.

Although Simpkins was already represented in collections with two touches, in each of which his surname was spelled out in full, this most recent find is also being attributed to him, though with considerable misgiving, because the same initials would apply equally well to Simpkins' older Boston contemporary, Thomas Smith.

Comment upon this newest of Semper Eadem touches will be deferred to pages 39–41, where the current installment of this fascinating mystery story will be continued.

ROBERT BONYNGE

In Volume One, on pages 66 and 67, were set down the two established facts in the life of a seemingly obscure Boston pewterer, as they had been recorded in the Boston Record Commissioners' Reports. Christened Robert, the pewterer's last name was variously spelled or misspelled Benning, Bonning, Bonynge, and Browning. We learned only that he had been married in Boston in 1731 to a Sarah Henderson and that he had applied for a lease on a shop in Dock Square in 1739 in which to carry on his pewtering.

Despite what seemed a further very careful search of Suffolk County Land Court, Probate and other public records, not another scrap of information could be found that seemed to apply to this man. This fruitless search was particularly disconcerting because Bonynge's career, beginning about 1730, seemed to correspond so closely with the estimated working years of an unidentified Boston pewterer, whose metal was marked with a small rose and crown and the initials R.B. in a circle, Plate LXIX, Fig. 292a.

Pewter stamped with this touch is more varied in form, more unusual in design, and more plentiful, though still very rare, than that of any Boston maker, whose career began before 1750. The touch has been found on church cups of early design with gadrooned decoration—cups that were made both with and without handles—on pint mugs in three different designs ([1] cylindrical drum with solid handle, [2] cylindrical drum with hollow handle, and [3] tulip-shaped body with hollow handle), on quart mugs with solid strap handle, 5 inch beakers, porringers with handles of unusual design in two different patterns—one with wavy-edge solid handle, identical to a handle attributed to Benjamin Day of Newport (Plate XIII, Fig. 70, in Volume One) and another with handle of open work design, Plate LXXXIV, Fig. 708, in this volume—that is almost identical with a handle that has been attributed to Thomas Byles of Newport and Philadelphia (though the handles differ greatly in the design of bracket or support), in pint and quart basins and in one quart tankard, as reported by the late Carl Jacobs, a tankard which I have been unable to trace to its owner.

The touch appears also on a number of plates and on at least one $11\frac{3}{8}$ inch dish. To the best of my recollection it never appears alone on plates, always in conjunction with a Semper Eadem touch, Plate LXIV, Fig. 290, with a Boston cartouche, Plate XLIV, Fig. 287, or with either one of two London place touches, Plate XLIV, Fig. 291 or Plate CIV, Fig. 835.

The Pewterers of Massachusetts Bay

The R.B. church cups, Figs. 231 and 232 of Plate XXXV, of a design that must have been discontinued in England before 1700, are unlike any other surviving Colonial cups. It seems difficult to believe that they could have been made in this country after 1740. Proof that R.B. of the rose and crown was working in the 1740's is evidenced by two surviving examples that had been engraved with their dates. The Yale University Art Gallery recently acquired a beaker that had descended in the family of Josiah Dwight, 1670–1748. This beaker is engraved "Dwight MDCCXXXX." The second example is a bellied pint mug in the author's collection which bears the inscription:

> The Gift of Mr. William
> Johnson to the Church
> in Southborough
> 1747

If, however, R.B. was the only user of the Semper Eadem touch, which his touch accompanies on a few plates, see Plate XLIV, Figs. 290b and 292, he must have been working for many years after 1749, because that Semper Eadem touch is the least rare of all pre-Revolutionary Boston marks.

For years collectors and dealers have been inquiring why the R.B. rose-and-crown touch had not been attributed, at least with reservations, to Bonynge. To begin with, just two known dates had been verified for Bonynge in Boston, 1731 and 1739. If we assume that all of the surviving R.B. pewter was made by one man, and not, in part, by others to whom his touch might have passed, his shop must have been one of the largest, if not the largest, in Boston at the middle of the eighteenth century. His principal competitors would probably have been Holyoke, Carnes, Cutler, and, towards the close of the period, Skinner and Thomas Green. All five of those men held one or more offices in the town government, all were property owners in Boston, three of the five advertised as pewterers in the Boston papers and three were members of the Ancient and Honorable Artillery Company, membership in which must have carried with it some social prestige. Even today we know of no identifiable examples of the work of John Holyoke or Thomas Green, just one plate that has been attributed to David Cutler and not more than half a dozen examples that bear the touch of Colonel Carnes. Skinner, who appeared last upon the scene, is the only one who has left us more marked pieces than "R.B."

How, under the circumstances, could one presume that a man, who never owned property in Boston, never held office in the town government, never advertised, and did not have the distinction of membership in the Artillery Company, could be expected to have been as big a factor in Boston's pewter-making as any of those more prominent competitors?

Reluctantly now, however, and with very real reservations, I am attributing the R.B. touch to Bonynge, for reasons as given below. Actually he is winning by default.

Suffolk County records were again combed not only for Bonynge but for any man with the initials R.B., who might be presumed to have made pewter. In both the Probate and Land Court offices the indexes were consulted and every entry of a name with those initials from the years 1730 to 1800 was examined. The same procedure was then followed at every county seat in eastern Massachusetts, as well as at Newport and Providence in Rhode Island. The only man who came close to qualifying was Richard Boylston, a brazier of Charlestown, Massachusetts. However, he was not born until 1722 and could not have made the Yale beaker, engraved with the date 1740, nor was he termed a pewterer in any of the many records in which his name appeared.

If therefore the initials, R.B., are those of a Boston pewterer, no possibility remains except Bonynge. Actually the case for this man is somewhat better than it seemed twenty-five years ago, because of the discovery in the Boston Selectmen's Minutes of two entries, which were somehow overlooked when material for the first edition was being collected.

At a meeting of the Selectmen on March 29, 1758, a list was presented of city firemen for whom request was made that they be excused from military duty. Included was "Robert Bonynge" of Engine No. 6. Again, at a meeting on January 5, 1763, John Brown, master of Engine No. 6 proposed John Foye as a member of his company "in the room of Robert Bonyne [sic] who has left." Note that the record reads "who has left" and not "who is deceased." Whether "left" meant that Bonynge had left Boston, or had merely withdrawn from the engine company, cannot be determined.

However these seemingly unimportant entries in the records do enable us to extend greatly the period of time when Bonynge was known to have been living in Boston, and presumably making pewter there, that is from 1731 to 1763. If Bonynge (and this now seems to have been the correct spelling of the name) was the maker of the R.B. pewter, it still remains a deep mystery as to why he never attained any position of prominence in the community. It is possible that, although he was an able pewterer, he was not able to operate his business successfully and, as a result, spent most of his working years as a journeyman in the employ of Holyoke or some other Boston pewterer, marking his pewter with his own R.B. die.

Attention is now called to what probably is just a coincidence but, if so, a most remarkable one. If Robert Bonynge had wished to identify for use in his own household any of the plates which he made, he would have impressed them with a triad of initials—B. over R. and S. Look at the combination of marks illustrated as Figs. 290a and 291 of Plate XLIV, Volume One!

JOSEPH RANDLE (OR RANDALL)

Joseph Randle, after all, may have been something more than a "lesser light of American pewter" as suggested in Volume One. It will be recalled that our last record of him in Boston was in 1739 when he and his wife sold property in Royal Exchange Lane.

J. K. Ott, in his search of old manuscripts for information about early Rhode Island craftsmen, recently came across a receipt which reads as follows:

> Providence.   Oct.ʳ 27th 1744
> Recᵈ of Mʳ John Thornton the sum of Six pounds
> Eighteen Shillings and two pence In full of
> all Accompts as witness my hand   6:18:2
>
>   Joseph Randle
>   Pewterer

It seems highly probable that the Boston pewterer sold his home in Boston in contemplation of an early move to Providence. His story will be continued on page 54 in a discussion of the Rhode Island makers.

"SEMPER EADEM"

The question of the identity of the eighteenth-century Boston pewterer, or pewterers, who used the enigmatic Semper Eadem touch (Plate XLIV, Fig. 290), has been one of the longest-unsolved problems of American pewter. Although proof may never be forthcoming that will settle the problem completely and definitely, several clues have turned up which permit deductions that the touch may, at different times, have been used in the shops of John Holyoke, Robert Bonynge, Thomas Simpkins (or Thomas Smith), and John Skinner.

Here are the pertinent facts as presently known, which might, upon study, provide the answers to our problem:

This puzzling touch is, by all odds, the least rare of all Boston pre-Revolutionary marks. It has been found on pint and quart basins and on a full range of plates and dishes from 7¾ inches to 16⅝ inches in diameter, including 9½ inch smooth-rim plates. There is no record of its having been found on hollow ware. On basins the die was struck just once but on plates and dishes there are usually two impressions. In some cases these are the only marks but more frequently they appear in one of the following combinations of touches:

1) with a Boston scroll (or cartouche), a die that was used by David Cutler, Thomas Badger, Richard Austin, and probably others (Figs. 287a, 290);
2) with an R.B. rose-and-crown touch, now tentatively attributed to Robert Bonynge, perhaps the rarest of these combinations (Figs. 290b, 292);
3) with a rounded-end rectangle, indented on top and bottom, enclosing the word London (Figs. 290a and 291);
4) with a larger London touch in a rather elaborate cartouche (Fig. 290c and Fig. 835 of Plate CIV in this volume).

"Semper Eadem"

The problem has been complicated further in recent years by the finding of two other Semper Eadem touches, very similar in design to one another, but bearing no resemblance to the better-known smaller mark. These later discoveries are illustrated, side by side, in Plate CIV. The rarer, and probably earlier, of the two touches, Fig. 836, has been reported thus far on only one piece of pewter, a $13\frac{1}{2}$ inch flat dish in the collection of Mr. and Mrs. Paul Glazier. The companion touch, Fig. 838, has been found on several quart mugs with solid strap handle of broken C design and double convolute terminals. It has been reported also on a few plates and dishes, including a $9\frac{1}{2}$ inch smooth-rim plate, a $15\frac{1}{8}$ inch shallow dish and two dishes measuring $16\frac{11}{16}$ and $16\frac{3}{4}$ inches, respectively, in diameter, two of the largest of Boston dishes, exceeded in size only by dishes attributed to two very early pewterers, John Baker and Edmund Dolbeare. There has also been a report of a 12 inch "I.S." dish, which I have not traced.

So, in addition to the problem of the identity of the user, or users, of the Semper Eadem rose-and-crown-in-gateway touch, we are faced with the determination of who "T.S." and "I.S." were, whose initials appear on the larger Semper Eadem touches. Was there some tie-in between T.S. and I.S. as the similarity of their touches would seem to indicate? May one or both of them have used the smaller Semper Eadem touch also?

Let us concentrate first on touch 290. On pages 34–35 in this volume reasons are presented for suggesting that John Holyoke may have been a user, perhaps the first user, of that mark. The principal evidence in support of the suggestion was furnished by the engraving on a set of $9\frac{1}{2}$-inch smooth-rim plates. On the bottom of each plate is the combination of touches that appeared as Figs. 290a–291 on Plate XLIV in Volume One. Engraved on the smooth brim of each plate is the Holyoke coat-of-arms and a cypher spelling out S Holyoke, presumably the monogram of a close relative of the pewterer, John Holyoke. Although it does not necessarily follow that John made the plates and owned the touch in question, that assumption seems logical but still lacks positive proof.

Another pewterer whose credentials, as an owner of the 290 die, seem even more impressive, is the "R.B." whose initial touch is found in conjunction with the Semper Eadem mark in Figs. 290b–292 on Plate LXIV. His claims which deserve serious consideration, have been set forward in the sketch of Robert Bonynge, pages 66–67 of Volume One and pages 36–38 in this volume.

Up to this point just two men have been put forward as likely users of the smaller Semper Eadem touch, John Holyoke and Robert Bonynge. Even if that assumption is correct, both lived so long ago that it seems unlikely that they were responsible for all of the metal so marked. Holyoke, born in 1687, probably was not active in business much after 1750; and Bonynge is not recorded as living in Boston after 1763. So much of this pewter has survived that it seems all but certain that a later pewterer was still using the die until perhaps 1780 or even after that.

Let us now return to the T.S. and I.S. Semper Eadem touches. Is there any evidence of a tie-in between T.S. or I.S. with the user or users of the better-known smaller Semper Eadem mark? There is indeed and with one another. An examination of touches shown in Figs. 836 and 838 of Plate CIV and 290–291 on Plate XLIV shows in each group of touches a London mark that appears to have been struck with exactly the same die in each group. It is also found on the 9½-inch plates that are engraved with the Holyoke cypher. Very evidently that London die served its time in a number of Boston shops and probably was used, year after year, for something like half a century. If, as may well have been the case, the small Semper Eadem die passed with the London die to each new owner, both T.S. and I.S. owned and perhaps used it.

Who were "T.S." and "I.S."? Although there may have been pewterers working in Boston in the eighteenth century whose initials were T.S. or I.S., men who are now unknown to us, our field of choice is limited to those pewterers whose names and records are known. In that category are two with the initials T.S.; one with I.S.

Thomas Smith, whose business career began about 1700 and Thomas Simpkins, who appeared upon the scene about 1727 and died in 1766, are possibilities. Either man, conceivably, could have been responsible for the T.S. Semper Eadem touch, but for reasons which will soon be apparent, Simpkins seems the logical choice.

John Skinner is the only recorded Boston pewterer of the eighteenth century with the initials, I.S. He must have begun the making of pewter shortly before 1760 and his career would have overlapped that of Simpkins by a very few years. The two touches are so very much alike in size, design, and character, that it would be difficult to believe that there had not been some close business relationship between the men who used them. Perhaps Skinner served his apprenticeship to Simpkins; maybe they were partners for a few years; or possibly Skinner acquired the older man's tools and dies upon the latter's retirement or death.

Although the I.S. Semper Eadem touch has been attributed to Skinner with very little questioning by collectors generally, it should be pointed out that Skinner's known touches bear no resemblance whatever, in design, feeling, or character to the I.S. Semper Eadem mark. Perhaps that is not significant but the writer is loath to award the touch to him without very real reservations.

The Semper Eadem mystery may be no closer to solution than it was forty or fifty years ago, but claims, tenuous to be sure, have been put forward in behalf of four Boston pewterers, Holyoke, Bonynge, Simpkins, and Skinner, one or all of whom may have used one or more of the three Semper Eadem touches.

PETER BLIN AND DAVID FLAGG

One brief fact may be added to David Flagg's history. In the Essex Gazette, August 25 to September 1, 1772 the following notice appeared:

Died at Boston, Mr. David Flagg, Pewterer

JOHN SKINNER

Much that might have been written here about John Skinner has already been presented in the discussion concerning "Semper Eadem" on pages 39–41 in this volume.

There is nothing new to add about this maker's history, but many more examples of his work, impressed with his touches that have been long-known to us, have been added to collections. The range of his work now includes plates with normal brim measuring from $7\frac{5}{8}$ to 9 inches in diameter, smooth-rim plates in the $8\frac{7}{8}$ to $9\frac{1}{2}$ inch range, semideep $12\frac{1}{2}$ inch dishes and flat dishes from 12 inches to $15\frac{1}{16}$ inches; also quart and three-pint basins. An unusual form with Skinner's lion touch is a tray, made of a $9\frac{1}{8}$ inch smooth brim plate, mounted on three bent-knee legs, just such legs as might have supported a small creamer. Still unreported is any hollow-ware, bearing any of Skinner's normal touches.

However two or three other touches are now being attributed to Skinner, on account of the discovery of pewter marked with a rose-and-crown touch showing the words "Semper Eadem" and the initials "I.S." (see Plate CIV, Fig. 838). Because we know of no Boston pewterer, other than Skinner, working in colonial times, whose first initial is I or J and second initial S, it has been assumed that he must have been the user of this touch, which has been found on at least one $9\frac{1}{2}$-inch plate, on a few flat dishes ranging in size from 12 inches to $16\frac{3}{4}$ inches and on several handsome quart mugs with an unusual broken C solid handle with double convolute terminals (see Plate LXXXVII, Fig. 727).

If it would be correct to attribute this touch to Skinner, would it not seem natural to believe that he must also have been the user of the far-better-known small Semper Eadem mark (Plate XLIV, Fig. 290)? Does it seem likely that two different shops in Boston would, contemporaneously, be using touches which included the same Latin motto? What's more, both Semper Eadem touches have been found in conjunction with a London touch, which also accompanies, occasionally, an R.B. rose-and-crown touch, attributed to Robert Bonynge (see Figs. 290b and 292 of Plate XLIV).

As explained in the discussion about Semper Eadem on page 39 the problem has been further confounded by the recent appearance of still another Semper Eadem touch. This new mark, Plate CIV, Fig. 836, is almost identical with the I.S. touch except that the initials are T.S. instead of I.S. So nearly alike are the designs that one wonders whether T.S. and I.S. were not members of the same family; either that, or one of them succeeded to the business of the other. Certainly there must be doubt that Skinner used either of the first two Semper Eadem touches.

Another cause for moving slowly in attributing Semper Eadem touches to Skinner is that the I.S. mark would then be the largest of all Skinner marks and yet it was used on the inside of quart mugs. Does it seem logical that the large die would have been employed in such cramped quarters when smaller dies were also available?

Last of the touches, which have been put forward as Skinner's, is one that was shown in Volume Two, Plate LXIX, Fig. 578, and recorded there as the mark of an unidentified maker. It shows what was then believed to have been a horse with one raised foreleg. It had been seen in a pint mug with early form of handle and in what was then the only known quart mug with broken C handle, of the same type as that in which the I.S. Semper Eadem touch has since been found. A much better impression of the touch discloses that what had seemed to have been a horse was in reality a rather crude portrayal of a stag, Plate CX, Fig. 578a. The only reason for attributing this mark to Skinner is that both the I.S. Semper Eadem touch and the stag mark are found in what appear to be identical quart mugs, vessels that might have come from the same set of moulds. However it should be remembered that moulds lasted a long time and passed from one pewterer to another. We need more convincing evidence before awarding the stag touch to Skinner.

So, with many collectors undoubtedly dissenting, the author will go no farther than to assert that the I.S. Semper Eadem touch is possibly, but by no means certainly, one of Skinner's touches; that the smaller Semper Eadem mark can be assigned to him only with very serious reservations; and that there is even less reason for thinking that he was the user of the stag touch.

EDWARD RAND

Edward Rand, son of Doctor Isaac Rand, was born in Charlestown, Massachusetts, September 4, 1750. Authority for listing him as a pewterer is derived from Lura Woodside Watkins' finding of two newspaper notices of this man's shop in the *Essex Journal and Merrimac Packet*, the first of which, dated January 5, 1774, reads in part as follows:

> Edward Rand
> Pewterer
>
> Informs his customers and others that he has to sell at his shop just to the westward of the Rev. Mr. Cary's Meeting House in Newburyport by Wholesale and Retail as cheap as can be bought at any shop or store in town, viz:
> Pewter Plates, Basons, Pots, Porringers, London Pewter Dishes and Plates, block-tin Tankards, Canns, Tea Pots and Spoons. . . .

together with a list of other items in brass, copper, iron, horn, etc. such as any hardware store of that day would have carried.

In another notice which appeared six months later he added, after listing the wares which he had for sale:

> . . . also
> He makes Pewter Plates, Pots, Basons, Porringers, Salts and all kinds of Tin Ware.

From the reading of these notices it would appear that Rand was equipped to manufacture only a comparatively few forms; no dishes, teapots, measures, or tankards. These latter forms he presumably bought from other domestic and English pewterers.

Because Nathaniel Austin's wife was an older sister of Edward Rand, it is but natural to assume that Edward was apprenticed to, and learned his trade from, his brother-in-law.

Rand was married to Ruth Sprague in 1781 and, after her death, to Martha Parsons. He had at least five children and died in Newburyport in 1829.

Sarah Ann Emery in *Reminiscences of a Nonagenarian* wrote that Rand had a shop and hardware business in the Market Square, Newburyport, and that these buildings burned in 1811. Because no one has reported the finding of any pewter, that could be attributed logically to this maker, it seems probable that his pewter-making career was comparatively brief and that in later years he was a general hardware merchant selling, among other commodities, pewter, but not pewter of his own manufacture.

EDWARD KNEELAND

In the files of the Henry F. du Pont Winterthur Museum is a letter written on October 20, 1783, by Edward Kneeland to the Tax Assessors of Boston begging release from taxes, a letter which throws further light on this man's straitened circumstances and the plight of the pewter industry in Boston at the close of the Revolution. The letter is reprinted here in its entirety:

To the Gentlemen Assessors

Edward Kneeland begs leave to inform the Gentlemen Assessors that he is taxed July 18th 1782 £7.12.3 March 14th 1783 £5.5.6 and July 24, 1783 £10.17.10 1/2 amounting in the whole to £23.15.7 1/2 all which remain unpaid.

I have spent much time and money in Public Service as an Officer of Militia and have sent into Actual Service not Less than Four hundred men for a Longer or Shorter time.

I have punctually adhered [to] the Several regulation Schemes — I have met with Losses by bad Debts & by Sea — The Peace has nearly destroyed My Present Business (a Pewterer) by the Great importations of Pewter from England — From all which Causes I have sunk Four Tons of Stock.

Finally I owe more money that I (at Present) am worth.

I am now depending on my Friends and my Own Exertions to Enter on some other Business in addition to my Own.

A vigorous Exaction of Taxes at this Time will severely Check my Exertions and perhaps incapacitate me from paying Taxes in future — I pray your attention to the above Circumstances, and that I may be relieved as in your Wisdom may seem meet.

I am Gentlemen your humble Servant

Edward Kneeland

The Pewterers of Massachusetts Bay

NATHANIEL AND RICHARD AUSTIN, SAMUEL GREEN AND THOMAS BADGER

When the stories about these men were presented in Volume One, each was given considerable space. In the intervening years many more examples of their work have come to light, but, in most cases these additions represented only duplications of what had already been found. Nor has anything of importance been discovered since about their personal lives. They are therefore lumped together here under one heading and a few notes are added concerning the range of their work.

To Nathaniel Austin's list of known forms can be added $7\frac{3}{4}$ inch plates with normal rim, $8\frac{3}{4}$ inch and 9 inch smooth brim plates, $11\frac{7}{8}$ inch smooth brim dishes and $9\frac{1}{4}$ inch (three-pint) basins.

Richard Austin made a smaller plate, $7\frac{1}{4}$ inches, than appears in his earlier list. Also, there is in existence a quart tankard that has this man's mark in its base. When the first two volumes of *Pewter in America* appeared, this particular tankard was in the collection of Edward L. Minor. Both Mr. Minor and I were a bit skeptical as to whether the tankard was "right." There seemed to be a possibility that a section of a marked Richard Austin plate might have been let into the base of an unmarked tankard to enhance greatly its value. That suspicion may be totally unwarranted, but the doubt persists, because such a prolific pewterer as Nathaniel Austin, who began his career long before Richard, has left us no marked tankard. It is doubtful indeed, whether such a form was still being made in Boston at the time when Richard Austin's business career began.

Nothing new can be reported about Samuel Green's limited range of known forms, but we are in position to illustrate one more of the man's touches, Plate CIV, Fig. 839, a slight variation of his touch, Plate XLVI, Fig. 302; in fact it may not be a variation at all—simply a clearer impression of 302.

The only additions to be made to Thomas Badger's recorded plate sizes are $7\frac{1}{2}$-inch plates with normal rim and $8\frac{7}{8}$-inch smooth brim plates. Reportedly he also made 8-inch and $8\frac{1}{2}$-inch smooth brim plates but I cannot verify that information.

One minor revision should be made in the captions for Plate XLVI as they appear in Volume One. In the third to last of those captions on the page facing the above-named plate, the figure numbers for the earlier touches of Thomas Badger should be 308 and 287a, instead of 308 and 287b.

JOHN GOOCH

In his *Guide to American Pewter*, Carl Jacobs introduced the name of a hitherto unrecorded pewterer, John Gooch. He reported of him merely that his locale was unknown, his working dates before 1750. On a tip from Jacobs and several important "assists" from Richard F. Upton of Concord, New Hampshire, John Gooch has been identified as a pewterer of Portsmouth, New Hampshire, who was working at his trade there in 1782 and possibly for some years before and after that date.

Strictly speaking Gooch is not a "Pewterer of Massachusetts Bay," but his father was a native of Boston, and, after all, Portsmouth is only just beyond the Massachusetts Bay area.

In November 1781, Seward and Gooch advertised in the New Hampshire Gazette the opening of a "Public Auction Room" where they proposed to sell at auction once a week all kinds of goods that might be consigned to them. Advertisements of the auction business, in much the same vein, were run in the paper until January 19, 1782. Then appeared, on that date, the following very brief notice.

> Cash given for Old Pewter by John Gooch, and one Pound of new Pewter for two pounds of old: Said Gooch makes and sells new Pewter. Portsmouth, Jan. 19, 1782.

Similar advertisements appeared until November 19, 1782. That is the only documentary evidence that we have of Gooch's entitlement to be added to our lists. What forms he was equipped to make and the extent of his business are unknown. No evidence could be found that he ever owned property in Portsmouth and no probate records for him or for his father, James, are on file in New Hampshire.

What further we know about this man and his family has been extracted from a genealogy entitled *The History of a Surname—The Line of John Gooch in New England*, by Frank A. Gooch.

The pewterer was descended from John Gooch, who settled, in 1640 or earlier, at Agamenticus, later known as Georgeana, and finally as York, Maine. His father, James Gooch, was born in Boston, June 17, 1719; married Mary Sherburne, daughter of Joseph Sherburne, "late of Portsmouth, N.H. and sister of Joseph Sherburne, merchant of Boston." James was a brazier of Boston, who moved, while still a young man, at first to Hopkinton, Massachusetts, and then to Portsmouth, where he had settled by 1747, or perhaps slightly earlier.

John Gooch, second son of James and Mary, was baptized at the North Church, Portsmouth, December 18, 1748. He married Mary, daughter of Michael and Mary (Hill) Whidden. In 1776 he took the oath to resist the British and in 1785 recognized the baptismal covenant and was mentioned as a very active lay member of the North Parish Congregational Church. The genealogy provides no information as to his occupation. He died in Portsmouth of "pulmonic fever" on March 20, 1824.

There is no evidence to indicate that John Gooch was more than a country pewterer with a small local trade.

LEE AND CREESY

In Fig. 770 of Plate XCIV is shown a handsome teapot of a Federal era design, formerly in the collection of the late Mark LaFountain. The teapot is marked on the outside bottom, Lee and Creesy, in a serrated rectangle, Plate CIV, Fig. 837. The close resemblance of this pot in design and decoration to the teapots of Israel Trask cried out its Beverly, Massachusetts, origin. As a result of the research of Mrs. Nancy Goyne Evans (see pages 171–172 of this volume) the identity of the senior member of this partnership has been established.

According to family tradition, as recorded in letters written in 1940 by a great-granddaughter of Philip Lee, he was born in 1786, probably on the island of Jersey, and was sent to this country by his father, before he had reached the age of twenty-one. Mistreated by a guardian, he ran away and started a britannia manufacturing shop in Beverly, Massachusetts. What his training was for such an undertaking is not known, nor could anything be learned about his partner, although there were a number of Creesys living in Beverly at the turn of the century.

If the family tradition may be trusted, the business was sold out to Israel Trask during a financial depression in 1812. This report fits in well with the statement of a Beverly historian, Edwin M. Stone, who wrote in 1843 that Israel Trask commenced the manufacture of britannia in 1812. No attempt was made to follow up Lee's later history.

THE RHODE ISLAND PEWTERERS

PERHAPS the most significant discoveries in recent years, in the field of Rhode Island pewter, are six or seven baluster-shaped measures, marked only with initials, initials however that have been attributed, variously and with reservations, to three different Newport shops. The earliest, and least questionable as to origin, are three measures, impressed with a touch showing the initials L.L. within an octagonal frame (Plate CV, Fig. 842) believed to have been a touch used by Lawrence Langworthy of Newport. Two or three more have a mark that, in each case, has been so badly erased that we can have no clear impression of the touch. The initials, in a rectangle, are purported to be I.F. and to indicate as the maker, John Fryers, younger contemporary in Newport of Langworthy. The last of the seven measures, with a touch that is also badly erased, is illustrated as Fig. 847 of Plate CV. Showing the initials T.M. in a rectangle, it is credited to a much later Newport pewterer, the elder Thomas Melville or to his nephew of the same name.

What is so surprising, about this flurry of measure discoveries, is the almost complete absence heretofore of marked American measures. In 1940 there was record of but one that had been made before 1800, and now, in Rhode Island alone, we have records of seven, all believed to have been made in the same town, Newport, but scattered in origin between three different shops.

One new name can now be added to our list of Colonial Rhode Island pewterers. A Joseph Randle (or Randall) was making pewter in Providence in 1744 and perhaps for a few years prior to that date. He thus becomes now our earliest maker of record in Providence.

Two later workers with Rhode Island training have been identified by the discovery of touches on plates that have come to light in recent years. One of these men, Ebenezer Crossman, although unquestionably trained in Newport or Providence, was a native of Taunton, Massachusetts, and, after a Rhode Island apprenticeship, worked in Hudson, New York. His story will be found with those of other Hudson Valley pewterers on page 116.

The second with his typically Rhode Island form of touch has been identified as a man named Tillinghast (see page 53 of this volume). He is presumed to have made pewter in Newport, but only for a very brief period, soon after 1800. What we have a right to hope for is that we may yet find records, if not metal, of pewterers who surely must have followed their trade in Rhode Island before Langworthy arrived in Newport.

[48]

The Rhode Island Pewterers

LAWRENCE LANGWORTHY

Of late years three lidded baluster measures, marked with an octagonal touch enclosing the letters L.L., have been reported. The late Dr. Madelaine Brown owned a quart specimen and later acquired one in the gill size. The quart measure, shown at an exhibition of Rhode Island pewter at the Rhode Island Historical Society in the summer of 1959, was illustrated in the Society's bulletin of that exhibition and appears again here, with the Society's permission, on Plate LXXXVIII. A third measure, in the pint size, is listed in Carl Jacobs' *Guide to American Pewter.*

The L.L. touch, Plate CV, Fig. 842, cannot be assigned positively to Langworthy, but no other pewterer of known record in England or the Colonies had the initials L.L. Furthermore the shape of the letter L, as it appears in that mark, is strikingly similar to the L.L. in Langworthy's full-name touch as found on the handle of a footed bell-metal skillet (Plate CV, Fig. 840). It is therefore with only slight reservations that these measures are attributed to this early Newport pewterer. It is particularly surprising that this mark has been preserved on such a rare form in American pewter as a measure, not once but three times.

During the spring of 1967 a 20⅜ inch dish or charger marked with Langworthy's English touch, Plate XLVII, Fig. 311, Volume One, turned up at an auction of an estate at Fairhaven, Massachusetts. Of course this dish may have been made in England, but Fairhaven is so near Newport that it seems quite likely that Langworthy made it at Newport and that it never moved far from its place of origin. If such is the case, which unfortunately cannot be proved, Langworthy would supplant his Philadelphia contemporary, Simon Edgell, as the maker of the largest of all surviving American dishes thus far recorded.

The most recent of Langworthy discoveries is a pint pot, or can, in the collection of Mrs. L. R. Schumann. This pot, with plain tapered drum, Plate LXXXIX, Fig. 743, has a solid handle of unusual form, unlike any previously reported on an American drinking vessel. Examination of the pot indicates that it may once have had a second handle. Handles of similar design are illustrated in Howard Cotterell's *Old Pewter* in Plates XXXV, Fig. c and XLVIII, Fig. a, as found on early eighteenth-century English examples.

The touch found in this pot, Plate CV, Fig. 841, has never been illustrated previously. Although heavily corroded and badly worn, its main features are sufficiently clear to permit ascription to Lawrence Langworthy, without much fear of contradiction. Not only does it bear that rare combination of initials, L.L., but, just as in Langworthy's large touch, Plate XLVII, Fig. 311, Volume One, two crossed weapons, perhaps a mace and a pike, beneath what appears to have been a crown or coronet, are the principal features in the touch's design. It is, in fact, exactly what we might have expected Langworthy's initial touch to look like.

PLATE CV — *Rhode Island and Connecticut Touches*

840. Cast name touch of Lawrence Langworthy, Newport, 1730–1739, as it appears on handle of iron skillet on three feet. Collection of Joseph K. Ott.

841. Initial touch of Lawrence Langworthy, Newport, 1730–1739, as found on a small cup which is illustrated as Fig. 743, Plate LXXXIX. Note that the touch is very similar to Fig. 311, Plate XLVII, Volume One, the touch used by Langworthy in England and possibly in Newport. Collection of Mrs. Lawrence R. Schumann.

842. Another L. L. initial touch, attributed with confidence to the same maker, as photographed near lip of a measure that was formerly in the collection of the late Dr. Madelaine R. Brown.

843. Early rose-and-crown touch of Samuel Hamlin, Hartford and Middletown, Connecticut, and Providence, 1767–1801. From a plate in the collection of the late Dr. Madelaine R. Brown.

844. Another early touch by the elder Hamlin, as found on 11½-inch-deep dish, also in the collection of the late Dr. Brown.

845 and 846. A touch which perhaps should be illustrated among the touches of unidentified pewterers, and this in spite of the fact that we know the man's name and the town in which he worked. The touch was photographed from a quart basin in the collection of John P. Remensnyder. The owner believes that Frink worked in Connecticut, but no record of any Northampton could be found in that state. It seems probable that the basin was made in Northampton, Massachusetts, but we have yet to find record of a Nathan Frink in that town before 1800. The design of the touch seems to point to a date prior to 1780.

847. Initials T.M. as found on a small measure in the collection of Joseph K. Ott. Attributed with some slight reservations to Thomas Melville, Newport, 1793–1806, or to his nephew of the same name, 1796–1824.

352c, 353a, and 365a. This combination of touches, as they appear on a dish in the collection of Mrs. J. Insley Blair and donated by her to the Metropolitan Museum, has reopened the controversy as to the proper attribution of the various touches of the three Thomas Danforths. (See page 67.)

848. Touch attributed, probably correctly, to Paris J. Tillinghast Jr. of Newport, *c.* 1802–1804. He moved soon thereafter to Fayetteville, North Carolina, where he sold a general line of merchandise. From a plate in the collection of Dr. Joseph H. Kler. Courtesy of the Smithsonian Institution, United States National Museum.

359a. A clearer impression of the eagle touch of Samuel Danforth of Norwich. (See Fig. 359, Plate LI, Volume One.) 1793–1802. From a porringer in the collection of Mr. and Mrs. Paul R. Glazier.

369a and 849. This combination of marks was photographed on a spoon excavated on the grounds of the Buttolph-Williams house, Wethersfield, Connecticut. The hallmarks (see Fig. 369, Plate LIII, Volume One) are those used by the third Thomas Danforth, Rocky Hill, Connecticut, and Philadelphia, 1777–*c.* 1818 or possibly by his father, Thomas Danforth 2nd, Middletown, Connecticut, 1755–1782. The other touch, Fig. 849, has been seen also on mugs but could not be identified as to user until this "Rosetta Stone" turned up. Courtesy of Arthur W. Leibundguth, Director, Antiquarian and Landmarks Society, Inc., of Connecticut.

377a, 380a, and 381a. A rare combination of Joseph Danforth touches including the lion touch of the elder Joseph, Middletown, Connecticut, 1780–1788, and two touches of Joseph Jr., Richmond, Virginia, 1807–1812. It is now known that Joseph's lion touch must have been used by his brothers Jonathan and William from about 1788 to 1807. Courtesy Henry Francis du Pont Winterthur Museum.

PLATE CV

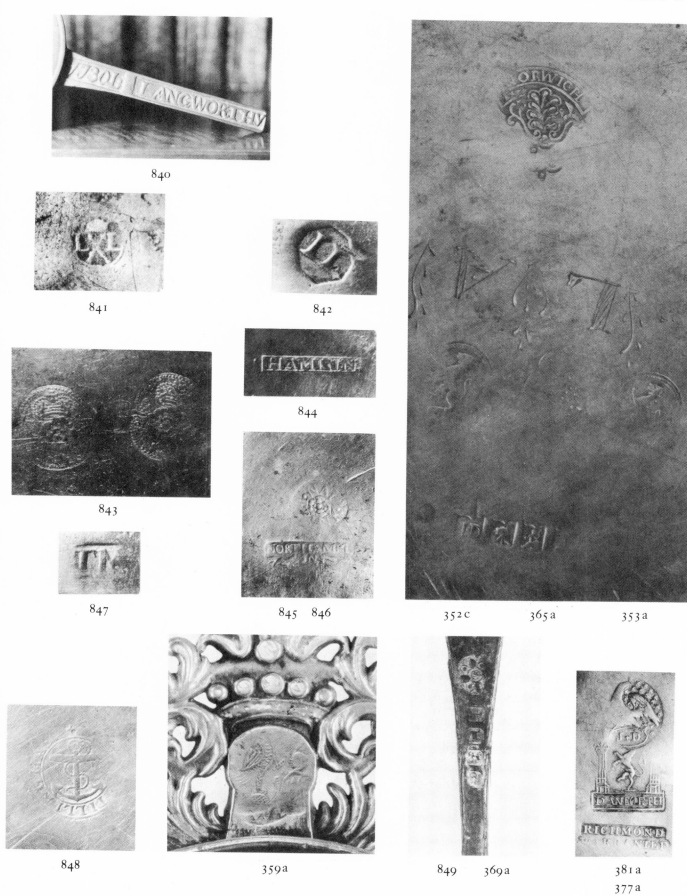

840

841

842

843

844

847

845　846

848

359a

352c　　　365a　　　353a

849　369a

381a
377a
380a

Benjamin Day

JOHN FRYERS

In Fig. 585 of Plate LXIX, Volume Two was shown a touch in a quart mug, formerly owned by the late Louis G. Myers, which mark he attributed with reservations to this Newport pewterer.

Recently Colonial Williamsburg acquired a tankard which had been fished out of the Ashley River near Dorchester, South Carolina. Although badly corroded as a result of its long immersion, the touch could still be definitely identified as this same Fig. 585. John M. Graham, Director of Collections at Williamsburg, wrote both to me and to Ronald Michaelis concerning the attribution of this touch. The latter replied, in part: "The mark is not recorded by Cotterell, but has been on my files for several years . . . [I am] certain it was English." This touch, therefore, should be eliminated from our lists.

At the Rhode Island Historical Society's exhibition of Rhode Island pewter, in the summer of 1959, a half-gallon measure, attributed to Fryers, was on display. This measure bore a different touch, a serrated rectangle, enclosing what purported to be the initials I.F., but the mark was so badly erased that only the F could be seen clearly, see Plate CX, Fig. 883. Attribution can be tentative at best. A half-pint measure with similar faint marking was in the late Dr. Madelaine Brown's collection.

BENJAMIN DAY

A touch with the initials B.D. enclosed in an octagonal frame, Fig. 312a of Plate XLVII in Volume One, was attributed with some slight misgivings to Benjamin Day, Newport pewterer, when the first two volumes of *Pewter in America* were published. Today those doubts still persist for reasons as given below:

What should have been noted and commented upon in 1940 is the marked similarity of two porringers with solid handles, that have an irregularly-scalloped outline. Compare, if you will, those handles, illustrated as Fig. 312a, mentioned above, and Fig. 292a of Plate LXIX in Volume Two. It should be at once apparent that the wavy edge outlines of the two porringers are not just similar, they are identical. The only evident difference in the two handles is in the size and shape of the hole from which the vessel was to be suspended and that opening may very well have been punched from the handle after casting. The point that is being made is that the two handles — and I have never seen another of the same design, marked or unmarked — assuredly came from the same mould.

So now we are plagued by a new problem. If we are correct in attributing the R.B. touch to Robert Bonynge in Boston and the B.D. touch to Benjamin Day in Newport, contemporaries of almost exactly the same age, what is the explanation for the use of the same mould by two men, whose shops were, roughly, one hundred miles apart? One possible explanation, that cannot be ruled out is that the B.D. touch was used by Benjamin Dolbeare of Boston, and not by Day. Dolbeare inherited his father's pewter and braziery business and may very well have made pewter in his early years before branching out into a general hardware business.

As Dolbeare enlarged his merchandising business, he apparently gave up metal manufacturing, for he called himself a merchant and is so styled in deeds. Bonynge might, at that time, have bought some or all of Dolbeare's equipment.

An argument, however, for the attribution of the B.D. touch to Day can be made on the basis of the design of the B.D. touch. There are just two American initial-in-octagon touches. The other is shown in Fig. 842 of Plate CV, attributed to Lawrence Langworthy, Newport pewterer. The same die-cutter may well have been responsible for these similar designs.

All that can be said is that we must keep an open mind about the touch attributed to Day. There is not now, and may never be, positive proof that he used it.

In the past twenty-five or thirty years only two more B.D. pieces of pewter have been reported, a second tankard with finial on domed cover and a third tankard, the cover of which never had a finial.

JOSEPH BELCHER, FATHER AND SON

A few more forms can be added to the 1940 listing of Belcher pewter. A number of $9\frac{3}{8}$-inch to $9\frac{1}{2}$-inch smooth rim plates, at least one of which bore the New London mark, have come to light. Reported also are a 6-inch plate, $11\frac{3}{16}$-inch dish, $13\frac{1}{2}$-inch deep dish, 5-inch porringer with crown handle, and pint mug.

To Melville T. Nichols we are indebted for uncovering a newspaper notice about the younger Belcher which appeared in the June 1, 1787, issue of the *Connecticut Gazette*, printed by Timothy Green in New London, which reads as follows:

Greene and Belcher
Pewterers

Inform the Public That they carry on the Pewterers Business at Mr. Isaiah Bolles' Shop in the Main-Street near the new Congregational Church, where they make all kinds of new Pewter in the neatest Manner — and sell on the most reasonable Terms, by Wholesale and Retail

All sorts of Ship Led [sic] Work done at said Shop.

N.B. New Pewter exchanged for old — and Cash given for old Pewter, Lead, Copper and Brass.

New London, May 28, 1787

On September 21st a sequel to this notice appeared in the same paper:

The partnership between Greene and Belcher, pewterers, was disolved [sic] the 15th day of August last.

Sept. 17, 1787

The reason for the dissolution is not known but the partnership lasted only two and one half months, just another indication of the instability of character of the younger Belcher.

Until the finding of these newspaper notices, no New London pewterer by the name of Greene had been known to collectors. His identity will be difficult to determine, because Connecticut public records fail to include the occupations of the individuals involved.

Mr. Nichols suggested that the pewterer may have been John Green, son of Timothy, printer and publisher of the newspaper in which the notices appeared and a cousin of the pewter-making Greens of Boston. This suggestion cannot be supported. The pewter-making family had no final *e* on their name. In the issues of the paper quoted above, the printer's name appears without a final *e*, whereas in both notices the senior partner of that short-lived business venture spelled his own name with a final *e*. Surely the printer, when editing the copy, would have eliminated that *e*, if the advertiser had been his own son. It might be pointed out too, that the Greenes of New London were a large and prominent family, whose most famous representative was General Nathanael Greene of Revolutionary War fame. The list of *Heads of Families for New London County in 1790* included twelve Greens or Greenes. Only two of the twelve were recorded as spelling their name without the final *e*—Timothy the printer and a Joseph Green. To prove who was Belcher's partner would require a more careful search of New London files.

Whether Belcher continued to make pewter in New London after 1787 is still not known, but in the census of 1790 he was living with his second wife, Hannah Wood, and one child at Lyme, Connecticut. He and his family were still residents of Lyme in the census of 1820. What his occupation was during those later years is not indicated in the census returns.

THE MELVILLES OF NEWPORT

The earlier lists of Melville shapes in pewter can be expanded to include 9-inch smooth-rim plates and quart mugs with solid strap handle made by David, pint basins with the marks of Samuel and Thomas, and tablespoons with the anchor mark that has been attributed to David's son, Thomas. This same touch has been found on a $14\frac{7}{8}$-inch dish which is also impressed with a much-worn New London rectangular touch. Photograph of this combination of marks is not available however. When, and for how long Thomas Melville worked in New London cannot be determined.

Of possibly greater interest is a half-pint baluster-shaped measure, Plate LXXXVIII, Fig. 740, in the collection of J. K. Ott. This is stamped with a badly-erased touch showing what appear to be the letters T.M. in a rectangular frame, Plate CV, Fig. 847. The mark is attributed to the elder Thomas Melville or to his nephew of the same name.

A David Melville porringer with flowered handle of unusual design is illustrated as Fig. 710 of Plate LXXXIV.

On Plate XLVII, Volume One, were shown what were believed, at that time, to be two different David Melville touches, each touch showing a porcupine as its central figure, Figs. 316 and 317. Examination under a magnifying glass leads to the conclusion that both impressions were struck with the same die. Incidentally no further examples of Melville's pewter similarly marked, have been reported in the past thirty years.

PARIS J. TILLINGHAST, JR.

In the April 1952 issue of the Pewter Collectors' Club of America *Bulletin* was a brief article by Dr. Adelbert C. Abbott about an 8-inch plate, which he had recently acquired, a plate impressed with a hitherto unknown mark of an American pewterer. Another impression of that touch from a second 8-inch plate, here illustrated as Fig. 848 of Plate CV shows an anchor in circle with the partially-erased name Tillinghast. The upper right-hand sector of the touch, where the Christian name would have appeared, had been completely obliterated on both plates.

The anchor was so reminiscent of the touches of the Melvilles of Newport, that the search for this unidentified pewterer turned at once to Rhode Island. There was once a large and prominent family of Rhode Island Tillinghasts, now spread far and wide, who were descended from the Reverend Pardon Tillinghast, who was born about 1622 in England, emigrated from Beachy Head, Sussex, and arrived at Providence in 1645. In that small settlement he is said to have become the town's wealthiest merchant, furnished the funds for the erection of the First Baptist Church and then became its pastor. He died in 1717 or 1718.

Despite diligent search by Dr. Abbott's agents and later by me, no record could be found in Rhode Island of any Tillinghast who was recorded as having worked in pewter. Each generation had at least one merchant, but none that gave evidence of pewter-making. For reasons which follow, the man who seemed to come closest to qualifying as a pewterer, was Paris J. Tillinghast, Jr.

One of the grandsons of the Reverend Pardon Tillinghast was Nicholas who became a Lieutenant Governor and Judge in Rhode Island. On December 26, 1754, he married, as his second wife, Joanna, daughter of Judge Daniel and Joanna Scott Jenckes. Born of this marriage in March 1757 was a son, Paris Jenckes Tillinghast, who, in surviving records, was termed a merchant.

In early life Paris had a house and shop in Providence. On November 13, 1777, he married Elizabeth Pearce and they proceeded to raise a large family. Their second son, Paris J., Jr., was born July 18, 1780. At some time before 1790 the family moved to Albany, New York, where this unusual name appears among the *Heads of Families in the Census of 1790*. The family could not have remained in Albany for long because a Providence deed for 1795 mentions Paris as a merchant of Uxbridge, Massachusetts, in that year. Soon thereafter the family returned to Providence, as proved by a deed of 1799.

It should be interjected here that another plate turned up with a badly erased Tillinghast mark, but accompanied by a Newport place name in rectangular touch. Unfortunately no photograph of this combination of touches was obtainable. Up to this point there had been no evidence of any ties of the Tillinghast family with Newport. But on August 14, 1802, the *Providence Gazette* announced the marriage of Paris J. Tillinghast, Jr., merchant and Mrs. Emma Hurley "both formerly of this town, at Newport." It is quite within the realm of possibility that young Tillinghast had been apprenticed to one of the Melvilles and had been living in Newport for a number of years prior to his marriage.

Soon after that marriage, Paris Tillinghast, Sr., and his family moved to Fayetteville, North Carolina, and the bride and groom must have followed soon thereafter. As early as April 1804 Paris, Sr., and Samuel Pearce, who may have been his brother-in-law, bought property in Fayetteville and just two months later Paris, Jr., bought a lot on Pearson Street.

On May 7, 1812, Jacob Eggleston of Middletown, Connecticut, Daniel Bass of Berlin, Connecticut, and Oliver Pearce and Paris J. Tillinghast, Jr., of Fayetteville sold property on Cold Spring Street. The evident business relationship between the pewterer, Eggleston, and young Tillinghast may be another straw in the wind indicating the probable maker of the Tillinghast pewter. All available records in North Carolina indicate that both Tillinghasts, father and son, were primarily merchants. There is no evidence that either one ever made pewter in North Carolina.

The first Mrs. Paris Tillinghast, Jr., must have died soon after moving to Fayetteville. The widower married, second, Eliza Voorhees Henley of Fayetteville. The elder Tillinghast died in Fayetteville in 1822. In what was known as "the great fire" in Fayetteville in 1831, Paris junior was listed as one of those whose property was destroyed. About 1838 he moved to Columbus, Georgia, where he died November 24, 1868.

There is still no evidence that Paris, Jr., was the pewterer, but his dates, his known residence in Newport and his business relationship with Jacob Eggleston, make his credentials far more acceptable than those of any other member of the Tillinghast family.

JOSEPH RANDLE

In the files of the Rhode Island Historical Society, Joseph K. Ott discovered a bill which reads as follows:

The Rhode Island Pewterers

Providence, Oct. 27, 1744

Received of Mr. John Thornton the sum of six pounds, eighteen shillings and two pence in full of all accounts as witness my hand.

Joseph Randle
Pewterer

With this discovery Randle becomes the earliest pewterer of whom we have record in Providence. When he first appeared there is not known, but at a meeting of the General Assembly on the last Wednesday of October 1744, "Joseph Randall, son of William" was one of five citizens of Providence who were admitted as Freemen of the Colony. On October 16, 1750 Joseph Randle, brazier, died in Providence.

If, as seems probable, this Joseph Randle (Randall) was the Boston brazier and pewterer (see Volume One, page 67), he was born in Boston, December 10, 1691, a son of William, a japanner, and Elizabeth Hall Randoll [sic]. On August 8, 1738, he was wed to Mary, only child of Samuel Plumer, cooper, a very late marriage, unless this was his second wife. Less than one month later, Joseph, termed a brazier, and his wife Mary sold property in Shrimpton's Lane and, in the following year (1740), "Joseph Randle, Puterer" and Mary disposed of property in Royal Exchange Lane, which she had inherited from her father. It seems altogether probable that these sales were made in anticipation of removal of Randle's shop to Providence, which may have occurred in 1740 or 1741 because the man's name disappears from Boston records after 1740.

SAMUEL HAMLIN AND SAMUEL E. HAMLIN

Because of the discovery of two early newspaper notices of the activities of the elder Hamlin, it is now possible to follow rather accurately his business career prior to the opening of his first shop in Providence.

The following advertisement in the *Connecticut Courant*, July 13, 1767, must have been the announcement of the opening of Hamlin's first shop at a time when he was just twenty-one years of age:

Henshaw & Hamlin
Braziers & Pewterers

Hereby inform the Public that they have lately set up their business at the shop of the Widow Hooker, near the North Meeting House in Hartford, where they make and have for sale Brass Kettles, Tea-Kettles, Coffee Pots, Quart and Point [sic] Potts, Basons, Plates, Dishes, Platters, Porringers &c on the most reasonable Terms for Cash, Country Produce, old Pewter, Brass, or old Copper. . . .

Later issues added the following:

N.B. He also gives the best Price for old Pewter, Brass, Copper and Lead.

Samuel Hamlin and Samuel E. Hamlin

It may be assumed, with little likelihood of contradiction, that this Hamlin was the Samuel of Middletown, Connecticut, and later of Providence, Rhode Island. But who was Henshaw, the senior partner?

To Miss Myrtle M. Jillson of Waterbury, Connecticut, the writer is indebted for the results of her research on the Henshaw family. It seems almost certain that the partner of young Hamlin was Benjamin Henshaw, next door neighbor of the Hamlins in Middletown.

About 1746 Josiah Henshaw moved to Middletown, probably from Dorchester, Massachusetts. In that year he purchased property abutting on tracts of Charles Hamlin, father of Samuel, and of Joseph Southmayd. Among Josiah's children was Benjamin, born about 1731, who married, first Elizabeth Lord in 1753 and second, in 1762, Huldah Summer.

On May 16, 1768 Benjamin Henshaw, at his store in Middletown, advertised in the *Courant:* "Tar, Pitch, Turpentine, soal [sic], Leather, Deer Skins" and other commodities. On November 13, 1769, a copy of a letter appeared in the *Courant* from a "Committee of Merchants in Middletown to Committee of Merchants in Hartford." It was signed by Benjamin Henshaw, Clerk.

Piecing together the available information about Benjamin Henshaw, one must assume that he was not a brazier or pewterer in his own right, but rather a general storekeeper. In less than a year after the opening of the Hartford shop Henshaw was back in Middletown, advertising the sale of general merchandise. It also may be significant that soon after the first Hartford notice appeared, the following issues said "N.B. He also gives the best Price," etc. The implication would seem to be that only one man was operating the shop. It may be that Henshaw, a general merchant, helped his young neighbor by lending his name and possibly capital to the Hartford venture.

Of passing interest is the statement in the vital records, at the time of Benjamin Henshaw's death, August 2, 1793, that he was "long subject to fits."

Another, and more significant, notice appeared in the *Connecticut Courant* for November 23, 1773:

> The Public are hereby inform'd
>
> that the Copartnership between Danforth and Hamlin is dissolv'd—and that the Pewterers and Braziers business is carried on in all their various branches by Samuel Hamlin at his Shop, next door to Mr. Jacob Whitman's, near the Great Bridge in Providence, where country traders shop keepers &c may be supply'd with any Quantity and Kind of Pewter ware on the shortest notice. He has nearly completed a set of moulds, of the newest and neatest fashions, and flatters himself that they will upon tryal give universal satisfaction. Any gentlemen that shall see cause to favor him with their custom, may depend upon having the goods as cheap as at any store in America, old pewter, brass and copper will be taken in exchange and where nothing new is wanted any person who has either of the above articles to sell, shall receive as great a price as is given in Boston in cash. Any gentlemen on [the] Connecticut river who may want any thing in this way, are informed that Capt. Jonathan Bozworth constantly sails from Providence to Hartford during the

summer season, and any order sent by him shall be duly executed, and the smallest favor will be greatfully acknowledged by their humble servant,

Samuel Hamlin

N.B. He has a number of brass Kettles of all sizes from one quart to a Barrell which he will sell cheap for cash.

Not only does this notice tell us that Hamlin was, for a brief period, possibly four or five years, a partner of the second Thomas Danforth in Middletown, but it pinpoints the date of his move to Providence. Even more important, it proves what we have long believed, but could not substantiate, that the better qualified of our makers, who were braziers as well as pewterers, made sets of moulds not only for their own use but also for sale to other pewterers.

Two early touches of the elder Hamlin have turned up since 1940 and both are illustrated here from impressions on plates in the collection of the late Dr. Madelaine Brown. The rose-and-crown touch, Plate CV, Fig. 843, is from an $8\frac{1}{8}$-inch plate and is the only known example of this mark. The name-in-rectangle touch is only less rare, Plate CV, Fig. 844. It has been found also inside a quart domed-top tankard, which, as might have been expected, resembles closely tankards made by Thomas, Edward and Samuel Danforth.

Other Hamlin forms, added to collections since 1940, are ladles, $5\frac{1}{2}$-inch butter plates, teapots, and small mugs with late double C form of handle. All of these appear to have been the product of the younger Hamlin's shop. However the father probably made teapots also, because J. K. Ott found in ledgers of a Providence turner, William Proud, charges against Samuel "Hamblen" in 1774 and 1775 for warming pan and coffee "pottes" handles.

GERSHOM JONES

To Wendell Hilt I am indebted for two newspaper notices which throw new light on Jones's activities and indicate how artisans in those days found it necessary to branch out into outside activities in order to "keep the wolf from the door."

In the Providence newspaper, *United States Chronicle*, of March 15, 1798, the following advertisement appeared:

Removal
Gershom Jones
Pewterer, Coppersmith and Brazier
Respectfully informs the Public That he has removed his Business from the old Stand in Westminister-Street, to his new Store in Pleasant-Street, directly back of his Dwelling-House. He takes this Opportunity to return his Thanks for all past Favors, and will be happy to wait upon all who may please in future to favor him with their Commands. At said Store he has for Sale, Excellent STONE-WARE, as cheap as can be purchased at New York or Boston.

[57]

To try to learn more about Jones's sideline of stoneware, Hilt worked backwards through Providence files and was rewarded with the discovery of the following notice in the May 12, 1791, issue of the same journal:

Wanted
A Labourer, to work in the STONE-WARE FACTORY of the Subscribers
Gershom Jones
John Dorrance
They have for sale (Wholesale and Retail) A great Variety of STONE-WARE.

To the earlier lists of pewter forms which Jones made can be added 9-inch smooth brim plates, porringers down to $3\frac{1}{4}$ inches in diameter, and pint mugs.

The suggestion was made in Volume One that the touch that was termed in Kerfoot's *American Pewter* as "Unidentified Eagle No. 1," and illustrated in Volume Two of this work as Fig. 600 of Plate LXX might be a touch of this man. The reasons advanced for that tentative attribution were: (1) that the touch had been found only on basins, and on a good many basins at that; (2) that although Jones has left us many plates, dishes and porringers, no basin, bearing his well-known touches had turned up; and (3) the crudeness of the eagle design was quite in character with the known Jones touches.

Since then J. K. Ott acquired a $9\frac{1}{8}$ inch basin, marked on the bottom, rather than in the well, with Jones normal touches, Figs. 339 and 340 of Plate L, very evidently an example of his early work. This discovery in no way invalidates the assumption that he may have used the "Unidentified Eagle No. 1" on his later basins. That attribution, however, must still be classified as doubtful.

WILLIAM BILLINGS

To be added to the earlier lists of Billings pewter are 8 to $11\frac{3}{4}$ inch basins, porringers down to $3\frac{1}{4}$ inches in diameter, tablespoons, and at least one quart mug.

Billings must have made ladles with wooden handles for J. K. Ott found entries in an account book of William Proud, Providence turner, of "long ladle handles" sold to Billings.

WILLIAM CALDER

The story of William Calder in Volume One (page 100) contained no information about his forebears. This was an oversight and, as it turns out, an unfortunate mistake, because an assumption has appeared in print that the father of the pewterer

The Rhode Island Pewterers

was also named William and also made pewter. So the record must be set straight here.

The Providence pewterer was descended from Alexander Calder, who was born in Aberdeen, Scotland, in 1660 and died in that city in 1715. Of his three sons, Alexander, William, and Robert, the second son, William, born in 1690 in Aberdeen, sailed for America and settled in Boston at some time prior to 1732. There he married Elizabeth Brooks, a native of Boston, who bore him five children of whom we have records. His occupation was that of a brewer. About 1766 he returned to Scotland, probably to settle family affairs there, and is said to have been lost at sea in 1768, while sailing back to America.

The third son of William and Elizabeth Calder, James, was born in February 1755. He served as a private in the early years of the Revolution. He learned his trade as a papermaker at the Milton Paper Works. With his wife Agnes Boies and their two small daughters he moved to Providence, Rhode Island, in 1780 to superintend the building of a paper mill. He continued in the paper-making business there until about 1815 and in later life was a miller and ran a grocery store. Although he removed from Providence, at first to New Bedford and later to Olneyville, Rhode Island, he had returned to Providence before 1840. He died in that city November 22, 1843, at the age of eighty-eight.

William Calder, the only pewterer in the family, was the seventh child of James and Agnes Calder. His history appears on pages 100–102, Volume One.

Although additional Calder forms have been found in the past twenty-five years, there have been no surprises among them. All, I believe, had been listed in the shop's extant day books.

Once more it should be stressed that pewter, marked with a rampant lion in archway and the name William Calder, is not American. It is the work of a pewterer of Bristol, England, who died in 1752.

THE PEWTERERS OF THE
CONNECTICUT VALLEY

ALTHOUGH the statement, that the story of Connecticut pewter is largely the history of the Danforths and their apprentices, still remains true, there must have been shops in that colony well before the first Thomas Danforth moved from Taunton to Norwich in 1733. Even before 1640, approximately one hundred years earlier, Hartford, Wethersfield, Windsor, New Haven, and Guilford had been settled, largely by colonists from Massachusetts. During the ensuing hundred years roads must have been few, compelling the settlers to depend largely upon what they themselves could produce, supplemented by occasional shipments received by water. It is difficult to believe that pewter-making shops had not been established well before the first Thomas Danforth settled in Norwich. Proof that there were earlier pewterers in Connecticut has been difficult to establish, because the public records of that colony rarely indicate the occupations of the principals involved. One such refugee from oblivion is Ivory Lucas, who was making pewter in New London at least as early as 1732. What little has been learned about this man will be found on pages 61–62. An examination of early inventories in the Connecticut State Library would probably uncover other, and earlier, makers.

Our judgment, however, about Connecticut pewterers and their work, must be based on the examples that we can see and handle. Collections today probably contain, in the aggregate, more pewter and britannia made within the narrow confines of that colony (and state) than in any other colony. Although the Danforths, who were responsible for our earliest identifiable Connecticut pewter, made good solid plates, dishes, basins, porringers, and to a limited extent other forms, their variety of shapes and designs is minimal. They gave very little indication of versatility, ingenuity, or artistic creativity. That so much of their metal has survived can be charged up to what has always been claimed for the "Nutmeg State"—that its merchants could sell anything, and did.

Many splendid early forms in American pewter, unknown thirty years ago, have been rediscovered, but not one of them bears the identifiable touch of a Connecticut pewterer. If the Colony ever had a pewterer with the capability of a Leddell, an Edgell, a Will, a Bassett, or a Heyne, evidence of such a man is still to be found. The lack of variety in form, of imagination in design, and, in many cases, of careful finish by the eighteenth-century Connecticut pewterers, points up the fact that they were, generally speaking, country makers with few moulds, catering to an unsophisticated clientele.

It is true, however, that, after 1810, Thomas D. Boardman and his brother Sherman, had no peers, with the possible exception of the Trasks in Beverly, Massachusetts, in variety and taste in design, as well as in quality and finish, while maintaining the Connecticut penchant for successful merchandising. Our knowledge of nineteenth-century pewter and britannia manufacture has been broadened by the study of three sets of records that had not been examined before 1940, namely: (1) a file of pertinent Thomas D. Boardman papers, some in his own handwriting in the Connecticut State Library; (2) the day books of Ashbil Griswold now in the custody of the International Silver Company at Meriden; and (3) Reed and Barton's very full company records that included much information about its predecessor companies.

The Boardman papers not only furnish information about the Hartford shop and its branches, but also give interesting sidelights concerning some of the Boardman competitors, stories which will be discussed in the comments about those shops.

Shortly before this volume went to press Abraham Brooks sent me photographs of a splendid flagon marked with an eagle touch of Samuel Danforth of Hartford which refutes impressively my statement above that Connecticut pewterers "gave very little indication of versatility, ingenuity or artistic creativity."

The body and cover of the flagon (Plate XCIXA) appear to have been made from the same moulds that Samuel Danforth normally used to fashion his church flagons. What gives such distinction to this flagon are its sweeping solid handle and early thumbpiece, designs that were common on English flagons of the seventeenth century which became outmoded by 1725 or earlier.

Whether Danforth acquired moulds for these parts of antiquated design or, perhaps, salvaged them from some flagon that had been brought in as damaged, to be remelted, is immaterial. The fact remains that the resulting composition is dignified and pleasing to the eye. No finer American flagon is known to have survived.

IVORY LUCAS

At least a few months before the first Thomas Danforth, in 1733, moved from Taunton to Norwich, Connecticut, another pewterer had set up shop in New London.

The story of this new claimant for the title of earliest Connecticut pewterer is taken largely from a note in the genealogical column of the *Hartford Times* for April 22, 1944. The man bore the rather unusual name of Ivory Lucas.

Lucas was in New London at least as early as 1732 when he bought a lot on Main Street, near the corner of the present Masonic Street. In the following year he married Mary, daughter of Solomon and Mary (Stow) Coit. Ivory and Mary were members of the First Church, in which five Lucas daughters were baptized between the years 1735 and 1742.

Perhaps the trade of pewtering in New London at that early date was not very lucrative or maybe Ivory sought adventure where he would be free of petticoat influence. In any event we have evidence of an interlude in his pewter-making. In a letter from New London dated the seventh of August 1741, addressed to the Hon. Joseph Talcott, Governor, at Hartford, written by George Phillips, Captain of the Colony Sloop, *Defiance*, a list of the crew is provided and includes "Avery [sic] Lucas, Armorer."

On May 6, 1747, Ivory leased a house in Delaware from William Hall of Ogles Town in the County of New-Castle-on-Delaware and on April 21, 1748, he sold the tools of his trade, along with a cow, to James Broom of Ogles Town. In these transactions his occupation is shown as "Pewterer and Founder" in one, "Pewterer and Brass Founder" in the other. Lucas' death must have occurred very soon thereafter, because on June 3, 1748, Mary Lucas, his widow, was appointed executrix of his estate.

In *Old Pewter* Howard Cotterell listed nine pewterers named Lucas, seven in London and two in York. None, however, was named Ivory. It is believed that Robert Lucas of London, who became Master Warden of the Company in 1667, may have been a progenitor, possibly grandfather of Ivory, because he, Robert, married a Mildred Prudden whose brother Edward married an Ivory.

Nothing that could be found in the Delaware records of the Broome family indicated that the purchaser of Ivory Lucas' pewter-making tools ever made pewter.

Among the touches that cannot be positively identified as that of any specific pewterer, is an I.L. initial touch, illustrated as Fig. 882 of Plate CX. It may have been a touch used by Lucas, an attribution based on the forms on which it appears. The touch has been found on at least three porringer handles of a design found occasionally in England, but, as far as now known, on only one marked American porringer handle. That handle is impressed with the I.D. lion touch (Plate LI, Fig. 356, Volume One), which was used by either John Danforth of Norwich or Joseph Danforth of Middletown. If Lucas was the user of this rare I.L. touch, he may have sold to Thomas or John Danforth, of nearby Norwich, the porringer handle mould from which the I.D. porringer handle was cast many years later. The I.L. touch has been reported on two other items, a large funnel and a porringer handle of most unusual design which, to the best of my knowledge, is not to be found on any other American porringer. The porringer is illustrated as Fig. 699 of Plate LXXXIII.

THOMAS DANFORTH, FIRST

The story of Thomas Danforth I, as it appeared on page 105 in Volume One contained the following sentence. "When he finally retired from business, presumably in 1773, his son John carried on the work of the shop." Thomas was then seventy years of age and the assumption seemed reasonable, but is refuted by the following newspaper notice, as copied from the *Norwich Packet* for October 28–November 4, 1773:

> The public are hereby informed that the co-partnership of Thomas Danforth and son is dissolved. Those that have any demands on said co-partnership are desired to bring in their accounts to Thomas Danforth that they may be settled, and those that are indebted to them are requested to make immediate payment. Said Danforth carries on the pewtering business, in all its branches, as usual, and will be much obliged to his customers for a continuance of their favours, and shall make it his study to merit the same, by a close application to business. N.B. He has at present on hand, a quantity of excellent onions which he will dispose of by the bushel for cash on very reasonable terms.
>
> Norwich, Nov. 1, 1773.

How much longer Thomas continued to turn out pewter cannot be determined, but, when he died in 1786 at the age of 83, there were still a few old moulds and a small amount of pewter in his shop.

Whether any of his marked pieces have survived is still an unsettled question. The problems of attributing correctly the different Danforth touches seem even more confused than they were thirty years ago. Once more they will be discussed under the heading Thomas Danforth Lion Marks on pages 67–70.

JOHN DANFORTH

When Thomas Danforth announced the dissolution of his partnership in Norwich in 1773 with his son John, it had been assumed that that was the occasion of the older man's retirement from active business, for he was then seventy years of age. But the wording of the newspaper announcement, in which Thomas states that he plans to continue the business alone, seems to indicate that there was a falling out between the two men. One wonders how John was able to set up a second pewtering shop in the town and where and how he acquired the necessary moulds, wheel, and tools.

A 12-inch dish, bearing John Danforth's touches was acquired by Mrs. J. Insley Blair soon after the first two volumes of *Pewter in America* were published. This dish, now in the Metropolitan Museum, is marked with John's hallmarks, the Norwich cartouche, and two impressions, somewhat worn, of the T.I. lion-in-oval touch, which can be seen in a good impression in Fig. 365 of Plate LIII, Volume One. This latter touch was assumed to have been used by the second Thomas Danforth and his son Joseph in Middletown. The marks as they appear on Mrs. Blair's dish are shown on Plate CV in this volume. So now there must be a new appraisal of the problem of how to allot properly to the different Thomas Danforths, the various T.D. lion marks. That problem will be discussed on pages 67–70 of this volume.

John Danforth

In the story of John Danforth in Volume One, page 106, two paragraphs were devoted to the attribution, with considerable reservation, to this pewterer, of two small lion touches with initials I.D., the design enclosed in a circular frame, see Figs. 356 and 357 of Plate LI. The same initials and the same lion symbol would have been equally appropriate for John's nephew, Joseph Danforth of Middletown.

In support of a John Danforth attribution was the knowledge that we already had another I.D.-and-lion touch, Fig. 368, and an I.D.-in-rectangle mark, Fig. 374 of Plate LIII, that had been identified positively as Joseph's marks. If we were to award to Joseph 356 and 357 as well, we would leave John, who had a longer working career than Joseph, with no initial touch of any kind.

It also seemed pertinent that touches 356 and 357 had been found only on porringer handles and that, in two instances, the handles were of most unusual designs; 356 was found on a rare openwork (or flowered) type (Plate XII, Fig. 57); 357 in a shield on a dolphin-handle porringer basin (Plate XII, Fig. 63). In 1940 no touch of any other American pewterer had been reported on a handle of either of those patterns.

One of the reasons put forward in 1940 for questioning the attribution of these touches to John was an entry in Joseph's inventory of what appeared to me to be a porringer basin mould, owned jointly with his brother Thomas. It now appears however that the entry was misread and that in no Danforth inventory has a porringer basin mould been found.

In recent years several porringer basins have come to light, vessels seemingly made from the same moulds as the I.D. example with the dolphin handle, but impressed with one of the small eagle initial touches, used by Samuel Danforth of Hartford. It seems more probable that Samuel would have acquired the moulds in question from the estate of his brother Joseph in nearby Middletown, than from his uncle John in the more distant town of Norwich, but what seems probable is not always what takes place.

One fact, discovered by Wendell Hilt, that might be pertinent here, is that, on April 15, 1786, John Danforth of Norwich mortgaged his house and property in Norwich to Daniel and Samuel Danforth of Hartford, minors. In debt to Samuel, John conceivably might have parted with some of his moulds to make his payments. Another possible clue is that, with the exception of one "new" pint basin mould in Joseph's inventory in 1788, all of his moulds had been inherited from his father's estate and were jointly owned with his brother Thomas or with his father Thomas and Jacob Whitmore. No dolphin-handle porringer basin has ever been reported bearing a touch of Thomas Danforth or Jacob Whitmore.

So, although there must be some doubt as to whether Figs. 356 and 357 were touches of John or of Joseph, there seems to be no good reason, on the basis of the available evidence, for altering the attribution to John that was first made by Louis G. Myers.

To our earlier list of forms made by John Danforth should be added 9 and $9\frac{3}{8}$ inch smooth brim plates.

The Pewterers of the Connecticut Valley

SAMUEL DANFORTH OF NORWICH

This maker's pewter is still exceedingly rare. The only forms not previously listed are $9\frac{3}{8}$ inch semideep plates, $12\frac{3}{16}$ inch flat dishes—a form that almost every Danforth made—and a $5\frac{1}{4}$ inch porringer with the so-called crown type of handle. The latter is impressed with Samuel's crude eagle die, Fig. 359. The handle and touch are illustrated on Plate CV. The dishes are impressed with the Norwich cartouche or the name in rectangular frame.

THOMAS DANFORTH, SECOND

Wendell Hilt's careful research into, and study of, the records of Connecticut pewterers, requires a re-examination and possibly a reappraisal of some of those makers and their work. This seems particularly true of Thomas Danforth of Middletown, the second Thomas.

The discovery that Jonathan Danforth, Thomas' fourth son, took over the pewter-making shop of his older brother, Joseph, when the latter died in 1788, raises to six the number of Thomas' sons, who became active pewterers with shops of their own, and makes Thomas the founder of the largest family of pewterers that this country produced.

Correction must be made also of the earlier statement (see page 107, Volume One) about the distribution of the moulds in the second Thomas' estate. It is true that the two older sons, the third Thomas and Joseph, received their father's share in the moulds that he and Jacob Whitmore owned jointly, but Thomas had owned outright a great many more moulds, and the administrators set off to three of the younger sons—Edward, Jonathan, and William—three lots of moulds and tools which weighed over two hundred pounds each.

It is not clear whether Thomas Danforth and Jacob Whitmore were, at one period, partners. It may be that they operated two separate businesses but under the same roof. They certainly were not partners in 1773, when Samuel Hamlin advertised that his partnership with Thomas Danforth was being dissolved and that he was moving his business to Providence. Nor is there any evidence now, as erroneously stated in Volume One, that Thomas was ever in business with his son Joseph. That statement had been postulated upon an assumption, that now seems very questionable, that is, that Thomas was the user of the lion-in-oval Danforth touch and that the particular die which shows on its face the initials T.I. naturally indicated a partnership between Thomas and Joseph.

It is Hilt's belief that the Middletown Thomas had a larger business than any of his sons ever enjoyed, including Thomas the third. This supposition is based on three factors that outwardly seem to support such a conclusion.

Thomas Danforth, Second

First of all, an examination of the schedules of distribution in the administration papers, rather than just in the inventory, shows that Thomas owned outright, or in conjunction with Whitmore, over one thousand pounds of moulds, more than have been reported in the estate of any other Connecticut pewterer. However we do not know how large a supply of moulds the third Thomas possessed at the height of his career.

The second indicator, which points to a large production, is the great number of surviving examples that are marked with the Thomas Danforth lion-in-gateway touch, the Middletown cartouche or the four T.D. hallmarks which usually accompany these larger marks. We are omitting here the T.D. and T.I. lion-in-oval pewter which this Thomas may or may not have made. Hilt points out also that the small lion-in-circle with initials T.D., the initials-in-rectangle and the set of small hallmarks, which the third Thomas is known to have used, before he adopted eagle touches, may have been used first by his father.

There are two very good reasons to support this probability. First of all, when the contents of the second Thomas' shop were distributed, his namesake, the third Thomas, very naturally received his father's pewter stamps, nine in all. To account for that many we must assume that the Middletown Thomas owned the lion-in-oval and/or some of the touches which we had believed to have been the marks of the third Thomas. The second reason is based on strong circumstantial evidence that the small lion-in-circle was used first in Middletown. That particular touch was illustrated in Jacobs, page 78, as found on the underside of a porringer handle, and I have in my collection a porringer stamped with the same touch in a similar location. This was a practice that must have gone out of fashion by 1770 or earlier. Thereafter porringers were invariably marked on the upper face of the handle. It would be surprising therefore if the third Thomas had been responsible for those porringers.

The third reason for believing that the second Thomas must have had a very large production is the fact that his lion-in-gateway pewter was so widely distributed and is still turning up far to the south and to the west of Middletown, as well as throughout New England.

But neither the second nor the third argument in support of the opinion, that the second Thomas had a larger business than Thomas the third, is very convincing. This is all because there is no way to know now which man used which dies and for what length of time. Although it is probable that some of the pewter, which previously was supposed quite definitely to be the work of the younger man, must now be considered the work of his father, Thomas the third's inheritance of all of his father's touch stamps may well mean that a great quantity of the lion-in-gateway pewter, which was assumed to have been definitely the work of the second Thomas, was actually made by his son. It is entirely possible, perhaps probable, that the younger Thomas in Rocky Hill was using those early dies for anywhere from five to ten years after his father's death.

In the light, therefore, of what we now know, it was rash indeed of me to have made the observation in 1940 that "of the many Danforths . . . probably none excelled the third Thomas in quality of work, none ever had a larger trade and certainly no one of them has left us so many examples of his handiwork." It would be equally rash however of anyone to assert in print now that the second Thomas was really the outstanding pewterer in the Danforth family. We just do not know, and probably never will, which man used which touches at any particular time.

If we must take from the second Thomas Danforth all the pewter that is marked with lion-in-oval touches, all as discussed below, he is still left with all the pewter marked with a Middletown cartouche and probably with the major portion of the Thomas Danforth lion-in-gateway pewter and pieces stamped with the large T.D. hallmarks. Known forms that would fall into that group would include $7\frac{3}{4}$ to $9\frac{1}{8}$ inch plates with normal rim, 9 to $9\frac{1}{2}$ inch smooth brim plates, $12\frac{1}{8}$ inch flat dishes, 11, $11\frac{1}{8}$, to $13\frac{1}{4}$ inch deep dishes, pint basins, a patch box, inkwell, and at least one quart tankard. To his list should be added also $3\frac{3}{8}$ and 4 inch porringers with the lion-in-circle touch, which he assuredly made, as explained above.

THE THOMAS DANFORTH LION MARKS

The puzzle as to which Thomas Danforth used which Thomas Danforth lion touch, or T.D. initial mark, seemed so very close to solution thirty years ago. Today we know not only that the true answers are farther from determination than ever, but that many pieces of Danforth-marked pewter can never be positively identified as the work of any one particular maker.

Let's see just where we do stand now. Our previous confusion has been compounded by two discoveries in recent years. The first was the acquisition by Mrs. J. Insley Blair of a dish, now in the Metropolitan Museum, on which were impressed the Norwich cartouche, Fig. 352, John Danforth's hallmarks, Fig. 353, and two impressions of the T.I. lion-in-oval, Fig. 365, all as reproduced on Plate CV. Up to that time the lion-in-oval touches had been presumed to have been used in Middletown by the second Thomas and his son Joseph. So, in spite of the fact that the touch appeared to be of later design than the lion-in-gateway, and although, generally speaking, the plates, on which the oval marks are found, seem to have had less wear and less evidence of age than those with the gateway mark, this combination of touches offered very strong evidence that the oval touches were the marks of Thomas and John Danforth of Norwich.

But how explain away the fact that those same lion-in-oval touches are usually found on plates and dishes in company with the set of large T.D. hallmarks, Fig. 363, which are found even more frequently with the lion-in-gateway mark, which in turn is sometimes accompanied by the "Middletown" cartouche, Fig. 361. The same set of hallmarks could not have been used in Norwich and Middletown at the same time. Is it possible that the oval touch may have been used first in Norwich and then discarded, but used later by the second Thomas in Middletown?

The problem does not end there. Wendell Hilt, who has studied Thomas Danforth touches on many plates and dishes under a magnifying glass, is convinced that the gateway touch is older than the lion-in-oval marks, and that the T.I. lion-in-oval preceded the similar T.D. mark, a conclusion that flies in the face of all of our preconceived ideas on the subject. His deductions are based on the fact that the die used for impressing the large T.D. hallmarks, which so frequently are found alongside both the gateway and oval touches had evidently been damaged at some time but continued in use long thereafter. The first hallmark, enclosing the initials T.D., shows, in many cases, the result of damage in the lower right-hand corner of the shield. This may be seen by a comparison on Plate LIII, Volume One, of Figs. 363 and 363a. Hilt writes that he has seen but one lion-in-gateway-marked plate that is accompanied by a damaged hallmark; that a number of the lion-in-oval with initials T.I. are found with similarly marred hallmarks and that it is normal to find damaged hallmarks with the T.D. lion-in-oval.

So, if you believe that there was but one set of large T.D. hallmarks, and that it would be difficult if not impossible for any die cutter to reproduce such a set so accurately that differences between the original and the reproduction could not be detected under a magnifying glass, one would have to believe that a touch showing marks of damage would necessarily be later than similar marks that are unmarred. If the Hilt examination covered a sufficiently large number of samples, the lion-in-gateway touch is older than the lion-in-oval, and the oval with initials T.I. was first used before the similar die with initials T.D.

The second discovery, that has upset our earlier determinations about the probable users of the different Thomas Danforth touches, resulted from the fact that Hilt noted that, when the second Thomas Danforth's estate was distributed (he died in 1782), his stamps for marking pewter, nine in all (undoubtedly his touch dies), were set off to the third Thomas, who had already been making pewter in his own shop in Rocky Hill for possibly four or five years. What touch or touches had the third Thomas been using before his father died? What were the nine dies which were then added to the dies which he already had? And to what extent did he make use of marks which had previously appeared on the product of his father's shop? Undoubtedly these acquisitions included the lion-in-gateway and the set of large hallmarks. Did they include also the set of small hallmarks, the T.D.-in-rectangle, the small T.D. lion-in-circle and the newly-found rosette, any or all of them, touches believed heretofore to have been used only by the third Thomas? And, is it possible that among the nine stamps were the extremely controversial T.D. and T.I. lion-in-oval marks?

Attention should be called to certain peculiarities in the practice of striking touches in different Danforth shops. Take first the normal procedure of marking plates and dishes in the shop of Thomas Danforth, Second, in Middletown. Almost invariably the lion-in-gateway was struck twice on each dish or plate, the bases of the impressions close together, the tops canted slightly away from one another. Now look at dishes or plates marked with either of the lion-in-oval touches. It must be immediately apparent that those touches were struck by a different hand and probably in a different shop. On the smaller plates there is usually but one impression and, on the dishes, where the die has been struck twice, the marks are never as close together as on the "gateway"; besides the lion appears to be in a fully upright position. This business of striking touches was a matter of habit and apparently journeymen and apprentices, if and when they were required to mark the pewter, had to follow the practice of the master, as developed in that particular shop. Undoubtedly there are exceptions to that generalization, but this seems pretty convincing proof that the second Thomas Danforth never used the lion-in-oval T.D. mark.

Where in this maze of contradictions do we stand now? Have we any firm basis for stating that this touch or that was positively used by any specific maker? The answer is "yes" but our certainties are fewer than once they seemed.

We still cannot say positively that the first Thomas Danforth ever used any of the known T.D. or T. Danforth touches. It is true that the T.I.-in-oval mark, Fig. 365, has been found in conjunction with the Norwich cartouche and with the hallmarks used by Thomas' son John, but only on one example. That however is not proof that the similar touch with initials T.D. was used by John's father. If then, those marks were not used in Norwich and if, as we have tried to show, they could not have been used by Thomas of Middletown, who were the users? Hilt, who is satisfied that the lion-in-gateway is older than the lion-in-oval, suggests that the oval T.I. mark may have been used by the third Thomas and his younger brother Joseph, right after Thomas Danforth, Second, died in 1782, and that later the T.I. die was recut, changing the second initial to a D and that the altered die was used by the third Thomas in Rocky Hill until his first eagle touch appeared. Any such explanation, however, must presuppose that the third Thomas was working in Middletown with his brother Joseph for several years after he had moved with his family to Rocky Hill. Frankly there is no satisfactory logical explanation of who the user or users of those oval touches may have been.

The picture is very much clearer of the lion-in-gateway and large T.D. hallmarks, Figs. 362 and 363. Both have been found with the "Middletown" cartouche. It can be stated with assurance that they were used by the second Thomas, probably throughout his working years. However he was not necessarily the only user, because all of his stamps passed, at his death, to Thomas of Rocky Hill. Either or both of those dies may have been used for a few years by the third Thomas. Nor have we any reasonable explanation of how that set of hallmarks could have been used by the owner of the lion-in-oval stamps.

The second Thomas may also have used one or all of the following four touches that are believed to have been normal touches of the third Thomas—the lion-in-circle

T.D., Fig. 368, small set of T.D. hallmarks, Fig. 369, initials in rectangle, Fig. 367, and small rosette, Fig. 849, Plate CV.

The third Thomas was the owner and, almost surely, the only user of all of the T.D. eagle touches. Because one or more of those eagles has been found in conjunction with Figs. 367 and 369, both of the latter were necessarily touches of the third Thomas, regardless of whether they had been used earlier by his father. The small lion in circle was almost surely used by both Thomas the second and Thomas the third. The rare rosette mark was probably a touch of the third Thomas, but it too may have been first used by the older man.

There, in a good many nutshells, is the status of the various Thomas Danforth lion marks as they appear from this corner. The longer we study the lion touches, the less certain do we become in our efforts to associate each one with a specific pewterer. The reader is warned that if and when he may have occasion to refer back to the touches on Plate LIII, Volume One, he should realize that every T.D., T.I., or I.D. lion touch as well as the two rectangular initial touches, Figs. 367 and 374, were probably used in more than one shop and cannot be attributed with any degree of confidence to any individual pewterer or pewterers.

THOMAS DANFORTH, THIRD

As explained in the discussion of the second Thomas and his pewter on pp. 65–67, it was rash to have stated as was done on page 111, Volume One, that the third Thomas probably had a larger trade and has left us more examples of his work than any other Danforth. This I still believe to be true but, because there is no certainty as to which Thomas Danforth used each of the different Thomas Danforth or T.D. touches and whether certain touches were used by more than one Thomas, there are comparatively few pieces — the Middletown-marked plates or dishes of the second Thomas and the eagle-marked pewter of the younger man — which can be positively allotted to one maker.

One other correction is needed in the statements about the third Thomas in Volume One. There it was noted that Charles and Hiram Yale had been apprentices of the third Thomas Danforth, a statement made on the authority of a volume entitled *Commemorative Biographical Record of Middlesex County.* However, Thomas Boardman wrote in his biographical notes, now in the Connecticut State Library, that the Yales, at the time when they bought pewter-making moulds from the estate of Samuel Danforth and set up in business, had had no previous experience in pewter-making. He was surely in position to know.

Fig. 849 of Plate CV illustrates a small rosette touch, known to collectors for some time but only in recent years identified as one used by one or more Thomas Danforths. Carl Jacobs in his *Guide to American Pewter*, page 89, illustrated the mark as it appeared on a tablespoon, which had been unearthed on the site of an early house at Wethersfield, Connecticut. On the spoon's handle were also the small hallmarks, which we formerly believed to have been used only by the third Thomas, but may have been used at an earlier date, as we now realize, by his father, the second Thomas. The touch on the spoon, Fig. 758 is illustrated here again with the kind permission of the Antiquarian and Landmarks Society, Inc., of Connecticut. Dr. Robert Mallory owns a pint mug which bears this same touch and near the handle on the lip of the mug is the T.D. initial touch, Fig. 367, Plate LIII, Volume One, which has been accredited to the third Thomas, but could as we know, have been used by his father.

Forms not recorded in the earlier edition as made by this pewterer, but since reported as bearing one of the touches which the third Thomas was known to have used, are pear-shaped teapots, small circular inkwells, shakers of a design hitherto unlisted (see Fig. 931 of Plate CXV), pint and quart lidded tankards, and tablespoons.

JACOB WHITMORE

Although Whitmore's pewter is not as scarce as was indicated twenty-five years ago, his range of forms is still very limited. The only new shapes reported for him are 3½ inch beakers and small lidded boxes, similar to the Thomas Danforth, Second, box, which appeared as Fig. 259 of Plate XL in Volume One. It seems quite reasonable to expect that we may yet find tall beakers and quart tankards bearing this man's touches.

HENSHAW AND HAMLIN

On July 13, 1767, an advertisement appeared in the *Connecticut Courant*, announcing the opening of the shop in Hartford, Connecticut, of Henshaw and Hamlin, Braziers and Pewterers. This story was told in the history of Samuel Hamlin on page 55 of this volume. The partners are believed to have been Benjamin Henshaw, Middletown merchant, and young Samuel Hamlin, who would have just about finished his apprenticeship when the notice appeared. It is thought that the partnership lasted only a few years at most, and possibly less than one year. Henshaw probably had had no training as a pewterer and merely supplied his name and capital to help start Hamlin in business.

AMOS TREADWAY

The pewter of this Middletown maker is still very rare and is still limited to plates and dishes. The only additions to the earlier lists are 13 inch dishes, two or three of which are known.

Joseph Danforth, Father and Son

JOSEPH DANFORTH, FATHER AND SON

When the second Thomas Danforth died in Middletown in 1782, he owned a one-half interest in a lot of moulds, which were jointly owned by Jacob Whitmore. His interest, at his death, was set off to his two oldest sons, Thomas and Joseph.

The moulds which the sons inherited jointly, one-half interest still vesting in Whitmore, were: 1 pint and 1 quart pot moulds, 1 wine pint, 1 three-gill and 1 two-gill beer measure porringers, 1 plate mould and 1 small plate mould, 1 quart basin mould and 1 "Babe porringer mold."

From the estate Thomas and Joseph each received a one-half interest in one other group of moulds, viz. one quart basin mould, pint basin mould, beer pint porringer mould and a "Supe plate mold."

It is now possible to explain, at least in part, why so much pewter bearing Joseph Danforth touches has survived, in spite of the fact that Joseph himself could not have been in business for more than nine or ten years at the most.

On February 7, 1789, only a month or two after Joseph's death, the following notice was printed in the Middlesex Gazette:

> The Pewterers, Braziers and Plumber's Business will be carried on at the shop of Joseph Danforth, Deceased, as usual, By Jonathan Danforth. . . .

When Wendell Hilt discovered this announcement Jonathan Danforth's history was unknown to collectors. It is related briefly on page 74. Very soon thereafter young Jonathan was joined by his still younger brother, William. Together they seem to have continued Joseph's business until 1794. Without any doubt Jonathan and William used Joseph's moulds and touches.

The son, Joseph, Jr., certainly learned the pewterer's trade from one of his uncles and probably, as the family genealogy states, from his uncle William. He could not have completed his training until 1803 or 1804. At just that time we find that he sold property in Middletown and probably moved to Richmond in the following year. He could have made very little pewter, if any, in Connecticut, before moving to Richmond.

Forms not reported earlier for the elder Joseph are 11 inch flat dishes with narrow rim, 8 inch and 12 inch basins, $4\frac{1}{4}$ and $5\frac{3}{16}$ inch beakers and 5 inch porringers with flowered handle.

If there was ever any doubt that Joseph, Jr., was the user of the large J.D. eagle touch, Fig. 379, and the "Richmond Warranted" mark, that doubt has been dispelled by the markings on a plate now at Winterthur, see Plate CV, Figs. 377a, 380a, and 381a. Marked originally with the senior Joseph's lion-in-gateway touch it has had superimposed thereon the younger Joseph's own eagle and below that the "Richmond Warranted" mark. Not only have a few $8\frac{3}{4}$ inch normal brim plates turned up bearing the Richmond eagles, but also at least one in the 9 inch diameter as well as $8\frac{3}{4}$ inch plates with smooth brim.

The Pewterers of the Connecticut Valley

EDWARD DANFORTH

In the brief account of Edward Danforth's career in Volume One (page 117) the suggestion was made that he probably turned out very little pewter after moving from Middletown to Hartford in 1788.

That suggestion has been thoroughly discredited from two different sources. As a matter of fact, Edward probably never made any pewter at all in Middletown, after his apprenticeship was completed. Shortly after his twenty-first birthday the following notice was printed in the *Connecticut Courant*, Hartford, June 5, 1786:

> Edward Danforth, Pewterer and Brasier Respectfully informs the public, that he has taken a shop nearly opposite Mr. Samuel Burr's Store, where he carries on his business in all its branches. Said Danforth has for sale a good assortment of new Pewter, by wholesale or retail, Brass Kettles of various sizes, brass skimmers and Ladles, lead Weights and all kinds of fish-net Leads. Also a small assortment of Tin and Iron ware.
>
> Hartford, June 1786.

In the following year, as a partner in the firm of Goodman and Danforth, he was selling a general line of merchandise including European and Indian goods as well as "New Pewter by wholesale and retail."

Although, in later years, he continued to advertise, he was usually in business by himself, offering a general line of dry goods with pewter as a sideline. After 1800 pewter was not mentioned at all.

Evidence from a different source confirms the suspicions raised by the newspapers that Edward made pewter only in a limited way after 1795.

To quote from Thomas D. Boardman's story of his own life:

> . . . came to Hartford in August 1795 in 1796 went to live with my Uncle Edward Danforth, a Pewterer by trade—worked at the trade part of the time until the fall of 1799—then with Uncle Samuel Danforth until July 21st 1804 at the age of 20 years & 6 months—Commencing business at once for myself in a small way—having hired the tools of Ed^d Danforth. . . .

This would indicate that Edward's pewtering business was so insignificant after 1796 that he could only provide the boy with part-time work. Since Boardman was using Edward's tools in 1804 the latter must have given up pewter-making prior to that time.

When Thomas Danforth, Second's, estate was divided in 1783, Edward received as his share of the shop equipment:

A number of Brazier's tools	wt. 323 lbs.
1 9 lb plate mold	wt. $21\frac{1}{4}$ lb.
1 Wine Pint Porringer	wt. 30. #
1 3 Pt Bason do	wt. $61\frac{1}{2}$ #

Jonathan Danforth

1 Flat Brim Plate	wt. 29½ #
1 Small Platter	wt. 68 #
1 Salt Seller Mold	
Old hooks etc.	

To the earlier list of forms bearing Edward's touches can now be added 9⅛ inch smooth brim plates, 8 and 9⅛ inch basins, porringers in five sizes from 3⅞ inches to 5 inches, an oval box with hinged lid similar to that illustrated in Plate XL, Fig. 259, in Volume One, a quart tankard with domed lid similar to those made by the second Thomas Danforth and by Samuel Hamlin (see Plate LXXXVII, Fig. 730) and another with a heavy cone-shaped finial such as has also been found on Samuel Danforth and Thomas D. Boardman tankards and flagons (Plate XXXIII, Fig. 223).

From newspaper files Wendell Hilt learned that Edward, in addition to selling dry goods and pewter, acted as an agent for the sale of land in 1793, was a "tax lister" in 1795, and a selectman in 1809.

His workmanship was so uniformly good that it is unfortunate that more examples have not been preserved.

JONATHAN DANFORTH

The following advertisement appeared in the *Middlesex Gazette* for February 7, 1789, directly below a notice concerning the settlement of the estate of Joseph Danforth, deceased, Edward Danforth, executor:

> The Pewterers, Braizers [sic] and Plumbers business will be carried on at the Shop of Joseph Danforth, Deceased, as usual By Jonathan Danforth. Those Persons who please to favor him with their Custom may depend on having their Work done in the best Manner and most reasonable Terms.

And so, thanks to Wendell Hilt's extensive research, we have one more Danforth to add to what had already been established as this country's largest family of pewterers.

Jonathan, born in 1766, was the fourth son of Thomas and Martha Danforth of Middletown. He may have commenced his apprenticeship in his father's shop, but almost surely completed it under his brother, Joseph, for whom he may have been working as a journeyman at the time of Joseph's death.

When the second Thomas' moulds were distributed to the sons, at the division of the estate in 1782 or 1783, the portion of Jonathan, still a minor, included one spoon mould, a chamber pot mould, a "Flat Brim" plate mould and moulds for pint and quart basins and two-gill and beer pint porringers.

In June 1790, Jonathan and William Danforth advertised "Cash given for old Pewter," and on December 6, 1794, the *Middlesex Gazette* carried a notice that the copartnership of Jonathan and William Danforth was dissolved by mutual consent. Presumably Jonathan's brief pewter-making career ended at that time.

In January 1796, Jonathan and his younger brother, Daniel, purchased property in Hartford. In the same month they offered for sale a "new elegant Canvas Top Chaise" and apparently were operating a general merchandising business, as confirmed by later newspaper notices. Jonathan married Lucy Ward of Ashford, Connecticut, at Guilford on October 27, 1793. He was lost at sea in September 1804, when just thirty-eight years of age.

There is no indication that Jonathan was a pewter-maker of any importance, and his period of activity seems to have been limited to the years 1787 to 1793. There is little likelihood that he had individual touches of his own. When he took over Joseph's business he almost surely used the dies of his late brother; those showing initials only would have been just as appropriate for Jonathan as for Joseph.

As stated on page 115, Volume One, it had seemed surprising that so much of Joseph's handiwork had survived, in view of the fact he could not have operated a shop of his own for a period of more than six or seven years. The Hilt discovery that Jonathan and William continued Joseph's business, probably using his touches, helps to explain why so much Joseph Danforth pewter is still to be seen.

WILLIAM AND JOSIAH DANFORTH

Whatever may be added here to our previous knowledge of William Danforth's career will be based entirely upon information uncovered by Wendell Hilt.

First of all we now know that after the death in 1788 of Joseph Danforth in Middletown, his pewtering business was carried on until 1794 by his two younger brothers, Jonathan and William (see page 74). Assuredly they used the moulds in Joseph's shop, supplemented by those which each of them had inherited from their father's estate. It seems reasonable to suppose that in carrying on Joseph's business they would have used his touches as well as his moulds. This would help to explain why so much pewter, stamped with that maker's marks, has survived.

While still in his minority, William had inherited from his father's estate six moulds for pewter forms as follows—spoon, #10 plate, "supe plater," "tancord" [sic], pint basin, and a dram cup. Up to this writing no William Danforth spoon, dram cup, or "tancord" has been reported.

Until 1809 William was presumably making pewter in Middletown and for several years served as sealer of weights and measures for the town and surrounding area. In that year William Nott advertised that he would carry on the business of "Mr. William Danforth" in the latter's shop. In March, 1809 Danforth advertised that all persons within the bounds of Middletown must bring in their measures during April to be "tryed and sealed according to law." One year later we find him resorting to the newspaper again to notify all concerned that he was leaving town for seven months. Surviving records seem to indicate that there was a gap of perhaps five years at this period, when Danforth was not making pewter in Middletown. Like his contemporary, Jacob Eggleston, he may have operated a shop for a few years in the Carolinas or in Georgia, but that is merely conjecture.

We know that Nott, who had been in charge of Danforth's shop in Middletown, bought a set of moulds from Eggleston's estate about 1814 and soon afterwards moved to Fayetteville, North Carolina. This may have been the occasion for Danforth's return to assume once more the management of his shop in Middletown. He died in the town of his birth in 1820.

Although William Danforth does not appear to have had a pewter-making business of any magnitude, the obituary notice quoted below, as copied from the *Middlesex Gazette* for December 14, 1820, records the very high esteem in which he was held by his fellow townsmen:

> Died. In this city on the 9th inst. Mr. William Danforth, aged 52 years, of Apoplexy. It seldom becomes our painful duty, to notice the death of an individual more worthy and respected than the one we have just named; nor one whose loss, especially to his family, would be more severely felt. The various duties appertaining to the several relations he sustained, to his family and community, he discharged, in some respects, in a manner almost unexampled. His disposition was uncommonly amiable and pleasant. To his wife and children, he was peculiarly affectionate, kind and indulgent; and the desolation which his death has made in their hearts, will be held in long and painful remembrance. As a neighbour, he was uniformly obliging and friendly; and it may be said of him, that in all his intercourse with his fellow men, he was strictly and conscientiously honest. The death of such a man is a public loss; and although his course through life has been modest, and unassuming, not marked by any of those striking incidents which give celebrity, yet his industry, his firm and tried Integrity, his peaceable, and upright conduct, deservedly placed him in high estimation, and cause us to mingle our tears and our sympathies with those of his afflicted family, over that sudden and awful visitation which has removed him forever from our sight.

Thanks to the Boardman papers, we now know that William's son, Josiah, took over his father's business in 1821, when he was still in his teens. Thomas Boardman tells us that, in order to help the youngster, he confided to him the Boardman formula for the composition of the new britannia metal and urged him not to divulge it to anyone. With the indiscretion of youth, Josiah disclosed the secret to his journeyman, Thomas Derby, and shortly thereafter Derby was hired away by Charles and Hiram Yale of Wallingford. The news was out and the dominance in the industry, which the Boardman brothers had enjoyed for more than a decade, was threatened.

In the July 1956 issue of the *Bulletin* of the Pewter Collectors' Club of America was illustrated a letter of October 27, 1842, which, as its heading, showed a "Price List of the Latest and Most Approved Patterns of Britannia Ware Manufactured by J. Danforth & Co., Middletown, Conn." The articles advertised were tea setts, teapots in five patterns, two forms of coffee pots, four of spitoons, cream cups, sugar bowles [sic], slop bowles [sic] stand and bed lamps, lather boxes, tumblers, and castors.

The Pewterers of the Connecticut Valley

Danforth had sold his lot and shop to Graham and Savage in 1837, all as recorded on page 118 of Volume One, but this letter indicates that he re-entered the field, presumably when the new proprietors failed in 1839 (see under Graham and Savage, page 103, Volume Two).

At some time after February 1839 this same shop was again in use by Josiah, for, on September 21, 1840, Ephraim Crofoot and Josiah Danforth quit-claimed the property, equipment, etc. back to William Savage.

On December 14, 1841, Josiah Danforth and Ephraim Crofoot operating as J. Danforth and Company leased from William and Benjamin Douglass of Middletown property on which to build.

The indenture was to run for five years, ending January 1, 1847, J. Danforth and Co. to pay $37.50 quarterly. "Said Danforth to have the right to errect a one story building . . . for the mfg. of Britannia ware" — William and Benjamin Douglass — "to furnish daily steam power to run 2, 3, or 4 pewterers lathes" the power to be furnished for "10 hours every day except Sunday." In 1845 Josiah branched out into the truss manufacturing business and probably made little britannia after that year. The revised estimate for his metal-making manufacture is from 1821 to 1845.

To the former list of Josiah's products, made in the early manner, should be added ladles and circular inkwells. Note should also be made that Josiah Danforth was not alone in making porringers with a tapered reinforcing rib down the underface of the handle. This same feature has been found on porringers of earlier manufacture, bearing the touches of Joseph Belcher and of David Melville, both of Newport.

SAMUEL DANFORTH OF HARTFORD

From Thomas D. Boardman's papers in the Connecticut State Library we have learned that Boardman completed his apprenticeship under his uncle, Samuel Danforth, and also that some of Samuel's moulds were sold by his estate to Charles and Hiram Yale of Wallingford, who had had no training at all in the manufacture of pewter.

Additional forms to be added to our earlier list of Danforth's recorded products are lidless quart tankards, $5\frac{5}{8}$-inch porringers, and porringer basins with handles of dolphin design, similar to that pictured in Plate XII, Fig. 63, of Volume One. Far more important than any of these, however, is a splended lidded flagon differing in handle and thumbpiece from Danforth's usual flagon design and illustrated in Plate XCIXA in this volume. A fuller description of this vessel, perhaps the finest surviving example of Connecticut pewter, appears on page 61. This fine flagon does much to raise the reputation of Samuel as a capable craftsman with a better sense of composition than had been demonstrated in his normal flagon and tankard designs.

Nathan and Prentice Frink

NATHAN AND PRENTICE FRINK

A quart basin, impressed with the touches illustrated as Figs. 845 and 846 of Plate CV is owned by John P. Remensnyder. As an examination of the touch shows, the name of the maker is Nath. Frink and the place where he worked Northampton. The design of the touch seems to indicate that it was in use in the third quarter of the eighteenth century. Given so much information about the maker, it should have been a simple matter to find the man's records and write up a brief history of his life. It was not.

The Frink family had moved to Connecticut during the seventeenth century and branches were established at Stonington, Pomfret, and elsewhere, prior to 1750. Unfortunately no published genealogy of the family, which might have helped in identifying the pewterer, could be found.

Although the present owner of the basin is convinced that it was made in Connecticut, such research as has been attempted, has failed to find even a very small hamlet in the state that is named Northampton.

The small city which is the site of Smith College in western Massachusetts seemed to offer the best promise for further inquiry. So a trip was made to Northampton, Massachusetts, but to little avail. The one small clue that was uncovered was the discovery at the Northampton Court House of a deed dated September 20, 1787 from Prentice Frink, yeoman, of Stonington, New London, to Cotton Hayden of Williamsburg, Massachusetts, of a piece of property at Williamsburg, Hampton County. Williamsburg is a village that is located about ten miles northwest of Northampton. No record could be found of how and when Prentice Frink gained title to that property.

One other clue, and an interesting one, was uncovered by Wendell Hilt. On June 14, 1792, the following notice appeared in the *Connecticut Gazette*, New London, Connecticut:

Stop Thief—Five Dollars Reward.

The subscribers shop in Stonington was broken open about the third instant, and a quart bason Mould stolen:—the mould is made chiefly of copper, and weighs forty three pounds. Whoever will take up the thief and the mould so that the thief shall be brought to justice and the mould recovered, shall have the above reward, or for the mould only, three dollars reward, and all necessary charges paid.

Prentice Frink, jun.

Was it just a coincidence that the one surviving piece of Frink pewter was a quart basin and that the mould which was stolen from Prentice was for exactly that same form? And what was it, that Prentice was accustomed to make in that shop into which a thief broke so long ago? Pewter, we should think, in at least a small way. But did Prentice make many other pewter forms besides quart basins? If so, how strange it was that the thief should have singled out the quart basin mould to steal, just to confound and confuse pewter collectors almost two hundred years later.

Prentice Frink, Jr., son of Prentice and Desire Frink, was born in Stonington, June 26, 1764. Strangely enough he married a Frink, Prudence by name, on March 4, 1784. Whether or not he was a pewterer and whether he was related in some way to Nathan Frink, pewterer, are new problems which must be left for solution to some more skillful, latter-day sleuth.

GREENE AND BELCHER

Among the stories of Rhode Island pewterers, under the heading Joseph Belcher, Father and Son, pages 51–52, report was made that Joseph, Jr., who had disappeared from Newport in 1784 or earlier, had relocated in New London, Connecticut. On June 1, 1787, Greene and Belcher (the senior partner's identity still undetermined) announced the opening of a pewtering business in New London. Two and one-half months later the partnership was dissolved. Whether Belcher made pewter in a shop of his own in New London before or after that venture is not known. He married Hannah Wood of Lyme, Connecticut, in 1788 and may have moved about that time to Lyme. His name does not appear at all in the Connecticut Census for 1790. He is recorded as living at Lyme in the Censuses for 1800, 1810, and 1820.

JACOB EGGLESTON

In the earlier account of Eggleston's history on pages 120–121 in Volume One, two errors crept in which require correction. The original inventory of the estate did, as reported, include 234 pounds of pewter moulds, but an additional inventory, not examined previously, added "46 lbs Pewter mould not before Inv." It is difficult, however, to reconcile those figures with two other entries in the same "Additional Inventory," which read as follows:

Gain on 144 lbs. Pewter moulds sold Wm & Samuel Yale $ 2.88
346 lbs Pewter moulds sold W. Nott   31c   107.26

Thus 380 pounds of moulds were inventoried, 490 pounds reported sold.

The second error was the statement that Nott accepted his payment in pewterers' moulds. A more careful reading of the administration files by Wendell Hilt shows that Eggleston's note for $100.00, which Nott held, was paid off with interest by the administrator just two months after Eggleston's death. The moulds were purchased by Nott for $107.26, an amount approximating that of the note, but apparently in a separate transaction.

Samuel Pierce

The one new form to be added to the previously listed products of Eggleston's shops, is a pear-shaped teapot. That discovery might have been expected because the inventory included twenty-one teapot handles at eight cents each.

There is also another eagle touch for this man, see Fig. 851 of Plate CVI, as found on a $7\frac{7}{8}$ inch plate in North Carolina and reported by Frank Horton. A similarly marked deep dish, discovered in the same area, is in the collection of Mr. and Mrs. Ralph P. Hanes. The touch is unquestionably the work of a Connecticut die-cutter. Note the similarity in design to touches of Eggleston's Connecticut-born contemporaries, Thomas Danforth, Third (Fig. 373), Joseph Danforth, Jr. (Fig. 381), and B. Barns (Fig. 557).

Additional information about Eggleston's southern shop will be found on page 158.

THE RICHARD LEES

Nothing more has been learned about the history of either Richard Lee, or his son Richard, Jr., but a few additional forms may be added to those previously listed. A number of porringers in the larger sizes, $4\frac{1}{4}$ inches to $5\frac{1}{4}$ inches in diameter have turned up and the late Carl Jacobs reported a tablespoon with beaded edge and a pear-shaped teapot. Also the Henry Francis du Pont Winterthur Museum has a small spoon with the name, R. Lee, cast in the handle, see Plate XC, Fig. 757.

SAMUEL PIERCE

To the list of Samuel Pierce's known forms may now be added $6\frac{1}{8}$ and $7\frac{3}{4}$ inch plates, $13\frac{1}{4}$ inch flat dishes, beakers in two sizes — $3\frac{5}{8}$ and $4\frac{1}{2}$ inches — pear-shaped and also lighthouse type teapots. The late Carl Jacobs also recorded porringers in two sizes — 4 and $5\frac{1}{4}$ inches — and an open salt, items which I have not run across.

In the Pewter Collector's Club of America *Bulletin* for May 1950 is a newspaper notice, found by Mrs. Oliver Deming, which reads as follows:

> The Copartnership heretofore existing between the Subscribers under the form of Pierce and Son is by mutual consent dissolved. All persons owing money to said firm are requested to make immediate payment.
>
> Samuel Pierce
> April 23, 1821   John J. Pierce

A study by Ross Levett of the account books and ledgers of Samuel Pierce and his sons indicates that pewtering was never Samuel's principal source of income. With many other young men, Pierce was probably attracted to Greenfield by the promotions of the town's first "booster" and entrepreneur, Colonel William Moore, who purchased a grist mill in 1791 and then built a six story building in which were installed a cotton factory, flouring mill, nail mill, cooper shop, potash works, tannery, tallow house, and slaughter house.

Pierce must have arrived in Greenfield with little or no capital and apparently worked until about 1799 for Colonel Moore. There is no evidence whatever in the Pierce records that he made or sold pewter during his early years in Greenfield.

In 1802 a great plague struck the town. Within the space of one month three of the five Pierce children died and another was stillborn. Surely these tragedies were the cause for the removal of the family to Colrain, a village a few miles northwest of Greenfield. In a Colrain deed of 1804 Pierce was termed a cooper. About three years later the family returned to Greenfield and perhaps at that time or soon thereafter Samuel was able to buy moulds and tools of the trade for which he had been trained.

In 1811 he formed a partnership with his son John Joyce in a general hardware merchandising business. During the ten years of that partnership Samuel must have turned out most of the surviving pewter which bears his touches. The demand for pewter dishes, plates, and basins was failing rapidly by 1821, but Samuel seems to have worked at the trade in a limited way until about 1831, as evidenced in the day books of his sons, which record purchases of small lots of pewter in exchange for old metal.

On the basis of the later research we should curtail Samuel Pierce's pewter-making to the period from the year 1807 (or later) until 1831 or 1832.

There is no documentation of the training of the Pierce sons as pewterers, and little reason for believing that Samuel Jr. would have used his father's dies after the latter's retirement about 1832.

EBENEZER SOUTHMAYD

Illustrated in Figs. 415a and 850 of Plate CVI are clearer impressions of Southmayd's large touch and the hallmarks which he occasionally used. Very little more of his work has turned up in recent years—a few $7\frac{7}{8}$ inch plates, 11 inch deep dishes, beakers, and one quart mug. Carl Jacobs reported a Southmayd communion flagon but I was unable to track it down for illustrating.

AMASA SIZER

This man is being given a place in the lists of Connecticut pewterers on the basis of a newspaper notice, found by Wendell Hilt, in which Sizer termed himself a pewterer. That notice, as it appeared in the *Middlesex Gazette* for November 29, 1799, reads as follows:

> The Subscriber Tin-plate Worker, Brazier and Pewterer Respectfully informs the public that he is carrying on said business at Staddlehill, one mile west of Middletown, opposite the Gristmill — where may be had all kinds of articles in the above mentioned branches, both for ship and household. He also makes Sheet Iron Stoves, and other articles — and repairs Brass and Copper Wares. He warrent's his work to be done in the best manner, and if any one should sustain damage either by badness of stock or lightness of work done by Subscriber, he promises to make it good to the purchaser. — Those who will favor him with their custom, may depend on having their work done with neatness and dispatch, by the public's humble servant.
>
> Amasa Sizer.

In later newspaper notices there is no mention of pewter-making and Sizer seems to have been essentially a tin-plate worker and brazier. He apparently moved about a great deal. Newspaper notices and census records show that he worked at Westerly, New London, Meriden, and Cheshire as well as at Middletown.

There is very little likelihood that he had a touch of his own and considerable doubt as to whether he belongs in our lists.

JAMES PORTER

Although there is nothing new to report about James Porter's pewter, Wendell Hilt has uncovered several clues which may identify the man who was listed as a pewterer in a Baltimore directory of 1803. The search for this man has been complicated by the fact that James Porters were plentiful in Connecticut in the eighteenth century.

Hilt discovered that in the Census for Connecticut for 1800 a James Porter of Middletown was listed right after William Danforth, indicating probably that he lived next door to Danforth. In his family was a male between the ages of 26 and 44 (no doubt himself), one male under 10, one female under 10, and one female between 16 and 25 (no doubt his wife). Then Hilt found that on November 20, 1794, Jonathan and William Danforth sold property adjoining that of William to a James Porter. Record was found also of a son born to James Porter in 1796 and another in 1803.

Further study of the land records shows that Porter sold his property next to Danforth in 1805 and on the fifth of June 1809 "James Porter, formerly of Middletown now of Baltimore in the state of Maryland" disposed of his last piece of real estate in Middletown for $1300.

This must definitely be our man and we can place him in Baltimore from 1803 until, at least, 1809, even though his name appeared but once in the city directories. It may be that his shop was just outside the city limits.

Although we still cannot be positive as to just which of the many James Porters this was, Hilt, by a process of elimination, is convinced that this must have been James, son of Dr. James and Lucy Porter of Waterbury, Connecticut, who was born on August 3, 1772. He would thus have been twenty-eight at the time of the Census in 1800. A James Porter, presumably this man, married Margery Stocking at Cromwell, Connecticut, on September 4, 1793, when he was just twenty-one. Cromwell is between the Danforth homes at Rocky Hill and Middletown and but fifteen miles from Waterbury. Margery was baptized at Cromwell, July 9, 1775, and accordingly would have been just under twenty-six at the census-taking in 1800.

Although we cannot be positive that the James Porter of Waterbury was the pewterer of Middletown and Baltimore, the dates correspond so closely to what we might have expected, that it is hard to believe that this is not the man whom we were seeking—a very excellent piece of detective work by Mr. Hilt.

ASHBIL GRISWOLD

The story of this man and his shop, as recorded in Volume One, pages 127–128, may now be amplified as a result of the fortuitous discovery and preservation of seven tattered leather-bound day books, filled with entries by Ashbil Griswold and his successors, dating from November 1807 until the settlement of accounts resulting from the formation of the Meriden Britannia Company in 1852.

For the first few months all the entries record sales to customers in Baltimore. At that time Griswold was only twenty-three years of age and may still have been in the employ of Thomas Danforth, Third, to whom he had been apprenticed. Danforth may have sent him to Baltimore as a peddler or salesman. It is doubtful that Griswold had a shop of his own at that time, for there are no records of cash paid to employees, for raw materials, or other shop outlays, such as are found later in his day books.

A very limited variety of forms was sold during his stay in Baltimore. Included were gallon "basons" at 91 cents each, half-gallon basons 61 cents, quart basons 31½ cents, pint basons 20 cents; plates $2.43 per dozen, large dishes 83 cents each, and small dishes 61 cents. There were also orders for dippers in three different sizes. After February 1808, most of the recorded sales were made in or near Meriden and, in November of that year, Griswold purchased from Ira Yale a small lot with shop thereon in Clarksville, a hamlet just north of Meriden. Additional forms, made in the next year or two, included large and small porringers, large and small teapots, and spoons. In succeeding years, quart and pint pots, soap boxes, sugar bowls, creamers, and "fassets" were added. I do not recall having seen any spoon, creamer, pint or quart pot, or faucet bearing Griswold's mark, but all the other forms listed above have been reported.

In the 1840's when Griswold was no longer active in the manufacturing end, the shop was making six different designs of teapots, coffee pots, spittoons, beakers, "as-trall" lamps, and hanging lamps.

The Boardmans

Very early Griswold was shipping large orders to dealers in Baltimore, New York, and Philadelphia. The extent of his business can be gauged by the fact that on December 17, 1842, he shipped to Foote and Thompson, hardware dealers in Philadelphia, twenty-eight dozen teapots, over eight dozen coffee pots, over ten dozen spittoons, more than seventeen dozen "lather boxes," fifty-seven dozen caster frames, and twelve and a half gross of teaspoons.

Griswold probably made little if any pewter himself after 1830 for, in that year, he was employing twelve hands and took Ira Couch in as a partner. A significant entry occurs in 1833 for "sundries for my shop which is under the supervision of Ira Couch and James A. Frary." From that time on, his duties must have been of a managerial and financial character only.

The books show record of cash payments to Couch, Frary, Enos H. Curtis, Lemuel J. Curtis, Luther Boardman, Jacob Whitmore, Jeptha Porter, Darius Benham, George Cowles, Burrage Yale, Thomas Mix, William W. Lyman, and others. Because the entries rarely state the reasons for the payments, we cannot be certain that these men were all Griswold employees, but most of them probably had their early training under Griswold. Except for the Boardman brothers of Hartford, Ashbil Griswold, more than any one other individual, was responsible for the tremendous growth of the britannia industry in Connecticut.

THE BOARDMANS

In the Connecticut State Library at Hartford is a collection of Boardman papers including manuscript notes, written by Thomas D. Boardman, concerning his own career, comments in another hand about the Boardman business, and correspondence with Lucius Hart concerning the New York branch. Although much of this has been published in recent years, certain excerpts will be reprinted again here because of the insight that they provide to the problems of pewterers just after the turn of the century.

The first excerpt is taken from Thomas D. Boardman's own notes, spelling and punctuation presented just as recorded.

Thomas Danforth Boardman Was born in Litchfield Con^t January 21st 1784. Came to Hartford in August 1795 in 1796 went to live with my uncle Edward Danforth, a Pewterer by trade — worked at the trade part of the time until the fall of 1799 — then with Uncle Samuel Danforth until July 21st 1804 at the age of 20 years & 6 months — Commencing business at once for myself in a small way — haveing hired the tools of Ed^d Danforth and a shop belonging to Father . . . previous to 1800 the pewterers were furnished with stock from the old worn out metal when new stock Tin in Blocks English banca V.V. came to Market it was found difficult to temper it fitt to cast well and the practice was to use a half new and half old London pewter then it would work well in 1805 I first heard the name of Regulus of antimony — what it was I knew not but enquired of all dealers in metals at length I found a Still & Worm manufacturer who had a few pounds — had it several years did not know what to do with it. I bought all he would sell 3 or 4 lb haf he had. I put some in a large Iron Ladle to melt over a furnace as soon as it melted it went throue the Ladle eat a hole right through melting the Iron — used some more with new tin, concluded it was not the thing & gave it up — The next year 1806 I recivd a lot of English tin from a puter [pewterer] in Philadelphia with orders to make it into teapots Just as it was. I cast the pots but could not turn them the metal was so soft the chips would — (?) — I melted them down and added 2 or 3 per ct. copper which had been try befor and as much R antimony — which proved to be the right thing — the pots were the best I had ever made — from what I could learn very few teapots had been made in New England & those verry clumsey with the propper preportion of Regulus of antimony and copper the ware would finish up equal to English bright around the soldering on of the trimmings so the Merchants who had imported the artickle considered them equal to English — of course we had orders from manufacturs of pewter ware to furnish with our teapots from Philadⁱa Providence Hartford and to Merchants in New York, Philadelphia, New Haven, Albany, Utica New Burgh, Providence, Newport, Boston. one House would order 50 Doz(?) at a time, one order 3,000 within 6 months.

. . . .

the use of antimony in the composition was kept a secret from 1806 by us TD & SB until after the death of S Danforth /1816/ & Wm Danforth /1820/ — our Journeymen and apprentices knew nothing of it. about 1821 to help a young friend undr age Just beg[gin]ing business I gave him the Secret, with the request that it should not be Communicated to the 3ᵈ person — but it was verry Soon to a Journey man & he was Soon employed by the Mess. Yales of Wallingford who had purchased the tools & moulds of the late Sam Danforth and they very soon bosted of new _____ (?) But they verry soon run the business down by sending more in the market then was demand & seling at 25 to 40 pct less than fair prices in Boston to a foreigner came with 3 sons & run the business down. . . .

From another paper we learn that the "young friend" to whom the secret of the composition was divulged was Boardman's cousin, Josiah, son of William Danforth, and that Josiah's journeyman, who learned the secret, was Thomas S. Derby.

To quote from the paper: Charles and Hiram Yale of Wallingford, who "never served an apprenticeship to the pewterers trade," purchased "the old tools of Mr. Saml. Danforth and went about hiring away the men from other shops — much to the annoyance of those having competent workmen — to teach and start them in the business! Among others, they hired away from Mr. Josiah Danforth, Thomas Derby from whom they learned the art of mixing the metals." The Yales "immediately came out with flaming advertisements, saying that they had discovered the art of Mixing Britannia metal and could make ware equal if not superior to the English manufacture. . . ."

Two facts of some importance emerge from these papers. The claims of the Yale family and of Wallingford and Meriden historians in their behalf, that Charles and Hiram Yale were the first to make britannia in this country, may be dismissed as completely unwarranted. Secondly, Boardman has made a very strong case for himself as the first successful manufacturer of the new alloy, at least in Connecticut, and probably in the country.

The comment on the Boardmans in Volume One requires correction of several assumptions. Although it remains true that Thomas Boardman completed his apprenticeship under his uncle, Samuel Danforth, his early years of training were in the shop of Samuel's older brother, Edward.

Secondly, the statement was made that Thomas Boardman almost certainly acquired Samuel Danforth's moulds when the latter died in 1816, because of the identity of design of flagons, teapots, and beakers made by the two shops. I still believe that assumption to be true even though Thomas Boardman himself stated that the "Mess Yales of Wallingford . . . purchased the tools and moulds of the late Sam Danforth." There is certainly no record of Yale flagons, teapots, or beakers that resemble at all the designs of those forms which bear the Samuel Danforth or Boardman marks. It is of course possible that Boardman acquired some of the Danforth moulds during Samuel's lifetime.

A third statement in Volume One which must be withdrawn is that the branch offices, Boardman & Company and Boardman & Hart in New York, as well as Boardman & Hall and successor companies in Philadelphia, were merely sales outlets for wares made in Hartford by the parent organization. Thomas Boardman's correspondence with Lucius Hart, as well as printed advertisements of Hall, Boardman and Company, prove conclusively that, both in New York and Philadelphia, a great deal of pewter and britannia ware was made on the premises, possibly all of the pewter bearing the New York and Philadelphia touches.

It is a great pity that, in his closing years, Thomas Boardman became embittered against his partner and long-time friend, Lucius Hart, accusing the latter of pocketing sums of money, that should have been accredited to the company's accounts. Hart's letters of protest have the ring of truth and one wonders whether Mr. Boardman's mind was not poisoned by the calumnies of some individual or individuals who were personal enemies of Hart.

In Volume Two it was stated that the business of the Boardmans was closed out in 1854. It may be that Boardman & Company ceased to function under that name in that year, but its founder, Thomas D. Boardman, continued to operate the plant, at least in a small way, for some years longer. Finally in September 1871 he offered for sale the "Old Britannia Manufactory" of Boardman & Company and in the advertisement stated that "advanced age of the subscriber renders him desirous of closing out business." Thomas D. Boardman was at that time eighty-six years of age, assuredly time to retire. He died two years later.

It would be tedious, and probably needless, to try to catalogue all the forms that were made by Thomas D. Boardman, his partners and successor firms. The Boardmans were undoubtedly equipped to make any article in pewter or britannia for which there was a demand and in any size desired.

Comment should be made about one shape, illustrated in Volume Two (Plate LXXVII, Fig. 671). This was an illustration of a handled flower vase or bucket, which was attributed to the Boardmans on the basis of a recollection of a great-granddaughter of Thomas D. Boardman. Perhaps the Boardmans did make such a vessel, but we now know for sure that an item of identical design was made and marked with the name, Flagg and Homan.

THE YALE FAMILY

Comment will be made first about the older Yale brothers, William and Samuel. Their eagle touch has been found on $6\frac{1}{8}$ inch butter plates and 11 inch deep dishes, as well as on forms previously listed.

Of the business activities of Charles and Hiram Yale new information has been gleaned from the papers of Thomas D. Boardman, which have been excerpted in some detail on pages 85–86 of this volume. From Boardman's statements we now know, contrary to a statement in Volume One (which had been based on an earlier statement in a volume entitled *Historical and Pictorial Description of the Town of Meriden, Connecticut*), that the Yales not only did not obtain their training in Captain Thomas Danforth's shop, but actually had had no previous experience in pewter-making, when they bought tools and moulds from Samuel Danforth's estate and set up in business for themselves. How they lured away Thomas Derby, Josiah Danforth's journeyman, with an offer of higher pay; through him learned Boardman's secret for the composition of britannia metal; and then advertised that they had learned the art of making the new metal, can be found in the Boardman records.

Comment should be made also about certain touches used by Hiram Yale. Plates have been found impressed with Hiram's eagle-head touch, Fig. 444, and also with touches depicting the bust of General Jackson, Fig. 441 and 442 all on Plate LVIII. The last two had been found previously either alone or in conjunction with T. S. Derby's name touch and had consequently been attributed to Derby. But on Plate CVI in this volume the Yale eagle 444a and the larger of the Jackson busts 442b are shown in conjunction, as they appear on a $13\frac{1}{8}$ inch deep dish in the collection of John H. McMurray. From the Boardman papers we know that Derby was merely a journeyman working for Josiah Danforth, when lured away by the Yales. So in all probability he acquired the Jackson dies only after they had been discarded by his master. They are now credited therefore to Hiram Yale with Derby as a secondary, and later user. The captions for Figs. 441 and 442 on Plate LVIII should be revised accordingly.

Hiram's early touches have been found on $8\frac{3}{8}$ inch plates, $11\frac{1}{8}$ and $13\frac{1}{8}$ inch deep dishes, 12 inch basins, and 8 inch teapots. The later uninteresting incised H. Yale and Co. is found on similar forms and also on communion flagons, chalices, beakers, teapots, coffee pots, and two-handled mugs. Illustrated as Fig. 812 of Plate CI is an unusual covered baptismal bowl, standing on a $7\frac{1}{2}$ inch tray which bears Yale's late touch.

PLATE CVI—*Connecticut Touches*

415a and 850. A clearer impression of the large touch (415) of Ebenezer Southmayd, Castleton, Vermont, 1802–1820, together with Southmayd's hallmarks as photographed on an 11½-inch-deep dish. Collection of William M. Goss Jr.

405a. Excellent impressions of the large touch 405 of Samuel Pierce, Greenfield, Massachusetts, 1807–1830. Collection of Dr. and Mrs. S. Harris Johnson III.

851. A different eagle touch used by Jacob Eggleston while working in Fayetteville, North Carolina, 1807–1813. Note the similarity of the design to 366, a touch of the third Thomas Danforth. Found on a 7⅞-inch plate and 13-inch-deep dish. Courtesy Museum of Early Southern Decorative Arts, Old Salem, Winston-Salem, North Carolina.

852. Rather badly worn touch which appears to have been made with a different die from that used for Jacob Eggleston's touch, Fig. 386, Plate LIV, Volume One. Collection of Mr. and Mrs. Charles W. Baughn.

449a. Better impression of 449 than that illustrated in Volume One, attributed to Jehiel Johnson, Middletown, Connecticut, and Fayetteville, North Carolina. From the collection of the Museum of Early Southern Decorative Arts, Old Salem.

450a. Clear impressions of the touch of William Nott, illustrated as 450 in Volume One, Middletown, Connecticut, and Fayetteville, North Carolina, 1813–1825. Courtesy of the Museum of Early Southern Decorative Arts, Old Salem.

444b and 442b. The discovery of the Hiram Yale eagle with the General Jackson touch is proof positive that the Jackson die was used by Hiram Yale and passed later to his one-time journeyman, T.S. Derby, Wallingford, Connecticut, 1822–1825. Collection of John H. McMurray.

PLATE CVI

415 a   850   405 a

851   852   449 a

450 a   444 b   442 b

THE NOTTS AND JOHNSONS

Careful research into the histories of Connecticut pewterers by Wendell Hilt seems to confirm the statements expressed in Volume One, page 133, that although two William Notts worked in pewter in Connecticut early in the nineteenth century, the maker whose pewter is marked with an eagle, a Masonic emblem, and the name W. Nott (see Plate CVI, Fig. 450a) is the man who was born in Middletown on February 10, 1789, and married Elizabeth Gaylord in April 1809.

On December 14, 1809, when Nott was still in his minority, the following notice appeared in the Middlesex Gazette:

William Nott

> Informs the Public that he has taken the Shop belonging to Mr. William Danforth, where the Pewtering, and all other business formerly done at that shop, will be continued in all its various branches, with punctuality and dispatch.
> N.B. Cash given for Old Pewter.

For several reasons that notice is of interest to us. Although we cannot know what sort of deal Danforth made with Nott, the wording does not seem to indicate that Nott bought out the older man's shop and business. It would, in fact, have been surprising, if Nott, at the age of twenty, could have raised the capital for any such venture. Rather, the implication seems to be that Nott was acting as agent and caretaker for Danforth, while the latter was absent on business elsewhere. That supposition is strengthened by the knowledge (see p. 75) that Danforth advertised, just a few months later, that he was leaving Middletown to be gone for seven months. The occasion for his absence is at best conjectural, but he may have learned from Eggleston, or from some of his own peddlers, that the opportunities for the sales of pewter in Georgia and the Carolinas warranted moving his shop into that area, and a firsthand exploration of such a move was warranted.

Another deduction, that can be made from this notice, is that Nott had probably served his apprenticeship to Danforth. The latter would surely have hesitated about entrusting his business to a twenty-year-old, unless he knew the boy well and had great confidence in the young man's training, ability, and judgment.

If the above surmises are correct, the pewter which Nott made in his early years would almost surely have come from Danforth moulds and, just as surely, would have been stamped with William Danforth's touches.

Late in 1813 Jacob Eggleston died in Fayetteville, North Carolina, and the major portion of his moulds for pewter casting, weighing 346 pounds, were sold to William Nott. Because final settlement of that estate did not occur until 1821, we cannot be sure how early Nott was able to operate a shop with his own moulds and equipment, but probably not before 1814 or 1815. As we know, he was making pewter in Fayetteville by 1817. The one known Nott touch (Fig. 450a), would probably have not been struck before August 1818, when he joined a Masonic lodge in Fayetteville. There is nothing additional to record about Nott's later history and just one form can be added to the list of products which he is known to have made, an 11$\frac{3}{16}$ inch flat dish.

Jehiel Johnson's history follows very closely the Nott pattern. His apprenticeship must have been completed about 1805, possibly under William Danforth or Eggleston. Very early, certainly by 1809, he was in close business association with Eggleston and when the latter died in 1813, he was appointed an administrator of the estate. A significant entry in the inventory under the heading of "Doubtful Notes," reads as follows:

> Ichabod Ward's in fav^r of Jacob Eggleston & Jehiel Johnson.
>   Date Sept. 14, 1809—$100.^{00}

This surely is an indication of a business connection between Eggleston and Johnson at that time.

Whether, as in the Danforth-Nott relationship, Johnson had been operating a shop for his older patron, or whether he was a partner in Eggleston's shop, cannot be determined from the estate records. It is of interest, though, that in the Census of Connecticut for 1810, Eggleston's name is on the Middletown lists and right next to it is that of Jehiel Johnson, indicating that Johnson probably lived with, or next door to, Eggleston.

Although Johnson must have had the first opportunity to buy moulds from Eggleston's estate, he failed to do so, perhaps because of lack of capital. So, when Eggleston's business was wound up, Johnson had to look for a new job and found this in a partnership with his brother, Constant, selling groceries in Middletown.

Jehiel Johnson's later history was discussed in Volume One on pages 134 and 135. Further comment about his activities in Fayetteville will be found on page 159 in this volume. A somewhat clearer impression of his touch 449 is shown on Plate CVI and there listed as Fig. 449a.

SIMEON STEDMAN

A maker named S. Stedman was listed in Volume Two among the men of the britannia period, because a ladle with birch handle, stamped with that name, had been reported.

Thanks to the investigations of J. C. Thomas, and particularly of Wendell Hilt, we can now put a little flesh on what had been just a name.

Thomas discovered that a patent on a ladle socket had been granted on July 25, 1818, to S. Stedman of Hartford, Connecticut. He pointed out that the name was not struck, as would be expected, normally, in the bowl of the ladle, but rather at the juncture of metal sleeve and wooden handle. The incised letters are large and thin as though intended for stamping on wood. The question then was raised whether Stedman simply made the handles and bought the bowls from the Boardmans or others.

The man's history, as ferreted out by Hilt is as follows: Simeon Stedman, son of Phineas and Sara (Howard) Stedman, was born May 25, 1782, either in Stafford, Connecticut, or Sturbridge, Massachusetts. He is presumed to have been apprenticed to a cabinet maker in Hartford. On November 24, 1808, he married Sally, sister of Thomas and Sherman Boardman. A few months earlier Simeon Stedman of Hartford, Connecticut, cabinetmaker, purchased an eighty-acre farm in Chicopee Parish, Springfield, Massachusetts, from Abel Chapin. Because Aaron Chapin, a now-well-known cabinetmaker, lived next door to the Boardmans in Hartford, and because Stedman bought property from a member of the Chapin family, he may have served his apprenticeship in Chapin's shop.

Although he is supposed to have moved with his family to Springfield soon after his marriage, there is record of property transactions in Hartford in the years 1816, 1820, 1822, and 1825. And since the patent in 1818 was made out to S. Stedman of Hartford, we must assume that much of his time was spent there even though his name was not found in Hartford, either in the Census of 1810 or of 1820. He probably moved permanently to Springfield soon after 1825, for there he died in 1842. In his inventory were "2 blocks of metal" and "187 sheets of tin."

Without much doubt Stedman made the wooden handles, fitted them into the pewter bowls and stamped them. Whether or not he made the pewter bowls himself or purchased them from his brothers-in-law cannot be determined now.

THOMAS S. DERBY

Thomas D. Boardman's brief autobiography in manuscript form and other Boardman papers on file in the Connecticut State Library throw a new light on Thomas Derby's career, as does the discovery of Hiram Yale's eagle touch in conjunction with the earlier of the General Jackson touches, Plate LVII, Fig. 441, which had been attributed to Derby.

Boardman related (see page 85, this volume) the story of his experiments and eventual success in developing a new alloy, which was, in practicality, the same composition as the English britannia. This secret he divulged at first only to his brother Sherman. Then—but let Thomas tell it in his own words—"about 1821 to help a young friend Just beg[inn]ing business [I] gave him the Secret—with the request that it should not be communicated to the 3ᵈ person."

The young friend was Boardman's cousin, Josiah Danforth, and, in a weak moment, young Danforth let his journeyman, Thomas Derby, into the secret. Soon thereafter Charles and Hiram Yale purchased the moulds and tools of Samuel Danforth of

Hartford and began hiring away the best workmen in other shops, including Thomas S. Derby, and immediately advertised that they had discovered the art of mixing britannia metal. It is therefore apparent that Derby did not have a shop of his own prior to 1822 at the earliest.

What's more Derby can have no credit at all for the design of the interesting General Jackson touches. Both were first used several years before he opened a shop. Now that pewter has been found with Hiram Yale's eagle and a Jackson touch on the same surface, it becomes evident that Derby must have acquired the second of the Jackson dies (Fig. 442) only after it had been discarded by the Yales.

In retrospect I am interested now in recalling that when I first saw a head-of-Jackson touch, back in 1927, on an 11½ inch basin, I had no idea who the maker was. This was in a dealer's shop in Baltimore. With it were three plates and a deep dish, bearing another mark, then new to me, Hiram Yale's eagle-head mark. I recall having been told that the basin, dish, and plates had all been found together in a Maryland farmhouse. This tends to confirm the fact that Hiram Yale, and not Derby, deserves credit for the first use of this patriotic mark.

And so perhaps Derby should be downgraded to a position not far above the lowly estate to which J. B. Kerfoot had assigned him.

J. CURTISS

Although the identity and place of work of this maker are still undetermined, we have one more bit of evidence that indicates that the man who used this touch was Joseph Curtiss of Albany. The mark has been found on a teapot which appears to be identical with that illustrated as Fig. 604 of Plate LXXI in Volume Two, a teapot made by Daniel Curtiss.

Besides small plates and this teapot, the Curtiss touch has been found on a pint basin, an 11⅛ inch deep dish and a coffee pot.

J. AND D. HINSDALE

The research of Wendell Hilt has developed the fact that the Hinsdale brothers formed their partnership on March 1, 1810, and has confirmed the statement, on page 137 in Volume One, that they failed in 1826.

Copy of a bill of sale from the Hinsdales to one Elias Stephens (address not shown) from "Augusta, 5th Augt. 1820" appeared in a bulletin of the Pewter Collectors' Club in February 1962.

The bill is interesting not only for the shipments recorded, but also for the date line. Was this Augusta, Maine, or Augusta, Georgia? It seems probable that the Hinsdales, like so many other Connecticut craftsmen and merchants, operated a shop for a brief period in the South. That however is still to be proved.

Included in the items sold to Stephens were "4 doz Table Spoons and 100 lb. of Pewter." If this latter item was old pewter, Elias Stephens may have been a pewterer. Where he lived and what his occupation was are matters still to be determined.

In 1940 nothing but 8¾ inch plates had been found that were stamped with the Hinsdale eagle. That touch has also been reported upon quart (8 inch) basins and upon a 13¼ inch deep dish.

SAMUEL CAMPBELL

Since 1940 we have learned that this maker's name was Campbell and not Campmell. And, thanks to the research of Miss Nancy Goyne, it has been established that he worked in Baltimore, Maryland—not in Connecticut, see page 159 in this volume. His name should be removed from the Connecticut list.

OTIS WILLIAMS

In the past thirty-five years just two more examples of Williams' work have been reported to me, a second 8 inch plate and, a rare form for any maker, a 12 inch basin. Oddly enough, one of these turned up in Illinois, the other in California.

THE PEWTERERS OF NEW YORK CITY

W HAT was written about New York pewter and pewterers for publication in 1940 is as true today as it was then. In the intervening years a few more makers have been uncovered, including Thomas Burroughs, whose activities began there in 1692 or earlier, making him now the city's earliest pewterer of record. Many more examples of the work of New York makers have been found, and those discoveries have merely confirmed and strengthened our earlier views of the capabilities of New York pewterers as a group.

Perhaps fate has been kinder to the New York pewterers, in preserving for us a more representative sampling of the product of their shops, than has been the case for the pewterers of any of the other colonies. In any event, a wider diversity of form, shape, and design can be found today in marked New York pewter, than in that of any other area in this country. Pennsylvania alone might have some grounds for attempting to dispute that distinction.

Take the matter of tankards. Only one such vessel can be identified positively today as the work of a Boston pewterer. In Connecticut several eighteenth-century tankards still exist, but they all appear to have been made from the same set of moulds, though impressed with the touches of several different men. Even Pennsylvania tankards, made before 1800, can be traced to only five different shops. Now compare New York's contribution.

At least ten different eighteenth-century pewtering establishments in New York City have left one or more tankards each and some are represented by a dozen or more examples. What is more, those tankards vary greatly in such details as the form of cover, design of lip and of handle terminal.

New York pewter of extreme rarity and importance, illustrated in this volume, includes an early sweetmeat dish, Fig. 692 of Plate LXXX, an early teapot, Fig. 761 of Plate XCII, attributed to the first Francis Bassett, another teapot of much the same early form by Frederick Bassett, Fig. 762 of Plate XCII, as well as a tremendous tankard by this same pewterer, Fig. 713 of Plate LXXXV, the West Haven, Connecticut, church chalice, shown in the frontispiece and made by the senior Joseph Leddell, two unusual tankards, Figs. 715 and 717 of Plate LXXXV, from the shop of John Will, a magnificent flagon bearing the hallmarks of Philip Will, Plate XCIX, and a fine baptismal bowl, Fig. 809 of Plate CI made by Philip's brother Henry.

Thomas Burroughs, Senior and Junior

THOMAS BURROUGHS, SENIOR AND JUNIOR

Just as might have been expected, evidence has turned up that pewter was made in New York prior to 1700. In a fascinating article, entitled "A New I B Silversmith and Two Unrecorded Pewterers" in the January 1968 issue of the *New York Historical Society Quarterly*, Helen Burr Smith has presented the story of three early New York artisans, a father and two sons, whose names were unknown to present day collectors. The men in question were Thomas Burroughs, pewterer, his older son, Thomas, Jr., also a pewterer, and a younger son, Joel, a silversmith.

The record, which uncovered the names of these long-forgotten craftsmen, was a New York conveyance, dated July 9, 1712, which begins "I, Joel Burroughs, Silversmith, lately the younger son of Thomas Burroughs, late of the City of New York, Pewterer, deceased and heir to my deceased elder brother, Thomas Burroughs. . . ."

This discovery called to Miss Smith's memory a description in Francis Bigelow's *Historic Silver of the Colonies and Its Makers* of a very handsome, elaborately decorated, covered silver porringer, which had been presented to the Metropolitan Museum by Sylvester Dering, great-great-great-grandson of Thomas Burroughs, Sr., with the pedigree of ownership descent, as recorded by Mr. Bigelow. The porringer was engraved B over T.M. in a triad for Thomas and Mary Burroughs, with the date 1680, thought to have been the year of their marriage. Although the maker of the porringer had not marked it with his own initial mark, Mr. Bigelow attributed it to the famous Boston silversmith, John Coney. This provided a clue that Burroughs had lived in Boston before settling in New York. The porringer is illustrated both in Miss Smith's article and on page 310 of Mr. Bigelow's volume.

What follows is a transcript of the brief biography of Thomas Burroughs, as developed by Miss Smith from surviving records.

Thomas Burroughs, Sr. was married twice and had three children of record, all of whom were mentioned in his will—Thomas, Joel, and Mary. The first wife, Mary (maiden name unknown) was the mother of the two boys, Thomas and Joel. Just when and where she died is not known, but on November 16, 1695, Thomas wed Mary Whitehead, widow of John Taylor in New York. Their only child was Mary, born about 1702.

If the Burroughs porringer was made by Coney and if the date engraved thereon was the year of Thomas' first marriage, his first wife was probably a Boston girl. The only record of the family in Boston was the date of baptism of Thomas, Jr., June 4, 1684. Since there is no record there of the birth or baptism of the second son Joel, the Burroughs family probably moved to New York soon after 1684.

The earliest record placing them in New York is in an administration, that reads in part as follows: "Major Richard Ingoldsby, Captain-General and Governor, &c. Whereas Thomas Slater, late of the County of Albemarle in Carolina, died on board his sloop, 'Hopewell,' upon the main ocean, in a voyage from Providence to Carolina,

The Pewterers of New York City

Letters of administration are granted to Thomas Burroughs, pewterer, as the principal creditor, May 13, 1692."

On September 29, of that year, the Common Council of the City of New York elected Thomas Burroughs Constable of the Dock Ward. In 1696 he was elected High Constable of the city and re-elected to the same post in 1697. From 1698 to 1700 he was an assessor of Dock Ward. He was still serving the city on December 1, 1702, when the mayor ordered the treasurer to pay Burroughs £1, 10 shillings for a beam for the city's use.

In Thomas Burroughs' will, dated August 18, 1703, he termed himself "of the City of New York, Merchant." It was filed for probate just a few weeks later, September 2, 1703. He bequeathed one third of his personal property to his wife and two thirds to his children. To his daughter Mary he left "a large silver Porthenger (porringer) with a cover to it."

To his elder son, Thomas, he bequeathed "all my working Tools belonging properly to the Pewterers' trade." On January 7, 1704, just four months after his father's death, Thomas, Jr., sold part of the tools to William Bickley, Merchant, "for the consideration of £60." The younger Thomas at that time would have been under twenty years of age, still probably an apprentice, and not qualified to set up in business for himself.

On July 9, 1712, after Thomas, Jr.'s death, the rest of the tools were sold for £50 to another merchant, Richard Willett, by Joel Burroughs, as administrator of his brother's estate.

We know nothing about the specific articles included in the second sale, but some of the more interesting items sold to Bickley in 1704 were:

> One quart pott mould with handles and bottoms. One quart tankard mould with handles, bottoms and joynts, two bellyed porringer moulds with handles, four flat porringer moulds with handles, one chamber pott mould with handles, one plate mould, one large two quart bason mould, one casting kettle, one caudle cup mould, two dram cup moulds, one salt cellar mould, two soldering irons, two burnishers, five vices [sic] one anvill, one border hammer, two planishing hammers, one spoon hammer and stamp, one iron stake, two ladles, one casting bench, two silver-smiths' turning lathes, one negro man named Frank.

Thomas, Jr. died intestate before April 17, 1712, at Jamaica, Long Island. No record of any marriage was found. Miss Smith believes that he was an invalid and may never have worked at his trade. He did however term himself a pewterer in his bill of sale of moulds to William Bickley in 1704.

There can be little doubt that Thomas Burroughs, Sr., is the Bristol, England, pewterer whom Howard Cotterell in *Old Pewter, Its Makers and Marks* listed as number 717. According to Cotterell, Thomas, son of William Burroughs, was apprenticed to Thomas Paschall, Bristol, and Jane his wife, 24 October 1671, and was elected to the freedom of the guild 2 December 1678.

For anyone who might be interested in tracing Burroughs' ancestry in England, it may be presumed that he was born in or near Bristol about 1657. If we are correct in believing that he was married in Boston in 1680, he must have left Bristol very soon after completing his apprenticeship. It is of interest that Burroughs, who now becomes the earliest New York pewterer of whom we have record, learned his trade from Thomas Paschall, Philadelphia's first pewterer.

DAVID LYELL

The following newspaper notice appeared in the *Boston News Letter* of August 23/30, 1714:

> This is to give notice that a Journeyman Pewterer, who is a good workman in Hollow-ware, may have constant work and good Wages, if they will go to New York, and apply themselves to Mr. David Lyell, or they may write to him and know further."

No careful study of this man's history has been made, but we do know that he was admitted as a freeman of New York on August 28, 1699. He was, by training, a silversmith and the making of pewter must have been very much of a sideline. It is of particular interest however that the journeyman was offered "constant work" and was expected to turn out hollow-ware, rather than just spoons or plates as might have been expected in a shop in which pewter-making was a secondary issue.

If Lyell's pewter was marked the touch was probably very similar to the mark which he used on silver.

THE LEDDELLS

Although the first piece of pewter that could be identified positively as the work of a Leddell did not appear until the late 1930's, that one example, a christening bowl or basin, with narrow rim (Plate XXXVIII, Fig. 247) was an extreme rarity, with no counterpart in American pewter. The design and workmanship of the bowl indicated that the Leddells, in their day, must have been unusually well equipped and qualified to furnish a very wide choice in pewter forms.

Since that first discovery, at least thirteen or fourteen more pieces of pewter have been identified as the work of Joseph or his son and, instead of just one Leddell touch, we have six different marks of positive attribution, as well as a seventh, showing initials only, which very probably was used by a Leddell. Today, with such an array of pewter available for examination, a fair appraisal of the Leddells as pewterers can be made. There seems to be every reason for believing that they were at least as capable and had just as large a percentage of the going pewter business in New York as any of those men whom we believe to have been their principal competitors — John

Bassett, the first Francis Bassett, or William Bradford. What is more, they were probably equipped and trained to furnish a wider variety of forms than any other shop in New York.

Seven Leddell touches are shown on Plate CVII. The "I.L. from Old England" die (Fig. 854) must surely have been one of the senior Joseph's earliest touches, though we know that it was still in use as late as 1744. The mark certainly would not have been used by the younger Leddell. Three different ship-design dies—Figs. 853, 855, and 857 were used. Figs. 855a and 854b and one of the initial touches (Fig. 856), were also in use in 1744. Because Robert Boyle, an apprentice of the elder Leddell, was just embarking—forgive the pun—on his pewtering career at the time of Joseph the elder's death and adopted as his mark a ship-in-archway (Plate LXII, Fig. 493, Volume Two), which is strikingly like Leddell's Fig. 855, it is probably safe to assume that the latter was the die in regular use when Leddel died. Plate LXIX, Fig. 579, Volume Two, shows another L.L. touch which can be attributed only tentatively to Leddell, because it has never been found in conjunction with a known Leddell mark.

Leddell forms reported to date are: 9 and $9\frac{5}{16}$ inch plates, flat dishes measuring 12, $13\frac{1}{2}$, and 15 inches in diameter, two baptismal basins of 13 inch diameter, at least two porringers in the $4\frac{7}{8}$ to $5\frac{1}{4}$ inch range, quart tankards with two different types of lid, one with flat top, the other domed, both with crenate lip, a large circular covered box and the largest—in some respects the finest—of all American chalices. This splendid vessel, frontispiece to this volume, formerly used in Christ Church, West Haven, Connecticut, now on loan at the New Haven Historical Society Museum, is $10\frac{1}{4}$ inches high. The bowl alone measures $5\frac{1}{2}$ inches in depth and $4\frac{3}{4}$ inches in diameter.

The lidded box mentioned above (not illustrated) with a $6\frac{1}{4}$ inch-top diameter, now in the Metropolitan Museum of Art, is a much larger container, but of exactly the same design as another box, Plate XL, Fig. 255, Volume One, which is impressed with another very rare touch, showing the initials W.B. and two stags' heads within an oval. The latter mark was attributed with reservations in 1940 to William Bradford, New York pewterer and contemporary of the elder Leddell. Discovery of the Leddell box strengthens the attribution of the stag-head touch to Bradford, because these two boxes, at least as far as I know, are the only recorded examples, American, English, or Continental, of what must have been a very specialized form in pewter. One wonders for what particular purpose this box was designed. Joseph, junior, advertised in 1752 that he ". . . makes . . . any uncommon Thing in Pewter, in any Shape or Form as shall be ordered. . . ."

As indicated above, surviving Leddell forms now include three of those "Uncommon Things"—a baptismal bowl, a lidded box, and a tall chalice. Perhaps other equally unusual shapes, bearing Leddell touches, are still in existence and will eventually emerge from obscurity.

It has been suggested—and the point may have been well taken—that, in our lists and records, the family name should be spelled *Leddel* just as it appears in the car-

PLATE CVII — *Touches of New York Pewterers*

853 and 854. Two touches of Joseph Leddell, New York, 1712–1753, as impressed on a 12-inch dish. Collection of Charles V. Swain.

855 and 854a. Another combination of Joseph Leddell marks as they appear on a 9-inch plate owned by Mrs. Frank Beaven.

855a and 854b. Impressions of exactly the same touches, as photographed on a plate now in the New Haven Colony Historical Society Museum, formerly used in the West Haven Congregational Church. The chalice that was with this paten, illustrated as the frontispiece of this volume, is engraved with the date 1744, indicating that these touches were used late in Leddell's career.

856. A Leddell initial touch from the bottom of the above-mentioned chalice. Courtesy New Haven Colony Historical Society.

455a and 857. Another combination of Joseph Leddell marks, photographed on a 15-inch dish in the collection of Stanley Paddock.

528a, 529a, and 858. The touches illustrated are from a 19-inch charger, possibly the largest of surviving American dishes. The piece is hammered all over and was unquestionably made in Philadelphia by Simon Edgell, two of whose touches are impressed here, 1713–1742. No reasonable explanation can be offered for the presence here of a touch of Andries Michel who is believed to have worked in New York, *c.* 1742–1752. Courtesy of Henry Francis du Pont Winterthur Museum.

859. Another Michel touch from a 9¼-inch plate in the collection of the author.

PLATE CVII

853 854

855 854a

855a 854b

856

858 528a 529a

857 455a

859

touche touch mark, Fig. 455. However spelling was free and easy in those days and in such records of the Leddells as could be found in New York, my notes show only one instance where the final *L* was not doubled.

THE BASSETTS

To the late Ralph Thomas, former curator and librarian of the New Haven Colony Historical Society, we are indebted for information which he found in a ledger of Roger Sherman, Connecticut statesman and patriot-to-be, who kept a store in Chapel Street, New Haven, across from what is now "the old campus." Beginning in June 1761 and running into 1765, Sherman listed twenty-six entries in an account with Mary Elizabeth Bassett, whose husband, the first Francis, had died in 1758. During this period he shipped more than a quarter of a ton of old pewter to Mrs. Bassett in New York and received, in return, quantities of new pewter and "sundries." In only three entries was the pewter itemized by form. The only shapes, there listed, that have not been found with a Francis Bassett touch, were chamber pots and quart measures.

Apparently Mrs. Bassett, like Mary Jackson in Boston and Mary Willett in Maryland, carried on her husband's business just as in his lifetime — in this case for at least six years after the husband's death. It does not seem probable that any of these wives did the physical work of pewter-making, but we would like very much to know who the journeymen or apprentices were, who continued, we presume, to use the touches of their former masters. It is still my own assumption, and only that, that the younger Francis had been an apprentice of the first Francis and probably remained, after his master's death, as the shop manager for Mary Elizabeth Bassett.

The later history of the activities of the second Francis have been amplified in a small way by the finding of two newspaper notices which follow, both of which were printed in the *New Jersey Journal*:

> The subscriber acquaints the public that he carries on the Pewterer's Business at Horse Neck, Essex County, near Mr. Caleb Hatfield's, where he makes and mends all sorts of pewter such as plates, basons, tankards, quart pots, etc. etc. provided they bring him old pewter.

> June 14, 1780   Francis Bassett

and again:

> The subscriber takes this method to acquaint the public that he has removed from Horse Neck to Crane Town, opposite Mr. William Crane's, where he continues to make and mend all sorts of pewter ware, with the provision they bring him old pewter,

> Francis Bassett

> N.B. Said Bassett gives cash for old pewter

> April 2, 1782

Horse Neck was in the present-day Caldwell and Crane Town is now in Montclair. At one time during the Revolution, William Crane's house was used as General Washington's headquarters. It was located at what is now the junction of Valley Road and Clairmont Avenue in Montclair. Bassett was still living in Crane Town on May 4, 1783, as proved by a third newspaper notice of that date. The British troops evacuated New York City in November 1783, and Francis probably returned to his shop there late in that year, or early in 1784.

A great many more examples of the work of the Bassetts have found their way into collections in the past thirty years.

Probably the most unusual, as well as the earliest, is a fluted and engraved sweetmeat dish, Plate LXXX, Fig. 692. Amazingly, a second dish of almost identical design came to light not many months after the first and is illustrated for comparison as Fig. 691. These plates have been described in detail and discussed at some length on page 8. Here it will be noted only that on the back of the 1732 dish is a worn but clearly identifiable impression of the circular lion-and-initials touch (Plate LIX, Fig. 461, Volume Two) of the first Francis Bassett. On the earlier, 1728 dish, any touch, that it may once have had, has been obliterated by wear. The maker cannot be identified.

Only less important, in the history of American pewter, is the finding of a Francis Bassett teapot, illustrated as Fig. 761 of Plate XCII. Earlier in design than any other marked American example, it is probably representative of the earliest form of teapot made in the Colonies. (See page 19 for further comment.)

Of special interest also are two tremendous Bassett tankards, one holding two quarts fifteen ounces, the second two full quarts. The larger vessel, owned by Dr. Adelbert C. Abbott, was described and illustrated in the Pewter Collectors' Club *Bulletin* for November 1955 and became the subject of a controversy in the following issue of July 1956. The tankard is marked with a badly worn F.B. touch, which seemed to differ from any known Bassett mark. So the question arose as to whether this was a Bassett piece or the work of an unidentified English pewterer. Since then the acquisition by William Goss of a two-quart tankard with an identical handle, of a design not previously reported on a Bassett tankard, and bearing Frederick Bassett's well-known initial touch, Plate LIX, Fig. 465, Volume Two, should settle the origin of the Abbott vessel. The two-quart tankard is illustrated as Fig. 713 of Plate LXXXV. No other marked American tankard, known to me, approaches in size Dr. Abbott's huge example. The flattened handle terminal of both tankards seems early in design for a pewterer who appeared on the scene as late as Frederick. Very probably the moulds for same had been owned and used many years earlier by his father, John Bassett.

Additions to John Bassett's list of known forms should include $8\frac{1}{2}$ and 9 inch plates with normal rim, $6\frac{1}{2}$ and 9 inch basins, $4\frac{7}{8}$ inch porringers, and an infusion pot.

For Francis Bassett, first or second, previously unrecorded forms, besides the sweetmeat dish and teapot mentioned above, are $8\frac{1}{2}$, 9 and $9\frac{1}{4}$ inch smooth brim plates, and $4\frac{5}{8}$ and $5\frac{5}{8}$ inch beakers.

PLATE CVIII — *New York and Albany Touches*

860. Touch of John Bassett, New York, 1720–1761; almost identical, except for the difference of the first initial, with touch 462, Plate LIX, Volume Two, which was there attributed to Francis Bassett, New York, 1718–1758 (brother of John) or to Francis Bassett 2nd, John's son, 1754–1799. From a 9-inch plate in the collection of Mr. and Mrs. Paul M. Young.

860a. Another impression of the same touch as found on an 8½-inch plate, this one in the collection of William M. Goss Jr. Here the initial I can be definitely distinguished from the F in 462. Other details also vary, as can be seen under a magnifying glass.

474a and 483a. A combination of John Will touches illustrated to show that the suspended sheep touch, 474, was used by John Will, New York, 1752–1774. Collection of Mr. and Mrs. Richard Rockwell, photograph courtesy of Charles D. Lyon.

476a, 475b, and 477a. This same group of touches was illustrated on Plate LXI, Volume Two, and there attributed to John Will. This illustration proves them to have been touches of John's son Philip, New York and Philadelphia, *c.* 1763–1787. As can be seen on Plate LXI, the New York touch was used by John as well as by Philip. Courtesy of Eric de Jonge and Harry Hirsch, owner of the plate.

504a. Another impression of William Elsworth's rarer large touch as found on a 15-inch dish, New York, 1767–1798. Collection of John J. D. Feyko.

495a. A touch which complements Fig. 495, Plate LXII, Volume Two, showing the hitherto unknown upper section of this Philadelphia touch of Cornelius Bradford, 1733–1770. From a quart tankard in the collection of Dr. Joseph H. Kler. Courtesy of Smithsonian Institution, United States National Museum.

861. A Bassett touch, probably used by Frederick, New York, 1761–1800, which resembles closely Frederick's initial touch, 468, as photographed from the under side of the porringer illustrated as Fig. 706, Plate LXXXIII, in this volume. Collection of Amory S. Skerry.

862 and 863. Touches of Ebenezer Crossman, Hudson, New York, *c.* 1790–1800, as photographed from a plate in the collection of John P. Remensnyder.

864, 865, and 520a. A group of touches as they appear on an 8-inch plate in the collection of Dr. and Mrs. Robert Mallory III. The maker is presumably Andrew Thompson, Albany, 1811–1817. The use here of the same Albany mark that is found on S. Stafford pewter may indicate that Stafford sold Thompson's pewter. No explanation can be offered for the small S. G. initial touch.

866. Another touch of Andrew Thompson, Albany, 1811–1817, as photographed on an 8-inch basin. Courtesy of Henry V. Button.

PLATE CVIII

860

860a

474a   483a

504a   495a

476a   475b   477a

861   862   863   864   865   520a   866

Frederick Bassett's already wide range of products has now been enlarged to include $16\frac{1}{2}$ inch deep dishes, basins up to $13\frac{1}{2}$ inches in diameter, $5\frac{5}{8}$ inch beakers, the huge tankards commented upon above, a teapot of early design, a double-flap inkstand, an infusion pot, and tablespoons.

At last we have a large touch for John Bassett, here illustrated as impressed on an $8\frac{1}{2}$ inch, and again on a 9 inch plate, Plate CVIII, Figs. 860 and 860a. As will be seen the touch is almost identical with one that has long been attributed to Francis Bassett, Sr., or to the younger Francis, Plate LIX, Fig. 462, Volume Two. It even repeats the reversed N of New York. There are slight variations in the curves of the curlicues in the two touches, but the only difference that is readily apparent is in the different first initial.

Another unrecorded Bassett touch is illustrated as Fig. 861 of Plate CVIII. This shows only a slight variation in design from Frederick Bassett's least rare initial touch, Plate LIX, Fig. 468.

For those who own copies of the first edition of Volumes One and Two of *Pewter in America*, attention is called to two errors in the earlier Bassett story. On page 6, Volume Two, in the fifth line from the bottom, the plate number should have read LXIX, instead of LXI. On page seven, line twenty-five, the figure number of the initial touch, there recorded, should have read 456 instead of 464.

THE BRADFORDS

In the 1940 edition, four touches, each of which included the initials W.B., Figs. 581, 582, 583, and 584, all on Plate LXIX, were classified as those of an unidentified maker or makers, but with the suggestion that any or all of them might have been used by William Bradford, Jr. The three smaller marks are in character with those of other New York pewterers and all four touches have been found on tankards, porringers, or other shapes that closely resemble similar forms made by Bradford's New York competitors. Of particular interest in this connection is the circular lidded box, which was illustrated as Fig. 255 of Plate XL in Volume One. The box was impressed with the W.B. stags' heads touch, Fig. 583, a touch that bore no close resemblance to any other American mark, and, up to that time, no other lidded box of that type had been reported. There was no assurance that it was even of American manufacture, much less that it had been made in New York. Since then a larger round container of the same general design has turned up and in it, providentially, is a touch of William Bradford's New York competitor, Joseph Leddell. In general there seem to be more grounds today, than twenty-five years ago, for attributing all four of those touches to William Bradford.

Two more examples of Bradford's handiwork are illustrated in this volume. One is a finely engraved quart tankard with flat lid and crenate lip, ram's-horn thumbpiece and fishtail terminal, Plate LXXXVI, Fig. 719. The second is an unusual basin, $5\frac{1}{2}$ inches in diameter. The sloping periphery of the bowl rises much more perpendicularly than in the normal pewter basin, Plate LXXXIII, Fig. 702.

The stag's head touch, one of the rarest of American touches, appears on a 9 inch plate and the initial touches on several more porringers and quart tankards.

Cornelius Bradford's pewter is still very scarce but a few more examples of his work have been found in the past twenty-five years. These include plates measuring $8\frac{1}{2}$, $8\frac{3}{4}$ and 9 inches, a three-footed pear-shaped teapot (Plate XCIII, Fig. 766) and a pint domed-top tankard (Plate LXXXVI, Fig. 722). Though pint tankards were made by most of the larger shops, old bills of sale indicate that there was never the same demand for them as for the quart size. Consequently, this is one of the scarcest of surviving forms in American pewter.

Illustrated as Fig. 495a of Plate CVIII is an impression of the upper half of Cornelius Bradford's Philadelphia touch, a portion of the mark which has not been shown previously.

THE WILLS OF NEW YORK

Since 1940 our knowledge of the capabilities and craftsmanship of John Will and his sons, Henry, Philip, and William, has been broadened by the finding of many Will forms, hitherto unknown to pewter collectors. At the same time we are now in position to fill in gaps in the Will family history, largely because of the research undertaken by Donald Noble, present owner of the remarkable John Will tankard illustrated in Figs. 717, 718 of Plate LXXXV, and described on page 14.

To the Burgomaster of Herborn, Noble wrote inquiring about the history of the family in Herborn, a town situated some forty or fifty miles east of Nieuwied on the Rhine, which latter was the hometown of Will and his family at the time that they emigrated to America. The information that follows is taken from a genealogical report prepared by Herr Walther Baumann at the request of Burgomaster Becker.

The forebears of the pewterer, Will, were traced back in Herborn to 1566, covering seven generations of the family. Most of his ancestors were tradesmen or craftsmen— bakers, butchers, dyers, weavers, etc.—though none are recorded as workers in metals. Several were guild masters, two of whom were leaders of a revolt in 1637, which demanded and obtained from the city the right of the guilds to a part in the governance of the town.

In general the Wills and allied families in Herborn seem to have been better educated than the masses, were prominent in the guilds, in the town government, and in the church. For instance, John Will's grandfather, of the same name, was a master baker and a warden in his church.

The pewterer was baptized in Herborn on May 10, 1696, and married Johanna

Judith Bömper of Herborn, on January 19, 1720. Children born in Herborn were Gertraud, November 15, 1720; Johann Jacob, August 13, 1724; Johannes, August 12, 1726; Martha Christina, October 1, 1728; Johann Wilhelm, October 29, 1731; Heinrich Bernhard, April 18, 1734; and Margaretha Elisabeth, November 1, 1736. Late in 1736, or early in 1737, the Wills moved to Nieuwied. Nothing more is known of Johann Jacob, Martha, or Johann Wilhelm, all of whom may have died in infancy or childhood. Gertraud was married in Nieuwied; Johannes preceded the family to New York; and Heinrich and Elisabeth were with their parents in Nieuwied and upon arrival in New York. So we now know that John Will was fifty-six years of age when he emigrated to New York with children ranging in age from eighteen to eight.

Herr Baumann reports that Johannes Will had an excellent record in Herborn "except that in the selection of his father-in-law he should have been more careful." The latter, John Jacob Bömper, had been a keeper of postal horses and, in 1710, became treasurer of the high school. Suddenly, in 1726, Bömper disappeared and rumors spread that money was missing from the school funds. An accounting disclosed a deficit of 476 Reich thalers. Some time later the wife made application for a reduction in this debt, charged to her, so that she might join her husband in New York.

Apparently John Will took over, in 1728, the administration of as much of the local postal business as his father-in-law had previously handled and is recorded in Herborn until 1731, as pewterer and postal officer. After 1734 he is termed citizen and pewterer and, in 1736, as a *Kannengiesser* or maker of hollow ware.

Through church records more has been learned also concerning John Will's later history in New York. In 1763 he was one of a group, probably its leader, that split away from the Reformed Dutch Church to establish the Reform German Congregation in New York. In that church's records from 1763 until 1772 his name invariably appeared first in the list of its three elders. His name is found for the last time in those records on April 15, 1774, when he and his wife were witnesses at a baptism. In 1775 or early in 1776 Henry Will moved to Albany and the church records show that many of the congregation moved to that city when the British landed in New York. Because no record of John Will's death could be found in New York, it seems probable that he too moved to Albany and died there during the Revolution. Since he would have been well up in his seventies, when we lose trace of him in New York, there is little likelihood that he made pewter during or after the Revolution.

To the earlier list of products made by John Will, as recorded in Volume Two, should be added $8\frac{7}{8}$ and $9\frac{5}{8}$ inch plates, creamers of at least two more designs, a tall beaker, and two quart tankards, differing widely in design from one another, neither of which has any exact counterpart in American pewter.

One of the creamers, on circular base, is illustrated in Fig. 778 of Plate XCV. Though unmarked, this piece has been attributed to John Will with considerable assurance, after a comparison of the handle and upper half of the vessel with marked I.W. creamers.

The Pewterers of New York City

The tall beaker, 6½ inches in height, Plate LXXXIX, Fig. 746, is very little smaller than the known examples made by John Bassett, Plate XXIII, Fig. 159, in Volume One, largest of American beakers. The touch in the Will piece is his rare early angel mark, Plate LXI, Fig. 482.

Two more examples of this man's hollow ware are illustrated as Figs. 715 and 716 of Plate LXXXV. The quart pot on the right has no rib or fillet, encircling the drum, whereas most New York pots were made with an unusually heavy rib. The tankard however is even more unusual. To the best of this writer's knowledge, it is the only New York tankard, thus far reported, with a bellied pot, and the only New York tankard with an acanthus-leaf-decorated double C handle. In fact this type of handle, used later by John Will's son, William, in Philadelphia on mugs, cups and tankards, is not known to have been employed by any other New York pewterer, or, for that matter, by any pewterer in New England.

Last of the John Will finds, and probably the most significant, is a flat-topped tankard, similar in design to Will tankards previously reported, but with a cover into which has been inserted a medallion illustrating a biblical story, Figs. 717 and 718, Plate LXXXV. In a depression in the center of the flat surface of the lid was impressed a cast religious picture in bas relief depicting an angel appearing to the prophet Elijah, as related in I Kings, 19:5–7. Whether made for use in a church or, as seems more probable, as a commemorative gift for an individual, this tankard was definitely designed and made on special order by a man, whom we now know to have been a prominent layman in his church, as well as an unusually able pewterer. That much abused and frequently misused adjective, unique, is truly applicable, to this tankard, which was probably the only one of its kind, even on the day that it was fashioned, some two hundred years ago.

Although John Will's stature has grown with the discoveries of new and unusual forms which he made, we are under compulsion to take away from him one touch and a set of hallmarks, which had been attributed to him with reservations in Volume Two. In Plate LXI are shown marks from an 8 inch plate then owned by the late Dr. Madelaine Brown (Figs. 475a, 476, and 477). Harry Hirsch acquired a pair of similar 8 inch plates in practically mint condition, with clear impressions of the 476 and 477 touches. These are now illustrated as 476a and 477a in Plate CVIII of this volume. It is immediately apparent that the user was Philip Will, and not his father, John. This raised a question as to whether the New York place touch, 475, which also appeared on the same plate, should not also be taken from John and given to Philip, as well as the suspended sheep mark, 474. The answer is no. On Plate CVIII are touches 474 and 483, illustrated together as 474a and 483a, as photographed on another 8 inch plate now owned by Mr. and Mrs. Richard Rockwell. So the suspended sheep remains in John Will's column, the rampant lion and hallmarks are taken from John and given to Philip and the New York place-of-work touch, 475, was evidently used by both John Will and his son Philip.

Before taking leave of John Will, attention should be called to an error in the text on page 13, Volume Two. I, in an absent-minded moment, wrote of John that he was an "agent for Amelung's ill-starred glass enterprise." Amelung's glass furnace was, of course, not in New York, but at Frederick, Maryland. Will, on this occasion, was acting for the Glass House Company of New York, known also as the Bayard-Bömper Glass Company. Since John Will's wife's name was Johanna Judith Bömper and one of the proprietors of the glass factory was Lodewyck Bömper it is altogether probable that a family as well as business relationship was involved here.

John Will's son, Henry, has left us a greater variety, in all probability, of unusual forms, than any other Colonial pewterer, with the possible exception of his younger brother, William, Philadelphia pewterer.

Although a long list of Henry's products was recorded in Volume Two, a few more varieties, unknown then, may be added now. These are $8\frac{1}{2}$ inch plates, $16\frac{3}{8}$ inch deep dishes, 8, 9, and $11\frac{1}{2}$ inch basins, 5 inch porringers, a ladle, $4\frac{5}{8}$ inch beakers, chalices, and at least one very fine christening bowl which is illustrated in Fig. 809 of Plate CI. Although the chalices, here attributed to Henry Will are unmarked, at least two such drinking vessels have been found in churches, which also owned marked Henry Will flagons, and, interestingly enough, the base of each of these chalices appears to have been cast from the same mold as the lid of the flagon. One such chalice is pictured as Fig. 813 of Plate CI. A Henry Will beaker is illustrated as Fig. 748, Plate LXXXIX. Henry Will advertised in 1786 that he made wine measures of all sizes but, thus far, no eighteenth-century measure, bearing the touch of any New York pewterer has been reported.

That Philip Will, despite the paucity of his pewter, was a well-trained maker, who may have been just as capable as his brothers, Henry and William, has been proved by the discovery of a Philip Will church flagon, marked with Philip's hallmarks. This remarkable vessel, owned by Mr. and Mrs. Oliver W. Deming, was the last important rarity to come to light before Volume Three went to press. It is illustrated as Fig. 806 of Plate XCIX.

Because Philip Will is believed to have been a journeyman working for his father, John, for a number of years after completing his apprenticeship, and because it is also thought that Philip may have inherited some of his father's moulds, it seems highly probable that if any of John Will's flagons should have survived and may come to light later, they may be expected to resemble closely Philip Will's masterpiece.

The measurements and description of the flagon will be found in the caption accompanying the illustration. It might be noted that the design and proportions of the body of the flagon closely resemble those of the Henry Will flagon illustrated as Plate XXXII, Volume One. However the fillet and the tooled decoration around lip and base of the drum are more elaborate and seem to this writer to enhance its beauty. The handle is better proportioned than Henry Will's tankard handle and its design has no counterpart in American pewter. If there be a weakness in Philip Will's design it is in the addition of a too heavy elaborate finial.

The Pewterers of New York City

PETER AND WILLIAM KIRBY

The only revision of the Kirby records as set forth in Volume Two consists in the addition to the lists of a few forms not recorded there, as well as some variations in size.

An $8\frac{7}{16}$ inch plate with Peter Kirby's initial touch has turned up, but we still have no large touch for this man. To be added to William Kirby's list are $8\frac{1}{2}$ and $8\frac{7}{8}$ inch plates with normal brim, porringers in four sizes from $4\frac{1}{4}$ to 5 inches, a slip-top round-bowl spoon, and a beaker, measuring $5\frac{3}{8}$ inches in height. A brass skimmer, bearing one of this maker's initial touches, has also been reported.

The following advertisement, which appeared in the *New York Daily Advertiser* for November 19, 1787, supplies a long list of products being made by Kirby at that date, most of which are still unaccounted for in today's collections.

William Kirby—Jersey Money

William Kirby, Pewterer, at No. 23 Great Dock-Street opposite the Old-Slip, and near Hanover-square has for sale a large and general assortment of Pewter Ware, Wholesale and retail, consisting of the following articles for which Jersey Paper-Money will be received without discount. . . . Dishes, Plates and Basons; Tankard, quart and pint pots, quart and pint and 1–2 Tea pots, straight and round dittos; pint and half pint porringers; soup, table and tea spoons, ditto laddles [sic] and round bowl spoons; large chamber pots; chair and bed pans; measures from a gallon to a gill; quart and pint bowls; infusing pots approved of in colds and consumptions; dish and basin callendars; hogshead, barrel and bottles cranes with many other articles in the Pewter way too tedious to mention. Old Pewter will be taken in exchange for new. . . .

ROBERT BOYLE

What became of Robert Boyle remains a mystery. It does not seem probable that he worked in New York for more than a very few years; otherwise, we would probably have found more of his handiwork. The only piece of pewter, marked with his touches, that has come to light in the past thirty years is a $16\frac{9}{16}$ inch dish, now in the Sleepy Hollow Restorations Collection, Tarrytown, New York, one of the largest of surviving New York dishes.

ANDRÉ MICHEL

A list of eight late New York workers, page 27, Volume Two, included André Michel, a tinsmith and pewterer, who was recorded in the city directories of 1795 and 1797 as working at 255 Broadway. It was assumed that these eight men were merely journeymen or menders of pewter, whose records scarcely warranted investigation.

Then Dr. Mallory acquired a 9 inch plate with a touch showing what appears to be a suspended sheep and, beneath it, in a rather badly erased touch, the letters MICH of what is unquestionably an incomplete name. The design of the touch clearly indicated its use long before 1795, perhaps twenty or thirty years earlier. But, if the name could be seen in a clear impression, would it be Michel?

The next development was the acquisition by the Henry F. du Pont Winterthur Museum of the largest (as far as now known) of all American dishes or platters, a 19 inch Simon Edgell dish. On the dish, flanking the Edgell name touch, are two badly worn impressions of a hitherto unknown mark, Plate CVII, Fig. 858. Just as in the suspended sheep touch, the name appears to be Michel. Above the name is a full-rigged ship, a design corresponding closely to that in touches of three other New York pewterers, Leddell, Boyle, and John Will. The period when the ship touches were in use in New York can be roughly estimated as from 1740 to 1760.

If the ship touch was used by the same André Michel, who was listed in New York directories as late as 1797, he must have been making pewter for over fifty years and would surely have been an old man at the only time when we found record of him as a pewterer. And how could it happen that the marks of a New York pewterer of the 1790's should be found on a Philadelphia dish made at least a half century earlier?

Whatever Michel's status was in the history of New York pewter, the new touches raised problems that warranted a search for their user. An examination of New York probate and land court records proved fruitless. Next church records were consulted. The French Church of New York seemed to offer the best chance for success, but no Michels were found there. Surprisingly, however, in the records of the Reformed Dutch Congregation, a Michel, who may have been the pewterer, was found.

On November 19, 1744, Andries Michael and Margareta Budern "uit Switserland" were admitted as members of the church and the following entries record baptisms of their children:

> February 28, 1742, Anna Margriet, daughter of Andries Michel and Margriet Puller
> March 4, 1744, Catharina, daughter of Andries Michel and Margareta Bultere
> January 12, 1746, Margareta, daughter of Andries Michel and Margaretta Dullering
> May 10, 1752, Johannes, son of Andries Michel and Margareta Buleren.

The clerk of the church seems to have been thoroughly confused by Madame Michel's maiden name. If the records have been read correctly, two of the children were baptized in the church before the parents were accepted as members. It was distressing to find that the family disappeared completely from the church's records after 1752.

In only one other New York record was this man's name found. There exists a list of "Persons Naturalized in New York Colony 1740–1769." The following entry appears therein:

> Michell, Andries, Dutch Reformed Church, New York City, labourer, April 21, 1748.

In Pennsylvania, and presumably in New York also, no foreigner could be naturalized until he had been in residence for seven years. We may assume, therefore, that he arrived in New York in April 1741, or slightly earlier. If this was our man, we wonder whether he had been trained as a pewterer in Switzerland.

There is no assurance that the Andries Michel of the Reformed Dutch Church from 1742 to 1752 was the André Michel of the directories of 1795 and 1797 but the names are strikingly similar. It could be that the André of 1795 was a son of Andries.

Because no record could be found in New York for an Andries or André Michel between the years from 1752 to 1795 and because his touch had been found on a Philadelphia dish, it was thought that he might have moved to Philadelphia, as Cornelius Bradford and two of the Wills had done, but a rather cursory search of the records there proved fruitless.

Since the above was written, a second 9 inch plate ($9\frac{1}{8}$ inches to be exact), with slightly clearer impressions of the suspended sheep touch, has come to light. The marks are illustrated as Plate CVII, Fig. 859. This particular example gives ample evidence that Michel, as a craftsman, could not be classified with Leddell, the Bassetts, or John Will. The plate is not very carefully finished, the booge was not hammered, as might well have been expected, and the metal is soft and of a dark color, no doubt because of a high lead content.

A comment of perhaps passing interest might be made about the design of Michel's touch. It seemed a rather odd combination of symbols, a suspended sheep above a fleur-de-lis. Cotterell's *Old Pewter* was consulted for a possible precedent. Sure enough, on page 301 is shown the touch of John Sedgwick, believed to have been of York, c. 1730, showing a dangling sheep above a fleur-de-lis. Surely Michel, seeing a plate of Sedgwick's, liked the design and took it to his diecutter as a proposed pattern for a touch of his own.

Although nothing can be stated with assurance about the user of these two touches, their character and design give every indication that they were in use in New York City at some time between 1740 and 1760.

CARY DUNN

Several years ago report was received of an eighteenth-century pewter creamer on three feet marked C — Dunn, N — York. I was unable to track down this piece but feel sure that it exists.

Without much doubt C — Dunn is the New York silversmith, Cary Dunn, who

Peter Young

was admitted as a freeman of the City of New York in 1765. He was essentially a worker in fine metals, but may have accepted old pewter in payment and, like such other New York silversmiths as David Lyell, occasionally hired a journeyman pewterer to come to his shop and work up the accumulation of old pewter.

In the 1770's Dunn's shop was at 23 Crown Street and in 1784 he advertised that he was "returning to this city from New Jersey after a seven years exile—that he carries on his business as usual at the old corner house where he formerly lived between the Fly Market and New-Dutch Church No 23 Crown-Street." Later he worked with a son at Smith Street and Maiden Lane and in 1791 and 1794 was at the corner of Maiden Lane and Liberty.

At what stage of his business career the pewter creamer was made cannot be determined.

WILLIAM J. ELSWORTH

The additions to the list of Elsworth marked forms are $8\frac{3}{8}$ and $8\frac{7}{8}$ inch plates, $11\frac{3}{4}$ inch flat dishes, $13\frac{1}{4}$ inch deep dishes and slip-top round-bowl spoons, the latter marked with the touch shown as Fig. 592, previously listed as that of an unidentified pewterer but now attributed to Elsworth with considerable confidence. Fig. 593, also listed as unidentified, but thought to be one that may have been used by Elsworth, is now attributed to an unidentified English pewterer.

PETER YOUNG

Two minor sidelights on Peter Young's history may be added to the earlier story. In 1775, when news of the battle of Lexington reached New York, a group of hotheads broke into City Hall, seized five hundred muskets and distributed them to known patriots. The New York Historical Society has a list of the men who gave receipts for their muskets, one of whom was Peter Young.

The second matter, of minor interest and conjecture, was occasioned by Dr. Adelbert C. Abbott's discovery of a Henry Will flagon and chalice in a church at Cambridge, New York. There he found in the church's records the following entry:

Mr. John McMullen

1797   To Peter Young Dr.
16 May

To 2 church cups @ 10/   £1 . . .0 . . .0

Rec'd payment for the above

                                                 her

Attest Henry Truax   Eva X Young
                                           mark

The church now has but one chalice. Unless they purchased from Young two chalices to add to the Henry Will service, chalices which have since been disposed of, this entry raises a few conjectures.

Henry Will had returned to New York in 1784. If the surviving chalice was one of the pair purchased in 1797 from Peter Young, then it may well be true, as we had surmised, that Young was no longer actively making pewter in 1797, but was acting as an agent for Will's shop in New York. Since the bill was receipted by Peter's wife, Eva, and since we know that Young was inflicted with an "imposthume" as a young man, the conjecture that he retired from active business in the early 1790's and later carried and sold Henry Will's products seems not unreasonable.

To our earlier list of Peter Young forms should be added quart mugs of a broad squat design, three-legged creamers of several types, sugar bowls, teapots and ladles. A fine sugar bowl is illustrated as Fig. 773 of Plate XCV. A ladle in almost mint condition which might serve almost as a Young touchplate is shown as Fig. 759 of Plate XC. It has clear impressions of three of his touches.

VAN DALSOM, VAN KLEECK, AND WILSON

What follows appeared first in an article entitled, "Three Embryo New York Pewterers" in the Pewter Collectors' Club *Bulletin* for January 1946.

In the New York Historical Society's *Bulletin* for July 1939 was printed a list of five hundred residents of New York City in 1775 with their occupations. The list was taken from a thin notebook dated July 8, 1775, found among the Alexander McDougall manuscripts. Dorothy C. Barck provided, with the list, an interesting commentary upon its *raison d' être*, which is presented here in abridged form.

News of the Battle of Lexington reached New York City on Sunday, April 23, 1775. That evening a number of hotheads broke into the City Hall and seized five hundred muskets belonging to the city. These were distributed to patriot sympathizers and, in most cases at least, receipts were signed by the recipients.

For several weeks, while a return to peaceful relations with the mother country hung in the balance, the self-appointed minutemen patrolled the streets, armed with their city-owned muskets. When, in July, the Second Continental Congress called upon New York to raise three thousand troops, the muskets were called in by the Provincial Congress.

It was then that the notebook was prepared on the basis of the receipts for muskets signed in April. Each page is ruled into four columns headed respectively: To Whom Delivered, No. of the Musket, Occupation, and Place of Abode.

The entries of particular interest to us, with the original spelling, follow:

McCuen, Malcomb	518	Plumber	18 Burling Slip
Van Kleeck, Peter	801	Pewterer	Partition St.
Van Dalsom, John	530	Pewterer	Cortland St.

| Wilson, Joseph | 699 | Pewterer | Dock St. |
| Young, Peter | 871 | [No occupation or address entered] | |

The list includes no New York pewterer with a well-established shop at that date and few men of mature age and established standing. McEuen and Young are, of course, well known to us, but were just starting their business careers in 1775. The majority appear to have been students, apprentices, and young journeymen and tradesmen — the materials of which rebellions are made.

A modest search was made for information about the later careers of Van Kleeck, Van Dalsom, and Wilson, but nothing was found to indicate that any one of the three made pewter in a shop of his own.

A "Peter Van Cleck, sergeant in 3rd Co. 2nd Regt. Philip Van Cortland, Colonel," died May 31, 1777, and on September 6, 1791, letters of administration upon the estate of "Peter Van Kleck of New York City, sergeant in Cortland's late regiment," were granted to Catharine Seaman, late Catharine Van Kleek, widow of the deceased. It seems reasonable to assume that the young patriot enlisted when war broke out and died in the service.

It may be recalled that William J. Elsworth, New York pewterer, married Ann Van Dalsam. According to the records of the Reformed Dutch Church in New York, John Van Dalsen was one of the witnesses at the wedding of "William Elswort and Annatje Van Dalsen." It is a natural supposition that John was a young brother-in-law of Elsworth, apprenticed to the older man to learn the pewterer's trade. He evidently did not follow the trade for long, for, in the city directory for 1791, the only man of that name was described as a ferryman, living at Cortland Street, the same street, incidentally, given as his address in 1775, and the location also of Elsworth's shop until 1798.

Of Joseph Wilson even less could be found. A man of that name married Sarah Hubbs June 22, 1775, and a Joseph Wilson, soapboiler and tallow chandler, had a shop on Beekman Street in 1792. It is pure conjecture whether either reference is to the musket-bearing pewterer.

MALCOLM McEUEN AND SON

In the history of the McEuens in Volume Two, it was pointed out that Malcolm was an "uncompromising patriot." Additional evidence has turned up that substantiates that statement.

On the evening of the arrival in New York of a messenger with news of the bloodshed at Lexington in April 1775, a group of young men broke into City Hall in New York and seized 500 muskets owned by the city. These were distributed to patriot sympathizers, who became self-appointed minutemen, who for several months patrolled the city. Two of the number who signed receipts for the muskets were Malcolm McEuen and Peter Young.

Just one more piece of McEuen pewter has been reported in the past thirty years, a $9\frac{1}{4}$ inch smooth rim plate with hammered bouge. The names D. and M. McEuen are clearly seen in this better impression of the touch previously attributed to the McEuens, Fig. 507 in Plate LXIII, Volume Two.

GEORGE COLDWELL AND MOSES LAFETRA

In Volume Two it was stressed that George Coldwell was an individualist, who did not run with the crowd. His work that has survived shows him to have been an artist, and what little we know of his private life indicates that he had problems of a kind that are frequently associated with men of artistic temperament.

Even the shapes which Coldwell made differed greatly from those of his competitors. This we know not only from his pewter that has survived, but also from his advertisements. Note for instance his offerings in the July 25, 1803, issue of the *Daily Advertiser* as quoted below:

George Coldwell

Ice Cream Moulds, a few pair of pewter Ice-Cream Moulds are now finished and now offered for sale at the subscriber's work-shop No 7 Beekman-street. They contain one gallon, are well made of the best materials, very strong and infinitely more durable than those made of Tinned Iron. Likewise for sale quart and pint Beer Pots, Seal'd Spirit Measures from a gallon to the half jill, Suckling Bottles for infants, Chamber Pots, Night Chair Pans, Bed do; Funnels, Sacrament vessels, common Toys, Plates for Music, with upwards of twenty different sizes Candle Moulds, plain, fluted and half fluted from threes to tens.

George Coldwell

Listed in William Will's inventory in 1799 were two "ice cream moulds." Nowhere else, except in this Coldwell advertisement, have I ever read of pewter ice cream moulds. No other American pewterer, to my knowledge ever advertised toys or "Plates for Music."

In another Coldwell advertisement of August 5, 1802, he offered for sale, among other items ". . . appropriate vessels &c for celebration of the Holy Sacrament, Ink Stands with glass bottles, Tea Pots, Turreen [sic] Ladles . . . Plates for Music prepared for Type . . . with sundry other articles. N.B. The Customers will not be asked at the first more than what the Goods will be sold for. George Coldwell." Even his advertising bespeaks the individuality of the man.

Of his antecedents and history before he first appeared in a New York directory in 1787 we know nothing. So different in form and feeling is his work from that of any of New York's eighteenth-century pewterers that we can feel all but certain that he was not a native and that he learned his trade elsewhere. Howard Cotterell in *Old Pewter* listed a George Coldwell who was mentioned as a pewterer in Cork, Ireland, in 1773. This may be our man.

Oddly, it seems, Coldwell did not advertise specifically those articles for which he is best known in collections today—japanned and engraved beakers and small lidded boxes, of various shapes and sizes. One such little container in the shape of a lady's slipper with lid, made perhaps as a patch box was japanned and engraved in the typical Coldwell manner. In addition a few of his "elegantly ornamented table and tea spoons," which he did advertise have turned up. A few also of his larger forms have at last been found. These include a ladle, teapots with boat-shaped bodies in two different designs, Plate XCIV, Figs. 771 and 772, and at least two teacaddies, one of which appears as Fig. 823 of Plate CIII.

Please turn to the illustration of that well-designed, neatly-engraved container. When Thomas D. Williams sent me, early in 1969, a photograph of the caddy, which he had recently acquired, I realized at once that somewhere I had seen strikingly similar engraved designs. A search through my files uncovered correspondence twenty-five years earlier with Mrs. Bertram K. Little of Brookline, Massachusetts, telling me about a pewter tea caddy which she had acquired, giving a description of it, its measurements, and pencil rubbings of the engraved patterns and of the touch which read Coldwell & Dean. The rubbings of the engraved designs were not only similar to those of the Williams caddy (which was marked G. Coldwell, N. York), they were identical, as were the measurements. Alas when I inquired from Mrs. Little about her caddy, she wrote me that she had determined that it was English and had disposed of it a number of years ago.

The next chapter in the Coldwell tea caddy mystery was the finding by Mr. Williams of another very similar caddy with exactly the same formalized leaf-pattern design of banding and similar decoration on the lids of both caddies. But this caddy was marked Thompson. (It is illustrated as Fig. 824 of Plate CIII.) Was this Thompson, the pewterer, who worked in Albany for a few years? It would seem probable, because Thompson first appeared in Albany directories in 1811, the year in which Coldwell died in New York. One would think that it would now be a very simple matter to link togehter Dean and Thompson with Coldwell. On the face of it the expectation would be that both had been apprentices or journeymen in Coldwell's shop. All that was needed was to check the Deans and Thompsons in the New York directories for the years between 1787 and 1811.

Well, that was done, but the so-promising clues led no place. For one year only in 1789 a Stewart Dean was listed at 144 Queen Street, no occupation shown. Once again, for one year only 1807–08 another Dean, first name Joseph, was recorded as a smith at 24 Sixth Street. The search for Thompson was almost as unsatisfactory. The only Andrew Thompson (the name of the Albany pewterer) in the New York directories for those years was termed a mason. There was, however, at different addresses on Water Street from 1802 until 1811, a Samuel Thompson, termed a tin and coppersmith, but not after 1811. Samuel might have been the maker of the Thompson tea caddy, but any such attribution would be mighty farfetched. If Coldwell had a shop either in this country or across the Atlantic, before he settled in New York, he may have been in business with a man named Dean. As matters stand however, his tea caddies have provided pewter collectors with just one more perplexing mystery to solve.

All that can be added to the Lafetra history is that one more pint mug bearing his touch and two small beakers measuring 3¼ inches and 3½ inches in height have been reported.

FOUR UNIMPORTANT NEW YORK PEWTERERS

In the earlier edition of *Pewter in America*, Volume Two, page 19, names were given of four men, Blaun, Bland, Henry, and Merryfield, termed pewterers at the time of enlistment, all as recorded in the Muster Rolls of New York Provincial Troops 1755–1764. None of the four would otherwise have appeared in our list of pewterers and probably none ever operated a shop of his own.

Overlooked earlier and called to my attention by Mrs. Lura Woodside Watkins in an article in the Pewter Collectors' Club of America *Bulletin* for July 1945 was a fifth name, that of "Edward Bennett, aet. 26, born Ireland, pewterer," who enlisted June 8, 1760. Mrs. Watkins believes, and I now concur, that Blaun and Bland were not one and the same and should be listed as separate individuals.

EIGHT LATE WORKERS

Mrs. Nancy Goyne Evans' recent examination of city directories, in a search for early nineteenth-century craftsmen, has extended the working dates for a few pewterers who had been known to us earlier, and has added a number of names that were not on our lists in 1940.

Of the "Eight Late Workers" who were named under that heading in Volume Two, the working dates of three of those men can now be extended as follows:

Anthony Allaire was recorded as working in 1815, one year earlier than the previous listing;
Luke Kiersted   1802/1803 to 1814;
Elijah Knapp   1796 and 1797.

Following are new names that should be added:

Edmund Nexsen, 3 James Slip, New York 1818, together with the following who were found in the Brooklyn directories:

Eight Late Workers

William Bokee   1817–1824;
Jonathan Bliss & Co. 11 Poplar St.   1822

In the following year Bliss was working alone at 11 Middagh Street, Brooklyn.

Henry Peal(e)   9 Poplar St.   1822–1823.

This may have been the same Henry Peale who was working in Philadelphia both before and after 1822.

Samuel G. Stanley—this man was listed as a pewterer at 91 Middagh Street from 1826 to 1829. In the 1830 directory the widow of Samuel Stanley is recorded as living at 190 Middagh Street.

ALBANY PEWTERERS

I T DOES not seem probable that, when Henry Will moved up the Hudson from New York City to Albany during the Revolution, he became Albany's first pewterer, but so far no trace of an earlier maker there has been found. Nor can much be added here about later makers. In the pages that follow will be found the history of one late eighteenth-century pewterer, Ebenezer Crossman, with a shop down the river at Hudson and a few unimportant nineteenth-century makers in Albany.

Nor are there any new forms to report that were distinctive of Albany. Her fame as a pewter-making center must rest on the church chalices of Peter Young and Timothy Brigden. A few Albany-made vessels have been illustrated in Volume Three and are commented upon in the sections devoted to the makers of those pieces.

HENRY WILL

A newspaper advertisement in the *New York Mercury*, which ran from April 15, 1776, to May 13, of the same year, gives us a reasonably accurate date for Henry Will's departure for Albany at the start of the American Revolution. In that notice "Henry Will, Pewterer, acquaints the Public that he is removed to Albany where he intends to carry on the Pewterer's Business in all its Branches. . . ."

PETER YOUNG

A bit of new information about Peter Young will be found in the additions to his earlier history, which additions appear under the section of New York City Pewterers on page 108.

It will be noted there that a ladle, teapot and sugar bowl, made by Young, have been illustrated in this volume as Fig. 759 of Plate XC, Fig. 769 of Plate XCIX and Fig. 773 of Plate XCV respectively.

Ebenezer Crossman
EBENEZER CROSSMAN

Although Ebenezer Crossman, a comparatively recent addition to our list of pewterers, worked in Hudson, New York, and not Albany, it seems more logical to include him with the Albany men than with any other grouping.

This new pewterer is represented today in two collections by one 8⅝ inch plate in each, and in Figs. 862 and 863 of Plate CVIII. I am privileged to illustrate the mark on J. P. Remensnyder's example. The first of these plates emerged from obscurity in 1951 and was described by Dean A. Fales, Jr., in the April 1952 issue of the Pewter Collectors' Club of America *Bulletin*. That particular plate showed in the touch the upper half of Crossman's mark and three of his hallmarks. The name and the eagle were clearly impressed but there was no indication of where the man worked, though it seemed logical from the design of the touch to assign him to Rhode Island in the first quarter of the nineteenth century.

Then in 1961 J. P. Remensnyder found, not far from his own home in the Hudson Valley, the second plate which clearly shows below the eagle the word Hudson. In the February 1962 issue of the *Bulletin* Mr. Remensnyder published the results of his investigation into Crossman's antecedents and activities. I can do no better than to reprint here the results of his research:

> Ebenezer was born in Taunton in 1768 into the family which gave New England so many gifted craftsmen. He probably left Taunton and learned his pewtering in Rhode Island.
>
> In 1783 the whalers of Nantucket, Martha's Vineyard and New Bedford had become weary of harassment by the British. Some forty ship-owners organized and appointed a small committee to locate a new and safer base for their whaling vessels. They explored the banks of the Hudson River and when they came to the sleepy riverside hamlet, called Claverack Landing, they decided this was their promised land. The river farms were purchased at once and by 1787 a new bustling whaling port had been constructed and incorporated as the city of Hudson, New York. They brought with them their fleet, with an army of skilled men to construct and operate wharves and shops even (says Carl Cramer) frames, ready built, of Nantucket style houses. Of course they needed a pewterer to produce the wares for ships and households, and it is easy to imagine the young and adventurous Ebenezer sailing with them from Providence with his molds and newly cut touch marks in his sea chest.
>
> How long he engaged in pewtering in Hudson is thus far unknown. Nowhere have I found any mention of him or his children as pewterers.
>
> The 1790 census lists Ebenezer as head of a household in Hudson consisting of "1 white male over 16, 1 under 16." Was he then a widower? In 1792 he married Polly Davis at Hudson, who bore him thirteen children. In 1802 the Hudson "Balance and Columbian Repository" carried the following notice: —

> For Sale
> A lot of land, 55 feet front and 120 feet deep, at the lower end of Diamond Street in Hudson, on which is a Building hitherto occupied as a school-house. The lot is conveniently located for building. For terms and particulars, enquire of
>
> Ebenezer Crossman

Ebenezer's death is given as May 30th 1835 and his wife, Polly, passed away in Hudson, July 17th 1846, aged 74 years.

TIMOTHY BRIGDEN

Nothing new is to be reported here about Brigden but one of his teapots, a new form to be added to his list, is illustrated as Fig. 769 of Plate XCIV.

ANDREW THOMPSON

When Henry V. Button found a quart basin marked "Thompson, Albany," (see Plate CVIII, Fig. 866) he made a search of Albany records to determine the identity of this hitherto unlisted pewterer. The results of that search were published by Clifton Blake in an article entitled "Andrew Thompson: Albany Pewterer" which appeared in the July 1951 issue of the magazine *Antiques.*

The gist of the findings was that the maker of the basin was almost surely a man named Andrew Thompson, who first appears in Albany records in 1811 and disappears therefrom after 1817. Where he came from and where he disappeared to, when he dropped from the Albany scene, are unanswered questions.

In July 1811 Mordecai Lester and wife sold to Andrew Thompson property on Lion Street that extended to Sand Street. He was listed as a coppersmith at 17 Lion Street in the Albany directory for 1813. During 1812 and 1813 he advertised the sale "at Thompson's Still Manufactory, Lion Street near Capitol" of tin plate, sheet iron, stills with copper and pewter worms, boilers, brass kettles, etc. It is apparent that Thompson was in the general wholesale hardware business and, like his Albany contemporary, Spencer Stafford, made and sold pewter only as a sideline.

In the 1814 directory Thompson was listed as a coppersmith at 115 State Street, and in 1815 and 1816 the listing reads Andrew and William Thompson, coppersmiths, 117 State Street.

On January 1, 1815, Andrew Thompson was married to Sally Musier of Albany. The last record of either Andrew or William Thompson in Albany was on January 2, 1817, when Andrew transferred his Lion Street property to George Hawkins. What the relationship of William Thompson to Andrew was, has not been determined.

At least three items of Thompson pewter have been reported, two quart basins and an 8 inch plate. Although these examples appear to have been well made, they furnish no reason for believing that this man ever had much of a business in pewter.

What was probably the normal Thompson touch, as it appears on a basin, is shown as Fig. 866 of Plate CVIII. The second touch, Fig. 864 of the same plate has been found, as here, with the incised Albany touch used on S. Stafford & Co. pewter. No guess can be made as to the significance of the small rectangular frame enclosing the initials S.G.

On page 112 there is lengthy comment about a pewter tea caddy, illustrated as Fig. 824 of Plate CIII, that is impressed with a worn touch "Thompson." Whether or not such a delicate form was made by the presumably little-qualified metal worker of many trades, Andrew Thompson, seems questionable on the basis of our limited knowledge of this man's work.

SPENCER STAFFORD

Although I have not seen any Stafford forms that had not been on the earlier lists, Carl Jacobs shows, in addition, 8 inch basins, quart mugs, drum-shaped and pear-shaped teapots, and bedpans.

THE CURTISSES

To earlier lists of pewter forms made by Daniel Curtiss should be added $9\frac{1}{2}$ inch semideep plates, $11\frac{1}{2}$ inch flat dishes, and pint and half-pint mugs.

THREE LATE ALBANY PEWTERERS

Mrs. Nancy Goyne Evans' list of previously unrecorded pewterers contained two names of Albany men of whom little or nothing was known previously. One of these was John Brigden, recorded in directories as working in Albany from 1823 to 1825. Nothing more is known about the man but he must have been a son or other close relative of Timothy Brigden who had died in Albany a few years earlier.

The second name is that of Shubel Cottam (the first name should probably have been spelled Shubael) who was listed in the 1815 Albany directory as a pewterer at 23 Capitol Street.

The third name is taken from an Albany Directory for 1822 in which the following advertisement was inserted:

Chauncey Whitney, 47 State Street, Albany, manufactures and keeps for sale all manner of Copper, Brass, Pewter and Tin Wares; and all articles of Kitchen Furniture, of the best quality and at the lowest prices.
Cash paid for old Copper and Pewter.

There have been no reports of any pewter that could be logically attributed to any of these men.

THE PEWTERERS OF PENNSYLVANIA

TO a handful of Pennsylvania pewterers of Continental extraction, we are indebted for a diversification in design of pewter forms and details, which could never have been possible in New England and failed to materialize in New York. But for these men, the story of American pewter might have been little more than a survey, on a small scale, of pewter of English design from 1700 onwards.

Until about the year 1740, emigration to Pennsylvania was very largely from England and Wales. The eight pewterers of record, working in or near Philadelphia before that year, were all of Anglo-Saxon stock and the pewter, which they fashioned, must surely have been typically English in design. Unfortunately all that remains of their handiwork are a few pieces made by Simon Edgell, including several large hammered dishes and a quart tankard. One of the dishes measures 19 inches in diameter, largest of all recorded examples of American flatware.

Before 1740 an influx of German emigrants had begun in earnest and at least three pewterers had settled, before 1760, in the largely Moravian settlement at Bethlehem. One of these men was Heyne the Saxon, who moved later to Lancaster; another, Hasselberg, a Swede, who left Bethlehem for Wilmington and eventually worked in Philadelphia; a third, who has not been identified by name, arrived in Bethlehem shortly before 1760. We may assume that pewter, made in Bethlehem, followed the designs that were familiar to Heyne and Hasselberg and that it differed radically from the English shapes, which had previously been the forms that were normally produced in Pennsylvania.

At about the same time that Hasselberg arrived in Philadelphia (*c.* 1762), William Will, a German, moved there from New York. From that date until Will's death at the end of the century, Pennsylvania's pewter industry seems to have been dominated by three shops, in which continental influence and training prevailed—the establishments of Heyne in Lancaster, that of the user or users of the "Love" touch (now believed to be Hasselberg and Brunstrom), and William Will's shop in Philadelphia.

During most of that period pewter was still being made in Philadelphia in the English tradition by such pewterers as Thomas Byles and Cornelius Bradford, but if their output compared favorably with that of William Will's shop, the evidence, in surviving examples of their work, is lacking. The German and Swedish backgrounds and training of our few Continental pewterers enabled them to enrich

Pennsylvania pewter with forms and details which were completely foreign to the pewter of the other colonies.

Particularly notable among recent discoveries in Pennsylvania pewter are several communion sets made by Colonel Will and four surprising tall altar candlesticks which bear Heyne touches, items which probably bear less resemblance to American forms than anything ever reported previously.

THOMAS PASCHALL

It is regrettable, but hardly surprising, that no identifiable example of the work of Philadelphia's earliest pewterer, Thomas Paschall, is known to have survived. For it must be remembered that when Paschall arrived in Pennsylvania in 1681, Philadelphia was only a city on paper, its site a wilderness. So during the first years of the settlement, the inhabitants were too busy in clearing the land, laying out streets, and building their houses to devote much time to trades such as pewter-making. Even by 1705, when Paschall would have been seventy years old, the city-to-be was still little more than a village and the demand for pewter must have been small.

What vessels Paschall made in this country we cannot know or how many moulds he may have been able to bring with him from Bristol, England. We are fortunate, however, in having some knowledge as to what Paschall made and sold in Bristol, some twenty years before he sailed for America.

The Henry Francis du Pont Winterthur Museum has in its files a number of loose pages from a day book of Thomas Paschall, recording his sales during the early years of his pewter-making, from 1660 to 1663. Listed among the forms sold were not only the stock shapes which we would expect, such as spoons, dishes, saucers, pint and quart pots, flagons, chamberpots, and stoolpans, but such curiosity-piqueing items as the following: "potadge dishes"; grand and small beakers; hammered, "quartern," gallon and hooped pots; "new fashion pott flagon"; new fashion spoons; half-pint and pint "botles"; sausage fillers; candlesticks; and "salsellers." Probably the moulds for some of these forms were left behind in England, but a Paschall candlestick, hooped pot, gallon pot, or flagon would be an addition beyond price to any collection, if it could be found and identified.

THOMAS LANGSHAW

One of the original settlers of Philadelphia, named Goodson, see Volume Two, page 38, wrote home to England in 1690 enumerating the varied occupations of the residents already established in the new city. Included in the list were two pewterers. We knew that Thomas Paschall was one of those men and assumed that the other was Thomas Badcocke, the record of whose death in Philadelphia in 1708, had been reported. Now Badcocke must be demoted to pewterer number three in Philadelphia history.

Mrs. Hannah B. Roach became interested in Goodson's list, did a great deal of delving into early Philadelphia records, and published in the *Pennsylvania Genealogical Magazine* a series of sketches of the lives of the town's merchants and craftsmen of that day. She learned that the pewterers were Thomas Paschall and Thomas Langshaw. I quote from her article "Two Pewterers" in Volume XXIII, Number 2, page 95:

> Thomas Langshaw, pewterer, in 1689 leased on ground rent from Griffith Jones a lot 25 by 100 feet in depth on the west side of Front at the southernmost corner of Jones' whole lot north of High Street. He was not rated here in 1693, probably having already moved to Chester County where he died in 1696."

Chester County records disclose that "T. Lonshaw" was a member of the petty jury "11th day 10th mo. 1695" and, as "Thomas Longshaw," was deceased by the tenth of June, 1696.

There is very little likelihood that any of this man's pewter has survived.

SIMON EDGELL

During the period when Simon Edgell was making pewter in Philadelphia, roughly from 1713 to 1742, there was probably no pewter-making shop in the Colonies, south of New York City, with a larger trade or a wider variety of forms. That observation is based on the inventory of Edgell's estate, the number of surviving examples of his work, and the range in size and shape which those examples cover.

Although there are probably not more than ten pieces in collections today that can be positively identified as Edgell's, that number, for a man who has been dead for over two hundred and twenty-five years, is a good indication of the size of the trade which he must have once had.

The most impressive Edgell find in recent years is the 19 inch hammered dish, now at Winterthur, largest of all known examples of American-made dishes, eloquent testimony to the ability of the shop to turn out special forms, not manufactured by the average pewterer. Like the two Edgell dishes reported earlier, one of which was illustrated as the frontispiece of Volume One, this specimen is hammered all over.

Oddly enough this magnificent charger bears not only Edgell's touches, but also two impressions of a badly-erased touch, not previously recorded, of a New York pewterer, André Michel, see plate CVII, Fig. 858. What, one wonders, is the explanation for the odd combination of Edgell and Michel touches?

Aaron Smith

EDMUND DAVIS

The following notice appeared in the *American Weekly Mercury* of Philadelphia in its issue of June 15-22, 1721:

> The Moulds and Tools of Edmund Davis, late of the City of Philadelphia, Pewterer, are to be sold by Owen Roberts and Thomas Tresse, His Executors.

A search of Philadelphia deeds shows that an Edmund Davis did acquire property in the city in 1720, but, in both deeds Davis is termed a tallow-chandler. It seems probable that these documents refer to the pewterer. The name was not found elsewhere among early Philadelphia records.

AARON SMITH

The following notice appeared in the *American Weekly Mercury*, published by Andrew Bradford in Philadelphia, in several issues for January and February 1736:

> Aaron Smith, lately Imported from London, To be Sold by Aaron Smith, Over against the George in Arch Street, All Sorts of Super fine Hard Metal Pewter, consisting of Large New fashion cisterns, Covers for Dishes of all sizes, Oval Peg Dishes, Fish Plates, Dishes and Plates of all sizes, Stool-Pans, Chamber Pots, Cullanders, Tea Kettles and Stands, Coffee Pots, Tea Pots, Quart and Pint Tankards, Punch Strainers, Porringers, Spoons and all other sorts of Pewter at very reasonable rates: where old Pewter or Brass is Bought or Changed. . . .

Smith's name was not included in the 1940 list of American pewterers because this notice indicated that he was an importer of pewter but not necessarily a pewterer. Another notice from the same paper, supplied by Charles Montgomery, which appeared in the issues of August 4 and 11, 1737, puts a new light on Smith's activities:

> Aaron Smith, Pewterer
>
> Designing to leave this Province in a few Days, gives this publick Notice thereof, that all Persons who have any Demands upon him, may bring in their Accompts to be adjusted; and those Persons who are indebted to him are hereby required to make speedy Payment, or they may expect Trouble.
> N.B. Said Smith now lives at the House of Andrew Edge, near the Baptist Meeting-House in Philadelphia.

Nothing further could be learned about this pewterer. His stay in Philadelphia was probably brief.

The Pewterers of Pennsylvania

THOMAS BYLES

Thomas Byles's large inventory of finished pewter and pewter moulds, as listed right after his death in 1770, is proof that he made a great quantity of pewter in a wide variety of forms. The comparatively few pieces, thought to have been his, which have survived, can still be only attributed to him with reservations, because the touch shows only the initials T.B. and not the full name.

Plates with the T.B. rose-and-crown mark, Fig. 586 of Plate LXIX, are found in the 8 and 9 inch sizes with normal brim and $8\frac{1}{4}$ and $8\frac{1}{2}$ inch with smooth brim. Dishes come in the following sizes—$10\frac{7}{8}$, 13, and $14\frac{7}{8}$ inches.

The correctness of the attribution gained further support from the discovery by Dr. Lola S. Reed of a 13 inch dish with hammered bouge, which not only is impressed with this T.B. touch, but also with a small lion-in-lozenge hallmark struck four times, just as it appears also on pewter made by that other Pennsylvania pewterer, who used the so-called Love touch and has yet to be positively identified. The new combination of marks is illustrated as Figs. 586b and 867 of Plate CIX.

In recent years a porringer has come to light with initials T.B. cast in the handle support, a support incidentally with a long narrow tongue, just as is found on the handles of those other, and later, Newport makers, the Melvilles. The porringer is illustrated as Fig. 709 of Plate LXXXIV and the initials on the bracket in Fig. 881 of Plate CX. With some reservation this porringer is attributed to Byles. The handle is of a rare type—compare Plate XII, Fig. 56, Volume One and Plate LXXXIII, Fig. 700, and Plate LXXXIV, Figs. 708 and 710, in this volume.

Another touch, not previously illustrated, is also being attributed here, and again with some reservation, to Thomas Byles. This touch, and the covered quart tankard in which it is found, should have been shown in 1940, for the writer had examined that tankard in Mrs. J. Insley Blair's collection. The tankard, now in the Blair Collection at the Metropolitan Museum, is illustrated here as Fig. 712 of Plate LXXXV and its touch as Fig. 878 of Plate CX.

There are several seemingly logical reasons for awarding this touch to Byles, though it might be the mark of an unidentified English pewterer. Five similar touches, showing initials with a year-date enclosed within a diamond-shaped frame, are found on the London touch plates. In four of the five the date is earlier than 1710, the date in this mark. The point that is being brought out here is that the design is one that would have been familiar to Byles, one that he might well have adopted.

Far more important, however, than the fact that the initials and design were appropriate, is the consideration that the date is precisely when we believe that Byles' business career began. In his father's will, written in 1704, the son Thomas was mentioned as under age and "apprenticed with Mr Man, Brazier." Furthermore a letter exists which was written by Thomas to a brother and sister in Boston, datelined Newport, January 11, 1711/1712. Presumably he was already established in business in Newport at that date. 1710 would consequently be just about when Byles' touch should have appeared.

To go back to the lion hallmarks on the T.B. dish, if our suspicions are correct that the "Love" pewter was made by one or more members of the so-called Hasselberg group (see pages 130–132), then the appearance of the lions on a "Love" tankard and upon the above-mentioned dish, gives strong support to the suggestion put forward by John J. Evans, Jr., that Byles's moulds and tools, at least in part, may have been sold to Hasselberg or to one of his successors.

SIMON WYER

Just one small bit of information can be recorded about Simon Wyer, obscure Philadelphia pewterer, who may have been only a mender of pewter.

When the ship, Loyal Judith, arrived at Philadelphia in November 1740, passenger list A included "Simon Vear 20 years old"; on list B there was a "Simmon Wehr." Both passengers (if there were two different men and not two different recordings of the same name) qualified for entry on November 25th. Both names are so similar to Wyer that it seems reasonable to assume that the pewterer arrived on the Loyal Judith. The date of arrival, after first glance, does seem to conflict with the date of Simon Wyer's marriage to Hannah Pearson—January 1, 1740. But that can probably be explained by the fact that the old style calendar was in use in 1740. January would have been the eleventh month of the year and, by the new reckoning, the marriage would have been in January 1741.

THE PEWTERERS OF BETHLEHEM

Until very recently Bethlehem has not appeared on any map of pewter-making centers in the Colonies. But now it can be stated, largely as a result of research undertaken by Eric de Jonge, that this Moravian settlement was probably an important outpost of the industry in the middle of the eighteenth century. Within one year of the town's settlement in 1741, it could boast one pewterer, Johann Christopher Heyne, known to us previously (see pages 44, 45, Volume Two) as a Lancaster maker, who did not, however, establish a shop in the latter town until after 1750. Just about the time that Heyne left Bethlehem, another pewterer, Abraham Hasselberg, who later moved to Philadelphia (see page 55, Volume Two), arrived in Bethlehem and, according to the Church records, two pewterers were in residence there in 1758, the third man still unidentified as to name.

The account of the settlement of Bethlehem is such a fascinating story of an early experiment in communal international living, that a brief digression into its history seems warranted here. Its founders were a group of dedicated Christians who, persecuted in their homelands, had banded together to seek a more rewarding life in a new land, where they might worship as they chose. They were members of a Protestant sect which had evolved in the states of Bohemia and Moravia in what is now East Germany, some years after John Huss was burned at the stake in 1415. They were known as the Brethren's Church or the *Unitas Fratrum*.

Just as the Lutheran Church had been formed in protest against the Roman Catholics for their rigid orthodoxy and persecution of all who deviated from their teachings, so now disaffected Lutherans were rising in opposition to their own church, as well as to the Papists, as both churches attempted to terrify, outlaw and scatter all those who refused to accept the established dogmas.

When, in the seventeenth century, the Romish Counter-Revolution swept over Bohemia and Moravia, the Brethren's Church was crushed and many of its adherents were driven into exile. But though crushed, the Church was never completely destroyed. In 1722 a young Saxon nobleman, Nicholas Ludwig, Count von Zinzendorf, deeply dissatisfied with the practices of the Lutheran Church of which he was a member, determined to devote his life to helping all those, regardless of religious training or background, who wished to live a life of Christian service to others. A man of considerable wealth and property, he opened a portion of his large estate at Berthelsdorf in Saxony as a center of Christian activity and built on his property the village of Herrnhut as a refuge for the persecuted of varied faiths. In 1727 he established a common order of worship there and from this beginning grew the revitalized Moravian Church.

From Herrnhut the Church sent out colonies of converts, teachers and missionaries to other German states, to Sweden, Holland, England, Ireland, Lapland, Greenland, to St. Thomas in the West Indies, and to Georgia. In 1740 agents of the Church were negotiating for the purchase of a site for a new settlement on the Lehigh River in northeastern Pennsylvania. At just that time the settlement in Georgia, near Savannah, had to be abandoned because of many misfortunes to the colonists, including sickness, deaths, desertions, and raids by Spaniards from Florida. A mere handful, less than two dozen, made their way north from the Georgian colony to the newly-purchased site in Pennsylvania. There, joined by a few Brethren already in Pennsylvania, they became the nucleus of the settlement on the banks of the Lehigh, soon to become the headquarters of the Moravian Church in the Western Hemisphere.

During 1741 there was great activity on the site of the town-to-be, clearing the land and building the first log house, while in Herrnhut plans went forward for sending overseas a large colony to establish this new outpost of the Church in the New World. Early in December Count von Zinzendorf, his daughter, Benigna, and several other prominent members of the faith arrived in New York. On Christmas Eve they reached the new settlement. There, in the new log house, with all the Brethren present, Christmas services were held, Holy Communion celebrated and a love feast of thanksgiving partaken. They sang of the "Little Town of Bethlehem" and by general consent, the new settlement was christened Bethlehem.

The Pewterers of Bethlehem

In March 1742 a group that was to become known as "The First Sea Congregation" gathered in London for the voyage to America. They had been recruited from various parts of Germany, with additions from England and a sprinkling from Switzerland, Holland, and Sweden. They set sail March 19 in the sloop *Catharine*, which had been chartered for this trip by the Church. After stops at Funchal in the Madeiras, at New Haven and, at New York, the *Catharine* finally arrived at Philadelphia on June 7. Joined there by a number of Pennsylvanians, recently converted to the Moravian Church, the entire "Congregation" moved overland to their new home, Bethlehem.

Included among the "Single Brothers" in the passenger list was the pewterer, Johann Christopher Heyne, whose story is related on pages 127–130. As recorded therein he was very active from the time of his arrival in the religious and educational work of the Church.

In 1750 Heyne and his wife Margaret severed their connections with the Bethlehem "Oeconomy" and moved to Margaret's former home in Tulpehocken, Pennsylvania. Although Heyne is presumed to have practiced his trade of pewterering while in Bethlehem, his church-centered activities were so extensive that one wonders how he could ever have found time to make pewter. Actually we have no positive record of his having done so.

Soon after the settlement of Bethlehem commenced, the Brethren undertook an experiment in communal craftsmanship which must have been without precedent either in Europe or America. In one shop were established all the metalworkers — silversmiths, braziers and bell-founders, pewterers, coppersmiths, tinsmiths, and blacksmiths. The work was under the general oversight of Abraham Bömper, a silversmith from Herborn, Germany, who divided his time between his interests in New York and Bethlehem. He was a contemporary, former townsman and relative by marriage of John Will, New York pewterer. The actual superintendent of the shop was Samuel Powell, a brazier and bell-founder from Whitechurch, Shropshire, England. Such an undertaking could never have been attempted either in England or in any of the states of western Europe, because the regulations of the craft guilds were so rigid. Just how successful the experiment was in Bethlehem we do not know, but it was of comparatively short duration, because in 1762 the Church determined to abolish the "General Economy," giving up most of the communal features of the settlement. Thereafter community of labor for the general welfare ceased and each individual was free to earn his livelihood as he might wish.

As noted earlier, just as Heyne was leaving Bethlehem, a second pewterer, Abraham Hasselberg, a native of Sweden, joined the community. He arrived in 1750 in the third large migration which was known as the "Henry Jorde Colony." Hasselberg's story will be found on pages 134–136. His stay in Bethlehem was longer than Heyne's and presumably he was able to give most of his time to his trade. He must have left Bethlehem in 1760 or 1761. On a still extant document a list was prepared on December 9, 1756, by the "Bethlehem Economy" for the constable of Bethlehem Township, giving the occupations of the members of the community. Included in the accounting was one pewterer, undoubtedly Hasselberg. Just two years later on a similar list, we find not only a pewterer, but a second man who is termed a "pewterer and tinman." Unfortunately we have no knowledge as to the identity of Bethlehem's third pewterer.

What can be said or surmised about the pewter made in Bethlehem? Has any of it survived? If so how may we identify it? No positive answers to these questions are possible, but I believe that there exists a goodly quantity of pewter, which was made by the pewterers of Bethlehem, some of it while they were still living in that settlement. This is the pewter marked with the so-called "Love" touch. In a section which follows, entitled "Love, Unidentified Pennsylvania Pewterer," reasons are presented for identifying the mysterious "Love" with one or more of the Bethlehem makers.

CORNELIUS BRADFORD

This man's story is told with that of the New York pewterers, but he spent so much of his pewter-making career in Philadelphia, that a paragraph should be carried here referring the reader to comments about him on page 101.

JOHANN CHRISTOPHER HEYNE

Christopher Heyne, Lancaster maker of Germanic-looking church flagons and chalices and, as we have recently learned, a prominent layman in the early history of the Moravian Church in America, has established his reputation as one of our most capable pewterers and as the Colonial pewterer, whose designs differ most markedly from the English tradition, in which the great majority of our makers were trained.

Since 1940 much more has been learned about this man's life and many more examples of his work have been identified, including four remarkable church candlesticks now in the Henry F. du Pont Winterthur Museum, candlesticks of a design so foreign to American practice, that no one would have suspected their origin had they not borne the touches of the Lancaster pewterer.

As set down in a record of burials of the Moravian Church of Lancaster, Heyne was born in the little village of Funtschen, Saxony, December 3, 1715. Where he served his apprenticeship has not been established, but, as a result of the research of Eric de Jonge, it is possible to trace in a general way the itinerary and activities of Heyne before he established himself in Lancaster about 1757.

As de Jonge has pointed out, under the rules and regulations of the guild in Saxony

Johann Christopher Heyne

in the early eighteenth century, an embryo pewterer was required to serve a four-year apprenticeship to a master pewterer and then three more years as a journeyman, working under other masters in other towns or cities, before his experience could be considered sufficient to qualify him to open a shop of his own.

Swedish records furnish some information about Heyne's activities as a journeyman pewterer. On August 8, 1735, "Heine, Johan Christoph von Rosswein" arrived at Stockholm from the Baltic port of Stettin. He would, presumably, have finished his apprenticeship in 1733 or 1734 and had set out on his required travels as a journeyman. Rosswein is a town in Saxony approximately twenty-five miles west of Dresden.

Soon after his arrival in Stockholm, Heyne secured employment in the shop of Maria Sauer, the recently widowed wife of a Stockholm pewterer, Jakob Sauer. That he quickly established himself among his peers as a competent craftsman of dependable character is testified to by his election in November 1736 as *ortsgeselle* of the guild of journeymen in Stockholm, the second highest position in that organization. As *ortsgeselle*, he was responsible for guiding young pewterers to the local masters for possible employment, for checking their working papers and otherwise helping and keeping track of them. The duties were many and undoubtedly Heyne would have known every master, journeyman, and apprentice in Stockholm during his term of office. His name appeared on the guild rolls only once more, in 1737. Thereafter a curtain drops upon his movements until March 1742, when he turned up in London, prepared to sail for America.

During those five uncharted years, he must have returned to his homeland, for, during that period, he became deeply involved in a religious movement, the United Brethren, which, from its base at Herrnhut in Saxony, was sending out colonies of converts and missionaries to other states and countries, even across the Atlantic. It was as a member of such a group, ever after known as the "First Sea Congregation," that Heyne set sail from London in the sloop *Catharine*, on March 15, 1742, arriving at Philadelphia June 7 of that year and moving overland to the new settlement at Bethlehem a few days later. A list, still extant of the settlers at Bethlehem on June 25, 1742, includes among the names of the single men, John Christopher Heyne.

It is evident from existing Moravian records that, even before Heyne had reached Bethlehem, church leaders had recognized in him unusual abilities, intelligence, and zeal, for within six weeks after his arrival, he was sent on three different trips as a missionary and lay helper to care for the spiritual needs of scattered settlements; and, in the following year, he made visits on church business to New York and Philadelphia and York, Pennsylvania. In 1746 he married Margaret Schaeffer of Tulpehocken, Berks County. (His wife's maiden name was Schaeffer but was incorrectly entered as Schiefeun in Church records at Lancaster.) Both Heyne and his wife taught and acted as supervisors in Moravian schools established at Germantown and elsewhere. He was licensed as a minister and frequently served as such, when the regular pastor was unavailable or in communities which had no regular supply. From

The Pewterers of Pennsylvania

1747 to 1749 he was absent in Ireland, acting as an assistant to Minister (later Bishop) Peter Boehler, who was sent to Dublin to establish a colony of the Church there. Soon after his return from that extended trip, in 1750, he and his wife left Bethlehem, for reasons now unknown, moving to Mrs. Heyne's former hometown, Tulpehocken.

When one considers the range of Heyne's church-centered activities and the time that must surely have been spent in such work, it is hard to believe that he ever could have made pewter in Bethlehem. Certainly such work would have been but sporadic at best and the amount of pewter made would have been small. Earlier the suggestion was put forward (see page 127) that the lovebird touch might have been designed for use on pewter made in the community metals shop in Bethlehem, possibly by Heyne before 1750. That remains a possibility but not a probability.

How soon after 1750 Heyne moved on from Tulpehocken to Lancaster is not known, but no record of him could be established in Lancaster prior to 1757. During those years from 1750 to 1757, however, he was definitely working at his trade, for the Museum at Hershey, Pennsylvania, owns a chalice bearing the inscribed date 1753, and a similar Heyne chalice in the Bindnagel Church at Palmyra, Pennsylvania, is dated 1754. Nothing of importance can be added to the account of Heyne's years in Lancaster beyond what was recorded on pages 44–48 in Volume Two.

Heyne's deep interest and involvement in church affairs carried over into his pewter-making. No other Colonial pewterer is represented in collections today by such a large number of church vessels. What is more, fully two thirds, and possibly three quarters, of his identifiable surviving pieces were made for use in churches, notably his flagons, chalices, and altar candlesticks.

To the best of my knowledge no one has yet reported an I.C.H. basin, pint or quart pot, or chamber pot, for all of which he is known to have had moulds; nor is there record of any Heyne dish or platter. Even the plates and saucers are exceedingly rare. Other surviving examples of his work that were made for domestic use included sugar bowls, one porringer, a 4⅛-inch beaker and a few dram bottles in two different sizes, 4½ inches and 5 inches in height.

Surviving Heyne flagons alone outnumber all examples of his domestic forms. These flagons, two of which are illustrated as Plate XXXIII, Figs. 220 and 222, in Volume One, and two others in the communion set in Plate XCVI, Figs. 786 and 790, in this volume, are all of the same general form and design, differing only in such minor details as to whether the body of the flagon was plain or ribbed and in the type of thumb piece used.

As rightly pointed out by Eric de Jonge in his instructive article entitled "Johann Christopher Heyne, Swedish Influence on American Pewter," which appeared in the March 1955 issue of the magazine *Antiques*, the design and method by which Heyne attached the ball thumbpiece on his flagons to the lid and handle was not an ingenious and original improvisation, as I had suggested in Volume Two, but was a copy or adaptation, of a design in common use in Sweden, one with which Heyne would have been thoroughly familiar.

PLATE CIX — *Touches of Pennsylvania, Maryland and the South*

586b and 867. Touches as found on a 13-inch dish, made by Thomas Byles, Newport, Rhode Island, and Philadelphia, 1710–1771. Because of space limitations a photograph of the entire back of the dish was cut into the two sections containing the two sets of marks, which sections were then butted together. The use of a single die, struck four times, was apparently customary in Massachusetts at the time when Byles' career began. See the touches of the Dolbeares, Figs. 831 and 832, Plate CIV. This same lion die was used later by the owner of the "Love" touch (Fig. 869) and by John A. Brunstrom, Philadelphia, 1781–1793. Collection of Dr. Lola S. Reed.

868 and 869. A touch of frequent incidence in eastern Pennsylvania as photographed on the outside bottom of a three-pint basin. Maker unidentified, but the "Love" touch is attributed with reservations to Abraham Hasselberg, Bethlehem, Pennsylvania, Wilmington, Delaware and Philadelphia *c.* 1750–1779. The accompanying crowned X quality mark is also found with the touch of John A. Brunstrom, Philadelphia 1781–1793. Collection of the author.

870 and 867a. Touches photographed in the interior of the quart tankard illustrated as Fig. 724, Plate LXXXVI. This group of touches links Brunstrom with the user of the "Love" touch (possibly Hasselberg) and with Thomas Byles. Museum of Early Southern Decorative Arts, Old Salem, North Carolina, photograph courtesy of Thomas D. Williams. Formerly in the collection of Mr. and Mrs. Ralph P. Hanes.

871. A combination of touches as they appear on the lip of a bellied quart tankard with double-dome lid (Fig. 725, Plate LXXXVI). Collection of Dr. and Mrs. Robert Mallory III. Inside the tankard is the "Love" touch (Fig. 869). The missing link in the Love-Brunstrom mystery is the still unreported discovery of a plate or vessel stamped with both the Love touch and Brunstrom's name touch. There is some doubt as to whether 871 is the same touch as 867. It may be that the same die was used for both and that what is here shown as 871 is but a sharper, clearer, less worn strike of the die illustrated above as 867. Photograph courtesy of Thomas D. Williams.

867a. The lion touches and crowned X as found on lip of bellied quart tankard; again with the Love bird touch 869 inside. Courtesy of the Brooklyn Museum.

873. Touch of Charles Plumly, Philadelphia, 1822–1833, used just before or just after his partnership with Bidgood. From a pint mug in the collection of Dr. and Mrs. Robert Mallory III.

565a. An impression of Olcott's touch that shows clearly that the name was Olcott, not Wolcott, from a plate in the Henry Francis du Pont Winterthur Museum.

453b. An impression that clarifies the spelling of Samuel Campbell's name. Listed erroneously in 1940 as probably from Connecticut, it has since been established that he worked in Baltimore, Maryland, 1814–1817. From a $5\frac{1}{4}$-inch saucer in collection of William M. Goss Jr.

601a. Formerly listed among the touches of unidentified pewterers (Fig. 601), the word Augusta in this impression identifies the maker as Giles Griswold, Augusta, Georgia, 1818–1820. Courtesy Henry Francis du Pont Winterthur Museum.

874. Another Giles Griswold touch, not previously illustrated, from a plate in the Henry Francis du Pont Winterthur Museum.

875. Touch of James Martine, Fayettesville, North Carolina, 1829–1835 as impressed on an $8\frac{7}{8}$-inch plate. Courtesy Museum of Early Southern Decorative Arts, Old Salem, North Carolina.

PLATE CIX

586b   867   868   869   870   867a

871   867a   873

565a   453b

874   601a   875

'Love,' Unidentified Pennsylvania Pewterer

Heyne's chalices are of just one general type with heavily knopped Germanic stems (see Figs. 238 and 239 of Plate XXXVI, Volume One and Fig. 788 of Plate XCVI in this volume). They are however found in two slightly different sizes, some with plain or ribbed cup and with or without lids. The stems vary quite a little in dimensions and design of the knop, indicating perhaps that they were cast in other than metal moulds. Heyne chalices, though rare, outnumber by a considerable margin his surviving flagons.

By far the most surprising and unusual Heyne discovery in recent years, was a pair of tall altar candlesticks, a find that was duplicated a few months later when two more such candlesticks came to light in the same area. One pair illustrating the raised decoration of religious symbols and also Heyne's touches is shown in Plate C. There is no reason to believe that candlesticks of similar design were ever made elsewhere in the Colonies or in England. The workmanship which they display enhances further Heyne's reputation as a pewterer of superior craftsmanship and training.

'LOVE,' UNIDENTIFIED PENNSYLVANIA PEWTERER

Illustrated as Figs. 868 and 869 of Plate CIX, is a combination of touches used by a pewterer, possibly by several pewterers, working in eastern Pennsylvania during the second half of the eighteenth century. Thirty or forty years ago this so-called lovebird pewter was found in antique shops and at country auctions in eastern Pennsylvania more frequently than that of any other pewterer, except Townsend and Compton of London, and successor Townsend firms. In 1931 in a small antique shop in Ephrata I saw fifteen or twenty Love-marked examples in a pile of pewter plates, dishes, and basins.

The first reaction upon seeing the Love marks would be to assume that the user's name was Love and that he made his pewter in London, a deduction that is almost certainly one hundred percent wrong.

Howard Cotterell in *Old Pewter* listed no British maker named Love. And yet so much London-stamped Love pewter has survived in Pennsylvania that the maker, if a London pewterer, must have had a tremendous export business, and both his name and touch should have been known to English collectors. As in the case of the "Semper Eadem" touch, when used in conjunction with a London mark on Boston pewter (see pages 39–41), the explanation must be that the mark "London" signified London quality and not London manufacture.

The 1790 United States Census showed men by the name of Love living in almost every county of southeastern Pennsylvania, but investigation, at the county court houses, failed to disclose any Love who was recorded as working in metals. Despite my feeling that "Love" had made his pewter in Pennsylvania, my own inability to identify and locate him in the state, coupled with his use of a London mark, restrained me from including his touch in the first two volumes of *Pewter in America*, when they appeared in 1940.

As more and more Love-marked pewter came to light and as examples were compared as to form and design with the work of other Pennsylvania pewterers, it became ever more certain that the user of the lovebird touch must have been a Pennsylvania pewterer. Might it be possible that Love was not the maker's name at all, but rather a symbol in a touch design that had some special meaning both for the user and for his prospective customers?

Eric de Jonge was the first, I believe, to uncover the information that Heyne and Hasselberg had both been members of the United Brethren and had lived at Bethlehem, before establishing shops in Lancaster and Philadelphia respectively, and it was he who suggested that there may have been some connection between the Love touch and the Bethlehem pewterers. In a communal settlement, such as Bethlehem was, where the importance of the individual was subordinated to the common good, it is not probable that a craftsman would have identified his work with a touch showing his name or initials. More appropriate would have been one which was emblematic of the community in which he worked. In that light the lovebird design seems eminently appropriate for a pewterer of the Moravian Church. The word Love and the lovebirds are symbolic of the tenets and beliefs of the Brethren, while the coronet may well have been included as recognition of the tremendous aid given to the settlement by its patron, Count von Zinzendorf.

Although such observations may seem but fanciful support for the idea that the lovebird touch originated with a pewterer of the Moravian faith, there is real evidence in pewter which strengthens such a supposition. In an article in the magazine *Antiques* for August 1959, entitled "Lovebirds and Lions," John J. Evans, Jr., presented a strong case for identifying John A. Brunstrom as the user of the lovebird touch.

Brunstrom, it will be recalled, was a native of Sweden, who arrived in Philadelphia about 1781, married a daughter of the recently deceased pewterer, Abraham Hasselberg, in 1783, was a member of the Moravian Church and died in Philadelphia in 1793. The piece of pewter which supplied the link between "Love" and Brunstrom was a Swedish-type tankard with flattened dome-top cover, then owned by Mr. and Mrs. Ralph P. Hanes, since presented by them to the Museum of Early Southern Decorative Arts, Winston-Salem, North Carolina. It is one of only two pieces of pewter of record, which carries Brunstrom's name touch. The touches as they appear inside that tankard are illustrated again in Figs. 870 and 867a of Plate CIX. The crowned X quality mark and the rampant lion hallmarks are found also on pewter that carries the Love touch, as illustrated in adjoining cuts on the same plate. Whether Brunstrom was actually a user, possibly the only user of the Love touch, we know for certain that he did own and use the dies which produced the same secondary marks that are frequently found in conjunction with the lovebird mark. Furthermore the inventory of Brunstrom's moulds, now on file in the H. F. du Pont Winterthur Museum, includes most of the forms on which the Love mark has been found.

It is to be doubted however that Brunstrom made all of the surviving Love-marked pewter. He was in business in Philadelphia for not over twelve years at the most, 1781–1793, and yet the Love pewter far exceeds in quantity the surviving examples of the work of that master pewterer, Colonel William Will, whose career began in Philadelphia in 1764 and continued until 1798. More significant is the evidence of the marks illustrated in Fig. 868, 869 of Plate CIX. These were photographed from the outside bottom of a 10¼ inch basin. Up until 1750, and possibly until a few years later, basins were usually marked on the outside base. Thereafter, at least in the Colonies, the place for the touch was invariably in the well inside. It is highly improbable that Brunstrom in 1781 or later would have applied his touch on the outside bottom of a basin. The evidence indicates that the Love touch was in use by 1760 or earlier.

Although proof is lacking, I believe that the lovebird touch was designed for use by the pewterers working in the community metal shop at Bethlehem, possibly even before Heyne left in 1750. Whether used in Bethlehem or not, it was probably designed by a member of the Moravian Church. A logical deduction is that Abraham Hasselberg took it with him from Bethlehem about 1759 or else had it made as his own touch, when he opened his shop in Wilmington in that year. Upon Hasselberg's death in Philadelphia in 1779, his tools, moulds, and touch die would have become the property of his widow and would have been used by her second husband, Adam Koehler, during the few years when he operated the shop. Finally, about 1783 after Brunstrom married a Hasselberg daughter, Mrs. Koehler presumably gave, or sold, to her son-in-law all the pewter-making equipment.

However controversial may be the arguments for attributing to Hasselberg, Koehler, and Brunstrom the use of the Love touch, it is possible to be completely factual in reporting the forms on which the Love touch or its quality mark has been found. The list follows; 6 to 8⅝ inch plates with normal brim including an 8⅝ inch deep plate; 6 to 8½ inch plates with smooth brim; 11 and 13 inch dishes of both the flat and deep varieties; 6⅝ to 12¾ inch basins; 4¾ inch porringers with the so-called crown type of handle (Plate LXXXIII, Fig. 704); pint and quart mugs, both straight-sided and bellied; quart tankards with cylindrical body and flattened dome cover (Plate LXXXVI, Fig. 724); bellied tankards with double-domed lid (Plate LXXXVI, Fig. 725); a quart measure, (Plate LXXXVIII, Fig. 741), the only marked Pennsylvania measure of record; at least three designs of teapots, the drum shape similar to teapots made by William Will, but of greater capacity (Plate XCIII, Fig. 768), bellied teapots on three feet, almost identical with those of Cornelius Bradford, see Fig. 766 of Plate XCIII, and bellied teapots without feet (Plate XCIII, Fig. 763).

The Pewterers of Pennsylvania

MUNGO CAMPBELL

Campbell apparently worked in Philadelphia for only a few years, four at the most. At least as early as 1756 he was living in Virginia. His later history, what little we know of it, will be found with the southern pewterers on page 152.

JOHN PHILIP ALBERTI

Just one brief addition can be made to Alberti's history. When he took the oath of allegiance in Philadelphia on December 12, 1754, his age was recorded as 32. He must have been born therefore in 1722.

PHILIP WILL

The addition to our knowledge of Philip Will's craftsmanship by the discovery of a splendid tall flagon and two more small plates will be found on pages 102–104 under the story of the Wills of New York, because these pieces were patently made in New York and not in Philadelphia.

COLONEL WILLIAM WILL

The stature of Colonel William Will, as man and craftsman, has grown with the years. The more that we see of his work, the more we are impressed with the evidence of ability of a high order, coupled with good taste, originality, and versatility in design.

When Will's story was presented in Volume Two, superlatives were used, and rightly, to describe the man and his craftsmanship. Nothing further of importance has been learned about his life or character, but catalogued examples of his work have grown from three dozen or so to well over one hundred; perhaps more than two hundred pieces of his manufacture have been found, if we include the chalices, creamers, sugar bowls, and salts which are unmarked, but can be attributed to this maker with very little reservation. Many of these pieces were cast in moulds which served also as parts of larger vessels, on which Will's touches have been found. For instance, Will's open salts on circular base appear to have been cast in the same moulds used to form part of the lid of his coffee pots. Compare Plate XXVII and Plate XXX, Fig. 210, both in Volume One. The same moulds furnished the lower section of a creamer pictured as Fig. 777 on Plate XCV in this volume.

Not only have we many more pieces of pewter today, by which we may judge

Will's ability as a pewterer, but a far wider variety of shapes and forms, together with variations in minor details of design, which have contributed to a better understanding of his versatility and originality.

The list of known forms made by the Colonel, not recorded in Volume Two, are tablespoons, ladles in two sizes, bed pans, commodes, 6 and $10\frac{5}{8}$ inch basins, hotwater plates, a teapot, similar to Fig. 189 in Volume One but larger, coffee pot on square plinth in this volume, Plate XCI, Fig. 760, a tankard with flattened dome lid, also in Volume Three, Plate LXXXVI, Fig. 723, similar to tankards made by his brother, Henry Will in New York, open salts, one of which was illustrated in Volume One as Fig. 210 of Plate XXX, but not attributed at that time to Will, sugar bowls (Plate XCV, Fig. 775), Volume Three, creamers of three different shapes, two of which are shown in Plate XCV, an inkwell, a ewer or jug, and a surprisingly large number of forms which were designed for use in churches.

Illustrated in Plates XCVI–XCVII are three fine communion services made by Will. Particularly noteworthy is the variety in shapes and designs which Will was able to provide; not one shape seen in any one of the three sets, is repeated in either of the others. It will be seen that there were two types of flagon of widely different pattern, two general forms of chalices which also differed greatly, the only known pair of Will church cups, an exceedingly handsome ewer or pitcher, which has no counterpart in American pewter, and a pair of dish top patens, another form which like the ewer, seems to have been original with Will. No similar shape has been illustrated in any of the books on English or Continental pewter, which I have been privileged to see.

We cannot know how wide was the variety of forms made by the more capable of the early pewterers, men such as Paschall or Edgell of Philadelphia, the elder Bassetts and Joseph Leddell in New York and some of the early Boston makers. They lived too long ago and nearly all of their work has vanished.

On the other hand we have what must be a fairly representative sampling of the forms made by the Colonel. If any of William Will's contemporaries made pewter of better quality than his, if any was equipped to make a wider variety of forms, if any showed greater taste or originality in design, evidence of such superiority is still to be presented.

Attention is called to an error in Volume Two. In the tenth line, page 54, mention was made of a pair of fine unmarked chalices (Plate XXVI, Fig. 240). The Roman numerals for the plate in question should have read XXXVI instead of XXVI.

THE HASSELBERG GROUP

Under the above caption, in Volume Two, appeared the brief histories of three Philadelphia pewterers, related to one another by marriage, but seemingly men of little importance in the pewter trade in Philadelphia. These makers of pewter were Abraham Hasselberg, Adam Kehler (or Koehler) who married Hasselberg's widow, and Johan A. Brunstrom, who married Hasselberg's daughter.

Since 1940 our knowledge of the activities of both Hasselberg and Brunstrom has widened, enough to indicate that both may have enjoyed a much larger business than our earlier information had indicated, sufficient also to warrant splitting their histories into two separate reports. Hasselberg's story will be considered first and with it, for convenience, will be added what little is now known about Kehler.

Abraham Hasselberg was born in Sweden, at a still undetermined place and date, early in the eighteenth century. His name is recorded between the years 1735 and 1745 in the three-volume work, *Stockholms Kaungjutareka*, by Albert Löfgren, the authoritative work on Swedish pewter. Hasselberg learned his trade at Norrköping and later worked as a journeyman in Stockholm. The last record of his activities in Sweden was dated June 1745. From then until May 1750, we know nothing of his movements, but, in the latter month, he sailed from London in the snow, *Irene*, with eighty-one immigrants to join other members of the United Brethren in Count Zinzendorf's Moravian settlement at Bethlehem, Pennsylvania. This shipload was the so-called "Henry Jorde Colony," which arrived in New York harbor June 22, 1750, and moved overland in small groups during the next ten days to their new home in northeastern Pennsylvania. For the most part these were young men, skilled in various trades, who had been recruited in Herrnhaag and Wetteravia, in what is now Czechoslovakia, and from United Brethren settlements in Holland.

What prompted Hasselberg to join that company? As related in the story of Johan Christian Heyne, that pewterer spent a number of years as a journeyman in Stockholm, was the executive officer of the journeymen's guild there in 1736 and, as such, would surely have known Hasselberg. Heyne was one of the earliest settlers in Bethlehem and may very well have influenced the young Swede to join the United Brethren and emigrate to America.

In a still-preserved census of the Bethlehem "Oeconomy," prepared in November 1756 by the Reverend Mr. Spangenburg for Governor Denny of Pennsylvania, Abraham Hasselberg was listed as one of the "Single Men." At almost exactly the same date, on December 9, 1756, a return of the various trades represented in the community was submitted to the Constable of Bethlehem Township, a copy of which is among the records of the United Brethren. Included in the returns is "Pewterer 1." Since we know that Heyne left Bethlehem in 1750, Hasselberg must have been the community's only pewterer in 1756. Two years later, a similar report showed not only a pewterer but also a "pewterer and tinman." The identity of Bethlehem's third pewterer has not been established but he may have been the maker with initials D.S., whose touches are shown in Figs. 886, 888 of Plate CXI.

In September 1759 Hasselberg advertised in the *Pennsylvania Gazette* that he was then living in Wilmington, Delaware, and proposed to carry on there the pewterer and tinman's trades. The stay in Wilmington must have been of short duration because, as reported in Volume Two, he was married in Philadelphia in 1762 at a time when he must have been over forty years of age. Also we know that he died in that city in 1779.

This man of whom so little was known twenty-five years ago, who seemed to have been an inconspicuous pewter-maker in Philadelphia for approximately seventeen years, has now been furnished with credentials which indicate that he may have been one of the leading pewterers in eastern Pennsylvania, during the third quarter of the eighteenth century.

Working in Bethlehem, Wilmington, and Philadelphia over a period of almost thirty years he should have left us some examples of his work. On pages 130–132 the suggestion was made that Hasselberg may have been a user, perhaps the first user, of the lovebird touch, Plate CIX, Fig. 869. This observation is based purely on conjecture, but no other Pennsylvania pewterer meets so closely the requirements and conditions, which we would have expected of the man who made the "Love" pewter.

Adam Koehler's story can be closed out in a few sentences. Just one scrap of information can be added to what was written about this man in Volume Two, page 55. In a list of the "Names of Persons who took the Oath of Allegiance to the State of Pennsylvania between 1777 and 1789" the following entry appears: "John Adam Koehler, a deserter from the British Army, now of Philada., Pewterer" took the oath of allegiance August 4, 1779.

That date probably antedates Hasselberg's death and is almost six months prior to Koehler's marriage to Elizabeth Hasselberg. It seems likely therefore that he had been an employee of Hasselberg and may even have been apprenticed to the trade in Germany, before becoming a Hessian mercenary.

As suggested in Volume Two, Koehler probably carried on Hasselberg's business only until about 1783, when his stepdaughter, Elizabeth Hasselberg, married John A. Brunstrom. At that time ownership of the business seems to have passed by purchase or by gift to young Brunstrom from his mother-in-law.

During the three years when Koehler is believed to have been making pewter, he would almost surely have continued to use whatever touch dies he may have found among Hasselberg's shop contents.

On pages 130–132 under the heading "Love," Unidentified Pennsylvania Pewterer, is a list of the forms that have been found, which are impressed with the lovebird touch or the quality marks which frequently accompany that touch.

WILLIAM BALL

One piece of pewter has been found that may have been made in the shop of William Ball. On May 29, 1775, William Ball advertised in the *Pennsylvania Packet* various pewter wares which he was prepared to furnish. Included in the list were inkstands.

Recently Thomas D. Williams acquired a pewter inkstand with double-flap, hinged covers, standing on four cup feet, very similar to the Henry Will inkstand pictured in Plate XLI. On the underside of the stand is a circular mark enclosing the initials W.B. and the letters PHILA (see Fig. 898 of Plate CXI). Block letters were used and the touch is incised. Although such forms of marking were found occasionally on German pewter, even as early as the seventeenth century, incised block letters have not been found, to the best of my knowledge, on any eighteenth-century pewter made in Great Britain or the American Colonies. So, although the inkstand is, in itself, of a design that Ball might have been expected to make, the mark is so late in form that there must be some reservation as to whether Ball actually was the maker.

GEORGE ELLICOTT

Back in 1902 Alice Morse Earle wrote in *Sun Dials and Roses of Yesterday:*

> There still exist in America, however, old soapstone moulds used for the casting of pewter sundials.
>
> . . . .
>
> The steatite mould of George Ellicott of Bucks County, Pennsylvania, is in good condition. He was a well-known maker of sundials and high case clocks. . . . Here is a pewter dial with base and gnomon in one piece, made recently in this cast. It is about five inches square; is marked "1779 G.E." The hours are in Roman numerals and "Lat. 40" is on the side of the gnomon. . . .

Just where that writer saw that mould and dial and where she obtained her knowledge of Ellicott's history is not now known.

However just such a dial as she described, though measuring $4\frac{1}{2}$ inches instead of 5 inches square, is illustrated as Fig. 923 of Plate CXV. Its owner, John P. Remensnyder, states that the back indicates that it was poured in an open mould face down.

Recently Bucks County deeds and probate records were searched at Doylestown, the County seat. At least as early as 1740 there were Ellicotts in Bucks County and in 1799 a Thomas Ellicott, wheelwright of Solebury, mentioned in his will three sons, one of whom was named George. But no further record of that George could be found nor were there any eighteenth-century deeds in which a George Ellicott was mentioned.

JOHN ANDREW BRUNSTROM

Little can be added to John Brunstrom's history as reported in 1940, but much should be stated about the forms which he made, the touches that he used, or is suspected of using, and his identification as a probable user of the "Love" touch.

John Andrew Brunstrom

Among the names of persons who took the oath of allegiance to the state of Pennsylvania there appears the following entry under date of October 10, 1785: "John Brunstrong from Sweden, resident in Philadelphia about four years." He therefore did not appear upon the scene until 1781, when he would have been about twenty-eight years of age. Hence it must be assumed that he obtained his early training as a pewterer in Sweden.

Two years after his arrival, Brunstrom married Elizabeth, daughter of the late pewterer, Abraham Hasselberg. Despite his close association with the Hasselberg family and business, he could never have seen or known his father-in-law, who died in 1779. There is reason for assuming that, soon after his marriage, Brunstrom succeeded to management of the Hasselberg business, for which his step-father-in-law had probably been acting as a caretaker only. Because of Brunstrom's early death in 1793, his career, with a shop of his own in Philadelphia, could have lasted for only about ten years.

Contrary to the statement made on page 56 in Volume Two that "he was probably a factor of little importance in the pewter trade of his adopted city," later information indicates that to have been a too hasty statement, based on an assumption that proved to be erroneous.

We now have a very accurate knowledge of what forms and shapes Brunstrom was equipped to make in quantity, at the time of his death in 1793, because of the acquisition by the Henry Francis du Pont Winterthur Museum of an inventory of the contents of Brunstrom's shop, as prepared by William Will and John Hera soon after Brunstrom's death.

In the shop were the usual wheel and spindle, anvils, bellows, quantities of old metals, a normal supply of pewterers' tools, blocks, patterns, etc. as well as a set of tinman's tools. Of particular interest among the hand tools were "4 Beading Tools." Such tools were apparently "a must" for every Philadelphia pewterer of any importance, during the closing years of the eighteenth century and the first two decades of the nineteenth. Beading is found on pewter of William Will, "Love," Parks Boyd, and Robert Palethorp, Jr., as well as on two pieces that can be identified positively as Brunstrom's work.

The inventory included an itemized list of finished pewter in the shop and the moulds from which articles could be made. Together they provide what must be a reasonably complete catalogue of what Brunstrom was making at the close of his career. In addition to the commoner stock forms which every pewterer was expected to make, Brunstrom supplied basins up to and including the gallon size, syringes in three sizes, porringers in three sizes, three types of teapots, designated as "straight," "bellied," and "old fashioned," coffee pots, sugar boxes, cream jugs, "jugs for freezing cream," "rum bottles," "challaces," small boxes, "salt sellars," measures in five sizes, tankards (for which there was but one set of moulds), and "watch cases." This last article has not been found in the lists or inventories of any other pewterer.

Surprisingly, Brunstrom had moulds for only one size of shallow plate and two sizes of soup plates. There is no indication from the inventory that he made butter plates or any large dishes or platters.

Although we have a reasonably clear picture of what forms Brunstrom made, and although there must be examples of his work in collections today, there are still unanswered questions as to how such pieces can be identified, exclusive of the two pieces which are impressed with his name touch.

But before discussing the touches which Brunstrom did use or may be presumed with reason to have used, it is necessary to correct one of the most regrettable errors that appeared in the first edition of *Pewter in America.* That was the ill-advised attribution to Brunstrom of an exceedingly crude touch of a rectangular frame enclosing the initials IAB illustrated as Fig. 548 of Plate LXVII in Volume Two. It is now generally acknowledged to be a modern fake and the reader is asked to correct accordingly the caption for same opposite Plate LXVII. The mark is usually found on new-cast pewter, which was not skimmed carefully, if skimmed at all, and not burnished on the wheel. Some pieces seem to have been blackened artificially to hide in part their crudity and to give the appearance of age. In some few cases the mark is found impressed on genuine antique pewter, but pewter which its real maker had failed to mark. Whatever the source of this spurious initial touch I am convinced that it is truly a fraud and regret my failure to recognize it as such before the original edition of my books appeared.

In place of this mark, which should be removed from our lists, we now have a legitimate name touch for Brunstrom (see Plate CIX, Fig. 870) as found in a tankard of Swedish design with coin-top lid and a body with wide banding—just such a tankard as was made by "Love" and, at a later date, by Boyd and Palethorp in Philadelphia (see Plate LXXXVI, Fig. 724). Significantly the new Brunstrom mark appears with the distinctive crowned X quality mark, that is found on so much of the "Love" pewter and also with a die impression, struck three times, of a rampant lion in diamond frame. A second piece, a quart mug with both the Brunstrom name touch and the "Love" quality mark has turned up also. The finding of the quality mark on the only two pieces that can be attributed positively to Brunstrom has led to the assumption which may, or may not, be warranted, that Brunstrom made some, if not all, of the Love-marked pewter.

Before I present arguments, pro and con, for the assumption that Brunstrom was a user of the "Love" touch, it is suggested that the reader turn back in this volume to the account of "Love," unidentified Pennsylvania Pewterer, pages 130–132 and then note on Plate CIX the combination of marks that appears most frequently on "Love" pewter. All of this is leading up to a demonstration, by examination of marks, which should help to determine whether Brunstrom was a user of the "Love" touch.

On Plate CIX in this volume are four combinations of marks as found on four different pieces of pewter, marks which indicate some connection between Brunstrom and Love, and between Brunstrom and Byles.

John Andrew Brunstrom

The first illustration, Fig. 870, shows the Brunstrom name touch as it appears on a tankard in Winston-Salem, North Carolina. Note that the Brunstrom name is accompanied by the identical crowned X quality mark used by "Love" and also three impressions of a diamond-shaped lozenge enclosing a rampant lion.

The second group of touches, Fig. 871, was found on the upper outside rim of an entirely different form of tankard, one with bellied body and double-domed lid owned by Dr. Robert Mallory. Here we have the same "Love" quality stamp and the same lion-in-diamond touch, the latter struck four times in this case. Inside the tankard is the well-known love-bird touch.

The third set of marks, Figs. 867a and quality mark, is from another tulip-shaped tankard, this one in the Brooklyn Museum, a tankard that appears to be very similar to the Mallory example. The only difference between the marking of this piece and that of the Mallory example is that the lion is here enclosed in a frame that is shaped more like a squared lozenge than like a diamond.

The fourth and last set of marks, Figs. 586b and 867 was found on a 13 inch dish owned by Dr. Lola S. Reed. Here the same lion-in-lozenge marks accompany the T.B. rose-and-crown touch that has long been attributed to Thomas Byles of Philadelphia.

A comparison of these four combinations of marks would seem at first thought to lead to the following conclusions: (1) that the identity of the user of the mysterious "Love" touch had been discovered at last—that "Love" and Brunstrom used identical secondary marks and must therefore be one and the same; and (2) that Brunstrom acquired, by purchase or otherwise, two rampant lion dies, one of which certainly, and the other probably, had been used earlier by Thomas Byles.

But the solution is not that simple. Worth consideration are the following observations which seem to point to a slightly different conclusion:

1) As explained in the comments about "Love," page 132, some pewter with the "Love" touch was so marked that it must have been made at a date before Brunstrom could have reached these shores.

2) The "Love" touch has been found on at least six different sizes and forms of flat plates. Yet at the time of Brunstrom's death there was listed in his inventory but one complete mould and half of another for making small plates.

3) Perhaps the most convincing argument against the belief that Brunstrom could have made all of the Love-marked pewter is again found in the inventory. So much "Love" pewter has survived that we can be certain that its maker, or makers, had a very large business. Yet the amount of finished pewter in that inventory is very small in comparison with the stock in William Will's inventory, which was appraised just five years later. For instance, Brunstrom had only fifteen teaspoons on hand, Will $44\frac{1}{2}$ gross of teaspoons; similarly Brunstrom had ten dishes, twelve plates, Will 210 pounds of dishes and 251 pounds of plates; Brunstrom one pint basin, Will $3\frac{1}{4}$ dozen pint basins; etc.

4) The possession and use by Brunstrom of a quality mark used by "Love," is no assurance that he also owned and used the lovebird mark.

From all that has gone before it must be apparent to the reader that the author believes the "Love" touch was used by more than one pewterer, that it was probably used first by Heyne or Hasselberg and that, after Hasselberg's death, it may have passed to Koehler and then to Brunstrom. Whether the latter ever did use the "Love" mark is still a matter of conjecture that can be solved only if and when pewter should be found that bears both Brunstrom's name touch and the lovebird mark.

THREE COUNTRY PEWTERERS OF PENNSYLVANIA

Under the above title a few paragraphs appeared in Volume Two about Elisha Kirk, Samuel Pennock, and John Shoff. There is nothing new to add about Shoff, whose only claim to fame is a plate with a touch that bears his name. Kirk and Pennock, however, have left us marked porringers, see Figs. 73 and 75 of Plate XIII. Because of the research of Francis D. Brinton, of Henry J. Kauffman, and of Arthur E. James, we now know a great deal more about the varieties of the Pennsylvania tab-handle porringers and the men who made them. This is a very specialized type of porringer, really a porringer basin, with a solid handle of simple design, that seems to have been cast in one unit with the bowl. Not only was the form made in no other colony but its manufacture and sale seem to have been restricted to one small section of Pennsylvania, in Chester and York Counties.

Interestingly enough this purely local product, with a purely local appeal, was made only by artisans who worked primarily at other trades and made pewter in a very limited way in a few simple forms as a sideline to their main activities.

In addition to Kirk and Samuel Pennock, at least three other part-time pewterers are believed to have made tab-handled porringers, namely Simon Pennock, son of Samuel, Robert Porter and Isaac Jackson.

Mr. Brinton, a collector, dealer and careful student of Pennsylvania antiques, who probably handled more tab-handled porringers than any man now living, stated that he had seen at least eight different varieties of this porringer, all very similar but from different moulds. One form bears Kirk's full name, three have S.P. touches attributed to the Pennocks, father and son, and one is impressed with a large P. which has been tentatively attributed to Robert Porter.

Now for the histories of these men. Perhaps the earliest, chronologically, was Isaac Jackson of New Garden Township, Chester County. Born in 1734 on his father's farm, known as Harmony Grove, near West Grove, he was the oldest child in a family of ten.

When twenty years of age Isaac was apprenticed to Benjamin Chandlee, Jr., of Nottingham Township, one of a family of clockmakers, silversmiths, and instrument makers. Presumably while living with Chandlee, Jackson gained some knowledge of pewter-making. In 1762 Jackson established his home on a 200-acre tract in New Garden Township, where he and his wife raised a family of twelve children.

In 1774 Elisha Kirk was apprenticed to Jackson to learn the clockmaker's trade.

Three Country Pewterers of Pennsylvania

Jackson was a devout Quaker and in deeds is variously termed a farmer, a clockmaker, and a silversmith. That he was also a pewterer is proved by his inventory taken in 1807. It included "tools for making pewter porringers" valued at $12.00, a spoon mould, set of crucibles, two small iron lathes, a vise, an anvil, letter stamps, polishing tools, nineteen pounds of lead, 167 pounds of brass, 259 pounds of pewter, and twenty pewter porringers.

Although no collection is known to have a Jackson porringer, when a sesquicentennial gathering of the Jackson family was held at Harmony Grove in 1875, a pewter porringer, made by Isaac Jackson and still preserved in the family, was on exhibition. Whether that porringer, or any made by Jackson, bore his own mark of identification is not known.

A contemporary of Jackson, but probably born a few years later, was Robert Porter of Caln Township, Chester County, who, incidentally, was the only one of these porringer-makers who was not a Quaker. Nothing was learned of his early history, but tax records for Caln Township indicate that, as early as 1770, he was boarding with Robert Valentine, renting a shop nearby, owned by Abiah Park, and was a carpenter as well as a pewterer. The records indicate that he was a single man and was probably not very old at the time of his death in 1785, for he willed articles of clothing to his father. His inventory, taken in December 1785, included eight pewter plates and forty-two porringers.

The Chester County Historical Society has a record, their manuscript #13612, of a vendue held soon after the taking of Porter's inventory. The sale included forty-five porringers, one brass porringer mould, a soapstone porringer mould, soldering irons and ladle, turning machine, three turning chisels, five turning hooks and a pair of bellows. The Society also owns one other pertinent document which reads as follows:

Received the 27th of the 4th month, 1786 from Thomas Pim, Executor of the Estate of Robert Porter, Deceased, two shillings for two pounds of Pewter delivered to him to make Porringers

Received by me   X   her mark

Mary Chrisman.

At least three tab-handled porringers, marked with a large "P," have been reported. These may be the work of this man.

Mr. Brinton's investigations turned up considerable new information about Elisha Kirk. The first member of the family to settle in America was Alphonsus, great-grandfather of the pewterer, who came from Ireland to New Castle, Delaware, in 1689. Elisha's grandfather, William, lived in East Nantmeal Township, Chester County, and his father, Caleb, a farmer and joiner, was married at Caln Meeting in 1756 to Elizabeth Coates, née Mendenhall, widow of Samuel Coates, a wealthy Quaker, for whose family Coatesville was named.

On Christmas Day, 1757, Elisha, oldest of three sons of this union, was born. Until

1770 the family continued to live in the Coates homestead, but in that year moved to York County.

At the age of seventeen, Elisha transferred to the Friends New Garden Meeting, Chester County, where he had himself apprenticed to Isaac Jackson, as stated above. He was looked upon with such favor by all of the Jackson family that, upon completion of his apprenticeship, he was offered and accepted a partnership in the business.

However in 1780 Elisha married Ruth, daughter of Solomon and Sarah Miller of Pipe Creek Meeting, Frederick, Maryland, and decided to settle with his bride in York. He bought a house and property on High Street. This house, still standing, is now recorded as 274 West Market Street.

Kirk was a devout and dedicated Quaker. In 1784 he was appointed Clerk of Warrington Monthly Meeting and in 1785 was recommended as a minister by York Meeting. He travelled extensively, visiting Quakers in Virginia, North Carolina, and New England. In Newport he stayed with John Townsend, well-known cabinet maker. While attending a yearly meeting in Philadelphia he caught "pulmonary consumption" and died April 11, 1790.

No indication of pewter-making was found in Kirk's inventory and presumably his chief occupation was clock-making, when he was not engaged in furthering the interests of the Church.

Of the marked tab-handled porringers, by far the easiest to find are those stamped with the initials S.P. These initials appear on porringers from three different moulds and there are two different S.P. touches. The better known touch is shown as Fig. 598 of Plate LXX, Volume Two, the other is not illustrated here.

According to Chester County traditions the makers of the S.P. porringers were Samuel Pennock of East Marlborough Township and his son, Simon. Actually there is nothing in the official records of either man to support the pewter-making claim, but the tradition in the family is strong, and, a few years ago, Henry J. Kauffman found in southern Lancaster County, in the possession of a great-grandson of Simon Pennock, one half of a porringer mould, a touch die with the initials S.P. within an elliptical frame, a curious spoon mould on tong-like handles and three pieces of pewter, marked with the S.P. touch. All of these items have since been presented to the Museum of the Chester County Historical Society, where may also be seen the die for the larger touch, and porringers with each of the marks. One porringer, bearing the larger mark, is stamped on the underside of the handle with the date 1807.

There is little reason to doubt that all of the S.P. porringers were made by a Pennock, but we are dependent upon hearsay evidence alone, in assuming that both father and son made porringers. It may well be that either individual was responsible for all of them. The fact that two different touches and three different moulds were used is possibly an argument in favor of the assumption that both men were pewterers.

The father, Samuel Pennock, born in 1754, was taxed, between 1785 and 1815, upon a seventy-acre farm in East Marlborough Township. In those records he is shown variously as operating a turning mill, yarn mill, saw mill, and carding mill, his occupation termed turner, wheelwright, spinning wheel maker, and chair, reel, and little wheel maker. In his will, dated 1843 he called himself a spinning wheel maker.

The son, Simon, born in 1783, apparently lived with and worked for his father at the latter's many trades. In 1806 he married Sarah Lamborn, and in 1810 he advertised in a local paper the manufacture of wool carding and spinning machinery. In 1818 Simon moved to a 192-acre farm in Drumore Township in Lancaster County and there he died in 1868. If Simon made any pewter porringers such activity probably occurred before he moved to Lancaster County.

Arthur E. James in his article on Chester County pewterers in the Pewter Collectors Club of America *Bulletin* for September 1962, included one other man, David Lamborn of London Grove Township, an uncle of Simon Pennock's wife. This listing is based on the fact that in a genealogy of the Lamborn family David was termed "a blacksmith and manufacturer of porringers and skillets." Iron porringers are still to be found occasionally at country auctions and since the man was primarily a blacksmith, I would assume that the porringers, as well as the skillets, were made of iron. Lamborn will consequently not be included here as a pewterer.

'D.S.'—UNIDENTIFIED PENNSYLVANIA PEWTERER

On some of his plates Cornelius Bradford used, in conjunction with one of his normal name touches, a set of hallmarks of crude design, the first of which contained the initials D.S. (see Figs. 496 and 497 of Plate LXII in Volume Two). Later the same hallmarks were found on plates made by Malcolm McEuen and his son Duncan. This was of course explained by the fact that Bradford formed a partnership with Malcolm McEuen in New York in 1772. Just how or why Bradford acquired, and then used, the D.S. hallmarks is not known.

There is, however, good cause for believing that a pewterer with those initials was working in Pennsylvania, during the third quarter of the eighteenth century. That assertion is made because quite a few pieces of pewter have come to light which are impressed with one of two touches which include the initials D.S. in the design. Neither the angel mark, Fig. 888, nor the rose-and-crown with D.S., Fig. 886, could be found in any of Erwin Hintze's books on German pewterers, although the design of these touches is definitely German.

Both touches have been found on 9¼ inch smooth rim plates as well as other plates with normal rims. The angel mark also appears on the bottom of sugar bowls similar to those made by William Will and Parks Boyd.

A careful search of Philadelphia records failed to uncover any man with the initials D.S., who might have made pewter, but I am convinced that there was such a pewterer in eastern Pennsylvania or southern New Jersey and that the discovery of his identity is just a matter of time.

GEORGE W. WILL

Another unfortunate error, in the first edition of *Pewter in America,* was to attribute to George Washington Will a touch illustrated as Fig. 552 of Plate LXVII, which in reality was not a maker's touch at all, but rather the impression of a George Washington commemorative button mould, stamped for some unexplainable reason on a B. Barns dish. The reader is asked to revise the caption for Plate LXVII, Fig. 552, accordingly.

There is no known touch for George Will. In all probability he used his father's touches, during the few years that he had a shop of his own.

THE YOUNGER HERAS

Nothing new can be added about the Hera family of pewterers. The $9\frac{1}{4}$ inch smooth rim plate is still the only form which has been found bearing the interesting Hera touch, and even that item is very scarce. This mark is probably the rarest of all the touches which J. B. Kerfoot illustrated, over forty years ago.

PARKS BOYD AND THE PALETHORPS

In the earlier listing of Boyd's surviving examples no record was made of basins. A check today shows that he made the normal range from $6\frac{1}{4}$ to 12 inch basins, and to the list of his plates should be added a smooth brim plate of $8\frac{3}{4}$ inches diameter. He not only made barrel-shaped quart mugs but also pint mugs in that design. He has left us also at least one drum-shaped teapot, similar to the William Will teapots in that shape. In Fig. 199 of Plate XXIX, a sugar bowl with lid was illustrated as the work of an unidentified Philadelphia pewterer. What should have been noted then, but was not pointed out until years later by Charles Swain, was the interesting fact that an identical lid capped the Boyd covered water pitcher, Plate XLII, Fig. 274. It is now possible therefore to attribute to Boyd with confidence several of these handsome lidded sugar bowls.

To the list of Robert Palethorp's known products should be added 11 inch flat and 11 inch deep dishes, pint and quart barrel mugs, such as Boyd made, 4 inch beakers, quart lidded tankards with flattened dome top, similar to those made by Brunstrom and Boyd (and, as in the case of Boyd's tankards, either with plain drum or wide ribs), a teapot of rather late design, and a footed bowl, perhaps a slop bowl, with a top diameter measuring $5\frac{3}{8}$ inches.

Nothing new can be added to the Boyd or Palethorp histories.

BLAKSLEE BARNES

B. Barnes was listed in Robinson's *Philadelphia Directory* for 1817 in this form:

Barnes, Blakslee & Porter — tin plate and pewter workers &c.

Porter has not been identified. The only additions to be made to our earlier list of Barnes's products are smooth brim plates in the $9\frac{1}{8}$ and $9\frac{1}{4}$ inch sizes.

PLUMLY AND BIDGOOD

Nothing further has been learned about either Plumly or Bidgood since the original comment on this firm appeared in 1940, but an 8 inch plate and a second pint mug bearing their touch have been found. In addition, a third pint mug, presumably from the same moulds, was acquired by Dr. Robert Mallory. This mug is impressed with a very similar eagle touch, but one in which only Plumly's name appears, see Plate CIX, Fig. 873. Evidently, during his brief pewter-making career in Philadelphia, Plumly at one period operated a shop by himself, either just before or after his association with Bidgood.

EIGHT OBSCURE PHILADELPHIA PEWTERERS

Of the eight men who were listed in Volume Two under the above title, known to us only because they were recorded as pewterers in early Philadelphia directories, proof has been presented that at least one had a shop of his own. Mrs. Neal Almgren owns two tablespoons that are marked E. LESLIE in a saw-toothed rectangular frame. Leslie's first name was probably Elkins as shown in a Philadelphia directory of 1821, though the name appears as Elkanah Leslie in a Philadelphia directory of 1823/1824. An E. Leslie, first name not spelled out, was listed in Brooklyn in 1825 and Elkins Leslie was employed as a journeyman in William Calder's shop in 1828 at Providence. Presumably there was but one E. Leslie making pewter at the time. Recently two more pairs of spoons, similarly marked, have been reported.

The Pewterers of Pennsylvania

Mrs. Nancy Goyne Evans, as a result of her study of early city directories, has provided additional information about another man in this group of eight — Henry Peal (also spelled Peel in some listings). His name appears first in the directory of 1820/1821, one year earlier than had been reported in Volume Two. He may have been identical with the Henry Peal, also spelled Piel, in one directory and listed as a pewterer in Brooklyn in 1822, 1823, and 1826. These listings overlap to some extent the Peel records in Philadelphia.

To the earlier list of eight men should be added four more pewterers as found by Mrs. Evans:

William Boker   1800,
Francis Rease   13th Street above Filbert   1820–1822,
Benjamin Scull   at 26 South Fourth Street in 1810 and at 160 South Third Street in 1811,
Reuben Ward   11 Franklin Court in 1825; Ward had been listed as a tinner from 1818 to 1822.

PEWTERERS OF THE SOUTH

WITH the passage of time it becomes increasingly evident that comparatively little pewter was made in the Southern Colonies prior to 1800 and that practically all that was turned out has long since disappeared. It will be surprising indeed, if even one example of hollow-ware, made south of the Mason and Dixon Line prior to the American Revolution, should be found and identified for what it is.

In recent years three $9\frac{1}{8}$ inch smooth brim plates have been found, which are marked on the underside of the brim with the raised letters, "E.W. Virginia," lettering that was cut in the mould and not impressed with a die after casting (see Fig. 885 of Plate CX). As will be explained on pages 149–150 these plates cannot, with justification, be attributed to Edward Willett, early Maryland pewterer. The real maker remains unidentified, but we can say with some confidence that the plates could hardly have been made before 1740. Aside from these plates, not one other pewter article has been found in the past thirty years that can be definitely established as made in the South prior to 1800.

Although we still find occasionally a plate, deep dish or basin made in Richmond, Virginia, Fayetteville, North Carolina, or Augusta, Georgia, after 1800 by some transplanted Yankee and although the work of two Baltimore makers, George Lightner and Samual Kilbourn, is far from rare, the latter is, as far as now known, the only pewterer, working south of the Mason and Dixon Line, who has left us any hollow-ware whatever.

Thanks to the careful and extensive research among the early records of Virginia by Harold B. Gill, Jr., Research Associate at Colonial Williamsburg, and a similar search of North Carolina files by James H. Craig, it is possible to present the names of a few more early pewterers whose brief records will be found in this section. In fact clues sent to me by Harold Gill led to the listing of five new Virginia pewterers — Andrews, Ballantyne, Bilbro, Haldane, and Pavey. There is little reason for thinking that any of them ever operated a pewter business that compared in size with the larger city shops in the northern Colonies.

EDWARD WILLETT

About twenty-five years ago Melville T. Nichols acquired a $9\frac{1}{8}$ inch smooth brim plate, which had the raised letters "E.W. Virginia" on the underface of the brim, see Plate CX, Fig. 885. In other words, the lettering was cut into the mould, not impressed with a die after casting. Very soon thereafter Marion and Oliver Deming found in Frederick, Maryland, two more similar plates.

In the April 1943 issue of the magazine *Antiques,* Dr. Edward A. Rushford, in an article entitled "Achievements in Pewter," described some of the outstanding rarities in the fine Nichols collection. One of the accompanying illustrations showed three rare dishes including the E.W. example. The caption covering that dish read in part as follows: "The maker of this plate has been identified by the owner as Edward Willett. . . . Possibly he made this plate in Maryland for sale in Virginia but more probably he lived and worked in Virginia at some time. The rim type suggests a date of 1740 or later. . . ."

The rim type does indeed suggest a date of 1740 or later, and for that reason I cannot accept Mr. Nichols' attribution, even though collectors generally may do so.

Let us examine the pertinent known facts in the case, starting with Willett's history. Edward Willett struck his touch in Pewterers' Hall, London, in 1684/85. To have been able to do so, he must needs have completed by that time a seven-year apprenticeship. Hence he was born not later than 1663 or 1664. When he left England has not been determined, but probably not later than 1690, because he first appears in Maryland records in 1692 when he was mentioned as "Clerk of the Vestry" at Charles Town, already well established there. No trace of any Edward Willett could be found in the early archives of Virginia. By 1696 he had bought land just outside Upper Marlboro, Maryland, property which he still owned at the time of his death in 1744 or 1745. There are many extant Maryland records, dated between the years 1697 and 1744, in which Edward Willett's name is mentioned and none that indicate that he ever left the vicinity of Upper Marlboro. So much for Willett's history!

Now what do the E.W. plates themselves tell us? Howard Cotterell in *Old Pewter, Its Makers and Marks,* illustrated on page 121 a composite plate showing all of the brim designs made in England, with the range in dates when each design was in vogue. Cotterell was a profound student of pewter and thousands of plates and dishes must have passed through his hands. His judgment was that the smooth brim plate with medium-width brim and a comparatively wide bead on the underface — the design of the E.W. plates — came into use in England about 1735. Surely it did not make its appearance in America until several years later, or as Dr. Rushford suggested about 1740.

In 1740 Willett was over seventy-five years old. It is possible that he might have still been able to ply his trade part-time at such an advanced age. But is it conceivable that after living in Maryland for close to half a century, he should move over into Virginia, have new moulds made in the newest fashion with the word Virginia cut into their surface, and, after that, return to his old home in Maryland to die? After all, what would a pewterer of seventy-five or more want with new moulds?

It is equally difficult to imagine that Willett, planning in 1685 to sail for Virginia and realizing that he would have no opportunity, in the wilderness to which he was going, to acquire moulds, had moulds made for him in England with "E.W. Virginia" cut in the face of each. Even if he had done so, how explain the fact that the design of the plate mould was one that did not appear in England until almost fifty years later? If the E.W. plates had been cast with a wide brim, such as on the E.D. dish shown in Plate LXXXI, Fig. 693 this might have been a logical explanation.

With the evidence what it is, the position will be taken here that we still have no Willett pewter and that the plates were probably made in Virginia, after 1740, by a presently unidentified pewterer with the initials E.W.

JOHN ANDREWS

Earliest of the Virginia pewterers, whom Harold B. Gill, Jr., discovered in his search for Virginia craftsmen in the Colonial records, was John Andrews.

According to a York County deed dated October 8, 1705, the Trustees of Portland in Yorktown transferred Lot 64 to John Andrews of Kickotan Parish, Elizabeth City County, Brazier. Again on February 1, 1706/7 the same grantors deeded Lot 65 to John Andrews, Brazier of Yorktown.

On the basis of those deeds alone there would be no occasion for listing Andrews as a pewterer. However, the inventory of his estate, appraised August 18, 1719, indicates that he did make pewter, though probably to a very limited extent.

The inventory contained the following entries:

A Sett of Smith's Tools	£ 5.10.0
A plate mold	1.10.0
A porringer mold	1. 0.0
A spoon mold	0.10.0
4 doz. spoons 6/ 6 porringers 6/1	
1 doz. plates 10/	1. 2.0
2 Soldering Irons & Sheres	0.16.0
7 lb. solder 1/	0. 7.0
A parcell Crucibles	0. 5.0

The entire estate was valued at £ 115.4.3.

At best Andrews' pewter-making must have been only a part-time operation on a small scale. His name is included here merely for the completeness of the records.

ADAM PAVEY

Here is another man who has been included in our list of pewterers, merely because his inventory, found by Harold Gill, indicates that he was a maker of pewter spoons. He was probably a founder or blacksmith essentially. We know from other records that his apprentice, William Ashwell, was a founder.

The inventory of the estate of Adam Pavey of Spottsylvania County, Virginia, recorded June 2, 1756, included the following entries:

3 barrs Iron wt 137 lb at 3d	1.14. 3
21 dozen pewter spoones 2/4	2. 9. 0
53 dozen & 10 rough cast Do 1/6	4. 0. 9
45 flesh forkes 22 ladles	3. 7. 0
19 Grubing hoes 2/6	2. 7. 6
17 Axes 2/6	2. 2. 6
5 trivetts 8 pr snuffers	0. 8. 0
14 Wedges 1/2	0.16. 4
124 1/2 lb pewter 5d lb	2.11.10 1/2
6 pr Shot moulds 4/	1. 4. 0
1 pr Bellows 3 anvils 2 vises & other Smith's Tools	10. 0. 0
Wm. Ashwell 11 months to serve	15. 0. 0
a parcel pewterers tools &c	3. 0. 0
one half of the schooner, Industry	40. 0. 0
one old house near the River 12 feet square	3. 0. 0
Total value	422.12. 5 1/2

JOHN CAMPBELL

The story of John Campbell, Annapolis pewterer, as it appeared in Volume Two, must now be revised and greatly shortened. In addition to the newspaper notice of 1749, information had been uncovered in Annapolis records that a John Campbell was a vestryman in St. Ann's Parish in 1767 and 1769, was an appointee of the Associators of the City of Annapolis at the outbreak of the Revolution, and died in Annapolis in 1777.

Later and more careful investigation proves that the John Campbell, wife Frances, who died in 1777, was a tailor and not a pewterer, which explains the fact that no evidence of pewter-making was found in his inventory. There must be doubt now whether the other John Campbell records, in regard to his activities in St. Ann's Parish and with the Annapolis Associators, may not also have applied to the tailor rather than the pewterer.

We are left therefore with but one certain fact concerning John Campbell, pewterer,

namely that Mungo Campbell, whose relationship, if any, to John is unknown, advertised groceries which he offered for sale in January 1749, "at the House of John
Campbell, Pewterer, in Annapolis." No deeds or probate records for the pewterer
in Annapolis can now be found.

MUNGO CAMPBELL

The earliest record that we have of Mungo Campbell was a newspaper notice in
the *Maryland Gazette* for January 4, 1749, when a man with this unusual name
offered various dry groceries for sale at the "House of John Campbell, Pewterer in
Annapolis."

Three years later, in 1752, he advertised in Philadelphia as a pewterer, lately arrived
from Dublin. His residence in Philadelphia must have been brief for, on September
7, 1756, his name was recorded as that of a witness to the wedding of Joseph Nisbet
and White Maye on a marriage bond for Norfolk County, Virginia. Mungo was
probably then living in or near Norfolk for it is recorded in a Minute Book of Princess
Anne County, Virginia, on December 18, 1759, that "Jonathan Huggins be bound
to Mungo Campbell for five years from this time, that he teach the said Orphan to
read & write & the Trade of a Pewterer & take Indentures to that purpose."

Again in a Princess Anne Minute Book under the date of September 20, 1763, the
following entry appears:

> Johnson Jenkins, an Orphan who was formerly by Order of this Court, Bound Apprentice to
> Anthony Walke Jr. Gent, and being unwilling to follow the Sea and chusing the Trade of a
> Pewterer, with the consent of the said Walke, it is ordered that the Church-Wardens of Lynhaven
> Parish Bind the said Orphan to Mungo Campbell, He learning him the Trade of a Pewterer and
> further complying with the Law.

According to the Records of Bruton Parish Church at Williamsburg, William, son
of Mungo and Sarah Campbell, was baptized in 1764.

Our last record of the man is found in York County Deed Book, No. 7. On
November 12, 1764, Mungo Campbell of York County, granted to Alexander Craig,
for £ 75 current money of Virginia, a mortgage on furniture and horses. This mortgage was recorded on February 18, 1765, and, on that day was acknowledged by
Campbell in York County Court.

No will or administration papers for Campbell were found in York County.
Where or when he died could not be discovered and none of his pewter is known to
be in existence.

Pewterers of the South

JOHN BILBRO

Bilbro is another man who is being given a place in our list of pewterers simply because of an entry in his inventory. According to a Surry County, Virginia, will book, the inventory of the estate of John Bilbro, deceased April 2, 1773, included the following item:

The Pewterers Tools   £ 7.10.0.

That is the only clue that has been found as to the man's occupation.

Bilbro's name is found in a number of entries in Surry County "Court Orders." In July 1755 a petition of John Bilbro against William and Henry Barness was dismissed. In 1756 and again in 1757 accounting was made of the estate of William Bilbro, orphan, by John Bilbro, his guardian. In a suit filed by John Bilbro against Thomas Jones and heard by a court convened on April 2, 1761, the suit was ordered dismissed, the defendant to pay the costs. Again at a hearing held on July 17, 1770, Bilbro sued George and Samuel Kerry. The court directed that the plaintiff should receive £ 12, 9d.

After John Bilbro's death, at a court convened November 22, 1773, Betty Bilbro relinquished all claims and rights that she might have under her husband's will.

What Bilbro was equipped to make in pewter and what the extent of his business may have been are questions that probably can never be answered.

JOHN BALLANTYNE (OR BALLENTINE)

In a deed dated May 20, 1763, and recorded May 21, 1768, James Campbell, Merchant of Norfolk, sold to John Ballantyne, Pewterer, of same place, two tracts of land, one of 200 acres and one of 50 acres.

On June 18, 1769, John Ballantyne, Pewterer, and Nora, his wife "sold to James Parker two tracts of land, one at the head of Julian's Creek west side of Southern Branch of Elizabeth River comprising two hundred acres more or less and another tract of approximately fifty acres on the south side of the Southern Branch, which tracts Ballantyne had purchased from Andrew Duche June 25, 1763."

These properties seem to be the same as those which, according to the deed first mentioned above, had been acquired by Ballantyne from James Campbell.

On January 4, 1769, John Ballantyne, Pewterer, "sold four negroes." His name was found for the last time on a deed of May 6, 1771, when William Cherry sold to "John Ballentine," occupation not recorded, ten acres on the south side of Deep Creek.

Norfolk probate records are now on films in the State Archives in the Virginia State Library and unfortunately a number of the books were filmed either without index or with an index that is illegible—at least in part. It would be too tedious, to be worth the time involved, to work through these unindexed films; otherwise it might be possible to learn when John Ballentine, John Norsworthy, and Mungo Campbell, one or all of them, died.

It is possibly worth noting that in Howard Cotterell's list of British pewterers a John Ballantyne received his freedom in Edinburgh, Scotland, in 1752 and no later record of his activities was listed there. It is conceivable that this man may have emigrated to Virginia between the years 1752 and 1763.

JAMES HALDANE

Herewith are two newspaper notices which appeared in the *Virginia Gazette:*

January 2, 1772
James Haldane, Copper Smith and Brass Founder from Philadelphia, in Church Street, near the Church, Norfolk, makes and sells all Sorts of Copper and Brass Work, namely Still, Brewing Coppers (etc) . . . at the most reasonable Rates . . . and gives the best Prices for old Copper, Brass, Pewter or Lead.—All Orders from the Country will be punctually attended to.

N.B. He deals for Cash or Country Produce.

July 13, 1776
The Subscriber is now settled in Petersburg, where he carries on the Copper Smith's, Brass-Founder's, Tinner's, Pewterer's and Plumber's Branches, in the best and most expeditious Manner, and on the lowest Terms, for ready Money. He makes and mends Stills, Pewter Worms, Kettles, Mill-Brasses &c. and repairs every Kind of Brass, Copper, Tin, Pewter or Lead and is in great Want of Spelter, or Spelter Solder, also Borax and Sal-Amoniac (for which he will give the highest price) and coarse and smooth Files. Any person having those Articles to dispose of are requested to let the Subscriber know thereof as soon as possible. . . .

James Haldane

Lost, by the Subscriber, at the Conflagration of Norfolk, a large Quantity of Copper Sheets and Bottoms. Whoever might have taken them from the situation they were in, thinking them lost to the Owner, will much oblige me if they will deliver the same to me at Petersburg, and I will give 1s 6d per lb. for them, or a reasonable Satisfaction to any Person who will inform me where they are, or any other Goods that were taken out of my House and Shops.

James Haldane

A check of Philadelphia deeds disclosed the fact that on May 1, 1765, William Moore, Merchant sold to James Haldane, occupation not shown, property on the east side of 2nd Street.

No other records could be found either in Philadelphia or Virginia which might have thrown light on Haldane's activities. Very evidently he was essentially a coppersmith and brazier, who did some work in pewter. Whether he rightfully belongs in a list of pewterers is difficult to determine on the basis of the meager evidence available.

JOHN NORSWORTHY

Because of an error in transcribing copy, before Volume Two went to print in 1940, this man's name was given as Norsworth, instead of Norsworthy, in recording an advertisement of the opening of his shop in Norfolk, Virginia in 1771. It should now be corrected accordingly on page 76, Volume Two. The reader is also asked to kindly change the spelling of the name in the list of American pewterers, page 147, in the Bibliography, p. 186, and the General Index, p. 231.

In spite of further search among Norfolk records, the name was not found for that period in any of the public records.

PETER HENLEY (OR HENDLEY)

In the Court Records for Rowan County, North Carolina, are two entries, which have preserved the information that a pewterer was at work in or near Salisbury, North Carolina, before the Revolution, at a time when northwestern North Carolina must have been very sparsely populated. The evidence appears in the Court Minutes as follows:

Nov. 1, 1774. Ordered by the Court that peter Henley (Henby?) take care of the Children of Margaret Haiden now in his possession, 'till next Court, then to be priduced [sic] to Court to be dealt with according to Law.

Feb. 10, 1775. The Bastard children of Margaret Headen are to be bound out as follows: John (age 6 years on Next June the 1st) to Peter Hendley to "Learn the Trade of a Tinner [Tinker?] and Pewterer"; Bennet, (age 4 years on November 1, last) to learn the same; & Hannah (age 8 years on last Oct. 1) to same until 18 years old.

No Peter Henley, Henly or Hendly could be found in the 1790 list of heads of families for North Carolina nor did a search of North Carolina probate or land court records disclose any further mention of this man. Living in a backwoods settlement, far from any source of supply, Henley could not have had much of a business in pewter.

FRANCIS HENDRICKS

In a loose-leaf page supplement to *Guide to American Pewter*, the late Carl Jacobs illustrated a drawing of a touch purported to be that of Francis G. Hendricks. The frame of the touch is a rectangle, taller than it is wide, but with a curved, rather than a horizontal, top line. The central design within the frame is a palm tree on one side of which are the initials F.G.; on the other the letter H, and, underneath, the date 1768.

What more appropriate design could be selected for a pewterer of the "Palmetto

Theodore Jennings

State" than a palm tree, flanked by his initials and a date that varied by but three years from the date when Francis Garlieb Hendricks first advertised his shop in Charleston? Jacobs can hardly be criticized for his attribution.

Soon after publication of this new mark, a dealer brought to me for identification a flagon of very Germanic design. It bore three touch marks, impressed in the form of a triad, with the base of each touch turned towards the center of the flagon base, as so often was done by German pewterers.

One of the three marks was shield-shaped, enclosing a rampant lion and, behind it, two wide vertical bars. The other two touches were identical, a small replica of the Jacobs drawing but with a fallen palm trunk at the base of the upright tree and with the date 1708 instead of 1768 as shown in the drawing. Presumably the touches which I saw were in better state of preservation than that from which the drawing was copied.

Both the design of the flagon and the methods of the marking were so typical of German practice that reference was made to Erwin Hintze's monumental work on German pewterers. In his volume, *Sächsische Zinngiesser*, page 83, pewterer no. 407, Friedrich Gottfried Hermann, was shown to have used the identical touches which I had seen on the flagon. The lion in the shield was the emblem used by Dresden pewterers. Of Hermann, Hintze wrote: ". . . vom Stosen, lernt in Leipzig. Wird Meister am 6 Oktober 1783, Dresden." What the significance of the date 1708 was, I cannot imagine.

And so, with apologies to the late Carl Jacobs, I am forced to deny to Hendricks what would have been an eminently appropriate touch.

THEODORE JENNINGS

In Volume Two a memorandum was presented of the arrival in Maryland in 1775 of an indentured servant named Theodore Jennings, termed in the passenger list a pewterer, aged forty, from Middlesex, England. Reference to Cotterell's *Old Pewter* showed that a Theodore Jennings had joined the yeomanry in London, March 24, 1757, possibly the pewterer who emigrated to Maryland. Search in this country failed to turn up any information about Jennings' later history.

However Dr. W. A. Monkhouse found a 9½-inch shallow smooth brim plate in Western Massachusetts about 1958, on which the touch indicated that the maker's name was Theodore Jennings. A few years later the Doctor found an identical plate in southern Maine. It seemed that the touches on these plates must be those of the London pewterer (Cotterell's no. 2616, page 244). The photographs of these touches were submitted to Mr. Ronald F. Michaelis, authority on English pewter, for his comments. He replied: "I agree that this is Theodore Jennings, London, but *not* the one suggested by you. I think it is T.J., Cott. no. 2615. The touch and all the supplementary marks and the crowned ownership initial, are typical of the *early* 18th Century rather than late 18th. . . ." If Mr. Michaelis is correct, as I believe him to be, Dr. Monkhouse's Jennings plates could not have been made in this country by the emigrant to Maryland.

J. W. OLCOTT

When the first two volumes of *Pewter in America* appeared, it was not known whether this obscure Baltimore pewterer was J. W. Olcott or J. Wolcott. The name is very clear on a 7¾-inch plate at Winterthur, see Plate CIX, Fig. 565a. The last name is definitely Olcott. In addition to small plates, at least one 11-inch deep dish, bearing this man's touch, has been reported. Nothing has been found to indicate the location of his shop in Baltimore or the exact dates of his pewter-making. The caption for Fig. 565 of Plate LXVIII in Volume Two should be noted to show that the correct name is J. W. Olcott.

When the first Olcott plate was reported, the appearance of the eagle in the design led to the suspicion that this unidentified pewterer, might, like Kilbourn and S. Griswold, be another transplanted Connecticut Yankee, who worked briefly in Baltimore. But no pewterer of that name could be located in Connecticut records.

However, Wendell Hilt's recent search of Connecticut records may very well have uncovered the man for whom we have been looking, even though we have no positive proof that the suspect ever made pewter.

On October 23, 1786, a Joel White Olcott was born at Litchfield, Connecticut to James and Mary Olcott. In 1802 Joel's father died and Joel's older brother Daniel was appointed his guardian. That is the last trace of the young man in Connecticut. He would presumably have been apprenticed about 1800 and would have come of age in 1807. In other words, the initials are correct and the age just what might be expected, because the eagle touch can be dated from its design as approximately 1805–1815. Olcott's name is not found in the Connecticut Census for 1810 or any later census in that state. Despite the absence of his name from any early Baltimore directory, it is possible that his shop was outside the city limits, and an examination of the Maryland Census for 1810 and again for 1820 might definitely locate in time and place this elusive pewterer.

SAMUEL KILBOURN

To be added to the earlier list of forms which had been found bearing impressions of one of Kilbourn's touches are teapots and bedpans, both of which articles were mentioned in Kilbourn's advertisement of 1819, which was printed in Volume Two. The teapots are of the tall type, similar in design to the T. D. Boardman pot, illustrated as Fig. 193 of Plate XXVIII.

On line 25, page 80, Volume Two, the Fig. no. on Plate XXII, Volume One, for the Kilbourn beaker should have read 150, instead of 155.

SYLVESTER GRISWOLD

Just one new form can be added to our earlier list of articles found bearing this man's touch—a pint (6⅝-inch) basin. Another careful check of available Baltimore records was unsuccessful in determining exactly when and where his pewter-making took place in that city.

JACOB EGGLESTON

The main accounts of Eggleston's pewter-making activities are to be found on pages 120–21 in Volume One and on page 79 in this volume. However new information is available about the Fayetteville operation and warrants presentation among the accounts of the Southern pewterers.

The following announcement appeared in the *North-Carolina Intelligencer*, Fayetteville, April 17, 1807:

> Eggleston & Bass Respectfully inform the Public they have commenced the Tin Plate Working, Pewter and Copper smith's Business, a few Rods south of the State House, on Person St. Fayetteville, where they have constantly on hand a large assortment of Pewter, Tin and Japanned Ware, which they will dispose of on the most reasonable terms. To Shopkeepers and others who purchase to sell again, their usual allowance will be made. . . .

The junior partner was Daniel Bass, a tinsmith, who had previously worked in Berlin, Connecticut. It is a matter of interest that Paris J. Tillinghast, Jr., a new name in the list of Rhode Island pewterers was also associated in some way in Eggleston's Fayetteville business, see pages 53–54.

On May 7, 1812, "Jacob Eggleston of Middletown, Conn, Daniel Bass of Berlin, Conn., Oliver Pearce and P. J. Tillinghast, Jr., of Fayetteville" sold property to William Terry of Fayetteville on Cold Spring Street in Fayetteville.

Since both Eggleston and Bass had apparently returned to Connecticut prior to the preparation of that deed the duration of their pewter-making activities in Fayetteville can be set with reasonable accuracy as just about five full years.

Pewterers of the South

WILLIAM NOTT AND JEHIEL JOHNSON

For information about these two Middletown pewterers, who followed Eggleston to Fayetteville, please see pages 133–135 in Volume One and pages 88–89 in this volume.

As was the case with Eggleston, we can determine very accurately when Jehiel Johnson opened a shop in Fayetteville. The notice which follows was taken from the Fayetteville *American* in its issue of November 10, 1815.

> The Subscribers Begs leave to inform their friends and the public, that they have rented the Store, formerly occupied by Messrs, Hogg & Ming, where they have on hand A General Assortment of Dry Goods: They intend commencing the Tin & Pewter Manufactory.
>
> Country Merchants and others can be supplied on reasonable terms by the quantity, Johnson, Hall & Co.

SAMUEL CAMPBELL

In 1940 nothing was known about the pewterer, Samuel Campbell; in fact it was not known whether his last name was Campbell or Campmell. But a few small plates bearing this name had turned up, and because the style and design of the touch seemed to indicate a Connecticut origin, comment about these plates was included with the stories of the pewterers of the Connecticut Valley.

Meanwhile the research of Mrs. Nancy Goyne Evans has uncovered the information that a pewterer of this name was working in Baltimore from 1814 to 1818, surely the user of the Samuel Campbell eagle touch, illustrated as Fig. 453 of Plate LVIII, Volume One. There are no directories for Baltimore for the years from 1811 to 1813. It is possible therefore that Campbell was working in Baltimore for one to three years before we find record of him as a pewterer at the corner of Bridge and Union Streets, Old Town, in the Baltimore Directory for 1814/1815. In 1816 he was at Potter near Union and in 1817/1818 at North Street. The name is not found in the succeeding directories.

It is quite possible that Samuel was a descendant, or at least a relative, of John or Mungo Campbell; both of whom were making pewter in Annapolis, Maryland, a generation or two earlier. No information about Samuel Campbell, other than the directory entries, could be learned about his activities in Baltimore.

One or two more 8-inch plates and butter plates in the $5\frac{1}{4}$-inch size have turned up in recent years. The name is now established as Campbell (not Campmell). See Plate CIX, Fig. 453a.

GILES GRISWOLD

When the first edition of *Pewter in America* was published an eagle touch, bearing the name Griswold, was illustrated as Fig. 601 of Plate LXX in Volume Two and classified as that of an unidentified pewterer, because the top portion of the touch, which might have shown the maker's given name, was badly erased and there was no way to determine whether the name was Ashbil, Sylvester, or Giles.

The H. F. du Pont Winterthur Museum now has an 8½-inch plate with a clear impression of the upper half of that touch, showing the word Augusta above the eagle's head (see Plate CIX, Fig. 601a, in this volume). The same museum also has an 11-inch deep dish with a hitherto unpublished touch which undoubtedly was used by the same maker and is so attributed here (see Plate CIX, Fig. 874).

FOUR LATE BALTIMORE PEWTERERS

The study of Baltimore city directories made by Mrs. Nancy Goyne Evans has turned up four men, listed as pewterers, who were hitherto unknown to present-day collectors. It is highly improbable that any of the four was a factor of any importance in the making of pewter in Baltimore but their names are given herewith:

Garey, Jeremiah and Hammond (probably Joseph) pewter and tinplate workers— Direc. of 1819. Garey was listed as a tinplate worker in 1817/18, 1822/23, 1824, and 1827; Hammond as a coppersmith and tinplate worker in 1822/23, 1824, and 1827.

Gehring, John G.—pewterer 1824; (in 1827 the same man was listed as a jeweller and watch-maker).

Johnson, Elijah—pewterer in directory of 1822/23. In 1819 he was recorded as a japanner.

Richardson, Jabez—pewterer in 1817/18. In 1816 and later in 1819 his occupation was given as plumber.

JAMES MARTINE

Chronologically this man's story probably should be included with the makers of the Britannia Period. However he was what Mr. Kerfoot termed an 8-inch plate maker. In other words, on the basis of his surviving work of record, an 8⅛-inch plate, a 10-inch dish and a 13-inch dish, he belongs to the earlier period and will be so listed here. His touch is shown as Fig. 875 of Plate CIX.

Pewterers of the South

Just when James Martine opened his first shop in Fayetteville, North Carolina, we do not know, but, thanks to the research of James H. Craig we know that on December 29, 1826, James Martine took William A. Bass, free Negro, as apprentice to the coppersmith's trade.

Three years later, in 1829, he advertised in the *North Carolina Journal* that he "had commenced the Tin Business in Fayetteville, a few doors east of Messrs Hall and Johnson." (This is our old friend Jehiel Johnson of Middletown, Connecticut, and Fayetteville, North Carolina.) He advertised "Brazier's Copper, Copper and Tin Ware, etc." and offered to buy old copper and pewter.

In 1832 he bought property in Fayetteville and in 1835 and again in 1836 he is recorded as having taken on apprentices to the coppersmith's and tinplate worker's trade. At no place in existing records could anything be found to indicate that Martine made pewter. Such pieces as bear his touch were probably made before 1832. By that date the demand for pewter plates and dishes must have dried up almost completely. Martine's history after 1836 was not traced.

UNIDENTIFIED AMERICAN TOUCHES

ON Plates LXIX and LXX, in Volume Two, were shown twenty-six touches, believed to have been used by American pewterers, but lacking the distinguishing characteristics which would permit their attribution to specific shops. Since 1940 many more of these unidentified marks have turned up. But, before the more recent finds are shown and discussed, a report is in order on the twenty-six unidentified touches of thirty years ago.

Fig. 578 was presumed to represent a horse with one foreleg raised. Several clearer impressions of this touch have since been found and the central figure is now seen to be a stag (of sorts). An unusually complete impression of the touch, as it appears in the bottom of a quart pot in the collection of Mrs. George A. Marks, is illustrated as Fig. 578a on Plate CX in this volume. The same touch has also been found on the underside of a flowered porringer handle. There can be very little doubt that the user was a pewterer of Boston or Newport, near the middle of the eighteenth century.

Nothing new can be added about Figs. 579 or 580 but several more examples of 579 have been found and the impression is growing that this is a Joseph Leddell touch. Please note here a correction that should be made in the comments about 580 as they appeared on page 88 in Volume Two. Eight lines from the bottom of that page the reference for the illustration of the dram bottle should have read, Plate XXXIX, 248 instead of XXXIX, 250.

Figs. 581–584 inclusive were thought to be touches of William Bradford, New York pewterer. As more examples bearing these touches are still coming to light, upon shapes and with details that are typical of New York workmanship, one is tempted to award, out of hand, all four to Bradford. A particularly strong case can be made for 583, the touch with two deer heads. That mark had been photographed from a large, round, lidded box, a form which, in 1940, was not known to have any counterpart in American pewter. The Metropolitan Museum now owns a slightly larger box of the same design and with similar tooled decoration which bears a known touch of Joseph Leddell, Bradford's neighbor and competitor.

Fig. 585, which had been attributed with reservations to John Fryers, Newport pewterer, probably should be removed from any list of American touches. Mr. Ronald Michaelis, eminent English authority, states that it has been found on several vessels in England.

Plates and dishes bearing the touch illustrated as Fig. 586 continue to come to light in Pennsylvania and it is pretty generally conceded by collectors that this is a touch of Thomas Byles, Newport and Philadelphia pewterer.

To the best of my knowledge, Figs. 587 and 588 are still the only known examples of those marks. The design and shape of the porringer handle on which 587 appears are discussed on page 11. The internal evidence points to a probable Boston or Newport origin.

Last of the touches on Plate LXIX was that in Fig. 292a, a touch which was undoubtedly used in Boston. Somewhat reluctantly I am prepared to accept the rather general assumption, that the touch is that of an obscure Boston pewterer, Robert Bonynge, 1731–1764, the only discoverable Boston maker with initials, R.B.

Let us turn now to Plate LXX. Thirty additional years of collecting have uncovered nothing new that need be added to the earlier comments upon Fig. 590–592 inclusive, 595, 596, or 599.

Although there is nothing new to be said about the touch illustrated as Fig. 589 on Plate LXX, an error should be corrected in the caption as it appeared opposite this plate in Volume Two. In the fourth line of the caption, the plate number should have read LXVI instead of LXV. Fig. 593 is now believed to be English and should be removed from our lists.

Fig. 594 must be removed from the list of American touches, despite the fact that a great quantity of pewter, marked with that touch has survived in this country. Ronald F. Michaelis has written me that he has frequently seen the same touch in England and on forms similar to those upon which it appears in this country. Even more recently an article by John Carl Thomas, entitled "H.I. an Answer and an End" in the Pewter Collectors Club of America *Bulletin* for June 1967 furnished what seems convincing proof that the user of the touch was Henry Joseph of London, *c.* 1757–1780.

Fig. 597, now identified as to user, proved to be even later than suspected. It has been found in conjunction with the name touch of William McQuilkin who was working in Philadelphia in the late 1830's and even into the 1850's.

Fig. 598 is almost certainly a touch of either Samuel or Simon Pennock of East Marborough Township, Chester County, Pennsylvania. Their history is given briefly on pages 141–142 of this volume.

Fig. 600 is still unidentified as to maker, but the belief persists that this touch was reserved for use on basins only by Gershom Jones of Providence. The only basin thus far reported with a known Jones touch bears his well-known early lion mark which of course preceded all of the American eagle touches.

A clear impression of Fig. 601, now illustrated as 601a on Plate CIX, this volume, was photographed from a plate in the Winterthur Museum. It identifies the user conclusively as Giles Griswold of Augusta, Georgia.

Last of the unidentified touches on Plate LXX was 602, showing an eagle with the initials A.B. Incidentally a pint basin has been reported, bearing this rare touch. Any thought that this might be a touch of Aaron Burdett of Baltimore should be banished. A more careful examination of that man's records shows that he was not working in Baltimore before 1838—much too late for this touch—and even then he was only a mender and plater of metals.

Now we may turn to the two new plates, CX and CXI, with illustrations of other touches which cannot be attributed with confidence to any specific pewterers.

The earliest of the group, Fig. 876 is a small shield-shaped mark, struck four times on the upper face of a smooth-brim dish, of similar design to and struck in the same manner as the touch attributed to Edmund Dolbeare, Plate CIV, Fig. 831. It may well be that this is a touch of Dolbeare's friend, and surety, John Baker of Boston, 1674–1696.

Not nearly as early is the next touch, but definitely that of a Boston pewterer, working during the first half of the eighteenth century. Just a faint impression can be seen of the same Boston cartouche that was employed by David Cutler, by "Semper Eadem," R.B. (believed to have been Robert Bonynge), and at a later date by Richard Austin and Thomas Badger. The user's name and record are probably already known to us.

Fig. 878 is typical of small London touches that were in general use slightly before 1700. It is being attributed here with definite reservations to Thomas Byles, Newport and Philadelphia pewterer. This attribution is made because of a number of seemingly valid reasons. In this country very few English tankards, made before 1750, have survived. The tankard upon which this touch appears was purchased by Mrs. J. Insley Blair many years ago, before English pewter had any vogue here as an antique.

The design of the touch is such as to lead one to say that this is just what might have been expected of Byles. As a boy he would have seen in Boston, and been familiar with, similar diamond-shaped initial touches. The initials, of course, fit the man and the date is equally appropriate. His father's will, written in 1704, spoke of Thomas as a minor, apprenticed to Mr. Mann, a brazier. We also know that in 1711 he had moved to Newport, presumably having opened a shop there. There is every reason to suppose that 1710—as shown on the touch—signified the date of opening of his first shop in Newport. It is of interest that not only does the touch not appear in Cotterell's *Old Pewter* but that Ronald F. Michaelis, Honorable Librarian of the Pewter Club of England, though stating that he thinks the mark English, agrees that there is no record of its having ever been seen on surviving English pewter.

Fig. 879 though a clear impression, gives no clues as to its maker and probably can never be identified unless found with a touch showing the name or initials of its maker, but it was photographed from the bottom of a typically Boston shallow dish and the touch itself has the general appearance of other Boston marks.

Figs. 880 and 881 have in common the initials T.B. and both have the initials in raised letters on the underside of porringer handles. Taking first Fig. 881, the general design of the handle is one that, so far, has been found only on Massachusetts and Rhode Island porringers. A discussion of this particular handle type is found on page 11. The support itself, with a narrow tongue extending below the support proper, is of a pattern peculiar to Newport pewterers. Consequently a case of sorts can be made, even though on circumstantial evidence, for attributing this porringer to Thomas Byles, Newport and Philadelphia, 1710 to 1771.

The third T.B. mark, Fig. 880, cannot be so easily classified as to probable origin. The handle is of the so-called crown (really coronet) type which was made with slight variations throughout the Colonies. This particular design, however, has no exact counterpart in this country. The support is also a variant from the norm. Though roughly triangular, it is unduly heavy and thick, with all edges slightly rounded. This is definitely an early porringer, the moulds for which were apparently not handed down to later generations, the more's the pity. Nothing about this porringer suggests a Newport origin. We would like to attribute it to Thomas Burroughs, earliest of New York pewterers, but, other than identity of initials, there is no evidence for such an assumption.

Our next new touch, Fig. 882, was also photographed from a porringer and is also unquestionably early, say first half of the eighteenth century. This porringer, and others of the same general pattern, were discussed on page 11. The same mark has been found on two similar porringers, on a porringer of earlier and even rarer handle design, Fig. 699, Plate LXXXIII, and upon a funnel. Because this particular handle has been found bearing only one other touch, the I.D. lion mark, Fig. 356, Plate LI, Volume I, attributed to John Danforth of Norwich, Connecticut, it has been suggested that I.L. may have stood for Ivory Lucas, who was working in New London, Connecticut, from 1732 to 1747. This is entirely possible, but proof is totally lacking.

Fig. 883 of Plate CX illustrates a worn impression of an initial touch that has been found on the lips of two measures, both of which came to light in Rhode Island. The first letter is completely erased in both touches and even the second letter cannot be seen in its entirety. However the mark has been attributed, perhaps correctly, to John Fryers of Newport, 1749–1768.

Fig. 884 showing a lamb and pennant, is so badly worn that any name, that may have encircled the design, has disappeared completely. The same religious symbol was the central motif in a touch of William Elsworth of New York, of Charles Jones and Samuel Smith of London and of several other English pewterers. But all of those touches were designed and cut by experts. In this touch the inability of the diecutter to produce a lamb of proportions approximating nature more closely, points to the likelihood of a country origin, either American or English. It has been reported thus far on just one plate.

Fig. 885 illustrates the raised cast letters E.W.: Virginia as found on the rim of an eighteenth-century $9\frac{1}{8}$ inch smooth brim plate. Two pairs of such plates have been reported. Because of the identity of initials, this plate and its fellows have been attributed to Edward Willett, Maryland's earliest pewterer of record. What's more, the attribution has been pretty generally accepted as correct, even though not a shred of evidence has been presented to place Willett in Virginia at any time in his life.

Unidentified American Touches

Not only did he not make these plates but it can be stated, beyond contradiction, that he could not have been their maker, all as explained on page 148–150 in this volume. The maker was an unidentified resident of Virginia, working somewhere in that colony about the middle of the eighteenth century.

The last illustration shown on Plate CX, Fig. 578a, was number one among the unidentified touches in Volume Two. This is the controversial stag touch, formerly thought to depict a horse, which has since been found on the underside of a flowered porringer handle, in pint mugs, and in quart pots with strap handles that are identical with similar pots made by Robert Bonynge and by "I.S. Semper Eadem." The user is still unidentified, but he must surely have been working in Boston or Newport about the middle of the eighteenth century. In all probability his name and history are well known to us.

Turning now to Plate CXI the first three touches—Figs. 886, 887, and 888—are, without much doubt, those of an unidentified pewterer, probably of German birth who was working in Eastern Pennsylvania during the third quarter of the eighteenth century. The same hallmarks with the initials D.S. were used later by Cornelius Bradford, Philadelphia pewterer. As more and more plates stamped with this crude rose and crown have appeared, the more likely did it seem that they must have been made by a local pewterer and not pewter that had been brought by the new settlers from the old country. The very fact that Bradford later used the die for the hallmarks would seem to substantiate that opinion. One wonders why Bradford would have wanted to use a die with such crudely cut designs. The angel touch, Fig. 888, to the best of my knowledge, has been found only on the bottom of two sugar bowls. I have yet to find the hallmarks in conjunction with either the angel touch or the rose and crown. So it is mere supposition that one man was responsible for all of these D.S. touches.

Figs. 889, 890, 891, and 892 were photographed on the upper rim of two smooth-rimmed plates. They are unusual in that they are not really touches. The initials and decoration were cut, in reverse, on the base of plate moulds so that, after casting, they would stand above the surface of the upper rim of the plate. Both plates are probably of New England origin, made about 1740–1780.

Figs. 893 and 894 are two small touches found on the bottom of a small beaker. One encloses the initials G.C., the other what appears to be an eagle's head. It may be that they are two more touches, not previously reported, that were used by George Coldwell, New York, 1784–1811.

Fig. 895, another small initial touch with letters R.E. in script within an oval, was found on a porringer handle of openwork design. The maker is unknown, probably late eighteenth or early nineteenth century.

Fig. 896, with initials W.H., is that of an unidentified maker, probably of the late eighteenth century. It was photographed from the handle of a well-made spoon the decoration of which resembles closely that of a similar smaller spoon illustrated in Volume One as Fig. 179 of Plate XXV.

Unidentified American Touches

In Fig. 897 is a rather badly worn touch showing the initials T.M. as they appear on the inside of a quart basin of presumably eighteenth-century manufacture. It may be that this mark is not American.

Fig. 898 is a puzzling touch as found on an ink chest with double-flap, hinged lids, a chest that has been attributed to William Ball of Philadelphia, 1775–1781. The chest appears to be all original and the touch original with it, but the design and type of the lettering are quite out-of-character with American touches of that period. On a few occasions German pewterers did use block letters in their touches even earlier than this, but I cannot be entirely happy in conceding that the native-born Philadelphian, William Ball, would have done so.

Our next touch, Fig. 899 is of a small eagle without name or initials, whose user is unknown to us. It has all the characteristics of a Connecticut origin and was probably a touch of a man already well known to us.

Fig. 900 shows what unquestionably is an American eagle, but in a design that is not at all characteristic of our other eagles. It may well have been one of the earliest eagle marks, say 1785–1800. The first name clearly is John and it would seem that enough of the surname has survived to identify the name. However, it would call for a decoder with greater perspicacity than mine to risk a guess as to what the missing letters are. This touch was found on an 8½-inch plate that came to light in the Pocono Mountains of Pennsylvania.

It should be possible to track down and identify, J.T.S., the user of the latest eagle touch to be reported, Fig. 901, with a beautifully clear impression of a hitherto unknown mark as found on a 7⅝-inch plate without reed. The mark resembles to some extent the eagle touches of Kilbourn and S. Griswold of Baltimore. The refinement of the composition and the precision of the cutting point to a more expert diecutter than the man who was responsible for so many of the Connecticut dies. The suggested date is 1810 to 1825.

Last of all among our unidentified touches, and quite possibly the latest chronologically, is the touch shown as Fig. 902. Here definitely is the mark of a Connecticut pewterer, probably one who removed to the South and set up shop in Augusta, Georgia, or Fayetteville, North Carolina. There is a close family resemblance between this eagle and the eagles of William Danforth of Middletown, Connecticut, and Jacob Eggleston of Fayetteville. The mark is from a 7¾-inch plate of rather thin, soft metal that had been used in the Purity Church at Chester, South Carolina. The only letters visible above the eagle's head are the CO of company. The name that once preceded it was short and may have been North or Rowe of Augusta, c. 1815–1825, men for whose touch or touches we have been looking.

PLATE CX—*Touches of Unidentified Pewterers*

876. A small touch impressed four times on rim of 17-inch dish—initials I. B. Maker unknown, but touch attributed with some reservations to John Baker, Boston, 1674–1696. Cf. touch of Baker's contemporary, Edmund Dolbeare, Fig. 831, Plate CIV. Courtesy of Dr. John H. Kler and the Smithsonian Institution, United States National Museum.

877 and 287c. Touches of an unidentified Boston pewterer, probably second quarter of eighteenth century. Note the faint Boston cartouche, used later by David Cutler, Thomas Badger, Richard Austin, and probably others. Courtesy of Henry Francis du Pont Winterthur Museum.

878. Touch attributed with some slight reservations to Thomas Byles, Newport, Rhode Island and Philadelphia, Pennsylvania, *c.* 1710–1771. The date 1710 is believed to be the year in which Byles opened his first shop. The touch is from a quart tankard, illustrated as Fig. 712, Plate LXXXV. Courtesy of the Metropolitan Museum of Art, gift of Mrs. J. Insley Blair, 1940, in memory of J. Insley Blair.

879. Touch of an unidentified pewterer, probably of Boston, *c.* 1750, as struck on a shallow plate with Boston characteristics. Courtesy Carl Jacobs.

880. The marks of an unidentified pewterer, initials T. B., as they appear beneath the handle of a very fine porringer illustrated as Fig. 701, Plate LXXXIII. Collection of William S. Wilcox.

881. Marks on the underside of another early porringer handle with initials T. B. Because this design of support with long tongue was used by Newport pewterers of a later date, the mark is attributed, with some reservations, to Thomas Byles. Newport and Philadelphia, 1710–1771. Collection of John H. McMurray.

882. Touch of an unidentified maker I. L. as found on two different early designs of porringer handle and on a funnel. Almost certainly New England. Attributed, but with definite reservations, to Ivory Lucas, New London, Connecticut, 1732–1747. Gift of Joseph France to William Penn Memorial Museum, Harrisburg, Pennsylvania.

883. Touch found on the lip of a lidded measure formerly in the collection of the late Dr. Madelaine R. Brown. Attributed with reservations to John Fryers, Newport, Rhode Island, 1749–1768.

884. Touch as found on plate of Lloyd W. Fowles. Mark of an unidentified pewterer, probably New England, 1750–1775, but it might be that of an English country pewterer.

885. Mark as found, cast on the under face of the brim of a 9⅛-inch plate in the collection of Dr. Joseph H. Kler. The maker is unidentified, the location of his shop in Virginia undetermined, probably mid-eighteenth century. Courtesy of Smithsonian Institution, United States National Museum.

578a. Here is a fine clear impression of a touch 578, which was believed to have a horse with upraised leg as its central motif. It is apparent now that the horse is a stag of sorts. The user of the touch is still unidentified, but worked almost certainly in Newport or Boston, *c.* 1750–1775. Collection of Mrs. George A. Marks, photograph courtesy of William O. Blaney.

PLATE CX

876

877 287c 878 879

880 881

882 883 885 884 578a

PLATE CXI—*Touches of Unidentified Pewterers*

886. A rather crude rose-and-crown design of a pewterer with the initials D. S., from a plate in the Henry Francis du Pont Winterthur Museum. Pewter so marked invariably turns up in eastern Pennsylvania or New Jersey. The pewterer is believed to have been German-American, working *c.* 1750–1775. It may have been this same D. S. whose equally crude hallmarks were used later by Cornelius Bradford; see Fig. 497, Plate LXII, Volume Two.

497b and 887. The initial touch D. S. in hallmarks used later by Cornelius Bradford, found here in conjunction with a London touch on a plate in the collection of Mr. and Mrs. Paul R. Glazier. On the plate the London touch is widely separated from the hallmarks. Therefore the photograph has been cut in two and the two areas showing the marks have been butted together to save space on the page.

888. Another touch with initials D. S., presumably used by the same pewterer. Photographed from the bottom of a sugar bowl illustrated as Fig. 774, Plate XCV. To date no one has reported any pewter that combines 497 with either 886 or 888. Collection of Charles V. Swain.

889, 890, and 891. The raised initials IG, a cup and a rosette, as they appear on the upper face of a smooth brim plate. Fig. 891 shows marking as found on brim of same plate, exactly across from the rosette and cup. Maker and place of work unknown; probably American, second half of eighteenth century. Courtesy of Dr. Joseph H. Kler and the Smithsonian Institution, United States National Museum, Washington.

892. Another example of raised lettering, as found on the upper face of a 9⅛-inch smooth-brim plate in the collection of Dr. Joseph H. Kler. The maker, initials H. S., is unidentified, his place of work unknown, probably mid-eighteenth century. Courtesy of the Smithsonian Institution, United States National Museum.

893 and 894. Touches as they appear in the bottom of a small beaker in the Henry Francis du Pont Winterthur Museum. The maker, G. C., cannot be identified but these may be additional marks of George Coldwell, New York, 1787–1811.

895. Script initial touch in oval on handle of a porringer. The maker, R. E., is unidentified. Probably New England, late eighteenth or early nineteenth century. Courtesy of Henry Francis du Pont Winterthur Museum.

896. Mark on the handle of a well-made spoon which resembles in shape and decoration a similar smaller spoon illustrated in Volume One as Fig. 179, Plate XXV. Maker unknown, probably late eighteenth century. Collection of Mr. and Mrs. Oliver W. Deming.

897. A touch as it appears in a quart basin in the collection of John H. McMurray. The mark may or may not be that of an American pewterer, working presumably in the eighteenth century.

898. Touch as found on an inkstand on four half-ball feet with two hinged flaps as covers on top. Attributed to William Ball, Philadelphia, 1775–1782. Courtesy of Thomas D. Williams.

899. A new eagle, whose user we may never be able to identify because it lacks name and initials, was undoubtedly used by a Connecticut pewterer, whether used in Connecticut or in the Southern states, *c.* 1810–1825. Courtesy of the Henry F. du Pont Winterthur Museum.

900. Touch from a plate formerly in the collection of John J. Evans Jr. Only the first name is clearly decipherable. This would appear to have been one of the earliest eagle touches, *c.* 1790–1800. Location probably New York or Philadelphia.

901. Excellent impression of a very well-preserved eagle touch as it appears on a plate in the collection of W. S. Wilcox. The initials J.T.S. do not fit any pewterer of whom we have record, a fact which may perhaps indicate that there are still a lot of American pewterers of whom we have no knowledge whatever.

902. Last of the eagle touches and probably one of the latest chronologically. Only the letters "& Co." can be deciphered above the eagle. A short name must have preceded that lettering. Suggested as possibilities are North or Rowe, both of whom worked in Augusta from 1818 to 1823. This mark was photographed on a 7¾-inch plate of thin metal, formerly in use in a church in Bethel, Alabama. Courtesy of the Historical Foundation, Southern Presbyterian Church, Montreat, North Carolina.

PLATE CXI

886

887 497 b

888

889 890

891

892

893 894

895

896

897

898

899

900

901

902

THE BRITANNIA PERIOD

WHEN the story of this period was prepared for Volume Two, no scholarly study of britannia, its composition and methods of manufacture, had been undertaken. As a result the subject was glossed over in an offhand way and should be rewritten in the light of more recent investigations and discoveries—in particular George Sweet Gibb's *The Whitesmiths of Taunton, a History of Reed and Barton, 1824–1943;* the undated autobiographical manuscript of the life and business career of Thomas Danforth Boardman, now in the Connecticut State Library at Hartford; and finally and definitively, "Britannia in America" by Nancy A. Goyne in *Winterthur Portfolio II,* 1965, published by The Henry Francis du Pont Winterthur Museum.

Miss Goyne's (now Mrs. Evans') scholarly story of britannia should be read by every student of the subject. What follows can be only an abbreviated outline of her authoritative work.

The alloy, britannia, probably evolved in England from a search for a pewter composition that would provide a harder metal, would have greater resistance to wear, could be cast into vessels with lighter walls, and hence could be manufactured more economically than the pewter then in use. At least as early as 1722 British pewterers were experimenting with a harder metal for plates, for in that year officials of the Pewterers Company in London confiscated plates made by Francis Whittle, "he having stamped them 'Superfine Hard Metal.'" In spite of the punishment, other British pewterers were soon using a similar stamp, a practice that continued well into the nineteenth century.

The search for a more satisfactory metal resulted in the 1760's in the manufacture of what was then termed "White Metal." Charles Dixon, a candlestick maker of Sheffield, England, in an extant document, stated that in 1769 John Vickers purchased a recipe for this metal and proceeded to manufacture spoons and forks by the new formula. These however proved to be too soft and only after further experimentation in Sheffield shops was a composition developed that gave the long-sought hardness and stiffness—a metal that was named britannia. In the 1797 Directory of Sheffield one firm was listed as "Manufacturers of Britannia Metal Goods," though the trade name of the new alloy was surely in general usage a number of years earlier. By 1800 the manufacture of britannia had become a thriving business not only in Sheffield but also in Birmingham and its environs.

The new metal, unlike pewter, contained no lead whatever. Its constituents were tin, copper, and antimony — the proportions of each varying slightly according to the treatments to which the metal was to be subjected. Miss Goyne presented a number of representative formulas under such titles as Good Britannia Metal, Britannia Metal for Casting, Britannia Metal for Spinning, Best Britannia for Spouts, Best Britannia for Spoons, Best Britannia for Handles, etc. Except in the composition recommended for spoons, the variations in the formulas are not great, the tin content varying from approximately ninety to ninety-five percent, copper from two to seven percent, and antimony from three and one-half to a little over six percent. For spoons the tin content was dropped to eighty-four percent with eight parts each of copper and antimony.

By eliminating lead and increasing the tin content, some strength may have been sacrificed, but it was now possible to fashion objects with much thinner walls and to impart to them a higher lustre and greater resistance to tarnishing. Copper added hardness and sonority while antimony, also a hardening agent, helped to improve the lustrous quality.

To quote from "Britannia in America":

> Although pewter and Britannia have been confused since the earliest days of the nineteenth century, objects made of these two similar alloys actually differ substantially in surface quality, fabrication, form and metal. Characteristic of Britannia is its lustrous silvery sheen, a quality sought and perfected by the craftsmen who first developed it. Pewter is bright but does not have the gleam of Britannia and is more quickly subject to the diminishing effects of tarnish. The process of casting in moulds was virtually the sole method of forming objects of pewter, but it was only one of several techniques employed in making Britannia. Stamping and spinning became equally important, because they facilitated the production of a wider variety of forms and shapes than it was possible to make easily and economically by casting. As a result, Britannia can frequently be distinguished from pewter by shape. Silhouettes of objects fashioned over a chuck on a lathe or shaped with a die in stamping press are characterized by angular and curvilinear lines or by fluted and paneled effects, all essential elements in the vocabulary of nineteenth-century design.

Before 1800 britannia was being imported into this country. As early as November 22, 1794, George Coldwell advertised that his stock included "British metal table, desert and tea spoons" and in the inventory of William Will's "Front Shop" in 1798 were "5 pr Bretania metal candlesticks." We do not know whether the sticks had been manufactured by Will or had been imported, but we do know that few if any American pewterers have given as marked evidence of keeping abreast of the fashions or of using so much ingenuity in providing new designs to please his public. Had he lived into the nineteenth century there can be little doubt that his would have been the first britannia factory in this country.

To whom should that honor go? In town histories, obituaries and other published documents, claims have been put forward by or in behalf of a great many makers including George Richardson in Boston, Thomas D. Boardman in Hartford, Israel Trask in Beverly, Massachusetts, the Yales in Wallingford, Connecticut and Babbitt and Crossman in Taunton, Massachusetts. We may promptly dismiss from consideration Richardson, the Yales, and Babbitt and Crossman, though it may well be true that the Yales were the first in this country to manufacture britannia made by the spinning process.

Thomas D. Boardman, who had just completed his apprenticeship under his uncles, Edward and Samuel Danforth, tells us in his autobiography that he began business in a small way in July 1804 "at the age of 20 years & 6 months." In 1805, he "first heard the name of Regulus of antimony." He managed to locate a few pounds of antimony after a few months and experimented mixing it with tin. At first he had little success but in the following year he had apparently solved the problem. Let Thomas tell it in his own vernacular:

> I recivd a lot of English tin from a pewter[er] in Philadelphia with orders to make it into teapots just as it was. I cast the pots but could not turn them the mital was so soft the chips would — ? — I melted them down and added 2 or 3 per ct. copper which had been try befor and as much R. antimony — which proved to be the right thing — the potts were the bestt I had ever made — from what I could learn very few teapots had been made in New England & those verry clumsey — with the propper proportions of Regulus of antimony and copper the ware would finish up equal to English bright around the soldering of the trimmings so the merchants who had imported the artickle considered them equal to English — of course we had orders from manufacturers of pewter ware to furnish them with our teapots from Philada . . . Providence, Hartford and to Merchants in New York, Philadelphia, New Haven, Albany, Utica, New Burgh, Providence, Newport [and] Boston. One house would order 50 Dos at a time — one order[ed] 3000 within 6 months.

Note that Boardman's success came in the year 1806. It is also of interest that a comparison of his formula with what later was considered the best composition for cast Britannia was just about the same as to copper content and only two or three percent low for antimony.

Since Richardson's first listing in the Boston directories was in 1818 and Babbitt and Crossman did not begin business in Taunton until 1824 their claims for being first in the field deserve no consideration.

Again we turn to Boardman's autobiography, this time to dispose of the Yales. He relates there that he shared his secret as to the formula only with his brother Sherman. Then "about 1821 to help a young friend under age just beg[gin]ing business [I] gave him the Secret — with the request that it should not be communicated to the 3ᵈ person." The "young friend" was his cousin, Josiah, son of William Danforth. Unfortunately Josiah gave away the information to his journeyman, Thomas Derby.

To quote from "Britannia in America": "[a]ccording to a brief anonymous sketch of Boardman's career, Charles and Hiram Yale of Wallingford, who 'never served an apprenticeship to the pewterer's trade' purchased 'the old tools of Mr. Saml. Danforth and went about hiring away the men from other shops — much to the annoyance of those having competent workmen — to teach and start them in the business!' Among others they hired away from Mr. Josiah Danforth, Thomas Derby, from whom they learned the art of mixing the metals. The Yales 'immediately came out with flaming advertisements, saying that they had discovered the art of mixing Britannia metal and could make ware equal if not superior to the English manufacture.' They 'very soon run the business down by sending more in the market than was demand[ed] & Seling at 25 to 40 p ct less than fair prices in Boston to a foreigner came [sic] with 3 sons.' " The foreigner was undoubtedly George Richardson, who had arrived in Boston from England a few years earlier.

Now let us consider the claim that Israel Trask of Beverly, Massachusetts, was the first American to make britannia. Edwin M. Stone in his *History of Beverly*, published in 1843, stated that "the manufacture of Britannia ware in this country was commenced in this town, in 1812 by Mr. Israel Trask." This statement is corroborated by the following entry, dated February 25, 1814, in the diary of the Reverend William Bentley of Salem, Massachusetts:

> Captain Bowditch living in Turner St. below Derby St. informed me this day that he had begun the work of the Britannia Ware, which had been carried on for several months with success in Beverly. The manufacture is of Zinc & tin & is rolled out. The articles to which the Manufacture is at present confined are teapots & cream cups, & the present demand makes it profitable. From this notice I passed to Beverly & visited Mr. Trask who introduced the manufacture into that place. He was a goldsmith & jeweller & employs about a dozen hands, & sells his work in Boston. Just above his [shop] works a Mr. [Eben] Smith, formerly a cabinet maker, who has gone to the same extent of the same business & the persons he employs are seamen & fishermen. They seem to be pleased with the present success & both of them sell to the same dealers in Boston.

It is thus pretty well established that Thomas Boardman was casting what he termed block-tin teapots at least six years earlier than Trask's first britannia teapots were made in Beverly. But Trask may not have started from "scratch" in 1812. There is reason to believe, as a result of Miss Goyne's research, that Israel Trask may have taken over the business of an earlier britannia maker in Beverly.

Soon after the publication of Volumes One and Two of *Pewter in America*, Mark LaFountain of Springfield, Vermont, sent me a photograph of a handsome oval teapot on ball feet, very similar in shape to the Trask example, illustrated in Fig. 615 of Plate LXXII and engraved in much the same style that Trask and Eben Smith employed. On the base was stamped in a saw-tooth rectangle, Lee and Creesy, all as set forth in an article entitled "Ramblings in Britannia-Land" in the April 1944 issue of the Pewter Collectors Club of America *Bulletin*. The Lee and Creesy teapot (no other examples so marked have been reported to me) is illustrated in Fig. 770 of Plate XCIV.

In the Beverly Historical Society's library Miss Goyne found a letter, written by Mrs. T. Henry Bott of Salem, a great-granddaughter of a man named Philip Lee, which indicates that Lee was one of the earliest producers of britannia in this country. The information about this man's life is very sketchy but he was born in 1786, probably on the island of Jersey, where he received a good education. Before he was of age his father sent him to America to escape from the turmoil of the Napoleonic wars. Mistreated by a guardian, he deserted that man and set up a

The Britannia Period

britannia ware factory. What qualifications he may have had for such a venture are not known. According to family tradition he and a man named Creesy operated the shop until a business decline in 1812, when they sold out to Israel Trask.

Pending the results of further research, Lee's credentials do not seem sufficient to warrant the assumption that he was making britannia in this country prior to Thomas D. Boardman. If his date of birth, as given by his descendant, is correct, he would have been but twenty years old in 1806 and only twenty-six when his firm was liquidated. Where in this country could he have mastered the techniques of this intricate business before he had even reached his majority and whence came his training that would enable him to engrave his finished product in a manner so reminiscent of the work of Israel Trask? The solution may be that the family historian was in error in believing that the firm of Lee and Creesy was liquidated in 1812. Far more probable is the assumption that Lee was one of Trask's early employees, set up in business as a competitor after he had learned the techniques of manufacturing and then sold out to his former boss, when unable to finance his venture adequately. I am inclined to accept Carl Jacobs' studied guess that Lee and Creesy's brief business career falls within the period from 1815 to 1820.

Regardless of where, when, and by whom britannia was first made in this country, the early success of the Boardmans in Hartford and the Trasks and Eben Smith in Beverly, soon encouraged others to enter the competition for a share of the fast-growing demand for the new alloy. Old-time pewterers such as Josiah Danforth in Middletown, Connecticut, Ashbil Griswold in Meriden, Calder and Hamlin in Providence, and J. H. Palethorp in Philadelphia added britannia wares to their stock in trade and converted their shops so as to make use of the new stamping and spinning processes. At the same time new shops were opened by men who had learned the business as workmen in the factories of the Boardmans, Trasks, and others. By 1835 New England was dotted with britannia shops and manufacturers were established as far west as Buffalo, New York, and Cincinnati, Ohio. Up until about 1850, when silver-plated wares began to replace britannia, the demand continued for tea sets, communion sets, pitchers, small beakers (or tumblers), lamps, candlesticks, spoons, ladles, casters, and spittoons. Miss Goyne tells us that the latter were made in at least four styles including the "Chinese pattern" and that Boardman and Hart advertised a type "suitable for parlors!"

Space will not be taken here to describe the various new techniques adopted in the manufacture of britannia. But that information may be studied in great detail in "Britannia in America" and *The Whitesmiths of Taunton*. From patent applications, manufacturers' broadsides, manuals, and other published records, Miss Goyne has presented very complete descriptions not only of the techniques of stamping, drop-pressing over dies, and spinning over chucks, but also seaming, soldering, burnishing, and buffing. Throughout the period some parts, such as handles and spouts, were still cast, much as the pewterers had been making them for over a hundred years, though now with an improved alloy. Even as late as 1854 a patent was taken out for a "Britannia Tea and Coffee Pot" fabricated by casting. By 1840, however, the larger shops, making a general line of wares, were equipped for pressing and spinning as well.

As long as the industry flourished the Boardmans of Hartford with branch shops in New York and Philadelphia maintained their leadership, a leadership shared with Reed and Barton of Taunton, eventual successors to the firm of Babbitt and Crossman. Other large-scale manufacturers were the Trasks in Beverly, Ashbil Griswold and successor firms in Meriden, Connecticut, Roswell Gleason in Dorchester, Massachusetts, William Calder in Providence, Rhode Island, George Richardson in Cranston, Rhode Island, and Rufus Dunham in Westbrook, Maine.

Despite the general decline in taste, during the second quarter of the nineteenth century, such forms as the teapots, chalices, and baptismal bowls made by Israel or Oliver Trask, the Boardman flagons, the Richardson sugar bowls, the lamps made by the Taunton Britannia Mfg. Co., by William Calder, or by Endicott and Sumner, the candlesticks of Henry Hopper and the Boardmans, the water pitchers of Daniel Curtiss, and the coffee urns of Roswell Gleason, to name but a few, are designs of distinction, worthy of a place in any collection.

PLATE CXII — *Candlesticks and Lamps*

903. Tall columnar candlestick with hexagonal drip tray and a base, now circular, which may have been cut down from a hexagonal shape. Height $7\frac{1}{8}$ inches, bottom diameter $4\frac{1}{2}$ inches. Touch badly worn with initials I.B. on bobeche. The IB touch is not a known John Bassett touch but may be, as the candlestick's owner believes, a previously unrecorded mark by him. It seems more probable that this is the work of an unidentified English pewterer, *c.* 1690–1720. Collection of Dr. and Mrs. Robert Mallory III.

904 and 905. Two small candlesticks, probably of Pennsylvania origin, 1790–1820. Neither bears a maker's touch. The stick on the left is $5\frac{5}{8}$ inches high, the base 4 inches in diameter. Engraved on the base in amateurish lettering is "H.C.K. 1812." Collection of the author. On the right the candlestick is $5\frac{7}{16}$ inches high with a base having a diameter of $4\frac{7}{16}$ inches. Collection of Charles V. Swain.

906 and 907. A pair of candlesticks of unusual design, height $7\frac{1}{2}$ inches, diameter of base $4\frac{1}{4}$ inches. James Weekes, New York, Brooklyn and Poughkeepsie, 1820–1843. Collection of Charles V. Swain.

908. Handsome lozenge-top lamp. Height 8 inches, bottom diameter $3\frac{3}{4}$ inches with simple, well-designed columnar stem. Maker J. B. Woodbury, Beverly, Massachusetts, and Philadelphia, 1830–1838. Formerly in the collection of Charles V. Davis.

909. Another lozenge-top lamp of pleasing design. Height 9 inches. Maker Oliver Trask, Beverly, Massachusetts, 1832–1839. Courtesy of Henry Francis du Pont Winterthur Museum.

910. Well-designed acorn-top lamp. Neither the name of the maker nor the measurements of the lamp were recorded. Present location and owner unknown. Formerly owned by Carl Jacobs, through whose courtesy the lamp is illustrated.

911. Another, smaller lamp of good design, once owned by Carl Jacobs. If the lamp was marked, no record of the maker has been preserved. Present location and measurements unknown.

PLATE CXII

907

906

911

910

905

904

909

903

908

PLATE CXIII — *Miscellaneous Forms*

912. Coffee urn. Fluted body, baluster column on circular foot. Height overall 14¾ inches, diameter of base 6⅞ inches, maximum diameter, exclusive of handles, 8¾ inches, Taunton (Massachusetts) Britannia Manufacturing Company, 1830–1834. Collection of Dr. William P. Shelton.

913. Ice-water pitcher with patented double-wall body, an interesting forerunner of the vacuum container. Marked "Jas. Stimpson Baltimore," 1851–1858. Listed in the 1858 Baltimore directory as "manufacturing chemist and patentee of ice pitcher." Collection of Dr. and Mrs. Robert Mallory III.

914. Hat mould used in manufacture of 6¾-inch Shaker hat with 3-inch brim. Found not far from the Shaker settlement at New Lebanon, New York. Maker unknown, probably early nineteenth century. Just such a hat is illustrated in Plate 39 of *Shaker Furniture* by Edward D. and Faith Andrews (New York, 1950). Collection of Mr. and Mrs. Paul M. Young.

915. Commode. Height 7¾ inches, bottom diameter 5¾ inches, top diameter 11¼ inches. Touch 593, attributed with serious reservations to William Elsworth, New York, 1767–1798, possibly English. Collection of the author.

PLATE CXIII

912

913

914

915

PLATE CXIV — *Britannia Teapots and Coffee Pots*

916. Calder percolator, assembled. Height 9¼ inches overall, bottom diameter of lower pot 4⅛ inches, bottom diameter of upper pot 3½ inches. Proof that very little is new under the sun. William Calder, Providence, Rhode Island, 1817–1856. Collection of Dr. Joseph H. Kler, courtesy Smithsonian Institution, United States National Museum.

917. An identical Calder percolator, disassembled. Collection of Dr. and Mrs. Robert Mallory III.

918. Tall teapot with fluted body. Height 10½ inches, bottom diameter, 4½ inches, Taunton (Massachusetts) Britannia Manufacturing Company, 1830–1834. One of the finer forms of the britannia period. Collection of Mrs. Ralph B. Post.

919. Tall teapot or coffee pot. Height overall 10½ inches. Boardman and Hart, New York, 1827–1847. Courtesy of Henry Francis du Pont Winterthur Museum.

920. Another tall teapot of approximately the same size, Hall, Boardman & Co., Philadelphia, 1846–1848. Courtesy of William Reid.

921. Smaller teapot, height 8 inches, bottom diameter 3¼ inches. Ephraim Capen, New York, 1847–1854. Collection of Mrs. Ralph B. Post.

922. Small teapot with wide base and screw cap on spout. Believed by its owner (probably correctly) to have been used on shipboard as a captain's teapot or coffee pot. Height overall 6¾ inches, diameter of base 5¾ inches, unmarked. Maker unknown, *c.* 1840–1860. Collection of Mr. and Mrs. Wendell Hilt.

PLATE CXIV

916

917

918

919

920

921

922

PLATE CXV — *Sundials, Miniatures, etc.*

923. Sundial 4$\frac{1}{2}$ inches square, marked "G.E." with date "1779" above; attributed to George Ellicott of Bucks County, Pennsylvania. The letters L40 no doubt indicate the latitude for which the dial was designed. Found in eastern Pennsylvania. Collection of John P. Remensnyder.

924. Sundial, 3$\frac{1}{2}$ inches square, marked "I.W." above "John Liscomb." I.W., who is unidentified, is believed to have been the maker. Liscomb may have been the distributor. At least two such dials are known. Collection of Mr. and Mrs. Oliver W. Deming.

925. Sundial, 4$\frac{9}{16}$ inches diameter, marked "Josiah Miller" above the numerals 42, which indicate the latitude for which the dials were made. Miller's place of work is unknown, but he may have been a member of the Millard (Miller) family, which was long established in Rehoboth, Massachusetts, and spread out north and west from there. There are also similar dials marked N.M., a maker believed to have been related to Josiah. The Rehoboth family contained several braziers, several Josiahs, as well as a Noah and several Nathaniels. This lead should be followed further. The illustrated dial is in the collection of John P. Remensnyder.

926. Early capstan-type salt with gadrooned decoration. Provenance unknown, possibly American, probably first quarter of eighteenth century. Height 2$\frac{1}{8}$ inches, top diameter 2$\frac{1}{2}$ inches, bottom diameter 3$\frac{1}{2}$ inches. Found on Cape Cod. Collection of the author.

927, 928, 929, and 930. Coin and medal, obverse and reverse. The medal at left measures 1$\frac{11}{16}$ inches in diameter and must be one of the earliest of surviving United States pewter medals. The wording on one side reads "Kittanning Destroyed by Colonel Armstrong," and at bottom "September 1756"; on the reverse "The Gift of the Corporation of the City of Philadelphia." The slightly smaller coin, measuring 1$\frac{9}{16}$ inches in diameter, shows the interconnected rings of the thirteen colonies and the words "American Congress/We are One"; on the reverse "Continental Currency, 1776"; and, in smaller letters, "Fugio/Mind Your Business/E.S. Fecit." Unfortunately, we have no idea as to who E.S. was. Both coin and medal are in the collection of John H. McMurray.

931. Shaker, 2$\frac{7}{8}$ inches high, bottom diameter 1$\frac{5}{8}$ inches. Touch 372, Thomas Danforth 3rd of Rocky Hill, Connecticut, and Philadelphia, 1777–1818. Collection of Joseph K. Ott.

932. Miniature box with hinged lid and decoration on lid, marked "B.G.S. and Co." Measures 2$\frac{5}{8}$ inches x 1$\frac{3}{4}$ inches. Makers unknown. Probably 19th century. Collection of Charles V. Swain.

933, 934, 935, 936, 937, and 938. Group of miniatures in the collection of Mr. and Mrs. Wendell Hilt. Reading from left to right, Figs. 933 and 934 were undoubtedly used for individual communion. The little chalice is 2 inches high with a top diameter of 1$\frac{3}{16}$ inches, bottom diameter 1$\frac{1}{16}$ inches; the footed cup is 1$\frac{7}{16}$ inches high, 1$\frac{5}{8}$ inches diameter at top and 1$\frac{1}{4}$ inches diameter at base. The funnel, Fig. 935, 1 inch in diameter, was probably used to fill small bottles or lamps. The other three miniatures, Figs. 936, 937 and 938, were toys or possibly salesmen's samples. They were all very carefully made and finished. The beaker, 936, is 1$\frac{7}{16}$ inches high, 1$\frac{3}{8}$ inches diameter at top and $\frac{7}{8}$ inch bottom diameter. The little pitcher or ewer, is 2$\frac{3}{8}$ inches high with 1$\frac{3}{16}$ inch base. The footed bowl, 938, is 1$\frac{3}{16}$ inches high with 3-inch top diameter and 1$\frac{13}{16}$ inches diameter at base. All pieces are unmarked.

939. Snuff- or patch-box in shape of a slipper with hinged lid, 4$\frac{1}{4}$ inches long. Engraved and japanned in dark green. Touch 508. George Coldwell, New York, 1787–1811, Courtesy of George Abraham.

940. Miniature candlestick, 3 inches high, unmarked, probably made about 1840 to 1850. Collection of Charles V. Swain.

941. Miniature pigeon-breasted teapot, 4$\frac{1}{2}$ inches high, bottom diameter 2$\frac{3}{8}$ inches. Unmarked, probably *c.* 1835–1845. Collection of Charles V. Swain.

942 and 943. Miniature teapot, drum-shaped with beaded edges on lid. Except for the handle it resembles closely larger Philadelphia teapots. Height to top of finial 3 inches, bottom diameter 2$\frac{3}{8}$ inches. Miniature lidded sugar bowl, height 2 inches to top of finial; bottom diameter 1$\frac{1}{2}$ inches. Neither piece is marked. Both were probably made in or near Philadelphia, *c.* 1800–1810. Collection of Charles V. Swain.

PLATE CXV

MAKERS OF THE BRITANNIA PERIOD

IN THIS supplement to the section with the same title in Volume Two, makers or firms in the earlier list will not be repeated here, except in those cases where new information for those shops has been reported. A very considerable number of new names will be included here.

Revisions and additions to the original list, arranged alphabetically, follow:

Adams, Henry W., New York City, 1857 — Jacobs listed a britannia lamp marked with this man's name.

Allison, Andrew, Philadelphia, 1837 to 1841 — Six teaspoons marked Allison are in the collection of Mrs. Oliver Adams. Whether the maker was Andrew Allison or John Allison cannot be determined now.

Andrews, Burr, Meriden, Connecticut, c. 1840–1846, New Haven, 1846 — This man is included in the lists of britannia manufacturers only because of one advertisement in 1846. In the *New Haven Palladium* of May 30, 1846, he advertised:

> New Manufactory of Britannia, Tin, Japan Ware &c.
> The Subscriber having removed his manufactory of plain and Japanned Tin, Britannia Ware &c from Meriden, is now prepared to offer the public a general assortment of the above goods....

In the city directories of New Haven thereafter he is listed as a manufacturer of tin and japanned ware, and by 1850 his main line was "Stoves, Sheet tin & Iron ware." His manufacture of britannia in Meriden or New Haven must have been a side issue of brief duration.

Armitages and Standish — The identity of Armitages is still undetermined but an Alexander Standish was an employee of Crossman, West and Leonard in Taunton from 1827 to 1831. By 1837 he was renting equipment from Leonard, Reed, and Barton, for his own shop, presumably in Taunton. A teapot and sugar bowl, marked with the names of this partnership are listed in Carl Jacobs' *Guide to American Pewter*.

Babbitt and Crossman, Taunton, Massachusetts, 1823–1827 — Because of an error in copying the manuscript for Volume Two in 1940, the date for the formation of this firm was erroneously recorded as 1814, instead of 1824. A very complete history of Babbitt and Crossman and successor firms, which culminated in the formation of Reed and Barton, still in business today, appears in George S. Gibb's *The Whitesmiths of Taunton*.

Makers of the Britannia Period

According to Gibb, Isaac Babbitt, a jeweler, was experimenting in 1823 on formulas and methods for making a satisfactory britannia metal. He was joined in that year in a shop at 3 Merchants Row by a mechanic, William W. Crossman, member of an old Taunton family.

Gibb tells us that Crossman, as a young man, went to Castleton, Vermont, to learn the clockmaker's trade; also that at the time of the formation of the partnership no one in their shop had had any previous training in metalworking. It seems highly probable that both statements are based on mistaken traditions, as handed down in the Crossman family, for reasons which follow.

Castleton today is still little more than a village. In 1810 it could hardly have boasted more than two or three shops. We know that the proprietor of one of those shops was Ebenezer Southmayd, a pewterer, brass founder, and block-tin manufacturer. Perhaps he also mended or made watches and clocks. In any event, if all the facts were known, it was probably Southmayd to whom Crossman was apprenticed. If such was the case it would be easy to understand why Babbitt, anxious to learn how to make britannia, should have allied himself with a young contemporary townsman, Crossman, who had probably become an experienced worker in metals.

Whatever the facts, the first sheet of britannia was rolled in 1824 with William W. Porter and William A. West as added members of the organization. In 1826 a new factory was built, with Babbitt as superintendent, and Porter as the foreman, in charge of fifteen hands. In 1827 West was admitted to partnership and the firm name was changed to Babbitt, Crossman and Company. (See below)

Babbitt, Crossman & Co., Taunton, Massachusetts, 1827–1829 — In 1827 the manufacture of tea sets commenced and in 1828 the product was first marked Babbitt, Crossman and Co. In February 1829 Babbitt sold out his interest in the company but stayed on as superintendent, while Porter continued as foreman. Among the apprentices at this time were Henry G. Reed, Charles E. Barton, and Alexander Standish. In 1829 Zephaniah A. Leonard purchased an interest in the concern and the firm name was changed to Crossman, West and Leonard.

Bailey and Brainard, Cobalt, Connecticut, 1840 or later — Carl Jacobs listed this previously unrecorded firm as makers of communion sets.

Baldwin, Charles Wyllis, New Britain, Connecticut, 1831 — This man was an older brother of Jesse G. Baldwin, see below. He was born November 4, 1792; married Sarah Stevens of Guilford, November 21, 1821. In 1831 he was listed in the *American Advertising Directory* as a maker of pewter spoons in New Britain. He was in Berlin in 1840 and back in New Britain in 1850. There he died on January 12, 1856. Both in the census of 1840 and that of 1850 he was listed as a manufacturer but we have no assurance that he worked in pewter or britannia after 1831.

Baldwin, D.S., Location of shop unknown, probably in Connecticut, *c.* 1840–1850 — The name has been found impressed on a tablespoon.

Makers of the Britannia Period

Baldwin, Jesse Guilford, Middletown and West Meriden, Connecticut, c. 1840–1850 — Jesse was a son of Charles and Susannah Hine Baldwin, born in Wallingford, March 17, 1804. He and his brother Seymour, trained as silversmiths, made silver spoons at Oxford, Connecticut, in the late 1820's. From there they moved to Middletown in 1832. In 1835 Seymour moved to Elyria, Ohio, and, about that time Jesse branched out into the manufacture of britannia and silverplated spoons. In 1849 he had shops in both Middletown and West Meriden. The Albany Institute of History and Art has a spoon said to be marked J. C. Baldwin. Without much doubt the middle initial should be read as a G.

Although not much of a factor in the history of britannia manufacturing, Baldwin was a prominent citizen of Middletown. He was an active antislavery man, running for governor on that party's ticket and, in 1876, ran as the Prohibition candidate for governor. He became President of the Central Bank of Middletown in 1858 and later of the Peoples Insurance Co. of Middletown. He died April 5, 1887.

Baldwin, L. G., Meriden, Connecticut, 1849 — Tablespoons stamped with this man's name are listed in Jacob's *Guide to American Pewter*. Possibly the name is confused with J. G. Baldwin.

Barton, Charles E., Taunton, Massachusetts, 1828–1867 — Barton was an apprentice and employee of Babbitt, Crossman and Co. and successor companies. In 1835 he became a partner in Leonard, Reed and Barton and its successor firm, Reed and Barton.

Benham, Darius, New York, New York, 1845–1847 — See under Simpson and Benham.

Bidwell, Solomon, Auburn, New York, 1842–1843 — Had a britannia factory in Auburn, New York. No records could be found of the products made there.

Boardman, Luther, South Reading, Massachusetts, Meriden, Connecticut, Chester, Connecticut, and East Haddam, Connecticut, 1833–1870 and later — William F. Kayhoe, owner of a number of Luther Boardman spoon moulds, one of which is illustrated in Plate LXXIX and commented upon on page 177, has had access to unpublished Boardman records, including a personal account book kept by Luther for the period from 1834 to 1842. Entries therein indicate that he gave up his operations in South Reading in October 1837 and moved to Meriden where he took up board with his former associate, James A. Frary, whose daughter, Lydia, he married.

In Meriden the business was operated under the firm name of Frary and Boardman until December 6, 1838, when a final accounting took place. Meanwhile he and his wife went to live at the home of Ira Couch, for whom Boardman seems to have worked until July 2, 1839.

On the latter date Luther recorded the formation of Luther Boardman & Co. of Chester, Connecticut. In that account book, there is no indication that he ever worked for Russell and Beach, as stated by Charlotte Goldthwaite in her *History of Middlesex County* and repeated by me in Volume Two, page 97, of *Pewter in America.*

In 1841 Boardman moved his operations to East Haddam and there built up what may have been the largest britannia spoon business in the country.

In 1850 he used one thousand pigs of tin valued at $12,000; employed thirty-three men and had an annual production of 12,000 gross of spoons. By 1860 he was using one hundred tons of block tin per year, employing one hundred and fifteen hands and turning out eighteen thousand gross of britannia spoons, valued at $90,000.00

A surviving Boardman trade card, now owned by Wendell Hilt, shows Boardman to have been a manufacturer of block tin and britannia wares, listing the following forms made in his shop; "Buff spoons, Coffee Pots, Tea Pots, Castors, Lamps, Shaving Boxes, Tumblers, Porringers, Coffin Plates &c."

Except for teapots and spoons none of those forms, bearing his marks, have been reported. After the move to East Haddam the shop's product was probably limited to spoons.

It is interesting to note that the elaborate spoon mould, illustrated on Plate LXXIX was not patented until 1870, indicating a continuing demand for Boardman's spoons long after most of his competitors had gone out of business.

Boardman and Hall, 436 High Street, Philadelphia, 1844–1845 — The statement was made in Volume Two that this firm sold the full Boardman line and probably made no pewter locally. An advertisement illustrated in Edwin T. Freedley's *Leading Pursuits and Leading Men, Philadelphia* shows the five-story sales office and factory of Hall and Boardman, successors to Boardman and Hall. On the front of the shop are signs which read "Hall and Boardman" and "Philadelphia Britannia Works." It is thus evident that the Philadelphia agents were manufacturers as well as distributors for the Boardman line.

Boardman and Hart, various addresses, New York City, 1828–1853 — What was true of Boardman and Hall in Philadelphia was almost certainly true of Boardman and Hart in New York, and possibly its predecessor firms, Timothy Boardman & Co. and Boardman and Company, i.e., pewter was manufactured locally as well as at the parent plant in Hartford. Although Thomas D. and Sherman Boardman sold their interests in the firm to Lucius Hart in 1847, the company operated by Hart continued under the Boardman and Hart name until 1853. See under Lucius D. Hart.

Bowditch, Captain, Salem, Massachusetts, 1814 — An entry in the diary of the Reverend William Bentley of Salem for February 25, 1814, began as follows: "Captain Bowditch informed me this day that he had begun the work of the Britannia Ware." When this interesting note was uncovered, it was assumed that it would be a simple matter to track down the Captain in the list of Salem Bowditches and probably to obtain a reasonable estimate of the extent of his britannia business. This did not prove to be the case.

Miss Nancy Goyne surmised that the man may have been Nathaniel Bowditch, self-educated astronomer and mathematician, born in 1773, who became a prominent citizen and spent his life in scientific activity.

Miss Ruth Hill, historian-librarian of the Beverly Historical Society, points out that an Ebenezer Bowditch, born about 1757, was a goldsmith in Salem, as listed in Belknap's *Artists and Craftsmen.* He died in Salem in 1836. It may be that this man, recognizing the success of his contemporary Israel Trask in converting this business from goldsmithing to britannia-making, may have attempted a similar conversion and is the unidentified captain. The problem of identifying the captain is, however, in all probability academic. Nothing whatever could be gleaned from Salem records about any such business venture and the odds are that britannia-making in Salem was a very short-lived venture.

Brainard, _____, Cobalt, Connecticut, 1840 or later — See Bailey and Brainard above.

Braman, Elijah, Warren, Rhode Island, 1832–1839 — The late Carl Jacobs reported having found the name E. Braman in a serrated rectangle on teapots and casters. Elijah Braman was an employee of Crossman, West and Leonard at Taunton, Massachusetts, in 1829 and of its successor firm, Taunton Britannia Manufacturing Company, in 1830 and 1831. About 1832 he left their employ to open a shop of his own in Warren, Rhode Island.

Britaw, _____, location unknown, *c.* 1850 — A spoon stamped with this name is in the collection of the Albany Institute of History and Art. Nothing has been learned about the maker.

Brook Farm, West Roxbury, Massachusetts, 1844–1847 — Ephraim Capen signed the constitution of the Brook Farm Association for Industry and Education on May 12, 1844, giving his place and date of birth as Dorchester, Massachusetts, March 6, 1813 and his profession as pewterer, the only member to register that occupation. It was undoubtedly Capen who was responsible for pewter marked "Brook Farm." Later he set up business in New York. See under Capen and Molineux on p. 99 of Volume Two.

Browe, William J. Jr., lampmaker, Newark, New Jersey, and New York City, 1843–1858 — Was a partner in Browe and Dougherty in Newark until 1852. Thereafter he had his own shop in New York until 1858.

Browe and Dougherty, lampmakers, Newark, New Jersey, 1844–1852 — The partners were William Browe Jr. and William M. Dougherty. They advertised lamps of all kinds, chandeliers, argands, china, glass and metal (including britannia lamps). Whether they actually made britannia lamps or had them made for them is not known. No lamp marked with this firm's name has been reported.

Brower, A., New York City, about 1820 — Carl Jacobs reported a candle mould with pewter tubes impressed with this man's name.

Brower, C. S., New Orleans, Louisiana, 1822 — This man was listed as a plumber and pewterer in the New Orleans directory for 1822.

Brown, E. & Co., location unknown (possibly Beverly-Salem area of Massachusetts),

Makers of the Britannia Period

c. 1820. The Ford Museum in Dearborn, Michigan owns a duck-bellied teapot on four feet. Its design and the engraving on its sides are reminiscent of the work of the Beverly makers. A second piece, a small creamer on ball feet, is in the collection of Charles V. Swain.

Burdett, Aaron, Baltimore, Maryland, 1838–1841 — This name should be removed from our lists. In the city directories he termed himself a repairer, not maker, of britannia.

Butler and Perkins, Boston, Massachusetts, 1852–1853 — Listed as manufacturers of britannia at 1½ Water Street in the Boston directory for 1852–1853. The partners were Thomas N. Butler and Daniel Perkins. Nothing is known about their product.

Caldwell, T. B., Boston, Massachusetts, 1853 — This man was a partner in Newell, Caldwell and Coffin. See under that heading.

Calverly, John, Philadelphia, Pennsylvania, 1840–1841 — At a 1969 auction at Reading, Pennsylvania, a pewter candle mould was sold which was marked J. Calverly, Philadelphia.

Capen, Ephraim, West Roxbury, Massachusetts, 1844–1847, New York City, 1849–1854 — See under Brook Farm and Capen and Molineux.

Carlstedt, J. M., Rockford, Illinois, after 1840 — A rectangluar lidded snuff box with rounded ends and sides marked "Manufactured by J. M. Carlstedt, Rockford, Ills." has been reported.

Cincinnati Britannia Co., Cincinnati, Ohio, about 1850 — Carl Jacobs reported a ladle stamped with this name.

Coburn, H. R., location unknown, after 1840 — The late Dr. Rushford listed this man as a maker of pewter lamps.

Coffin, G. J., Boston, Massachusetts, 1853 — A partner in Newell, Caldwell and Coffin. See under that listing.

Cotton, _____, Middlefield, Connecticut, *c.* 1840–1845 — A man named Cotton, first name unknown, was the junior partner of Hall and Cotton. See under that listing.

Cowles, George C., Meriden, Connecticut, 1834–1836 — Cowles was a partner of Isaac C. Lewis in the firm of Lewis and Cowles. See under that listing.

Crossman, West and Leonard, Taunton, Massachusetts, 1829–1830 — This firm succeeded Babbitt, Crossman and Co. The partners were William W. Crossman, William A. West, and Zephaniah A. Leonard. The partnership was formed early in 1829 and in July of that year the plant was mortgaged to Horatio Leonard.

In August, 1830, the partnership was dissolved and a joint stock company, The Taunton Britannia Manufacturing Co., was formed to take over the assets of Crossman, West, and Leonard.

Curtiss, Edwin E., Meriden, Connecticut, *c.* 1838–1845 — The name of Edwin and his brothers, Enos and Lemuel, was misspelled Curtis in Volume Two, page 100. From 1838 to 1840 his younger brother, Lemuel was his partner.

He was born in Meriden, September 1, 1805, and married Aurelia Benham, December 24, 1826. He was at one time president of the Meriden Savings Bank, and very active in St. Andrew's Church, to which he left the bulk of his estate at the time of his death in 1885.

Curtiss, Enos Hall, Meriden, Connecticut, *c.* 1845 — Born in Meriden, September 12, 1796, son of Elisha and Abigail Hall Curtiss. Older brother of Edwin. Represented Meriden in General Assembly in 1833 and was the first president of the Meriden Savings Bank. Is said to have had a britannia factory for a few years in the 1840's.

Curtiss, E. and L., Meriden, Connecticut, 1838–1840 — The partners were Edwin and his younger brother Lemuel. Oliver Deming reports having seen a teapot marked E&L.C. in a straight-sided rectangle with rounded ends, probably the mark of this partnership.

Curtiss, Frederick, Glastonbury, Connecticut, *c.* 1850 — Carl Jacobs recorded a ladle marked F. Curtiss. The maker was probably Frederick Curtiss, who purchased property in Glastonbury, Connecticut in 1846 and 1847. In the Industrial Census of Connecticut for 1850 he was listed as a manufacturer of German silver and plated goods. He advertised not only such wares but also "Britannia Spoons." He had an office at 55 Cedar Street, New York, and a store and office at 1 Asylum Street, Hartford.

Curtiss, Lemuel J., Meriden, Connecticut, 1836–1852 — Born January 15, 1814, in Meriden, a younger brother of Enos and Edwin. On December 24, 1835, he married Bedotha P. Burton, was a director and officer in many companies in Meriden and was Warden of St. Andrew's Church. In 1883 he founded an orphanage and a home for elderly women and upon his death left an endowment of $700,000 for the home.

Derby, Albert H., Middletown, Connecticut, 1835–1850; New Haven, Connecticut, 1851–1854 — Albert Derby may have been a son of Thomas S. Derby, but of this no definite proof was found. He was born October 17, 1815, and married Calista D. Burr of Middletown April 10, 1848. He died December 21, 1865, and is buried in Meriden, Connecticut. He was probably associated with Thomas S. Derby from the 1830's until 1851. In New Haven he had a britannia business of his own at High and Grove Streets from 1851 to 1854.

Derby, Thomas S., Jr. — An error was made in Volume Two, where it was stated that Thomas, junior, was born in 1820. The source or cause for this misstatement cannot be found now, but his birth occurred in 1809 or 1810. The issue of the *Connecticut Herald* for April 6, 1850, reports his death at the age of forty-one.

Dickinson, Charles, Britannia Metal, Crane, North of Caroline, Newark, 1850–1857 — After 1855 address was 39 Roseville Avenue, Newark. See also under William Hattersley.

Makers of the Britannia Period

Dougherty, William M., lampmaker, 156 Plain Street, Newark, 1843–1844 — Junior partner of Browe and Dougherty, Newark (see under that heading), 1844–1853. Working in New York City, 1854 and later.

Dunlap, J. & Co., Philadelphia, Pennsylvania, after 1830 — Mr. and Mrs. Paul Brunner own a $10\frac{5}{16}$ inch dish of soft pewter marked "J. Dunlap & Co. Philadelphia." No pewterer with that name could be found in Philadelphia directories.

Eldridge, Eli, Taunton, Massachusetts, 1848–1860 — The correct spelling is Eldridge (not Eldredge, as shown in Volume Two). This man was on the payroll of the Taunton Britannia Manufacturing Co. and successor companies from 1831 to 1841. He left Taunton to become a foreman for Roswell Gleason in Dorchester, Massachusetts. Although he is listed at 15 Hawley Street in the Boston directory for 1849 a brief genealogy of the family in *Representative Men and Old Families of Southeastern Massachusetts* states that Eli and his son returned to Taunton in 1848 and there started their own business under the name of Eldridge & Co. which continued until 1860. I have record of a small pitcher stamped with this name.

Engel, Gotlieb, 120 North Sixth Street, Philadelphia, 1858 — Listed as a britannia ware manufacturer for that one year only.

Farnam, D. L., Location unknown, probably Connecticut or Rhode Island, after 1825 — a britannia teapot, owned by Dr. E. H. Whitaker is stamped with this name in a rectangle. Above the name is a rather crude eagle mark impressed intaglio.

Feltman, J. C., Jr., 35 Dean Street, Albany, New York, 1847–1848 — Junior partner in the firm of Sheldon and Feltman. See under that listing, page 112, Volume Two.

Flagg and Homan, Cincinnati, Ohio, 1842–1854 — This firm and its successor, Homan and Co. made many forms not listed in Volume Two, including mugs of late design, porringers, syrup pitchers, goblets, sauce boats, candlesticks, and lamps. One of their designs was a handled flower bowl or ice bucket, formerly attributed to the Boardmans and illustrated as Fig. 671 of Plate LXXVII in Volume Two.

Foote, Henry C., Wallingford, Connecticut, 1850 — In the Industrial Census of Connecticut for 1850 Henry and James Foote were both listed as spoon manufacturers. Henry may have been associated at that time with his older brother, James, in the firm of James Foote & Co.

Foote, James & Co., Wallingford, Connecticut, 1850–1851 — In the 1850 Industrial Census this concern was listed as a manufacturer of blocktin spoons, using 600 pigs of blocktin per year, employing fifteen men and one woman. They turned out $25,000.00 worth of spoons per year. In an advertisement Foote stated that his best spoons were stamped "Hall's Patent." See also under Almer Hall. This was a patent on a wire-reinforced spoon. The wire was flattened at the ends to prevent it from slipping in the metal. In 1851 James Foote advertised as a maker of blocktin spoons and was there listed as "Late Foote and Co." We have no information as to how early James Foote commenced the spoon-making business.

He was born in Wallingford, August 15, 1811, a son of Benjamin and Betsey Foote.

Forbes, E. B., location unknown, after 1830 — at one time Charles F. Montgomery owned a two-quart covered pitcher, similar to Boardman pitchers, but stamped with this man's name in a rectangle with saw-tooth border.

Frary and Boardman, Meriden, Connecticut, 1837–1838 — The partners were James A. Frary and Luther Boardman. See under Luther Boardman, p. 176.

Fuller and Smith, Pequonoc Bridge, New London Co., Connecticut, *c.* 1850–1854 — The senior partner was Aaron Chauncey Fuller, born at East Haddam, June 27, 1815, married Eunice Avery of Groton, Connecticut, November 24, 1851. The firm used 1000 pounds of blocktin and two hundred dollars worth of antimony in 1850. Their product was valued at $3,300 per year. Because so many Fuller and Smith candlesticks have survived it must be assumed that the business increased rapidly after that slow beginning.

Gerhardi and Company, location unknown after 1840 and probably as late as the 1850's — This firm has been listed heretofore as Gerhardt and Co. In recent years a sugar bowl and creamer made by this firm have been reported. The creamer is clearly marked in a very small oval frame "Gerhardi & Co. Manufacturers, Britannia Metal Goods," with a pattern or catalogue number, a very late, even modern, form of marking.

Gleason, Roswell, Dorchester, Massachusetts, 1822–1871 — Nothing new can be added to our knowledge of this man's extensive business or the wares that he made; although an unusual Gleason mug is illustrated as Fig. 733 of Plate LXXXVII. But the following entertaining anecdote, taken from Gibb's *Whitesmiths of Taunton* provides an insight into the lives of apprentices of that day.

In 1848, B. F. Knox decided to leave the employ of Gleason. An offer at the munificent wage of $8.00 per week reached Knox at a most opportune time, for the Gleason apprentices, of which he was one, were in great disfavor with their master. Allegedly, in protest over the quality of Mrs. Gleason's cooking, the boys, with a sense of the spectacular, rolled a large chopping block down the Gleason front stairs and out through the closed front door.

Graves, J. B. — Joshua B. Graves is listed in Troy, New York, directories for 1847 and 1848 as a britannia Manufacturer at 5 River Street, next door to the britannia ware plant of J. H. Whitlock. In 1848 Graves and Whitlock formed a partnership under the name of Graves and Whitlock, operating at the site of Whitlock's factory, 6 River Street. In 1849 Graves's name appears in a Troy directory for the last time with no occupation given. Presumably he returned in that year to Middletown, Connecticut (see pages 103 and 104 in Volume Two). The G. and W. Troy mark, shown at the top of page 104 in Volume Two, was undoubtedly used by this partnership for one year only in 1848.

Hall, Almer, Wallingford, Connecticut, 1827–1834; 1847–1860 and later — Son of David, Jr., and Thankful Hall, born September 10, 1793, in Wallingford, married

(1) to Lois Twiss of Meriden; (2) to Fanny Ives; (3) Clarissa Cook, a widow, née Hall. He died January 15, 1865.

He began the manufacture of britannia spoons in 1827 and so continued until about 1834. He then ventured into other businesses but in 1847 returned to the manufacture of britannia spoons, with William Elton; branching out later into making German Silver and plated wares and so continued until after 1860. The Albany Institute of History and Art has reported a teaspoon with a pattern of a shell at the juncture of bowl and handle. The spoon is stamped Hall's Patent, a patent for which Almer Hall may have been the grantee.

Hall, Boardman & Co., Philadelphia, Pennsylvania, 1846 to 1848 — This company, and its successor firm, Hall and Boardman, were not only distributors for the Boardmans of Hartford, but actually manufactured britannia goods in Philadelphia. See under Boardman and Hall. Until recently no examples were known that bore a specific Hall, Boardman and Co. mark, but a tall teapot, illustrated in the May 1944 *Bulletin* of the Pewter Collectors' Club of America, shown again here as Fig. 920 of Plate CXIV has the name in raised letters. Incised on the bowl are the words, "Best Britannia Metal."

Hall, Elton Co., Wallingford, Connecticut, 1847 to 1860 and later — See under Almer Hall above. The junior partner was William Elton.

Hall, Nelson, Middlefield, Connecticut, *c.* 1840–1845 — See under Hall and Cotton.

Hall and Cotton, Middlefield, Connecticut, *c.* 1840–1845 — Through the records of the International Silver Co. it has been learned that the senior member of this firm was Nelson Hall and that their shop in the 1840's was in Middlefield. R. H. Ellenberger reported a ladle, superior to most of the late ladles, which bears their mark. Jacobs listed teapots, pint mugs, and sanders in addition to forms previously reported.

Harrison, Joseph, Philadelphia, Pennsylvania, 1829–1852 — Until recently nothing made by Harrison had been reported. However Stanley Goldsmith, now owns a teapot marked Harrison, Phila. Pa. which is attributed to this man.

Hart, Lucius, New York, New York, 1825 to 1853 — Lucius Hart was born in Rocky Hill, Connecticut, June 14, 1803. The date previously given for his birth on page 104, Volume One, was actually the date of his baptism. He was apprenticed to Thomas D. Boardman, June 1, 1819. After the death of Timothy Boardman on March 1, 1825, Hart was sent to New York as local manager of Boardman & Co. which, on January 1, 1828, became Boardman and Hart. The partnership was dissolved on February 1, 1847, and thereafter Hart operated the shop alone until 1853 and perhaps later. After 1847 Hart may have been largely an agent for other companies, because, in 1851 in the *Merchants' Ledger*, New York, for December 6, he advertised as a manufacturer and importer of britannia ware at 6 Burling Slip. After listing various forms that he could supply, he added ". . . a full assortment of Dixon's Sheffield Britannia goods, Reed and Barton's celebrated Plated & Britannia Goods."

Makers of the Britannia Period

Among the Boardman manuscripts in the Connecticut State Library at Hartford is a tragic letter written in 1860 by Hart to his former benefactor and partner, which apparently was in reply to a letter from Boardman, which latter must have accused Hart of double-dealing, at a time when he had been with Boardman and Hart. The letter has the ring of truth and one fears that Thomas Boardman, in his old age, must have listened to calumnies uttered by enemies of Hart, who intended to injure him. Unfortunately Thomas' reply to the Hart letter was not preserved.

Hattersley, Joseph, 126 State Street, Newark, New Jersey, 1850–51 — Listed as a britannia metal smith in that one directory only. Thereafter listed as a silversmith at the same address until 1860 and later.

Hattersley, William, Crane Street, North of Caroline, Newark, New Jersey, 1849–1852; 141 Quarry Street, Newark, New Jersey, 1852–1853; Washington Factory, Newark, New Jersey, 1854–1861 — Listed as a silversmith in 1849–50, as britannia metal works at same address 1850–52, as britannia metal works at Quarry Street, 1852–1853; as partner in Hattersley and Dickinson at Washington Factory in 1854–56 and as of Hattersley and Son J. at Washington Factory, britannia metal workers, 1856–1861.

Hattersley and Dickinson, Washington Factory, Newark, New Jersey, 1854–1856 — Partners William Hattersley and Charles Dickinson.

Hattersley and Son J., Washington Factory, Newark, New Jersey, 1856–1861 — Presumably William Hattersley and a son with initial J.

H. D. and H., Newark, New Jersey, probably 1851–1856 — In 1943 Douglas Curry reported a neatly made small pewter box marked "H. D. and H. Newark N. J." Without much doubt the initials stood for Hattersley, Dickinson and Hattersley and dates from 1850–51 when both William Hattersley and Charles Dickinson were working at the same address on Crane Street or from 1854–56 when they were partners at Washington Factory. The second H. probably stood for William Hattersley's son.

Henshaw, Joseph B., Wallingford, Connecticut, 1835 — A partner of Edwin R. Yale in the firm of Yale and Henshaw. (See under that listing.)

Hersey, S. S., Belfast, Maine, probably c. 1840–1860 — In the Maine register of 1855 Samuel S. Hersey is listed as "Britannia Ware" in Belfast. How much earlier his shop had been established there is not now known. After 1860 he, and his son Samuel, Jr., were listed as tinsmiths in Belfast. The name is found on teapots, coffeepots, large pitchers, small beakers and on at least one communion set.

Homan Manufacturing Co., Cincinnati, Ohio, 1847–1890 and later — Fig. 671 of Plate LXXVII in Volume Two shows a vessel with movable handle, designed to hold flowers or ice or to serve any one of a number of other purposes. It was there attributed to the Boardmans. However the late Mrs. Edwin L. Rothschild owned an identical vessel that was stamped with an anchor in a circle with

"Homan Manufacturing Company" above and "Made in U.S.A." below. The Boardman ascription is therefore withdrawn.

Humiston, Hiram, Troy, New York—Probably a son or brother of Willis, 1850–1853.

Humiston, Willis, Troy, New York, 1841–1852.

Janney, N. E. & Co., St. Louis, Missouri, 1845—Sales agents for Archer and Janney. See under that listing, page 96, Volume Two.

Johnson, G. W., Greenfield, Massachusetts, 1834—Johnson was a partner in Pierce and Johnson. See under that listing on page 189 in this volume.

Kaufman, Earnest, Philadelphia, Pennsylvania, 1855—For one year only this man was listed as "brit-tin" at 669 No. 2nd Street, Philadelphia.

Knowles, Henry, Providence, Rhode Island, 1826–1831—Listed as a pewterer in Providence directories over this five-year period. Since one of the two addresses shown for him was the same as that for Samuel E. Hamlin, Knowles may have been a journeyman in Hamlin's employ.

Lake, John D., Middletown, Connecticut, 1850—In the Industries Census of Connecticut for 1850, this man is listed as a manufacturer of teapots in Middletown who used $5,000.00 worth of blocktin per year in a shop run by steam power and employing five males at $200.00 per month. Nothing more is known about this maker.

Lawrence, William, Meriden, Connecticut, 1831–1834—Carl Jacobs reported a lamp with this name which had been patented in 1831.

Leas and Beastall, New York, New York, 1825–1826—This partnership was listed in just one New York city directory as "Manufacturers of Britannia metal goods." Nothing has been learned about either partner or about the firm's product.

Leonard, Gustavus, Taunton, Massachusetts, 1837–1845—Gustavus was a son of Horatio. In 1837 he took over his father's interest in Leonard, Reed and Barton, becoming an active partner. He died in 1845.

Leonard, Horatio, Taunton, Massachusetts, 1830–1837—Horatio Leonard, son of Zephaniah, was a partner in the Taunton Britannia Manufacturing Co. 1830–1833 and the majority stockholder of its successor company, Leonard, Reed and Barton.

Leonard, Reed and Barton, Taunton, Massachusetts, 1835–1840—After the Taunton Britannia Manufacturing Company failed in November 1834, three former employees, Benjamin Pratt, company agent, Henry G. Reed, spinner and Charles E. Barton, solderer, decided to lease space and tools in the old shop from its owner, Horatio Leonard. The new concern was not a legal entity, but apparently it prospered and Horatio Leonard, watching with interest its success, decided to buy an interest and set up his son, Gustavus, in business with two of the owners, Reed and Barton. The T.B.M. Co. remained only as a landlord, while the operating concern was known as Leonard, Reed and Barton. Leonard handled the selling and the financial end of the business while Reed and Barton ran the factory. Gustavus Leonard remained with the firm until his early death in 1845, but in

1840 he sold his financial interest and the name of the company was changed to Reed and Barton. (See under that title.)

Leonard, Zephaniah, Taunton, Massachusetts, 1830–1837 — Zephaniah Leonard was the junior partner of Crossman, West and Leonard in 1829. See under that listing, page 179 in this volume.

Lewis and Holt, Meriden, Connecticut, 1831 — This firm was listed in the *American Advertising Directory for Manufacturers and Dealers in American Goods*, 1831, as manufacturers of britannia spoons. The junior partner was Thomas R. Holt, see under that listing in Volume Two. Lewis has not been identified. This could hardly have been Isaac C. Lewis who was but nineteen years of age in 1831.

Lincoln, _____, place of work not known, probably *c.* 1800–1830 — Carl Jacobs reported a quart basin marked with the name Lincoln in a rectangular frame.

Marshall, Joseph, New York, New York, 1821–1822 — This man was listed in just one directory, 1821/1822 as a britannia spoon manufacturer at Greenwich, corner Cedar Street. Thereafter he was termed a plumber or laborer.

Mix, G. I. and Co., Yalesville, Connecticut, *c.* 1845 to 1860 and later — Garry I. Mix, born in 1819, was a nephew of William Mix (see below). Before 1850 he was associated with Charles Parker in Wallingford. In 1854 he established his own company in Yalesville. As late as 1861 he was granted a patent for "Improvement in Wiring and strengthening Cast-Metal Spoons." His spoons are plentiful.

Mix, Thomas — Meriden district, Connecticut, 1827 and later — At least two spoons have turned up that are marked with a raised T in a square box and the name Mix in a separate frame. They have been attributed to the Thomas Mix who was employed as a spoon maker by Ashbil Griswold in 1826.

Mix, William, Prospect, Connecticut, 1827 to 1850 and later — Known to his contemporaries as Captain Mix. He started his business career as a blacksmith, but, about 1827, commenced the manufacture of britannia spoons. In the period from 1827 to 1831, Charles Parker and Robert Wallace, who later had large spoon-making shops of their own, were Mix's apprentices. In 1848 and 1849 Mix was issued papers of patent for improved methods of casting wire-strengthened spoons. In his day he must have had one of the largest spoon factories in the country. Many spoons marked W. Mix in a serrated rectangle or stamped Wm. Mix Patent have survived. A nephew of the same name, who, in later years, was employed by the Meriden Britannia Company, may also have had a shop of his own and may indeed have made some of the spoons marked with a William Mix touch.

Molineux, George, 132 William Street, New York, 1848 to 1854 — Molineux was the junior partner in the firm of Capen and Molineux. See under that listing in Volume Two, page 99.

Morey, David B., Charlestown and Boston, Massachusetts, 1841–1856 — This man's story has been told, in part, under Smith and Morey, page 113, Volume Two. For one year, in 1845, Morey must have left his partners, Smith and Ober, because, in that year, he was listed in the Charlestown, Massachusetts, directory, as proprietor of a blocktin manufactory on Town Hill. The firms, with which Morey was connected, made teapots, coffeepots, half pint and pint mugs, shaving mugs, beakers, candlesticks, and lamps.

Newell, Caldwell and Coffin, Boston, Massachusetts, 1853 — J. Carl Thomas owned a small bell-shaped camphene lamp marked J. C. Newell's Patent. His investigation developed the information that J. C. Newell was granted a patent for a camphene lamp October 4, 1853, and that the above-named firm was listed in the Boston directory for that year as "Lamp Manufacturers and Dealers." The other partners were T. B. Caldwell and G. J. Coffin.

Nichols, O., probably New England, *c.* 1810–1820 — This man was listed by Jacobs as a pewterer on the evidence of a quart basin marked O. Nichols in a rectangle. Nothing more is known of him.

Ober, R. H., Haverhill Stréet, Boston, Massachusetts, 1849–1856 — A partner in Smith, Ober and Co. and successor firms. See Volume Two, pages 107–108, 113–114.

Palmer, W., 2nd, location and dates undetermined — Reginald French reported finding a quart basin with this name stamped intaglio on it.

Parker, Charles, Wallingford, Connecticut, *c.* 1835–1844 — Charles Parker & Co. was listed in Volume Two, page 109, as a manufacturer of spoons in Meriden. Wendell Hilt's investigations however indicate that there were at least two, and possibly three, spoon-making shops in the Wallingford-Meriden area in the mid-nineteenth century, that were listed under the name of Charles Parker or Charles Parker & Co. It is difficult, if not impossible, to determine today to which shop any specific spoon, marked C. Parker or C. Parker & Co. should be attributed.

The earliest of these spoonmakers was Charles, son of Charles and Charity Parker, who was born in Wallingford, January 27, 1797, married Harriet Sherman of Wallingford, January 23, 1834, and died September 8, 1844.

It was presumably this Charles Parker who was apprenticed to William Mix in his spoon-making shop in Prospect, Connecticut. Later Parker was in business in Wallingford with William Mix's nephew, Garry I. Mix. At the time of his death, Parker's inventory listed moulds for tablespoons and teaspoons as well as stocks of blocktin, old metal, and antimony. This did not seem to have been a large operation.

Parker, Charles (another), Meriden, Connecticut, *c.* 1850–1860 and later — This is the Charles Parker who was listed under the heading C. Parker and Co. in Volume Two. This man was not essentially a maker of spoons but his shop turned out a great quantity of britannia spoons as part of a general hardware manufacturing business.

Son of Stephen and Rebecca Ray Parker, this Charles was born January 2, 1809, in Cheshire, Connecticut. On October 6, 1831, he married Abby L. Eddy of Berlin, Connecticut. He is said to have served his apprenticeship to a button-caster in Southington, Connecticut. In 1828 he hired out with Patrick Lewis to make coffee mills in Meriden. In 1832 he started his own business manufacturing various kinds of hardware. By 1850 he was operating a large factory, employing 240 men. The shop was using annually 500 tons of iron, 100 of blocktin, 100 boxes of tin plate, as well as brass and copper, its product valued at $225,000. No mention of spoons was made in the 1850 census but by 1860 the plant was turning out 26,000 gross of britannia spoons per year, valued at $110,000.00, a tremendous output, of which very few examples are in existence today. The manufacture of spoons must have commenced about 1850 and continued until 1860. This same company is still in business today, known most widely as a maker of shotguns.

Parker, C. and Co., Wallingford, Connecticut, *c.* 1855–1860 — This name does not appear in the census of 1850 for Wallingford, but in 1860 they were listed as manufacturers of britannia and German silver spoons, employing sixty workers and using annually two hundred tons of blocktin and sixty-five tons of antimony. They made 13,140 gross of tablespoons and an equal number of teaspoons per year, valued at over $118,000. They may have been the makers of the spoons that bear the C. Parker & Co. mark. Whether they had any connection with either of the C. Parkers listed above has not been determined.

Parkin, William — This name was listed erroneously on page 109, Volume Two, as an American maker. It should now be deleted. In Frederick Bradbury's *History of Old Sheffield Plate*, Parkin was termed a britannia maker, working at Sheffield in 1821. At a much later date he (or possibly a son of the same name) emigrated to America, and, in the 1850's was a die-sinker foreman, in the employ of Reed and Barton at Taunton, Massachusetts. We have no information that any man of this name ever had a shop of his own in this country.

Pelton, F. W. and O. Z., Middletown, Connecticut, *c.* 1852–1860 — The partners were Frederic W. and Oliver Z. Pelton, sons of Ebenezer and Prudence Pelton of Portland, Connecticut. This concern was listed in the New England Business Directory of 1856 and the Industries Census of 1860. In the latter year they used twelve tons of blocktin and one thousand pounds of antimony. They made tea sets, pitchers, castors, and lamps. The britannia products were valued at $15,000.00 per year; plated ware at $2,500.00 per year.

Pelton, William, Portland, Connecticut, 1849 and possibly earlier until *c.* 1852 — In an Industries Census for Connecticut for 1850 this man was listed as a britannia manufacturer who used 7000 pounds of tin per year, employed three men in a shop run by horsepower and made 1200 dozen candlesticks per year, valued at $3,000.00. In other words his candlesticks were valued at approximately twenty-one cents each. Pelton was born in Chatham, Connecticut, in 1817, married Hannah E. Hopkins in 1843. He was living in Portland at least as early as 1849, moved about 1852 to Middletown, later to Wallingford and eventually to Dallas County, Iowa. To Wendell Hilt I am indebted for this man's history.

Makers of the Britannia Period

Perkins, Daniel, Boston, Massachusetts, 1852–1853 — See under Butler and Perkins.

Pierce and Johnson, Greenfield, Massachusetts, 1834 — In a Greenfield newspaper for June 27, 1834, a notice appeared that "the connexion in business between Samuel Pierce Jr. and G. W. Johnson under the firm of Pierce & Johnson was by mutual consent dissolved on the 23rd inst."

Pierce, J. & S., Greenfield, Massachusetts, 1834 — John J. Pierce and Samuel Pierce Jr. were sons of Samuel Pierce, whose history is found on page 124, Volume One. The same newspaper notice of 1834, quoted above, continues with the following statement: "Business will hereafter be carried on by John J. Pierce and Samuel Pierce Jr. under the firm name of J. & S. Pierce, who manufacture and will keep constantly for sale a general assortment of Tin, Sheet Iron, Pewter & Copper Wares ... also Lead Aqueduct Pipes.... Cash paid for old Copper and Brass...."

Plumly and Felton, location unknown, c. 1840 — Jacobs reported a teapot stamped with the name of this firm. This may have been the Charles Plumly (see page 109, Volume Two) who sold out his business in Middletown, Connecticut in 1844.

Pomroy, William C., 69 East Fifth Street, Cincinnati, Ohio, 1853–1856 — This man was a partner in the firm of J. H. Stalkamp and Co. See under that listing, page 114, Volume Two.

Reed and Barton, Taunton, Massachusetts, 1840 until the present — Successors to Leonard, Reed and Barton. For a very complete and interesting history of Reed and Barton and its predecessor companies the reader is referred to George S. Gibb's *The Whitesmiths of Taunton*.

Riley, Michael, Brooklyn, New York, 1830–1838 — From 1830 to 1834, Riley was associated with a man named Rogers in the firm of Riley and Rogers. They manufactured britannia ware at York near Main Street until 1832 and thereafter at 96 High Street. In 1836–37 Riley worked alone at 154 Sands Street and in the following year at 104 Gold Street.

Riley and Rogers, Brooklyn, New York, 1830–1834 — See above. Stanley Paddock owns a teapot similar to pots made by D. Curtiss, see Fig. 604 of Plate LXXI, Volume Two, which bears a mark in a circular frame with the name Rei___ & Rogers, with N.Y. in a rectangle in the center of the circle.

Rogers, Smith & Co., Mechanic Street, Hartford, Connecticut, 1856–1862, East Street, New Haven, Connecticut, 1862–1876 — The partners were William Rogers and George W. Smith. William Hazen Rogers, born May 12, 1801, in Hartford, was a silversmith in his early years and in 1847 was President of the firm of Rogers Brothers in which Simeon and Asa Rogers were partners. In 1856 he joined with George W. Smith to manufacture britannia ware in great variety and of superior quality. George W. Smith was born in New Haven, September 8, 1808, and died there on January 1, 1875. Prior to joining with Rogers, he had been in Albany, New York in the firm of Smith and Felton, later in Smith and Co. See under those listings.

After the business was closed out in Hartford, a shop was opened in New Haven about 1862, although Rogers continued to live in Hartford. During the time that the company was in New Haven, they were listed as manufacturers of silver plated ware and after 1857 practically all of the product of the Hartford shop was plated also.

Most of the surviving examples are parts of communion services—plates, chalices, flagons, and baptismal bowls.

Rust, H. N., probably New York, c. 1840—Carl Jacobs recorded an 8 inch basin, cast in the early manner and marked in small incised letters "H. N. Rust," indicating a very late date for such a form.

Shaw, _____, 33 N. Fourth Street, Philadelphia, 1849–1850—A partner in the firm of Sickel and Shaw. See under that listing on page 112, Volume Two.

Simpson and Benham, 272½ Pearl Street, New York, 1845–1847—The junior partner in this firm was not Morris Benham, as stated on page 112, Volume Two, but Darius Benham, who may have been closely related to Morris.

Smith, Ebenezer, Jr., Beverly, Massachusetts, 1814–1856—Reference is again made to the diary of the Reverend William Bentley of Salem, Massachusetts, in 1814 (see page 171). "I passed to Beverly and visited Mr. Trask who introduced the manufacture [of britannia] into that place . . . just above him works a Mr. Smith, formerly a cabinet maker, who has gone to the same extent of the same business & the persons he employs are seamen and fishermen. . . ."

Parson Bentley may have been correct in his statement that Smith was formerly a cabinet maker, but it would seem that it would have been a difficult jump to go directly from cabinet work into britannia manufacturing. It seems very much easier to believe, as stated by J. B. Kerfoot in *American Pewter*, that Eben Smith had some training under Israel Trask. Certainly the forms that he made bear close resemblance to those of Trask.

Bentley's statement however pushes back to a very much earlier date, than previously believed, the date when Eben Smith began to make britannia.

Ebenezer Smith, Jr., son of Ebenezer and Emme Smith was born in Beverly, Massachusetts, in 1773. He married Lydia Rea on January 8, 1797, and would have been forty-one years of age when Bentley found him making britannia in Beverly. So it is quite possible that he started as a cabinet maker and later worked for Trask, before operating a britannia shop of his own. His son, the third Eben, born in 1802, joined his father in the business and carried it on after his father died of cholera in 1848. Regardless of where Eben, Jr., got his training he became a very capable maker of britannia.

Smith, George W., Albany, New York, 1849–1856; Hartford, Connecticut, 1856–1857—See Smith and Feltman and Smith and Co., page 113, Volume Two and Rogers, Smith & Co., page 189 in this volume.

Standish, Alexander, probably Taunton, Massachusetts, c.1835–1840—See also Armitages and Standish, page 174 this volume. From the *Whitesmiths of Taunton* we learn that in 1829 Alexander Standish was on the payroll of Crossman, West and Leonard, receiving the princely wage of thirty-eight cents per day, seven cents more than Charles E. Barton, who would later become a partner and owner of the successor firm, Reed and Barton. At some time prior to 1837 Standish had set up in business for himself, probably in Taunton, for in that year he was recorded as renting equipment from Leonard, Reed and Barton.

Stimpson, James H., Baltimore, Maryland, 1851–1857 — Address, 267 Fayette Street, Baltimore. This man's occupation, when listed at all in the Baltimore directories, appeared variously as inventor, Zink [sic] works, chemical works and in 1857 "manufacturing chemist and patentee of ice pitcher." The name James Stimpson has been found on a large double-walled britannia pitcher and Carl Jacobs listed also a flagon and teapot. The directories do not indicate that Stimpson made britannia and it is possible that wares, marked with his name, were made for him elsewhere.

B. G. S. & Co., unidentified as to name or location, probably *c.* 1810–1830 — Charles V. Swain owns a small snuff box and two $4\frac{3}{4}$ inch beakers, stamped B. G. S. & Co. in a rectangular frame, all three pieces decorated tastefully with bright-cut work.

Taunton Britannia Manufacturing Company, Taunton, Massachusetts, 1830–1834 — This company succeeded Crossman, West and Leonard, which was dissolved in 1830. The new organization was a joint stock company, in which the former partners owned slightly less than fifty percent of the stock. The new stockholders were James W. Crossman, Haile Wood, Horatio Leonard, Daniel S. Cobb, and Haile N. Wood. In 1832, Crossman, West, and Leonard sold out their interests to Horatio Leonard for fifteen thousand dollars. In 1833 the company was incorporated with Horatio Leonard as president and principal stockholder. At about this time Isaac Babbitt left the company in a huff and in November 1834, the company failed. It was succeeded later by Leonard Reed and Barton (see under that title on page 185, this volume).

Thomas, John, Philadelphia, Pennsylvania, 1841 — Carl Jacobs reported having seen teapots and spoons bearing this man's name.

Tomlinson, Harvey, Geneva, New York, 1843 — Notation was made in Volume Two of the existence of a lamp marked Tomlinson's Patent 1843. Through the research of J. Carl Thomas, record was found that on September 1, 1843, a patent on a lard lamp was granted to Harvey Tomlinson of Geneva, New York.

Trask, Israel, Beverly, Massachusetts, *c.* 1813–*c.* 1856 — Assuredly one of the most capable of all American britannia manufacturers, and one of the first to enter the business, was Israel Trask, who deserves more credit and space than was accorded to him in Volume Two.

Born in Beverly, Massachusetts, October 28, 1786, he was the second of the thirteen children born to Jeremiah and Hannah Wallis Trask. There is a good deal of conflicting testimony in the stories of Trask's early business career, as handed down in the family traditions, in the similar traditions of the family of Philip Lee of Beverly and in that town's histories.

There seems to be no reason to doubt the family belief that in 1797 Israel was apprenticed to John W. Ellington, a young goldsmith and jeweller, just five years older than Trask. Ellington, unhappy in his work, decided to study for the ministry and is said to have sold out his business to Trask about 1807 or 1808.

Another story, unrecorded however among the Trask traditions, was that a young man named Philip Lee, also born in 1786, came to this country about 1807, presumably from the island of Jersey, settled in Beverly and made there the first britannia ever manufactured in this country. That would have been just about the time when Trask opened shop as a silversmith. Because of the War of 1812 and the general stagnation of business, Lee found his work unprofitable and is said to have sold out to Trask about 1812.

Our first verifiable date for Trask's working in britannia is furnished by a previously mentioned entry, in the Diary of the Rev. William Bentley of Salem, Massachusetts, dated February 25, 1814. I quote: "Capt. Bowditch . . . informed me this day that he had begun the work of the Britannia Ware, which had been carried on for several months with success in Beverly. . . . I passed to Beverly & visited Mr. Trask who introduced the manufacture into that place. He was a goldsmith & jeweller & employs about a dozen hands, & sells his work in Boston. . . ."

We are told that Eben Smith, a cabinet-maker, who worked on the floor above Trask, made the wooden handles for Trask's teapots and, at the time of Bentley's visit, had already begun the manufacture of britannia in his own shop.

According to tradition Trask made silver spoons for Jones, Low and Ball (the present Shreve, Crump and Low) in Boston, and from them he obtained his first order for britannia teapots.

It is difficult now to sift the truth from the mere hearsay in these stories, but the beautiful bright-cut work, found on much of Trask's product, argues strongly for his training as a silversmith. Similarly the reported connection with Philip Lee would seem to explain how Trask learned to make britannia. It is possible that Lee was employed for a few months by Trask, or possibly Trask by Lee, before the sale of Lee's business was negotiated. At the time of the Rev. Bentley's visit, Trask was engraving his metal with tools which he had designed himself.

We can now be certain that Trask—and for that matter Eben Smith also—was making britannia in Beverly much earlier than either Mr. Kerfoot or I had supposed; to be exact, in 1813, rather than 1825.

Trask's first teapots were probably much like the Lee and Creesy example illustrated as Fig. 770 of Plate XCIV. He later developed other designs including what Mr. Kerfoot termed the "pigeon-breasted" pot. One of his most successful designs was his "light-house" coffeepot, of which, fortunately, many examples have survived to enrich our collections. He made many other forms including communion sets, complete tea sets, lamps, castors, beakers, sanders, etc. His wares rank with the best of the period.

Vartklop's Britannia Ware, Newark, New Jersey, 1831 — This firm is listed as one of the industries of Newark in 1831 in Atkinson's *History of Newark*.

Walker, _____, New York, New York, probably after 1840 — A lamp has been reported that is marked "Walker's Safety Lamp" within a circular frame. Below that mark is a small N.Y. in rectangular frame.

Wallace, R., Wallingford, Connecticut, *c.* 1838–1855 and later — This man was an apprentice to William Mix, as was Charles Parker of Wallingford, in Mix's spoon factory at Prospect, Connecticut, in 1831. He probably made spoons in a shop of his own, perhaps in partnership with Parker, before he embarked on his successful silver-plating enterprise.

Ward, H. B. & Co., Wallingford, Connecticut, 1849–1850 and later — The partners were three brothers, Henry Beebe, J. Smith, and Lowden Baily Ward. In 1850 they used 200 pigs of blocktin per year and turned out products valued at $10,000.00 per year.

Warner, James M., Providence, Rhode Island, 1828–1848 — For twenty years this man was listed as a pewterer in Providence directories. For the first ten years his address was recorded as 109 North Main Street, the address of Samuel E. Hamlin. In all probability Warner was one of Hamlin's employees.

Warren, John B., Boston, Massachusetts, 1825, 1827–28 — No other information.

Warren, Josiah, Cincinnati, Ohio, 1821 — On February 20, 1821, letters of patent were granted to Josiah Warren of Cincinnati on a lamp for burning fat. He may have been the maker of the Warren's Hard Metal Lamp, which was mentioned on page 115 of Volume Two.

Wayne, Caleb P. & Son, Philadelphia, Pennsylvania, 1840–1849 — In Volume Two the suggestion was made that britannia marked with Wayne's name was probably made about 1835. That date is probably too early. From at least as early as 1825 until 1839 Wayne was the proprietor of a "Looking Glass and Fancy store." Thereafter the establishment, at Fourth and High Streets, was described in directories as a "Hardware and Looking Glass" store. The britannia was therefore made in the period from 1840–1849.

Webb, W., New York, probably after 1810 — Carl Jacobs recorded the information that he had owned two candlemolds with Webb's name on the metal tubes.

Weekes, James & Co., Poughkeepsie, New York, 1842–1843 — This firm is listed as "Britannia Ware Manufacturers" in the Western Business Directory for 1842–1843. Without much doubt this is the same firm that was listed on pages 115–116, Volume Two, under the name of James Weekes.

Wendeln, John F., Cincinnati, Ohio, 1853–1855 — A partner of J. H. Stalkamp. See under that listing, page 114, Volume Two.

Whitcomb, A. G., Boston, Massachusetts, nineteenth century — One never enjoys down-grading one of his own examples, but that is what must be done with the little inkchest illustrated as Fig. 263 of Plate XLI in Volume One. The chest itself is, as I believed it, an eighteenth or early nineteenth-century product but the lid covering the hole for the ink is perhaps one hundred years later in manufacture.

William O. Blaney made a real search for this man Whitcomb, as I had never done, and came up with the information that from 1873 to 1875 Amasa G. Whitcomb was a salesman for William G. Shattuck, a manufacturer of chairs and school furniture at 73 Fulton Street, Boston. From 1876 to 1891 Whitcomb himself was a manufacturer of "settees, school, and church furniture." At some time, evidently, someone removed the cap of an inkwell in one of Whitcomb's school desks and soldered it to the top of an old ink chest, probably without any intention whatever of forming a synthetic antique to pass off to some gullible collector. So, off with his head! Whitcomb's name should be removed from any list of pewter makers.

White, Henry, Boston, Massachusetts, 1842–1849 — White was one of the partners of Smith and Morey, Thomas Smith & Co., and successor firms. See under those listings on page 113, Volume Two.

White, James, New York, New York, 1822–1834 — This man was listed as a pewterer and plumber at 334 Water Street for twelve years. None of his pewter has been identified.

Whitlock, J.H. — Although John H. Whitlock is recorded in Troy, New York directories as proprietor of a store as early as 1836, he is first recorded as a britannia manufacturer in 1847. In the following year he formed a short-lived partnership with Joshua B. Graves which lasted but a year. His manufacturing plant was at 6 River Street. He appears at other River Street addresses until 1852. After that the name became John H. Whitlock and Company, makers of "Britannia and White Metal," listed for the last time in the directory of 1856.

Contrary, therefore, to my and J. B. Kerfoot's belief, Whitlock was a britannia maker in his own right and not a distributor for the Boardmans of Hartford.

Whitney, Chauncey, Albany, New York, 1822 — In the Albany Directory for 1822 this man advertised that he manufactured copper, brass, pewter, and tin wares. Nothing further can be reported about him.

Wilcox, H. C. & Co., Meriden, Connecticut, *c.* 1848–1852 — The partners were Horace C. and Dennis C. Wilcox. Horace was born in Westfield Parish, Middletown, Connecticut, January 26, 1824; married Charlotte A. Smith of Middletown, August 9, 1848. Is said to have been a travelling salesman for James A. Frary for a year or two. Dennis, believed to have been a younger brother, married Mary E. Peck of Meriden, December 23, 1852.

In 1851 H. C. Wilcox & Co. of West Meriden advertised as manufacturers of various britannia wares, including coffeepots, teapots, pitchers, tumblers, beer mugs, spoons, etc. Thus far, nothing but an occasional teapot has turned up marked with this name. Both Wilcoxes were among the incorporators of the Meriden Britannia Company in 1852.

Wildes, Thomas, Hester Street, New York, 1833–1840—Probably the latest of all surviving American tankards is that illustrated as Fig. 732 of Plate LXXXVII. Now in the collection of Charles V. Swain, it is impressed with a previously unreported mark, a circle enclosing the name T. Wildes above, with N.York at base of circle. Although dignified in general appearance, the design is marred by a thumbrest which is merely a thin strip of metal cut from a sheet of britannia. The handle is also made from a sheet. To Wildes's earlier list of products, small beakers should be added.

Williams, Lorenzo L., Philadelphia, Pennsylvania, 1838–1842—Although Williams' name and place of work are normally found stamped intaglio on his metal, one of his baptismal bowls has been found with a place touch of earlier design. The mark, similar to one used by J. H. Palethorp is "Philadᵃ" in serrated rectangle.

Wood, N.G., & Sons, Boston, Massachusetts, *c.* 1882—This entry seems almost too late for inclusion in this history.

Nathaniel G. Wood was born in Leominster, Massachusetts, in 1824 and was trained as a jeweller. He worked in Saco and Biddeford, Maine, and moved to Boston about 1850. For many years he was listed as N. G. Wood or N. G. Wood & Co, jewellers, at 9 Hanover Street. About 1870 his son Albert was associated with him in N. G. Wood and Son and about 1882 a second son joined the firm and it became known as N. G. Wood & Sons. Beakers, mugs, a tankard, and what was listed as a jardiniere have been found marked N.G. Wood and Sons. These, of course, are very late and cannot even be classified as antiques, if we accept the U.S. Customs definition that an antique must be one hundred years old.

Woodbury, J. B.—Probably Beverly, Massachusetts, *c.* 1830–1835, Philadelphia, 1835–1838—According to the Vital Records for Beverly, John Baker Woodbury was born in Beverly, October 3, 1805, son of Thomas and Hepzibah Baker Woodbury. He probably learned his trade from Israel Trask or Eben Smith and may have had a shop of his own in or near Beverly before moving to Philadelphia in 1835.

Yale, Burrage, South Reading, Massachusetts, 1808–1835—According to the U.S. Secretary of the Treasury's *Documents Relative to the Manufactures in the United States, 1833,* Burrage Yale employed fifty-five men in that year and must have had a very large shop. Strangely nothing has survived that can be identified as of his manufacture.

Yale, Charles & Co., Wallingford, Connecticut, 1817–1835—To the list of surviving forms made by this firm should be added lidded measures. Dr. Robert Mallory owns a half-pint measure marked "Charles Yale, Wallingford, Conn."

Yale, H. & Co., Wallingford, Connecticut, 1824–1835—For further information about Charles and Hiram Yale refer to page 87 in this volume.

Makers of the Britannia Period

Yale and Henshaw, Wallingford, Connecticut, 1835–1837 — The partners were Edwin R. Yale, son of William and Mary Yale, born in Meriden, Connecticut, August 8, 1804, and Joseph B. Henshaw. Yale married Eliza Ives of Meriden, March 14, 1824. Soon after that he opened a shop in Meriden where he manufactured japanned lamps and tinware.

On August 1, 1835 Yale and Henshaw leased for two years from Charles Yale, "the upper turning room" and other rooms used for casting, "lately occupied by Thomas S. Derby," for the sum of $2,000.00. That figure covered the use of tools, moulds, etc., which were required to be kept in good condition. In 1836 and 1837 they had a shop in New York where they were termed "Commission Merchants and Importers and Manufacturers of Japanned Tin and Britannia Ware." In 1838 Yale advertised "Japanned Tin" at the New York store for the last time. The firm apparently lasted but two years.

Four rather well-made tablespoons marked in incised letters "Yale & Henshaw" are the only known surviving products of this shop.

DETHRONED PEWTERERS

WHEN the original edition of *Pewter in America* was in preparation, a decision was made to include a section in which would be listed men, whose names had appeared in print in the past as American pewterers, but without, so I felt, real justification for such classification and with little or no documentation of their claims to pewter-making. That section was termed, rather facetiously, Dethroned Pewterers.

It was hoped, with what now appears to have been unwarranted optimism, that such an exposure of the errors of careless attribution in the past, would encourage future writers in the field of pewter to abjure wishful thinking and to weigh carefully the credentials of any new candidate for our lists, before rushing into print with his name.

A discouraging phase of the preparation of this third volume has been the need to spend so much time and effort in trying to authenticate, one by one, a twenty-five-year accumulation of hitherto unlisted American pewterers and touches which, in quite a few cases, would have been withheld from print, had their sponsors made but minimum efforts to substantiate or document those listings.

It may be asked: "Why worry? Why bother again to remove from the lists names of men and touches that do not belong there?" The answer is that once a statement appears in print, no matter how erroneous it may be, the average reader, with no opportunity to check its accuracy, will naturally accept it as fact, and errors caused by ill-considered statements, faulty attribution, careless proofreading, incorrect spelling, etc. will be considered true, unless and until they are corrected in print.

It is a painful task to expose the unreliability of certain printed statements by collectors and dealers, who were honestly trying to further our knowledge of American pewter—men whose friendships I still hope to retain—but the authenticity of our lists seems important. So a new list of pewterers to be "dethroned" will be presented below and the chips must be allowed to fall where they may.

In the foregoing pages and in the list of dethroned pewterers which will follow, not all of the new names of makers and not all of the new touches, reputed to be American, that have appeared in print since 1940, have been or will be accounted for in this volume. There are some which, for one reason or another, could not be, or at least were not investigated with sufficient care to warrant either endorsement or "dethronement."

Perhaps the most important examples in this category are J. M. Ufen and M. B.

Dethroned Pewterers

Uven, whose very similar touches were certainly used by two members of the same family, despite the differences in spelling. These marks have been reported upon several occasions as found on spoons with fig-shaped bowls and trifid handles, spoons of early design such as were made in England and on the Continent during the seventeenth century and earlier. The name is not found in any early Colonial records searched by the author nor, if the makers were American, did either of them leave descendants, whose names could be found in the census of 1790. Whether the Ufen or Uven pewter was made in the Colonies or on the continent of Europe cannot be determined at this time. Similarly there are other names suggested as pewterers whose claims I have had no opportunity to verify.

However those men, reported to be American pewterers in publications appearing between 1940 and the present day who, in my considered opinion cannot be substantiated as belonging in such lists, will be considered below in alphabetical order and, in each case, reasons will be presented for recording, as at least suspect, the inclusion of that particular name or touch in any authenticated record of American pewterers and their marks. The newly dethroned names follow:

Name	Place	Probable Dates	Comments
Applebee, J.	Probably New England or Albany district	1820	This name has been found in a scalloped rectangular frame touch on at least two flat dishes and one plate, which latter the author once owned. On at least one of the dishes the touch is flanked by impressions, largely erased, of a rose and crown touch that is reminiscent of a mark of an English pewterer, John Dolbeare of Ashburton, who died c. 1760. Applebee is an unusual name. Despite a search through many Colonial and Federal sources, including the Census of 1790, the name was found in the Colonies only at Coeymans and Greenbush in Albany County, New York. A search of records there indicated that the Applebees were farmers with no evidence of pewtermaking. Although Applebee may yet be established as an American pewterer, the chances of such an outcome seem very slim. If his place of work is ever determined, it seems likely that it will prove to be in Bristol or one of the West Country English towns, such as Ashburton, Plymouth, or Bideford.
Beck and Thomas (Thomas Beck and William Thomas)	Trenton, N.J.	1780–1790	A fiddle-back pewter spoon, marked Beck and Thomas, attributed to these two Trenton silversmiths was to have been illustrated in this volume. Then in the Pewter Collectors' Club of America *Bulletin* for December 1969 appeared a list of pewterers and britannia makers of Birmingham, England. By an odd coincidence one of the firms listed there was Beck and Thomas, of whom the following

Dethroned Pewterers

Name	Place	Probable Dates	Comments
			was recorded: "White metal buttons and tutania and Britannia metal spoon makers, 64 Coleshill Street, 1833, 1835, 1839, 1841–43; Britannia Metal ware manufacturers 1845." There had never been any proof that the Trenton silversmiths had also worked in pewter. Under the circumstances they are being removed from our lists.
Bonzigues	Philadelphia	Early 1800's	Printer's error. The name should read Bouzigues.
Bowdith "Captain"	Salem, Mass.	1814	Spelling error. The name should be Bowditch.
Brickley, T.M.	Troy, N.Y.	1835	Undoubtedly confused with Townsend M. Buckley, Troy lampmaker, 1853–1857.
Broom, James	Oglestown (New Castle), Del.	1748	In 1748 a James Broom purchased the moulds of Ivory Lucas (see under that name, page 62), but nothing in Broom's surviving records indicates that he ever made pewter.
Brunstrom, I. A.	Philadelphia	1783–1793	John Brunstrom, of course, belongs in our lists but I was guilty of attributing to him in Volume Two, page 56, an initial touch, Fig. 548 of Plate LXVII, which should have been suspect at the time and is now generally discredited as a fake, see page 139 of this volume.
Burdett, Aaron	Baltimore, Md.	1838–1841	A more careful examination of Baltimore directories shows that this man was never listed therein as a pewterer or britannia manufacturer. He worked in Baltimore from 1840 to 1855 described as "Repairer of silver-plated and Britannia ware."
Burdett, Aaron	Baltimore, Md.	Early 1800's	Listed in *A Guide to American Pewter*. A touch of an eagle with initials *AB* is there shown as Burdett's. The man's name does not appear in any Baltimore directory prior to 1835 in which directory his occupation is not given. See above.
Calder, William	Providence, R.I.	Eighteenth Century	Despite the fact that a William Calder with lion touch was included among the "dethroned pewterers" in Volume Two, as long ago as 1940, with the statement that he had been a pewterer in Bristol, England who died in 1752, the same touch has been illustrated in recent years with the following comments: "Two marks of a William Calder, probably working in Providence, R.I. The pre-Revolutionary types of touches would seem to indicate the father of the known William Calder, who worked in the 19th Century." The father of William Calder, Providence pewterer, was not named William and did not make pewter, see page 58–59 of this volume. Although Howard Cotterell had not seen, and could not illustrate, the Bristol Calder's touch, he did show that of Calder's apprentice, Thomas Bennett, no. 385. That touch is almost identical with the design of the William Calder lion mark, differing only in the names of the users.

Dethroned Pewterers

Name	Place	Probable Dates	Comments
Campmell, S.	Unknown	c. 1820	When the first two volumes of *Pewter in America* appeared it was not possible to determine from the partially-erased impression of the one known touch of this man whether his name was Campbell or Campmell. Later discoveries prove that the correct spelling is Campbell.
Clunn, Matthew	Trenton, N.J.	1769	In the Pewter Collectors' Club of America *Bulletin* for November 1953 names of two men were presented as pewterers, who had not been on earlier lists. One of these was Matthew Clunn of Trenton, N.J. Record was found of Clunn's marriage in Trenton in 1768 and of his service during the Revolution in the 2nd Battalion, New Jersey Militia. A history of Trenton mentions him as a tinsmith in 1776 and, in a volume entitled *Silversmiths of New Jersey*, the author, Carl M. Williams, writing of John Fitch, steamboat inventor, says: "When he arrived in Trenton [he] was befriended by a tinsmith named Matthew Clunn, for whom he made brass buttons and cleaned watches...." Clunn may have made pewter as well as tinware, but, in all probability, the reason for his being listed as a pewterer was that someone found that he had advertised for old pewter in a newspaper notice, a practice common to braziers, coppersmiths and tinmen as well as pewterers. Until real evidence of pewtermaking can be presented he should not be on our lists.
Compaire, Claudius	Charleston, S.C.	1736	In the South Carolina Gazette for May 22, 1736 Compaire advertised that he "mends all sorts of Pewter, Copper and Brass Work." Had he been equipped to newmould old pewter, his notice would surely have so stated. Without much doubt he was a tinker, not a pewterer.
Dolbeare, John	Devonshire, England and Boston	1690–1740	Criticism is made here, not for listing John Dolbeare as a Boston pewterer, but for confusing him with a relative who worked in Devonshire, England, and for illustrating as a touch, used by the Boston John Dolbeare, the normal touch of John Dolbeare of Ashburton, Devonshire, no. 1408 in Cotterell's *Old Pewter*. Although Mr. Cotterell did not know the exact working dates for the Ashburton man, he stated that a John Dolbeare, presumably this maker, died in 1765. In a publication that illustrates this English touch as a mark of John Dolbeare of Boston, a photograph of a plate and basin appears alongside with the following caption: "A quart basin and a small plate, both bearing the marks of John Dolbeare of Devonshire, England and Boston. Both pieces show evidence of American manufacture." Fortunately more is known about the life of John Dolbeare of Boston than about any early Colonial pewterer, thanks to the preservation

Dethroned Pewterers

of so many Dolbeare papers and records, see pages 54–56 in Volume One. Herewith are quoted the first paragraphs of a letter that was briefly mentioned in Volume One:

> Boston, New England
> 28th August 1772

Mr. Benjn Dolbeare
at Ashurton in O. England

Sir:

I have lately been informed by one Mr. Row, who lives about 20 miles from your Town, that you were alive & well when he left home, & you being the only relation that I have heard anything of in England, am desirous of having a Correspondence with you if it will be agreeable to you. Therefore take this opportunity to acquaint you as far as I know, how the relationship came about. Viz. my late father, Mr. John Dolbeare came from Ashburton into this Country with my Grandfather Mr Edmund Dolbeare, my Grandmother & Uncle Joseph, about the year 1664. My father & uncle Joseph served their times with my Grandfather to the pewterers Trade in which business my father set up & added to it the Ironmongery Trade, both which he carried on to the year 1740 when he died in about the 76th year of his age. . . .

> Yr unknown kinsman,
> Benjamin Dolbeare

One added note on the latter reads as follows: "I Rec^d a letter from him & his Name is John instead of Benjn." Benjamin would never have written such a letter if his father had returned to England for a period and had made pewter there. One other bit of evidence argues against the attribution of this controversial touch to the Boston pewterer. On the rim of the plate, that was illustrated as the work of the Boston John Dolbeare, are impressed two sets of initials and a year date, presumably stamped there at time of purchase. The date is 1751. John Dolbeare died in Boston in 1740!

Name	Place	Probable Dates	Comments
Dunlop, H. & Co.	Philadelphia	1830	In error for I. Dunlap & Co., Philadelphia.
Fischer, John	Pennsylvania	Late eighteenth century	An illustration has appeared of a partially reconstructed touch found on a tab-handled porringer and on a deep dish. Visible within a circular or oval outline are the letters FISCH of a patently incomplete name and below the letters GER of another unfinished word. On the dish also are four worn hall marks, one of which shows the letters I.F. This touch may be American, but, with equal or better cause, it could be attributed to a Continental pew-

Dethroned Pewterers

Name	Place	Probable Dates	Comments
			terer. With no supporting documentary evidence one can only wonder what the basis was for determining that the man's name was John Fischer.
Fischer I. and T.	Pennsylvania	Late eighteenth century	A touch showing a rectangle enclosing in large letters I&TF, as they appear on a plate and on a beaker, has also been ascribed to the above mentioned John Fischer, but with hesitant attribution. Recently a pint mug has turned up impressed with this mark. Its hollow handle ends in a graceless flat spade-shaped terminal soldered flush to the drum, a form of handle that is commonplace on very late English hollow-ware, rarely, if ever, found on American pieces. What's more it is marked with the W.R. excise mark to the left of the handle, near the rim indicating manufacture during the reign of William IV (1830–1837). The touch has no place in American lists.
Gerhardt & Co.	Unknown	After 1840	In error for Gerhardi & Co. — See page 183 in this volume.
Hall, Elton & Co.	Wallingford, Conn.	1860	Listed under Dethroned Pewterers as "too late" on page 120, Volume Two in *Pewter in America* (first edition). However their story is given on page 183 in this volume.
Hooker, "The Widow"	Hartford, Conn.	1767	This name has been included in a list of American pewterers with the comment: "Perhaps she was the wife of a pewterer or brazier." Undoubtedly the cause for her listing was the knowledge that she had rented a shop to Henshaw and Hamlin, (see page 55 this volume) in 1767. This seems a very slender clue on which to build a case for placing her name in any list of pewterers.
Linthwaite, William	Charleston, S.C.	1736	This name has appeared on more than one list of American pewterers, presumably on the basis of a newspaper notice in the *South Carolina Gazette* for July 24, 1736, which notice reads, in part as follows: "... The Said Linthwaite has a fine assortment of Indian Trading Kettles and Pewter by him and makes and mends all sorts of old ones. . . ." However on March 12, 1737, in the same medium, he advertised "... William Linthwaite has just imported a fresh assortment of iron and pewter Wares, which he will sell Wholesale or Retail at a reasonable price for ready money, he designing to leave off Shop-Keeping and to sell only such goods as he makes himself viz. all sorts of Brass, Copper and Tinwares. . . ." Taken together these two notices indicate that Linthwaite was equipped to mend but not new-mould pewter.
Longstreet, Bartholomew	Warminster, Bucks Co., Philadelphia	Second Quarter, eighteenth century	Here is another man who was "dethroned" in 1940 and is about to go down for a second time, unless real evidence is presented to warrant his listing. On page 120, Volume Two, causes were presented for

Dethroned Pewterers

removing from any list of American pewterers, the name of the nebulous Bartholomew Longstreet. And yet a drawing has appeared since then in a publication showing the initials B.L. in a rectangle with the accompanying caption "Longstreet Bartholomew, Warminster, Bucks Co., Pa, 2nd Qr. 18th C." There is no accompanying explanation as to the reason for the attribution. If this man belongs in our lists we should have the evidence for such inclusion.

Melville, William L.   Newport, R.I.   1805–1810

As set down on page 95, Volume Two, William Melville was trained as a pewterer and perhaps, for a few years, worked at that trade in his brother's shop, but existing records indicate that practically his entire business career was devoted to engraving. There seems little reason for believing that he ever had a pewter-making shop or touch of his own. However it has been recorded in print that his work is marked with "an extremely rare Anchor touch." Then follows a sketch of the word Newport in a rectangle and a drawing of a very small segment of what must have been a very badly worn touch, as it appeared on an 8 inch plate. That sketch shows the bottom of what might have been an anchor and, within the border banding of the design, the consecutive letters ILL. Apparently it was taken for granted that these letters were part of the name, William. A photograph or rubbing of that touch, badly worn though it may be, would probably prove it to be the touch of the recently discovered Newport pewterer, Tillinghast, see Fig. 848 of Plate CV. Unless and until a plate is found showing not only the letters ILL but at least part of the name Melville, there seems little justification for awarding the mark to William Melville.

Mix, G. I. & Co.   Yalesville, Conn.   After 1860
Spoons

Listed under Dethroned Pewterers as "too late" on page 120, Volume Two in *Pewter in America*. However their story is given on page 186 in this volume.

Parkin, W.   Unknown   Nineteenth century

I am responsible for listing this man erroneously as an American maker, page 109, Volume Two. This mistake could have been avoided, if I had read Frederick Bradbury's *History of Old Sheffield Plate*. In that volume William Parkin is recorded as an English maker of britannia in 1821. Interestingly enough George Gibb, in *The Whitesmiths of Taunton*, stated that by 1854, Reed and Barton of Taunton had set up a designing room ". . . and placed [it] under the direction of William Parkin who was brought from England to make dies for the department. . . ." As late as 1875 Parkin was still on the Reed and Barton payrolls as a boss diesinker.

Dethroned Pewterers

Name	Place	Probable Dates	Comments
			Whether this was the same William Parkin or a son of that man, who had made britannia in England several decades earlier, is not known. In any event metal marked W. Parkin was probably made in Sheffield, England.
Norsworth, John	Norfolk, Va.	1771	This man's name is Norsworthy, and not Norsworth, as recorded incorrectly on page 76, Volume Two in *Pewter in America* (first edition).
Russell and Beach	Chester, Conn.	1838	Said to have been britannia makers for whom Luther Boardman worked. Boardman's own day books do not indicate that he ever was employed by them, though he had business dealings with them. His records indicate that they were iron founders and not pewterers.
Smith, Aaron	Philadelphia	1729	This name appeared in the original list of dethroned pewterers. It should now be removed. See page 198, Volume Three.
Thomas, William	Trenton, N.J.	1780–1790	See under Beck and Thomas.
Tutin, William	Unknown	c. 1800–1830	A pewter or britannia teapot of late federal design, decorated with an eagle on each side and a circle of stars, was reported to me some twenty or more years ago—present location unknown. It was marked W. Tutin in a rectangle and was assumed to be American. Later several spoons and a ladle, similarly marked, have come to light. However the previously mentioned list of Birmingham, England, pewterers and britannia makers includes the following: "Tutin [William] and Co. manufacturers of tutania and pewter spoons; Coleshill St. 1805; tutania spoon manufactures, 1823; tutania spoon manufacturers and white metal smiths 1825."
Van Norden, Peter	Bound Brook, N.J.	1782	A man of this name is recorded as a New Jersey pewterer in the Pewter Collector's Club of America *Bulletin*, November 1953, but no evidence was presented to support such listing. A search of New Jersey records indicates that at Bound Brook there was a Peter Van Norden, son of Tobias. The father was a prominent and patriotic citizen of the town, a baker, storekeeper and Justice of the Peace. In his will, written in 1798 he left to son, Peter, "Notes and book accounts I hold against him; also use of shop, now in his possession during his life. . . ." What Peter did in that shop is not known. If, like Michael Clunn, he worked in metals and advertised in a newspaper for old pewter, that still would be far from conclusive proof of pewter-making. On the basis of records found to date he can be termed only a hearsay pewterer.
Whitehouse, E.	Unknown	c. 1800–1825	Spoons marked E. Whitehouse or just plain Whitehouse have been turning up in this country for years and were believed to be of American manufacture. In fact one collector thought that they had been

Dethroned Pewterers

Name	Place	Probable Dates	Comments
			made for use in the new White House at Washington and were consequently marked in that manner. Directories of Birmingham, England list seven different Whitehouses who were making pewter, tutania, or britannia in that city during the years from 1809 to 1856. One of the number was Edmund listed as a tutania spoon maker at Aston Road in 1816. So— "off with their heads."
Will, George W.	Philadelphia	1798–1804	George Will should remain in our records as a Philadelphia pewterer, but the touch that was attributed to him in Volume Two of this work, Fig. 552 on Plate LXVII, without sufficiently careful study, should now be deleted with cause from our records of American touches, see page 145 of this volume.
Wolcott, J.	Baltimore, Md.	c. 1800	In Fig. 565 of Plate LXVIII, Volume Two, was shown a touch of a Baltimore pewterer, whose name was not found in any of the city directories. In the one known impression of the man's mark it was impossible to determine whether the name was J. W. Olcott or J. Wolcott. Now that a second plate has come to light bearing the same touch, it is apparent, Fig. 565a of Plate CIX that the name is J. W. Olcott. Wolcott should therefore be deleted from our lists.

CHECKLIST OF AMERICAN MAKERS OF PEWTER, BRITANNIA, OR BLOCK TIN

In the list which follows should be found the names of all men in my lists who are recorded as having made pewter, britannia, or blocktin prior to 1860, who had or might conceivably have had shops of their own. A star has been placed against the name of each man or shop known to have left marked examples that can be attributed to that man or shop with reasonable confidence. This list supersedes a similar list in Volume Two.

NAME OF INDIVIDUAL OR FIRM	LOCATION OF SHOP	APPROXIMATE WORKING DATES
*Adams, Henry W.	New York City	1857
Alberti, Johann Philip	Philadelphia, Pa.	1754–1780
Alberti and Höran (Philip Alberti and Christian Höran)	Philadelphia, Pa.	1758–1764
Allaire, Anthony, Jr.	New York, N.Y.	1815–1821
*Allison, Andrew	Philadelphia, Pa.	1837–1841
Allison, John	Philadelphia, Pa.	1835–1836
Andrews, Burr	Meriden, Conn.	1840–1846
	New Haven, Conn.	1846
Andrews, John	Elizabeth City, Va.	1706
	Yorktown, Va.	1707
Archer, Benjamin	St. Louis, Mo.	1847
*Archer, Ellis S.	Philadelphia, Pa.	1842–1850
*Archer and Janney (Benjamin Archer and N. E. Janney)	St. Louis, Mo.	1847
*Armitages and Standish	Location unknown	1837 or later
Austin, John	Boston, Mass.	1785
*Austin, Nathaniel	Charlestown, Mass.	1763–1807
*Austin, Richard	Boston, Mass.	1793–1807
*Babbitt, Crossman and Co. (Isaac Babbitt and William W. Crossman)	Taunton, Mass.	1827–1829
*Babbitt and Crossman (same partners)	Taunton, Mass.	1824–1827
Badco(c)ke, Thomas	Philadelphia, Pa.	1707
*Badger, Thomas	Boston, Mass.	1787–1815
Bailey, Timothy	Malden, Mass.	1830–1840
*Bailey and Brainard	Cobalt, Conn.	After 1840
*Bailey and Putnam (Timothy Bailey and James H. Putnam)	Malden, Mass.	1830–1835
Baker, John	Boston, Mass.	1674–1696
Baldwin, Charles W.	New Britain, Conn.	1831
*Baldwin, D. S.	Probably Conn.	c. 1840–c. 1850

Checklist of American Makers

Name of Individual or Firm	Location of Shop	Approximate Working Dates
*Baldwin, J. C. (possibly confused with J. G.)	Probably Conn.	*c.* 1840–*c.* 1850
*Baldwin, Jesse G.	Middletown and West Meriden, Connecticut	*c.* 1840–*c.* 1850
*Baldwin, L. G.	Meriden, Conn.	1849
*Ball, William	Philadelphia, Pa.	1775–1781
Ballantyne, John	Norfolk, Va.	1763–1769
*Barn(e)s, Blak(e)slee	Philadelphia, Pa.	1812–1817
*Barns, Stephen	Probably Conn.	*c.* 1791–1800
*Bartholdt, William	Williamsburgh, N.Y.	1850–1854
Barton, Charles E. (Partner in Leonard, Reed and Barton and successor companies)	Taunton, Mass.	1835–1867
Bass, Daniel (of Eggleston & Bass)	Fayetteville, N.C.	1807–*c.* 1813
*Bassett, Francis	New York, N.Y.	1718–1758
*Bassett, Francis, Second	New York, N.Y.	1754–1780 and 1785–1799
	Horseneck and Cranetown, N.J.	1780–1785
*Bassett, Frederick	New York, N.Y.	1761–1780 and 1785–1799
	Hartford, Conn.	1780–1785
*Bassett, John	New York, N.Y.	1720–1761
Beastall (Partner in Lees and Beastall)	New York, New York	1825–1826
*Beebe (see Sage and Beebe)	St. Louis, Mo.	After 1840
*Belcher, Joseph	Newport, R.I.	1769–1776
*Belcher, Joseph, Jr.	Newport, R.I.	1776–1784
	New London, Conn.	1784–*c.* 1787
Benedict, Lewis (see Stafford Spencer & Co.)	Albany, N.Y.	1815–1824
Benham, Darius (a partner of Simpson and Benham)	New York, N.Y.	1845–1847
*Benham, Morris	West Meriden, Conn.	1849
Benham and Whitney	New York, N.Y.	1849
Bennett, Edward	New York, N.Y.	1760
*Bidgood (see Plumly and Bidgood)	Philadelphia, Pa.	*c.* 1825
Bidwell, Solomon	Auburn, N.Y.	1842–1843
Bilbro, John	Surry County, Va.	1773 and earlier
*Billings, William	Providence, R.I.	1791–1806
Billings and Danforth (William Billings and Job Danforth)	Providence, R.I.	1798–1801
Bird, James	New York, N.Y.	1820–1821
Bland, James	Westchester County, N.Y.	1761
Blaun, James	Westchester County, N.Y.	1759
Blin, Peter	Boston, Mass.	1757–1759
Bliss, Jonathan & Co.	Brooklyn, N.Y.	1822–1823
*Boardman, Henry S.	Hartford, Conn.	1841
	Philadelphia, Pa.	1844–1861
Boardman, J. D.	Hartford, Conn.	1828

Checklist of American Makers

Name of Individual or Firm	Location of Shop	Approximate Working Dates
*Boardman, Luther	South Reading, Mass.	1834–1837
	Meriden, Conn.	1837–1839
*Boardman, Luther & Co.	Chester, Conn.	1839–1842
	East Haddam, Conn.	1842–1870 and later
Boardman, Sherman (see T. D. and S. Boardman)	Hartford, Conn.	1810–1850
*Boardman, Thomas D.	Hartford, Conn.	1804–1860 and later
*Boardman, T. D. and S. (Thomas D. and Sherman Boardman)	Hartford, Conn.	1810–1850
*Boardman, Timothy & Co. (Timothy Boardman and Lucius Hart, agents for T. D. & S. Boardman)	New York, N.Y.	1822–1825
*Boardman & Co.	New York, N.Y.	1825–1827
*Boardman and Hall (Henry S. Boardman and Franklin D. Hall)	436 High Street Philadelphia, Pa.	1844–1845
*Boardman and Hart (Thomas D. Boardman and Lucius Hart)	New York, N.Y.	1828–1853
Bokee, William	Brooklyn, N.Y.	1817–1824
Boker, William (possibly same as above)	Philadelphia, Pa.	1800
*Bonynge, Robert	Boston, Mass.	1731–1763
Bouis, John	Baltimore, Md.	1829–1834
Bouis, John and Son	Baltimore, Md.	1831–1832
Bouis, Joseph	Baltimore, Md.	1834
Bouzigues, _____	Philadelphia, Pa.	1810
Bowditch, Capt.	Salem, Mass.	1814
Bowles, Samuel	Boston, Mass.	1787–1788
Bowman, Nathaniel	Charlestown, Mass.	1806–1814
Bowman, _____ (Partner in Manning Bowman & Co.)	Middletown, Conn.	After 1850
*Boyd, Parks	Philadelphia, Pa.	1795–1819
*Boyle, Robert	New York, N.Y.	1752–1758
*Bradford, Cornelius	New York, N.Y.	1752–1753 and 1770–1785
	Philadelphia, Pa.	1753–1770
Bradford, John	Boston, Mass.	1784–1788
*Bradford, William, Jr.	New York, N.Y.	1719–1758
Bradford and McEuen (Cornelius Bradford and Malcolm McEuen)	New York, N.Y.	1772–1785
Brainard (See Bailey and Brainard)	Cobalt, Conn.	1840 or later
*Braman, Elijah	Warren, R.I.	1832–1839
Brigden, John	Albany, N.Y.	1823–1825
*Brigden, Timothy	Albany, N.Y.	1816–1819
*Britaw, _____	Unknown	c. 1850
*Brook Farm	West Roxbury, Mass.	1844–1847
Brooks, David S.	Hartford, Conn.	1828

Checklist of American Makers

Name of Individual or Firm	Location of Shop	Approximate Working Dates
Browe and Dougherty (William Browe, Jr. and William M. Dougherty)	Newark, N.J.	1845–1853
*Brower, A.	New York, N.Y.	c. 1820
Brower, C. S.	New Orleans, La.	1822
*Brown, E. & Co.	Location unknown	c. 1820
*Brunstrom, John Andrew	Philadelphia, Pa.	1781–1793
*Buckley, Townsend M.	Troy, N.Y.	1854–1857
Bull, Lyman & Couch (_____ Bull, William Lyman, Ira Couch)	Meriden, Conn.	1845–1849
Bumste(a)d, Thomas	Roxbury, Mass.	1640–1643
	Boston, Mass.	1643–1677
Burroughs, Thomas	Boston, Mass.	c. 1684
	New York, N.Y.	c. 1685–1703
Burroughs, Thomas, Jr.	New York, N.Y.	c. 1705–1712
Butler and Perkins (Thomas N. Butler and Daniel Perkins)	Boston, Mass.	1852–1853
*Byles, Thomas	Newport, R.I.	1711–1712
	Philadelphia, Pa.	1738–1771
*Cahill, J. W. & Co.	Location unknown	After 1830
*Calder, William	Providence, R.I.	1817–1856
Caldwell, T.B. (A partner in Newell, Caldwell & Coffin)	Boston, Mass.	1853
*Calverley, John	Philadelphia, Pa.	1840–1841
Camp, William E.	Middletown, Conn.	1849
Campbell, John	Annapolis, Md.	1749
Campbell, Mungo	Philadelphia, Pa.	1749–1752
	Norfolk, Virginia	1756–1764
*Campbell, Samuel	Baltimore, Md.	1814–1818
*Capen, Ephraim	West Roxbury, Mass.	1844–1847
	New York, N.Y.	1847–1854
*Capen and Molineux (Ephraim Capen and George Molineux)	New York, N.Y.	1848–1854
*Carlstedt, J. N.	Rockford, Ill.	After 1840
*Carnes, John	Boston, Mass.	1723–1760
Carter, Samuel	Boston, Mass.	1712–1747
*Cincinnati Britannia Co.	Cincinnati, Ohio	c. 1850
Clark(e), Jonas	Boston, Mass.	1715–1737
Clark(e), Thomas	Boston, Mass.	1674–1720
*Coburn, H. R.	Location unknown	Probably after 1840
Coffin, G. J. (see Newell, Caldwell and Coffin)	Boston, Mass.	1853
*Coldwell, George	New York, N.Y.	1787–1811
*Colton, Oren (see Woodbury and Colton)	Philadelphia, Pa.	1835–1838
Comer, John	Boston, Mass.	1674–1721
Comer, John, Jr.	Boston, Mass.	1700–1706
Cone, S. L.	Meriden, Conn.	1849

Checklist of American Makers

Checklist of American Makers

NAME OF INDIVIDUAL OR FIRM	LOCATION OF SHOP	APPROXIMATE WORKING DATES
*Danforth, Thomas (3rd)	Stepney, Conn.	1777–1818
	Philadelphia, Pa.	1807–1813
Danforth, Thomas (4th)	Philadelphia, Pa.	1812
	Augusta, Georgia	1818
*Danforth, William	Middletown, Conn.	1792–1820
Danforth and Hamlin (Thomas Danforth, 2nd and Samuel Hamlin)	Middletown, Conn.	c. 1767–1773
Davis, Edmund	Philadelphia, Pa.	1720–1721
*Day, Benjamin	Newport, R.I.	1744–1757
Derby, Albert H.	Middletown, Conn.	1835–1850
	New Haven, Conn.	1851–1854
*Derby, Thomas S.	Middletown, Conn.	1822–1850
Derby, Thomas S., Jr.	Middletown, Conn.	1840–1850
Derby, Thomas S. and Son	Middletown, Conn.	1849
*DeRiemer, Cornelius B. & Co.	Auburn, N.Y.	1833
*Dickinson, Charles	Newark, N.J.	1850–1857
Digg(e)s, William	New York, N.Y.	1801–1802
Dolbeare, David	Boston, Mass.	c. 1736–c. 1770
*Dolbeare, Edmund	Boston, Mass.	c. 1671–c. 1684
		c. 1692–c. 1706
	Salem, Mass.	c. 1684–c. 1692
Dolbeare, James	Boston, Mass.	1727–1740
Dolbeare, John	Boston, Mass.	1690–1740
Dolbeare, Joseph	Boston, Mass.	c. 1690–c. 1704
Dougherty, William M. (see Browe and Dougherty)	Newark, N.J.	1845–1849
*Dunham, E.	Location unknown	After 1825
*Dunham, Rufus	Westbrook, Maine	1837–1860
*Dunham, R. & Sons	Portland, Maine	1861
*Dunlap, J. & Co.	Philadelphia, Pa.	Probably after 1830
*Dunn, Cary	New York, N.Y.	c. 1770–1790
Durninger, Daniel	Boston, Mass.	1722–1723
*Eadem, Semper	Boston, Mass.	c. 1740–c. 1780
*Eadem, Semper, I.S.	Boston, Mass.	Mid-18th century
*Eadem, Semper, T.S.	Boston, Mass.	Mid-18th century
*Edgell, Simon	Philadelphia, Pa.	1713–1742
Edgell, William	Boston, Mass.	1724
*Eggleston, Jacob	Middletown, Conn. and Fayetteville, N.C.	c. 1796–1813
Eggleston and Bass (Jacob Eggleston and Daniel Bass)	Fayetteville, N.C.	1807–1812
Eldridge, Eli	Taunton, Mass.	1848–1860
*Ellicott, George	Bucks County, Pa.	1779
Ellison, John	Philadelphia, Pa.	1837
*Elsworth, William J.	New York, N.Y.	1767–1798
Elton, William (see Hall, Elton & Co.)	Wallingford, Conn.	1849–1850

Checklist of American Makers

Checklist of American Makers

Checklist of American Makers

Checklist of American Makers

Checklist of American Makers

Checklist of American Makers

Name of Individual or Firm	Location of Shop	Approximate Working Dates
*Lowe, I.	Location unknown	After 1800
Lucas, Ivory	New London, Conn.	1732–1747
	Ogles Town, Del.	1747–1748
Lyell, David	New York, N.Y.	1714
*Lyman, William W. (see also Curtiss and Lyman)	Meriden, Conn.	1844–1852
Lyman and Couch (W. W. Lyman and Ira Couch)	Meriden, Conn.	1844–1845
McEuen, Duncan	New York, N.Y.	1793–1803
McEuen, Malcolm (see also Bradford and McEuen)	New York, N.Y.	1765–1803
*McEuen, Malcolm and Son (Malcolm and Duncan McEuen)	New York, N.Y.	1793–1803
McIlmoy, John	Philadelphia, Pa.	1793
*McQuilkin, William	Philadelphia, Pa.	1839–1853
Mann, William	Boston, Mass.	1690–1738
*Manning, E. B.	Middletown, Conn.	After 1840
Manning, Thaddeus	Middletown, Conn.	1849
*Manning, Bowman & Co.	Middletown, Conn.	After 1850
Marshall, Joseph	New York, N.Y.	1821–1822
*Marston, _____	Baltimore, Md.	After 1830
*Martine, James	Fayetteville, N.C.	c. 1826–1835
Maton, Marcus	Hartford, Conn.	1828
Melville, Andrew	Newport, R.I.	1804–1810
*Melville, David	Newport, R.I.	1776–1793
*Melville, Samuel	Newport, R.I.	1793–1800
*Melville, S. and T. (Samuel and Thomas Melville)	Newport, R.I.	1793–1800
*Melville, Thomas	Newport, R.I.	1793–1796
*Melville, Thomas, Second	Newport, R.I.	1796–1824
	New London, Conn.	c. 1820
Melville, William L.	Newport, R.I.	1807–1810
*Meriden Britannia Co.	Meriden, Conn.	1852 and later
Merryfield, Robert	New York, N.Y.	1760
Metcalf, Michael	Dedham, Mass.	1691
*Michel, Andre	New York, N.Y.	1742–c. 1752
Michel, Andre (perhaps son of above)	New York, N.Y.	1795–1797
*Miller, Josiah	Probably Rhode Island or Connecticut	18th century
Minze, James (see Stafford & Minze)	Albany, N.Y.	1794–1796
Mix, Garry I.	Wallingford, Conn.	c. 1845–1854
	Yalesville, Conn.	1854–1861 and later
*Mix, G. I. and Co.	Yalesville, Conn.	1854–1861 and later
*Mix, Thomas	Meriden area, Conn.	1827 and later

Checklist of American Makers

*Mix, William	Prospect, Conn.	1827–1850 and later
Mix, William (another)	Meriden area, Connecticut	c. 1845 and later
Molineux, George (see Capen and Molineux)	New York, N.Y.	1848–1854
Moore, Luke	Philadelphia, Pa.	1819–1822
Morey, David B. (see Smith & Co. and successor firms)	Boston, Mass.	1841–1845
		1847–1864 and later
	Charlestown, Mass.	1845
*Morey and Ober (D. B. Morey and R. H. Ober)	Boston, Mass.	1852–1855
*Morey, Ober and Co. (D. B. Morey, R. H. Ober, Thomas Smith)	Boston, Mass.	1855–1857
*Morey and Smith (D. B. Morey and Thomas Smith)	Boston, Mass.	1857–1860 and later
Morgan, Henry	Groton, Conn.	1849
*Munson, John	Yalesville, Conn.	1846–1852
*M., N.	Probably Rhode Island or Connecticut	18th century
*Neal, I.	Location unknown	1842
Nexsen, Edmund	New York, N.Y.	1818–1819
*Newell, J. C.	Boston, Mass.	1853
*Newell, Caldwell and Coffin (J. C. Newell, T. B. Caldwell, G. J. Coffin)	Boston, Mass.	1853
*Nichols, O.	Location unknown	Early 19th century
Norris, George (see Ostrander and Norris)	New York, N.Y.	1848–1850
Norsworthy, John	Norfolk, Va.	1771
North, John	Augusta, Ga.	1818–1823
North and Rowe (John North, Adna S. Rowe)	Augusta, Ga.	1818–1823
Northey, David	Salem, Mass.	1732–1778
Northey, William	Lynn, Mass.	1764–1804
Nott, William	Philadelphia, Pa.	1812
*Nott, William [another (see Johnson and Nott)]	Middletown, Conn.	1809–1817
	Fayetteville, N.C.	1817–1825
Nott, Babcock and Johnson (William Nott, Samuel Babcock, Jehiel Johnson)	Middletown, Conn.	1817
Ober, R. H. (see Smith, Ober and Co.)	Boston, Mass.	1849–1856
*Olcott, J. W.	Baltimore, Md.	c. 1800
*Ostrander, Charles	New York, N.Y.	1848–1854
*Ostrander and Norris (Charles Ostrander and George Norris)	New York, N.Y.	1848–1850
*Palethorp, John H.	Philadelphia, Pa.	1820–1845
*Palethorp, J. H. & Co. (J. H. Palethorp and Thomas Connell)	Philadelphia, Pa.	1839–1841

Checklist of American Makers

Checklist of American Makers

Checklist of American Makers

NAME OF INDIVIDUAL OR FIRM	LOCATION OF SHOP	APPROXIMATE WORKING DATES
Rust, Leonard M.	New York, N.Y.	1849
*Rust, Samuel	New York, N.Y.	1837–1845
*Sage, Timothy	St. Louis, Mo.	1847–1848
Sage, T. and Co.	St. Louis, Mo.	1847
*Sage and Beebe	Location unknown	After 1840
Savage, William	Middletown, Conn.	1838–1839
*Savage, William H. (see Graham and Savage)	Middletown, Conn.	1837–1840
*Savage and Graham (William H. Savage and John B. Graham)	Middletown, Conn.	1837–1838
Scull, Benjamin	Philadelphia, Pa.	1810–1811
Seip, Jacob	Philadelphia, Pa.	1820–1822
*Sellew and Company (Enos, Osman and William Sellew)	Cincinnati, Ohio	1832–1860
Seltzer, Abraham	Philadelphia, Pa.	1793
Shaw, _____ (see Sickel and Shaw)	Philadelphia, Pa.	1849–1850
*Sheldon and Feltman (Smith Sheldon and J. C. Feltman, Jr.)	Albany, N.Y.	1847–1848
*Shoff, I.	Eastern Pennsylvania	Late 18th century
Shrimpton, Henry	Boston, Mass.	1639–1666
Sickel, H. G.	Philadelphia, Pa.	1849–1853
*Sickel and Shaw (H. G. Sickel and _____ Shaw)	Philadelphia, Pa.	1849–1850
*Simpkins, Thomas	Boston, Mass.	1727–1766
*Simpson, Samuel	Yalesville, Conn.	1835–1852
*Simpson and Benham (Samuel Simpson and Darius Benham)	New York, N.Y.	1845–1847
Sizer, Amasa	Middletown, Conn.	1799
*Skinner, John	Boston, Mass.	1760–1790
Smith, Aaron	Philadelphia, Pa.	1736–1737
*Smith, Eben, Jr.	Beverly, Mass.	1814–1856
*Smith, George W. (see Smith & Feltman)	Albany, N.Y.	1849–1856
(Rogers, Smith & Co.)	Hartford, Conn.	1856–1857
Smith, James E.	Maryland?	After 1775
*Smith, Ober and Co. (Thos. Smith, R. H. Ober, and D. B. Morey)	Boston, Mass.	1849–1852
Smith, Thomas	Boston, Mass.	1700–1742
Smith, Thomas (see Morey and Smith)	Boston, Mass.	1841–1862
Smith, Thomas and Co. (Thomas Smith, D. B. Morey, and Henry White)	Boston, Mass.	1842–1847
Smith, William R.	Middletown, Conn.	1848
*Smith & Co. (Thomas Smith, D. B. Morey and Henry White)	Boston, Mass.	1847–1849
Smith & Co. (another) (George W. Smith and associates)	Albany, N.Y.	1853–1856
*Smith and Feltman (G. W. Smith and J. C. Feltman, Sr.)	Albany, N.Y.	1849–1852

Checklist of American Makers

Checklist of American Makers

Name of Individual or Firm	Location of Shop	Approximate Working Dates
*Trask, Israel	Beverly, Mass.	*c.* 1813–*c.* 1856
*Trask, Oliver	Beverly, Mass.	1832–1839
*Treadway, Amos	Middletown, Conn.	*c.* 1760–*c.* 1790
Tyler, John	Boston, Mass.	1720–1756
Tymiesen, Sebastian (a partner in S. Stafford & Co.)	Albany, N.Y.	1815–1817
Van Dalsam, John	New York, N.Y.	1775
Van Kleeck, Peter	New York, N.Y.	1775
Vartklop's Britannia Ware	Newark, N.J.	1831
*Vose and Co.	Albany, N.Y.	After 1840
Wadsworth, Lester	Hartford, Conn.	1838
*Walker, _____	New York, N.Y.	After 1840
*Wallace, R. & Co.	Wallingford, Conn.	*c.* 1838–1855 and later
*Ward, H. B. & Co. (Three brothers, Henry Beebe Ward, J. Smith Ward and Lowden Bailey Ward)	Wallingford, Conn.	1849 and later
Ward, Reuben	Philadelphia, Pa.	1825
Warner, James M.	Providence, R.I.	1828–1848
Warren, John B.	Boston, Mass.	1825–1828
*Warren, Josiah	Cincinnati, Ohio	1821
*Wayne, C. P. and Son	Philadelphia, Pa.	1840–1849
*Webb, W.	New York, N.Y.	Probably after 1810
*Weekes, James	Brooklyn, N.Y.	After 1830
*Weekes, J. (probably same as above)	New York, N.Y.	After 1820
*Weekes, J. & Co. (probably same as above)	Poughkeepsie, N.Y.	1833–1835
Weekes, James & Co. (probably same as above)	Poughkeepsie, N.Y.	1842–1843
Wells, D. B. (see I. C. Lewis & Co.)	Meriden, Conn.	1839–1852
Wendeln, John F. (see J. H. Stalkamp & Co.)	Cincinnati, Ohio	1853–1855
West, William A. (see Crossman, West and Leonard)	Taunton, Mass.	1828–1830
White, Henry (see Smith and Morey and successor firms)	Boston, Mass.	1842–1849
White, James	New York, N.Y.	1821–1834
Whitfield, George B.	New York, N.Y.	1828–1865
*Whitfield, G. and J.	New York, N.Y.	1836–1865
*Whitlock, John H. (see also Graves and Whitlock)	Troy, N.Y.	1847–1856
Whitlock, J. H. & Co.	Troy, N.Y.	1854–1856
*Whitmore, Jacob	Middletown, Conn.	1758–1790
Whitmore, Lewis	Rocky Hill, Conn.	1841
Whitmore and Francis (_____ Whitmore, and Daniel Francis)	Buffalo, N.Y.	1833
Whitney, Chauncey	Albany, N.Y.	1822
Whitney, _____ (see Benham and Whitney)	New York, N.Y.	1849

Checklist of American Makers

Name of Individual or Firm	Location of Shop	Approximate Working Dates
*Wilcox, H. C. & Co. (Horace C. and Dennis C. Wilcox)	Meriden, Conn.	c. 1848–1852
*Wildes, Thomas	New York, N.Y.	1833–1840
Wilds, Thomas, possibly same as above	Philadelphia, Pa.	1829–1833
Will, Christian	New York, N.Y.	1770–1789
Will, George W.	Philadelphia, Pa.	1799–1807
*Will, Henry	New York, N.Y.	1761–1775
		1783–1793
	Albany, N.Y.	1776–1783
*Will, John	New York, N.Y.	1752–1774
*Will, Philip	New York, N.Y.	1766 and later
	Philadelphia, Pa.	1763–1787
*Will, William	Philadelphia, Pa.	1764–1798
Willett, Edward	Upper Marlboro, Md.	1692–1743
Willett, Mary	Upper Marlboro, Md.	1773
Willett, William	Upper Marlboro, Md.	1744–1772
*Williams, Lorenzo L.	Philadelphia, Pa.	1838–1842
*Williams, Otis	Buffalo, N.Y.	1826–1831
Williams, Richard	Stepney, Conn.	1793–1800
*Williams and Simpson (Lorenzo L. Williams and Samuel Simpson)	Yalesville, Conn.	1837–1838
Willis, Thomas	Philadelphia, Pa.	1829–1833
Wilson, Joseph	New York, N.Y.	1775
Witherle (or Weatherly), Joshua	Boston, Mass.	1784–1793
Wolfe, John	Philadelphia, Pa.	1801
*Wood, N. G. and Sons	Boston, Mass.	About 1870
*Woodbury, J. B.	Mass. — probably Beverly	c. 1830–1835
	Philadelphia, Pa.	1835–1838
*Woodman Cook and Co.	Portland, Me.	After 1830
Wyer, Simon	Philadelphia, Pa.	1740–1752
E. W.	Virginia	18th century
Yale, Burrage	South Reading, Mass.	1808–1835
*Yale, Charles	Wallingford, Conn.	1817–1835
Yale, Charles (probably same as above)	New York, N.Y.	1832
Yale, C. and S. (Charles and Selden Yale)	Wallingford, Conn.	1817–1823
	Richmond, Va.	
Yale, Henry (see Yale and Curtis)	New York, N.Y.	1858–1867
*Yale, Hiram	Wallingford, Conn.	1822–1831
*Yale, H. & Co. (Hiram and Charles Yale)	Yalesville, Conn.	1824–1835
	Richmond, Va.	
Yale, Samuel (see W. and S. Yale)	Meriden, Conn.	1813–1820
Yale, Selden (see C. and S. Yale)	Wallingford, Conn.	1817–1823
	Richmond, Va.	
Yale, William	Meriden, Conn.	1813–1820
Yale, William (probably same as above)	New York, N.Y.	1830–1832
*Yale, W. and S. (William and Samuel Yale)	Meriden, Conn.	1813–1820
*Yale and Curtis (Henry Yale and Stephen Curtis)	New York, N.Y.	1858–1867

Checklist of American Makers

Name of Individual or Firm	Location of Shop	Approximate Working Dates
*Yale and Henshaw (Edwin R. Yale and Joseph B. Henshaw)	Wallingford, Conn.	1835
*Youle, George	New York, N.Y.	1793–1828
Youle, Thomas	New York, N.Y.	1813–1819
Young, Abraham	New York, N.Y.	1796
*Young, Peter	New York, N.Y.	1775
	Albany, N.Y.	1785–1795

INDEX OF SYMBOLS AND INITIALS IN
THE EARLY TOUCHMARKS
Volume Three

Index of Symbols and Initials in the Early Touchmarks

INDEX OF MAKERS OF PEWTER
SHOWN IN PLATES
Volume Three

Index of Makers of Pewter Shown in Plates

Index of Makers of Pewter Shown in Plates

BIBLIOGRAPHY
Volume Three

PROBLEMS OF THE AMERICAN PEWTERER

N. Whittock, J. Bennett, J. Badcock, C. Newton, et al. *The Complete Book of Trades*, London, John Bennett, 1837, pp. 443 xxx, 444 xxx and 446.

The Domestic Encyclopaedia: or A Dictionary of Facts and Useful Knowledge. A. F. M. Willich, London, 1802, vol. 4.

The Cyclopaedia, or, Universal Dictionary of Arts, Sciences and Literature. Abraham Rees, Philadelphia, Samuel Bradford, 1802–1819, vol. XXXVIII—tin.

Shorter Oxford English Dictionary. Second Edition, Vol. II, Oxford at the Clarendon Press, 1939, p. 2421.

THE BUSINESS OF A PEWTERER

J. Carl Thomas, An Improvement in Spoon Moulds, *Pewter Collectors Club of America Bulletin*, No. 50, March 1964, p. 16, vol. V. (This source will hereafter be abbreviated to *P.C.C.A. Bulletin*.)

THE MARKS ON PEWTER

John F. Ruckman, Two More Forms Attributable to Peter Young, *P.C.C.A. Bulletin* 47, September 1962, p. 127, vol. IV.

Charles V. Swain, Varying Forms from one Mold, *P.C.C.A. Bulletin* 48, March 1963, p. 147, vol. IV.

Charles V. Swain, Two Lids from the Same Mold, *P.C.C.A. Bulletin* 49, September 1963, pp. 176, 177, vol. IV.

HOUSEHOLD PEWTER

Porringers

Ronald F. Michaelis, *A short history of The Worshipful Company of Pewterers of London* and *a catalogue of pewter in its possession*, Court of Assistants, Pewterers Hall, Oak Lane, London, E.C. 2, 1968, p. 68.

Tankards, Pots and Measures

J. B. Kerfoot, *American Pewter*, Houghton Mifflin Company, Riverside Press, Cambridge, 1924, p. 46.

Spoons, Ladles and Dippers

Dr. James Deetz, Howland Spoon, *The Howland Quarterly*, published by The Pilgrim John Howland Society, vol. XXXIII, pp. 2, 3.

The Buttolph-Williams House, Its History, Restoration and Furnishings, published by the Antiquarian and Landmarks Society, Inc. of Connecticut, Hartford, 1969, p. 14.

Coffee Pots, Teapots, Creamers and Sugar Bowls

Louis G. Myers, *Some Notes on American Pewterers*, Country Life Press, Garden City, New York, 1926, opp. p. 57.

[233]

Bibliography

Charles V. Swain, On the Collecting of Teapots, Part I, *P.C.C.A. Bulletin* 53, December 1965, pp. 81–85 and Part II, *Bulletin* 55, December 1966, pp. 122–124, vol. 5.

Agnes Hayes Post, Teapots, *P.C.C.A. Bulletin* 55, December 1966, pp. 117–118, vol. 5.

Inventory of the Goods and Chattels of John Brunstrom, Henry Francis du Pont Winterthur Museum, Joseph Downs Manuscript Collection No. 56X14.2.

J. Carl Thomas, H. I. An Answer and an End, *P.C.C.A. Bulletin* 56, June 1967, pp. 132–134, vol. 5.

ECCLESIASTICAL PEWTER

Paul M. Auman, New Finds in Old Pewter by William Will, The Aaronsburg Communion Service, *Antiques*, April 1950, pp. 274–275.

THE PEWTERERS OF MASSACHUSETTS BAY

Dr. Reginald F. French, The Dolbeares, *P.C.C.A. Bulletin* 33, May 1954, pp. 57–59, vol. 3.

Carl Jacobs, 17th Century Boston Pewter Identified, *P.C.C.A. Bulletin* 35, November 1955, pp. 99–100, vol. 3.

Account Book of Benjamin Clarke, Boston Brazier, 1760–1819 in Henry Francis du Pont Winterthur Museum.

Richard Graves

Boston Record Commissioners Reports, Births, Baptisms and Marriages, 1630–1699, Rockwell and Churchill, Boston, 1883, pp. 58, 81.

Vital Records of Salem, Massachusetts, Essex Institute, Salem, Massachusetts, Vol. I, pp. 380–381.

The Dolbeare Family

Winifred Lovering Holman, Early Dolbeares, *New England Historic Genealogical Register*, vol. CXII, 1958, pp. 170–178.

Dolbeare Records. Copied from the Parish Registers by Rev. G. A. B. Jones, Vicar of Ashburton, Devon, *New England Historic Genealogical Register*, Notes, vol. CV, p. 74.

Dr. Reginald F. French, "The Dolbeares," *op. cit.*

Suffolk County, Massachusetts Deeds, vol. 95, pp. 78, 131.

Suffolk County Probate Records, John Dolbeare, Docket 7458.

John Baker

Carl Jacobs, 17th Century Boston Pewter Identified, *op. cit.*

Two New Pewterers and a Scandal

C. H. Paige, Two New Pewterers and a Scandal, *P.C.C.A. Bulletin* 27, November 1950, pp. 154–156.

Suffolk County, Massachusetts, Court House. A mineographed book of abstracts entitled, The Inferior Court of Pleas, Suffolk County Court, 1680–1698.

John Holyoke

Andrew Nichols, *Genealogy of the Holyoke Family*, Essex Institute Historical Collections, vol. 3, pp. 55–79.

Ledlie I. Laughlin, Semper Eadem, *P.C.C.A. Bulletin* 57, December 1967, pp. 164–167, vol. 5.

Robert Bonynge

Report of the Record Commissioners, City of Boston, vol. 19. Selectmen's Minutes 1754–1763, pp. 80, 243.

Carl Jacobs, *Guide to American Pewter*, The McBride Co., Inc., New York, 1957, p. 26.

Bibliography

Joseph Randle

    See under The Pewterers of Rhode Island.

Semper Eadem

    John J. Evans, Jr., More Light and Shadow on John Skinner, Boston Pewterer, *P.C.C.A. Bulletin* 38, July 1957, pp. 128–131, vol. 3.

    Ledlie I. Laughlin, Semper Eadem, *op. cit.*

Peter Blin and David Flagg

    Essex Gazette, Salem, Massachusetts, August 28, 1772.

John Skinner

    John J. Evans, Jr., More Light and Shadow on John Skinner, Boston Pewterer, *op. cit.*

    Thomas D. Williams, Horse Grows Horns, *P.C.C.A. Bulletin* 44, February 1961, pp. 72–73, vol. 4.

    J. Carl Thomas, Stag Marked Porringer, *P.C.C.A. Bulletin* 46, February 1962, pp. 107–108, vol. 4.

Edward Kneeland

    Letter of Edward Kneeland to the Tax Assessors of Boston, File 53, 158; Manuscripts. Henry F. du Pont Winterthur Museum, Winterthur, Delaware.

Edward Rand

    Lura Woodside Watkins, Edward Rand, Pewterer, *P.C.C.A. Bulletin* 12, June 1943, pp. 5, 6.

John Gooch

    Carl Jacobs, *A Guide to American Pewter, op. cit.*, p. 98.

    Frank A. Gooch, *The History of a Surname, The Line of John Gooch in New England*, privately printed, New Haven, Connecticut, 1926, pp. 63–64 and 109–112.

    Suffolk County Deeds, Suffolk County Court House, vol. 47, p. 72; vol. 61, p. 253.

    New Hampshire Gazette, State Journal and General Advertiser, August 6, 1781 to September 15, 1781; January 19, 1782–November 9, 1782.

Lee and Creesy

    Nancy A. Goyne, *Britannia in America*, Winterthur Portfolio, vol. II, 1965, p. 165.

    Memoranda of Mrs. T. Henry Bott, Beverly Historical Society, Beverly, Massachusetts.

THE RHODE ISLAND PEWTERERS

    Rhode Island Pewter, 1711–1856, Bulletin Covering Exhibition of the Rhode Island Historical Society, July 1–Oct. 30, 1959.

    Joseph K. Ott, Dr. Brown's Recent Finds, *P.C.C.A. Bulletin* 44, Feb. 1961, pp. 75, 76, vol. IV.

    Paine-Thornton-Waterman Papers, Miscellaneous Manuscripts, p. 161 in the Rhode Island Historical Society, Providence, Rhode Island.

    Dr. Adelbert C. Abbott, A New American Touch, *P.C.C.A. Bulletin* 30, April 1952, p. 21, vol. III.

    Dean A. Fales, Jr., Another New American Pewterer, *P.C.C.A. Bulletin* 30, April 1952, p. 22, vol. III.

    John P. Remensnyder, Ebenezer Crossman, Pewterer to River Whalemen, *P.C.C.A. Bulletin* 46, February 1962, pp. 110, 111, vol. IV.

Lawrence Longworthy

    Rhode Island Pewter, 1711–1856, *op. cit.*

    Howard H. Cotterell, F. R. S., *Old Pewter, Its Makers and Its Marks*, B. T. Botsford, Ltd., London, 1929, pp. 115–116.

Bibliography

John Fryers

    Carl Jacobs, *Guide to American Pewter, op. cit.*, p. 95.

    Rhode Island Pewter, 1711–1856, *op. cit.*

    Joseph K. Ott, Dr. Brown's Recent Finds, *op. cit.*

    William O. Blaney, Rhode Island Holloware at the Newport, P.C.C.A. Meeting, *P.C.C.A. Bulletin* 55, December 1966, pp. 103, 104, vol. V.

Joseph Belcher, Father and Son

    Melville T. Nichols, A Challenge in Pewter, *Antiques*, vol. XLIV, December 1943, p. 292.

    The Connecticut Gazette, June 1, 1787 and September 28, 1787.

    Heads of Families at the First Census of the United States Taken in the Year 1790. Connecticut, U.S. Government Printing Office, Washington, D.C., 1908.

    Census of Lyme, Connecticut, 1820, vol. 3, p. 1413–86, Connecticut State Library, Hartford.

Paris J. Tillinghast, Jr.

    Dr. Adelbert C. Abbott, A New American Touch, *op. cit.*

    New England Historic Genealogical Register, The Reverend Pardon Tillinghast, vol. 13, p. 282.

    William B. Browne, The Jenks Family of America, Rumford Press, Concord, New Hampshire, 1952, p. 38.

    Vital Records of Rhode Island, 1636–1850, James N. Arnold, Providence, Narragansett Historical Publishing Co., 1898, Providence Marriages, p. 390, Newport Gazette, August 14, 1802.

    Cumberland County Court House, Fayetteville, North Carolina, Deed Books, vol. 20, pp. 162, 216, 220; vol. 23, pp. 122–123, vol. 37, p. 152.

    Representative Men and Old Families of Rhode Island, J. H. Beers & Co., Chicago, Illinois, 1908, vol. I, p. 546.

Joseph Randle

    Paine-Thornton-Waterman Papers, Miscellaneous Manuscripts, p. 161, Rhode Island Historical Society, Providence, R. I.

    Vital Records of Rhode Island, *op. cit.*, vol. II, Providence Deaths, p. 273.

    Records of the Colony of Rhode Island and Providence Plantations, printed by Order of the General Assembly, edited by John Russell Bartlett, Secretary of State, Providence, Knowles, Anthony and Company, vol. 5, 1751–1756, p. 98.

Samuel Hamlin and Samuel E. Hamlin

    Joseph France, Two Advertisements, *P.C.C.A. Bulletin* 20, September 1947, pp. 13, 14, vol. II.

    The Connecticut Courant, July 13, 1767, April 3, 1769, November 23, 1773.

    Middletown Connecticut Vital Records, vol. 2, p. 297.

    Middletown Church Records, vol. I, p. 129; 2S-2, p. 24.

Gershom Jones

    Joseph K. Ott, A Gershom Jones Basin and a Whodunit, *P.C.C.A. Bulletin* 38, July 1957, pp. 136–138, vol. III.

    United States Chronicle, Providence, Rhode Island, May 12, 1791; March 15, 1798.

William Calder

    Representative Men and Old Families of Rhode Island, op. cit., vol. II, pp. 1142–1143.

THE PEWTERERS OF THE CONNECTICUT VALLEY

    The Hartford, Connecticut, Times, Genealogical column, April 22, 1944.

Bibliography

Ivory Lucas

The Hartford, Connecticut, Times, Genealogical column, April 22, 1944.

Percy E. Raymond, Another Pewterer Discovered on the Genealogical Page, *P.C.C.A. Bulletin* 14 October 1944, p. 6.

Connecticut Historical Society Collections, vol. 5, p. 358.

Wilmington, Delaware, Court House, Deeds Q1-pp. 227, 273, Administrations G1, p. 132; Wills O1, p. 14.

Thomas Danforth, first

Norwich, Connecticut, Packet, issue of October 28-November 4, 1773.

Probate File 3094, Thomas Danforth, Norwich, 1787, at Connecticut State Library, Hartford.

John Danforth

Norwich, Connecticut, Land Records, vol. 30, p. 55.

Middletown Probate Records at Connecticut State Library, File 1147, Joseph Danforth; file 1149, Thomas Danforth Estate Distribution.

Thomas Danforth, second

Middlesex Gazette, Middletown, February 7, 1789.

Connecticut Courant, Hartford, issue of November 23, 1773.

Middletown Probate Records, Connecticut State Library, File 1149, 1782, Thomas Danforth Inventory and Distribution.

Middletown, Connecticut, Vital Records, vol. 2, p. 353.

Thomas Danforth, third

Thomas D. Boardman Manuscripts in Connecticut State Library.

Carl Jacobs, *A Guide to American Pewter, op. cit.*, p. 82.

Henshaw and Hamlin

The Connecticut Courant, Hartford, issue of July 13, 1767.

Middletown Vital Records, vol. 2, p. 297.

Middletown Church Records, vol. 1, p. 129.

Middletown Families, Compiled by Edwin Stearns—Unpublished Manuscripts of Connecticut Historical Society, Hartford, Stack T (Middletown) vol. 4, p. 164. Henshaw Family.

Joseph Danforth, Father and Son

Middletown Probate Records, Connecticut State Library, File 1149, 1782, Thomas Danforth Estate Distribution.

Middlesex Gazette, Middletown, issue of February 7, 1789.

Middletown Land Records, Connecticut State Library, vol. 37, p. 311.

Edward Danforth

Connecticut Courant, Hartford, issues of June 5, 1786, October 15, 1787 and December 14, 1789.

Thomas D. Boardman Manuscripts, Connecticut State Library.

Middletown Probate Records, Connecticut State Library, File 1149, 1782, Thomas Danforth Estate Distribution.

Connecticut Gazette, New London, vol. XXX 1567, issue of November 21, 1793.

American Mercury, Hartford, Connecticut, vol. XII, 581, issue of August 24, 1795.

Connecticut Courant, vol. XLVI, 2239, issue of November 22, 1809.

Bibliography

Jonathan Danforth

John Joseph May, *Danforth Genealogy*, Charles H. Pope, Boston, 1901, p. 101.

Middletown, Connecticut, Vital Records, vol. 2, p. 353.

Middlesex Gazette, Middletown, issue of February 7, 1789.

Middletown Probate Records, Connecticut State Library, File 1149, Thomas Danforth Estate Distribution.

Middlesex Gazette, issues of June 26, 1790 and December 6, 1794.

William and Josiah Danforth

Middletown Probate Records, Connecticut State Library, File 1149, Thomas Danforth Estate Distribution.

Middlesex Gazette, Middletown, issues of June 26, 1790; December 6, 1794; March 23 and December 14, 1809; September 13, 1810; December 14, 1820.

Middletown Probate Records, Connecticut State Library, File 1288, Jacob Eggleston, Additional Inventory.

Manuscript Notes of Thomas D. Boardman, *op. cit.*

Dean A. Fales, Jr., T.D.B. Tells All, *P.C.C.A. Bulletin* 46, February 1962, pp. 109, 110, vol. 4.

Walton Deckelman, The Last of the Danforths, *P.C.C.A. Bulletin* 36, July 1956, pp. 109, 110, vol. 3.

Middletown Deeds, vols. 66, p. 438; vol. 70, p. 221; vol. 76, p. 77.

Samuel Danforth of Hartford

Manuscript Notes of Thomas D. Boardman, *op. cit.*

Nathan and Prentice Frink

Northampton County, Massachusetts Deeds, vol. 1, p. 151.

Connecticut Gazette, New London, January 14, 1792.

Stonington, Connecticut, Vital Records, vol. 3, pp. 225, 275.

Greene and Belcher

Melville T. Nichols, A Challenge in Pewter, *op. cit.*

Connecticut Gazette, New London, issues of June 1, 1787 and September 11, 1787.

Census of 1800, Lyme, Connecticut, vol. 3, p. 576.

Census of 1810, Lyme, Connecticut, vol. 3, p. 1537.

Census of 1820, Lyme, Connecticut, vol. 3, p. 1413.

Jacob Eggleston

Middletown Probate Records, Connecticut State Library, File 1288, Jacob Eggleston, Inventory and Additional Inventory.

Cumberland County Court House, Fayetteville, North Carolina Deeds, vol. 23, pp. 122, 123; vol. 27, p. 152.

James H. Craig, *The Arts and Crafts in North Carolina, 1699–1840*, The Museum of Early Southern Decorative Arts, Winston-Salem, North Carolina, 1965, p. 108.

The Richard Lees

Carl Jacobs, *Guide to American Pewter, op. cit.*, p. 125.

Samuel Pierce

Marion Deming, Samuel Pierce and a Note, *P.C.C.A. Bulletin* 26, May 1950, p. 133.

Francis M. Thompson, *History of Greenfield, Shire Town of Franklin County, Massachusetts*, Greenfield, Massachusetts, 1904.

Bibliography

Ross Levett (unpublished), Samuel Pierce, a Study Through Related Account Books, 1967.

Pierce Account Books, *Ledgers I and II, Day Book I*, Hall Tavern, Deerfield, Massachusetts.

Pierce Family Diaries (unpublished) in possession of Miss Gladys Pierce, Greenfield, Massachusetts.

Ebenezer Southmayd

Carl Jacobs, *op. cit.*, p. 163.

Dr. Adelbert C. Abbott, Ebenezer Rates the Accolade, *P.C.C.A. Bulletin* 34, May 1955, pp. 79–81, vol. 3.

Amasa Sizer

Middlesex Gazette, Middletown, Connecticut, vol. XV, no. 732, November 29, 1799.

New London Bee, vol. V, no. 211, January 20, 1802.

Census of 1810, Middletown, Connecticut, vol. 7, p. 990.

Census of 1820, New London, Connecticut, vol. 3, p. 1279.

James Porter

Waterbury, Connecticut, Vital Records, vol. 1, p. 84.

Records of the First Congregational Church of Cromwell, Connecticut, vol. 1, p. 114.

Census of Middletown, Connecticut, 1800, vol. 7, p. 459.

Middletown, Connecticut, Land Records; vol. 30, p. 571; vol. 33, p. 125; vol. 37, pp. 365, 367, 566; vol. 41, p. 213.

First Church Records, Middletown, Connecticut, vol. 2S-2, pp. 47 and 73.

Ashbil Griswold

Ledlie I. Laughlin, Ramblings in Britannia Land, *P.C.C.A. Bulletin* 13, April 1944, pp. 13–17.

George Holmes Edwards, Ashbil Griswold, Pewterer, *P.C.C.A. Bulletin* 24, March 1949, vol. 2, pp. 89–92.

Daybooks of Ashbil Griswold, 1808–1844, Historical Department, International Silver Co., Meriden, Connecticut.

The Boardmans

Manuscript Notes of Thomas D. Boardman, Connecticut State Library, Hartford.

John F. Ruckman, A Boardman Loving Cup, *P.C.C.A. Bulletin* 28, June 1951, vol. 2, p. 175.

Dean A. Fales, Jr., T.D.B. Tells All, *P.C.C.A. Bulletin* 46, February 1962, vol. 4, pp. 109–113.

J. Carl Thomas, Homan Takes One from the Boardmans, *P.C.C.A. Bulletin* 48, March 1963, vol. 4, p. 146.

Wendell Hilt, The Boardman Group, *P.C.C.A. Bulletin* 52, May 1965, vol. 5, pp. 52–59.

The Yale Family

Manuscript Notes of Thomas D. Boardman, *op. cit.*

John F. Ruckman, Nineteenth Century Chalices, *P.C.C.A. Bulletin* 48, March 1963, vol. 4, pp. 148–150.

The Notts and Johnsons

Middlesex Gazette, Middletown, Connecticut, issues of December 14, 1809 and September 13, 1810.

Middletown Probate Records, Connecticut State Library, File 1288, Jacob Eggleston, Additional Inventory.

Middletown Census of 1810, vol. 7, p. 995.

Bibliography

Simeon Stedman

J. Carl Thomas, Additions to the Record, *P.C.C.A. Bulletin* 49, September 1963, vol. 4, pp. 184–185.

Charlotte Goldthwaite, *Boardman Genealogy*, published by W. F. J. Boardman, Lockwood and Brainerd Co., Hartford, 1895, pp. 446, 447.

John J. May, *Danforth Genealogy, op. cit.*, pp. 56, 57.

Hampden County, Massachusetts, Registry of Deeds, vol. B48, p. 165.

Hartford, Connecticut, Land Records, Municipal Building, vol. 29, p. 52; vol. 36, p. 2; vol. 40, p. 81, 395; vol. 43, p. 392.

Springfield County, Massachusetts Court House, Vol. G., 331, Simeon Stedman Estate, case 10747, 1842.

Thomas S. Derby

Manuscript Notes of Thomas D. Boardman, Connecticut State Library.

J. & D. Hinsdale

John J. Evans, Jr., Important Document, *P.C.C.A. Bulletin* 46, February 1962, vol. 4, pp. 108, 109.

Samuel Campbell

Nancy A. Goyne, New Pewterers and More Information, *P.C.C.A. Bulletin* 58, August 1968, vol. 5, p. 199.

THE PEWTERERS OF NEW YORK CITY

Helen Burr Smith, A New IB Silversmith and Two Unrecorded Pewterers, The New York Historical Society Quarterly, vol. LII, Number 1, pp. 81–85.

Thomas Burroughs, Senior and Junior

Helen Burr Smith, *op. cit.*

New York Conveyances, Liber 25, p. 248; Liber 26, p. 543, Register's Office, City of New York.

Francis H. Bigelow, *Historic Silver of the Colonies and Its Makers*, The MacMillan Co., New York, 1925, p. 311.

A Report of the Record Commissioners Containing Boston Births, Baptisms, Marriages and Deaths, 1630–1699, Boston, 1883, p. 162.

"Supplementary List of Marriage Licenses," State Library Bulletin No. 1, Albany 1898, p. 12.

Abstracts of Wills, vol. 1, p. 198 and vol. 7, p. 134. Historical Documents Collection, Queens College, New York.

Minutes of the Common Council of the City of New York, New York, 1917, vol. I, pp. 286, 423, 424; vol. II, pp. 56, 58, 210.

Howard Cotterell, *op. cit.*, p. 172.

David Lyell

George Francis Dow, *The Arts and Crafts in New England, 1704–1775*, The Wayside Press, Topsfield, Massachusetts, 1927, p. 73.

The Leddells

Stanley Paddock, A Leddell Item for Study, *P.C.C.A. Bulletin* 32, p. 4.

John J. Evans, Jr., A Discovery in American Pewter, *P.C.C.A. Bulletin* 45, p. 84.

The Bassetts

Oliver Deming, A Bassett Discovery, *Antiques*, January 1949, p. 40.

Bibliography

Dean A. Fales, Jr., Pewter at the New Haven Colony Historical Society, *P.C.C.A. Bulletin* 30, pp. 19–20.

Eric de Jonge, The Pewter Institute—Examples, *P.C.C.A. Bulletin* 32, p. 43.

Dr. Adelbert C. Abbott, Bassett out-Bassett's Bassett, *P.C.C.A. Bulletin* 35, p. 95.

Ronald F. Michaelis, Dr. Abbott's Giant Tankard, *P.C.C.A. Bulletin* 36, pp. 102–105.

Dean A. Fales, Jr., Patriot and Pewteress, *P.C.C.A. Bulletin* 37, p. 122.

New Jersey Journal, Issues of June 14, 1780; April 3, 1782 and May 14, 1783.

The Wills of New York

Correspondence of Donald Noble, 18 Orchard Road, Chatham, N.J. with Herr Becker, Burgermeister of Herborn, Dillkreis, West Germany.

Ecclesiastical Records of the State of New York, published 1905 by the State under the supervision of Hugh Hastings, State Historian, vol. VI, pp. 3901, 3913, 3924, 3982, 3999, 4240, 4242.

Records of Baptism, Reformed German Congregation in the City of New York, pp. 2, 3, 9, 11, 14, 15, 26, 27, 31, 38, 39, 40, 48 and 63. New York Historical Society, Manuscript Department.

Eric de Jonge, Philip's Whose Touch Harmonious, *P.C.C.A. Bulletin* 34, May 1955, vol. 3, p. 83.

Percy E. Raymond, Wine Measures Made in Pewter, *P.C.C.A. Bulletin* 27, November 1950, vol. 2, p. 158.

Helen and George S. McKearin, *Two Hundred Years of American Blown Glass*, Doubleday & Co., Inc., Garden City, New York, 1950, pp. 9–11 and 33–40.

Frederick W. Hunter, *Stiegel Glass*, Dover Publications, Inc. New York, 1950, pp. 146–147, 152–154.

André Michel

Records of the Reformed Dutch Church in the City of New York, Church Members' List, New York Genealogical and Biographic Record, vol. 60, p. 35.

Records of the Reformed Dutch Church, Baptisms, New York Genealogical and Biographic Record, vol. 3, pp. 93, 108, 121.

The Colonial Naturalization Act of 1740 with a List of Persons Naturalized in New York Colony, 1740–1769, contributed by Richard J. Wolfe, New York Genealogical and Biographic Record, vol. 94, p. 138.

Blaun, Bland, Henry and Merrifield, Four Unimportant New York Pewterers

Lura Woodside Watkins, Another Pewterless Pewterer, *P.C.C.A. Bulletin* 16, July 1945, p. 9.

Enlistments in New York Muster Rolls of Provincial Troops, 1755–1764, New York Historical Society Publications, vol. XXIV.

Cary Dunn

Stephen G. C. Eusko, *American Silversmiths and Their Marks*, privately printed by the Southworth Press, Portland, Maine, New York, 1927, p. 84.

New York Packet and American Advertiser, January 5, 1784.

Malcolm McEuen and Son

Ledlie I. Laughlin, Three Embryo New York Pewterers, *P.C.C.A. Bulletin* 17, January 1946, p. 8.

Peter Young

Ledlie I. Laughlin, Three Embryo New York Pewterers, *op. cit.*

Van Dalsam, Van Kleeck and Wilson

Ledlie I. Laughlin, Three Embryo New York Pewterers, *op. cit.*

Bibliography

Coldwell and Lafetra

Rita S. Gottesman, *The Arts and Crafts in New York, 1800–1804* in *New York Historical Society Collections*, vol. LXXXII, 1965 Advertisements, 541, 542, 543.

Eight Late Workers

Nancy A. Goyne, New Pewterers and More Information, *P.C.C.A. Bulletin* 58, August 1968, vol. 5, pp. 198, 199.

ALBANY PEWTERERS

Clifton Blake, Andrew Thompson, Albany Pewterer, *Antiques*, July 1951, p. 51.

John P. Remensnyder, Ebenezer Crossman, Pewterer to Hudson River Whalers, *P.C.C.A. Bulletin* 46, February 1962, vol. 4, pp. 110–111.

Ebenezer Crossman

Dean A. Fales, Jr., Another New American Pewterer, *P.C.C.A. Bulletin* 30, April 1952, vol. 3, p. 22.

John P. Remensnyder, *op. cit.*, pp. 110–111.

Andrew Thompson

Clifton Blake, Andrew Thompson, Albany Pewterer, *Antiques*, July 1951, p. 51.

Three Late Albany Pewterers

Nancy A. Goyne, New Pewterers and More Information, *P.C.C.A. Bulletin* 58, August 1968, vol. 5, pp. 198–199.

Thomas Paschall

Pages from a *Day Book of Thomas Paschall*, Bristol, England, 1660–1663, Henry F. du Pont Winterthur Museum, Manuscript files.

Thomas Langshaw

Hannah B. Roach, Philadelphia Business Directory, 1690 and Two Pewterers, *Pennsylvania Genealogical Magazine*, vol. XXII, No. 2, pp. 95, 117.

Philadelphia Deeds, vol. E25, p. 126.

Chester County, Pennsylvania, Court Records, files 363, 385.

Edmund Davis

American Weekly Mercury of Philadelphia, June 15, 1721.

Philadelphia Deeds, vol. F3, p. 196; vol. G3, p. 121.

Aaron Smith

American Weekly Mercury of Philadelphia, several issues of January and February, 1736; August 4 and 11, 1737.

Thomas Byles

John J. Evans, Jr., Speculations, *P.C.C.A. Bulletin* 43, September 1960, vol. 4, p. 59.

Lola S. Reed, More About Lions, *P.C.C.A. Bulletin* 51, December 1964, vol. 5, p. 36.

Simon Wyer

Ralph B. Strassburger, *The Pennsylvania German Pioneers*, Norristown, Pa., 1934, pp. 282–284.

The Pewterers of Bethlehem

Joseph Mortimer Levering, Bishop of the Moravian Church, *A History of Bethlehem, Pennsylvania, 1741–1892*, Times Publishing Company, Bethlehem, Pennsylvania, 1903, pp. 7, 16–19, 21–22, 29–31, 70–79, 123, 136, 207, 253–254.

John Hall Martin, *Historical Sketch of Bethlehem in Pennsylvania with Some Account of the Moravian Church*, printed by the author, Philadelphia, 1873, pp. 5–7, 15, 45–47.

Bibliography

Unpublished Records of the Moravian Church, Moravian Archives, Bethlehem.

Notes and Queries, *Pennsylvania Magazine* vol. 39, p. 244.

Johann Christopher Heyne

Moravian Burial Records at Lancaster, Lancaster Historical Society, p. 14.

Albert Loefgren, *Svenska Tenngjutare Lantverkets Historia*, 3 vols., vol. 3, Nordiska Maseet, Stockholm, 1950, pp. 343, 483.

Unpublished Letters and Account Books, Moravian Archives, Bethlehem, Pennsylvania.

Diarium Bethlehem, vol. 1, 1742, Moravian Archives, Bethlehem.

Cash Books, 1743–1749, Moravian Archives, Bethlehem.

Joseph M. Levering, *op. cit.*, pp. 122, 136, 207.

Eric de Jonge, Swedish Influence on American Pewter, *Antiques*, March 1955, pp. 230–232.

Eric de Jonge, Johann Christopher Heyne, Swedish Influence on American Pewter, *P.C.C.A. Bulletin* 34, May 1955, vol. 3, pp. 71–76.

Love, Unidentified American Pewterer

Ledlie I. Laughlin, Love, Pennsylvania Pewterer, *P.C.C.A. Bulletin* 18, June 1946, pp. 5–10.

John F. Ruckman, Two Letters about Pewter, *P.C.C.A. Bulletin* 19, December 1946, pp. 11–13.

Eric de Jonge, Swedish Influence on American Pewter, *Antiques*, *op. cit.*

Eric de Jonge, Johann Christopher Heyne, Swedish Influence on American Pewter, *P.C.C.A. Bulletin* 34, *op. cit.*

Walton Deckelman, The Love Enigma, *P.C.C.A. Bulletin* 41, September 1959, vol. 4, pp. 27–29.

John J. Evans, Jr., Love . . . That Man! *P.C.C.A. Bulletin* 43, September 1960, vol. 4, pp. 63–64.

Eric de Jonge, We're in Love Again, *P.C.C.A. Bulletin* 44, February 1961, vol. 4, pp. 73–75.

John J. Evans, Jr., Lovebirds and Lions—A Pewter Mystery Solved, *Antiques*, August 1959, p. 142.

Lola S. Reed, More About Lions, *P.C.C.A. Bulletin* 51, December 1964, vol. 5, p. 36.

John F. Ruckman, More about Love, *Antiques*, May 1954, p. 388.

Pennsylvania Magazine, Notes and Queries, vol. 39, p. 244.

Joseph M. Levering, *op. cit.*, pp. 123, 136, 207, 253–254.

Mungo Campbell

Princess Anne County, Va., *Minute Book 7*, 1753–1762, p. 371.

John Philip Alberti

Ralph B. Strassburger, *Pennsylvania German Pioneers*, Pennsylvania German Society, Norristown, Pennsylvania, 1934, 3 vols., vol. 1, p. 672.

Colonel William Will

Charles V. Swain, Varying Forms From One Mold, *P.C.C.A. Bulletin* 48, March 1963, vol. 4, p. 147.

The Hasselberg Group

John Hill Martin, *op. cit.*, pp. 15, 45–47.

Joseph M. Levering, *op. cit.*, pp. 253–255.

Pennsylvania Archives, vol. 3, p. 70.

Pennsylvania Magazine, Notes and Queries, vol. 39, p. 244.

Unpublished leather-bound *Notebook*, Moravian Archives, Bethlehem.

Albert Loefgren, *op. cit.*, pp. 323, 331.

Bibliography

John F. Ruckman, More About Love, *Antiques*, May 1954, p. 388.

Eric de Jonge, Swedish Influence on American Pewter, *op. cit.*

The Pennsylvania Gazette, Philadelphia, September 6, 1759.

Thompson Westcott, *Names of Persons Who Took the Oath of Allegiance to the State of Pennsylvania Between 1777 and 1789*, Philadelphia 1865, pp. 59, 108.

George Ellicott

Alice Morse Earle, *Sun Dials and Roses of Yesterday*, Macmillan Co., Norwood, Massachusetts, 1902, p. 24.

Dr. Reginald F. French, About Time, *P.C.C.A. Bulletin* 46, February 1962, vol. 4, pp. 104–107.

Index to Estates, Doylestown, Bucks County, Pennsylvania, No. 455, 1741, Andrew Ellicott, Jr.; 2886, 1799, Thomas Ellicott, Wheelwright of Solebury.

John Andrew Brunstrom

Thompson Westcott, *op. cit.*, p. 108.

Inventory of the Estate of John Brunstrom, Manuscript files of the Henry F. du Pont Winterthur Museum, Winterthur, Delaware.

Eric de Jonge, Johann Christoph Heyne, Swedish Influence on American Pewter, *op. cit.*

Walton Deckelman, The Love Enigma, *op. cit.*

John J. Evans, Jr., Speculations, *op. cit.*

John J. Evans, Jr., Love . . . That Man, *op. cit.*

Eric de Jonge, We're in Love Again, *op. cit.*

Lola S. Reed, More About Lions, *op. cit.*

John F. Ruckman, More About Love, *op. cit.*

Three Country Pewterers of Pennsylvania

Francis D. Brinton, New Light on Elisha Kirk, *Antiques*, April 1947, p. 253.

Henry J. Kauffman, Simon Pennock, Pewterer, *Antiques*, April 1948, p. 196.

Francis D. Brinton, Tab-Handled Porringers, *P.C.C.A. Bulletin* 28, June 1951, vol. 2, p. 174.

Dean A. Fales, Jr., Robert Porter?, *P.C.C.A. Bulletin* 30, April 1952, vol. 3, p. 23.

Arthur E. James, Chester County Pewter and Pewterers, *P.C.C.A. Bulletin* 47, September 1962, vol. 4, pp. 128–130.

John J. Evans, Jr., Provident Preservation, *P.C.C.A. Bulletin* 48, March 1963, vol. 4, pp. 145, 146.

Friends Miscellany, Vol. VI, Memoirs of Elisha Kirk, John and Isaac Comly, Byberry, Pennsylvania, 1835.

Chester County Historical Society, Chester, Pennsylvania, Manuscript 13612.

D.S. Unidentified American Pewterer

Leather-bound Notebook in Moravian Archives, Bethlehem.

Parks Boyd and The Palethorps

Charles V. Swain, Two Lids from the Same Mold, *P.C.C.A. Bulletin* 49, September 1963, vol. 4, pp. 176, 177.

Plumly and Bidgood

Walton Deckelman, A Few Auction Notes, *P.C.C.A. Bulletin* 41, September 1959, vol. 4, p. 33.

Eight Obscure Philadelphia Pewterers

Nancy A. Goyne, New Pewterers and More Information, *P.C.C.A. Bulletin* 58, August 1968, vol. 5, pp. 198, 199.

Bibliography

THE PEWTERERS OF THE SOUTH

Harold B. Gill, Jr., Research Associate, Colonial Williamsburg, Virginia, Unpublished Records of Research in Virginia Archives.

James H. Craig, *The Arts and Crafts in North Carolina, 1699–1840*, The Museum of Early Southern Decorative Arts, Winston-Salem, North Carolina, 1965.

Edward Willett

Dr. E. A. Rushford, Achievements in Pewter, *Antiques*, April 1943, vol. LXIII, p. 171.

Howard H. Cotterell, Old Pewter, *op. cit.*, p. 121.

John Andrews

York County, Virginia Deeds, Bonds No. 2, 1701–1713, pp. 172, 221.

York County Orders, Wills, vol. 15, 1716–1720, pp. 490, 491.

Adam Pavey

Spotsylvania County, Virginia, Will Book, 1749–1759, pp. 293, 294.

John Campbell

Anne Arundel County, Maryland, Wills EV. No. 1, p. 40.

Anne Arundel County Deeds, B.B., No. 3, p. 214.

Mungo Campbell

Norfolk County, Virginia, Abstracts of Marriage Bonds, 3N, p. 127.

Princess Anne County, Virginia, Minute Book 7, 1753–1762, p. 371, vol. 8, 1762–1796, page reference missing.

York County, Virginia, Judgments and Orders, 1763–1765, p. 227.

York County Deeds, No. 7, 1763–1769, pp. 83, 84.

Records of Bruton Parish Church, Williamsburg, Virginia, p. 151.

John Bilbro

Surrey County, Virginia, Wills and Deeds, 1769–1779, pp. 407–410.

John Ballantyne

Norfolk County Deeds, vol. 24, 1767–1770, pp. 39, 124, 194, 197.

Lower Norfolk County, Virginia, Antiquarian, vol. 5, part 4, p. 135.

Howard H. Cotterell, *Old Pewter, op. cit.*, p. 153.

James Haldane

Virginia Gazette, issues of January 2, 1772, July 13, 1776.

Philadelphia County Deeds, City Hall, Philadelphia, Vol. II, p. 375.

Peter Henley

James H. Craig, *op. cit.*, p. 107.

Francis G. Hendricks

Carl Jacobs, *op. cit.*, loose leaf supplement.

Erwin Hintze, *Sachsische Zinngieser*, Karl W. Hierseman, Leipzig, 1921, p. 83.

Theodore Jennings

Howard H. Cotterell, *op. cit.*, p. 244.

Jacob Eggleston

James H. Craig, *op. cit.*, p. 108.

Cumberland County, North Carolina Deeds, vol. 27, p. 152.

Bibliography

William Nott and Jehiel Johnson

    James H. Craig, *op. cit.*, p. 109.

Samuel Campbell

    Nancy A. Goyne, New Pewterers and More Information, *op. cit.*, Bulletin 58, p. 199.

J. W. Olcott

    Litchfield, Connecticut, Vital Records, vol. 1, p. 69.

    Connecticut State Library, Probate Records, Litchfield District 1802, nos. 4250, 4251.

Samuel Kilbourn

    W. A. Monkhouse, A Rare Kilbourn Form, *P.C.C.A. Bulletin* 33, May 1954, vol. 3, p. 65.

Four Late Baltimore Pewterers

    Nancy A. Goyne, New Pewterers and More Information, *P.C.C.A. Bulletin*, *op. cit.*, pp. 198, 199.

James Martine

    James H. Craig, *op. cit.*, pp. 114, 116, 117, 124.

    Cumberland County, North Carolina Deeds, vol. 39, p. 592; vol. 42, p. 43; and vol. 46, p. 310.

Unidentified Touches

    Thomas D. Williams, Horse Grows Horns, *P.C.C.A. Bulletin* 44, February 1961, pp. 72, 73.

    J. Carl Thomas, Stag-Marked Porringer, *P.C.C.A. Bulletin* 46, February 1962, pp. 107, 108.

    J. Carl Thomas, H.I. An Answer and an End, *P.C.C.A. Bulletin* 56, June 1967, vol. 5, p. 132.

    Carl Jacobs, 17th Century Boston Pewter Identified, *P.C.C.A. Bulletin* 35, November 1955, vol. 3, pp. 99, 100.

    Dr. E. A. Rushford, Achievements in Pewter, *Antiques*, April 1943, vol. LXIII, p. 171.

    John J. Evans, Jr., A New Touch?, *P.C.C.A. Bulletin* 32, November 1953, vol. 3, p. 47.

THE BRITANNIA PERIOD

    Nancy A. Goyne, Britannia in America, *Winterthur Portfolio* II, 1965.

    George S. Gibb, *The Whitesmiths of Taunton, a History of Reed and Barton, 1824–1943*, Harvard Studies in Business History, Cambridge, Massachusetts, Harvard University Press, 1943.

    Business Manuscripts of Thomas D. Boardman, Connecticut State Library, Hartford.

MAKERS OF THE BRITANNIA PERIOD

Adams, Henry W., New York City Directory, 1857.

Andrews, Burr

    New Haven Palladium, May 30, 1846.

    New Haven, Connecticut, Directories, 1846–7, 1853–4, 1857.

    Industrial Census of Connecticut for 1850, p. 217, Connecticut State Library, Hartford.

Armitages and Standish

    George S. Gibb, *op. cit.*, pp. 39, 70, 147.

Babbitt and Crossman

    George S. Gibb, *op. cit.*, pp. 23–34.

    Nancy A. Goyne, Britannia in America, *op. cit.*, p. 170.

    John P. Remensnyder, William W. Crossman, Apprentice to Ebenezer Southmayd, *P.C.C.A. Bulletin* 46, February 1962, pp. 111–112.

Babbitt, Crossman and Co.

    George S. Gibb, *op. cit.*, pp. 34–36.

Bibliography

Bailey and Brainard

Carl Jacobs, *op. cit.*, p. 27.

Baldwin, Charles W.

Charles C. Baldwin, *Baldwin Genealogy*, Cleveland, Ohio, 1881.

Guilford, Connecticut Vital Records, vol. 2, p. 280.

American Advertising Directory for 1831, Jocelyn Darling & Co., New York, 1831.

Census of Connecticut, 1840, Berlin, vol. 1, pp. 220, 221 in Connecticut State Library.

Census of Connecticut, 1850, New Britain, vol. 2, pp. 68, 135.

Industries Census of Connecticut, 1850, p. 93.

Connecticut State Library — Cemeteries, New Britain, 1118 Inscriptions, Cemetery 1, p. 54.

Baldwin, D.S.

Carl Jacobs, *op. cit.*, p. 27.

Baldwin, Jesse G.

Charles Candee Baldwin, *op. cit.*

Connecticut State Library, File on Cemeteries, Middletown 711 Inscriptions, Cemetery 1, p. 1.

New England Business Directory, 1849, Pratt and Co., New York.

Connecticut Business Directory for 1851, printed and published by J. H. Benham, New Haven, Connecticut.

Baldwin, L.G.

Carl Jacobs, *op. cit.*, p. 27.

Barton, Charles E.

George S. Gibb, *op. cit.*, pp. 37, 71, 81 and others through 379.

Bidwell, Solomon

Nancy A. Goyne, New Pewterers and More Information, *op. cit.*

Boardman, Luther

Unpublished Account Book, 1834–1842, of Luther Boardman, owned in the Boardman family.

J. Carl Thomas, An Improvement in Spoon Moulds, *P.C.C.A. Bulletin* 50, March 1964, vol. 5, p. 16.

Industrial Census of Connecticut, 1850, p. 215; 1860, p. 78; 1870, p. 127 — Connecticut State Library.

Charlotte Goldthwaite, *Boardman Genealogy*, published by W. F. J. Boardman, Case Lockwood and Brainerd Co., Hartford 1895, pp. 495, 496.

Boardman and Hall

Edwin T. Freedley, *Leading Pursuits and Leading Men*, Philadelphia, Edward Young, 1856, p. 501.

Nancy A. Goyne, Britannia in America, *op. cit.*, p. 177.

Boardman and Hart

New York City Directories, 1847–1850.

Bowditch, Captain Nathaniel

The Diary of William Bentley, D. D. Salem, Massachusetts, The Essex Institute 1914, vol. IV, p. 237.

Nancy A. Goyne, Britannia in America, *op. cit.*, p. 166.

Braman, Elijah

George S. Gibb, *op. cit.*, pp. 147, 155.

Bibliography

Brook Farm

Ledlie I. Laughlin, Ramblings in Britannia Land, *P.C.C.A. Bulletin* 13, April 1944, p. 16.

Browe, William, Jr., Newark, New Jersey, Directories, 1844–1852.

Browe and Dougherty, Newark, New Jersey, Directories, 1844–1852.

Brower, C.S.

Carl Jacobs, *op. cit.*, p. 48.

Nancy A. Goyne, New Pewterers and More Information, *P.C.C.A. Bulletin* 58, *op. cit.*, p. 198.

Burdett, Aaron

Baltimore, Maryland, Directories, 1838–1854.

Butler and Perkins

Boston, Massachusetts, Directories, 1852, 1853.

J. Carl Thomas, Two New Britannia Firms, *P.C.C.A. Bulletin* 50, March 1964, vol. V, p. 19.

Capen, Ephraim

See under Brook Farm

Cincinnati Britannia Company

Carl Jacobs, *op. cit.*, p. 55.

Coburn, H. R.

Edward A. Rushford, M.D. American Pewter Lamps, *P.C.C.A. Bulletin* 13, April 1944, p. 9.

Crossman, West and Leonard

George S. Gibb, *op. cit.*, pp. 36–48.

Curtiss, Edwin E.

Frederick Haines Curtiss, *A Genealogy of the Curtiss Family*, Rockwell and Churchill Press, Boston, 1903.

Meriden, Connecticut, Vital Records, vol. 1, pp. 7, 29.

Curtiss, Enos H.

Frederick H. Curtiss, *op. cit.*

Curtiss, Frederick

Carl Jacobs, *op. cit.*, p. 60.

Glastonbury, Connecticut, Land Records, vol. 27, pp. 370, 411, 412, 449, 450 and vol. 29, p. 68, 148; vol. 30, p. 121.

Industrial Census of Connecticut, 1850, p. 113; 1860, p. 108.

Curtiss, Lemuel J.

Frederick H. Curtiss, *op. cit.*

Meriden, Connecticut, Vital Records, vol. 1, p. 52.

Derby, Albert H.

Connecticut State Library, file on cemeteries, Meriden 211, Inscriptions, Cemetery 3, p. 31.

Middletown Vital Records, vol. 4, pp. 32, 102, 103.

Census of Connecticut, 1850, vol. 10, p. 592.

New Haven Directories, 1852–53, 1853–54, etc. to 1859–60.

Derby, Thomas S., Jr.

Connecticut Herald, April 6, 1850.

Bibliography

Dickinson, Charles
Newark, New Jersey, Directories, 1850 to 1857.

Dougherty, William M.
Newark, New Jersey, Directories, 1843 to 1854.

Eldridge, Eli
Boston Directory, 1849.
George Gibb, Letter to the author, dated December 16, 1941, which will be filed in the manuscript archives at Henry Francis du Pont Winterthur Museum.
Old Families of Southeastern Massachusetts, vol. 1, pp. 494–5.

Engel, Gotlieb
Philadelphia Directory, 1858.

Farnam, D. L.
Ellis H. Whitaker, New Maker, *P.C.C.A. Bulletin* 41, September 1959, vol. 4, p. 32.

Foote, Henry C.
Industrial Census of Connecticut for 1850, p. 271.

Foote, James and Co.
Industrial Census of Connecticut, 1850, p. 271.
Connecticut Business Directory, 1851.
Wallingford, Connecticut, Vital Records, vol. 1, p. 55.

Fuller and Smith
William H. Fuller, *Fuller Genealogy*, 1914, vol. 3, pp. 52–55.
Connecticut Industries Census, 1850, p. 317.
Groton, Connecticut, Vital Records, vol 1, p. 93.

Gerhardi and Co.
Formerly listed as Gerhardt & Co.
Eric de Jonge, Gerhardt & Co., Touch Discovered, *Antiques*, April 1950, p. 293.

Gleason, Roswell
George S. Gibb, *op. cit.*, p. 136.

Graves, J. B.
Troy, New York, Directory, J. C. Kneeland & Co., publisher, 1847.
Troy, New York, Directory, Prescott and Wilson, 1847–1848, 1848–1849, 1849–1850.

Graves and Whitlock
Troy, New York, Directories, 1847 to 1849.

Hall, Almer
David A. Hall, *The Halls of New England*, Joel Munsell's Sons, Albany, New York, 1883.
American Advertising Directory, 1831, Jocelyn Darling & Co., New York, 1831.
Industries Census of Connecticut, 1850, p. 271.
Industries Census of Connecticut, 1860, p. 359.

Hall, Boardman and Co.
Edwin T. Freedley, *Leading Pursuits and Leading Men, Philadelphia*, p. 501.
Nancy A. Goyne, Britannia in America, *op. cit*, p. 177.
Dean A. Fales, Hall, Boardman and Co., *P.C.C.A. Bulletin* 34, May 1955, vol. 3, p. 82.

Bibliography

Hall, Elton and Co.
American Advertising Directory, op. cit., 1831.

Hall and Cotton
Ledlie I. Laughlin, Ramblings in Britannia Land, *op. cit.*, pp. 15–16.

Hart, Lucius
New York Directories, 1828–1860.
Thomas D. Boardman Manuscripts in Connecticut State Library.

Hattersley, Joseph
Newark, New Jersey, Directories, 1850–1860.

Hattersley, William
Newark, New Jersey, Directories, 1849–1861.

Hattersley and Dickinson
Newark, New Jersey, Directories, 1854–1856.

Hattersley and Son, J.
Newark, New Jersey, Directories, 1856–1861.

Henshaw, Joseph B. (See under Yale and Henshaw)

Hersey, S. S.
Dean A. Fales, Samuel S. Hersey, *P.C.C.A. Bulletin* 30, April 1952, vol. 3, p. 24.
Maine Register, 1855.

Homan Manufacturing Co.
J. Carl Thomas, Homan Takes One from the Boardmans, *P.C.C.A. Bulletin* 48, March 1963, vol. IV, p. 146.

Kaufman, Earnest
Philadelphia Directory, 1855.

Knowles, Henry
Nancy A. Goyne, New Pewterers and More Information, *op. cit.*, p. 198.

Lake, John D.
Industries Census of Connecticut for 1850.

Lawrence, William
Carl Jacobs, *op. cit.*, p. 194.

Lees and Beastall
New York Directory, 1825–1826.

Leonard, Gustavus
George S. Gibb, *op. cit.*, pp. 87–88, 92–98, 103–108.

Leonard, Horatio
George S. Gibb, *op. cit.*, pp. 48–49, 52–53, 76–77, 81, 83, 87, 95, 106.

Leonard Reed and Barton
George S. Gibb, *op. cit.*, pp. 92–99, 102–108, 112–114.

Leonard, Zephaniah
George S. Gibb, *op. cit.*, pp. 36–37, 47–52.

Lewis and Holt
American Advertising Directory for Manufacturers and Dealers in American Goods, 1831.

Bibliography

Lincoln, _____.
   Carl Jacobs, *op. cit.*, p. 129.

Marshall, Joseph
   New York Directory, 1821–1822.

Mix, G. I. & Co.
   Nancy A. Goyne, Britannia in America, *op. cit.*, pp. 174, 175.

Mix, Thomas
   Nancy A. Goyne, *op. cit.*, p. 192.
   Reginald F. French, William Mix I, *P.C.C.A. Bulletin* 28, June 1951, pp. 176, 177.

Mix, William
   Nancy A. Goyne, *op. cit.*, pp. 172–174.
   Reginald F. French, William Mix I, *op. cit.*, pp. 176–177.

Morey, David B.
   Charlestown, Massachusetts Directory, 1845.

Newell, Caldwell and Coffin
   J. Carl Thomas, Two New Britannia Firms, *op. cit.*, p. 19.

Nichols, O.
   Carl Jacobs, *op. cit.*, p. 140.

Parker, Charles
   Reginald F. French, William Mix I, *op. cit.*, p. 177.
   Wallingford, Connecticut, Vital Records, vol. 22, p. 416.
   New Haven, Connecticut, Vital Records, vol. 4, p. 143.
   Wallingford Estate Records, 1844, no. 1303.

Parker, Charles (another)
   Peter H. Johnson, *Parker, America's Finest Shotgun*, The Stackpole Company, Harrisburg, Pa.,
      1961, p. 243.
   Berlin, Connecticut, Vital Records, vol. 1, p. 44.
   A brochure without page numbers prepared in 1940 by the Charles Parker Company.
   Industrial Census of Connecticut, 1850, Meriden, p. 273 and for 1860, p. 175.

Parker, Charles and Co.
   Industrial Census of Connecticut, 1860, Wallingford, p. 359.

Parkin, W.
   Frederick Bradbury, *History of Old Sheffield Plate*, Pawson and Brailsford, Sheffield, 1912, p. 497.
   George S. Gibb, *op. cit.*, pp. 132–133, 142, 250.

Pelton, F. W. and O.Z.
   J. M. Pelton, *Pelton Family in America*, Joel Munsell's Sons, Albany, New York, 1892, pp. 368, 369.
   Industrial Census of Connecticut 1860, p. 181.
   New England Business Directory, George Adams, Boston, 1856, p. 562.

Pelton, William C.
   J. M. Pelton, *op. cit.*, pp. 256, 367–8, 376.
   Industrial Census of Connecticut, Portland, 1850, p. 195.
   Chatham, Connecticut, Vital Records, vol. 1, p. 172.

Bibliography

Population Census of Connecticut—Portland, vol. 10, p. 65.

Pierce and Johnson

Marion Deming, Samuel Pierce and a Note, *P.C.C.A. Bulletin* 26, May 1950, vol. 3, p. 133.

Pierce, J. & S.

Marion Deming, Samuel Pierce and a Note, *op. cit.*, p. 133.

Plumly and Felton

Carl Jacobs, *op. cit.*, p. 147.

Reed and Barton

George S. Gibb, *op. cit.*, pp. 81 to the end.

Riley, Michael

Nancy A. Goyne, New Pewterers and More Information, *op. cit.*, p. 198.

Brooklyn, New York, Directories, 1830–1840.

Riley and Rogers

Nancy A. Goyne, New Pewterers, etc., *op. cit.*, p. 198.

Brooklyn, New York, Directories, 1830–1834.

Rogers Smith & Co.

Industrial Census of Connecticut, 1860, p. 133.

Hartford, Connecticut, Directories, 1857–1863.

Cemetery Inscriptions, New Haven, vol. 1, p. 215; vol. 2, p. 653, in Connecticut State Library.

James Swift Rogers, *James Rogers and his Descendants*, Boston, 1902.

New Haven Directory and Annual Advertiser, 1861–62 to 1876.

Rust, H. N.

Carl Jacobs, *op. cit.*, p. 152.

Smith, Eben

The Diary of William Bentley, D.D., *op. cit.*

Nancy A. Goyne, Britannia in America, *op. cit.*, p. 166.

J. B. Kerfoot, *American Pewter*, Houghton Mifflin Co., Boston, 1924, p. 150.

Beverly, Massachusetts, Vital Records, vol. I, Topsfield Historical Society, 1906, p. 295; vol. II, pp. 277 and 554.

Smith, George W.

Elihu Geer, Hartford City Directories 1857–8 to 1862.

Industrial Census of Connecticut, 1860, p. 133.

New Haven City Directory, 1863–1864.

Standish, Alexander

George S. Gibb, *op. cit.*, pp. 39, 70, 147.

Stimpson, James H.

Carl Jacobs, *op. cit.*, p. 165.

Baltimore, Maryland, Directories, 1851–1857.

Taunton Britannia Manufacturing Company

George S. Gibb, *op. cit.*, pp. 48–88.

Thomas, John

Carl Jacobs, *op. cit.*, p. 166.

Bibliography

Tomlinson, Harvey
J. Carl Thomas, Additions to the Record, *P.C.C.A. Bulletin* 49, September 1963, vol. 4, p. 185.

Trask, Israel
The Diary of William Bentley, D.D., *op. cit.*
Nancy A. Goyne, Britannia in America, *op. cit.*, p. 166.
Memoranda of Miss Edith Webber at Beverly Historical Society, Beverly, Massachusetts.

Vartklop's Britannia Ware
Joseph Atkinson, *History of Newark*, William B. Guild, Newark, 1878, p. 188.

Wallace, R.
Reginald F. French, William Mix I, *op. cit.*, p. 177.

Ward, H. B. & Co.
Meetings 1940. *P.C.C.A. Bulletin* 9, April 1941, p. 1.
Wallingford, Connecticut, Vital Records, pp. 120, 121.
Industrial Census of Connecticut, 1850, p. 271.

Warner, James M.
Nancy A. Goyne, New Pewterers and More Information, *op. cit.*, p. 199.

Warren, John B.
Nancy A. Goyne, same reference as above.

Warren, Josiah
J. Carl Thomas, Additions to the Record, *op. cit.*, p. 185.

Wayne, Caleb P.
Philadelphia Directories, 1825–1849.

Webb, W.
Carl Jacobs, *op. cit.*, p. 173.

Weekes, James and Co.
Nancy A. Goyne, New Pewterers and More Information, *op. cit.*, p. 199.

White, James
Nancy A. Goyne, same reference as above, p. 199.
New York Directories, 1822–1834.

Whitlock, J. H.
Troy, New York Directory, 1847–48. Published by J. C. Kneeland & Co.
Troy, New York Directory, 1847–48. Published by Prescott and Wilson; also directories for 1848–49 and 1849–50.
Troy, New York, Directories from 1851 to 1859 published by C. L. MacArthur.

Whitney, Chauncey
Albany, New York Directory, 1822.

Wilcox, H. C. & Co.
Carl Jacobs, *op. cit.*, p. 176.
Ancestral Register of Roy Cromwell Wilcox, compiled by Algot G. Stenborg, Hartford, Connecticut, 1934, in Connecticut State Library.
Census of 1850, Meriden, Connecticut, vol. 14, p. 17.
Connecticut Business Directory, 1851.

Bibliography

Wildes, Thomas

John F. Ruckman, The Latest American Tankard, *P.C.C.A. Bulletin* 47, September 1962, vol. 4, p. 162.

Wood, N. G. and Sons

George T. Heussner, N. G. Wood and Sons, A New Mark—A New Form, *P.C.C.A. Bulletin* 59, December 1968, vol. 5, pp. 223, 224.

Boston Directories, 1850–1885.

Vital Records, Leominster, Massachusetts, p. 158.

William S. Wood, *Descendants of Jeremiah and John Wood*, Press of Charles Hamilton, Worcester, Massachusetts, 1885, pp. 269–273.

Woodbury, J. B.

Beverly, Massachusetts, Vital Records, vol. 1, Births, p. 379, Topsfield Historical Society, 1906.

Yale, Burrage

United States, Secretary of the Treasury, Documents Relative to the Manufactures in the United States, 1833.

Yale and Henshaw

Meriden, Connecticut, Vital Records, vol. 1, p. 325.

Middletown Church Records, Christ Church, vol. C., p. 59.

Wallingford Land Records, vol. 41, p. 651.

Connecticut State Library Mss. 974.62 — M547 Bill of Sale.

Wallingford Probate Records, Charles Yale, 1835, file 1654.

Longworth's American Almanac, New York Register and City Directory, 1836–1837, 1837–1838, 1838–1839.

DETHRONED PEWTERERS

J. M. Ufen and M. B. Uven

Vernon Jay Morse, A Complete American Trifid. *P.C.C.A. Bulletin* 39, March 1958, vol. 3, p. 153.
Carl Jacobs, *op. cit.*, p. 172.

J. Applebee

Carl Jacobs, *op. cit.*, p. 21.
Ellis H. Whitaker, New Applebee Touch, *P.C.C.A. Bulletin* 49, Sept. 1963, vol. 4, p. 193.

Beck and Thomas

Nancy Goyne Evans, A Directory Survey of Pewter and Britannia Craftsmen Working in Birmingham, England, until 1860, *P.C.C.A. Bulletin* 61, December 1969, vol. 6, p. 29.

Broom, James

Wilmington, Delaware, Court House, Will Book 01, p. 14, Deeds Q1, pp. 433, 439.

Burdett, Aaron

Baltimore, Maryland, Directories, 1835–1857
Carl Jacobs, *op. cit.*, p. 49.

Calder, William

Howard H. Cotterell, *op. cit.*, p. 159.
Representative Men and Old Families of Rhode Island, *op. cit.*, vol. II, pp. 1142, 1143.

Bibliography

Clunn, Matthew

New Jersey Marriage Records, State House, Trenton, Liber C, p. 45.

Official Register of Officers and Men in the Revolutionary War, Trenton 1872, p. 103.

A History of Trenton, published by Trenton Historical Society, Princeton University Press, 1929, vol. I, p. 110.

Carl M. Williams, *Silversmiths of New Jersey.* George S. McManus Co., Philadelphia, 1949, p. 132.

Dolbeare, John

Carl Jacobs, *op. cit.*, pp. 87, 88.

Dolbeare Family Manuscripts, Massachusetts Historical Society particularly letter of Benjamin Dolbeare, August 28, 1772 to a cousin Benjamin Dolbeare in England.

H. H. Cotterell, *op. cit.*, p. 197.

Fischer, John

Carl Jacobs, *op. cit.*, p. 93.

Fischer, I. and T.

Robert Mallory, 3rd, M.D., Fakes and Falsies, *P.C.C.A. Bulletin* 45, September 1961, vol. 4, p. 97.

Linthwaite, William

South Carolina Gazette, March 12, 1737.

Parkin, William

Frederick Bradbury, *History of Old Sheffield Plate, op. cit.*, p. 497.

Van Norden, Peter

First Houses of Bound Brook, in Princeton University Library, New Jersey Archives, vol. XXXVIII, Abstracts of Wills, vol. IX, 1798, October 4, Tobias Van Norden.

GENERAL INDEX

Aaronsburg, Pa., 22

Abbott, Dr. Adelbert C., xii; article on P. J. Tillinghast, 53; on F. Bassett tankard, 99; discovered Henry Will flagon, 108

Aberdeen, Scotland, 59

Abraham, George, xiii

"Achievements in Pewter" by Dr. E. A. Rushford, 149

Adams, Henry W., 174

Adams, Mrs. Oliver, 174

Agamenticus, Maine, 46

Ahlborn, Richard E., xiv

Albany, N.Y., Paris J. Tillinghast in Census of 1790 for Albany, 53; incised touch on S. Stafford pewter, 118

Albany Institute of History and Art, xii; has spoon marked Britaw, 178; has spoon marked Hall's Patent, 183; has spoon marked J.C. Baldwin, 176

Alberti, John Philip, 133

Alderwick, Mrs. Peter H., xiii

Allaire, Anthony, 113

Allison, Andrew, 174

Allison, John, 174

Almgren, Mrs. Neal, xii; owns E. Leslie spoons, 146

Amelung's Glass Works, 104

American Advertising Directory; listed Charles W. Baldwin as spoonmaker, 175; listed Lewis and Holt as spoonmakers, 186

American Pewter, see Kerfoot, J.B.

American Weekly Mercury, Philadelphia, advertised offer of sale of Edmund Davis' moulds, 122; published advertisements of Aaron Smith, 122

Ancient and Honorable Artillery Company, 37

Andrews, Burr, 174

Andrews, John, 148; inventory, 150

Angel of the Lord, 103

Annapolis, Md., John Campbell, pewterer in, 151; Mungo Campbell, pewterer in, 152

Antimony, use of by Thomas D. Boardman, 84; in britannia, 169

Antiquarian and Landmarks Society of Connecticut, xiii

Antiques, xi, Aaronsburg Church Service, 22; "Lovebirds and Lions," 131; "Achievements in Pewter" by Dr. Rushford, 149

Applebee, J., 198

Armitages and Standish, 174

Ashburton, Devon, England, Lawrence Langworthy of, 9; Edmund Dolbeare of, 25; St. Andrews Church, 201

Ashwell, William, 151

Asner, Norton, xii

Atkinson's History of Newark, lists Vartklop's britannia ware, 193

Auburn, N.Y., 176

Augusta, Ga., plates made in, 148; name on plate in Winterthur Museum, 160; J. and D. Hinsdale, 1820, 91

Auman, Paul M., xii; on Aaronsburg church service, 22

Austin, Nathaniel, quart pots, 13, 27; sold porringers to Benjamin Clarke, brazier, 27; additional information about, 44, 45

Austin, Richard, 27, 45; Boston scroll touch used by, 39

Avery, Eunice, 182

Babbitt, Isaac, 175; left Crossman, West and Leonard, 191

Babbitt, Crossman and Co., 175

Babbitt and Crossman, not first to make britannia in U.S., 169–170; 174

Babcock, Thomas, possible maker of T.B. porringer, 12; recorded in error as original settler of Philadelphia, 121

Badger, Thomas, 27; Boston scroll touch used by, 39; additional forms made by, 45

Bailey and Brainard, shop at Cobalt, Conn., 175; Brainard was junior partner, 178

Baker, John, dish attributed to, 8; touch attributed to, 26, 164; dish acquired by Dr. Kler, 31; went surety to Town for Edmund Dolbeare, 26; may have employed Dolbeare, 32

Baldwin, Charles, 176

Baldwin, Charles W., 175

Baldwin, D. S., 175

Baldwin, J. C., 176

Baldwin, Jesse G., 176

Baldwin, L. G., 176

Ball, William, 136–137

Ballantyne, John, Harold Gibb found record of, 148; 153–154.

Ballantyne, Nora, wife of John, 153

Baluster type measures, 48

Barck, Dorothy C., 109

Barns, Blakslee, Jacob Eggleston touch similar to one of, 80; in business in 1817 with Jeptha Porter, 146

Barns, B. and Porter, 146

Barre Publishing Co., xiv

Barry, John L., Jr., xii

Barton, Charles E., apprentice at Babbitt Crossman and Co., 175; partner in Leonard Reed and Barton, 176; solderer for Taunton Britannia Manufacturing Co., 185; wages at Crossman, West and Leonard, 191

Bass, Daniel, in business with Paris J. Tillinghast, 54; partner of Jacob Eggleston, 158

Bassetts, the, A. Michel cannot be classed with, 107

Bassett, Francis first, touch on sweetmeat dish, 8; touch possibly used by, 14; teapot attributed to, 19, 93; shapes by, 99

Bassett, Francis second, 98–99

Bassett, Frederick, two-quart tankard made by, 14; teapot with mark of, 19, 93; additional forms and touch of, 99–100

Bassett, John, porringer by, 18; additional forms, 99; new touch, 100

Bassett, Mary Elizabeth, 98

Baughn, Mr. and Mrs. Charles W., xiii

Baumann, Herr Walther, 101

Bayard-Bömper Glass Co., 104

B.D., 50

Beachy Head, Sussex, England, 53

Beading tools, 138

Beastall, 185

Beaven, Mrs. Charles, xiii

Beck, Thomas, 198

Beck and Thomas, fiddle-back spoon by, 198; britannia makers of Birmingham, England, 199

Becker, Herr, Bürgermeister of Herborn, Germany, xii, 101

Belcher, Joseph, 12

Belcher, Joseph, Jr., 51–52

Belfast, Me., 184

Belknap's *Artists and Craftsmen*, 178

Belson, John, 22

Benedict, Lewis, 208

Benham, Darius, cash paid to by A. Griswold, 84; of Simpson and Benham, New York, 176, 190

Benham, Morris, 190

Benham and Whitney, 208

Bennett, Alexander J., xii

Bennett, Edward, 113

Bennett, Thomas, 199

Bentley, Reverend William, 190

Berlin, Conn., Daniel Bass worked in, 54, 158

Berthelsdorf, Saxony, 125

Bethlehem, Pa., Moravian settlement, 119; pewterers, 124; pewterers may have used lovebird touch, 132

Beverly, Mass., Israel Trask's shop at, 23, 191; shop of Lee and Creesy at, 47; shop of Eben Smith at, 190; J. B. Woodbury born at, 195

Beverly, Mass., Historical Society, xii; letter of Mrs. T. Henry Bott in, 171

B.G.S. & Co., 191

Biddeford, Me., 195

Bidgood, *see* Plumly and Bidgood, 146

Bidwell, Solomon, 176

Bigelow, Francis, 94

Bilbro, Betty, 153

Bilbro, John, record of found by H. B. Gill, 148; life of, 153

Bilbro, William, 153

Billings, William, 58

Bindnagel Church, Palmyra, 129

Birmingham, England, britannia manufacturing thrived at, 168; Beck and Thomas britannia in, 198; W. Tutin spoons in, 204

Blair, Mrs. J. Insley, owned John Danforth dish

General Index

E.W. Virginia on plate, 148, 165

The Fairbanks Family in America, 33
Fairbanks, George, 33
Fairbanks, Jonathan, 33
Fairbanks, Jonathan (another), of Sherborn, Mass., 32–34
Fairbanks, Lorenzo S., 33
Fairbanks, Margaret, 32, 33
Fairhaven, Mass., 9, 49
Fales, Dean A., Jr., xii; described E. Crossman plate, 116
Farnam, D. L., 181
Fayetteville, N.C., Paris J. Tillinghast and family moved to, 54; Jacob Eggleston died in, 88; Jehiel Johnson worked in, 159; Martine shop in, 161
Fayetteville American, 159
Feltman, J. C., Jr., 181
Felton, 189
Ferguson, Hugh S., xii
Feyko, John J. D., xiii
First Sea Congregation, gathered in London in 1742, 126; Heyne member of, 126, 128
Fischer, John, 201–202
Fischer I. and T., 202
Fitch, John, 200
Fitzgerald, Mrs. Stephen S., xiii
Flagg, David, 41
Flagg and Homan, forms made by, 86, 87, 181
Foote, Henry C., 181
Foote, James & Co., 181
Forbes, E. B., 182
Fowles, Lloyd W., xiii
France, Joseph, xiii
Franklin, the late Mrs. Paul J., xii
Frary, James A., with Ira Couch managed Griswold's shop, 84; father-in-law of Luther Boardman, 176; H. C. Wilcox travelling salesman for, 194
Frary and Boardman, 176, 182
Freedly, Edwin T., 177
French, Dr. Reginald F., xii; wrote "The Dolbeares," 25, 26; reported quart basin marked W. Palmer, 2nd, 87
Frink, Nathan, 78
Frink, Prentice, 78
Frink, Prentice, Jr., 78, 79
Fryers, John, Newport maker, 16; measure at-
tributed to, 17; touch attributed to, 50, 165; attributed touch may be English, 162
Fuller, Aaron Chauncey, 182
Fuller and Smith, 182
Funtschen, Saxony, 127

Gardiner, Rockwell, xii; found Semper Eadem plates marked with Holyoke cypher, 34
Garey, Jeremiah, 160
Garey and Hammond, 160
Garrett, Wendell D., xii
Garvan and allied collections, xiv
Gaylord, Elizabeth, 88
G.C., 166
G.E., 137
Geesey, Titus C., xii
Gehring, John G., 160
General Assembly of the United Presbyterian Church, Phila., xiv
Geneva, N.Y., 191
Georgeanna, Me., 46
Georgia, 125
Gerhardi and Co., marks of, 182; formerly listed as Gerhardt and Co., 202
Gerhardt and Co., 202
Germantown, Pa., 128
Gibb, George S., xii; mention of his "Whitesmiths of Taunton," 168; his history of Babbitt and Crossman, 174, 175; anecdote about Gleason's apprentices, 182
Giffen, Mrs. Daniel H., xii
Gill, Harold B., Jr., xii; discovered records of pewterers in Virginia, 148
Glass House Company of New York, 104
Glastonbury, Conn., 180
Glaze, Mary, xiii
Glazier, Mr. and Mrs. Paul, xiii; own dish with T.S. Semper Eadem mark, 40
Gleason, Roswell, shop in Dorchester, Mass., 173; coffee urns, 173; Eli Eldridge foreman for, 181; B. F. Knox apprentice of, 182
Goelet, Robert G., xii
Goldsmith, Stanley, xii; reported teapot by J. Harrison, 183
Goldthwaite, Charlotte, 176
Gooch, Frank A., 46
Gooch, James, 46
Gooch, John, 45–46
Gooch, Mary S., 46
Goodman and Danforth, 73

General Index

pages from day book of Thomas Paschall, 120; has copy of Brunstrom inventory, 138; owns J. W. Olcott plate, 157; published Nancy Goyne's *Britannia in America*, 168

Henry Ford Museum, Dearborn, xiii; owns duck-bellied teapot marked E. Brown & Co., 179

Henry Jorde Colony, third migration to Bethlehem, 126; Abraham Hasselberg with, 135

Henshaw, Benjamin, 56

Henshaw, Joseph B., *see* Yale and Henshaw

Henshaw and Hamlin, advertised in *Connecticut Courant*, 55, 71; widow Hooker rented shop to, 55

Hera, C. and J., 145

Hera, John, took inventory of Brunstrom's shop, 20, 138

Herborn, Germany, former home of John Will, 101; Abraham Boemper from, 126

Hermann, Fredrick Gottfried, 155, 156

Herrnhaag, 135

Herrnhut, village built by Count von Zinzendorf, 125; plans at to send colony to Pennsylvania, 125, 128

Hersey, S. S., 184

Hersey, Samuel S., Jr., 184

Hershey, Pa., 129

Heussner, George T., xii

Heyne, Johann Christian, a Saxon who settled at Bethlehem, xi, 119; altar candlesticks by, 21; communion service in church at Cleona, Pa., by, 22; variations in chalices of, 24; moved to Lancaster, 119; history of, 127–130; left Bethlehem in 1750, 135

Heyne, Margaret, 126

H.I., an answer and an end, 20

Hill Evangelical Church, Cleona, Pa., 21, 22

Hill, John, xiii

Hill, Ruth, xii; suggested that Ebenezer Bowditch may have been the Capt. Bowditch of the Rev. Bentley's diary, 178

Hilt, Wendell, xii, xiii; furnished advertisements of Gershom Jones, 57; discovered mortgage of John Danforth's house, 64; opinion of Thomas Danforth marks, 65–68; found Jonathan Danforth's records, 74; found Prentice Frink advertisement, 78; found newspaper notice of Amasa Sizer, 82; studied genealogy of the Porters in Connecticut, 82; research on William Nott, 88; studied S. Stedman history, 89;

probable origin of J. W. Olcott found, 157; found trade card of Luther Boardman, 177; learned that Hinsdales began business in 1810, 91; new information on William and Josiah Danforth, 75; history of William Pelton, 188

Hinsdale, J. & D., 91, 92

Hinshaw, C. P., xii

Hintze, Erwin, German author who did not list D.S. touches of Pennsylvania maker, 144; illustrated marks of F. G. Hermann, 156

Hirsch, Harry, xiii

Historic Silver of the Colonies and its Makers, 94

Historical Foundation of the Presbyterian and Reformed Churches, xiii

Historical and Pictorial Description of the Town of Meriden, Conn., 87

History of Beverly, Mass., 47

History of Old Sheffield Plate, 188

History of a Surname, 46

Holman, Winifred Lovering, 28

Holt, Thomas R., 186

Holyoke, Edward, 35

Holyoke, John, 34–35; Semper Eadem touch may have been used by, 40

Holyoke, Samuel, brother of John Holyoke, 34

Holyoke, Samuel (another), nephew of John Holyoke, 34

Holyoke, Sarah, sister of John Holyoke, 34

Holyoke, Sarah (another), niece of John, married John Skinner, 34

Holyoke, S., cypher on Holyoke plates, 34

Homan Manufacturing Co., 184–185

Hommel, the late Rudolf P., xii

Hood, Graham, xiv

Hooker, widow, rented shop to Henshaw and Hamlin, 55; no reason for listing as pewterer, 202

Hopkins, Hannah E., 188

Hopper, Henry, 173

Horse Neck, N.J., 98

Horton, Frank L., xii, xiii; reported new touch of Eggleston, 80

Howland, Joseph, house 17

Howland spoon, 17

Hudson, N.Y., 116

Hugo, Harold, xiv

Hull, John, 26

Humiston, Hiram, 185

Humiston, Willis, 185

Hurley, Mrs. Emma, 54

General Index

Kingsbury, Mrs. Amos Clark, xiii
Kingston, Mass., 17
Kirby, Peter, 105
Kirby, William, 105
Kirk, Alphonsus, 142
Kirk, Caleb, 142–143
Kirk, Elisha, 141–143
Kler, Dr. Joseph H., xiii; acquired dish attributed to John Baker, 31
Knapp, Elijah, 113
Kneeland, Edward, 44
Knowles, Henry, 185
Knox, B. F., 182
Koehler, Adam, possible user of lovebird touch, 132; married Hasselberg's widow, 134; history of, 136

Lafetra, Moses, 113
La Fountain, Mark, xiii; owned teapot marked Lee and Creesy, 46, 171
Laidacker, Sam, xiii
Lake, John D., 185
Lamb and pennant, 165
Lamborn, David, 144
Lancaster, Pa., Heyne pewterer of, 21; Heyne established in 1757 at, 127
Lancaster County, 144
Lancaster Historical Society, xii
Langshaw, Thomas, 120–121
Langworthy, Lawrence, maker of large dish, 9; two-handled cup by, 15; measure by, 16, 17, 48; touches by, 49–51; history of, 49
Laughlin, Roberta H., xiv
Lawrence, William, 185
Leading Pursuits and Leading Men, 177
Leas and Beastall, 185
Leddell, Joseph, possible user of I.L. touch on rare porringer, 11; maker of West Haven chalice, 21, 93; touches of, 96; forms by, 96, 97; circular lidded box by, 97, 162; Michel cannot be classed with, 107
Leddell, Joseph, Jr., possible user of I.L. touch on rare porringer, 11
Lee, Philip, 47
Lee, Richard, 80
Lee and Creesy, Beverly, Mass., 46; made teapots similar to those of Israel Trask, 46, 192; teapot illustrated Plate LXXII, 171; supposedly sold business to Israel Trask, 172, 192
Lehigh River, 125

Leibundguth, Arthur W., xiii
Leipzig, 156
Leominster, Mass., 195
Leonard, Gustavus, 185
Leonard, Horatio, Crossman, West and Leonard plant mortgaged to, 179; majority stockholder of Leonard, Reed and Barton, 191
Leonard, Zephaniah A., partner in Crossman, West and Leonard, 175–179; Horatio Leonard son of, 185
Leonard, Reed and Barton, 185, 186; Alexander Standish rented equipment from, 191
Leslie, Elkanah, 146
Leslie, Elkins, 146
Levett, Ross, 80
Levy, Aaron, 22
Lewis, Isaac C., partner of George C. Cowles, 179; too young to have been the Lewis of Lewis and Holt, 186
Lewis and Cowles, 179
Lewis and Holt, 186
Lightner, George, 148
Lincoln, 186
Linthwaite, William, 202
Litchfield, Conn., 157
Little, Mrs. Bertram K., xiii; owned Coldwell and Dean tea caddie, 112
Löfgren, Albert, 135
London touches, on Semper Eadem pewter, 41; on lovebird pewter, 130
Longstreet, Bartholomew, 202–203
Lost Creek, Pa., Presbyterian Church, 23
Love, men named in 1790 census, 130
Lovebird touch, users, 5; on bellied quart tankard, 15; on measure, 16; Brunstrom possible user of, 16; Hasselberg possible user of, 131; lion marks accompanying, 132; forms bearing, 132; identical secondary touches used by Brunstrom and user of, 140
"Lovebirds and Lions," 131
Lucas, Ivory, possible maker of rare porringer with I.L. touch, 11; of New London, Conn., 61; history of, 60–62; touches attributed to, 61, 165
Lucas, Mary, 61
Lyell, David, 96
Lyman, William W., 84
Lyme, Conn., Joseph Belcher, Jr., lived in, 79; home of Hannah Wood, 52
Lyon, Charles W., xiii
Lyons, Louis, xiii

General Index

General Index

least rare of early Boston touches, 39; touches found with, 39–41
Seward and Gooch, 46
S.G., 118
Shattuck, William G., 194
Shaw, 190
Sheep, suspended, above fleur-de-lis touch, 107
Sheffield, England, Charles Dixon britannia manufacturer in, 168; W. Parkin made britannia in, 188
Shelley, Donald A., xiii
Shelton, Dr. William P., xiv
Sherborn, Mass., 32
Sherburne, Mary, 46
Sherman, Harriet, 187
Sherman, Roger, 98
Shoff, John, 141
Shreve, Crump and Low, 192
Sickel and Shaw, 190
Silversmiths of New Jersey, 200
Simpkins, Thomas, no pots by? 27; Semper Eadem touch attributed to, 35, 41
Simpson and Benham, 190
Sittig, Mr. and Mrs. Edgar, xiv
Sizer, Amasa, 82
Skerry, Amory S., xiv
Skinner, John, pots attributed to, 27; married Sarah Holyoke, 34; probably competitor of R. Bonynge, 37; Semper Eadem touch may have been used by, 41; forms by, 42; I.S. Semper Eadem touch attributed to, 42; stag touch used by? 43
Sleepy Hollow Restorations Collection, xiii; has large Robert Boyle dish, 105
Smith, Aaron, Phila. pewterer, 122; once listed as dethroned pewterer, 204
Smith, Charlotte A., 194
Smith, Ebenezer, 190
Smith, Ebenezer, Jr., early success, 172; history of, 190
Smith, Emma, 190
Smith, George W., 189, 190
Smith, Helen Burr, xiii; article about Thomas Burroughs, 94
Smith, Ober & Co., 187
Smith, Samuel, 165
Smith, Thomas, older contemporary of Thomas Simpkins, 36; may have used Semper Eadem die, 41
Smith, Thomas & Co., 194

Smith and Morey, 194
Smithsonian Institution, xiv; custodian for I.B. dish, 31
Snow, Julia D. S., xiii
Snow, the late William G., xiii
Society of Pewter Collectors, London, 26
Solebury, Bucks County, Pa., 137
Some Notes on American Pewterers, 18
Southborough, Mass., 37
South Carolina Gazette, Claudius Compaire advertised in, 200; William Linthwaite advertised in, 202
Southington, Conn., 187
Southmayd, Ebenezer, 81
Southmayd, Joseph, 56
South Reading, Mass., L. Boardman shop in, 176; Burrage Yale shop in, 195
S.P., 141–143
Spangenburg, Reverend Mr., 135
Spencer, T. H., Jr., xiii
Spittoons, made in four patterns, 76; made by A. Griswold, 83
Spottsylvania County, Va., 151
Sprague, Ruth, 44
Stafford, Spencer, 117, 118
Stafford, S. & Co., 118
Stag touch, on quart pot, 16; on porringers, 166
Stalkamp, J. H. & Co., William C. Pomroy partner in, 189; John F. Wendeln partner in, 193
Standish, Alexander, apprentice at Babbitt Crossman & Co., 175; history of, 174, 190, 191
Stanley, Samuel G., 114
Stedman, Phineas, 90
Stedman, Sally Boardman, 90
Stedman, Sara Howard, 90
Stedman, Simeon, 89, 90
Stettin, East Germany, 128
Stevens, Sarah, 175
Stevenson, Celia, xii
Stimpson, James H., 191
Stockholm, Sweden, Heyne worked in, 128; Hasselberg worked in, 135
Stockholm's Kaungjutareka, 135
Stocking, Margery, 83
Stone, Edwin M., 47
Stone, Warren, xiv
Stone-ware, 58
Stonington, Conn., 78, 79
Summer, Huldah, 56
Sun Dials and Roses of Yesterday, 137

[273]

General Index

Vartklop's Britannia Ware, 193

Vear, Simon, 124

Vickers, John, 168

Virginia Gazette, 154

Voluntown Church, 15

von Zinzendorf, Benigna, 125

von Zinzendorf, Nicholas Ludwig, opened estate to oppressed Christians, 125; arrival in New York, 125; coronet in Love touch may have been in recognition of, 131; settlement in Bethlehem, 135

Walker, 193

Wallace, R., apprentice of William Mix, 186; history of, 193

Wallingford, Conn., Henry and James Foote made spoons at, 181; Almer Hall worked at, 182; Hall, Elton and Co. shop at, 183; Charles Parker and Gary Mix made spoons in, 186; R. Wallace in, 193; H. B. Ward and Co. made britannia at, 193; Hiram Yale shop in, 195; Yale and Henshaw in, 196

Ward, Henry Beebe, 193

Ward, H. B. & Co., 193

Ward, J. Smith, 193

Ward, Lowden Bailey, 193

Ward, Lucy, 75

Ward, Reuben, 147

Warminster, Bucks County, Pa., 202

Warner, James M., 193

Warren, John B., 193

Warren, Josiah, 193

Warren, R. I., 178

Washington, General George, 99

Watch cases, 138

Waterbury, Conn., 83

Watkins, C. Malcolm, xiv

Watkins, Lura Woodside, xiii; listed Edward Rand as pewterer, 43; called attention to Edward Bennett on New York Provincial Troop Muster Rolls, 113

Watts, Melvin H., xiii

Wayne, Caleb P. & Co., 193

W.B. and two stags in touch, 100

W.B. on inkstand may be mark of Wm. Ball, Phila., 167

Webb, W., 193

Weekes, James and Co., 193

Wehr, Simmon, 124

Weil, Jack H., xiii

Wendeln, John F., 193

Wenham Historical Association and Museum, xiii

West, William A., 175

Westbrook, Me., 173

Westerly, R.I., 82

Western Business Directory, 193

Westfield Parish, Middletown, Conn., 194

West Haven, Conn., site of Christ Church Parish, 21; chalice from, 93, 97

West Roxbury, Mass., 178

Wethersfield, Conn., Buttolph-Williams House, 18

Wetteravia, 135

W.H., 166

Whidden, Mary, 46

Whidden, Michael, 46

Whitaker, Dr. E. H., 181

Whitcomb, A. G., 193

White, Henry, 194

White, James, 194

Whitechurch, Shropshire, 126

Whitehead, Mary, 94

Whitehouse, E., 205

White metal, 2, 3

Whitesmiths, 3

Whitesmiths of Taunton by George S. Gibb, 168; history of Babbitt and Crossman, 174; see for complete history of Reed and Barton, 189; William Parkin designer for Reed and Barton, 188

Whitlock, John H., partner of J. B. Graves, 182; shops in Troy, N.Y., 194; was not Boardman distributor, 194

Whitmore, Jacob, no record of dolphin-handle porringers by, 64; owned moulds jointly with Thomas Danforth, 2nd, 70; additional forms, 71; cash paid to by Ashbil Griswold, 84

Whitney, Chauncey, 118, 194

Whittemore, Capt. Robert N., xiii

Whittle, Francis, 168

Wilcox, Dennis C., 194

Wilcox, Horace C., 194

Wilcox, H. C. & Co., 194

Wilcox, William S., xiv

Wildes, Thomas, 195

Will, George W., 145, 205

Will, Gertraud, 102

Will, Henry, baptismal bowl by, 93; history of, 101–103; great variety of forms, 104; flagon

General Index

found by Dr. Adelbert C. Abbott, 108; returned to New York City in 1784, 109; moved to Albany, 115

Will, Johanna Judith Bömper, 101–102

Will, John, tankard with Bible scene in medallion, 14; tankard and quart pot, 14; creamer by, 20; tall beakers by, 23; two unusual tankards by, 93; history of, 101–104; ship touch similar to A. Michel's, 106

Will, Johannes, 102

Will, Margaretha Elisabeth, 102

Will, Philip Daniel, flagon by, 23, 93, 133; German background, 101–102; plates with touch, 103

Will, William, lids of coffeepots, 6; coffee pots by, 19; took inventory of Brunstrom's shop, 20; forms by, 20; church services by, 22–24; moved to Phila. from New York, 119; communion sets particularly notable, 120; teapots similar to those of "Love," 132; history of, 133, 134; beading on forms, 138; ice cream moulds, 111; inventory included "Bretania Metal" candlesticks, 169

Willett, Edward, E.W. Virginia plates attributed erroneously to, 148–149, 165

Willett, Mary, 98

William Penn Memorial Museum, xi, xiv; church service of Hill Evangelical Lutheran Church, Cleona, Pa., 21

Williams, Carl M., 200

Williams, Lorenzo L., 195

Williams, Otis, 92

Williams, Mr. and Mrs. Thomas D., xiv; found Coldwell and Thompson tea caddies, 112; found inkstand marked "W.B. Phila," 137

Williamsburg, Mass., 78

Williamsburg, Va., 152

Wilmington, Del., 135

Wilson, Joseph, 110

Winchester, Alice, xi

Winterthur Museum, *see* Henry F. du Pont Winterthur Museum

Winston-Salem, N.C., 140

Winterthur Portfolio, xii; *Britannia in America* in, 168

Withington, Lothrop, Jr., xiv; owns mould in which Howland spoon was cast, 18

Wolcott, J., 157

Wood, Haile, 191

Wood, Haile N., 191

Wood, Hannah, 52

Wood, N. G. & Sons, 195

Woodbury, Hepzibah B., 195

Woodbury, J. B., 195

Woodbury, Mrs. Peter, xiv

Woodbury, Thomas, 195

Worshipful Company of Pewterers, 12

Wyer, Simon, 124

Yale, Burrage, cash paid to by A. Griswold, 84; employed 55 men in South Reading, 195

Yale, Charles, made measures, 195; Yale and Henshaw leased shop from, 196

Yale, Charles and Hiram, not apprenticed to Capt. Danforth, 70, 87; bought Samuel Danforth moulds, 77, 85, 87; Thomas S. Derby worked for, 84, 87; not the first to make britannia in U.S., 85, 170; forms by include measures, 195

Yale, Edwin R., 196

Yale, Hiram, used Gen. Jackson touch, 9, 90; touches and forms, 87

H. Yale and Company, 195

Yale, Ira, 83

Yale, Mary, 196

Yale, William, 196

Yale, William and Samuel, 87

Yale and Henshaw, 196

Yale University Art Gallery, xiv; acquired beaker with R.B. rose and crown touch, 37

Yalesville, Conn., 186

York, Me., 46

York County, Pa., tab-handled porringers in, 141; Caleb Kirk family moved to, 143

York County, Va., deed to John Andrews found in, 150; Mungo Campbell granted mortgage in, 152

Yorktown, Va., John Andrews brazier in, 150

Young, Eva, 108

Young, Mr. and Mrs. Paul M., xiv

Young, Peter, signed receipt for musket, 108, 111; sold church cups, 108; agent for Henry Will in Albany, 109; additional forms, 109, 115